Lecture Notes in Artificial Intelligence   4578

Edited by J. G. Carbonell and J. Siekmann

Subseries of Lecture Notes in Computer Science

Francesco Masulli   Sushmita Mitra
Gabriella Pasi (Eds.)

Applications of Fuzzy Sets Theory

7th International Workshop on Fuzzy Logic
and Applications, WILF 2007
Camogli, Italy, July 7-10, 2007
Proceedings

 Springer

Series Editors

Jaime G. Carbonell, Carnegie Mellon University, Pittsburgh, PA, USA
Jörg Siekmann, University of Saarland, Saarbrücken, Germany

Volume Editors

Francesco Masulli
University of Genoa
DISI - Department of Computer and Information Sciences
Via Dodecaneso 35, 16146 Genova, Italy
E-mail: masulli@disi.unige.it

Sushmita Mitra
Indian Statistical Institute
Machine Intelligence Unit, 203 B.T. Road, Kolkata 700 108, India
E-mail: sushmita@isical.ac.in

Gabriella Pasi
Università degli Studi di Milano Bicocca
Dipartimento di Informatica Sistemistica e Comunicazione
Via Bicocca degli Arcimboldi 8, 20133 Milano, Italy
E-mail: gabriella.pasi@unimib.it

Library of Congress Control Number: 2007929541

CR Subject Classification (1998): I.2.3, I.5, F.4.1, F.1, F.2, G.2, I.2, I.4

LNCS Sublibrary: SL 7 – Artificial Intelligence

ISSN   0302-9743
ISBN-10   3-540-73399-X Springer Berlin Heidelberg New York
ISBN-13   978-3-540-73399-7 Springer Berlin Heidelberg New York

Springer is a part of Springer Science+Business Media

springer.com

© Springer-Verlag Berlin Heidelberg 2007
Printed in Germany

Typesetting: Camera-ready by author, data conversion by Scientific Publishing Services, Chennai, India
Printed on acid-free paper   SPIN: 12085170   06/3180   5 4 3 2 1 0

Preface

The 7th International Workshop on Fuzzy Logic and Applications (WILF 2007), held at Ruta di Camogli, Genova (Italy) on July 7-10, 2007 covers topics related to theoretical, experimental and applied fuzzy techniques and systems. This event represents the continuation of an established tradition of biennial interdisciplinary meetings, aimed at bringing together researchers and developers from both academia and industry, to the aim of reporting on the latest scientific and theoretical advances in this scientific context as well as to demonstrate the state of the art of applications and systems.

Previous WILF workshops have been held, with an increasing number of participants, in Naples (1995), Bari (1997), Genoa (1999), Milan (2001), Naples again (2003), and Crema (2005). Each event has focused on distinct main thematic areas of fuzzy logic and related applications.

This, the 7th WILF meeting, hosts four specials sessions namely the Fourth International Meeting on Computational Intelligence Methods for Bioinformatics and Biostatistics (CIBB 2007), the Third International Workshop on Cross-Language Information Processing (CLIP 2007), Intuitionistic Fuzzy Sets: Recent Advances (IFS), and Soft Computing in Image Processing (SCIP). These special sessions extend and deepen the main topics of WILF, thus allowing a cross-fertilization among different, but interdependent, scientific communities.

WILF 2007 received 147 paper submissions from all over the world. A rigorous peer-review selection process was applied to ultimately select 84 high quality manuscripts from the submissions. These were accepted for presentation at the conference, and have been published in this volume. Moreover, the volume also includes three presentations from keynote speakers.

The success of this conference is to be credited to the contributions of many people. In the first place, we would like to thank the organizers of the special sessions for the effort they put into attracting so many good papers. Moreover, special thanks are due to the Program Committee members and reviewers for their commitment to the task of providing high-quality reviews. Last, but not least, we would like to thank the invited speakers Joaquín Dopazo (CIPF, Spain), Rada Mihalcea (University of North Texas, USA), Witold Pedrycz (University of Alberta, Canada), Alessandro Villa (University Joseph Fourier, France), and Ronald Yager (Iona College, USA), and the tutorial presenters Giovanni Garibotto (Elsag SpA, Genova, Italy), Marina Resta (University of Genova, Italy), and Gennady M. Verkhivker (University of Kansas, USA).

July 2007

Francesco Masulli
Sushmita Mitra
Gabriella Pasi

Organization

WILF 2007 has been jointly organized by the DISI, University of Genova, Italy, the IEEE Computational Intelligence Society - Italian Chapter, the International Neural Network Society (INNS) SIGs Italy and Bioinformatics, the Bioinformatics ITalian Society (BITS), the Italian Neural Networks Society (SIREN), the SCIP Working Group Soft Computing in Image Processing (SCIP), the DSI, Università degli Studi di Milano, Italy, and the DMI, University of Salerno, Italy.

Conference Chairs

Francesco Masulli	(University of Genoa, Italy)
Sushmita Mitra	(Indian Statistical Institute, Kolkata, India)
Gabriella Pasi	(University of Milan Bicocca, Italy)

Program Committee

Jim Bezdek	(University of West Florida, USA)
Isabelle Bloch	(ENST-CNRS, France)
Gloria Bordogna	(IDPA CNR, Italy)
Mohand Boughanem	(University Paul Sabatier, Toulouse, France)
Giovanna Castellano	(University of Bari, Italy)
Gianpiero Cattaneo	(University of Milan Bicocca, Italy)
Giulianella Coletti	(University of Perugia, Italy)
Mario Fedrizzi	(University of Trento, Italy)
Brunella Gerla	(University of Insubria, Italy)
Antonio Gisolfi	(University of Salerno, Italy)
Ugur Halici	(METU, Ankara, Turkey)
Enrique Herrera Viedma	(University of Granada, Spain)
Katsuhiro Honda	(Osaka Prefecture University, Japan)
Janusz Kacprzyk	(Polish Academy of Sciences, Warsaw, Poland)
Nik Kasabov	(Auckland Univ. Technology, New Zealand)
Etienne Kerre	(Ghent University, Belgium)
Erich P. Klement	(J. Kepler University, Linz, Austria)
Sankar Pal	(Indian Statistical Institute, India)
Witold Pedrycz	(University of Alberta, Canada)
Germano Resconi	(Catholic University of Brescia, Italy)
Elie Sanchez	(Université Aix-Marseille II, France)
Michio Sugeno	(Doshisha University, Kyoto, Japan)
Umberto Straccia	(ISTI CNR, Pisa, Italy)
Settimo Termini	(University of Palermo and CNR, Italy)
Ronald Yager	(Iona College, New York, USA)

WILF Steering Committee

Andrea Bonarini	(Politecnico di Milano, Italy)
Vito Di Gesù	(University of Palermo, Italy)
Antonio Di Nola	(University of Salerno, Italy)
Francesco Masulli	(University of Genoa, Italy)
Gabriella Pasi	(University of Milan Bicocca, Italy)
Alfredo Petrosino	(University of Naples Parthenope, Italy)

Special Session Organizers

R. Tagliaferri and G. Valentini	*CIBB 2007 - Fourth International Meeting on Computational Intelligence Methods for Bioinformatics and Biostatistics*
P. Rosso and S. Rovetta	*CLIP 2007 - Third international workshop on Cross-Language Information Processing*
G.D. Sergiadis and I.K. Vlachos	*Intuitionistic Fuzzy Sets: Recent Advances*
I. Bloch and A. Petrosino	*Soft Computing in Image Processing*

Referees

(in addition to members of the other committees)

J. Abonyi	S. Hadjitodorov	F. Pla
A. Achs	E. Herrera-Viedma	A. Popov
M. Alexandrov	M. Suzuri Hitam	R.M. Suresh
S. Alonso	C.-S. Lee	P. Salgado
P. Amato	E. Levner	D. Sánchez
K. Atanassov	G. Lo Bosco	S. Sessa
A. Ban	M. Reza Malek	P. Shivakumara
H. Banka	F. Martínez Santiago	A. Staiano
A. Barriga	P. Martinez-Barco	G. Stamou
R. Berlanga-Llavori	M. Matteucci	C. Strapparava
M. Biba	C. Mencar	E. Szmidt
P. Brox Jimenez	M. Montes	A.G.B. Tettamanzi
L. Castellana	L. Moreno	D. Tufis
A. Ciaramella	M. Nachtegael	B. Turchiano
O. Colot	A. Nijholt	L.A. Ureña-López
M. De Cock	O. Okun	V. Varma
F. Di Martino	D. Ortiz-Arroyo	L.G. Nayagam Velu
M. Errecalde	M. Panella	L. Villasenor-Pineda
A. Gelbukh	V. Patrascu	G. Vincenti
S. Giove	A. Peñas	D. Vivona
G. Giraldi	C. Pereira	L. Wang
P.M. Goebel	L. Peterson	B. Wyns

Local Scientific Secretary

Maurizio Filippone	(University of Genoa, Italy)
Stefano Rovetta	(University of Genoa, Italy)
Marina Resta	(University of Genoa, Italy)

Congress Management

Promoest, Genoa (Italy)

Financing Institutions

GNCS, Gruppo Nazionale Calcolo Scientifico, Italy
INNS, International Neural Network Society
DSI, Università degli Studi di Milano, Italy
DMI, University of Salerno, Italy

Table of Contents

Advances in Fuzzy Set Theory

Fuzzy Information Access and Retrieval

Fuzzy Machine Learning

Fuzzy Architectures and Systems

Special Session on Intuitionistic Fuzzy Sets: Recent Advances

Special Session on Soft Computing in Image Processing

Special Session Third International Workshop on Cross-Language Information Processing (CLIP 2007)

Special Session Fourth International Meeting on Computational Intelligence Methods for Bioinformatics Biostatistics (CIBB 2007)

From Fuzzy Beliefs to Goals

Célia da Costa Pereira and Andrea G.B. Tettamanzi

Università degli Studi di Milano
Dipartimento di Tecnologie dell'Informazione
Via Bramante 65, I-26013 Crema (CR), Italy
pereira@dti.unimi.it, andrea.tettamanzi@unimi.it

Abstract. In this paper, we propose a new approach to deal with beliefs by supposing that a rational agent has a *degree of trustiness* for each information it disposes of. We propose (i) a new framework for dealing with imprecise beliefs and desires; (ii) two algorithms for updating the mental state of an agent in this new setting; (iii) three ways for comparing the resulting fuzzy set of desires and (iv) two postulates which the goal election function must obey.

1 Introduction

A rational agent changes its goals if something changes in its mental state. In this work, the mental state is represented by three components: a set of beliefs; a set of desires/motivations; and a set of relations between beliefs and desires. In [2], the concept of belief is considered as an all-or-nothing concept: either an agent believes something or it does not. It has been argued this is not the best way to represent the concept of belief [5]. In this paper a more realistic approach to representing beliefs is taken. We assume an agent has a *degree of trustiness* which expresses how strongly it believes a piece of information. Two well-known theories are suitable to dealing with such a situation, namely probability and fuzzy set theory. However, probability theory requires statistical information on the frequency of events, which in many applications is hard or even impossible to obtain. A sensible choice is thus to regard the degree of trustiness of a belief as a fuzzy degree of truth. As a consequence, the set of current desires of an agent is fuzzy. Therefore, a new method to change the goal set of an agent given new information or a new desire must be considered. We propose (i) a new framework for dealing with imprecise beliefs and desires; (ii) two algorithms for updating the mental state of the agent in this new setting; (iii) three ways for comparing the resulting fuzzy sets of desires and (iv) two postulates which the goal election function, which determines the set of desires an agent decides to pursue as goals, must obey.

2 Preliminaries

In this section, we propose a fuzzy logic-based formalism which will be used throughout the paper, as well as the three components of the mental state of an agent.

F. Masulli, S. Mitra, and G. Pasi (Eds.): WILF 2007, LNAI 4578, pp. 1–8, 2007.

Desires (obligations or motivations) are necessary but not sufficient conditions for action. When a desire is met by other conditions that make it possible for an agent to act, that desire becomes a *goal*. Therefore, given this technical definition of a desire, all goals are desires, but not all desires are goals.

We distinguish two crisp sets of atomic propositions (or atoms): the set $\mathcal{D}$ of all possible desires and the set $\mathcal{K}$ of all possible knowledge items. For the sake of simplicity, we make the assumption that desires and knowledge items are on completely different levels: a desire is not a piece of knowledge and *vice versa*. However, desires can depend on knowledge, while knowledge never depends on desires.

2.1   A Fuzzy Representation Formalism

Unlike [2], we assume here that an agent does not always trust its beliefs completely. This may depend on the reliability of its information sources. Here we are not interested in the computation of such reliabilities; we merely assume that, for an agent, a belief has a truth degree in $[0, 1]$.

The fuzzy counterpart of a desire-generating rule defined in [2] is defined as follow:

Definition 1 (Desire-Generating Rule). *A desire-generating rule is an expression of the form $b_\wedge \ldots \wedge b_n \wedge d_1 \wedge \ldots \wedge d_m \rightarrowtail d$, or $\delta \rightarrowtail d$, where $b_i \in \{p, \neg p\}$ for some $p \in \mathcal{K}$, $d_j \in \{q, \neg q\}$ for some $q \in \mathcal{D}$, $d \in \mathcal{D}$, $d \neq d_j$ for all j, and $\delta \in (0, 1]$.*

The meaning of the first type of desire-generating rule is "if an agent believes $b_1, \ldots, b_n$ and desires $d_1, \ldots, d_m$, then an agent possibly desires d as well". The meaning of the second type of rule is "the agent unconditionally desires d to degree δ".

Given a desire-generating rule R, we shall denote lhs(R) the set of literals that make up the conjunction on the left-hand side of R, and rhs(R) the atom on the right-hand side of R. Furthermore, if S is a set of rules, we define rhs(S) = $\{$rhs(R) : $R \in S\}$.

Definition 2 (State of an Agent). *The state of an agent is completely described by a triple $\mathcal{S} = \langle \mathcal{B}, \mathcal{R}_J, \mathcal{J} \rangle$, where*

- $\mathcal{B}$ *is a fuzzy set of atoms (beliefs) on the universe of discourse $\mathcal{K}$;*
- $\mathcal{J}$ *is a fuzzy set of atoms (desires) on the universe of discourse $\mathcal{D}$;*
- $\mathcal{R}_J$ *is a set of desire-generating rules, such that, for each desire d, $\mathcal{R}_J$ contains at most one rule of the form $\delta \rightarrowtail d$.*

The membership degree of an atom in $\mathcal{B}$ is the degree to which an agent believes the information represented by the atom. $\mathcal{R}_J$ contains the rules which generate desires from beliefs and other (more basic) desires. $\mathcal{J}$ contains all desires which may be deduced from the agents's desire-generating rule base, given the agent's beliefs and the agent's desires.

Definition 3 (Degree of Activation of a Desire-Generating Rule). *Let R be a desire-generating rule. The degree af activation of R, Deg(R), is given by* $\mathrm{Deg}(R) = \min\{\mathcal{B}(b_1), \ldots, \mathcal{B}(b_n), \mathcal{J}(d_1), \ldots, \mathcal{J}(d_m)\}$ *for rules of the first type, and by* $\mathrm{Deg}(R) = \delta$ *if* $R = \delta \longmapsto d$.

Finally, we do not expect a rational agent to formulate desires out of whim, but based on some rational argument. To model that state of affairs, desire-generating rules play the role of rational arguments. We define the degree to which a desire is justified as follows.

Definition 4 (Degree of justification of a desire). *The degree of justification of desire d,* $\mathcal{J}(d) = \max_{R \in \mathcal{R}_{\mathcal{J}} : \mathrm{rhs}(R)=d} \mathrm{Deg}(R)$, *represents how rational it is the fact that an agent desires d.*

3 Changes in the State of an Agent

The acquisition of a new belief with a given degree of trustiness in state $\mathcal{S}$, may cause a change in the belief set $\mathcal{B}$ and this may also cause a change in the desire set $\mathcal{J}$ with the variation of the justification degree of desires. Likewise, the arising of a new desire with a given degree may also cause changes in the desire set $\mathcal{J}$.

3.1 Changes in the Set of Beliefs Caused by a New Belief

To account for changes in the belief set $\mathcal{B}$ caused by the acquisition of a new belief, we define a new operator for belief change, noted $*$, which is an adaptation of the well known AGM operator for belief revision [1] to the fuzzy belief setting, in the spirit of [6].

Definition 5 (Belief Change Operator). *Let* $*$ *be the belief change operator. Let* $b \in \mathcal{K}$ *be an atomic knowledge item and* $\frac{\alpha}{l}$, *with* $l \in \{b, \neg b\}$, *a piece of information concerning b, with a trustiness degree of* $\alpha \in [0,1]$. *Let* $\mathcal{B}$ *be a fuzzy set of beliefs. The new fuzzy set of beliefs* $\mathcal{B}' = \mathcal{B} * \frac{\alpha}{l}$ *is such that:*

$$\mathcal{B}'(b) = \begin{cases} \mathcal{B}(b).(1-\alpha) + \alpha, & \text{if } l = b; \\ \mathcal{B}(b).(1-\alpha), & \text{if } l = \neg b. \end{cases} \tag{1}$$

Proposition 1. *If* $l = b$, *i.e., if the new piece of information does not contradict b, applying the operator* $*$ *makes the truth degree of b increase, i.e.,* $\mathcal{B}'(b) \geq \mathcal{B}(b)$.

Proof. If $\mathcal{B}(b) = 0$ the result is obvious. Otherwise, if $\mathcal{B}(b) > 0$, since $0 \leq 1 - \alpha \leq 1$, we have $0 \leq \mathcal{B}'(b) - \mathcal{B}(b) \leq \alpha$. α is greather or equal than zero and then $\mathcal{B}'(b) - \mathcal{B}(b) \geq 0$.

Proposition 2. *If* $l = \neg b$, *i.e., if the new piece of information contradicts b, applying the operator* $*$ *makes the truth degree of b decrease, i.e.,* $\mathcal{B}'(b) \leq \mathcal{B}(b)$.

Proof. $\mathcal{B}'(b') - \mathcal{B}(b') = \mathcal{B}(b) * (1-\alpha) - \mathcal{B}(b) = -\mathcal{B}(b) * \alpha \leq 0$.

The semantics of our belief change operator is defined by the following propperties. Here $\mathcal{B}$ represents a fuzzy belief set, l an acquired trusted information, Sup is the function which returns the support of a fuzzy set, and $\cup$, $\cap$, $\subseteq$ and $\supseteq$ are fuzzy operators.

- **(P * 1)**(Stability) The result of applying * in $\mathcal{B}$ with l is always a fuzzy set of beliefs: $\mathcal{B} * \frac{\alpha}{l}$ is a fuzzy set of beliefs.
- **(P * 2)**(Expansion) If $l = b$, the fuzzy set of information expands: $\mathrm{Sup}(\mathcal{B} * \frac{\alpha}{l}) \supseteq \mathrm{Sup}(\mathcal{B})$.
- **(P * 3)**(Shrinkage) If $l = \neg b$, the fuzzy set of beliefs shrinks: $\mathrm{Sup}(\mathcal{B} * \frac{\alpha}{l}) \subseteq \mathrm{Sup}(\mathcal{B})$.
- **(P * 4)**(Invariance) If the new information is completely untrusted, i.e., $\alpha = 0$, invariance holds: $(\alpha = 0) \Rightarrow (\mathcal{B} * \frac{\alpha}{l} = \mathcal{B})$.
- **(P * 5)**(Predictability) The result of applying * contains all beliefs in $\mathrm{Sup}(\mathcal{B} \cup \{\frac{\alpha}{l}\})$: $\mathrm{Sup}(\mathcal{B} * \frac{\alpha}{l}) \supseteq \mathrm{Sup}(\mathcal{B} \cup \{\frac{\alpha}{l}\})$.
- **(P * 6)**(Identity) The result of applying * does not depend on the particular information. If $l_1(\in \{b_1, \neg b_1\}) = l_2(\in \{b_2, \neg b_2\})$ and $\alpha_1 = \alpha_2$: $\mathcal{B} * \frac{\alpha_1}{l_1} = \mathcal{B} * \frac{\alpha_2}{l_2}$.

3.2   Changes in the Fuzzy Desire Set Caused by a New Belief

The acquisition of a new belief may induce changes in the justification degree of some desires. More generally, the acquisition of a new belief may induce changes in the belief set of an agent which in turn may induce changes in its desire set. Let $\frac{\alpha}{l}$, with $l \in \{b, \neg b\}$, be a new belief which is trusted by an agent to degree α. To account for the changes in the desire set caused by this new acquisition, we must consider each rule $R \in \mathcal{R}_{\mathcal{J}}$ such that $b \in \mathrm{lhs}(R)$ or $\neg b \in \mathrm{lhs}(R)$, in order to update the justification value of the desire $\mathrm{rhs}(R)$. In other words, the new desire set $\mathcal{J}'$ is such that $\mathcal{J}' = f(\mathcal{B}', \mathcal{R}_{\mathcal{J}}, \mathcal{D})$, with $\mathcal{B}' = \mathcal{B} * \frac{\alpha}{l}$. The set $\mathcal{R}_{\mathcal{J}}$ does not change.

Let C_k be the set containing all desires such that their justification degree changes in the step k, i.e., $\forall d \in C_k$, $\mathcal{J}'_k(d) \neq \mathcal{J}'_{k-1}(d)$. The algorithm to compute the new desire set $\mathcal{J}'$ is given in Figure 1.

Observation 1. *If the new information is not contradictory:*

$$\mathcal{J}' = \bigcup_{k=0}^{\infty} \mathcal{J}'_k.$$

Proof. According to Proposition 1, for all b we have $\mathcal{B}'(b) \geq \mathcal{B}(b)$. Therefore, the degree of all desires d in the new desire set $\mathcal{J}'$ may not decrease, i.e., for all k, $\mathcal{J}'_k(d) \geq \mathcal{J}'_{k-1}(d)$.

Observation 2. *If the new information is contradictory:*

$$\mathcal{J}' = \bigcap_{k=0}^{\infty} \mathcal{J}'_k.$$

1. $\mathcal{B}' \leftarrow \mathcal{B} * \frac{\alpha}{\tau}; \; k \leftarrow 1; \; C_0 \leftarrow \emptyset;$
2. For each $d \in \mathcal{D}$ do
    (a) consider all $R_i \in \mathcal{R}_{\mathcal{J}}$ such that $\mathrm{rhs}(R) = d$;
    (b) calculate their respective degrees $\mathrm{Deg}(R_i)$ considering $\mathcal{B}'$;
    (c) $\mathcal{J}'_0(d) \leftarrow \max_{R_i} \mathrm{Deg}(R_i)$;
    (d) if $\mathcal{J}'_0(d) \neq \mathcal{J}(d)$ then $C_0 \leftarrow C_0 \cup \{d\}$.
3. repeat
    (a) $C_k \leftarrow \emptyset;$
    (b) for each $d \in C_{k-1}$ do
        i. for all $R_j \in \mathcal{R}_{\mathcal{J}}$ such that $d \in \mathrm{lhs}(R_j)$ do
            A. calculate their respective degrees $\mathrm{Deg}(R_j)$ considering $\mathcal{J}'_{k-1}(d)$;
            B. $\mathcal{J}'_k(\mathrm{rhs}(R_j)) \leftarrow \max_{R_i \mid \mathrm{rhs}(R_i) = \mathrm{rhs}(R_j)} \mathrm{Deg}(R_i)$;
            C. if $\mathcal{J}'_k(\mathrm{rhs}(R_j)) \neq \mathcal{J}'_{k-1}(\mathrm{rhs}(R_j))$ then $C_k \leftarrow C_k \cup \{\mathrm{rhs}(R_j)\}$.
        ii. $k \leftarrow k + 1$.
4. until $C_{k-1} = \emptyset$.
5. for all d, $\mathcal{J}'(d)$ is given by the following equation:

$$\mathcal{J}'(d) = \begin{cases} \mathcal{J}(d), & \text{if } d \notin C; \\ \mathcal{J}'_i(d), & \text{otherwise,} \end{cases} \qquad (2)$$

where i is such that $d \in C_i$ and $\forall j \neq i$ if $d \in C_j$ then $j \leq i$, i.e., the justification degree of a "changed" desire is the last degree it takes.

Fig. 1. An algorithm to compute the new desire set upon arrival of a new belief. The set of "changed" desires is $C = \bigcup_{k=0}^{\infty} C_k$.

Proof. According to Proposition 2, for all b we have $\mathcal{B}'(b) \leq \mathcal{B}(b)$. Therefore, the degree of all desires d in the new desire set $\mathcal{J}'$ may not increase, i.e., for all k, $\mathcal{J}'_k(d) \leq \mathcal{J}'_{k-1}(d)$.

3.3 Changes Caused by a New Desire

The acquisition of a new desire may cause changes in the fuzzy desire set and in the desire-generating rule base. In this work, for the sake of simplicity, we consider only new desires which are not dependent of beliefs and/or other desires. A new desire, justified with degree δ, implies the addition of the desire-generation rule $\delta \rightarrowtail d$ into $\mathcal{R}_J$, resulting in the new base $\mathcal{R}'_J$. By definition of a desire-generating rule base, $\mathcal{R}'_J$ must not contain another $\delta' \rightarrowtail d$ with $\delta \neq \delta'$. How does $\mathcal{S}$ change with the arising of the new desire (d, δ)?

- Any rule $\delta' \rightarrowtail d$ with $\delta \neq \delta'$ is retracted from $\mathcal{R}_J$,
- $\delta \rightarrowtail d$ is added to $\mathcal{R}_J$,

It is clear that the arising of a new desire does not change the belief set of the agent.

The new fuzzy set of desires $\mathcal{J}' = g(\mathcal{B}, \mathcal{R}'_J)$ is computed by the follwing algorithm:

4 Comparing Fuzzy Sets of Desires

An agent may have many desires. However, it is essential to be able to represent the fact that not all desires have the same importance or urgency for a rational

1. if $\{\delta' \rightarrowtail d\} \in \mathcal{R}_{\mathcal{J}}$ then $\mathcal{R}'_{\mathcal{J}} \leftarrow (\mathcal{R}_{\mathcal{J}} \setminus \{\delta' \rightarrowtail d\}) \cup \{\delta \rightarrowtail d\}$;
   else $\mathcal{R}'_{\mathcal{J}} \leftarrow \mathcal{R}_{\mathcal{J}} \cup \{\delta \rightarrowtail d\}$;
2. $k \leftarrow 1$; $C_0 \leftarrow \{d\}$; $\mathcal{J}'_0(d) \leftarrow \delta$;
3. repeat
   (a) $C_k \leftarrow \emptyset$;
   (b) for each $d \in C_{k-1}$ do
       i. for all $R_j \in \mathcal{R}'_{\mathcal{J}}$ such that $d \in \text{lhs}(R_j)$ do
          A. calculate their respective degrees $\text{Deg}(R_j)$ considering $\mathcal{J}'_{k-1}(d)$;
          B. $\mathcal{J}'_k(\text{rhs}(R_j)) \leftarrow \max_{R_i | \text{rhs}(R_i) = \text{rhs}(R_j)} \text{Deg}(R_i)$;
          C. if $\mathcal{J}'_k(\text{rhs}(R_j)) \neq \mathcal{J}'_{k-1}(\text{rhs}(R_j))$ then $C_k \leftarrow C_k \cup \{\text{rhs}(R_j)\}$.
       ii. $k \leftarrow k + 1$.
4. until $C_{k-1} = \emptyset$.
5. for all d, $\mathcal{J}'(d)$ is given by Equation 2.

Fig. 2. An algorithm to compute the new desire set upon the arisal of a new desire

agent. A natural choice for representing the importance of desires would be to adopt the notion of utility. A utility function for desires is a function $u : \mathcal{D} \to \mathbb{R}$ which associates a real value, utility, to all desires.

We can extend this notion to the case of desire sets. In this paper, we distinguish three cases. In the first case we dispose of qualitative utilities; in the second case we dispose of qualitative utilities; in the last case we do not dispose of utilites. In all three cases, the preference relation between two fuzzy sets of desires is noted $\succeq$.

4.1   Comparing Sets of Desires Under Qualitative Utility

We adopt the notion of pessimistic utilities [4] and optimistic utilities [7] for the purposes of our work.

Definition 6 (Pessimistic Utility). *Let $\mathcal{J}$ be a fuzzy set of desires, and $u : \mathcal{D} \to [0, 1]$ the function wich maps a desire to a qualitative utility. The pessimistic utility of $\mathcal{J}$, $U^{\text{Pes}}(\mathcal{J})$, is given by:*

$$U^{\text{Pes}}(\mathcal{J}) = \min_d \max(1 - \mathcal{J}(d), u(d))$$

If all desires d in $\mathcal{J}$ are completetly justified, i.e., $\mathcal{J}(d) = 1 \ \forall d$, the pessimistic utility of $\mathcal{J}$ is equal to the utility of the less important desire.

Definition 7 (Optimistic Utility). *Let $\mathcal{J}$ be a fuzzy set of desires, and $u : \mathcal{D} \to [0, 1]$ the function wich maps a desire to a qualitative utility. The optimistic utility of $\mathcal{J}$, $U^{\text{Opt}}(\mathcal{J})$, is given by:*

$$U^{\text{Opt}}(\mathcal{J}) = \max_d \min(\mathcal{J}(d), u(d))$$

If all desires d in $\mathcal{J}$ are completetly justified, the optimistic utility of $\mathcal{J}$ is equal to the utility of the most important desire.

Definition 8 (Preference between Fuzzy Sets of Desires). *Given two fuzzy sets of desires $\mathcal{J}_1$ and $\mathcal{J}_2$, JD_1 is preferred to $\mathcal{J}_2$, in symbols $\mathcal{J}_1 \succeq \mathcal{J}_2$, iff $U^{\text{Pes}}(\mathcal{J}_1) > U^{\text{Pes}}(\mathcal{J}_2)$; or $U^{\text{Pes}}(\mathcal{J}_1) = U^{\text{Pes}}(\mathcal{J}_2)$ and $U^{\text{Opt}}(\mathcal{J}_1) \geq U^{\text{Opt}}(\mathcal{J}_2)$.*

4.2   Comparing Sets of Desires Under Quantitative Utility

In case we dispose of quantitative utilities, the utitily of a fuzzy set of desires may be calculated as follows.

Definition 9 (Quantitative Utility). *Let $\mathcal{J}$ be a fuzzy set of desires, and $u : \mathcal{D} \to \mathbb{R}$ a function wich maps a desire to a real value. The utility of $\mathcal{J}$ is*

$$\mathrm{U}(\mathcal{J}) = \sum_{d \in \mathcal{J}} u(d) \cdot \mathcal{J}(d).$$

Definition 10 (Preference between Fuzzy Sets of Desires). *A fuzzy set of desire $\mathcal{J}_1$ is prefered to $\mathcal{J}_2$, in symbols $\mathcal{J}_1 \succeq \mathcal{J}_2$, iff $\mathrm{U}(\mathcal{J}_1) \geq \mathrm{U}(\mathcal{J}_2)$.*

4.3   Comparing Sets of Desires Without Utilities

In case we do not dispose of utilities, we can still compare sets of desires by using the justification degrees of their elements. We consider two parameters: the possibility $\Pi(\mathcal{J})$ and the necessity $N(\mathcal{J})$ that the fuzzy set $\mathcal{J}$ is justified.

$\Pi(\mathcal{J}) = \max_d \mathcal{J}(D)$ represents how possibly justified is the fuzzy set $\mathcal{J}$. $\Pi(\mathcal{J}) = 0$ means that $\mathcal{J}$ is certainly not a desire set of the agent. $\Pi(\mathcal{J}) = 1$ means that it would not be surprising at all if $\mathcal{J}$ were the desire set of the agent.

$N(\mathcal{J}) = 1 - \max_{d \in \mathrm{rhs}(\mathcal{R}_{\mathcal{J}})}(1 - \mathcal{J}(d))$ represents how surely justified is the set $\mathcal{J}$. That is because we consider only desires which are justified, i.e., desires in the right hand side of a desire-generation rule with a nonzero justification degree, instead of the entire set of possible desires. $N(\mathcal{J}) = 0$ means that it would not be surprising at all if $\mathcal{J}$ were not a set of desires of the agent. $N(\mathcal{J}) = 1$ means that it is certainly true that $\mathcal{J}$ is a set of desires of the agent.

Definition 11 (Preference between Fuzzy Sets of Desires). *A fuzzy set of desire $\mathcal{J}_1$ is preferred to a fuzzy set of desires $\mathcal{J}_2$, in symbols $\mathcal{J}_1 \succeq \mathcal{J}_2$, iff $N(\mathcal{J}_1) > N(\mathcal{J}_2)$; or $N(\mathcal{J}_1) = N(\mathcal{J}_2)$ and $\Pi(\mathcal{J}_1) \geq \Pi(\mathcal{J}_2)$.*

5   Goal Sets

The main point about desires is that we expect a rational agent to try and manipulate its surrounding environment to fulfill them. In general, considering a planning problem $\mathcal{P}$ to solve, not all desires can be fulfilled at the same time, especially when there is not a solution plan which allows to reach all of them at the same time. We assume we dispose of a $\mathcal{P}$-dependent function $\mathcal{F}_{\mathcal{P}}$ wich, given a fuzzy set of beliefs $\mathcal{B}$ and a set of desires $\mathcal{J}$, returns a degree γ which corresponds to the certainty degree of the most certain solution plan found [3]. We may call γ the *degree of feasibility* of $\mathcal{J}$ given $\mathcal{B}$, i.e., $\mathcal{F}_{\mathcal{P}}(\mathcal{B}, \mathcal{J}) = \gamma$. In general, a rational agent will try to reach a set of desires which first of all has a suitable degree of feasibility. The preference criterion comes into play in a second time.

Definition 12 (γ-Goal Set). *A γ-goal set, with $\gamma \in [0, 1]$, in state $\mathcal{S}$ is a fuzzy set of desires $\mathcal{G}$ such that:*

1. $\mathrm{Sup}(\mathcal{G}) \subseteq \mathrm{Sup}(\mathcal{J})$;
2. $\mathcal{F}_{\mathcal{P}}(\mathcal{B}, \mathcal{G}) \geq \gamma$.

Postulates of a γ-Goal Set Election Function

In general, given a fuzzy set of desires $\mathcal{J}$, there may be more than one possible γ-goal sets $\mathcal{G}$. However, a rational agent in state $\mathcal{S} = \langle \mathcal{B}, \mathcal{J}, \mathcal{R}_J \rangle$ will elect as the set of goals it is pursuing one precise goal set $\mathcal{G}^*$, which depends on $\mathcal{S}$.

Let us call G_γ the function which maps a state $\mathcal{S}$ into the γ-goal set elected by a rational agent in state $\mathcal{S}$: $\mathcal{G}^* = G_\gamma(\mathcal{S})$. A goal election function G_γ must obey two fundamental postulates:

- **(G $\odot$ 1)** $\forall \mathcal{S}, G_\gamma(\mathcal{S})$ is a γ-goal set;
- **(G $\odot$ 2)** $\forall \mathcal{S}$, if $\mathcal{G}$ is a γ-goal set, then $G_\gamma(\mathcal{S}) \succeq \mathcal{G}$, i.e., a rational agent always selects the most preferrable γ-goal set.

6   Conclusion

A new framework for dealing with imprecise beliefs and desires in rational agents has been proposed, based on an AGM-like belief change operator; two algorithms for updating the mental state of an agent in this new setting and three ways for comparing the resulting fuzzy set of desires have been given. Finally, two fundamental postulates any rational goal election function should obey have been stated. This work is the natural fuzzy extension of previous work carried out in the field of BDI (belief-desire-intention) agents.

References

1. Alchourrón, C.E., Gärdenfors, P., Makinson, D.: On the logic of theory change: Partial meet contraction and revision functions. J. Symb. Log. 50(2), 510–530 (1985)
2. da Costa Pereira, C., Tettamanzi, A.: Towards a framework for goal revision. In: Proceedings of 18th BeNeLux Conference on Artificial Intelligence, BNAIC'06. pp. 99–106, Namur, Belgium (2006)
3. da Costa Pereira, C., Garcia, F., Lang, J., Martin-Clouaire, R.: Planning with graded nondeterministic actions: a possibilistic approach. International Journal of Intelligent Systems 12, 935–962 (1997)
4. Dubois, D., Prade, H.: Possibility theory as a basis for qualitative decision theory. In: IJCAI, Montreal, pp. 19–25 (1995)
5. Hansson, S.O.: Ten philosophical problems in belief revision. J. Log. Comput. 13(1), 37–49 (2003)
6. Witte, R.: Fuzzy Belief Revision. In: 9th Intl. Workshop on Non-Monotonic Reasoning (NMR'02), April 19–21 2002, pp. 311–320, Toulouse, France (2002) http://rene-witte.net
7. Yager, R.: An approach to ordinal decision making. International Journal of Approximate Reasoning 12, 237–261 (1995)

Information Entropy and Co–entropy of Crisp and Fuzzy Granulations

Daniela Bianucci, Gianpiero Cattaneo, and Davide Ciucci

Università degli Studi di Milano–Bicocca
Dipartimento di Informatica, Sistemistica e Comunicazione,
Via Bicocca degli Arcimboldi 8, 20126 Milano (Italy)
{bianucci, cattang, ciucci}@disco.unimib.it

Abstract. The standard approach to information entropy applied to partitions of a universe is equivalently formulated as the entropy of the corresponding crisp identity resolutions, interpreted as crisp granulations, by the corresponding characteristic functionals. Moreover, in this crisp context the co–entropy notion is introduced. The extension to the case of fuzzy identity resolutions, a particular case of fuzzy granulation, is studied.

1 Entropy of Abstract Discrete Probability Distributions

In this section we briefly discuss the *abstract* approach to information theory, involving suitable finite sequences of numbers from the real unit interval $[0, 1]$, each of which can be interpreted as a probability of occurrence of something, without any reference to a concrete universe X. To be precise, a length N *probability distribution* is a vector $\boldsymbol{p} = (p_1, p_2, \ldots, p_N)$ in which: (pd-1) every $p_1 \geq 0$ and (pd-2) $\sum_{i=1}^{n} p_i = 1$. In this abstract context, a length N *random variable* is a real vector $\boldsymbol{a} = (a_1, a_2, \ldots, a_N)$ in which each component is a real number: $a_i \in \mathbb{R}$ for any i. For a fixed length N random variable $\boldsymbol{a}$ and a length N probability distribution $\boldsymbol{p}$, the numbers a_i are interpreted as *possible values* of $\boldsymbol{a}$ and the quantities p_i as the probability of occurrence of the event "$\boldsymbol{a} = a_i$" (thus, p_i can be considered as a simplified notation of $p(a_i)$) (see [1, p.5]).

Hence, the *average* (or *mean*) value of the random variable $\boldsymbol{a}$ with respect to a probability distribution $\boldsymbol{p}$ is given by $Av(\boldsymbol{a}, \boldsymbol{p}) = \sum_{i=1}^{N} a_i \cdot p_i$.

In particular, to any probability distribution $\boldsymbol{p} = (p_1, p_2, \ldots, p_N)$ it is possible to associate the *information random variable* $\boldsymbol{I}[\boldsymbol{p}] = (I(p_1), I(p_2), \ldots, I(p_N))$, where for every $p \in (0, 1]$ it is $I(p) := -\log(p)$, whose mean value with respect to the probability distribution $\boldsymbol{p}$, called the *entropy* of the probability distribution and denoted by $H(\boldsymbol{p})$, is explicitly expressed by the formula (with the convention $0 \log 0 = 0$):

$$H(\boldsymbol{p}) = -\sum_{i=1}^{N} p_i \log p_i \qquad (1)$$

with $0 \leq H(\boldsymbol{p}) \leq \log N$. Let us recall that the real number $I(p) := -\log(p)$ is a measure (called the Hartley *measure* [2]) of the *uncertainty* due to the knowledge

F. Masulli, S. Mitra, and G. Pasi (Eds.): WILF 2007, LNAI 4578, pp. 9–19, 2007.
© Springer-Verlag Berlin Heidelberg 2007

of a probability since if the probability is 1, then there is no uncertainty and so its corresponding measure is 0. Moreover, any probability different from 1 (and 0) is linked to some uncertainty whose measure is greater than 0 in such a way that the lower is the probability, the greater is the corresponding uncertainty measure. Hence, the entropy of a probability distribution $\boldsymbol{p}$ can be considered as a quantity which in a reasonable way measures the *average amount of uncertainty* associated with this distribution, expressed as the mean value of the corresponding information random variable $\boldsymbol{I}[\boldsymbol{p}]$.

2   Entropy and Co–entropy of Partitions

Now we apply the just discussed notion of *information entropy* to the concrete case of partitions of a *finite* nonempty universe X. A partition of X is a finite collection $\pi = \{A_1, A_2, \ldots, A_N\}$ of nonempty subsets A_i of X which are pairwise disjoints and whose set theoretic union is X. Elements A_i forming the partition π are considered as *granules* of some knowledge associated with the partition. As it is well known, a partition π is equivalently described by an equivalence (reflexive, symmetric and transitive) relation on X formally written as $(x, y)\mathcal{R}$ iff $\exists A_j \in \pi : x, y \in A_j$, and this equivalence relation expresses the fact that two objects x and y of the universe cannot be *distinguished* relatively to the knowledge supported by the partition. The equivalence relation is in this way interpreted as an *indistinguishability* relation (see [5], [6], [7]). In this sense a partition furnishes a *granulation* of the universe X by "crisp" granules, also if in the sequel we adopt a weaker notion of granulation linked to a measure distribution assigned to every equivalence class A_i of the partition.

Given a partition π, the subsets $A_i \in \pi$ are the *elementary events* of the *measure distribution* $\boldsymbol{m}(\pi) = (|A_1|, |A_2|, \ldots, |A_N|)$, where the measure of the event A_i is an application to it of the so–called *counting measure* $m_c(Y) := |Y|$ (the cardinality measure) for any arbitrary subset Y of X. This measure distribution satisfies the conditions: (md-1)   every $|A_i| > 0$; (md-2)   its *total measure* is $M(\pi) := \sum_{i=1}^{N} |A_i| = |X|$. The *probability of occurrence* of the event A_i is then given by $p(A_i) = \frac{|A_i|}{|X|}$. In this way we have generated the *probability distribution* $\boldsymbol{p}(\pi) := (p(A_1), p(A_2), \ldots, p(A_N))$, depending from the partition π. This probability distribution satisfies the conditions: (pd-1)   every $p(A_i) > 0$; (pd-2)   its *total probability* is $P(\pi) := \sum_{i=1}^{N} p(A_i) = 1$. According to (1), the entropy of this probability distribution, simply written as $H(\pi)$ instead of $H(\boldsymbol{p}(\pi))$, is then

$$H(\pi) = -\sum p(A_i) \log p(A_i) = -\sum_{i=1}^{N} \frac{|A_i|}{|X|} \log \frac{|A_i|}{|X|} \tag{2}$$

In particular, we can consider the *trivial* partition $\pi_t = \{X\}$ (consisting of the unique set X) and the *discrete* partition $\pi_d = \{\{x_1\}, \{x_2\}, \ldots, \{x_{|X|}\}\}$ (the collection of all singletons from the universe $X = \{x_1, x_2, \ldots, x_{|X|}\}$ of cardinality $|X|$). In these two particular partitions the associated entropies are

$H(\pi_t) = 0$ and $H(\pi_d) = \log|X|$ and for any other partition π of the same universe X one has the following inequalities: $0 = H(\pi_t) \leq H(\pi) \leq H(\pi_d) = \log|X|$, with $H(\pi) = 0$ iff $\pi = \pi_t$ and $H(\pi) = \log|X|$ iff $\pi = \pi_d$.

Note that the entropy (2) associated with a probability distribution π assumes also the following form:

$$H(\pi) = \log|X| - \frac{1}{|X|}\sum_{i=1}^{N}|A_i|\log|A_i| \qquad (3)$$

Hence, if one introduces the *co–entropy* of the partition π defined as

$$E(\pi) := \frac{1}{|X|}\sum_{i=1}^{N}|A_i|\log|A_i| \qquad (4)$$

then the (3) leads to the identity:

$$\forall \pi, \quad H(\pi) + E(\pi) = \log|X| \qquad (5)$$

i.e., the quantity $E(\pi)$ is the "entropy" which *complements* $H(\pi)$ with respect to the constant value $\log|X|$. Let us stress, with particular regard to the fuzzy generalization discussed in the sequel, that since any $|A_i| \geq 1$ also the co–entropy is a non negative quantity whatever be the involved partition: formally, for every partition π, $E(\pi) \geq 0$. Moreover, also in this case we have the inequalities: $\forall \pi, 0 = E(\pi_d) \leq E(\pi) \leq E(\pi_t) = \log|X|$, with $E(\pi) = 0$ iff $\pi = \pi_d$ and $E(\pi) = \log|X|$ iff $\pi = \pi_t$.

It is possible to consider two (non–negative) discrete random variables generated by a partition π:

(G-RV). The *granularity random variable* $G(\pi) = (\log|A_1|, \log|A_2|, \ldots, \log|A_N|)$, each component of which $G(A_i) := \log|A_i|$ expresses the *measure of the granularity* supported by the *granule* A_i of the partition π.

(U-RV). The *uncertainty random variable* $I(\pi) = (-\log p(A_1), -\log p(A_2), \ldots, -p(A_N))$, each component of which $I(A_i) := -\log p(A_i)$ expresses (according to the general discussion of section 1) the *uncertainty measure* related to the probability of occurrence of the *event* A_i of the partition π.

The relationship between the uncertainty measure and the granularity measure of A_i is similar to the (5): $\forall A_i, G(A_i) + I(A_i) = \log|X|$, with $G(A_i)$ (resp., $I(A_i)$) increasing (resp., decreasing) mapping. With respect to the now introduced random variables, we have that $E(\pi) = \sum_{i=1}^{N} G(A_i) \cdot p(A_i)$, i.e., the co–entropy furnishes the *average granularity measure*, and $H(\pi) = \sum_{i=1}^{N} I(A_i) \cdot p(A_i)$, i.e., the entropy furnishes the *average uncertainty measure* related to π.

2.1   Partitions Induced from Information Systems

Let us recall that in the context of partitions of a concrete universe, as the support structure of the Pawlak approach to rough set theory, the above co–entropy has been introduced in [4]. In particular, these considerations can be applied to the case of a (complete) *Information System* (IS), formalized by a triple $IS := \langle X, Att, F \rangle$ consisting of a nonempty finite set X of objects, a nonempty finite set of attribute Att, and a mapping $F : X \times Att \rightarrow V$ which assigns to any object $x \in A$ the value $F(x, a)$ assumed by the attribute $a \in Att$ [5], [7], [3]. Indeed, in the IS case the partition of the universe of objects X generated by a set of attributes $\mathcal{A}$, denoted by $\pi_{\mathcal{A}}(IS)$, consists of the equivalence classes of objects which are *indistinguishable* with respect to the information furnished by the attributes in $\mathcal{A}$, formalized by the equivalence relation: $(x, y) \in R_{\mathcal{A}}$ iff $\forall a \in \mathcal{A}$, $F(x, a) = F(y, a)$.

Example 1. Consider the (complete) information system based on the finite universe $X = \{1, 2, 3, 4\}$ and finite set of attributes $Att = \{a_0, a_1, a_2\}$. The information system is given by the following *information table*:

$x \in X$	$f_{a_0}(x)$	$f_{a_1}(x)$	$f_{a_2}(x)$
1	A	G	S
2	A	R	S
3	T	G	M
4	T	G	L

The meaning of the attributes of this example could be the following: a_0 is the *shape* of the object (A as *arched* and T as *thin*), a_1 is the *color* (G as *green* and R as *red*), a_2 is the *dimension* (S as *small*, M as *medium* and L as *large*). We have the following partitions, one for each possible collection of attributes:

$$\pi(a_0) = \{\{1, 2\}, \{3, 4\}\}, \quad \pi(a_1) = \{\{1, 3, 4\}, \{2\}\},$$
$$\pi(a_2) = \{\{1, 2\}, \{3\}, \{4\}\} = \pi(a_0, a_2),$$
$$\pi(a_0, a_1) = \{\{1\}, \{2\}, \{3, 4\}\}, \quad \pi(a_1, a_2) = \{\{1\}, \{2\}, \{3\}, \{4\}\} = \pi(a_0, a_1, a_2)$$

2.2 Partition Entropy on a Finite Measure Space

Let us see now some generalizations of the partition entropy notion, making the following

Notational Convention: *From now on, if no confusion is likely, the counting measure m_c (resp., probability p_c) will be simply denoted by m (resp., p).*

This notational convention is very useful from the general point of view. Indeed, the treatment of the entropy partition performed in the previous section is formally based on the structure of the measure space $\langle X, \mathcal{E}_\pi(X), m_c \rangle$ in which the universe is constrained to the strong condition of being a *finite* set and the involved measure is the very particular counting measure assigning to any (finite) measurable subset $E \in \mathcal{E}_\pi(X)$ the corresponding cardinality $m_c(E) = |E|$.

This approach can be extended to the more general case of a measurable space with finite measure $\langle X, \mathcal{E}(X), m \rangle$ where X is a (non necessarily finite) universe, $\mathcal{E}(X)$ a fixed σ–algebra of its measurable subsets, and $m : \mathcal{E}(X) \mapsto \mathbb{R}_+$

a *finite* measure on $\mathcal{E}(X)$, i.e., such that $m(X) < \infty$. Note that this condition imply (for the standard monotonicity property of a generic measure) that for any $E \in \mathcal{E}(X)$, $m(E) \leq m(X) < \infty$. Indeed, all the results previously proved, and all the results which we shall prove in the sequel, are formulated in such a way that they hold in this general framework, instead of the very narrow situation of a finite universe with the counting measure. It is only necessary to consider the so–called *measurable partitions* of X, i.e., *finite* (or in general, with a slight modification about convergence, *countable*) families $\pi = \{E_1, E_2, \ldots, E_N\}$ of measurable subsets of X (for any i, $E_i \in \mathcal{E}(X)$) such that: (pp-1) $m(E_i) > 0$ (strictly positiveness); (pp-2) $m(E_i \cap E_j) = 0$ (measurable disjointness); (pp-3) $m(\cup_i E_i) = \sum_{i=1}^{N} m(E_i) = m(X)$ (normalization). Of course, any standard partition π of X is also a measure partition, i.e., we have an enrichment of the usual notion of partition.

Given a probability partition π, the corresponding vector $\boldsymbol{p}(\pi) = \left(\frac{m(E_1)}{m(X)}, \frac{m(E_2)}{m(X)}, \ldots, \frac{m(E_N)}{m(X)} \right)$ is a probability distribution. More generally, we have the probability space $\langle X, \mathcal{E}(X), p_m \rangle$, where $p_m(E) = \frac{m(E)}{m(X)}$ is a probability measure on the σ–algebra $\mathcal{E}(X)$ generated by the finite measure m.

As examples of this general situation, let us mention any Lebesgue measurable subset X of $\mathbb{R}^n$ of finite Lebesgue measure $\mu(X) < \infty$. For instance, a bounded interval of $\mathbb{R}$, a bounded rectangle and a circle of $\mathbb{R}^2$, a bounded parallelepiped or a sphere in $\mathbb{R}^3$, and so on.

Let us stress that also in the case of a *finite* universe the just defined notion of probability partition leads to an enrichment of the usual family of partitions.

Example 2. Let us consider a *biased die* modelled by a probability space $\langle X, \mathcal{A}(X), p \rangle$ with $X = \{1, 2, 3, 4, 5, 6\}$, $\mathcal{A}(X) = \mathcal{P}(X)$, and the probability function generated on $\mathcal{A}(X)$ by the probabilities defined for any elementary event $\{i\}$ of the involved universe X by the probability distribution $\boldsymbol{p} = (p(\{1\}) = 2/6, p(\{2\}) = 1/6, \ p(\{3\}) = 1/6, \ p(\{4\}) = 1/6, \ p(\{5\}) = 1/6, \ p(\{6\}) = 0)$. The probability of the generic subset (event) A of X is given by the rule: $p(A) = \sum_{i \in A} p(\{i\})$. We have in particular that $p(X) = \sum_{i \in X} p(\{i\}) = 1$. Then the families of events $\pi_1 = \{A_1 = \{1, 2, 6\}, \ A_2 = \{4, 6\}, \ A_3 = \{5, 6\}\}$ and $\pi_2 = \{B_1 = \{1, 2, 3\}, B_2 = \{4, 5\}\}$ are probability partitions which are not standard. The former π_1 is a covering of X and the latter π_2 is not a covering, but its two subsets are disjoint.

2.3   Partitions as Identity Resolutions by Crisp Sets (Sharp Granulations)

In this section we show that any partition can be identify with an "*identity resolution* by crisp sets. To be precise, given a partition $\pi = \{A_1, A_2, \ldots, A_N\})$, if one introduces the characteristic functional $\chi_{A_i} : X \longmapsto \{0, 1\}$ of any set A_i defined for any point $x \in X$ as $\chi_{A_i}(x) = 1$ if $x \in A_i$ and $= 0$ otherwise, then the collection of characteristic functionals $\mathcal{C}(\pi) := \{\chi_{A_1}, \chi_{A_2}, \ldots, \chi_{A_N}\}$ associated with the partition π is a *crisp (sharp) identity resolution,* i.e., a family of crisp sets such that the following property holds: $\forall x \in X, \quad \sum_{i=1}^{N} \chi_{A_i}(x) = 1$. Denoting by $\mathbf{1}$ the identity mapping assigning to any point $x \in X$ the value $\mathbf{1}(x) = 1$, we can also say that the family of crisp sets $\mathcal{C}(\pi)$ satisfies the *functional crisp identity resolution* condition:

$$\sum_{i=1}^{N} \chi_{A_i} = \mathbf{1} \tag{6}$$

Of course, partitions and identity resolutions can be identified by the one-to-one and onto correspondence

$$\pi = \{A_1, A_2, \ldots, A_N\} \longleftrightarrow \mathcal{C}(\pi) := \{\chi_{A_1}, \chi_{A_2}, \ldots, \chi_{A_N}\} \tag{7}$$

The condition (6) defines the identity resolution by crisp sets $\mathcal{C}(\pi) = \{\chi_{A_i} \in \{0,1\}^X : i = 1, 2, \ldots, N\}$ as a *crisp granulation* of the universe X, in which any crisp set χ_{A_i} is a *granule.* Then, the *counting measure* of the *elementary event* A_i by its *crisp granule* representation χ_{A_i} is given by

$$m(A_i) = \sum_{x \in X} \chi_{A_i}(x) = |A_i| \tag{8}$$

The probabilities associated to any event A_i can also be expressed as a probability of the corresponding crisp granule χ_{A_i} by the equation

$$p(A_i) = \frac{1}{m(X)} m(A_i) = \frac{1}{m(X)} \sum_{x \in X} \chi_{A_i}(x) \tag{9}$$

and the entropy (2) and co–entropy (4) generated by π are given now by

$$H(\pi) = \log m(X) - \frac{1}{m(X)} \sum_{i=1}^{N} m(A_i) \log m(A_i) \tag{10a}$$

$$E(\pi) = \frac{1}{m(X)} \sum_{i=1}^{N} m(A_i) \log m(A_i) \tag{10b}$$

with the standard result $\forall \pi, \quad H(\pi) + E(\pi) = \log m(X)$.

3   Fuzzy (Unsharp) Granulations

An immediate generalization of crisp identity resolution (as a finite collection of crisp sets $\mathcal{C} := \{\chi_i \in \{0,1\}^X : i = 1, 2, \ldots, N\}$ whose sum is, according to (6), the identity mapping $\sum_{i=1}^{N} \chi_i = \mathbf{1}$) is the notion of *fuzzy identity resolution* as a finite collection of fuzzy sets $\mathcal{F} := \{w_i \in [0,1]^X : i = 1, 2, \ldots, N\}$ such that the functional identity resolution condition $\sum_{i=1}^{N} w_i = \mathbf{1}$ holds. Generalizing the (8), the measure of a generic fuzzy set $w \in [0,1]^X$ of a *finite* universe X can be defined as follows

$$m(w) := \sum_{x \in X} w(x) \tag{11}$$

Definition 1. *A fuzzy (also* unsharp*) granulation of the universe X is defined as a collection of fuzzy sets $\mathcal{F} = \{\omega_i \in [0,1]^X : i = 1, 2, \ldots, N\}$, whose elements ω_i are said to be* fuzzy granules, *under the condition of* total measure $M(\mathcal{F}) := \sum_{i=1}^{N} m(\omega_i) = |X|$.

Thus, the condition of fuzzy granulation is dependent from the measure $m(\omega_i)$ of each *fuzzy granule* $\omega_i \in \mathcal{F}$ given by (11), provided its total measure is the cardinality of the universe. Let us stress that in practical applications some further regularity conditions are usually (hiddenly, in the sense of non explicitly formalized) involved. Let us quote two of them which in this paper are tacitly assumed.

Non–redundancy of the granulation, formally expressed by the fact that if in a fuzzy granulation $\mathcal{F}$ two fuzzy granules $\omega_i, \omega_j \in \mathcal{F}$ are such that $\omega_i \leq \omega_j$ (in the pointwise ordering, i.e., for every $x \in X$ one has $\omega_i(x) \leq \omega_j(x)$), then $\omega_i = \omega_j$.

Covering of the universe X, i.e., for any point $x \in X$ there must exists at least a fuzzy granule $\omega_i \in \mathcal{F}$ such that $\omega_i(x) \neq 0$.

Let us note that any fuzzy identity resolution, $\mathcal{F} = \{\omega_i \in \{0,1\}^X : i = 1, 2, \ldots, N\}$ is necessarily a fuzzy granulation since $\sum_{i=1}^{N} m(\omega_i) = \sum_{i=1}^{N} \sum_{x \in X} \omega_i(x) = \sum_{x \in X} \sum_{i=1}^{N} \omega_i(x) = |X|$. The vice versa in general is not true as the following example shows.

Example 3. In the finite universe $X = \{1, 2, 3, 4, 5\}$, let us consider the fuzzy granulation consisting of the two fuzzy sets ω_i, $i = 1, 2$, defined by the table

	1	2	3	4	5	$m(\omega_i)$
ω_1	1	1/2	1/2	1/2	0	5/2
ω_2	1/2	0	1/2	1	1/2	5/2

Then $m(\omega_1) = m(\omega_2) = 5/2$, from which $\sum_{i=1,2} m(\omega_i) = 5 = |X|$. But, for instance, $\omega_1(4) + \omega_2(4) = 3/2 \neq 1$.

Moreover, any fuzzy identity resolution is a covering fuzzy granulation, but in general there is no certainty about the non–redundancy condition.

Example 4. In the case of the universe $X = \{1, 2, 3\}$ the following fuzzy identity resolution of two fuzzy sets furnishes a fuzzy granulation of X which is redundant.

	1	2	3	$m(\omega_i)$
ω_1	1/2	1	1/2	2
ω_2	1/2	0	1/2	1

Indeed, $m(\omega_1) + m(\omega_2) = 3$, but $\omega_2(x) \leq \omega_1(x)$ whatever be x.

3.1 Entropy and (Possible Negative) Co–entropy for Fuzzy Granulation

In the case of a fuzzy granulation, for any of its fuzzy granule w_i it is possible to assign the non–negative number (and compare with (9)):

$$p(w_i) = \frac{1}{M(\mathcal{F})} m(w_i) = \frac{1}{M(\mathcal{F})} \sum_{x \in X} w_i(x) \tag{12}$$

whose collection $\boldsymbol{p}(\mathcal{F}) = (p(w_1), p(w_2), \ldots, p(w_N))$ is a *probability distribution* since trivially: (pd-1) for any i it is $p(w_i) \geq 0$ and (pd-2) $\sum_{i=1}^{N} p(w_i) = 1$. The *entropy* of the fuzzy granulation $\mathcal{F}$ is then the one generated by this probability distribution, which as usual is given by the real non–negative quantity

$$0 \leq H(\mathcal{F}) = -\sum_{i=1}^{N} p(w_i) \log p(w_i) \leq \log N \tag{13}$$

Trivially, by (12) and recalling that the total measure of the fuzzy covering $\mathcal{F}$ is $M(\mathcal{F}) = |X|$, one gets that

$$H(\mathcal{F}) = -\frac{1}{M(\mathcal{F})} \sum_{i=1}^{N} m(w_i) \log \frac{m(w_i)}{M(\mathcal{F})} \tag{14}$$

and so also in this case we can introduce the *co–entropy* of the fuzzy granulation $\mathcal{F}$ as the quantity

$$E(\mathcal{F}) = \frac{1}{M(\mathcal{F})} \sum_{i=1}^{N} m(w_i) \log m(w_i) \tag{15}$$

obtaining from (14) the following identity which is true whatever be the fuzzy granulation $\mathcal{F}$:

$$H(\mathcal{F}) + E(\mathcal{F}) = \log M(\mathcal{F}) = \log |X| \tag{16}$$

This identity is an extension to fuzzy granulations of the identity (5) previously seen in the case of partitions (crisp granulations). Also in this case the "co–entropy" $E(\mathcal{F})$ complements the original entropy $H(\mathcal{F})$ with respect to the constant quantity $\log |X|$, invariant relatively to the choice of the granulation $\mathcal{F}$. This co–entropy refers to the *measure distribution* $\boldsymbol{m}(\mathcal{F}) = \big(m(w_1), m(w_2), \ldots, m(w_N)\big)$ for which the following hold: (md-f1) every $m(w_i) \geq 0$; (md-f2) its *total measure* is $M(\mathcal{F}) := \sum_{i=1}^{N} m(w_i) = |X|$. Of course, the entropy of a fuzzy granulation, from (13), is always non–negative, but in the present fuzzy case notwithstanding the expected link expressed by (16), the co–entropy could be negative.

Example 5. In the universe $X = \{1, 2, 3\}$ let is consider the fuzzy granulation consisting of the fuzzy sets defined according to the following tabular representation:

	1	2	3	$m(\omega_i)$
ω_1	1/2	0	0	1/2
ω_2	1/2	1/3	0	5/6
ω_3	0	1/3	1	4/3
ω_4	0	1/3	0	1/3

Of course, this is a fuzzy identity resolution (and so also a fuzzy granulation) since trivially $\sum_{i=1}^{4} \omega_i(x) = 1$ for every point $x = 1, 2, 3$. But in this example the entropy is $H \cong 1.8163$, whereas the co–entropy is negative $E \cong -0.2314$ with $H + E \cong 1.5850 \cong \log 3$.

As shown by this example, the possible negativity of co–entropy (15) rises from the fact that some of the measures $m(\omega_i)$ could be number in the real unit interval $[0, 1]$ producing in this way a $\log m(\omega_i)$ term which is negative. In the case of a fuzzy granulation $\mathcal{F}$ it is possible to consider the two following discrete random variables:

(FG-RV). The *fuzzy granularity random variable* $G(\mathcal{F}) = (\log m(\omega_1), \log m(\omega_2), \ldots, \log m(\omega_N))$, each component of which $G(\omega_i) := \log m(\omega_i)$ expresses the *granularity measure* supported by the *fuzzy granule* ω_i of the fuzzy granulation $\mathcal{F}$. Note that some of these fuzzy granules could have negative measure, precisely under the condition $G(\omega_i) < 1$.

(FU-RV). The non–negative *fuzzy uncertainty random variable* $I(\mathcal{F}) = (-\log p(\omega_1), -\log p(\omega_2), \ldots, -p(\omega_N))$, each component of which $I(\omega_i) := -\log p(\omega_i) = \log M(\mathcal{F}) - \log m(\omega_i)$ expresses (according to the general discussion of section 1) the *uncertainty measure* related to the probability of occurrence of the *fuzzy event* ω_i of the fuzzy granulation $\mathcal{F}$.

The relationship between these uncertainty and granularity measures of ω_i is now (compare with the (16)): $\forall \omega_i,\ G(\omega_i) + I(\omega_i) = \log |X|$. With respect to the now introduced random variables, we have that $E(\mathcal{F}) = \sum_{i=1}^{N} G(\omega_i) \cdot p(\omega_i)$, i.e., it is the *average fuzzy granularity measure*, and $H(\mathcal{F}) = sum_{i=1}^{N} I(\omega_i) \cdot p(\omega_i)$, i.e., it is the *average fuzzy uncertainty measure* related to the fuzzy granulation.

3.2   A Normalized Non–negative Co–entropy for Fuzzy Granulation

In order to avoid the previously stressed negativity of co–entropy of a fuzzy granulation $\mathcal{F}$, due to the fact that the measure distribution $m(\mathcal{F}) = (m(\omega_1), m(\omega_2), \ldots, m(\omega_N))$ some of its components could be less that 1, it is possible to introduce the minimum measure $\hbar(\mathcal{F}) := \min\{m(\omega_1), m(\omega_2), \ldots, m(\omega_N)\}$, and then to construct the new fuzzy granulation $\mathcal{F}_\hbar = \mathcal{F}/\hbar := (\omega_1/\hbar(\mathcal{F}), \omega_2/\hbar(\mathcal{F}), \ldots, \omega_N/\hbar(\mathcal{F}))$, where the generic component is $\omega_i/\hbar(\mathcal{F}) \geq 1$. The measure distribution corresponding to the new fuzzy granulation $\mathcal{F}_\hbar$ is $m_\hbar(\mathcal{F}) =$

$(m(\omega_1)/\hbar(\mathcal{F}), m(\omega_2)/\hbar(\mathcal{F}), \ldots, m(\omega_N)/\hbar(\mathcal{F}))$, whose total measure is $M_\hbar(\mathcal{F}) = \sum_{i=1}^{N} m(\omega_i)/\hbar(\mathcal{F}) = |X|/\hbar(\mathcal{F})$, and with generic component denoted by $m_\hbar(\omega_i)$ $:= m(\omega_i)/\hbar(\mathcal{F})$. The probability distribution generated by the normalization of the new measure distribution $\boldsymbol{m}_\hbar(\mathcal{F})$ by its total measure $M_\hbar(\mathcal{F})$ is $\boldsymbol{p}_\hbar :=$ $\boldsymbol{m}_\hbar(\mathcal{F})/M_\hbar(\mathcal{F}) = \boldsymbol{m}(\mathcal{F})/|X| = \boldsymbol{p}$, i.e., the probability distribution does not change as to this change of the measure distribution. As a consequence of this result, also the entropy does not change: $H(\mathcal{F}_\hbar) = H(\mathcal{F})$. It is the co–entropy which strongly changes (compare with (15)):

$$E(\mathcal{F}_\hbar) = \frac{1}{M_\hbar(\mathcal{F})} \sum_{i=1}^{N} m_\hbar(\omega_i) \cdot \log m_\hbar(\omega_i) \qquad (17)$$

In particular $E(\mathcal{F}_\hbar) = E(\mathcal{F}) - \log \hbar(\mathcal{F})$, and so with respect to the new quantities we have that (and compare with (16)):

$$H_\hbar(\mathcal{F}) + E_\hbar(\mathcal{F}) = \log \frac{M(\mathcal{F})}{\hbar(\mathcal{F})} = \log \frac{|X|}{\hbar(\mathcal{F})} \qquad (18)$$

In particular, from $[H_\hbar(\mathcal{F}) + \log \hbar(\mathcal{F})] + E_\hbar(\mathcal{F}) = \log M(\mathcal{F})$, we can introduce a new entropy for fuzzy granulation, $H'_\hbar(\mathcal{F}) = H_\hbar(\mathcal{F}) + \log \hbar(\mathcal{F})$, for which trivially one has the expected "invariance" $H'_\hbar(\mathcal{F}) + E_\hbar(\mathcal{F}) = \log M(\mathcal{F}) = \log |X|$. Explicitly it turns out that this new entropy has the form (and compare with (14)):

$$H'_\hbar(\mathcal{F}) = -\frac{1}{M_\hbar(\mathcal{F})} \sum_{i=1}^{N} m_\hbar(\omega_i) \cdot \log \frac{m_\hbar(\omega_i)}{M_\hbar(\mathcal{F})} \frac{1}{\hbar(\mathcal{F})} \qquad (19)$$

4   Conclusions and Open Problems

The extension of the crisp granulation notion to the fuzzy case is investigated. In particular the two usual *measures* of average granulation (co–entropy) and average uncertainty (entropy) is deeply treated, eliminating a first drawback of possible negativity of the co–entropy.

As an open problem it remains to study the behavior of the fuzzy co–entropy and entropy with respect to the monotonicity.

References

1. Ash, R.B.: Information theory, Dover Publications, New York, 1990, (originally published by John Wiley & Sons, New York, 1965).
2. Hartley, R.V.L.: Transmission of information. The Bell System Technical Journal 7, 535–563 (1928)
3. Komorowski, J., Pawlak, Z., Polkowski, L., Skowron, A.: Rough sets: A tutorial, Rough Fuzzy Hybridization. In: Pal, S., Skowron, A. (eds.), pp. 3–98 Springer–Verlag, Singapore (1999)

4. Liang, J., Shi, Z.: The information entropy, rough entropy and knowledge granulation in rough set theory. International Journal of Uncertainty, Fuzziness and Knowledge-Based Systems 12, 37–46 (2004)
5. Pawlak, Z.: Information systems - theoretical foundations. Information Systems 6, 205–218 (1981)
6. Rough sets, Int. J. Inform. Comput. Sci. 11, 341–356 (1982)
7. Rough sets: Theoretical aspects of reasoning about data. Kluwer Academic Publishers, Dordrecht (1991)

Possibilistic Linear Programming in Blending and Transportation Planning Problem

Bilge Bilgen

Dokuz Eylul University, Department of Industrial Engineering, 35100, Izmir, Turkey
bilge.bilgen@deu.edu.tr

Abstract. This paper presents a possibilistic linear programming model for solving the blending and multi-mode, multi-period distribution planning problem with imprecise transportation, blending and storage costs. The solution procedure uses the strategy of simultaneously minimizing the most possible value of the imprecise total costs, maximizing the possibility of obtaining lower total costs, minimizing the risk of obtaining higher total costs. An illustration with a data set from a realistic situation is included to demonstrate the effectiveness of the proposed model.

1 Introduction

In real world distribution planning problems, input data or related parameters, such as market demand, capacity, and relevant operating costs, frequently are fuzzy owing to some information being incomplete or unobtainable. Therefore crisp data are inadequate to model real-life situations. Fuzzy set theory was proposed by Zadeh [23] and has been found extensive applications in various fields. Fuzzy mathematical programming (FMP) is one of the most popular decision making approach based on fuzzy set theory. Fuzzy sets theory has been implemented in mathematical programming since 1970 when Bellman and Zadeh [1] introduced the basic concepts of fuzzy goals, fuzzy constraints, and fuzzy decisions. A detailed discussion of the FMP procedures can be found in [11,17].

Zadeh [24] presented the theory of possibility, which is related to the theory of fuzzy sets by defining the concept of possibility distribution as a fuzzy restriction. After pioneering work of Zadeh [24], possibility theory has found gradual acceptance in the literature. Several research efforts have concentrated on possibilistic linear programming [2,3,5,6,9,10,12,15,22]. For an extensive theory oriented discussion of possibilistic programming, the interested reader is referred to several research works by [2,3,9,10,15]. Although there are many research works in the possibilistic linear programming (PLP), application oriented papers are relatively scarce. Only a few PLP approach of practical relevance have been made. Application oriented studies on PLP problems include [5,9,22].

The objective of the paper is to develop a possibilistic decision model to solve the blending and multi-mode, multi-period distribution planning problem in a

F. Masulli, S. Mitra, and G. Pasi (Eds.): WILF 2007, LNAI 4578, pp. 20–27, 2007.

wheat supply chain. The remainder of this work is organized as follows. Section 2 describes the problem, and formulates the original blending and multi-mode, multi-period distribution planning problem. Section 3 develops the PLP model for solving the problem. In Section 4, an illustration with a data set from a case company is included to demonstrate the effectiveness of the solution approach. Finally, we provide conclusions regarding the effectiveness of the possibilistic approach in Section 5.

2   Problem Definition

The supply chain network considered in the model consists of the multiple up-country storage sites, and a set of customers. The planning horizon ranges from 1 month to 3 months. Different transportation modes are used between the sites. Each storage site has limited out-loading capacity for each transportation mode. Products stored in the storage sites are then transported to the customers by rail and/or road transport. Destination sites also have limited in-loading capacity for each transportation mode. The following details are added: Possible transportation links are defined between the storage sites and the customers, including the transport modes. The transportation between the storage sites and the customers is done by haulage companies using different types of transportation modes. It is assumed that, customer's demand for a product and the shipment of that product must take place at the same period.

In real-life situation for a distribution planning problem, many input information related to the blending and distribution process are not known with certainty. Fuzzy and/or imprecise natures of the problem can not be described adequately by the conventional approach. Probability theory has long been studied to reflect the imprecise nature. But applying probability theory to some optimization problems may have a negative effect on the computational efficiency. Alternatively, PLP approach not only provides more computational efficiency, but also supports possibilistic decision environment [12,22,24]. Possibility distribution offers an effectual alternative for proceeding with inherent ambiguous phonemia in determining environmental coefficients and related parameters [12]. Therefore a possibilistic programming model is constructed to determine the optimum transportation amount between storage site and customer by transportation mode. Then, a possibilistic linear programming model is transformed into a crisp multi-objective programming model. Finally, Zimmermann's fuzzy programming method [25] is applied to obtain composite single objective. Related studies on the use of fuzzy programming method to solve the fuzzy transportation problems include [8,13,14,19,21]. In this study, blending, storage and transportation costs are represented by triangular possibility distributions. The parameters of a triangular possibility distribution are given as the optimistic, the most possible, and the pessimistic values, which were estimated by a decision maker.

3   Possibilistic Programming Model Development

The following notation is used.

Indices

j	set of original grains $\{j = 1, 2, \ldots, J\}$
i	set of blended grains $\{i = 1, 2, \ldots, I\}$
s	set of storage sites $\{s = 1, 2, \ldots, S\}$
m	set of transportation modes $\{m = RL, RD\}$
k	set of customers $\{k = 1, 2, \ldots, K\}$
t	set of time periods $\{t = 1, 2, \ldots, T\}$
P	set of original and blended products $\{I\} + \{J\}$

Parameters

The full set of parameters is as follows:

D_{ikt}	demand for grain i ($i \in \{I, J\}$), by customer k, during time period t,
Supply_{js}	the amount of original grain j supplied to storage site s,
LCap_{sm}	out loading capacity at storage site s, by using transportation m,
InCap_{km}	in loading capacity at customer k, by using transportation mode m,
ComCap_s	combined out loading capacity for storage site s,
ComCap_k	combined in loading capacity for customer k,
$\mathrm{MinBlnd}_{ij}$	minimum ratio of original grain j in blended grain i,
$\mathrm{MaxBlnd}_{ij}$	maximum ratio of original grain j in blended grain i,
BCap_s	maximum blending capacity at storage site s,
$\tilde{\mathrm{TC}}_{skm}$	freight cost for route from storage site s to customer k, by using transportation mode m,
$\tilde{\mathrm{HC}}_s$	unit storage cost at each storage site s,
$\tilde{\mathrm{BC}}_s$	unit blending cost at each storage site s.

Variables

z_{iskmt}	the amount of product i transported from storage site s to customer k by using transportation mode m during time period t, $i \in M$, $s \in S$, $k \in P$, $m \in M$, $t \in T$,
w_{ijst}	the amount of original grain j used to make blended grain i at storage site s during time period t, $i \in I$, $j \in J$, $s \in S$, $t \in T$,
b_{ist}	the amount of grain i blended at site s during time period t, $i \in I$, $s \in S$, $t \in T$,
I_{jst}	quantity of remaining stock of original grain j at storage site s at the end of period t, $j \in J$, $s \in S$, $t \in T$,
IB_{ist}	quantity of remaining stock of blended grain j at site s at the end of period t, $i \in I$, $s \in S$, $t \in T$.

The distribution system, formulated as a linear program, can be expressed as follows:

Minimize

$$\sum_{i,s,k,m,t} \tilde{\mathrm{TC}}_{skm} z_{iskmt} + \sum_{i,s,t} \tilde{\mathrm{BC}}_s b_{ist} + \sum_{j,s,t} \tilde{\mathrm{HC}}_s I_{jst} \tag{1}$$

subject to

$$I_{js0} = \mathrm{Supply}_{js} \qquad \forall j, s \tag{2}$$

$$\sum_j w_{ijst} = b_{ist} \qquad \forall i, j, s, t \tag{3}$$

$$\begin{aligned} w_{ijst} - \text{MaxBlnd}_{ij} b_{ist} \leq 0 \qquad \forall i, j, s, t \\ w_{ijst} - \text{MinBlnd}_{ij} b_{ist} \geq 0 \qquad \forall i, j, s, t \end{aligned} \tag{4}$$

$$\sum_i b_{ist} \leq \text{BCap}_s \qquad \forall s, t \tag{5}$$

$$\sum_{k,m} z_{jskmt} + \sum_{i \in I} w_{ijst} - I_{jst-1} + I_{jst} = 0 \qquad \forall j, s, t \tag{6}$$

$$\sum_{k,m} z_{iskmt} - b_{ist} - \text{IB}_{ist-1} + \text{IB}_{ist} = 0 \qquad \forall i, s, t \tag{7}$$

$$\sum_{i,k} z_{iskmt} \leq \text{OutCap}_{sm} \qquad \forall s, m, t \tag{8}$$

$$\sum_{i,s} z_{iskmt} \leq \text{InLoad}_{km} \qquad \forall k, m, t \tag{9}$$

$$\sum_{i,k,m} z_{iskmt} \leq \text{ComCap}_s \qquad \forall s, t \tag{10}$$

$$\sum_{i,s,m} z_{iskmt} \leq \text{ComCap}_k \qquad \forall k, t \tag{11}$$

$$\sum_{s,m} z_{iskmt} = D_{ikt} \qquad \forall i, k, t \tag{12}$$

In this model, the unit transportation cost, blending cost and storage cost are approximately known, and are represented by the triangular possibility distribution. The objective function (1) is to minimize the sum of the transportation, blending and storage costs. Constraints (2) assure that the initial amount of product j at storage site s is equal to the inventory for that product j at storage site s at the end of the time period zero. Constraint sets (3) and (4) are required to meet the blended product specifications. Constraints (5) ensure that the blending capacity at each site. Constraints (6) and (7) assure the availability of the original and blended products at each storage site, and during each time period, respectively. Constraints (8) assure that the out-loading capacity for storage site s and transportation mode m. Constraints (9) enforce the in-loading capacity at the customers. Constraints (10)-(11) embodied that the combined out-loading capacity for each storage site, and combined in-loading capacity for each customers, respectively. Finally demand constraints are imposed by equations (12).

4 Model the Imprecise Data with Triangular Possibility Distribution

There are many studies to tackle with the imprecise cost coefficients in the objective function in the literature. We refer the interested reader to several research papers for more information [4,12,15,16,18,20]. According to Lai and Hwang's [12] method, the imprecise objective function of our model in the previous section has a triangular possibility distribution. Geometrically, this imprecise objective is fully defined by three corner points $(c^m, 1)$, $(c^p, 0)$, $(c^o, 0)$. Consequently, solving the imprecise objectives requires minimizing c^m, c^p, c^o simultaneously. Using Lai and Hwang's approach [12], we substitute minimizing c^m, maximizing $(c^m - c^o)$, and minimizing $(c^p - c^m)$. That is, the approach used in this work involves minimizing the most possible value of the imprecise costs, c^m, maximizing the possibility of lower costs $(c^m - c^o)$, and minimizing the risk of obtaining higher cost $(c^p - c^m)$. The three replaced objective functions can be minimized by pushing the three prominent points towards left. In this way, our problem can be transformed into a multi-objective linear programming as follows:

$$\min z_1 = \sum_{j,s,k,m,t} T\tilde{C}^m_{skm} z_{jskmt} + \sum_{i,s,t} B\tilde{C}^m_s b_{ist} + \sum_{j,s,t} H\tilde{C}^m_s I_{jst} \tag{13}$$

$$\max z_2 = \sum_{j,s,k,m,t} T\tilde{C}^{m-o}_{skm} z_{jskmt} + \sum_{i,s,t} B\tilde{C}^{m-o}_s b_{ist} + \sum_{j,s,t} H\tilde{C}^{m-o}_s I_{jst} \tag{14}$$

$$\min z_3 = \sum_{j,s,k,m,t} T\tilde{C}^{p-m}_{skm} z_{jskmt} + \sum_{i,s,t} B\tilde{C}^{p-m}_s b_{ist} + \sum_{j,s,t} H\tilde{C}^{p-m}_s I_{jst} \tag{15}$$

In this study, we suggest Zimmermann's fuzzy programming method with normalization process [25]. Initially, the positive ideal solutions (PIS) and negative ideal solutions of the three objective functions should be obtained to construct the linear membership functions of the objectives [12].

For each objective function, the corresponding linear membership function is computed as:

$$\mu_{z_1} = \begin{cases} 1 \text{ if } z_1 < z_1^{PIS}, \\ \frac{z_1^{NIS} - z_1}{z_1^{NIS} - z_1^{PIS}} \text{ if } z_1^{PIS} < z_1 < z_1^{NIS}, \\ 0 \text{ if } z_1 > z_1^{NIS} \end{cases} \qquad \mu_{z_2} = \begin{cases} 1 \text{ if } z_2 > z_2^{PIS}, \\ \frac{z_2 - z_2^{NIS}}{z_2^{PIS} - z_2^{NIS}} \text{ if } z_2^{NIS} < z_2 < z_2^{PIS}, \\ 0 \text{ if } z_2 < z_2^{NIS} \end{cases}$$

$$\mu_{z_3} = \begin{cases} 1 \text{ if } z_3 < z_3^{PIS}, \\ \frac{z_3^{NIS} - z_3}{z_3^{NIS} - z_3^{PIS}} \text{ if } z_3^{PIS} < z_3 < z_3^{NIS}, \\ 0 \text{ if } z_3 > z_3^{NIS} \end{cases}$$

Finally, we solve Zimmermann's following equivalent single-objective linear programming model to obtain the overall satisfaction compromise solution [25].

$$\begin{aligned} \max \lambda \\ \text{s. t. } \lambda \le \mu_{z_i} \quad i = 1, 2, 3, \\ x \in X, \end{aligned} \tag{16}$$

where x represents the constraint sets (2)-(14).

5 Computational Experiments

An industrial case is presented to demonstrate the feasibility of applying possibilistic linear programming to real blending and transportation planning problem. The proposed blending and multi-mode, multi-distribution planning model described above were tested on a real life project of a company that exports wheat to the customers. The company has 3 grain types, 1 blended product, four storage sites, two customers, two transportation modes and three time periods.

The illustrated problem has been solved by ILOG OPL Studio Version 3.7 [7]. We made all test runs on a personal computer based on a 1.4 GHz Pentium IV processor equipped with 1 GB RAM. In our model, the decision maker must specify an appropriate set of PIS and NIS of the objective function for making transportation planning decisions to set the right linear membership function for each objective function. For specifying the appropriate set of PIS and NIS values, it is useful to consult the computational result of crisp linear programming problem. The summary results, including positive and negative ideal solutions, as well as the compromise solutions of z_i and resulting overall satisfaction level, are displayed in Table 1.

Table 1. Results of the objective function

	PIS	NIS
z_1	640 000	1 240 000
z_2	290 000	100 000
z_3	135 000	235 000
$\lambda = 0.7860$		
$z_1^* = 768368,\ z_{m-o} = z_2^* = 247211,\ z_{p-m} = z_3^* = 156395$		
$z = (768368, 521157, 924763)$		

Total cost is imprecise and has a triangular possibility distribution of $\tilde{z} = (z_1^*, z_1^* - z_2^*, z_1^* + z_3^*)$.

6 Conclusion

This paper proposed a possibilistic decision model for the blending and multi-mode, multi-period distribution planning problem. The proposed model attempts to minimize total costs with reference to supply, blending, capacity and demand restrictions. We provide an auxiliary multiple objective linear programming problem with three objectives to solve a linear programming problem with imprecise cost coefficients. These objectives are: minimize the most possible value of the imprecise total costs, maximize the possibility of obtaining lower total costs, and minimize the risk of obtaining higher total costs. The effectiveness of the possibilistic model is demonstrated through an illustrative example on the data set adapted from a case company.

References

1. Bellman, R.E., Zadeh, L.A.: Decision making in a fuzzy environment. Management Science 17, 141–164 (1970)
2. Buckley, J.J.: Possibilistic programming with triangular fuzzy numbers. Fuzzy Sets and Systems 26, 135–138 (1988)
3. Buckley, J.J.: Solving possibilistic linear programming problems. Fuzzy Sets. and Systems 31, 329–341 (1989)
4. Delgado, M., Verdegay, J.L., Vila, M.A.: Imprecise costs in mathematical programming problems. Control and Cybernetics 16, 113–121 (1987)
5. Hsu, H.-M., Wang, W.-P.: Possibilistic programming in production planning of assembly-to-order environments. Fuzzy Sets. and Systems 119, 59–70 (2001)
6. Hussein, M.L., Wang, W.P.: Complete solutions of multiple objective transportation problems with possibilistic coefficients. Fuzzy Sets and Systems 93, 293–299 (1998)
7. ILOG OPL Studio 3.7.: Language Manual. Gentilly, France: ILOG SA (2003)
8. Jimenez, F., Verdegay, J.L.: Solving fuzzy solid transportation problems by an evolutionary algorithm based parametric approach. European Journal of Operational Research 117, 485–510 (1999)
9. Inuiguchi, M., Ramik, J.: Possibilistic linear programming: a brief review of fuzzy mathematical programming and a comparison with stochastic programming in portfolio selection problem. Fuzzy Sets and Systems 111, 3–28 (2000)
10. Julien, B.: An extension to possibilistic linear programming. Fuzzy Sets and Systems 64, 195–206 (1994)
11. Lai, Y.J., Hwang, C.L.: Fuzzy mathematical programming-methods and applications. Lecture Notes in Economics and Mathematical Systems 394 (1992)
12. Lai, Y.J., Hwang, C.L.: A new approach to some possibilistic linear programming problems. Fuzzy Sets and Systems 49, 121–133 (1992)
13. Liang, T.F.: Distribution planning decisions using interactive fuzzy multi-objective linear programming. Fuzzy Sets and Systems 157, 1303–1316 (2006)
14. Liu, S-T., Kao, C.: Solving fuzzy transportation problems based on extension principle. European Journal of Operational Research 153, 661–674 (2004)
15. Luhandjula, M.K.: Multiple objective programming with possibilistic coefficients. Fuzzy Sets and Systems 21, 135–146 (1987)
16. Rommelganger, H., Hanuscheck, R., Wolf, J.: Linear programming with fuzzy objectives. Fuzzy Sets and Systems 29, 31–48 (1989)
17. Rommelganger, H.: Fuzzy linear programming and applications. European Journal of Opertaional Research 92, 512–527 (1996)
18. Sakawa, M., Yano, H.: Interactive fuzzy satisfying method for multiobjective nonlinear programming problems with fuzzy parameters. Fuzzy Sets and Systems 30, 221–238 (1989)
19. Shih, L.H.: Cement transportation planning via fuzzy linear programming. International Journal of Production Economics 58, 277–287 (1999)
20. Tanaka, H., Ichihashi, H., Asai, K.: A formulation of fuzzy linear programming problem based on comparison of fuzzy numbers. Control and Cybernetics 13, 185–194 (1984)
21. Tzeng, G.H., Teodorovic, D., Hwang, M.J.: Fuzzy bicriteria multi-index transportation problems for coal allocation planning of Taipower. European Journal of Operational Research 95, 62–72 (1996)

22. Wang, R.C., Liang, T.-F.: Applying possibilistic linear programming to aggregate production planning. International Journal of Production Economics 98, 328–341 (2005)
23. Zadeh, L.A.: Fuzzy sets. Information and Control 8, 338–353 (1965)
24. Zadeh, L.A.: Fuzzy sets as a basis for a theory of possibility. Fuzzy Sets and Systems 1, 3–28 (1978)
25. Zimmermann, H.-J.: Fuzzy programming and linear programming with several objective functions. Fuzzy Sets and Systems 1, 45–55 (1978)
26. Bilgen, B.: Modelling of a blending and marine transportation planning problem with fuzzy mixed-integer programming. International journal of advanced manufacturing Technology (DOI: 10.1007/s00170-006-0919-2)

Measuring the Interpretive Cost
in Fuzzy Logic Computations[*]

Pascual Julián[1], Ginés Moreno[2], and Jaime Penabad[3,**]

[1] Dep. Information Technologies and Systems, UCLM, 13071 Ciudad Real, Spain
[2] Dep. Computing Systems, UCLM, 02071 Albacete, Spain
[3] Dep. Mathematics, UCLM, 02071 Albacete, Spain
Tel: +34 967 599200, Fax: +34 967599224
{Pascual.Julian, Gines.Moreno, Jaime.Penabad}@uclm.es

Abstract. Multi-adjoint logic programming represents an extremely flexible attempt for introducing fuzzy logic into logic programming (LP). In this setting, the execution of a goal w.r.t. a given program is done in two separate phases. During the operational one, *admissible steps* are systematically applied in a similar way to classical resolution steps in pure LP, thus returning an expression where all atoms have been exploited. This last expression is then interpreted under a given lattice during the so called interpretive phase. In declarative programming, it is usual to estimate the computational effort needed to execute a goal by simply counting the number of steps required to reach their solutions. In this paper, we show that although this method seems to be acceptable during the operational phase, it becomes inappropriate when considering the interpretive one. Moreover, we propose a more refined (interpretive) cost measure which fairly models in a much more realistic way the computational (special interpretive) a given goal.

Keywords: Cost Measures, Fuzzy Logic Programming, Reductants.

1 Introduction

Logic Programming [9] has been widely used for problem solving and knowledge representation in the past. Nevertheless, traditional LP languages do not incorporate techniques or constructs to treat explicitly with uncertainty and approximated reasoning. On the other hand, *Fuzzy Logic Programming* is an interesting and still growing research area that agglutinates the efforts to introduce fuzzy logic into LP. During the last decades, several fuzzy logic programming systems have been developed [1,2,3,8,12], where the classical inference mechanism of SLD–Resolution is replaced with a fuzzy variant which is able to handle partial truth and to reason with uncertainty. This is the case of *Multi-adjoint*

---

[*] This work has been partially supported by the EU, under FEDER, and the Spanish Science and Education Ministry (MEC) under grant TIN 2004-07943-C04-03.
[**] Corresponding author.

F. Masulli, S. Mitra, and G. Pasi (Eds.): WILF 2007, LNAI 4578, pp. 28–36, 2007.

logic programming [11,10]. Informally speaking, a multi–adjoint logic program can be seen as a set of rules each one annotated by a truth degree and a goal is a query to the system plus a substitution (initially the empty substitution, denoted by *id*). Given a multi–adjoint logic program, goals are evaluated in two separate computational phases. During the *operational* one, *admissible steps* (a generalization of the classical *modus ponens* inference rule) are systematically applied by a backward reasoning procedure in a similar way to classical resolution steps in pure logic programming, thus returning a computed substitution together with an expression where all atoms have been exploited. This last expression is then interpreted under a given lattice during what we call the *interpretive* phase, hence returning a pair ⟨*truth degree*; *substitution*⟩ which is the fuzzy counterpart of the classical notion of computed answer used in pure logic LP.

The most common approach to analyzing the efficiency of a program is measurement of its execution time and memory usage. However, in order to (theoretically) analyze the efficiency of programs, computing strategies or program transformation techniques, it is convenient to define abstract approaches to cost measurement. In a declarative programming framework, it is usual to estimate the computational effort needed to execute a goal in a program by simply counting the number of derivation steps required to reach their solutions. In the context of multi-adjoint logic programming, we show that although this method seems to be acceptable during the operational phase, it becomes inappropriate when considering the interpretive one. Therefore, in this paper, we define a more refined (interpretive) cost measure based on counting the number of connectives and primitive operators appearing in the definition of the aggregators which are evaluated in each (interpretive) step of a given derivation. Also, as an application of these cost criteria, we compare the efficiency of two semantically equivalent notions of reductant (the original one introduced in [11] and a refined version, that we call $PE-$reductant, formally introduced in [7]).

2   Procedural Semantics of Multi-adjoint Logic Programs

This section summarizes the main features of multi-adjoint logic programming[1]. We work with a first order language, $\mathcal{L}$, containing variables, constants, function symbols, predicate symbols, and several (arbitrary) connectives to increase language expressiveness: implication connectives ($\leftarrow_1, \leftarrow_2, \ldots$); conjunctive operators (denoted by $\&_1, \&_2, \ldots$), disjunctive operators ($\vee_1, \vee_2, \ldots$), and hybrid operators (usually denoted by $@_1, @_2, \ldots$), all of them are grouped under the name of "aggregators". Although these connectives are binary operators, we usually generalize them as functions with an arbitrary number of arguments. So, we often write $@(x_1, \ldots, x_n)$ instead of $@(x_1, \ldots, @(x_{n-1}, x_n), \ldots)$. By definition, the truth function for an n-ary aggregation operator $[\![@]\!] : L^n \to L$ is required to be monotonous and fulfills $[\![@]\!](\top, \ldots, \top) = \top$, $[\![@]\!](\bot, \ldots, \bot) = \bot$.

---

[1] We send the interested reader to [11] for a complete formulation of this framework.

Additionally, our language $\mathcal{L}$ contains the values of a multi-adjoint lattice[2], $\langle L, \preceq, \leftarrow_1, \&_1, \ldots, \leftarrow_n, \&_n \rangle$, equipped with a collection of adjoint pairs $\langle \leftarrow_i, \&_i \rangle$, where each $\&_i$ is a conjunctor which is intended to the evaluation of *modus ponens* [11]. A *rule* is a formula $H \leftarrow_i \mathcal{B}$, where H is an atomic formula (usually called the *head*) and $\mathcal{B}$ (which is called the *body*) is a formula built from atomic formulas $B_1, \ldots, B_n - n \geq 0$ —, truth values of L, conjunctions, disjunctions and aggregations. A *goal* is a body submitted as a query to the system. Roughly speaking, a multi-adjoint logic program is a set of pairs $\langle \mathcal{R}; \alpha \rangle$ (we often write $\mathcal{R}$ *with* α), where $\mathcal{R}$ is a rule and α is a *truth degree* (a value of L) expressing the confidence of a programmer in the truth of the rule $\mathcal{R}$. By abuse of language, we sometimes refer a tuple $\langle \mathcal{R}; \alpha \rangle$ as a "rule".

In the following, $\mathcal{C}[A]$ denotes a formula where A is a sub-expression which occurs in the –possibly empty– context $\mathcal{C}[]$. Moreover, $\mathcal{C}[A/A']$ means the replacement of A by A' in context $\mathcal{C}[]$, whereas $\mathcal{V}ar(s)$ refers to the set of distinct variables occurring in the syntactic object s, and $\theta[\mathcal{V}ar(s)]$ denotes the substitution obtained from θ by restricting its domain to $\mathcal{V}ar(s)$.

The procedural semantics of the multi–adjoint logic language $\mathcal{L}$ can be thought as an operational phase followed by an interpretive one [6].

Definition 1 (Admissible Steps). *Let $\mathcal{Q}$ be a goal and let σ be a substitution. The pair $\langle \mathcal{Q}; \sigma \rangle$ is a state and we denote by $\mathcal{E}$ the set of states. Given a program $\mathcal{P}$, an admissible computation is formalized as a state transition system, whose transition relation $\rightarrow_{AS} \subseteq (\mathcal{E} \times \mathcal{E})$ is the smallest relation satisfying the following admissible rules (where we always consider that A is the selected atom in $\mathcal{Q}$):*

1) $\langle \mathcal{Q}[A]; \sigma \rangle \rightarrow_{AS} \langle (\mathcal{Q}[A/v \&_i \mathcal{B}])\theta; \sigma\theta \rangle$ *if $\theta = mgu(\{A' = A\})$, $\langle A' \leftarrow_i \mathcal{B}; v \rangle$ in $\mathcal{P}$ and $\mathcal{B}$ is not empty.*

2) $\langle \mathcal{Q}[A]; \sigma \rangle \rightarrow_{AS} \langle (\mathcal{Q}[A/v])\theta; \sigma\theta \rangle$ *if $\theta = mgu(\{A' = A\})$, and $\langle A' \leftarrow_i; v \rangle$ in $\mathcal{P}$.*

3) $\langle \mathcal{Q}[A]; \sigma \rangle \rightarrow_{AS} \langle (\mathcal{Q}[A/\bot]); \sigma \rangle$ *if there is no rule in $\mathcal{P}$ whose head unifies to A.*

were $mgu(E)$ denotes the most general unifier *of an equation set E.*

Note that 3th case is introduced to cope with (possible) unsuccessful admissible derivations. As usual, rules are taken renamed apart. We shall use the symbols $\rightarrow_{AS1}, \rightarrow_{AS2}$ and $\rightarrow_{AS3}$ to distinguish between computation steps performed by applying one of the specific admissible rules. Also, the application of a rule on a step will be annotated as a superscript of the $\rightarrow_{AS}$ symbol.

Definition 2. *Let $\mathcal{P}$ be a program and let $\mathcal{Q}$ be a goal. An admissible derivation is a sequence $\langle \mathcal{Q}; id \rangle \rightarrow_{AS}^* \langle \mathcal{Q}'; \theta \rangle$. When $\mathcal{Q}'$ is a formula not containing atoms, the pair $\langle \mathcal{Q}'; \sigma \rangle$, where $\sigma = \theta[\mathcal{V}ar(\mathcal{Q})]$, is called an admissible computed answer (a.c.a.) for that derivation.*

Example 1. Let $\mathcal{P}$ be the following program and let $([0, 1], \preceq)$ be the lattice where $\leq$ is the usual order on real numbers.

$$\mathcal{R}_1 : p(X, Y) \leftarrow_\mathsf{P} @_1(\&_\mathsf{L}(q(X), r(X)), \vee_\mathsf{G}(s(Y), t(Y))) \quad \text{with } 0.9$$

---

[2] In general, the set of truth values L may be the carrier of any complete bounded lattice but, for readability reasons, in the examples we shall select L as the set of real numbers in the interval $[0, 1]$ (which is a totally ordered lattice or chain).

$$\mathcal{R}_2 : q(a) \leftarrow \quad \text{with} \quad 0.8 \qquad \mathcal{R}_3 : r(X) \leftarrow \quad \text{with} \quad 0.7$$
$$\mathcal{R}_4 : s(b) \leftarrow \quad \text{with} \quad 0.9 \qquad \mathcal{R}_5 : t(Y) \leftarrow \quad \text{with} \quad 0.6$$

where $[\![@_1]\!](x,y) = (x+y)/2$ (average aggregator) and the labels L, G and P mean respectively for *Łukasiewicz logic*, *Gödel intuitionistic logic* and *product logic*, that is, $[\![\&_L]\!](x,y) = max\{0, x+y-1\}$, $[\![\vee_G]\!](x,y) = max\{x,y\}$ and $[\![\&_P]\!](x,y) = x \cdot y$. Now, we can generate the following admissible derivation (we underline the selected expression in each admissible step):

$\langle \underline{p(X,Y)};\ id \rangle$ $\qquad\qquad \rightarrow_{AS1}{}^{\mathcal{R}_1}$
$\langle \&_P(0.9, @_1(\&_L(\underline{q(X_1)}, r(X_1)), \vee_G(s(Y_1), t(Y_1)))); \{X/X_1, Y/Y_1\}\rangle$ $\qquad \rightarrow_{AS2}{}^{\mathcal{R}_2}$
$\langle \&_P(0.9, @_1(\&_L(0.8, \underline{r(a)}), \vee_G(s(Y_1), t(Y_1)))); \{X/a, Y/Y_1, X_1/a\}\rangle$ $\qquad \rightarrow_{AS2}{}^{\mathcal{R}_3}$
$\langle \&_P(0.9, @_1(\&_L(0.8, \overline{0.7}), \vee_G(\underline{s(Y_1)}, t(Y_1)))); \{X/a, Y/Y_1, X_1/a, X_2/a\}\rangle$ $\ \rightarrow_{AS2}{}^{\mathcal{R}_4}$
$\langle \&_P(0.9, @_1(\&_L(0.8, 0.7), \vee_G(\overline{0.9}, \underline{t(b)}))); \{X/a, Y/b, X_1/a, X_2/a, Y_1/b\}\rangle$ $\rightarrow_{AS2}{}^{\mathcal{R}_5}$
$\langle \&_P(0.9, @_1(\&_L(0.8, 0.7), \vee_G(0.9, 0.6)); \{X/a, Y/b, X_1/a, X_2/a, Y_1/b, Y_2/b\}\rangle$
Here, the a.c.a. is the pair: $\langle \&_P(0.9, @_1(\&_L(0.8, 0.7), \vee_G(0.9, 0.6)); \theta\rangle$, where $\theta = \{X/a, Y/b, X_1/a, X_2/a, Y_1/b, Y_2/b\}[Var(\mathcal{Q})] = \{X/a, Y/b\}$.

If we exploit all atoms of a goal, by applying admissible steps as much as needed during the operational phase, then it becomes a formula with no atoms which can be then directly interpreted in the multi–adjoint lattice L as follows.

Definition 3 (Interpretive Step). *Let $\mathcal{P}$ be a program, $\mathcal{Q}$ a goal and σ a substitution. We formalize the notion of interpretive computation as a state transition system, whose transition relation $\rightarrow_{IS} \subseteq (\mathcal{E} \times \mathcal{E})$ is defined as the least one satisfying: $\langle Q[@(r_1, r_2)]; \sigma\rangle \rightarrow_{IS} \langle Q[@(r_1, r_2)/[\![@]\!](r_1, r_2)]; \sigma\rangle$, where $[\![@]\!]$ is the truth function of connective @ in the lattice $\langle L, \preceq \rangle$ associated to $\mathcal{P}$.*

Definition 4. *Let $\mathcal{P}$ be a program and $\langle Q; \sigma\rangle$ an a.c.a., that is, $\mathcal{Q}$ is a goal not containing atoms. An interpretive derivation is a sequence $\langle Q; \sigma\rangle \rightarrow_{IS}^* \langle Q'; \sigma\rangle$. When $Q' = r \in L$, being $\langle L, \preceq\rangle$ the lattice associated to $\mathcal{P}$, the state $\langle r; \sigma\rangle$ is called a fuzzy computed answer (f.c.a.) for that derivation.*

Example 2. If we complete the previous derivation of Example 1 by executing the necessary interpretive in order to obtain the final fuzzy computed answer $\langle 0.63; \{X/a, Y/b\}\rangle$, we generate the following interpretive derivation $\mathcal{D}_1$:
$\langle \&_P(0.9, @_1(\underline{\&_L(0.8, 0.7)}, \vee_G(0.9, 0.6)); \theta \rangle \rightarrow_{IS} \langle \&_P(0.9, @_1(0.5, \underline{\vee_G(0.9, 0.6)}); \theta\rangle$
$\rightarrow_{IS} \langle \&_P(0.9, \underline{@_1(0.5, 0.9)}); \theta\rangle \rightarrow_{IS} \langle \underline{\&_P(0.9, 0.7)}; \theta\rangle \rightarrow_{IS} \langle 0.63; \theta\rangle$

3   Computational Cost Measures

A classical, simple way for estimating the computational cost required to built a derivation, consists in counting the number of computational steps performed on it. So, given a derivation D, we define its:

- *operational cost*, $\mathcal{O}_c(D)$, as the number of admissible steps performed in D.
- *interpretive cost*, $\mathcal{I}_c(D)$, as the number of interpretive steps done in D.

So, the operational and interpretive costs of derivation D_1 performed in the previous section are $\mathcal{O}_c(D_1) = 5$ and $\mathcal{I}_c(D_1) = 4$, respectively. Intuitively, $\mathcal{O}_c$ informs us about the number of atoms exploited along a derivation. Similarly, $\mathcal{I}_c$ estimates the number of aggregators evaluated in a derivation. However, this last statement is not completely true: $\mathcal{I}_c$ only takes into account those aggregators appearing in the bodies of program rules, but no those recursively *nested* in the definition of other aggregators. The following example highlights this fact.

Example 3. A simplified version of rule $\mathcal{R}_1$, whose body only contains an aggregator symbol is $\mathcal{R}_1^* : p(X, Y) \leftarrow_P @_1^*(q(X), r(X), s(Y), t(Y))$ with 0.9, where $[\![@_1^*]\!](x, y, z, w) = ([\![\&_L]\!](x, y) + [\![\vee_G]\!](z, w))/2$. Note that $\mathcal{R}_1^*$ has exactly the same meaning (interpretation) that $\mathcal{R}_1$, although different syntax. In fact, both of them have the same sequence of atoms in their head and bodies. The differences are regarding the set of aggregators which explicitly appear in their bodies since in $\mathcal{R}_1^*$ we have moved $\&_L$ and $\vee_G$ from the body (see $\mathcal{R}_1$) to the definition of $@_1^*$. Now, we use rule $\mathcal{R}_1^*$ instead of $\mathcal{R}_1$ for generating the following derivation D_1^* which returns exactly the same f.c.a that D_1:

$$
\begin{array}{ll}
\langle p(X, Y);\ id \rangle & \rightarrow_{AS1}{}^{\mathcal{R}_1^*} \\
\langle \&_P(0.9, @_1^*(q(X_1), r(X_1), s(Y_1), t(Y_1)); \{X/X_1, Y/Y_1\} \rangle & \rightarrow_{AS2}{}^{\mathcal{R}_2} \\
\langle \&_P(0.9, @_1^*(0.8, \overline{r(a)}, s(Y_1), t(Y_1)); \{X/a, Y/Y_1, X_1/a\} \rangle & \rightarrow_{AS2}{}^{\mathcal{R}_3} \\
\langle \&_P(0.9, @_1^*(0.8, \overline{0.7}, \underline{s(Y_1)}, t(Y_1)); \{X/a, Y/Y_1, X_1/a, X_2/a\} \rangle & \rightarrow_{AS2}{}^{\mathcal{R}_4} \\
\langle \&_P(0.9, @_1^*(0.8, 0.7, \overline{0.9}, \underline{t(b)}); \{X/a, Y/b, X_1/a, X_2/a, Y_1/b\} \rangle & \rightarrow_{AS2}{}^{\mathcal{R}_5} \\
\langle \&_P(0.9, @_1^*(0.8, 0.7, 0.9, \overline{0.6}); \{X/a, Y/b, X_1/a, X_2/a, Y_1/b, Y_2/b\} \rangle & \rightarrow_{IS} \\
\langle \&_P(0.9, \overline{0.7}); \{X/a, Y/b, X_1/a, X_2/a, Y_1/b, Y_2/b\} \rangle & \rightarrow_{IS} \\
\langle 0.63; \{X/a, Y/b, X_1/a, X_2/a, Y_1/b, Y_2/b\} \rangle &
\end{array}
$$

Note that, since we have exploited the same atoms with the same rules (except for the first steps performed with rules $\mathcal{R}_1$ and $\mathcal{R}_1^*$) in both derivations, then $\mathcal{O}_c(D_1) = \mathcal{O}_c(D_1^*) = 5$. However, although aggregators $\&_L$ and $\vee_G$ have been evaluated in both derivations, in D_1^* such evaluations have not been explicitly counted as interpretive steps, and consequently they have not been added to increase the interpretive cost measure $\mathcal{I}_c$. This unrealistic situation is reflected by the abnormal result: $\mathcal{I}_c(D_1) = 4 > 2 = \mathcal{I}_c(D_1^*)$. It is important to note that $\mathcal{R}_1^*$ can not be considered an optimized version of $\mathcal{R}_1$: both rules have a similar computational behaviour, even when the wrong measure $\mathcal{I}_c$ seems to indicate the contrary.

In order to solve this problem, we redefine $\mathcal{I}_c$ in terms of the connective and *primitive operators*[3] appearing in the definition of the aggregators which are evaluated in each admissible step of a given derivation. So, let $@$ be an n-ary aggregator, defined as $[\![@]\!](x_1, \dots, x_n) = E$ where the (possibly empties) sequences of primitive operators and aggregators (including conjunctors and disjunctors) appearing in E are respectively $op_1, \dots, op_r$ and $@_1, \dots, @_s$. The weight of aggregator $@$ is recursively defined as $\mathcal{W}(@) = r + \mathcal{W}(@_1) + \cdots + \mathcal{W}(@_s)$. Now, our

---

[3] That is, arithmetic operators such as $+, -, *, /, max, min, root, \dots$

improved notion of *interpretive cost*, denoted $\mathcal{I}_c^+(D)$, is the sum of the weights of the aggregators evaluated in every interpretive step of derivation D.

Example 4. Looking at the definitions given before for aggregators $\&_P, \vee_G, \&_L, @_1$ and $@_1^*$, it is easy to see that: $\mathcal{W}(\&_P) = 1, \mathcal{W}(\&_L) = 3, \mathcal{W}(\vee_G) = 1, \mathcal{W}(@_1) = 2$ and $\mathcal{W}(@_1^*) = 2 + \mathcal{W}(\&_L) + \mathcal{W}(\vee_G) = 2 + 3 + 1 = 6$. Consequently, we have that $\mathcal{I}_c^+(D_1) = \mathcal{W}(\&_L) + \mathcal{W}(\vee_G) + \mathcal{W}(@_1) + \mathcal{W}(\&_P) = 3 + 1 + 2 + 1 = 7$, and $\mathcal{I}_c^+(D_1^*) = \mathcal{W}(@_1^*) + \mathcal{W}(\&_P) = 6 + 1 = 7$. Now, both the operational and interpretive cost of derivations D_1 and D_1^* do coincide, which is quite natural and realistic if we have into account that rules $\mathcal{R}_1$ and $\mathcal{R}_1^*$ have the same semantics and, consequently they must also have the same computational behaviour.

The previous example shows us that the way in which aggregators are introduced in the body or in the definition of other aggregators of a program rule, might only reflect syntactic preferences, without negative repercussions on computational costs, as our improved definition of the interpretive cost reflects.

4   Reductants and Cost Measures

Reductancts were introduced in the context of multi-adjoint logic programming to cope with a problem of incompleteness that arises for some lattices. It might be impossible to operationally compute the greatest correct answer (the supremum of the set of correct answers), if a lattice $(L, \preceq)$ is partially ordered [11]. This problem can be solved by extending the original program with the set of all its reductants. The classical notion of reductant was initially adapted to the multi-adjoint logic programming framework in the following terms:

Definition 5 (Reductant [11]). *Let $\mathcal{P}$ be a program, A a ground atom, and $\{\langle C_i \leftarrow_i \mathcal{B}_i; v_i \rangle\}$ be the set of rules in $\mathcal{P}$ whose head matches[4] with A. A reductant for A in $\mathcal{P}$ is a rule $\langle A \leftarrow @(\mathcal{B}_1, \dots, \mathcal{B}_n)\theta; \top \rangle$ where $\theta = \theta_1 \cdots \theta_n$, $\leftarrow$ is any implication with an adjoint conjunctor, and the truth function for the intended aggregator $@$ is defined as $[\![@]\!](b_1, \dots, b_n) = sup\{[\![\&]\!]_1(v_1, b_1), \dots, [\![\&]\!]_n(v_n, b_n)\}$.*

Obviously, the extension of a multi-adjoint logic program with all its reductants increases both the size and execution time of the final *"completed"* program. In [7] we defined a refinement to the notion of reductant based on partial evaluation techniques [4], that we call $PE-reductant$. The new concept of $PE-$reductant is aiming at the reduction of the aforementioned negative effects. Since $PE-$reductants are partially evaluated before being introduced in the target program, the computational effort done (once) at generation time is saved (many times) at execution time. Intuitively, given a program $\mathcal{P}$ and a ground atomic goal A, a $PE-$reductant can be constructed following these steps: i) Construct an *unfolding tree[5]*, τ, for $\mathcal{P}$

---

[4] That is, there exists a θ_i such that $A = C_i \theta_i$.

[5] An *unfolding tree* is a possible incomplete search tree. That is, a search tree, of the atom A in the program $\mathcal{P}$, built using a breath-first search strategy where some nodes may be let unexpanded (See [7] for a formal definition of this concept, that we omit by the lack of space).

and A. ii) Collect the set of leaves $S = \{\mathcal{D}_1, \ldots, \mathcal{D}_n\}$ in τ. iii) Construct the rule $\langle A \leftarrow @_{sup}\{\mathcal{D}_1, \ldots, \mathcal{D}_n\}; \top\rangle$, which is the PE−reductant of A in $\mathcal{P}$ with regard to τ. Formally:

Definition 6 (*PE*−**Reductant [7]**). *Let $\mathcal{P}$ be a program, A a ground atom, and τ an unfolding tree for A in P. A PE−reductant for A in $\mathcal{P}$ with respect to τ, is a rule $\langle A \leftarrow @_{sup}(\mathcal{D}_1, \ldots, \mathcal{D}_n); \top\rangle$, where the truth function for the intended aggregator $@_{sup}$ is defined as $[\![@]\!]_{sup}(d_1, \ldots, d_n) = sup\{d_1, \ldots, d_n\}$, and $\mathcal{D}_1, \ldots, \mathcal{D}_n$ are, respectively, the leaves of τ.*

A PE^k−reductant is a PE−reductant which is obtained building a depth k unfolding tree.

In this section we apply the cost measures just introduced to compare the efficiency of these two semantically equivalent notions of reductants. We start with an example showing the appropriateness of our cost criteria.

Example 5. Given the lattice $([0, 1], \preceq)$, where "$\preceq$" is the usual order on real numbers, consider the following multi-adjoint logic program $\mathcal{P}$:

$$\mathcal{R}_1 : \langle p(a) \leftarrow_{\text{L}} q(a, b); 0.7\rangle \qquad \mathcal{R}_3 : \langle p(X) \leftarrow_{\text{G}} q(X, b); 0.4\rangle$$
$$\mathcal{R}_2 : \langle p(a) \leftarrow ; \qquad 0.5\rangle \qquad \mathcal{R}_4 : \langle q(a, b) \leftarrow ; \qquad 0.9\rangle$$

The reductant for $\mathcal{P}$ and $p(a)$ is: $\mathcal{R} \equiv \langle p(a) \leftarrow @(q(a, b), 1, q(X_1, b)); 1\rangle$. On the other hand, the PE^1−reductant for program $\mathcal{P}$ and atom $p(a)$ is: $\mathcal{R}' \equiv \langle p(a) \leftarrow @_{sup}(0.7 \&_{\text{L}} q(a, b), 0.5, 0.4 \&_{\text{G}} q(X_1, b)); 1\rangle$, where $[\![@_{sup}]\!](x, y, z) = sup\{x, y, z\}$ and $[\![@]\!](x, y, z) = sup\{[\![\&_{\text{L}}]\!](0.7, x), [\![\&_G]\!](0.5, y), [\![\&_{\text{G}}]\!](0.4, z)\}$. Now, with reductant $\mathcal{R}$ we can build derivation D:

$$\langle p(a); id\rangle \rightarrow^{\mathcal{R}}_{AS} \langle @(q(a, b), 0.5, q(X_1, b)); id\rangle \rightarrow^{\mathcal{R}_4}_{AS} \langle @(0.9, 0.5, q(X_1, b)); id\rangle \rightarrow^{\mathcal{R}_4}_{AS}$$
$$\langle @(0.9, 0.5, 0.9); \{X_1/a\}\rangle \rightarrow_{IS} \langle 0.6; \{X_1/a\}\rangle$$

On the other hand, if we use reductant $\mathcal{R}'$, we can generate derivation D':

$$\langle p(a); id\rangle \rightarrow^{\mathcal{R}}_{AS} \langle @_{sup}(0.7 \&_{\text{L}} q(a, b), 0.5, 0.4 \&_{\text{G}} q(X_1, b)); id\rangle \rightarrow^{\mathcal{R}_4}_{AS} \langle @(0.9, 0.5, 0.4$$
$$\&_{\text{G}} \ q(X_1, b)); id\rangle \rightarrow^{\mathcal{R}_4}_{AS} \langle @_{sup}(0.7 \&_{\text{L}} 0.9, 0.5, 0.4 \&_{\text{G}} 0.9); \{X_1/a\}\rangle \rightarrow_{IS} \langle @_{sup}(0.6,$$
$$0.5, 0.4 \&_{\text{G}} 0.9); \{X_1/a\}\rangle \rightarrow_{IS} \langle @_{sup}(0.6, 0.5, 0.4); \{X_1/a\}\rangle \rightarrow_{IS} \langle 0.6; \{X_1/a\}\rangle$$

Both derivations lead to the same f.c.a. and we are going to see that their operational/interpretive costs are also the same. Indeed: $\mathcal{O}_c(D) = 3 = \mathcal{O}_c(D')$. On the other hand $\mathcal{I}^+_c(D) = \mathcal{W}(@) = 5$ and $\mathcal{I}^+_c(D') = \mathcal{W}(\&_L) + \mathcal{W}(\&_G) + \mathcal{W}(@_{sup}) = 3 + 1 + 1 = 5$, that is, $\mathcal{I}^+_c(D) = \mathcal{I}^+_c(D')$. Therefore, the PE^1−reductant $\mathcal{R}'$ has the same efficiency than the reductant $\mathcal{R}$ when we count all the (connective and primitive) operators evaluated during the interpretive phase. Moreover, if we only consider the number of interpretive steps, we would wrongly measure that a derivation performed using $\mathcal{R}$ (i.e., the original notion of reductant) was more efficient. This justify the adoption of our more refined cost criterion $\mathcal{I}^+_c$.

In general, it is possible to prove that the reductant and the PE^1−reductant have the same efficiency.

Theorem 1. *Let* $\mathcal{R} \equiv \langle A \leftarrow @(\mathcal{B}_1\theta_1, \ldots, \mathcal{B}_n\theta_n); \top \rangle$ *be a reductant (w.r.t. Def. 5) and let* $\mathcal{R}' \equiv \langle A \leftarrow @_{sup}(v_1 \& _1 \mathcal{B}_1\theta_1, \ldots, v_n \& _n \mathcal{B}_n\theta_n); \top \rangle$ *a* PE^1-*reductant for a ground atom* A *in a program* $\mathcal{P}$. *Then,* $D \equiv [\langle A; id \rangle \to_{AS}^{\mathcal{R}} \langle E; id \rangle \to_{AS/IS}^* \langle r; \sigma \rangle]$ *iff* $D' \equiv [\langle A; id \rangle \to_{AS}^{\mathcal{R}'} \langle E'; id \rangle \to_{AS/IS}^* \langle r; \sigma \rangle]$, *where* $r \in L$. *Moreover,* $\mathcal{O}_c(D) = \mathcal{O}_c(D')$, *and* $\mathcal{I}_c^+(D) = \mathcal{I}_c^+(D')$.

5   Conclusions and Future Work

In this paper we were concerned with the introduction of cost measures for computations performed in the multi-adjoint logic programming framework. We have highlighted the fact that the usual method of counting the number of computational steps performed in a derivation, may produce wrong results when estimating the computational effort developed in the interpretive phase of a multi-adjoint derivation. The problem emerges when we consider aggregators on the body of program rules whose definitions also invokes other aggregators. Obviously, the evaluation of this last kind of aggregators consumes computational resources at execution time. However, a naive measurement forgets to add these consumptions to the final cost, since they don't explicitly produce interpretive steps. We have solved this problem by simple assigning weights to aggregators in concordance with their complexity. We have applied these cost measures to compare the efficiency of two semantically equivalent notions of reductants.

In the near future, we also plan to take advantage of these cost criteria to formally prove the efficiency of the fuzzy fold/unfold [5] and partial evaluation techniques [7] we are developing.

References

1. Baldwin, J.F., Martin, T.P., Pilsworth, B.W.: Fril-Fuzzy and Evidential Reasoning in Artificial Intelligence. John Wiley & Sons, Inc, West Sussex, England (1995)
2. Guadarrama, S., Muñoz, S., Vaucheret, C.: Fuzzy prolog: A new approach using soft constraints propagation. Fuzzy Sets. and Systems 144(1), 127–150 (2004)
3. Ishizuka, M., Kanai, N.: Prolog-ELF Incorporating Fuzzy Logic. In: Joshi, A.K. (ed.) (IJCAI'85).Proc. of the 9th International Joint Conference on Artificial Intelligence, Los Angeles, USA, pp. 701–703. Morgan Kaufmann, Seatle,Washington,USA (1985)
4. Jones, N.D., Gomard, C.K., Sestoft, P.: Partial Evaluation and Automatic Program Generation. Prentice-Hall, Englewood Cliffs, NJ (1993)
5. Julián, P., Moreno, G., Penabad, J.: On Fuzzy Unfolding. A Multi-adjoint Approach. Fuzzy Sets and Systems 154, 16–33 (2005)
6. Julián, P., Moreno, G., Penabad, J.: Operational/Interpretive Unfolding of Multi-adjoint Logic Programs. Journal of Universal Computer Science 12(11), 1679–1699 (2006)
7. Julián, P., Moreno, G., Penabad, J.: Efficient Reductants Calculi using Partial Evaluation Techniques with Thresholding. In: Lucio, P. (ed.) Electronic Notes in Theoretical Computer Science, p. 15. Elsevier, Amsterdam (2007)

8. Li, D., Liu, D.: A fuzzy Prolog database system. John Wiley & Sons, Inc, West Sussex, England (1990)
9. Lloyd, J.W.: Foundations of Logic Programming, 2nd edn. Springer-Verlag, Berlin (1987)
10. Medina, J., Ojeda-Aciego, M., Vojtáš, P.: Multi-adjoint logic programming with continuous semantics. In: Eiter, T., Faber, W., Truszczyński, M. (eds.) LPNMR 2001. LNCS (LNAI), vol. 2173, pp. 351–364. Springer, Heidelberg (2001)
11. Medina, J., Ojeda-Aciego, M., Vojtáš, P.: Similarity-based Unification: a multi-adjoint approach. Fuzzy Sets and Systems 146, 43–62 (2004)
12. Vojtáš, P.: Fuzzy Logic Programming. Fuzzy Sets and Systems 124(1), 361–370 (2001)

A Fixed-Point Theorem for Multi-valued Functions with an Application to Multilattice-Based Logic Programming

Jesús Medina[*], Manuel Ojeda-Aciego[**], and Jorge Ruiz-Calviño[***]

Dept. Matemática Aplicada. Universidad de Málaga
{jmedina,aciego,jorgerucal}@ctima.uma.es

Abstract. This paper presents a computability theorem for fixed points of multi-valued functions defined on multilattices, which is later used in order to obtain conditions which ensure that the immediate consequence operator computes minimal models of multilattice-based logic programs in at most ω iterations.

1 Introduction

Following the trend of generalising the structure of the underlying set of truth-values for fuzzy logic programming, multilattice-based logic programs were introduced in [7] as an extended framework for fuzzy logic programming, in which the underlying set of truth-values for the propositional variables is considered to have a more relaxed structure than that of a complete lattice.

The first definition of multilattices, to the best of our knowledge, was introduced in [1], although, much later, other authors proposed slightly different approaches [4,6]. The crucial point in which a complete multilattice differs from a complete lattice is that a given subset does not necessarily have a least upper bound (resp. greatest lower bound) but some minimal (resp. maximal) ones.

As far as we know, the first paper which used multilattices in the context of fuzzy logic programming was [7], which was later extended in [8]. In these papers, the meaning of programs was defined by means of a fixed point semantics; and the non-existence of suprema in general but, instead, a set of minimal upper bounds, suggested the possibility of developing a non-deterministic fixed point theory in the form of a multi-valued immediate consequences operator.

Essentially, the results presented in those papers were the existence of minimal models below any model of a program, and that any minimal model can be attained by a suitable version of the iteration of the immediate consequence operator; but some other problems remained open, such as the constructive nature of minimal models or the reachability of minimal models after at most countably many iterations.

---

[*] Partially supported by Spanish project TIC2003-09001-C02-01.
[**] Partially supported by Spanish project TIN2006-15455-C03-01.
[***] Partially supported by Andalusian project P06-FQM-02049.

The aim of this paper is precisely to present conditions which ensure that minimal models for multilattice-based logic programs can be reached by a "bounded" iteration of the immediate consequences operator, in the sense that fixed points are attained after no more than ω iterations. Obviously, the main theoretical problem can be stated in the general framework of multi-valued functions on a multilattice. Some existence results in this line can be found in [2,3,9,10,5], but they worked with complete lattices instead of multilattices.

The structure of the paper is as follows: in Section 2, some preliminary definitions and results are presented; later, in Section 3, we introduce the main contribution of the paper, namely, reachability results for minimal fixed points of multi-valued functions on a multilattice; then, in Section 4, these results are instantiated to the particular case of the immediate consequences operator of multilattice-based logic programs; the paper finishes with some conclusions and prospects for future work.

2 Preliminaries

In order to make this paper self-contained, we provide in this section the basic notions of the theory of multilattices, together with a result which will be used later. For further explanations, the reader can see [7,8].

Definition 1. *A* complete multilattice *is a partially ordered set, $\langle M, \preceq \rangle$, such that for every subset $X \subseteq M$, the set of upper (resp. lower) bounds of X has minimal (resp. maximal) elements, which are called* multi-suprema *(resp.* multi-infima*).*

The sets of multi-suprema and multi-infima of a set X are denoted by $\text{multisup}(X)$ and $\text{multinf}(X)$. It is straightforward to note that these sets consist of pairwise incomparable elements (also called *antichains*).

An upper bound of a set X needs not be greater than any minimal upper bound (multi-supremum); such a condition (and its dual, concerning lower bounds and multi-infima) has to be explicitly required. This condition is called *coherence*, and is formally introduced in the following definition, where we use the Egli-Milner ordering , i.e., $X \sqsubseteq_{EM} Y$ if and only if for every $y \in Y$ there exists $x \in X$ such that $x \preceq y$ and for every $x \in X$ there exists $y \in Y$ such that $x \preceq y$.

Definition 2. *A complete multilattice M is said to be* coherent *if the following pair of inequations hold for all $X \subseteq M$:*

$$LB(X) \sqsubseteq_{EM} \text{multinf}(X)$$
$$\text{multisup}(X) \sqsubseteq_{EM} UB(X)$$

where $LB(X)$ and $UB(X)$ denote, respectively, the sets of lower bounds and upper bounds of the set X.

Coherence together with the non-existence of infinite antichains (so that the sets multisup(X) and multinf(X) are always finite) have been shown to be useful conditions when working with multilattices. Under these hypotheses, the following important result was obtained in [7]:

Lemma 1. *Let M be a coherent complete multilattice without infinite antichains, then any chain[1] in M has a supremum and an infimum.*

3   Reaching Fixed Points for Multi-valued Functions on Multilattices

In order to proceed to the study of existence and reachability of minimal fixed points for multi-valued functions, we need some preliminary definitions.

Definition 3. *Given a poset P, by a multi-valued function we mean a function $f \colon P \longrightarrow 2^P$ (we do not require that $f(x) \neq \varnothing$ for every $x \in P$).*
We say that $x \in P$ is a fixed point of f if and only if $x \in f(x)$.

The adaptation of the definition of isotonicity and inflation for multi-valued functions is closely related to the ordering that we consider on the set 2^M of subsets of M. We will consider the Smyth ordering among sets, and we will write $X \sqsubseteq_S Y$ if and only if for every $y \in Y$ there exists $x \in X$ such that $x \preceq y$.

Definition 4. *Let $f \colon P \longrightarrow 2^P$ be a multi-valued function on a poset P:*

- *We say that f is isotone if and only if for all $x, y \in P$ we have that $x \preceq y$ implies $f(x) \sqsubseteq_S f(y)$.*
- *We say that f is inflationary if and only if $\{x\} \sqsubseteq_S f(x)$ for every $x \in P$.*

As our intended application is focused on multilattice-based logic programs, we can assume the existence of minimal fixed points for a given multi-valued function on a multilattice (since in [7] the existence of minimal fixed points was proved for the $T_{\mathbb{P}}$ operator). Regarding reachability of a fixed point, it is worth to rely on the so-called *orbits* [5]:

Definition 5. *Let $f \colon M \longrightarrow 2^M$ be a multi-valued function an orbit of f is a transfinite sequence $(x_i)_{i \in I}$ of elements $x_i \in M$ where the cardinality of M is less than the cardinality of I ($|M| < |I|$) and:*

$$x_0 = \bot$$
$$x_{i+1} \in f(x_i)$$
$$x_\alpha \in \text{multisup}\{x_i \mid i < \alpha\} \text{ , for limit ordinals } \alpha$$

Note the following straightforward consequences of the definition:

---

[1] A chain X is a totally ordered subset. Sometimes, for convenience, a chain will be denoted as an indexed set $\{x_i\}_{i \in I}$.

1. In an orbit, we have $f(x_i) \neq \varnothing$ for every $i \in I$.
2. As $f(x_i)$ is a nonempty set, there might be many possible choices for x_{i+1}, so we might have many possible orbits.
3. If $(x_i)_{i \in I}$ is an orbit of f and there exists $k \in I$ such that $x_k = x_{k+1}$, then x_k is a fixed point of f.
   Providing sufficient conditions for the existence of such orbits, we ensure the existence of fixed points. Note that the condition $f(\top) \neq \varnothing$ directly implies the existence of a fixed point, namely $\top$.
4. Any increasing orbit eventually reaches a fixed point (this follows from the inequality $|M| < |I|$).
   This holds because every transfinite increasing sequence is eventually stationary, and an ordinal α such that $x_\alpha = x_{\alpha+1} \in f(x_\alpha)$ is a fixed point.

Under the assumption of f being non-empty and inflationary, the existence of increasing orbits can be guaranteed; the proof is roughly sketched below:

The orbit can be constructed for any successor ordinal α by using the inequality $\{x_\alpha\} \sqsubseteq_S f(x_\alpha)$, which follows by inflation, since any element $x_{\alpha+1} \in f(x_\alpha)$ satisfies $x_\alpha \preceq x_{\alpha+1}$. The definition for limit ordinals, directly implies that it is greater than any of its predecessors.

As a side result, note that when reaching a limit ordinal, under the assumption of f being inflationary, the initial segment is actually a chain; therefore, by Lemma 1 it has only one multi-supremum (the supremum of the chain); this fact will be used later in Propositions 1 and 2.

Regarding minimal fixed points, the following result shows conditions under which any minimal fixed point is attained by means of an orbit:

Proposition 1. *Let $f \colon M \longrightarrow 2^M$ be inflationary and isotone, then for any minimal fixed point there is an orbit converging to it.*

Proof. Let x be a minimal fixed point of f and let us prove that there is an increasing orbit $(x_i)_{i \in I}$ satisfying $x_i \preceq x$. We will build this orbit by transfinite induction:

Trivially $x_0 = \bot \preceq x$.

If $x_i \preceq x$, by isotonicity $f(x_i) \sqsubseteq_S f(x)$. Then for $x \in f(x)$ we can choose $x_{i+1} \in f(x_i)$ such that $x_{i+1} \preceq x$ and obviously $x_i \preceq x_{i+1}$ by inflation.

For a limit ordinal α, as stated above, $x_\alpha = \sup_{i<\alpha} x_i$; now, by induction we have that $x_i \preceq x$ for every $i < \alpha$, hence $x_\alpha \preceq x$.

The transfinite chain $(x_i)_{i \in I}$ constructed this way is increasing, therefore there is an ordinal α such that $x_\alpha = x_{\alpha+1} \in f(x_\alpha)$, so x_α is a fixed point and $x_\alpha \preceq x$ but by minimality of the fixed point x, we have that $x = x_\alpha$. $\square$

The usual way to approach the problem of reachability is to consider some kind of 'continuity' in our multi-valued functions, understanding continuity in the sense of preservation of suprema and infima. But it is obvious that we have to state formally what this preservation is meant, since in complete multilattices we only have for granted the existence of *sets of multi-infima* and *sets of multi-suprema*. This is just another reason to rely on coherent complete multilattices M

without infinite antichains so that, at least, we have the existence of suprema and infima of chains.

Definition 6. *A multi-valued function $f\colon M \longrightarrow 2^M$ is said to be* sup-preserving *if and only if for every chain $X = (x_i)_{i \in I}$ we have that:*

$$f(\sup\{x_i \mid i \in I\}) = \{y \mid \text{ there are } y_i \in f(x_i) \text{ s.t. } y \in \text{multisup}\{y_i \mid i \in I\}\}$$

Note that, abusing a bit the notation, the definition above can be rephrased in much more usual terms as $f(\sup X) = \text{multisup}(f(X))$ but we will not use it, since the intended interpretation of $\text{multisup}(f(X))$ is by no means standard.

Reachability of minimal fixed points is granted by assuming the extra condition that our function f is sup-preserving, as shown in the following proposition.

Proposition 2. *If a multi-valued function f is inflationary, isotone and sup-preserving, then at most countably many steps are necessary to reach a minimal fixed point (provided that some exists).*

Proof. Let x be a minimal fixed point and consider the approximating increasing orbit $(x_i)_{i \in I}$ given by Proposition 1. We will show that x_ω is a fixed point of f and, therefore, x_ω equals x.

As f is sup-preserving we have that $f(x_\omega)$ is the set

$$\{y \mid \text{ there are } y_i \in f(x_i) \text{ s.t. } y = \text{multisup}\{y_i \mid i < \omega\}\}$$

In order to prove that x_ω is a fixed point, on the one hand, recall that we have, by definition, that $x_\omega = \sup\{x_i \mid i < \omega\}$. On the other hand, we will show that this construction can be also seen as a multi-supremum of a suitable sequence of elements $y_i \in f(x_i)$.

To do this we only have to recall that, by construction of the orbit, we know that $x_{i+1} \in f(x_i)$, therefore for every $0 \le i < \omega$ we can consider $y_i = x_{i+1}$. Hence the element x_ω can be seen as an element of $f(x_\omega)$. Thus, x_ω is a fixed point of f and $x_\omega \preceq x$ and by minimality of x, we have that $x = x_\omega$.   □

4   Application to Fuzzy Logic Programs on a Multilattice

In this section we apply the previous results to the particular case of the immediate consequences operator for extended logic programs on a multilattice, as defined in [7, 8]. To begin with, we will assume the existence of a multilattice (coherent and without infinite antichains) M as the underlying set of truth-values, that is, our formulas will have certain degree of truth in M. In order to build our formulas, we will consider a set of computable n-ary isotone operators $M^n \longrightarrow M$ which will be intended as our logical connectors. Finally, we will consider a set Π of propositional symbols as the basic blocks which will allow to build the set of formulas, by means of the connector functions.

Now, we can recall the definition of the fuzzy logic programs based on a multilattice:

Definition 7. *A fuzzy logic program based on a multilattice M is a set $\mathbb{P}$ of rules of the form $A \leftarrow B$ such that:*

1. *A is a propositional symbol of Π, and*
2. *B is a formula built from propositional symbols and elements of M by using isotone operators.*

Now we give the definition of interpretation and model of a program:

Definition 8

1. *An interpretation is a mapping $I : \Pi \longrightarrow M$.*
2. *We say that I satisfies a rule $A \leftarrow B$ if and only if $\hat{I}(B) \leq I(A)$, where $\hat{I}$ is the homomorphic extension of I to the set of all formulae.*
3. *An interpretation I is said to be a model of a program $\mathbb{P}$ iff all rules in $\mathbb{P}$ are satisfied by I.*

Example 1. Let us consider an example of a program on a multilattice. The program consists of the four rules below to the left, whereas the underlying multilattice is the six-element multilattice depicted below to the right:

$$E \leftarrow A$$
$$E \leftarrow B$$
$$A \leftarrow a$$
$$B \leftarrow b$$

It is easy to check that the program does not have a least model but two minimal ones, I_1 and I_2, given below:

$$
\begin{array}{ll}
I_1(E) = c & I_2(E) = d \\
I_1(A) = a & I_2(A) = a \\
I_1(B) = b & I_2(B) = b
\end{array}
$$ □

A fixed point semantics was given by means of the following consequences operator:

Definition 9. *Given a fuzzy logic program $\mathbb{P}$ based on a multilattice M, an interpretation I and a propositional symbol A; the immediate consequences operator is defined as follows:*

$$T_{\mathbb{P}}(I)(A) = \mathrm{multisup}\left(\{I(A)\} \cup \{\hat{I}(B) \mid A \leftarrow B \in \mathbb{P}\} \right)$$

Note that, by the very definition, the immediate consequences operator is an inflationary multi-valued function defined on the set of interpretations of the program $\mathbb{P}$, which inherits the structure of multilattice. Moreover, models can be characterized in terms of fixed points of $T_{\mathbb{P}}$ as follows:

Proposition 3 (see [7]). *An interpretation I is a model of a program if and only if $I \in T_{\mathbb{P}}(I)$.*

Although not needed for the definition of either the syntax or the semantics of fuzzy logic programs, the requirement that M is a coherent multilattice without infinite antichains turns out to be essential for the existence of minimal fixed points, see [7]. Hence, a straightforward application of Proposition 2 allows us to obtain the following result.

Theorem 1. *If $T_{\mathbb{P}}$ is sup-preserving, then ω steps are sufficient to reach a minimal model.*

5 Conclusions

Continuing the study of computational properties of multilattices initiated in [7], we have presented a theoretical result regarding the attainability of minimal fixed points of multi-valued functions on a multilattice which, as an application, guarantees that minimal models of multilattice-based logic programs can be attained after at most countably many iterations of the immediate consequence operator. We recall that, in this paper, the existence of such fixed points has been assumed because of the intended application in mind (that is, the existence of minimal models for multilattice-based logic programs was proved in [7]).

As future work, this initial investigation on fixed points of multi-valued functions on a multilattice has to be completed with the study of sufficient conditions for the existence of (minimal) fixed points.

Another interesting line of research, which turns out to be fundamental for the practical applicability of the presented result, is the study of conditions which guarantee that the immediate consequences operator is sup-preserving.

References

1. Benado, M.: Les ensembles partiellement ordonnés et le théorème de raffinement de Schreier, II. Théorie des multistructures. Czechoslovak Mathematical Journal 5(80), 308–344 (1955)
2. d'Orey, V.: Fixed point theorems for correspondences with values in a partially ordered set and extended supermodular games. Journal of Mathematical Economics 25, 345–354 (1996)
3. Echenique, F.: A short and constructive proof of Tarski's fixed-point theorem. International Journal of Game Theory (2005)
4. Hansen, D.: An axiomatic characterization of multi-lattices. Discrete Mathematics 33(1), 99–101 (1981)
5. Khamsi, M.A., Misane, D.: Fixed point theorems in logic programming. Annals of Mathematics and Artificial Intelligence 21, 231–243 (1997)
6. Martínez, J., Gutiérrez, G., de Guzmán, I., Cordero, P.: Generalizations of lattices via non-deterministic operators. Discrete Mathematics 295, 107–141 (2005)

7. Medina, J., Ojeda-Aciego, M., Ruiz-Calviño, J.: no. Multi-lattices as a basis for generalized fuzzy logic programming. In *Proc. of WILF*. In: Bloch, I., Petrosino, A., Tettamanzi, A.G.B. (eds.) WILF 2005. LNCS (LNAI), vol. 3849, pp. 61–70. Springer, Heidelberg (2006)
8. Medina, J., Ojeda-Aciego, M., Ruiz-Calviño, J.: Fuzzy logic programming via multilattices. Fuzzy Sets and Systems 158(6), 674–688 (2007)
9. Stouti, A.: A generalized Amman's fixed point theorem and its application to Nash equilibrium. Acta Mathematica Academiae Paedagogicae Nyíregyháziensis 21, 107–112 (2005)
10. Zhou, L.: The set of Nash equilibria of a supermodular game is a complete lattice. Games and economic behavior 7, 295–300 (1994)

Contextualized Possibilistic Networks with Temporal Framework for Knowledge Base Reliability Improvement

Marco Grasso, Michèle Lavagna, and Guido Sangiovanni

Politecnico di Milano, Dipartimento di Ingegneria Aerospaziale, Via la Masa 34,
20156 Milano, Italy
{grasso,lavagna,sangiovanni}@aero.polimi.it

Abstract. Possibilistic abductive reasoning is particularly suited for diagnostic problem solving affected by uncertainty. Being a Knowledge-Based approach, it requires a Knowledge Base consisting in a map of causal dependencies between failures (or anomalies) and their effects (symptoms). Possibilistic Causal Networks are an effective formalism for knowledge representation within this applicative field, but are affected by different issues. This paper is focused on the importance of a proper management of explicit contextual information and of the addition of a temporal framework to traditional Possibilistic Causal Networks for the improvement of diagnostic process performances. The necessary modifications to the knowledge representation formalism and to the learning approach are presented together with a brief description of an applicative test case for the concepts here discussed.

1 Introduction

An engineering diagnostic problem consists in the identification of the explanation (or an ordered set of explanations) for a given set of observed manifestations which have been recognized to be symptoms of a failure or of an anomalous behaviour in a dynamical system. The inference mechanism requires a Knowledge Base (KB) consisting in a map of causal dependencies between failures (or anomalies) and their effects (symptoms). In real complex applications the assessment of the existence of such causal dependencies might be affected by uncertainty and Possibilistic Causal Networks (PCN) [1] are a very effective formalism for representing this kind of uncertain knowledge, given their capability of graphically capturing the propagation of the effects of an event within the problem domain and the qualitative approach to uncertainty handling. This paper presents the advantages of explicitly representing contextual information and temporal framework in PCNs; the knowledge management strategy is presented together with the results of some practical applications.

F. Masulli, S. Mitra, and G. Pasi (Eds.): WILF 2007, LNAI 4578, pp. 45–52, 2007.

2   Knowledge Islands for Abductive Diagnosis

Diagnostic abductive inference [2] requires a KB consisting in a map of causal dependencies between failures and their effects. Therefore the KB can be defined as a set of Knowledge Islands (KIs) consisting in PCNs, each one representing the uncertain causal correlations between each failure and its detectable symptoms. The nature of events captured in the KB depends on the applicative domain, and in case of engineering diagnostic problems it's constituted by dynamical systems.

A dynamical system can be represented by means of a set of variables $V = \{v_1, ..., v_H\}$, whose possible states can be defined by a set of qualitative (fuzzy) attributes $S(v_h) = \{e_1(v_h), ... s_K(v_h)\}$. Then, let $E = \{v_1, ..., e_n\}$ be the *universe of events* which can be represented in the KB, where $e_i = \langle v_h, s_k(v_h) \rangle$, i.e. an event corresponds to a specific state (attribute) of a given variable (e.g. low pressure, trigger off, etc...). In particular, in a diagnostic problem, events can be divided into nominal events, symptom events, and failure (or disorder) events. A PCN is a Directed Acyclic Graph (DAG) that can be represented by the 3-tuple $\langle N, C^f, \Pi \rangle$, where:

- $N = \{n_1, ..., n_m\}$ is the nonempty set of the network nodes; nodes without parents are called "header nodes". Each node $n_i \in N$ corresponds to an event $e_j \in E$, and therefore $N \subseteq E$. Events corresponding to header nodes are called "header events".

- $C^f \subseteq N \times N$ is the causal framework of the network, which is a set of causal correlations $c_i^f = \langle n_h, n_k \rangle$, $c_i^f \in C^f$, such that node n_h corresponds to an event which is a direct cause for the event corresponding to node n_k.

- $\Pi : C^f \to [0,1]$ is the possibility distribution, which associates a linguistic weight (a qualitative measure of the intrinsic uncertainty), corresponding to a value belonging to set $[0,1]$, to each causal correlation [3].

PCNs used in abductive diagnosis are networks with only one header node corresponding to a single failure (or disorder) event, under the assumption of effects superimposition principle [4] (the case hereafter considered), or to a set of contemporaneous failures otherwise. Therefore learning PCN consists in defining a map between each failure event $f_i \in F$ and the 3-tuple $\langle N, C^f, \Pi \rangle$, where F is the universe of possible failures. In order to be operatively exploited by the inference mechanism, any PCN must be formalized in terms of fuzzy sets [3]. $M(f_i)^+$ and $M(f_i)^-$ are respectively the fuzzy sets of the manifestations (more or less) certainly and (more or less) impossibly caused by the failure event f_i. For each node $\tilde{n} \in N$, its membership functions to those sets are defined: respectively $\mu_{M(f_i)^+}(\tilde{n})$ and $\mu_{M(f_i)^-}(\tilde{n})$.

3   Issues in Knowledge Representation

PCNs as knowledge representation formalism are particularly suitable for manual KB compilation, due to the graphical nature and the qualitative uncertainty management; the reliability of a manually acquired KB, however, depends exclusively on the experience of the human expert who generated it. It is thus necessarily incomplete, imprecise and dependant on the human expert confidence on event occurrence. These limitations drive the development of algorithms for automatic learning of PCNs from data [1], [5]. However, even if a complete and fully reliable KB is acquired (manually or with an automatic learning process), if represented as shown in Section 2 it will be always characterized by a low reliability in every diagnostic problems applied to complex dynamical systems working in dynamically changing environments, due to the lack of two fundamental pieces of information: the explicit contextualization of KIs and the temporal framework. The acquisition of these two knowledge components is a necessary step for the improvement of diagnosis and, possibly, of recovery performances, and for the increase of the diagnostic system robustness with respect to non deterministic failure dynamics and non deterministic interactions with environment and changes in the system internal state.

4   Contextualized Possibilistic Networks

The representation of causal correlations between events or variables of a problem is contextual in nature. Both the existence of a correlation between two events and the confidence in its existence, in fact, might be function of the contexts in which the events can occur. In most cases a failure, disorder or anomaly can't be correctly and reliably identified if no information about the context in which symptoms and manifestations have been detected and observed is available. Moreover, failure criticality is strongly correlated to the context (e.g. a battery failure on a satellite during an eclipse is more critical than the same failure during light period) and different recovery procedures can be planned depending on current context. The explicit representation of contextual information within the KB is therefore a necessary step in the learning process.

The universe of possible contexts C^* can be defined as the power set of the universe of events $E : C^* = 2^E$. A generic context $c_k \in C^*$ is the minimum set of events whose contemporaneous manifestation is a necessary condition for the univocal characterization of a KI, in terms of set of symptoms $N(c_k)$, set of causal correlations $C^f(c_k)$, and possibility distribution $\Pi(c_k)$; if a condition is not satisfied (e.g. an event belonging to c_k is actually false), a different KI must be associated to the same failure. Therefore a given set of events $E^* \subseteq E$ can be considered a context ($E^* = c_k$) within KB only when it is associated to a specific KI. Learning contextualized PCNs consists in defining a map between the couple $\langle f_i | c_k \rangle$, with $f_i \in F$ and $c_k \in C^*$, and the 3-tuple $\langle N, C^f, \Pi \rangle$. A KB represented in this way allows to associate to each contextualized KI a criticality parameter and, possibly, a recovery procedure. The fuzzy sets formalization must then be changed defining $M(f_i | c_k)^+$ and $M(f_i | c_k)^-$ as, respectively, the fuzzy set of the manifestations more or less certainly and more or less impossibly caused by the failure event f_i in context c_k. For each node $\widetilde{n} \in N$, the membership functions are: $\mu_{M(f_i | c_k)^+}(\widetilde{n})$ and $\mu_{M(f_i | c_k)^-}(\widetilde{n})$.

5   Temporal Framework Management

A representation of the knowledge in form of PCN such as the one described in Section 2 does not contain any temporal information, and the causal framework is not sufficient to completely represent the dynamical correlations between failures and symptoms. In order to complete the knowledge domain, the temporal framework must be considered and represented, too. In systems characterized by complex dynamics, the symptoms of a failure might not be observed as instantaneous manifestations once the failure has occurred, but only after a certain delay. If no information about this delay is available, neither the numerical knowledge associated to each PCN, nor the entire diagnostic process can be considered completely reliable. The proposed strategy for the integration of a temporal framework in the KB consists in associating to each KI a Temporal Constraint Map (TCM) defined as the couple $\langle Order, Gap \rangle$ where, for any couple of events $e_1, e_2 \in E$ associated to nodes $n_1, n_2 \in N, Order : N \times N \to \{-1, 0, +1\}$ is such that:

- $Order(e_1, e_2) = +1$ if an event e_1 is expected to occur certainly before the event e_2,
- $Order(e_1, e_2) = -1$ if an event e_2 is expected to occur certainly before the event e_1,
- $Order(e_1, e_2) = 0$ if no information about the temporal constraint between e_1 and e_2 is available;

while $Gap : N \times N \to \mathbb{R}^+$ is, instead, the quantitative information about the minimum delay, if it does exist, expected between the manifestations of the two events. Note that if e_1 and e_2 are causally correlated, the temporal constraint is already known; causality, in fact, necessarily implies a temporal sequence. Therefore, learning contextualized PCNs with temporal framework consists in defining a map between the couple $\langle f_i | c_k \rangle$, with $f_i \in F$ and $c_k \in C^*$, and the 4-tuple $\langle N, C^f, \Pi, TCM \rangle$. For the acquisition of the TCM during the learning process, temporal data must be available in the reference data set. The most important aspect of a KB represented in this way is that its formalization in terms of fuzzy sets depends on the temporal variable, e.g. membership functions are function of time (i.e. given two events $e_1, e_2 \in E$ such that $Order(e_1, e_2) = +1$ and which are both certainly caused by a given failure f_i, until e_1 is absent, e_2 must belong to impossibly expected effects of f_i, and it must be considered a certainly expected effect only after the manifestation of e_1).

A contextualized PCN with temporal framework can be formalized in terms of fuzzy sets by defining:

- $M(f_i | c_k; f)^+$, the fuzzy set of the manifestations more or less certainly caused by the failure event c_k at the time t since f_i occurrence.
- $M(f_i | c_k; f)^-$, the fuzzy set of the manifestations more or less impossibly caused by the failure event c_k at the time t since f_i occurrence.

At generic time step $\tilde{t}$ the membership functions $\overline{\mu}_{M(f_i | c_k; \tilde{t})^+}(e_j)$ and $\overline{\mu}_{M(f_i | c_k; \tilde{t})^-}(e_j)$ of a given event $e_j \in E$ are defined as follows: If $\exists e_j \in E$ such that $e_j \notin M(\tilde{t})^+ \wedge e_j \in M(f_i | ck)^+$, then:

$$\overline{\mu}_{M(f_i|c_k;\tilde{t})^+}(e_j) =$$
$$\begin{cases} \mu_{(f_i|c_k)^+}(e_j), & \text{if } \exists \hat{e} \in E \wedge \hat{e} \in M(\tilde{t})^+ \setminus Order(e_j, \hat{e}) = +1 \vee Order(e_j, \hat{e}) = 0 \\ 0, & \text{if } \forall \hat{e}_0 \in M(t_0)^+, Order(e_j, \hat{e}_0) = -1 \wedge min_{\hat{e}_0}(Gap(e_j, \hat{e}_0)) > (\tilde{t} - t_0) \end{cases}$$
$$\text{(1)}$$

$$\overline{\mu}_{M(f_i|c_k;\tilde{t})^-}(e_j) =$$
$$\begin{cases} \mu_{(f_i|c_k)^-}(e_j), & \text{if } \exists \hat{e} \in E \wedge \hat{e} \in M(\tilde{t})^+ \setminus Order(e_j, \hat{e}) = +1 \vee Order(e_j, \hat{e}) = 0 \\ 1, & \text{if } \forall \hat{e}_0 \in M(t_0)^+, Order(e_j, \hat{e}_0) = -1 \wedge min_{\hat{e}_0}(Gap(e_j, \hat{e}_0)) > (\tilde{t} - t_0) \end{cases}$$
$$\text{(2)}$$

Else, if $\exists e_j \in E$ such that $e_j \in M(\tilde{t})^+ \wedge e_j \in M(f_i|c_k)^+$, then:

$$\overline{\mu}_{M(f_i|c_k;\tilde{t})^+}(e_j) = \mu_{M(f_i|c_k)^+}(e_j) \text{ and } \overline{\mu}_{M(f_i|c_k;\tilde{t})^-}(e_j) = \mu_{M(f_i|c_k)^-}(e_j) \quad \text{(3)}$$

Where:

- $M(\tilde{t})^+$ and $M(\tilde{t})^-$ are respectively the fuzzy sets of manifestations more or less certainly observed and more or less certainly absent at time $\tilde{t}$, with membership functions $\mu_{M(\tilde{t})^+}(e_j)$ and $\mu_{M(\tilde{t})^-}(e_j)$ for each event $e_j \in E$,
- t_0 is the time corresponding to the observation of the first symptom (or of the first symptoms in case of multiple observations at the same time), once the diagnostic process has been started.

6   Examples and Applications

A simulator of a bio-regenerative plant for human life support designed for a Lunar Base will be used to provide some examples of the necessity of a proper contextual information and temporal framework management for diagnostic knowledge representation. Fig. 1 shows a schematic view of the main components of the plant.

The scenario considered for the plant design is referred to a mission at the Lunar South Pole. The power generation and storage system consists in a solar array composed by four fixed panels, a battery and a fuel cell. Solar arrays (and the battery for power peaks) are used during light period, while the fuel cell is used during lunar night (with battery as backup solution). Plants in the greenhouse require CO_2 during 12 - 14 hours per day of photoperiod, and O_2 for the remaining time. Table 1 shows that a failure on the O_2 tank output line causes different effects depending on operative context. For simplicity hereafter only certain effects have been considered and linguistic weights have been omitted in Fig. 2, which shows two different strategies for representing the contextual information in KIs for the considered failure scenario: solution A is the one described in this paper, while solution B is the only plausible alternative for explicit representation of PCNs.

In case of solution B at each symptom acquisition step during diagnostic process the entire KB must be explored and each logical condition (associated to single nodes) must be verified. Moreover, in more complex situations, also the linguistic weights associated to networks branches might depend on contexts,

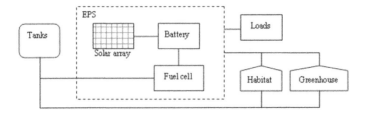

Fig. 1. Schematic view of the life support plant for a Lunar base

Table 1. Contextualization of effects of a failure in oxygen tank output line

Symptoms ID	Description	Context
$\downarrow W_{fr}$	Reduction of power generated by fuel cell	Lunar night
Batt_act	Reduction of power generated by fuel cell	Lunar night
$\downarrow SOC$	Reduction of battery state of charge	Lunar night
$H_2 block$	Stop of hydrogen supply towards the fuel cell	Lunar night
$\downarrow Hab.O_2$	Reduction of percentage of oxygen in habitat module	Always
$\downarrow Green.O_2$	Reduction of percentage of oxygen input in greenhouse module	Out of plants photoperiod
$\downarrow Green.CO_2$	Reduction of CO_2 produced by greenhouse	Out of plants photoperiod

Table 2. Contextualization of effects of a failure in oxygen tank output line

Symptoms ID	Failure	Description	Temporal Constraint
$\downarrow W_{sa}$	String loss, panel loss	Reduction of power generated by solar array	
$\downarrow SOC$	String loss, panel loss	Reduction of battery state of charge	After $\downarrow W_{sa}$ Minimum delay=11s
SOC_alarm	Panel loss	Battery state of charge under threshold	After $\downarrow SOC$ Minimum delay=7s

with the result of a further increase of the number of logical conditions to be checked at each step. The approach proposed in this paper (solution A), instead, allows the utilization of a reduced portion of KB at each diagnostic step, i.e. the one consistent with current context. While in case B six logical conditions must be verified to define the search space of potential explanations, in case A they are reduced to four, and until no change in the system state or in the external condition is detect, the subset of contextual KIs is kept, without checking its

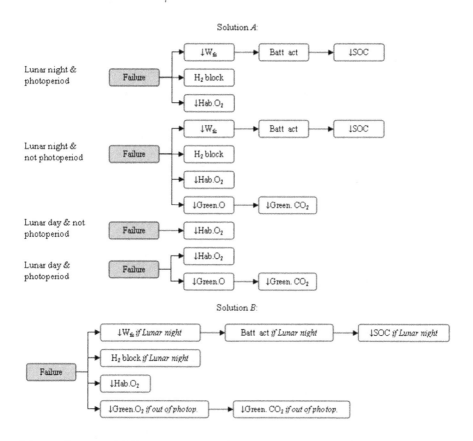

Fig. 2. Contextual KI representation: the proposed approach (solution A) vs. an approach for contextual specification within a signle KI (solution B)

consistency at each step. Other two failure scenarios (f_1: loss of a string of solar array, and f_2: loss of an entire solar panel) are presented in Table 2, in order to demonstrate the need for a temporal framework in the KB.

Failures f_1 and f_2 cause the same symptoms within a time window of seven minutes, e.g. until symptom SOC_alarm can't be detected. The knowledge of this temporal information allows to know that these two failures can't be distinguished before that time: such information can be exploited during the system design phase in order to add a checkable effect which can help the failure distinction during diagnosis process.

7   Conclusions

Automatic learning of PCN from data can be an effective approach for the increase of KB completeness and reliability in diagnostic applications. The presented examples and applications, however, demonstrate that further kinds of information must be explicitly included in the knowledge representation formalism for diagnosis improvement: contextual information and a temporal framework.

The advantages of the proposed approach for a proper management of this kinds of information in KB have been discussed and a strategy for the formalization of these concepts in KIs used in abductive diagnosis problems applied to dynamical systems has been proposed.

References

1. Sanguesa Solé, R., Fabregat, J.C., Garcia, U.C.: Possibilistic Conditional Independence: a Similarity-Based Measure and its Application to Causal Network Learning. International Journal of Approximate Reasoning 18(1), 145–169 (1998)
2. Peng, Y., Reggia, J.A.: Abductive Inference Models for Diagnostic Problem-Solving. Springer-Verlag, Heidelberg (1990)
3. Cayrac, D., Dubois, D., Prade, H.: Handling Uncertainty with Possibility Theory and Fuzzy Sets in a Satellite. Fault Diagnosis Application IEEE Trans. On Fuzzy Systems 4(3), 251–269
4. DeKleer, J., Williams, B.C.: Diagnosing Multiple Faults. Artificial Intelligence 32, 97–130 (1987)
5. Gebhardt, J., Kruse, R.: Learning Possibilistic Networks from Data. Computational Statistics and Data Analysis 38, 449–463 (2002)

Reconstruction of the Matrix of Causal Dependencies for the Fuzzy Inductive Reasoning Method

Guido Sangiovanni and Michèle Lavagna

Politecnico di Milano, Dipartimento di Ingegneria Aerospaziale, Via la Masa 34,
20156 Milano, Italy
{sangiovanni,lavagna}@aero.polimi.it

Abstract. Fuzzy Inductive Reasoning (FIR) methodology is a very
powerful tool for creating a mixed qualitative-quantitative model of any
dynamical system by using its input and output signals. One of the
key issue of this methodology is the creation of the *mask*, i.e. a matrix
that contains the causal dependencies among the signals of the systems
for particular time steps. This paper describes the ARMS – Automatic
Reconstruction of the Mask Scheme – methodology that gives the opportunity of creating a sub-optimal mask with very good performances
without an exhaustive search in the space of all the possibilities. This
methodology has been validated on a wide class of dynamical system
(from LTI systems to chaotic time series) and it has been compared to
other methods proposed in literature.

1 Introduction

The Fuzzy Inductive Reasoning (FIR) methodology is a very powerful tool for
creating a mixed qualitative-quantitative model of any dynamical system. The
first key concept of this methodology is Fuzzy Logic that is used for managing qualitative values, after the *fuzzification* of the most relevant signals, and
for reproducing the qualitative dependencies between system variables, thus increasing the capability of reproducing the behaviour of a system affected by
uncertainty, vagueness, or imprecision. The other key issue is the utilization of
the Inductive Reasoning that is used for inferring general (qualitative) rules from
passed observation. FIR is well known and detailed literature is available on that
topic [1][2][3]. A very general description of the concepts of this methodology for
creating models of dynamical systems is given in this short introduction, in order
for better understanding the problems associated with it, and with the definition
of the inductive rules. The signals coming from the system are firstly sampled
and then they are fuzzified, i.e. converted into a triple of data: class, side, value:
class is the name of the Gaussian membership function that is associated to the
variable (e.g.: *x is high*), whereas, side and value are two parameters that allow
the user to define the membership degree of the considered sampled data to the
set (e.g.: *0,8*); in general the class is indicated with an integer that stands for

F. Masulli, S. Mitra, and G. Pasi (Eds.): WILF 2007, LNAI 4578, pp. 53–60, 2007.
© Springer-Verlag Berlin Heidelberg 2007

a linguistic value (e.g.: "*1*" means "*high*" whereas "*2*" means "*low*"). In the second phase of the methodology, these signals are exploited for creating the qualitative if-then rules: the so called *mask*, a matrix that contains the causal dependencies among the signals of the systems in particular time steps, is applied to the series of qualitative (fuzzified) signals. As an example, the system described in (1):

$$y_1(t) = f(u_3(t - 2 \cdot \Delta t), u_1(t - \Delta t), u_4(t - \Delta t), y_1(t - \Delta t), u_1(t)) \quad (1)$$

where f is a general non-linear function, y are the outputs of the system, and u are its inputs, could be reproduced by the mask M presented in (2). The value '+1' in the mask is related to the value to be forecasted, a '−1' is inserted in the time steps of the variables that are highly related to the value to be forecasted, whereas '0' means that no dependency exists.

$$M = \begin{bmatrix} u_1 & u_2 & u_3 & u_4 & y_1 \\ 0 & 0 & -1 & 0 & 0 \\ -1 & 0 & 0 & -1 & -1 \\ -1 & 0 & 0 & 0 & +1 \end{bmatrix} \begin{matrix} t - 2 \cdot \Delta t \\ t - \Delta t \\ t \end{matrix} \quad (2)$$

Applying the mask to the fuzzyfied data, it is possible to construct the qualitative causal rules that represent the model of the system; this process produces the three matrices of the *pseudo-static relations* (one for the classes, one for the sides, and one for the membership values), as depicted in Fig. 1 where the mask (2) is used. These rules are interpreted in the standard if-then formalism by linking each number to the linguistic membership class; as an example, the rule highlighted in Fig. 1 could be read in the following way:

If u_3 at time $t - 2 \cdot \Delta t$ is '*high*', and u_1 at time $t - \Delta t$ is '*low*',   ...   and u_1
at time t is '*medium*', then y_1 at time t is '*low*'.

The number of rows of the mask matrix is called the *depth* of the mask, whereas the number of non-zero elements in the mask is called the *complexity* of the mask; as an example, in (2) depth is equal to 3 and complexity is equal to 6. In the FIR methodology, the off-line modelling phase deals with the identification of the best mask among all the possible ones; in order to achieve this target, the quality of the mask is judged using the index $Q_m = H_r \cdot O_r$. O_r is the observation ratio, it could takes values in the interval [0,1] and it is equal to 1 when in the values extracted by the training set using the mask, there are at least five observations for each of the possible state. H_r is the entropy reduction and it derives by the Shannon's entropy, i.e., a measure of the uncertainty related with the forecasting of an output given any possible state vector (for more details on the quality index see [2]). Under the same value of complexity, the mask with the quality index nearest to 1 should be preferred for extracting the behaviour of the system. The forecasting process basically consists in the superimposition of the mask on the qualitative data collected by sensors at each sample time. The current obtained qualitative vector is compared with the antecedent of all the pseudo-static rules, in order to identify the 5 nearest one on the basis of a pre-defined metric; this operation is performed with the so-called 5NN algorithm (Five Nearest Neighbour – for a definition see [1] and [2]). The consequent parts of these 5 pseudo-static rules gives a qualitative forecasting of the current value of the output signal; the forecasted output ultimately undergoes a defuzzification process that gives the numerical value. In Section 2 the ARMS algorithm for constructing the mask in an autonomous way is described: it gives the opportunity of creating a sub-optimal mask with very good performances without an exhaustive search in the space of all the possibilities. Next section proves that is very advantageous the search for a sub-optimal mask instead of the one with the highest value of the quality index. Moreover, in Section 4 some tests are described whose goal is to prove the efficacy of the proposed methodology because it reduces the amount of calculation required for creating the mask.

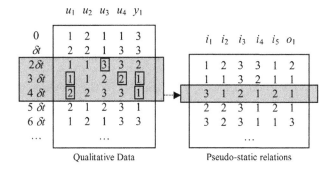

Fig. 1. Creation of the pseudo-static relations using the FIR

2   The ARMS Algorithm

The most simple way for finding the best mask of a dynamical system is represented by performing an exhaustive search in the mask space. In order to compare all the masks it is possible to look at the value of their quality index Q_m obtained with the application of the FIR methodology on the chosen training set: the highest Q_m is associated with the preferred mask. Therefore it is necessary to study different techniques that can speed up the generation of the system's model. In this section an algorithm called ARMS, similar to the hill climbing method, is presented. The purpose of the algorithm is to find out the mask with the highest quality with a user-defined value of complexity. The first step of the algorithm is an exhaustive search of the element with the highest quality index in the subset of the mask space characterized by complexity 2, i.e. with only one '-1' in the matrix. The second step is the same search performed in the sub-space of masks with complexity equal to 3, that could be obtained by adding an element to the best-quality mask identified at the previous step. This passage is repeated for the next steps, from complexity 3 to 4, from 4 to 5, and so on, until the user defined maximum complexity is reached. Fig. 2 gives a visual description of the tree of the masks chosen step by step. It is evident that this algorithm that exploits a bottom-top approach reduces the number of the masks whose quality index must be evaluated in comparison with the exhaustive research, thus improving the performance of the search method.

The ARMS methodology belongs to the class of hill climbing algorithms, and it is quite similar to the approach proposed by Van Welden in [4]; in this Ph.D. thesis an exhaustive list of methods for building the structure of the mask is provided together with a lot of comments and evaluations. The main difference with the Van Welden method, is that ARMS starts from empty masks, i.e. masks with the lowest complexity, and then it increases the value of the complexity parameter, whereas the other method starts from a full masks, i.e. the complexity has the highest value, and at each step it removes the causal link, i.e. the '-1' in the mask, associated with the minimum value of the quality index. In the remaining part of the paper, a comparison between the two methodologies will be given and an evaluation of ARMS will be provided on the basis of some tests performed on a wide class of dynamical systems reported in [5] that are:

- a linear time invariant (LTI) system, in particular a mass-spring-damper with sinusoidal forcing functions;
- a linear time invariant (LTV) system, similar to the previous one with variable spring stiffness;
- non linear systems, such as the Duffing and the Van der Pol oscillators and the Lotka-Volterra system;
- the Henon and the Mackey-Glass chaotic time series.

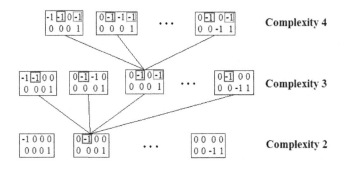

Fig. 2. Functional diagram of the ARMS algorithm

3   Using the Suboptimal Mask

In order to justify the decision of searching for a suboptimal mask instead of the one with the maximum value of the quality index, some preliminary tests have been performed on all the cases introduced in Section 2. As an example, the results obtained on the aforementioned LTI system are reported in Table 1 (see also [5] for details on this system): the five masks with the highest quality indexes have been selected and their mean squared error (MSE - for its definition see [1] and [2]) in forecasting 1500 sampling data have been evaluated with a complexity that goes from 3 to 5. The five best quality masks analysis confirms that the highest values of the quality index correspond to the minimum MSE values, justifying the utilization of one of the suboptimal masks. Moreover, it is not guaranteed that the highest quality mask has the minimum error for the same complexity values, but in general it is very close to the absolute minimum value. The same consideration has been given by Van Welden in [4], so it is very useful to use a suboptimal mask for system identification. Moreover, this issue gives the possibility not to search for the optimal mask with an exhaustive search, thus justifying the efficacy of the ARMS algorithm in reducing the number of the masks evaluated.

Table 1. Evaluation of the MSE of the five best quality masks

Complexity	M_1	M_2	M_3	M_4	M_5	
3	0,7490	0,7490	0,7321	0,7168	0,7168	Q_m
3	0,3012	0,3458	0,2881	0,3027	0,4390	MSE
4	0,7365	0,7050	0,6817	0,6701	0,6578	Q_m
4	0,3436	0,3911	0,2944	0,3113	0,3122	MSE
5	0,6100	0,6094	0,6094	0,5905	0,5905	Q_m
5	0,3273	0,3828	0,3515	0,3707	0,4103	MSE

4   Performances of the ARMS Algorithm

This ARMS approach has been validated on the wide class of systems presented in Section 3 in order to prove the correctness of the following statement:

"passing from a complexity level to the next one, from the highest quality mask it is possible to reach masks with highest quality" and vice versa.

Fig. 3 depicts this situation for the LTI case: the circles represent the values of the quality index of all the mask for the complexity parameter that goes from 2 to 8, whereas the lines connect all the best quality mask obtained with the ARMS search with the children masks. It has to be noticed that, except for complexity equal to 7, in general ARMS gives the mask that could be obtained with the exhaustive search for a predefined complexity value. It is possible to demonstrate now the counterpart of the aforementioned rule; in Fig. 4 this situation is well represented, always on the LTI system. All the children masks that are generated from the worst quality matrix of the previous complexity value possess very slow quality values, so it is better to avoid to follow this path. The same results have been obtained on all the other test benches, even if they are not here reported for lack of space.

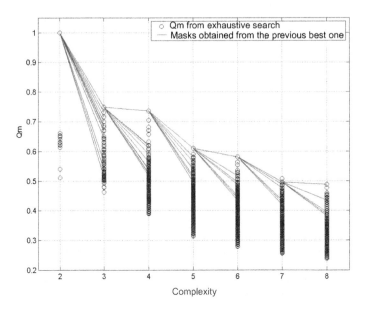

Fig. 3. Quality of the mask studied with the ARMS algorithm with growing complexity

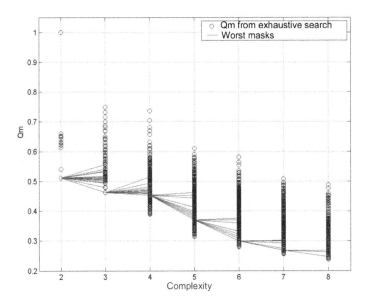

Fig. 4. Quality index of the mask selected by augmenting the complexity of the worst one

The relevance of the ARMS algorithm is its efficacy in reducing the time required for obtaining the suboptimal mask that could be used for reproducing the dynamical system under observation. In the LTI case, the ARMS algorithm

Table 2. Number of masks evaluated with the exhaustive search and ARMS (LTI system)

Complexity	2	3	4	5	6	7	8
Exhaustive search	17	136	680	2380	6188	12376	18448
ARMS Method	17	16	15	14	13	12	11

evaluates only 98 mask instead of the 41225 of the exhaustive search, with a reduction factor of 420 (Table 2).

The analogous result could be observed by measuring the time for computation required in the LTI case. All the calculations have been performed on a machine endowed with a Pentium 4 (2.8 GHz) and 512 Mb of RAM. For the ARMS algorithm there is a linear trend that never exceeds 1 second in the chosen interval of complexity [2 – 8]; on the contrary, the exhaustive search shows an exponential behaviour that reaches more than 650 seconds when the complexity index is 8.

The ARMS algorithm confirms its good quality in reducing the number of evaluated mask on all the other test cases described in Section 2; in particular, Table 3 reports the values obtained for the Duffing non linear system. In this case, the mask has an higher depth and there are more variables, i.e. the matrix is bigger than in the LTI case, so the reduction factor is higher than in the previous case: it has a value of about 1400 (with the evaluation of 145 masks instead of 206367).

Table 3. Number of masks evaluated with the exhaustive search and ARMS (Duffing)

Complexity	2	3	4	5	6
Exhaustive search	31	465	4495	31465	169911
ARMS Method	31	30	29	28	27

Some other tests have been performed in order to evaluate the differences between the ARMS algorithm and the one proposed by Van Welden. The first relevant result is that in all the considered cases, ARMS obtained masks with a quality index higher than the one obtained with the Van Welden method. Secondly, masks with a low degree of complexity better describes the most important frequencies, instead masks of high complexity better describes the lest important frequencies. The proposed approach, passing from masks with low complexity to masks with high complexity, consents to capture directly the most important behaviour of the system and then to add secondary information.

5   Conclusions

One of the most difficult task to be faced when applying FIR for solving the problem of creating the model of a dynamical system, is the reconstruction of the matrix of causal dependencies that is called mask. In this paper the ARMS algorithm has been described together with the very good results obtained: it allows to reduce the amount of time required for calculation of the best mask with very high factors. The obtained suboptimal mask has showed its very good properties in a wide class of dynamical systems (from LTI to chaotic series), thus increasing the confidence in the ARMS algorithm [5]. With the proposed ARMS algorithm, the utilization of the Fuzzy Inductive Reasoning becomes easier because it inserts some autonomy in the process of creation of the internal model of the system. The other parameters to be selected in the FIR methodology, together with the rules defined in order to best exploit its capabilities, are currently under investigation.

References

1. Nebot, A., Cellier, F., Vallverdu, M.: Mixed quantitative/qualitative modelling and simulation of the cardiovascular system. Journal of Computer Methods and Programs in Biomedicine (1997)
2. Mirats Tur, J. M.: Qualitative Modelling of Complex Systems by Means of Fuzzy Inductive Reasoning. Variable Selection and Search Space Reduction. Ph. D. Dissertation, Instituit de Robòtica i Informàtica Industrial, Universitat Politècnica de Catalunya. Barcelona, Spain (2001)
3. Li, D., Cellier, F. E.: Fuzzy Measure in Inductive Reasoning. In: Proc. 1990 Winter Simulation Conference, New Orleans, pp. 527–538 (1990)
4. Van Welden, D.F.: Induction of Predictive Models for Dynamical Systems Via Datamining. Ph. D. Dissertation, Toegepaste Wiskunde en Biometrie, Universiteit Ghent, Belgium (1999)
5. Cavallini, F., Lavagna, M., Sangiovanni, G.: Using Fuzzy Inductive Reasoning for Model Creation and Failures Detection in Dynamical Systems. In: Proc. DCSSS 2006, Greenwich, London, England, July 16-20 (2006)

Derivative Information from Fuzzy Models

Paulo Salgado and Fernando Gouveia

Universidade de Trás-os-Montes e Alto Douro, Quinta de Prados,
Apartado 1013, 5001–801 Vila Real, Portugal
{psal, fgouveia}@utad.pt

Abstract. Universal approximation is the basis of theoretical research and practical application of fuzzy systems. The ability of fuzzy models to model static information has been successfully proven and tested, while on the other hand their limitations in simultaneously modelling dynamical information are well known. Generally, the fuzzy model is a correct zero-order representation of a process or function. However the derivative of its mathematical expression is not necessarily a derivative fuzzy model of the process or function. A perturbed fuzzy system, as a generalization of the traditional fuzzy system, is proposed. It has the ability to uniformly approximate continuous functions and their derivatives on arbitrarily compact sets to the desired degree.

Keywords: Derivative approximation, Fuzzy modelling, Fuzzy System.

1 Introduction

Models are needed for various purposes such as simulation, design and system analysis, decision making, process control, diagnosis, monitoring, and supervision. One of the most popular approaches to model these processes is the fuzzy system based on fuzzy set theory, which makes it possible to work with natural vagueness and incompleteness of information while using exact mathematical structures. Usually the fuzzy logic is introduced as a way of formally describing and manipulating linguistic information.

In most situations the systems have derivative information expressing tendencies, motions, agitations, perturbations, etc. However, contrarily to the analytical mathematical models, fuzzy systems have not the ability to apprehend this type of information. To remedy that, this work proposes a new fuzzy system, a perturbed fuzzy system that is capable of modelling the derivative information, while maintaining the inference mechanism and structure model of a traditional fuzzy system.

In the traditional fuzzy modelling process, fuzzy rules are collected as photos in a photo album (not as a movie). Thus, the natural linguistically dynamical process is not captured by static fuzzy rules and consequently the derivative information is lost.

In this paper we consider several general families of functions, including some of the most popular fuzzy systems, and for all it is shown that the resulting fuzzy system has the ability to uniformly approximate continuous functions and their derivatives on

F. Masulli, S. Mitra, and G. Pasi (Eds.): WILF 2007, LNAI 4578, pp. 61–68, 2007.
© Springer-Verlag Berlin Heidelberg 2007

arbitrarily compact sets to the desired degree, with linguistic interpretability of the approximation. This result is independent of the fuzzy set's shape, continuity and derivative. To do this, we investigate the relationship between the potential translations of fuzzy sets within the fuzzy relationships, which are capable of describing local trend of the fuzzy models (temporal or positional derivatives).

2 The Fuzzy System

Various structures and learning algorithms are capable of implementing fuzzy models that can be perturbed in order to model the derivative information, as presented in the next section. Without any loss of generalization, in this paper we use the fuzzy system resulting from the following algorithm.

Consider a system $y = f(x)$, where y is the output variable and $x = [x_1, \cdots, x_n]^T \in R^n$ is the input vector. Let $U = [\alpha_1, \beta_1] \times \cdots \times [\alpha_n, \beta_n]$ be the domain of input vector x. The problem we are going to solve is the following. Consider the input-output data pairs $(x_k, y_k^{(i)})$, $k = 1, 2, \cdots, n_p$, where $x_k \in U$ and $y_k^{(i)} \in V = R$ is the derivative value, with $i = 1, 2, \cdots, r$. This data is assumed to be generated by an unknown nonlinear function $y = f(x)$ and our objective is to design a fuzzy system $g(x)$ based on these input-output pairs that approximates the unknown function $f(x)$.

Typically, the expert knowledge expressed in a verbal form is translated into a collection of if-then rules of the type:

$$R_{i_1, i_2, \cdots, i_n} : \text{IF } x_1 \text{ is } A_{i_1}^1 \text{ and } x_2 \text{ is } A_{i_2}^2 \text{ and } \cdots \text{and } x_n \text{ is } A_{i_n}^n \text{ THEN } y \text{ is } C_{i_1, i_2, \cdots, i_n} \tag{1}$$

where $A_{i_j}^j$ in U_j and $C_{i_1, i_2, \cdots, i_n}$ in V are linguistic terms characterized, respectively, by fuzzy membership functions $A_{i_j}^j(x_j)$ and $C_{i_1, i_2, \cdots, i_n}(y)$, and the index set is defined by

$$I = \left\{ i_1, i_2, \cdots, i_n \mid i_j = 1, 2, \cdots, N_j; j = 1, 2, \cdots, n \right\} \tag{2}$$

Fuzzy system $g(x)$ is constructed through the following steps:

Step1: Partition of the input space — For each j, $j = 1, 2, \cdots, n$ define N_j fuzzy sets in $[\alpha_j, \beta_j]$ using the following triangular membership functions: $A_r^j(x_j) = \mu(x_j; \overline{x}_j^{r-1}, \overline{x}_j^r, \overline{x}_j^{r+1})$, for $r = 1, \cdots, N_j$, $\alpha_j = \overline{x}_j^1 < \cdots < \overline{x}_j^{N_j} = \beta_j$, with $\mu(x; a, b, c)$ a triangular membership given by $\mu(x; a, b, c) = \{(x-a)/(b-a)$, for $a \leq x \leq b; (c-x)/(c-b)$, for $b \leq x \leq c$; 0 otherwise$\}$ and $a < b < c$. After completing this task, the domain space is partitioned by a grid of triangular membership functions. The antecedent of fuzzy rule $R_{i_1, i_2, \cdots, i_n}$ in (1) can be viewed as the fuzzy set

$A_{i_1,\cdots,i_n} = \underset{j}{\overset{n}{\times}} A_{i_j}^j \in U$, with the membership functions $A_{i_1,\cdots,i_n}(x) = A_{i_1}^1(x_1) * \cdots * A_{i_n}^n(x_n)$,

where $*$ is the min or product T-norm operator and $i_1,\cdots,i_n \in I$.

Step 2: Learning of the Rule base — For each antecedent, with index $i_1,\cdots,i_n \in I$, find

the subsets of the training data where the membership function $A_{i_1,\cdots,i_n}(x)$ is not null.

If the number of points found is not zero, then rule $R_{i_1,\cdots,i_n}$ is added to the rule base,

represented by a table of indexes: $RB = \left\{ i_1,\cdots,i_n \in I : A_{i_1,i_2,\cdots,i_n}(x_k) > 0, k = 1,\cdots,n_p \right\}$.

Step 3: The fuzzy system — Here we assume the use of the singleton fuzzifier, the product inference engine and the centre-average defuzzifier. The fuzzy system can thus be represented by:

$$g(x,\theta) = p^T(x) \cdot \theta \tag{3}$$

where $p(x) = \left[p_1(x),\cdots,p_M(x) \right]^T$ and $\theta = \left[\theta_1,\cdots,\theta_M \right]^T$ are the vectors of fuzzy basis functions (FBF's) and the constant consequent constituents, respectively. θ_l is the point in V at which $C_l(y)$ achieves its maximum value and $l \in RB$ is the index of the rule. Each fuzzy basis function (FBF) of the fuzzy system is given by $p_l(x) = A_l(x) \Big/ \sum_{l=1}^{M} A_l(x)$.

The Fuzzy Model (FM) described by (3) has been clearly recognized as an attractive alternative to functional approximation schemes, since it is able to perform nonlinear mappings of any continuous function [1]-[5].

3 The Perturbed Fuzzy System

In this section, we consider the approximation of a function and its derivative functions by a specific family of perturbed fuzzy systems, based on the "potential" perturbation of membership functions.

We can interpret the derivative of a function $f(x)$ as a measure of the effect of a perturbation due to its translation in the domain space:

$$\frac{df(x)}{dx} \triangleq \lim_{h \to 0} \frac{F(x,h) - f(x)}{h} \tag{4}$$

where $F(x,h) = f(x+h)$ is the perturbed version of $f(x)$, due to a translation process, and h is the perturbation vector. This type of perturbed function, belonging to a set of perturbed functions presented in Definition 1, obey to Theorem 1.

Definition 1. Let $F(x,h)$ be a perturbed version of $f(x)$, both real functions, where x is in the real interval (a,b) and h is in $\Omega = \{ h \in \mathbb{R} : -\Delta < h < \Delta \}$, with Δ a fixed positive real number. We say that for $\varepsilon > 0$ there is a $\|h\| < \Delta$ such that $\|F(x,h) - f(x)\| < \varepsilon$ and $F(x,0) = f(x)$.

If $F(x,h)$ is a continuous and differentiable function with respect to the perturbation variable $h \in \Omega$, the derivative of the perturbed function can also be a perturbed version of the derivative function of $f(x)$. This result is present on the following theorem, whose proof is here omitted.

Theorem 1. Let $f(x) \in C_x^v(\mathbb{R})$ and $F(x,h) \in C_h^v(\Omega)$ be continuous and differentiable functions with respect to x and h, respectively. If $f(x)$ is a v-times continuously differentiable function then, then there is a perturbed function $F(x,h)$ that verifies:

$$f(x) = \lim_{h \to o} F(x,h) \qquad \text{and} \qquad \frac{d^{(i)} f(x)}{dx^{(i)}} = \lim_{h \to 0} \frac{d^{(i)} F(x,h)}{dh^{(i)}}, \quad i = 1, \cdots, v$$

Here, our goal is to prove that it is possible to create a fuzzy system G capable of approximating function F, and so capable of approximating function f and its analytical derivatives, i.e.

$$G(x,h) \approx F(x,h) \quad \text{and} \quad \frac{d^{(i)} G(x,h)}{dh^{(i)}} \approx \frac{d^{(i)} F(x,h)}{dh^{(i)}}, \quad i = 1, \cdots, r$$

For the problem of estimating the derivative approximation, we propose a fuzzy system with perturbations of fuzzy sets $A_l(x)$ and $C_l(y)$. So, perturbation parameters of various fuzzy sets could be estimated in order to catch the linguistic derivative information to the fuzzy model. This perturbed fuzzy system will be able to approximate the perturbed version of $f(x)$, as presented in Definition 1. In the absence of any perturbation factor, this function should be identical to $f(x)$.

Definition 2. The perturbed fuzzy set of $A \in U$ of order v, denoted as $A(x,h)$ or as A_h, is the fuzzy set on the product space given by $(x,h) \in U \times H$, with

    i) $A(x) = \lim_{h \to 0} A_h(x)$

    ii) A_h a continuous function of variable $h \in H$, differentiable up to order v,
where h is the perturbation vector that belongs to the perturbation space.

Two types of perturbed fuzzy set will be used in this work: the translation fuzzy set and the additive fuzzy set, presented on Definitions 3 and 4, respectively.

Definition 3. A_h is a perturbed fuzzy set resulting from a translation process of a fuzzy set A of U when its membership function is given by:

$$A_h(x) = A(x - \phi(h))$$ (5)

Perturbation $\phi(h)$ moves fuzzy set A from its natural position to another position in the neighbourhood.

Definition 4. Let A be a fuzzy set defined on U and A_h the fuzzy set on U that results from the perturbation of A by h:

$$A_h(x) = A(x)(1 + \sigma(h, x))$$ (6)

where $\sigma(h, x) = \sigma_x(h)$ is the additive perturbation function with values in such a way that $\sigma_x(h) \leq (1 - A(x))/A(x)$ in order to preserve de normality of $A_h(x)$.

Definition 5. Let $g(x)$, the fuzzy system given by (3), and $G(x, h)$, its perturbed version, be real-valued functions defined when x is in a closed real region $U = [\alpha_1, \beta_1] \times \cdots \times [\alpha_n, \beta_n]$ and h is in the real region Ω, which contains the null value, i.e. $\Omega \supset \mathbf{0}$. Then we have $\lim_{h \to 0} G(x, h) = g(x)$.

In the context of this work, the perturbed fuzzy system $G(x, h)$ of fuzzy system $g(x)$ results only from the perturbation of both the antecedent and the consequent fuzzy sets of fuzzy rules. Naturally, various types of perturbations can be used by the model, resulting in perturbed fuzzy systems with different behaviours and properties. We chose perturbed fuzzy sets of the additive type for the antecedents, with the same perturbation process for all of them, i.e. $\sigma_i(h, x) = \sigma_j(h, x)$ for $\forall i, j$, and of the translation type for consequents, with distinct perturbations, i.e. $\phi_i(h, x) \neq \phi_j(h, x)$ for $\forall i \neq j$. Under these conditions, the perturbed version of fuzzy system (3) is given by:

$$G(x, h) = \frac{\sum_{l=1}^{M} A_{l,h}(x) y_k(h)}{\sum_{l=1}^{N} A_{l,h}(x)}$$ (7)

where $y_k(h) = y_k + \sigma_{y_k}(h)$.

The following theorem establishes that under certain mild conditions on the basis function A, fuzzy system represented by (7) is capable of approximating arbitrarily well any function in $L^p(U)$, where $U \subset \mathbb{R}^n$ is an arbitrarily chosen L-measurable bounded set whose measure is nonzero.

Theorem 2. Let $f(x)$ be a continuous and differentiable scalar function, $g(x)$ its approximation by fuzzy model (3), and $G(x, h)$ a perturbed fuzzy system of type (7). Consider that one perturbation process is used for all antecedent fuzzy sets A,

$\sigma_i(h,x) = \sigma_j(h,x)$ for $\forall i, j$, and further consider an appropriate continuous and v-times differentiable translation function $\phi_i(h,x) \neq \phi_j(h,x)$ for $\forall i \neq j$, for consequent sets $C_i(y)$. Then for any $x \in U$:

i) $g(x) = \lim_{h \to 0} G(x,h)$

ii) $\displaystyle \sup_{x \in \text{supp}(f)} \left(\lim_{h \to 0} \| f(x) - G(x,h) \| \right) < \varepsilon$

iii) $\displaystyle \sup_{x \in \text{supp}(f)} \lim_{h \to 0} \left\| \frac{\partial^{(i)} f(x)}{\partial x^{(i)}} - \frac{\partial^{(i)} G(x,h)}{\partial h^{(i)}} \right\| < \varepsilon$, for $i = 1, \ldots, n$

The proof of Theorem 2 can be found in [4].

Lemma 2. Let $\phi_{y_k}(h)$ be the perturbation function affecting k^{th} consequent membership function's centre, and $\sigma_x^k(h)$ the potential translation function of the kth antecedent membership function. For $\phi^k(h)$ a polynomial function of order n,

$$y_k(h) = y_k + \sum_{j=1}^{r} b_{k,j}\, h^j / j! = P_k^r(h), \text{ and } \sigma_x^k(h) \text{ an additive function, which is the}$$

same for all antecedents, then we have:

$$G(x,h) = \sum_{k=1}^{N} A_i(x) P_k^r(h) \Big/ \sum_{k=1}^{N} A_i(x) \tag{8}$$

where $P_k^r(h) = \sum_{j=0}^{r} b_{k,j} h^j / j!$ (with $b_{k,0} = y_k$). Fuzzy system (8) is an approximate function of function $f(x)$ and its derivative functions, up to the rth-order derivative.

4   The Derivatives Learning Algorithm

Let $f(x)$ be a function in $\mathbb{R}^n$. Suppose that the noisy scattered data y_i is collected at points $x_k \in \mathbb{R}^n$, $k = 1, 2, \ldots, n$. The problem is to find a function such that its partial derivatives approximate the exact partial derivatives of function $f(x)$. Let $\{x_1, \cdots, x_k, \cdots, x_n\}$ be a set of finite distinct points in $\mathbb{R}^n$ that are not collinear and Ω its convex hull. Suppose S_i^r is a sphere in Ω with centre in node x_i and with radius r. Let s_i^r be the total number of points included in sphere S_i^r and s be the total number of points in domain Ω.

The present algorithm considers the following optimization problem:

$$J(k) = \arg\min_{\theta} \sum_{j=1}^{k} \sum_{i=1}^{k} \varphi_{i,j} \frac{s}{s_i^r} \left(d_i - G(x_i, h_{i,j}, \theta) \right)^2 + \rho \|\theta\|_G \tag{9}$$

with $\varphi_{i,j} = \{1 \text{ if } x_j \in S_i^r; 0 \text{ otherwise}\}$, where $\boldsymbol{h}_{i,j} = \boldsymbol{x}_j - \boldsymbol{x}_i$, $\rho \geq 0$ is a regularization parameter, $\|\boldsymbol{\theta}\|_G = \boldsymbol{\theta}^T \boldsymbol{G} \boldsymbol{\theta}$ and $\boldsymbol{\theta}$ is the parameters vector of the consequents' polynomial. This is a Tikhonov-like regularization problem [5]. This performance criterion leads to the minimum of a non-negative quadratic function, giving the optimal weight vector $\boldsymbol{\theta} = (\boldsymbol{R} + \rho \boldsymbol{G})^{-1} (\boldsymbol{A}^T \boldsymbol{d})$.

5 Numerical Results

In this experiment, we use the interpolation of data from a known function. We use data corrupted by white noise with variance 0.05. For validation purposes, assume that the function is

$$f(x) = 0.02(12 + 3x - 3.5x^2 + 7.2x^3) \times (1 + \cos(4\pi x)) \times (1 + 0.8\sin(3\pi x)) \qquad (10)$$

and its derivative function is obtained by the known mathematics derivative rules.

The input interval [0; 1] is made discrete using a resolution step $T = 0.01$, which yields a set of 101 points $\{x_i\}$, $i=1,\ldots,101$. Equation (10) is used to compute the corresponding output, and the training set for the proposed algorithm is generated by randomly selecting half of these points from this set of input–output pairs. In the first step, the domain space is partitioned by a grid of triangular memberships with $N_j = 12$, where the extremes of the memberships are meeting with the centre of the adjacent membership function. After this, the rule base has 24 fuzzy rules.

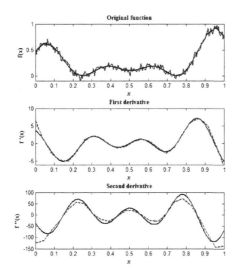

Fig. 1. Approximation of the original, the first derivative and the second derivative of function (10) with corrupted data. Solid line: exact function; dashed line: fuzzy model.

Table 1. Square error of the approximation

Order of derivative	Fuzzy model
0	0,040
1	0,395
2	14.12

Figure 1 shows the approximation of function (10) by the perturbed fuzzy system (8), where the fuzzy rules' consequents are second-order polynomial functions, with corrupted data. Curves show good agreement between function values and the estimated model's output, as well as for the first and second derivatives' values. The performance of the learning algorithm is shown in Table 1.

6   Conclusions

The ability of Fuzzy Systems to approximate any sufficiently smooth function, reproducing its derivatives up to any order, has been demonstrated, assuming that the fuzzy sets of input and output fuzzy spaces are sensitive to the perturbations. This work establishes a formal analysis of the estimation processes involved in automatic rule generation mechanisms of simultaneous estimation of functions and their derivatives using information contained in finite numerical samples extracted from modelled systems.

Acknowledgments. This work was supported by the Portuguese Fundação para a Ciência e a Tecnologia (FCT) under grant POSI/SRI/41975/2001.

References

1. Zeng, X.J., Singh, M.G.: Approximation theory of fuzzy systems–SISO case. IEEE Trans. Fuzzy Syst. 2, 162–176 (1994)
2. Mao, Z.-H., Li, Y.-D., Zhang, X.-F.: Approximation Capability of Fuzzy Systems Using Translations and Dilations of One Fixed Function as Membership Functions. IEEE Trans. Fuzzy Syst. 5(3), 468–473 (1997)
3. Rovatti, R.: Fuzzy Piecewise Multilinear and Piecewise Linear Systems as Universal Approximators in Sobolev Norms. IEEE Trans. Fuzzy Syst., 6(2), 235–248 (1998)
4. Salgado, P., Gouveia, F.: Multi-Dimensional Derivative approximation capability of the Fuzzy system (to be published)
5. Tikhonov, A.N., Arsenin, V.Y.: Solutions of Ill-Posed Problems. Wiley, Washington, DC, Winston, New York (1977)

The Genetic Development of Uninorm-Based Neurons

Angelo Ciaramella[1,*], Witold Pedrycz[2], and Roberto Tagliaferri[3]

[1] Dept. of Applied Sciences University of Naples "Parthenope",
via A. de Gasperi, I-80133 Napoli (Na), ITALY,
Tel.: +390815476520; Fax: +39089963303
ciaramella@uniparthenope.it
[2] Dept. of Electrical and Computer Engineering
University of Alberta, Edmonton AB, Canada
pedrycz@ee.ualberta.ca
[3] Dept. of Mathematics and Computer Science, University of Salerno,
via Ponte Don Melillo, I-84084, Fisciano, Salerno
robtag@unisa.it

Abstract. In this study, we are concerned with a new category of logic connectives and logic neurons based on the concept of uninorms. Uninorms are a generalization of t-norms and t-conorms used for composing fuzzy sets. We discuss the development of such constructs by using genetic algorithms. In this way we optimize a suite of parameters encountered in uninorms, especially their identity element. In the sequel, we introduce a class of logic neurons based on uninorms (which will be refereed to as unineurons). The learning issues of the neurons are presented and some experimental results obtained for synthetic and benchmark data are reported.

1 Introduction

Triangular norms (t-norms) and the corresponding t-conorms play a fundamental role in several branches of mathematics [7], e.g., in probabilistic metric spaces, the theory of generalized measures, game theory, and fuzzy logic [7,9]. Let us recall that t-norms are considered to be special semigroup operations on $[0, 1]$ with neutral element equal to 1. Observe that we can use strictly increasing bijections from the unit interval onto itself in order to construct new t-norms from a given one [9]. The semantics of logic operators (logic connectives) in fuzzy sets is enormously rich. Some of the most recent conceptual developments along this line involve uninorms [8,5,6,10] nullnorms [1] and ordinal sums [3] of t-norms, just to name a few of them.

Logic operators are the crux of the fundamentals of the fuzzy sets or granular computing in general. Quite commonly, more advanced models of logic connectives come with a suite of adjustable parameters whose role is to customize the operator to available experimental data. This flexibility should come hand in hand with a viable method of optimizing these parameters. Subsequently, the optimization should be efficient enough and supported through some architectural realizations of the operators. This tendency

---

* Corresponding author.

F. Masulli, S. Mitra, and G. Pasi (Eds.): WILF 2007, LNAI 4578, pp. 69–76, 2007.

is quite visible in case of Neural Network (NN) implementations of AND and OR operators with weights, AND/OR logic hybrids [8,6] and ordinal sums [4,3].

The main objective of this study is to introduce a new category of logic connectives and logic neurons based on the concept of uninorms. We note that in [8] an approach to define the structure of both AND and OR neurons by using uninorms is proposed and a gradient descend algorithm to learn the parameters has been introduced. Moreover in [3,4] the generalization of t-norms is obtained by using the ordinal sums and to learn the parameters Genetic Algorithms (GAs) were considered. Here we discuss the development of the uninorms by using GAs. In the sequel, we introduce a class of logic neurons based on uninorms, that are a generalization of the neurons introduced in [8] and that use the same learning mechanism based on GAs. The learning aspects of the neurons are discussed. Experimental results are shown on synthetic and benchmark data.

The paper is organized as follows. In Section 2, we describe the uninorms-based generalization of norms. In Section 3, we focus our attention on the genetic optimization of uninorms and uninorm-based logical neurons. In Section 5, we present several experimental results obtained when using uninorms and unineurons on benchmark data sets.

2   Uninorms - A Brief Summary

We start our discussion by recalling that both the neutral element 1 of a t-norm and the neutral element 0 of a t-conorm are boundary points of the unit interval. A *uninorm* is a binary operation $u : [0,1]^2 \rightarrow [0,1]$ which satisfies the properties of *Commutativity*, *Monotonicity*, *Associativity* and it has a *neutral element* $e \in]0,1[$ (see Figure 1). Noticeably we allow the values of the identity element e to vary in-between 0 and 1. As a result of this, we can implement switching between pure AND and OR properties of the logic operators occurring in this construct. In this study we confine ourselves to the following family of constructs that seem to be highly interpretative and thus intuitively appealing:

Let t be a t-norm, s be a t-conorm and $e \in]0,1[$. In the spirit of the construction of Ordinal Sums [4,3] the following operation $\mathbf{u}_{t,s,e,\alpha} : [0,1]^2 \rightarrow [0,1]$ ($\alpha = \min$ or $\alpha = \max$) make $[0,1]$ into fully ordered semigroups with neutral element e:

$$\mathbf{u}_{t,s,e,\alpha}(x,y) = \begin{cases} e \cdot t(\frac{x}{e}, \frac{y}{e}) & \text{if } (x,y) \in [0,e]^2 \\ e + (1-e) \cdot s(\frac{x-e}{1-e}, \frac{y-e}{1-e}) & \text{if } (x,y) \in [e,1]^2 \\ \alpha(x,y) & \text{otherwise} \end{cases} \quad (1)$$

Obviously, $\mathbf{u}_{t,s,e,\min}$ is a conjunctive, and $\mathbf{u}_{t,s,e,\max}$ is a disjunctive uninorm.

Interestingly, we observe that the two intermediate regions deliver some flexibility to the specific realization of the uninorm [8]. Conceptually, this realization favors different slant of the logic aggregation with the dominant nature of the AND or OR character. As indicated, a certain value of the identity element implies some mixture of the logic operations. Considering the area occupied by some t-norm (and minimum) and t-conorm (and maximum, respectively), we can quantify the or-ness and and-ness character of

Fig. 1. The structure of a uninorm with neutral element e

the uninorm by computing the following integrals that reflect the corresponding areas of the unit square:

- or-ness degree: $(1 - e)^2$ for AND dominance and $1 - e^2$ for OR dominance
- and-ness degree : $1 - (1 - e)^2$ for AND dominance and e^2 for OR dominance

This helps us to understand the character of the logic aggregation completed by some uninorm and expressed in terms of the generic logic connectives. The case of $e = 0.5$ places the uninorm in a neutral position with an equal balance of the OR and AND properties.

3   Uninorms and Genetic Algorithms

In the previous section, we showed how the uninorms form an interesting generalization of t-norms and t-conorms. To effectively construct a uninorm, one has to come up with a numeric value of the neutral element and to choose some models (realizations) of t-norms and t-conorms.

Furthermore one has to choose one of the lattice operators (min or max). Given the combinatorial character of the optimization, we consider the usage of the genetic optimization.

The essential component to be defined when using GAs is to come up with a suitable format of a chromosome. An intuitive appealing alternative could be to consider the following string

$$\boxed{t}\boxed{\tilde{s}}\boxed{\tilde{e}}\boxed{\alpha}$$

where the entries are defined in the $[0, 1]$ range.

More specifically, denoting by m the number of t-norms to be considered in the optimization then we associate certain t-norm $t_k(k = 1, 2, \ldots, m)$

$$\tilde{t} \in \left[\frac{k - 1}{m}, \frac{k}{m} \right] \to t_k. \tag{2}$$

In the same way we can construct the t-conorms based upon the values of the $\tilde{s}$. The identity parameter e in equation 1 is the third element of the chromosome, $\tilde{e}$, and the fourth parameter α helps to choose between max ($\alpha > 0.5$) or min ($\alpha \leq 0.5$). We also consider that the *fitness function* guides the GA optimization. Let us consider two n-dimensional vectors, $\mathbf{x} = [x_1, x_2, \ldots, x_n]$ and $\mathbf{y} = [y_1, y_2, \ldots, y_n]$, respectively. The optimized fitness function is introduced as follows (Sum-of-Squares Error (SSE))

$$J = \min \frac{1}{2} \|\mathbf{o} - \mathbf{t}\|_2^2 \tag{3}$$

where $\mathbf{t} = [t^1, t^2, \ldots, t^n]$ is an n-dimensional target vector with values t^i and $\mathbf{o} = [o^1, o^2, \ldots, o^n]$ is the n-dimensional vector that contains the outputs of the uninorms

$$o^i = \mathbf{u}_{t,s,e,\alpha}(x_i, y_i). \tag{4}$$

We mark that the other operators used in the genetic optimization have not changed. Mainly we consider [3,4,2]: *recombination*, *mutation* and *fitness-based reinsertion*.

4   A Generic Construct of a Uninorm-Based Logic Neuron

Now we note that from the previous studies carried out in the realm of logic-based neurocomputing, we can distinguish between two general categories of neurons that are OR and AND neurons. Some extensions of these operators were proposed in the literature [4,8].

Let $\mathbf{x}$ be a vector in the unit hypercube, $\mathbf{x} \in [0,1]^n$ and y denote an element in $[0,1]$. Formally speaking, the underlying logic processing is governed by a composition between the individual inputs and the corresponding connections (weights) $\mathbf{w} \in [0,1]^n$. In detail, $L_1 : (x_i, w_i) \rightarrow [0,1]$ followed by some overall logic aggregation L_2 giving rise to the output y, that is

$$y = L_2[L_1(x_1, w_1), L_1(x_2, w_2), \ldots, L_1(x_n, w_n)] \tag{5}$$

In the OR neuron, the semantics of L_1 is concerned with any realization of the and operator (t-norm), $L_1 = $ AND. L_2 concerns the realization of the or operator (s-norm), $L_2 = $ OR. In contrast, in the AND neuron we have these two operations reversed, that is $L_1 = $ OR and $L_2 = $ AND.

By using the uninorms, that admit more flexibility into the overall aggregation, we arrive at the expression (see Figure 2)

$$y = u[u_1(x_1, w_1, e_1, \alpha_1), u_2(x_2, w_2, e_2, \alpha_2), \ldots, u_n(x_n, w_n, e_n, \alpha_n), e] \tag{6}$$

where $u_i = \mathbf{u}_{t_i, s_i, e_i, \alpha_i}$ is the i-th uninorm with parameters t_i, s_i, e_i and α_i that are estimated by the optimization process. Moreover, $u = \mathbf{u}_{t,s,e,\alpha}$ is the uninorm that permits to obtain the overall composition

In this case the format of the chromosome describing the structure of the neuron is:

$\tilde{t}_1$	...	$\tilde{t}_n$	$\tilde{s}_1$	...	$\tilde{s}_n$	$\tilde{e}_1$	...	$\tilde{e}_n$	...
α_1	...	α_n	w_1	...	w_n	$\tilde{t}$	$\tilde{s}$	$\tilde{e}$	α

where the values are confined to the $[0,1]$ range and n is the number of input neurons.

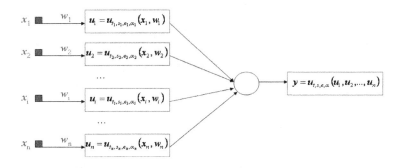

Fig. 2. The structure of the unineuron

In detail, the parameters have these features:

- $\widetilde{t}_i$ and $\widetilde{s}_i$ are the t-norm and t-conorm of the i-th uninorm. In detail we have that $\widetilde{t}_i$ and $\widetilde{s}_i$ are used in the uninorm to connect the input x_i with the weight w_i;
- the parameters $\widetilde{e}_i$ are the identities of the uninorms;
- the parameters α_i are used to define the min ($\alpha_i \leq 0.5$) or max ($\alpha_i > 0.5$) operator;
- $\widetilde{t}, \widetilde{s}, \widetilde{e}, \alpha$ are the parameters of the extern uninorm connective.

At this point, to obtain the parameters of the uninorms, we apply the same transformations previously argued for each uninorm.

5   Experimental Results

We completed a series of experiments with uninorms and unineurons by carrying out the genetic optimization. The suite of t-norms (and the dual t-conorms) from which one optimize connectives is chosen between several t-norms commonly used (t_{M} (minimum), t_{P} (product), t_{L} (L ukasiewicz), t_{W} (drastic product)).

In the first experiment, we are concerned with a "reconstruction" of a certain uninorm. Given the uninorm and its parameters we generate input-output data (1000 samples). Data are now processed by using the proposed optimization approach to obtain the estimation of the parameters of the original uninorm.

The target data vector $\ell = [\widetilde{o}^1, \widetilde{o}^2, \ldots, \widetilde{o}^n]$ is obtained by using the composition (i-th element) $\widetilde{o}^i = \mathbf{u}_{t,s,e,\alpha}(\mathbf{x}, \mathbf{y})$, where $\mathbf{x} = [x_1, x_2, \ldots, x_n]$ and $\mathbf{y} = [y_1, y_2, \ldots, y_n]$ are two random vectors having values in the $[0, 1]$ range. In this case also the parameters are randomly chosen and they are: $t = t_{\mathbf{W}}$, $s = s_{\mathrm{M}}$, $\alpha = \min$ and $e = 0.68128$.

In essence, our aim is to show the effectiveness of the genetic optimization and so we know that ideally the error should be equal to zero. In fact, this has been accomplished (see Figure 3). The learning is quite fast and the method was able to pick up the same t-norms used in the original case. We stress that similar experiments have been conduced by using different data sets and by considering the unineurons and also in these cases we obtain good results.

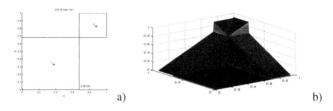

Fig. 3. Uninorm reconstruction: a) uninorm parameters; b) 3D plot of the boundary

In the second experiment we study a data set coming from Zimmermann and Zysno [11]. It consists of 24 pairs of membership values $A(x)$ and $B(x)$ along with the experimentally collected results of their aggregation.

We start showing in Figure 4a the mapping obtained by using the estimated parameters of an uninorm. In this case the SSE is of 0.2617. We also note that estimated uninorm describes an AND-dominant connective. In fact, after computing the level of and-ness and or-ness we have 0.9922 and 0.0078, respectively.

Now we apply to the same data set the uninorm-based neuron. In figure 4b we show the obtained 3-dimensional boundary. In this case the SSE is of 0.0527. Moreover we show in Table 1 the estimated parameters. In this Table we also describe the or-ness and the and-ness of the connectives. We stress that the connectives on the input are all OR-dominant and the connective on the output is AND-dominant.

We however have to note that the benchmark data set is very scarce hence a *leave-one-out* procedure is most appropriate. The results obtained by using a single uninorm are shown in figure 5. The minimum error of the SSEs on the training sets is 0.2124 and 0 on the test sets. We also note that the average SSE performance indeces are of 0.2508 and 0.0109 on the training and test sets, respectively. Looking the comparison of the SSEs in figure 5a we note that since it is difficult to define the minimum of both error performance indeces than we chosen the point where both the errors are closed the average (SSE of 0.2489 for the training set and of 0.0128 for the test set). The associated estimated parameters are shown in Table 2. Also in this case we have that the estimated connective is AND-dominant. In figure 5b we plot the SSEs obtained applying the leave-one-out technique, by using the uninorm-based neuron. We note that the minimum error on the SSEs of the training sets is 0.0276 and 0 on the test sets. We also note that the average SSE performance indeces are 0.0430 and 0.0020 on the training and test sets, respectively. Moreover the estimated parameters, that correspond to the minimum of the error on both training and test sets, are described in Table 3. We stress in this case that the output is described by an AND-dominant connective as in the previous case but the connectives between inputs and weights are one AND-dominant and another OR-dominant.

We consider that for the considered data set the unineuron presents better performance than the uninorm. This simple conclusion gives us the possibility to confirm that the input-output mapping is non-linear. In fact, the mapping underlining the Zimmermann Zysno data set is not so simple and cannot be described by using simple norms. This issue has been discussed and the model experimentally quantified using various generalized connectives (i.e. Ordinal Sums [3]).

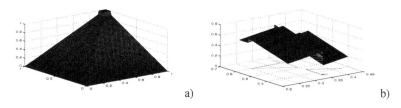

Fig. 4. Boudary obtained on the Zimmermann Zysno data set: a) by using uninorm ; b)by using the uninorm-based neuron

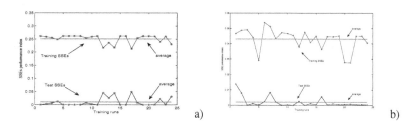

Fig. 5. SSEs obtained by using the leave-one-out method: a) with uninorm; b) with uninorm-based neuron

Table 1. Parameters of the uninorm-based neuron

I/O	t-norm	s-norm	e	α	or-ness	and-ness
I_1	t_P	s_L	0.2409	max	0.9420	0.0580
I_2	t_M	s_M	0.0068	max	1	$4.6e-005$
O	t_L	s_L	0.6074	min	0.1541	0.8459

Table 2. Estimated parameters with the use of the leave-one-out method with uninorms and GA

I/O	t-norm	s-norm	e	α	or-ness	and-ness
$I(x,y)$	t_M	s_M	0.8346	min	0.0274	0.9726

Table 3. Estimated parameters with the use of the leave-one-out method with uninorm-based neuron and GA

I/O	t-norm	s-norm	e	α	or-ness	and-ness
I_1	t_M	s_L	0.4854	max	0.2648	0.7352
I_2	t_M	s_W	0.1	min	0.99	0.01
O	t_W	s_P	0.4995	min	0.2505	0.7495

6   Conclusions

In this study, we have investigated a new category of logic connectives and logic neurons based on the concept of uninorms. We offered a genetic scheme of learning showing how it helps us to estimate the values of the parameters as well as to pick up a specific realization of t-norms and t-conorms from a predefined family of connectives.

The experimental studies show that the optimization approach can be used to automatically learn the parameters of the uninorms and of the unineurons. For small data sets it becomes advisable to use a leave-one-out technique.

We verified that the uninorm obtained by using the genetic optimization on a known benchmark data set, give us a better result if compared with single t-norms.

Moreover, the unineuron allows us to obtain better performance than the uninorm. In fact, the mapping of the Zimmermann Zysno data set is obtained by using complex aggregations. For this reason we obtain better results by considering an uninorm-based neuron.

In the future the authors will focus their attention to develop a Multi-Layer Neural Network and to compare the uninorm-based logical connectors with the Ordinal Sums-based logical operators.

References

1. Calvo, T., Mesiar, R.: Continuous Generate Associative Aggregation Operators. Fuzzy Sets and Systems 126, 191–197 (2002)
2. Chipperfield, A., Fleming, P., Pohlheim, H., Fonseca, C.: Genetic Algorithms Toolbox for Use with Matlab, Dept. of Automatic Control and Systems Engineering, University of Sheffield http://www.shef.ac.uk/acse/research/ecrg/gat.html
3. Ciaramella, A., Pedrycz, W., Tagliaferri, R.: The Genetic Development of Ordinal Sums. Fuzzy Sets and Systems 151, 303–325 (2005)
4. Ciaramella, A., Pedrycz, W., Tagliaferri, R.: OR/AND Neurons for Fuzzy Set Connectives Using Ordinal Sums and Genetic Algorithms. In: Bloch, I., Petrosino, A., Tettamanzi, A.G.B. (eds.) WILF 2005. LNCS (LNAI), vol. 3849, pp. 188–194. Springer, Heidelberg (2006)
5. Fodor, J.C., Yager, R.R., Rybalov, A.: Structure of Uninorms. Int. J. of Uncertainty, Fuzziness and Knowledge-Based Systems 5, 411–427 (1997)
6. Hirota, K., Pedrycz, W.: OR/AND Neuron in Modeling Fuzzy Set Connectives. IEEE Transaction on Fuzzy Systems 2, 151–161 (1994)
7. Klement, E.P., Mesiar, R., Pap, E.: Triangular Norms. Kluwer Academic Publishers, Dordrecht (2001)
8. Pedrycz, W.: Logic-Based Fuzzy Neurocomputing with Unineurons. IEEE Transaction on Fuzzy Systems 14(6), 860–873 (2006)
9. Trillas, E., Alsina, C., Jacas, J.: On Logical Connectives for a Fuzzy Set Theory with or without Non-Empty Self-Contradictions. Int. Journal of Intelligent Systems 15(1), 155–164 (2000)
10. Yager, R.R.: Uninorms in Fuzzy Systems Modeling. Fuzzy Sets and Systems 122, 167–175 (2001)
11. Zimmermann, H.H., Zysno, P.: Latent Connectives in Human Decision Making. Fuzzy Sets and Systems 4, 37–51 (1980)

Using Visualization Tools to Guide Consensus in Group Decision Making

Sergio Alonso[1], Enrique Herrera-Viedma[2], Francisco Javier Cabrerizo[2], Carlos Porcel[3], and A.G. López-Herrera[4]

[1] Software Engineering Dept., University of Granada (Spain)
[2] Computer Science and Artificial Intelligence Dept., University of Granada (Spain)
[3] Computer Science and Numerical Analysis Dept., University of Córdoba (Spain)
[4] Computer Science Dept., University of Jaén (Spain)
{salonso,viedma}@decsai.ugr.es,cabrerizo@ugr.es,
carlos.porcel@uco.es,aglopez@ujaen.es

Abstract. In the resolution of group decision making problems where the consensus process can not be held *face to face* by the experts it is usually difficult for them to be able to identify the closeness of the opinions of the rest of the experts, and thus, it is difficult to have a clear view of the current state of the consensus process. In this paper we present a tool that creates consensus diagrams that can help experts to easily comprehend the current consensus state and to easily identify the experts that have similar or very different opinions. Those diagrams are based on several new similarity and consistency measures.

Keywords: Consensus, Visualization, Consistency, Group Decision Making.

1 Introduction

Usually, to solve Group Decision Making problems, that is, problems where a set of experts $E = \{e_1, \ldots, e_m\}$ have to choose the best alternative or alternatives from a feasible set of alternatives $X = \{x_1, \ldots, x_n\}$, two different processes have to be carried out: the *consensus process* and the *selection process*. The former consists on obtaining the highest consensus level among experts, that is, to obtain a state were the opinions of the different experts are as close as possible one to another. The latter process consists on obtaining the final solution to the problem from the opinions expressed by the experts in the last round of the consensus process.

While the selection process can be almost fully automatized using different Soft Computing techniques [4,5,9,10,12,17], the consensus process [2,3,11,14,16,22] involves the communication and discussion among experts and between the experts and the moderator, which is usually encharged to guide the consensus process in order to obtain the final solution for the problem with a high level of consensus. Thus, to fully automatize the consensus process is a more difficult task. However, several new different approaches and tools to adapt classical consensus processes

F. Masulli, S. Mitra, and G. Pasi (Eds.): WILF 2007, LNAI 4578, pp. 77–85, 2007.

and models to new environments and making use of new technologies (mainly web-based technologies) can be found in the literature [1,18,19,21].

The application of these new technologies allow to carry out consensus processes in situations which previously could not be correctly addressed. For example, nowadays it is possible to carry out consensus processes among several experts which are located in different countries around the world. Though, it is important to remark that even with the adoption of new communication technologies (video-conference, chat rooms, instant messaging, e-mail and so on) there is still an important need of new collaboration and information tools for the experts being able to solve decision making problems where they cannot meet together with the other experts.

In this work we center our attention in a particular problem that arises in many consensus processes for group decision making when experts do not have the possibility of gathering together: experts may not have a clear idea about the current consensus status among all the experts involved in the decision process. In usual decision making models, where experts gather together to discuss their opinions about the different alternatives, it is relatively easy to determine which experts have similar opinions, and thus, experts may join or form different groups to better discuss and to reason out about the pros and cons of every alternative. Additionally, when experts are able to determine the consensus state of the decision making process it is more easy for them to influence the other experts [8]. However, in the cases where direct communication is not possible, experts will probably need some assistance to stablish connections among them and to obtain a clear view of the consensus process progress.

To ease the perception of the consensus state to the experts, we propose to use a novel visualization tool which generates simple consensus diagrams of the current consensus state in the decision making problem that is being solved by drawing a graph in which the experts are nodes which are separated from each other depending on the affinity of their preferences about the alternatives in the problem. Visual elements do have a great protential to influence experts in decision processes [20] and thus, these consensus diagrams, when presented to the experts, will allow them to have a more profound and clear view about the consensus process and about which experts have similar or different opinions about the alternatives. To develop the visualization tool we take into account several factors as the consistency of the information expressed by each expert and the similarity of the opinions of the experts at three different levels. This visualization tool can be easily integrated into existing consensus models.

The structure of this contribution is as follows: In section 2 we present fuzzy preference relations as the representation model that the experts will use to provide their preferences about the alternatives and some consistency properties and measures about them. In section 3 we present some similarity masures that can be computed from the preferences expressed by the experts. Section 4 describes the visualization tool that using the previous similarity and consistency measures generates some consensus diagrams that can be used by the experts to obtain a clear picture of the current consensus state in the problem. Finally, some conclusions and future works are outlined in section 5.

2 Preliminaries

In this section we present fuzzy preference relations as the representation model that the experts will use to express their preferences about the alternatives in the problem. Additionally, some consistency measures for the preference relations at three different levels (pair of alternatives, alternatives and preference relation levels) are presented.

There exists many different representation formats that can be used by experts to provide their preferences about the alternatives in a group decision making problem. One of the most used formats is *fuzzy preference relations* due to their effectiveness as a tool for modelling decision processes and their utility and easiness of use when we want to aggregate experts' preferences into group ones [13,15,23]:

Definition 1. *A fuzzy preference relation P^h given by expert e^h on a set of alternatives X is a fuzzy set on the product set $X \times X$, i.e., it is characterized by a membership function $\mu_{P^h} : X \times X \longrightarrow [0, 1]$.*

When cardinality of X is small, the preference relation may be conveniently represented by the $n \times n$ matrix $P^h = (p_{ik}^h)$, being $p_{ik}^h = \mu_{P^h}(x_i, x_k)$ ($\forall i, k \in \{1, \dots, n\}$) interpreted as the preference degree or intensity of the alternative x_i over x_k: $p_{ik}^h = 1/2$ indicates indifference between x_i and x_k ($x_i \sim x_k$), $p_{ik}^h = 1$ indicates that x_i is absolutely preferred to x_k, and $p_{ik}^h > 1/2$ indicates that x_i is preferred to x_k ($x_i \succ x_k$). Based on this interpretation we have that $p_{ii}^h = 1/2$ $\forall i \in \{1, \dots, n\}$ ($x_i \sim x_i$).

Consistency [13], that is, lack of contradiction, is usually a very desirable property for preference relations (information without contradiction is usually more valuable than contradictory information). In [12] we developed some consistency measures for fuzzy preference relations which are based on the additive consistency property, whose mathematical definition was provided by Tanino in [23]:

$$(p_{ij}^h - 0.5) + (p_{jk}^h - 0.5) = (p_{ik}^h - 0.5) \ \forall i, j, k \in \{1, \dots, n\} \tag{1}$$

that can be rewritten as:

$$p_{ik}^h = p_{ij}^h + p_{jk}^h - 0.5 \ \forall i, j, k \in \{1, \dots, n\} \tag{2}$$

We consider a fuzzy preference relation P^h to be *additive consistent* when for every three alternatives in the problem $x_i, x_j, x_k \in X$ their associated preference degrees $p_{ij}^h, p_{jk}^h, p_{ik}^h$ fulfil (2).

Additionally, expression (2) can be used to calculate an estimated value of a preference degree using other preference degrees in a fuzzy preference relation. Indeed, the preference value p_{ik}^h ($i \neq k$) can be estimated using an intermediate alternative x_j in three different ways:

1. From $p_{ik}^h = p_{ij}^h + p_{jk}^h - 0.5$ we obtain the estimate

$$(cp_{ik}^h)^{j1} = p_{ij}^h + p_{jk}^h - 0.5 \tag{3}$$

2. From $p_{jk}^h = p_{ji}^h + p_{ik}^h - 0.5$ we obtain the estimate

$$(cp_{ik}^h)^{j2} = p_{jk}^h - p_{ji}^h + 0.5 \tag{4}$$

3. From $p_{ij}^h = p_{ik}^h + p_{kj}^h - 0.5$ we obtain the estimate

$$(cp_{ik}^h)^{j3} = p_{ij}^h - p_{kj}^h + 0.5 \tag{5}$$

The overall estimated value cp_{ik}^h of p_{ik}^h is obtained as the average of all possible $(cp_{ik}^h)^{j1}$, $(cp_{ik}^h)^{j2}$ and $(cp_{ik}^h)^{j3}$ values:

$$cp_{ik}^h = \frac{\sum_{j=1; i \neq k \neq j}^{n} (cp_{ik}^h)^{j1} + (cp_{ik}^h)^{j2} + (cp_{ik}^h)^{j3}}{3(n-2)} \tag{6}$$

When the information provided is completely consistent then $(cp_{ik}^h)^{jl}=p_{ik}^h \, \forall j, l$. However, because experts are not always fully consistent, the information given by an expert may not verify (2) and some of the estimated preference degree values $(cp_{ik}^h)^{jl}$ may not belong to the unit interval $[0, 1]$. We note, from expressions (3–5), that the maximum value of any of the preference degrees $(cp_{ik}^h)^{jl}$ ($l \in \{1, 2, 3\}$) is 1.5 while the minimum one is -0.5. Taking this into account, we define the error between a preference value and its estimated one as follows:

Definition 2. *The error between a preference value and its estimated one in* $[0, 1]$ *is computed as:*

$$\varepsilon p_{ik}^h = \frac{2}{3} \cdot |cp_{ik}^h - p_{ik}^h| \tag{7}$$

Thus, it can be used to define the consistency level between the preference degree p_{ik}^h and the rest of the preference values of the fuzzy preference relation.

Definition 3. *The consistency level associated to a preference value* p_{ik}^h *is defined as*

$$cl_{ik}^h = 1 - \varepsilon p_{ik}^h \tag{8}$$

When $cl_{ik}^h = 1$ then $\varepsilon p_{ik}^h = 0$ and there is no inconsistency at all. The lower the value of cl_{ik}^h, the higher the value of εp_{ik}^h and the more inconsistent is p_{ik}^h with respect to the rest of information.

Easily, we can define the consistency measures for particular alternatives and for the whole fuzzy preference relation:

Definition 4. *The* consistency level associated to a particular alternative x_i *of a fuzzy preference relation* P^h *is defined as*

$$cl_i^h = \frac{\sum\limits_{\substack{k=1 \\ i \neq k}}^{n}(cl_{ik}^h + cl_{ki}^h)}{2(n-1)} \tag{9}$$

with $cl_i^h \in [0,1]$.

Definition 5. *The* consistency level of a fuzzy preference relation P^h *is defined as follows:*

$$cl^h = \frac{\sum\limits_{i=1}^{n} cl_i^h}{n} \tag{10}$$

with $cl^h \in [0,1]$.

3   Computing Similarity Measures

In this section we present some new similarity measures among experts that can be computed from the fuzzy preference relations expressed by experts. These new measures, as the consistency measures presented in section 2, are computed in three different levels (pair of alternatives, alternatives and preference relations levels) for every pair of experts in the problem.

To do so, for each pair of experts (e_h, e_l) $(h < l)$ we define a similarity matrix $SM^{hl} = \left(sm_{ik}^{hl}\right)$ where

$$sm_{ik}^{hl} = 1 - |p_{ik}^h - p_{ik}^l| \tag{11}$$

Definition 6. *The measure of similarity of the preference experts* e_h *and* e_l *about the alternative* x_i *over* x_k *is* sm_{ik}^{hl}.

The closer sm_{ik}^{hl} is to 1, the more similar is the opinion of the experts about alternative x_i over x_k.

We can now compute similarity measures at the alternatives and preference relation levels:

Definition 7. *A similarity measure for experts* e_h *and* e_l *for a particular alternative* x_i *is computed as:*

$$sm_i^{hl} = \frac{\sum\limits_{\substack{k=1 \\ i \neq k}}^{n}(sm_{ik}^{hl} + sm_{ki}^{hl})}{2(n-1)} \tag{12}$$

Definition 8. *A global similarity measure for experts* e_h *and* e_l *(taking into account the whole preference relations) is computed as:*

$$sm^{hl} = \frac{\sum\limits_{i=1}^{n} sm_i^{hl}}{n} \tag{13}$$

4   A Tool to Visualize the Consensus State for Group Decision Making Problems

In this section we present a novel visualization tool that generates consensus diagrams in which the experts on the problem are drawn in different locations depending on the similarity of their opinions, that is, experts with similar opinions will be drawn near to each other, while the experts whose opinions differ greatly will be drawn far away from each other.

To draw the consensus diagrams we use a spring model graph drawing algorithm [7] in which the experts correspond to the nodes of the graph and a similarity measure between each pair of experts act as the length of the spring associated to each edge of the graph. These kind of algorithms simulate a system of springs defined on the graph and output a locally minimum energy configuration.

As we have defined several different similarity measures the tool can use different similarity measures depending on the information that we want to visualize. For example, if we need a general overview of the consensus state for the problem, we can choose to use the global similarity measures sm^{hl}, but if we want to visualize the consensus state about a particular alternative x_i we can choose to use the similarity measures sm_i^{hl}.

As consistency of the information is also an important issue to take into account (inconsistent experts are usually far away from the opinions of the other experts) we have introduced in the visualization tool the possibility of incorporating the consistency measures presented in section 2 to improve the consensus diagrams. This improvements are reflected in two different ways:

- The most consistent experts are drawn bigger. Thus, it is easy to recognize the most consistent experts and those who provide contradictory information.
- The similarity measures are altered according to the consistency of the experts involved:

$$\overline{sm}_{ik}^{hl} = \frac{sm_{ik}^{hl}}{(cl_{ik}^h + cl_{ik}^l)/2} \quad ; \quad \overline{sm}_i^{hl} = \frac{sm_i^{hl}}{(cl_i^h + cl_i^l)/2} \quad ; \quad \overline{sm}^{hl} = \frac{sm^{hl}}{(cl^h + cl^l)/2}$$

In figure 1 we have a snapshot of the tool where the global consensus state is depicted for a group decision making problem with 4 different alternatives and 7 different experts involved. As it can be seen, there are three experts (*Enrique*, *Francisco* and *Francisco C.*) with similar opinions -they are close to each other-. On the other hand, *Sergio*'s opinions seem to be far from all the other experts,

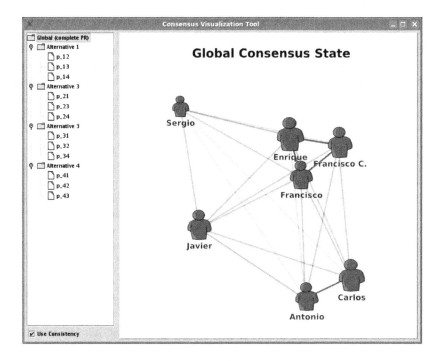

Fig. 1. Snapshot of the Visualization Tool

and moreover, his opinions are the most inconsistent (contradictory) -he is drawn smaller due to that contradictions-. Additionally it can be seen that *Antonio* and *Carlos* have similar opinions about the problem, but these opinions are different than the opinions expressed by all the other experts.

5   Conclusions

In this paper we have presented a tool that allows to visualize the status of a consensus process. It makes use of consistency and similarity measures in order to generate some consensus diagrams were experts are drawn nearer when their opinions are similar. Thus, we provide a powerful tool for experts that participate in consensus processes where there is no possibility of gathering together (for example if the consensus process is held by means of web technologies) and consecuently, where is difficult to obtain a clear overview of the consensus state.

In future works we will improve this visualiztion tool in order to be able to represent more useful information in the consensus diagrams, as the position of the current solution of consensus or the automatic detection of groups of experts with similar alternatives.

References

1. Alonso, S., Herrera-Viedma, E., Herrera, F., Cabrerizo, F.J., Chiclana, F.: An Interactive Support System to Aid Experts to Express Consistent Preferences. In: Proceddings of the 7th International FLINS Conference on Applied Artificial Intelligence (FLINS, Genova (Italy) pp.425–432 (2006)
2. Bordogna, G., Fedrizzi, M., Pasi, G.: A linguistic modeling of consensus in group decision making based on OWA operators. IEEE Transactions on Systems, Man and Cybernetics, Part A 27, 126–133 (1997)
3. Bryson, N.: Group decision-making and the analytic hierarchy process: exploring the consensus-relevant information content. Computers and Operational Research 23, 27–35 (1996)
4. Chiclana, F., Herrera, F., Herrera-Viedma, E.: Integrating Three Representation Models in Fuzzy Multipurpose Decision Making Based on Fuzzy Preference Relations. Fuzzy Sets and Systems 97, 33–48 (1998)
5. Chiclana, F., Herrera, F., Herrera-Viedma, E.: Integrating multiplicative preference relations in a multipurpose decision-making model based on fuzzy preference relations. Fuzzy Sets and Systems 122(2), 277–291 (2001)
6. Choudhury, A.K., Shankar, R., Tiwari, M.K.: Consensus-based intelligent group decision-making model for the selection of advanced technology. Decision Support Systems 42(3), 1776–1799 (2006)
7. Eades, P.: A heuristic for graph drawing. Congress Numerant. 42, 149–160 (1984)
8. Erb, H.P., Bohner, G.: Mere Consensus Effects in Minority and Majority Influence. In: De Dreu, C.K.W., De Vries, N.K. (eds.) Group Consensus and Minority Influence, Implications for Innovation, Blackwell Publishers, Oxford (UK) (2001)
9. Evangelos, T.: Multi-Criteria Decision Making Methods: A Comparative Study. Kluwer Academic Publishers, Dordrecht (2000)
10. Herrera, F., Herrera-Viedma, E., Verdegay, J.L.: A sequential selection process in group decision making with linguistic assessments. Information Sciences 85, 223–239 (1998)
11. Herrera-Viedma, E., Alonso, S., Herrera, F., Chiclana, F., Consensus, A.: Model for Group Decision Making with Incomplete Fuzzy Preference Relations. IEEE Transactions on Fuzzy Systems (2006) (in press)
12. Herrera-Viedma, E., Chiclana, F., Herrera, F., Alonso, S.: A Group Decision Making Model with Incomplete Fuzzy Preference Relations Based on Additive Consistency. IEEE Transactions on Systems, Man and Cybernetics B37(1), 176–189 (2007)
13. Herrera-Viedma, E., Herrera, F., Chiclana, F., Luque, M.: Some issues on consistency of fuzzy preference relations. Europ. J. of Operational Research 154, 98–109 (2004)
14. Herrera-Viedma, E., Martínez, L., Mata, F., Chiclana, F.: A consensus support system model for group decision-making problems with multi-granular linguistic preference relations. IEEE Transactions on Fuzzy Systems 13(5), 644–658 (2005)
15. Kacprzyk, J.: Group decision making with a fuzzy linguistic majority. Fuzzy Sets and Systems 18, 105–118 (1986)
16. Kacprzyk, J., Fedrizzi, M., Nurmi, H.: Group decision making and consensus under fuzzy preferences and fuzzy majority. Fuzzy Sets and Systems 49, 21–31 (1992)
17. Kahraman, C., Ruan, D., Dogan, I.: Fuzzy group decision-making for facility location selection. Infomation Sciences 157, 135–153 (2003)

18. Kersten, G., Noronha, S.: Negotiation via the World Wide Web: A Cross-cultural Study of Decision Making. Group Decision and Negotiation 8(3), 251–279 (1999)
19. Kersten, G.: e-democracy and participatory decision processes: lessons from e-negotiation experiments. Journal of Multi-Criteria Decision Analysis 12, 127–143 (2004)
20. Messaris, P.: Visual Persuasion. The Role of Images in Advertising. SAGE Publications, London (UK) (1997)
21. O'Keefe, R.M., McEachern, T.: Web-based customer decision support systems. Communications of the ACM 41(3), 71–78 (1998)
22. Szmidt, E., Kacprzyk, J.: A consensus reaching process under intuitionistic fuzzy preference relations. Int. Journal of Intelligent Systems 18(7), 837–852 (2003)
23. Tanino, T.: Fuzzy preference orderings in group decision making. Fuzzy Sets and Systems 12, 117–131 (1984)

Reconstruction Methods for Incomplete Fuzzy Preference Relations: A Numerical Comparison

Matteo Brunelli[1], Michele Fedrizzi[1], and Silvio Giove[2]

[1] Dipartimento di Informatica e Studi Aziendali, Università di Trento,
Via Inama 5, TN 38100 Trento, Italy
Tel. +39 0461 882148
michele.fedrizzi@unitn.it
[2] Dipartimento di Matematica Applicata, Università di Venezia Dorsoduro,
3825/E, Venezia, Italy
silvio.giove@unive.it

Abstract. In this paper we compare, by means of numerical simulations, seven different methods for reconstructing incomplete fuzzy preference relations. We consider the case of highly inconsistent preference relations as well as the case of preference relations close to consistency. We compare the numerical results on the basis of the consistency of the reconstructed preference relations.

1 Introduction

Fuzzy preference relations, *FPR* in the following, are a flexible tool for pairwise comparing n alternatives [12] [16]. Incomplete *FPR* may occur, for instance, when the number n of the alternatives is large or when it can be convenient/necessary to skip some direct critical comparison between alternatives, even if the total number of alternatives is small [8]. Given an incomplete *FPR* $R = [r_{ij}]$, it is possible to compute the corresponding priority vector for the alternatives in two equivalent ways. The first one is to directly use one of the few methods proposed in the literature for incomplete *FPR* [7] [11] [24] [25] . The second one is to use, as explained in section 3, one of the methods proposed for the same problem in the *multiplicative* framework [3] [8] [9] [13] [15] [20] [21] [23]. For the numerical simulations presented in this paper we have chosen three methods of the first kind and four of the second one. The paper is organized as follows: in section 2 we introduce the necessary definitions and notations on *FPR* and incomplete *FPR*. In Section 3 we describe the various numerical simulations and we present the obtained results. In section 4 we apply the seven methods to an example proposed in 2001 by T. Saaty. In section 5 we conclude with some comments and remarks.

2 Reconstruction of Incomplete Fuzzy Preference Relations

We assume that the reader is familiar with *FPR*s and we only recall that they are nonnegative relations $R : \Lambda \times \Lambda \rightarrow [0,1]$ on a set of alternatives $\Lambda =$

F. Masulli, S. Mitra, and G. Pasi (Eds.): WILF 2007, LNAI 4578, pp. 86–93, 2007.
© Springer-Verlag Berlin Heidelberg 2007

$\{A_1, A_2, ..., A_n\}$. Additive reciprocity is assumed, $r_{ji} = 1 - r_{ij}$, $i, j = 1, ..., n$, where $r_{ij} := R(A_i, A_j)$. The $n \times n$ matrix $R = [r_{ij}]$ is also called *additive pairwise comparison matrix* or *additive preference matrix*. A *FPR* $[r_{ij}]$ is called *consistent* in additive sense if and only if

$$(r_{ih} - 0.5) + (r_{hj} - 0.5) = (r_{ij} - 0.5), \quad i, j, h = 1, ..., n. \tag{1}$$

If one or more comparisons r_{ij} are missing, the *FPR* is called incomplete. In the simulations presented in section 3 we consider three methods, denoted in the following by M5–M7, proposed in the literature to compute the missing entries r_{ij} of an incomplete *FPR*, as well as four methods (M1–M4) proposed to compute the missing entries a_{ij} of an incomplete pairwise comparison matrix in the multiplicative framework. More precisely, we use the term *multiplicative* to refer to Saaty's approach, assuming that the reader is familiar with it. In this framework, a_{ij} estimates the ratio between the priorities, $a_{ij} \approx \frac{w_i}{w_j}$ and the *multiplicative pairwise comparison matrix* $A = [a_{ij}]$, also called *multiplicative preference matrix*, is positive and reciprocal ($a_{ji} = 1/a_{ij}$) [18]. A multiplicative matrix is called *consistent* if and only if $a_{ih}a_{hj} = a_{ij}$, $i, j, h = 1, ...n$.

It is also possible to considered the methods proposed in the multiplicative approach because it can be shown that each multiplicative matrix $A = [a_{ij}]$ can be easily transformed into the corresponding matrix $R = [r_{ij}]$ associated to a *FPR* and vice versa. The simple function introduced in [6],

$$r_{ij} = f(a_{ij}) = \frac{1}{2}(1 + \log_9 a_{ij}) \tag{2}$$

transforms the a_{ij} values into the r_{ij} values in such a way that all the relevant properties of $A = [a_{ij}]$ are transformed into the corresponding properties for $R = [r_{ij}]$ in the additive sense. In particular, multiplicative reciprocity is transformed into additive reciprocity and multiplicative consistency is transformed into additive consistency. Clearly, if we need to transform a *FPR* $R = [r_{ij}]$ into a multiplicative matrix $A = [a_{ij}]$, it is sufficient to use the inverse f^{-1} of (2). This means that the two ways of eliciting preferences are equivalent and every result obtained in one of the two frameworks can immediately be reformulated in the other one, see for instance, [1] [4] [10] [26].

The methods considered in section 3 are listed below. For easy reference, we have assigned a tag and a name to each method,

M1 Least Squares method 1	**M5** Xu goal programming
M2 Least Squares method 2	**M6** Xu eigenproblem
M3 Harker	**M7** Fedrizzi – Giove ρ
M4 Shiraishi et al. c_3	

In the following we describe very briefly the methods M1–M7. Please refer to the original papers for a more complete description.

Method M1 – Least squares 1

The priorities w_i for a complete matrix $A = [a_{ij}]$ can be computed by solving, with respect to $w_1, ..., w_n$, the problem (see [5])

$$\min_{w_1,\ldots,w_n} \sum_{i=1}^{n}\sum_{j=1}^{n}\left(a_{ij} - \frac{w_i}{w_j}\right)^2 \quad \text{s.t.} \sum_{i=1}^{n} w_i = 1, \quad w_i > 0. \qquad (3)$$

If $A = [a_{ij}]$ is incomplete, the only change needed in (3) is to skip, in the objective function, the terms corresponding to missing comparisons [3].

Method M2 – Least squares 2

In some cases, method M1 can have serious problems in numerical computation, due to the presence of the variable w_j in the denominator. Therefore it has been modified, obtaining

$$\min_{w_1,\ldots,w_n} \sum_{i=1}^{n}\sum_{j=1}^{n}(a_{ij}w_j - w_i)^2 \quad \text{s.t.} \sum_{i=1}^{n} w_i = 1, \quad w_i > 0.$$

Details can be found in [3], [5].

Method M3 – Harker

This method, proposed by P.T. Harker in 1987 [8], is not based on the optimization of a function, but refers to the eigenvector approach of Saaty. Harker extends the Saaty's approach to nonnegative quasi reciprocal matrices, in order to apply it to the case of incomplete preferences.

Method M4 – Shiraishi et al. c_3

The name c_3 refers to the coefficient of λ^{n-3} in the characteristic polynomial of the matrix A. Shiraishi et al. [20] observe that c_3 can be considered as an index of consistency for A. Then, in order to maximize the consistency of A, the authors consider the (let be m) missing entries in A as variables $x_1,\ldots,x_m$ and propose to maximize $c_3(x_1,\ldots,x_m)$ as a function of these variables.

Method M5 – Xu goal programming

In [24], Xu proposes a model, based on goal programming and denoted by (LOP2), to calculate the priority vector $w = [w_i]$ of an incomplete *FPR*. This method is based on a characterization of consistent *FPR* introduced by Tanino in [22] and thus it aims to minimize the errors $\varepsilon_{ij} = |r_{ij} - 0.5(w_i - w_j + 1)|$ for all the known entries (i,j). Note that, in order to obtain satisfactory results, we removed from the proposed model an unnecessary normalization constraint, which conflicts with the requested optimization [2].

Method M6 – Xu eigenproblem

In his second proposal, Xu [25] develops a method, for incomplete fuzzy preference relations, similar to M3. In [25] the priority vector $w = [w_i]$ is calculated by solving a system of equations which corresponds to the auxiliary eigenproblem developed by Harker in the multiplicative framework.

Method M7 – Fedrizzi–Giove ρ

The method proposed in [7] for incomplete FPR, considers, as in M4, the m missing comparisons as variables $x_1, \dots, x_m$ and compute their optimal values by minimizing an (in)consistency index $\rho(x_1, \dots, x_m)$ based on consistency condition (1),

$$\min \rho = \min \sum_{i,j,h=1}^{n} (r_{ih} + r_{hj} - r_{ij} - 0.5)^2 \quad \text{s.t.} \ \ 0 \leq x_j \leq 1. \tag{4}$$

3   Numerical Simulations

The objective of the numerical simulations presented in this section is to study how well the seven methods mentioned above are able to reconstruct an incomplete FPR and to compare the results obtained in the different considered cases.

It should be preliminarily noted that methods M1, M2, M3, M5 and M6 give, as a result, not directly the missing comparisons, but a priority vector, say w^*. Nevertheless, each missing comparison can be estimated by $a_{hk} = w_h^*/w_k^*$ or by $r_{hk} = 0.5 + 0.5(w_h^* - w_k^*)$, respectively in the multiplicative [18] and in the additive case [22]. Thus, for every considered method, the final result is a complete (reconstructed) preference matrix.

The results of the various methods are compared on the basis of the consistency of the reconstructed preference matrices. Many different methods have been proposed to measure the inconsistency level of a preference matrix. We chose to use the most old and popular: the consistency ratio, CR, introduced by Saaty [18]. The smaller is the CR, the more consistent is the preference matrix, with $CR = 0$ only for full consistent matrices. We assume that the more consistent is a reconstructed matrix, the better is the method, as the computed missing comparisons are coherent with the known entries. Since the CR can be calculated for multiplicative matrices $A = [a_{ij}]$ only, we have first transformed the FPR $[r_{ij}]$ reconstructed with the methods M5–M7 by means of the inverse f^{-1} of the function (2). The CR has been then calculated on the obtained multiplicative matrices.

In order to study the performances of the methods in different consistency situations, we use two classes of matrices: random matrices – which are very inconsistent – and consistent matrices slightly modified by a gaussian noise. The results of the simulations are summarized in Tab 1 and in Fig. 1 (a)–(d). We proceed as follows. First, we randomly generate 1000 6×6 matrices. For each matrix we randomly choose three comparisons to be considered missing; due to the reciprocity, six entries of the matrix are missing. We apply the seven methods, obtaining, for each matrix, seven different reconstructed matrices. We compute the CR of the obtained matrices. Finally, we compute, for each method, the average value of the CR on the 1000 simulations. We report this average value in the first column of Tab. 1. The values in the second column are obtained in the same way, with the only difference that, instead of random matrices, we use randomly generated consistent matrices which are then modified with gaussian

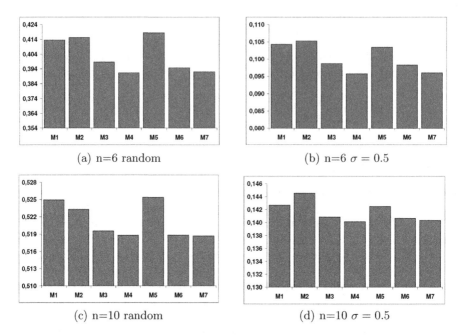

(a) n=6 random

(b) n=6 $\sigma = 0.5$

(c) n=10 random

(d) n=10 $\sigma = 0.5$

Fig. 1. Consistency Ratio of the reconstructed preference relations

random noise. The parameter σ represents the standard deviation of the gaussian distribution. Also in this case the reported average values are obtained from 1000 simulations.

Columns three and four of Tab 1 are obtained with the same kind of simulations, but with 10×10 matrices. Column two is interesting because the CR values are close to Saaty's threshold 0.1 for acceptability. Some methods succeed in respecting it, while others do not.

The last row of Tab 1 reports the average CR of the original matrices, before having considered three entries (plus the reciprocals) as missing. Note that, as expected, all the considered methods improve in average the consistency of the original complete matrices.

The results of the simulations are shown in Fig. 1 (a)–(d) by means of bar charts.

It can be observed that the best results are obtained by using the optimization methods M4 and M7, where the missing entries are directly computed, followed by the methods where the priority weights w_i are first computed. Good results are also obtained by using M3 and M6, which are methods based on eigenvalue approach. The two least squares based methods M1 and M2 form the last group, together with M5.

By varying the dimension n of the preference matrices and the number of missing comparisons, the relative performances of the methods do not significantly change. Given this stability with respect of these parameters, we have omitted to report other tables and bar charts.

Tab. 1 Consistency Ratio				
	n = 6		n = 10	
	random	noise $\sigma = 0.5$	random	noise $\sigma = 0.5$
M1	0.4130	0.1043	0.5249	0.1427
M2	0.4147	0.1053	0.5233	0.1445
M3	0.3981	0.0987	0.5195	0.1408
M4	0.3908	0.0958	0.5188	0.1401
M5	0.4180	0.1035	0.5254	0.1425
M6	0.3943	0.0983	0.5188	0.1406
M7	0.3916	0.0960	0.5187	0.1403
original	0.5599	0.1395	0.5621	0.1531

4 An Example of Reconstruction

We briefly consider an example proposed by T. Saaty in [19], page 14. The problem concerns the choosing of a house on the basis of eight criteria. We assume that three comparisons are missing, so that the obtained matrix $A_{inc} = [a_{ij}]$ has the following form, with a_{12}, a_{28}, a_{37} and their reciprocals being missing entries,

$$
A_{inc} = \begin{pmatrix}
1 & x_1 & 3 & 7 & 6 & 6 & 1/3 & 1/4 \\
1/x_1 & 1 & 1/3 & 5 & 3 & 3 & 1/5 & x_2 \\
1/3 & 3 & 1 & 6 & 3 & 4 & x_3 & 1/5 \\
1/7 & 1/5 & 1/6 & 1 & 1/3 & 1/4 & 1/7 & 1/8 \\
1/6 & 1/3 & 1/3 & 3 & 1 & 1/2 & 1/5 & 1/6 \\
1/6 & 1/3 & 1/4 & 4 & 2 & 1 & 1/5 & 1/6 \\
3 & 5 & 1/x_3 & 7 & 5 & 5 & 1 & 1/2 \\
4 & 1/x_2 & 5 & 8 & 6 & 6 & 2 & 1
\end{pmatrix}.
$$

Different reconstruction methods complete the matrix with different levels of consistency. We summarize the results in a vector $c = (c_1, \cdots, c_7)$, with c_i representing the CR achieved by using the i-*th* method,

$$ c = (0.07855, 0.07681, 0.07460, 0.07463, 0.08432, 0.07777, 0.07457). $$

It can be seen that the performances of the seven methods are substantially on line with the results described in the previous section.

5 Final Remarks

In this paper we have chosen to consider seven reconstruction methods. In our future research work we will extend the present approach, since other proposals for the problem of incomplete preferences are known, see for instance [3] [9] [11] [13] [15] [21] [23].

Moreover, the CR could be substituted by any other index proposed in the literature to measure the (in)consistency of a preference matrix, see for instance [1]

[3] [7] [17] [20]. Here we have chosen the CR of Saaty for two main reasons: the first one is that it is the oldest and most popular one; the second reason is its *neutrality*: some other possible consistency indices, as c_3 and ρ, are precisely the objective function of the corresponding reconstruction method, and would unfairly favorite the method itself. Note that each optimization–based method implicitly defines a consistency index and vice versa. Nevertheless, alternative ways for evaluating the various reconstruction methods could be taken into account.

References

1. Barzilai, J.: Consistency measures for pairwise comparison matrices. J. Multi–Crit. Decis. Anal. 7, 123–132 (1998)
2. Brunelli, M., Fedrizzi, Michele: A note on the paper Goal programming models for obtaining the priority vector of incomplete fuzzy preference relation, submitted to International Journal of Approximate Reasoning (2007)
3. Chen, Q., Triantaphyllou, E.: Estimating Data for Multi–Criteria Decision Making Problems: Optimization Techniques. In: Pardalos, P.M., Floudas, C. (eds.) Encyclopedia of Optimization, vol. 2, Kluwer Academic Publishers, Boston, MA (2001)
4. Chiclana, F., Herrera, F., Herrera–Viedma, E.: Integrating multiplicative preference relations in a multipurpose decision–making model based on fuzzy preference relations. Fuzzy Sets and Systems 122, 277–291 (2001)
5. Chu, A.T.W., Kalaba, R.E., Springarn, K.: A comparison of two methods for determining the weights of belonging to fuzzy sets. J. Optim. Th. Appl. 27, 321–538 (1979)
6. Fedrizzi, Michele: On a consensus measure in a group MCDM problem. In: Kacprzyk, J., Fedrizzi, M. (eds.) Multiperson Decision Making Models using Fuzzy Sets and Possibility Theory (Theory and Decision Library, series B: Mathematical and Statistical Methods, Vol. 18), Kluwer Academic Publishers, Dordrecht, The Netherlands (1990)
7. Fedrizzi, Michele, Giove, S.: Incomplete pairwise comparison and consistency optimization. European Journal of Operational Research (2006) doi: 10.1016/j.ejor.2006.09.065
8. Harker, P.T.: Alternative modes of questioning in the analytic hierarcy process. Mathl Modelling 9(3-5), 353–360 (1987)
9. Harker, P.T.: Incomplete pairwise comparisons in the analytic hierarcy process. Mathl Modelling 9(11), 837–848 (1987)
10. Herrera–Viedma, E., Herrera, F., Chiclana, F., Luque, M.: Some Issues on Consistency of Fuzzy Preference Relations. European Journal of Operational Research 154, 98–109 (2004)
11. Herrera–Viedma, E., Chiclana, F., Herrera, F., Alonso, S.: Group decision-making model with incomplete fuzzy preference relations based on additive consistency. IEEE Trans. Syst. Man. Cybern. B. Cybern. 37(1), 176–189 (2007)
12. Kacprzyk, J., Roubens, M.: Non–Conventional Preference Relations in Decision–Making. Springer, Berlin (1988)
13. Kwiesielewicz, M.: The logaritmic least squares and the generalized pseudoinverse in estimating ratios. European Journal of Operational Research 93, 611–619 (1996)
14. Kwiesielewicz, M., van Uden, E.: Ranking Decision Variants by Subjective Paired Comparisons in Cases with Incomplete Data. In: Kumar, V. (ed.) ICCSA 2003. LNCS, vol. 2667, Springer, Heidelberg (2003)

15. Nishizawa, K.: Estimation of unknown comparisons in incomplete AHP and it's compensation. Report of the Research Institute of Industrial Technology, Nihon University (77) (2004)
16. Orlovsky, S.A.: Decision–making with a fuzzy preference relation. Fuzzy Sets and Systems 1, 155–167 (1978)
17. Peláez, J.I., Lamata, M.T.: A new measure of consistency for positive reciprocal matrices. Computers and Mathematics with Applications 46, 1839–1845 (2003)
18. Saaty, T.L.: The Analytical Hierarchy Process. McGraw-Hill, New York (1980)
19. Saaty, T.L., Vargas, L.G.: Models, methods, concepts & applications of the analythical hierarchy process. Kluwer Academic, Boston (2001)
20. Shiraishi, S., Obata, T., Daigo, M.: Properties of a positive reciprocal matrix and their application to AHP. J. Oper. Res. Soc. Japan 41, 404–414 (1998)
21. Takeda, E., Yu, P.L.: Assessing priority weights from subsets of pairwise comparisons in multiple criteria optimization problems. European Journal of Operational Research 86, 315–331 (1995)
22. Tanino, T.: Fuzzy preference orderings in group decision making. Fuzzy Sets and Systems 12, 117–131 (1984)
23. van Uden, E.: Estimating missing data in pairwise comparison matrices. In: Bubnicki, Z., Hryniewicz, O., Kulikowski, R. (eds.) Operational and Systems Research in the Face to Challenge the XXI Century, Methods and Techniques in Information Analysis and Decision Making, Academic Printing House, Warsaw (2002)
24. Xu, Z.S.: Goal programming models for obtaining the priority vector of incomplete fuzzy preference relation. International Journal of Approximate Reasoning 36, 261–270 (2004)
25. Xu, Z.S.: A procedure for decision making based on incomplete fuzzy preference relation. Fuzzy Optimization and Decision Making 4, 175–189 (2005)
26. Xu, Z.S.: A least deviation method to obtain a priority vector of a fuzzy preference relation. European Journal of Operational Research 164, 206–216 (2005)

Web User Profiling Using Fuzzy Clustering

Giovanna Castellano[1], Fabrizio Mesto[2], Michele Minunno[2],
and Maria Alessandra Torsello[1]

[1] CILab - Computational Intelligence Laboratory
Computer Science Department, University of Bari,
Via E. Orabona, 4 - 70126 Bari, Italy
{castellano, torsello}@di.uniba.it
http://www.di.uniba.it/~cilab/
[2] Tel.net - Telecomunicazioni e Networking
Via Fanelli 226/13 - 70124 Bari, Italy
info@telnetsrl.com
http://www.telnetsrl.com

Abstract. Web personalization is the process of customizing a Web site
to the preferences of users, according to the knowledge gained from usage
data in the form of user profiles. In this work, we experimentally evaluate a fuzzy clustering approach for the discovery of usage profiles that can
be effective in Web personalization. The approach derives profiles in the
form of clusters extracted from preprocessed Web usage data. The use of
a fuzzy clustering algorithm enable the generation of overlapping clusters
that can capture the uncertainty among Web users navigation behavior
based on their interest. Preliminary experimental results are presented to
show the clusters generated by mining the access log data of a Web site.

Keywords: Web mining, Fuzzy clustering, access log, Web personalization, user profiling.

1 Introduction

The explosive growth in the information available on the Web has prompted the
need for developing Web Personalization systems that understand and exploit
user preferences to dynamically serve customized content to individual users
[9]. Web server access logs contain substantial data about user access patterns.
Hence, if properly exploited, the logs can reveal useful information about the
navigational behavior of users in a site. Therefore, a Web personalization system
can take advantage of anonymous Web usage data contained in log files to derive
profiles of users and compute recommendations for new users according to the
discovered profiles.

To reveal information about user preferences from Web log data, Data Mining
techniques can be naturally applied, leading to the so-called Web Usage Mining
(WUM). In general, a WUM approach involves the application of any Data
Mining algorithm on usage data gathered from one or more Web sites in order
to discover interesting patterns in the navigational behavior of visitors [6], [8],

F. Masulli, S. Mitra, and G. Pasi (Eds.): WILF 2007, LNAI 4578, pp. 94–101, 2007.
© Springer-Verlag Berlin Heidelberg 2007

[4], [11]. Among data mining approaches, clustering seems to be an effective way to group users with common browsing behavior [13], [15]. Several well-known clustering approaches have been employed to discover usage profiles, such as the EM algorithm [1], the Belief functions [17] or the SOFMs [14].

In the choice of the clustering method for WUM, one important constraint to be considered is the possibility to obtain overlapping clusters, so that a user can belong to more than one group. Another key feature to be addressed is vagueness and imprecision inherent Web usage data [5]. To deal with the ambiguity and the uncertainty underlying Web interaction data, as well as to derive overlapping clustering, fuzzy clustering appears to be an effective tool [10], [7], [12].

In this paper, we use fuzzy clustering for the discovery of usage profiles from web log data. To this aim, we firstly preprocess Web log files in order to derive user sessions. Then user sessions are mapped into a multi-dimensional space as a matrix of interest degrees. Finally the standard fuzzy C-means is applied to partition this space into groups of similar behavior patterns. Hence each cluster represents a user profile, i.e. a group of users with similar navigational behavior. The obtained user profiles can be exploited to implement different personalization functions, such as dynamic suggestion of links to Web pages retained interesting for the user.

The rest of the paper is organized as follows. Section 2 describes the steps of log data preprocessing aimed to identify user sessions. Section 3 deals with the employment of FCM to derive user profiles. Section 4 presents preliminary simulation results. Section 5 draws final conclusions.

2   User Session Identification by Log Data Preprocessing

A web log file contains information on the access of all visitors to a particular web site in chronological order. According to the Common Log Format [16], a log file contains, for each request, the client's host name or IP address, the request's date and time, the operation type (GET, POST, HEAD, and so on), the requested resource name (URL), a code indicating the status of the request, the size of the requested page (if the request is successful). Based on such information, we have to determine for each visitor, the sequence of URLs accessed during a certain time period. This process, called *sessionization* is performed through LODAP, a Log Data Preprocessor [3] that processes a Web log file through three main steps: data cleaning, data structuration and data filtering.

The data cleaning removes redundant and useless records (e.g. accesses to multimedia objects, robots' requests, etc.) so as to retain only information concerning accesses to pages of the Web site. We formally define the set of all distinct pages as $P = \{p_1, p_2, ..., p_{n_P}\}$.

Data structuration consists in grouping the unstructured requests for different pages into user sessions. A user session is defined as a finite set of URLs accessed by the same user within a particular visit. Identifying user sessions from the log data is a difficult task because many users may use the same computer and the same user may use different computers. For Web sites requiring user registration, the log file contains the user login that can be used for user identification. When the user login is not available, we simply consider each IP address as a different user (being aware that an IP address might be used by several users). We define $U = \{u_1, u_2, ..., u_{N_U}\}$ as the set of all the users (IP) that have accessed that web site. A user session is the set of accesses originating from the same user within a predefined time period. In LODAP such time period is fixed at 25 min. Formally, we define a user session as a triple $\mathbf{s}_i = \langle u_i, t_i, \mathbf{p}_i \rangle$ where $u_i \in U$ represents the user identifier, t_i is the access time of the whole session, $\mathbf{p}_i$ is the set of all pages (with corresponding access information) requested during the i-th session. Namely, $\mathbf{p}_i = \langle (p_{i1}, t_{i1}, N_{i1}), (p_{i2}, t_{i2}, N_{i2}), ..., (p_{i,n_i}, t_{i,n_i}, N_{i,n_i}) \rangle$ with $p_{ik} \in P$, where N_{ik} is the number of accesses to page p_k during the i-th session and t_{ik} is the total access time to that page. Summarizing, after the data structuration phase, a collection of n_S sessions is identified from the log data. We denote the set of all identified sessions by $S = \langle \mathbf{s}_1, \mathbf{s}_2, ..., \mathbf{s}_{n_S} \rangle$.

After the identification of user sessions, LODAP performs data filtering to retain only relevant URLs in each user session. This is done by removing requests for very low support URLs (i.e. requests to URLs which do not appear in a sufficient number of sessions) and requests for very high support URLs (i.e. requests to URLs which appear in nearly all sessions). This type of support-based filtering is useful to eliminate URLs having minimal knowledge value for the purpose of modeling the visitor behavior. As a consequence, all user sessions that comprise only very-low-support URLs or only very-high-support URLs are also removed. In addition, all user sessions including less than 3 visited URLs are removed. In this way, the size of data is even more reduced. We denote by $n < n_S$ the final number of sessions and by $m < n_P$ the final number of distinct URLs.

The statistics concerning the identified user sessions are used to create a model of the visitor behavior. The proposed model is based on a measure expressing the degree of interest for each page the user accessed during her/his navigation. We define the degree of interest to a page as a function of two variables: the overall time the user spends on the page during navigation and the number of accesses to the page within the session. Formally, given a page p_{ik} accessed in the i-th user session, we estimate the interest degree for that page as the average time of visit, i.e. $ID_{ik} = \frac{t_{ik}}{N_{ik}}$.

According to the definition of user session, the number of Web pages accessed by different users may vary. As a consequence, any two different session vectors $\mathbf{s}_i \neq \mathbf{s}_l$ may have different dimension, i.e. $n_i \neq n_l$. In order to create a homogeneous model for all visitors, we need to create vectors with the same number of components. Being m the number of different pages required in all the user sessions, we model the navigational behavior of a user $u_i (i = 1, ..., n)$ through a vector $\mathbf{b}_i = (b_{i1}, b_{i2}, ..., b_{im})$ where

$$b_{ij} = \begin{cases} ID_{ij} & \text{if page } p_j \text{is accessed in session } \mathbf{s}_i \\ 0 & \text{otherwise} \end{cases}$$

Summarizing, we represent the final usage data as a $n \times m$ matrix $\mathbf{B} = [b_{ij}]$ where each entry represents the interest degree of the i-th user for the j-th page. Based on this matrix, visitors with similar preferences can be successively clustered together into user profiles useful to personalize the content/structure of the Web site.

3   User Profiling by Fuzzy Clustering

Once the matrix of interest degrees has been derived, a clustering process is applied in order to identify user profiles. Each user profile will include users exhibiting a common browsing behavior and hence similar interests. In this work, the well-known Fuzzy C-Means (FCM) clustering algorithm [2] is applied in order to group vectors $\mathbf{b}_i$ in overlapping clusters which represent user profiles. Briefly, the FCM algorithm finds C clusters based on the minimization of the following objective function:

$$F_\alpha = \sum_{i=1}^{n} \sum_{c=1}^{C} u_{ic}^{\alpha} \parallel \mathbf{b}_i - \mathbf{v}_c \parallel^2, 1 \leq \alpha \leq \infty$$

where α is any real number greater than 1, u_{ic} is the degree of membership of the behavior vector $\mathbf{b}_i$ to the c-th cluster, $\mathbf{v}_c$ is the center of the c-th cluster. The FCM algorithm works as follows:

1. $\mathbf{U} = [u_{ic}]_{i=1,\ldots,n}^{c=1,\ldots,C}$ matrix, $\mathbf{U}^{(0)}$
2. At τ-th step: calculate the center vectors $\mathbf{V}^{(\tau)} = (\mathbf{v}_c)_{c=1,\ldots,C}$ as

$$\mathbf{v}_c = \frac{\sum_{i=1}^{n} u_{ic}^{\alpha} \mathbf{b}_i}{\sum_{i=1}^{n} u_{ic}^{\alpha}}$$

3. Update $\mathbf{U}^{(\tau)}$ according to:

$$u_{ic} = \frac{1}{\sum_{k=1}^{C} \left(\frac{\parallel \mathbf{b}_i - \mathbf{v}_c \parallel}{\parallel \mathbf{b}_i - \mathbf{v}_k \parallel} \right)^{\frac{2}{\alpha-1}}}$$

4. If $\parallel \mathbf{U}^{(\tau)} - \mathbf{U}^{(\tau-1)} \parallel < \epsilon$ with $0 < \epsilon < 1$, STOP; otherwise return to step 2.

As a result, FCM provides:

- C cluster prototypes represented as vectors $\mathbf{v}_c = (v_{c1}, v_{c2}, ..., v_{cm})$ for $c = 1, ..., C$.
- a fuzzy partition matrix $\mathbf{U} = [u_{ic}]_{i=1...n}^{c=1...C}$ where u_{ic} represents the membership degree of the visitor behavior vector $\mathbf{b}_i$ to the c-th cluster.

Summarizing, the FCM mines a collection of C clusters from navigational behavior data, representing profiles of users that have accessed to the Web site under analysis. Each profile $\mathbf{v}_c = (v_{c1}, v_{c2}, ..., v_{cm})$ describes the typical navigational behavior of a group of users with similar interests about the most visited pages of the web site.

4   Simulation Results

We carried out preliminary simulations to demonstrate the applicability of FCM for clustering Web users with similar interests. We used the access logs from a Web site targeted to young users (average age 12 years old), i.e. the italian Web site of the Japanese movie Dragon Ball (www.dragonballgt.it). This site was chosen because of its high daily number of accesses (thousands of visits each day).

The LODAP system described in section 2 was used to identify user sessions from the log data collected during a period of 24 hours. After data cleaning, the number of requests were reduced from 43,250 to 37,740, that were structured into 14,788 sessions. The total number of distinct URLs accessed in these sessions was 2268. Support-based data filtering was used to eliminate requests for URLs having a number of accesses less than 10% of the maximum number of accessess, leading to only 76 distinct URLs and 8040 sessions. Also, URLs appearing in more than 80% of sessions (including the site entry page) were filtered out, leaving 70 final URLs and 6600 sessions. The adopted values for the thresholds involved in page filtering were chosen by committing to past experience, accumulated during previous applications of LODAP to log files concerning different Web sites. We found that with a value less than 10% for the first threshold LODAP retained many pages rarely visited. Likewise, when a value greater than 80% was used for the second threshold, LODAP retained even those pages visited by almost all the users, that do not contribute to distinguish among user categories. In a further filtering step, LODAP eliminated short sessions, leaving only sessions with at least 3 distinct requests. We obtained a final number of 2422 sessions. The 70 pages in the Web site were labelled with a number (table 1) to facilitate the analysis of results.

Once user sessions were identified, visitor behavior models were derived by calculating the interest degrees of each user for each page, leading to a 2422x70 behavior matrix.

Next, the FCM algorithm (implemented in the Matlab environment 6.5) was applied to the behavior matrix in order to obtain clusters of users with similar navigational behavior. We carried out several runs with different number of clusters ($C = 30, 20, 15, 10$). In each run the parameter α of FCM was fixed to 2 and the maximum number of iterations was set to 1000. For each trial, we analyzed the obtained cluster center vectors and we observed that many of them were identical. Hence, an actual number of 3 clusters were found in each trial. This demonstrated that three clusters were enough to model the behavior of all the considered users. Table 2 describes the clusters found by FCM. For each cluster, the cardinality[1] and the first 8 (most interesting) pages are displayed. It can be noted that some pages (e.g. pages 12, 22 and 28) appear in more than one cluster, thus showing the importance of producing overlapping clusters. In

---

[1] The cardinality of a cluster c is defined as the cardinality of the set $\{\mathbf{b}_i | \parallel \mathbf{b}_i - \mathbf{v}_c \parallel < \parallel \mathbf{b}_i - \mathbf{v}_k \parallel \ \forall c \neq k\}$.

Table 1. Description of the pages in the Web site

Pages	Content
1	Home page
2	Comments by users
3,..., 12	Various kind of pictures related to the movie
13,..., 18	Pictures of characters
19, 26, 27	Matches
20, 21, 36, 47, 48	Services (registration, login, ...)
22, 23, 25, 28, ..., 31, 50, 51	General information about the movie
32, ..., 35, 55	Entertainment (games, videos,...)
37, ..., 46, 49, 52, ..., 54, 56	Description of characters
57, ..., 70	Galleries

Table 2. Clusters of visitor behavior

Cl.	Card.	Visited pages	Interest degrees
1	906	(28, 12, 15, 43, 17, 22, 13, 50)	(11.1, 7.3, 6.9, 6.6, 6.59, 5.14, 4.5, 4.4)
2	599	(28, 26, 22, 55, 12, 33, 49, 32)	(80.8, 43.3, 30.1, 25.9, 24.5, 19.2, 18.1, 14.3)
3	917	(28, 12, 26, 13, 22, 9, 19, 16)	(5.3, 4.0, 3.4, 3.1, 2.6, 2.60, 2.3, 2.2)

particular, page 28 (i.e. the page that lists the episodes of the movie) appears in all the three clusters with the highest degree of interest.

An interpretation of the three clusters revealed the following profiles:

- Profile 1. Visitors in this profile are mainly interested in pictures and descriptions of characters.
- Profile 2. These visitors prefer pages that link to entertainment objects (games and video)
- Profile 3. These visitors are mostly interested in matches among characters.

A qualitative analysis of these profiles made by designer of the considered Web site confirmed that they correspond to real user categories reflecting the interests of the typical site users.

5   Conclusions

We investigated the applicability of fuzzy clustering to discover user profiles from Web log data. To this aim, the first task was to preprocess log data in order to identify user sessions. Then, visitor behavior models were derived by estimating the interest degrees of each user for each page. Finally, the FCM algorithm was applied on the behavior matrix in order to obtain a number of clusters representing user profiles. Different runs of FCM provided always the same number of user profiles leading to the conclusion that the number of extracted profiles was sufficient to characterize the actual interests of the typical visitors, as confirmed by the designer of the considered Web site. The extracted user profiles will be used to implement personalization functions in the considered Web site, which is the ultimate goal of our research activity. In particular, our work in progress is oriented to develop a personalization module that dynamically suggests links to pages considered interesting for a current user, according to his profile.

References

1. Anderson, C.R., Domingos, P., Weld, D.S.: Adaptive Web navigation for wireless devices. In: Proc. of the 17th International Joint Conference on Artificial Intelligence(IJCAI-01), pp. 879–884 (2001)

2. Bezdek, J.C.: Pattern recognition with fuzzy objective function algorithms. Plenum Press, New York (1981)

3. Castellano, G., Fanelli, A.M., Torsello, M.A.: LODAP: A Log Data Preprocessor for mining Web browsing patterns. In: Proc. of The 6th WSEAS International Conference on Artificial Intelligence, Knowledge Engineering and Data Bases (AIKED '07), Corfu Island, Greece (2007)

4. Facca, F.M., Lanzi, P.L.: Mining interesting knowledge from weblogs: a survey. Data and Knowledge Engineering 53, 225–241 (2005)

5. Frias-Martinez, E., Magoulas, G., Chen, S., Macredie, R.: Modeling human behavior in user-adaptive systems: Recent advances using soft computing techniques. Expert Systems with Applications 29, 320–329 (2005)

6. Garofalakis, M.N., Rastogi, R., Seshadri, S., Shim, K.: Data mining and the web: past, present and future. In: Proc. of the second international workshop on web information and data management, ACM, New York (1999)

7. Joshi, A., Joshi, K.: On mining Web access logs. In: ACM SIGMOID Workshop on Research issues in Data Mining and Knowledge discovery, pp. 63–69 (2000)

8. Mobasher, B., Cooley, R., Srivastava, J.: Automatic personalization based on Web usage mining. TR-99010, Department of Computer Science. DePaul University (1999)

9. Nasraoui, O.: World Wide Web Personalization. In: Wang, J. (ed.) Encyclopedia of Data Mining and Data Warehousing, Idea Group (2005)

10. Nasraoui, O., Frigui, H., Joshi, A., Krishnapuram, R.: Mining Web access log using relational competitive fuzzy clustering. In: Proc. of the Eight International Fuzzy System Association World Congress (1999)

11. Pierrakos, D., Paliouras, G., Papatheodorou, C., Spyropoulos, C.D.: Web usage mining as a tool for personalization: a survey. User Modeling and User-Adapted Interaction 13(4), 311–372 (2003)

12. Suryavanshi, B.S., Shiri, N., Mudur, S.P.: An efficient technique for mining usage profiles using Relational Fuzzy Subtractive Clustering. In: Proc. of WIRI 05, Tokyo, Japan (2005)

13. Vakali, A., Pokorny, J., Dalamagas, T.: An Overview of Web Data Clustering Practices. In: EDBT Workshops, pp. 597–606 (2004)

14. Velasquez, J.D., Yasuda, H., Aoki, T., Weber, R., Vera, E.: Using Self Organizing Feature Maps to Acquire Knowledge about Visitor Behavior in a Web Site. In: Palade, V., Howlett, R.J., Jain, L. (eds.) KES 2003. LNCS, vol. 2773, pp. 951–958. Springer, Heidelberg (2003)
15. Wang, X., Abraham, A., Smith, K.A.: Intelligent web traffic mining and analysis. Journal of Network and Computer Applications 28, 147–165 (2005)
16. W3C. Logging Control in W3C httpd, `http://www.w3.org/Daemon/User/Config/Logging.html`
17. Xie, Y., Phoha, V.V.: Web user clustering from access log using belief function. In: Proc. of the First International Conference on Knowledge capture (K-CAP 2001), pp. 202–208. ACM Press, New York (2001)

Exploring the Application of Fuzzy Logic and Data Fusion Mechanisms in QAS

Daniel Ortiz-Arroyo and Hans Ulrich Christensen

Computer Science Department
Aalborg University Esbjerg
Niels Bohrs Vej 8, 6700 Denmark
do@cs.aaue.dk, huc1405@student.aaue.dk

Abstract. In this paper we explore the application of fuzzy logic and data fusion techniques to improve the performance of passage retrieval in open domain *Question Answering Systems (QAS)*. Our experiments show that our proposed mechanisms provide significant performance improvements when compared to other similar systems.

Keywords: Information Retrieval, Question Answering Systems, Passage Retrieval, Fuzzy Logic.

1 Introduction

A *Question Answering System (QAS)* is one type of information retrieval (IR) system that attempts to find exact answers to user's questions expressed in natural language. In *Open-Domain Question Answering Systems (ODQAS)*, answers to questions have to be found within an unstructured document collection containing different topics. *Passage Retrieval (PR)* is one component of a QAS that extracts text segments from a group of retrieved documents and ranks these passages in decreasing order of computed likelihood for containing the correct answer to a question. The overall performance of a QAS is determined, in large part, by the performance of its PR system.

Data Fusion is the combined ranking performed by a variety of IR systems on a document's relevance to a user's information need. When applied to QAS, the goal of the fusing process is to improve performance by combining the relevance scores obtained by a diversity of PR systems participating in an ensemble.

This paper describes an efficient language-independent, fuzzy logic-based model PR system, together with data fusion mechanisms for QAS. The paper is organized as follows. Section 2 briefly describes related work on passage retrieval systems and data fusion. Section 3 describes the main component mechanisms of the fuzzy logic based PR system and its performance results. Section 4 briefly describes the data fusion methods employed and presents the final performance results obtained by our system. Finally, Section 5 presents some conclusions and future work.

F. Masulli, S. Mitra, and G. Pasi (Eds.): WILF 2007, LNAI 4578, pp. 102–109, 2007.
© Springer-Verlag Berlin Heidelberg 2007

2 Related Work

JIRS is a PR system based on a n-gram model introduced by Gómoz-Soriano et al. in [1] that was adapted to the special needs of QA. JIRS supports two extensions to the basic n-gram matching mechanism (called *Simple Model*): *Term Weights* model and the *Distance Model* that include both term weights and a distance measure. JIRS ranks higher passages containing larger sequences of the terms contained in the questions. A related work is Web QA system [2] that builds queries constructed as permutations of the terms employed in the questions.

Several studies have investigated the application of Data Fusion to QA systems achieving in general promising results e.g. [3] reported a consistent improvements in terms of precision as high as 20%. However, few have investigated the potentially beneficial application of Data Fusion to the task of PR within a QAS. One example is [4] where a consistent significant improvement in Coverage@n is achived on the TREC11 collection. However, the machine learning techniques employed in [4] require an extra training step to learn the features of answering passages. Finally, Tellex et. al. experimentally fused three PR systems achieving a slight increase in performance in terms of MRR [5] using a simple voting mechanism.

Other studies on the application of Data Fusion to document retrieval (e.g. [6] and [7]) have reported important improvements in performance but on ad-hoc document retrieval systems and not specifically within PR for QAS.

3 A Fuzzy Logic-Based PR System

In QAS *the question reformulation intuition* stated as: "*a passage p is relevant to the user's question q if many question terms or variations of these question terms occur in close proximity*" is a commonly used technique to retrieve answering passages to a question. Fuzzy Logic is especially suited to model this intuition. The feature *"many (important) question terms"* can be modeled by the fuzzy subset: *The degree to which candidate passages contain all question terms.* "*Close proximity*" can be modeled by the fuzzy subset: *The degree to which the question terms contained in a candidate passage are juxtaposed* i.e. the more distributed the terms are, the lower the degree of proximity will be. The third vague concept that can be used to model the reformulation intuition is *term matching*. The fuzzy logic interpretation of binary term similarity is the fuzzy subset: *The degree to which two terms are identical.*

The reformulation intuition was modeled and implemented within *FuzzyPR*. *FuzzyPR* consists of two components: 1) a question–passage similarity measure module and 2) a passage identification and extraction mechanism adapted to the special needs of QAS. *FuzzyPR* uses a similarity measure based on the fuzzy logic interpretation of the *reformulation intuition* described by Equation 1.

$$\mu_{rel}(p,q) = wMin\left((v_1, \mu_f(p,q)), (v_2, \mu_p(p,q))\right). \tag{1}$$

The similarity measure combines lexical and statistical data extracted at *term-level* into two fuzzy measures: $\mu_f(p,q)$ the weighted fraction of question terms q occurring in the passage p and $\mu_p(p,q)$ the proximity of question terms q within the passage. $\mu_f(p,q)$ and $\mu_p(p,q)$ are defined in equations 2 and 3.

$$\mu_f(p,q) = h_{\alpha_f}\left((v_1^f, sat(t_{q_1}, p))\ldots(v_n^f, sat(t_{q_n}, p))\right). \tag{2}$$

where h is the AIWA importance weighted averaging operator [8] with an AND-ness of $\alpha_f = 0.65$, t_{q_i} is a question term, $v_i^f = NIDF(t_{q_i}) = 1 - \frac{log(n_i)}{1+log(N)}$ [1], n=frequency of t_{q_i} in Ω the set of documents, $N = |\Omega|$. $sat(p, t_{q_i})$ measures the degree to which p contains t_{q_i} using the normalized longest common subsequence (nLCS), i.e. $sat(p, t_{q_i}) = \max\limits_{\forall t_p \in p}\left(\mu_{sim}^{nLCS}(t_p, t_{q_i})\right)$, where $\mu_{sim}^{nLCS}(t_p, t_{q_i}) = \frac{|LCS(t_p, t_{q_i})|}{max(|t_p|, |t_{q_i}|)}$, LCS being the longest common subsequence. Finally,

$$\mu_p(p,q) = \frac{s(p,q)}{\max\limits_{\forall p_i \in \Omega} s(p_i, q)}. \tag{3}$$

where $\mu_p(p,q)$ is a max-normalization of Mercier and Beigbeder's *fuzzy proximity* method [9] described by $s(p,q) = \int_1^n \mu_t^p(x)dx$, $t \in q$ with the term influence function $\mu_t^p(x) = \max\limits_{i \in Occ(t,p)}\left(\max\left(\frac{k - |x - i|}{k}, 0\right)\right)$, where the parameter adjusting the support $k = 70$. The values of v_1, v_2, α_f and k were determined experimentally. Aggregating these two fuzzy measures using the weighted minimum gives the overall relevance score $wMin$, which is defined as:

$$wMin(v_1, v_2, \mu_f, \mu_p) = \min\left(\max(1 - v_1, \mu_f(p,q)), \max(1 - v_2, \mu_p(p,q))\right). \tag{4}$$

with the importance weights $v_1 = 1$, $v_2 = 1$ and both the passage p and the question q represented as sets of terms: $\{t_{p_1}, t_{p_2}, ..., t_{p_n}\}$ and $\{t_{q_1}, t_{q_2}, ..., t_{q_m}\}$, respectively. $wMin$ aggregates $\mu_f(p,q)$ and $\mu_p(p,q)$ into a single fuzzy value $\mu_{rel}(p,q)$ as described by Equation 1. $\mu_{rel}(p,q)$ is the fuzzy subset of passages providing a correct answer to the question q, where p is a specific passage. $\mu_{rel}(p,q)$ has the advantage of being *language-independent*.

FuzzyPR also employs a fuzzified variation of the concept *arbitrary passages*[2]. Details on the membership function employed to describe an arbitrary passage can be found in [10].

We measured the effectiveness of *FuzzyPR* comparing its ability to find correct answers to questions with JIRS' PR system [1] and an adapted PR system that we have integrated within Lucene using two different document corpora. The adapted PR system allows Lucene to be used as the PR module in a QAS, employing a simple query expansion method that keeps removing the question term with the lowest IDF until ≥ 20 passages are retrieved from the index of

---

[1] NIDF is an abbreviation of normalized inverse document frequency.

[2] Arbitrary passages are defined as: "*any sequence of words of any length starting at any word in the document*".

Table 1. MRRs obtained with TREC12's and CLEF04's QA test data

PR system / QA test data	TREC12	%Impr.	CLEF04	%Impr.
FuzzyPR	0.3394	-	0.3726	-
JIRS Distance Model	0.3180	6.73%	0.3721	0.13%
JIRS Simple Model	0.2724	24.60%	0.3771	−1.19%
Lucene	0.2910	16.63%	0.3399	9.62%

Table 2. The PR systems' coverages tested with (a) TREC12 and (b) CLEF04 data

(a)

	FuzzyPR	Lucene	JIRS_SM	JIRS_DM
1	0.250	0.224 (11.8%)	0.222 (12.5%)	0.243 (2.7%)
2	0.358	0.305 (17.2%)	0.270 (32.7%)	0.320 (11.8%)
3	0.418	0.350 (19.5%)	0.299 (40.0%)	0.384 (9.1%)
4	0.450	0.371 (21.3%)	0.347 (29.8%)	0.421 (7.0%)
5	0.487	0.403 (20.9%)	0.370 (31.4%)	0.450 (8.2%)
6	0.518	0.424 (22.4%)	0.405 (28.1%)	0.479 (8.3%)
7	0.542	0.434 (24.9%)	0.431 (25.7%)	0.492 (10.2%)
8	0.568	0.453 (25.6%)	0.447 (27.1%)	0.508 (11.9%)
9	0.582	0.479 (21.4%)	0.479 (21.5%)	0.532 (9.4%)
10	0.595	0.495 (20.2%)	0.489 (21.5%)	0.548 (8.6%)
11	0.611	0.505 (20.8%)	0.495 (23.4%)	0.558 (9.4%)
12	0.616	0.524 (17.6%)	0.505 (21.9%)	0.569 (8.3%)
13	0.621	0.529 (17.4%)	0.521 (19.2%)	0.579 (7.2%)
14	0.624	0.537 (16.2%)	0.527 (18.5%)	0.590 (5.7%)
15	0.624	0.547 (13.9%)	0.529 (17.9%)	0.595 (4.8%)
16	0.626	0.550 (13.9%)	0.532 (17.8%)	0.603 (3.8%)
17	0.632	0.558 (13.2%)	0.548 (15.3%)	0.609 (3.8%)
18	0.637	0.561 (13.6%)	0.556 (14.6%)	0.611 (4.2%)
19	0.637	0.561 (13.6%)	0.564 (13.0%)	0.616 (3.3%)
20	0.645	0.563 (14.5%)	0.571 (12.8%)	0.619 (4.2%)

(b)

	FuzzyPR	Lucene	JIRS_SM	JIRS_DM
1	0.283	0.272 (4.1%)	0.322 (−12.1%)	0.300 (−5.6%)
2	0.378	0.372 (1.5%)	0.389 (−2.9%)	0.372 (1.5%)
3	0.439	0.394 (11.3%)	0.411 (6.8%)	0.444 (−1.2%)
4	0.494	0.422 (17.1%)	0.450 (9.9%)	0.483 (2.3%)
5	0.533	0.439 (21.5%)	0.472 (12.9%)	0.494 (7.9%)
6	0.556	0.456 (21.9%)	0.494 (12.4%)	0.528 (5.3%)
7	0.561	0.472 (18.8%)	0.522 (7.4%)	0.544 (3.1%)
8	0.572	0.472 (21.2%)	0.528 (8.4%)	0.567 (1.0%)
9	0.572	0.483 (18.4%)	0.533 (7.3%)	0.572 (0.0%)
10	0.594	0.489 (21.6%)	0.561 (5.9%)	0.583 (1.9%)
11	0.600	0.489 (22.7%)	0.561 (6.9%)	0.583 (2.9%)
12	0.617	0.489 (26.1%)	0.567 (8.8%)	0.594 (3.8%)
13	0.622	0.489 (27.3%)	0.567 (9.8%)	0.600 (3.7%)
14	0.628	0.500 (25.6%)	0.578 (8.7%)	0.606 (3.7%)
15	0.628	0.506 (24.2%)	0.578 (8.7%)	0.617 (1.8%)
16	0.639	0.506 (26.4%)	0.578 (10.6%)	0.617 (3.6%)
17	0.639	0.506 (26.4%)	0.578 (10.6%)	0.617 (3.6%)
18	0.639	0.517 (23.7%)	0.578 (10.6%)	0.622 (2.7%)
19	0.644	0.522 (23.4%)	0.583 (10.5%)	0.628 (2.6%)
20	0.650	0.533 (21.9%)	0.583 (11.4%)	0.633 (2.6%)

3 sentence passages. Both, the PR system and JIRS implement an index of 3 sentence passages with 1 sentence overlapping since as it is reported in [11] this approach achieves good results.

As test data we used TREC12's set of 495 questions and the corpus called AQUAINT consisting of 1,033,461 documents of English news text together with CLEF04's 180 question and the AgenciaEFE corpus of 454,045 Spanish newswire documents. To check for correct answers automatically we used Ken Litkowsky's regular expression patterns of correct answers for TREC12 and the patterns supplied with JIRS.[3] As evaluation metrics we used *Mean Reciprocal Rank (MRR)* and *coverage*. Finally, the TREC12 question set was reduced to 380, since 115 questions do not have a recognizable pattern.

In Table 3, a parenthesized value is *FuzzyPR*'s performance improvement, expressed as a percentage, compared to other PR systems. Tables 3 and 2(b) show that *FuzzyPR* consistently performs better than Lucene's vector space PR system independently of the number of top-ranked passages consulted tested with both TREC12 and CLEF04 QA test data. MRR is improved at least 9.62% and coverage@20 at least 14.5%. Our results also show that FuzzyPR performs better than JIRS_SM and JIRS_DM (simple and distance model respectively) on the

---

[3] Patterns of correct answers to CLEF QA test data are available from JIRS' web site http://jirs.dsic.upv.es/

TREC copora, but slightly worst than JIRS_SM on the CLEF corpora. One explanation for this is that answers sometimes do not conform to the reformulation intuition.

4   Data Fusion Methods

In this section we present a brief description of the data fusion methods employed in our experiments[4]. The *Condorcet-fuse* method is a generalization of the Condorcet election process, where the winner of an election is the candidate that beats or ties with every other candidate in a pair-wise comparison, such that the result is a ranked list of documents rather than a single winner. *Borda-Fuse*, introduced in [12], is an adaptation of the Borda Count election process, where voters give candidates a certain amount of points and the winner is the one who makes more points. Tellex et al. [5] propose a method that combines passages rank and a simple vote: the total number of passages retrieved by all component PR systems with a specific document ID fused into a relevance score. Based on the observation that frequently when Tellex et al.'s Fusion method boosted low ranked passages, those passages in fact were non-relevant, we propose a new Fusion method called *Tellex Modified*, where the union of top m passages retrieved by all component PR systems is re-ranked. Fox and Shaw [13] introduce and evaluate the 6 simple Fusion methods depicted in Table 3.

Table 3. The six Fusion Methods introduced by Fox and Shaw (adapted from [13])

CombMAX	$r_f(d_i) = \max\limits_{\forall s_j \in S} \left(r_{s_j}(d_i) \right)$
CombMIN	$r_f(d_i) = \min\limits_{\forall s_j \in S} \left(r_{s_j}(d_i) \right)$
CombSUM	$r_f(d_i) = \sum\limits_{\forall s_j \in S} \left(r_{s_j}(d_i) \right)$
CombANZ	$r_f(d_i) = CombSUM/t$
CombMNZ	$r_f(d_i) = CombSUM * t$
CombMED	The median of a document's similarities

In table 3, $r_f(d_i)$ is the fused relevance score (similarity) of the document d_i, $r_{s_j}(d_i)$ document d_i's similarity at the IR system $s_j \in S$, the set of IR systems to be fused, and t the number of IR systems retrieving d_i.

Borda-fuse can be extended to a weighted variant: *Weighted Borda-fuse* by multiplying the points, which a PR system S_i assigns to a candidate passage with an overall system weight α_i [12].

In *weighted Condorcet-fuse*, Condorcet-fuse is extended to take importance weights into account, where each component PR system provides an importance weighted vote. These importance weights are used in binary candidate elections,

---

[4] A complete description can be found in [10].

where the sum of weights rather than votes is compared, giving preference to the highest sum.

The *Linear combination* (LC) Data Fusion method combines the relevance scores and training data of two or more component IR systems into a combined relevance score per document [14]. In LC, training data are used for calculating *importance weights* based on standard IR metrics, thus reflecting the overall ability of the system to provide relevant documents. The aggregated relevance score of a document is calculated in equation 5 using individual relevance scores and performance weights.

$$s_{LC}(d) = \sum_{\forall s_i \in S} \alpha * s_i(d) \tag{5}$$

where $S_{LC}(d)$ is the fused relevance score assigned to the document d, s_i is the ith system of the set S of PR systems whose relevance score will be combined, and a_i the importance weight assigned to the ith PR systems. In LC, if an IR system does not retrieve a particular document, then the IR system is assumed to consider it non-relevant by assigning a relevance score of 0. Additionally to the 9 Data Fusion methods previously described, we applied in our experiments subclass weighting to *weighted Condorcet-Fuse*, *weighted Borda-Fuse*, *LC* and *weighted Maximum Entropy OWA (MEOWA)*, comprising a total of 13 different methods.

Since IR systems use different scales for relevance scores it is necessary to normalize them. For this task and based on the evaluation of 7 different performance weights, we selected max-normalized MRR (nMRR). Lastly, we found it necessary to exclude the Condorcet-fuse method with question type weights because it consistently worsened overall performance. In our experiments we used the following 8 component PR systems: JIRS [15] using both the Simple Model and the Distance Model, FuzzyPR, FuzzyPRS+LucenePRS, LucenePRS, Swish-e, Terrier PL2 [16] using In expC2 probabilistic model, and Zettair.

As test data we used TREC12's set of 495 questions and the corpus called AQUAINT consisting of $1,033,461$ documents of English news text and CLEF04's 180 question and the AgenciaEFE corpus of $454,045$ Spanish newswire documents. We used Ken Litkowsky's regular expression patterns of correct answers to check answers automatically for TREC12 and for CLEF4 we used the pattern supplied with JIRS[5] The TREC12 question set was reduced to 380, since 115 questions do not have a recognizable pattern. As evaluation metrics we used MRR, Coverage, and Redundancy.

Table 4 shows the results obtained using from 2 up to 6 of the best performing PR mechanisms combined. These results show that the Data Fusion methods were able to improve performance measured as MRR by a maximum of 6.43% and Coverage@20 by 11.39%. This result was obtained fusing 4 of the best performing PR system with the *Tellex Modified* fusion method. *Tellex Modified*

---

[5] Patterns of correct answers to CLEF QA test data are available from JIRS' website: http://jirs.dsic.upv.es/

Table 4. The MRR and Coverage@20 of Tellex Modified compared to the 2nd best Fusion methods tested with TREC12 and CLEF04 QA test data

(a) TREC12 QA test data

Performance metric	MRR					Coverage@20				
No. of PR4QA systems combined	2	3	4	5	6	2	3	4	5	6
Avg. of best PR4QA systems	0.300	0.309	0.316	0.321	0.324	0.590	0.607	0.617	0.623	0.627
Tellex Modified (best)	0.317	0.329	0.336	0.341	0.344	0.642	0.675	0.687	0.694	0.696
Relative performance in %	5.54%	6.41%	6.43%	6.33%	6.25%	8.77%	11.32%	11.39%	11.30%	10.91%
LC	0.300	0.316	0.327	0.332	0.335	0.613	0.636	0.651	0.659	0.664
Relative performance in %	0.00%	2.15%	3.46%	3.55%	3.43%	3.85%	4.79%	5.51%	5.66%	5.89%

(b) CLEF04 QA test data

Performance metric	MRR					Coverage@20				
No. of PR4QA systems combined	2	3	4	5	6	2	3	4	5	6
Avg. of best PR4QA systems	0.352	0.362	0.369	0.375	0.379	0.590	0.607	0.617	0.623	0.627
Tellex Modified (best)	0.357	0.367	0.371	0.376	0.379	0.622	0.658	0.673	0.681	0.685
Relative performance in %	1.28%	1.26%	0.59%	0.39%	−0.03%	5.45%	8.40%	9.07%	9.19%	9.10%
LC w. quest. class weights	0.350	0.362	0.370	0.377	0.385					
LC						0.615	0.642	0.655	0.664	0.671
Relative performance in %	−0.7%	−0.11%	0.12%	0.54%	1.60%	4.24%	5.83%	6.15%	6.52%	6.92%

required neither relevance scores of passages nor importance weights assigned to the fused PR systems.

5   Conclusions and Future Work

Our experiments show that *FuzzyPR* achieves higher MRR and coverage than other similar systems on the TREC corpora. Furthermore it performs better in terms of coverage than JIRS on the CLEF corpora at ranks 4 to 20 but also slightly worse than JIRS simple model in terms of MRR on the same collection. Additionally, we investigated the application of a total of 13 Data Fusion methods, eight of these utilizing importance weights and importance weight per subclass of questions. We found that our proposed modification to Tellex et. al.'s method is able to improve MRR by a maximum of 6.43% and Coverage@20 by 11.39% fusing 4 different PR systems. However, contrary to our initial expectations, we found that the use of importance weights and importance weights per subclass of questions did not provide any improvement in data fusion performance.

As future work we consider addressing some of the weaknesses we found in our approach, namely handling questions with answers not conforming to the reformulation intuition and investigating optimal ways to include relevance scores in the data fusion mechanisms.

References

1. Gómez-Soriano, J.: A passage retrieval system for multilingual question answering. In: Matoušek, V., Mautner, P., Pavelka, T. (eds.) TSD 2005. LNCS (LNAI), vol. 3658, pp. 443–450. Springer, Heidelberg (2005)
2. Brill, E., Lin, J., Banko, M., Dumais, S., Ng, A.: Data-intensive question answering. In: Proceedings of the Tenth Text REtrieval Conference (TREC 2001), Gaithersburg, Maryland (November 2001) pp. 443–462 (2001)

3. H., et al.: Employing two question answering systems in trec-2005. In: proceedings of The Fourteenth Text REtrieval Conference (TREC 2005) (2005)
4. Unsunier, N., Amini, M., Gallinari, P.: Boosting weak ranking functions to enhance passage retrieval for question answering. In: IR4QA workshop of SIGIR 2004 (2004)
5. Tellex, S., Katz, B., Lin, J., Marton, G., Fernandes, A.: Quantitative evaluation of passage retrieval algorithms for question answering. In: Proceedings of the 26th Annual International ACM SIGIR Conference on Research and Development in Information Retrieval (SIGIR 2003) (July 2003)
6. Lee, J.H.: Combining multiple evidence from different properties of weighting schemes. In: proceedings of the 18th annual international ACM SIGIR conference on Research and development in information retrieval (July 1995)
7. Montague, M.: Metasearch: Data fusion for document retrieval. PhD thesis, Dartmouth College (2002)
8. Larsen, H.L.: Efficient andness-directed importance weighted averaging operators. International Journal of Uncertainty, Fuzziness and Knowledge-Based Systems, pp. 67–82 (2003)
9. Beigbeder, M., Mercier, A.: An information retrieval model using the fuzzy proximity degree of term occurrences. In: Proceedings of the 2005 ACM symposium on Applied computing (March 2005)
10. Christensen, H.U.: Exploring the use of fuzzy logic and data fusion techniques in passage retrieval for question answering. Master's thesis, Aalborg University Esbjerg (December 2006)
11. Llopis, F., Ferrandez, A., Vicedo, J.L.: Text segmentation for efficient information retrieval. In: Gelbukh, A. (ed.) CICLing 2002. LNCS, vol. 2276, pp. 373–380. Springer, Heidelberg (2002)
12. Aslam, J., Montague, M.: Models for metasearch. In: The 24th Annual ACM Conference on Research and Development in Information Retrieval (SIGIR '01), New Orleans, LA (2001)
13. Fox, E.A., Shaw, J.A.: Combination of multiple searches. In: The Second Text REtrieval Conference (TREC-2), Gaithersburg, MD, USA, pp. 243–249 (March 1994)
14. Vogt, C.C., Cottrell, G.W.: Fusion via a linear combination of scores. Information Retrieval 1(1), 151–173 (1999)
15. Gómez-Soriano, J.: y Gómez, M.M.: Jirs—the mother of all the passage retrieval systems for multilingual question answering?, http://www.dsic.upv.es/workshops/euindia05/slides/jgomez.pdf
16. Ounis, I., Amati, G., Plachouras, V., He, B., Macdonald, C., Johnson, D.: Terrier information retrieval platform. In: Losada, D.E., Fernández-Luna, J.M. (eds.) ECIR 2005. LNCS, vol. 3408, pp. 517–519. Springer, Heidelberg (2005)

Fuzzy Indices of Document Reliability

Célia da Costa Pereira[1] and Gabriella Pasi[2]

[1] Università degli Studi di Milano, DTI
Via Bramante 65, 26013 Crema (CR), Italy
pereira@dti.unimi.it
[2] Università degli Studi di Milano Bicocca, DISCO
Via Bicocca degli Arcimboldi 8, 20126 Milano (MI), Italy
pasi@disco.unimib.it

Abstract. This paper presents a first step toward the formalization of the concept of document reliability in the context of Information Retrieval (and Information Filtering). Our proposal is based on the hypothesis that the evaluation of the relevance of a document can also depend on the concept of reliability of a document. This concept has the following properties: (i) it is user-dependent, i.e., a document may be reliable for a user and not reliable for another user; (ii) it is source-dependent, i.e., the source which a document comes from may influence its reliability for a user; and (iii) it is also author-dependent, i.e., the information about who wrote the document may also influence the user when assessing the reliability of a document.

1   Introduction

The problem of information overload on the Web leads to a demand for effective systems able to locate and retrieve information relevant to user's individual interests. Usual systems for the content-based access to huge information repositories produce a ranked list of documents to be presented to the user. The rank is made possible by the estimate, by the system, of the so called "retrieval status value" (RSV). The usual evaluation criterion is relevance assessment, based on a formal representation and comparison of documents contents and the user's query content. In this case the RSV represents the system's estimate of the relevance of a document to the user's information needs. However, several additional properties of documents could be considered to assess their RSVs to users' needs [12]. Among these criteria, the *reliability* is a quite interesting one, which we try to approach and analyze in this paper. We present both a first analysis and some possible formalizations of the document reliability concept. Starting from a philosophical standpoint, we propose a fuzzy formalism for taking into account some different dimensions which concern the reliability of a document with respect to a particular user. More precisely, we attempt to give formal answers to the following questions:

- how the trust of the user in the source from which a document comes from, may determine document reliability?

F. Masulli, S. Mitra, and G. Pasi (Eds.): WILF 2007, LNAI 4578, pp. 110–117, 2007.
© Springer-Verlag Berlin Heidelberg 2007

- may the document reliability concept be corroborated by other sources?
- might other information like the author of the document and the date in which the document was been published contain useful information to enhance evaluation of document relevance?

To answer these questions, we have taken an inspiration from a philosophical approach [6]. We propose then some fuzzy indices which may be combined in distinct ways and which can be used in the process of document ranking.

The paper is organized as follows. In Section 2, we propose two fuzzy indices for evaluating the reliability of a document from the trust the user has for its source. In Section 3, we propose a third index for evaluating the reliability of a document. Thanks to this index, the case in which the information provided by the document is shared by other sources is also considered. In Section 4, we propose two other criteria as possible components in the process of evaluating document relevance. In section 5, we propose a simple way to combine the abovementioned indices into a unique index representing the overall reliability of a document. Finally, Section 6 concludes.

2 Evaluating the Reliability of a Document from the User Trust of Its Source

There are two different dimensions in the process of evaluating the user trust of a source. The first one, more intuitive and easily tractable, is when the user has had in the past a significant amount of relevant information from a given source. The second dimension is when the user either does not know at all or does not dispose of enough information to be allowed to evaluate the source. We will approach in a separate way either situation in the next sections.

2.1 When the Source is Known

In this case the user has a clear idea of the contents of the source, and she/he has been able to judge the information coming from that source as relevant. Therefore, when the source is *known*, the user can associate a trust degree with it; as a consequence the reliability degree of a document for the user i, noted $T_i^k(d)$, may be computed in the basis of the degree to which the user trusts the source from which the document d comes from, i.e.,

$$T_i^k(d) = T_i(s(d)), \tag{1}$$

where index k stands for *known* source, $s(d)$ represents the source of document d, and $T_i(s(d))$ represents the trust degree of the source for user i.

In the case in which the user may dispose of information describing the preferences of other users (such in the case of some collaborative filtering approaches) it would also be judicious to base the document reliability evaluation on the opinion of other users the user trusts. Thus doing, we may suppose that the user explicitly associates with a source a trust degree which depends also (i.e. it is influenced) on the ones specified by the colleagues she/he trusts. The degree of trust a user i has in document d, originated from a known source, $T_i^k(d)$, may in this case be given by:

$$T_i^k(d) = \gamma * T_i(s(d)) + (1 - \gamma) * T(s(d)) \tag{2}$$

where $\gamma \in]0, 1]$ is the degree of self trust of the user and $T(s(d))$ represents the average degree on source $s(d)$ for all the users who user i trusts. It may be given by:

$$T(s(d)) = \begin{cases} \frac{\sum_{j \in Users} t(i,j)*T_j(s(d))}{\sum_j t(i,j)} & \text{if } \exists j \text{ such that } t(i,j) \neq 0, \\ 0 & \text{Otherwise,} \end{cases}$$

where $t(i, j)$ representes the degree of trust user i has for user j.

2.2   When the Source is Unknown

Things are more complicated in the case in which the Web is the considered document repository, or in the case in which the information source is unknown. In fact, there is a huge number of information sources in the Web and, in most cases, when using for example a search engine, a user obtains information from quite different and "unknown" sources (sources she/he sees for the first time). By information sources we may here intend Web sites. Thus, it would be not possible to evaluate the user trust of a source "seen" for the first time; in this case "past track records" do not exist. When information is provided by Internet sources or other sources which do not have a well-established reputation, a possible approach for evaluating user trust is link analysis, i.e. to determine whether the information source is "strongly" endorsed by others by looking at how many Web sites link to that Web site. In the case of other kinds of unknwon sources, we may act in an analogous way, depending on the type of considered documents. For example in the case of information source containing scientific documents the impact of a document could be evaluated by using citation counts. A possible model of this interpretation is inspired by the formula used by *Citeseer* [8] for calculating the impact of a scientific article in a given year. Let $\bar{n}$ be the average number of citations for each document published in a given period, and n be the number of citations for the document d, published in that period. We define the impact of d, impact(d), as

$$\text{impact}(d) = \log_2(\frac{n}{\bar{n}} + 1). \tag{3}$$

The impact index of d, $\mathcal{I}(d)$, is given by:

$$\mathcal{I}(d) = 1 - 2^{-\text{impact}(d)} \tag{4}$$

The degree of reliability of document d for user i is then given by:

$$T_i^u(d) = \mathcal{I}(d), \tag{5}$$

where index u stands for *unknown* source.

The above proposition for computing the impact of a document does not take into accout the "weight" of each citation. In fact, a citation which comes from a much cited document counts like the citation which comes from a little cited document and this is not reasonable. To take the "weight" of citations into account, we propose a function inspired by the notion of *PageRank* proposed by [2] for ranking pages on Google, which makes the calculation of the weighted value of a citation possible.

Let $d_1, \ldots, d_m$ be m documents which cite a document d, and $o(d_i)$ the number of citations pointing out from d_i. The *weighted value of citations* of d, $n(d)$, may be computed by using the following iterative procedure:

$$n(d) = \frac{n(d_1)}{o(d_1)} + \ldots + \frac{n(d_m)}{o(d_m)} \tag{6}$$

where $n(d_i)$ is the weighted value of citations to document d_i. The intuitive justification of this formula is that a document has a higher citation value if many other documents point to it. This value may increase if there are high-scoring documents pointing to it.

3   When Information Is Corroborated Can It Help in Evaluating the Reliability of a Document?

In the previous section, we looked at ways to determine the reliability of a document by considering a single source of information. In this section, we attempt to evaluate the reliability of a document by also considering the case in which the information provided by that document is shared by other sources. In fact,

> in addition to the character of the "witness", we may pay attention to the "number of witnesses". This is because it is much more likely that one individual will "deceive or be deceived" than that several individuals will "deceive or be deceived" in exactly the same way [6]

(a remarkable counterexample is when the majority of the electors of a country is deceived by the false promises of a politician).

> For this reason, several philosophers have noted that the agreement of a number of experts on a topic can be an important indicator of accuracy. This suggests that another technique for verifying the accuracy of a piece of information is to see if other information sources corroborate the original source of the information [6].

Of course,

> information sources do not always agree with each other. In fact, it is fairly easy to find conflicting information. If sources do conflict, then people simply have to determine which source is more reliable [6]

(or use some of the other techniques for verifying the accuracy of the information).

Notably, however, agreement between information sources is not always an indication that their information is accurate. It depends on how these different sources got their information. In particular, if they all got their information from the same place, then ten sources saying the same thing is no better evidence than one source saying it. This issue turns out to be especially important on the Internet since it is so easy for the very same information to be copied by several different Web sites. However, the fact that all of these sites corroborate each other still does nothing to help us verify that the information is accurate. Agreement between sources should not increase our degree of confidence in the accuracy of a piece of information unless those sources are independent. Obviously, here what is required is only a *conditional independence* and not full independence. In fact, if two information sources are reliable, their reports will be correlated with each other simply because their reports will both be correlated with the truth. Thus, it is very difficult to calculate the reliability of a piece of information based on the fact that it is or not corroborated by other sources without making some trade-off [6].

Here, we propose to evaluate the accuracy of a piece of information by checking if such information is shared by other sources.

Let d be a new document and d' be a document obtained from source s' which is such that:

- d' is the document more similar to document d, i.e. $\neg \exists d''$ with $s(d'') = s' \neq s(d)$ such that $\operatorname{sim}(d, d'') > \operatorname{sim}(d, d')^1$;
- $\operatorname{sim}(d, d') \geq \alpha$, where α is the similarity degree after which two documents are considered similar.

The degree of trust a user i has for document d, $T_i^c(d)$, may be defined as follows:

$$T_i^c(d) = \frac{\sum_{s' \in Sources} T_i(s') * \operatorname{sim}(d, d')}{\sum_{s'} T_i(s')}, \qquad (7)$$

where $\operatorname{sim}(d, d')$ is set to 0 if $\operatorname{sim}(d, d') < \alpha$, i.e., we consider only documents similar to d. This allows us to take also into account the number of sources sharing documents similar to d. Another possibility is

$$T_i^c(d) = \max_{s' \in Sources} \min(T_i(s'), \operatorname{sim}(d, d')) \qquad (8)$$

In both cases, if there is no source in which the user trusts, or if there is no source containing at least a document more or less similar to document d, the user concludes that the information in document d is not corroborated by any source she/he trusts and, consenquently, she/he does not trust d.

---

[1] Sim is a function which returns the similarity degree between two documents.

4 Other Information Which Could Enhance Evaluation of Document Relevance

In this section, we propose two other criteria, namely the author of the document and the publication date of the document, as possible components in the process of evaluation of document relevance. In fact, in the case in which the source contains, for example, scientific documents, information about who wrote the document may be useful for determining the relevance of the document. In a similar way, if the piece of information has a temporary "truth value", e.g., it is merely relevant during a certain period, the date in which the document was written may strongly contribute to evaluating its relevance.

4.1 Information About the Author of the Document

As we have said previously, information about the author of a document may also be useful to determine the reliability of the document for a user. This information may include:

- the author's name, N_a ($\in \{0,1\}$). More precisely, $N_a = 1$ if the document contains the name of the author and 0 otherwise;
- the author's education or experience, $E_a(\in [0,1])$ which represents how the author experience is relevant to the interest group of the document. The calculation of this degree may be made based on a comparison between the interest theme of the document and the interest theme of the author's qualification, degree, or scholarship on one hand and, on the other hand, it may be based on an evaluation made by the user of past documents written by the same author;
- contact information, I_a ($\in \{0,1\}$). More precisely, $I_a = 1$ if the document contains a contact information of the author and 0 otherwise;
- the name of the organization for which she/he works, O_a ($\in \{0,1\}$). More precisely, $O_a = 1$ if the document contains the name of the author's organization and 0 otherwise.

The following importance order may be established according to common sense: $N_a = I_a > E_a > O_a$. This order means that the most important piece of information is the name of the author and her/his contact information, followed by the author experience and the least important piece of information is the organization for which she/he works. Therefore, the trust degree of document d for user i, considering information about the author, may be calculated as follows:

$$T_i^a(d) = \lambda_1 \cdot (N_a + I_a)/2 + \lambda_2 \cdot E_a + \lambda_3 \cdot O_a \tag{9}$$

with $\lambda \in [0,1]$ and $\sum_{i=1}^3 \lambda_i = 1$ and $\lambda_1 > \lambda_2 > \lambda_3$.

4.2 Date of the Document

The presence or absence of the date ($D \in \{0,1\}$) on which a document was written may also help in determining its reliability. For some themes, the information contained in a document with an old date may become irrelevant/obsolete/not true. For example, in the sport theme, information that "Juventus plays in premier league, 2005", is not reliable in 2006. Instead, information that "Dante Alighieri was born in Florence in 1265", is always reliable. Thus, an old date on information known to be changeable is a sign of irrelevance.

We propose to take this fact into account by combining all user's interests into two groups, namely, those in which the date influences their relevance and those in which it does not. The reliability degree of document d for author i, considering the presence or absence of the date in which the document was written, may be calculated as follows:

$$T_i^d(d) = (1 - \beta) + \beta * D. \tag{10}$$

$\beta \in [0, 1]$ is high if the document belongs to the first group, and low otherwise.

5   Combining Reliability Degrees

Each of the user trust degrees proposed in the previous sections corresponds to different trust degrees the user may give to a document. We propose to combine all of these degrees to obtain the overall *degree of reliability* of a document d for a user i, $\mathcal{R}_i(d)$, as follows:

$$\mathcal{R}_i(d) = \delta_1 * T_i^j(d) + \delta_2 * T_i^c(d) + \delta_3 * T_i^a(d) + \delta_4 * T_i^d(d), \tag{11}$$

$j = k$ if the source is known otherwise $j = u$; $\delta_i \in [0, 1]$ and $\sum_i^4 \delta_i = 1$. Of course, the above overall *degree of reliability* will then have to be combined with some conventional document-similarity measure and other criteria to obtain the RSV of a document.

6   Conclusion

To answer a number of questions stated in the Introduction, an extensive critical survey of the literature about relevance and trustiness, in particular in the philosophical domain, has been carried out. The material gathered has been elaborated on and formalized, resulting in the proposal of several fuzzy measurements of user trust which were combined to obtain the overall reliability of a document for a user. Since the relevance of a document for a user depends also on the reliability of that document for that user, we believe that this proposal may be useful in automated methods to locate and retrieve information with respect to individual user interests.

References

1. Alexander, J.E., Tate, M.A.: Web Wisdom; How to Evaluate and Create Information Quality on the Webb. Lawrence Erlbaum Associates, Inc, Mahwah, NJ, USA (1999)
2. Brin, S., Page, L.: The anatomy of a large-scale hypertextual Web search engine. Computer Networks and ISDN Systems 30(1–7), 107–117 (1998)

3. Bruce, B.: Credibility of the web: Why we need dialectical reading. Journal of Philosofy of Education 34, 97–109 (2000)
4. Burbukes, N.C.: Paradoxes of the web: The ethical dimensions of credibility. Library Trends 49, 441–453 (2001)
5. Dubois, D., Prade, H.: Possibility Theory – An approach to Computerized processing of Uncertainty. Plenum Press, New York (1988)
6. Fallis, D.: On verifying the accuracy of information: Philosophical perspectives. Library Trends 52(3), 463–487 (2004)
7. Ketelaar, E.: Can we trust information? International Information and Library Review 29, 333–338 (2004)
8. Ley, M.: Estimated impact of publication venues in computer science (2003)
9. Lynch, C.A.: When documents deceive: Trust and provenance as new factors for information retrieval in a tangled web. Journal of the American Society for Information Science and Technology 52(1), 12–17 (2001)
10. Matthew, R., Agrawal, R., Domingos, P.: Trust management for the semantic web (2003)
11. Tomlin, J.A.: A new paradigm for ranking pages on the world wide web. In: WWW '03. Proceedings of the 12th international conference on World Wide Web, New York, NY, USA, pp. 350–355. ACM Press, New York, NY, USA (2003)
12. (Calvin) Xu, Y., Chen, Z.: Relevance judgment: What do information users consider beyond topicality? J. Am. Soc. Inf. Sci. Technol. 57(7), 961–973 (2006)
13. Zadeh, L.A.: Fuzzy sets. Information and Control 8, 338–353 (1965)

Fuzzy Ontology, Fuzzy Description Logics and Fuzzy-OWL

Silvia Calegari and Davide Ciucci

Dipartimento di Informatica Sistemistica e Comunicazione
Università di Milano – Bicocca
Via Bicocca degli Arcimboldi 8, I–20126 Milano (Italia)
{calegari,ciucci}@disco.unimib.it

Abstract. The conceptual formalism supported by an ontology is not sufficient for handling vague information that is commonly found in many application domains. We describe how to introduce fuzziness in an ontology. To this aim we define a framework consisting of a fuzzy ontology based on Fuzzy Description Logic and Fuzzy–Owl.

1 Introduction

In recent years ontologies played a major role in knowledge representation. For example, applications of the Semantic Web [1] (i.e., e-commerce, knowledge management, web portals, etc.) are based on ontologies. In the Semantic Web an ontology is a formal conceptualization of a domain of interest, shared among heterogeneous applications. It consists of *entities, attributes, relationships* and *axioms* to provide a common understanding of the real world [2, 3]. With the support of ontologies users and systems can communicate through an easy information exchange and integration. Unfortunately, the conceptual formalism supported by the ontology structure is not sufficient for handling imprecise information that is commonly found in many application domains. Indeed, humans use linguistic adverbs and adjectives to describe their requests. For instance, a user can be interested in finding topics about "an expensive item" or "a fun holiday" using web portals. The problem that emerges is how to represent these non-crisp data within the ontology definition.

Fuzzy sets theory, introduced by L. A. Zadeh [4], allows to deal with imprecise and vague data, so that a possible solution is to incorporate fuzzy logic into ontologies. In [5] we gave a first definition of fuzzy ontology. Here we present a better formalization which can be mapped to a suitable Fuzzy Description Logic. Let us note that also [6] gives a formalization of a fuzzy ontology, but it does not investigate its relationship to Fuzzy DL and Fuzzy–OWL. This is of great importance due to the central role that Description Logic and OWL play in the Semantic Web.

Further, $\mathcal{SHOIN}(\mathcal{D})$ is the theoretical counterpart of the OWL Description Logic. Thus, in the current paper, we define a fuzzy extension of the OWL language considering fuzzy $\mathcal{SHOIN}(\mathcal{D})$ [7]. We have extended the syntax and semantic of fuzzy $\mathcal{SHOIN}(\mathcal{D})$ with the possibility to add a concept modifier to a relation and introducing a new constructor which enable us to define a subset of objects belonging to a given concept with a membership value greater or lower that a fixed value.

F. Masulli, S. Mitra, and G. Pasi (Eds.): WILF 2007, LNAI 4578, pp. 118–126, 2007.

Our idea is to map the fuzzy ontology definition (presented in this paper) into the corresponding Fuzzy-OWL language through the syntax and semantic of fuzzy $\mathcal{SHOIN(D)}$. Finally, we propose an extension of the KAON project [8] in order to directly define some axioms of the fuzzy ontology through graph-based and tree-based metaphors.

2 Fuzzy Ontology

In this section, we formally introduce the notion of Fuzzy Ontology. Our definition is based on the vision of an ontology for the Semantic Web where knowledge is expressed in a DL-based ontology. Thus, a fuzzy ontology is defined in order to correspond to a DL knowledge base as we will give in Section 3 [9].

Definition 1. *A Fuzzy Ontology is defined as the tuple* $\mathbf{O_F} = \{\mathbf{I}, \mathbf{C}, \mathbf{R}, \mathbf{F}, \mathbf{A}\}$ *where:*
- $\mathbf{I}$ is the set of individuals, also called instances of the concepts.
- $\mathbf{C}$ is the set of concepts. Each concept $C \in \mathbf{C}$ is a fuzzy set on the domain of instances $C : \mathbf{I} \mapsto [0, 1]$. The set of entities of the fuzzy ontology will be indicated by $\mathbf{E}$, i.e., $\mathbf{E} = \mathbf{C} \cup \mathbf{I}$.
-$\mathbf{R}$ is the set of relations. Each $R \in \mathbf{R}$ is a n-ary fuzzy relation on the domain of entities, $R : \mathbf{E}^n \mapsto [0, 1]$. A special role is held by the taxonomic relation $\mathcal{T} : \mathbf{E}^2 \mapsto [0, 1]$ which identifies the fuzzy subsumption relation among the entities.
- $\mathbf{F}$ is the set of the fuzzy relations on the set of entities $\mathbf{E}$ and a specific domain contained in $\mathcal{D} = \{integer, string, ...\}$. In detail, they are n-ary functions such that each element $F \in \mathbf{F}$ is a relation $F : \mathbf{E}^{(n-1)} \times P \mapsto [0, 1]$ where $P \in \mathcal{D}$.
- $\mathbf{A}$ is the set of axioms expressed in a proper logical language, i.e., predicates that constrain the meaning of concepts, individuals, relationships and functions.

Let us note that any concept and any relation is fuzzy. In particular the taxonomic relationship $\mathcal{T}(i, j)$ indicates that the child j is a conceptual specification of the parent i with a certain degree. For example, in an ontology of the "animals" an expert can have some problems on how to insert the "platypus" instance, since it is in part a "mammal" and in part an "oviparous". Using the fuzzy subsumption relationships $\mathcal{T}(mammal, platypus) = x$ and $\mathcal{T}(oviparous, platypus) = y$, where x, y are two arbitrary fuzzy values, it is possible to declare partial relations in order to better specify the ontology knowledge. The same holds for non-taxonomic relationships. For instance, a way to describe the fact "Paul lives sometimes in London and sometimes in Rome" could be $Lives(Paul, London) = 0.6$, $Lives(Paul, Rome) = 0.5$.

Of course, since fuzzy sets are a sound extension of classical boolean sets, it is always possible to define crisp (i.e, non-fuzzy) concepts (resp., relations) by using only values in the set $\{0, 1\}$.

A particular interest in our work is held by the non-taxonomic fuzzy relationship "correlation" defined as $Corr : \mathbf{E}^2 \mapsto [0, 1]$ (see [10, 11]). The correlation is a binary and symmetric fuzzy relationship that allows to specify the semantic link among the entities of the fuzzy ontology. The values of correlation between two objects can be assigned not only by the expert of the domain, but also considering the knowledge based on how the two objects are used together (for instance, in the queries or in the documents definition). For example, it is possible to state that "sun and yellow" are semantically correlated with value 0.8, i.e., $Corr(sun, yellow) = 0.8$. Furthermore, it is possible to have the special case where an entity x is itself correlated. For instance, we can affirm that $Corr(sun, sun) = 0.3$. In the implementation phase, for the fuzzy relationship $Corr$ is necessary to define the attribute "count" that allows to storage how many times the entities are searched together.

Properties of relations. In the fuzzy ontology the properties on the relations we are interested in are symmetry and transitivity. Given a fuzzy ontology $\mathbf{O_F}$, a binary relation $R : \mathbf{E} \times \mathbf{E} \mapsto [0, 1]$ is *Symmetric* if $\forall i, j \in \mathbf{E}$, $R(i, j) = R(j, i)$ and *Transitive* if $\forall i, j \in \mathbf{E}$, $\sup_{k \in \mathbf{E}}\{t(R(i, k), R(k, j))\} \leq R(i, j)$, where t is a t-norm. Further, given a binary relation $R : \mathbf{E} \times \mathbf{E} \mapsto [0, 1]$, its *inverse* relation is defined as $R^-(i, j) := R(j, i)$. Thus, we have that a relation is symmetric if and only if $\forall i, j \in \mathbf{E}$, $R(i, j) = R^-(i, j)$.

3 Fuzzy Description Logic

Our next step in the description of a complete framework for a fuzzy ontology is the definition of a fuzzy description logic. Let us note that in literature there are several approaches to this topic. The most complete and coherent one is [7]. Stoilos et. al [12] have also presented a Fuzzy-OWL language version based only on $\mathcal{SHOIN}$ discarding datatypes and concept modifiers. We take inspiration mainly from Straccia's work [7], adding a complete formalization of fuzzy axioms and introducing some differences:

- we add the possibility to have fuzzy relations with modifiers, and not only modified fuzzy concepts. This can be helpful to express a sentence as "there is a *strong* correlation between sun and yellow" where strong is a modifier and "correlation" a fuzzy relation;
- we give a different semantic of cardinality restriction;
- we add a new possibility to define a concept: $\leq_\alpha C$ (and similarly $\geq_\alpha$, $<_\alpha$, $>_\alpha$) which enable us to define, for instance, the fuzzy set of "people which are tall with value lower than 0.3" or the "wines which have a dry taste with a value at least of 0.6".

Decidability and computability issues of these modifications will be investigated in a forthcoming paper.

3.1 Syntax

The alphabet of the logic is (C, R_a, R_c, I_a, I_c) where C is the set of concept names, R_a (resp., R_c) is the set of abstract (resp., concrete) role names, I_a (resp., I_c) the set of abstract (resp., concrete) individual names. All these sets are non-empty and they are pair-wise disjoint. A concrete domain is a pair $\langle \Delta_D, \Phi_D \rangle$ where Δ_D is an interpretation domain and Φ_D the set of concrete fuzzy relations p on the domain Δ_D with interpretation $p^D : \Delta_D^n \mapsto [0, 1]$. The set of modifier names is denoted as M and to each element $m \in M$ is associated its interpretation $f_m : [0, 1] \mapsto [0, 1]$.

Finally, using the following notation: $A \in C$ is a concept, $R \in R_a$ an abstract relation name, $T \in R_c$ a concrete relation name, $S \in R_a$ an abstract simple relation name (a relation is simple if it is not transitive and it has not transitive sub-relations), $m \in M$ a modifier name, $p \in \Phi_D$ a concrete predicate name, $a \in I_a$ an abstract instance name,

$c \in I_c$ a concrete instance name, $n \in \mathbf{N}$, we can define a fuzzy-$\mathcal{SHOIN}(D)$ concept according to the following rules.

$$C \rightarrow \top|\bot|A|C_1 \sqcup C_2|C_1 \sqcap C_2|\neg C|\forall P.C|\exists P.C|(\leq n S)|(\geq n S)|\{a_1, \dots, a_n\}|mC|$$
$$|(\leq n T)|(\geq n T)| <_\alpha C| \leq_\alpha C| >_\alpha C| \geq_\alpha C|\forall T_1 \dots T_n.D|\exists T_1 \dots T_n.D|$$
$$D \rightarrow p|\{c_1, \dots, c_n\} \qquad P \rightarrow R|R^-|mR$$

Now, we introduce the axioms, which, as usual, are divided in three categories. From now on, by $\star$ we mean a symbol in $\{<, \leq, >, \geq, =, \neq\}$ and by α a value in $[0, 1]$.

TBox. Let A, B be concepts. A fuzzy inclusion axiom is $(A \sqsubseteq B) \star \alpha$. Let us note that non-fuzzy inclusion axioms can be obtained as $(A \sqsubseteq B) = 1$
RBox. Let $R_1, R_2 \in R_a$ and $T_1, T_2 \in R_a$. Fuzzy role inclusion axioms are $(R_1 \sqsubseteq R_2) \star \alpha$ and $(T_1 \sqsubseteq T_2) \star \alpha$. Further, we can have transitivity axioms $\text{TRANS}(R)$.
ABox. Let $a, b \in I_a$, $c \in I_c$ and C a concept. Then, ABox axioms are $\langle a : C \rangle \star \alpha$, $\langle (a, b) : R \rangle \star \alpha$, $\langle (a, c) : T \rangle \star \alpha$, $a = b$ and $a \neq b$.

A *Knowledge Base* is a triple $\langle \mathcal{T}, \mathcal{R}, \mathcal{A} \rangle$ with $\mathcal{T}$, $\mathcal{R}$ and $\mathcal{A}$ respectively a TBox, RBox and ABox.

3.2 Semantics

The interpretation is given by a pair $\langle \Delta^\mathcal{I}, \cdot^\mathcal{I} \rangle$ where $\Delta^\mathcal{I}$ is a set of objects with empty intersection with the concrete domain Δ_D: $\Delta^\mathcal{I} \cap \Delta_D = \emptyset$. An individual $a \in I_a$ is mapped to an object in $\Delta^\mathcal{I}$: $a^I \in \Delta^\mathcal{I}$. An individual $c \in I_c$ is mapped to an object $c^\mathcal{I} \in \Delta_D$. A concept $A \in C$ is interpreted as a fuzzy set on the domain $\Delta^\mathcal{I}$, $A^\mathcal{I}$: $\Delta^\mathcal{I} \mapsto [0, 1]$. Abstract roles $R \in R_a$ and concrete roles $T \in R_c$ are interpreted as fuzzy binary relations, respectively: $R : \Delta^\mathcal{I} \times \Delta^\mathcal{I} \mapsto [0, 1]$ and $T : \Delta^\mathcal{I} \times \Delta_D \mapsto [0, 1]$. The interpretation of the concepts is given according to table 1, where t is a t-norm, s a t-conorm, $\rightarrow$ a (residual) implication, N a negation, $m \in M$ a modifier, $x, y \in \Delta^\mathcal{I}$ and $v \in \Delta_D$. For the sake of simplicity we omit the semantic of $\leq n S$ which is dual to $\geq n S$ and of $<_\alpha, \leq_\alpha, >_\alpha$ which are similar to $\geq_\alpha$.

Let us note that the semantic of cardinality restrictions $\geq n S$ and $\leq n S$ is different from both [7] and [12]. Indeed, we do not fuzzify them, since, in our opinion, the property $\forall x$ "there are at least n distinct elements that satisfy to some degree" [7] $S(x, y)$, i.e, the semantic of $\geq nS$, is satisfied or not, in a Boolean fashion. For instance, a "Tortoiseshell cat" is characterized by having three colours. This can be expressed in fuzzy DL as $\geq 3HasColor \sqcap \leq 3HasColor$ which is a crisp concept. That is, a cat is a "Tortoiseshell" if it has exactly three colours, each of them to some (fuzzy) degree. Further, the *classical* relationship $\leq nS \equiv \neg(\geq (n+1)S)$ is satisfied and, as showed below, the semantic of a function is coherent with the idea that a function assigns to any instance only one value, in this fuzzy environment with a certain degree.

In Table 2 the interpretation of axioms is given. Further important axioms derivable in fuzzy $\mathcal{SHOIN}(D)$ from the primitive ones are the requirement that a relation is symmetric and that a relation is a function. They can be respectively expressed as $R \equiv R^-$ and $(\top \sqsubseteq\leq 1S) = 1$ whose semantic, according to Table 2, is $\forall a, b \in \Delta^\mathcal{I}$, $R^\mathcal{I}(a, b) = (R^-)^\mathcal{I}(a, b)$ and $\forall x \in \Delta^\mathcal{I}, |\{y \in \Delta^\mathcal{I} : S(x, y) \geq 0\}| \leq 1$.

Table 1. Interpretation of concepts in fuzzy $\mathcal{SHOIN}(D)$

$\perp^{\mathcal{I}}(x)$	0
$\top^{\mathcal{I}}(x)$	1
$(C_1 \sqcap C_2)^{\mathcal{I}}(x)$	$t(C_1^{\mathcal{I}}(x), C_2^{\mathcal{I}}(x))$
$(C_1 \sqcup C_2)^{\mathcal{I}}(x)$	$s(C_1^{\mathcal{I}}(x), C_2^{\mathcal{I}}(x))$
$(\neg C)^{\mathcal{I}}(x)$	$(N(C^{\mathcal{I}}))(x)$
$(mC)^{\mathcal{I}}(x)$	$f_m(C^{\mathcal{I}}(x))$
$(R^-)^{\mathcal{I}}(x, y)$	$R^{\mathcal{I}}(y, x)$
$(mR)^{\mathcal{I}}(x, y)$	$f_m(R^{\mathcal{I}}(x, y))$
$(\forall P.C)^{\mathcal{I}}(x)$	$\inf_{y \in \Delta^{\mathcal{I}}} \{P^{\mathcal{I}}(x, y) \rightarrow C^{\mathcal{I}}(y)\}$
$(\exists P.C)^{\mathcal{I}}(x)$	$\sup_{y \in \Delta^{\mathcal{I}}} \{t(P^{\mathcal{I}}(x, y), C^{\mathcal{I}}(y))\}$
$(\geq nS)^{\mathcal{I}}(x)$	$\begin{cases} 1 & \text{if } \|\{y \in \Delta^{\mathcal{I}} : S(x,y) > 0\}\| \geq n \\ 0 & \text{otherwise} \end{cases}$
$(\geq_\alpha C)^{I}(x)$	$\begin{cases} C(x) & \text{if } C(x) \geq \alpha \\ 0 & \text{otherwise} \end{cases}$
$\{a_1, \ldots, a_n\}^{\mathcal{I}}(x)$	$\begin{cases} 1 & \text{if } x \in \{a_1, \ldots, a_n\} \\ 0 & \text{otherwise} \end{cases}$
$\{c_1, \ldots, c_n\}^{\mathcal{I}}(v)$	$\begin{cases} 1 & \text{if } v \in \{c_1, \ldots, c_n\} \\ 0 & \text{otherwise} \end{cases}$
$(\forall T_1 \ldots T_n.D)^{\mathcal{I}}(x)$	$\inf_{y_i \in \Delta_D} \{t_{i=1}^n T_i^{\mathcal{I}}(x, y_i) \rightarrow D^{\mathcal{I}}(y_1, \ldots, y_n)\}$
$(\exists T_1 \ldots T_n.D)^{\mathcal{I}}(x)$	$\sup_{y_i \in \Delta_D} \{t(t_{i=1}^n T_i^{\mathcal{I}}(x, y_i), D^{\mathcal{I}}(y_1, \ldots, y_n))\}$

Table 2. Interpretation of axioms in fuzzy $\mathcal{SHOIN}(D)$

$(C \equiv D)^{\mathcal{I}}$	$\forall x \in \Delta^{\mathcal{I}} \; C^{\mathcal{I}}(x) = D^{\mathcal{I}}(x)$
$((C \sqsubseteq D) \star \alpha)^{\mathcal{I}}$	$(\inf_{x \in \Delta^{\mathcal{I}}} \{C^{\mathcal{I}}(x) \rightarrow D^{\mathcal{I}}(x)\}) \star \alpha$
$(R_1 \equiv R_2)^{\mathcal{I}}$	$\forall x, y \in \Delta^{\mathcal{I}} \; R_1^{\mathcal{I}}(x, y) = R_2^{\mathcal{I}}(x, y)$
$((R_1 \sqsubseteq R_2) \star \alpha)^{\mathcal{I}}$	$(\inf_{x,y \in \Delta^{\mathcal{I}}} \{R_1^{\mathcal{I}}(x, y) \rightarrow R_2^{\mathcal{I}}(x, y)\}) \star \alpha$
$((T_1 \sqsubseteq T_2) \star \alpha)^{\mathcal{I}}$	$(\inf_{x \in \Delta^{\mathcal{I}}, v \in \Delta_D} \{T_1^{\mathcal{I}}(x, v) \rightarrow T_2^{\mathcal{I}}(x, v)\}) \star \alpha$
$(\langle a : C \rangle \star \alpha)^{\mathcal{I}}$	$C^{\mathcal{I}}(a^{\mathcal{I}}) \star \alpha$
$(\langle (a, b) : R \rangle \star \alpha)^{\mathcal{I}}$	$R^{\mathcal{I}}(a^{\mathcal{I}}, b^{\mathcal{I}}) \star \alpha$
$Trans(R)$	$\forall a, b, c \in \Delta^{\mathcal{I}}$
	$\sup_{b \in \Delta^{\mathcal{I}}} t(R^{\mathcal{I}}(a, b), R^{\mathcal{I}}(b, c)) \leq R^{\mathcal{I}}(a, c)$
$(a = b)^{\mathcal{I}}$	$a^{\mathcal{I}} = b^{\mathcal{I}}$
$(a \neq b)^{\mathcal{I}}$	$a^{\mathcal{I}} \neq b^{\mathcal{I}}$

As an example let us consider the property HasColor with value white, In fuzzy $\mathcal{SHOIN}(D)$ it can be expressed as $(\exists HasColor.\{white\})$ which, once applied to the individual Silvester, becomes $(\exists HasColor.\{white\})(Silvester) = \sup_y\{t(HasColor(Silvester, y), \{white\}(y))\}$. According to the given semantics, $\{white\}(y)$ is different from 0 (and in particular equal to 1) only when $y = white$. Thus, the above statement $(\exists HasColor.\{white\})(Silvester)$ is equivalent to $HasColor(Silvester, white)$. Finally, it is possible to define the set of "white cats which are white with a degree at least of 0.3" as the axiom $(White - Cat \sqsubseteq \geq_{0.3} (\exists HasColor.\{white\})) = 1$. Indeed, the semantics of the last statement is

$$\left(\inf_{x \in \Delta^{\mathcal{I}}} \left\{ White - Cat(x) \rightarrow \begin{cases} HC(x, white) & HC(x, white) \geq 0.3 \\ 0 & \text{otherwise} \end{cases} \right\} \right) = 1$$

and considering that $\rightarrow$ is a residual implication, we must have that

$$\forall x \, White - Cat(x) \leq \begin{cases} HC(x, white) & HC(x, white) \geq 0.3 \\ 0 & \text{otherwise} \end{cases}$$

Thus, if for a cat x, $HasColor(x, white) = 0.2$, it must be $White - Cat(x) = 0$, i.e., it does not belong to the set of white cats.

4 Fuzzy-OWL

Once we have defined a fuzzy ontology and after to have showed how to extend $\mathcal{SHOIN}(D)$, the next step is to define the new fuzzy language suitable to implement the fuzzy ontology. In order to achieve this goal, the logical framework of the KAON project has been extended .

4.1 Defining Fuzzy Ontology in KAON

The KAON project is a meta-project carried out at the Institute AIFB, University of Karlsruhe and at the Research Center for Information Technologies (FZI) [13]. KAON includes a comprehensive tool suite allowing easy creation, maintenance and management of ontologies. An important user-level application supplied by KAON is an ontology editor called OI-modeler whose most important features are its support for manipulation of large ontologies and for user-directed evolution of ontologies. In the last years, KAON has been applied to the Semantic Web [14].

An ontology in KAON consists of concepts (sets of elements), properties (specifications of how objects may be connected) and instances grouped in reusable units called OI-models (ontology-instance models) [13]. The conceptual model proposed allows to define an entity in different ways, depending on the point of view of the observer. That is, an entity can be interpreted as a concept, as well as an instance.

Fuzzy ontologies in KAON. Our aim is to enrich KAON language adding the proposed fuzzy-sets approach. In order to integrate our framework in the KAON project we have developed a suited "Fuzzy Inspector". The Fuzzy Inspector is composed by a table representing fuzzy entity, a membership degree and a number of updates Q. This new panel allows to the expert an easy fuzzy logic integration.

Furthermore, the Fuzzy Inspector allows to assign the fuzzy values in two ways in order to handle the trade off between understandability and precision [15]. In the first case, he/she can assign a precise value (between 0 and 1) to define an high degree of accuracy according to his/her experience. Whereas, in the second case, he/she can assign a linguistic value defining an high degree of interpretability. He/she can choose a linguistic value by a combo-list where automatically a numerical value is assigned. The choice of this list has been made arbitrarily, an expert can choose the linguistic values suitable to the context, and the numerical values relative to the labels can be calculated by the Khang et al.'s algorithm [16].

Fuzzy-OWL language. KAON's ontology language is based on RDFS [17] with proprietary extensions for algebraic property characteristics (symmetric, transitive and

Table 3. Constructor

Fuzzy constr.	Example for Fuzzy-OWL
$\geq_\alpha \exists R.\{x\}$	\<fowl:Restriction\> \<fowl:onProperty rdf:resource="♯R"/ \> \<fowl:hasValue rdf:resource="♯x"/ \> \<fowl:moreOrEquivalent fowl:degree=α/ \> \< /fowl:Restriction\>

Table 4. Axioms and fuzzy constraint between concepts

Fuzzy axioms	Example for Fuzzy-OWL
$A \sqsubseteq B \star \alpha$	\<fowl:Class rdf:ID="A"\> \<fowl:subClassOf rdf:resource=♯B/ \> \<fowl:ineqType fowl:degree=α/ \> \< /fowl:Class\>
$(\top \sqsubseteq (\leq 1S)) = 1$	\<fowl:ObjectProperty rdf:ID="S"\> \<rdf:type rdf:resource="FunctionalProperty"/ \> \<rdfs:domain rdf:resource="♯A"/ \> \<rdfs:range rdf:resource="♯B"/ \> \<fowl:ObjectProperty/ \>
$A(a) \star \alpha$	\<fowl:Thing rdf:ID="a"/ \> \<fowl:Thing rdf:about="♯a"/ \> \<rdf:type rdf:resource="♯A"/ \> \<fowl:ineqType fowl:degree=α/ \> \< /fowl:Thing \>
$R(a,b) \star \alpha$	\<fowl:Thing rdf:ID="a"\> \<R rdf:resource="♯b"/ \> \<fowl:ineqType fowl:degree=α/ \> \< /fowl:Thing \>

Fuzzy constraints	Example for Fuzzy-OWL
$R(c,d) \star \alpha$	\<rdf:Description rdf:about="c"\> \<R rdf:resource="♯d" fowl:ineqType fowl:degree=α / \> \< /rdf:Description\>

inverse), cardinality, modularization, meta-modelling and explicit representation of lexical information. But it is possible to export the fuzzy ontology file in the OWL [18] format. OWL DL is the language chosen by the major ontology editors because it supports those users who want the maximum expressiveness without losing computational completeness (all conclusions are guaranteed to be computed) and decidability of reasoning systems (all computations will finish in finite time) [18]. However, OWL DL does not allow to handle the information represented with a not precise definition. Our aim is to present an extension of OWL DL, named Fuzzy-OWL, by adding a fuzzy value to the entities and relationships of the ontology following the fuzzy $\mathcal{SHOIN}(\mathcal{D})$ syntax of Section 3 and the fuzzy ontology definition given in Section 2. In Table 3 is reported only the new constructor $\geq_\alpha$ defined in Section 3 (here the namespace is "fowl"), where $\alpha \in [0,1]$ allows to state the fuzzy values into the two ways previously described (i.e. by a combo-list or directly editing the value). Other constructors are defined analogously (see also [19]).

Table 4 reports the major axioms of Fuzzy-OWL language, where "a,b" are two individuals and "ineqType"= "moreOrEquivalent | lessOrEquivalent | moreThan | lessThan | Exactly". The fuzzy constraint between concepts "c" and "d" is useful for defining the non-taxonomic relationship "Corr" (see Section 2). In order to represent this, we adopt the solution proposed in [20] using RDF/XML syntax in Fuzzy OWL's DL language.

5   Conclusions

We outlined a complete framework for building a fuzzy ontology for the Semantic Web. Apart from defining a fuzzy ontology this required a coherent definition of Fuzzy

Description Logic and Fuzzy-OWL. With this new framework is possible to introduce and handle vagueness, an intrinsic characteristic of the web (and of human reasoning in general). From the applicative point of view some work is still needed. Indeed KAON is based on RDF(S) and all its limits with respect to OWL DL are well-known [21]. Although KAON language is based on own extension, this is not sufficient for representing all the constructors and axioms of OWL DL. For example, it is not possible to define the union, intersection and complement constructor between classes. A possible solution is to export the KAON file in the Fuzzy-OWL language. This will also enable the use of the fuzzy ontology in a fuzzy inference engine (for example KAON2 [22]).

References

[1] Berners-Lee, T., Hendler, T., Lassila, J.: The semantic web. Scientific American 284, 34–43 (2001)

[2] Gruber, T.: A Translation Approach to Portable Ontology Specifications. Knowledge Acquisition 5, 199–220 (1993)

[3] Guarino, N., Giaretta, P.: Ontologies and Knowledge Bases: Towards a Terminological Clarification. In: Mars, N. (ed.) Towards Very Large Knowledge Bases: Knowledge Building and Knowledge Sharing, pp. 25–32. IOS Press, Amsterdam (1995)

[4] Zadeh, L.A.: Fuzzy sets. Inform. and Control 8, 338–353 (1965)

[5] Calegari, S., Ciucci, D.: Integrating Fuzzy Logic in Ontologies. In: Manolopoulos, Y., Filipe, J., Constantopoulos, P., Cordeiro, J. (eds.) ICEIS, pp. 66–73. INSTICC press (2006)

[6] Sanchez, E., Yamanoi, T.: Fuzzy ontologies for the semantic web. In: Larsen, H.L., Pasi, G., Ortiz-Arroyo, D., Andreasen, T., Christiansen, H. (eds.) FQAS 2006. LNCS (LNAI), vol. 4027, pp. 691–699. Springer, Heidelberg (2006)

[7] Straccia, U.: A fuzzy description logic for the semantic web. In: Sanchez, E., ed.: Fuzzy Logic and the Semantic Web. Capturing Intelligence. Elsevier, pp. 73–90 (2006)

[8] KAON: Karlsruhe Ontology and Semantic Web Tool Suite (2005), http://kaon.semanticweb.org

[9] Baader, F., Calvanese, D., McGuinness, D.L., Nardi, D., Patel-Schneider, P.F. (eds.): The Description Logic Handbook: Theory, Implementation, and Applications. Cambridge University Press, Cambridge (2003)

[10] Calegari, S., Loregian, M.: Using dynamic fuzzy ontologies to understand creative environments. In: Larsen, H.L., Pasi, G., Ortiz-Arroyo, D., Andreasen, T., Christiansen, H. (eds.) FQAS 2006. LNCS (LNAI), vol. 4027, pp. 404–415. Springer, Heidelberg (2006)

[11] Calegari, S., Farina, F.: Fuzzy ontologies and scale-free networks analysis. In: RCIS, IEEE (2007) (in printing)

[12] Stoilos, G., Stamou, G., Tzouvaras, V., Pan, J.Z., Horrocks, I.: Fuzzy OWL: Uncertainty and the Semantic Web. In: International Workshop of OWL: Experiences and Directions (OWL-ED2005), Galway, Ireland (2005)

[13] AA.VV.: Developer's Guide for KAON 1.2.7. Technical report, FZI Research Center for Information and WBS Knowledge Management Group (2004)

[14] Oberle, D., Staab, S., Studer, R., Volz, R.: Supporting application development in the semantic web. ACM Trans. Inter. Tech. 5, 328–358 (2005)

[15] Casillas, J., Cordon, O., Herrera, F., Magdalena, L.: Accuracy improvements to find the balance interpretability–accuracy in linguistic fuzzy modeling:an overview. In: Accuracy Improvements in Linguistic Fuzzy Modeling, pp. 3–24. Physica-Verlag, Heidelberg (2003)

[16] Khang, T.D., Störr, H., Hölldobler, S.: A fuzzy description logic with hedges as concept modifiers. In: Third International Conference on Intelligent Technologies and Third Vietnam-Japan Symposium on Fuzzy Systems and Applications, pp. 25–34 (2002)

[17] RDFS: Resource Description Framework Schema (2004) http://www.w3.org/TR/PR-rdf-schema

[18] OWL: Ontology Web Language (2004) http://www.w3.org/2004/OWL/

[19] Gao, M., Liu, C.: Extending OWL by Fuzzy Description Logic. In: IEEE-ICTAI05 (2005)

[20] Stoilos, G., Nikos Simou, G.S., Kollias, S.: Uncertainty and the Semantic Web. IEEE Intelligent System 21, 84–87 (2006)

[21] Jeff, Z., Pan, I.H.: RDFS(FA):Connecting RDF(S) and OWL DL. IEEE Transactions on Knowledge and Data Engineering 19, 192–2006 (2007)

[22] KAON2: Karlsruhe Ontology and Semantic Web Tool Suite 2 (2005), http://kaon2.semanticweb.org

An Improved Weight Decision Rule Using SNNR and Fuzzy Value for Multi-modal HCI

Jung-Hyun Kim and Kwang-Seok Hong

School of Information and Communication Engineering, Sungkyunkwan University, 300, Chunchun-dong, Jangan-gu, Suwon, KyungKi-do, 440-746, Korea
kjh0328@skku.edu, kshong@skku.ac.kr
http://hci.skku.ac.kr

Abstract. In this paper, we suggest an improved weight decision rule depending on SNNR (Signal Plus Noise to Noise Ratio) and fuzzy value for simultaneous multi-modality including a synchronization between audio-gesture modalities. In order to insure the validity of the suggested weight decision rule, we implement a wireless PDA-based Multi-Modal Fusion Architecture (hereinafter, MMFA) by coupling embedded speech and KSSL recognizer, which fuses and recognizes 130 word-based instruction models that are represented by speech and KSSL (Korean Standard Sign Language), and then translates recognition result into synthetic speech (TTS) and visual illustration in real-time. In the experimental results, the average recognition rate of the MMFA fusing 2 sensory channels based on wireless PDA was 96.54% in clean environments (e.g. office space), and 93.21% in noisy environments, with the 130 word-based instruction models.

1 Introduction

Intelligent HCI for more advanced and personalized PC system such as wearable computer and PDA based on wireless network and wearable computing, may require and allow new interfaces and interaction techniques such as tactile interfaces with haptic feedback methods, and gesture interfaces based on hand gestures, to serve different kinds of users. In other words, for perceptual experience and behavior to benefit from the simultaneous stimulation of multiple sensory modalities that are concerned with a human's the (five) senses, fusion and fission technologies of the information from these modalities are very important and positively necessary [1], [2].

Consequently, we implement a wireless PDA-based MMFA that fission the handling of haptic and aural modalities by coupling embedded speech and KSSL recognizer, for clear instruction processing in noisy environments, and suggest an improved fusion and fission rules depending on SNNR and fuzzy value for a simultaneous multi-modality between audio-gesture information. In contrast to other proposed multi-modal interaction approaches, our approach is unique in two aspects: First, because the MMFA provides different weight and feed-back function at individual (speech or gesture) instruction recognizer, according to SNNR and fuzzy value, it may select an optimal instruction processing interface under a given situation or noisy environment. Second, according as the MMFA fuses and recognizes 130 word-based

F. Masulli, S. Mitra, and G. Pasi (Eds.): WILF 2007, LNAI 4578, pp. 127–135, 2007.
© Springer-Verlag Berlin Heidelberg 2007

instruction models that are represented by speech and KSSL, then translates recognition results that is fissioned according to a weight decision rule into synthetic speech and visual illustration in real-time, it performs certain features, such as a remote control and a instruction input function more correctly and can allow more interactive communication functions in noisy environment, for the next generation PC.

2 CHMM and Viterbi Search-Based Embedded Speech Recognizer

We implement a wireless PDA-based embedded Vocabulary-Independent Speech Recognizer (VISR) composing standard models such as CV, VCCV, VC. In embedded VISR, a sampling rate is 8 KHz, and a frame length is 10ms (we allow the 50% overlapping). To extract feature vectors at each frame from given various speech data, we applied the MFCC (Mel Frequency Cepstral Coefficient). MFCC coefficient uses 12 vectors, and because frame log energy is used additionally, characteristic vector that is used by input of speech recognition amounts to the 13th vectors (whole the 39th feature vectors: MFCC the 13th, Delta and Delta-Delta). In addition, we used a Continuous Hidden Markov Model (CHMM) and the Viterbi algorithm as a recognition and search algorithm for embedded VISR. A HMM is an extended stochastic model from a Markov chain to find a sequence of states with observation value, a probabilistic function of a state, and the HMM parameters are given in Eq. (1).

$$\lambda = \{A, B, \pi\} \tag{1}$$

Where, $A = \{a_{ij}\}$ is the set of transition probability from state i to state j, $B = \{b_j(k)\}$ is the set of observation probability given the current state j, and $\pi = \pi_i$ is the set of initial state probability. However, in CHMM, $b_j(x)$ in Eq. (2) is substituted for $B = \{b_j(k)\}$ in Eq. (1) [3].

$$b_j(x) = \sum_{K=1}^{M} c_{jk} b_{jk}(x) = \sum_{K=1}^{M} c_{jk} N(x, \mu_{jk}, \sum_{jk}) \tag{2}$$

Where, x is the observation vector being modeled, C_{jk} is the mixture coefficient for the k-th mixture in state j, and N is the Gaussian pdf with mean vector μ_{jk} and co-variance matrix $\sum_{jk}$ for the k-th mixture component in state j. The flowchart of embedded VISR is shown in Fig. 3 (in section 4).

3 Fuzzy Logic -Based Embedded KSSL Recognizer

For an implementation of a wireless PDA-based embedded KSSL recognizer, we constructed the 130 word-based instruction models according to an associability of prescribed hand gestures and basic KSSL motion gestures, according to "Korean Standard Sign Language Tutor (KSSLT) [4]". KSSL motion gestures and hand gestures are classified by an arm's movement, hand shape, pitch and roll degree by RDBMS [5]. In addition, for acquisition of KSSL gesture, we used 5DT company's wireless data gloves and Fastrak® which are popular input devices in the haptic application field, and utilized bluetooth module for the wireless sensor network [6]. As the fuzzy logic for KSSL recognition, we applied trapezoidal shaped membership functions for representation of fuzzy numbers-sets, and utilized the fuzzy max-min composition. In this paper, we utilized the fuzzy max-min composition to extend a crisp relation concept to relation concept with fuzzy proposition and to reason approximate conclusion by composition arithmetic of fuzzy relation. Two fuzzy relations R and S are defined on sets A, B and C (we prescribed the accuracy of hand gestures and basic KSSL gestures, object KSSL recognition models as the sets of events that are happened in KSSL recognition with the sets A, B and C). That is, $R \subseteq A \times B$, $S \subseteq B \times C$. The composition $S \bullet R = SR$ of two relations R and S is expressed by the relation from A to C, and this composition is defined in Eq. (3) [7], [8].

$$For\ (\,x,\,y\,) \in A \times B,\ (\,y,\,z\,) \in B \times C,$$

$$\mu_{S \bullet R}\ (\,x,\,z\,) = \underset{y}{Max}\ [Min\ (\,\mu_R(\,x,y\,),\ \mu_S\,(\,y,z\,)\,)] \tag{3}$$

$S \bullet R$ from this elaboration is a subset of $A \times C$. That is, $S \bullet R \subseteq A \times C$. If the relations R and S are represented by matrices M_R and M_S, the matrix $M_{S \bullet R}$ corresponding to $S \bullet R$ is obtained from the product of M_R and M_S; $M_{S \bullet R} = M_R \bullet M_S$. That is, we can see the possibility of occurrence of B after A, and by S, that of C after B in Table 1, 2. For example, by matrices M_R, the possibility of "Best" $\in B$ after "Best" $\in A$ is 0.9.

Table 1. The matrices M_R for the relations R between the fuzzy set A and B

R	Accuracy of basic KSSL gestures				
Accuracy of hand gestures	Best	Good	Normal	Bad	Very_bad
Very_bad	0.0	0.1	0.2	0.6	0.9
Bad	0.0	0.2	0.3	0.8	0.6
Normal	0.2	0.3	0.6	0.4	0.3
Good	0.7	0.9	0.5	0.3	0.2
Best	0.9	0.7	0.5	0.2	0.1

Table 2. The matrices M_R for the relations R between the fuzzy set B and C

S	Accuracy of 25 basic KSSL gestures				
Accuracy of basic KSSL gestures	Insignificance	Bad_YOU	Normal_YOU	Good_YOU	Best_YOU
Best	0.1	0.2	0.4	0.6	0.9
Good	0.2	0.3	0.5	0.8	0.7
Normal	0.3	0.4	0.6	0.3	0.2
Bad	0.7	0.8	0.4	0.2	0.1
Very_bad	0.9	0.6	0.3	0.1	0.0

Table 3. The matrix $M_{S \bullet R}$ corresponding to the relations $S \bullet R$

S • R	KSSL recognition model : "YOU"				
Accuracy of basic KSSL gestures	Insignificance	Bad_YOU	Normal_YOU	Good_YOU	Best_YOU
Very_bad	0.9	0.6	0.3	0.2	0.1
Bad	0.6	0.7	0.4	0.2	0.2
Normal	0.3	0.4	0.4	0.3	0.3
Good	0.3	0.3	0.5	0.8	0.7
Best	0.2	0.3	0.4	0.6	0.9

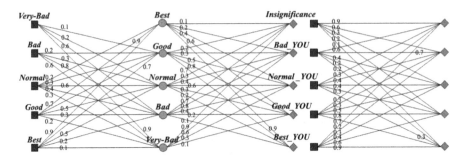

Fig. 1. Composition of fuzzy relation

Also, by matrices M_S, the possibility of occurrence of "Good_YOU" after "Best" is 0.6. Also, the matrix $M_{S \cdot R}$ in Table 3 represents max-min composition that reason and analyze the possibility of C when A is occurred and it is also given in Fig. 1. Embedded KSSL recognizer calculates and produces a fuzzy value from the user's dynamic KSSL via a fuzzy reasoning and composition process, and then decides and recognizes various KSSL according to produced fuzzy value. The flowchart of KSSL recognizer is shown in Fig. 3 (in section 4) together with the flowchart of the MMFA.

4   The Fusion Architecture for a Wireless PDA-Based MMFA

The fusion principle, which is featured in this paper, is based on the understanding, that there are two aspects of the integration process: 1) achieving the synergistic integration of two or more sensor modalities and 2) actual combination (fusion) of the various information streams at particular moments of their processing. All the recognizers produce time-stamped hypotheses, so that the fusion process can consider various temporal constraints. The key function of modality fusion is the reduction of the overall uncertainty and the mutual disambiguation of the various analysis results. By fusing symbolic and statistical information derived from the recognition and analysis components for speech, gesture and double-touching, MMFA can correct various recognition errors of its uni-modal input components and thus provide a more robust dialogue than a uni-modal system. In principle, modality fusion can be realized during various processing stages like multimodal signal processing, multimodal parsing, or multimodal semantic processing. In MMCR, fusion could be 1) done early or late in the interpretation process; 2) some modes could be principal and others auxiliary.

The fusion and fission schemes consists of six major steps: 1) the user inputs prescribed speech and KSSL data to a wireless PDA-based MMFA, Simultaneously, 2) inputted 2 sensory information are recognized and recorded by the embedded VISR and KSSL recognizer, and then ASR and gesture recognition results are saved to the MMDS (Multi-Modal Database Server; The MMDS is a responsible database for synchronizing data between speech and KSSL gesture), 3) at this point, the user's KSSL and speech data are synchronized depending on the internal SQL logic in the MMDS, and then 4) while suggested MMFA runs a validity check function on ASR and KSSL recognition results with prescribed instruction models, the NAT(Noise

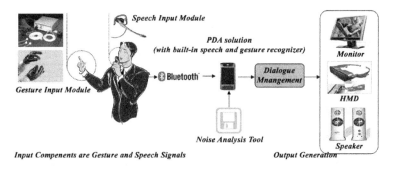

Fig. 2. The architecture of the MMFA for simultaneous multi-modality

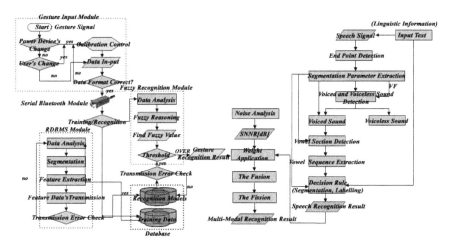

Fig. 3. The flowchart of the MMFA fusing 2 sensory channels with speech and gesture

Analysis Tool) analyzes a noise for user's speech data which is recorded in the second step, 5) according to analyzed noise and a validity check result, the MMFA gives weight into an individual embedded recognizer by improved fusion and fission rules in section 5, 6) finally, user's intention is provided to the user through TTS and visualization. The suggested architecture and flowchart of the MMFA are shown in Fig. 2 and 3, respectively.

5   An Improved Weight Decision Rule for Fusion and Fission

In noisy environments, speech quality is severely degraded by noises from the surrounding environment and speech recognition systems fail to produce high recognition rates. Consequently, we designed and implemented Noise Analysis Tool (NAT) for weight decision in individual (gesture or speech) recognizer. The NAT calculates average energy (mean power; [dB]) for a speech signal that recorded by wave-format in embedded VISR; and then computes SNNR by Eq. (4), where, P is a mean power.

Table 4. Weight value according to the SNNR and critical value for a feed-back function; in case SNNR critical value for weight decision is ambiguous, The MMFA calls a feed-back function that requests re-input (speech and KSSL) to user

xSNNR Critical value	Weight value (%)		Average speech recognition rates for the 20 test recognition models (%)						
	Speech (W_S)	KSSL(W_G)	Reagent 1	Reagent 2	Reagent 3	Reagent 4	Reagent 5	Average(S)	Differ-ence
more than 40 [dB]	99.0	1.0	98.2	98.4	97.9	98.5	98.2	98.2	0.9
35 [dB] ≤ SNNR < 40 [dB]	98.0	2.0	97.8	97.3	96.6	97.1	97.5	97.3	0.3
30 [dB] ≤ SNNR < 35 [dB]	96.0	4.0	97.5	96.5	96.6	97.0	97.4	97.0	0.2
25 [dB] ≤ SNNR < 30 [dB]	94.0	6.0	97.2	96.5	96.5	96.9	96.9	96.8	0.2
20 [dB] ≤ SNNR < 25 [dB]	92.0	8.0	96.9	95.9	96.4	96.8	96.8	96.6	2.2
15 [dB] ≤ SNNR < 20 [dB]	Feed-Back		92.4	96.2	93.8	95.2	94.1	94.3	11.1
10 [dB] ≤ SNNR < 15 [dB]	6.0	94.0	83.6	83.4	83.5	82.6	83.2	83.3	8.8
5 [dB] ≤ SNNR < 10 [dB]	4.0	96.0	71.9.	72.5	70.2	79.5	75.6	74.5	22.4
0 [dB] ≤ SNNR < 5 [dB]	2.0	98.0	53.4	51.3	52.6	51.6	51.3	52.0	14.0
less than 0 [dB]	1.0	99.0	38.5	37.6	37.5	38.2	38.5	38.1	-

$$SNNR(dB) = 10\log_{10}\frac{P\,signal + noise}{P\,noise} \tag{4}$$

We utilized an average speech recognition rate as speech probability value for a weight decision, and to define speech probability value depending on SNNR, we repeatedly achieved speech recognition experiments 10 times with the 20 test recognition models in noisy and clean environments, for every 5 reagents. The average speech recognition rates for 20 test recognition models are given in Table 4.

$$P\_W = W_S \times S + W_G \times G \tag{5}$$

- P_W : a probability value after weight application
- W_S : Defined Weight for Speech recognition mode in Table 4.
- W_G : Defined Weight for KSSL recognition mode in Table 4.
- S : speech probability (an average speech recognition rate)
- G : KSSL probability (the critical value depending on normalized fuzzy value)

$$G = \frac{Fuzzy\,Value\_Current}{Fuzzy\,Value\_Max} = \frac{Fuzzy\,Value\_Current}{3.5} \tag{6}$$

- *Fuzzy Value_Current : Fuzzy value to recognize current gesture(KSSL)*

Table 5. In case *Fuzzy Value_Current* is 3.2, *P_W* values using the Eq. (5) and (6)

SNNR	Speech		KSSL		P_W
	W_S	S	W_G	G	
more than 40 [dB]	0.99	0.982	0.01	0.914	0.981
35 [dB] ≤ SNNR < 40 [dB]	0.98	0.973	0.02	0.914	0.972
30 [dB] ≤ SNNR < 35 [dB]	0.96	0.970	0.04	0.914	0.968
25 [dB] ≤ SNNR < 30 [dB]	0.94	0.968	0.06	0.914	0.965
20 [dB] ≤ SNNR < 25 [dB]	0.92	0.966	0.08	0.914	0.917
15 [dB] ≤ SNNR < 20 [dB]	Feed-Back				
10 [dB] ≤ SNNR < 15 [dB]	0.06	0.833	0.94	0.914	0.909
5 [dB] ≤ SNNR < 10 [dB]	0.04	0.745	0.96	0.914	0.907
0 [dB] ≤ SNNR < 5 [dB]	0.02	0.520	0.98	0.914	0.906
less than 0 [dB]	0.01	0.381	0.99	0.914	0.909

For an improved weight decision rule depending on SNNR and fuzzy value, we defined *P_W* that is a probability value after weight application and the *KSSL probability (G)* of the embedded KSSL recognizer in Eq. (5) and (6). This *P_W* value depending on SNNR and fuzzy value gives standard by which to apply weights, and because *KSSL probability (G)* is changed according to *Fuzzy Value_Current*, the *P_W* is changed justly. (*The maximum fuzzy value* for KSSL recognition is *3.5*, and *the minimum critical value* is *3.2*, in our application). As a result, if *P_W* value is greater than 0.917, the MMFA fissions and returns recognition result of embedded VISR, while the MMFA fissions the embedded KSSL recognizer in case *P_W* value is less than 0.909. The *P_W* values depending on SNNR and fuzzy value are given in Table 5.

6 Experiments and Results

The experimental set-up is as follows. The distance between the KSSL input module and a wireless PDA with a built-in KSSL recognizer approximates radius 10M's ellipse form. In KSSL gesture and speech, we move the wireless data gloves and the motion tracker to the prescribed position. For every 10 reagents, we repeat this action 10 times in noisy and clean environments. While the user inputs KSSL using data gloves and a motion tracker, and speaks using the blue-tooth headset in a wireless PDA. These experiments were achieved on below experimental conditions and weights.

- *As a noisy environment, the average SNNR using actual waveform data is recorded in laboratory space, including the music and the mechanical noise, was about 13.59[dB], and the average SNNR using actual waveform data that remove noise elements for a clean environment was about 38.37[dB].*

- *If the SNNR changes by experimental conditions such as the music and the mechanical noise, because weight also is changed, experiment result can be changed.*

Table 6. Recognition results for the130 word-based instruction models

Evaluation Reagents	Uni-modal Language Processing Interface			The MMFA	
	KSSL (%)	Speech (%)		KSSL + Speech (%)	
	Noise	Noise	Clean	Noise	Clean
Reagent 1	92.8	83.6	98.1	92.8	98.1
Reagent 2	93.8	83.5	95.4	93.8	95.4
Reagent 3	94.1	82.4	95.6	94.0	95.6
Reagent 4	92.9	85.1	96.3	92.9	96.3
Reagent 5	93.1	85.6	96.7	93.2	96.6
Reagent 6	91.8	84.6	95.9	91.8	95.9
Reagent 7	92.7	84.3	95.7	92.6	95.8
Reagent 8	94.6	82.6	96.8	94.6	96.7
Reagent 9	93.4	83.4	97.5	93.4	97.6
Reagent10	93.1	84.9	97.3	93.0	97.4
Average	93.23	84.00	96.53	93.21	96.54

Experimental results, the uni-modal and the MMFA's average recognition rates in noisy and clean environment for the130 word-based instruction models, are shown in Table 6 respectively.

7 Conclusions

Human's senses information processing technology and new UI (User Interface) technology connected with various input/output devices as well as a touch screen and a virtual keyboard that is shown on the touch screen are required, for more efficient HCI than the old one in the next generation PC. This study combines natural language and artificial intelligence techniques to allow HCI with an intuitive mix of speech, gesture and sign language based on a wireless PDA. The MMFA's average recognition rates for the 130 word-based instruction models were 96.54% in clean environments (e.g. office space), while 93.21% were shown in noisy environments. In addition, the MMFA supports two major types of multi-modality for language recognition based on embedded and ubiquitous computing:

- *Simultaneous multi-modality allows users to move seamlessly between speech and KSSL (gesture) recognition modes. Simultaneous multi-modality offers real value when different steps of a single application are more effective or efficient in one mode than the other. The swap between speech and KSSL (gesture) recognition modes in this paper may be initiated (or selected) by the application or by the user.*

- *Sequential multi-modality, where the device has both modes active, empowers the user to use speech and sign language communication simultaneously, depending on noise. Results can be delivered in speech, KSSL (gesture) recognition modes, or both-giving positive confirmation of the transaction*

In further work, we will concentrate on increasing the robustness of the multi-modal recognition algorithms and on different modalities of combination with the acoustic part (e.g., the mouth detection-based lip reading using a vision technology or E-nose).

Acknowledgement

This research was supported by MIC, Korea under ITRC IITA-2006-(C1090-0603-0046).

References

1. Jacko, J.A., et al.: Handbook for Human Computer Interaction. Lawrence Erlbaum & Associates, Mahwah (2003)
2. Wooldridge, M.J., Jennings, N.R.: Intelligent agents: Theory and practice, Know. Eng. Review 10(2), 115–152 (1995)
3. Rabiner, L.R.: A Tutorial on Hidden Markov Models and Selected Applications in Speech Recognition. In: Proceedings of the IEEE, February 1989, vol. 77 (2), pp. 257–286 (1989)
4. Kim, S.-G.: Korean Standard Sign Language Tutor, 1st. Osung Publishing Company, Seoul (2000)
5. Kim, J.-H., et al.: An Implementation of KSSL Recognizer for HCI Based on Post Wearable PC and Wireless Networks KES 2006. In: Gabrys, B., Howlett, R.J., Jain, L.C. (eds.) KES 2006. LNCS (LNAI), vol. 4251, pp. 788–797. Springer, Heidelberg (2006)

6. Kim, J.-H., et al.: Hand Gesture Recognition System using Fuzzy Algorithm and RDBMS for Post PC. In: Wang, L., Jin, Y. (eds.) FSKD 2005. LNCS (LNAI), vol. 3614, pp. 170–175. Springer, Heidelberg (2005)
7. Vasantha kandasamy, W.B.: Smaranda Fuzzy Algebra. American Research Press, Seattle (2003)
8. Chen, C.H.: Fuzzy Logic and Neural Network Handbook. 1st. McGraw-Hill, New York (1992)

DWT-Based Audio Watermarking Using Support Vector Regression and Subsampling

Xiaojuan Xu, Hong Peng, and Chengyuan He

School of Mathematics & Computer Science,
Xihua University, Chengdu, Sichuan, 610039, China
laony@163.com

Abstract. How to protect the copyright of digital media over the Internet is a problem for the creator/owner. A novel support vector regression (SVR) based digital audio watermarking scheme in the wavelet domain which using subsampling is proposed in this paper. The audio signal is subsampled and all the sub-audios are decomposed into the wavelet domain respectively. Then the watermark information is embedded into the low-frequency region of random one sub-audio. With the high correlation among the sub-audios, accordingly, the distributing rule of different sub-audios in the wavelet domain is similar to each other, SVR can be used to learn the characteristics of them. Using the information of unmodified template positions in the low-frequency region of the wavelet domain, the SVR can be trained well. Thanks to the good learning ability of SVR, the watermark can be correctly extracted under several different attacks. The proposed watermarking method which doesn't require the use of the original audio signal for watermark extraction can provide a good copyright protection scheme. The experimental results show the algorithm is robust to signal processing, such as lossy compression (MP3), filtering, resampling and requantizing, etc.

1 Introduction

In recent years, efforts are made to take advantage of machine learning techniques for watermark embedding and extraction. In [1], neural networks are introduced into a nonblind audio watermarking scheme, which is used to estimate the watermark scaling factor intelligently from the host audio signal. Support vector machine (SVM), as another kinds of new machine learning method based on the statistical learning theory, could overcome the over-fitting of neural networks. Moreover, according to Vapnik's structure risk minimization principle[2], SVM algorithm is a convex optimization problem, so that the local optimal solution is sure to be the global optimal solution. Due to these advantages, watermarking scheme based on SVM is magnetic. Wang et al.[3] introduce SVM for audio watermark detection in DWT domain, which considers the watermark extraction as a two-class problem. In [4], it presents an audio watermark decoding process based on SVM, which combines the watermark decoding and detection problems into a single classification problem.

F. Masulli, S. Mitra, and G. Pasi (Eds.): WILF 2007, LNAI 4578, pp. 136–144, 2007.
© Springer-Verlag Berlin Heidelberg 2007

In this paper, a novel support vector regression (SVR) based digital audio watermarking scheme in the wavelet domain which using subsampling is proposed. The SVR is regression version of SVM used to solve the regression or estimation problem. Because several sub-audios obtained from the original audio signal by subsampling technique have the similarity, the distribution rule of the DWT coefficients corresponding to different sub-audios also has the high correlation. Here, SVR is used to model the relationship between random one of the sub-audios and the other three in the same position in the wavelet domain. The SVR-based model can improve robustness of the watermarked audio signal, and help to finish the watermark extraction without the original audio signal.

2 Proposed Watermarking Scheme Based on SVR

SVR is a universal regression algorithm applied to the problems of function approximate and regression. Here, the problem of determining the relationship among the different sub-audios which using subsampling technique to divide the original audio into, regarded as a nonlinear regression problem. Accordingly, the distributing rule of the sub-audios in the wavelet domain have the same regression problem, so we can use SVR to model the relationship between one of the randomly selected sub-audios and the other three in the wavelet domain. Then, the watermark is embedded or extracted by the trained SVR. In this paper, the watermark data is a binary logo image, and the embedding/extraction algorithm is performed in the low-frequency wavelet coefficients obtained from L-level wavelet decomposition. Because it does not need the original signal while retrieving the watermark, so it is a blind watermarking technique.

2.1 Subsampling in Audio Signal

With the time-variable characteristic of audio signal is a slow change process, the characteristic of the signal in short-time is invariable. Here, we could use a new sampling technique - the subsampling method to divide the audio signal into four different sub-audios.

Given the audio signal $A(n), n = 0, 1, \ldots, N-1$, in which N denotes the total sample numbers of audio signal. Then,

$$\begin{cases} A_1(m) = A(4m), \\ A_2(m) = A(4m+1), \\ A_3(m) = A(4m+2), \\ A_4(m) = A(4m+3). \end{cases} \tag{1}$$

for $m = 0, 1, \ldots, N/4 - 1$, are the mth samples in the sub-audios. $A_i(m)$ refers to the amplitude (temporal domain) of the mth samples in the ith sub-audios, which is obtained by subsampling.

Since these four sub-audios A_i are highly correlated with each other, it is expected that, for the different sub-audios, $A_i \approx A_j$, where $i \neq j$. This is indeed the case in practice for many audio signals of interest. (e.g. shown in Fig.1)

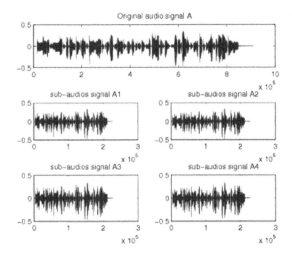

Fig. 1. Subsampling in The Original Audio

2.2   Watermark Embedding

Let $A(n)$ be the original audio with the length N, A_i in Eq.(1) be the sub-audios, where $i = 1, 2, 3, 4$.

Step1. Permute the Original Watermark
The binary logo watermark with size $M1 \times M2$ is permuted into one-dimensional sequence. Then, we scramble and encrypt it in order to ensure security. Define the watermark set as follows:

$$W = \{w(t) | w(t) \in \{0, 1\}, t = 1, 2, \dots, M\} \tag{2}$$

where $M = M1 \times M2$ is the length of one-dimensional sequence of watermark.

Step2. DWT Transforming
Each sub-audio A_i is decomposed into L-levels DWT transforming respectively. Let $\{D_1, D_2, D_3, D_4\}$ be the DWT low-frequency coefficients set of the different sub-audios, and D_i can be expressed as:

$$D_i = \{c_t^i | c_t^i = C_i(t)_{A_L}, t = 1, 2, \dots, T\} \tag{3}$$

where $i = 1, 2, 3, 4$, $C_i(t)_{A_L}$ is the value of the tth low-frequency coefficients in the ith sub-audios, and T is the total numbers of low-frequency coefficients in each sub-audio.

Step3. Selecting the Template and Embedding Position
Suppose $\overline{D}_i = \{c_t^i = C_i(t)_{A_L} | t = 1, 2, \dots, P + M\}, i = 1, 2, 3, 4$, be the randomly selected low-frequency coefficients in each D_i, which according to the randomly

selected position sequence, generated by the secret key K. The $\overline{D}_i$ is composed of two part, one part $\overline{D}_{i1} = \{c_t^i = C_i(t)_{A_L} | t = 1, 2, \ldots, P\}$ is the low-frequency coefficients set in $\overline{D}_i$ which corresponding to template position sequence. And $\overline{D}_{i1}$ is used as the set of training patterns, and not modified in the embedding procedure. The remaining part $\overline{D}_{i2} = \{c_t^i = C_i(t)_{A_L} | t = P+1, P+2, \ldots, P+M\} \subset \overline{D}_i$ is corresponding to embedding positions which is used for embedding the watermark. The reason for using the information of unmodified template positions in the low-frequency region of the wavelet domain is to maintain the same trained SVR in the embedding and extraction procedure.

Step4. Training the SVR

With the similarity of the distributing rule of the low-frequency region in each sub-audio A_i, whose relationship could be modelled between random one of the sub-audios and the other three in the same position with SVR.

For each template position, we select one set $\overline{D}_{j1} |_{j \in \{1,2,3,4\}}$ randomly from $\{\overline{D}_{11}, \overline{D}_{21}, \overline{D}_{31}, \overline{D}_{41}\}$ by another secret key $k1$ as the output vector set of SVR (T_{out}), the remaining three sets are regarded as inputs vectors of SVR (T_{in}). Define the training patterns dataset as follows:

$$\begin{cases} \{(d_t^{in}, d_t^{out}) \mid t = 1, 2, \ldots, P\}, \\ d_t^{in} = (d_t^1, d_t^2, d_t^3) \in T_{in}, d_t^{out} \in T_{out}, \\ T_{in} = [\{\overline{D}_{11}, \overline{D}_{21}, \overline{D}_{31}, \overline{D}_{41}\} - \{\overline{D}_{j1}\}], \\ T_{out} = \overline{D}_{j1}. \end{cases} \tag{4}$$

Applying the dataset given, the SVR can be trained:

$$f(x) = \sum_{t=1}^{P} (\alpha_t - \hat{\alpha}_t) K(d_t^{in}, x) + b \tag{5}$$

where α_t, $\hat{\alpha}_t$ are trained coefficients, b is the bias, and $K(\cdot, \cdot)$ is the kernel function.

Then, we could use the trained SVR for the embedding procedure.

Step5. Watermark Embedding

For each embedding position, we can obtain input vector set of SVR (T_{in}) from $\{\overline{D}_{12}, \overline{D}_{22}, \overline{D}_{32}, \overline{D}_{42}\}$ by the same secret $k1$, which is the same combination as using in the SVR training process.

Then, using the trained SVR in Eq.(5), we can calculate the desired output $\{y_t\}|_{t=P+1,P+2,\ldots,P+M}$ corresponding to the original value of $\overline{D}_{j2} = \{c_t^j | c_t^j = C_j(t)_{A_L}, t = P+1, P+2, \ldots, P+M\}$ at each embedding position, i.e.:

$$\begin{cases} y_t = f(d_t), t = P+1, P+2, \ldots, P+M \\ d_t \in T_{in} = [\{\overline{D}_{12}, \overline{D}_{22}, \overline{D}_{32}, \overline{D}_{42}\} - \{\overline{D}_{j2}\}] \end{cases} \tag{6}$$

According to the desired values, the watermark bits are embedded in the following manner:

$$C'_j(t)_{A_L} = y_t + \alpha \times (2w_t - 1), t = P + 1, P + 2, \ldots, P + M \qquad (7)$$

where α is the embedding strength, whose role is keeping a good tradeoff between the robustness and the watermarked audio quality.

Step6. Last, each sub-audio is reconstructed by applying the inverse DWT transform respectively, and then four different sub-audios (temporal domain) are combined into the final watermarked audio signal.

2.3   Watermark Extraction

For the decoder, watermark can be extracted from the tested audio signal in the similar way, without the original audio.

For the watermarked audio signal, the randomly selected low-frequency coefficients set $\overline{D'}_i = \{c'^i_t = C'_i(t)_{A_L} | t = 1, 2, \ldots, P + M\} \subset D'_i, i = 1, 2, 3, 4$, is obtained according to the randomly selected position sequence, which is composed of $\overline{D'}_{i1}$ and $\overline{D'}_{i2}$, generated again by the same secret K as used in the embedding procedure. Then, another same secret $k1$ is used to obtain the output vector set T'_{out} and inputs vector set T'_{in} from $\{\overline{D'}_1, \overline{D'}_2, \overline{D'}_3, \overline{D'}_4\}$ as in the embedding process. The watermark extraction process is described as follows:

Step1. DWT Transforming
Input audio is divided by the subsampling technique and then four sub-audios are decomposed into the DWT domain respectively in the same manner as in the embedding process.

The low-frequency coefficients set of the different sub-audios A'_i is given as:

$$D'_i = \{c'^i_t | c'^i_t = C'_i(t)_{A_L}, t = 1, 2, \ldots, T\} \qquad (8)$$

Step2. Training the SVR
For each template position, we can define the training dataset from the unmodified part as follows:

$$\begin{cases} \{(d'^{in}_t, d'^{out}_t) \mid t = 1, 2, \ldots, P\}, \\ d'^{in}_t = (d'^1_t, d'^2_t, d'^3_t) \in T'_{in}, d'^{out}_t \in T'_{out}, \\ T'_{in} = [\{\overline{D'}_{11}, \overline{D'}_{21}, \overline{D'}_{31}, \overline{D'}_{41}\} - \{\overline{D'}_{j1}\}], \\ T'_{out} = \overline{D'}_{j1}, \end{cases} \qquad (9)$$

where $\overline{D'}_{i1} \subset \overline{D'}_i, i = 1, 2, 3, 4$.

Applying the training dataset given, the SVR can be trained:

$$f(x) = \sum_{t=1}^{P} (\alpha_t - \hat{\alpha}_t) K(d'^{in}_t, x) + b \qquad (10)$$

Step3. Watermark Extraction

For each embedding position, using the trained SVR in Eq.(10), we can calculate the desired output $\{y'_t\}|_{t=P+1,\ldots,P+M}$ at each embedding position, *i.e.*:

$$\begin{cases} y'_t = f(d'_t), t = P+1, P+2, \ldots, P+M \\ d'_t \in T'_{in} = [\{\overline{D'}_{12}, \overline{D'}_{22}, \overline{D'}_{32}, \overline{D'}_{42}\} - \overline{D'}_{j2}] \end{cases} \tag{11}$$

In Eq.(11), $\overline{D'}_{i2} \subset \overline{D'}_i, i = 1, 2, 3, 4$, and $\{y'_t\}|_{t=P+1,\ldots,P+M}$ is the predictive value of the original low-frequency coefficients, which can be compared with the actual value $\overline{D'}_{j2} = \{c'^j_t | c'^j_t = C'_j(t)_{A_L}, t = P+1, P+2, \ldots, P+M\}$ at each embedding position for extracting the watermark in the follow manner:

$$w'_t = \begin{cases} 1, \; C'_j(t)_{A_L} > y'_t; \\ 0, \; \text{otherwise.} \end{cases} t = P+1, \ldots, P+M \tag{12}$$

Step4. Lastly, we decrypt the extracted watermark sequence $\{w'_t\}|_{t=P+1,\ldots,P+M}$, and do the reverse scrambling. Then, the one-dimensional watermark sequence is converted into the two-dimensional logo watermark image.

3 Experimental Results

In our experiments, the simulated experiment and the result analysis of the robustness using our method is taken in Windows 2000 and MATLAB 7.0 environment.

The original audio what we tested is the "*svega.wav*" file[5], a female singing, with $44.1KHz$ sampling rate and 16 bits/sample (length=20.67s, mono), shown in $Fig.2(a)$. The signal svega is significant because it contains noticeable periods of silence, the watermark should not be audible during these silent periods. The Haar 3-Levels wavelet is used for DWT decomposition of each sub-audio respectively.

The watermark is a binary image of size 32×32, showing in $Fig.2(b)$.

Some necessary parameters used in our watermarking scheme include watermark strength $\alpha = 0.0095$, and the kernel function "$RBF\ kernels$" for SVR, which shows better performance in the testing than other kernel functions, such as "$Polynomial$" and "$Linear$".

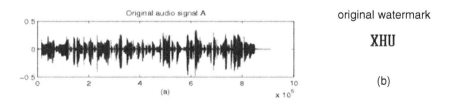

Fig. 2. Digital watermark embedding process (a) Original audio signal. (b) Original watermark.

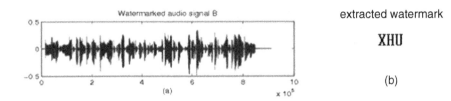

Fig. 3. Digital watermark extracting process (a) Watermarked audio signal. (b) Extracted watermark.

Table 1. The Table of Experiment Results for Resist Attacks

Signal Processing and Attacking	PSNR(dB)	BER	NC	CORR
No processing	64.4132	0	1	1
Echo	30.0122	4.0000E-004	1	0.9994
Blow-up(50%)	22.9691	0	1	1
Reduce(50%)	26.8411	0	1	1
Blow-up/Reduce(50%)	62.4132	0	1	1
Resampling(32KHz)	38.2972	0.0508	0.8821	0.9227
Requantizing(8bit)	40.9445	4.0000E-004	1	0.9994
Sampling 32KHz,8bit	36.4205	0.0576	0.8573	0.9116
MP3compression(128kb)	55.0756	0.0168	0.9623	0.9750
Lowpass(10KHz)	30.6719	0.0188	0.9587	0.9720
Gauss White Noise	41.6463	0.0148	0.9611	0.9780

XHU	XHU	XHU	XHU	XHU	XHU
(a)	(b)	(c)	(d)	(e)	(f)

Fig. 4. Experiment results for resist attacking. (a) Echo; (b) Blow-up/Reduce; (c) Resampling; (d) MP3 compress; (e) Lowpass; (f) Gaussian white noise.

*Fig.*3(*a*) depicts the watermarked audio signal with PSNR = 62.4132*dB*, which could not be distinguished from the original signal by the testing listeners. *Fig.*3(*b*) shows the watermark signature that is extracted exactly from the watermarked audio signal by using our method in the attack-free case, which at NC= 1, BER= 0, CORR=1 compared with the original watermark image.

The audio watermarking scheme are evaluated from robustness against unintentional or intentional common attacks as MP3 compression, filtering, resampling, additive noise, echo, etc.

Experiment results under different attacks are tabulated in $Table1$, while $Fig.4(a)-(f)$ illustrate the extracted watermark under various attacks. Fig.4(a)-(b) is the extracted watermark image after adding the echo and blowing-up/ reducing by using the tape recorder program that Window 2000 brings; Fig.4(c) is the extracted watermark image under the operation of resampling (changed from 44.1 KHz, 16 bit to 32KHz, 8 bit); Fig.4(d) shows the extracted watermark image after the MP3-compress processing at 128kBits compression ratio; Fig.4(e) is the extracted watermark image after low pass filtering (the cut off frequency is 10 KHz); Fig.4(f) is the extracted watermark image for watermarked audio signal with additive Gaussian white noise.

As can be seen, our proposed method ensures a good response of the detector under the different test attacks, which also illustrates good robustness.

4 Conclusions

In this paper, we have proposed a novel blind audio watermarking scheme based on SVR in the wavelet domain, referred to the subsampling method. Since the high correlation among the sub-audios which using the subsampling method to divide the original audio into, the distribution rule of the DWT coefficients corresponding to different sub-audios also have the similarity,and this relationship can be learnt by the training of SVR. To achieve the goal of blind watermark extraction, with the aids of the information comes from the unmodified template positions, we insert the watermark into random one of the sub-audios in the DWT low-frequency region while the other three sub-audios are unmodified in the whole watermarking scheme. Due to the good generalization ability of SVR, the watermark can be exactly recovered unless the watermarked audio signal is attacked severely. The experimental results under several attacks show that our proposed method can be immune against many different types of attacks.

Acknowledgements

This work is supported by the importance project foundation of the education department of Sichuan province, China (No.2005A117, 2005A121).

References

1. Yang, H.J., Patra, J.C., Chan, C.W.: An Artificial Neural Network-Based Scheme For Robust Watermarking of Audio Signals, ICASSP 02, 1 I-1029–1032 (2002)
2. Vapnik, V.: The Nature of Statistical Learning Theory. Springer-Verlag, New York (2001)
3. Wang, J., Lin, F.Z.: Digital Audio Watermarking Based on Support Vector Machine. Journal of Computer Research and Development 42(9), 1605–1611 (2005)
4. Kirbiz, S., Gunsel, B.: Robust Audio Watermark Decoding by Supervised Learning, In: Proceedings of ICASSP 2006, 5 V-761- V-764 (2006)
5. http://www.petitcolas.net/fabien/steganography/mp3stego/index.html

6. Chu, W.C.: DCT Based Image Watermarking Using Subsampling. IEEE Transactions on Multimedia 5, 34–38 (2003)
7. Fu, Y.G., She, R.M., et al.: SVR-Based Oblivious Watermarking Scheme, ISNN 2005. In: Wang, J., Liao, X.-F., Yi, Z. (eds.) ISNN 2005. LNCS, vol. 3497, pp. 789–794. Springer, Heidelberg (2005)
8. Wang, C., Ma, X.: An Audio Watermarking Scheme with Neural Network. In: Wang, J., Liao, X.-F., Yi, Z. (eds.) ISNN 2005. LNCS, vol. 3497, pp. 795–800. Springer, Heidelberg (2005)

Improving the Classification Ability of DC* Algorithm

Corrado Mencar*, Arianna Consiglio, Giovanna Castellano,
and Anna Maria Fanelli

Department of Informatics, University of Bari, Italy
mencar@di.uniba.it

Abstract. DC* (Double Clustering by A*) is an algorithm for interpretable fuzzy information granulation of data. It is mainly based on two clustering steps. The first step applies the LVQ1 algorithm to find a suitable representation of data relationships. The second clustering step is based on the A* search strategy and is aimed at finding an optimal number of fuzzy granules that can be labeled with linguistic terms. As a result, DC* is able to linguistically describe hidden relationships among available data. In this paper we propose an extension of the DC* algorithm, called DC*$_{1.1}$, which improves the generalization ability of the original DC* by modifying the A* search procedure. This variation, inspired by Support Vector Machines, results empirically effective as reported in experimental results.

Keywords: DC*, Interpretability, Fuzzy Information Granulation.

1 Introduction

Fuzzy information granulation is the process of summarizing data into *information granules*, i.e. fuzzy aggregates of data kept together by some similarity relationship. Fuzzy information granules are knowledge pieces used for describing hidden relationships among data, as well as for making inference on newly observed data. Therefore, fuzzy information granules can be employed in decision support systems to help users in formulating decisions, planning, etc. [1]

However in many applicative contexts, such as medical diagnosis, decision support systems should be not only accurate but also *reliable*, in the sense that users (e.g. physicians) should be *convinced* about the validity of the inferred decisions [5,7]. In other words, information granules should be *interpretable*. The interpretability condition is verified when users can understand the semantics of the knowledge base driving the decision support system [13] and can be achieved when a set of interpretability constraints is imposed on the granulation process [12,9].

The DC* (Double Clustering by A*) algorithm [2] performs an information granulation process so that interpretability of resulting granules is verified. DC*

---

* Corresponding author.

F. Masulli, S. Mitra, and G. Pasi (Eds.): WILF 2007, LNAI 4578, pp. 145–151, 2007.
© Springer-Verlag Berlin Heidelberg 2007

is based on a double clustering process and is specifically suited for classification problems. It returns highly interpretable information granules that can be employed in a fuzzy rule-based classifier with satisfactory accuracy.

In the next Section we describe a variation of the DC*, called DC*$_{1.1}$, which is inspired by separation hyperplanes of Support Vector Machines [4] to improve classification accuracy. As reported in Section 3, DC*$_{1.1}$ outperforms on the average DC* in classification accuracy, still maintaining high interpretability of derived information granules. The paper ends with some conclusive remarks in Section 4.

2   The DC*$_{1.1}$ Algorithm

DC* is an implementation of the Double Clustering framework (also known as DCf [3]), which is mainly centered on a double clustering process. A first clustering identifies prototypes in the multidimensional data space so as to summarize similar data. Then the projections of these prototypes are further clustered along each dimension to provide a granulated view of data. Finally, the extracted granules are described in terms of fuzzy sets that meet a number of interpretability constraints so as to provide a qualitative description of the information granules (see fig. 1).

DC* is specifically suited for granulating data tagged by class labels. The objective of DC* is twofold: performing interpretable information granulation and minimizing the number of granules that describe the input space. The main rationale of the second objective is that a small number of information granules provide for a compact – hence understandable – description of data relationships.

These objectives are achieved by exploiting class information provided with input examples in the first step of clustering, implemented by the LVQ1 algorithm [6], and performing the second clustering step with an informed search procedure based on the A* strategy [10].

Starting from a collection of input data supplied with class labels, LVQ1 returns a user-defined number c of multidimensional prototypes with class labels reflecting classes of nearby data. Since LVQ1 is a well-known technique, we only describe the second step of DC*. In this stage multidimensional prototypes obtained from the first clustering step are projected on each dimension and then clustered so as to obtain a number of one-dimensional clusters on each dimension.

The A* clustering operates an informed search in a *state space* so as to minimize the number of information granules describing data. The search is applied on a a priority queue, i.e. a sequence of states sorted by a priority value. The priority value of a state is given by the sum of the *cost function* and the *heuristic function*.

At each iteration, a state **S** is removed from the head of the queue. A *test function* is applied to **S** in order to verify if it is a final state or not. If the state is final then the procedure stops and the state **S** is returned as the minimal-cost solution for the considered problem. If the state is not final, the successors of **S** are generated. Each successive state is put in the queue according to its priority value and the entire process is reiterated.

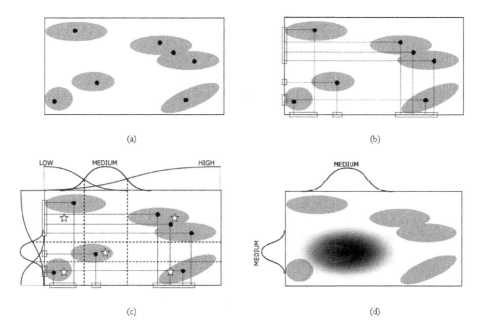

Fig. 1. The three steps of DCf. The available data (gray ellipses), are clustered to provide multidimensional prototypes (a). Such prototypes are then projected onto each dimension and clustered (b). Fuzzy sets are derived for each dimension (c), which are properly combined to generate information granules (d).

The search space $\mathbb{S}$ is defined as the set of all possible granulated views of the input domain. Hence, any state in $\mathbb{S}$ is defined by a possible combination of *valid cuts* on the n dimensions. A valid cut on dimension $i = 1, 2, \ldots, n$ is an element that separates two adjacent prototypes' projections of different class, lying between them (see fig. 2). A state $\mathbf{S}'$ is a successor of $\mathbf{S}$ if and only if $\mathbf{S}'$ has one valid cut more than $\mathbf{S}$.

Each region of the input domain that is delimited by valid cuts is a *hyper-box*. We call it *pure* if it contains only prototypes belonging to the same class. A state is *final* if all hyper-boxes induced by its valid cuts are pure. It is noteworthy observing that final states may not have valid cuts on some dimensions. If this happens the corresponding attributes are represented with a single degenerate granule corresponding to the entire domain. Such attributes are not useful in describing data and can be removed. As a result, an automatic feature selection is performed, which improves the interpretability of the information granules.

The cost function is defined by the number of valid cuts in a state. By minimizing the cost function, the number of valid cuts – and hence of hyper-boxes – is reduced and hence the number of resulting information granules is minimal. However, the A* search procedure is mainly driven by the heuristic function. Given a state $\mathbf{S}$ the heuristic function estimates (by defect) the cost function of the nearest final state that can be reached by A* through the generation of

---

148   C. Mencar et al.

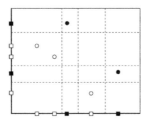

Fig. 2. The valid cuts. A cut is *valid* when it lays between two prototypes belonging to different classes.

an appropriate search path from **S**. The heuristic function of DC* counts the number of valid cuts to be added to a given state that are necessary (albeit not sufficient) in order to generate a final state.

At any iteration of the A* search procedure in DC*, several states with the same highest priority value may be present in the priority queue. In this situation (quite common as empirically observed) A* selects one of such states randomly to verify if it is final and eventually to generate its successors. The selection is random because there is no further information to distinguish between states with same priority value. Nevertheless, different choices may lead to different final states with different classification accuracies.

To overcome this problem we introduce DC*$_{1.1}$, which differs from DC* in the selection criterion when several states have the same highest priority value. The objective of DC*$_{1.1}$ selection criterion is to choose states in order to improve the classification accuracy of the derived information granules. More specifically, when a state successor **S** is generated by adding a new valid cut t, the distance $D(\mathbf{S})$ of t from the nearest one-dimensional prototype is computed. States with same priority value are sorted in descending order according to their corresponding values $D(\mathbf{S})$. In a sorted set of states with same priority, the first state has all its valid cuts well separated from all one-dimensional projections. The criterion implemented in DC*$_{1.1}$ has been inspired by separation hyper-planes of linear SVMs, which are defined so as to maximize their distance from available data to provide highly accurate classifications.

At the end of a DC*$_{1.1}$ run, a collection of fuzzy information granules with class label $(G_1, c_1), (G_2, c_2), ..., (G_n, c_n)$ is available. Such granules can be used for designing a rule-based classifier. Each granule corresponds to one rule with the following schema:

IF x IS G_i THEN CLASS $= c_i$

When an input value is presented to the classifier, classification is performed according to 0th-order Takagi-Sugeno inference:

$$class_k(x) = \sum_i G_i(x)\delta(c_i, k)/\sum_i G_i(x)$$

being δ the Kronecker symbol.

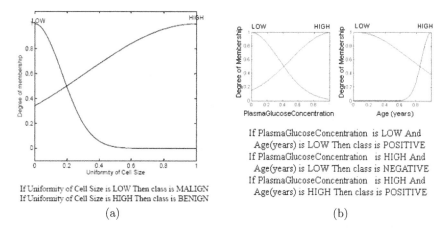

If Uniformity of Cell Size is LOW Then class is MALIGN
If Uniformity of Cell Size is HIGH Then class is BENIGN

(a)

If PlasmaGlucoseConcentration is LOW And
Age(years) is LOW Then class is POSITIVE
If PlasmaGlucoseConcentration is HIGH And
Age(years) is LOW Then class is NEGATIVE
If PlasmaGlucoseConcentration is HIGH And
Age(years) is HIGH Then class is POSITIVE

(b)

Fig. 3. Fuzzy rule bases discovered by DC*$_{1.1}$ and corresponding fuzzy sets. Results for WBC (a) and for PID (b), both obtained using 20 prototypes.

3   Experimental Results

A comparative study between DC* and DC*$_{1.1}$ has been performed in order to evaluate differences in classification accuracy. More specifically, two medical datasets have been considered, the Wisconsin Breast Cancer dataset (WBC) and the Pima Indians Diabetes dataset (PID), both publicly available. Ten-fold stratified cross-validation has been adopted, in order to achieve statistically significant results. Furthermore, examples with missing attributes have been removed. We performed several simulation sessions, corresponding to different number of multidimensional prototypes (denoted by c) discovered in the first clustering step.

In each session, we apply both DC* and DC*$_{1.1}$ to extract fuzzy granules and derive corresponding fuzzy classification rules. To appreciate the interpretability of the rules discovered by DC*$_{1.1}$, in fig. 3 we report the fuzzy sets generated in a simulation run with 20 multidimensional prototypes, and the corresponding rule base.

As we are more concerned in comparing classification ability of DC* and DC*$_{1.1}$, we report average classification errors both on the training and test set for WBC and PID dataset in table 1.

We firstly observe that the classification errors achieved by DC* and DC*$_{1.1}$ are slightly higher than average classification errors attained with numerical intensive techniques (about 4% for WBC and about 24% for PID, see [11]). This is due to the bias introduced by interpretability constraints that restrict the choice of fuzzy sets describing data. Interpretability and accuracy are indeed conflicting features and an appropriate trade-off of them is an important design issue beyond the scope of the paper.

Table 1. Average results obtained on WBC and PID Datasets

WBC	DC*			$DC^*_{1.1}$		
c	Train. set	Test set	no. rules	Train. set	Test set	no. rules
10	15.6%	16.5%	2	8.9%	13.5%	2
20	7.7%	8.1%	2	7.9%	7.7%	2
30	9.2%	10.2%	2	7.3%	7.5%	2
40	9.4%	10.6%	3.8	8.5%	10.9%	4.8
PID	DC*			$DC^*_{1.1}$		
c	Train. set	Test set	no. rules	Train. set	Test set	no. rules
6	32.7%	31.2%	2	27%	26.8%	2.1
10	30.5%	29.8%	2.3	26%	26.9%	2.4
20	29.5%	29.2%	5.2	26.1%	27.1%	3.7

The reported table show a significant reduction of the classification error, both on the training set and the test set. Also, the number of rules generated by $DC^*_{1.1}$ is quite stable and similar to DC*. Some variability, observed when the value of c is very high, is due to the dependency of LVQ1 (employed in the first step of $DC^*_{1.1}$) from initial conditions.

4   Final Remarks

DC* is a promising technique for deriving interpretable information granules from data. Classification ability of DC* is acceptable, considering that interpretability and accuracy are often conflicting features. However there is space for accuracy improvements. $DC^*_{1.1}$ goes in this direction by modifying the selection procedure in the priority queue in order to drive the granulation procedure toward a better solution in terms of accuracy. Even further improvements are possible, which however are more focused on making the first clustering step more robust w.r.t initial conditions. Also, multi-level granulation is a promising approach for balancing accuracy and interpretability. A preliminary study is reported in [8]. Research on the application of the multi-level approach to DC* is in progress.

References

1. Bargiela, A., Pedrycz, W.: Granular Computing: An Introduction. Kluwer Academic Publishers, Boston, MA (2003)
2. Castellano, G., Fanelli, A.M., Mencar, C., Plantamura, V.L.: Classifying data with interpretable fuzzy granulation. In: Proc Of SCIS & ISIS 872–876 (2006)
3. Castellano, G., Fanelli, A.M., Mencar, C.: DCf: A Double Clusterng framework for fuzzy information granulation. In: Proc. of IEEE GrC-2005, Beijing, China (2005)
4. Cristianini, N., Shawe-Taylor, J.: An introduction to support vector machines (and other kernel-based learning methods). Cambridge University Press, New York, NY, USA (2000)

5. Giboin, A.: ML Comprehensibility and KBS explanation: stating the problem collaboratively. In: Proc. of IJCAI '95 Workshop on Machine Learning and Comprehensibility, pp. 1–11 (1995)
6. Kohonen, T.: Self Organizing Maps. Springer Verlag, Heidelberg (1995)
7. Kuncheva, L.I., Steimann, F.: Fuzzy Diagnosis (Editorial). Artificial Intelligence in Medicine 16(2), 121–128 (1999)
8. Mencar, C., Castellano, G., Fanelli, A. M.: Balancing Interpretability and Accuracy by Multi-Level Fuzzy Information Granulation. In: Proc. of WCCI 2006, Vancouver, Canada, pp. 2157–2163 (2006)
9. Mencar, C.: Theory of Fuzzy Information Granulation: Contributions to Interpretability Issues, Ph.D. Thesis, University of Bari, (2005)
   available at www.di.uniba.it/~mencar/phdthesis.html
10. Russel, S.J., Norvig, P.: Artificial Intelligence: a modern Approach. Prentice-Hall Inc, New Jersey (1995)
11. Ster, B., Dobnikar, A.: Neural Networks in medical diagnosis: comparison with other methods. In: Proc. of EANN, pp. 427–430 (1996)
12. Valente de Oliveira, J.: Semantic Constraints for Membership Function Optimization. in IEEE Transactions on Systems, Man and Cybernetics, part A 29(1), 128–138 (1999)
13. Zhou, Z.-H.: Comprehensibility of Data Mining Algorithms. In: Encyclopedia of Data Warehousing and Mining, Wang, J.(ed.), pp. 190–195 (Hershey, PA: IGI, 2005)

Combining One Class Fuzzy KNN's

Vito Di Gesù[1,2] and Giosuè Lo Bosco[2]

[1] Università di Palermo, C.I.T.C., Italy
[2] Università di Palermo, DMA, Italy

Abstract. This paper introduces a parallel combination of $N > 2$ one class fuzzy KNN ($FKNN$) classifiers. The classifier combination consists of a new optimization procedure based on a genetic algorithm applied to $FKNN$'s, that differ in the kind of similarity used. We tested the integration techniques in the case of $N = 5$ similarities that have been recently introduced to face with categorical data sets. The assessment of the method has been carried out on two public data set, the Masquerading User Data (www.schonlau.net) and the badges database on the UCI Machine Learning Repository (http://www.ics.uci.edu/~mlearn/). Preliminary results show the better performance obtained by the fuzzy integration respect to the crisp one.[1]

Keywords: Fuzzy classification, genetic algorithms, similarity.

1 Introduction

An algorithm to integrate several one class $FKNN$'s is proposed in this paper. One-class classifiers have been introduced in order to discriminate a target class from the rest of the feature space [1]. This approach is mandatory when only examples of the target class are available and it can reach an high performance if the cardinality of the target class is much greater than the other one; so that too few training examples of the smallest class are available in order to compute valid statistics. Recently, Wang and Stolfo [2] have shown that a one class training algorithm can perform equally well as two class training approaches in the specific problem of masquerader detection.

Here, we introduce a parallel Integrated Fuzzy Classification (IFC) algorithm that is grounded on the weighted combination of classifier Cl_i with $1 < i \leq N$. The accuracy and the precision of each classifier can be represented by a weight, π, defined in the interval $[0, 1]$. In the last decade, several methods for the integration of multiple classifier have been developed [3,4]. Recently, the *fusion* of classifiers has been performed by weighting the training samples, where a training sample with a high weight has a larger probability of being used

---

[1] "This work makes use of results produced by the PI2S2 Project managed by the Consorzio COMETA, a project co-funded by the Italian Ministry of University and Research (MIUR) within the Piano Operativo Nazionale "Ricerca Scientifica, Sviluppo Tecnologico, Alta Formazione" (PON 2000-2006). More information is available at http://www.ii2s2.it and http://www.consorzio-cometa.it"

F. Masulli, S. Mitra, and G. Pasi (Eds.): WILF 2007, LNAI 4578, pp. 152–160, 2007.
© Springer-Verlag Berlin Heidelberg 2007

in the training of the next classifier. Adaptive Boosting [5,6] is an example of such integration algorithms. Other approaches assign different feature subsets to each single classifier [7], integrate individual decision boundaries (e.g. mixture of experts [8], do ensemble averaging [9]).

The paper is organized as follow: Section 2 describes the $FKNN$ classifiers; the five definitions of similarity are introduced in Section 3; the fuzzy combination algorithm is described in Section 4; method validation is performed in Section 5 by using two different experimental data sets; final remarks and discussion are given in Section 6.

2   One Class Training FKNN

A KNN classifier [10] for an M classes problem is based on a training set $T^{(m)}$ for each class m, $1 \leq m \leq M$. The assignment rule for an unclassified element $\mathbf{x} \in \mathbf{X}$ is:

$$j = \underset{1 \leq m \leq M}{argmax} \mid T_K^{(m)}(x) \mid$$

where, $T_K^{(m)}(x)$ are the training elements of class m in the K nearest neighbors of x. A $FKNN$ assigns to each $x \in \mathbf{X}$ a membership function $\gamma : \mathbf{X} \times \{1, 2, ..., M\} \rightarrow [0, 1]$. One possible straight definition is the proportional one:

$$\gamma(x, m) = \frac{\mid T_K^{(m)}(x) \mid}{K}$$

This definition does not consider the proximity between x and training elements. Let $0 \leq \delta \leq 1$ be a normalized distance between elements in $\mathbf{X}$, then the following membership function can be defined:

$$\gamma(x, m) = 1 - \frac{1}{K} \sum_{y \in T_K^{(m)}(x)} \delta(x, y)$$

Definitions of normalized distances, suitable for non numerical data, will be given in Section 3.

In the case of binary classifiers ($M = 2$), one-class training means that in the decision rule we use the training examples of only one class. In the following T_U denotes the training set of the target class U and, for each $x \in \mathbf{X} - T_U$, $T_\phi(x) \equiv \{y \in T_U \mid \delta(y, x) \leq \phi\}$, where $0 \leq \phi \leq 1$. Here, we propose a new one class training $FKNN$ based on the membership function of an unknown element, x, computed as it follows:

$$\gamma(x, 1) = \begin{cases} 1 - \frac{1}{H} \sum_{y \in T_\phi(x)} \delta(x, y) & \text{if } H = |T_\phi(x)| > K \\ 1 - \frac{1}{K} \sum_{y \in T_K(x)} \delta(x, y) & \text{otherwise} \end{cases}$$

where $T_K(x)$ are the training elements of U in the K nearest neighbors of x. This rule tells that the membership of x increases with the number of elements in T_U distant from x at most ϕ. For the second class we set $\gamma(x, 2) = 1 - \gamma(x, 1)$.

The choice of the *best* K, and ϕ are usually obtained minimizing the misclassification rate in validation data. Both of them can be determined from the *Receiver Operating Characteristic ROC* curve [11] obtained in the pre-classification phase. Here, the pre-classification phase includes the one class training phase and the computation of the *ROC* curves from a test set, T_s, that is separated from the training set, T_U, but smaller than the whole data set ($|T_s| \ll |\mathbf{X}|$).Note that, in order to calculate the *ROC* curve T_s must contain also example of the no target class.

A *ROC* curve is a two dimensional visualization of the false no target(FA) rate versus the true no target ($Hits$) rate for various values of the classification threshold, ϕ, and a given K imposed on the one-class $FKNN$. The definition of FA and $Hits$ can be generally stated as follow:

$$FA = \frac{False positive}{False Positives + True Negatives}$$

$$Hits = \frac{True Positives}{True Positives + False Negatives}$$

Here, we consider as positive (negative) no target elements (target elements).

A specific operating condition coincides with a point, corresponding to a given ϕ, on the *ROC*. The goal is to find values of ϕ and K that improve the accuracy of the classification. The optimization consists in finding a function $\mathcal{F}$ that measures the distance between the worst *ROC*-curve and the current one. The determination of (ϕ^*, K^*) can be now stated as an optimization problem:

$$Find \ (\phi^*, K^*) = arg\max\{\mathcal{F}(FA, Hits; \phi, K)\} \ ; \ Subj \begin{cases} FA + Hits \leq 2 \\ 1 \leq K \leq N \\ 0 \leq \phi \leq 1 \end{cases}$$

In general, ϕ and K are not independent and this makes very heavy the computation of finding (ϕ^*, K^*). Here, K is in the interval $[1, 30]$ and for each K we find the optimal ϕ^* on the corresponding *ROC*. The optimization procedure finds threshold value that maximize the distance of the experimental *ROC* curve from the worst one (the one with slope $45°$). It can be easily seen that this value will satisfy the condition also unique:

$$(\phi^*, K^*) = arg\min\{FA(\phi, K) + 1 - Hits(\phi, K)\}$$

3   Similarity Measures

In this Section five SM's are considered; they are suitable to handle non-numerical features spaces often present in several problems. In the following we consider finite sequence of symbols $\mathbf{x} \in X$, in the alphabet, A, representing a non numerical feature space, $\mathbf{x} \equiv (x_1, x_2, \ldots, x_d)$, with $x_h \in A$, for $h = 1, \ldots, d$.

SM's of two instances $\mathbf{x}_i, \mathbf{x}_j \in X$, can be built using the operators $\cup$, $\cap$, $\otimes$, and S (*support*) introduced in [12,13] and reported briefly below. In order to simplify the notation, $\mathbf{x}_{i \cup j}$, $\mathbf{x}_{i \cap j}$, $\mathbf{x}_{i \otimes j}$, and $S_{i,j}$ will denote the union, the intersection$_1$, the intersection$_2$, and the *support* of $\mathbf{x}_i$ and $\mathbf{x}_j$ respectively. Moreover we introduce the support as a normalization factor equal to the juxta-position of $\mathbf{x}_i$ and $\mathbf{x}_j$. The *occurrence* of a symbol y in a sequence $\mathbf{x}$ is denoted by $\#\mathbf{x}(y)$, and the corresponding *fragment* is denoted by $\%\mathbf{x}(y)$ (e.g. $\mathbf{x} = aabac$, $y = a$, $\#\mathbf{x}(y) = 3$, $\%\mathbf{x}(y) = aaa$). Given two instances, $\mathbf{x}_i \equiv (x_1^{(i)}, x_2^{(i)}, \ldots, x_l^{(i)})$ and $\mathbf{x}_j \equiv (x_1^{(j)}, x_2^{(j)}, \ldots, x_m^{(j)})$, the following definitions hold:

$$Intersection_1 \ \mathbf{x}_{i \cap j} = \bigcup_{\forall x \in \mathbf{x}_i \wedge x \in \mathbf{x}_j} \min(\%\mathbf{x}_i(x), \%\mathbf{x}_j(x))$$

$$Intersection_2 \ \mathbf{x}_{i \otimes j} = \bigcup_{\forall x_h \in \mathbf{x}_i \wedge x_h \in \mathbf{x}_j} x_h \ for \ h = 1, \ldots, \min(l, m)$$

$$Union \qquad \mathbf{x}_{i \cup j} = \bigcup_{\forall x \in \mathbf{x}_i \vee x \in \mathbf{x}_j} \max(\%\mathbf{x}_i(x), \%\mathbf{x}_j(x))$$

$$Support \qquad S_{i,j} = x_1^{(i)} x_2^{(i)} \ldots x_l^{(i)} x_1^{(j)} x_2^{(j)} \ldots x_m^{(j)}$$

The operators $\cap$, $\cup$, and S are insensitive to the position of symbols in the string. The operator $\otimes$ could be introduced to consider also the position of elements in a string in the definition of σ's. Using these definitions, the following SM's are introduced:

$\sigma_1(\mathbf{x}_i, \mathbf{x}_j) = \frac{|\mathbf{x}_{i \otimes j}|}{|\mathbf{x}_{i \cup j}|}$ [14].

$\sigma_2(\mathbf{x}_i, \mathbf{x}_j) = C \cdot \left[1 - \frac{|\mathbf{x}_{i \cup j}|}{|S_{i,j}|}\right] \cdot e^{-\frac{|\mathbf{x}_{i \cap j}|}{|S_{i,j}|}}$ C is a normalization constant.

$\sigma_3(\mathbf{x}_i, \mathbf{x}_j) = D \cdot \frac{|\mathbf{x}_{i \cup j}| \cdot |\mathbf{x}_{i \cap j}|}{|S_{i,j}|^2}$ D is a normalization constant.

$\sigma_4(\mathbf{x}_i, \mathbf{x}_j) = \frac{1 + \eta_{ij}}{2}$ and $\eta_{ij} = \frac{|S_{i,j}| \cdot |\mathbf{x}_{i \cap j}| - |\mathbf{x}_i| \cdot |\mathbf{x}_j|}{\sqrt{|\mathbf{x}_i| \cdot |\mathbf{x}_j| \cdot (|S_{i,j}| - |\mathbf{x}_i|) \cdot (|S_{i,j}| - |\mathbf{x}_j|)}}$

$\sigma_5(\mathbf{x}_i, \mathbf{x}_j) = \frac{match(\mathbf{x}_i, \mathbf{x}_j)}{\max(|\mathbf{x}_i|, |\mathbf{x}_j|)}$ [15].

where, $match(\mathbf{x}, \mathbf{y})$ is a function that returns the maximum number of symbols having the same value and position in the strings $\mathbf{x}$ and $\mathbf{y}$.

All σ's are normalized in [0,1]. It can be demonstrated that for the set-operators, previously described, holds $\sigma(\mathbf{x}_i, \mathbf{x}_j) \geq 0$ (positivity) and $\sigma(\mathbf{x}_i, \mathbf{x}_j) = \sigma(\mathbf{x}_j, \mathbf{x}_i)$ (symmetry). Moreover, the normalization condition $0 \leq \sigma \leq 1$ ($\sigma(\mathbf{x}_i, \mathbf{x}_j) = 1 \leftrightarrow \mathbf{x}_i \equiv \mathbf{x}_j$) can be added. Usually, nothing can be said about the triangular inequality. Note that, a distance function, δ, can be induced by a σ by putting $\delta = 1 - \sigma$.

4   The Genetic-IFC

The above described similarities, using a nearest neighbor decision rule, provide different classification results in terms of global confusion matrix. In the following we describe an extension of a classifiers integration method recently introduced and tested on different kind of data [16]. Let us consider to have N membership functions γ_i, $i = 1, \cdots, N$ and M classes. The combined classifier $\Gamma(\Pi, X, m)$ is defined as:

$$\Gamma(\Pi, X, m) = \sum_{i=1}^{N} \pi_m^{(i)} \times \gamma_i(X, m)$$

In this work, each γ_i is obtained by each similarities σ_i described in Section 3. Thus, $\Gamma(\Pi, X, m)$ is a linear combination of γ_i by means of the vector of weighting coefficients $\Pi = \{\pi_m^{(i)}\}$. Then the genetic optimization (GO) procedure is applied as follows:

$$\text{Find } \Pi = \{\pi_m^{(i)}\} \text{ such that } \mathbf{max}(\textstyle\sum_{m=1}^{M} A_\Pi(m,m)) \quad \sum_{i=1}^{N} \pi_m^{(i)} = 1$$

where A_Π is the global confusion matrix obtained using $\Gamma(\Pi, X, k)$ as membership function; the decision rule to assign an element X to the class j is:

$$\text{Assign } X \text{ to class } j = 1, \cdots, M \Leftrightarrow j = arg(max_{m=1, \cdots M} \Gamma(\Pi, X, m)) \quad (1)$$

In the following, chromosomes are vectors of floating point values of length $M \times N$ (number of classes $\times$ number of classifiers) that are exactly the values of Π's. A key point is the choice of the *fitness function* that is used to solve the global optimization problem. In our case it corresponds to the sum of the diagonal elements of A_Π:

$$f(\Pi) = \sum_{m=1}^{M} A_\Pi(m,m)$$

and the matrix A_Π is build using the decision rule in Eq. 1. The evolution of the population is determined by the classical *single point crossover* and a *mutation* operator that differs from classical ones because it is non uniform with the iterations; it has been used to reduce the disadvantage of random mutation in the floating point representation of chromosomes [17].

Consider the chromosome $\Pi(g) = \{\pi_1^{(1)}(g), \pi_1^{(2)}(g), ..., \pi_M^{(N)}(g)\}$ at the generation g, and suppose that $\pi_r^{(h)}(g)$ has been selected for mutation, the new chromosome $\Pi'(g)$ is then evaluated as follows:

$$\pi_r^{(h)'}(g) = \begin{cases} \pi_r^{(h)}(g) + \Delta(g, 1 - \pi_r^{(h)}(g)) & \text{if a random digit is 0} \\ \pi_r^{(h)}(g) - \Delta(g, \pi_r^{(h)}(g)) & \text{if a random digit is 1} \end{cases}$$

where $\Delta(t, y) = y * (1 - rand^{(1 - \frac{g}{G})})$, G is the maximum number of iteration, and $rand$ is a random number in the interval $[0, 1]$.

In the case of the floating point representation the cross-over operator does not change the global content of each chromosome, while the mutation is the main responsible for changing the population space. Here, we use an adaptive mutation rule that generate a wider kind of chromosomes initially and very selected ones in the later stages. After the application of crossover and mutation, we select the chromosomes using the *binary tournament method*. The genetic operator and the selection process are applied until maximum fixed number G of iteration is reached.

5   Method Validation

We have tested the similarity measures and the integration algorithm on two data-set, the Masquerading User Data (www.schonlau.net) and the badges database on the UCI Machine Learning Repository (http://www.ics.uci.edu/~mlearn/).

The first data-set consists of UNIX commands collected from 50 users. Each user is represented by 150 blocks each of 100 UNIX commands defined in an alphabet of 856 commands. The first 50 are legal user commands, the remaining 100 blocks may contain masquerader commands (commands from an intruder). A more detailed description about the data can be found in [19]. This data-set has been collected in order to face with the *masquerader problem*. Intuitively a masqueraded user is an interloper that, assumes control of the keyboard, and enters commands, using privileges and access to programs and data of the legit-imate user, temporarily absent from his/her working place. The interloper may also access to legitimate user accounts, through a stolen password or a hackers break in. The main issue is to discover the masqueraded users of an operating system, (in our case UNIX), on the basis of their *typical* sequence of commands. The assumption is that their behavior is characterized by their frequency, the context, and the redundancy. In order to apply our SMs and integration method we have established a biunique correspondence between each one of the 856 com-mands and 856 literals. The masquerader problem has been deeply faced in the recent literature by means of different techniques [20,21], also based on one class classifiers [2].

The second data-set has been created during the 1994 Machine Learning Con-ference and 1994 Computational Learning Theory Conference. Every partici-pants (the total number is 294) received a badge labelled with a "+" or "-", the labelling was due to some function known only to the badge generator, and it depended only on the attendee's name. The goal is to discover the unknown func-tion used to generate the +/- labelling. Also for this data-set we have codified each letter of the name by its corresponding ASCII value.

In table 1 the performances of the $FKNN$ on the masquerading user data are presented. In the first 4 rows the results of the $FKNN$ on each single SMs are shown while in the last row the result of the Genetic-IFC combination is re-ported. In this experiment, 50 blocks of 100 commands for each users have been considered as the training set T_U. The test set T_s is composed by 100 blocks of commands for each users. The considered single $FKNN$ have been obtained by estimating before the *optimal* parameters (ϕ_i, K_i) for each user separately, as described in Section 2. Therefore the results in table 1 regard the recognition of the total number of users (masqueraders) in the whole data-set. The genetic-IFC optimize the combination of the $FKNN$ for each user separately using a population size of $N = 300$ chromosomes, a crossover probability rate $p_c = 0.9$ and a mutation probability rate $p_m = 0.06$. The total number of generation has been fixed to 2000. The results for this data-set show that the Genetic-IFC combination has improved the FA recognition, while the masquerader recogni-tion rate is comparable to the one of the best $FKNN$ ($FKNN - \sigma_1$). Note that

Table 1. Performances on the masquerading user data

Method	Hits %	FA %
$FKNN - \sigma_1$	77	1
$FKNN - \sigma_2$	18	0.2
$FKNN - \sigma_3$	78	1
$FKNN - \sigma_4$	74	1
$FKNN - \sigma_5$	47	0.5
$FKNN - Genetic - IFC$	75	0.6

Table 2. Performances on the masquerading user data of methods recently reported in literature

Method	Hits %	FA %
$N.Bayes(Upd.)$	62	1
$N.Bayes(noUpd.)$	66	5
$Uniqueness$	39	1
$Hybrid\ Markov$	49	3
$Bayes\ 1 - Step\ Markov$	69	7
$IPAM$	41	3
$Sequence\ Matching$	37	4
$Compression$	34	5

Table 3. Performances on the badges database

Method	Hits %	FA %
$FKNN - \sigma_1$	44	24
$FKNN - \sigma_2$	82	22
$FKNN - \sigma_3$	20	15
$FKNN - \sigma_4$	28	18
$FKNN - \sigma_5$	80	52
$FKNN - Genetic - IFC$	72	14

results shown in Table 1 are competitive with those given in the literature [19] as shown in Table 2.

In table 3 the performances of the $FKNN$ on the badges database data are reported. In this experiment, 100 elements have been considered for the training set T_U. The remaining 194 elements are used as test set T_s. We have considered the $FKNN$ obtained by estimating before the *optimal* parameters, (ϕ, K) and the Genetic-IFC to optimize the combination of these $FKNN$ using a population size of $N = 100$ chromosomes, a crossover probability rate $p_c = 0.9$ and a mutation probability rate $p_m = 0.06$. The total number of generation has been fixed to 1000. In this case, the Genetic-IFC combination has a $Hits$ recognition rates comparable with those of $FKNN - \sigma_2$ and $FKNN - \sigma_5$ but the FA has been clearly improved.

The Genetic-IFC has been implemented in Matlab, the average CPU time per generation for both the two experiments has been $1, 6$ seconds on an Intel Dual Xeon $2, 80$ Ghz Platform running windows XP professional.

6   Conclusions

The paper discusses the role of distances in classifications and strategies to combine them in one-class classifiers. We shown experimentally that the fuzzy integration of one class classifiers may improve the overall recognition rate whenever optimal working parameters are found. At this purpose a genetic algorithm has been developed and tested on two non numerical data-sets. The distances we have introduced are suitable in the case of non-numeric data grouping and further work will be done in order to validate our approach to biological data-sets.

References

1. Tax, D.M.J.: One-class classification, Ph.D. thesis, Delft University of Technology (June 2001) http://www.ph.tn.tudelft.nl/davidt/thesis.pdf
2. Wang, K., Stolfo, S.J.: "One-Class Training for Masquerade Detection", in Workshop on Data Mining for Computer Security, Melbourne, Florida, pp. 10–19, November 19-22 (2003)
3. Dietterich, T.G.: Ensemble methods in machine learning. In: Kittler, J., Roli, F. (eds.) MCS 2000. LNCS, vol. 1857, pp. 1–15. Springer, Cagliari, Italy (2000)
4. Valentini, G., Masulli, F.: Ensembles of learning machines. In: Marinaro, M., Tagliaferri, R. (eds.) Neural Nets. LNCS, vol. 2486, pp. 3–19. Springer, Heidelberg (2002)
5. Freund, Y., Schapire, R.E.: A decision-theoretic generalization of on-line learning and an application to boosting. In: Second European Conference on Computational Learning Theory (March 1995)
6. Shapire, R.E., Freund, Y., Barlett, P., Lee, W.: Boosting the margin. A new explanation for the effectiveness of voting methods. The annals of statistics 26(5), 1651–1686 (1998)
7. Kuncheva, L.I., Jain, L.C.: Designing Classifier Fusion Systems by Genetic Algorithms. IEEE Transactions on Evolutionary computation 4(4), 327–336 (2000)
8. Jordan, M.I., Jacobs, R.A.: Hierarchical mixture of experts and the EM algorithm. Neural Computation 6, 181–214 (1994)
9. Hashem, S.: Optimal linear combination of neural networks. Neural computation 10, 519–614 (1997)
10. Jain, A.K., Dubes, R.C.: Algorithms for clustering data. Prentice-Hall, New York (1988)
11. Swets, J., Pickett, R.: Evaluation of Diagnostic Systems: Methods from Signal Detection Theory. Academic Press, New York (1992)
12. Di Gesú, V., Friedman, J.H., Lo Bosco, G.: Similarity measures: an application to an intrusion systems problem. In: Workshop on Data Mining and decision theory, Pavia (2006)
13. Di Gesú, V., Friedman, J.H.: New similarity rules for mining data. In: Apolloni, B., Marinaro, M., Nicosia, G., Tagliaferri, R. (eds.) WIRN 2005 and NAIS 2005. LNCS, vol. 3931, Springer, Heidelberg (2006)

14. Tenenbaum, J.B.: Rules and Similarity in Concept Learning. In: Solla, S.A., Leen, T.K., Müuller, K.-R. (eds.) Advances in Neural Information Processing Systems, vol. 12, pp. 59–65. MIT Press, Cambridge (2000)
15. Hamming, R.W.: Error-detecting and error-correcting codes. Bell System Technical Journal 29(2), 147–160 (1950)
16. Di Gesú, V., Lo Bosco, G.: A Genetic Integrated Fuzzy Classifier, Pattern Recognition Letters, Elsevier, vol. 26, pp. 411–420 (2005)
17. Janikowa, C.Z., Michalewicz, Z.: An experimental comparison of binary and floating point representations in genetic algorithms. In: Proceedings of the Fourth International Conference Genetic Algorithms, Belew, R.K., Booker, J.B. (eds.), pp.31–36 (1991)
18. Vapnik, V.: The Nature of Statistical Learning Theory. Springer-Verlag, Heidelberg (1999)
19. Maxion, R.A., Townsend, T.N.: Masquerade Detection Using Truncated Command Lines. In: Proc. International Conference on Dependable Systems and Networks (DSN-02), pp. 219–228 (2002)
20. Schonlau, M., Theus, M.: Detecting masquerades in intrusion detection based on unpopular commands. Information Processing Letters 76(1-2), 33–38 (2000)
21. Schonlau, M., DuMouchel, W., Ju, W.H., Karr, A.F., Theus, M., Vardi, Y.: Computer intrusion: Detecting masquerades. Statistical Science 16(1), 58–74 (2001)

Missing Clusters Indicate Poor Estimates or Guesses of a Proper Fuzzy Exponent

Ulrich Möller

Leibniz Institute for Natural Product Research and Infection Biology - Hans Knöll Institute, 07745 Jena, Germany

Abstract. The term 'missing cluster' (MC) is introduced as an undesirable feature of fuzzy partitions. A method for detecting persistent MCs is shown to improve the choice of proper fuzzy parameter values in fuzzy C-means clustering when compared to other methods. The comparison was based on simulated data and gene expression profiles of cancer.

1 The Problem of Choosing the Fuzzy Exponent

Fuzzy clustering (FC) [1] is a frequently used approach for data exploration, class discovery and the generation of decision rules and hypotheses. FC requires the definition of the fuzzy parameter m. With m close to one, FC degenerates to hard clustering. If m exceeds a value $m_\wedge$, FC partitions degenerate as well: all fuzzy memberships become equally large. The optimal fuzzy partition requires the use of a value $m_{opt} \in (1, m_\wedge)$. However, a unique theoretically justified optimality criterion is lacking, and so the optimal choice of m is still an open problem [2].

Previous applications mostly relied on general heuristic guidelines (e.g., set $m = 2$ or choose m from the interval [1.5, 2.5]). In practice, these guidelines often led to reasonable results. However, emerging applications of FC to data from genomic high-throughput technologies pose a fundamentally new challenge. For gene expression data from DNA microarrays, Dembélé and Kastner [3] found that the recovery of meaningful structures may require the choice of data-specific values of m clearly smaller than 1.5. For that purpose, effective methods are desired. A hypothesized optimality criterion for m has been used in geosciences [4,5]; however, the method is based on empirical observations for data which are presumably less challenging than genomic data. Two recently proposed methods estimate $m_\wedge$ and suggest a value $m < m_\wedge$ [2,3] (section 2). This strategy helps avoiding poor estimates $m \in [m_\wedge, \infty]$. However, due to the gradual change of the fuzzy memberships with increasing m, accurate estimation of $m_\wedge$ is difficult; moreover, it is unclear *how much* smaller than $m_\wedge$ the value of m should be.

We present a method for obtaining at least a partial answer to that question: a value $m_\odot$ above which FC provides poor models even though $m_\odot < m_\wedge$. Constraining the search interval to $(1, m_\odot]$ increases the chance for finding a proper value. Estimates m_i of other methods $i = 1, 2, ..$ can be characterized as being likely inappropriate if $m_i > m_\odot$. In our method, the inappropriateness of a value m_i is determined by the persistent occurrence of so-called missing clusters in partitions obtained when using m_i.

F. Masulli, S. Mitra, and G. Pasi (Eds.): WILF 2007, LNAI 4578, pp. 161–169, 2007.
© Springer-Verlag Berlin Heidelberg 2007

2   Methods

Clustering. Let $X = \{x_{ij}\}$, $i = 1, ..., N$, $j = 1, ..., p$, be a data set of size N and dimension p. As the result of applying an FC method to X we consider fuzzy partition matrix $U = [u_{ik}]_{N \times C}$, where $0 \le u_{ik} \le 1$ $\forall$ $i = 1, ..., N$; $k = 1, ..., C$. u_{ik} denotes the degree of membership of object i in cluster k and C is the pre-specified number of clusters.

We used the following algorithm and algorithmic parameters: fuzzy C-means (FCM) algorithm [1], Euclidean metric for the FCM objective function E, random initialization of U with $\sum_{k=1}^{C} u_{ik} = 1$ $\forall$ $i = 1, ..., N$, FCM termination if the decrease of E between the last two iterations fell below 10^{-6} or after at most 300 iterations. For estimating fuzzy parameter m, a partition $U_{q,C}$ was generated for pairs $\{m_{q,C}\}$, $1 < m_1 < ... < m_q < ... < m_M$ and $C = 2, ..., 13$. Each partition $U_{q,C}$ represented the smallest value of E obtained from 100 runs of FCM for the simulated data and from 30 runs for the gene expression data.

Empty clusters in defuzzified partitions. For assessing cluster stability in previous FC analyses of gene expression data (e.g., [6]), we generated defuzzified (hard) partitions: $U \to U^d = [u_{il}^d]_{N \times C}$, where $u_{il}^d = 1$ if $u_{il} = \max_{k=1,...,C} u_{ik}$ and $u_{il}^d = 0$ otherwise. When checking the power $S_k^d = \sum_{i=1}^{N} u_{ik}^d$ of each cluster in U^d, we found so-called *empty clusters* (ECs), characterized by $S_k^d = 0$ for some k. Hard partitions with ECs are considered as poorly fitting models and strategies are used to avoid them (e.g., implemented in Matlab's k-means algorithm). However, these strategies did not succeed in our case. ECs occurred with increasing persistence for increasing values of C. Inspired by the finding that gene expression data may require smaller values of m [3], we decreased m and ECs systematically diminished. Therefore, we hypothesized that persistent EC occurrence is a feature that can be utilized to identify inappropriate values of m, or – consequently – inappropriate combinations $\{m, C\}$. We justified this idea by visual inspection in a two-dimensional (2D) example (a sample of a 2D gaussian mixture model, $C_{true} = 3$, $N = 60$): partitions with ECs from multiple runs of FCM ($m \ge 8, C \ge 10$) were inconsistent and the final cluster seed points poorly represented the clusters assigned to these seed points (results not shown). Below we will justify by theoretical considerations that ECs in *defuzzified* partitions determine the inappropriateness of the underlying fuzzy partitions.

Missing clusters in fuzzy partitions. We can initialize U so that $S_k > 0$ $\forall$ $k = 1, ..., C$, where $C > N$ and $S_k = \sum_{i=1}^{N} u_{ik}$. Hence, if we called each column in U a (fuzzy) cluster, no cluster is 'empty' — in a set-theoretic meaning. However, it is not conceivable to model $C > N$ object classes based on only N objects (i.e., at most N clusters can exist). To identify poor results, a criterion for the *existence* of a fuzzy cluster should be established. Then we can check whether an obtained partition has the pre-specified number of clusters. A sufficient condition that restricts the number C^* of actual clusters in U to $C^* \le N$ is defined as follows: column l of partition U constitutes a cluster if at least one object i has its top membership degree in column l ($u_{il} = \max_{k=1,...,C} u_{ik}$). We interpret the subordinate memberships as the expression of cluster overlap. The above criterion for the existence of fuzzy clusters is identical to the criterion for the non-emptiness of the corresponding defuzzified clusters. In other words, an EC in U^d corresponds to a *missing cluster* (MC) in U. From the practical point of view, an EC is not a real cluster so that MC is a reasonable term for characterizing both fuzzy and hard partitions.

An estimate of the fuzzy parameter that avoids MCs. The number of objects that constitute a fuzzy cluster l based on their top membership degree is $S_l^t = \sum_{i=1}^{N} I(u_{il} = \max_k u_{ik})$, where I denotes the indicator function. (S_l^t equals the power of the defuzzified cluster l.) Accordingly, the number of constituent clusters of the fuzzy partition is obtained by $C_\odot = \sum_{k=1}^{C} I(S_k^t \geq 1)$. Based on FC results for C fixed and a set of candidate values $m_1 < ... < m_q < ... < m_M$, we determine an upper bound for a suitable choice of m,

$$m_\odot = \max_{q=1,...,M}\{m_q, C_\odot(m_r) = C \ \forall \ r \leq q\}.$$

The symbol $\odot$ was used to mimic the required minimal occupancy of the clusters.

Other estimates used. We investigated the potential usefulness of $m_\odot$ for the validation of other estimates of m: m_{2+} and $m_{2\times}$ [2], $m_{3\diamond}$ and $m_{3\square}$ [3], and $m_{4\triangle}$ [4]. For convenience, the subscript number equals the reference number of the original paper, and the subscript symbol indicates the symbol that was used for plotting the results of this method in Figures 2 and 3.

m_{2+} results from the analytical rule β in [2] that provides an upper bound of m, where U with equal memberships u_{ik} is not a stable fixed point of FCM. $m_{2\times}$ is an approximation of m_{2+} based on the size N and dimension p of the data. $m_{3\diamond}$ is an estimate of $m_\wedge$ (the smallest value of m that leads to equal memberships), and $m_{3\square}$ denotes a heuristic estimate of a proper value of m: $m_{3\square} = 2$ if $m_{3\diamond} > 10$ and $m_{3\square} = 1 + m_{3\diamond}/10$ otherwise. Whereas the above measures are derived from the data only, the method in [4] depends on FC results: $m_{4\triangle}(C) = \text{argmax}_{q=1,...,M} f_C(m_q)$, where $f_C(m) = -[(\delta E/\delta m)C^{0.5}]$, $\delta E/\delta m$ as originally defined in [1] (p. 73), and E being the FCM objective function.

Validation of the results. The true estimation error of m cannot be calculated, because the optimal value of m is unknown (section 1). However, we can speak of a suitable or a poor value of m, if the corresponding (defuzzified) partitions agreed fairly or poorly with a reference partition. This partition is justified by external knowledge (i.e., the class label vector obtained from either the model simulation or external knowledge about the considered tumor classes; see Figure 1 and section 3). For this purpose, the adjusted Rand index (ARI) (see [7]) was used. ARI = 1 indicates perfect partition agreement, ARI = 0 is the expectation for a random relationship between the two partitions.

3   Simulated Data and Gene Expression Data Analyzed

The subsequent data sets were obtained from the supplementary website to [7] (http://www.broad.mit.edu/cgi-bin/cancer/datasets.cgi).

Sim6. High-dimensional data ($N \ll p$) with a known structure (Figure 1).

CNS5 and *Novartis4* are DNA microarray data sets comprising expression values of $p = 1000$ genes for tumor samples of sizes $N \ll p$. Original references, data preprocessing and a normalization step are described in [7].

CNS5. $N = 42$ embryonal tumors of the central nervous system. 5 classes: 10 medulloblastomas, 8 primitive neuroecto-dermal tumors, 10 atypical teratoid/rhabdoid tumors, 10 malignant gliomas, 4 normal cerebellum.

Novartis4. $N = 103$ samples from tumor tissues. 4 classes: 26 breast, 26 prostate, 28 lung, 23 colon.

For the microarray data, the optimum partition and the optimum value of C are not definitly known, because the tumor class definition is based on phenotype information. Nevertheless, the data sets can be used for algorithm benchmarking, because the data represent the expression of selected genes which are known to be related to the phenotype and the phenotype classes were largely recovered in previous clustering studies [6,7].

4   Results

Figures 2 and 3 show which combinations of m and C enabled the most adequate recovery of the reference classes.

1a) For *Sim6* and *Novartis4* the transition from suitable to poor values of m is sharp so that a clear upper bound for a proper m exists. $m_\odot$ equalled this upper bound for the most adequate values of C. 1b) For *CNS5* the transition is not as sharp. So it is not as clear where the optimal upper bound may be. In fact, $m_\odot$ here represents a compromise between excluding and retaining sub-optimal results. Nevertheless, the set of partitions obtained for $m \leq m_\odot$ included all partitions that best represented the reference classes.

2) For the most adequate pairs $\{m, C\}$, $m_{4\triangle}$ was rather close (≤ 0.1) to the largest m-values for which no MCs occurred. Even though, a number of partitions contained MCs when using $m_{4\triangle}$.

3a) m_{2+} clearly overestimated the range of m for a reasonable class recovery. 3b) After all, m_{2+} was always close to the largest m-value that prevented MCs in partitions with fewer (three) clusters than classes had to be recovered.

4) $m_{2\times}$ was consistently much smaller than the largest suitable m-values and rather close to 1.0, the value for hard clustering.

5) The result of $m_{3\square}$ for *CNS5* is missing, because the method for calculating $m_{3\diamond}$, based on a dichotomous search strategy, did not converge with its default parameters. For the other data sets the value of $m_{3\square}$, suggested for practical use, was even larger than the underlying estimated upper bound $m_{3\diamond}$.

6) The range of m that enabled the highest class recovery depended on the number of clusters, best recognizable for *CNS5*. Moreover, the m-range that prevented MC occurrence and $m_{4\triangle}$, an FC-based estimate of the optimal m, also varied with C.

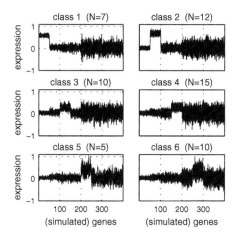

Fig. 1. Data set Sim6. $N = 59$ simulated gene expression profiles. Only the first $p = 400$ dimensions of the original data set [7] were used. In each class 50 genes are specifically up-regulated. The values 301-400 represent noise (the variables have the same distribution in all classes). These variables simulate genes with no or little discriminatory power which appear in real data when the inclusion of all discriminatory genes was given higher priority.

Fig. 2. Results for Sim6: $m_\odot$, $m_{2\times}$, m_{2+}, $m_{3\diamond}$, $m_{3\square}$, $m_{4\triangle}$; the subscript symbols were also used in the figure. The fat solid line separates the results with MCs (upper area) and without MCs. Background: bright gray: best class recovery ($ARI = 1$), dark gray: worst class recovery ($ARI = 0.18$), white: results obtained without FC (no ARI available). Reasonable class recovery for $5 \leq C \leq 7$ and $m \leq 1.3$.

7) The curve of the estimate $m_{4\triangle}$ for increasing values of C approached or intersected with the curve of the proposed upper bound $m_\odot$ near the true value of C (also for other data not shown).

8) A number of partitions – with C larger than the number of reference classes – agreed considerably with the reference classes *because* some ('overproduced') columns in the partiton matrix were MCs.

5   Discussion

Our results demonstrate a clear relationship between the transition from successful to failing class recovery and the transition from lacking to persistent MCs. Hence, our hypothesis that persistent MCs in fuzzy partions indicate a too large value of m was practically confirmed. The trustworthiness of the (unsupervised) class recovery results in this confirmation is justified, because the classes were known and have been recovered from the same data also by other clustering methods than FCM [7].

The MC-based measure $m_\odot$ was an optimal upper bound for proper values of m (Result 1a) or, at least, the criterion of a reasonable upper bound was fulfilled (Result 1b). We never observed the overall best class recovery for values of m

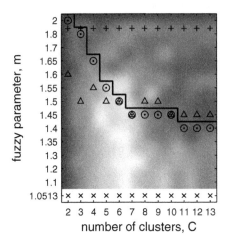 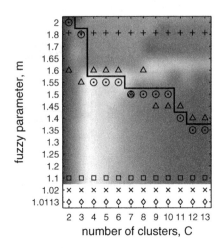

Fig. 3. Results for the gene expression data. Left: *CNS5*, ARI from 0.67 (bright gray) down to 0.23 (dark gray). Reasonable class recovery for $6 \leq C \leq 7$ and $m \leq 1.55$; $C = 5$ and $1.4 \leq m \leq 1.45$; $C = 8$, $m = 1.2$. Right: *Novartis4*, ARI from 0.92 (bright gray) down to 0.31 (dark gray). Reasonable class recovery for $4 \leq C \leq 6$ and $m \leq 1.55$. For further explanations see Figure 2.

larger than $m_{\odot}$. $m_{4\triangle}$ provided a good orientation for the choice of m, but was not reliable enough to be considered as a stand-alone method for estimating the optimal m (Result 2). Result 3 indicates the potential and limitation of a method for estimating m without using FC results: m_{2+} was possibly a reasonable upper bound for recovering coarse structures (Result 3b), but it was inappropriate for optimal class recovery (Result 3a). For very high-dimensional data of a reasonable sample size, $m_{2\times}$ is near 1.0 (Result 4) by definition (section 2). In this case, the use of $m_{2\times}$ is counterintuitive when aiming at a genuine fuzzy model. Result 5 suggests that the method underlying $m_{3\diamond}$ and $m_{3\square}$ did not work properly in our applications.

The performance of the methods with subscripts 2 and 3 may be related to the scenarios under which these methods have been configured and tested. The authors in [2,3] describe functional relationships between the dimension p, or the N/p ratio, and the proper range of m. The N/p ratios ranged from 2.5 to 238 [2], 12 to 184 [3], but only 0.04 to 0.15 in our study. Possibly, these methods show higher performance if they can be tuned for lower N/p ratios.

The use of the MC method identified inappropriate estimates of m obtained by the other methods. Apart from the theoretical justification of the MC criterion, the correctness of this identification was confirmed by the recovery of known classes.

Result 6 and others [4,5] suggest that – regardless of estimator performance – the proper value of m may have to be estimated specifically for each desired value of C. This would make FC analysis more demanding. The results show that such an extended FC analysis can be a great benefit. Moreover, estimates of m obtained for increasing C may contain useful information to assist methods for estimating the true number of clusters (Result 7). Estimates of m obtained from the data alone may be reasonable for certain values of C (Result 3b); however, it is unclear whether these values of C include the true number of clusters. If not, class discovery may become less successful.

The sharp transition from suitable to poor values of m may be related to the distinctness of the data structures which is high for $Sim6$ (Figure 1) and $Novartis4$ (indicated by high class recovery in our study and by using other methods [7]). For $CNS5$, where the transition was not as sharp, the (phenotype) classes are not so easily recovered from gene expression as previously found by other methods [7]. We may also consider that the N/p ratio of $CNS5$ (0.04) was the worst pre-requisite for building a model upon the data sets used.

Some authors adapted the term EC: a fuzzy cluster k was called an EC if $u_{ik} < \varepsilon \ \forall \ i = 1, ..., N$, where $0 < \varepsilon \leq 0.5$ [8,9]. However, whereas $emptiness$ is a correct term for characterizing missing cluster occupancy in hard clustering, we regard it as a misleading category for fuzzy clusters, because in FC we may expect $S_k > 0$ for $k = 1, ..., C$. The use of the MC criterion avoids the problem of (heuristically) choosing parameter ε (e.g., $\varepsilon = 10^{-5}$ [8] or $\varepsilon = 0.5$ [9]). When using the above (fuzzy) EC criterion, $\varepsilon = 0.5$ is the weakest condition to ensure that the MC criterion can not be violated for any value of C. Precisely, using $\varepsilon = 0.5$ corresponds to the MC criterion for the special case of $C = 2$. However, the requirement $u_{ik} > 0.5$ may be too strong for practically relevant values of C clearly larger than two (e.g., when $C = 7$, a top membership of 0.4 may justify establishing a fuzzy cluster, if the other six membership degrees of that object are about 0.1). Nevertheless, in order to avoid that a poor top membership constitutes a cluster (e.g., 0.34 for $C = 3$ with two subordinate memberships of 0.33), we may additionally apply a reasonable ε that properly decreases with increasing C.

Result 8 seems to be an argument against the rejection of MCs: if class recovery improves $due\ to$ an increasing number of MCs for increasing overpartitioning, the optimal choice of the cluster number becomes less problematic (see [9] for the same finding). However, the relationship is not strict enough to ensure accurate class recovery: increasing overpartitioning also increased the number of non-empty clusters in our study and [9]. A (possibly undetected) MC occurrence likely hinders the correct estimation of C based on the usual concepts for quantifying the validity and stability of genuine clusters.

The findings described in this paper are supported by more results for other simulated and gene expression data including the frequent task of gene clustering. These results are presented elsewhere in more detail [12].

6   Conclusions

The measure $m_\odot$, derived from the notion of missing clusters (MCs) in fuzzy partitions, is a useful upper bound for proper values of the fuzzy exponent m

in fuzzy clustering. This particularly applies i) if sample data are very high-dimensional, ii) if the sample size is relatively small, iii) if a number of variables contain no or little discriminatory power, and iv) if $m_\odot$ is smaller than commonly used m-values such as 2 or 1.5. $m_\odot$ restricts the search space for the optimal m by rejecting an inappropriate range of m that is not yet excluded by the more conservative upper bound $m_\wedge$ (section 1).

Accurate class discovery in complex data via clustering is desired in various fields (e.g., [10]), where FC may be attractive and the choice of m is a non-trivial problem. In this regard the MC method may be a general tool for validating estimates of m obtained from other methods. Our results show that applications exist, where the output of other methods deserves an extra validation. The MC method has theoretical justification, is intuitively comprehensible, easily applied and robust.

We recommend an estimation of m based on FC results across different values of the number of clusters C, because the optimal m may depend on C and vice versa. An approach for the simultaneous optimization of m and C is also available [11]. In addition, randomized data can be analyzed to estimate these parameters [9]. The costs of computing power for this estimation will often be low compared to the costs required for obtaining the data (e.g., DNA microarrays or long-term observations in astronomy). More importantly, advanced estimation of m provides the user with confidence in the effective utilization of the potential inherent to the FC approach.

Acknowledgement

This work was supported by the German BMBF, 0312704D.

References

1. Bezdek, J.C.: Pattern recognition with fuzzy objective function algorithms. Plenum Press, New York (1981)
2. Yu, J., Cheng, Q., Huang, H.: Analysis of the weighting exponent in the FCM. IEEE Trans. Syst., Man Cybern. 34, 634–639 (2004)
3. Dembélé, D., Kastner, P.: Fuzzy C-means method for clustering microarray data. Bioinformatics 19, 973–980 (2003)
4. McBratney, A.B., Moore, A.W.: Application of fuzzy sets to climatic classification. Agricultural and Forest Meteorology 19, 165–185 (1985)
5. Amini, M., Afyuni, M., Fathianpour, N., Khademi, H., Fluhler, H.: Continuous soil pollution mapping using fuzzy logic and spatial interpolation. Geoderma 124, 223–233 (2005)
6. Möller, U., Radke, D.: A cluster validity approach based on nearest neighbor resampling. In: Proc. of the ICPR 2006, Hong Kong, IEEE Computer Society Press, on CD, ISBN 0-7695-2521-0 or http://ieeexplore.ieee.org
7. Monti, S., Tamayo, P., Mesirov, J., Golub, T.: Consensus clustering: A resampling-based method for class discovery and visualization of gene expression microarray data. Machine Learning 52, 91–118 (2003)

8. Hall, L.O., Ozyurt, I.B., Bezdek, J.C.: Clustering with a genetically optimized approach. IEEE Trans. Evolut. Comput. 3, 103–112 (1999)

9. Futschik, M.E., Carlisle, B.: Noise-robust soft clustering of gene expression time course data. J. Bioinformatics Comput. Biol. 3, 965–988 (2005)

10. Djorgovski, S.G., Donalek, C., Mahabal, A., Williams, R., Drake, A.J., Graham, M.J., Glikman, E.: Some pattern recognition challenges in data-intensive astronomy. In: Proc. of the ICPR 2006, Hong Kong, IEEE Computer Society Press; on CD, ISBN 0-7695-2521-0

11. Yang, W., Rueda, L., Ngom, A.: A simulated annealing approach to find the optimal parameters for fuzzy clustering microarray data. In: Proceedings of the 25th Int. Conf. of the Chilean Computer Science Society (SCCC05), Valdivia, Chile (2005) doi: 10.1109/SCCC.2005.1587865

12. Möller, U., Gerasyuk, A.: How fuzzy is good for fuzzy clustering? Six methods and results for simulated and gene expression data (submitted)

An Analysis of the Rule Weights and Fuzzy Reasoning Methods for Linguistic Rule Based Classification Systems Applied to Problems with Highly Imbalanced Data Sets

Alberto Fernández[1], Salvador García[1], Francisco Herrera[1],
and María José del Jesús[2]

[1] Dept. of Computer Science and A.I., University of Granada
{alberto,salvagl,herrera}@decsai.ugr.es
http://sci2s.ugr.es
[2] Dept. of Computer Science, University of Jaén, Spain
mjjesus@ujaen.es
http://wwwdi.ujaen.es

Abstract. In this contribution we carry out an analysis of the rule weights and Fuzzy Reasoning Methods for Fuzzy Rule Based Classification Systems in the framework of imbalanced data-sets with a high imbalance degree. We analyze the behaviour of the Fuzzy Rule Based Classification Systems searching for the best configuration of rule weight and Fuzzy Reasoning Method also studying the cooperation of some pre-processing methods of instances. To do so we use a simple rule base obtained with the Chi (and co-authors') method that extends the well-known Wang and Mendel method to classification problems.

The results obtained show the necessity to apply an instance pre-processing step and the clear differences in the use of the rule weight and Fuzzy Reasoning Method.

Finally, it is empirically proved that there is a superior performance of Fuzzy Rule Based Classification Systems compared to the 1-NN and C4.5 classifiers in the framework of highly imbalanced data-sets.

Keywords: Fuzzy Rule Based Classification Systems, Over-sampling, Imbalanced Data-sets, rule weight, Fuzzy Reasoning Method.

1   Introduction

In the last years the data-set imbalance problem has demanded more attention by researchers in the field of classification [3]. This problem occurs when the number of instances of one class overwhelms the others. In this contribution we focus on the two class imbalanced data-sets, where there are only one positive and one negative class. We consider the positive class as the one with the lower number of examples.

We may distinguish between three degrees of imbalance: a *low imbalance degree* when the instances of the positive class are between the 25 and 40% of

F. Masulli, S. Mitra, and G. Pasi (Eds.): WILF 2007, LNAI 4578, pp. 170–178, 2007.

the total instances, a *medium imbalance degree* when the number of the positive instances is between the 10 and 25% of the total instances and a *high imbalance degree* where there are no more than the 10% of positive instances in the whole data-set compared to the negative ones.

To solve the imbalance data-set problem there are two main types of solutions: solutions at the data level which is achieved balancing the class distribution and solutions at the algorithmic level, for example adjusting the cost per class.

In this work we study the performance of the Fuzzy Rule Based Classification Systems (FRBCSs) [8] in the field of high imbalanced data-sets. In order to deal with the class imbalance problem we analyze the cooperation of some pre-processing methods of instances.

Our aim is to locate the best configuration of rule weight and Fuzzy Reasoning Method (FRM) for imbalanced data-sets with a high degree of imbalance. To do so we use a simple rule base obtained with the Chi (and co-authors') method [4] that extends the well-known Wang and Mendel method [11] to classification problems. We use triangular membership functions with five labels per variable.

Finally we will compare our results with the classic KNN and C4.5 classifiers to prove the higher performance of our model.

In order to do that, this contribution is organized as follows. In Section 2 we introduce the FRBCS, the inductive learning algorithm used and the rule weights and FRMs. Then in Section 3 we propose some preprocessing techniques for imbalanced data-sets. Section 4 shows the experimental study carried out with seven different data-sets. Finally, in Section 5 we present some conclusions about the study done.

2   Fuzzy Rule Based Classification Systems

Any classification problem consists of m training patterns $x_p = (x_{p1}, \ldots, x_{pn})$, $p = 1, 2, \ldots, m$ from M classes where x_{pi} is the ith attribute value ($i = 1, 2, \ldots, n$) of the p-th training pattern. In this work we use fuzzy rules of the following form for our FRBCSs:

Rule R_j : If x_1 is A_{j1} and ... and x_n is A_{jn} then Class = C_j with RW_j (1)

where R_j is the label of the jth rule, $x = (x_1, \ldots, x_n)$ is an n-dimensional pattern vector, A_{ji} is an antecedent fuzzy set, C_j is a class label, and RW_j is a rule weight. As antecedent fuzzy sets we use triangular fuzzy sets with 5 partitions per variable.

To generate the fuzzy Rule Base we use the method proposed in [4] that extends the Wang and Mendel method [11] to classification problems. This FRBCS design method determines the relationship between the variables of the problem and establishes an association between the space of the features and the space of the classes by means of the following steps:

1. *Establishment of the linguistic partitions.* Once determined the domain of variation of each feature A_i, the fuzzy partitions are computed.

2. *Generation of a fuzzy rule for each example* $x_p = (x_{p1}, \ldots, x_{pn}, C_p)$. To do this is necessary:

    2.1 To compute the matching degree $\mu(x_p)$ of the example to the different fuzzy regions using a conjunction operator (usually modeled with a minimum or product T-norm).

    2.2 To assign the example x_p to the fuzzy region with the greatest membership degree.

    2.3 To generate a rule for the example, which antecedent is determined by the selected fuzzy region and with the label of class of the example in the consequent.

    2.4 To compute the rule weight.

In the following of this section we will first explain the use of rule weights for fuzzy rules and the different types of weights analyzed in this work and then we will introduce the two FRMs employed: classification via the winning rule or via a voting procedure.

2.1 Rule Weights for Fuzzy Rules

Rule weights are used in FRBCSs in order to improve their performance [7]. In the literature different mechanisms have been employed to compute the rule weight. In [9] we can find some heuristics methods for rule weight specification, where the most common one is the Certainty Factor (CF) [5]:

$$CF_j^I = \frac{\sum_{x_p \in Class C_j} \mu_{A_j}(x_p)}{\sum_{p=1}^{m} \mu_{A_j}(x_p)} \qquad (2)$$

In addition, in [9] another definition for the rule weight is proposed:

$$CF_j^{IV} = CF_j^I - \frac{\sum_{x_p \notin Class C_j} \mu_{A_j}(x_p)}{\sum_{p=1}^{m} \mu_{A_j}(x_p)} \qquad (3)$$

This new definition may be named as the Penalized CF.

A third rule weight is used in this work. In [10], Mansoori et al., using weighting functions, modify the compatibility degree of patterns to improve the classification accuracy. Their approach specifies a positive pattern (i.e. pattern with the true class) from the covering subspace of each fuzzy rule as splitting pattern and uses its compatibility grade as threshold. All patterns having compatibility grade above this threshold are positive so any incoming pattern for this subdivision should be classified as positive. When using rule weights, the weighting function for R_j is computed as:

$$\mu_{A_j}^{out}(x_p) \cdot CF_j = \begin{cases} \mu_{A_j}^{in}(x_p) \cdot CF_j & \text{if } \mu_{A_j}^{in}(x_p) < n_j \\ \left(\frac{p_j - n_j \cdot CF_j}{m_j - n_j}\right) \cdot \mu_{A_j}^{in}(x_p) - \left(\frac{p_j - m_j \cdot CF_j}{m_j - n_j}\right) \cdot n_j & \text{if } n_j \leqslant \mu_{A_j}^{in}(x_p) < m_j \\ CF_j \cdot \mu_{A_j}^{in}(x_p) - CF_j \cdot m_j + p_j & \text{if } \mu_{A_j}^{in}(x_p) \geqslant m_j \end{cases}$$

$$\qquad (4)$$

where $\mu^{out}_{A_j}(x_p) \cdot CF_j$ is the output degree of association used in the FRM, $\mu^{in}_{A_j}(x_p)$ is the compatibility grade of x_p, CF_j is the rule weight and the parameters n_j, m_j, p_j are obtained as:

$$n_j = t_j \sqrt{\frac{2}{1+CF_j^2}}$$
$$m_j = \{t_j \cdot (CF_j + 1) - (CF_j - 1)\}/\sqrt{2CF_j^2 + 2} \qquad (5)$$
$$p_j = \{t_j \cdot (CF_j - 1) - (CF_j + 1)\}/\sqrt{2CF_j^2 + 2}$$

where t_j is the compatibility grade threshold for Rule R_j. For more details of this proposal please refer to [10]

2.2 Fuzzy Reasoning Methods

We study the performance of two different FRMs for classifying new patterns by the rule set. We use the classic fuzzy reasoning method or maximum matching, where every new pattern is classified as the consequent class of a single winner rule which is determined as

$$\mu_{A_w}(x_p) \cdot CF_w = max\{\mu_{A_q}(x_p) \cdot CF_q | R_q \in S\} \qquad (6)$$

where S is the set of fuzzy rules of the form in (1) and $x_p = (x_{p1}, \ldots, x_{pn})$ is the pattern example. We also use a weighted vote method or additive combination method where each fuzzy rule casts a vote for its consequent class. The total strength of the vote for each class is computed as follows:

$$V_{Class_h}(x_p) = \sum_{R_q \in S; C_q = h} \mu_{A_q}(x_p) \cdot CF_q, h = 1, 2, \ldots, M. \qquad (7)$$

The pattern x_p is classified as the class with maximum total strength of the vote.

3 Preprocessing Imbalanced Data-Sets

In order to deal with the imbalanced data-set problem we can distinguish between two kind of solutions: those applied at the data level such as instance selection and those applied at the algorithmic level. In this work we evaluate different instance selection based on oversampling and hybrid techniques to adjust the class distribution in the training data. Specifically we have chosen the following methods which have been studied in [2]:

- Oversampling methods:
  - **Random Over-Sampling.** Is a non-heuristic method that aims to balance class distribution through the random replication of minority class examples.
  - **"Synthetic Minority Over-Sampling Technique (Smote)".** Its main idea is to form new minority class examples by interpolating between several minority class examples that lie together. Thus, the overfitting problem is avoided and causes the decision boundaries for the minority class to spread further into the majority class space.

- Hybrid methods: Oversampling + Undersampling:
  - **"Smote + Tomek links"**. In order to create better-defined class clusters, Tomek links may be applied to the over-sampled training set as a data cleaning method. Instead of removing only the majority class examples that form Tomek links, examples from both classes are removed.
  - **"Smote + ENN"**. After applying the Smote mechanism, ENN is used to remove examples from both classes. Any example that is misclassified by its three nearest neighbors is removed from the training set.

For a further explanation please refer to [2]. The preprocessing methods chosen are the ones based on oversampling because they are proved to provide a good performance for imbalanced data-sets when using FRBCSs [6].

4 Experimental Study

In this section we introduce our experimentation framework. First we will describe the data-sets we have chosen for this work and all the parameters used. Then we will present our results and we will make a brief analysis according to our objetives.

4.1 Data-Sets and Parameters

In this study we have considered seven data sets from UCI with a high imbalance degree. Table 1 summarizes the data employed in this study and shows, for each data set the number of examples (#Examples), number of attributes (#Atts.), class name of each class (majority and minority) and class attribute distribution.

Table 1. Data Sets summary descriptions

Data set	#Examples	#Atts.	Class (min., maj.)	%Class(min.,maj.)
Abalone9-18	731	8	(18, 9)	(5.65,94.25)
Abalone19	4174	8	(19, remainder)	(0.77,99.23)
EcoliMO	336	7	(MO, remainder)	(6.74,93.26)
Glass	214	9	(Ve-win-float-proc, remainder)	(8.78,91.22)
Vowel0	988	13	(hid, remainder)	(9.01,90.99)
YeastCYT-POX	482	8	(POX,CYT)	(4.15,95.85)
Yeast5	1484	8	(ME5, remainder)	(3.4,96.6)

In order to develop a comparative study, we use a five fold cross validation approach, that is, five partitions where the 80% is used for training and the 20% for test. For each data-set we consider the average results of the five partitions. We consider the following parameters for the Chi et al. algorithm:

- Membership Function: Linear triangular membership function.
- Number of labels per fuzzy partition: 5 labels.
- Computation of the compatibility degree: Minimum and Product T-norm.

- Combination of compatibility degree and rule weight: Product T-norm.
- Inference method: Classic method (winning rule) and additive combination among rules classification degree per class (voting procedure).

Table 2. Percentage of classes after balancing for the seven data-sets

Balancing Method	% Positives	% Negatives
None (Original Data-Sets)	5.5	94.5
RandomOverSampling	50.0	50.0
SMOTE	50.0	50.0
SMOTE-TomekLinks	45.78	54.22
SMOTE-ENN	46.1	53.9

In Table 2 the percentages of examples for each class after balancing are shown, together with the original percentage.

As we are in the imbalanced data-set field a properly evaluation measure must be used. We employ the geometric mean metric (8), suggested in [1] where acc^+ is the accuracy classification on the positive instances, and acc^- the accuracy on the negative ones.

$$GM = \sqrt{acc^+ \cdot acc^-} \tag{8}$$

4.2 Results and Analysis

Our study is oriented to compare and find the best configuration for FRBCSs in the framework of highly imbalanced data-sets. In this section we present the average results for the FRBCSs obtained by the Chi et al. method for the different rule weight, T-norm and FRM used. Then we demonstrate the necessity to apply a preprocessing step to transform the data into a more balanced set and we analyze the best configuration (T-norm, rule weight and FRM) found. Finally we make a comparison between the classic algorithms and the FRBCSs used in this work in order to prove the validity of this model.

In Table 3 we show a comparative of the average results obtained with the FR-BCS method (Chi et al.) with the C4.5 decision tree model and 1-NN algorithms for the 7 data-sets chosen in this work.

The following information is showed by columns:

- The first colum "Weight" is the rule weight used in the FRBCS. CF stands for the classic Certainty Factor, P-CF stands for the Penalized CF and M-CF stands for the Mansoori weighting system.
- Inside column "t-norm" we note if the results correspond to minimum or product T-norm.
- In the third column "FRM" we distinguish between each type of FRM, where WR stands for the Winning Rule method and AC stands for the Additive Combination method

Table 3. Global comparison of the average results for FRBCSs with different Rule Weigths, T-norm and FRM. Including the results for C4.5 and 1-NN algorithms.

			None		RandomOS		SMOTE		SMOTE-TL		SMOTE-ENN	
Weight	T-norm	FRM	GM_{Tr}	GM_{Tst}	GM_{Tr}	GM_{Tst}	GM_{Tr}	GM_{Tst}	GM_{Tr}	GM_{Tst}	GM_{Tr}	GM_{Tst}
CF	Minimum	WR	51.03	40.21	84.25	73.59	83.52	74.4	83.06	*75.17*	83.01	75.05
CF	Product	WR	53.96	40.51	85.74	73.1	84.56	74.68	84.17	75.07	84.09	*75.17*
P-CF	Minimum	WR	45.83	37.0	83.7	<u>75.07</u>	82.98	*75.11*	82.32	74.73	82.12	74.79
P-CF	Product	WR	51.72	39.76	84.48	73.99	83.78	**76.32**	83.36	<u>76.13</u>	83.28	<u>76.09</u>
M-CF	Minimum	WR	45.87	34.9	81.54	69.78	80.77	70.21	80.54	*71.25*	80.9	71.01
M-CF	Product	WR	50.69	35.93	83.85	70.98	82.55	71.5	82.16	*72.17*	82.25	72.14
CF	Minimum	AC	46.39	36.8	74.54	60.99	81.4	66.31	81.16	*68.18*	81.44	67.95
CF	Product	AC	51.25	40.06	81.01	64.84	83.77	70.72	83.43	*70.93*	83.76	70.22
P-CF	Minimum	AC	43.15	34.43	83.08	72.39	82.4	72.99	81.84	*73.11*	81.65	73.01
P-CF	Product	AC	50.24	36.89	84.3	72.76	83.7	74.3	83.15	74.68	83.09	*75.17*
M-CF	Minimum	AC	30.55	21.58	79.36	68.57	79.44	69.3	79.32	69.75	79.35	*69.9*
M-CF	Product	AC	36.41	21.43	80.87	68.42	79.61	68.48	79.01	*69.12*	79.1	68.88
C4.5	—	—	59.07	40.52	99.57	62.89	93.46	60.27	93.47	*68.16*	93.58	67.86
1-NN	—	—	58.69	<u>57.45</u>	58.69	57.45	97.56	67.6	97.17	67.95	96.96	*68.39*

- Finally in the rest of the columns the average results for the geometric mean in training (GM_{Tr}) and test (GM_{Tst}) are showed for each type of preprocessing method, where None indicates that the data-set employed in the experiment is the original one (without preprocessing).

We focus our analysis on the generalization capacity via the test partition. In **bold** the best results for test are stressed. In <u>underline</u> the best results in columns, that is, for each preprocessing method, are marked. In *italics* we may observe the best results in rows, that is, for the different configurations for FR-BCSs and for C4.5 and 1-NN.

As we can see in Table 3 there is a huge difference in the results when we apply a preprocessing mechanism to balance the data comparing with the results without preprocessing. The performance achieved with the FRBCS with the original data-sets is roughly 30 points below the performance in the case of preprocessed data-sets via oversampling, which confirms the necessity to transform the data-sets into a more balanced format. Since there is a clear over-fitting with Random-Oversampling, we select as most appropriate the methods based in the SMOTE family.

The use of the Penalized CF obtains the best results for both types of T-norms and FRMs. Specifically the highest performance is achieved in the case of Penalized CF with product T-norm and FRM of the Winning Rule.

Regarding the use of the T-norms applied in this work we found that in most cases the product T-norm is more effective. Comparing the two FRMs applied in this work, it is clear that the one based in the Winning Rule is much better than the one based in the Additive Combination.

When we compare our results obtained with FRBCSs with the classic reference algorithms (C4.5 and 1-NN) we can conclude that, for highly imbalanced data-sets, our methods outperforms these algorithms. We can observe a high over-fitting in the classic algorithms, with a difference in almost 30 points between the training and test results.

5   Concluding Remarks

In this work we have analyzed the performance of the FRBCSs searching for the best configuration of rule weight and FRM in the framework of highly imbalanced data-sets. Also we have studied the cooperation of some pre-processing methods of instances.

Our results shown the necessity of using pre-processing instances methods to improve the balance between classes before the use of the FRBCS method. We have found a kind of mechanism (SMOTE) that provides very good results as a preprocessing technique for FRBCSs. It helps fuzzy methods (Chi et al. in this case) to became a very competitive model in high imbalanced domains.

We have also studied the differences for the most appropriate configuration for rule weight and FRM in highly imbalanced data-sets, concluding that the Penalized CF is the most accurate for the rule weight and the Winning Rule is the best selection for the FRM.

Finally we have found a superior behaviour of the FRBCSs against the classic algorithms 1-NN and C4.5. In this way we can see fuzzy methods as a promising technique in the highly imbalanced data-sets framework.

Acknowledgements

Supported by Spanish Projects TIN-2005-08386-C05-01 & TIC-2005-08386-C05-03.

References

1. Barandela, R., Sánchez, J.S., García, V., Rangel, E.: Strategies for learning in class imbalance problems. Pattern Recognition 36(3), 849–851 (2003)
2. Batista, G.E.A.P.A., Prati, R.C., Monard, M.C.: A study of the behaviour of several methods for balancing machine learning training data. SIGKDD Explorations 6(1), 20–29 (2004)
3. Chawla, N.V., Japkowicz, N., Kolcz, A.: Editorial: special issue on learning from imbalanced data sets. SIGKDD Explorations 6(1), 1–6 (2004)
4. Chi, Z., Yan, H., Pham, T.: Fuzzy algorithms with applications to image processing and pattern recognition. World Scientific, Singapore (1996)
5. Cordón, O., del Jesús, M.J., Herrera, F.: A proposal on reasoning methods in fuzzy rule-based classification systems. International Journal of Approximate Reasoning 20(1), 21–45 (1999)
6. del Jesús, M.J., Fernández, A., García, S., Herrera, F.: A First Study on the Use of Fuzzy Rule Based Classification Systems for Problems with Imbalanced Data Sets. FSCS06, Magdeburg , Germany, pp. 63–72 (2006)
7. Ishibuchi, H., Nakashima, T.: Effect of Rule Weights in Fuzzy Rule-Based Classification Systems. IEEE Transactions on Fuzzy Systems 9(4), 506–515 (2001)
8. Ishibuchi, H., Nakashima, T., Nii, M.: Classification and modeling with linguistic information granules: Advanced approaches to linguistic Data Mining. Springer, Heidelberg (2004)

9. Ishibuchi, H., Yamamoto, T.: Rule Weight Specification in Fuzzy Rule-Based Classification Systems. IEEE Trans. on Fuzzy Systems 13, 428–435 (2005)
10. Mansoori, E.G., Zolghadri, M.J., Katebi, S.D.: A Weigthing Function for Improving Fuzzy Classification Systems Performance. Fuzzy Sets and Systems 158(5), 583–591 (2007)
11. Wang, L.X., Mendel, J.M.: Generating fuzzy rules by learning from examples. IEEE Transactions on Systems, Man, and Cybernetics 25(2), 353–361 (1992)

Fuzzy Clustering for the Identification of Hinging Hyperplanes Based Regression Trees

Tamas Kenesei, Balazs Feil, and Janos Abonyi

University of Pannonia, Department of Process Engineering,
P.O. Box 158, H-8201 Veszprem, Hungary
Phone: +36-624-209
abonyij@fmt.uni-pannon.hu
www.fmt.uni-pannon.hu/softcomp

Abstract. This article deals with the identification of hinging hyperplane models. This type of non-linear black-box models is relatively new, and its identification is not thoroughly examined and discussed so far. They can be an alternative to artificial neural nets but there is a clear need for an effective identification method. This paper presents a new identification technique for that purpose based on a fuzzy clustering technique called Fuzzy c-Regression Clustering. To use this clustering procedure for the identification of hinging hyperplanes there is a need to handle restrictions about the relative location of the hyperplanes: they should intersect each other in the operating regime covered by the data points. The proposed method recursively identifies a hinging hyperplane model that contains two linear submodels by partitioning of the operating region of one local linear model resuling in a binary regression tree. Hence, this paper proposes a new algorithm for the identification of tree structured piecewise linear models, where the branches correspond to linear division of the operating regime based on the intersection of two local linear models. The effectiveness of the proposed model is demonstrated by a dynamic model identification example.

Keywords: Neuro-fuzzy systems, Clustering, Hinging Hyperplane, Regression Tree, NARX model.

1 Introduction

The problem of nonlinear function approximation has attracted much attention during the past years [3], because in real life data sets the relationship between the input and output variables is often nonlinear, which can be obtained via nonlinear regression. A lot of nonlinear regression techniques have been worked out so far (splines, artificial neural networks etc). This article proposes a method for piecewise linear model identification applying hinging hyperplanes as linear submodels. Hinging hyperplane model is proposed by Breiman [7], and several application examples have been published in the literature, e.g. it can be used in model predictive control [5], or identification of piecewise affine systems via

F. Masulli, S. Mitra, and G. Pasi (Eds.): WILF 2007, LNAI 4578, pp. 179–186, 2007.

mixed-integer programming [4]. The original identification algorithm developed by Bremain is much more simple and easily implementable, but it suffers from convergency and range problems [5,6].

The motivation of this paper is to provide a new, robust and easily implementable and computationally effective algorithm for hinge identification. The proposed technique uses the Fuzzy c-Regression Clustering, where the cluster prototypes are functions instead of geometrical objects. Therefore, if the number of prototypes c is equal to two, FCRM can be used to identify hinging hyperplanes, if the relative location of the two linear regression models correspond to a hinge function, in other words: they should intersect each other in the current operating region filled by the data point available. Hence, in this paper a method is proposed that allows the incorporation of constrains in the clustering procedure.

In the application example the proposed hinge function based model will be used for the modeling of a dynamical system. The Non-linear AutoRegressive with eXogenous input (NARX) model is frequently used with many non-linear identification methods, such as neural networks and fuzzy models (see in [1]). Neural networks are in relation with hinging hyperplanes. We have found that the proposed technique highly improves the original identification method, and makes hinge hyperplanes commensurable with neural networks even in such a hard tests like a free-run measurement. This paper is organized as follows. Section 2 discusses hinge function approximation, and how the constrains can be incorporated into the FCRM identification approach. After that the resulted tree structured piecewise linear model is described. In Section 3 an application example is presented, and Section 4 concludes the paper.

2   Non-linear Regression with Hinge Functions and Fuzzy c-Regression Clustering

This section gives a brief description about what the hinging hyperplane approach means on the basis of [3], followed by how the constrains can be incorporated into FCRM clustering.

2.1   Function Approximation with Hinge Functions

Suppose two hyperplanes are given by: $y_k = \mathbf{x}_k^T \theta^+, y_k = \mathbf{x}_k^T \theta^-$, where $\mathbf{x}_k = [x_{k,0}, x_{k,1}, x_{k,2}, \dots, x_{k,n}]$ ($x_{k,0} \equiv 1$) is the kth regressor vector and y_k is the kth output variable ($k = 1, \dots, N$). These two hyperplanes are continuously joined together at $\{\mathbf{x} : \mathbf{x}^T (\theta^+ - \theta^-) = 0\}$ as can be seen in Figure 2.4. As a result they are called *hinging hyperplanes*. The joint $\triangle = \theta^+ - \theta^-$, multiples of $\triangle$ are defined *hinge* for the two hyperplanes, $y_k = \mathbf{x}_k^T \theta^+$ and $y_k = \mathbf{x}_k^T \theta^-$. The solid part of the two hyperplanes explicitly given by $y_k = \max(\mathbf{x}_k^T \theta^+, \mathbf{x}_k^T \theta^-)$ or $y_k = \min(\mathbf{x}_k^T \theta^+, \mathbf{x}_k^T \theta^-)$.

For a sufficiently smooth function $f(\mathbf{x}_k)$, the approximation with hinge functions can get arbitrarily close if sufficiently large number of hinge functions are used. The sum of the hinge functions $\sum_{i=1}^{K} h_i(\mathbf{x}_k)$ constitutes a continuous piecewise linear function. The number of input variables n in each hinge function and the number in hinge functions K are two variables to be determined. The explicit form for representing a function $f(\mathbf{x}_k)$ with hinge functions becomes

$$f(\mathbf{x}_k) = \sum_{i=1}^{K} h_i(\mathbf{x}_k) = \sum_{i=1}^{K} \langle \max | \min \rangle \left(\mathbf{x}_k^T \theta_i^+, \mathbf{x}_k^T \theta_i^- \right) \qquad (1)$$

where $\langle \max | \min \rangle$ means max or min.

2.2   Hinge Search as an Optimization Problem

The essential hinge search problem can be viewed as an extension of the linear least-squares regression problem. Given N data pairs as $\{\mathbf{x}_1, y_1\}, \{\mathbf{x}_2, y_2\}, \dots, \{\mathbf{x}_N, y_N\}$ from a function (linear or non-linear) $y_k = f(\mathbf{x}_k)$, the linear least-squares regression aims to find the best parameter vector $\widehat{\theta}$, by minimizing a quadratic cost function

$$\widehat{\theta} = \arg\min_{\theta} \sum_{k=1}^{N} \left(y_k - \mathbf{x}_k^T \theta \right)^2 \qquad (2)$$

with which, the regression model gives the best linear approximation to y. For nonsingular data matrix $\mathbf{X} = [\mathbf{x}_1 \mathbf{x}_2 \dots \mathbf{x}_N]^T$ the linear least squares estimate $y = \mathbf{x}^T \theta$ is always uniquely available.

The hinge search problem, on the other hand, aims to find the two parameter vectors θ^+ and θ^-, defined by

$$[\theta^+, \ \theta^-] = \arg\min_{\theta^+, \ \theta^-} \sum_{k=1}^{N} \left[y_k - \langle \max | \min \rangle \left(\mathbf{x}_k^T \theta^+, \mathbf{x}_k^T \theta^- \right) \right]^2 . \qquad (3)$$

A brute force application of Gauss-Newton method can solve the above optimization problem. However, two problems exist [3]:

1. High computational requirement. The Gauss-Newton method is computationally intensive. In addition, since the cost function is not continuously differentiable, the gradients required by Gauss-Newton method can not be given analytically. Numerical evaluation is thus needed which has high computational demand.
2. Local minima. There is no guarantee that the global minimum can be obtained. Therefore appropriate initial condition is crucial.

The proposed identification algorithm applies a much simpler optimization method, the so called alternating optimization which is is a heuristic optimization technique and has been applied for several decades for many purposes, therefore it is an exhaustively tested method in non-linear parameter and structure identification as well. Within the hinge function approximation approach, the two linear submodels can be identified by the weighted linear least-squares approach, but their operating regimes (where they are valid) are still an open question. For that purpose the FCRM method was used which is able to partition the data and determine the parameters of the linear submodels simultaneously. In this way, with the application of the alternating optimization technique and taking advantage of the linearity in $(y_k - \mathbf{x}_k^T \theta^+)$ and $(y_k - \mathbf{x}_k^T \theta^-)$, an effective approach is given for hinge function identification (Problem 1). The proposed procedure is attractive in the local minima point of view (Problem 2) as well, because in this way although the problem is not avoided but transformed into a deeply discussed problem, namely the cluster validity problem. In the following section this method is discussed briefly in general, and in Section 2.4 the hinge function identification and FCRM method are joined together.

2.3   Constrained Prototype Based FCRM

Fuzzy c-regression models, deeply discussed in the literature, yield simultaneous estimates of parameters of c regression models together with a fuzzy c-partitioning of the data. It is an important question how to incorporate constrains into the clustering procedure. These constrains can contain prior knowledge, or like in the hinge function identification approach, restrictions about the structure of the model (the relative location of the linear submodels).

This section deals with prototypes linear in the parameters. Therefore the parameters can be estimated by linear least-squares techniques. When linear equality and inequality constraints are defined on these prototypes, quadratic programming (QP) has to be used instead of the least-squares method. This optimization problem still can be solved effectively compared to other constrained nonlinear optimization algorithms.

The parameter constraints can be grouped into three categories:

- **Local constrains** are valid only for the parameters of a regression model, $\Lambda_i \theta_i \leq \omega_i$.
- **Global constrains** are related to all of the regression models, $\Lambda_{gl} \theta_i \leq \omega_{gl}$, $i = 1, \ldots, c$.
- **Relative constrains** define the relative magnitude of the parameters of two or more regression models,

$$\Lambda_{rel,i,j} \begin{bmatrix} \theta_i \\ \theta_j \end{bmatrix} \leq \omega_{rel,i,j} \tag{4}$$

For a throughout discussion how these constrains can be incorporated into the identification approach, see [1].

2.4   Improvements of Hinge Identification

For hinge function identification purposes, two prototypes have to be used by FCRM ($c = 2$), and these prototypes must be linear regression models. However, these linear submodels have to intersect each other within the operating regime covered by the known data points (within the hypercube expanded by the data). This is a crucial problem in the hinge identification area [3]. To take into account this point of view as well, constrains have to be taken into consideration as follows. Cluster centers $\mathbf{v}_i$ can also be computed from the result of FCRM as the weighted average of the known input data points

$$\mathbf{v}_i = \frac{\sum_{k=1}^{N} \mathbf{x}_k \mu_{i,k}}{\sum_{k=1}^{N} \mu_{i,k}} \tag{5}$$

where the membership degree $\mu_{i,k}$ is interpreted as a weight representing the extent to which the value predicted by the model matches y_k. These cluster centers are located in the 'middle' of the operating regime of the two linear submodels. Because the two hyperplanes must cross each other (see also Figure 2.4), the following criteria can be specified as relative inequality constraints:

$$\Lambda_{rel,1,2} \begin{bmatrix} \boldsymbol{\theta}_1 \\ \boldsymbol{\theta}_2 \end{bmatrix} \leq 0 \text{ where } \Lambda_{rel,1,2} = \begin{bmatrix} \mathbf{v}_1 & -\mathbf{v}_1 \\ -\mathbf{v}_2 & \mathbf{v}_2 \end{bmatrix} \tag{6}$$

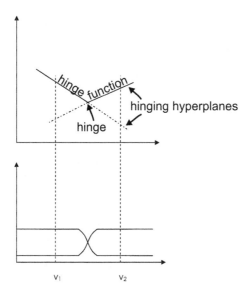

Fig. 1. Basic definitions and hinge identification restrictions

2.5   Tree Structured Piecewise Linear Models

So far, the hinge function identification method is presented. The proposed technique can be used to determine the parameters of one hinge function. In general, there are two method to construct a piecewise linear model: additive and tree structured models [3]. In this paper the later will be used since the resulting binary tree structured hinge functions can have a simpler form to interpret and more convenient structure to implement.

The basic idea of the binary tree structure is as follows. Divide the data set into an estimation set and validation set. With the estimation data set, based on certain splitting rules, grow and sufficiently large binary tree. Then use the validation data set to prune the tree into a right size. The estimation data is recursively partitioned into subsets, while each subset leads to a model. As a result, this type of model is also called the recursive partitioning model. For example given a simple symmetrical binary tree structure model, the first level contains one hinge function, the second level contains 2 hinge functions, the third level contains 4 hinges, and in general the kth level contains $2^{(k-1)}$ hinge functions.

3   Application Example

In this example, the proposed method is used to approximate a Hammerstein system that consists of a series connection of a memoryless nonlinearity and linear dynamics. For transparent presentation, the Hammerstein system to be identified consists of a first-order linear part, $y(k+1) = 0.9y(k) + 0.1v(k)$, and a static nonlinearity represented by a polynomial, $v(k) = u(k)^2$. The identification data consists of 500 input-output data generated with random input $u(k)$ in the range of $[0, 1.3]$.

In this simple example a hinge function based tree with 4 leaves were generated. For the robust testing of the performance of the model building algorithm, 10 fold cross validation method is used. For comparison the nonlinear identification toolbox of Jonas Sjoberg [2] has been used and global hinging hyperplane models with 4 hinges have been identified based on the same training data. Surprisingly, the resulted classical models gave extremely bad modeling performance (see Table 3). As the results show in Table 3, the identified models give excellent performance. For comparison, a feedforward neural net was also trained and tested using the same data. The neural net contains one hidden layer with 4 neurons using tanh basis functions. As can be seen from the results, the training and test error is comparable with the errors of the proposed method. A very rigorous test of NARX models is free run simulation because the errors can be cumulated. It can be also seen on Figure 2 that the identified models (the proposed ones and the neural nets) perform very good also in free run simulation (the system output and the simulated ones can hardly be distinguished). However, the neural net seems to be more robust in this example, the proposed hinge model is much more interpretable than the neural net. This confirms that both the proposed clustering based constrained optimization strategy and the hierarchial

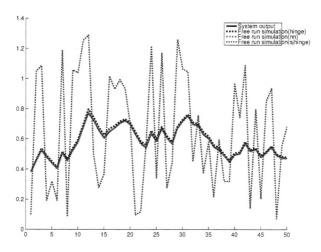

Fig. 2. Free run simulation by the Hammerstein system (proposed hinge model, neural network, hinge model by Sjoberg)

Table 1. Mean square errors of the hinging hyperplane models

	Training error	Test error	Free run
Sjoberg	0.3601	0.3596	0.3598
Neural network	0.0039	0.0040	0.0033
This paper	0.0045	0.0046	0.0143

model structure has advantages over the classical gradient-based optimization of global hinging hyperplane models.

4   Conclusion

Hinging hyperplane models are an alternative to artificial neural nets. The motivation of the research presented in this paper was to provide a new algorithm to handle convergence problems of the classical hinging hyperplane identification algorithms. A clustering technique has been proposed that applies linear models as prototypes. The identification of a hinge function is applied recursively, so the hinge functions recursively partition the input space of the model. Since hyperplanes should intersect each other in the operating regime covered by the data points a constrained version of the fuzzy c-regression clustering has been developed. A comparisons were made with the neural networks. Neural networks are in relation with hinging hyperplanes, therefore this comparison is quite adequate. We have found that the proposed technique highly improves the original identification method, and makes hinge hyperplanes commensurable with neural networks even in such a hard tests like a free-run measurement.

In our further research the benefits of hinging hyperplanes (piecewise linear models, tree structure) up to the neural networks will be further emphasized, especially, the advantages in model based process control will be studied.

Hence, further validation could be the application of the proposed identification algorithm in more complex identification problems, and even in model based control tasks. Hence, in this case the performance of the model would be also validated from the point of the control performance of the model used to design a model predictive controller.

In our further research we are going to emphasize the benefits of hinging hyperplanes (piecewise linear models, tree structure) up to the neural networks. We are working constantly on the improvement and adaptability of the method, but the limited length of the paper didn't allow us to present further, more complex examples, but we would like to utilize the advantages of this method on as many fields as possible (e.g. in process control or classification).

Acknowledgements

The authors would like to acknowledge the sup-port of the Cooperative Research Centre (VIKKK) (project 2004-I) and Hungarian Research Found (OTKA T049534). Janos Abonyi is grateful for support of the Bolyai Fellowship of the Hungarian Academy of Sciences and the veges Fellowship of National Office of Re-search and Technology.

References

1. Abonyi, J.: Fuzzy model identification for control. Birkhauser, Boston (2003)
2. Sjoberg, J.: Nonlinear Toolbox, Version 1.0
3. Niu, S., Pucar, P.: Hinging hyperplanes for non-linear identification (1995), http://www.control.isy.liu.se
4. Roll, J., Bemporad, A., Ljung, L.: Identification of piecewise affine systems via mixed-integer programming. Automatica 40, 37–50 (2004)
5. Ramirez, D.R., Camacho, E.F., Arahal, M.R.: Implementation of min-max MPC using hinging hyperplanes. Application to a heat exchanger. Control Engineering Practice 12, 1197–1205 (2004)
6. Pucar, P., Sjoberg, J.: Parameterization and conditioning of hinging hyperplane models. Technical Report LiTH-ISY-R-1809, Department of Electrical Engineering, Linkoping University, Linkoping, Sweden (ftp 130.236.24.1.) (1995)
7. Breiman, L.: Hinging hyperplanes for regression, classification and function approximation. IEEE Transactions on Information Theory 39(3), 311–325 (1993)

Evaluating Membership Functions for Fuzzy Discrete SVM

Carlotta Orsenigo[1] and Carlo Vercellis[2]

[1] Dip. di Scienze Economiche, Aziendali e Statistiche, Università di Milano, Italy
carlotta.orsenigo@unimi.it
[2] Dip. di Ingegneria Gestionale, Politecnico di Milano, Italy
carlo.vercellis@polimi.it

Abstract. A vast majority of classification problems are characterized by an intrinsic vagueness in the knowledge of the class label associated to each example. In this paper we propose a classifier based on fuzzy discrete support vector machines, that takes as input a binary classification problem together with a membership value for each example, and derives an optimal separation rule by solving a mixed-integer optimization problem. We consider different methods for computing the membership function: some are based on a metric defined in the attribute space; some derive the membership function from a scoring generated by a probabilistic classifier; others make use of frequency voting by an ensemble classifier. To evaluate the overall accuracy of the fuzzy discrete SVM, and to investigate the effect of the alternative membership functions, computational tests have been performed on benchmark datasets. They show that fuzzy discrete SVM is an accurate classification method capable to generate robust rules and to smooth out the effect of outliers.

1 Introduction

In a *classification* problem we are required to analyze a set of *examples*, generally expressed as n-dimensional vectors, whose associated *class label* is supposed to be known, in order to identify a function that accurately describes the relationship between each input vector and the associated class label. For instance, the examples may represent customers of a company which have to be labeled as loyal or churners. The input vectors can include socioeconomic information about customers, such as age, income and number of children, and transactional data, such as the spending of the individuals.

Several mathematical methods have been successfully applied for binary classification: among others, support vector machines (SVM), neural networks, classification trees and logistic regression. All these methods are based on the assumption that the class label is known with certainty for each example. However, most applications of classification are characterized by a certain degree of vagueness, since the input vector, representing the values of the explanatory variables, is usually insufficient to univocally determine the class label for each

F. Masulli, S. Mitra, and G. Pasi (Eds.): WILF 2007, LNAI 4578, pp. 187–194, 2007.
© Springer-Verlag Berlin Heidelberg 2007

example. For instance, in marketing applications the examples describe individuals whose subjective attitude towards decision making, generally unknown to the analyst, may significantly influence the behavior of a customer and the corresponding class label.

In order to relax the assumption that the class label is perfectly known for each example, one might resort to *fuzzy logic*, that requires to define a fuzzy function regulating the membership of an example to more than one class. Fuzzy approaches to classification have been first considered in connection to neural networks (5). Subsequently, fuzzy extensions of SVM have been considered in (6; 3; 15; 4; 14), where a fuzzification of the input data was performed by a membership function, in most cases assumed inversely proportional to the distance from the centroid of the corresponding class.

In this paper we propose to combine a fuzzy discrete support vector machines for classification (12) with several methods for computing the membership function. Some of them are based on a metric defined in the attribute space; some derive the membership function from a scoring generated by a probabilistic classifier; others make use of frequency voting by an ensemble classifier. Discrete SVM are a successful alternative to SVM, originally introduced in (8; 9), that is based on the idea of accurately evaluating the number of misclassified examples instead of measuring their distance from the separating hyperplane. Starting from the original formulation, discrete SVM have been successfully extended in several directions, to deal with multi-class problems (10) or to learn from a small number of training examples (11). To evaluate the overall accuracy of the fuzzy discrete SVM, and to investigate the effect of the different membership functions, computational tests have been performed on benchmark datasets. They show that fuzzy discrete SVM is an accurate classifier capable to generate robust rules and to smooth out the effect of outliers.

2   SVM, Discrete SVM and Fuzzy Discrete SVM

In a binary classification problem we are required to distinguish between examples belonging to two different classes. From a mathematical point of view, the problem can be stated as follows. Suppose we are provided with a training set $\mathcal{S}_m = \{(\mathbf{x}_i, y_i),\ i \in \mathcal{M} = \{1, 2, \ldots, m\}\}$ of examples, where $\mathbf{x}_i \in \Re^n$ is an input vector of predictive variables, and $y_i \in \mathcal{D} = \{-1, +1\}$ is the categorical class value associated to $\mathbf{x}_i$. Each component x_{ij} of an example $\mathbf{x}_i$ is a realization of a random variable $\mathbf{A}_j, j \in \mathcal{N} = \{1, 2, \ldots n\}$, that will be referred to as an *attribute* of $\mathcal{S}_m$. Let $\mathcal{H}$ denote a set of functions $f(\mathbf{x}) : \Re^n \mapsto \mathcal{D}$ that represent hypothetical relationships between $\mathbf{x}_i$ and y_i. A classification problem consists of defining an appropriate hypotheses space $\mathcal{H}$ and a function $f^* \in \mathcal{H}$ which optimally describes the relationship between the examples and their class values.

In the theory of support vector machines (SVM) the hypotheses space $\mathcal{H}$ is based on the set of separating hyperplanes in $\Re^n$ (13). Hence, the generic hypothesis is given by $f(\mathbf{x}) = \text{sgn}(\mathbf{w}'\mathbf{x} - b)$, where $\mathbf{w}$ defines the orientation of the hyperplane in the space and b its offset from the origin. In order to select an optimal hypothesis $f^* \in \mathcal{H}$, SVM relies on the *structural risk minimization principle* (SRM), which establishes the concept of reducing the empirical error as well as the generalization error in order to achieve a high prediction accuracy on future examples. Formally, this is obtained by minimizing the following risk functional

$$\hat{R}(f) = \frac{1}{m} \sum_{i=1}^{m} V(y_i, f(\mathbf{x}_i)) + \lambda \|f\|_K^2, \tag{1}$$

where the first term, based on the *loss function* V, represents the empirical error on the training set $\mathcal{S}_m$, and the second term is related to the generalization capability of f. Here, $K(\cdot, \cdot)$ is a given symmetric positive definite function named *kernel*, $\|f\|_K^2$ denotes the norm of f in the reproducing kernel Hilbert space induced by K, and λ is a parameter that controls the trade-off between the two terms. According to the SRM principle, the first term in (1) expresses the misclassification rate of the examples in the training set. However, for computational reasons, SVM replace this term with a continuous proxy of the sum of the distances of the misclassified examples from the separating hyperplane. More specifically, for SVM the loss function V takes the form

$$V(y_i, f(\mathbf{x}_i)) = |1 - y_i (\mathbf{w}'\mathbf{x}_i - b)|_+ \tag{2}$$

where $|t|_+ = t$ if t is positive and zero otherwise. The best separating hyperplane is determined by the solution of a quadratic optimization problem.

A different family of classification models, termed *discrete* SVM, has been introduced in (8; 9) and is motivated by an alternative loss function that, according to the SRM principle, counts the number of misclassified examples instead of measuring their distance from the separating hyperplane. The rational behind discrete SVM is that a precise evaluation of the empirical error could possibly lead to a more accurate classifier. In this case, the loss function is given by

$$V(y_i, f(\mathbf{x}_i)) = c_i \theta(1 - y_i (\mathbf{w}'\mathbf{x}_i - b)), \tag{3}$$

where $\theta(t) = 1$ if t is positive and zero otherwise, and c_i is a penalty for the misclassification of the example $\mathbf{x}_i$. The inclusion of the loss (3) into the risk functional (1) leads to the formulation of a mixed-integer linear programming problem, whose solution provides the optimal separating hyperplane in the context of discrete SVM.

A fuzzy variant of discrete SVM, which can be used for solving binary classification problems when the class values are affected by an intrinsic vagueness, is proposed in (12). In order to describe class uncertainty, according to a fuzzy logic, the model considers a membership value assigned to each example in the training set by means of a generic fuzzy function, such as those described in the next section. In particular, let $f_i \in [0, 1]$ and $(1 - f_i), i \in \mathcal{M}$, denote the membership values of $\mathbf{x}_i$ for the positive and the negative class, respectively. Hence, if $f_i = 1$ the example $\mathbf{x}_i$ is assigned with certainty to the positive class, whereas it is labeled as negative if $f_i = 0$.

The concept of empirical error must be redefined, since each example in the training set contributes to the total error in a proportion expressed by the corresponding membership value f_i. By this way, the loss function (3) can be redefined as

$$V(y_i, f(\mathbf{x}_i)) = c_i f_i \vartheta \left(1 - (\mathbf{w}'\mathbf{x}_i - b)\right) + c_i \left(1 - f_i\right) \vartheta \left((\mathbf{w}'\mathbf{x}_i - b) - 1\right). \qquad (4)$$

As a consequence, in order to formalize the double misclassification status of each example, fuzzy discrete SVM require to introduce two families of binary variables by letting

$$p_i = \begin{cases} 0 & \text{if} \quad \mathbf{w}'\mathbf{x}_i - b \geq 1 \\ 1 & \text{if} \quad \mathbf{w}'\mathbf{x}_i - b < 1 \end{cases}, \quad r_i = \begin{cases} 0 & \text{if} \quad \mathbf{w}'\mathbf{x}_i - b \leq -1 \\ 1 & \text{if} \quad \mathbf{w}'\mathbf{x}_i - b > -1 \end{cases}, \quad i \in \mathcal{M}.$$

The separating hyperplane can be obtained by solving a new optimization problem, termed *fuzzy discrete support vector machines*,

$$\min \quad \frac{\alpha}{m} \sum_{i=1}^{m} c_i(f_i p_i + (1 - f_i) r_i) + \beta \sum_{j=1}^{n} u_j + \gamma \sum_{j=1}^{n} h_j q_j \qquad \text{(FZDVM)}$$

$$\begin{aligned}
\text{s.t.} \quad & \mathbf{w}'\mathbf{x}_i - b \geq 1 - S p_i & i \in \mathcal{M} \qquad (5) \\
& \mathbf{w}'\mathbf{x}_i - b \leq -1 + S r_i & i \in \mathcal{M} \qquad (6) \\
& \mathbf{w}'\mathbf{x}_i - b \leq 1 - \varepsilon + S(1 - p_i) & i \in \mathcal{M} \qquad (7) \\
& \mathbf{w}'\mathbf{x}_i - b \geq -1 + \varepsilon + S(r_i - 1) & i \in \mathcal{M} \qquad (8) \\
& u_j \leq R q_j & j \in \mathcal{N} \qquad (9) \\
& -u_j \leq w_j \leq u_j & j \in \mathcal{N} \qquad (10)
\end{aligned}$$

$$\mathbf{u} \geq \mathbf{0}, \quad \mathbf{p}, \mathbf{r}, \mathbf{q} \text{ binaries}; \quad \mathbf{w} \text{ and } b \text{ free}.$$

The objective function of problem (FZDVM) is composed by the weighted sum of three terms, expressing a trade-off between accuracy and potential of generalization, regulated by the parameters α, β, γ. The first term represents the revised version of the empirical error(4) in the presence of class uncertainty. The second term is a variant of the smoothing regularizer $\|f\|_K^2$ that appears in (1) to restore well-posedness and increase the predictive capability of the classifier. Specifically, it corresponds to the 1-norm computed with respect to a linear kernel. Finally, the third term further supports the generalization capability of the model, by minimizing the number of attributes used in the classification rule. Constraints (5), (6), (7) and (8) are required to set the binary variables $\mathbf{p}$ and $\mathbf{r}$ at the appropriate value, in order to correctly evaluate the empirical error. Here S is an appropriate large constant, whereas $\varepsilon > 0$ is a small constant required since lower halfspaces in the definition of p_i and r_i are open. In practice, its value can be set equal to the zero precision used in the solution algorithm. Constraints (9) imply that the binary variable q_j takes the value 1 whenever $\mathbf{w}_j \neq 0$, that is whenever the j-th attribute is actively used in the optimal classification rule. Constraints (10) set the bounding relationships between variables w_j and u_j. A feasible suboptimal solution to model (FZDVM) can be derived by solving a sequence of linear programming problems (12).

3   Defining a Class Membership Function

In this section, we consider several membership functions, that can be grouped into three main categories: distance-based, score-based and frequency-based. Each proposed function will be used for generating the membership values for different datasets in connection to both fuzzy SVM and fuzzy discrete SVM, in order to compare the overall effectiveness when combined with a fuzzy classifier. Let $V = \{i : y_i = -1\}$ and $W = \{i : y_i = 1\}$ be the sets of indices of the examples whose class label is negative and positive, respectively, and denote by $v = \mathrm{card}(V)$ and $w = \mathrm{card}(W)$ the cardinalities of the two sets.

Distance-based membership functions

In order to reduce the effect of the outliers, some authors perform a fuzzification of the examples by setting the membership as a function of the Euclidean distance in $\Re^n$. Here the idea is to assign to each example a membership value that is inversely proportional to the distance from the centroid of its class label, so as to soften the influence of the farthest examples in the training process.

More precisely, define the centroids $\mathbf{h}$ and $\mathbf{k}$ for the negative and positive classes, respectively, as

$$\mathbf{h} = \frac{1}{v} \sum_{i \in V} \mathbf{x}_i, \quad \mathbf{k} = \frac{1}{w} \sum_{i \in W} \mathbf{x}_i.$$

A first membership function can be defined as

$$1 - f_i = 1 - \frac{\|\mathbf{x}_i - \mathbf{h}\|}{\max\limits_{t \in V} \|\mathbf{x}_t - \mathbf{h}\|} \text{ if } y_i = -1; \quad f_i = 1 - \frac{\|\mathbf{x}_i - \mathbf{k}\|}{\max\limits_{t \in W} \|\mathbf{x}_t - \mathbf{k}\|} \text{ if } y_i = 1. \quad (11)$$

Clearly, membership values range in the interval $[0, 1]$, approaching 1 when the example is labeled as 1 and is close to the the centroid of its class or is labeled as -1 and is far from the centroid of its class, and approaching 0 when the opposite conditions are met.

A second distance-based membership function, adapted from (5) and parameterized with respect to δ, can be defined as

$$1 - f_i = 0.5 + \frac{e^{\delta(\|\mathbf{x}_i - \mathbf{k}\| - \|\mathbf{x}_i - \mathbf{h}\|)/\|\mathbf{k} - \mathbf{h}\|} - e^{-\delta}}{2(e^{\delta} - e^{-\delta})}, \qquad y_i = -1 \qquad (12)$$

$$f_i = 0.5 + \frac{e^{\delta(\|\mathbf{x}_i - \mathbf{h}\| - \|\mathbf{x}_i - \mathbf{k}\|)/\|\mathbf{k} - \mathbf{h}\|} - e^{-\delta}}{2(e^{\delta} - e^{-\delta})}, \qquad y_i = 1, \qquad (13)$$

However, the adoption of membership functions based on the notion of Euclidean distance is debatable when some of the explanatory variables are categorical. This appears a severe limitation in the classification of real world datasets, naturally described in terms of variables of different types.

Score-based membership functions

In a completely different perspective, a membership function can be derived from a classification algorithm trained in a preprocessing phase, avoiding the pitfalls due to the improper treatment of categorical attributes. For instance, in (14) a score is assigned to each example by means of a generic classification algorithm, and then it is mapped into a membership value using either a linear, logistic or probit function.

Here, we propose to use a traditional (non fuzzy) discrete SVM as a base classifier in order to assign a score to each example. More precisely, let $\mathbf{w}'\mathbf{x}_i - b = 0$ be the optimal separating hyperplane derived by training the discrete SVM, and define the score as $s_i = y_i\,(\mathbf{w}'\mathbf{x}_i - b)$. Clearly, a high positive score indicates that the corresponding example falls within the hyperspace associated to the class label and is far from the separating hyperplane, whereas a negative score means that the example falls in the wrong hyperspace and has been misclassified.

In order to convert the score function into a membership function, we apply a *logit* function parameterized by τ, by setting

$$1 - f_i = \frac{e^{\tau s_i}}{1 + e^{\tau s_i}} \text{ if } y_i = -1; \quad f_i = \frac{e^{\tau s_i}}{1 + e^{\tau s_i}} \text{ if } y_i = 1. \tag{14}$$

Frequency-based membership functions
As a third alternative, proposed in (12), we consider an ensemble method which can be used to assess the class membership of the training examples in the presence of both numeric and categorical predictive variables. The predictions are generated on the training examples by a set of L classification models, each obtained by the solution of a discrete SVM problem. This leads to the definition of a new fuzzy membership function which returns, for the generic example, a class membership according to the frequency of the labels assigned by the L component classifiers. In particular, if $\mathbf{w}'_k\mathbf{x} - b_k = 0$ denotes the optimal separating function for the k-th component classifier, the membership value of the generic example $\mathbf{x}_i$ with respect to the positive class can be defined as follows:

$$f_i = \frac{1}{L} \sum_{k=1}^{L} \vartheta\,(\mathbf{w}'_k\mathbf{x} - b_k). \tag{15}$$

4   Computational Tests

Several computational tests have been performed in order to evaluate the effectiveness of the membership functions considered in this paper. The aim of these tests was manyfold. From one side, we were interested in investigating the dependence of fuzzy discrete SVM from the particular choice of the membership function. On the other side, we desired to understand whether one of the functions dominates the others on an empirical basis, both for fuzzy SVM and fuzzy discrete SVM. Finally, we wanted to assess the usefulness of the membership functions based on discrete SVM when combined with fuzzy SVM.

The computational tests concerned the classification of five datasets available from the UCI Machine Learning Repository (2): Pima indians diabetes (*Diabetes*), Haberman's survival data (*Haberman*), Cleveland heart disease (*Heart*), hepatitis domain (*Hepatitis*) and Bupa liver disorders (*Liver*). Among these datasets, *Diabetes*, *Haberman* and *Liver* contain only numerical attributes, whereas *Hepatitis* and *Heart* include also categorical predictive variables, that were converted to numerical values before computing the distance-based membership values.

Eight different classification methods have been compared on the five datasets in terms of overall accuracy and *sensitivity*, defined as the percentage of correctly classified positive examples. These methods were derived by combining fuzzy SVM and fuzzy discrete SVM with the four membership functions considered: the first based on the distance between the examples and the centroid of their own class (DB_1), as in (11); the second combining the distances from the centroids of both classes (DB_2), as in (12) and (13); the third based on the scores derived by means of discrete SVM (SB), as in (14); the fourth using the frequency assignment provided by the discrete SVM ensemble method (FB), as in (15).

Table 1. Accuracy (%) and sensitivity [%] results with five and ten-fold cross-validation

	Method							
	Fuzzy discrete SVM				Fuzzy SVM			
Dataset	DB_1	DB_2	SB	FB	DB_1	DB_2	SB	FB
Diabetes	**81.5**	81.0	80.5	81.2	77.6	76.8	78.2	79.8
	[74.1]	[**77.2**]	[74.1]	[73.3]	[62.4]	[72.3]	[68.0]	[68.0]
Haberman	77.5	**77.8**	77.2	77.5	74.8	74.2	75.8	75.8
	[46.0]	[**60.3**]	[58.4]	[52.2]	[32.2]	[47.1]	[38.9]	[33.5]
Heart	**84.1**	83.8	82.6	83.5	83.1	82.9	81.6	83.5
	[79.5]	[79.3]	[**80.0**]	[79.8]	[77.0]	[77.6]	[78.5]	[78.5]
Hepatitis	84.5	83.0	83.2	**84.5**	76.0	73.0	82.7	**84.5**
	[65.0]	[70.0]	[72.1]	[**78.0**]	[69.0]	[54.0]	[69.4]	[70.0]
Liver	68.8	74.9	75.5	**76.1**	69.1	72.9	71.8	71.8
	[70.0]	[59.7]	[66.7]	[62.3]	[**71.3**]	[5.7]	[55.0]	[57.3]

Table 1 shows the accuracy and the sensitivity obtained for each method using ten-fold cross-validation for *Diabetes*, *Heart* and *Liver*. Due to their limited size, five-fold cross-validation was applied on *Haberman* and *Hepatitis*. For all methods a preliminary search was applied in order to select the most promising combination of the parameters. The results for fuzzy SVM and fuzzy discrete SVM were derived using the heuristic procedures proposed in (8; 12). Moreover, the membership function (FB) was based on the class values predictions performed by an ensemble classifier composed by ten discrete SVM models.

From the results presented in table 1 some interesting issues can be pointed out. With respect to fuzzy SVM, fuzzy discrete SVM appeared to be more accurate. This remarks holds true for all the functions used to compute the membership values, except for the first distance-based function in the classification of the *Liver* dataset. Hence, we may conclude that the effectiveness of fuzzy discrete SVM has a mild dependence on the membership function adopted. In terms of sensitivity analysis, on the *Liver* dataset fuzzy SVM performed better using DB_1. As one might expect, none of the membership functions appeared to be dominant, even if the functions relying on the Euclidean distance, DB_1 and DB_2, seemed to achieve the best trade-off between accuracy and sensitivity for both fuzzy SVM and fuzzy discrete SVM. Notice that sometimes the use of DB_1 leads to a greater accuracy, whereas the highest sensitivity is obtained using DB_2, and viceversa. However, if we confine the attention to the overall accuracy, the tests showed that the membership functions based on discrete SVM, SB and FB, outperformed the distance-based ones, leading to a higher quality classification for most datasets. Thus, they represent a powerful alternative to the distance-based functions also for fuzzy SVM.

References

[1] Chang, C.C., Lin, C.J.: LIBSVM: a library for support vector machines (2001)
[2] Hettich, S., Blake, C., Merz, C.: UCI repository of machine learning databases, URL (1998), http://www.ics.uci.edu/mlearn/MLRepository.html
[3] Huang, H.-P., Liu, Y.-H.: Fuzzy support vector machines for pattern recognition and data mining. International Journal of Fuzzy Systems 3, 826–835 (2002)
[4] Jiang, X., Yi, Z., Lv, J.C.: Fuzzy svm with a new fuzzy membership function. Neural Comput. Appl. 15, 268–276 (2006)
[5] Keller, J., Hunt, D.: Incorporating fuzzy membership functions into the perceptron algorithm. IEEE Trans. Pattern Anal. Mach. Intell. 7, 693–699 (1985)
[6] Lin, C.-F., Wang, S.-D.: Fuzzy support vector machines. IEEE Transactions on Neural Networks 13, 464–471 (2002)
[7] Liu, H.-B., Niu, S.-W.X.X.-X.: Fuzzy support vector machines based on spherical regions. Lectures Notes on Computer Science, pp. 949–954 (2006)
[8] Orsenigo, C., Vercellis, C.: Multivariate classification trees based on minimum features discrete support vector machines. IMA Journal of Management Mathematics 14, 221–234 (2003)
[9] Orsenigo, C., Vercellis, C.: Discrete support vector decision trees via tabusearch. Journal of Computational Statistics and Data Analysis 47, 311–322 (2004)
[10] Orsenigo, C., Vercellis, C.: Multicategory classification via discrete support vector machines. Computational Management Science (to appear, 2007a)
[11] Orsenigo, C., Vercellis, C.: Accurately learning from few examples with a polyhedral classifier. Computational Optimization and Applications (to appear, 2007b)
[12] Orsenigo, C., Vercellis, C.: Regularization through fuzzy discrete SVM with applications to customer ranking (submitted, 2007c)
[13] Vapnik, V.: The nature of statistical learning theory. Springer, New York (1995)
[14] Wang, Y., Wang, S., Lai, K.K.: A new fuzzy support vector machine to evaluate credit risk. IEEE Transactions on Fuzzy Systems 13, 820–831 (2005)
[15] Xiong, S., Liu, H., Niu, X.: Fuzzy support vector machines based on lambda-cut. Lectures Notes on Computer Science, pp. 592–600 (2005)

Improvement of Jarvis-Patrick Clustering Based on Fuzzy Similarity

Agnes Vathy-Fogarassy[1], Attila Kiss[2], and Janos Abonyi[3]

[1] University of Pannonia, Department of Mathematics and Computing
[2] Eötvös Lóránd University, Department of Information Systems
[3] University of Pannonia, Department of Process Engineering
P.O. Box 158,Veszprem, H-8201 Hungary
abonyij@fmt.uni-pannon.hu
Phone: +36/88/624209
www.fmt.uni-pannon.hu/softcomp

Abstract. Different clustering algorithms are based on different similarity or distance measures (e.g. Euclidian distance, Minkowsky distance, Jackard coefficient, etc.). Jarvis-Patrick clustering method utilizes the number of the common neighbors of the k-nearest neighbors of objects to disclose the clusters. The main drawback of this algorithm is that its parameters determine a too crisp cutting criterion, hence it is difficult to determine a good parameter set. In this paper we give an extension of the similarity measure of the Jarvis-Patrick algorithm. This extension is carried out in the following two ways: (i) fuzzyfication of one of the parameters, and (ii) spreading of the scope of the other parameter. The suggested fuzzy similarity measure can be applied in various forms, in different clustering and visualization techniques (e.g. hierarchical clustering, MDS, VAT). In this paper we give some application examples to illustrate the efficiency of the use of the proposed fuzzy similarity measure in clustering. These examples show that the proposed fuzzy similarity measure based clustering techniques are able to detect clusters with different sizes, shapes and densities. It is also shown that the outliers are also detectable by the proposed measure.

Keywords: fuzzy similarity measure, neighborhood relation, Jarvis-Patrick clustering, VAT, MDS.

1 Introduction and Related Works

Cluster analysis is a powerful method of exploratory data analysis. The main goal of clustering is to divide objects into well separated groups so that the objects lying in the same group are more similar to one other than to the objects in other groups. A large number of clustering techniques have been developed based on different theories. Several approaches utilize the concept of cluster center or centroid (k-means, k-medoid algorithms), other methods build clusters based on the density of the objects (e.g. DBSCAN [6], OPTICS [2], LSDBC [4]) and a lot of methods represent the objects as the vertices of graphs (e.g. Chameleon[11], ROCK [7], Jarvis-Patrick algorithm [10]).

F. Masulli, S. Mitra, and G. Pasi (Eds.): WILF 2007, LNAI 4578, pp. 195–202, 2007.

1.1   Neighborhood Relations and the Jarvis-Patrick Clustering

Neighborhood graphs connect nearby points with a graph edge. There are many clustering algorithms that utilize the neighborhood relationships of the objects. For example, the use of minimal spanning trees (MST) [13] for clustering was initially proposed by Zahn [12]. The approach presented in [1] utilizes several neighborhood graphs to find the groups of objects. Jarvis and Patrick [10] extended the nearest neighbor graph with the concept of the shared nearest neighbors. In [5] Doman et al. iteratively utilize the Jarvis-Patrick algorithm for creating crisp clusters and then they fuzzify the previously calculated clusters. In [8] a node structural metric has been chosen making use of the number of shared edges.

In the Jarvis-Patrick (JP) clustering two objects are placed in the same cluster whenever they fulfill two conditions: (i) they must be in the set of each other's k-nearest neighbors; (ii) they must have at least l nearest neighbors in common. The parameters (k and l) are determined by the users. If these parameters are chosen inadequately, the clustering algorithm fails. Although, the Jarvis-Patrick method is a non-iterative clustering algorithm, it is suggested to be run repeatedly with different k and l values to get a reasonable number and structure of clusters. The main drawbacks of this method are: (i) decision criterion is very rigid (the value of l) and (ii) it is constrained only by the local k-nearest neighbors. To avoid these disadvantages we suggest a new similarity measure based on the shared neighbors. The suggested *fuzzy similarity measure* takes not only the k nearest neighbors into account, and it gives a nice tool to tune this l parameter based on visualization and hierarchical clustering methods that utilize the proposed fuzzy similarity.

1.2   Visualization

It is a difficult challenge to determine the number of clusters. While cluster validity measures give numerical information about the number of the clusters, a low dimensional graphical representation of the clusters could be much more informative. In the second case the user can cluster by eye and qualitatively validate conclusions drawn from clustering algorithms.

Objects to be clustered are most often characterized by many parameters. The multidimensional scaling methods (MDS) map the high-dimensional data objects into a low-dimensional vector space by preserving the similarity information (e.g. pairwise distance) of the objects. Applying an MDS on the objects makes it possible to pick out the clusters visually.

Visual Assessment of Cluster Tendency (VAT) [3] is an effective visualization method to reveal the number and the structure of clusters. It visualizes the pairwise dissimilarity information of N objects as a square image with N^2 pixels. VAT uses a digital intensity image of the reorganized inter-data distance matrix, and the number of the dark diagonal blocks on the image indicates the number of clusters in the data. The VAT algorithm includes the following main steps: (i) reordering the dissimilarity data, (ii) displaying the dissimilarity image based on the previously reordered matrix, where the gray level of a pixel is in connection with the dissimilarity of the actual pair of points. Although VAT becomes intractable for large data sets, the bigVAT [9] as a modification of VAT allows the visualization for larger data sets, too.

The organization of this paper is as follows. In Section 2.1 and 2.2 the fuzzy similarity measure is described. Section 2.3 outlines some application possibilities of the fuzzy similarity measure. Section 3 contains application examples based on synthetic and real life data sets to illustrate the usefulness of the proposed similarity measure. Section 4 concludes the paper.

2   Fuzzy Similarity Measure Based on Cascade Shared Neighbors

Let $\mathbf{X} = \{\mathbf{x}_1, \mathbf{x}_2, \ldots, \mathbf{x}_N\}$ be the set of the data. Denote $\mathbf{x}_i$ the i-th object, which consists of n measured variables, grouped into an n-dimensional column vector $\mathbf{x}_i = [x_{1,i}, x_{2,i}, ..., x_{n,i}]^T$, $\mathbf{x}_i \in \mathbb{R}^n$. Denote $m_{i,j}$ the number of the common k-nearest neighbors of $\mathbf{x}_i$ and $\mathbf{x}_j$. Furthermore, denote the set A_i the k-nearest neighbors of $\mathbf{x}_i$. The Jarvis-Patrick clustering groups $\mathbf{x}_i$ and $\mathbf{x}_j$ in the same cluster, if Equation (1) holds.

$$\mathbf{x}_i \in A_j \quad and \quad \mathbf{x}_j \in A_i \quad and \quad m_{i,j} > l \tag{1}$$

Because $m_{i,j}$ can be expressed as $|A_i \cap A_j|$, where $|\bullet|$ denotes the cardinality, the $m_{i,j} > l$ formula is equivalent with the expression $|A_i \cap A_j| > l$.

2.1   Fuzzy Similarity Measure

To refine this decision criterion we suggest a new similarity measure between the objects. The proposed *fuzzy similarity measure* is calculated in the following way:

$$s_{i,j} = \frac{|A_i \cap A_j|}{|A_i \cup A_j|} = \frac{m_{i,j}}{2k - m_{i,j}} \tag{2}$$

Equation (2) means that the fuzzy similarity measure characterizes the similarity of a pair of objects by the fraction of the number of the common neighbors and the number of the total neighbors of that pair. The fuzzy similarity measure is calculated between all pairs of objects, and it takes a value from $[0, 1]$. The $s_{i,j} = 1$ value indicates the strongest similarity between the objects, and the $s_{i,j} = 0$ denotes that objects $\mathbf{x}_i$ and $\mathbf{x}_j$ are very different from each other. By this similarity measure we have fuzzyfied the crisp parameter l.

2.2   Transitive Fuzzy Similarity Measure

To extend the scope of the k-nearest neighbors the calculation of the similarity takes not only the directly connected k-nearest neighbors of $\mathbf{x}_i$, $\mathbf{x}_j$ into account, but it calculates with the cascade chain of the neighbors, too. Besides parameter k, which determines the number of the neighbors to examine the computation of the fuzzy similarity measure includes another parameter t indicating the degree of the spread. The $t = 1$ value means that only the k-nearest neighbors are considered. The $t = 2$ indicates that the second-order neighbors (k-nearest neighbors of the k-nearest neighbors of the object) are also taken into account, and so on. The effect of the higher degree shared neighbors become less and less.

The calculation of the *transitive fuzzy similarity measure* is an iterative process. In each iteration step there is a t-order similarity measure $(s_{i,j}^{(t)})$ calculated of two sets of objects. In the case of $t = 1$ the $s_{i,j}^{(1)}$ is calculated as the fraction of the number of shared neighbors of the k-nearest neighbors of objects $\mathbf{x}_i$ and $\mathbf{x}_j$ and the total number of the k-nearest neighbors of objects $\mathbf{x}_i$ and $\mathbf{x}_j$. In this case Equation (2) is obtained. Generally, $s_{i,j}^{(t)}$ is calculated in the following way:

$$s_{i,j}^{(t)} = \frac{|A_i^{(t)} \cap A_j^{(t)}|}{|A_i^{(t)} \cup A_j^{(t)}|},\tag{3}$$

where set $A_i^{(t)}$ denotes the t-order k-nearest neighbors of object $\mathbf{x}_i$, and $A_j^{(t)}$ respectively for $\mathbf{x}_j$.

In each iteration step the pairwise calculated fuzzy similarity measures are updated based on the following formula:

$$s_{i,j}^{'(t+1)} = (1 - \alpha)s_{i,j}^{'(t)} + \alpha s_{i,j}^{(t+1)},\tag{4}$$

where α is the first-order filter parameter. The iteration process is proceeded until t achieves the predefined value.

As a result of the whole process a *fuzzy similarity matrix* ($\mathbf{S}$) will be given, which summarizes the pairwise fuzzy similarity of the objects. The *fuzzy distance matrix* ($\mathbf{D}$) of the objects is obtained by the formula: $\mathbf{D} = 1 - \mathbf{S}$. As the fuzzy similarity measure is special case of the transitive fuzzy similarity measure we would use these terms as equivalent.

2.3   Application of the (Transitive) Fuzzy Similarity Measure

There are several ways to apply the previously introduced fuzzy similarity/distance matrix. For example, the hierarchical clustering methods work on similarity or distance matrices. Generally, these matrices are obtained from the Euclidian distances of pairs of objects. Instead of the other similarity/distance matrices, the hierarchical methods can also utilize the fuzzy similarity/distance matrix. The dendrogram not only shows the whole iteration process, but it can also be a useful tool to determine the number of the data groups and the threshold of the separation of the clusters. To separate the clusters we suggest to draw the fuzzy similarity based dendrogram of the data, where the long nodes denote the proper thresholds to separate the clusters.

The visualization of the objects may significantly assist in revealing the clusters. Many visualization techniques are based on the pairwise distance of the data. Because multidimensional scaling methods work on dissimilarity matrices, this method can also be based on the fuzzy distance matrix. The VAT is an effective tool to determine the number of the clusters. Because VAT works with the dissimilarities of the data, it can be also based on the fuzzy distance matrix.

The computation of the proposed fuzzy similarity measure includes three parameters. The choice of the value of these parameters has affect on the separation of clusters. Lower values of parameter k (e.g $k = 3$) separate the clusters better. By increasing value k clusters that overlap in some objects become more similar. The higher the value of parameter t is, the higher the similarity measure of similar objects become. The increase of the value t results in more compact clusters. The lower the value of α, the less the affect of neighbors far away.

3   Application Examples

In this section some examples are presented to show the application of the proposed fuzzy similarity measure. The first example is based on a synthetic data set, and the second example deals with the visualization and clustering of the well-known wine data set.

The synthetic data set contains 100 2-dimensional data objects. 99 objects are partitioned in 3 clusters with different sizes (22, 26 and 51 objects), shapes and densities, and it also contains an outlier. Figure 1(a) shows a relatively good result of the Jarvis-Patrick clustering applied on the normalized data set ($k=8, l=4$). The objects belonging to different clusters are marked with different markers. It can be seen that the algorithm was not able to identify the outlier object, and therefore the cluster denoted with '+' markers is split into 2 clusters. To show the complexity of this data set in Fig. 1(b) the result of the well-known k-means clustering ($k = 4$) is also presented. The proposed fuzzy similarity was calculated with different k, t and α parameters. Different runs with parameters $k = 3 \ldots 25$, $t = 2 \ldots 5$ and $\alpha = 0.1 \ldots 0.4$ have been resulted in good clustering outcomes. In these cases the clusters were easily separable and the clustering rate (the number of well clustered objects/total number of objects) of $99 - 100\%$ was obtained. If a large value is chosen for parameter k, it is necessary to keep parameter t on a

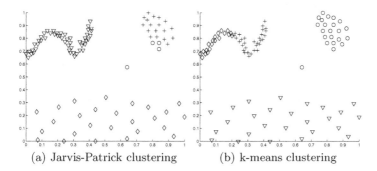

(a) Jarvis-Patrick clustering   (b) k-means clustering

Fig. 1. Result of k-means and Jarvis-Patrick clustering on the normalized synthetic data set

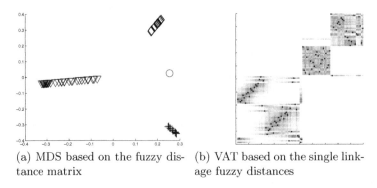

(a) MDS based on the fuzzy distance matrix

(b) VAT based on the single linkage fuzzy distances

Fig. 2. Different graphical representations of the fuzzy distances (synthetic data set)

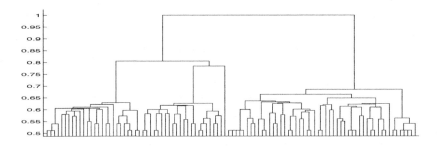

Fig. 3. Single linkage dendrogram based on the fuzzy distances (synthetic data set)

small value to avoid merging the outlier object with one of the clusters. The result of the MDS presentation based on the fuzzy distance matrix is shown in Fig. 2(a). The parameter settings here were $k = 7$, $t = 3$ and $\alpha = 0.2$. It can be seen that the calculated pairwise fuzzy similarity measures separate the 3 clusters and the outlier well. Figure 2(b) shows the VAT representation of the data set based on the single linkage fuzzy distances. The three clusters and the outlier are also easily separable in this figure. To find the proper similarity threshold to separate the clusters and the outlier we have drawn the single linkage dendrogram based on the fuzzy distance values of the objects (Fig. 3). The dendrogram shows that the value $d_{i,j} = 0.75$ ($d_{i,j} = 1 - s_{i,j}$) is a suitable choice to separate the clusters and the outlier from each other. Applying the single linkage agglomerative hierarchical algorithm based on the fuzzy similarities, and halting this algorithm at the threshold $d_{i,j} = 0.75$ results in a 100% clustering rate. This toy example illustrates that the proposed fuzzy similarity measure is able to separate the clusters with different sizes, shapes and densities, furthermore it is able to identify outliers.

The wine database (http://www.ics.uci.edu) consists of the chemical analysis of 178 wines from three different cultivars in the same Italian region. Each wine is characterized by 13 attributes, and there are 3 classes distinguished. Figure 4 shows the MDS projections based on the Euclidian and the fuzzy distances (k=6,

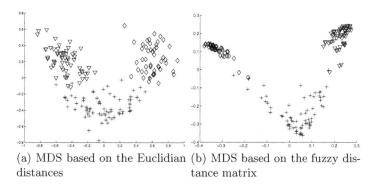

(a) MDS based on the Euclidian distances (b) MDS based on the fuzzy distance matrix

Fig. 4. Different MDS representations of the wine data set

$t=3$, $\alpha=0.2$). The figures illustrate that the fuzzy distance based MDS separates the 3 clusters better. To separate the clusters we have drawn dendrograms based on the single, average and the complete linkage similarities. Using these parameters the best result (clustering rate 96.62%) is given by the average linkage based dendrogram, on which the clusters are uniquely separable.

4 Conclusion

In this paper we introduced a new fuzzy similarity measure that extends the similarity measure of Jarvis-Patrick algorithm in two ways: (i) it takes into account the far neighbors partway and (ii) it fuzzifies the crisp decision criterion of the JP algorithm. We demonstrated through application examples that clustering methods based on the proposed fuzzy similarity measure can discover outliers and clusters with arbitrary shapes, sizes and densities.

Acknowledgements

The authors acknowledge the financial support of the Hungarian Research Found (OTKA 49534), the Bolyai Janos fellowship of the Hungarian Academy of Science and the Öveges fellowship.

References

1. Anders, K.H.: A Hierarchical Graph-Clustering Approach to find Groups of Objects. In: Proceedings 5th ICA Workshop on Progress in Automated Map Generalization, IGN, Paris, France, 28–30 April, 2003.
2. Ankerst, M., Breunig, M.M., Kriegel, H.-P., Sander, J.: Optics: ordering points to identify the clustering structure. In: SIGMOD 99: Proceedings of the 1999 ACM SIGMOD International Conference on Management of Data, ACM Press, New York, pp. 49–60 (1999)

3. Bezdek, J.C., Hathaway, R.J.: VAT: A Tool for Visual Assessment of (Cluster) Tendency. In: Proc. IJCNN 2002, pp. 2225–2230. IEEE Press, Piscataway, N.J (2002)

4. Bicici, E., Yuret, D.: Locally Scaled Density Based Clustering. In: Roddick, J.F., Hornsby, K. (eds.) TSDM 2000. LNCS (LNAI), vol. 2007, Springer, Heidelberg (2001)

5. Doman, T.N., Cibulskis, J.M., Cibulskis, M.J., McCray, P.D., Spangler, D.P.: Algorithm5: A Technique for Fuzzy Similarity Clustering of Chemical Inventories. Journal of Chemical Information and Computer Sciences 36(6), 1195–1204 (1996)

6. Ester, M., Kriegel, H.-P., Sander, J., Xu, X.: A density-based algorithm for discovering clusters in large spatial databases with noise. In: KDD, pp. 226–231 (1996)

7. Guha, S., Rastogi, R., Shim, K.: ROCK: a robust clustering algorithm for categorical attributes. In: Proc. of the 15th Intl Conf. On Data Eng. pp.512–521 (1999)

8. Huang, X., Lai, W.: Clustering graphs for visualization via node similarities. Journal of Visual Languages and Computing 17, 225–253 (2006)

9. Huband, J.M., Bezdek, J.C., Hathaway, R.J.: bigVAT: Visual assessment of cluster tendency for large data sets. Pattern Recognition 38(11), 1875–1886 (2005)

10. Jarvis, R.A., Patrick, E.A.: Clustering Using a Similarity Measure Based on Shared Near Neighbors. IEEE Transactions on Computers C22, 1025–1034 (1973)

11. Karypis, G., Han, E.-H., Kumar, V.: Chameleon: Hierarchical Clustering Using Dynamic Modeling. IEEE Computer 32(8), 68–75 (1999)

12. Zahn, C.T.: Graph-theoretical methods for detecting and describing gestalt clusters. IEEE Transaction on Computers C20, 68–86 (1971)

13. Yao, A.: On constructing minimum spanning trees in k-dimensional spaces and related problems. SIAM Journal on Computing, pp. 721–736 (1982)

Fuzzy Rules Generation Method for Pattern Recognition Problems

Dmitry Kropotov and Dmitry Vetrov

Dorodnicyn Computing Centre of the Russian Academy of Sciences, 119991, Russia, Moscow, Vavilov str. 40
dkropotov@yandex.ru, vetrovd@yandex.ru
http://vetrovd.narod.ru

Abstract. In the paper we consider the problem of automatic fuzzy rules mining. A new method for generation of fuzzy rules according to the set of precedents is suggested. The proposed algorithm can find all significant rules with respect to wide range of reasonable criterion functions. We present the statistical criterion for knowledge quality estimation that provides high generalization ability. The theoretical results are complemented with the experimental evaluation.

Keywords: Data-mining, Artificial intelligence, Fuzzy sets, Knowledge generation, Rules optimization.

1 Introduction

To the present time fuzzy logic has been applied in many areas of human knowledge [15]. Fuzzy expert systems mainly operate in linguistic terms [11] which often provide better understanding and managing the investigated process [18]. Such systems traditionally use a number of fuzzy sets and a knowledge base which consists of fuzzy inference rules. System's performance depends on the lucky choice of fuzzy sets and rules appropriate for the current research field. It often happens that experts can't fully solve the problem with forming of fuzzy sets and rules and hence we need an automatical routine for doing this. For this purpose methods using neural networks [10,9], genetic algorithms [7,6], clustering [5] and others have been proposed. Unfortunately, these approaches have some drawbacks:

- Most of those methods generate large sets of rules with relatively low significance that may overfit the data;
- The rules are generally of large dimension that leads to poor knowledge interpretation and prevents an expert from deep understanding the process being investigated;
- Neuro-fuzzy techniques are characterized by the dependence from initial approximation and large computation time needed for training;
- For clustering approach there is a need to determine number of clusters or number of rules beforehand;

F. Masulli, S. Mitra, and G. Pasi (Eds.): WILF 2007, LNAI 4578, pp. 203–210, 2007.

- In genetic approach there is a great number of parameters to be adjusted by user and again large computation time (or even infinite time in case of non-convergence) is demanded.

Also the following algorithms for fuzzy rules generation as decision lists [13] and boosting [4,3] can be mentioned. In these algorithms rules are used consequently for decision making. In practice consequent scheme makes the interpretation of acquired knowledge for expert harder. The algorithms based on decision trees [1,12,2] show good performance and are frequently used in practice. However, presentation of tree structure as a set of rules leads to great number of long rules with very similar sumptions [12].

The goal of this paper is to establish an algorithm for rules generation which avoids the mentioned drawbacks and constructs a little set of short informative rules. In the next section different ways of representing fuzzy rules are considered. Section 3 investigates criterion functions for determination of significant rules and presents our algorithm. In section 4 experimental results and conclusion are given.

2   Knowledge Presentation

Hereinafter suppose we are given objects with d real-valued features (independent variables) and one unobserved dependent variable, which either takes values in $\{1, \ldots, l\}$ for classification problem with l classes or takes real values for regression problem. Suppose we are given training set $\{\boldsymbol{x}_i, y_i\}_{i=1}^q$, where $\boldsymbol{x}_i \in \mathbb{R}^d$ and $y_i \in \{1, \ldots, l\}$ or $y_i \in \mathbb{R}$, and we need to construct decision function and a knowledge base about the process being studied.

Usually for knowledge presentation a set of "IF , THEN" rules is used [15]. Sumption of such rule is some logical expression with respect to fuzzy sets of features. Let $\mu_A(x)$ be a membership function of fuzzy set A. Consider some real-valued feature. From expert's point of view this feature can be described as ordered set of fuzzy sets, where each of them corresponds to some linguistic value. For example, feature "patient's body temperature" can be represented by three fuzzy sets with labels "Low", "Medium" and "High". In general case suppose that for expert there exists some partition of feature axis which determines approximate borders between different states. Each state corresponds to some fuzzy set which is given by parametric membership function. Unimodal functions such as trapeziums, bell-shaped functions and Gaussians are of popular choice.

Trapezium-shaped characteristic functions are simple and have intuitive interpretation. However, such functions are not smooth, that makes difficult optimization of approximate borders by using precedent information. To solve this problem a set of Gaussians or bell-shaped functions can be used. A bell-shaped function is given by the following expression:

$$\mu(x; l, r, \alpha, \beta) = \frac{1}{1 + \left(\frac{1}{\alpha} - 1\right)\left(\frac{x - (l+r)/2}{(r-l)/2}\right)^{2\beta}}, \alpha \in (0,1), \beta \in \mathbb{N}, l, r, x \in \mathbb{R}, l < r.$$

$$(1)$$

Here parameters l and r determine approximate borders of fuzzy set, coefficient β controls fuzziness degree and α gives function value at borders l and r. When β tends to infinity bell-shaped membership function determines characteristic function of crisp set $\{x | l \leq x \leq r\}$.

In the following $\mu(x)$ can be considered as any unimodal characteristic function such as trapezium- or bell-shaped function.

3   Rule Generation

3.1   Significance Criterion Functions

Consider fuzzy rule R of the following form:

$$\text{IF } x_{i_1} \in M_{i_1}^{j_1} \& \dots \& x_{i_r} \in M_{i_r}^{j_r}, \text{THEN } y \in N^k \tag{2}$$

Here $\text{Sump}(R) = \{M_{i_1}^{j_1}, \dots, M_{i_r}^{j_r}\}$ is sumption of the rule R, number $r = \text{Ord}(R)$ is called order of the rule, and $\text{res}(R) = N^k$ is result set of the rule R. Denote $\mathcal{R}^*$ the set of all possible rules of type (2). The problem of rule generation is in separation of some subset of rules $\tilde{\mathcal{R}}$ from $\mathcal{R}^*$ with respect to some criterion function. Many known criterion functions can be formulated using notions of representativeness and effectiveness.

Definition 1. *Representativeness of rule R is the following value:*

$$rep(R) = \frac{1}{q} \sum_{i=1}^{q} \min \left(\mu_{M_{i_1}^{j_1}}(x_{i_1}^k), \dots, \mu_{M_{i_r}^{j_r}}(x_{i_r}^k) \right)$$

Definition 2. *Effectiveness of rule R is the following value:*

$$eff(R) = \frac{\sum\limits_{i=1}^{q} \min \left(\mu_{M_{i_1}^{j_1}}(x_{i_1}^k), \dots, \mu_{M_{i_r}^{j_r}}(x_{i_r}^k), \mu_{N^k}(y^k) \right)}{rep(R)q}$$

In other words representativeness is implicitly the rate of precedents, which satisfy sumption of the given rule while effectiveness is the rate of precedents from sumption, which satisfy the rule itself. We intend to generate rules, which have both high representativeness and effectiveness. More formally, a rule $R \in \tilde{\mathcal{R}}$, if $C(rep(R), eff(R)) = 1$, where $C : [0,1]^2 \to \{0,1\}$ is a predicate of form:

$$C(v, w) = \begin{cases} 1, & \text{if } F(v, w) \geq F_0 \\ 0, & \text{otherwise,} \end{cases}$$

here $F : [0,1]^2 \to \mathbb{R}$ is criterion function and F_0 is some threshold. The simplest heuristic criterion function uses constant thresholds for representativeness and effectiveness:

$$C^h(v, w) = \begin{cases} 1, & \text{if } v \geq c_r, w \geq c_e \\ 0, & \text{otherwise} \end{cases} \tag{3}$$

In general it is clear that if a rule has low representativeness, it must have high effectiveness in order to be significant and vice versa. Criterion function which takes this assumption into account can be formulated using statistical significance levels. The rule R is insignificant if the information that object satisfies sumption of the rule provides no knowledge on its affiliation to the result set of the rule. Check the following statistical hypothesis:

$$\mathbb{P}\{y \in N^k | x \in \mathrm{Sump}(R)\} = \mathbb{P}\{y \in N^k\}$$

Without loss of generality suppose uniform prior probabilities: $\mathbb{P}\{y \in N^1\} = \cdots = \mathbb{P}\{y \in N^l\} = 1/l$. Examine the value $q\mathrm{rep}(R)\mathrm{eff}(R)$. If the hypothesis is right, we have $n = \mathrm{rep}(R)q$ Bernoulli trials with the probability of success equal to $s = 1/l$. If ns is large enough, then according to Moivre-Laplace theorem this distribution can be approximated with a normal distribution with mean ns and variance $ns(1 - s)$:

$$\mathrm{eff}(R) \sim \mathcal{N}\left(s, \frac{s(1 - s)}{n}\right)$$

Thus statistical criterion function becomes $F^s(\mathrm{rep}, \mathrm{eff}) = (l\mathrm{eff} - 1) \Big/ \left(\sqrt{\frac{l-1}{q\mathrm{rep}}}\right)$. The necessary significance threshold F_0 for some level of significance α is a fractile of standard normal distribution z_α. Statistical criterion as well as other known criterions for determination of significant rules are presented on figure 1.

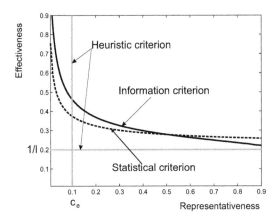

Fig. 1. Different criterion functions can be expressed in terms of representativeness and effectiveness. Rules lying above the presented curves are supposed to be significant due to corresponding criterion.

Statistical criterion has a strong theoretical ground in case of crisp sets, i.e. when characteristic functions of all sets equal to either 1 or 0. In fuzzy case this criterion is supposed to be true but its justification requires larger efforts.

However, in practice it shows good results and thus can be used effectively for constructing fuzzy rules as well.

In order to obtain a valid criterion for fuzzy case suppose a distribution of characteristic function values for some rule R

$$G(t) = \mathbb{P}\{\mu_R(\boldsymbol{x}) < t\}.$$

Then we may construct empirical cumulative distribution functions $G'(t)$ and $G''(t)$ using training objects with $y_i \in \text{res}(R)$ and $y_i \notin \text{res}(R)$ respectively. Kolmogorov-Smirnov non-parametric statistical test allows us to check if there is sufficient reason to suppose that $G'(t)$ and $G''(t)$ correspond to different distributions with predefined confidence level.

Many other possible predicates for identification of significant rules based on effectiveness and representativeness notions can be found in literature . Entropy-based criterion and exact Fisher test [17] can serve as examples.

Definition 3. *Criterion function F satisfies monotonicity condition if $\forall(v_0, w_0)$: $F(v_0, w_0) \geq F_0$ the following is true:*

- $\forall v > v_0 \quad F(v, w_0) \geq F(v_0, w_0),$
- $\forall w > w_0 \quad F(v_0, w) \geq F(v_0, w_0).$

Monotonicity condition is some natural restriction for criterion function selection. Suppose some significant rule with representativeness v and effectiveness w has quality $F(v, w)$. A rule with the same representativeness and higher effectiveness must have at least the same quality. In the same manner a rule which provides the same effectiveness but at higher representativeness level must have at least the same quality as $F(v, w)$. However, the following theorem is true:

Theorem 1. *Heuristical, statistical, Kolmogorov-Smirnov, entropy-based, and exact Fisher criterion functions satisfy monotonicity condition.*

So all considered criterion functions satisfy natural monotonicity restriction.

3.2   Effective Restrictions Method for Rule Generation

Definition 4. *Value $\alpha \geq 0$ is called a characteristic of predicate $C : [0, 1]^2 \rightarrow [0, 1]$, if the following is true:*

- $\forall(v, w) \in [0, 1]^2 : C(v, w) = 1 \Rightarrow vw \geq \alpha$
- $\forall \varepsilon > 0 \; \exists(v, w) \in [0, 1]^2 : C(v, w) = 1, vw < \alpha + \varepsilon$

Definition 5. *Predicate $C^\alpha : [0, 1]^2 \rightarrow [0, 1]$ with characteristic α is called a maximal one, if for any other predicate $C' : [0, 1]^2 \rightarrow [0, 1]$ with characteristics $\alpha \; \forall(v, w) \in [0, 1]^2 : C'(v, w) = 1 \Rightarrow C^\alpha(v, w) = 1.$*

Definition 6. *Rule R_b is a restriction of rule R_a ($R_b \subset R_a$) if two conditions are satisfied:*

- $res(R_a) = res(R_b)$
- $Sump(R_a) \subset Sump(R_b)$

During restriction of a rule representativeness becomes lower while the effectiveness may increase. In latter case we will call restriction an effective one.

Suppose we are given fuzzy partitions of all features $\mathcal{I}_1, \ldots, \mathcal{I}_d$, rules' result set N^k and some predicate C with characteristics $\alpha \geq \alpha_0 > 0$. Denote

$$c_r^* = \inf\{v \in [0,1] | \exists w \in [0,1] : C(v,w) = 1\}$$

An algorithm given below (effective restrictions method) finds all significant rules of minimal possible order according to training set with respect to any criterion function with positive characteristics. The algorithm is based on linear search over the rules order.

Step 1. Construct all possible rules of the first order

$$\mathcal{R}^{(1)} = \{R \in \mathcal{R}^* | res(R) = N^k, Sump(R) = M_i^{j_i}, j_i = \overline{1, n_i}, i = \overline{1, d}\}$$

Step 2. Reject all rules with low representativeness, i.e. $\mathcal{R}^{(2)} = \{R \in \mathcal{R}^{(1)} | rep(R) \geq c_r^*\}$.

Step 3. Reject all rules that will not become significant even after the most effective restriction:

$$\mathcal{R}^{(3)} = \{R \in \mathcal{R}^{(2)} | C^{\alpha_0}(rep(R), eff(R)) = 1\}$$

where C^{α_0} is maximal predicate with characteristic α_0.

Step 4. If no rules remained then go to step 6. Otherwise examine the effectiveness of residuary rules. If $C(rep(R), eff(R)) = 1$ then the rule is significant and should be moved to the list of final rules:

$$\tilde{\mathcal{R}} = \tilde{\mathcal{R}} \cup \{R \in \mathcal{R}^{(3)} | C(rep(R), eff(R)) = 1\}$$
$$\mathcal{R}^{(4)} = \{R \in \mathcal{R}^{(3)} | C(rep(R), eff(R)) = 0\}$$

Step 5. All other rules (if any) are used for restrictions in the following way. Sumption of any rule being restricted should be a subset of any other two rules, which are being restricted to the same rule of higher order:

$$\mathcal{R}^{(5)} = \{R \in \mathcal{R}^* | res(R) = N^k, Sump(R) = Sump(R_1) \cup Sump(R_2), R_1, R_2 \in \mathcal{R}^{(4)},$$
$$Ord(R) = Ord(R_1) + 1, \forall R_+ : R \subset R_+, Ord(R_+) = Ord(R) - 1 \Rightarrow R_+ \in \mathcal{R}^{(4)}\}$$
$$(4)$$

In other words, the union of sumptions of any two rules, which are restricted to the same rule of higher order, is exactly the sumption of this new rule. If no new rules got, then go to step 6. Otherwise set $\mathcal{R}^{(1)} = \mathcal{R}^{(5)}$ and go to step 2.

Step 6. If all result sets were examined then stop working, otherwise increase k by one and go to step 1.

Theorem 2. *Effective restrictions method constructs all significant rules of minimal order for any predicate C with positive characteristic, i.e.*

$$\tilde{\mathcal{R}} = \{R \in \mathcal{R}^* | C(rep(R), \mathit{eff}(R)) = 1, \forall R' \supset R \Rightarrow C(rep(R'), \mathit{eff}(R')) = 0\}$$

The use of trapezium-shaped membership functions leads to continuous outputs with respect to continuous inputs. In case of bell-shaped functions the outputs are smooth (i.e. second derivative of output with respect to the inputs can be computed). These properties of outputs make it possible to optimize fuzzy partition adjusting it to the training data using first (in case of continuous outputs) and second order (in case of smooth outputs) optimization methods.

4   Experiments

The proposed algorithm was tested on a set of classification problems. For knowledge presentation bell-shaped membership functions with further borders optimization using training set were used. Results of proposed technique (ExSys) were compared with q-nearest neighbors (QNN), support vector machines (SVM) [16], committee of linear classificators (LM) [14], test algorithm (TA) [19], linear Fisher discriminant (LDF), multi-layer perceptron (MLP) and neuro-fuzzy approach ANFIS [8,9] on 4 classification problems. The first was melanoma diagnostics (3 classes, 33 features, 48 objects in the training set, 32 objects in the test set), the second problem was speech phoneme recognition (2 classes, 5 features, 2200 objects in the training sample, 1404 in the testing set), the third task was drug intoxication diagnostics (2 classes, 18 features, 450 objects in the training sample and 450 in the testing set) and the last one was artificial task with mixture of Gaussian distributions (2 classes, 2 features, 200 objects in the training set, 5000 objects in the test set). The results of experiments (percent of correctly classified objects in the independent test sample) are shown in Table 1. For ANFIS and ExSys also number of generated rules are given in brackets. For Melanoma task ANFIS failed to train due to out of memory error.

Table 1. Accuracy on test set for several problems

Method	Melanoma	Phoneme	Drug intoxication	Mixture
MLP	65.6	78.2	77.5	29.4
LDF	56.3	77.4	77.5	26.7
TA	62.5	65.5	65.7	25.3
LM	50.0	77.2	79.3	26.8
SVM	59.4	77.4	83.1	27.6
QNN	62.5	74.6	80.2	21.9
ANFIS	NaN $(> 10^8)$	77.2 (3125)	78.4 $(\sim 10^6)$	24.0 (25)
ExSys	68.7 (186)	77.5 (15)	84.4 (44)	26.1 (20)

Based on experiments we may conclude that our method provides comparable performance with popular classification algorithms. It can also be used for understanding the nature of process by analyzing the set of generated rules. The effective restrictions method is applicable to the wide range of criterion functions with the only requirement to have positive characteristics.

Acknowledgements

The work was supported by the Russian Foundation for Basic Research (projects numbers 06-01-08045, 05-01-00332, 05-07-90333, 07-01-00211).

References

1. Breiman, L., Friedman, J.H., Olshen, R.A., Stone, C.J.: Classification and Regression Trees (1984)
2. Breslow, L.A., Aha, D.W.: Simplifying decision trees: a survey. Knowledge Engineering Review 12(1), 1–40 (1997)
3. Cohen, W.W., Singer, Y.: A Simple, Fast and Effective Rule Learner.In: Proc. 16th Nat. Conf. Artif. Intell (1999)
4. Freund, Y., Schapire, R.E.: Experiments with a new boosting algorithm. In: Proc. 13th Intern. Conf. Mach. Learn,pp.148–156 (1996)
5. Gomez-Scarmeta, A.F., Jimenez, F.: Generating and Tuning Fuzzy Rules Using Hybrid Systems.In: Proc. 6th IEEE Intern. Conf. Fuzzy Syst. vol. 1, pp. 247–252 (1997)
6. Inoue, H., Kamei, K., Inoue, K.: Rule Pairing Methods for Crossover in GA for Automatic Generation of Fuzzy Control Rules (1998), http://citeseer.ist.psu.edu/200265.html
7. Ishibuchi, H., Nozaki, K., Yamamoto, N., Tanaka, H.: Construction of Fuzzy Classification Systems with Rectangular Fuzzy Rules Using Genetic Algorithms. Fuzzy Sets and Systems 65(2/3), 237–253 (1994)
8. Jang, J.-S.R.: ANFIS: Adaptive-Network-based Fuzzy Inference Systems. IEEE Trans. on Syst. Man and Cyber. 23(3), 665–685 (1993)
9. Jang, J.-S.R., Sun, C.-T., Mizutani, E.: Neuro-Fuzzy and Soft Computing. Prentice-Hall, Englewood Cliffs (1997)
10. Ojala, T.: Neuro-Fuzzy Systems in Control. MSc thesis, Tampere, Finland (1994)
11. Perfilieva, I.: Applications of fuzzy sets theory. In: Itogi nauki i techniki, vol. 29,pp. 83–151 (1990)
12. Quinlan, J.R.: C4.5: Programs for machine learning. Morgan Kaufmann, San Francisco (1993)
13. Rivest, R.L.: Learning Decision Lists. Machine Learning 2(3), 229–246 (1987)
14. Ryazanov, V.V., Obukhov, A.S.: On using of relaxation algorithm for optimization of linear decision rules.In: Proc. 10th Conf. Math. Methods Pattern Recogn. (2001)
15. Terano, T., Asai, K., Sugeno, M.: Applied Fuzzy Systems (1993)
16. Vapnik, V.N.: Statistical Learning Theory. Wiley, Chichester, UK (1998)
17. Vorontsov, K.V.: Lectures on logical classification algorithms (2006), http://www.ccas.ru/voron/download/LogiclAlgs.pdf
18. Zadeh, L.: The Concept of a linguistic variable and its application to approximate reasoning. Elsevier Pub. Co., Amsterdam (1973)
19. Zhuravlev, Y.I.: Selected Scientific Works. Magistr. (1998)

Outliers Detection in Selected Fuzzy Regression Models

Barbara Gładysz and Dorota Kuchta

Institute of Industrial Engineering and Management, Wrocław University of Technology, Wybrzeże Wyspiańskiego 27, 50-370 Wrocław, Poland
{barbara.gladysz,dorota.kuchta}@pwr.wroc.pl

Abstract. The paper proposes three fuzzy regression models - concerning temperature and electricity load - based on real data. In the first two models the monthly temperature in a period of four years in a Polish city is analyzed. We assume the temperature to be fuzzy and its dependence on time and on the temperature in the previous month is determined. In the construction of the fuzzy regression models the least square methods was used. In the third model we analyze the dependence of the daily electricity load (assumed to be a fuzzy number) on the (crisp) temperature. Outliers, i.e. non-typical instances in the observations are identified, using a modification of an identification method known from the literature. The proposed method turns out to identify the outliers consistently with the real meaning of the experimental data.

1 Introduction

In this paper we propose to apply fuzzy regression to temperature and electricity load. Because of the variability of these data, fuzzy approach seems quite suitable. The models we construct, using real data, can be used to predict temperature and electricity load for analogous periods in the future.

While constructing regression models, one encounters often the problem of outliers - non-typical observations, which may distort the model, especially if they occurred only single time and should have no influence on future prediction. It is thus very important to identify the outliers and then try to explain their occurrence, trying to find out whether they have a chance to repeat themselves or rather not. There are several methods of outliers identification. Here we propose a modification of a method known from the literature. In two models clear outliers are identified. In one of the cases it is possible to see clearly their nature, in the other case more historical data would be necessary to interpret them.

2 Basic Notions

In the paper we will use the notions of a fuzzy number, representing an unknown magnitude, which can take on various values with various possibility degrees. *A*

F. Masulli, S. Mitra, and G. Pasi (Eds.): WILF 2007, LNAI 4578, pp. 211–218, 2007.

fuzzy number will be denoted by means of capital letters with a ˜ (e.g. $\widetilde{A}$). It is defined by its membership function $\mu_{\widetilde{A}} : \Re \rightarrow [0,1]$, [4].

We will use a special type of fuzzy numbers: *triangular fuzzy numbers* $\widetilde{A}$ defined by the following membership function

$$\mu_{\widetilde{A}}(t) = \begin{cases} 0 & \text{for } x < \underline{a} \\ 1 - \frac{a-x}{a-\underline{a}} & \text{for } \underline{a} \leq x < a \\ 1 - \frac{x-a}{\overline{a}-a} & \text{for } a \leq x < \overline{a} \\ 0 & \text{for } x > \overline{a} \end{cases} \tag{1}$$

Triangular fuzzy numbers $\widetilde{A}$ with membership function (1) will be denoted as a triple $(\underline{a}, a, \overline{a})$. Number a will be called *centre* of $\widetilde{A}$ and values $p = a - \underline{a}$ and $q = \overline{a} - a$ left and right *spread*, respectively.

Addition of two triangular fuzzy numbers, of a triangular fuzzy number and a crisp number and *scalar multiplication* of a triangular fuzzy number can be defined as follows:

$$\widetilde{A} + \widetilde{B} = (\underline{a}, a, \overline{a}) + (\underline{b}, b, \overline{b}) \, ; r + \widetilde{A} = (r + \underline{a}, r + a, r + \overline{a}) \, ; r\widetilde{A} = (r\underline{a}, ra, r\overline{a})$$

In the literature there are several definitions of *the mean value* (*m*) of a fuzzy number. We will use the one of Yager [1]. For a triangular fuzzy number $\widetilde{A} = (\underline{a}, a, \overline{a})$ the Yager's mean value is defined as

$$m = a + [(a - \underline{a}) - (\overline{a} - a)] \, /4 \tag{2}$$

There are several *distance measure between two fuzzy numbers* . We will use the following one for two triangular fuzzy numbers $\widetilde{A} = (\underline{a}, a, \overline{a})$, $\widetilde{B} = (\underline{b}, b, \overline{b})$:

$$d^2\left(\widetilde{A}, \widetilde{B}\right) = w_1 \left[(a - \underline{a}) - (b - \underline{b})\right]^2 + w_2 \left[a - b\right]^2 + w_3 \left[(\overline{a} - a) - (\overline{b} - b)\right]^2 \tag{3}$$

where: w_1, w_2, w_3 are given positive weights.

3   Fuzzy Regression Analysis of Air Temperature in a Polish City

3.1   Input Data

The climate in Poland belongs to the temperate zone with the average of 97 insolation days annually (which gives 2328 hours). The average annual temperature in Wroclaw ranges from $-30^{\circ}C$ to $19^{\circ}C$. The hottest month is September and the coldest is January. The temperature increases from January till September to take the reverse course from September to January.

The temperature from January 2000 to September 2004 has been analysed. The observed monthly temperature throught this period have been assumed to fuzzy. The data has already been pre-processed to get the observed data in the fuzzy form $\widetilde{Y}_t = \left(\underline{y}_t, y_t, \overline{y}_t\right)$. The original data (taken from statistical annuals of the city of Wroclaw [12]) comprised the minimal temperature value in moment t, $(t = 1, 2, ..., 57)$ $(\underline{y}_t$), the maximal temperature value in moment t $(\overline{y}_t$) and a mean value of the temperature of the moment t $(m_t$). We assumed the temperature in a moment t to be a triangular fuzzy number $\left(\underline{y}_t, y_t, \overline{y}_t\right)$. The centre y_t has been calculated from (2).

In the next sections three polynomial fuzzy regression models of temperature with fuzzy output and crisp input will be presented. The forth degree of the polynomial was selected because it gave the best results. The parameters of models will vary from one model to another.

Throughout the paper we will use the following notation: x_t - number of month in year in moment t (crisp input data), k - the polynomial's degree, t - time' index, $n = 57$- number of observations.

3.2 "Ordewise" Polynomial Regression Model of Temperature

Here we consider the model proposed by D'Urso and Gastaldi and its modification with respect to the criterion used. The model proposed in [13] has the following form:

- center polynomial model: $\hat{y}_t = a_0 + a_1 x_t + a_2 x_t^2 + \ldots + a_k x_t^k + \epsilon_t$,
- left spread polynomial model: $\hat{y}_t - \hat{\underline{y}}_t = d + c\left(a_0 + a_1 x_t + \ldots + a_k x_t^k\right) + \lambda_t$,
- right spread polynomial model: $\hat{\overline{y}}_t - \hat{y}_t = h + g\left(a_0 + a_1 x_t + \ldots + a_k x_t^k\right) + \rho_t$,
  where: $a_0, a_1, \ldots, a_k, c, d, h, g$ - crisp regression parameters,
  $\epsilon_t, \lambda_t, \rho_t$- residuals.

The parameters of regression model are found by minimizing the sum of distances between the observations and aapproximated temperature over the whole period for which we have the historic data:

$$D^2\left(a_0, a_1, \ldots, a_k, c, d, h, g\right) = \sum_{t=1}^{57} w_1 \epsilon_t^2 + w_2 \lambda_t^2 + w_3 \rho_t^2 = \sum_{t=1}^{57} d^2\left(\widetilde{Y}_t, \hat{\widetilde{Y}}_t\right) \quad (4)$$

subject to:

$$d + c\left(a_0 + a_1 x_t + \ldots + a_k x_t^k\right) \geq 0, h + g\left(a_0 + a_1 x_t + \ldots + a_k x_t^k\right) \geq 0$$

where: $\hat{\widetilde{Y}}_t = \left(\hat{\underline{y}}_t, \hat{y}_t, \hat{\overline{y}}_t\right) =$
$\left(-d + (1 - c)\left(a_0 + \ldots + a_k x_t^k\right), a_0 + \ldots + a_k x_t^k, h + (g - 1)\left(a_0 + \ldots + a_k x_t^k\right)\right)$-
approximated temperature $\widetilde{Y}_t = \left(\underline{y}_t, y_t, \overline{y}_t\right)$ in moment t.

The minimal value of $D^2\left(a_0, a_1, \ldots, a_k, c, d, h, g\right)$ over $a_0, a_1, \ldots, a_k, c, d, h, g$ is called the distance fuzzy least square.

Solving (4) with $w_1, w_2, w_3 = 1/3$ gives the following approximate of parameters (center and spreads) of fuzzy temperature $\hat{\widetilde{Y}}_t$ in month $x_t \in \{1, 2, \ldots, 12\}$ [6]:

$$\hat{y}_t = 4,17 - 6,6x_t + 3,45x_t^2 - 0,42x_t^3 + 0,015x_t^4,$$
$$\hat{y}_t - \underline{\hat{y}}_t = -14,69 + 0,58\left(4,17 - 6,6x_t + 3,45x_t^2 - 0,42x_t^3 + 0,015x_t^4\right),$$
$$\overline{\hat{y}}_t - \hat{y}_t = 11 - 0,785\left(4,17 - 6,6x_t + 3,45x_t^2 - 0,42x_t^3 + 0,015x_t^4\right).$$

The polynomial degree was determined on the basis of the determination coefficient value $R^2 = \sum_{t=1}^{n} d^2\left(\hat{\tilde{Y}}_t, \overline{\tilde{Y}}\right) / d^2\left(\tilde{Y}_t, \overline{\tilde{Y}}\right)$, where $\overline{\tilde{Y}} = 1/n \sum_{t=1}^{n} \tilde{Y}_t$. For the forth degree polynomial it assumed the largest value: $R^2 = 0,63$. From the polynomial regression form it follows that the January temperature can be modelled as a triangular fuzzy number $(-13.9°C, 0.6°C, 11.3°C)$, and the changes of the temperature which is certain to the highest degree (1) can be described with a 4th degree polynomial. The spreads widths of the fuzzy number which models the temperature depend linearly on this most certain temperature. The width of the left spread is $-14,69+0,58\hat{y}_t$, that of the right one: $11-0,785\hat{y}_t$. Thus, the spread widths are between the values 10,2 oC do 14,5 oC, where the left spread is the widest for the winter months and the narrowest for the summer ones, and the right spread the other way round. Figure 1 (the diagram on the left-hand side) shows the corresponding data for 12 months, showing $\left(\underline{\hat{y}}_t, \hat{y}_t, \overline{\hat{y}}_t\right)$ (the three curves) and gathering for each month the respective values observed(the maximal, centre and minimal) from all the years.

Analyzing the influence of the weights w_1, w_2, w_3 on the model form and on the adaptation of the model to the observations it was stated that the determination coefficient is the higher the higher is the value of the weight w_1, i.e. the weight linked to the fuzzy number center.

3.3   Autoregressive Model with Fuzzy Data of Temperature

In this section we will build the autoregressive linear model of temperature using fuzzy input and output data. Here the temperature of a month will be made dependent on the temperature in the previous month.

$$\hat{\tilde{Y}}_t = a_0 + a_1 \tilde{Y}_{t-1} \tag{5}$$

where: $\hat{\tilde{Y}}_t = \left(\underline{\hat{y}}_t, \hat{y}_t, \overline{\hat{y}}_t\right)$ - approximated fuzzy output data of temperature for t-moment, $t = 2, 3, ..., 57$; a_0, a_1 - crisp parameters.

The parameters of regression model are found by minimizing the distance between the observations and their approximations, [3].

$$D^2(a_0, a_1) = \sum_t d^2\left(\tilde{Y}_t, a_0 + a_1\tilde{Y}_{t-1}\right) \tag{6}$$

In this model two types of segments can be distinguished: the first one for the periods from February to August and the second one for the periods from September to January. Such a segmentation of the model is a consequence of a different temperature behaviour (increasing and decreasing tendency) in those periods. The resulting regression model takes the following form:

$$\hat{\tilde{Y}}_t = \begin{cases} 3,94 + 0,91\tilde{Y}_{t-1}, \text{ for } t \in T_1 \\ -4,21 + 0,93\tilde{Y}_{t-1}, \text{ for } t \in T_2 \end{cases}$$

where:
$T1 = \{t : t = 2 + 12k, 3 + 12k, 4 + 12k, 5 + 12k, 6 + 12k, 7 + 12k, 8 + 12k\}$,
$T2 = \{t : t = 9 + 12k, 10 + 12k, 11 + 12k, 12 + 12k, 1 + 12k, 57; \}$,k=0, 1, 2, 3, 4

The determination coefficient for the autoregressive model of temperature equals $0,77$ for the months since February till August and $R^2 = 0,61$ for the months since September till January. In Figure 1 (the diagram on the right-hand side) we can see the results of the model. Of course, in the above model we

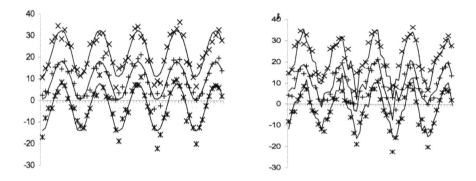

Fig. 1. The results obtained by means of polynomial and autoregressive models of temperature: the three curves represent $\left(\underline{\hat{y}}_t, \hat{y}_t, \overline{\hat{y}}_t\right)$ - the approximated fuzzy temperature, the backgrounds show the observed values

get various $\hat{\tilde{Y}}_t$ for the given month for different years. We use triangular fuzzy numbers, thus the prediction for a given month of the year takes the form of a triple (minimal possible value, center value, maximal possible value). The center value and the values around it are those whose occurrence is highly possible, the extreme values show the limits - the values which are possible to a low degree.

4   Regression Model of Electricity Load as a Function of Temperature for December

The problem of fuzzy regression of electricity loadwas considered among others in [5], [8], [11]. From the results presented above it follows that the temperature in the period September - December shows a descending tendency. In this section we will examine what influence, if any, has the temperature decrease on the electricity load. The calculations will be carried out for December 1998.In this case the data in the model are as follows:

- $\widetilde{Y}_t = \left(\underline{y_t}, y_t, \overline{y_t}\right)$ - the electricity load during the t-th day in December: the fuzzy number approximated on the basis of the minimal, maximal and average daily electricity load, similarly as the fuzzy number for the temperature in section 3.1,
- x_t - the minimal temperature during the t-th day - crisp number
- $t = 1, 2, \ldots, 31$ - the consecutive days of December

Estimating the linear fuzzy regression model according to (4) with $w_1, w_2, w_3 = 1/3$ we get the following equation

$$\hat{y}_t = 256333, 37 - 1212, 92 x_t$$
$$\hat{y}_t - \underline{\hat{y}}_t = 42444, 0 + 0, 03 \left(256333, 37 - 1212, 92 x_t\right)$$
$$\overline{\hat{y}}_t - \hat{y}_t = 11258, 6 + 0, 24 \left(256333, 37 - 1212, 92 x_t\right) \qquad (7)$$

The determination coefficient for this model equals $0, 63$. The input data and

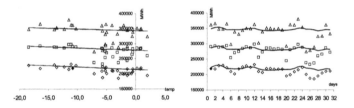

Fig. 2. Dependency of electricity load on the temperature and electricity load in the consecutive days of December(the data and their extrapolation)

the extrapolation results are presented in Figure 2. The diagram on the left-hand side presents the regression model of the dependency of the electricity load on temperature and the observation values $\left(\underline{y_t}, y_t, \overline{y_t}\right)$. In the diagram in the right-hand side the observed electricity load values and their extrapolation in consecutive December days are shown.

5   Outliers Detection

It can be observed in Figure 2 that the fitting of the model is not identical in various days of the month. Thus, let us try to determine the outliers. The problem of outliers in fuzzy regression is treated in many papers. In [7], [9], [10] the multicriteria programming was used to identify a regression which would be insensitive to outliers. Here, like in [2], we will determine the outliers basing ourselves on a measure which measures the non-typicality of an observation for a ready regression. In [2] a complex non-typicality measure for a single observation

was used, we will use three indicators: for the modal, the left and the right spread.
We say that an observation is an outlier if

$$|y_t - \hat{y}_t| > m\bar{s}_y \text{ or}$$

$$\left|\left(y_t - \underline{y}_t\right) - \left(\hat{y}_t - \underline{\hat{y}}_t\right)\right| > m\bar{s}_L \text{ or}$$

$$\left|\left(\bar{y}_t - y_t\right) - \left(\hat{\bar{y}}_t - \hat{y}_t\right)\right| > m\bar{s}_R \tag{8}$$

where: $\bar{s}_y = \sqrt{\sum_{t=1}^{n} (y_t - \hat{y}_t)^2 / n}$, $\bar{s}_L = \sqrt{\sum_{t=1}^{n} \left[\left(y_t - \underline{y}_t\right) - \left(\hat{y}_t - \underline{\hat{y}}_t\right)\right]^2 / n}$,

$\bar{s}_R = \sqrt{\sum_{t=1}^{n} \left[\left(\bar{y}_t - y_t\right) - \left(\hat{\bar{y}}_t - \hat{y}_t\right)\right]^2 / n}$,

m - a parameter, which can assume values 2, 2.5, 3.

In our example, taking m=2, the Christmas days (the 25 and 26 of December), all the December Sundays and the days just before Christmas (the 22 and 23 of December) and just before the New Year's Eve (the 30 of December) were identified as outliers. The results show that the method of outliers identification proposed here is effective: holidays and Sundays are non-typical days of the year with respect to the electricity load (small electricity load), and the days just before holidays have a high electricity load . If we assume two additional explanatory variables: h_t, taking value 1 for Sundays and the Christmas days and 0 for the other December days and s_t, taking value 1 for the days immediately preceding holidays and 0 for the other December days, we obtain the following model for the electricity load:

$$\hat{y}_t = 268802, 5 - 393, 1x_t - 46516, 1h_t + 13400, 6s_t$$

$$\hat{y}_t - \underline{\hat{y}}_t = -115243, 6 + 0, 6 \left(268802, 5 - 393, 1x_t - 46516, 1h_t + 13400, 6s_t\right)$$

$$\hat{\bar{y}}_t - \hat{y}_t = 3261, 1 + 0, 3 \left(268802, 5 - 393, 1x_t - 46516, 1h_t + 13400, 6s_t\right) \tag{9}$$

The determination coefficient R^2 for this model is equal to 0,62, while for the model (7) $R^2 = 0, 08$.

The application of the same non-typicality measures to identify outliers in polynomial regression model lead to the conclusion that January 2003 had a non-typical temperature (the left spread of the fuzzy number). For m=3 January 2003 remained an outlier for various values of the coefficients w1, w2, w3. In the case of the autoregression model of temperature no outliers were identified for m=3.

6   Conclusions

Three fuzzy regression models were considered. In the first two ones the temperature variability in the period of four years was examined, in the third one the temperature influence on electricity load. In all the three models the problem of outliers was considered. They were identified using a modification of a method known from the literature. The modification consists in using three parameters instead of two - the additional parameter is the modal of the fuzzy number. Further research is planned to provide more evidence of the reliability of the proposed method, concerning above all the problems of electricity load.

Of course, many other methods can be used to idetity outliers: other regresion models or e.g. neutral neutworks. The authors have tried the classical and robust regression, but they did not identify the outliers correctly in the case discussed here. Further research is needed to find out which otliers detection method would be the best.

References

1. Chanas, S., Nowakowski, M.: Single value simulation of fuzzy variable. Fuzzy Sets and Systems 25, 43–57 (1988)
2. Chen, Y.S.: Outliers detection and confidence interval modification in fuzzy regression. Fuzzy Sets and Systems 119, 259–272 (2001)
3. Diamond, P.: Least squares and maximum likelihood regression for fuzzy linear models. In: Kacprzyk, J., Fedrizzi, M. (eds.) Fuzzy Regression Analysis, pp. 137–151. Omnitech Press Warsaw and Physica-Verlag Heidelberg, Warsaw (1992)
4. Dudois, D., Prade, H.: Fuzzy Sets and Systems: Theory and Applications. Academic Press, San Diego CA (1980)
5. Gładysz, B.: The electric power load fuzzy regression mode. In: Hryniewicz, O., Kacprzyk, J., Kuchta, D. (eds.) Issues in Soft Computing Decisions of Operations Research, pp. 171–180. Academic Publishing House EXIT, Warsaw (2005)
6. Gładysz, B., Kuchta, D.: Polynomial least squares fuzzy regression models for temperature. In: Cader, A., Rutkowski, L., Tadeusiewicz, R., Zurada, J. (eds.) Artificial Intelligence and Soft Computing, pp. 118–124. Academic Publishing House EXIT, Warsaw (2006)
7. Nasrabadi, M.M., Nasrabadi, E., Nasrabadi, A.R.: Fuzzy linear regression analysis: A multi-objective programming approach, Applied Mathematics and Computation, vol. 163, pp. 245-251 (2005)
8. Nazarko, M., Zalewski, W.: The fuzzy regression approach to peak load estimation in power distribution systems. IEEE Transactions on Powr Systems 8(3), 809–814 (1999)
9. Özelkan, E.C., Duckstein, L.: Multi-objective fuzzy regression: a general framework. Computers and Operations Research 27, 635–652 (2000)
10. Sakawa, M., Yano, H.: Multiobjective fuzzy linear regression analysis for fuzzy input-output data. Fuzzy Sets and Systems 47, 173–181 (1992)
11. Shen, R.: Fuzzy causal relation analysis in time series. In: Kacprzyk J., Fedrizzi M. (eds.) Fuzzy Regression Analysis, Omnitech Press Warsaw and Physica-Verlag Heilderberg, Warsaw, pp. 181-193 (1992)
12. Statistic Annuals. Regional Statistical Office, Wrocław (2000-2004)
13. D'Urso, P., Gastaldi, T.: An ordewise polynomial regression procedure for fuzzy data. Fuzzy Sets and Systems 130, 1–19 (2002)

Possibilistic Clustering in Feature Space

Maurizio Filippone, Francesco Masulli, and Stefano Rovetta

Dipartimento di Informatica e Scienze dell'Informazione, Università di Genova, and
CNISM, Via Dodecaneso 35, I-16146 Genova, Italy
{filippone,masulli,rovetta}@disi.unige.it

Abstract. In this paper we propose the Possibilistic C-Means in Feature Space and the One-Cluster Possibilistic C-Means in Feature Space algorithms which are kernel methods for clustering in feature space based on the possibilistic approach to clustering. The proposed algorithms retain the properties of the possibilistic clustering, working as density estimators in feature space and showing high robustness to outliers, and in addition are able to model densities in the data space in a non-parametric way. One-Cluster Possibilistic C-Means in Feature Space can be seen also as a generalization of One-Class SVM.

1 Introduction

In the last few years, some applications of kernel methods [1] to clustering tasks have been proposed. Kernel approach allows us to implicitly map patterns into a high feature space where the cluster structure is possibly more evident than in the original data space. In the literature, kernels have been applied in clustering in different ways. We can be broadly classify these approaches in three categories, which are based respectively on the: (a) *kernelization of the metric* (see, e.g., [9,12]); (b) *clustering in feature space* (see, e.g., [11]); (c) *description via support vectors* (see, e.g., [4]). The first two keep the concept of centroid as a prototype of a cluster as it is in K-Means. Methods based on kernelization of the metric look for centroids in input space and the distance between patterns and centroids is computed through kernels. Clustering in feature space is made by mapping each pattern in feature space and then computing centroids in this new space. The description via support vectors is used in the One-Class Support Vector Machine (One-Class SVM) algorithm [4] that finds a hypersphere with minimal radius in the feature space able to enclose almost all data excluding outliers. When we go back to the input space, this hypersphere corresponds to a non-linear and possibly non-connected surface separating clusters. A labeling procedure is then applied in order to group the patterns lying in the same cluster in data space.

In this paper we present the Possibilistic C-Means in Feature Space (PCM-FS) and the One-Cluster Possibilistic C-Means in Feature Space (One-Cluster PCM-FS) algorithms, which are two novel kernel methods for clustering in feature space based on the possibilistic approach to clustering [5,6]. The proposed

F. Masulli, S. Mitra, and G. Pasi (Eds.): WILF 2007, LNAI 4578, pp. 219–226, 2007.

algorithms retain the properties of the possibilistic approach to clustering, working as density estimators in feature space and showing high robustness to outliers, and in addition they are able to model densities in the data space in a non-parametric way. Note that previous kernel approaches to possibilistic clustering [12,10,7] are based on the kernelization of the metric.

One-Cluster PCM-FS can be seen also as a generalization of One-Class SVM as it is able to find a family of minimum enclosing hyperspheres in feature space; each of such hyperspheres can be obtained by simply thresholding the memberships.

The paper is organized as follows: Section 2 sketchs the main aspects of the PCM algorithm, in Sections 3 and 4 we introduce the PCM-FS and the One-Cluster PCM-FS while in Sections 5 and 6 we present some experimental results and the conclusions.

2   Possibilistic C-Means

Let U be the *membership matrix*, where each element u_{ih} ($u_{ih} \in [0,1]$) represents the membership of the h-th pattern ($h = 1, 2, \ldots, n$) to the i-th cluster ($i = 1, 2, \ldots, c$). In the possibilistic clustering framework [5], memberships u_{ih} can be interpreted of as degrees of typicality of patterns to clusters. To this aim, in the possibilistic clustering framework we do we relax the usual *probabilistic constraint* on the sum of the memberships of a pattern to all clusters (i.e., $\sum_{i=1}^{c} u_{ih} = 1$) that applies, e.g., to the Fuzzy C-Means (FCM) [3], to this minimal set of constraints:

$$u_{ih} \in [0,1] \quad \forall i, h \tag{1}$$

$$0 < \sum_{h=1}^{n} u_{ih} < n \quad \forall i \tag{2}$$

$$\bigvee_i u_{ih} > 0 \quad \forall h. \tag{3}$$

Roughly speaking, these requirements simply imply that clusters cannot be empty and each pattern must be assigned to at least one cluster.

There are two formulations of the Possibilistic C-Means (PCM) algorithm [5], [6]. Here we consider the latter which attempts to minimize the following functional:

$$J(U,V) = \sum_{h=1}^{n} \sum_{i=1}^{c} u_{ih} \|\mathbf{x}_h - \mathbf{v}_i\|^2 + \sum_{i=1}^{c} \eta_i \sum_{h=1}^{n} (u_{ih} \ln(u_{ih}) - u_{ih}) \tag{4}$$

with respect to U and the set of centroids $V = \{\mathbf{v}_1, \ldots, \mathbf{v}_c\}$. The first term of $J(U,V)$ is the expectation of distortion, while the latter is an entropic term which allows us to avoid the trivial solution with all memberships equal to zero.

Setting the gradient of $J(U, V)$ with respect to the u_{ih} and $\mathbf{v}_i$ to zero we obtain:

$$u_{ih} = \exp\left(-\frac{\|\mathbf{x}_h - \mathbf{v}_i\|^2}{\eta_i}\right) \tag{5}$$

$$\mathbf{v}_i = \frac{\displaystyle\sum_{h=1}^{n} u_{ih}\mathbf{x}_h}{\displaystyle\sum_{h=1}^{n} u_{ih}} \tag{6}$$

To perform the optimization of $J(U, V)$ we apply the Picard iterations method, by simply iterating Eq.s 5 and 6. Each iteration consists of two parts: in the first one the centroids are kept fixed and the memberships are modified using Eq. (5), while in the second one we keep the memberships fixed and update the centroids using Eq. (6). The iteration ends when a stop criterion is satisfied, e.g., memberships change less than an assigned threshold, or when no significant improvements of $J(U, V)$ are noticed. The constraint on the memberships $u_{ih} \in [0, 1]$ is satisfied given the form of Eq. 5.

The parameter η_i regulates the tradeoff between the two terms in Eq. 4 and is related to the width of the clusters. In [5,6], the authors suggest to estimate η_i using a weighted mean of the intracluster distance of the i-th cluster:

$$\eta_i = \gamma\frac{\displaystyle\sum_{h=1}^{n} u_{ih}\|\mathbf{x}_h - \mathbf{v}_i\|^2}{\displaystyle\sum_{h=1}^{n} u_{ih}} \tag{7}$$

where the parameter γ is typically set to one. The parameter η_i can be updated at each step of the algorithm or can be fixed for all iterations. The former approach can lead to instabilities since the derivation of the algorithm have been obtained considering η_i fixed. In the latter a good estimation of η_i can be obtained only when starting from a preliminary solution of the clustering solution, given, e.g., from an algorithm based on the probabilistic constraint, such as the FCM. For this reason often the PCM is usually applied as a refining step for a clustering procedure.

Note that the lack of of competitiveness among clusters due to the relaxation of the probabilistic constraints makes the PCM approach equivalent to a set of c independent estimation problems that can be solved one at a time through c independent Picard iterations of Eq. 5 and Eq. 6, i.e., one for each cluster.

The main drawback for the possibilistic clustering, as well as for most central clustering methods, is its inability to model in a non-parametric way the density of clusters of generic shape (parametric approaches such as Possibilistic C-Spherical Shells [5], instead, have been proposed).

3   Possibilistic Clustering in Feature Space

In order to overcome this limit, we propose the Possibilistic C-Means in Feature Space (PCM-FS) algorithm. It is based on a kernelization of the PCM obtained by applying a mapping Φ from the input space S to a high dimensional feature space $\mathcal{F}$ ($\Phi : S \to \mathcal{F}$) to the patterns, and applying the PCM to them in the new space $\mathcal{F}$. The objective function to be minimized becomes:

$$J^{\Phi}(U, V^{\Phi}) = \sum_{h=1}^{n} \sum_{i=1}^{c} u_{ih} \|\Phi(\mathbf{x}_h) - \mathbf{v}_i^{\Phi}\|^2 + \sum_{i=1}^{c} \eta_i \sum_{h=1}^{n} (u_{ih} \ln(u_{ih}) - u_{ih}). \quad (8)$$

Note that the centroids $\mathbf{v}_i^{\Phi}$ of PCM-FS algorithm lie in the feature space. We can minimize $J^{\Phi}(U, V^{\Phi})$ by setting its derivatives with respect to $\mathbf{v}_i^{\Phi}$ and u_{ih} equal to zero, obtaining:

$$\mathbf{v}_i^{\Phi} = \frac{\sum_{h=1}^{n} u_{ih} \Phi(\mathbf{x}_h)}{\sum_{h=1}^{n} u_{ih}} = b_i \sum_{h=1}^{n} u_{ih} \Phi(\mathbf{x}_h), \qquad b_i \equiv \left(\sum_{h=1}^{n} u_{ih} \right)^{-1} \quad (9)$$

$$u_{ih} = \exp \left(-\frac{\|\Phi(\mathbf{x}_h) - \mathbf{v}_i^{\Phi}\|^2}{\eta_i} \right). \quad (10)$$

In principle, Eq.s 9 and 10 can be used for a Picard iteration minimizing $J^{\Phi}(U, V^{\Phi})$, but as Φ is not known explicitly, we cannot compute directly them. Despite this, if we consider Mercer Kernels [2] (symmetric and semidefinite kernels) which can be expressed as a scalar product:

$$K(\mathbf{x}_i, \mathbf{x}_j) = \Phi(\mathbf{x}_i) \cdot \Phi(\mathbf{x}_j), \quad (11)$$

this relation holds (*kernel trick* [1]):

$$\|\Phi(\mathbf{x}_i) - \Phi(\mathbf{x}_j)\|^2 = K(\mathbf{x}_i, \mathbf{x}_i) + K(\mathbf{x}_j, \mathbf{x}_j) - 2K(\mathbf{x}_i, \mathbf{x}_j). \quad (12)$$

This allows us to obtain an update rule for the memberships by substituting Eq. 9 in Eq. 10:

$$u_{ih} = \exp \left[-\frac{1}{\eta_i} \cdot \left(k_{hh} - 2b_i \sum_{r=1}^{n} u_{ir} k_{hr} + b_i^2 \sum_{r=1}^{n} \sum_{s=1}^{n} u_{ir} u_{is} k_{rs} \right) \right]. \quad (13)$$

Note that in Eq. 13 we introduced the notation $k_{ij} = K(\mathbf{x}_i, \mathbf{x}_j)$. The Picard iteration then reduces to the iterative update of the memberships only using Eq. 13, ending when an assigned stopping criterion is satisfied (e.g., when memberships change less than an assigned threshold, or when no significant improvements of $J^{\Phi}(U, V^{\Phi})$ are noticed).

Concerning the parameters η_i, we can applying in the feature space the same criteria suggested for the PCM (Eq. 7) obtaining in such a way:

$$\eta_i = \gamma\, b_i \sum_{h=1}^{n} u_{ih} \left(k_{hh} - 2b_i \sum_{r=1}^{n} u_{ir} k_{hr} + b_i^2 \sum_{r=1}^{n} \sum_{s=1}^{n} u_{ir} u_{is} k_{rs} \right) \qquad (14)$$

The parameters η_i can be estimated at each iteration or once at the beginning of the algorithm. In the latter case the initialization of the memberships, that allows to provide a good estimation of the η_i, can be obtained as a result of a Kernel Fuzzy c-Means [11].

Note that if we chose a linear kernel $k_{ij} = \mathbf{x}_i \cdot \mathbf{x}_j$ the PCM-FS reduces to the standard PCM, i.e., using a linear kernel is equivalent to put $\Phi \equiv I$, where I is the identity function. In the following, we will use a Gaussian kernel:

$$k_{ij} = \exp\left(-\frac{\|\mathbf{x}_i - \mathbf{x}_j\|^2}{2\sigma^2} \right) \qquad (15)$$

for which

$$\|\Phi(\mathbf{x}_i)\|^2 = \Phi(\mathbf{x}_i) \cdot \Phi(\mathbf{x}_i) = k_{ii} = 1. \qquad (16)$$

As a consequence, patterns are mapped by the Gaussian kernel from data space to the surface of a unit hypersphere in feature space.

Centroids in the feature space $\mathbf{v}_i^{\Phi}$ are not constrained to the hyperspherical surface as mapped patterns; therefore, centroids lie inside this hypersphere, and due to the lack of competitiveness between clusters (that characterizes the possibilistic clustering framework), centroids of PCM-FS often collapse into a single one, with slight dependency on the value of the cluster spreads η_i.

Note that PCM-FS retains the principal characteristics of PCM, including the capability of estimating hyperspherical densities, this time in the feature space. In the data space this corresponds to the capability to model clusters of more general shape, a significant improvement with respect the original PCM.

4   One-Cluster Possibilistic C-Means in Feature Space Algorithm

We propose now the One-Cluster Possibilistic C-Means in Feature Space (One-Cluster PCM-FS) algorithm aimed to model all data points in a single cluster in features space. We assume the presence of a unique cluster in feature space, with no regard to the number of clusters we expect to model in the data space. In the following, we will denote with u_h the membership of the h-th pattern to the cluster. It is made up by three main steps: *Core*, *Defuzzification*, and *Labeling*.

The *Core* step is the "*fuzzy*" part of the algorithm, aimed to producing a fuzzy-possibilistic model of densities (membership function) in the feature space. It is initialized by selecting a *stop criterion* (e.g., when memberships change less than an assigned threshold, or when no significant improvements of $J^{\Phi}(U, V^{\Phi})$ are noticed), setting the value of σ for the Gaussian kernel (in order to define the spatial resolution of density estimation), and initializing the memberships u_h (usually as $u_h = 1$). Then, after estimating the value of η using Eq. 14, we perform the Picard iteration using Eq. 13.

The *Defuzzification* steps filters outliers from data points by selecting a threshold $\alpha \in (0, 1)$ and using it to define an α-*cut* (or α-*level set*) on data points:

$$A_\alpha = \{\mathbf{x}_h \in X \mid u_h > \alpha\} \tag{17}$$

Note that given the form of u_h(Eq. 10) the threshold α defines a hypercircle which encloses a hyperspherical cap. A_α is then the set of data points whose mapping in feature space lies on the cap, whose base radius depends on α. Points outside the α-cut are considered to be outliers.

The *Labeling* step separates the data points belonging to the single cluster in feature space, in a number of "*natural*" clusters in data space. It uses a convexity criterion derived from the one proposed for One-Class SVM [4] assigning the same label to a pair of points only if all elements of the linear segment joining the two points in data space belong to A_α.

The *Defuzzification* and *Labeling* steps can be iterated with different values of α, thus performing a very lightweight *model selection*, without involving new runs of the *Core* step. Often, such as in the case of experiments presented in next section, an a-priori analysis of the memberships histogram permits to obtain a good evaluation of α without performing a true model selection. Indeed, the presence of multiple modes in the membership histogram indicates the presence of different structures of data in feature space, and allows us to find several levels of α discriminating the different densities of data in feature space.

5   Experimental Results and Discussion

In this section we present some results obtained on a synthetic second data set (Fig. 1) consisting in three disjoint dense regions (black dots) on a 10x10 square: two rectangular regions, each of them corresponding to 1.24 % of the square and composed by 100 patterns uniformly distributed, and a ring shaped region, corresponding to 7.79 % of the square, that contains 300 patterns uniformly distributed. An uniformly distributed noise of 1000 grey dots is superimposed to the square.

We used a Gaussian kernel with standard deviation $\sigma = 0.5$ estimated as the order of magnitude of the average inter-data points distance. The memberships u_h were initialized to 1. The stop criterion was $\sum_h \Delta u_h < \varepsilon$ with $\varepsilon = 0.01$.

In the *Defuzzification* step we evaluated α using the histogram method. As shown in Fig. 1(a), choosing $\alpha = .3667$ that is the value of membership separating the two modes of the histogram, we obtain a good separating surface in the data space (Fig. 1(b)), with no need to perform any iteration for model selection.

As shown in the experiment, One-Cluster PCM-FS shows a high robustness to outliers and a very good capability to model clusters of generic shape in the data space (modeling their distributions in terms of fuzzy memberships). Moreover it is able to find *autonomously* the *natural* number of clusters in the data space.

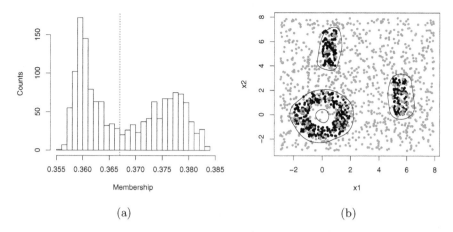

(a)   (b)

Fig. 1. (a) Histogram of the memberships obtained by One-Cluster PCM-FS with $\sigma = 0.5$. The dotted line gets through to membership value .3667 that separates the two modes of the graph; the value of α is then taken as $\alpha = .3667$. (b) Data space: black dots belong to the dense regions and the grey ones are the noisy patterns. The contours correspond to points with membership equal to .3667.

The outliers rejection ability is shared also by the standard PCM, but is limited to the case of globular clusters. The standard PCM shows also a good outliers rejection ability, but it works only with globular clusters.

One-Class SVM [4] is also able to find the "natural" number of clusters of generic shape in the data space, but it doesn't model their distribution. Moreover, One-Class SVM needs a complete *model selection* procedure involving many time consuming runs from scratch of the full algorithm.

In all the runs of One-Cluster PCM-FS the *Core* step, which involves the minimization of $J^{\Phi}(U, V^{\Phi})$ (Eq. 8), resulted to be very fast, as only less than a tenth of iterations of Eq. 13 where enough.

6   Conclusions

In this paper we have proposed the kernel possibilistic approach to clustering and two clustering algorithms, namely the Possibilistic C-Means in Feature Space and the One-Cluster Kernel Possibilistic C-Means in Feature Space algorithms which are novel kernel methods for clustering in feature space based on the possibilistic approach to clustering [5,6]. The proposed algorithms retain the properties of the possibilistic approach to clustering, working as density estimator in feature space and showing high robustness to outliers, and in addition are able to model densities in the data space in a non-parametric way.

One-Cluster PCM-FS can be seen also as a generalization of One-Class SVM as it is able to find a family of minimum enclosing hyperspheres in feature space; each of such hyperspheres can be obtained by simply thresholding the memberships. Note that, after fixed the value of the σ of the Gaussian kernel, the *model selection* does not involve the optimization step of One-Cluster PCM-FS, a.k.a. *Core* step, and can be performed very quickly. Moreover, often this is not necessary, and an analysis of the histogram of memberships can easily permit to find an optimal value for the threshold α, as in the case of the experiment shown.

Acknowledgements

Work funded by a grant from the University of Genova.

References

1. Aizerman, M., Braverman, E., Rozonoer, L.: Theoretical foundations of the potential function method in pattern recognition learning. Automation and Remote Control 25, 821–837 (1964)
2. Aronszajn, N.: Theory of reproducing kernels. Transactions of the American Mathematical Society 68(3), 337–404 (1950)
3. Bezdek, J.C.: Pattern Recognition with Fuzzy Objective Function Algorithms. Kluwer Academic Publishers, Norwell, MA, USA (1981)
4. Hur, A.B., Horn, D., Siegelmann, H.T., Vapnik, V.: Support vector clustering. Journal of Machine Learning Research 2, 125–137 (2001)
5. Krishnapuram, R., Keller, J.M.: A possibilistic approach to clustering. IEEE Transactions on Fuzzy Systems 1(2), 98–110 (1993)
6. Krishnapuram, R., Keller, J.M.: The possibilistic c-means algorithm: insights and recommendations. IEEE Transactions on Fuzzy Systems 4(3), 385–393 (1996)
7. Mizutani, K., Miyamoto, S.: Possibilistic Approach to Kernel-Based Fuzzy c-Means Clustering with Entropy Regularization. In: Torra, V., Narukawa, Y., Miyamoto, S. (eds.) MDAI 2005. LNCS (LNAI), vol. 3558, pp. 144–155. Springer, Heidelberg (2005)
8. Nasraoui, O., Krishnapuram, R.: Crisp interpretations of fuzzy and possibilistic clustering algorithms. vol. 3, pp. 1312–1318, Aachen, Germany (1995)
9. Wu, Z.D., Xie, W.X., Yu, J.P.: Fuzzy c-means clustering algorithm based on kernel method.In: Fifth International Conference on Computational Intelligence and Multimedia Applications, pp. 49–54 (2003)
10. Wu, X.H., Zhou, J.-J.: Possibilistic Fuzzy c-Means Clustering Model Using Kernel Methods. Proceedings of the Int. Conf. Computational Intelligence for Modelling, Control and Automation and Int. Conf.Intelligent Agents, Web Technologies and Internet Commerce, vol. 2, pp. 465–470 (2005)
11. Zhang, D.Q., Chen, S.C.: Fuzzy clustering using kernel method. In: The 2002 International Conference on Control and Automation, ICCA 2002 , pp. 162–163 (2002)
12. Zhang, D.Q., Chen, S.C.: Kernel-based fuzzy and possibilistic c-means clustering. In: Proceedings of the International Conference on Artificial Neural Networks, pp. 122–125 (2003)

OpenAdap.net: Evolvable Information Processing Environment

Alessandro E.P. Villa[1,2] and Javier Iglesias[1,2]

[1] Grenoble Institute of Neuroscience GIN, Centre de Recherche
Inserm U 836-UJF-CEA-CHU, Neuroheuristic Research Group,
University Joseph Fourier, Grenoble, France
[2] Information Systems Department, University of Lausanne, Switzerland
{Alessandro.Villa,Javier.Iglesias}@ujf-grenoble.fr
http://www.neuroheuristic.org/

Abstract. OpenAdap.net is an Open Source project aimed at breaking the barriers existing in the flow of information access and information processing. The infrastructure makes it possible the dissemination of resources like knowledge, tools or data, their exposure to evaluation in ways that might be unanticipated and hence support the evolution of communities of users around a specific domain. The architecture is designed by analogy with a virtual distributed operating system in which the dynamic resources are presented as files in a structured virtual file system featuring ownership and access permissions.

1 Introduction

The Cyberspace has become the main site of information exchange and its extension in terms of bandwidth is opening the way equally to all media of information. However, most of this information flow still remains associated to a 'declarative' approach, i.e. associated to the knowledge of 'what', as illustrated by the access of web portals built around search engines of any kind. Internet has still a huge unexploited potential in applying the 'procedural' approach, complementary to the declarative one, based on the knowledge of 'how'. The procedural approach necessarily relies on a *trial-and-error* paradigm that may be achieved more efficiently when the results are shared within a community of agents, independently of their human or non-human nature.

The benefits in terms of education, business developments, market diversification and creation of employment generated by the fast circulation and ease of access to the results of trial-and-error procedures clearly emphasizes the importance of the society, beyond the community of agents. Knowledge sharing leads to share the methods of information processing and the socialware [Hattori et al., 1999] becomes the vehicle for user adaptive collaboration support. Despite the immediate worldwide availability of new information published at Internet, the tools of information processing (e.g., software programs and methods of data analysis developed and provided by research laboratories

F. Masulli, S. Mitra, and G. Pasi (Eds.): WILF 2007, LNAI 4578, pp. 227–236, 2007.
© Springer-Verlag Berlin Heidelberg 2007

and businesses) are generally released in small niches delimited by the readers of specialized journals as well as by specific software environments and computer platforms.

Potential meaningful contributions may remain unexploited, or even forgotten, within the same field of competence and their availability is severely restricted in particular for cross-fertilized applications to other fields. This situation often leads to the delayed re-invention of similar (if not the same) methods of information processing and, to some extent, the re-discovery of the same knowledge. Despite the fact that the development of event-delivery middleware based on publish-subscribe communication allows high-performance computing [Eisenhauser et al., 2006], the development of added-value activities created by knowledge sharing is not yet widespread. The current situation tends to create an artificial 'distance' between the authors and developers of original information processing methods (i.e., the providers of the 'how' knowledge) and the users (i.e., the testers of *trial-and-error*) with the risk of erroneous applications of the methods and false evaluation of its value.

In the OpenAdap.net structure we have designed brokers playing a pivotal role, being responsible for dynamically decomposing and routing end-user tasks to appropriate resource sharers for execution. The negotiation between brokers (and workers) is inspired by the way how the brain processes information. In the present paper we present an event timing driven rule for adapting the connections between brokers belonging to the same network of community-related applications.

2   Functional Structure

OpenAdap.net is a distributed system composed by three types of interconnected components: brokers, workers and OAN-aware applications (see Figure 1). A broker is a process permanently running on a server in charge of managing a community of users and dispatching tasks and results on their behalf. Workers are processes shared by community members in charge of giving secured distant access to contributed resources like programs or data. OAN-aware applications are pieces of software (standalone applications, web portals, command line tools, etc.) providing access for an end-user to the community shared resources through identified connections to a broker.

The components are running on a network of computers, each of them defined by their specific CPU architecture, operating system (OS), amount of memory and available programs. Their resources are partially shared in a dynamic way. OpenAdap.net is designed by analogy with a virtual distributed OS in which all the resources are presented in a structured virtual file system. Using this high-level paradigm, resources are assigned to files in the file system tree. Security is enforced through ownership and access permissions defined on a per-file basis. OpenAdap.net goes beyond a traditional OS as the configuration is highly volatile. The file system structure and contents are the result of the constant runtime aggregation of several sources of information: the user database, the

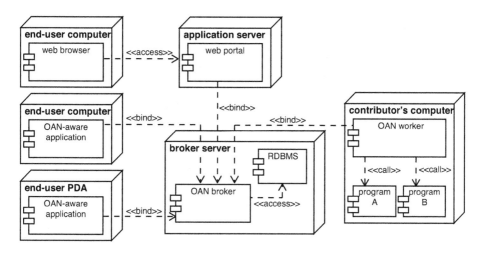

Fig. 1. Deployment diagram for the OpenAdap.net components. Boxes represent different computers, rectangles represent processes, and arrows represent inter-process communications over Internet.

inter-process message queues status, the worker status, etc. A dedicated URL name scheme (oan://) is proposed to identify each file in a transparent and interoperable way.

The Java 2 Platform was chosen for the implementation of the project, based on portability and platform neutrality requirements. Brokers, workers and OAN-aware applications are loosely coupled, distributed components that asynchronously communicate through a message-oriented middleware (MOM) as defined by the Java Message Service (JMS) API. The use of established industrial standards such as JMS allowed reusing existing Open Source software as a starting point for the project. It can also be expected that JMS implementations available for other platforms will allow applications written by third parties to connect to OpenAdap.net brokers and interoperate seamlessly [Laufer, 2005].

For OpenAdap.net the security is addressed transversally by defining rules on how to handle data at any point in the system, providing the required profiles for identification and authentication of the entities, and offering strongly encrypted connections when communicating through the Internet. Standards and models of the field were applied from the start of the project [Zhang et al., 2005].

3 Internet Application

3.1 Software Architecture

OpenAdap.net stands in the area of complexity and aims at providing a distributed environment where tools of all kinds (applications, data, knowledge, ...) can be accessed transparently via the Internet. At this time, three architectures are used in this field: Grid, Web-services (WS), and Peer-to-Peer (P2P). The peculiar strongholds of these architectures are briefly described here and synthesized in Table 1.

Grid: *"Each user has a large dataset to manipulate with one application distributed on a set of computers."* The problem addressed by the Grid is to distribute the processing of large data sets. The required application is copied to distinct computers over a network with each treating a portion of the data. The results are recomposed from all the partial results at the end of the treatment. End-users have control on both data and applications, but little information on remote execution hosts.

Web-services: *"Many users exploit the same services permanently provided through a centralized authority."* Web Services provide a secured and controlled access to applications, usually to collaborators in the same company or institution. The goal is to provide distributed access to the same references, databases or applications. The system is articulated around a repository where the service interfaces are published in a self-contained form. The architecture is rather static, as services seldom change and are expected to be permanently available. End-users have no control over the applications and little information on remote execution hosts.

Peer-to-Peer: *"Many users exchanging pieces of data in an unsupervised way."* P2P (peer-to-peer) systems address the data-sharing problem. Copies of the applications installed on end-users computers keep open connections from one computer to peers, forwarding queries and results back and forth until a match is found somewhere on the network. The architecture is open and competing implementations coexist on a self-organized network. End-users have control over their data and information on the peer hosts. It is interesting to note that end-users tolerate incredibly poor service quality and that this architecture raises social as well as technical issues.

OpenAdap.net (OAN) falls somewhere between these three architectures exploiting several of their interesting aspects, but with the intention to address a two-way problem: To provide to a community of users in the same domain a means to interchange their resources in an open, dynamic and secured way and to provide to a community of users the access to the exploitation of information processing solutions contributed by users belonging to other communities. End-users have control over their data, but do not need to manage the resources, nor do they have complete information on remote execution hosts. Collaboration within the OpenAdap.net network allows the dynamic integration of these resources, possibly yielding new or previously unexpected composite resources. This can be summarized as follows: *Many users interchanging resources (data, applications, knowledge in general) dynamically provided by interconnected domain-oriented brokers.*

Individual users of OpenAdap.net can be classified as either contributors of shared resources, or end-users of such. People who develop and provide new methods of data analyses are able to share their contribution and people interested in processing their own data or access data stored elsewhere (e.g. in a community database) can extract the results of their analysis. In addition to

Table 1. Comparison of OpenAdap.net with the other approaches over Internet

	Data treatment distribution	Hardware resource allocation	Hidden execution hosts	Application sharing	Published application interface	Data sharing	Highly dynamic system	Transparent user/resource connection
Grid	×	×	×					
WS		×	×	×	×			
P2P					×	×	×	
OAN	×	×	×	×	×	×	×	×

individual use, OpenAdap.net is open to exploitation by networked organisations and alliances, by providing an infrastructure with which they can share and integrate resources and develop new business solutions and opportunities.

It is important to emphasize that users' privacy is as important as contributors traceability. The information sent by an end-user for manipulation by a contributors resource is anonymized, despite the fact that all the transactions are identified and that the activity is tracked like in any computer system. In contrast, meta-information concerning the contributed resource like program authorship and version number should be made available to the end-user, as a mark of diligence to the contributor, but also to point the responsibilities in the information processing chain and enhance quality assessment and reproducibility. Each task submitted to the system is returned to the submitter with a record attesting where the information travelled, which processes were applied and who was responsible for the computers and the programs.

Contributors will keep complete control over their authorship as well as the source and binary codes for the software. At the same time, they will be responsible for maintaining and checking the quality of the results that the community will use and validate.

3.2 Demonstrator Testbed

In the last few years, we have been developing, running and testing a prototype for OpenAdap.net. The concept proof was checked in a preliminary study aimed at the analysis of multivariate time series corresponding to spike trains, i.e. time series of neuronal discharges [Villa et al., 2001]. In 2006, the middleware was re-implemented from scratch (Figure 2) based on the experience and remarks we have acquired along the prototyping phase [Villa et al., 2006]. Several applications related to the preliminary study have raised interest in the Neural Coding community and are in production via the website http : //www.neuralcoding.org. This community is composed by academicians, students and researchers who investigate the neural coding schemes within the brain.

OpenAdap.net being an Open Source project released under the GPL and LGPL licences, contributions are welcomed from developers and interested professionals. This is encouraged by the availability of publicly accessible development tools like a version control system, mailing lists and a bug tracker. There is enough experience on the impact of such coordinated and distributed development scheme on the quality of the resulting software to embrace it.

During the prototyping phase, the need appeared to have a portable and user-friendly tool that could provide a fast glimpse on the numerical output of unrelated programs. We searched for a generic front-end for plotting a wide range of graphics obtained through the web, and none could be found that was able to run on multiple platforms without requiring complicated installation procedures, and capable of producing journal-quality graphics output for free. XY-Viewer is a Java application that is being developed for that purpose as a by-product of the main project, featuring a dedicated XML data format. This standalone application can be launched directly from the OpenAdap.net portal to visualize files in the appropriate format that can be produced with the help of libraries made available to interested contributors in C and Java under the LGPL licence.

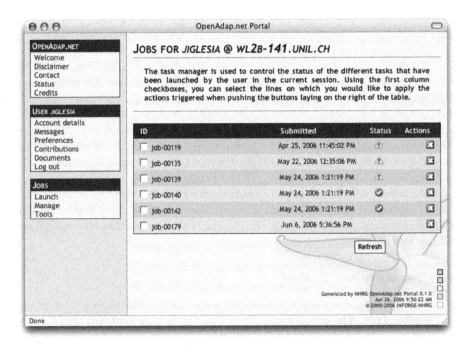

Fig. 2. Screenshot of the OpenAdap.net web portal using Mozilla Firefox on Apple MacOS X (as of October 2006 - beta version)

4   Inter-Broker Connection Dynamics

We consider that brokers handling the same data formats belong to the same network of community-related applications. A key element consists in making brokers adaptive and dynamically interconnected into an OpenAdap.net network (like a neuronal network) [Iglesias et al., 2005]. These brokers form a dynamic network of inter-brokers connections characterized by a connection strength. Internally, brokers are responsible for decomposing and routing end-user tasks to

appropriate workers for execution. The requests for resources will be processed
and dispatched among the components of the system following a set of learning
rules dynamically modifying the routing according to, for example, the computing load generated by specific tasks, availability of the resources, or the number
of accesses. We introduce a particular feature based on a critical window for
modification of the strength of inter-brokers connections incorporating a simple
event timing driven model.

Let us assume that any connection between brokers j and i is characterized
by a characteristic value of its strength w_{ij} that may depend only on the type
of interconnected brokers. A state variable X is introduced to model the modification rule governing the strength of the connection. It is assumed *a priori* that
X has N equilibrium configurations (attractor states) $X_1 < X_2 < \cdots < X_N$
to which it will decay with time constant $1/\tau$ in the absence of any requests
received by brokers j and i. It appears that $X(t)$ is governed by the family of
equations

$$\tau \frac{dX}{dt} = -(X - X_k), \qquad B_{k-1} < X \leq B_k, \quad k = 1, \cdots N \qquad (1)$$

in which $-\infty = B_0 < B_1 < B_2 < \cdots < B_{N-1} < B_N = \infty$ are user-defined
boundaries of attraction satisfying $B_{k-1} < X_k < B_k$ for $k = 1, \cdots, N$. For
example one can set $B_k = (X_k + X_{k+1})/2$. At any time t, the connection strength
w_{ij} is determined by the state to which X is attracted.

An event timing driven rule defines how the current value of X is changed
by the arrival of requests to broker i, by the arrival of requests to broker j
and, in particular, through the correlation existing between these events. On
the generation of requests on broker i, the state X is *incremented* which is a
decreasing function of the elapsed time from the previous requests received by
the interconnected brokers. The rule used here is

$$\left[X\right] = X_{i-j}\, e^{-\delta t/\tau_{i-j}} \qquad (2)$$

where $[X]$ indicates the jump in X, X_{i-j} is the magnitude of the jump in X occurring when broker i receives a request after broker j received the same request,
δt is the interval between the last requests received by the two interconnected
brokers, and τ_{i-j} is the decay constant of the reinforcement of the link.

Similarly, when the order of the requests received by the brokers is reversed
in time, the state X is *decremented* which is likewise a decreasing function of
the elapsed time of the last requests received by the two interconnected brokers.
The rule used in this case is

$$\left[X\right] = -X_{j-i}\, e^{-\delta t/\tau_{j-i}} \qquad (3)$$

where τ_{j-i} is the decay constant of the weakening of the link. In the example
illustrated by Fig 3 all connections are initially set at level $[X_3]$. This figure
illustrates also the fact that after a jump of $[X]$ occurred at time t, the real-
valued variable B_{ij} is reset to $B_{ij} = (X_k + X_{k+1})/2$.

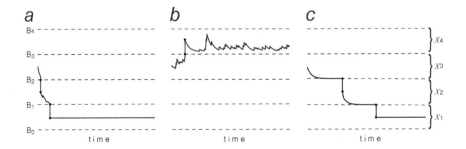

Fig. 3. Dynamic change of inter-brokers connectivity strength. *(a):* fast weakening of inter-btokers connections down to its minimal level; *(b):* reinforcement of inter-brokers connection with an increase in strength that is stabilized on the long term; *(c):* example of a link that is neither strengthened nor weakened, but whose strength decays down to its minimal level $[X_1] = 0$ according to the time constant τ.

The rules themselves will evolve and optimize in an unsupervised manner, thus allowing the emergence of unexpected dynamics. In that sense, the required negotiation between brokers (and workers) may be compared to agent interaction. The OpenAdap.net network will also be able to self-adapt via learning processes derived from neural and artificial life learning. Such learning might result in new broker-broker connections, reassessments of the value of such connections, specialisation or generalisation of broker behaviour, etc.

5   Discussion

This paper has presented the main features of OpenAdap.net, which is an intelligent network infrastructure supporting the use of shared resources, such as data, knowledge, tools, expertise, etc. aimed at providing the latest published versions by the original authors and developers to a broad audience over Internet. OpenAdap.net is an Open Source project designed as an open architecture. Anyone is invited to contribute their own enhancements to the system, via a set of libraries and tools provided by the consortium. Such an initiative is aimed at increasing the impact of the project with all the contributions that competent contributors will imagine and realize within their specific domains.

Individual users can be classified as either contributors of shared resources, or end-users of such resources. End-users are provided with the ability to browse and apply shared resources, and dynamically compose and integrate existing resources to leverage new research insights. From the viewpoint of contributors, OpenAdap.net makes possible the dissemination of resources, and their exposure to application and evaluation by a broader user community. The support for broader evaluation of programs and data sets is particularly important in the research arena, as is the ability of other researchers to reproduce computational results [Villa et al., 2006].

The ability to tackle a scientific problem from a new perspective relies on both the past experience and new skills adopted by an individual. This is the feature of the *trial-and-error* paradigm and characterizes the 'procedural' approach (to know 'how') vs. the 'declarative' approach (to know 'what'). The OpenAdap.net project is based on the collaboration between information scientists, electronic engineers, computer scientists and neuroscientists having diverse scientific interests and very specialized backgrounds. We feel that such a transdisciplinary approach is a necessary way for the achievement of real advances in producing impacts in the Information Society Technologies. A key point for the success of OpenAdap.net dissemination is the build-up of Communities who share common data formats tailored to their interest. In the prototype that we implemented the multivariate time series format is well known and accepted by leading institutions and researchers in the field.

The adaptive and behavioural models for the broker implementation represent major innovations of the OpenAdap.net project. This is definitely a novelty and a plus to the existing architectures for distributed environments like grids and web services that points out the project expected income to the networked computing field. Pushing existing paradigms like neuronal network inspired learning rules for the adaptable information processing or the operating system paradigm for the overall communication layout, and the lessons learned for 10 years on the self, dynamically, openly organized content on the web are key aspects of the OpenAdap.net philosophy and architecture for resource sharing.

When completed, the OpenAdap.net project network will be able to self-adapt via learning processes that could give rise to modifiable broker-broker connections, specialisation or generalisation of broker behaviour, etc. Thus, the nonlinear dynamics that will emerge from our approach makes OpenAdap.net closer to the complexity of a living organism and the socialware will benefit of the full range of advances achieved in the fast-growing fields of cognitive computation and computational intelligence.

References

[Eisenhauser et al., 2006] Eisenhauser, G., Bustamante, F.E., Schwan, K.: Publish-subscribe for high-performance computing. IEEE Internet computing, 10(1), 407 (2006)

[Hattori et al., 1999] Hattori, F., Ohguro, T., Yokoo, M., Matsubara, S., Yoshida, S.: Socialware: Multiagent systems for supporting network communities. Comm. ACM 42(3), 55–61 (1999)

[Iglesias et al., 2005] Iglesias, J., Eriksson, J.L., Pardo, B., Tomassini, M., Villa, A.E.P.: Emergence of oriented cell assemblies associated with spike-timing-dependent plasticity. In: Duch, W., Kacprzyk, J., Oja, E., Zadrożny, S. (eds.) ICANN 2005. LNCS, vol. 3696, pp. 127–132. Springer, Heidelberg (2005)

[Laufer, 2005] Laufer, K.: A hike through post-ejb j2ee web application architecture. Computing in Science and Engineering, 7(5), 808 (2005)

[Villa et al., 2006] Villa, A.E.P., Iglesias, J., Ghernaouti-Helie, S.: openadap.net: A collaborative sharing environment. In: Exploiting the Knowledge Economy: Issues, Applications, Case Studies, pp. 753–760. IOS Press, Amsterdam (2006)

[Villa et al., 2001] Villa, A.E.P., Tetko, I.V., Iglesias, J.: Computer assisted neurophysiological analysis of cell assemblies. Neurocomputing 38-40, 1025–1030 (2001)

[Zhang et al., 2005] Zhang, X., Chen, S., Sandhu, R.: Enhancing data authenticity and integrity in p2p systems. IEEE Internet computing 9(6), 429 (2005)

Binary Neuro-Fuzzy Classifiers Trained by Nonlinear Quantum Circuits

Massimo Panella and Giuseppe Martinelli

INFO-COM Dpt., University of Rome "La Sapienza"
Via Eudossiana 18, 00184 Rome, Italy
panella@infocom.uniroma1.it

Abstract. The possibility of solving an optimization problem by an exhaustive search on all the possible solutions can advantageously replace traditional algorithms for learning neuro-fuzzy networks. For this purpose, the architecture of such networks should be tailored to the requirements of quantum processing. In particular, it is necessary to introduce superposition for pursuing parallelism and entanglement. In the present paper the specific case of neuro-fuzzy networks applied to binary classification is investigated. The peculiarity of the proposed method is the use of a nonlinear quantum algorithm for extracting the optimal neuro-fuzzy network. The computational complexity of the training process is considerably reduced with respect to the use of other classical approaches.

1 Introduction

Quantum processing allows the solution of an optimization problem through the exhaustive search undertaken on all the possible solutions of the problem itself. The reason for this possibility is the existence of two relevant properties of quantum processing: *parallelism* and *entanglement*. Because of the first property, it is simple to take into account simultaneously in every problem the several alternatives to be explored, included the best one. The second property allows the association to each solution of its performance, on the basis of which the best choice is undertaken.

For this reason, several applications of quantum processing are available in the technical literature [1]; many of them regard training or implementation of neural networks. Recently, it was suggested to extend the research to the entire field of computational intelligence [2]. In the present paper we will focus our attention to Neuro-Fuzzy Networks (NFN), which differ from neural networks because of their structure based on fuzzy rules instead of neurons. Using the flexibility of fuzzy logic and fuzzy inference systems, NFNs are particularly suited to solve many real-world problems, such as robust control, problem inversion, estimation, classification, and so on [3,4,5,6,7]. We will describe in Sect.2 a particular architecture of NFN tailored to hardware implementation and to the nature of quantum processing.

The use of quantum computing to train such NFNs will be introduced in Sect.3, in the case of general classification problems defined by a set of examples. The underlying idea is to represent any NFN architecture by a quantum

F. Masulli, S. Mitra, and G. Pasi (Eds.): WILF 2007, LNAI 4578, pp. 237–244, 2007.

state entangled with an appropriate label describing its performance. We will demonstrate in Sect.4 that, using parallelism, the optimal NFN will be efficiently extracted from a superposition of states, by means of quantum search algorithms based on nonlinear quantum gates. Finally, our conclusions will be drawn in Sect.5.

2 Binary Neuro-Fuzzy Networks

Nowadays, the diffusion of NFNs for industrial and consumer applications is still constrained to their efficient, reliable and cost-effective implementations, which are commonly based on digital computing hardware. A particular subclass of NFN particularly suited to such implementations is represented by Binary Neuro-Fuzzy Networks (BNFN), in which the variables assume only integer values (coded by binary digits). Nevertheless, we will see in this paper that BNFNs can also exploit the peculiarities of quantum processing.

Although the proposed approach can be generalized to any problem, as the ones previously mentioned, in the following we will consider BNFNs for classification. In this case a BNFN is constituted by a set of R rules, where the k-th rule, $k = 1 \dots R$, has the following form:

$$\text{if } x_1 \text{ is } A_{k1} \text{ and } x_2 \text{ is } A_{k2} \text{ and} \dots x_N \text{ is } A_{kN} \text{ then class is } C_k. \qquad (1)$$

Each input variable x_j, $j = 1 \dots N$, assumes integer values only and it is represented by $B_j^{(\text{in})}$ bits. Each input fuzzy quantity A_{kj} is associated with a Membership Function (MF) $\mu_{kj}(\cdot)$ centered around an integer value $\bar{a}_{kj}$, which is coded by $B_j^{(\text{in})}$ bits as well[1]. We outline that the values of $\mu_{kj}(\cdot)$ must be defined only in correspondence of the normalized differences between the integer numbers representing x_j and $\bar{a}_{kj}$. Let $\mathcal{L} = \{L_1, L_2, \dots, L_W\}$ be the set of labels representing the W different classes involved in the problem to be solved. The output quantity C_k is one of these class labels, i.e. $C_k \in \mathcal{L}$. Thus, the rule output can assume only fuzzy quantities associated with singleton MFs, each related to a different class. Evidently, the overall number of bits necessary to code each class label, and hence each rule output, is $B^{(\text{out})} = \lceil \log_2 W \rceil$. In conclusion, the BNFN can be univocally represented by a string of $B^{(\text{net})}$ bits, where

$$B^{(\text{net})} = R\left(B^{(\text{in})} + B^{(\text{out})}\right), \qquad B^{(\text{in})} = \sum_{j=1}^{N} B_j^{(\text{in})}. \qquad (2)$$

When a pattern $\underline{x}_o = [x_{o1} \, x_{o2} \dots x_{oN}]$ is presented to the BNFN, a fuzzy inference mechanism is invoked in order to assign the pattern a specific class label. Several options are possible for the fuzzy reasoning (i.e., T-norms, T-conorms, compositions, implications, etc.); we will consider the commonly adopted choices,

---

[1] We are considering a fixed shape for MFs; the generalization to any kind of MF is easily achieved by adding further bits associated with other shape parameters.

which determine the class label $C(\underline{x}_o)$ of $\underline{x}_o$, $C(\underline{x}_o) \in \mathcal{L}$, using one among the rule outputs:

$$C(\underline{x}_o) = C_q, \quad q = \arg\max_{k=1...R}\{\gamma_k\}, \tag{3}$$

where γ_k is the *reliability degree* of the k-th rule depending on the chosen T-norm (e.g. 'min', 'product', etc.):

$$\gamma_k = \bigwedge_{j=1}^{N} \mu_{kj}(x_{oj}). \tag{4}$$

3   Training BNFNs Using Quantum Computing

To train a BNFN means to determine the number R of its rules, the centroid $\bar{a}_{kj}$ of each MF and the output class label C_k of each rule. The right number of rules is essential in order to obtain a good generalization capability of the BNFN. The optimization of R can be carried out using well-known constructive or pruning methods, starting from a small/large number of rules up/down to the optimal number guided, for example, by early-stopping, cross-validation or any other procedure based on learning theory [8]. In the following we will focus on the basic step of the entire learning procedure, i.e. the training for a fixed number of rules.

The data-driven procedure to train a BNFN is based on a Training Set (TS) of numerical examples of the process to be modeled. The TS is based on a collection of P patterns $\xi_i = (\underline{x}_i, T_i)$, $i = 1 \ldots P$, where $\underline{x}_i$ is the joint vector of the input variables and $T_i \in \mathcal{L}$ is the class label of the pattern. Thus, each sample ξ_i can be coded as a string of $\left(B^{(\text{in})} + B^{(\text{out})}\right)$ bits. Based on the TS, the determination of a BNFN for a fixed R is equivalent to find the string of $B^{(\text{net})}$ bits representing the whole set of network parameters. Several approaches can be followed in this regard: a first family comes from the adaptation to binary integer programming of classical derivative-based methods (such as clustering and back-propagation); conversely, the family of direct search methods (such as genetic or swarm-based algorithms) can be directly applied to BNFN training.

For both the previous categories the computational complexity is strictly linked to the number of different BNFNs whose performance is evaluated on the TS. Since no assumptions are usually made about the structure of the search problem, a $O(M)$ complexity is mandatory to find an optimal BNFN, being $M = 2^{B^{(\text{net})}}$ the total number of possible solutions. The more complexity is reduced, the more increased the probability to find a suboptimal (and unsatisfactory) solution. Unfortunately, the value of M can be very large even for very simple architectures; for instance, a BNFN with four rules, three 8-bit antecedents and two classes has $M = 2^{4 \cdot (8+8+8+1)} \cong 10^{30}$ possible solutions!

For all the previous reasons, we propose in this paper the use of quantum computing in order to improve and speedup the training process of BNFNs. As shown in the following, quantum processing and *quantum circuits* (i.e., the physical systems by which the relevant quantum information is processed) allow the exhaustive search of all the solutions in a time drastically reduced with respect to the previous approaches. It is important to remark that exhaustive search yields the best BNFN given R and TS. Consequently, the accuracy in solving the classification problem will depend only on the number of bits used to quantize the input variables, on how the TS represents well the underlying problem and on the global optimization of the number of rules. Such problems can be investigated separately in future research works.

The aim of the proposed approach is to train a BNFN, whose parameters are represented by B bits[2], by searching the optimal one in the set of M possible solutions. Quantum computing is particularly suited to solve this kind of search problems and, from what discussed so far, it can be readily applied to BNFN training. In fact, the bit string $\underline{\psi}_h = b_{h,B-1} \cdots b_{h,1} b_{h,0}$ representing the integer h and thus the h-th BNFN, $h = 0 \ldots M - 1$, can be associated with the h-th basis vector $\left| \underline{\psi}_h \right\rangle$ of a B-qubit quantum system [9]. For example, if $B = 3$ the seventh basis vector is $\left| \underline{\psi}_6 \right\rangle = \left| 110 \right\rangle$ and hence $\underline{\psi}_6 = b_{6,2} \, b_{6,1} \, b_{6,0} = 110$.

The use of quantum computing in this context has been deeply investigated in the literature: we have to solve an unstructured search problem that can be reformulated as 'find some $\underline{\psi}$ in a set of possible solutions such that a statement $S(\underline{\psi})$ is true (i.e., the related BNFN is optimal since it satisfies the TS above a given accuracy)'. The latter condition can be represented by a classically computable boolean function $f(\cdot)$ with B input bits and one output bit. The truth table of $f(\cdot)$ has M entries: each of them associates with the input $\underline{\psi}_h$ the output bit $\delta_h = f(\underline{\psi}_h)$, corresponding to the value of the statement $S(\underline{\psi}_h)$ for that BNFN. The truth table depends on the TS in use; it can be obtained using the following steps:

1. consider the BNFN defined by the generic entry $\underline{\psi}_h$;
2. for each pattern ξ_i of the TS apply the fuzzy reasoning of BNFNs, as for example the one defined by (3) and (4), and evaluate if the resulting class label $C(\underline{x}_i)$ matches the class T_i of the training pattern;
3. evaluate the overall classification error (i.e., the percentage of patterns not correctly assigned) and set $\delta_h = 1$ if this error is lower than a given threshold or $\delta_h = 0$ otherwise.

As illustrated in [10], it is always possible to design linear quantum gates that map any boolean function into the quantum field. It is not necessary to know a priori the boolean mapping. The gate is just a quantum physical system realizing the same operation for every truth table's input, in order to determine the corresponding output as specified, for example, by previous steps 2 and 3.

Once the boolean function $f(\cdot)$ has been defined into the quantum field, it can be implemented by the linear gate U_f represented in Fig. 1: when inputs are qubit basis vectors $\left| \underline{\psi}_h \right\rangle$ instead of classical bit strings, the output will be a qubit $\left| \delta_h \right\rangle = \left| f(\underline{\psi}_h) \right\rangle$ entangled to $\left| \underline{\psi}_h \right\rangle$. In other words, there exists a $(B+1)$-qubit basis vector $\left| \underline{\omega}_h \right\rangle = \left| \underline{\psi}_h, \delta_h \right\rangle$, whose amplitude probability is directly related to

---

[2] In the following we will use for simplicity the symbol B in place of $B^{(\text{net})}$.

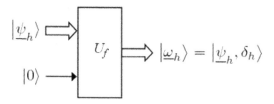

Fig. 1. Linear quantum gate used to solve quantum search problems. Wide arrows indicate entangled qubits in strings $|\underline{\psi}_h\rangle$ and $|\underline{\omega}_h\rangle$.

that of $|\underline{\psi}_h\rangle$. The further qubit present at the input, which is always set to $|0\rangle$, allows representing U_f by a unitary matrix of order $(B+1)$ for any function $f(\cdot)$ [9].

The definition of U_f is the basic step, which any quantum search problem is based on. In fact, measuring the output $|\delta_h\rangle$ for a particular input $|\underline{\psi}_h\rangle$ is equivalent to evaluate the BNFN performance on the TS and hence, if it is a solution of the problem or not. A fundamental result of quantum computing is that, using U_f and suitable linear quantum gates, the lower bound for the number of evaluations necessary to find a solution can be reduced to $O(\sqrt{M})$ [11]. However, the implementation of such algorithms on a quantum hardware may still require a huge computational time even for very simple BNFN architectures. Considering the previous example, where $M \cong 10^{30}$, the overall complexity would be reduced to about 10^{15} possible evaluations. Thus, linear quantum gates only are not sufficient to make feasible the exhaustive BNFN training.

4   Exhaustive Search by Nonlinear Quantum Circuits

The complexity of search problems is heavily reduced with respect to classical quantum algorithms when nonlinear quantum circuits are used. This result follows from the discussion reported in [12] regarding the implication of a nonlinear regime in quantum processing. Moreover, specific nonlinear quantum gates have been proposed in this regard as, for example, reported in [13]. We will introduce firstly some basic notations and processing elements.

Let us consider the B-qubit system generated by the basis vectors $\underline{\psi}_h$ and the generic subspace of dimension 2^{B-Q}, which is generated by the set of basis vectors $|\underline{\psi}_{\overline{k},t}\rangle$, $0 \leq \overline{k} \leq 2^Q - 1$, $t = 0 \ldots 2^{(B-Q)} - 1$, in which the first Q qubits are identical and associated with the fixed integer $\overline{k}$. This means that the bit substring $b_{h,B-1} \cdots b_{h,B-Q}$ of $\underline{\psi}_h$ is the binary representation of $\overline{k}$. An example for this notation is summarized in Table 1.

Using the previous notations, the algorithm proposed in this paper is founded on a basic iteration, which is implemented by the quantum circuit in Fig. 2, along with a suitable initialization.

Table 1. Basis vectors for subspaces generated when $B = 4$ and $Q = 2$

| 1st subsp. ($\overline{k} = 0$) | 2nd subsp. ($\overline{k} = 1$) | 3rd subsp. ($\overline{k} = 2$) | 4th subsp. ($\overline{k} = 3$) |
$b_{h,3}\, b_{h,2} = 00$	$b_{h,3}\, b_{h,2} = 01$	$b_{h,3}\, b_{h,2} = 10$	$b_{h,3}\, b_{h,2} = 11$
$\lvert\psi_{0,0}\rangle = \lvert 0000\rangle$	$\lvert\psi_{1,0}\rangle = \lvert 0100\rangle$	$\lvert\psi_{2,0}\rangle = \lvert 1000\rangle$	$\lvert\psi_{3,0}\rangle = \lvert 1100\rangle$
$\lvert\psi_{0,1}\rangle = \lvert 0001\rangle$	$\lvert\psi_{1,1}\rangle = \lvert 0101\rangle$	$\lvert\psi_{2,1}\rangle = \lvert 1001\rangle$	$\lvert\psi_{3,1}\rangle = \lvert 1101\rangle$
$\lvert\psi_{0,2}\rangle = \lvert 0010\rangle$	$\lvert\psi_{1,2}\rangle = \lvert 0110\rangle$	$\lvert\psi_{2,2}\rangle = \lvert 1010\rangle$	$\lvert\psi_{3,2}\rangle = \lvert 1110\rangle$
$\lvert\psi_{0,3}\rangle = \lvert 0011\rangle$	$\lvert\psi_{1,3}\rangle = \lvert 0111\rangle$	$\lvert\psi_{2,3}\rangle = \lvert 1011\rangle$	$\lvert\psi_{3,3}\rangle = \lvert 1111\rangle$

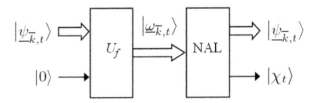

Fig. 2. Quantum circuit implementing the generic iteration of the proposed algorithm. Qubits $\lvert\psi_{\overline{k},t}\rangle$ and $\lvert\chi_t\rangle$ are disentangled at the output of NAL quantum gate.

- **Initialization.** Set $Q = 1$ and $\overline{k} = 0$ (i.e., $b_{h,B-1} = 0$ for each basis vector), and start the algorithm with the first iteration.

- **Iteration.** Considering the current values for Q and $\overline{k}$, and using the procedure illustrated in [9], all the basis vectors $\lvert\psi_{\overline{k},t}\rangle$ are inserted into a superposition $\lvert\Psi\rangle$ of states having a same probability $1/M_Q$, where $M_Q = 2^{B-Q}$:

$$\lvert\Psi\rangle = \frac{1}{\sqrt{M_Q}} \sum_{t=1}^{M_Q} \lvert\psi_{\overline{k},t}\rangle. \tag{5}$$

The qubit string $\lvert\Psi\rangle$ is applied to the input of gate U_f in Fig. 2, obtaining the superposition $\lvert\Omega\rangle$ of the basis vectors $\lvert\omega_{\overline{k},t}\rangle = \lvert\psi_{\overline{k},t}, \delta_t\rangle$:

$$\lvert\Omega\rangle = \frac{1}{\sqrt{M_Q}} \sum_{t=1}^{M_Q} \lvert\omega_{\overline{k},t}\rangle = \frac{1}{\sqrt{M_Q}} \sum_{\substack{t=1 \\ t\notin\mathcal{O}}}^{M_Q} \lvert\psi_{\overline{k},t}, 0\rangle + \frac{1}{\sqrt{M_Q}} \sum_{t\in\mathcal{O}} \lvert\psi_{\overline{k},t}, 1\rangle, \tag{6}$$

where $\mathcal{O}$ is the set of indexes for which the BNFN is optimal.

Once the superposition $\lvert\Omega\rangle$ has been generated, it can be processed by the nonlinear gate associated with the algorithm proposed in [12]. Such a gate, denoted as Nonlinear Abrams & Lloyd (NAL), is able to return a superposition in which the last qubit $\lvert\chi_t\rangle$ is disentangled from $\lvert\psi_{\overline{k},t}\rangle$. More precisely, $\lvert\chi_t\rangle = \lvert 1\rangle$ for every element of the superposition if there exists at least one element $\left|\omega_{\overline{k},t}\right\rangle$ of $\left|\Omega\right\rangle$ for which $\left|\delta_t\right\rangle$ is $\left|1\right\rangle$, that is if at least one $\left|\psi_{\overline{k},t}\right\rangle$ represents an optimal BNFN. Otherwise $\left|\chi_t\right\rangle = \left|0\right\rangle$ for every element of the superposition.

The qubit $\left|\chi_t\right\rangle$ can be measured at the output of the NAL gate; based on this result, the final value of bit $b_{h,B-Q}$ in $\overline{k}$ can be determined by distinguishing the following situations:

- $\left|\chi_t\right\rangle = \left|1\right\rangle$. There exist some solutions having $b_{h,B-Q} = 0$.

- $\left|\chi_t\right\rangle = \left|0\right\rangle$. In this case there exist no solutions of the search problem having the bit $b_{h,B-Q} = 0$ and hence, it is switched to $b_{h,B-Q} = 1$. A further distinction is necessary:

  * $Q = 1$. The previous procedure is applied with $b_{h,B-1} = 1$ (i.e. $\overline{k} = 1$). If also in this case $\left|\chi_t\right\rangle = \left|0\right\rangle$, then the problem admits no solutions and hence no BNFNs satisfy the TS for the given accuracy. In this case the algorithm is stopped and we should consider if the threshold used for generating the boolean mapping $f(\cdot)$ has been set too low and it may be increased. Conversely, if $\left|\chi_t\right\rangle = \left|1\right\rangle$, then there exist some solutions of the search problem with $b_{h,B-1} = 1$.

  * $Q > 1$. Since the algorithm has not been stopped when $Q = 1$, then we are sure that some solutions there exist in which $b_{h,B-Q} = 1$.

At this point the final value of bit $b_{h,B-Q}$ has been determined. If $Q = B$, the algorithm is completed and the optimal solution is given by the bit string associated with the final values of bits $b_{h,B-1}, \ldots, b_{h,0}$ obtained during the previous iterations. If $Q < B$, the value of Q is increased by one and the iteration is restarted. The new value of $\overline{k}$ is obtained using the final values of bits $b_{h,B-1}, \ldots, b_{h,B-Q+1}$ previously determined and letting $b_{h,B-Q} = 0$.

Exploiting the power of NLA quantum gates, the proposed algorithm is able to find an optimal BNFN using B or $B + 1$ iterations. In fact, each iteration requires one evaluation only of the BNFN performance, i.e. one use of the U_f gate in the processing chain of Fig. 2, but for the first iteration that may need one or two evaluations. Thus, the resulting complexity for the proposed algorithm is $O(B) = O(\log_2 M)$. Considering the previous example, for which $M \cong 10^{30}$ and $B = 100$, the search problem would be completed after about 100 evaluations, therefore in much less time than required by using linear quantum gates only.

5   Conclusion

The possibility of quantum processing of solving an optimization problem by an exhaustive search on all the possible solutions can advantageously replace all the known algorithms proposed for learning from a TS. In order to pursue this possibility, it is necessary to tailor the specific architectures used for solving the problems of interest to the requirements of quantum processing. In particular, it is necessary to introduce superposition for pursuing parallelism and entanglement for associating the performance with each solution present in the superposition. In the present paper we investigate the use of quantum processing for NFNs applied to classification. Since these networks are based on the use of rules, preliminarily the rules must be tailored to quantum processing. This result is attained by using a particular type of NFN called Binary Neuro-Fuzzy Network. The superposition of quantum states is undertaken by transforming into quantum operators suitable boolean functions. This superposition contains the optimal solutions marked by a dedicated qubit. The extraction of these optimal solutions is carried out by using a specific nonlinear quantum algorithm. The resulting learning procedure can determine the optimal solution from the superposition of an exponential number of different BNFNs.

References

1. Los Alamos preprint server: available at http://xxx.lanl.gov/archive/quant-ph
2. Perkowski, M.: Multiple-valued quantum circuits and research challenges for logic design and computational intelligence communities. IEEE Connections 3, 6–12 (2005)
3. Frayman, Y., Wang, L.: Data mining using dynamically constructed recurrent fuzzy neural networks. In: Wu, X., Kotagiri, R., Korb, K.B. (eds.) PAKDD 1998. LNCS, vol. 1394, pp. 122–131. Springer, Heidelberg (1998)
4. Held, C., Heiss, J., Estevez, P., Perez, C., Garrido, M., Algarin, C., Peirano, P.: Extracting fuzzy rules from polysomnographic recordings for infant sleep classification. IEEE Trans. on Biomedical Engineering 53, 1954–1962 (2006)
5. Jang, J.S.: ANFIS: Adaptive-network-based fuzzy inference system. IEEE Trans. on Systems, Man and Cybernetics 23, 665–685 (1993)
6. Wang, L., Fu, X.: Data Mining with Computational Intelligence. Springer, Berlin (2005)
7. Wang, W., Ismail, F., Golnaraghi, F.: A neuro-fuzzy approach to gear system monitoring. IEEE Trans. on Fuzzy Systems 12, 710–723 (2004)
8. Haykin, S.: Neural Networks, a Comprehensive Foundation, 2nd edn. Prentice-Hall, Englewood Cliffs, NJ, USA (1999)
9. Rieffel, E., Polak, W.: An introduction to quantum computing for non-physicists. ACM Computing Surveys 32, 300–335 (2000)
10. Deutsch, D.: Quantum theory, the Church-Turing principle and the universal quantum compute. In: Proc. of the Royal Society of London. vol. A 400, pp. 97–117 (1985)
11. Grover, L.: A fast quantum mechanical algorithm for database search. In: Proc. of the 28th Annual ACM Symposium on the Theory of Computing, Philadelphia, Pennsylvania, USA, pp. 212–219 (1996)
12. Abrams, D., Lloyd, S.: Nonlinear quantum mechanics implies polynomial-time solution for NP-complete and #P problems. Phys. Rev. Lett. 81, 3992–3995 (1998)
13. Gupta, S., Zia, R.: Quantum neural networks. Journal of Computer and System Sciences 63, 355–383 (2001)

Digital Hardware Implementation of High Dimensional Fuzzy Systems

Pablo Echevarria, M. Victoria Martínez, Javier Echanobe,
Inés del Campo, and Jose M. Tarela

University of the Basque Country, Apartado 644. 48080 Bilbao, Spain
webecfep@ehu.es

Abstract. This paper presents an algorithm to compute high dimensional piecewise linear (PWL) functions with simplicial division of the input domain, and introduces the circuit scheme for its implementation in a FPGA. It is also investigated how to modify this algorithm and implementation to compute a class of PWL fuzzy systems.

1 Introduction

Complex systems are dynamic, nonlinear and multivariable. Therefore, dealing with such systems in a feasible manner involves some considerations. First, nonlinear dynamic systems can be separated so that nonlinearities are entirely confined to static blocks. Then, nonlinearities can be tackled by applying approximation techniques. Piecewise-linear (PWL) based methods possess interesting properties that make them broadly used in every engineering and scientific field. This leads to selecting convenient models that yet must deal with high dimensional inputs.

Fuzzy systems, are frequently used for solving or approximating nonlinear problems. Some classes of fuzzy systems present PWL characteristics derived from the type of their membership functions, and so these systems provide the required nonlinearities of the represented problem.

When using PWL techniques, simplicial partitions exhibit advantageous approximating properties. In this paper we show an efficient hardware implementation of PWL simplicial functions of high dimensionality. The proposed algorithm, design and architecture can be adapted to configure fundamental blocks of PWL fuzzy systems by incorporating only minor changes. This is the case of the systems based on the fuzzy inference mechanisms introduced by Ueno [1] and Rovatti [2].

Section 2 briefly presents the state of the art in the computation of simplicial PWL functions. In Section 3 a new algorithm to compute this class of functions is proposed. In Section 4 a hardware design of the proposed algorithm and its implementation are described. Finally, some concluding remarks are made.

F. Masulli, S. Mitra, and G. Pasi (Eds.): WILF 2007, LNAI 4578, pp. 245–252, 2007.

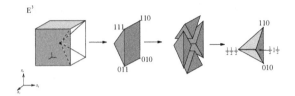

Fig. 1. Simplicial division of a PWL fuzzy system, $n=3$

2   Simplicial PWL Functions

Most of the simplicial PWL functions in PWL literature use the partition of the input domain proposed by [3]. This kind of partition divides each axis into m_i segments, where $i = 1, ...n$ and n is the dimension of the input space. For an easier computation of the PWL functions the use of a certain homeomorphism transforms the original domain, D, into another domain, C, where the segments of each axis are unitary, [3].

If we assume that all the axes are divided into the same number of unitary segments, m, the partiton of the new domain C_m consists of m^n hypercubes. Each hypercube is identified by a set of $(m+1)^n$ vertices noted as $V_m = \{\mathbf{I} \in \mathbb{Z}_+^n \mid 0 \le I_i \le m, i = 1, \ldots, n\}$. After this tessellation and transformation, each hypercube is divided into $n!$ non-overlapping simplices, each of them defined by $(n+1)$ vertices, $\{\mathbf{I}_0, ..., \mathbf{I}_n\}$. The arrangement of the vertices of V_m in a proper order guarantees that the simplices do not overlap, [3]. The values of the function on the vertices will determine the function in the rest of the domain. Therefore, as the vertices of the simplicial regions are vertices of the hypercubes, $(m+1)^n$ data must be sampled to identify the function.

In the field of fuzzy systems, the model introduced by Rovatti, [2], presents a simplicial PWL output. These fuzzy systems are defined by a set of rules *if-then* where the consequents are singletons, the membership functions are normalized, triangular and overlapped by pairs, and also by the use of the center of gravity defuzzification. In [4] was proven that, as a result of these specifications, the domain of these fuzzy systems is partitioned into hypercubes, but additionally each of them is divided into $2^{n-1}n!$ non-overlapping simplices. These simplicial regions are defined by vertices of the corresponding hypercube and by the centers of gravity of k-dimensional subcells of the hypercube $(k < n)$, [5]. Figure 1 depicts the simplicial division of a cube, i.e. the simplicial partition of a fuzzy system like the explained above with $n=3$.

In order to compute a simplicial PWL function, Julian showed that, taking in account that the set of PWL functions with simplicial partitions of their input domains is a Hilbert space, each PWL function can be expressed as a linear combination of a set of basis functions, [6]. Regarding the geometric characteristics of the simplices, and with a proper set of basis functions, in [7] it is shown that the computation of a simplicial PWL function, f, is just

$$f(\mathbf{z}) = \sum_{j=0}^{q} c_j \mu_j \qquad (1)$$

where c_j are the values of the function f on the vertices of the simplex where $\mathbf{z}$ lies, and μ_j are the barycentric coordinates of point $\mathbf{z}$ with respect to the vertices of that simplex. If point $\mathbf{z}$ lies within the simplex then $q=n$, otherwise, the point lies on an edge of the simplex and $q < n$.

In [3] an algorithm to find the simplicial region where a given input lies is presented. This algorithm is slightly modified in [7] in order to make it more suitable for a parallel implementation and a very simple mixed-signal architecture of this algorithm is proposed. This architecture presents however an important drawback when it is implemented in a fully digital platform, as it will be explained below.

3   Proposed Algorithm

In this work we propose an alternative algorithm to compute the output of a simplicial PWL function. It has been designed keeping in mind high dimensional cases and PWL fuzzy systems as those described above. It is very similar in complexity to the algorithm presented in [7]. But the computation of the proposed algorithm requires one multiplication less, and it is besides quite more intuitive. Instead of calculating the barycentric coordinates of the point, we exploit piecewise-linear characteristic of the function: inside each simplex the function is just an affine plane. Thus, once the simplicial region is found, the slopes and the independent term of the corresponding hyperplane are calculated. The algorithm and its implementation require minor changes to compute the output of a PWL fuzzy system. The steps of the method are explained below:

Step 1. First we must make the input domain transformation $(D \rightarrow C_m)$ in such way that each hypercube is unitary. Now, given an input point, $\mathbf{z}$, we define two vectors: $\lfloor \mathbf{z} \rfloor = (\lfloor z_1 \rfloor, ..., \lfloor z_n \rfloor)^T$ and $\delta\mathbf{z} = (z_1 - \lfloor z_1 \rfloor, ..., z_n - \lfloor z_n \rfloor)^T$. Vector $\lfloor \mathbf{z} \rfloor$ identifies the corresponding hypercube and coincides with $\mathbf{I}_0$. The vector $\delta\mathbf{z}$ will be used to find the simplicial region where $\mathbf{z}$ lies.

Step2. Next, we need to sort the vector $\delta\mathbf{z}$ in a decreasing order. After this sorting, we get a permutation $p : \{1, ..., n\} \rightarrow \{1, ..., n\}$ such that $\delta z_{p(1)} \geq \cdots \geq \delta z_{p(n)}$.

Step 3. Now we must calculate the vertices of the corresponding simplex. These vertices will be of the form $\mathbf{I}_i = \mathbf{I}_0 + v_i$, where each v_i is a n-dimensional binary vector. We will denote all the vectors v_i which have k 1's as $v^{(k)}$. As a result of the arrangement of the vertices of the hypercubes, vertices $\mathbf{I}_0 = \mathbf{I}_0 + v^{(0)}$ and $\mathbf{I}_0 + v^{(n)}$ will always be vertices of the corresponding simplex. In order to find the next vector, the $p(n)$-th coordinate of $v^{(n)}$ must be replaced by a '0', so we get a $v^{(n-1)}$ type vertex. Then the $p(n-1)$-th coordinate of $v^{(n-1)}$ is replaced by a '0'. This step must be repeated until the $v^{(0)}$ is reached. Table 1 shows how to get the coordinates of the $n+1$ vertices.

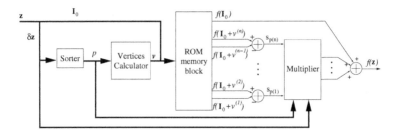

Fig. 2. Proposed circuit scheme

Step 4. As we said above, regarding the piecewise-linear characteristic of the function, inside each region of the domain the function is just an affine plane and it can be derived that:

$$f(\mathbf{z}) = f(\mathbf{I}_0 + \delta \mathbf{z}) = \sum_{i=1}^{n} s_i \delta z_i + f(\mathbf{I}_0) \tag{2}$$

where s_i are the slopes of the plane. As the hypercubes are unitary, the calculation of the n slopes is just $s_{p(i)} = f\left(v^{(i)}\right) - f\left(v^{(i-1)}\right)$ where $i=1,...,n$.

When dealing with PWL fuzzy systems we must consider not only the values of the function on the vertices of the hypercubic cells, but also the values corresponding to other points, as those resulting from the defuzzification method. For example, for systems based on the inference mechanisms of Ueno and Rovatti the centers of gravity of lower dimensional subcells must be considered. The computation algorithm for PWL fuzzy systems is very similar to that presented above, by only including a previous change of variables.

4   Circuit Scheme and Hardware Implementation

In order to implement the algorithm proposed above, we will suppose that the transformation of the input domain, $D \rightarrow C_m$, has been previously done. Figure 2 shows the top blocks of the proposed architecture.

Table 1. This table shows how to get the $n+1$ different $v^{(k)}$, $k=0,...,n$

	$\delta z_{p(1)}$	$\delta z_{p(2)}$	$\cdots$	$\delta z_{p(n-1)}$	$\delta z_{p(n)}$
$v^{(n)}$	1	1	$\cdots$	1	1
$v^{(n-1)}$	1	1	$\cdots$	1	0
$v^{(n-2)}$	1	1	$\cdots$	0	0
$\vdots$	$\vdots$	$\vdots$	$\cdots$	$\vdots$	$\vdots$
$v^{(1)}$	1	0	$\cdots$	0	0
$v^{(0)}$	0	0	$\cdots$	0	0

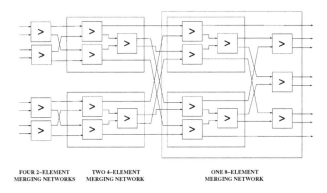

Fig. 3. Sorting network based om merging networks ($n=8$)

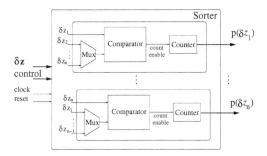

Fig. 4. Sorter scheme: each module compares one input with the others. If it is bigger increases the counter at the output.

We will set the number of segments of each axis to $m = 2^b - 1$, with $b < n$. This makes the first step very simple, due to the fact that each component will be encoded by a b-bit number. Thus, the b most significant bits of $\mathbf{z}$ will be its integer part, and if P stands for the precision in bits of the input, the $(P\text{-}b)$ less significant bits of $\mathbf{z}$ will be the decimal part.

The sorter block calculates the permutation obtained after the sorting of the decimal part, δz, of the input vector $\mathbf{z}$. For the implementation of this circuit component different schemes can be used, [8]. The fastest solution is the network based on *merging networks*. Figure 3 depicts this kind of network for an input with $n=8$. This network has a temporal complexity of $t(n) = O\left(log^2 n\right)$, therefore it is much faster than, for example, the Quicksort algorithm $(O\left(nlogn\right))$. However, the scheme of *merging networks* needs a high number of comparators $(O\left(n\,log^2 n\right))$ and this is just when the input is a power of two. Moreover we would need additional logic to compute the required permutation.

As an alternative we propose the *modular sorting network* depicted in figure 4. It is built using n modules, which allow an easy implementation for any dimension n of the input vector. Each module compares one of the coordinates with all the others and when it is bigger, it increases the counter at the output.

Table 2. This table shows the clock cycles and operations needed for the different architectures of a simplicial PWL function

Architectures based on:	Clock cycles	Operations
Current ramp	2^{P-n}	1 counter n comparisons n 1-bit additions 1 memory block 1 acummulator
Merging network	$O\left(log^2 n\right)$	$O\left(nlog^2 n\right)$ comparators n n-bit subtractions 1 memory block n multiplications 1 n-term subtraction
Modular sorting network	$n+5$	n comparators n n-bit subtractions 1 memory block n multiplications 1 n-term subtraction

Once the permutation is found the calculation of the vertices $v^{(k)}$ is made by a parallel combinational circuit. These vertices together with $\mathbf{I_0}$ define the simplex of the input, and they are used to address a memory block, which stores the value of the function in all the $(m+1)^n$ vertices of the input domain. Then the corresponding outputs of the memory are used to compute the slopes of the PWL function. Finally, the slopes are multiplied by the inputs and the results and the independent term are added in parallel. The whole circuit is controlled by a finite state machine.

The hardware requirements of this scheme are n comparators, one memory block, n subtracters, n multipliers and one n-input adder. The time required to complete the calculation is $n+5$ clock cycles.

Regarding the algorithm presented by Julian, the architecture proposed in [7] is based on a *current ramp*, a set of comparators, a memory block and an integrator. The comparison is carried out by comparing each input with the value of the ramp in each instant. This method has an important drawback when it is implemented in a fully digital circuit: a digital ramp (just a counter) needs to sweep all the possible values of the input. This means many clock cycles to make the calculation of the output. For example, if the inputs of the function f are 8-bit precision data, the digital ramp would need $2^8 = 256$ clock cycles to sweep all the possible values of the input. Moreover, this algorithm is not valid when dealing with PWL fuzzy systems. On the other hand it is a simpler architecture in terms of complexity. Table 2 shows the clock cycles an the operations of different architectures regarding their sorting methods.

The use of VHDL code, as well as the modularity of the proposed circuit, allow a simple modification of several important parameters by only changing a few lines of code. These parameters are the precision (P), the dimension of the

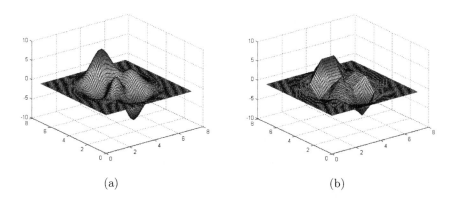

$$(a) \qquad\qquad\qquad (b)$$

Fig. 5. (a) Matlab peaks function and (b) circuit's PWL output

input (n) and the number of segments of the division of each input axis. The use of VHDL code also allows to program the ROM block from a text file, making possible the generation of the programming files from computing environments like Matlab.

As an example we have implemented a two-dimensional 8-bit precission input, (P=8). Each axis of the domain has been divided into $m = 7$ segments, so the b=3 most significative bits of the input are used to codify the corresponding segment. The ROM memory block is programmed with data extracted from the *peaks* function of Matlab. Figure 5 depicts the Matlab peaks function and the corresponding simplicial PWL output of the circuit. The implementation platform is a Virtex II Pro, FPGA of Xilinx. This FPGA offers several resources such as embedded multipliers and memory blocks. The use of these resources makes possible an operation frequency of 140 MHz. The current controller is designed to activate each module of the architecture sequentially, but if we slightly modify the state machine, it would be possible a pipeline mode and the circuit could achieve a sampling rate of 70 MHz. Moreover, this FPGA integrates on-chip PowerPCs so this proposed PWL architecture can be used as a co-processor block communicated with the PowerPC by the On-chip Peripheral Bus.

The modification of this implementation to compute PWL fuzzy system as those referred in this work would require the addition of a combinatorial block to make the change of variables and some other minor changes in the *vertices calculator*. It would also be necessary the use of the output of the fuzzy system at the centers of gravity of each subcell. There are two possibilities regarding this aspect. The first one consists in storing in the ROM memory the centers of gravity previously calculated off-line. This solution needs $(2m + 1)^n$ data words to be stored into the memory block, which is a considerable amount of memory but it wouldn't increase the clock cycles of the computation. The other possibility consists in including the design of extra blocks to calculate the centers of gravity. In this case the addition of n adders (each of them with different number of inputs) and at least one more clock cycle are required. In the selection of one of the possibilities a trade-off between speed and area occupation arises, depending on the application in which it will be used.

5   Conclusions

An algorithm has been presented for the computation of PWL simplicial functions of high dimensionality. A hardware design and architecture has been proposed based on that algorithm. The procedure and the implementation are more efficient than other remarkable methods found in the literature, and they can be adapted to be used in PWL fuzzy systems.

This work was financed by the University of the Basque Country by the projects UPV224.310-E-15871/2004 and EHU06/106 and by the Basque Country Government by the project SA-2006/00015.

References

1. Sasaki, M., Ueno, F.: A novel implementation of fuzzy logic controller using new meet operation. In: 3 IEEE Int. Conf. Fuzzy Sys., Orlando, FL, pp.1676-1681 (June 1993)
2. Rovatti, R.: Fuzzy multilinear and piecewise linear systems as universal approximators in Sobolev norms. IEEE Trans. on Fuzzy Systems 6, 235–249 (1998)
3. Chien, M.J, Kuh, E.S.: Solving Nonlinear Resistive Networks Using Piecewise-Linear Analysis and Simplicial Subdivision, IEEE Transactions on Circuits and Systems, Cas-24(6) (June 1977)
4. Echanobe, J., del Campo, I., Tarela, J.M.: Issues concerning the analysis and implementation of a class of fuzzy controllers Fuzzy Sets and Sys., 2, 252-271 (2005)
5. Echevarriai, P., Martinez, M.V., Echanobe, J., del Campo, I., Tarela, J.M.: Design and Hw/Sw Implementation of a Class of Piecewise-Linear Fuzzy System, Seminario de automatica y electrica industrial, Santander (SAAEI 2005), 2005
6. Julian, P., Desages, A., Agamennoni, O.: High-level canonical piecewise linear representation using a simplicial partition. IEEE Transactions on Circuits and Systems-I 46, 463–480 (1999)
7. Parodi, M., Storace, M., Julian, P.: Synthesis of multiport resistors with piecewise-linear characteristics: a mixed-signal architecture. International Journal of Circuit Theory and Applications
8. Akl, S.G.: The design and analysis of parallel algorithms. Prentice-Hall, Englewood Cliffs (1989)

Optimization of Hybrid Electric Cars by Neuro-Fuzzy Networks

Fabio Massimo Frattale Mascioli[1], Antonello Rizzi[1],
Massimo Panella[1], and Claudia Bettiol[2]

[1] INFO-COM Dpt., University of Rome "La Sapienza"
Via Eudossiana 18, 00184 Rome, Italy
mascioli@infocom.uniroma1.it
[2] University of Rome "Tor Vergata",
Via della Ricerca Scientifica 1, 00133 Rome, Italy
bettiol@ing.uniroma2.it

Abstract. In this paper, the problem of the optimization of energetic flows in hybrid electric vehicles is faced. We consider a hybrid electric vehicle equipped with batteries, a thermal engine (or fuel cells), ultracapacitors and an electric engine. The energetic flows are optimized by using a control strategy based on the prediction of short-term and medium-term vehicle states (energy consumption, vehicle load, current route, traffic flow, etc.). The prediction will be performed by a neuro-fuzzy control unit, where the predictive model exploits the robustness of fuzzy logic in managing the said uncertainties and the neural approach as a data driven tool for non-linear control modeling.

1 Introduction

During the last two decades, governments have become more and more sensitive to the topic of sustainability and the ecological future of our planet. Any correct strategy for the sustainable development must involve proper solution to the problem of people transportation systems in urban areas. As a consequence, vehicle manufacturers are developing suited technologies towards the use of electric-based propulsion, in particular Hybrid Electric Vehicles (HEVs) as a bridge technology towards pure electric solutions [1]. However, the feasibility of mass production of these vehicles, besides problems due to marketing and logistic issues, is constrained to the maintenance and operating costs to the final user [2]. From this point of view it is very important to improve the efficiency of the energy management by adopting a suited control strategy for the energetic flows between batteries, thermal engine (or fuel cells), ultracapacitors and the electric engine [3].

We will consider HEVs using two or more of such energy sources. The main control task in a HEV is accomplished by the Control Unit (CU) that supervises the energy partition between the different sources with the aim to maximize the energetic efficiency. For instance, in order to reach the minimization of both fuel

F. Masulli, S. Mitra, and G. Pasi (Eds.): WILF 2007, LNAI 4578, pp. 253–260, 2007.

and battery consumption, several control strategies can be implemented, either static or dynamic, according to different control algorithms and design procedures [4]. This methodology allows computing the sequence of control actions (i.e. power splitting) over a time horizon as a function of the vehicle load. When the vehicle load and the route schedule is known in advance, a global optimal solution can be obtained so that the CU can be suitably programmed. However, if the vehicle load or its route change in real time, the optimality of the control sequence is not assured. In this case a prediction of the unknown factors must be pursued.

Traditional predictive models have a critical behavior since there are several exogenous variables (e.g. driver behavior, traffic congestions) that are not predictable in a deterministic fashion. We propose to optimize in real-time the energetic flows between electrical energy sources and engines by a neuro-fuzzy predictor, able to forecast the short-term and medium-term energy consumption on the basis of the actual conditions (such as the route computed by an on-board GPS system and navigation software). Neuro-fuzzy predictors make use of the flexibility of fuzzy logic to manage the hard task of complex system modeling. Moreover, the neural approach allows the synthesis of a suited model on the basis of a set of examples derived by past observations of the system to be controlled [5, ?]. Other neuro-fuzzy approaches to the energy management in hybrid vehicles have been already proposed in the technical literature as, for instance, in [7, 8]. The dynamic prediction of the energy consumption can be achieved as a function of the previous consumption states. Based on the predicted values of energy consumption, it is possible to generate suited control signals to the actuators of energy sources.

We will ascertain the effectiveness of the proposed approach by considering the simulation of a neuro-fuzzy CU, which will be tested on energy consumption series collected by a HEV prototype. Basic details about energetic flows in the simulation models adopted in this context will be illustrated in Sect. 2. The implementation of the prediction core in the proposed neuro-fuzzy CU will be introduced in Sect. 3, while the performance of the proposed control strategy will be simulated in Sect. 4 considering different prediction models as well.

2   Characterization of Energetic Flows

In the following we will consider the common problem of a HEV working in a urban context; thus, it should be a sufficiently small and light car. Nevertheless, such a vehicle should be cost-effective with respect to other thermal (traditional) vehicles in the same category, without considerable penalties for the acceleration performance and achieving an apex speed compatible with traditional motorization (i.e., 120 Km/h in suburban cycles). Although we cannot reproduce accurately the HEV's performances in every possible situation, we will consider its performances in some reference working tests, in which it should satisfy the minimal requirements.

In order to design the energy sources of a HEV it is necessary to define a prototype mission, by which it is possible to specify the control strategy of the energy consumption in order to obtain the highest autonomy of the vehicle. In this regard, we will consider the standard operation cycles defined by the government agencies as, for instance, the NEDC for Europe (and the urban version called ECE-15), the FTP-74 for United States, etc.

Such cycles were not defined to design traditional or hybrid vehicles, since they were specifically intended to evaluate pollutant emissions and fuel consumption in different route and traffic conditions. Successively, the test cycles were used to test electric and hybrid vehicles, so that they could be compared in well-definite situations. Consequently, the operation cycles have been defined by considering different driving styles on urban and suburban routes. In the following we will consider the repetition of a sufficient number of NEDC cycles, which are defined by the 94/12 European Regulation.

The characteristics of a typical NEDC cycle are illustrated in Fig. 1; they consist essentially of the mechanical power necessary to satisfy the required work, which is evidently related to the energy consumption with a given efficiency, at the corresponding mechanical force and velocity. As the HEV should be used prevalently in a urban context, the whole cycle will be composed of four urban elementary cycles (ECE-15) and only one suburban cycle. The cycles are separated in Fig. 1 by dotted vertical lines. In its first part, the whole cycle consists of two urban cycles in a flat slope route, each lasting 195 seconds with different speeds up to 50 Km/h. The third part is a suburban cycle of 400 seconds, with an apex speed of 120 Km/h. Successively, there are two other urban cycles, similar to the previous ones but with a 10% slope. The whole cycle has a duration of 1180 seconds and, since data are sampled every 0.5 seconds, it will be made of 2360 samples.

The cycle represented in Fig. 1 is typically used to detect the pollutant emissions of thermal engines equipping vehicles having a mass not exceeding 2500Kg. We ascertained that the corresponding model for energy consumption describes a wide range of situations in which HEVs are involved too. Thus, it will be adopted for designing the CU of such vehicles. More precisely, the specific task to be pursued is the prediction of the mechanical power as the one illustrated in Fig. 1(a). Based on this prediction, and assuming a given autonomy due to a fixed amount of energy available in the HEV, it possible to define the specifications for energy sources, such as type and dimensions of fuel cells, batteries and supercapacitors. Moreover, the prediction unit will assure the largest autonomy by providing an efficient switch among these sources in correspondence to the particular state (instantaneous power requirement) of the HEV.

3 Optimization by a Neuro-Fuzzy Control Unit

The basic operation of a CU is the prediction of the energy consumption of the HEV under control. Such sequences are characterized by repetitive trends, each one in correspondence of a particular vehicle's state (depending on load, course,

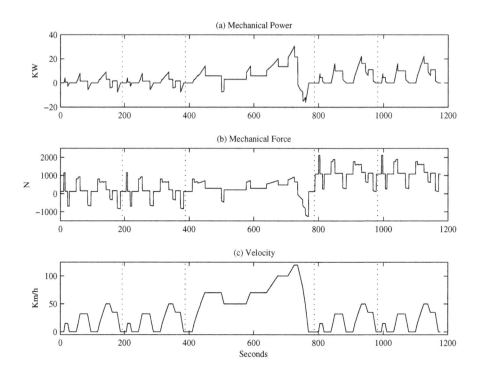

Fig. 1. Mechanical characteristics of a NEDC cycle: (a) power requirement; (b) mechanical force; (c) vehicle's speed

driver, etc.). Thus, the energy consumption is often a chaotic sequence, in which similar subsequences appear irregularly during the HEV employment. This claim will be ascertained in the following simulation tests.

A chaotic sequence $S(n)$ can be considered as the output of a chaotic system that is observable only through $S(n)$. Using a suitable embedding technique, the sequence is predicted by means of the reconstructed (unfolded) state-space attractor of the underlying system [9]:

$$\underline{x}_n = \begin{bmatrix} S(n) & S(n-T) & S(n-2T) & S(n-(D-1)T) \end{bmatrix}, \tag{1}$$

where $\underline{x}_n$ is the reconstructed state at time n, D is the embedding dimension of the reconstructed state-space attractor and T is the time lag between the embedded past samples of $S(n)$. The prediction of $S(n)$ can be considered as the determination of the function $f(\cdot)$, which approximates the link between the reconstructed state $\underline{x}_n$ and the output sample at the prediction distance q, i.e. $S(n+q) = f(\underline{x}_n)$, $q > 0$. In the following we will use the default value $q = 1$ without loss of generality.

Because of the intrinsic non-linearity and non-stationarity of a chaotic system, $f(\cdot)$ should be a non-linear function, which can be determined only by using data driven techniques [10]. Thus, the prediction of $S(n)$ can be accomplished by the function approximation of $f(\underline{x})$. We propose in this regard the use of neuro-fuzzy networks, which are particularly suited to the solution of function approximation problems by using a training set of samples. Nevertheless, the use of fuzzy logic is suited to manage robustly the transition of the system between the different states encountered while using the HEV. A control unit performing the prediction of energy consumption using neuro-fuzzy networks will be referred to in the following as Neuro-Fuzzy Control Unit (NFCU).

In this paper, we will consider as reference for neuro-fuzzy models the Adaptive Neuro-Fuzzy Inference Systems (ANFIS), composed by a set of R rules of Sugeno first-order type [?]. The k-th rule, $k = 1 \ldots R$, has the following form:

$$\text{If } x_1 \text{ is } B_1^{(k)} \text{ and } \ldots x_m \text{ is } B_m^{(k)} \text{ then } y^{(k)} = \sum_{j=1}^{m} a_j^{(k)} x_j + a_0^{(k)} , \qquad (2)$$

where $\underline{x} = [x_1 \; x_2 \ldots x_m]$ is the input pattern and $y^{(k)}$ is the output associated with the rule. The latter is characterized by the MFs $\mu_{B_j^{(k)}}(x_j)$ of the fuzzy input variables $B_j^{(k)}$, $j = 1 \ldots m$, and by the coefficients $a_j^{(k)}$, $j = 0 \ldots m$, of the crisp output. Several alternatives are possible for the fuzzification of crisp inputs, the composition of input MFs, and the way rule outputs are combined [?]. Usually, the structure of the fuzzy inference system is the following one:

$$\tilde{y} = \frac{\sum_{k=1}^{R} \mu_{\underline{B}^{(k)}}(\underline{x}) \, y^{(k)}}{\sum_{k=1}^{R} \mu_{\underline{B}^{(k)}}(\underline{x})} , \qquad (3)$$

where $\underline{B}^{(k)}$ is the overall fuzzy input variable, $\mu_{\underline{B}^{(k)}}(\underline{x})$ the corresponding MF, and $\tilde{y}$ the prediction, for a given input $\underline{x}_n$, of the actual value $S(n + q)$.

The approximation of the process $f(\underline{x})$ is obtained by means of a training set of P input-output pairs, being each pair the association of the reconstructed state $\underline{x}_n$ with the value to be predicted $S(n + q)$. The crucial problem during the learning process of ANFIS networks is to obtain a good generalization capability, which assures a satisfactory approximation when different HEV's conditions appear from those represented by the training set. This problem has been deeply investigated in the literature [?, 13]; usually, the generalization capability of ANFIS networks is optimized by checking data set for overfitting model validation [?, ?].

4   Illustrative Tests

In order to ascertain the capability of NFCUs to control efficiently the energetic flow in HEVs, we will consider in this Section different implementations of the prediction units. As explained, such predictors are used in the CU in order to forecast the energy consumption with a suitable margin so that it will be possible to switch among the different energy sources available for that vehicle. In this regard, the prediction of the power consumption is pursued by following the method proposed in the previous Section.

The prediction performances of the resulting CUs are compared by considering different approximation models $f(\cdot)$. The first one is a simple 'Linear' model determined by the least-squares technique. A neural CU is obtained by training a Radial Basis Function (RBF) neural network using the 'Neural Network' toolbox of the Matlab software package. Two different types of NFCU are obtained using ANFIS networks as approximation models: the first one is based on rule initialization using a grid partition on the input space of the training set ('Genfis1' routine of the Matlab 'Fuzzy Logic' toolbox); the second ANFIS model makes use of a subtractive clustering method [14] for rule initialization ('Genfis2' routine of the Matlab 'Fuzzy Logic' toolbox). Both ANFIS models are successively tuned by using a hybrid learning method based on a combination of least-squares estimation with back-propagation [?]. All the neural models are validated to prevent overfitting and thus to optimize their generalization capability.

In the following tests, the reference model for power consumption has been obtained as explained in Sect. 2. More precisely, the power sequence illustrated in Fig. 1(a) has been split in two subsequences: the first one is used as training set from sample 1 to 1000; the next one, from sample 1001 to 2360, is used as test set. The training sequence is also used to compute the time lag T and the embedding dimension D by means of, respectively, the Average Mutual Information (AMI) and the False Nearest Neighbors (FNN) methods [9]. The level of chaos present in the sequences is evaluated by means of the Spatio-Temporal Entropy (STE), which is defined and measured using the 'VRA' software package [15]. The STE index takes on values close to 50% in the case of chaotic signals and tends to 100% in the case of pure noise. We obtained for the training sequence the following values: $T = 35$, $D = 2$ and STE $= 64\%$. As expected, on the basis of the several tests we carried out in this regard, the power sequences possess a prevalent chaotic behavior, which is also affected by the spurious noise due to the stochastic factors affecting the HEV's operation.

Table 1. Prediction results obtained using different approximation models

Prediction Model	Training Error	Test Error
Linear	0.930	1.307
RBF	0.922	1.334
Genfis1	0.899	3.812
Genfis2	0.918	1.270

The prediction results of the considered models are illustrated in Table 1 in terms of Mean Squared Error (MSE) for both the training and the test sequence. The use of the standard neural model based on the RBF is not much effective for this application. In fact, it performs on the test set similarly to the very simple linear model. The use of fuzzy logic in ANFIS networks allows obtaining better prediction results and, consequently, a better control of the HEV's energy. However, this is actually achieved only by the Genfis2 method, where a suitable

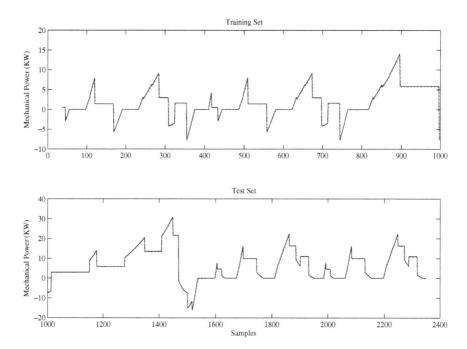

Fig. 2. Prediction results using the Genfis2 method to train the ANFIS network: continuous lines represent the actual sequences; dotted lines represent the predicted sequences

initialization of fuzzy rules is obtained using a proper clustering technique. The poor results of ANFIS using the Genfis1 method confirms the roughness of its rule initialization, which is further evidenced when different learning problems are investigated.

The behavior of sequences predicted by the Genfis2 ANFIS network is illustrated in Fig. 2: it is evident that we have obtained an adequate prediction accuracy since dotted lines, corresponding to predicted sequences, are almost identical to the actual ones for both training and test set. Thus, the high accuracy obtained in the training phase does not imply overfitting phenomenons.

5 Conclusion

In this paper we have proposed a neuro-fuzzy approach for the design of energy control units in HEVs. In this regard, we have considered the optimization of energetic flows in such vehicles, usually equipped with batteries, thermal engine, fuel cells, ultracapacitors and an electric engine. The energetic flows are optimized by using a control strategy based on the prediction of the vehicle states and, in particular, of their energy consumption. We have ascertained that prediction obtained by a NFCU exploits the robustness of fuzzy logic in managing the underlying uncertainties and the neural approach as a data driven tool for non-linear control modeling. The results illustrated for some simulations are encouraging in order to improve the neuro-fuzzy prediction system and to obtain a hardware implementation for 'on-the-road' validations.

References

1. Arsie, I., Graziosi, M., Pianese, C., Rizzo, G., Sorrentino, M.: Control strategy optimization for hybrid electric vehicles via provisional load estimate. In: Proc. of 1st International Symposium on Advanced Vehicle Control (AVEC), Arnhem, The Netherlands, Vol. 7 (2004)
2. Boccaletti, C., Fabbri, G., Mascioli, F.M.F., Santini, E.: Technical and economical feasibility study of a small hybrid vehicle for urban transportation. In: Proc. of 1st Workshop on Hybrid and Solar Vehicles, Salerno, Italy, pp. 57–62 (2006)
3. Arsie, I., Marotta, M., Pianese, C., Rizzo, G., Sorrentino, M.: Optimal design of a hybrid electric car with solar cells. In: Proc. of 1st AUTOCOM Workshop on Preventive and Active Safety Systems for Road Vehicles, Istanbul, Turkey (2005)
4. Arsie, I., Pianese, C., Rizzo, G., Santoro, M.: Optimal energy management in a parallel hybrid vehicle. In: Proc. of 6th Biennial Conference on Engineering Systems Design and Analysis (ASME-ESDA), Turkey, pp. 8–11 (2002)
5. Panella, M., Rizzi, A., Mascioli, F.M.F., Martinelli, G.: A neuro-fuzzy system for the prediction of the vehicle traffic flow. In: Di Gesù, V., Masulli, F., Petrosino, A. (eds.) WILF 2003. LNCS (LNAI), vol. 2955, pp. 110–118. Springer, Heidelberg (2006)
6. Haykin, S.: Neural Networks, a Comprehensive Foundation, 2nd edn. Prentice-Hall, Englewood Cliffs, NJ, USA (1999)
7. Mohebbi, M., Charkhgard, M., Farrokhi, M.: Optimal neuro-fuzzy control of parallel hybrid electric vehicles. In: IEEE Vehicle Power and Propulsion Conference, Chicago, USA (2005)
8. Cerruto, E., Raciti, A.C.A., Testa, A.: Energy flows management in hybrid vehicles by fuzzy logic controller. In: Proc. of MELECON'94, Antalya, Turkey, Vol. 3, pp. 1314–1317 (1994)
9. Abarbanel, H.: Analysis of Observed Chaotic Data. Springer, Verlag, Inc., New York, USA (1996)
10. Panella, M., Rizzi, A., Martinelli, G.: Refining accuracy of environmental data prediction by MoG neural networks. Neurocomputing 55, 521–549 (2003)
11. Jang, J.S.: ANFIS: Adaptive-network-based fuzzy inference system. IEEE Transactions on Systems, Man and Cybernetics 23, 665–685 (1993)
12. Jang, J.S., Sun, C., Mizutani, E.: Neuro-Fuzzy and Soft Computing: a Computational Approach to Learning and Machine Intelligence. Prentice Hall, Upper Saddle River, NJ, USA (1997)
13. Panella, M., Rizzi, A.,Mascioli, F.M.F., Martinelli, G.: ANFIS synthesis by hyperplane clustering. In: Proc. of IFSA/NAFIPS. Vol. 1, Vancouver, Canada, pp. 340–345 (2001)
14. Chiu, S.: Fuzzy model identification based on cluster estimation. Journal of Intelligent & Fuzzy Systems 2, 267–278 (1994)
15. Kononov, E.: Visual Recurrence Analysis (VRA), version 4.2 (1999), http://www.myjavaserver.com/ nonlinear/vra/download.html

Fuzzy k-NN Lung Cancer Identification by an Electronic Nose

Rossella Blatt[1], Andrea Bonarini[1], Elisa Calabró[2], Matteo Della Torre[3],
Matteo Matteucci[1], and Ugo Pastorino[2]

[1] Politecnico di Milano, Department of Electronics and Information, Milan, Italy
blatt@elet.polimi.it, bonarini@elet.polimi.it, matteucci@elet.polimi.it
[2] Istituto Nazionale Tumori of Milan, Toracic Surgery Department, Milan, Italy
ugo.pastorino@istitutotumori.mi.it, elisa.calabro@istitutotumori.mi.it
[3] Sacmi Imola S.C., Automation & Inspection Systems, Imola (BO), Italy
matteo.della.torre@sacmi.it

Abstract. We present a method to recognize the presence of lung cancer in individuals by classifying the olfactory signal acquired through an electronic nose based on an array of MOS sensors. We analyzed the breath of 101 persons, of which 58 as control and 43 suffering from different types of lung cancer (primary and not) at different stages. In order to find the components able to discriminate between the two classes 'healthy' and 'sick' as best as possible and to reduce the dimensionality of the problem, we extracted the most significative features and projected them into a lower dimensional space, using Nonparametric Linear Discriminant Analysis. Finally, we used these features as input to a pattern classification algorithm, based on Fuzzy k-Nearest Neighbors (Fuzzy k-NN). The observed results, all validated using cross-validation, have been satisfactory achieving an accuracy of 92.6%, a sensitivity of 95.3% and a specificity of 90.5%. These results put the electronic nose as a valid implementation of lung cancer diagnostic technique, being able to obtain excellent results with a non invasive, small, low cost and very fast instrument.

Keywords: Electronic Nose, E-Nose, Olfactory Signal, Pattern Classification, Fuzzy k-NN, MOS Sensor Array, Lung Cancer.

1 Motivation and Methodology

It has been demonstrated that the presence of lung cancer alters the percentage of some volatile organic compounds (VOCs) present in the human breath [7], which may be considered as markers of this disease. This substances can be detected by an electronic nose, that is an instrument that allows to acquire the olfactory signal. The electronic nose includes an array of electronic chemical sensors with partial specificity and an appropriate pattern recognition system able to recognize simple or complex odors [1].

The main objective of this paper is to demonstrate that it is possible to recognize individuals affected by lung cancer, analyzing the olfactory signal of

F. Masulli, S. Mitra, and G. Pasi (Eds.): WILF 2007, LNAI 4578, pp. 261–268, 2007.
© Springer-Verlag Berlin Heidelberg 2007

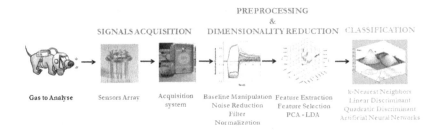

PREPROCESSING
&
SIGNALS ACQUISITION   DIMENSIONALITY REDUCTION   CLASSIFICATION

Gas to Analyse   Sensors Array   Acquisition   Baseline Manipulation   Feature Extraction   k-Nearest Neighbors
                                     system   Noise Reduction   Feature Selection   Linear Discriminant
                                                     Filter   PCA - LDA   Quadratic Discriminant
                                                     Normalization   Artificial Neural Networks

Fig. 1. Block scheme of an electronic nose

their breath, by the use of an electronic nose and an appropriate classification algorithm.

The experiment has been developed within the Italian MILD (Multicentric Italian Lung Detection) project, promoted by the Istituto Nazionale Tumori of Milan, Italy. The study has been approved from the Ethical Committee of the Institute and we asked all volunteers to sign an agreement for the participation to the study. We analyzed the breath of 101 volunteers, of which 58 healthy and 43 suffering from different types of lung cancer. In particular 23 of them have a primary lung cancer, while 20 of them have different kinds of pulmonary metastasis. Control people do not have any pulmonary disease and have negative chest CT scan. The breath acquisition has been made by inviting all volunteers to blow into a nalophan bag of approximately $400 cm^3$. Considering that the breath exhaled directly from lung is contained only in the last part of exhalation, we decided to consider only this portion of the breath. We used a spirometer to evaluate each volunteer exhalation capacity and, at the end of the exhalation, we diverted the flow into the bag. Finally, the air contained in the bag has been input to the electronic nose and analyzed. From each bag we took two measures, obtaining a total of 202 measurements, of which 116 correspond to the breath of healthy people and 86 to diseased ones.

2 Processing and Classification of the Olfactory Signal

An electronic nose is an instrument able to detect and recognize odors, namely the volatile organic compounds present in the analyzed substance. It consists in three principal components (Figure 1): a *Gas Acquisition System*, a *Preprocessing and Dimensionality Reduction phase* and a *Classification Algorithm*. In particular the acquisition of the olfactory signal is done through a sensor array that converts a physical or chemical information into an electrical signal. MOS sensors are characterized by high sensitivity (in the order of ppb), low cost, high speed response and a relatively simple electronics. Considering that most of the VOCs markers of lung cancer are present in the diseased people's breath in very small quantities, varying from parts per million to parts per billion, we chose to use this kind of sensors rather than others. In particular, we used an array composed of six MOS sensors (developed by SACMI s.c.), that react to gases

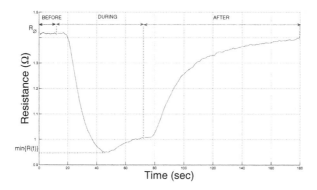

Fig. 2. Example of a typical sensor response

with a variation of resistance. The VOCs interact with a doped semiconducting material deposited between two metal contacts over a resistive heating element, which operates from 200 °C to 400 °C. As a VOC passes over the doped oxide material, the resistance between the two metal contacts changes in proportion to the concentration of the VOC. The registered signal corresponds to the change of resistance through time produced by the gas flow [3]. In Figure 2 it is possible to see a typical response of a MOS sensor. In particular, each measure consists of three main phases:

1. **Before**: during this time the instrument inhales the reference air, showing in its graph a relatively constant curve;
2. **During**: it is the period in which the electronic nose inhales the analyzed gas, producing a change of the sensors' resistance. It is the most important part of the measurement because it contains informations about how sensors react to the particular substance;
3. **After**: during this phase the instrument returns to the reference line.

After the electronic nose has acquired the olfactory signal, the pre-processing phase begins; its purpose is to reduce the effect of humidity, to normalize the obtained signal and to manipulate the baseline. The latter transforms the sensor response w.r.t. its baseline (e.g., response to a reference analyte) for the purposes of contrast enhancement and drift compensation [2].

After pre-processing, we performed dimensionality reduction to extract the most relevant information from the signal. We reached this objective through *Features Extraction*, *Features Selection* and *Features Projection* in a lower dimensional space. The first operation extracts those descriptors from the sensors' responses able to represent data characteristics in the most efficient way. Feature selection finds, among all possible features, those ones that maximize the informative components and, thus, the accuracy of classification. In particular, we applied the non-parametric test of Mann-Whitney-Wilcoxon [11] with a significance level equal to $\alpha = 0.0001$ to select only discriminant descriptors. In order to evaluate the discriminative ability of the combination of more features, we performed an Analysis of Variance (ANOVA) [11] and several scatter plots. Let define $R(t)$ the curve representing the resistance variation during the measurement and R_0 the value of the resistance at the beginning of the measurement (as indicated in Figure 2), we found as the most discriminative features between the two classes 'healthy' and 'sick':

- **Single Point**. It is the minimum value of resistance reached during the measurement: $S = \min(R(t))$;
- **Delta**. It corresponds to the resistance change of sensors during the measurement: $\delta = R_0 - \min(R(t))$;
- **Classic**. It is the ratio between the reference line and the minimum value of resistance reached during the measurement: $C = R_0 / \min(R(t))$;
- **Relative Integral**. It is calculated as: $I = \int R(t)/(t \cdot R_0)$;
- **Phase Integral**. It represents the closed area determined by the plot of the state graph of the measurement [8]: $x = R, \quad y = dR/dt$.

After feature selection we performed data projection: we considered Principal Component Analysis (PCA) [10] and Nonparametric Linear Discriminant Analysis (NPLDA) [12], that is based on nonparametric extensions of commonly used Fisher's linear discriminant analysis [10]. PCA transforms data in a linear way projecting features into the directions with maximum variance. It is important to notice that PCA does not consider category labels; this means that the discarded directions could be exactly the most suitable for the classification purpose. This limit can be overcome by NPLDA, which looks for the projection able to maximize differences between different classes and minimize those intra-class. In particular, NPLDA removes the unimodal gaussian assumption by computing the between scatter-matrix S_b using local information and the k nearest neighbors rule; as a result of this, the matrix S_b is full-rank, allowing to extract more that c-1 features (where c is equal to the number of considered classes) and the projections are able to preserve the structure of the data more closely [12]. As evident from Figure 3, NPLDA is able to separate the projected features more clearly than PCA, which plot shows a more evident overlap of samples. This means that NPLDA is more suitable, for the problem considered, in terms of classification performance. Moreover, the plot and the obtained eigenvalues clearly indicated that only one principal component is needed.

Once the most representative characteristics are found, it is possible to perform the analysis of the data, that, in this case, consists in a *pattern recognition* algorithm. In particular, we considered Fuzzy k-Nearest Neighbors (Fuzzy k-NN) classifier, a variation of the classic k-NN, based on a fuzzy logic approach [13]. The basic idea of k-NN is to assign a sample to the class of the k closest samples in the training set. This method is able to do a non linear classification, starting from a small number of samples. The algorithm is based on a measure of the distance (in this case, the Euclidean one) between the normalized features and it has been demonstrated [10], that the k-NN is formally a non parametric approximation of the Maximum A Posteriori MAP criterion. The asymptotic performance of this simple and powerful algorithm, is almost optimum: with an infinite number

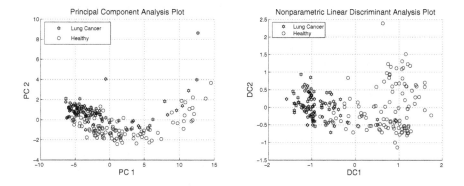

Fig. 3. The result of dimensionality reduction through PCA on the left and NPLDA on the right

of samples and setting $k=1$, the minimum error is never higher than the double of the Bayesian error (that is the theoretical lower bound reachable) [10]. One of the most critical aspects of this method regards the choice of parameter k with a limited number of samples: if k is too large, then the problem is too much simplified and the local information loses its relevance. On the other hand, a too small k leads to a density estimation too sensitive to outliers. For this reason, we decided to consider the Fuzzy k-NN, a variation of the classic k-NN that assigns a fuzzy class membership to each sample and provides an output in a fuzzy form. In particular, the membership value of unlabeled sample x to i^{th} class is influenced by the inverse of the distances from neighbors and their class memberships:

$$\mu_i(x) = \frac{\sum_{j=1}^{k} \mu_{ij} (\|x - x_j\|)^{\frac{-2}{m-1}}}{\sum_{j=1}^{k} (\|x - x_j\|)^{\frac{-2}{m-1}}} \tag{1}$$

where μ_{ij} represents the membership of labeled sample x_j to the ith class. This value can be crisp or it can be calculated according to a particular fuzzy rule: in this work we defined a fuzzy triangular membership function with maximum value at the average of the class and null outside the minimum and maximum values of it. In this way, the closer the sample j is to the average point of class i, the closer its membership value μ_{ij} will be to 1 and vice versa. The parameter m determines how heavily the distance is weighted when calculating each neighbor's contribution to the membership value [14]; we chose $m = 2$, but almost the same error rates have been obtained on these data over a wide range of values of m.

3   Results and Conclusion

The performance of the classifier has been evaluated through the obtained confusion matrix and performance indexes. Being 'TruePositive' (TP) a sick sample classified as sick, 'TrueNegative' (TN) a healthy sample classified as healthy,

'FalsePositive' (FP) a healthy sample classified as sick and 'FalseNegative' (FN) a sick sample classified as healthy, performance indexes are defined as:

- Accuracy (Non Error Rate NER)$=(TP+TN)/(TP+FP+TN+FN)$;
- Sensitivity (True Positive Rate TPR)$=(TP)/(TP+FN)$;
- Specificity (True Negative Rate TNR)$=(TN)/(TN+FP)$;
- Precision w.r.t. diseased people $(PREC_{POS})=(TP)/(TP+FP)$;
- Precision w.r.t. healthy people $(PREC_{NEG})=(TN)/(TN+FN)$.

To obtain indexes able to describe in a reliable way the performances of the algorithm, it is necessary to evaluate these parameters on new and unknown data, validating the obtained results. Considering the not so big dimension of population and that for every person we had two samples, we opted for a modified Leave-One-Out approach: each test set is composed by the pair of measurements corresponding to the same person, instead of a single measure as would be in the normal Leave-One-Out method. Doing this way, we avoided that one of these two measures could belong to the training set, while using the other in the test set. In order to deeply understand the relevance of the obtained performance indexes, we calculated the corresponding confidence intervals, which lower and upper bounds are defined as:

$$\bar{X} - t_{\frac{\alpha}{2}} \frac{\sigma}{\sqrt{n}} \leq \mu_x \leq \bar{X} + t_{\frac{\alpha}{2}} \frac{\sigma}{\sqrt{n}} \tag{2}$$

where $\bar{X}$ is the registered index value, n is the number of the degrees of freedom, σ is the standard deviation and $t_{\frac{\alpha}{2}}$ is the quantile of the t-student distribution corresponding to the degrees of freedom-1 of the problem.

Results obtained by Fuzzy k-NN are very satisfactory, leading to an accuracy of 92.6%. The confusion matrix obtained by this algorithm is shown in Table 1(a), where elements along the principal diagonal represent respectively the TruePositive and the TrueNegative values, while those off-diagonal are respectively the FalseNegative and the FalsePositive values. Performance indexes and their corresponding confidence intervals (set CI=95%), are reported in Table 1(b). A relevant consideration regards the robustness of Fuzzy k-NN to k changes: we considered different values of k, but the algorithm demonstrated to be very robust to these changes, keeping its results invariant.

In order to prove the effectiveness of Fuzzy k-NN for the considered problem, we evaluated also other families of classifiers: in particular we considered performance achieved by the classic k-NN, by a feedforward artificial neural network (ANN) and by two classifiers based, respectively, on linear and quadratic discriminant functions. All obtained results were comparable or worst than those achieved by Fuzzy k-NN in terms of average accuracy. Considering the single indexes we noticed that sensitivity and precision w.r.t healthy people were higher using Fuzzy k-NN classifier. This consideration is very important because in diagnosis sensitivity is more relevant than specificity because it is more important to recognize correctly a sick person instead of a healthy one; in the same way, precision w.r.t. negative samples is more relevant than precision w.r.t. positive

Table 1. Confusion matrix (a) and performance indexes (b) obtained from Fuzzy k-NN algorithm (k=1,3,5,9,101)

(a)

CONFUSION MATRIX		ESTIMATED LABELS	
		Positive	Negative
TRUE LABELS	Positive	82	4
	Negative	11	105

(b)

Indexes	Average Index	Confidence Interval ($CI = 95\%$)
Accuracy	92.6%	[88.5-96.7]
Sensitivity	95.3%	[91.8-98.9]
Specificity	90.5%	[86.0-95.0]
PREC$_{POS}$	88.2%	[82.3-94.1]
PREC$_{NEG}$	96.3%	[93.2-99.4]

Table 2. Comparison of lung cancer diagnosis performance and corresponding confidence intervals (set CI=95%) reached by the electronic nose presented in this work and current diagnostic techniques. Data from [9]. Note that results regarding CAT and PET have been obtained from a different dataset than the one analyzed by the E-Nose.

	Accuracy	Sensitivity	Specificity	PREC$_{POS}$	PREC$_{NEG}$
CAT	Nd	75%	66%	Nd	Nd
Confidence Interval		[60-90]	[55-77]		
PET	Nd	91%	86%	Nd	Nd
Confidence Interval		[81-100]	[78- 94]		
E-Nose	92.6%	95.3%	90.5%	88.2%	96.3%
Confidence Interval	[88.5-96.7]	[91.8-98.9]]	[86.0-95.0]	[82.3-94.1]	[93.2-99.4]

ones, because it is worse to classify a person as healthy when he or she is actually sick, than the opposite. Moreover the robustness showed by the Fuzzy k-NN's to k changes is not verified in the classic k-NN, that lead to different results according to different values of k. However, performing a Student's t-test between all pair of classifiers, no relevant differences emerged; this means that implemented classifiers' results are comparable for the problem considered.

The use of an electronic nose as lung cancer diagnostic tool is reasonable if it gives some advantage compared to current lung cancer diagnostic techniques, namely Computed Axial Tomography (CAT) and Positron Emission Tomography (PET). Not only this is verified in terms of performance, as illustrated in Table 2, but also because the electronic nose, unlike the classical approaches, is a low cost, robust, small (and thus, eventually portable), very fast and, above all, non invasive instrument.

In literature there are three other main research works regarding lung cancer diagnosis by an electronic nose [4,5,6]. Accuracy indexes obtained from these works were respectively equal to 90.32%, 88.16% and 80%. Moreover, in [5] and [6], no cross-validation techniques has been applied to obtain such results; this means that results have been obtained from one realization and, therefore, they are not necessarily representative of the real generalization capability of the classifier.

An ambitious research prospective regards the individuation of risk factors connected to lung cancer (as smoke or food). Involving a larger population and partitioning it according to different disease stages, it would be possible to study the possibility of early diagnosis, that is the most important prospective of research that this work should follow.

References

1. Gardner, J.W., Bartlett, P.N.: Electronic noses. Principles and applications. Oxford University Press, Oxford (1999)
2. Osuna, R.G., Nagle, H.T., Shiffman, S.S.: The how and why of electronic nose, IEEE Spectrum, pp. 22-34 (September 1998)
3. Pardo, M., Sberveglieri, G.: Electronic Olfactory Systems Based on Metal Oxide Semiconductor Sensor Arrays. Material Research Society Bullettin, 29(10) (October 2004)
4. Di Natale, C., Macagnano, A., Martinelli, E., Paolesse, R., D'Arcangelo, G., Roscioni, C., Finazzi-Agro, A., D'Amico, A.: Lung cancer identification by the analysis of breath by means of an array of non-selective gas sensors. Biosensors and Bioelectronics 18(10), 1209–1218 (2003)
5. Machado, R.F., Laskowski, D., Deffenderfer, O., Burch, T., Zheng, S., Mazzone, P.J., Mekhail, T., Jennings, C., Stoller, J.K., Pyle, J., Duncan, J., Dweik, R.A., Erzurum, S.: Detection of Lung Cancer by Sensor Array Analyses of Exhaled Breath, American Journal of Respiratory and Critical Care Medicine. American Journal of Respiratory and Critical Care Medicine 171, 1286–1291 (2005)
6. Chen, X., Cao, M., Li, Y., Hu, W., Wang, P., Ying, K., Pan, H.: A study of an electronic nose for detection of lung cancer based on a virtual SAW gas sensors array and imaging recognition method. Measurement science & technology 16(8), 1535–1546 (2005)
7. Phillips, M.D., Cataneo, R.N., Cummin, A.R.C., Gagliardi, A.J., Gleeson, K., Greenberg, J., Maxfield, R.A., Rom, W.N.: Detection of lung cancer with volatile markers in the breath. Chest 123(6), 2115–2123 (2003)
8. Martinelli, E., Falconi, C., D'Amico, A., Di Natale, C.: Feature Extraction of chemical sensors in phase space. Sensors and Actuators B:Chemical 95(1), 132–139 (2003)
9. Pieterman, R.M., Van Putten, J.W.G., Meuzelaar, J.J., Mooyaart, E.L., Vaalburg, W., Koter, G.H., Fidler, V., Pruim, J., Groen, H.J.M.: Preoperative staging of non-small-cell lung cancer with positron-emission tomography. The New England journal of medicine 343(4), 254–261 (2000)
10. Fukunaga, K.: Introduction to statistical pattern recognition, 2nd edn. Academic Press, San Diego (1990)
11. Lyman Ott, R., Longnecker, M.T.: An Introduction to Statistical Methods and Data Analysis, 5th edn., Duxbury Press (2001)
12. Fukunaga, K., Mantock, J.M.: Nonparametric discriminant analysis. IEEE Transactions on pattern analysis and machine intelligence PAMI 5(6), 671–678 (1983)
13. Zadeh, L.: Fuzzy sets. Information and Control 8, 338–353 (1965)
14. Keller, J.M., Gray, M.R., Givens, J.A.: A fuzzy k-Nearest neighbor algorithm,In: IEEE Transactions on systems, man and cybernetics, 15(4), 580-585 (July-August 1985)

Efficient Implementation of SVM Training on Embedded Electronic Systems

Paolo Gastaldo, Giovanni Parodi, Sergio Decherchi, and Rodolfo Zunino

Dept. of Biophysical and Electronic Engineering (DIBE), Genoa University
Via Opera Pia 11a, 16145 Genoa, Italy
{paolo.gastaldo, giovanni.parodi, rodolfo.zunino}@unige.it

Abstract. The implementation of training algorithms for SVMs on embedded architectures differs significantly from the electronic support of trained SVM systems. This mostly depends on the complexity and the computational intricacies brought about by the optimization process, which implies a Quadratic-Programming problem and usually involves large data sets. This work presents a general approach to the efficient implementation of SVM training on Digital Signal Processor (DSP) devices. The methodology optimizes efficiency by suitably adjusting the established, effective Keerthi's optimization algorithm for large data sets. Besides, the algorithm is reformulated to best exploit the computational features of DSP devices and boost efficiency accordingly. Experimental results tackle the training problem of SVMs by involving real-world benchmarks, and confirm both the computational efficiency of the approach.

Keywords: Support Vector Machine, SMO, embedded systems, DSP.

1 Introduction

Support Vector Machines (SVMs) [1] are one of the most effective tools for tackling classification and regression problems in complex, nonlinear data distributions [1, 2]. Indeed, SVM has been recently successfully applied to the fuzzy methodology [3, 4]. The training of SVMs is characterized by convex optimization problem; thus local minima can be avoided by using polynomial-complexity Quadratic Programming (QP) methods. Besides, kernel-based representations allow SVMs to handle arbitrary distributions that may not be linearly separable in the data space. The ability to handle huge masses of data is indeed an important feature; in such significant cases, SVM training algorithms [5-7] typically adopt an iterative selection strategy: first, limited subsets of (supposedly) critical patterns are identified and undergo partial optimization; then the local solution thus obtained is projected onto the whole data set to verify consistency and global optimality. Such a process iterates until convergence.

The success of SVMs in real-world domains motivates continuing research toward embedded implementations on low-cost machinery. Programmable digital devices often represent the basic choice for the run-time support of trained SVMs [8], but FPGA technology may not prove efficient when dealing with systems that

F. Masulli, S. Mitra, and G. Pasi (Eds.): WILF 2007, LNAI 4578, pp. 269–276, 2007.

require training capabilities. In these cases, the target hardware platforms should be endowed with: 1) agile memory handling for easy support of the pattern-selection strategies described in the previous section; 2) buffering and caching capabilities, for managing large sets of high-dimensional data effectively; 3) specialized arithmetic features to speed up computations and maximize efficiency; 4) limited cost, to ensure maximal market impact of the embedded technologies. Hence, the basic features of the SVM training model make the family of Digital Signal Processors (DSPs) possibly more appropriate. Therefore, this paper describes a methodology for the embedded support of SVM training by means of DSP-based architectures. The research reconsiders the overall training problem and privileges the viewpoint of embedded implementations. This resulted in a hardware-oriented version of Keerthi's well-known optimization algorithm [6]. A reformulation of the basic local-optimization steps allows the algorithm to exploit the architectural features of the target processors at best, thus attaining highest efficiency. The method has been tested on a set of standard benchmarks, to verify the algorithm's effectiveness and the computational efficiency of the embedded system.

2   Support Vector Machines for Classification

A binary classification problem involves a set of patterns $Z = \{(\mathbf{x}_l, y_l); l=1,..,n_p\}$ where $y_l \in \{-1,+1\}$. To perform such task, SVM [1] requires the solution of the QP problem:

$$\min_{\alpha} \left\{ \frac{1}{2} \sum_{l,m=1}^{np} \alpha_l \alpha_m y_l y_m K(\mathbf{x}_l, \mathbf{x}_m) - \sum_{l=1}^{np} \alpha_l \right\} \text{ subject to: } \begin{cases} 0 \leq \alpha_l \leq C, \forall l \\ \sum_{l=1}^{np} y_l \alpha_l = 0 \end{cases}$$

(1)

where α_l are the SVM parameters setting the class-separating surface and the scalar quantity C upper bounds the SVM parameters; $K()$ is a kernel function such that $K(\mathbf{x}_1, \mathbf{x}_2) = \langle \Phi(\mathbf{x}_1), \Phi(\mathbf{x}_2) \rangle$, where $\Phi(\mathbf{x}_1)$ and $\Phi(\mathbf{x}_2)$ are the points in the "feature" space that are associated with $\mathbf{x}_1$ and $\mathbf{x}_2$, respectively. An SVM supports a linear class separation in that feature space; the classification rule for a trained SVM is:

$$f(\mathbf{x}) = \sum_{l=1}^{np} \alpha_l y_l K(\mathbf{x}, \mathbf{x}_l) + b$$

(2)

where b is a bias. The n_{SV} patterns for which non-null parameters α_l are found by solving (1) are called support vectors. For a thorough presentation of SVM, see [1, 2].

The problem setting (1) involves a QP problem with linear constraints; thus, the solution is unique and it can be found in polynomial time. Since the problem formulation depends on the sample cardinality, n_p, an effective strategy for selecting the eventual support vectors is critical in the presence of large training sets. In such cases, the widely accepted approach consists in focusing the optimization algorithm on subsets of training patterns in turns. Sequential Minimal Optimization (SMO) [6, 7] proved to be one of the most effective approaches for that purpose. It belongs to the class of "Decomposition" methods [5]; hence, the overall QP problem is decomposed into fixed size QP sub-problems. In particular, SMO involves the smallest possible subset of vectors, and considers pairs of patterns sequentially. The crucial advantage is that the solution of (1) when $n_p=2$ can be computed analytically and explicitly.

Lin's LibSVM [7] represents a highly efficient implementation of the SMO approach in terms of convergence speed. LibSVM applies Keerthi's SMO [6] on "working sets" of patterns that can be selected iteratively by a shrinking process. This approach tackles the convergence problem by measuring the cost gradient, ∇f_l, at the l-th pattern $\mathbf{x}_l$. The selection strategy identifies the pair of patterns whose Lagrange coefficients $\{\alpha_i, \alpha_j\}$ most violate the Karush-Kuhn-Tucker conditions (KKTs) [6]. Two quantities are associated with these patterns, and rule the stopping criterion:

$$g_i \equiv \begin{cases} -\nabla f(\alpha)_i \text{ if } y_i = 1, \alpha_i < C \\ \nabla f(\alpha)_i \quad \text{ if } y_i = -1, \alpha_i > 0 \end{cases}, \quad g_j \equiv \begin{cases} -\nabla f(\alpha)_j \text{ if } y_j = -1, \alpha_j < C \\ \nabla f(\alpha)_j \quad \text{ if } y_j = 1, \alpha_j > 0 \end{cases};$$
(3)

the stopping condition that ensures convergence is written as $g_i \leq g_j$. Empirical practice shows that it is one of the most successful strategies to minimize the number of iterations in QP optimization.

3   SVM Training on DSP-Based Architectures

The basic algorithm for SVM training described in LibSVM involves three main procedures (Fig.1) : 1) the selection of the working set, 2) the verification of stopping criteria, and 3) the update of the crucial quantities, namely, α_i, α_j, and $\nabla f(\alpha)$. The first two steps clearly play a crucial role to the ultimate effectiveness of the training algorithm.

Nevertheless, one should note that the optimization efficiency of decompositions algorithms is conventionally measured by the involved reduction in the number of iterations until QP convergence. When implemented on specific embedded devices, however, selection-based algorithms might exhibit peculiar features that ultimately tend to limit the computational efficiency of the overall system.

The crucial issue is that the implemented strategy should also take into account the internal architecture of the target electronic device. Toward that end, the research presented in this paper proposes a hardware-oriented reformulation of the optimization algorithm [6] for DSP-based embedded electronics, which provide a suitable tradeoff between computational power and cost efficiency. Besides, in the specific context of SVMs, hardware-looping capabilities and SIMD architectures well fit the features of training algorithms, which are typically characterized by deeply nested loop cycles.

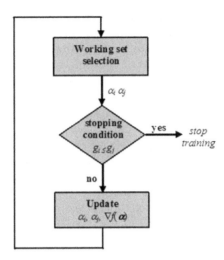

Fig. 1. The basic steps of the SVM training algorithm

3.1   Training Algorithm: Reformulation and Optimization

Keerthi's algorithm can be adapted by means of specific reformulations in the basic local-optimization steps, and the eventual optimization algorithm exploits a slightly modified heuristic. With respect to the original criterion formulated in the LibSVM library [7], the new heuristic proposed in this work replaces (3) with:

$$
g_i \equiv \begin{cases} -\nabla f(\alpha)_i \text{ if } y_i = 1, \alpha_i < C \\ \nabla f(\alpha)_i \quad \text{if } y_i = -1, \alpha_i = C \end{cases},
\tag{4}
$$

Thus, the new pattern-selection heuristic implied by (4) improves on computational efficiency by accepting the risk that a few patterns might violate one KKT condition. From a hardware-oriented viewpoint, the rationale behind this approach is that fulfilling entirely the KKTs results in a computationally demanding task. On the other hand, one runs the risk that the method might reach a sub-optimal solution. The reformulation (4) specifically aims to balance solution accuracy and computational efficiency.

From a cognitive viewpoint, one might justify the above modified heuristic in terms of region representation. The heuristic implied by (4) replaces the condition $\alpha_i > 0$ with $\alpha_i = C$; hence, only multipliers that are bounded support vectors are considered violators. In principle, one doesn't know how bounded support vectors and true support vectors are placed; however, in practice, a considerable percentage of the bounded support vectors that are violators with the original heuristic (3) will be subject to optimization process implied by (4). Indeed, true support vectors are not used in the optimization process; as a result, a loss of generalization ability is expected. Experimental evidence actually showed that the new heuristic embeds a sort of early stopping criterion.

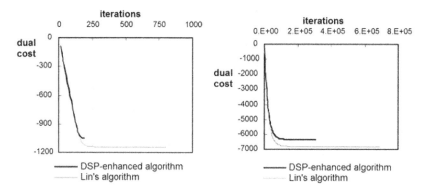

Fig. 2. Results on the "Diabetes" and "Sonar" datasets using the LibSVM criterion and the DSP-enhanced heuristic

The graphs in Fig.2 plot the dual cost (1) on the y-axis versus the number of iterations for two training sessions. The graphs compare the results obtained by training an SVM with the original criterion (gray line) with those resulting from the DSP-enhanced heuristic (4) (black line). Fig. 2a presents the costs for the "Pima-Indians Diabetes" testbed [9], whereas Fig. 2b is associated with tests on the "Sonar" testbed [10]. In both cases, the graphs show that the algorithm based on the DSP-enhanced selection strategy supports an early stopping criterion, as it terminates in a number of iterations that is significantly smaller than that required by the original criterion. Indeed, one notes that the training cost attained by the proposed algorithm is quite close to the optimal solution reached by the original algorithm. Further experiments on other testbeds confirmed these conclusions.

3.2 Training Algorithm: Basic Porting

Step 3) indeed involves some critical aspects for the DSP implementation, as updating $\nabla f(\alpha)$ requires the access to the Hessian matrix Q. In general, the Hessian matrix needs an amount of memory that is available only in the memory external to the DSP. Thus, to implement the updating task efficiently, bandwidth becomes a critical aspect in transferring data from external RAM to the on-DSP memory.

The specific internal architectures of DSP devices allow one to attain optimal performance, as the Harvard schema provides separate, independent memory sections for program and data buses. Moreover, DMA channels allow independent memory loading from external to internal memory. Hence, in the proposed implementation, the DSP-internal RAM operates as a fast caching device, where matrix subsections are copied in turns. The eventual design strategy follows the architectural approach sketched in Fig. 2. The working set selection defines the columns of the Hessian matrix involved in the update procedure; then, DMA-channels support data loading from external to internal memory. As a result,

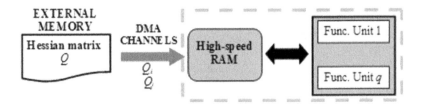

Fig. 3. The design strategy supporting data loading from the Hessian matrix

data transfer from the cache proceeds in parallel with ongoing computations. DMA channels are then used for data transfer from the external to the on-chip memory, so that the core can operate with limited latency. These features allow embedded implementations to exploit properly the limited amount of on-chip memory even when large data sets are involved. Incidentally, one notes that such a characteristic is hardly found on conventional microprocessors, which do not support directly addressable on-chip memory.

4   Experimental Results

The proposed training algorithm has been implemented on an "ADSP-BF533 Blackfin" Analog Devices® DSP (denoted, in the following, as 'Blackfin' for brevity), running at a clock speed of 270 MHz. This device combine a 32-bit RISC instruction set with a dual 16-bit multiply accumulate (MAC) digital signal processing functionality. The memory architecture is hierarchical and provides a fast on chip memory (L1) and a slower off-chip memory. This platform supports DMA data transfer between internal and external data memory, thereby fulfilling the bandwidth condition for optimal data-transfer rates. Fixed-point representation brings about some loss in precision, as compared with the performance that could be attained by the higher resolutions provided by floating-point representations. Preliminary analysis pointed out that a 16-bit quantization level conveyed an acceptable degradation for the problem at hand. At the same time, the Q15 format representation allowed one to exploit the available 16-bit multipliers in parallel within the Blackfin DSP core.

The results presented in Table I compare the performances of the original training algorithm with the enhanced version implemented on the target DSP platform. To allow a fair comparison, training sessions were always performed by using the following parameter settings: $C=1$, $2\sigma^2=100$. Table 1 (a) and (b) compare the performances of the two algorithms on a random subset ($n_p = 100$) of four different testbeds: "Spam," "Ionosphere," "Banana," and "Pima-Indians Diabetes" [9, 11]. The following quantities are reported: the number of iterations required by the training procedure, the dual cost (1) attained at convergence, the classification performance of error percentage (CE), the number of support

Table 1. Performance comparison between the enhanced algorithm and LibSVM

	Spam Testbed			Ionosphere Testbed		
	Proposed heuristic (DSP)	LibSVM criterion (DSP)	LibSVM criterion (PC)	Proposed heuristic (DSP)	LibSVM criterion (DSP)	LibSVM criterion (PC)
Iterations	86	172	55	54	69	47
Dual cost	-31.894	-31.978	-31.916	-49.514	-49.707	-49.606
CE	1	1	1	12	12	12
SV	63	65	66	73	72	71
Clock cycles	598010	3194066	-	378150	1301331	-

	Banana Testbed			Diabetes Testbed		
	Proposed heuristic (DSP)	LibSVM criterion (DSP)	LibSVM criterion (PC)	Proposed heuristic (DSP)	LibSVM criterion (DSP)	LibSVM criterion (PC)
Iterations	52	97	51	49	49	49
Dual cost	-96.772	-96.649	-96.863	-92.043	-92.043	-91.828
CE	49	51	51	51	51	50
SV	99	98	98	98	98	98
Clock cycles	357755	1799341	-	334770	1254342	-

vectors (SV), and the clock cycles required. The last column gives the results obtained by completing the SVM training on a high-end PC supporting the original heuristic included in LibSVM.

Empirical evidence confirms that the DSP-enhanced heuristic improves computational efficiency by attaining satisfactory performances in term of dual cost and digital cost. Experimental evidence shows that when implemented on a DSP LibSVM requires a computational effort that is five times larger than the effort required by the proposed heuristic. The proposed heuristic always outperforms the original heuristic in term of computational efficiency. Nonetheless, the dual cost and the classification error are very close to the reference values obtained by running LibSVM on a PC.

References

1. Vapnik, V.: Statistical Learning Theory. Wiley, New York (1998)
2. Cristianini, N., Shawe-Taylor, J.: An introduction to Support Vector Machines. Cambridge University Press, Cambridge, U.K (2000)
3. Chen, Y., Wang, J.Z.: Support vector learning for fuzzy rule-based classification systems. IEEE Trans. Fuzzy System 11, 716–728 (2003)
4. Chaves, Ad.C.F., Vellasco, M.M.B.R., Tanscheit, R.: Fuzzy rule extraction from support vector machines. In: Proc. HIS05 (2005)
5. Joachims, T.: Making large-Scale SVM Learning Practical. In: Scholkopf, B., Burges, C.J.C., Smola, A.J. (eds.) Advances in Kernel Methods - Support Vector Learning, MIT Press, Cambridge (1999)

6. Keerthi, S., Shevade, S., Bhattacharyya, C., Murthy, K.: Improvements to Platt's SMO algorithm for SVM classifier design. Neural Computation 13, 637–649 (2001)
7. Chang, C.-C., Lin, C.-J.: LIBSVM: a Library for Support Vector Machines. Available at: http://www.csie.ntu.edu.tw/cjlin/libsvm
8. Anguita, D., Boni, A., Ridella, S.: A digital architecture for support vector machines: theory, algorithm and FPGA implementation. IEEE TNN 14, 993–1009 (2003)
9. Rätsch, G., Onoda, T., Müller, K.-R.: Soft margins for AdaBoost. Machine Learning 42, 287–320 (2001)
10. Torres-Moreno, J.M., Gordon, M.B.: Characterization of the sonar signals benchmark. Neural Processing Lett. 7, 1–4 (1998)
11. Newman, D.J., Hettich, S., Blake, C.L., Merz, C. J.: UCI repository of machine learning databases. Available at: http://www.ics.uci.edu/ mlearn/ MLRepository.html

A Possible Approach to Cope with Uncertainties in Space Applications

Michèle Lavagna and Guido Sangiovanni

Dipartimento di Ingegneria Aerospaziale, Politecnico di Milano
Via La Masa 34
20156 Milano, Italia
{lavagna,sangiovanni}@aero.polimi.it

Abstract. The paper shows methods that could be suitably applied to manage uncertainties in space systems design and modeling. Attention is focused on the Interval Analysis, as one of the most promising methods. In this research two issues typical faced in space-related researchs have been treated: optimization and ordinary differential equations (ODEs) solving taking into account possible uncertainties included in the models; the first is generally related to space system design phases while the second deals with systems dynamics analysis. Because of lack of space this paper presents results from the first area only: more specifically, the optimization of a control system design to accomplish robust reconfiguration manoeuvre is achieved taking into account uncertainties on the technological parameters of the propulsion unit to obtain a robust design from the beginning of the study. Results turned out that the Interval Analysis is effective and efficient to handle these classes of uncertainties.

1 Introduction

This paper presents the very preliminary results of a research project focused on identifying problems concerning Space in which uncertainty has a key role, and on finding out methodologies, as general as possible, that allow handling uncertainties with a significant benefit for the problem solving. Any engineering application entails some undefined quantities not perfectly known at the beginning of the project and typically inferred by the designers - thanks to their expertise - with a certain degree of confidence. It is noteworthy that as soon as a project got its maturity and every single component is optimized, even very small variations around the nominal values assumed along the design process could lead to low performances or, more drastically, to catastrophic events for the safety of the system itself: for example very little truncation errors (of the order of 10^{-8}) on the onboard 24 bit computer compromised the Patriot missiles' control system in the Gulf War [1]. If such a small error leads to the failure of a whole project, it is easy to understand that bigger errors, given by the absence of knowledge, would bring to unreliable results. That makes quite meaningful to look for methods that can manage the unavoidable uncertainties from the very beginning of any kind of project. In this way assumptions, made to guess those

F. Masulli, S. Mitra, and G. Pasi (Eds.): WILF 2007, LNAI 4578, pp. 277–284, 2007.

numbers that are not perfectly known, would affect the system performance at the minimum, giving the solution the precious feature to be robust. Recently a growing interest of the scientific and technological community to this kind of problems has been registered. The NASA Langley Research Center too identified a critical need in applying uncertainty-based methodologies for application to aerospace vehicles [2]. The uncertainty-based design is a design problem that has a vague and imprecise formulation; that is some essential components of the problem, like parameters used to describe either the phenomenon or the nominal mathematical model that captures its physics, have not a clear analytical representation. There are two main interesting problems in which uncertainty has a preeminent role: the robust design and the reliability-based design [2]. The robust design tries to output a system that is unsensible to little variations around the nominal value of all those data that are not precisely known; as a result a high quality system that has high performances in everyday fluctuations of the parameters during its operative life is obtained. The reliability-based design's target is a system that correctly works even when unknown data are very far from their nominal value; the result is an highly safe system that can avoid catastrophe even in extreme operating conditions. The same mathematical formulation can be employed to manage both the aforementioned approaches. In this paper the Interval Analysis has been selected to face uncertainty-based design problems. The following sections are dedicated to present and deeper discuss an optimal control problem solving with a robust approach: a rendez-vous manoeuvre to change the orbit of a spacecraft controlled by means of electric thrusters; uncertainties relate to the selected control devices performances; that simple test case is representative for a class of actual problems related to the identification of stable control solutions, even in the very first designing phase, through the choice of a technological class of products; the choice, however, is connected to the different technical performances the alternative products have, which -at the design process beginning - are undefined,being the outputs of the design process itself.

The ODE system solving in presence of uncertainties- that represents the other class of typical problems aerospace engineers have to deal with - is not discussed because of lack of space, although the research done so far revealed the Interval Analysis to be a suitable tool to solve some of those problems too. A deep presentation of Interval Analysis could be found in [3][4][5]. Furthermore useful instructions to implement Interval Analysis in MatLab could be find in [6] with some others numerical techniques developed to solve many classical problems [7][8].

2   Robust Optimal Control

Interval Analysis exploited in studies focused on enhancing the robustness features for control systems has the aim to guarantee the stability of the controller with respect to the uncertainties included in the mathematical description of the process that has to be controlled. That technique can be applied twofold within this research area: *stability analysis*: the controller is obtained by means of usual real and crisp techniques; its performances in terms of stability are then measured through the Interval Analysis; *control system design*: the Interval Analysis is here applied from the very beginning of the controller design process to directly make it stable according to the considered uncertainties. Literature offers some examples for both the applications [4][9][10]. The first application is becoming more widespread, while very few works can be retrieved as far as the second scenario is concerned, according to the uncertainties management. In the following a *control system design* application is presented. Differently from applications offered in literature, the Optimal Control Theory is here preferred to solve the control problem.The control design is based upon the mathematical description of the phenomenon that has to be controlled: as a consequence the control is greatly affected by the model quality. No matter of the model precision some discrepancies always keep existing between the model and the real world. The Interval Analysis is here exploited as an effective tool to keep trace of those discrepancies and their effects on the results while synthesizing the control law. Discrepancies may be introduced as parametric and nonparametric perturbations: parametric perturbations account for the inexact knowledge of some parameters selected to settle the model; nonparametric perturbations concern with the unmodeled dynamics. The application showed in this paper is focused on the first class of possible perturbations, since nonparametric uncertainties are already included in the Robust and Optimal Control Theory.

2.1   Problem Formulation

TThe procedure to follow to design a control system under uncertainties is here described. The specific example is treated in the next paragraph. Given a linear system perfectly known with no uncertain parameter, it is well known that the control parameters domain is a limited interval [**c**]. The technology that is used for the control system restricts the value of the parameters to lie in a feasible interval [**c**]. The target is to find the values of the parameters for which the closed loop poles lie on the left semi-plane of the complex space,having its origin in $x = -\delta$, whit $\delta > 0$; δ is the required stability margin. By building the Routh table for the translated system, it is possible to define the Routh vector by taking into account the first column of the table, $r = r(\mathbf{c}, \delta)$. The designer asks for the maximum degree of stability in the feasible set:

$$\mathbf{c} = \arg \max_{\substack{\mathbf{c} \in [\mathbf{c}] \\ \mathbf{r}(\mathbf{c},\delta) \geq 0}} \delta \tag{1}$$

Let now insert a vector of uncertain parameters, **p**, that refers to the transfer function and lies in a set that can be easily represented with an interval vector, [**p**]. The control vector has to be stabilized for every parameter value included in the uncertain vector. The obtained solution space is:

$$\mathcal{S}_c = \arg \max_{\mathbf{c} \in [\mathbf{c}]} \left(\min_{\mathbf{p} \in [\mathbf{p}]} \max_{\mathbf{r}(\mathbf{p},\mathbf{c},\delta) \geq 0} \delta \right) \tag{2}$$

The target stays in finding at least a solution that lies in the solution space, $\mathcal{S}_c$. The problem leads to a system of non linear inequalities that can be solved by applying one of the several Interval Analysis Global Optimization techniques, known as branch and bound [3][5][6]. Others than the stability degree constraint can be considered, such as constraints on the dumping coefficient, the static gain and the stability margin, just adding more inequalities to the system. The computational cost of the designing process grows exponentially with the **p** and **c** vectors dimensions. For this reason only controllers with a simple structure can be designed and the research field is still very open.

2.2 Control System for a Reconfiguration Manoeuvre

The former procedure is here applied to the design of an optimal control system for a reconfiguration manoeuvre in space. It is assumed that the spacecraft mounts low thrust devices to control its own centre of mass dynamics. The reconfiguration manoeuvre is aimed to move the space system from a slightly circular to a perfectly circular orbit [11][12]. That is a typical reconfiguration manoeuvre for orbiting systems; figure 1reports a sketch of the manoeuvre. The equations of motion for the spacecraft and the target point can be respectively expressed - in an inertial frame - as follows:

$$\frac{d^2 r_1}{dt^2} = -\frac{\mu}{r_1^3} r_1 \tag{3}$$

$$\frac{d^2 r_2}{dt^2} = -\frac{\mu r_2^3 r_2}{+} f \tag{4}$$

where f and μ are the vector of accelerations given by the control system and the planetary constant respectively. It is possible to express the inertial dynamics with respect to the relative position vector ϱ:

$$\frac{d^2 \varrho}{dt^2} = \frac{d^2 r_2}{dt^2} - \frac{d^2 r_1}{dt^2} = \frac{\mu}{r_1^3}\left[r_1 - \frac{r_1^3}{r_2^3} r_2 \right] + f \tag{5}$$

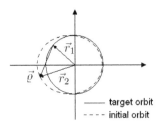

Fig. 1. Reconfiguration manoeuvre scheme

Eq.(5) can be expressed according to an orbiting reference system: by neglecting higher order terms, thanks to a very low eccentricity, the Hill-Clohessy-Wilshire equations are obtained [12]:

$$\ddot{x} - 2n\dot{y} - 3n^2 x = f_x$$
$$\ddot{y} + 2n\dot{x} = f_y$$
$$\ddot{z} + n^2 z = f_z \tag{6}$$

n is the mean angular velocity, equal to $\sqrt{\mu/r_1^3}$

The third equation in Eqs.(6) is uncoupled from the others; it should be reminded that the z axis the third equation refers to, is normal to the orbital plane; therefore that third equation is representative for the out-of-plane motion. The nature of the free dynamics equation (i.e. $f_z = 0$) reveals an oscillatory behaviour that makes the spacecraft swings around the orbit plane twice a orbit; indeed, as soon as the spacecraft crosses the target orbit plane, an orbital maneuver should occur to input the satellite on the desired final plane. The controller is designed taking into account the $x - y$ in-plane coupled dynamics only. The system is preferably written at the states. The state variables vector, $\mathbf{q}$, and the control forces vector, $\mathbf{u}$, are defined as:

$$\mathbf{q}^T = \{\, x\ \dot{x}\ y\ \dot{y}\,\} \tag{7}$$
$$\mathbf{u}^T = \{\, f_x\ f_y\,\} \tag{8}$$

By having in mind Eqs.(7) and (8) the system can be settled as follows:

$$\{\dot{q}\} = [A]\{q\} + [B]\{u\} \tag{9}$$

To design the controller, the theory of Optimal Control with infinite horizon is applied[20]; therefore the minimization of the following functional was aimed:

$$F = \frac{1}{2} \int \left(q^T Q q + \rho u^T R u \right) dt \tag{10}$$

The Q matrix has been settled to have equally weighted states; a min-max approach has been applied to get the R matrix. The Riccati equation can be written:

$$PA + A^T P + Q - \rho P B R^{-1} B^T P = 0 \tag{11}$$

the P matrix is obtained by solving Eq.(11). The gain matrix G can be, then, computed from Eq.(12), and the Eq.(11) can be formalized as a system of non linear equations.

$$G = R^{-1} B^T P \tag{12}$$

The uncertainty is introduced in terms of maximum thrust the propulsion unit can supply: a 2 N nominal thrust is assumed, with an uncertainty span of ±10%;

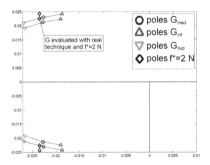

Fig. 2. Poles obtained with nominal thrust

that is the typical range offered by data sheets of electrical thrusters. The R matrix is clearly affected by the inserted uncertainty on the actuator performances: it is no more a crisp but an interval matrix. Therefore the nonlinear equations system that allows computing the P matrix asks for interval computation.

2.3   Results

To solve the system of interval non linear equations an algorithm, based on the *branch and bound* technique [3],[10] has been developed. The resulting P is an interval matrix, and generates an interval gain matrix:

$$[G] = [R]^{-1}B^T[P] \qquad (13)$$

The potential of the Interval Analysis allows taking into account the thrusters uncertain performances directly in the gain matrix computation: the suitability of the selected actuators category - in terms of controller robustness - can be stated through a single analysis that spreads all over the thrusters performance interval. Figure 2 shows the closed loop poles obtained by the matrices G_{inf}, G_{med}, and G_{sup} respectively; matrices refer to the lower bound, the middle point, and the upper bound of every interval of the G matrix evaluated in Eq.(13).

The designed control system is stable for every choice of the gain matrix values within the bounds obtained with the Interval Analysis. A comparison between these results and the closed loop poles obtained with a classical crisp approach is also highlighted in figure 2. The crisp analysis has been accomplished by considering a nominal thrust level of 2 N. The crisp controller is stabler than the controller synthesized while taking into account possible thrust uncertainties. The effects of the worst propulsion unit performances occurrence are shown in figure 3: location of the controller poles, identified by solving the Riccati equation for nominal condition, whenever the thrust is actually of 1.8 N are presented: the obtained controller is less stable than the worst controller obtained by considering the uncertainty till the beginning of the design process, exploiting the Interval Analysis methodology. The average performances - in term of stability

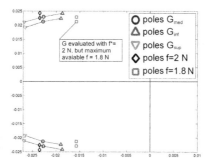

Fig. 3. Poles obtained with the lowest available thurst

- of the interval controller are very close to those of the typically applied crisp technique; as an added value, it is noteworthy that the interval controller performs more robustly according to parametric uncertainties the system may have. A SWLQR (Sensitivity Weighted Linear Quadratic Regulator) designing method may lead to similar results: less stable with respect to nominal values, but with more robust performances around the nominal case. However, it is important to note that the SWLQR method cannot be applied to the proposed scenario as the state vector is independent from the uncertain parameter [13].

3   Conclusions

All engineering projects are affected by uncertainties; therefore a methodology that helps taking into account those imprecisions from the very beginning of the process would certainly represents a powerful and effective tool to increase both the reliability and the quality of the final product. At the time being to cope with the problem the Monte Carlo simulations are largely applied, but they present some drawbacks. First of all they are very time and resource consuming. Further they need assumptions on the probability density functions of the uncertain data. For this reason they often lead to the most probable solution, not taking into account the tails of the probability density functions and so those conditions that actually size the problem. Last, but not least, computerized computations introduce rounding, truncation and conversion errors. The Interval Analysis has been developed to overcome all those limitations, giving rise to a guaranteed result. In this paper an example from typical problems in which uncertainty holds a key role in space system analysis is presented. A critical analysis of the obtained results leads to state that the Interval Analysis seems to be a promising technique - to be wider tested on similar benchmarks - to get rid of problems significantly affected by some relevant quantities uncertainties. By taking advantage of Global Optimization techniques based on Interval Analysis [5], the design of an optimal controller affected by uncertainties in the actuators technical parameters has been achieved. Thanks to the Interval Analysis exploitation a controller stabler than the controller synthesized by means of a traditional approach is obtained;

that translates into a better knowledge of the system behaviour during different operative conditions with a reduced analysis effort. Interval Analysis seems to efficiently behave whenever uncertainties are strictly connected with ODEs solving too: although here not presented for lack of space, effects of both initial conditions and parameters uncertainties on the final state vector of a dynamic system can be obtained. Again, the increase of knowledge is evident: the actual uncertainties typically unmodeled can be taken into account while analyzing the system behavior, catching important information about each quantity sensitivity according to those uncertainties. It has to be said that the computational need of Interval Analysis is greater than the Real Algebra computational effort. To overcome this drawback other new techniques have been developed; the Taylor Models method to be surely mentioned. This method improves Interval Analysis potential and is useful also to solve integration problems affected by wrapping effect.

References

1. Wolpe, H.: Patriot missile defense - software problem led to failure at Dhahran, Saudi Arabia. Tech. Rep. B-247094, United States General Accounting Office, Washington D. C (1992)
2. Zang, T.A., Hemsch, M.J., Hilburger, M.W., Kenny, S.P., Luckring, J.M., Maghami, P., Padula, S.L., Stroud, W.J.: Needs and Opportunities for Uncertainty-Based Multidisciplinary Design Methods for Aerospace Vehicles. Tech. Rep.TM-2002-211462, NASA Langley Research Center (2002)
3. Caprani, O., Madsen, K., Nielsen, H. B.: Introduction to interval analysis. DTU (2002)
4. Jaulin, L.: Applied Interval Analysis: with example in parameter and state estimation, robust control and robotics. Springer, London (2001)
5. Hansen, E.: Global optimization using interval analysis. Marcel Dekker, inc., New York (1992)
6. Hargreaves, G.I.: Interval analysis in MATLAB. Tech. rep.,University of Manchester, UMIST (2002)
7. Schichl, H.,Neumaier, A.: Interval Analysis. Tech. rep., University of Vienna (2000)
8. Kearfott, R.B., Ning, S.: A Comparison of some Methods for Solving Linear Interval Equations. SIAM Journal (1997)
9. Malan, S., Milanese, M., Taragna, M.: Robust Analysis and Design of Control Systems Using Interval Arithmetic. Automatica 33(7), 1363–1372 (1997)
10. Jaulin, L., Walter, E.: Guaranteed Tuning, with Application to Robust Control and Motion Planning. Automatica 32(8), 1217–1221 (1996)
11. Wertz, J.R., Larson, W.J.: Space Misssion Analysis and Design. El Segundo, Microcosm Press, California (2003)
12. Kaplan, M.H.: Modern Spacecraft Dynamics and Control, New York. John Wiley & sons, West Sussex, England (1976)
13. Meirovitch, L.: Dynamics and Controls of Structures. John Wiley & Sons, West Sussex, England (1990)

Fuzzy Measures: Collectors of Entropies

Doretta Vivona and Maria Divari

Sapienza - Universitá di Roma
Facoltá di Ingegneria
Dipartimento di Metodi e Modelli Matematici per le Scienze Applicate
v.A.Scarpa n.16 - 00161 ROMA(ITALIA)

Abstract. In the fuzzy setting we define a collector of entropies, which allows us to consider the reliability of observers. This leads to a system of functional equations. We are able to find the general solution of the system for collectors, which are compatible with a law of the kind "Inf" in [2]. Finally we give a class of solutions for a collector for which we dont'n take into account a law of compositivity for entropies.

1 Introduction

In the subjective theory of information without probability, according with J.Kampé de Feriet and B.Forte [7], one supposes that each group of observers is provided with an amount of information for the same event. Every group has a reliability coefficient, which enjoys some characteristic properties, as Baker, Forte and Lamb have proposed in [1,4,5,6]. We have already studied the same problem for fuzzy events [8,9]. In this paper we shall give an entropy of fuzzy partitions which is influenced by a group of observers. The collector is the entropy computed taking into account of the different opinions of the groups of observers in the framework of an axiomatic theory.

For example: let F be the fuzzy set of ill grey-haired men between 40 and 60 years. The partition $\mathcal{P}(F)$ has two atoms, F_1 and F_2 : the ill grey-haired men $40-50$ years old and $51-60$, respectively. The groups of observers are the crisp sets E_1 and E_2 of the dentists and the surgeons, respectively. Our collector allows us to estimate the entropy through the reability ascribed to the different groups of observers.

2 Preliminaires

In the fuzzy setting, we consider the following model:

1) X is an abstract space, $\mathcal{F}$ is a family of fuzzy sets $F \subset X$ with membership function $f(x) \in [0,1]$, $\forall x \in X$; we refer to [11] for the operations among fuzzy sets.

A fuzzy partition of the set F, called support, is a family [3] of fuzzy sets, called atoms $\mathcal{P}(F) = \{F_1, ..., F_i, ..., F_n / F_i \cap F_h = \emptyset, \Sigma_{i=1}^n f_i(x) = f(x)\}$. We refer to [3] for the concepts conserning the fuzzy partitions. $\mathcal{G}$ is the family of all partitions. We indicate with $\{F\}$ the fuzzy set F thought as a partition.

F. Masulli, S. Mitra, and G. Pasi (Eds.): WILF 2007, LNAI 4578, pp. 285–290, 2007.

As in [10], given two partitions $\mathcal{P}(F)$ and $\mathcal{P}(G)$, with $F \cap G = \emptyset$ and $f(x) + g(x) \leq 1 \ \forall \ x \ \in X$ the union $\mathcal{P}(F) \cup^+ \mathcal{P}(G)$ is the partition whose atoms are all elements of $\mathcal{P}(F)$ and $\mathcal{P}(G)$ and whose support set is $F \cup G$.

2) $\mathcal{O}$ is another space and $\mathcal{E}$ an algebra, which contains $E \subset \mathcal{O}$ called group of observers.

3) A $\vee$-additive measure μ is defined on the measurable space $(\mathcal{O}, \mathcal{E}) : \mu(\emptyset) = 0, \mu(\mathcal{O}) = \overline{\mu} \in (0, +\infty]$, μ is non-decreasing with respect to the classical inclusion and $\mu(E_1 \cup E_2) = \mu(E_1) \vee \mu(E_2)$. If $E \subset \mathcal{O}$, $\mu(E)$ is called reliability coefficient.

4) An entropy H, without a fuzzy measure, evaluated by the group E i.e. linked to the group of observers, is a map $H : \mathcal{G} \times \mathcal{E} \longrightarrow [0, +\infty]$ which is monotone with respect to classical order for fuzzy partitions and fixed $E \subset \mathcal{O}, \mathrm{E} \neq \emptyset, \neq \mathcal{O}$, for all $\mathcal{P}(F), \mathcal{P}(F') \in \mathcal{G}$ it is $H(\{X\}, E) = 0$ and $H(\{\emptyset\}, E) = +\infty$ [3].

5) Every entropy H evaluated by the group is compositive with respect to the law $\wedge$:

$$H\left(\mathcal{P}(F) \cup^+ \mathcal{P}(G), E\right) = H\left(\mathcal{P}(F), E\right) \wedge H\left(\mathcal{P}(G), E\right). \tag{1}$$

3   Collector of Entropies

In previous papers [8,9] we have defined a collectors for crisp and fuzzy sets.

We call a **collector of entropies evaluated by the group** $E_1 \cup E_2$ of observers, $E_1 \cap E_2 = \emptyset$, with reliability coefficient $\mu(E_1)$ and $\mu(E_2)$, respectively, the entropy of the partition $\mathcal{P}(F)$ evaluated by $E_1 \cup E_2, E_1 \cap E_2 = \emptyset$: $H\left(\mathcal{P}(F), E_1 \cup E_2\right)$ and we define it in the following way:

$$H\left(\mathcal{P}(F), E_1 \cup E_2\right) = \Phi\left[\mu(\mathrm{E}_1), \mu(\mathrm{E}_2), \mathrm{H}\left(\mathcal{P}(F), E_1\right), \mathrm{H}\left(\mathcal{P}(F), E_2\right)\right], \tag{2}$$

where $\mathcal{P}(\mathrm{F}) \in \mathcal{G}, \mathrm{E}_1, \mathrm{E}_2 \in \mathcal{E}$, $H\left(\mathcal{P}(F), E_1\right)$ and $H\left(\mathcal{P}(F), E_2\right) \in [0, +\infty], \mu(\mathrm{E}_1)$ and $\mu(E_2) \in [0, +\infty]$, and $\Phi : [0, +\infty] \times [0, +\infty] \times [0, +\infty] \times [0, +\infty] \longrightarrow [0, +\infty]$.

We recognize that, $\forall \ \mathcal{P}(\mathrm{F}) \in \mathcal{G}, E_1, E_2, E_3 \in \mathcal{E}, E_1 \cap E_2 = \emptyset, E_1 \cap E_2 \cap E_3 = \emptyset$, the collector is:
- commutative: $H\left(\mathcal{P}(\mathrm{F}), \mathrm{E}_1 \cup \mathrm{E}_2\right) = H\left(\mathcal{P}(\mathrm{F}), \mathrm{E}_2 \cup \mathrm{E}_1\right)$,

- associative: $H\left(\mathcal{P}(\mathrm{F}), (\mathrm{E}_1 \cup \mathrm{E}_2) \cup \mathrm{E}_3\right) = H\left(\mathcal{P}(\mathrm{F}), \mathrm{E}_1 \cup (\mathrm{E}_2 \cup \mathrm{E}_3)\right)$,

- with universal values: $H\left(\{\emptyset\}, E_1 \cup E_2\right) = +\infty, H\left(\{X\}, E_1 \cup E_2\right) = 0$.

Moreover, if the entropy of the group of observers is $\wedge$-compositive in the sense of (1) we can add another property:
- compatibility condition between the $\wedge$-compositivity of H and the collector Φ:

$$H\left(\mathcal{P}(F) \cup^+ \mathcal{P}(G), E_1 \cup E_2\right) = H\left(\mathcal{P}(F), E_1 \cup E_2\right) \wedge H\left(\mathcal{P}(G), E_1 \cup E_2\right). \tag{3}$$

By the definition (2), $\forall\ \mathcal{P}(F), \mathcal{P}(G) \in \mathcal{G}, E_1, E_2, E_3 \in \mathcal{E}, E_1 \cap E_2 = \emptyset, E_1 \cap E_2 \cap E_3 = \emptyset, \forall\ \mathcal{P}(F) \in \mathcal{G}$ we can traslate the properties seen above by using the function Φ :

$(A_1)\quad \Phi\left[\mu(E_1), \mu(E_2), H\left(\mathcal{P}(F), E_1\right), H\left(\mathcal{P}(F), E_2\right)\right] =$

$$\Phi\left[\mu(E_2), \mu(E_1), H\left(\mathcal{P}(F), E_2\right), H\left(\mathcal{P}(F), E_1\right)\right],$$

$(A_2)\quad \Phi\left[\mu(E_1) \vee \mu(E_2), \mu(E_3), H\left(\mathcal{P}(F), E_1 \cup E_2\right), H\left(\mathcal{P}(F), E_3\right)\right] =$

$$\Phi\left[\mu(E_1), \mu(E_2) \vee \mu(E_3), H\left(\mathcal{P}(F), E_1\right), H\left(\mathcal{P}(F), E_2 \cup E_3\right)\right],$$

$(A_3)\quad \Phi\left[\mu(E_1), \mu(E_2), +\infty, +\infty\right] = +\infty$

$(A_4)\quad \Phi\left[\mu(E_1), \mu(E_2), 0, 0\right] = 0$.

By (2) and (3), we have also:

$(A_5)\Phi\left[\mu(E_1), \mu(E_2), H\left(\mathcal{P}(F), E_1\right) \wedge H\left(\mathcal{P}(G), E_1\right), H\left(\mathcal{P}(F), E_2\right) \wedge H\left(\mathcal{P}(G), E_2\right)\right] =$

$$\Phi\left[\mu(E_1), \mu(E_2), H\left(\mathcal{P}(F), E_1\right), H\left(\mathcal{P}(F), E_2\right)\right]$$

$$\wedge\ \Phi\left[\mu(E_1), \mu(E_2), H\left(\mathcal{P}(G), E_1\right), H\left(\mathcal{P}(G), E_2\right)\right].$$

4   System of Functional Equations for the Collector

Now we put $\mu(E_1) = x, \mu(E_2) = y, \mu(E_3) = z, H\left(\mathcal{P}(F), E_1\right) = u, H\left(\mathcal{P}(F), E_2\right) = v, H\left(\mathcal{P}(F), E_3\right) = w, H\left(\mathcal{P}(G), E_1\right) = u', H\left(\mathcal{P}(F), E_2\right) = v'$ with $x, y, z, u, v, w,$
$u', v' \in [0, +\infty]$. Now we rewrite the conditions $[(A_1) - (A_5)]$ in order to obtain a system of functional equations. The equations are:

$$
\begin{cases}
(A'_1) \quad \Phi\left(x, y, u, v\right) = \Phi\left(y, x, v, u\right) \\[2mm]
(A'_2) \quad \Phi\left(x \vee y, z, \Phi(x, y, u, v), w\right) = \Phi\left(x, y \vee z, u, \Phi(y, z, v, w)\right) \\[2mm]
(A'_3) \quad \Phi\left(x, y, +\infty, +\infty\right) = +\infty \\[2mm]
(A'_4) \quad \Phi\left(x, y, 0, 0\right) = 0 \\[2mm]
(A'_5) \quad \Phi\left(x, y, u \wedge u', v \wedge v'\right) = \Phi\left(x, y, u, v\right) \wedge \Phi\left(x, y, u', v'\right) \quad .
\end{cases}
$$

For the first time, in crisp setting, an analogous system was studied and solved by Benvenuti-Divari-Pandolfi in [2], when the reliability coefficients are defined in a probabilistic space. Later, we have found the same system for information measures [8,9].

Proposition 1. *The class of solution of the system* $[(A'_1) - (A'_5)]$ *is:*

$$
\Phi(x, y, u, v) = h\left(x \vee y \ , \ h^{-1}(x, u) \wedge h^{-1}(y, v)\right) \tag{4}
$$

where $h : [0, +\infty] \times [0, +\infty] \to [0, +\infty]$ *is a continuous function satisfying the following conditions:* $1) h(x, \cdot)$ *is non-decreasing, with* $h(x, 0) = 0$ *and* $h(x, +\infty) = +\infty, \ \forall x \in [0, +\infty],$ $2) h(0, u) = u, \ \forall u \in [0, +\infty]$ *,* $3) h(x, u) = h(x, v) \implies h(y, u) = h(y, v), \ \forall \ y > x.$

For the proof, we refer back to [2,8,10].

Moreover, we give a class of solution for collectors, which don't satisfy the condition (A_5).

First of all, we remark that a class of solution is the function (4) seen above. Now, we look for other solutions. If we put

$$
\Phi(x, y, u, v) = F_{(x,y)}(u, v), \tag{5}
$$

where $F_{[0,1] \times [0,1]} : [0, 1] \times [0, 1] \to [0, +\infty]$, the condition (A'_2) becomes:

$$
(A''_2) \quad F_{(x,y+z)}\left(u, F_{(y,z)}(v, w)\right) = F_{(x+y,z)}\left(F_{(x,y)}(u, v), w\right) ;
$$

and we recognize that the function F enioyes a form of associativity, when we highlight the link between the entropies of the partitions and the reliability of the group of observers. With the position (5), $\forall \ x, y, z, u, v, w \in [0, +\infty]$ the system $[(A'_1) - (A'_4)]$ is

$$
\begin{cases}
(A''_1) \quad F_{(x,y)}(u, v) = F_{(x,y)}(u, v) \\[1mm]
(A''_2) \quad F_{(x \vee y \ , \ z)}\left(F_{(x,y)}(u, v), \ w\right) = F_{(x \ , \ y \vee z)}\left(u, F_{(y,z)}(v, w)\right) \\[1mm]
(A''_3) \quad F_{(x,y)}(+\infty, +\infty) = +\infty \\[1mm]
(A''_4) \quad F_{(x,y)}(0, 0) = 0 \quad .
\end{cases}
$$

We can give the following

Proposition 2. *A class of solutions of the sistem* $[(A_1'') - (A_4'')]$ *is:*

$$F_{(x,y)}^{k,\vee}(u,v) = k\left(\frac{x\ k^{-1}(u) \vee y\ k^{-1}(v)}{x \vee y}\right), \tag{6}$$

where $k : [0,+\infty] \to [0,+\infty]$ *is any strictly increasing function with* $k(0) = 0$ *and* $k(+\infty) = +\infty$.

Proof. The proof is immediate.

REMARK : 1) The Proposition 1 is valid even when $(\mathcal{O}, \mathcal{E})$ is a probabilistic space. In this case, the measure μ is additive and $range(\mu) \subset [0,1]$, only in (A_2) and (A_2') we must replace the operation $\vee$ with $+$. The corresponding solutions (4) and (6) are, respectively:

$$\Phi(x,y,u,v) = h\left(x+y, h^{-1}(x,u) \wedge h^{-1}(y,v)\right) \text{ and}$$

$$\Phi(x,y,u,v) = F_{(x,y)}^{k,+}(u,v) = k\left(\frac{x\ k^{-1}(u) + y\ k^{-1}(v)}{x+y}\right), \tag{7}$$

where h and k are functions from Propositions 1 and 2, respectively. In (7) the quantity $\dfrac{x\ k^{-1}(u) + y\ k^{-1}(v)}{x+y}$ can be considered the *weighted average* of the entropies $H\left(\mathcal{P}(F), E_1\right) = u$, $H\left(\mathcal{P}(F), E_2\right) = v$ with weights the measures $\mu(E_1) = x, \mu(E_2) = y$.

2) It is easy to prove that all considerations are satisfied also in the crisp setting.

3) A collector of the entropy for fuzzy partitons evaluated by group of obververs has the following expressions: - from (2) and (4):

$$H\left(\mathcal{P}(F), E_1 \cup E_2\right) =$$

$$h\left[\mu(E_1) \vee \mu(E_2), h^{-1}\left(\mu(E_1), H(\mathcal{P}(F))\right) \wedge h^{-1}\left(\mu(E_2), H(\mathcal{P}(F))\right)\right]$$

where $h : [0,1] \times [0,+\infty] \to [0,+\infty]$ is any function seen in Proposition 1; - from (2), (3), (6) and (7):

$$H\left(\mathcal{P}(F), E_1 \cup E_2\right) = k\left[\frac{\mu(E_1)\ k^{-1}\left(H(\mathcal{P}(F), E_1)\right) \vee \mu(E_2)\ k^{-1}\left(H(\mathcal{P}(F), E_2)\right)}{\mu(E_1) \vee \mu(E_2)}\right],$$

$$H\left(\mathcal{P}(F), E_1 \cup E_2\right) = k\left[\frac{\mu(E_1)\ k^{-1}\left(H(\mathcal{P}(F), E_1)\right) + \mu(E_2)\ k^{-1}\left(H(\mathcal{P}(F), E_2)\right)}{\mu(E_1) + \mu(E_2)}\right]$$

where $k : [0,+\infty] \to [0,+\infty]$ is any function seen in Proposition 2.

References

1. Baker, J.A., Forte, B., Lam, L.F.: On the existence of a collector for a class of information measures. Util. Math. 1, 219–239 (1972)
2. Benvenuti, P., Divari, M., Pandolfi, M.: Su un sistema di equazioni funzionali proveniente dalla teoria soggettiva della informazione. Rend.Mat. 3(5), 529–540 (1972)
3. Benvenuti, P., Vivona, D., Divari, M.: Fuzzy partions and entropy. In: Klement, P., Weber, S. (eds.) Proc. III Linz Seminar on Fuzzy Set Theory: Uncertainty Measures, pp.14–18 (1991)
4. Forte, B.: Measures of information: the general axiomatic theory. R.A.I.R.O pp.63–90, (1969)
5. Kampé de Fériet, J.: Mesures de l'information par un ensemble d'observateurs. C.R. Acad. Sc. Paris. 269, 1081–1085 (1969). 271, 1017-1021 (1970)
6. Kampé de Fériet, J.: La Theorie Generale de L'Information et La Misure Subjective de L'Information. In: Lectures Notes in Mathematics, vol. 398, pp. 1–35. Springer-Verlag, Heidelberg (1974)
7. Kampé de Fériet, J., Forte, B.: Information et Probabilité. C.R. Acad. Sc. Paris, 265A, 110–114(a), 142–146(b), 350–353(c) (1967)
8. Vivona, D., Divari, M.: On a collector of ∧-compositive informations. In: Proc. IPMU 04, pp. 1199–1203 (2004)
9. Vivona, D., Divari, M.: A collector for information without probability in a fuzzy setting. Kybernetika 45, 389–396 (2005)
10. Vivona, D., Divari, M.: Entropies of fuzzy compositive partitions. In: Proc. IPMU 06, pp. 1811–1815 (2006)
11. Zadeh, L.A.: Fuzzy sets. Information and Control 8, 338–353 (1965)

Some Problems with Entropy Measures for the Atanassov Intuitionistic Fuzzy Sets

Eulalia Szmidt and Janusz Kacprzyk

Systems Research Institute, Polish Academy of Sciences
ul. Newelska 6, 01–447 Warsaw, Poland
{szmidt, kacprzyk}@ibspan.waw.pl

Abstract. This paper is a continuation of our previous papers on entropy of the Atanassov intuitionistic fuzzy sets (A-IFSs, for short)[1]. We discuss the necessity of taking into account all three functions (membership, non-membership and hesitation margin) describing A-IFSs while considering the entropy.

Keywords: Intuitionistic fuzzy sets, entropy.

1 Introduction

Fuzziness, a feature of imperfect information, results from the lack of a crisp distinction between the elements belonging and not belonging to a set (i.e. the boundaries of a set under consideration are not sharply defined). A measure of fuzziness often used and cited in the literature is called an entropy (first mentioned by Zadeh [27]).

De Luca and Termini [4] introduced some requirements which capture our intuitive comprehension of a degree of fuzziness. Kaufmann (1975) (cf. [11]) proposed to measure a degree of fuzziness of a fuzzy set A by a metric distance between its membership function and the membership (characteristic) function of its nearest crisp set. Yager [26] viewed a degree of fuzziness in terms of a lack of distinction between the fuzzy set and its complement. Higashi and Klir [3] extended Yager's concept to a general class of fuzzy complements. Yager's approach was also further developed by Hu and Yu [8]. Indeed, it is the lack of distinction between sets and their complements that distinguishes fuzzy sets from crisp sets. The less the fuzzy set differs from its complement, the fuzzier it is. Kosko [10] investigated the fuzzy entropy in relation to a measure of subsethood. Fan at al. [5], [6], [7] generalized Kosko's approach.

Here we discuss measures of fuzziness for intuitionistic fuzzy sets which are a generalization of fuzzy sets. We recall a measure of entropy we introduced (Szmidt and Kacprzyk [16], [22]). We compare our approach with Zeng and Li [28] approach. We discuss the reasons of differences and the counter-intuitive results obtained in the case of Zeng and Li's entropy which boils down to entropy given by Hung [9] (cf. Szmidt and Kacprzyk [22] for further discussion).

---

[1] There is currently a discussion on the appropriateness of the name *intuitionistic fuzzy set* introduced by Atanassov. However, this is beyond the scope of this paper which is just concerned with an application of the concept.

F. Masulli, S. Mitra, and G. Pasi (Eds.): WILF 2007, LNAI 4578, pp. 291–297, 2007.

2   A Brief Introduction to A-IFSs

One of the possible generalizations of a fuzzy set in X (Zadeh [27]), given by

$$A^{'} = \{< x, \mu_{A'}(x) > | x \in X\} \tag{1}$$

where $\mu_{A'}(x) \in [0, 1]$ is the membership function of the fuzzy set $A^{'}$, is an A-IFS, i.e. Atanassov's intuitionistic fuzzy set, (Atanassov [1], [2]) A given by

$$A = \{< x, \mu_A(x), \nu_A(x) > | x \in X\} \tag{2}$$

where: $\mu_A : X \to [0, 1]$ and $\nu_A : X \to [0, 1]$ such that

$$0 \leq \mu_A(x) + \nu_A(x) \leq 1 \tag{3}$$

and $\mu_A(x)$, $\nu_A(x) \in [0, 1]$ denote a degree of membership and a degree of non-membership of $x \in A$, respectively.

Obviously, each fuzzy set may be represented by the following A-IFS

$$A = \{< x, \mu_{A'}(x), 1 - \mu_{A'}(x) > | x \in X\} \tag{4}$$

For each A-IFS in X, we will call

$$\pi_A(x) = 1 - \mu_A(x) - \nu_A(x) \tag{5}$$

an *intuitionistic fuzzy index* (or a *hesitation margin*) of $x \in A$, and it expresses a lack of knowledge of whether x belongs to A or not (cf. Atanassov [2]). It is obvious that $0 \leq \pi_A(x) \leq 1$, for each $x \in X$.

In our further considerations we will use the complement set A^C [2]

$$A^C = \{< x, \nu_A(x), \mu_A(x) > | x \in X\} \tag{6}$$

In our further considerations we will use the normalized Hamming distance between fuzzy sets A, B in $X = \{x_1, \ldots, x_n\}$ Szmidt and Baldwin [13], [14], Szmidt and Kacprzyk [15], [21]:

$$l_{IFS}(A, B) = \frac{1}{2n} \sum_{i=1}^{n} (|\mu_A(x_i) - \mu_B(x_i)| + |\nu_A(x_i) - $$
$$+ \nu_B(x_i)| + |\pi_A(x_i) - \pi_B(x_i)|) \tag{7}$$

For (7) we have: $0 \leq l_{IFS}(A, B) \leq 1$. Clearly the normalized Hamming distance (7) satisfies the conditions of the metric. In Szmidt and Kacprzyk [15], Szmidt and Baldwin [13], [14], and especially in Szmidt and Kacprzyk [21] it is shown why when calculating distances between IFSs we should take into account all three functions describing A-IFSs.

Applications of A-IFSs to group decision making, negotiations, etc. are presented in (Szmidt and Kacprzyk [17,19,20]).

3   Entropy

The entropy measures the whole missing information which may be necessary to have no doubts when classifying an element, i.e. to say that an element fully belongs or fully does not belong to a set considered.

3.1   Zeng and Li's Entropy Measure

We cite here Zeng and Li's entropy measure [28] for an A-IFSs A (notation used in [28] is changed so that they are consistent with those in this paper):

$$E_{ZL}(A) = 1 - \frac{1}{n} \sum_{i=1}^{n} (|\mu_A(x_i) + \mu_A(x_i) + \pi_A(x_i) - 1| \tag{8}$$

Having in mind that for A-IFSs we have $\mu.(x_i) + \nu.(x_i) + \pi.(x_i) = 1$, Zeng and Li's entropy measure (8) becomes

$$E_{ZL}(A) = 1 - \frac{1}{n} \sum_{i=1}^{n} (|\mu_A(x_i) - \nu_A(x_i)| \tag{9}$$

In other words, Zeng and Li's similarity measure (9) does not take into account the values of $\pi_A(x_i)$. Only the values of the memberships and non-memberships are taken into account.

In Szmidt and Kacprzyk [22] we discussed in more detail the above measure (9). Although all the mathematical "constructions" of this measure are correct, the question arises if we may use any mathematically correct approach to represent the measures which by definition are to render some properties that have a concrete semantic meaning, and are in most cases to be useful. It seems that the mathematical correctness is in this context for sure a necessary but not a sufficient condition. The same conclusions are drawn in Szmidt and Kacprzyk [23] for similarity measures.

Now we will recall briefly another approach (cf. Szmidt and Kacprzyk [22] which is not only mathematically correct but at the same time rendering the sense of entropy not as a pure mathematical construction but as a measure to be useful in practice.

3.2   Szmidt and Kacprzyk's Entropy for A-IFSs

In Szmidt and Kacprzyk [22] we gave a motivation and revised some conditions for entropy measures for A-IFSs. Here we only recall one of the possible entropy measures fulfilling the new conditions (cf. Szmidt and Kacprzyk [22]) and rendering the very meaning of entropy.

Entropy for an A-IFS A with n elements may be given as (Szmidt and Kacprzyk [16]):

$$E(A) = \frac{1}{n} \sum_{i=1}^{n} \frac{d(F_i, F_{i,near})}{d(F_i, F_{i,far})} \tag{10}$$

where $d(F_i, F_{i,near})$ is a *distance* from F_i to its the nearer point $F_{i,near}$ among $M(1,0,0)$ and $N(0,1,0)$, and $d(F_i, F_{i,far})$ is the *distance* from F_i to its the farer point $F_{i,far}$ among $M(1,0,0)$ and $N(0,1,0)$.

A ratio-based measure of entropy (10) satisfies the entropy axioms formulated in Szmidt and Kacprzyk [22]. For the detailed explanations we refer an interested reader to Szmidt and Kacprzyk [15], [16], [18], [22].

4   Results

Now we will verify if the results produced by (9) and (10) are consistent with our intuition. We examine entropy of single elements x_i of an A-IFS, each described via (μ_i, ν_i, π_i), namely:

$$x_1 : (0.7, 0.3, 0) \tag{11}$$
$$x_2 : (0.6, 0.2, 0.2) \tag{12}$$
$$x_3 : (0.5, 0.1, 0.4) \tag{13}$$
$$x_4 : (0.4, 0, 0.6) \tag{14}$$

We assume that x_i represents the $i - th$ house we consider to buy. On the one extreme, for house x_1 the first house 70% of the attributes have desirable values, and 30% of attributes have undesirable values. On the other extreme, for house x_4 we only know that it has 40% of the desirable attributes and we do not know about 60% of the attributes we are interested in. The entropy calculated due to (9) gives the following results:

$$E_{ZL}(x_1) = 1 - |0.7 - 03| = 0.6 \tag{15}$$
$$E_{ZL}(x_2) = 1 - |0.6 - 0.2| = 0.6 \tag{16}$$
$$E_{ZL}(x_3) = 1 - |0.5 - 0.1| = 0.6 \tag{17}$$
$$E_{ZL}(x_4) = 1 - |0.4 - 0| = 0.6 \tag{18}$$

Results (15)–(18) suggest that the entropy of all $x_1, \ldots, x_4$ is the same though this is counter-intuitive! It seems that the entropy of the situation expressed by x_1, i.e., 70% positive attributes, 30% negative attributes is less than the entropy of x_4, i.e., 40% of positive attributes, and 60% unknown. Case (x_1) is "clear" in the sense that we know for sure that 30% negative attributes prevents house x_1 to be our "dream house" while in case of (x_4) we only know for sure that it has 40% of desirable attributes, and 60% is unknown. So we may conclude that it is quite possible that (x_4) may: fulfill in 100% our demands (if all 60% of the unknown attributes happen to be desirable), or may fulfill in 40% our demands and does not fulfill 60% of our demands (if 60% of unknown attributes turn out to be undesirable), or in general – 40%+α can fulfill and 0%+β does not fulfill our demands where $\alpha + \beta = 60\%$ and $\alpha, \beta \geq 0$. So we intuitively feel that it is easier to classify house x_1 as fulfilling our demands (30% is missing) than to classify house x_4 to the set of houses fulfilling (worth buying) or not fulfilling (not worth buying) our demands.

The entropy calculated from (10) gives the following results:

$$E(x_1) = \frac{|1 - 0.7| + |0 - 0.3| + |0 - 0|}{|0 - 0.7| + |1 - 0.3| + |0 - 0|} = 0.43 \qquad (19)$$

$$E(x_2) = \frac{|1 - 0.6| + |0 - 0.2| + |0 - 0.2|}{|0 - 0.6| + |1 - 0.2| + |0 - 0.2|} = 0.5 \qquad (20)$$

$$E(x_3) = \frac{|1 - 0.5| + |0 - 0.1| + |0 - 0.4|}{|0 - 0.5| + |1 - 0.1| + |0 - 0.4|} = 0.56 \qquad (21)$$

$$E(x_4) = \frac{|1 - 0.4| + |0 - 0| + |0 - 0.6|}{|0 - 0.4| + |1 - 0| + |0 - 0.6|} = 0.6 \qquad (22)$$

Results (19)–(22) seem to better reflect our intuition - the purchase decision is the easiest in the first case (entropy is the smallest) and the most difficult in the fourth case (the biggest entropy). This may be depicted as in Fig. 1. It is worth stressing that entropy (10) is a special case of a similarity measure (we refere an interested reader to Szmidt and Kacprzyk [18] for more details). Certainly, Fig. 1 a) and b) represent A-IFS entropy only for such $\mu(x)$ and $\nu(x)$ for which $\mu(x) + \nu(x) \leq 1$ (in Figures 1 a) and b) we illustarted the shape of (9) and (10) for $\mu(x) \in [0, 1]$ and $\nu(x) \in [0, 1]$ so to better render the shape differences of the two functions – a more general case of the situation discussed in the example above on buying a house).

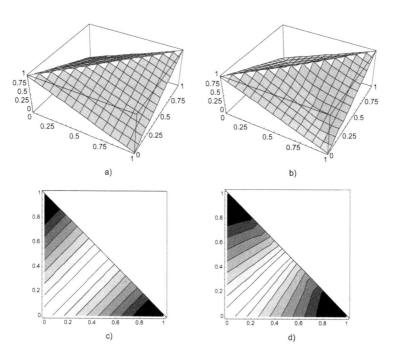

Fig. 1. Entropy calculated from (9): a) and c)– countour plot, entropy calculated from (10): b) and d) – countour plot

It seems that when calculating entropy of A-IFSs one should take into account all three functions (membership, non-membership and hesitation margin) describing an A-IFSs. Only then full information preventing from univocal classification of an element as belonging or not belonging to a set is taken into account (due to the very sense of entropy). This point of view has been also justified in, e.g., image processing via A-IFSs (cf. Vlachos and Sergiadis [25]).

5 Concluding Remarks

We considered the problem of measuring entropy for A-IFSs. It turns out that just the same as it was while considering the possible representations of A-IFSs (Szmidt and Kacprzyk [15], Tasseva at al. [24]), distances between A-IFSs (Szmidt and Kacprzyk [15], [21])), and similarity (Szmidt and Kacprzyk [23]), while considering entropy one should take into account all three functions (membership, non-membership and hesitation margin). Omitting e.g., hesitation margin may lead to counter-intuitive results.

References

1. Atanassov, K.: Intuitionistic Fuzzy Sets. VII ITKR Session. Sofia (Centr. Sci.-Techn. Libr. of Bulg. Acad. of Sci., 1697/84) (in Bulgarian) (1983)
2. Atanassov, K.: Intuitionistic Fuzzy Sets: Theory and Applications. Springer, Heidelberg (1999)
3. Higashi, M., Klir, G.: On measures of fuzziness and fuzzy complements. Int. J. Gen. Syst. 8, 169–180 (1982)
4. De Luca, A., Termini, S.: A definition of a non-probabilistic entropy in the setting of fuzzy sets theory. Inform. and Control 20, 301–312 (1972)
5. Fan, J., Xie, W.: Distance measure and induced fuzzy entropy. Fuzzy Sets and Systems 104, 305–314 (1999)
6. Fan, J-L., Ma, Y-L., Xie, W-X.: On some properties of distance measures. Fuzzy Sets and Systems 117, 355–361 (2001)
7. Fan, J-L., Ma, Y-L.: Some new fuzzy entropy formulas. Fuzzy Sets and Systems 128, 277–284 (2002)
8. Hu, Q., Yu, D.: Entropies of fuzzy indiscernibility relation and its operations. Int. J. of Uncertainty, Knowledge-Based Systems 12(5), 575–589 (2004)
9. Hung, W-L.: A note on entropy of intuitionistic fuzzy sets. Int. J. of Uncertainty, Fuzziness and Knowledge-Based Systems 11(5), 627–633 (2003)
10. Kosko, B.: Fuzzy entropy and conditioning. Inform. Sciences 40, 165–174 (1986)
11. Pal, N.R., Bezdek, J.C.: Measuring fuzzy uncertainty. IEEE Trans. on Fuzzy Systems 2(2), 107–118 (1994)
12. Pal, N.R., Pal, S.K.: Entropy: a new definition and its applications. IEEE Trans. on Systems, Man, and Cybernetics 21(5), 1260–1270 (1991)
13. Szmidt, E., Baldwin, J.: New Similarity Measure for Intuitionistic Fuzzy Set Theory and Mass Assignment Theory. Notes on IFSs 9(3), 60–76 (2003)
14. Szmidt, E., Baldwin, J.: Entropy for Intuitionistic Fuzzy Set Theory and Mass Assignment Theory. Notes on IFSs 10(3), 15–28 (2004)

15. Szmidt, E., Kacprzyk, J.: Distances between intuitionistic fuzzy sets. Fuzzy Sets and Systems 114(3), 505–518 (2000)
16. Szmidt, E., Kacprzyk, J.: Entropy for intuitionistic fuzzy sets. Fuzzy Sets and Systems 118(3), 467–477 (2001)
17. Szmidt, E., Kacprzyk, J.: An Intuitionistic Fuzzy Set Base Approach to Intelligent Data Analysis (an application to medical diagnosis). In: Abraham, A., Jain, L., Kacprzyk, J. (eds.) Recent Advances in Intelligent Paradigms and Applications, pp. 57–70. Physica-Verlag, Heidelberg (2002)
18. Szmidt, E., Kacprzyk, J.: Similarity of intuitionistic fuzzy sets and the Jaccard coefficient. IPMU 2004, pp. 1405–1412 (2004)
19. Szmidt, E., Kacprzyk J.: A Concept of Similatity for Intuitionistic Fuzzy Sets and its use in Group Decision Making. In: 2004 IEEE Conf. on Fuzzy Systems, Budapest pp. 1129–1134 (2004)
20. Szmidt, E., Kacprzyk, J.: A New Concept of a Similarity Measure for Intuitionistic Fuzzy Sets and its Use in Group Decision Making. In: Torra, V., Narukawa, Y., Miyamoto, S. (eds.) MDAI 2005. LNCS (LNAI), vol. 3558, pp. 272–282. Springer, Heidelberg (2005)
21. Szmidt, E., Kacprzyk, J.: Distances Between Intuitionistic Fuzzy Sets: Straightforward Approaches may not work. In: 3rd Int. IEEE Conf. Intelligent Systems, pp. 716–721 (2006)
22. Szmidt, E., Kacprzyk, J.: Entropy and similarity of intuitionistic fuzzy sets. IPMU 2006 pp. 2375–2382 (2006)
23. Szmidt, E., Kacprzyk, J.: A new similarity measure for intuitionistic fuzzy sets: straightforward approaches may not work (Submitted)
24. Tasseva, V., Szmidt, E., Kacprzyk, J.: On one of the geometrical interpretations of the intuitionistic fuzzy sets. Notes on IFSs 11(3), 21–27 (2005)
25. Vlachos, I.K., Sergiadis, G.D.: The Role of Entropy in Intuitionistic Fuzzy Contrast Enhancement (Accepted, 2007)
26. Yager, R.R.: On measures of fuzziness and negation. Part I: Membership in the unit interval. Int. J. Gen. Syst., 5, 221–229 (1997)
27. Zadeh, L.A.: Fuzzy sets. Information and Control 8, 338–353 (1965)
28. Zeng, W., Li, H.: Relationship between similarity measure and entropy of interval valued fuzzy sets. Fuzzy Sets and Systems 157, 1477–1484 (2006)

Twofold Extensions of Fuzzy Datalog

Ágnes Achs

Department of Computer Science, Faculty of Engineering, University of Pécs,
Pécs, Boszorkany u. 2, Hungary
achs@witch.pmmf.hu

Abstract. In this work we present several possible extensions of fuzzy Datalog. At first the concept of fuzzy Datalog will be summarized, then its extension for intuitionistic- and interval-valued fuzzy logic is given and the concept of bipolar fuzzy Datalog is introduced.

Keywords: intuitionistic fuzzy Datalog, interval-valued fuzzy Datalog, bipolar fuzzy Datalog.

1 Introduction

The dominant portion of human knowledge can not be modeled by pure inference systems, because this knowledge is often ambiguous, incomplete and vague. The study of inference systems is tackled by several - and often very different - approaches. When knowledge is represented as a set of facts and rules, this uncertainty can be handled by means of fuzzy logic. A few years ago in [8, 9] a possible combination of Datalog-like languages and fuzzy logic was presented. In these works the concept of fuzzy Datalog has been introduced by completing the Datalog-rules and facts by an uncertainty level and an implication operator. The level of a rule-head from the level of the body, and the level of the rule can be inferred by the implication operator of the rule. Based upon our previous works, later on a possible fuzzy knowledge-base was developed [1]. In this paper we present other possible extensions of fuzzy Datalog: we extend it to intuitionistic- and interval-valued fuzzy logic and joining to the discussion in [2, 3] we introduce the concept of bipolar fuzzy Datalog. On the next pages we summarize the concept of fuzzy Datalog, and then its new extensions will be presented.

2 Fuzzy Datalog

A Datalog program consists of facts and rules. In fuzzy Datalog (fDATALOG) we can complete the facts by an uncertainty level, the rules by an uncertainty level and an implication operator. This means that evaluating the fuzzy implication connecting to the rule, its truth-value according to the implication operator is at least the given uncertainty level. We can infer the level of a rule-head from

F. Masulli, S. Mitra, and G. Pasi (Eds.): WILF 2007, LNAI 4578, pp. 298–305, 2007.

the level of the body, and the level of the rule by the implication operator of the rule. The notion of fuzzy rule is given in definition below.

Definition 1. *An fDATALOG rule is a triplet $r; \beta; I$, where r is a formula of the form*

$$A \leftarrow A_1, ..., A_n (n \geq 0).$$

A is an atom (the head of the rule), $A_1, ..., A_n$ are literals (the body of the rule); I is an implication operator and $\beta \in (0, 1]$ (the level of the rule).

For getting finite result, all the rules in the program must be safe. An fDATALOG rule is safe if all variables occurring in the head also occur in the body, and all variables occurring in a negative literal also occur in a positive one. An fDATALOG program is a finite set of safe fDATALOG rules. There is a special type of rule, called fact. A fact has the form $A \leftarrow; \beta; I$. From now on, we refer to facts as (A, β), because according to implication I, the level of A easily can be computed. The semantics of fDATALOG is defined as the fixed points of consequence transformations. Depending on these transformations, two semantics for fDATALOG can be defined. The deterministic semantics is the least fixed point of the deterministic transformation DT_P, the nondeterministic semantics is the least fixed point of the nondeterministic transformation NT_P. According to the deterministic transformation, the rules of a program are evaluated in parallel, while in the nondeterministic case the rules are considered independently and sequentially. These two transformations are the following:

Definition 2. *Let BP be the Herbrand base of the program P, and let $F(B_P)$ denote the set of all fuzzy sets over B_P. The consequence transformations DT_P : $F(B_P) \rightarrow F(B_P)$ and $NT_P : F(B_P) \rightarrow F(B_P)$ are defined as*

$$DT_P(X) = \{\cup\{(A, \alpha_A)\}\} \cup X \tag{1}$$

and

$$NT_P(X) = \{(A, \alpha_A)\} \cup X \tag{2}$$

where $(A \leftarrow A_1, ..., A_n; \beta; I) \in ground(P)$, $(|A_i|, \alpha_{A_i}) \in X$, $1 \leq i \leq n$; $\alpha_A = \max(0, \min\{\gamma \mid I(\alpha_{body}, \gamma) \geq \beta\})$. $|A_i|$ denotes the kernel of the literal A_i, (i.e., it is the ground atom A_i, if A_i is a positive literal, and $\neg A_i$, if A_i is negative) and $\alpha_{body} = \min(\alpha_{A_1}, ..., \alpha_{A_n})$.

In [8] it is proved that starting from the set of facts, both DT_P and NT_P have fixed points which are the least fixed points in the case of positive P. These fixed points are denoted by lfp(DT_P) and lfp(NT_P). It was also proved, that lfp(DT_P) and lfp(NT_P) are models of P, so we could define lfp(DT_P) as the deterministic semantics, and lfp(NT_P) as the nondeterministic semantics of fDATALOG programs. For a function- and negation-free fDATALOG, the two semantics are the same, but they are different if the program has any negation. In this case the set lfp(DT_P) is not always a minimal model, but the nondeterministic semantics – lfp(NT_P) – is minimal under certain conditions. These conditions are referred to as stratification. Stratification gives an evaluating sequence in which the negative literals are evaluated first [9]. To compute the level of rule-heads, we need the next concept:

Definition 3. *The uncertainty-level function is:*

$$f(I, \alpha, \beta) = \min(\{\gamma \mid I(\alpha, \gamma) \geq \beta\}).$$

According to this function the level of a rule-head can be computed. In the former papers there were detailed several implications (the operators treated in [10]), but now we take out of them only three ones. The values of theirs uncertainty-level function can be easily computed. They are the following:

Gödel	$I_G(\alpha, \gamma) = \begin{cases} 1 & \alpha \leq \gamma \\ \gamma & \text{otherwise} \end{cases}$	$f(I_G, \alpha, \beta) = \min(\alpha, \beta)$
Lukasiewicz	$I_L(\alpha, \gamma) = \begin{cases} 1 & \alpha \leq \gamma \\ 1 - \alpha + \gamma & \text{otherwise} \end{cases}$	$f(I_L, \alpha, \beta) = \max(0, \alpha + \beta - 1)$
Kleene-Dienes	$I_K(\alpha, \gamma) = \max(1 - \alpha, \gamma)$	$f(I_K, \alpha, \beta) = \begin{cases} 0 & \alpha + \beta \leq 1 \\ \beta & \alpha + \beta > 1 \end{cases}$

Further on during the extensions of fDATALOG we deal only with these operators.

3   Extensions of Fuzzy Datalog

In intuitionistic-(IFS) and interval-valued (IVS) fuzzy logic the uncertainty is represented by two values, $\boldsymbol{\mu} = (\mu_1, \mu_2)$, while in "normal" fuzzy logic it is represented by a single value (μ). In the intuitionistic case the two elements must satisfy the condition $\mu_1 + \mu_2 \leq 1$, while in the interval-valued case the condition is $\mu_1 \leq \mu_2$. In IFS μ_1 is the degree of membership, and μ_2 is the degree of non-membership, while in IVS the membership degree is between μ_1 and μ_2. It is obvious that the relation $\mu'_1 = \mu_1$, $\mu'_2 = 1 - \mu_2$ create a mutual connection between the two systems. In both cases an ordering relation can be defined, and according to this ordering a lattice is taking shape:

Definition 4.

$L_F = \{(x_1, x_2) \in [0,1]^2 \mid x_1 + x_2 \leq 1\}, (x_1, x_2) \leq_F (y_1, y_2) \Leftrightarrow x_1 \leq y_1, x_2 \geq y_2$

and

$L_V = \{(x_1, x_2) \in [0,1]^2 \mid x_1 \leq x_2\}, (x_1, x_2) \leq_V (y_1, y_2) \Leftrightarrow x_1 \leq y_1, x_2 \leq y_2$

are lattices of IFS and IVS respectively.

It can be proved that both L_F and L_V are complete lattices [4]. In both cases the extended fDATALOG is defined on these lattices, and the necessary concepts are generalizations of the ones presented in Definition 1 and Definition 2.

Definition 5. *The extended fDATALOG program (efDATALOG) is a finite set of safe efDATALOG rules $(r; \beta; \mathbf{I}_{FV})$;*

- *the extended consequence transformations eDT_P and eNT_P are formally the same as DT_P and NT_P in (1), (2) except:*
$\alpha_A = \max(\mathbf{0}_{FV}, \min\{\gamma \mid \mathbf{I}_{FV}(\alpha_{body}, \gamma) \geq_{FV} \beta\})$ *and*
- *the extended uncertainty-level function is*
$f(\mathbf{I}_{FV}, \alpha, \beta) = \min(\{\gamma \mid \mathbf{I}_{FV}(\alpha, \gamma) \geq_{FV} \beta\}),$

where α, β, γ are elements of L_F, L_V respectively, $\mathbf{I}_{FV} = \mathbf{I}_F$ or $\mathbf{I}_V$ is an implication of L_F or L_V, $\mathbf{0}_{FV}$ is $\mathbf{0}_F = (0,1)$ or $\mathbf{0}_V = (0,0)$ and $\geq_{FV}$ is $\geq_F$ or $\geq_V$.

As eDT_P and eNT_P are inflationary transformations over the complete lattices L_F or L_V, thus according to [11] they have an inflationary fixed point denoted by lfp(eDT_P) and lfp(eNT_P). If P is positive (without negation), then $eDT_P = eNT_P$ is a monotone transformation, so lfp(eDT_P) = lfp(eNT_P) is the least fixed point. The next theorem for extended fDATALOG can be proved in a way similar to the way for fDATALOG in [8, 9].

Theorem 1. *Both eDT_P and eNT_P have a fixed point, denoted by lfp(eDT_P) and lfp(eNT_P). If P is positive, then lfp(eDT_P) = lfp(eNT_P) and this is the least fixed point. lfp(eDT_P) and lfp(eNT_P) are models of P; for negation-free fDATALOG this is the least model of P.*

A number of intuitionistic implications are established in [4, 6] and other papers, four of them are chosen for now, these are the extensions of operators presented in the table above. For these operators we have deduced the suitable interval-value operators, and for both kinds of operators we have deduced the uncertainty-level functions. Pressed for space, the computations can not be shown, only the starting points and results are presented:

The connection between $\mathbf{I}_F$ and $\mathbf{I}_V$ and the extended versions of uncertainty-level functions are given below:

$$\mathbf{I}_V(\alpha, \gamma) = (I_{V1}, I_{V2}) \text{ where}$$

$$I_{V1} = I_{F1}(\alpha', \gamma'), \qquad \alpha' = (\alpha_1, 1 - \alpha_2),$$
$$I_{V2} = 1 - I_{F2}(\alpha', \gamma')); \qquad \gamma' = (\gamma_1, 1 - \gamma_2).$$

$$f(\mathbf{I}_F, \alpha, \beta) = (\min(\{\gamma_1 \mid I_{F1}(\alpha, \gamma) \geq \beta_1\}), \max(\{\gamma_2 \mid I_{F2}(\alpha, \gamma) \leq \beta_2\}));$$

$$f(\boldsymbol{I}_V, \boldsymbol{\alpha}, \boldsymbol{\beta}) = (\min(\{\gamma_1 \mid I_{V1}(\boldsymbol{\alpha}, \boldsymbol{\gamma}) \geq \beta_1\}), \min(\{\gamma_2 \mid I_{V2}(\boldsymbol{\alpha}, \boldsymbol{\gamma}) \geq \beta_2\})).$$

The studied operators and the related uncertainty-level functions are the following:

3.1 Extension of Kleene-Dienes Implication

One possible extension of Kleene-Dienes implication for IFS is:

$$\boldsymbol{I}_{FK}(\boldsymbol{\alpha}, \boldsymbol{\gamma}) = (\max(\alpha_2, \gamma_1), \min(\alpha_1, \gamma_2)).$$

The appropriate computed elements are the followings:

$$\boldsymbol{I}_{VK}(\boldsymbol{\alpha}, \boldsymbol{\gamma}) = (\max(1 - \alpha_2, \gamma_1), \max(1 - \alpha_1, \gamma_2));$$

$$f_1(\boldsymbol{I}_{FK}, \boldsymbol{\alpha}, \boldsymbol{\beta}) = \begin{cases} 0 & \alpha_2 \geq \beta_1 \\ \beta_1 & \text{otherwise} \end{cases}, \quad f_1(\boldsymbol{I}_{VK}, \boldsymbol{\alpha}, \boldsymbol{\beta}) = \begin{cases} 0 & 1 - \alpha_2 \geq \beta_1 \\ \beta_1 & \text{otherwise} \end{cases},$$

$$f_2(\boldsymbol{I}_{FK}, \boldsymbol{\alpha}, \boldsymbol{\beta}) = \begin{cases} 1 & \alpha_1 \leq \beta_2 \\ \beta_2 & \text{otherwise} \end{cases}; \quad f_2(\boldsymbol{I}_{VK}, \boldsymbol{\alpha}, \boldsymbol{\beta}) = \begin{cases} 0 & (1 - \alpha_1 \leq \beta_2 \\ \beta_2 & \text{otherwise} \end{cases}.$$

3.2 Extension of Lukasiewicz Implication

One possible extension of Lukasiewicz implication for IFS is:

$$\boldsymbol{I}_{FL}(\boldsymbol{\alpha}, \boldsymbol{\gamma}) = (\min(1, \alpha_2 + \gamma_1), \max(0, \alpha_1 + \gamma_2 - 1)).$$

The appropriate computed elements are the followings:

$$\boldsymbol{I}_{VL}(\boldsymbol{\alpha}, \boldsymbol{\gamma}) = (\min(1, 1 - \alpha_2 + \gamma_1), \min(1, 1 - \alpha_1 + \gamma_2));$$

$$f_1(\boldsymbol{I}_{FK}, \boldsymbol{\alpha}, \boldsymbol{\beta}) = \min(1 - \alpha_2, \max(0, \beta_1 - \alpha_2)),$$
$$f_2(\boldsymbol{I}_{FK}, \boldsymbol{\alpha}, \boldsymbol{\beta}) = \max(1 - \alpha_1, \min(1, 1 - \alpha_1 + \beta_2));$$

$$f_1(\boldsymbol{I}_{VK}, \boldsymbol{\alpha}, \boldsymbol{\beta}) = \max(0, \alpha_2 + \beta_1 - 1),$$
$$f_2(\boldsymbol{I}_{VK}, \boldsymbol{\alpha}, \boldsymbol{\beta}) = \max(0, \alpha_1 + \beta_2 - 1).$$

3.3 Extensions of Gödel Implication

There are several alternative extensions of Gödel implication, now we present two of them:

$$\boldsymbol{I}_{FG1}(\boldsymbol{\alpha}, \boldsymbol{\gamma}) = \begin{cases} (1, 0) & \alpha_1 \leq \gamma_1 \\ (\gamma_1, 0) & \alpha_1 > \gamma_1, \alpha_2 \geq \gamma_2 \\ (\gamma_1, \gamma_2) & \alpha_1 > \gamma_1, \alpha_2 < \gamma_2 \end{cases}; \quad \boldsymbol{I}_{FG2}(\boldsymbol{\alpha}, \boldsymbol{\gamma}) = \begin{cases} (1, 0) & \alpha_1 \leq \gamma_1, \alpha_2 \geq \gamma_2 \\ (\gamma_1, \gamma_2) & \text{otherwise} \end{cases}.$$

The appropriate computed elements are:

$$I_{VG1}(\boldsymbol{\alpha},\boldsymbol{\gamma})=\begin{cases} (1,1) & \alpha_1 \leq \gamma_1 \\ (\gamma_1,1) & \alpha_1 > \gamma_1, \alpha_2 \geq \gamma_2 \\ (\gamma_1,\gamma_2) & \alpha_1 > \gamma_1, \alpha_2 < \gamma_2 \end{cases} ; \quad I_{VG2}(\boldsymbol{\alpha},\boldsymbol{\gamma})=\begin{cases} (1,1) & \alpha_1 \leq \gamma_1, \alpha_2 \leq \gamma_2 \\ (\gamma_1,\gamma_2) & \text{otherwise} \end{cases}.$$

$$f_1(\boldsymbol{I}_{FG1},\boldsymbol{\alpha},\boldsymbol{\beta}) = \min(\alpha_1,\beta_1), \qquad f_1(\boldsymbol{I}_{FG2},\boldsymbol{\alpha},\boldsymbol{\beta}) = \min(\alpha_1,\beta_1),$$

$$f_2(\boldsymbol{I}_{FG1},\boldsymbol{\alpha},\boldsymbol{\beta}) = \begin{cases} 1 & \alpha_1 \leq \beta_2 \\ \max(\alpha_2,\beta_2) & \text{otherwise} \end{cases}; \quad f_2(\boldsymbol{I}_{FG2},\boldsymbol{\alpha},\boldsymbol{\beta}) = \max(\alpha_2,\beta_2);$$

$$f_1(\boldsymbol{I}_{VG1},\boldsymbol{\alpha},\boldsymbol{\beta}) = \min(\alpha_1,\beta_1), \qquad f_1(\boldsymbol{I}_{VG2},\boldsymbol{\alpha},\boldsymbol{\beta}) = \min(\alpha_1,\beta_1),$$

$$f_2(\boldsymbol{I}_{VG1},\boldsymbol{\alpha},\boldsymbol{\beta}) = \begin{cases} 0 & \alpha_1 \leq \beta_2 \\ \min(\alpha_2,\beta_2) & \text{otherwise} \end{cases}; \quad f_2(\boldsymbol{I}_{VG2},\boldsymbol{\alpha},\boldsymbol{\beta}) = \min(\alpha_2,\beta_2).$$

An extremely important question is whether the resulting degrees satisfy the conditions referring to IFS and IVS respectively. Unfortunately, for implications other than G2, the resulting degrees do not fulfill these conditions in all cases. (It is possible, that as a result of further research the current results can be used for eliminating the contradiction between the facts and rules of the program.) For now, the next proposition can easily be proven:

Proposition 1. *For* $\boldsymbol{\alpha} = (\alpha_1,\alpha_2)$, $\boldsymbol{\beta} = (\beta_1,\beta_2)$
if $\alpha_1 + \alpha_2 \leq 1$, $\beta_1 + \beta_2 \leq 1$ *then* $f_1(\boldsymbol{I}_{FG2},\boldsymbol{\alpha},\boldsymbol{\beta}) + f_2(\boldsymbol{I}_{FG2},\boldsymbol{\alpha},\boldsymbol{\beta}) \leq 1$;
if $\alpha_1 \leq \alpha_2$, $\beta_1 \leq \beta_2$ *then* $f_1(\boldsymbol{I}_{VG2},\boldsymbol{\alpha},\boldsymbol{\beta}) \leq f_2(\boldsymbol{I}_{VG2},\boldsymbol{\alpha},\boldsymbol{\beta})$.

4 Bipolar Extension of Fuzzy Datalog

The above mentioned problem of extended implications and the results of certain psychological researches have led to the idea of bipolar fuzzy Datalog. The intuitive meaning of intuitionistic degrees is based on psychological observations, namely on the idea that concepts are more naturally approached by separately envisaging positive and negative instances [2, 6, 8]. Taking a further step, there are differences not only in the instances but also in the way of thinking as well. There is difference between positive and negative thinking, between using modus ponens (positive inference) and using modus tollens (negative inference) [5]. The idea of bipolar Datalog is based on the previous observation: we use two kinds of ordinary fuzzy implications for positive and negative inference, i.e. we define a pair of consequence transformations instead of single one. Since in the original transformations lower bounds are used with degrees of uncertainty, therefore starting from IFS facts, the resulting degrees will be lower bounds of membership and non-membership respectively, instead of the upper bound for non-membership. However, if each non-membership value μ is transformed into membership value $\mu' = 1 - \mu$, then both members of head-level can be inferred similarly. Therefore, two kinds of bipolar evaluations have been defined.

Definition 6. *The bipolar fDATALOG program (bfDATALOG) is a finite set of safe bfDATALOG rules* $(r; (\beta_1, \beta_2); (I_1, I_2))$;

- *in variant "A" the elements of bipolar consequence transformations* $bDT_P = (DT_{P1}, DT_{P2})$ *and* $bNT_P = (NT_{P1}, NT_{P2})$ *are the same as* DT_P *and* NT_P *in (1), (2),*
- *in variant "B" in* DT_{P2} *and* NT_{P2} *the level of rule's head is:*
$\alpha'_{A2} = \max(0, \min\{\gamma'_2 | I_2(\alpha'_{body2}, \gamma'_2) \geq \beta'_2\}); \alpha'_{body2} = \min(\alpha'_{A_1 2}, \ldots, \alpha'_{A_N 2})$

According to the two variant, the uncertainty-level functions are:

$$\boldsymbol{f}_A = (f_{A1}, f_{A2}); \quad \boldsymbol{f}_B = (f_{B1}, f_{B2});$$

$$f_{A1} = f_{B1} = \min\{\gamma_1 \mid I_1(\alpha_1, \gamma_1) \geq \beta_1\};$$

$$f_{A2} = \min\{\gamma_2 \mid I_2(\alpha_2, \gamma_2) \geq \beta_2\};$$

$$f_{B2} = 1 - \min\{1 - \gamma_2 \mid I_2(1 - \alpha_2, 1 - \gamma_2) \geq 1 - \beta_2\}.$$

It is evident, that applying the transformation $\mu'_1 = \mu_1$, $\mu'_2 = 1 - \mu_2$, for each IFS levels of the program, the B variant can be apply to IVS degrees as well. Contrary to the results of efDATALOG, the resulting degrees of most variant of bipolar fuzzy Datalog satisfy the conditions referring to IFS and IVS respectively.

Proposition 2. *For* $\boldsymbol{\alpha} = (\alpha_1, \alpha_2)$, $\boldsymbol{\beta} = (\beta_1, \beta_2)$ *and for* $(I_1, I_2) = (I_G, I_G)$; $(I_1, I_2) = (I_L, I_L)$; $(I_1, I_2) = (I_L, I_G)$; $(I_1, I_2) = (I_K, I_K)$; $(I_1, I_2) = (I_L, I_K)$
if $\alpha_1 + \alpha_2 \leq 1$, $\beta_1 + \beta_2 \leq 1$ *then* $f_{A1}(I_1, \boldsymbol{\alpha}, \boldsymbol{\beta}) + f_{A2}(I_2, \boldsymbol{\alpha}, \boldsymbol{\beta}) \leq 1$
and $f_{B1}(I_1, \boldsymbol{\alpha}, \boldsymbol{\beta}) + f_{B2}(I_2, \boldsymbol{\alpha}, \boldsymbol{\beta}) \leq 1$;
further on

$$f_{A1}(I_G, \boldsymbol{\alpha}, \boldsymbol{\beta}) + f_{A2}(I_L, \boldsymbol{\alpha}, \boldsymbol{\beta}) \leq 1; \quad f_{A1}(I_G, \boldsymbol{\alpha}, \boldsymbol{\beta}) + f_{A2}(I_K, \boldsymbol{\alpha}, \boldsymbol{\beta}) \leq 1;$$
$$f_{A1}(I_K, \boldsymbol{\alpha}, \boldsymbol{\beta}) + f_{A2}(I_G, \boldsymbol{\alpha}, \boldsymbol{\beta}) \leq 1; \quad f_{A1}(I_K, \boldsymbol{\alpha}, \boldsymbol{\beta}) + f_{A2}(I_L, \boldsymbol{\alpha}, \boldsymbol{\beta}) \leq 1.$$

Example: Consider the next program:

$(p(a), (0.6, 0.25))$. $(q(a); (0.7, 0.1))$.

$(r(a), (0.7, 0.3))$. $q(x) \leftarrow p(x), r(x); I; (0.8, 0.15)$.

Let $\boldsymbol{I} = \boldsymbol{I}_{FK}(\boldsymbol{\alpha}, \boldsymbol{\gamma}) = (\max(\alpha_2, \gamma_1), \min(\alpha_1, \gamma_2))$, then as $\alpha_{body} = \min((0.6, 0.25), (0.7, 0.3)) = (0.6, 0.3)$, so $f_1(I_{FK}, \boldsymbol{\alpha}, \boldsymbol{\beta}) = \beta_1 = 0.8$, $f_2(I_{FK}, \boldsymbol{\alpha}, \boldsymbol{\beta}) = \beta_2 = 0.15$, that is the level of rule's head is $(0.8, 0.15)$. Allowing the other levels of q(a), its resulting levels are: $\max((0.8, 0.15), (0.7, 0.1)) = (0.8, 0.1)$. So the fixed point of the program is:

$$\{(p(a), (0.6, 0.25)), (r(a), (0.7, 0.3)), (q(a), (0.8, 0.1))\}$$

Now let the program be evaluated in bipolar manner and let $I = (I_L, I_G)$, then in variant "B" $\alpha_{body1} = \min(0, 6, 0, 7) = 0.6$, $\alpha_{body2} = 1 - \min(1 - 0.3, 1 - 0.25) = 0.3$; $f_{B1}(I_L, \alpha_1, \beta_1) = \max(0, \alpha_1 + \beta_1 - 1) = 0.8 + 0.6 - 1 = 0.4$; $f_{B2}(I_G, \alpha_2, \beta_2) = 1 - \min(1 - \alpha_2, 1 - \beta_2) = 1 - \min(0.7, 0.85) = 0.3$, allowing the other levels of q(a), its resulting levels are $(\max(0.4, 0.7), \max(0.3, 0.1))$, so the fixed point is:

$$\{(p(a), (0.6, 0.25)), (r(a), (0.7, 0.3)), (q(a), (0.7, 0.3))\}.$$

5 Conclusions

In this paper we have presented several possible extensions of fuzzy Datalog to intuitionistic- and interval-valued fuzzy logic, and the concept of bipolar fuzzy Datalog has been introduced. Our propositions were proven for negation-free fDATALOG. The extension of stratified fDATALOG and the terminal conditions of fixed point algorithm will be the subject of further research as well.

References

1. Achs, A.: Creating and evaluating of fuzzy knowledgebase, Journal of Universal Computer Science, 12–9 (2006) http://www.jucs.org/jucs_12_9
2. Dubois, D., Gottwald, S., Hajek, P., Kacprzyk, J., Prade, H.: Terminological difficulties in fuzzy set theory. The case of "Intuitionistic Fuzzy Sets", Fuzzy Sets and Systems 156, 485–491 (2005)
3. Atanassov, K., Dubois, D., Gottwald, S., Hajek, P., Kacprzyk, J., Prade's papers, H.: Terminological diffculties in fuzzy set theory-the case of "Intuitionistic Fuzzy Sets. Fuzzy Sets and Systems 156, 496–499 (2005)
4. Cornelis, C., Deschrijver, G., Kerre, E.E.: Implication in intuitionistic fuzzy and interval-valued fuzzy set theory: construction, classification, application. International Journal of Approximate Reasoning 35, 55–95 (2004)
5. Új észjárások, M.L.: Tercium Kiadó, Budapest (2001)
6. Dubois, D., Hajek, P., Prade, H.: Knowledge-Driven versus Data-Driven Logics. Journal of Logic, Language, and Information 9, 65–89 (2000)
7. Atanassov, K., Gargov, G.: Elements of intuitionistic fuzzy logic. Part I, Fuzzy Sets and Systems 95, 39–52 (1998)
8. Cacioppo, J.T., Gardner, W.L., Berntson, G.G.: Beyond bipolar conceptualization and measures: the case of attitudes and evaluative spaces. Personality and Social Psychol. Rev. 1, 3–25 (1997)
9. Achs, A., Kiss, A.: Fixed point query in fuzzy Datalog, Annales Univ. Sci. Budapest. Sect. Comp. 15, 223–231 (1995)
10. Achs, A., Kiss, A.: Fuzzy extension of Datalog. Acta Cybernetica Szeged 12, 153–166 (1995)
11. Dubois, D., Prade, H.: Fuzzy sets in approximate reasoning, Part 1: Inference with possibility distributions. Fuzzy Sets and Systems 40, 143–202 (1991)
12. Ceri, S., Gottlob, G., Tanca, L.: Logic Programming and Databases. Springer-Verlag, Berlin (1990)

Combs Method Used in an Intuitionistic Fuzzy Logic Application

Jon E. Ervin[1] and Sema E. Alptekin[2]

[1] Apogee Research Group, Los Osos, CA 93402, USA
[2] California Polytechnic State University, San Luis Obispo, CA 93407, USA
apogee@alumni.calpoly.edu, salpteki@calpoly.edu

Abstract. In this paper, we describe the optimization of membership functions in an Intuitionistic Fuzzy Logic application developed in the Matlab software environment. A unique formulation, known as Combs method, is used to control the problem of 'exponential rule expansion' in the rule base. The optimization is performed using a Particle Swarm Optimization (PSO) algorithm to adjust the geometry of trapezoidal membership functions. The technique is tested against the Wisconsin Breast Cancer Database. The use of Combs method shows great promise in significantly expanding the range and complexity of problems that can be addressed using Intuitionistic Fuzzy Logic.

Keywords: Intuitionistic Fuzzy Logic, Particle Swarm Optimization, Combs Method.

1 Introduction

Fuzzy Logic has proven to be a very useful tool in a number of niche applications, particularly in automated control and decision-making. However, a major drawback of expanding the use of the fuzzy algorithm to more complex problems is that the rule-base generally grows exponentially as the number of input membership functions increases. In Intuitionistic Fuzzy Logic (IFL), introduced by Atanassov [1], this problem is exacerbated further by the introduction of non-membership functions in addition to the usual membership functions for some or all of the input variables. This shortcoming of Fuzzy Logic and IFL has severely limited its use to relatively small, specialized applications.

A number of authors have developed techniques to mitigate this problem by various means [2-4]. However, in most cases the underlying issue of rule-base expansion remains as the number of inputs increases. In contrast, a unique methodology, developed by William Combs, addresses this 'exponential rule expansion' problem directly [5-9]. Combs method changes the problem from one of an exponential dependence to a linear dependence, thus making the solution of systems with a large number of inputs and associated membership functions much more tractable. The use of Combs method can also help simplify the automated tuning process of a fuzzy system, by fixing the structure of the rule-base at the beginning of the tuning process. Tuning can then proceed by only adjusting membership functions while maintaining the same rule-base throughout the process.

F. Masulli, S. Mitra, and G. Pasi (Eds.): WILF 2007, LNAI 4578, pp. 306–312, 2007.
© Springer-Verlag Berlin Heidelberg 2007

We have chosen to use a Particle Swarm Optimization (PSO) algorithm to optimize the membership functions for this purpose. PSO, introduced by Kennedy and Eberhart [10], is a population-based algorithm inspired by the coordinated group behaviors of animals such as fish and birds. The initial PSO population of candidate solutions or "particles" is usually distributed randomly over the allowable N-dimensional solution space. The solution represented by the position of each particle in this N-space is then evaluated using an appropriate fitness function.

The Wisconsin Breast Cancer Database (WBCD) was used as the test case for the algorithm [11]. This instance of the dataset consists of 9 different, real valued input variables used in the diagnosis of whether a given suspect tissue mass is a benign or a malignant cancerous growth. These input variables ranges in value from 0 to 10 and are associated with a single binary output that can take the value of benign or malignant.

In the following section a brief background of Combs method is provided followed by a section describing the methodology of the optimization process. Results from the optimization runs are discussed in section 4 and some final remarks are given in the Conclusion.

2   Combs' URC Method

William Combs, himself refers to his method as the union rule configuration (URC) versus what he calls the intersection rule configuration (IRC) of the traditional fuzzy rule-base construct [6]. The main difference in appearance between the URC and IRC is that every rule in the rule-base of the URC has only one antecedent for every consequent. Initially, this may sound counter-intuitive as a means of reducing the number of rules, however by imposing this restriction it requires that each membership function of all the input variables is used only once in the antecedent of a rule in the rule base. Each of these rules are joined by a logical OR in the rule-base, hence the designation union rule configuration.

To illustrate, suppose you have a fuzzy system of 5 inputs with 7 membership functions each and you wish to design a complete rule-base that covers all possible contingencies. In the simplest approach to building a rule base, a separate rule is formed for each of the possible combinations of the input membership functions, which will result in 16,807 (7^5) rules in the conventional technique. In contrast the URC method will have only 5x7=35 rules for the same number of inputs and membership functions. The URC has advantages over other rule trimming methods in simplicity and ease of definition as well as lending itself to a straight forward tuning process.

Combs and his various co-authors show that the entire problem space can be just as well modeled by implementing the URC as it can when using the IRC. A spirited debate can be found in the literature discussing the validity of the claims made for the URC and the interested reader is referred to the references [6-9] for detail on this topic. In our own experience in a prior practical application [12] the URC provided equivalent performance to the IRC with a much smaller rule-base.

The Intuitionistic Fuzzy system for this project was developed using the Fuzzy Logic Toolbox in Matlab. An initial set of membership and non-membership functions were developed for each of the 9 input variables of the WBCD. It was these functions that were later optimized in the PSO tuning process. The sum of the membership and non-membership functions was forced to remain less than one resulting in a hesitation margin that ranged in value over the interval [0,1].

The WBCD was chosen for this study because it provides a larger number of inputs than many benchmark datasets, providing an opportunity to appreciate the rule-base size savings afforded by using the URC method. The entire rule-base consisted of 36 rules (9 inputs x 4 membership/non-membership functions) versus the 262,144 (4^9) maximum number of rules that could be used in the IRC method.

3 Optimization

Particle Swarm Optimization (PSO), like the Genetic Algorithm is a population-based stochastic optimization method inspired by biological phenomena. In the case of PSO the inspiration comes from flocking behaviors of birds or schooling of fish. An optimization run is usually initialized by dispersing a population of solutions at random throughout the N-dimensional problem space. A new position for each of the solutions or "particles" is then calculated based on the equations:

$$V_{id}^{+1} = V_{id} + c_1 r_1 (X_{id}^{best} - X_{id}) + c_2 r_2 (G_d^{best} - X_{id}) \tag{1}$$

$$X_{id}^{+1} = X_{id} + V_{id}^{+1} \quad i = 1,...M \text{ Population} \quad d = 1,...N \text{ Dimensions} \tag{2}$$

where X_{id} is the particle position vector and V_{id} is an associated "velocity" vector. The predetermined constant coefficient c_1 is often referred to as the cognitive parameter and c_2 as the social parameter in the velocity vector. The random numbers r_1 and r_2 are selected from a uniform distribution on the interval [0,1] and X_{id}^{best} and G_d^{best} are the previous personal best position for each individual particle and the global best position of the population, respectively.

A number of improvements and variations on these original equations have been made by a number of authors [13], but in general the formulation remains relatively simple and easy to implement in software. Fortunately for us, an excellent add-on to the Matlab suite, the PSO Toolbox is distributed free for use on the internet [14]. We modified the source code of this package to interface with the Fuzzy Logic Toolbox that is also an add-on to Matlab software suite [15]. These software elements were combined with the Wisconsin Breast Cancer Dataset (WBCD) to develop an optimized Intuitionistic Fuzzy System for diagnosing tumor malignancy. A flow diagram of the optimization process is shown in Fig. 1.

The output from the IFL system was a continuous number between [0,1] for each set of input data values. Any value in the range [0, 0.5] was assigned a diagnosis of benign, while a value in the range [0.5, 1] was considered malignant. The fitness function for the optimizer was constructed in such a way as to minimize the absolute number of breast cancer misdiagnoses. A secondary term in the fitness function served to minimize the ambiguity in correct diagnoses by penalizing values that came

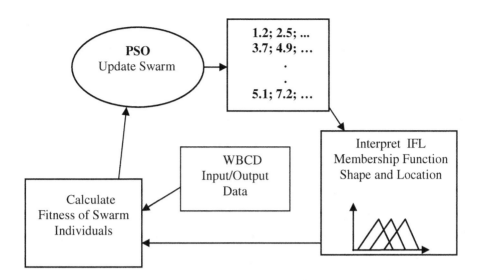

Fig. 1. IFL Membership Function Optimization

close to a value of 0.5. A scaling coefficient was applied to the secondary term to ensure that it served only as a tie-breaker for solutions that provided the same number of correct diagnoses.

Figure 2 shows the improvement in the fitness function versus the number of epochs executed for a variety of PSO formulations.

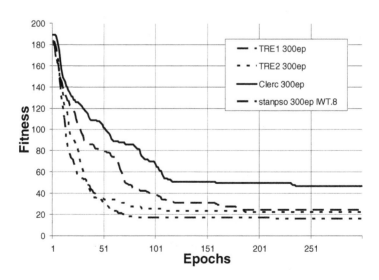

Fig. 2. Convergence of Various PSO Formulations

Although some formulations exhibited faster convergence than others, they all performed well when allowed to run for thousands of epochs. The improvement in the fitness function during an optimization run followed an exponential decay, showing rapid improvement early on and much slower gains with increasing numbers of epochs. However, slight improvement was noticeable throughout the runs in the secondary fitness objective of moving correct diagnoses away from a value of 0.5 to less ambiguous values of 0 or 1.

The PSO method provided convergence in a reasonable amount of time on a relatively modest computing platform. The method also was easy to formulate and code into a working program in a short amount of time.

4 Results

The optimization process successfully produced an intuitionistic fuzzy system that provided results similar to that found by other authors [16]. The best outcome produced a system that gives a correct diagnosis 98.83% of the time or 8 misdiagnoses out of 683 cases. Several separate optimization runs, with different parameter values and different PSO formulations were able to achieve this result. There was significant variation in the membership functions developed from separate optimization runs, resulting in differences in the secondary fitness criterion that determined the level of system ambiguity. A typical optimization run with a population of 90 particles running for 12,000 epochs would finish in 8 hours on a Dell Latitude laptop with an 850 MHz CPU.

Figure 3 shows the distribution of the values of the input "bare nuclei" with respect to benign/malignancy of the tissue mass. On the chart a diagnosis of benign is marked as an "x" and a diagnosis of malign is marked with an "o". The distribution shows a strong correspondence between low values and a diagnosis of benign, however there are a number of exceptions to this generalization. This distribution is characteristic to a greater or lesser degree in all of the input variables.

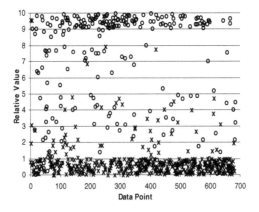

Fig. 3. Distribution of Input "Bare Nuclei"

The membership and non-membership functions for the same input variable "Bare Nuclei" are shown in figure 4. The thin lines in this figure are non-membership functions and the thick lines are the membership functions. From this figure it is clear that the computed (non)membership functions are not simple complements of each other. Membership and non-membership functions for the other input variables have a similar geometry to those shown in figure 4. The membership functions generated by the process exhibited varying values of hesitation margin ranging from 0 to nearly 1. The non-membership functions appeared to play an important role in tuning the system to provide better diagnostic accuracy.

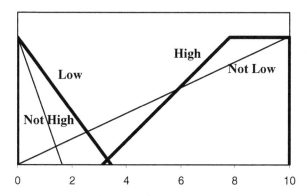

Fig. 4. Membership and Non-membership functions for Input "Bare Nuclei"

5 Conclusions

An intuitionistic fuzzy system was optimized to produce a correct breast cancer diagnosis with an accuracy that rivaled that of the best systems to date. The IFL employed Combs URC rule construction methodology to limit rule-base growth to a linear relationship with increasing numbers of inputs and membership functions. This is a significant improvement over the standard formulation that suffers from an exponential growth of rules with increasing inputs/membership functions. These results suggest that it may be possible to apply fuzzy logic in general, and intuitionistic fuzzy logic in particular, to complex problems with large numbers of inputs and (non)membership functions.

In this research we used Particle Swarm Optimization to tune the geometry and location of (non)membership functions. We made no attempt to optimize the performance of the optimizer, yet we were able to achieve a satisfactory result within a reasonable amount of CPU time on a fairly modest computing platform.

References

1. Atanassov, Krassimir T.: Intuitionistic Fuzzy Sets: Theory and Applications, Springer-Verlag New York, LLC
2. Guvenc, M.K., Passino, K.M.: Avoiding Exponential Parameter Growth in Fuzzy Systems. IEEE Transactions on Fuzzy Systems 9(1) (February 2001)

3. Linkens, D.A., Nyongesa, H.O.: A Hierarchical Multivariable Fuzzy Controller for learning with Genetic Algorithms. Int. J. Control 63(5), 865–883 (1996)

4. Raju, G.V.S., Zhou, J.: Adaptive Hierarchical Fuzzy Controller. IEEE Transactions on Systems, Man, and Cybernetics 23(4), 973–980 (1993)

5. Cox, E.: The Fuzzy Systems Handbook: A Practitioner's Guide to Building, Using, and Maintaining Fuzzy Systems – Appendix A. Academic, Boston, MA (1994)

6. Combs, W.E., Andrews, J.E.: Combinatorial Rule Explosion Eliminated by a Fuzzy Rule Configuration. IEEE Transactions on Fuzzy Systems 6(1), 1–11 (1998)

7. Weinschenk, J. J., Combs, W.E. , Marks II, R. J.: Avoidance of rule explosion by mapping fuzzy systems to a disjunctive rule configuration, 2003 In: International Conference on Fuzzy Systems (FUZZ-IEEE), St. Louis, (May 25-28, 2003)

8. Dick, S., Kandel, A.: A comment on Combinatorial Rule Explosion Eliminated by a Fuzzy Rule Configuration by Combs, W.E., Andrews, J., IEEE Transactions on Fuzzy Systems, vol. 7(4), pp. 475–477 (1999)

9. Mendel, J.M., Liang, Q.: Comments on Combinatorial Rule Explosion Eliminated by a Fuzzy Rule Configuration. IEEE Transactions on Fuzzy Systems 7(3), 369–373 (1999)

10. Eberhart, R., Kennedy, J.: A New Optimizer Using Particle Swarm Theory, In: Proc. of the Sixth Int. Symposium on Micro Machine and Human Science, MHS '95, pp. 39–43 (4-6 Oct 1995)

11. Wolberg, W. H.: Wisconsin Breast Cancer Database (last accessed on Jan 26, 2007) http://www.ailab.si/orange/datasets.asp?Inst=on&Atts=on&Class=on&Values=on&Description =on& sort=Data+Set

12. Ervin, J. C., Alptekin, S., DeTurris, D. J.: Optimization of the Fuzzy Logic Controller for an Autonomous UAV, In: Proceedings of the Joint 4th European Society of Fuzzy Logic and Technology (EUSFLAT) Conference, Barcelona, Spain, (7-9 September) pp. 227–232 (2005)

13. Clerc, M.: Particle Swarm Optimization, ISTE Publishing Company (2006)

14. Birge, B.: Particle Swarm Optimization Toolbox, (last accessed on Jan 26, 2007) http://www.mathworks.com/matlabcentral/fileexchange/loadFile.do?objectId=7506

15. Jang, J. S., Gulley, N.: Fuzzy Logic Toolbox User's Guide, version 1, The MathWorks, Natick Mass (1997)

16. Pena-Reyes, C.A., Sipper, M.: Fuzzy CoCo: A Cooperative Coevolutionary Approach to Fuzzy Modeling. IEEE Transactions on Fuzzy Systems 9(5), 727–737 (2001)

Intuitionistic Fuzzy Spatial Relationships in Mobile GIS Environment

Mohammad Reza Malek[1, 3], Farid Karimipour[2], and Saeed Nadi[2]

[1] Department of GIS, Faculty of Geodesy and Geomatics Engineering,
KN Toosi University of Technology, Tehran, Iran
malek@ncc.neda.net.ir
[2] Department of Surveying and Geomatics Engineering, Faculty of Engineering,
University of Tehran, Tehran, Iran
{fkarimipr, snadi}@ut.ac.ir
[3] Research center, National Cartographic Center, Tehran, Iran

Abstract. The paper aimed to establish a framework for handling the relationships between different agents in mobile environments. In such environments, objects are vague due to incompleteness and local nature of sensed data. The lack of relevant data stimulated us to use intuitionistic fuzzy (IF) logic for modeling spatial relationships between them. In this paper uncertainty modeling of spatial relationships are analyzed from the view point of intuitionistic fuzzy (IF) logic and in order to provide a paradigm that treats with uncertain topological relationships in mobile GIS environments, a logical framework is presented in which the concept of spatial influenceability is combined with the IF logic.

1 Introduction

Mobile computing is a new revolutionary style of technology emerging of the advances in the development of portable hardware and wireless communications. It enables us to access information anywhere and anytime. Advances in location-based engines and on-board positioning sensors lead to mobile geospatial information system (GIS). Mobile GIS as an integrating system of mobile computing and some GIS capabilities has fostered a great interest in the GIS field [15]. It becomes a new branch of GIS and brings the GIS into a new stage of development.

Although the mobile computing has been increasingly grown in the past decade, there still exist some important constraints which complicate the design of mobile information systems. The limited resources on the mobile computing would restrict some features available on the traditional computing. Describing spatial phenomena in a mobile GIS suffers from uncertainty. Sources of uncertainty are the inexact or incomplete definition of objects, and the inability to observe precise and complete relevant data (see [6]). The description of objects- static or dynamic- is not only uncertain in the above mentioned sense, but also contradictory in different contexts [16]. As an example, consider the navigation services for tourist. It is not enough to focus on technical parameters, but navigation services in this environment need to be dynamically generated according to a wider range of variables from user preferences and

F. Masulli, S. Mitra, and G. Pasi (Eds.): WILF 2007, LNAI 4578, pp. 313–320, 2007.
© Springer-Verlag Berlin Heidelberg 2007

interests, the given task, cultural aspects to communicative goals and actual context and location. Therefore a mobile GIS environment is an uncertain prone environment.

Although fuzzy logic methods are of great interest in many GIS applications to handle the uncertainty, the traditional fuzzy logic has two important deficiencies which make it irrelevant for mobile GIS environments [17],[18],[19],[20]: First, to apply the fuzzy logic we need to assign, to every property and for every value, a crisp membership function and second, it does not distinguish between the situation in which there is no knowledge about a certain statement and a situation that the belief to the statement in favor and against is the same. In a mobile GIS environment, however, sensors of user side could not access all relevant information about other users (not complete data) and they are concerned to the user and its neighbors (not global data). Fortunately, abovementioned characteristics can be handled using intuitionistic fuzzy (IF).

One of the most important characteristics of qualitative properties of spatial data and perhaps the most fundamental aspect of space is topology and topological relationship which are invariant with respect to specific transformations due to homeomorphism. The study of topological relationships is firmly evolving as an important area of research in the mobile GIS in both temporal and spatial aspects [8] and [12],[13]. In this direction, the concept of influenceability seems promising. Influenceability which stands for spatial causal relations, i.e. objects must come in contact with one another; is primary order relation. Although influenceability as a primary relation does not need to prove, it has some exclusive properties which show why it is selected. Influenceability supports contextual information and can be served as a basis for context aware mobile computing.

In this paper, uncertainty modeling of spatial relationships are analyzed from the view point of intuitionistic fuzzy (IF) logic. In order to provide a paradigm that treats with uncertain topological relationships in mobile GIS environment, a logical framework is presented in which the concept of spatial influenceability is combined with the IF logic. The remainder of the paper is structured as follows: Section 2 reviews related works on temporal and spatial relationships and also using fuzzy and IF in GIS applications. Section 3 presents the fundamental concepts of influenceability and introduces an algebraic logical framework for it. In section 4, the concepts of influenceability and IF are integrated to create a framework to handle the Mobile environment situation. Finally, section 5 contains some conclusions and ideas for future works.

2   Related Works

There are some spatial and temporal topological models for spatial objects among which thirteen topological relations between two temporal intervals by Allen [1] and 9-intersection approach for spatial topological relations by Egenhofer [10],[11],[12] have been widely used in the GI communities. The other significant approach known as RCC (Region-Connection Calculus) which has been provided by Cohn [8] is a pointless topology based upon a single primitive contact relation, called connection, between regions. In this logic-based approach the notion of a region as consisting of a set of points is not used at all.

The intersection model is extended to vague regions by three main approaches: the work of Clementini and Di Felice [7] on regions with "broad boundary" and Tang and Kainz [23] that provided a 3*3, a 4*4, and a 5*5 intersection matrix based on different topological parts of two fuzzy regions. Two fuzzy generalization of the RCC to define spatial relations between vague regions are defined in [14] and [22]. Furthermore Schneider conducts a series of researches including the definition of fuzzy spatial objects, fuzzy topological relationships and etc. [e.g. 21].

The notion of intuitionistic fuzzy sets (IFS) was introduced by Atanassov [2],[3],[4] as a generalization of fuzzy sets. Later the concept of intuitionistic fuzzy topology was introduced by Coker [9]. Malek [17],[18],[19] in his works provided a theoretical framework for defining a simple geographic object and discussed the process of creating intuitionistic thematic maps using remote sensing satellite imagery.

3   Influenceability and Its Algebraic Logical Framework

Causality is widely known and esteemed concept. There is much literature on causality, extending philosophy, physics, artificial intelligence, cognitive science and so on (see for example [5]). In our view, influenceability stands for spatial causal relation, i.e. objects must come in contact with one another. In the relativistic physics based on the postulate that the vacuum velocity of light c is constant and maximum velocity, the light cone can be defined as a portion of space-time containing all locations which light signals could reach from a particular location.

With respect to a given event, its light cone separates space-time into three parts, inside and on the future light cone, inside and on the past light cone, and elsewhere. An event 'A' can influence (or influenced by) another event 'B'; only when B (A) lies in the light cone of A (B). In a similar way, the aforementioned model can be applied for moving objects. Henceforth, a cone is describing an agent in mobile GIS environment for a fixed time interval. This cone is formed of all possible locations that an individual could feasibly pass through or visit. The current location or apex vertex and speed of object is reported by navigational system or by prediction. The hyper surface of the cone becomes a base model for spatio-temporal relationships, and therefore enables analysis and further calculations in space-time.

Let us take influenceability as an order relation (symbolized by $\prec$) to be the primitive relation. It is natural to postulate that influenceability is irreflexive, antisymmetric, but transitive:

$$(A \prec B) \wedge (B \prec C) \Rightarrow A \prec C \tag{1}$$

Thus, it can play the role of 'after'.

Definition 1 (Temporal order). Let A and B be two moving objects with t_a and t_b corresponding temporal orders, respectively. Then

$$(A \prec B) \Rightarrow (t_a < t_b) \tag{2}$$

Connection as a reflexive and symmetric relation can be defined by influenceability as follows:

Definition 2 (Connect relation). Two moving objects are connected if the following equation holds:

$$(\forall xy)C(x,y) \overset{def}{=} [(x \prec y) \vee (y \prec x)] \wedge \{\neg(\exists a)[(x \prec a \prec y) \vee (y \prec a \prec x)]\} \tag{3}$$

Consequently, all other exhaustive and pairwise disjoint relations in region connected calculus (RCC) [8] can be defined (Table 1).

Although the above algebra can be used for relations for spatial, temporal or spatio-temporal objects, it does not consider any kind of uncertainty which is important to be modeled in mobile environments. In the next section, we will develop the model to support relations between objects with uncertainty elements.

Table 1. Relations extracted from "Connect" relation [8]

Relation	Interpretation	Definition
DC(x, y)	x is disconnected from y	$\neg C(x,y)$
P(x, y)	x is a part of y	$\forall z[C(z,x) \rightarrow C(z,y)]$
PP(x, y)	x is a proper part of y	$P(x,y) \wedge \neg P(y,x)$
EQ(x, y)	x is identical with y	$P(x,y) \wedge P(y,x)$
O(x, y)	x overlaps y	$\exists z[P(z,x) \wedge P(z,y)]$
DR(x, y)	x is discrete from y	$\neg O(x,y)$
PO(x, y)	x partially overlaps y	$O(x,y) \wedge \neg P(x,y) \wedge \neg P(y,x)$
EC(x, y)	x is externally connected to y	$C(x,y) \wedge \neg O(x,y)]$
TPP(x, y)	x is a tangential proper part of y	$PP(x,y) \wedge \exists z[EC(z,x) \wedge EC(z,y)]$
NTPP(x, y)	x is a non-tangential proper part of y	$PP(x,y) \wedge \neg \exists z[EC(z,x) \wedge EC(z,y)]$

4   Intuitionistic Fuzzy Influenceability

As it was mentioned before, in a mobile GIS environment, information is local and incomplete which is the case of intuitionistic fuzzy theory. In this section, the fundamental concepts of the intuitionistic fuzzy will be present and then the idea will be used to construct an IF influenceability.

Definition 3. Let X be a nonempty fixed set. An intuitionistic fuzzy set (IFS) A in X is an object having the following form [2]

$$A := \{< x, \mu_A(x), \nu_A(x) > \mid x \in X\} \tag{4}$$

Where the function $\mu_A : X \rightarrow [0,1]$ and $\nu_A : X \rightarrow [0,1]$ define the degree of membership and the degree of non-membership of the element $x \in X$, respectively. For every $x \in X$, μ_A and ν_A satisfy $0 \leq \mu_A(x) + \nu_A(x) \leq 1$. In contrary of traditional fuzzy, the addition of μ_A and ν_A does not necessarily have to be 1. This is particularly useful when system may lack complete information. We follow based on operations defined for every two IFSs like logical and ($\wedge$) and logical or ($\vee$) [2].

Let $X \times X$ be the Cartesian product X with itself as defined in. Then, influence-ability can be defined for every $x, y \in X$ as:

$$x \prec y := R_{In} = \{< (x,y), \mu_{In}(x,y), \nu_{In}(x,y) >| (x,y) \in X \times X \} \tag{5}$$

Using the relation R_{In} and IF logical rules, an IF version of influenceability can be calculated:

$$
\mu_C(x,y) = \min[\max(\vec{\mu},\overleftarrow{\mu}), \min_{a_i}(\min(\overrightarrow{\max},\overleftarrow{\max}))]
$$
$$
\nu_C(x,y) = \max[\min(\vec{\nu},\overleftarrow{\nu}), \max_{a_i}(\max(\overrightarrow{\min},\overleftarrow{\min}))]
\tag{6}
$$

where

$\vec{\mu} = \mu(x,y), \vec{\nu} = \nu(x,y), \overleftarrow{\mu} = \mu(y,x), \overleftarrow{\nu} = \nu(y,x),$

$\overrightarrow{\max} = \max(\vec{\nu}_x, \vec{\nu}_y), \overrightarrow{\min} = \min(\vec{\mu}_x, \vec{\mu}_y), \overleftarrow{\max} = \max(\overleftarrow{\nu}_y, \overleftarrow{\nu}_x), \overleftarrow{\min} = \min(\overleftarrow{\mu}_y, \overleftarrow{\mu}_x),$

$\vec{\mu}_x = \mu(x,a_i), \vec{\mu}_y = \mu(y,a_i), \overleftarrow{\mu}_x = \mu(a_i,x), \overleftarrow{\mu}_y = \mu(a_i,y),$

$\vec{\nu}_x = \nu(x,a_i), \vec{\nu}_y = \nu(y,a_i), \overleftarrow{\nu}_x = \nu(a_i,x), \overleftarrow{\nu}_y = \nu(a_i,y).$

The translation of the remaining crisp relations to IF relations are straightforward and illustrated in table 2. Figure 1 shows the influenceability relationship between two IF cones.

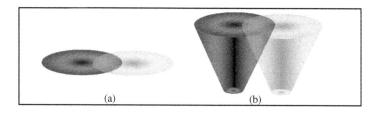

Fig. 1. (a) Topological relation between two IF spatial Objects, (b) Influenceability relation between two IF spatial Objects

Furthermore, some other new relations can be defined, such as which termed as speed-connection (SC) which did not defined either by RCC or by 9-intersection methods (see Figure 2):

$$SC(x,y) \overset{def}{=} \neg EQ(x,y) \wedge \{[C(x,y) \wedge (\forall ab)\, (C(x,a) \wedge (C(x,b) \wedge C(y,a) \wedge C(y,b)] \Rightarrow C(a,b)\} \tag{7}$$

We are not going into detail; just say that SC relation could be considered as a basis relation to define a qualitative geometry.

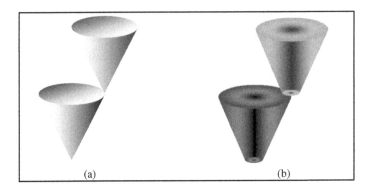

(a)   (b)

Fig. 2. Speed-connection relation between two agents (a) Crisp agents, (b) IF agents

Table 2. IF version of the Influenceability

IF Relation	Crisp relation
$DC(x,y) = \{< (x,y), v_C(x,y), \mu_C(x,y) >\mid (x,y) \in X \times X \}$	$DC(x,y) = \neg C(x,y)$
$P(x,y) = \{< (x,y), \min\limits_{z \in X}[\max(v_C(z,x), \mu_C(z,y))],$ $\max\limits_{z \in X}[\min(\mu_C(z,x), v_C(z,y))] >\mid (x,y) \in X \times X \}$	$P(x,y) = \forall z[C(z,x) \Rightarrow C(z,y)]$
$PP(x,y) = \{< (x,y), \min(\mu_P(x,y), v_P(x,y)),$ $\max(v_P(x,y), \mu_P(x,y)) >\mid (x,y) \in X \times X \}$	$PP(x,y) = P(x,y) \wedge \neg P(y,x)$
$EQ(x,y) = \{< (x,y), \min(\mu_P(x,y), v_P(x,y)),$ $\max(v_P(x,y), \mu_P(x,y)) >\mid (x,y) \in X \times X \}$	$EQ(x,y) = P(x,y) \wedge P(y,x)$
$O(x,y) = \{< (x,y), \max\limits_{z \in X}[\min(\mu_P(z,x), \mu_P(z,y))],$ $\max\limits_{z \in X}[\min(v_P(z,x), v_P(z,y))] >\mid (x,y) \in X \times X \}$	$O(x,y) = \exists z[P(x,z) \wedge P(z,y)]$
$DR(x,y) = \{< (x,y), v_O(x,y)), \mu_O(x,y)) >\mid (x,y) \in X \times X \}$	$DR(x,y) = \neg O(x,y)$
$PO(x,y) = \{< (x,y), \min(\mu_O(x,y), v_P(x,y), v_P(y,x)),$ $\max(v_O(x,y), \mu_P(x,y), \mu_P(y,x)) >\mid (x,y) \in X \times X \}$	$PO(x,y) = O(x,y) \wedge \neg P(x,y) \wedge$ $\neg P(y,x)$
$EC(x,y) = \{< (x,y), \min(\mu_C(x,y), v_O(x,y)),$ $\max(v_C(x,y), \mu_O(x,y) >\mid (x,y) \in X \times X \}$	$EC(x,y) = C(x,y) \wedge \neg O(x,y)$

5   Conclusions and Further Works

In contrary to the traditional fuzzy logic, IF logic is well equipped to deal with missed data. By employing IFSs in spatial data models, we can express a hesitation concerning the object of interest. Because it distinguishes between the situations in which there is no knowledge about a certain statement and a situation that the belief to the statement in favor and against is the same. This article has gone a step forward in developing methods that can be used to define spatial relationships between fuzzy spatial regions.

This paper has demonstrated that concerns to mobile GIS theory can profitably be addressed in terms of influenceability relation and Intuitionistic fuzzy logic. Of particular significance is the fact that the spatio-temporal relationships for fuzzy objects can be given in a way that a unique framework is prepared for moving agents.

The main contributions of the paper is defining influenceability as a new basis for spatio-temporal relationships and translating the result relations to IF logic. This paper has demonstrated that fuzzy spatial object may profitably be addressed in terms of intuitionistic fuzzy logic. We leave the finding spatial relationships and defining complex regions as well as other spatial objects as our future work.

Acknowledgements. The first author is partially supported by KN Toosi university of Technology under grant M-P/1046. Also all authors would like to thank Prof. Dr. A. U. Frank (Technical University of Vienna) for their valuable comments.

References

1. Allen, J.F.: Maintaining Knowledge about Temporal Intervals. Communications of the ACM 26(11), 832–843 (1983)
2. Atanassov, K.T.: Intuitionistic Fuzzy Sets. Fuzzy Sets and Systems 20, 87–96 (1986)
3. Atanassov, K.T.: More on Intuitionistic Fuzzy Sets. Fuzzy sets and Systems 33, 37–45 (1989)
4. Atanassov, K.T.: Intuitionistic Fuzzy Sets: Theory and Application. Studies in Fuzziness and Soft Computing, Springer-Verlag, Telos (1999)
5. Born, M.: Natural Philosophy of Cause and Chance. Dover Publications, New York (1949)
6. Burrough, P.A., Frank, A.U. (eds.): Geographic Objects with Indeterminate Boundaries. In: Masser, I., Salgé, F. (eds.): GISDATA Series, vol. II, Taylor & Francis, London (1996)
7. Clementini, E., Di Felice, P.: An Algebraic Model for Spatial Objects with Indeterminate Boundaries. In: Masser, I., Salgé, F. (eds.): GISDATA Series, vol. II, pp. 155–169, Taylor & Francis, London (1996)
8. Cohn, A.G., Bennett, B., Gooday, G., Gotts, N.M.: Qualitative Spatial Representation and Reasoning with the Region Connection Calculus. Geoinformatica 3, 275–316 (1997)
9. Coker, D.: An introduction to intuitionistic fuzzy topological space. Fuzzy sets and Systems 88, 81–89 (1997)
10. Egenhofer, M.J.: A Formal Definition of Binary Topological Relationships. In: Third International Conference on Foundations of Data Organization and Algorithms (FODO), Paris, France. Springer-Verlag, Berlin Heidelberg Germany (1989)
11. Egenhofer, M.J., Franzosa, R.D.: Point-set topological spatial relations. International Journal of Geographical Information Systems 5(2), 161–174 (1991)
12. Egenhofer, M.J., Herring, J.R.: Categorizing Binary Topological Relationships Between Regions, Lines, and Points in Geographic Databases. Technical report. Department of Surveying Engineering. University of Maine. Orono (1991)
13. Egenhofer, M.J.,Golledge, R.G.: Time in geographic space. Report on the specialist meeting of research initiative, National Center for Geographic Information and Analysis. Santa Barbara, CA (1994)
14. Esterline, A., Dozier, G., Homaifar, A.: Fuzzy Spatial Reasoning. In: Proceeding of the International Fuzzy Systems Association Conference, Prague, pp. 162–167 (1997)

15. Gis-Lounge, Mobile and Field GIS. 2003, (Accessed, January 2007) http://gislounge.com/ll/mobilegis.shtml

16. Kokla, M., Kavouras, M.: Fusion of Top-level and Geographic Domain Ontologies based on Context Formation and Complementarity. International Journal of Geographical Information Science 15(7), 679–687 (2001)

17. Malek, M.R.: Spatial Object Modeling in Intuitionistic Fuzzy Topological Spaces, Lecture Notes in Computer Science. In: Tsumoto, S., Słowiński, R., Komorowski, J., Grzymała-Busse, J.W. (eds.) RSCTC 2004. LNCS (LNAI), vol. 3066, pp. 427–434. Springer, Heidelberg (2004)

18. Malek, M.R., Twaroch, F.: An Introduction to Fuzzy Spatial Region. In: Frank, A.U., Grum, E. (compilers): ISSDQ '04, Vienna, Dept. for Geoinformation and Cartography, Vienna University of Technology (2004)

19. Malek, M.R., Karami, J., Aliabady, S.: Classification with Intuitionistic Fuzzy Region in Geospatial Information System. In: Ruan, D., D'hondt, P., Fantoni, P.F., De Cock, M., Nachtagael, M., Kerre, E.E. (eds.) Applied Artificial Intelligence, world Scientific, Singapore (2006)

20. Roy, A.J.: A Comparison of Rough Sets, Fuzzy sets and Non-monotonic Logic. University of Keele. Staffordshre (1999)

21. Schneider, M.: Fuzzy Spatial Data Types and Predicates: Their Definition and Integration into Query Languages. In: Spatio-Temporal Databases: Flexible Querying and Reasoning, Springer-Verlag, Heidelberg (2004)

22. Schockaert, S., Cornelis, C., De Cock, M., Kerre, E.E.: Fuzzy Spatial relations between vague regions. In: Proceeding of 3rd IEEE Conference on Intelligent Systems, pp. 221–226 (2006)

23. Tang, X., Kainz, W.: Analysis of Topological relations between Fuzzy Regions in a General Fuzzy Topological space. In: Proceeding of Symposium on Geospatial Theory, Processing and Applications. Ottawa (2002)

A Two-Dimensional Entropic Approach to Intuitionistic Fuzzy Contrast Enhancement

Ioannis K. Vlachos and George D. Sergiadis

Aristotle University of Thessaloniki
Faculty of Technology
Department of Electrical & Computer Engineering, Telecommunications Division
University Campus, GR–54124, Thessaloniki, Greece
ivlachos@mri.ee.auth.gr, sergiadi@auth.gr
http://mri.ee.auth.gr

Abstract. This paper presents a generalized approach to the intuitionistic fuzzification of gray-scale images. Parametric membership and non-membership functions are applied in order to derive the optimal representation of the image in the intuitionistic fuzzy domain. A two-dimensional intuitionistic fuzzy entropy measure is employed as the optimization criterion for driving the aforementioned procedure. Finally, experimental results demonstrate the ability of the proposed method to efficiently enhance low-contrasted gray-scale images.

1   Introduction

Atanassov's intuitionistic fuzzy sets (A–IFSs) [1] are one of the various extensions of fuzzy sets (FSs) theory [2]. A–IFSs are characterized by their ability to attribute, apart from degrees of membership, degrees of hesitancy to elements belonging to a set. It is this additional degree of freedom that allows for the efficient modelling of imprecise or/and imperfect information. Images, on the other hand, are susceptible of bearing imprecision mainly due to various factors, such as the acquisition chain, the non-linear nature of the mapping mechanisms, and the quantization noise. Therefore, A–IFSs turn out to be flexible tools for dealing with the imprecision often present in digital images.

In this paper we propose a generalized method for constructing the A–IFS that optimally describes the image intensity levels in the intuitionistic fuzzy domain. The modelling of gray levels is carried out using parametric membership and non-membership functions, derived using the concepts of involutive fuzzy complements and intuitionistic fuzzy generators. The process is driven by optimization criteria based on the index of fuzziness and on the intuitionistic fuzzy entropy of the image in a two-dimensional parameter space. Finally, we demonstrate that the proposed scheme successfully enhances highly low-contrasted images.

F. Masulli, S. Mitra, and G. Pasi (Eds.): WILF 2007, LNAI 4578, pp. 321–327, 2007.
© Springer-Verlag Berlin Heidelberg 2007

2   Atanassov's Intuitionistic Fuzzy Sets

In this section, we briefly introduce the basic notions, concepts, and definitions of A–IFSs theory. Throughout this paper the notation $\tilde{A}$ is used to represent an FS, while A describes an A–IFS. Moreover, by $\mathscr{IFS}(X)$ we denote the set of all A–IFSs defined on X. Correspondingly, $\mathscr{FS}(X)$ is the set of all FSs on X.

Definition 1. *An A–IFS A defined on a universe X is given by [1]*

$$A = \{\langle x, \mu_A(x), \nu_A(x)\rangle | x \in X\} \ , \tag{1}$$

where

$$\mu_A(x) : X \to [0,1] \qquad and \qquad \nu_A(x) : X \to [0,1] \ ,$$

with the condition

$$0 \leqslant \mu_A(x) + \nu_A(x) \leqslant 1 \ , \tag{2}$$

for all $x \in X$.

The values of $\mu_A(x)$ and $\nu_A(x)$ denote the *degree of belongingness* and the *degree of non-belongingness* of x to A, respectively. For an A–IFS A in X we call the *intuitionistic fuzzy index* of an element $x \in X$ in A the following expression

$$\pi_A(x) = 1 - \mu_A(x) - \nu_A(x) \ . \tag{3}$$

Finally, one of the operators, proposed by Atanassov [1], for converting an A–IFS into an FS is given by the following definition.

Definition 2. *If $A \in \mathscr{IFS}(X)$, then $D_\alpha : \mathscr{IFS}(X) \to \mathscr{FS}(X)$, where*

$$D_\alpha(A) = \{\langle x, \mu_A(x) + \alpha\pi_A(x), \nu_A(x) + (1 - \alpha)\pi_A(x)\rangle | x \in X\} \ , \tag{4}$$

with $\alpha \in [0,1]$.

3   Generalized Intuitionistic Fuzzification

In [3], a method for automatically constructing the A–IFSs that optimally models the gray levels of an image was introduced. Moreover, the authors demonstrated that this analysis results in efficiently enhancing the contrast of images [3]. In this paper, we propose a generalized approach to intuitionistic fuzzification, based on a two-dimensional intuitionistic fuzzy entropy optimization scheme. We also demonstrate that the proposed framework successfully enhances low-contrasted images.

3.1   Generalized Intuitionistic Fuzzification – From Images to Sets

Let us consider an image A of size $M \times N$ pixels having L gray levels g ranging between 0 and $L - 1$. Generalizing the definition of an image of Pal and Pal [4,5,6] using FSs, the image in the intuitionistic fuzzy domain can be considered as an array of intuitionistic fuzzy singletons, with each element of the array denoting the degrees of membership (belongingness) and non-membership (non-belongingness) attributed to a pixel with respect to an image property. Therefore, the definition of a digital image in the intuitionistic fuzzy setting is given as follows [3].

Definition 3. *An image A is described by the A–IFS*

$$A = \{\langle g_{ij}, \mu_A(g_{ij}), \nu_A(g_{ij})\rangle | g_{ij} \in \{0, \ldots, L-1\}\} \ , \tag{5}$$

with $i \in \{1, \ldots, M\}$ and $j \in \{1, \ldots, N\}$, where $\mu_A(g_{ij})$ and $\nu_A(g_{ij})$ denote respectively the degrees of membership and non-membership of the (i, j)-th pixel to the set A associated with an image property.

The first stage of intuitionistic fuzzy image processing, involves the fuzzification of the image according to the following scheme

$$\mu_{\tilde{A}}(g) = \frac{g - g_{min}}{g_{max} - g_{min}} \ , \tag{6}$$

where g_{min} and g_{max} are the minimum and maximum gray levels of the image, respectively. The construction of the A–IFS that represents the intensity levels of the image in an optimal way is carried out using parametric membership and non-membership function, derived directly from $\mu_{\tilde{A}}$ using intuitionistic fuzzy generators [7]. The shapes of the aforementioned functions are controlled through corresponding parameters. A simple method for parameterizing the membership function $\mu_{\tilde{A}}$ can be derived by considering parametric involutive fuzzy complements. Employing the Yager fuzzy complement with $w > 0$, yields

$$\mu_A(g; w) = 1 - \left(1 - \mu_{\tilde{A}}^w(g)\right)^{\frac{1}{w}} \ . \tag{7}$$

Based on the concept of intuitionistic fuzzy generators [7] the following non-membership function is also generated from $\mu_A(g; w)$ as

$$\nu_A(g; \lambda, w) = \varphi\left(\mu_A(g)\right) = \left(1 - \mu_{\tilde{A}}^w(g)\right)^{\frac{\lambda}{w}} \ , \tag{8}$$

where the intuitionistic fuzzy generator $\varphi(x)$ is given by

$$\varphi(x) = (1 - x)^\lambda \ , \tag{9}$$

with $x \in [0, 1]$ and $\lambda \geqslant 1$.

By varying the free parameters λ and w of (7) and (8) different representations of the image in the intuitionistic fuzzy domain can be obtained. Therefore, an optimization criterion must be employed to select the optimal parameter set. Using the definition of entropy of an A–IFS by Szmidt and Kacprzyk [8], the entropy of image A is given by

$$E(A; \lambda, w) = \frac{1}{MN} \sum_{g=0}^{L-1} h_{\tilde{A}}(g) \frac{1 - \max\left\{1 - \left(1 - \mu_{\tilde{A}}^w(g)\right)^{\frac{1}{w}}, \left(1 - \mu_{\tilde{A}}^w(g)\right)^{\frac{\lambda}{w}}\right\}}{1 - \min\left\{1 - \left(1 - \mu_{\tilde{A}}^w(g)\right)^{\frac{1}{w}}, \left(1 - \mu_{\tilde{A}}^w(g)\right)^{\frac{\lambda}{w}}\right\}} , \tag{10}$$

where $h_{\tilde{A}}$ is the histogram of the fuzzified image $\tilde{A}$. It is evident that the entropy can also be considered as a function of the parameters λ and w. Fig. 1(a) illustrates the intuitionistic fuzzy entropy of (10) in the two-dimensional space of parameters λ and w. One may observe that for constant w, the entropy $E(A; \lambda, w)$ attains a maximum for a specific value of λ, which will be denoted as $\lambda_{opt}(w)$, and can be derived according to the following criterion

$$\lambda_{opt}(w) = \arg \max_{\lambda \geqslant 1} \{E(A; \lambda, w)\} , \tag{11}$$

with $w > 0$. Consequently, for every set of parameters $(\lambda_{opt}(w), w)$, a different representation of the image in the intuitionistic domain can be obtained, described in general as the A–IFS

$$A(\lambda_{opt}(w), w) = \{\langle g, \mu_A(g; w), \nu_A(g; \lambda_{opt}(w), w)\rangle | g \in \{0, \dots, L-1\}\} \tag{12}$$

for $w > 0$.

3.2 Intuitionistic Defuzzification: From A–IFSs to Images

Intuitionistic defuzzification refers to the sequence of operations carried out in order to transfer the image to the fuzzy domain. Moreover, contrast enhancement of images requires in general the increment of grayness ambiguity by increasing the number of intensity levels. Images with high fuzziness are considered to be more suitable in term of human brightness perception. Motivated by this observation, the *maximum index of fuzziness defuzzification* scheme was proposed in [3], in order to de-construct the A–IFS describing the image into its optimal FS. In view of performing this task, the Atanassov's operator of (4) is employed. It should be mentioned that different values of parameter α generate different FSs and therefore different representations of the image in the fuzzy plane are possible.

For an FS $\tilde{A}$ defined on a universe X, the *index of fuzziness*, using the product operator to implement the intersection, is given by

$$\gamma(\tilde{A}) = \frac{1}{4|X|} \sum_{i=0}^{|X|} \mu_{\tilde{A}}(x_i) \left(1 - \mu_{\tilde{A}}(x_i)\right) , \tag{13}$$

where $|X| = Cardinal(X)$. Consequently, for the FS $D_\alpha(A(\lambda_{opt}(w), w))$ derived using Atanassov's operator of (4), the index of fuzziness may be written as

$$\gamma\left(D_\alpha(A(\lambda_{opt}(w), w))\right) = \frac{1}{4MN} \sum_{g=0}^{L-1} h_{\tilde{A}}(g) \mu_{\tilde{A}}(g)(1 - \mu_{\tilde{A}}(g)) . \tag{14}$$

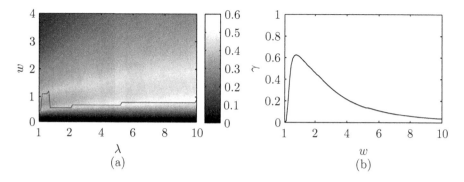

Fig. 1. (a) The intuitionistic fuzzy entropy for the image of Fig. 3(a) in the two-dimensional space of parameters λ and w. The curve $\lambda_{opt}(w)$ is also annotated (red line). (b) The index of fuzziness as a criterion for selecting w_{opt}.

According to the maximum index of fuzziness defuzzification, the optimal parameter is derived analytically, by solving the equation

$$\frac{d\gamma\left(D_\alpha(A(\lambda_{opt}(w), w))\right)}{d\alpha} = 0 \ , \tag{15}$$

which yields that

$$\alpha_{opt}(\lambda_{opt}(w), w) = \begin{cases} 0, & \text{if } \alpha'_{opt}(\lambda_{opt}(w), w) < 0 \\ \alpha'_{opt}(\lambda_{opt}(w), w), & \text{if } 0 \leqslant \alpha'_{opt}(\lambda_{opt}(w), w) \leqslant 1 \\ 1, & \text{if } \alpha'_{opt}(\lambda_{opt}(w), w) > 1 \end{cases} \ , \tag{16}$$

with

$$\alpha'_{opt}\left(\lambda_{opt}(w), w\right) = \frac{\sum_{g=0}^{L-1} h_{\tilde{A}}(g)\pi_A(g; \lambda_{opt}(w), w)\left(1 - 2\mu_A(g; w)\right)}{2\sum_{g=0}^{L-1} h_{\tilde{A}}(g)\pi_A^2(g; \lambda_{opt}(w), w)} \tag{17}$$

where $\alpha_{opt}(\lambda_{opt}(w), w)$ is the parameter of Atanassov's operator obtained for each parameter set $(\lambda_{opt}(w), w)$. It should be stressed out that (16) guarantees that $\alpha_{opt}(\lambda_{opt}(w), w)$ will lie in the $[0, 1]$ interval.

3.3   Parameter Selection Through Optimization of Image Fuzziness

Using the maximum index of fuzziness defuzzification scheme, a set of candidate fuzzy images can be derived for all $w > 0$. Since increasing the fuzziness of an image is a desired property for contrast enhancement, the following optimization criterion based on the index of fuzziness is employed in order to derive the optimal parameter w_{opt}

$$w_{opt} = \arg\max_{w \geqslant 0}\left\{\gamma\left(D_{\alpha_{opt}(\lambda_{opt}(w), w)}(A\left(\lambda_{opt}(w), w)\right)\right)\right\} \ . \tag{18}$$

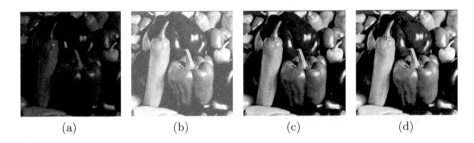

(a)   (b)   (c)   (d)

Fig. 2. (a) Initial low-contrasted image. Images obtained using (b) the histogram equalization technique, (c) the one-parametric intuitionistic fuzzification scheme of [3] ($\lambda_{opt} = 0.6$), and (d) its proposed generalized extension ($\lambda_{opt} = 0.5$, $w_{opt} = 0.5$).

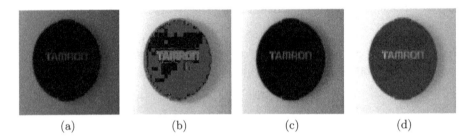

(a)   (b)   (c)   (d)

Fig. 3. (a) Initial low-contrasted image. Images obtained using (b) the histogram equalization technique, (c) the one-parametric intuitionistic fuzzification scheme of [3] ($\lambda_{opt} = 1.2$), and (d) its proposed generalized extension ($\lambda_{opt} = 0.6$, $w_{opt} = 0.8$).

Finally, using the optimal parameter set $(\lambda_{opt}(w_{opt}), w_{opt})$, the enhanced image in the gray-level domain is obtained as

$$g' = (L-1)\left(\mu_A(g; w_{opt}) + \alpha_{opt}(\lambda_{opt}(w_{opt}), w_{opt})\pi_A(g; \lambda_{opt}(w_{opt}), w_{opt})(g)\right) , \tag{19}$$

where g and g' are the initial and the modified gray-levels, respectively. It should be stressed out that if $\lambda = w$, then the proposed generalized intuitionistic fuzzification scheme degenerates to the approach introduced by the authors in [3]. Fig. 1(b) illustrates the curve of the index of fuzziness used for selecting the optimal parameter w_{opt}.

4   Experimental Results

In order to assess the performance of the method for contrast enhancement, we applied the proposed approach to various real-world and computer-generated low-contrasted images. For the experimental evaluation we considered gray-scale images of size 256×256 pixels, having 8 bits-per-pixel gray-tone resolution. For real-world images, their brightness was manually altered to produce images exhibiting very low contrast. Figs. 1 and 2 demonstrate the results obtained using the proposed generalized intuitionistic fuzzification scheme, as well as the ones derived using its one-parametric counterpart and also the histogram equalization technique. One may observe that the proposed generalized intuitionistic fuzzy approach produces images in which constant intensity regions and high-frequency edges have been drastically enhanced, resulting in images that are more suitable in terms of human brightness perception, compared to the ones derived using the one-parametric intuitionistic fuzzification method.

5 Conclusions

In this paper we presented a generalized approach to intuitionistic fuzzification of gray-scale images, using optimization criteria based on the index of fuzziness and on the intuitionistic fuzzy entropy of the image in a two-dimensional parameter space. Application of the proposed scheme demonstrated its ability to efficiently enhance highly low-contrasted images.

References

1. Atanassov, K.T.: Intuitionistic Fuzzy Sets: Theory and Applications. In: Studies in Fuzziness and Soft Computing, Physica–Verlag, Heidelberg (1999)
2. Zadeh, L.A.: Fuzzy sets. Inf. Control 8, 338–353 (1965)
3. Vlachos, I.K., Sergiadis, G.D.: Intuitionistic Fuzzy Image Processing. In: Soft Computing in Image Processing: Recent Advances. Studies in Fuzziness and Soft Computing, vol. 210, pp. 385–416. Springer, Heidelberg (2007)
4. Pal, S.K., King, R.A.: Image enhancement using fuzzy set. Electron. Lett. 16, 376–378 (1980)
5. Pal, S.K., King, R.A.: Image enhancement using smoothing with fuzzy sets. IEEE Trans. Syst. Man Cybern. 11, 495–501 (1981)
6. Pal, S.K., King, R.A.: A note on the quantitative measure of image enhancement through fuzziness. IEEE Trans. Pattern Anal. Mach. Intell. 4, 204–208 (1982)
7. Bustince, H., Kacprzyk, J., Mohedano, V.: Intuitionistic fuzzy generators—Application to intuitionistic fuzzy complementation. Fuzzy Sets Syst. 114, 485–504 (2000)
8. Szmidt, E., Kacprzyk, J.: Entropy for intuitionistic fuzzy sets. Fuzzy Sets Syst. 118, 467–477 (2001)

Intuitionistic Fuzzy Histogram Hyperbolization for Color Images

Ioannis K. Vlachos and George D. Sergiadis

Aristotle University of Thessaloniki
Faculty of Technology
Department of Electrical & Computer Engineering, Telecommunications Division
University Campus, GR–54124, Thessaloniki, Greece
ivlachos@mri.ee.auth.gr, sergiadi@auth.gr
http://mri.ee.auth.gr

Abstract. In this paper an extension of the Intuitionistic Fuzzy Image Processing (IFIP) framework from gray-scale to color images is presented. Analysis and synthesis of images into their corresponding intuitionistic fuzzy components is demonstrated using a suitable color model. Additionally, application of the proposed framework to histogram hyperbolization is also shown. Finally, experimental results demonstrate the efficiency of the proposed scheme.

1 Introduction

Since Zadeh conceived the notion of fuzzy sets (FSs) [1], many theories treating the imprecision originating out of imperfect information have been proposed. Among the various extensions of FSs theory, Atanassov's intuitionistic fuzzy sets (A–IFSs) [2] provide a flexible, yet solid, mathematical framework that mimics aspects of human decision making. A–IFSs successfully handle the inherent imprecision of information by modeling efficiently its very essence by assigning to each element of the universe besides membership and non-membership functions also the corresponding lack of knowledge (hesitation, indeterminacy).

Exploiting the potential of A–IFSs, Vlachos and Sergiadis [3] introduced the Intuitionistic Fuzzy Image Processing (IFIP) framework for handling the intrinsic imprecision of gray-scale images, by means of heuristic and analytical models. A heuristic modelling of the hesitancy carried by the pixels of color images was also demonstrated by the authors, by considering the factors that introduce imprecision in a color image [4].

The main purpose of this work is to extend the analytical model of the IFIP framework to the context of color images. Having established a unified representation of color images in the intuitionistic fuzzy domain, an application of the proposed framework to intuitionistic fuzzy histogram hyperbolization is presented using the $L*a*b$ color space. Finally, experimental results demonstrate the ability of the proposed method to enhance efficiently the contrast of real-world color images.

F. Masulli, S. Mitra, and G. Pasi (Eds.): WILF 2007, LNAI 4578, pp. 328–334, 2007.

2 Elements of Intuitionistic Fuzzy Sets Theory

In this section, we briefly introduce the basic notions, concepts, and definitions of A–IFSs theory. Throughout this paper the notation $\tilde{A}$ is used to represent an FS, while A describes an A–IFS. Moreover, by $\mathscr{I}\mathscr{F}\mathscr{S}(X)$ we denote the set of all A–IFSs defined on X. Correspondingly, $\mathscr{F}\mathscr{S}(X)$ is the set of all FSs on X.

Definition 1. *An A–IFS A defined on a universe X is given by [2]*

$$A = \{\langle x, \mu_A(x), \nu_A(x)\rangle | x \in X\} \ , \tag{1}$$

where $\mu_A(x) : X \rightarrow [0,1]$ and $\nu_A(x) : X \rightarrow [0,1]$, with the condition $0 \leqslant \mu_A(x) + \nu_A(x) \leqslant 1$ for all $x \in X$.

The values of $\mu_A(x)$ and $\nu_A(x)$ denote the *degree of membership* (*belongingness*) and the *degree of non-membership* (*non-belongingness*) of x to A, respectively. For an A–IFS A in X we call the *intuitionistic fuzzy index* of an element $x \in X$ in A the expression $\pi_A(x) = 1 - \mu_A(x) - \nu_A(x)$. We can consider $\pi_A(x)$ as a *hesitancy degree* of x to A. It is evident that $0 \leqslant \pi_A(x) \leqslant 1$ for all $x \in X$.

Finally, one of the operators, proposed by Atanassov [2], for converting an A–IFS into an FS is given by the following definition.

Definition 2. *If $A \in \mathscr{I}\mathscr{F}\mathscr{S}(X)$, then $D_\alpha : \mathscr{I}\mathscr{F}\mathscr{S}(X) \rightarrow \mathscr{F}\mathscr{S}(X)$, where*

$$D_\alpha(A) = \{\langle x, \mu_A(x) + \alpha\pi_A(x), \nu_A(x) + (1-\alpha)\pi_A(x)\rangle | x \in X\} \ , \tag{2}$$

with $\alpha \in [0,1]$.

3 IFIP Framework for Color Images

Motivated by the definition of a gray-scale image using FSs of Pal and Pal [5,6,7], Vlachos and Sergiadis [3] proposed the following representation of a digital image in terms of elements of A–IFSs theory.

Definition 3. *A gray-scale image A is described by the A–IFS*

$$A = \{\langle g_{ij}, \mu_A(g_{ij}), \nu_A(g_{ij})\rangle | g_{ij} \in \{0, \dots, l-1\}\} \ , \tag{3}$$

with $i \in \{1, \dots, M\}$ and $j \in \{1, \dots, N\}$, where $\mu_A(g_{ij})$ and $\nu_A(g_{ij})$ denote respectively the degrees of membership and non-membership of the (i,j)-th pixel to the set A associated with an image property, and l is the number of gray levels.

IFIP involves in general a sequence of operations carried out using the concepts of A–IFSs theory, in view of performing image processing tasks. Fig. 1 illustrates an overview of the aforementioned framework for gray-scale images. Generally, in the first stage the gray-levels of the image are transferred into the fuzzy domain and then into the intuitionistic fuzzy domain by a suitable selection of corresponding membership and non-membership functions. After the modification of the intuitionistic fuzzy components according to the desired image operation, the inverse procedure is carried out to obtain the image in the pixel domain.

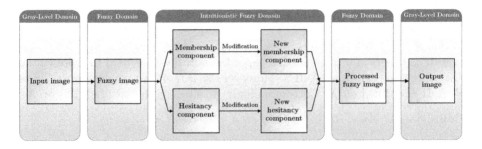

Fig. 1. Overview of the Intuitionistic Fuzzy Image Processing (IFIP) framework

4   Contrast Enhancement of Color Images by A–IFSs

Color images can be represented in various ways using different color spaces. A color space is the mean for representing the colors and their relationship among them. One of the most commonly used color spaces is the RGB that utilizes an additive model, in which the primary colors *red*, *green*, and *blue* are combined in different amounts to produce the different colors. However, and despite its simplicity, the RGB color model is not suitable for contrast enhancement procedures since the color components are not decoupled. Consequently, modifying independently the R, G, and B channels has the effect of altering the hue and saturation of colors, resulting in images that often appear to be not natural. Therefore, in most cases, when contrast enhancement is considered, alternative color spaces are employed, such as the HSV and the $L*a*b$ color spaces. In the proposed approach we utilize the $L*a*b$ color model, in which L is the *luminance*, while a and b are the chromatic components. By preserving the chromatic components a and b, one may enhance the contrast of a color image by processing independently the luminance channel. Therefore, in the proposed method only the luminance will be considered.

4.1   Intuitionistic Fuzzification of Color Images

Intuitionistic fuzzification is the first and, presumably, the most important stage of the IFIP framework, since it involves the construction of suitable membership and non-membership functions that describe the intensity values of image pixels efficiently. In order to transfer the luminance component L to the intuitionistic fuzzy domain, we apply the method of *maximum intuitionistic fuzzy entropy principle* [3], which involves the selection of an appropriate combination from a family of parametric membership and non-membership functions, in such a way that the intuitionistic fuzzy entropy of the luminance component of the image is maximized.

By varying a common free parameter $\lambda \geqslant 0$, that controls the shape of the membership and non-membership functions, different representations can be derived. Therefore, the optimal representation of luminance, in terms of A–IFSs, is obtained according to the following optimization criterion

$$\lambda_{opt} = \arg \max_{\lambda \geqslant 0} \{E(A; \lambda)\} \ , \tag{4}$$

where E is the intuitionistic fuzzy entropy, according to Szmidt and Kacprzyk's definition [8], of the L component defined as

$$E(A; \lambda) = \frac{1}{MN} \sum_{g=0}^{L-1} h_{\tilde{A}}(x_L) \frac{1 - \max \left\{ 1 - (1 - \mu_{\tilde{A}}(x_L))^{\lambda}, (1 - \mu_{\tilde{A}}(x_L))^{\lambda(\lambda+1)} \right\}}{1 - \min \left\{ 1 - (1 - \mu_{\tilde{A}}(x_L))^{\lambda}, (1 - \mu_{\tilde{A}}(x_L))^{\lambda(\lambda+1)} \right\}} \ , \tag{5}$$

where $\mu_{\tilde{A}}$ is the membership function of the fuzzified L component and is given by

$$\mu_{\tilde{A}}(x_L) = \frac{x_L - x_{L_{min}}}{x_{L_{max}} - x_{L_{min}}} \ , \tag{6}$$

with $x_{L_{min}}$ and $x_{L_{max}}$ being the minimum and maximum values of luminance, respectively, while $h_{\tilde{A}}$ is the histogram of the fuzzified luminance component. After the intuitionistic fuzzification, the luminance component of the color image A is optimally represented using the following A–IFS

$$A_{opt} = \{\langle x_L, 1 - (1 - \mu_{\tilde{A}}(x_L))^{\lambda_{opt}}, (1 - \mu_{\tilde{A}}(x_L))^{\lambda_{opt}(\lambda_{opt}+1)} \rangle | x_L \in \{0, \dots, l-1\}\}, \tag{7}$$

where l is the number of luminance levels.

4.2 Intuitionistic Fuzzy Luminance Histogram Hyperbolization

One of the most common approaches to contrast enhancement of gray-scale images is histogram equalization (HEQ), in which we seek for a gray-level transformation in order for the histogram of the resulting image to approximate to a uniform distribution over the gray-level range. However, due to the nonlinear nature of human brightness perception, the requirement of a uniform histogram is not always suitable. Based on this fact, Frei [9] proposed the idea of histogram hyperbolization, where the underlying model for equalization is logarithmic. Extending the histogram hyperbolization into the fuzzy setting, Tizhoosh and Fochem [10] proposed the method of fuzzy histogram hyperbolization (FHH).

For A–IFSs the following operator is defined $A^n : \mathscr{IFS}(X) \to \mathscr{IFS}(X)$ given by

$$A^n = \{\langle x, (\mu_A(x))^n, 1 - (1 - \nu_A(x))^n \rangle | x \in X\} \ , \tag{8}$$

where n is any positive real number. Using the aforementioned operator, the FHH approach is extended into the intuitionistic fuzzy setting by modifying the luminance component according to

$$A'_{opt} = A^{\beta}_{opt} \ , \tag{9}$$

where $\beta \geqslant 0$. It should be stressed out that the chromatic components a and b are left unaltered during this operation.

4.3   Intuitionistic Defuzzification

In order to transfer the luminance component of the image in the fuzzy domain, we employ the *maximum index of fuzziness intuitionistic defuzzification* approach described in [3], which involves the application of Atanassov's operator of (2) on the modified luminance component A_{opt}^{β}. However, different representations of the luminance component in the fuzzy domain can be obtained, depending on the parameter α selected. According to the *maximum index of fuzziness defuzzification* approach the selection of the optimal parameter α_{opt} is carried out according to the following scheme

$$
\alpha_{opt} = \begin{cases} 0, & \text{if } \alpha'_{opt} < 0 \\ \alpha'_{opt}, & \text{if } 0 \leqslant \alpha'_{opt} \leqslant 1 \\ 1, & \text{if } \alpha'_{opt} > 1 \end{cases}, \tag{10}
$$

where

$$
\alpha'_{opt} = \frac{\sum_{x_L=0}^{l-1} h_{\tilde{A}}(x_L) \pi_{A_{opt}^{\beta}}(x_L)\left(1 - 2\mu_{A_{opt}^{\beta}}(x_L)\right)}{2\sum_{x_L=0}^{l-1} h_{\tilde{A}}(x_L)\pi_{A_{opt}^{\beta}}^{2}(x_L; \lambda_{opt})}. \tag{11}
$$

Therefore, the luminance component in the pixel domain is obtained as

$$
x'_L = \frac{l-1}{e^{-1}-1}\left(e^{-\mu_{D_{\alpha_{opt}}(A_{opt}^{\beta})}(x_L)} - 1\right), \tag{12}
$$

where x'_L are the new levels of luminance of the image. Finally, the modified luminance channel and the chromatic components a and b are combined to produce the processed image back in the *RGB* color space.

5   Experimental Results

For experimental evaluation we considered both real-world and synthetic color images with 8 bits-per-channel color resolution. Figs. 2–4 illustrate the results obtained using the HEQ approach, as well as the FHH technique and its proposed intuitionistic fuzzy counterpart. Experimental results demonstrated that the proposed intuitionistic fuzzy approach successfully enhances even highly low-contrasted color images. Lower values of the parameter β are more suitable for highly low-contrasted images as the one of Fig. 4. For this image the brightness was manually altered to produce an image with very low contrast. One may observe that the image obtained using the color intuitionistic fuzzy luminance histogram hyperbolization (CIFLHH) approach possesses successfully balanced colors. One may also observe that the proposed intuitionistic fuzzy approach produces images in which constant intensity regions and high-frequency edges have been drastically enhanced, resulting in images that are more suitable in terms of human brightness perception. Finally, it should be mentioned that similarly to the proposed CIFLHH technique, the HEQ and the FHH methods have applied solely on the luminance component of the image in the *L*a*b* color space.

(a) Initial image   (b) HEQ   (c) FHH   (d) CIFLHH

Fig. 2. (a) Initial color image and images obtained using (b) the HEQ technique, (c) the FHH method, and (d) the CIFLHH approach

(a) Initial image   (b) HEQ   (c) FHH   (d) CIFLHH

Fig. 3. (a) Initial color image and images obtained using (b) the HEQ technique, (c) the FHH method, and (d) the CIFLHH approach

(a) Initial image   (b) HEQ   (c) FHH   (d) CIFLHH

Fig. 4. (a) Initial color image and images obtained using (b) the HEQ technique, (c) the FHH method, and (d) the CIFLHH approach

6 Conclusions

In this work we presented an extension of the IFIP framework to color image processing. An approach to intuitionistic fuzzy histogram hyperbolization in the $L*a*b$ color space was presented. Finally, our future work involves a detailed study of the proposed approach using different color models.

References

1. Zadeh, L.A.: Fuzzy sets. Inf. Control 8, 338–353 (1965)
2. Atanassov, K.T.: Intuitionistic Fuzzy Sets: Theory and Applications. Studies in Fuzziness and Soft Computing, Physica–Verlag, Heidelberg (1999)
3. Vlachos, I.K., Sergiadis, G.D.: Intuitionistic Fuzzy Image Processing. In: Soft Computing in Image Processing: Recent Advances. Studies in Fuzziness and Soft Computing, vol. 210, pp. 385–416. Springer, Heidelberg (2007)
4. Vlachos, I.K., Sergiadis, G.D.: A heuristic approach to intuitionistic fuzzification of color images. In: Proc. 7th International FLINS Conference on Applied Artificial Intelligence, Genova, Italy (2006)
5. Pal, S.K., King, R.A.: Image enhancement using fuzzy set. Electron. Lett. 16, 376–378 (1980)
6. Pal, S.K., King, R.A.: Image enhancement using smoothing with fuzzy sets. IEEE Trans. Syst. Man Cybern. 11, 495–501 (1981)
7. Pal, S.K., King, R.A.: A note on the quantitative measure of image enhancement through fuzziness. IEEE Trans. Pattern Anal. Mach. Intell. 4, 204–208 (1982)
8. Szmidt, E., Kacprzyk, J.: Entropy for intuitionistic fuzzy sets. Fuzzy Sets Syst. 118, 467–477 (2001)
9. Frei, W.: Image enhancement by histogram hyperbolization. "Comput. Graphics Image Process. 6(3), 286–294 (1977)
10. Tizhoosh, H.R., Fochem, M.: Image enhancement with fuzzy histogram hyperbolization. In: Proc. of EUFIT'95. vol. 3, pp. 1695–1698 (1995)

Computer Vision and Pattern Recognition in Homeland Security Applications

Giovanni B. Garibotto

Elsag spa
Genova, Italy
giovanni.garibotto@elsagdatamat.com

Abstract. The tutorial will summarize the status of research and innovation in the field of Security of Computer Vision and Pattern Recognition Technology. Two main research areas are considered: intelligent scene analysis in video-surveillance, and mobile Automatic Number Plate recognition ANPR, for investigation and crime prevention. The lecture will refer the most recent advances of mobile ANPR solutions on board of patrol car as well as portable hand-held devices to improve mobility and flexibility. From the patrol car it is possible to collect vehicle information within the traffic flow with a performance that far exceeds human detection and recognition capabilities in all weather conditions and 24 h operation. Such a solution is currently used by most advanced police departments in the world.

Keywords: Computer Vision, Pattern Recognition, Video Surveillance & Security Applications.

1 Intelligent Video Analysis Systems

A common objective of new advanced Video Analysis System is the possibility to describe in a synthetic high-level what happens in the framed scene. Basic components of such description are the objects that are found in the scene and their movement (trajectories) during time. Another essential requirement is the possibility of reasoning in a 3D reference coordinate system and using a volumetric representation of objects (size and shape) beside radiometric color features. Such a representation should be quite similar to the human description in terms of basic primitives like the appearance of a target (when and where) its trajectory (in a reference plane), its persistence in the scene coordinates (how long). Based on such low-level primitives it is possible to build any higher level interpretation of the overall behavior and sequence of the main events in the scene, depending on the specific content and application objectives. The accuracy of people/object detection and tracking is particularly important for a variety of situations like people flow or density estimation, detection of objects (of a certain size and shape), and their condition, to be left or removed from the scene. In this research field, people modeling is a key issue for the description of flexible and complex objects to be detected and tracked. There is a wide literature dealing with such problem. A recent interesting discussion of the problem and the most advance proposed solution can be found in the special issue [1]. Among other

F. Masulli, S. Mitra, and G. Pasi (Eds.): WILF 2007, LNAI 4578, pp. 335–341, 2007.

important initiatives in this area, it is worth to remark the Performance Evaluation workshop PETS that is organized on a regular basis (the last event has been hold in New York last June 18, 2006 [2]), where most advanced research labs in the world are involved to present the last achievements of their studies. Moreover, this topic of people detection and tracking has a great interest also in the industrial domain [3] for a variety of applications from security and crime prevention, to statistical commercial analysis, up to entertainment and sports applications.

2 3D Model-Based Target Tracking

The main processing steps of a vision system for target detection and tracking are briefly summarized in the following.

1. Calibration of the involved cameras (possibly multi-camera systems) w.r.t the 3D world coordinates, with strong requirements to be robust, fast and easy to use, in practical installations. It is also required to provide the system with a sufficient level of self-awareness to immediately detect and possibly correct any deviation from the initial installation conditions.
2. Foreground/background segmentation and background updating with adaptive control to compensate the variability of light and environmental noise (shadows, highlights, etc.). A highly sensitive event detection system is of the required, even in very low contrast conditions (this is particularly important for intruder detection).
3. Target tracking using a variety of geometric and radiometric features with a suitable 3D target model and an appropriate state model including position and motion parameters
4. New target detection process for the localization of potential new objects and targets in the scene at any stage of the process (including the boot-strap situation).
5. Low-level data fusion to remove local ambiguities and minimize the number of false alarms and missed targets.
6. High-level data integration and event detection; this processing step is highly dependent on the current application with some specific constraints and contextual information.

The proposed solution is based on a simple volumetric representation of the targets and their detection, prediction and tracking in the reference 3D system, by using multiple camera views. An essential component of the process is camera calibration including both intrinsic as well as extrinsic parameters.

The area to be inspected may be quite large and it may require the installation and activation of multiple cameras to cover the scene from different multi-view positions to guarantee the correct detection and tracking of multiple objects (of different classes) in the 3D scene.

The considered application is wide-field target detection and tracking, where the targets are supposed to be quite small with poor details. In high resolution applications with close-up video recording, human body representations require a much complex model scheme to describe their non-rigid properties.

In the proposed approach new candidate objects are detected at each new time step in the different camera views according to their projected silhouettes of the foreground map (color segmentation is performed, with shadow detection and removal). A local search is performed around the predicted position to refine the object estimate using color feature representation [6], of the different class of objects (from the larger to the smaller and from the closer to the farthest).

Fig. 1. vanishing geometry on the camera view

Fig. 2. People tracking from outdoor scene with strong highlight Some of the targets are temporarily lost during the video sequence

The automatic detection of abnormal behavior represents one of the main objectives of any new intelligent video surveillance system to drive the human attention only when relevant actions take place. An essential component of an advance video analysis system is the detection and tracking of people in a video sequence in all environmental conditions.

Fig. 2 shows an example of people detection and tracking by using a 3D model based approach. An essential component of the process is the accurate calibration of the scene and the video camera system since the tracking process is performed in the 3D scene.

The target models are then re-projected into the image plane to verify their correct position in the image view. The use of a very simple symmetric 3D target model has proved to be appropriate for people counting with a sufficient precision even in very crowded and complex situations.

The accuracy of target position in the 3D reference coordinate system is highly dependent on the image resolution in wide-field cameras and it may be definitely improved by multi-camera configuration. Further research efforts will be devoted to improve the robustness of the full processing chain.

The final goal is the design of an easy to use, self-consistent system to be managed by security personnel, in real applications, in both indoor and out-door environments.

3 License Plate Recognition in Security Applications

Increasing traffic density and congestion represents one of the main problems of everyday life. Motorists lose time and money in the cues, and safety and security are often compromised. License-plate recognition (LPR) technology, often represents a solution to save time and alleviate congestion by allowing motorists to pass toll plazas or weigh stations without stopping. It can improve safety and security by helping control access to secured areas or assisting patrol in law enforcement. LPR is a consolidated technology (see the tutorial in (1)), widely used in a variety of ITS applications since License plates are the only universal identification device from vehicles to roadside. From the long list of suppliers it is possible to identify two different types of products, i.e. software packages of Optical Character Recognition (OCR), mainly oriented to system developers, and integrated systems, where OCR is a component of complete solutions, including image sensors and lighting, and special image processors, for Traffic Control or Police Security applications. Most referred applications are based on fixed installations for access control, electronic pay-toll collection and law-enforcement (red-light violation, average speed control) and security control (stolen-car detection and crime investigation). Currently, the new challenge in ITS applications is based on mobile LPR systems, installed on standard patrol vehicles, to increase data-collection capabilities and extend the inspection field during normal patrol missions. The mobile system may identify particular vehicles of interest which may be hidden amongst the huge volume of traffic using our roads today. The recognition task of a moving platform is much more complex than for fixed urban or highway traffic control installations, and represents a real challenge for Computer Vision. In fact all critical situations are concurrently present, like sudden, unpredictable changes of lighting conditions during patrols (transition from sunlit to shadow areas, tunnels, night patrols, etc.), arbitrary license plate 3D orientation, fast real-time processing requirements.

4   Mobile ANPR System

Auto-Detector [8] is a new mobile Automatic Number Plate Recognition system, installed on board of any kind of patrol vehicle (car, motor-vehicle), to automatically detect and read the license plates of the vehicles falling in its field of view.

Fig. 3. Example of Auto-Detector installation for the Italian Carabinieri-Arm, the Italian Road Police, and USA State Highway Patrol forces

The innovation content of Auto-Detector is twofold: it is a new service solution for security and surveillance monitoring; moreover it represents a significant innovation of integrated Computer Vision solutions by continuous high-rate number plate recognition from a moving sensor in all possible environmental conditions.

Auto-Detector is actually an independent intelligent sensor that is continuously inspecting what happens around the patrol vehicle and is able to detect automatically the presence of a license plate irrespective of its orientation in the field of view. As such the proposed system represents a revolutionary contribution to patrol crew, working in background and without affecting normal patrol duties.

The continuous recognition of plates in the scene is a performance far exceeding any practical possibility by the human eye and the on-line response feature of Auto-Detector (by on-board real-time checking the recognized plate against a search list size of more than millions of plates) provide a great economical value for all security and surveillance applications. Technology innovation is provided also in the Computer Vision process and Optical Character Recognition to achieve a detection performance better than 90% of all license plates in the field of view and a correct recognition rate greater than 99% among all detected license plates. Moreover the system provides a great flexibility in terms of learning tools, to achieve successful performance for all international number plates in all countries.

Another important innovation contribution is the miniaturization of the imaging sensor case, that must be installed on-board within a very small space (lighting bar, roof of the car, interior, etc.). To achieve such goals the proposed solution is an effective optimization of existing technology components in the area of digital cameras (LVDS and Camera-Link standard) and infrared illumination sources (using a very innovative LED-on-chip technology that was originally developed and used for automation inspection and Machine Vision). Finally, the selected Auto-Detector on-board processing unit is an effective network processor using a local LAN connection between dedicated processors devoted to each camera and data storage and search, with low-power consumption, and automotive constraints. The decision to adopt fixed camera positions is a compromise to acquire as much data as possible (license plate strings and images) during patrol. This capillary data collection system can rapidly alert patrols (through the onboard navigation system) and the operations centre when blacklisted numbers are detected. The system has been designed for low consumption to fit with existing power supply onboard. It integrates perfectly with existing on-board systems without adding any extra effort to the workload of patrol personnel, who is free to operate as usual in his/her patrol missions. It can be easily defined as "an auxiliary officer on-board of the car", with a reading and recognition performance that highly exceeds human capabilities, being able to detect immediately any appearance of selected number plates in the neighbourhood of the patrol car. As such it strongly enhances the capabilities of the patrol crew.

5 Conclusions

The paper provides a summary of advanced research and innovation in the field of Security. The automatic detection of abnormal behavior represents one of the main objectives of any new intelligent video surveillance system to drive the human attention only when relevant actions take place. An effective video surveillance system should be an active tool towards crime prevention rather the most common "after the fact" investigation. People detection and tracking is one of the most representative computer vision tasks, using multi-camera integration and fusion of information.

Another relevant application area is considered. It is the exploitation of License Plate Recognition technology in mobile applications for Homeland Security, to provide security forces the most efficient tools for a wide and thorough vehicle data collection and the possibility to early detect potential criminal behavior. Recent studies confirm that most relevant crime events are closely connected with the use of a car and the identification and tracking of all vehicles along the road and in downtown has proved to be an essential tool for investigation and crime prevention.

References

1. Special Issue on Modeling People: Vision based Understanding of a Person's shape, appearance, movement and behavior, Computer Vision and Image Understanding, vol. 104(2-3) (November/December 2006)
2. PETS2006, (th Int. Conf. on Performance Evaluation of Tracking and Surveillance, June 18, 2006, New York www.cvg.cs.reading.ac.uk
3. Lowe, D.: The computer vision Industry http://www.cs.ubc.ca/spider/lowe/vision.html
4. Garibotto, G., Corvi, M.: Landmark-based Stereo Vision. In: Roli, F., Vitulano, S. (eds.) ICIAP 2005. LNCS, vol. 3617, pp. 6–8. Springer, Heidelberg (2005)
5. Garibotto, G., Cibei, C.: 3D Scene Analysis by Real-Time Stereovision. In: Proc of the IEEE Int. Conf. On Image Processing, ICIP-05, Genova (September 12-15, 2005)
6. Horpraset, T., Harwood, D., Davis, L.S.: A Statistical Approach for Real-Time Robust Background Subtractiuon and Shadow Detection. In: Proc. IEEE Frame Rate Workshop, pp. 1–19, Kerkya, Greece (1999)
7. Garibotto, G., et al.: Detection of Abnormal Behavior of people and vehicles in a parking lot; an outcome of the ISCAPS project on Security, submitted to the Int. Conference on Image Analysis and Processing, ICIAP07, Modena (September 2007)
8. Garibotto, G.: Auto-Detector: Mobile Automatic Number Plate Recognition. In: Chen, C.H., Wang, P.S.P.(eds.): Handbook of Pattern Recognition and Computer Vision, ch. 5.6, pp. 601–618 (2005)

A Genetic Algorithm Based on Eigen Fuzzy Sets for Image Reconstruction

Ferdinando Di Martino and Salvatore Sessa

Università degli Studi di Napoli "Federico II"
Dipartimento di Costruzioni e Metodi Matematici in Architettura
Via Monteoliveto, n. 3, 80134 Napoli, Italy
{fdimarti, sessa}@unina.it

Abstract. By normalizing the values of its pixels, any image is interpreted as a fuzzy relation whose the greatest eigen fuzzy set with respect to the $\max - \min$ composition and the smallest eigen fuzzy set with respect to the $\min - \max$ composition are used in a genetic algorithm for image reconstruction scopes. Image-chromosomes form the population and a fitness function based on the above eigen fuzzy sets of each image-chromosome and of the related original image is used for performing the selection operator. The reconstructed image is the image-chromosome with the highest value of fitness.

Keywords: $\max - \min$ composition, $\min - \max$ composition, eigen fuzzy set, genetic algorithm, image reconstruction.

1 Introduction

By normalizing the values of its pixels with respect to (for short, w.r.t.) to the length of the gray scale used, any image of sizes $m \times m$ is interpreted as a square fuzzy relation R. So the fuzzy relation calculus for image compression (e.g, [2], [6], [10]) is a natural tool for dealing with this topic. For instance, the usage of the greatest eigen fuzzy set of R ([1], [11], [12]) w.r.t. the $\max - \min$ composition (for short, GEFS) and the smallest eigen fuzzy set of R w.r.t. the $\min - \max$ composition (for short, SEFS) is applied to problems of image information retrieval [3], image analysis [7] and image reconstruction [8]. Some authors (e.g., [4], [9]) have used genetic algorithms (for short, GA) for coding/decoding images. Indeed we have tested the use of GA to reconstruct an image by using GEFS and SEFS of the original image as input data. In Section 2 we recall the definitions of GEFS and SEFS of a fuzzy relation R, in Section 3 we describe our genetic algorithm by using a fitness function based on GEFS and SEFS and in Section 4 we show the results of our experiments.

2 Eigen Fuzzy Sets

Let $A \in F(X) = \{B : X \to [0,1]\}$ be a fuzzy set defined on a referential finite set X and $R \in F(X \times X) = \{S : X \times X \to [0,1]\}$ be a fuzzy relation such that

$$R \circ A = A \tag{1}$$

F. Masulli, S. Mitra, and G. Pasi (Eds.): WILF 2007, LNAI 4578, pp. 342–348, 2007.

where $\circ$ stands for the $\max - \min$ composition. In terms of membership functions, we write (1) as

$$A(y) = \max_{x \in X}\{\min(A(x),\ R(x,y)\} \tag{2}$$

for all $x, y \in X$ and A is said an eigen fuzzy set of R. Let $A_i \in F(X)$, $i = 1, 2, \ldots$ be given recursively by

$$A_1(z) = \max_{x \in X} R(x, z) \quad \forall z \in X, A_2 = R \circ A_1, \ldots, A_{n+1} = R \circ A_n, \ldots . \tag{3}$$

We know (e.g., [1], [11], [12]) that there exists an integer $p \in \{1, \ldots, \mathrm{card}X\}$ such that $R \circ A_p = A_p$ and $A_p \geq A$ for all $A \in F(X)$ satisfying the Equation (1), that is A_p is the GEFS of R. By dualizing the Equation (2), we also consider the following equation:

$$R \bullet B = B \tag{4}$$

where $\bullet$ denotes the $\min - \max$ composition. In terms of membership functions, we write the Equation (4) as

$$B(y) = \min_{x \in X}\{\max(B(x),\ R(x,y)\} \tag{5}$$

for all $x, y \in X$ and B is also said an eigen fuzzy set of R w.r.t. the $\min - \max$ composition. Let $B_i \in F(X)$, $i = 1, 2, \ldots$ be given recursively by

$$B_1(z) = \min_{x \in X} R(x, z) \quad \forall z \in X, B_2 = R \bullet B_1, \ldots, B_{n+1} = R \bullet B_n, \ldots . \tag{6}$$

By duality, it is easily seen that there exists an integer $q \in \{1, \ldots, \mathrm{card}X\}$ such that $R \bullet B_q = B_q$ and $B_q \leq B$ for all $B \in F(X)$ satisfying the Equation (4), that is B_q is the SEFS of R.

The following example illustrates the above concepts. Indeed, let $\mathrm{card}X = 3$ and we consider the following fuzzy relation:

$$\mathcal{R} = \begin{pmatrix} 0.8 & 0.2 & 0.7 \\ 0.1 & 0.3 & 0.7 \\ 0.5 & 0.4 & 0.3 \end{pmatrix}$$

By using the sequence (3), we have that $A_1 = (0.8, 0.4, 0.5)$ and $A_2 = R \circ A_1 = (0.8, 0.4, 0.7)$, hence $A_3 = R \circ A_2 = A_2$, that is A_2 is the GEFS of R w.r.t. the $\max - \min$ composition (2). Further, by using the sequence (6), we see that $B_1 = (0.1, 0.2, 0.3)$ and $B_2 = R \bullet B_1 = (0.2, 0.2, 0.3)$, hence $B_3 = R \bullet B_2 = B_2$ and then B_2 is the SEFS of R w.r.t. the $\min - \max$ composition (5).

We have used formulas (3) and (6) in our algorithms for calculating GEFS and SEFS of the fuzzy relations involved in this paper.

3 The Genetic Algorithm

The GA method [5] encodes a potential solution to a specific problem on a simple chromosome like data structures and applies recombination operators to these structures. Genetic algorithms are often viewed as optimization functions although the range of problems to which they have been applied is quite broad. We use the GA approach for the reconstruction of an image by using its GEFS and SEFS in the fitness function of a chromosome. It is well known that the principal step in developing a GA is the definition of a solution coding: in other words, a chromosome must contain information about the solution that it represents. The coding process depends mainly on the problem under consideration (e.g., binary strings, integers, real numbers, parsing trees, etc.). In our approach we use a population of N chromosomes formed by random images; the gene of a chromosome is a pixel. The allele value of a gene is an integer value in the set $X = \{0, 1, \ldots, 255\}$ since in our experiments we use gray images of sizes 256×256. We applied the selection operator by calculating for each image chromosome the value of fitness given by

$$F(R, R_j) = \frac{1}{\mathrm{MSE}_{\mathrm{GEFS+SEFS}}(R, R_j)} \qquad (7)$$

where $j = 1, 2, \ldots, N$ and MSE stands for Mean Square Error defined as

$$\mathrm{MSE}_{\mathrm{GEFS+SEFS}}(R, R_j) =$$

$$\frac{1}{256} \sum_{x \in X} \left[(A(x) - A_j(x))^2 + (B(x) - B_j(x))^2 \right], \qquad (8)$$

being $A, B \in F(X)$ the GEFS and SEFS, respectively, of the fuzzy relation R obtained by normalizing the pixels of the input original image (that is if $P(x, y)$ is the pixel value in $(x, y) \in X \times X$, there we assume $R(x, y) = P(x, y)/255$) and $A_j, B_j \in F(X)$ the GEFS and SEFS, respectively, of the fuzzy relation R_j obtained by normalizing the pixels of the j-th image-chromosome of the population. The crossover operator defines the procedure for generating a child from two parent genomes. For the crossover operation we applied a fixed-length bi-dimensional array Single Point Crossover with a probability p_{cros} to two images in the mating pool. After the crossover operator is performed, we have applied a mutation operator to each chromosome with probability p_{mut}. In order to accelerate the convergence of the algorithm, the mutation operator performs a random change of a genes value in a chromosome by choosing a random value very close to the previous value of the gene. In the GA we have prefixed several values of the number I of generations and we have determined as reconstructed image the image-chromosome with the highest value of fitness.

4   Experimental Results

We have used in our experiments 10.000 gray images of sizes 256×256 extracted from SIDBA data set (http://www.cs.cmu.edu/ cil/vision.html). In our experiments we used the $C++$ library class GALIB (http://lancet.mit.edu/ga/ dist/) in a $C++$ project. We have used a crossover probability $p_{\mathrm{cros}} = 0.6$ and a mutation probability $p_{mut} = 0.01$ by testing the GA with different values of the population number N and the number I of generations. For brevity, we only give some results for the well known image $R = \mathrm{Lena}$ (Figure 1a) and $R = \mathrm{Bird}$ (Figure 1b), whose reconstructed images under several values of N and I are shown in the Figures $2a \div 5a$ and in the Figures $2b \div 5b$ respectively.

Fig. 1a.

The sample image $R = \mathrm{Lena}$

Fig. 1b.

The sample image $R = \mathrm{Bird}$

Fig. 2a.

Reconstruction $S1$ (N=40, I=10^3)

Fig. 3a.

Reconstruction $S2$ (N=40, I=10^4)

Table 1. Values of the PSNR for the reconstructed images

PSNR for Lena	PSNR for Bird
$(\mathrm{PSNR})_1 = \;\;9.80$ (Fig. 2a)	$(\mathrm{PSNR})_1 = \;\;9.68$ (Fig. 2b)
$(\mathrm{PSNR})_2 = 11.22$ (Fig. 3a)	$(\mathrm{PSNR})_2 = 10.93$ (Fig. 3b)
$(\mathrm{PSNR})_3 = 13.35$ (Fig. 4a)	$(\mathrm{PSNR})_3 = 14.25$ (Fig. 4b)
$(\mathrm{PSNR})_4 = 19.37$ (Fig. 5a)	$(\mathrm{PSNR})_4 = 21.41$ (Fig. 5b)

From above tests, it is evident that the better performance of the GA algorithm is achieved for $N = 100$ and $I = 100000$. Indeed, in Table 1 we report the values of the Peak Signal Noise Ratio $(\mathrm{PSNR})_c$ for each reconstructed image $S_c (c = 1, 2, 3, 4)$ given by

$$(PSNR) = 20\log_{10} \frac{255}{\sqrt{\frac{\sum_{x \in X} \sum_{y \in X} [R(x,y) - S_c(x,y)]^2}{256 \times 256}}}$$

being $X = \{0, 1, \ldots, 255\}$ and $R, S_c \in F(X \times X)$.

Fig. 4a.

Reconstruction $S3(N=40, I=5 \times 10^4 I=10^5)$

Fig. 5a.

Reconstruction $S4$ ($N=100$, $I=10^5$)

Fig. 2b.

Reconstruction $S1$ ($N=40$, $I=10^3$)

Fig. 3b.

Reconstruction $S2$ ($N=40$, $I=10^4$)

Fig. 4b.

Reconstruction $S3(N=40, I=5 \times 10^4)$

Fig. 5b.

Reconstruction $S4$ ($N=100$, $I=10^5$)

For sake of completeness, in the Figures 1 and 2 are shown the GEFS and SEFS of the original image R of Figure 1a and of the reconstructed image S_4 of Figure 5a respectively, on which is evaluated the fitness value (7).

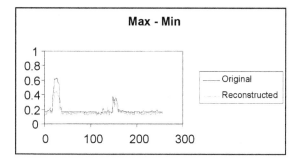

Fig. 1. GEFS of the images R and S_4

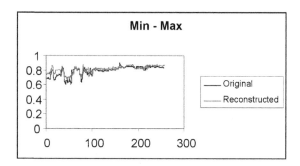

Fig. 2. SEFS of the images R and S_4

5   Conclusions

Two types of eigen fuzzy sets, that is the max-min and min-max compositions are used to calculate the fitness value in a GA used for image reconstruction scopes. We have applied the GA over many random gray images by using several population dimensions and generation numbers and we have assumed as reconstructed image that one with the greatest value of fitness, that is having GEFS and SEFS very close to those ones of the original image. Here we have not discussed on time coding, nor we have studied optimization tasks for improving the performance of the GA algorithm.

References

1. Bourke, M.M., Grant Fisher, D.: Convergence, Eigen Fuzzy Sets and Stability Analysis of Relation Matrices. Fuzzy Sets and Systems 81, 227–234 (1996)
2. Di Martino, F., Loia, V., Sessa, S.: A method for coding/decoding images by using fuzzy relation equation. In: De Baets, B., Kaynak, O., Bilgiç, T. (eds.) IFSA 2003. LNCS, vol. 2715, pp. 436–441. Springer, Heidelberg (2003)

3. Di Martino, F., Nobuhara, H., Sessa, S.: Eigen Fuzzy Sets and Image Information Retrieval. In: Proceedings of the International Conference on Fuzzy Information Systems (Budapest). vol. 3, pp. 1385–1390 (2004)

4. Faround, K.M., Boukelif, A.: Speeding Up Fractal Image Compression by Genetic Algorithm. Multidimensional Systems and Signal Processing 16(2), 217–236 (2005)

5. Goldberg, D.E.: Genetic Algorithms in Search, Optimization and Machine Learning. Addison-Wesley Longman Publishing Co., Inc, Boston (1989)

6. Nobuhara, H., Hirota, K., Pedrycz, W.: Fast Solving Method of Fuzzy Relational Equations and Its Application to Lossy Image Compression. IEEE Transactions of Fuzzy Systems 8(3), 325–334 (2000)

7. Nobuhara, H., Iyoda, E.M., Bede, B., Hirota, K.: A Solution for Generalized Eigen Fuzzy Sets Equations by Genetic Algorithm and its Application to Image Analysis, In: Proceedings of IEEE International Conference Intelligent Systems (Varna, Bulgaria), Vol. 1, pp. 208–212 (2004)

8. Nobuhara, H., Bede, B., Hirota, K.: On Various Eigen Fuzzy Sets and Their Application to Image Reconstruction. Information Sciences 176, 2988–3010 (2006)

9. Pedrycz, W., Reformat, M.: Genetic Optimization with Fuzzy Coding. In: Herrera, F., Verdegay, J. (eds.) Genetic Algorithms and Soft Computing. Studies in Fuzziness and Soft Computing, vol. 8, pp. 51–67. Physica Verlag, Heidelberg New York (1996)

10. Pedrycz, W., Hirota, K., Sessa, S.: A Decomposition of Fuzzy Relations. IEEE Transactions on Systems, Man, and Cybernetics, Part B 31(4), 657–663 (2001)

11. Sanchez, E.: Resolution of Eigen Fuzzy Sets Equations. Fuzzy Sets and Systems 1, 69–74 (1978)

12. Sanchez, E.: Eigen Fuzzy Sets and Fuzzy Relations. J. Math. Anal. Appl. 81, 399–342 (1981)

Fuzzy Metrics Application in Video Spatial Deinterlacing

Julio Riquelme, Samuel Morillas*, Guillermo Peris-Fajarnés, and Dolores Castro

Universidad Politécnica de Valencia, E.P.S. de Gandia,
Departamento de Expresión Gráfica en la Ingeniería,
Carretera Nazaret-Oliva s/n, 46730 Grao de Gandia (Valencia), Spain

Abstract. Spatial methods play a relevant role in the deinterlacing matter. Common spatial algorithms often introduce artifacts like crawling, alias and blur in the output signal. In this paper a new spatial deinterlacing method for color image sequences that introduces less artifacts than other common methods is proposed. It uses fuzzy metrics to select the current pixel from a group of the nearest pixels taking into account how much *chromatically similar* and *spatially close* are these pixels to each other. Experimental results show that the proposed algorithm outperforms common spatial algorithms in various video sequences.

1 Introduction

Interlace video format does not display complete frames but half-frames. Many deinterlacing methods have appeared as a necessary tool for transforming the scan format from interlace to progressive [1]. The most recent and complex deinterlacing methods use motion vectors for compensating the motion on the scene. However they need spatial methods when the sequence presents motion and it can not be compensated [1,2,3,4,5]. Spatial methods that have the lowest implementation cost are line repetition and line averaging. Edge-based line averaging (ELA) and its modifications select the most suitable direction and interpolate along that direction. Nevertheless, these methods produce mistakes when edges are not sharp enough or in the presence of noise [6,7,8,9].

In this paper we present a new spatial deinterlacing method which uses a fuzzy metric to select the current pixel from a group of the nearest pixels taking into account how much *chromatically similar* and *spatially close* are these pixels to each other. The use of fuzzy metrics is considered because they provide an appropriate way to represent multiple criteria simultaneously, as it will be described.

In the following, Section 2 presents fuzzy metrics concepts used and defines the new spatial deinterlacing method. Section 3 shows the obtained experimental results and finally in Section 4 some conclusions are drawn.

2 Proposed Deinterlacing Method

The deinterlacing method proposed in this paper uses a fuzzy metric to compare and select one pixel from the nearest pixels embedded in the processing window W defined

---

* The author acknowledges the support of Spanish Ministry of Education and Science under program "Becas de Formación de Profesorado Universitario FPU".

F. Masulli, S. Mitra, and G. Pasi (Eds.): WILF 2007, LNAI 4578, pp. 349–354, 2007.

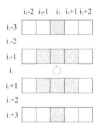

Fig. 1. Processing window for the pixel at position $\mathbf{i} = (i_1, i_2)$

as in Figure 1. The color vectors in the processing window W will be ordered using the commented fuzzy metric as distance criterion in a reduced ordering procedure [10] such that the vector being the most *chromatically similar* and *spatially close* with respect to the rest of the pixels in W will be the output pixel of the process and will be identified in an extreme of the ordering as it will be explain below.

2.1 Measuring Fuzzy Metrics

In order to measure the *chromatic similarity* between color vectors and according to the studies made in [11,12] we should consider the difference in direction between the RGB color vectors. Then, we will consider the unitary vector associated to each color vector which characterizes its direction in the vector space.

Let $\mathbf{F_i} = (F_i(1), F_i(2), F_i(3))$ denote the color vector of the $\mathbf{F}$ image located at position $\mathbf{i} = (i_1, i_2)$ comprised of its R, G and B components. The unitary vector $\mathbf{F'_i}$ characterizing the direction in the vector space of the color vector $\mathbf{F_i}$ is obtained as

$$\mathbf{F'_i} = \frac{\mathbf{F_i}}{\|\mathbf{F_i}\|_2} \tag{1}$$

where $\|\cdot\|_2$ denotes the Euclidean norm. Gray-scale vectors in RGB correspond to the vectors with the form $V_a = (a, a, a)$ where $a \in [0, 255]$ and that for any $a > 0$, $\|V_a\|_2 = a\sqrt{3}$ and $V'_a = (\frac{1}{\sqrt{3}}, \frac{1}{\sqrt{3}}, \frac{1}{\sqrt{3}})$, then we will extend the above function by defining the unitary vector $Z' = (\frac{1}{\sqrt{3}}, \frac{1}{\sqrt{3}}, \frac{1}{\sqrt{3}})$ for black and white vector images.

Given this, we propose to measure the *chromatic similarity* by using the fuzzy metric M_K introduced in [13,14,15] between these unitary vectors as follows

$$M_K(\mathbf{F'_i}, \mathbf{F'_j}) = \prod_{l=1}^{3} \frac{min\{F'_i(l), F'_j(l)\} + K}{max\{F'_i(l), F'_j(l)\} + K} \tag{2}$$

Then $M_K(\mathbf{F'_i}, \mathbf{F'_j})$ will be the *fuzzy chromatic similarity* between the color vectors $\mathbf{F_i}$ and $\mathbf{F_j}$. According to [13,14,15,16,17], the K parameter should be set accordingly to the range of the vector component values so that in our case $K = 4$ is an appropriate value.

For the *spatial distance* between pixels it will be considered the so-called standard fuzzy metric deduced from the L_1 metric M_{L_1} in [18]. Then, the *fuzzy spatial closeness* between the pixels $\mathbf{F_i}$ and $\mathbf{F_j}$ is given by

$$M_{L_1}(\mathbf{i}, \mathbf{j}, t) = \frac{t}{t + L_1(\mathbf{i}, \mathbf{j})} \tag{3}$$

where L_1 denotes the L_1 metric. The t parameter may be interpreted as a parameter to adjust the importance given to the spatial criterion since according to [18] $M_{L_1}(\mathbf{i}, \mathbf{j}, t)$ measures the distance between $\mathbf{i}$ and $\mathbf{j}$ with respect to t.

2.2   A Fuzzy Metric for Chromatic Similarity and Spatial Closeness

For our purpose it will be considered a fuzzy metric combining the *fuzzy chromatic similarity* M_K (2) and the *fuzzy spatial closeness* M_{L_1} (3). So, it will considered the following combined fuzzy metric

$$CFM_{K,L_1}(\mathbf{F_i}, \mathbf{F_j}, t) = M_K(\mathbf{F'_i}, \mathbf{F'_j}) \cdot M_{L_1}(\mathbf{i}, \mathbf{j}, t) \tag{4}$$

which, according to [19], can be proved to be a fuzzy metric, as well. Then, the expression in 4 is a fuzzy measure of the *fuzzy chromatic similarity and fuzzy spatial closeness* between the color vectors $\mathbf{F_i}$ and $\mathbf{F_j}$.

2.3   Proposed Spatial Deinterlacing Method

The proposed method will select as output the pixel which is simultaneously the most *chromatically similar and spatially close* to all the other vector pixels in the processing window. To realize the selection, a reduced vector ordering [10] using the combined fuzzy metric CFM_{K,L_1} as distance criterion will be performed as follows.

Let $\mathbf{F}$ represent a multichannel interlaced image and let W be the N length processing sliding window in Figure 1. The image vectors in W are denoted as $\mathbf{F_j}, \mathbf{j} \in W$. The *fuzzy chromatic similarity and fuzzy spatial closeness* between two vectors $\mathbf{F_k}$ and $\mathbf{F_j}$ is denoted by $CFM_{K,L_1}(\mathbf{F_k}, \mathbf{F_j}, t)$. For each vector in W, an accumulated measure of the *fuzzy chromatic similarity and fuzzy spatial closeness* to all the other vectors in the window has to be calculated. The scalar quantity $R_{\mathbf{k}} = \sum_{j \in W, \mathbf{j} \neq \mathbf{k}} CFM_{K,L_1}(\mathbf{F_k}, \mathbf{F_j}, t)$, is the accumulated measure associated to the vector $\mathbf{F_k}$. The reduced ordering [10] establishes that the ordering of the $R_{\mathbf{k}}$'s: $R_{(0)} \leq R_{(1)} \leq ... \leq R_{(N-1)}$, implies the same ordering of the vectors $\mathbf{F_k}$'s: $\mathbf{F}_{(0)} \leq \mathbf{F}_{(1)} \leq ... \leq \mathbf{F}_{(N-1)}$. Then the output of the selection process is $\mathbf{F}_{(N-1)}$ since it is the vector which maximizes the accumulated measure and then it is the most *chromatically similar and spatially close* to all the other vector pixels in W.

The t parameter allows to adjust the importance of the spatial criterion such that when $t \longrightarrow \infty$ the spatial criterion is not taken into account; for lower values of t, pixels far from the central pixel help to decide the output but they are not likely to be the output as they are not *spatially close* to all the other pixels in the window. Moreover, the proposed method is robust in the presence of noise since noisy pixels will usually occupy high ranks in the ordering and thus they can hardly be the output of the method.

3   Experimental Results

The proposed method is evaluated using the video sequences *Flower Garden* and *Table Tennis* in front of the most common spatial methods. In this paper we make use of the conventional ELA algorithm and two modifications, an extended ELA (ELA-5) which searches the interpolation direction between five possible ones and EDI algorithm which usually have a visually better performance than other spatial methods [7,9].

The well-known *Mean Absolute Error* (MAE) and *Peak Signal to Noise Ratio* (PSNR) quality measures have been used to assess the performance of the proposed method and are defined in [10]. Table 1 shows comparisons in terms of the objective quality measures for the sequence *Flower* and two different scenes of the sequence *Table-Tennis*.

The proposed method has a good performance for a wide range of values of the t parameter. Values in $[0, 1]$ provided the better numerical results, getting worse for higher value of t. We set the parameter $t = 0.1$ empirically. It is possible to choose another processing window W configuration with more pixels almost without differences in the visual results but that would increase the computational load.

Table 1. Comparison of the methods performance

Method	flower		tennis1		tennis2	
Measure	MAE	PSNR	MAE	PSNR	MAE	PSNR
Line repetition	7.36	32.47	2.86	34.87	4.76	34.32
Line averaging	6.09	32.86	2.34	35.54	4.09	34.53
EDI	6.09	32.88	2.42	35.17	4.08	34.47
ELA	5.85	33.05	2.32	35.34	3.61	34.84
ELA-5	5.79	32.12	2.27	35.27	3.49	34.96
Proposed	5.16	33.45	2.25	35.41	3.04	35.31

The detail of deinterlaced Tennis-Table sequences depicted in Figure 2 shows some outputs of the considered deinterlacing methods. All spatial methods introduce artifacts when deinterlacing. Some of these artifacts can be only observed by seeing the animated sequence. Numerical results are an estimation of the original signal recovering but it does not necessarily correspond with artifacts appearance. The proposed method has a good balance between signal recovering (best numerical results) and artifacts generation (no new artifacts appearance).

4   Conclusion

In this paper, a new spatial deinterlacing method has been proposed. It makes use of a fuzzy metric in order to select the output pixel from a group by performing a reduced vector ordering.

The proposed fuzzy metric simultaneously measures the *chromatic similarity* and *spatial closeness* between two color pixels such that the proposed method performs a chromaticity based selection. The use of fuzzy metrics has been considered since they provide an appropriate way to simultaneously model multiple criteria.

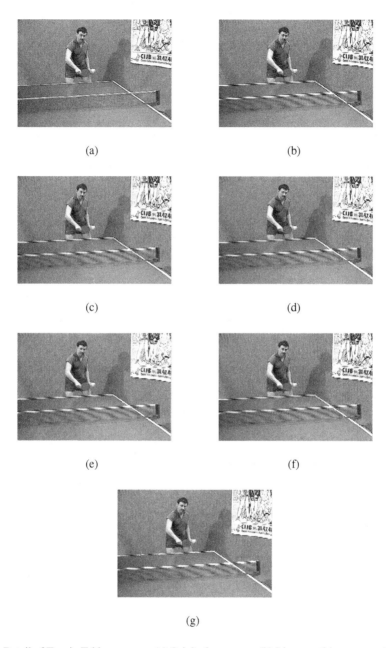

(a)

(b)

(c)

(d)

(e)

(f)

(g)

Fig. 2. Detail of Tennis-Table sequence (a) Original sequence, (b) Line repetition output, (c) Line averaging output, (d) ELA output, (e) ELA-5 output, (f) EDI output, (g) Proposed method output

Experimental results show that the proposed method can outperform other state-of-the-art spatial methods in terms of performance.

References

1. de Haan, G., Bellers, E.B.: Deinterlacing - an overview. In: Proceedings of the IEEE, vol. 86, pp. 1839–1857 (September 1998)
2. Jeon, G., Jeong, J.: Designing takagi-sugeno fuzzy model-based motion adaptive deinterlacing system. IEEE Trans. on Consumer Electronics 52(3), 1013–1020 (2006)
3. Huang, Q., Gao, W., Zhao, D., Sun, H.: An efficient and robust adaptive deinterlacing technique. IEEE Trans. on Consumer Electronics 52(3), 888–895 (2006)
4. Wang, D., Vincent, A., Blanchfield, P.: Hybrid de-interlacing algorithm based on motion vector reliability. IEEE Trans. on Circuits and Systems for Video Technology 15(8), 1019–1025 (2005)
5. Chang, Y.L., Lin, S.F., Chen, C.Y., Chen, L.G.: Video de-interlacing by adaptive 4-field global/local motion compensated approach. IEEE Trans. on Circuits and Systems for Video Technology 15(12), 1569–1582 (2005)
6. Kuo, C.J., Liao, C., Lin, C.C.: Adaptive interpolation technique for scanning rate conversion, IEEE Trans. on Circuits and Systems for Video Technology, 6(3) (1996)
7. Oh, H.S., Kim, Y., Jung, Y.Y., Morales, A.W., Ko, S.J.: Spatio-temporal edge-based median filtering for deinterlacing. In: Digest of the Int. Conf. on Consumer Electronics, pp. 52–53 (June 2000)
8. Yoo, H., Jeong, J.: Direction-oriented interpolation and its application to de-inderlacing, IEEE Trans. on Consumer Electronics, 28(4) (November 2002)
9. Park, M.K., Kang, M.G., Nam, K., Oh, S.G.: New edge dependent deinterlacing algorithm based on horizontal edge pattern, IEEE Trans. on Consumer Electronics, 49(4) (November 2003)
10. Plataniotis, K.N., Venetsanopoulos, A.N.: Color Image processing and applications. Springer-Verlag, Berlin (2000)
11. Trahanias, P.E., Venetsanopoulos, A.N.: Vector directional filters-a new class of multichannel image processing filters, IEEE Trans. Image Process, 2(4), 528–534 (1993)
12. Trahanias, P.E., Karakos, D., Venetsanopoulos, A.N.: Directional processing of color images: theory and experimental results. IEEE Trans. Image Process 5(6), 868–880 (1996)
13. Morillas, S., Gregori, V., Peris-Fajarnés, G., Latorre, P.: A new vector median filter based on fuzzy metrics. In: Kamel, M., Campilho, A. (eds.) ICIAR 2005. LNCS, vol. 3656, pp. 81–90. Springer, Heidelberg (2005)
14. Morillas, S., Gregori, V., Peris-Fajarnés, G., Latorre, P.: A fast impulsive noise color image filter using fuzzy metrics. Real-Time Imaging 11(5-6), 417–428 (2005)
15. Morillas, S., Sánchez, A.J., Latorre, P., Peris-Fajarnés, G.: A new fuzzy similarity measure for multichannel image processing. In: Simposio sobre Lógica Fuzzy y Soft Computing, LFSC 2005, Granada, Spain, pp. 29–35 (2005)
16. Morillas, S., Gregori, V., Sapena, A.: Fuzzy Bilateral Filtering for Color Images. In: Campilho, A., Kamel, M. (eds.) ICIAR 2006. LNCS, vol. 4141, pp. 138–145. Springer, Heidelberg (2006)
17. Morillas, S.: Fuzzy Metrics and Peer Groups for Impulsive noise reduction in Color Images. In: Proc. of 14th European Signal Processing Conference EUSIPCO 2006, 4-8 Sep (2006)
18. George, A., Veeramani, P.: On Some results in fuzzy metric spaces. Fuzzy Sets and Systems 64(3), 395–399 (1994)
19. Sapena, A.: A contribution to the study of fuzzy metric spaces. Appl. Gen. Topology 2(1), 63–76 (2001)

Fuzzy Directional-Distance Vector Filter

Samuel Morillas*, Valentín Gregori, Julio Riquelme, Beatriz Defez,
and Guillermo Peris-Fajarnés

Universidad Politécnica de Valencia, E.P.S. de Gandia,
Carretera Nazaret-Oliva s/n, 46730 Grao de Gandia (Valencia), Spain

Abstract. A well-known family of nonlinear multichannel image filters uses the ordering of vectors by means of an appropriate *distance or similarity measure* between vectors. In this way, the *vector median filter* (VMF), the *vector directional filter* (VDF) and the *distance directional filter* (DDF) use the relative magnitude differences between vectors, the directional vector difference or a combination of both, respectively. In this paper, a novel *fuzzy metric* is used to measure magnitude and directional *fuzzy distances* between image vectors. Then, a variant of the DDF using this *fuzzy metric* is proposed. The proposed variant is computationally cheaper than the classical DDF. In addition, experimental results show that the proposed filter receives better results in impulsive noise suppression in colour images.

1 Introduction

Nonlinear vector filters based on the theory of robust statistics [6,10], commonly use the reduced ordering principle amongst vectors in a predefined sliding window [12,17]. When the vectors are ranked using the reduced ordering principle by means of a suitable *distance or similarity measure*, the lowest ranked vectors are those which are *close* to all the other vectors in the window according to the *distance or similarity measure* used. On the other hand, atypical vectors, susceptible to be considered as noisy or outliers, occupy the highest ranks. The output of these filters is defined as the lowest ranked vector as follows.

Let $\mathbf{F}$ represent a multichannel image and let W be a window of finite size $n+1$ (filter length). The image vectors in the filtering window W are denoted as $\mathbf{F}_j, j = 0, 1, ..., n$. The *distance* between two vectors $\mathbf{F}_k, \mathbf{F}_j$ is denoted as $\rho(\mathbf{F}_k, \mathbf{F}_j)$. For each vector in the filtering window, a global or accumulated distance to all the other vectors in the window has to be calculated. The scalar quantity $R_k = \sum_{j=0, j \neq k}^{n} \rho(\mathbf{F}_k, \mathbf{F}_j)$, is the accumulated distance associated to the vector $\mathbf{F}_k$. The ordering of the R_k's: $R_{(0)} \leq R_{(1)} \leq ... \leq R_{(n)}$, implies the same ordering of the vectors $\mathbf{F}_k$'s: $\mathbf{F}_{(0)} \leq \mathbf{F}_{(1)} \leq ... \leq \mathbf{F}_{(n)}$. Given this order, the output of the filter is $\mathbf{F}_{(0)}$.

---

* The author acknowledges the support of Spanish Ministry of Education and Science under program "Becas de Formación de Profesorado Universitario FPU".

F. Masulli, S. Mitra, and G. Pasi (Eds.): WILF 2007, LNAI 4578, pp. 355–361, 2007.
© Springer-Verlag Berlin Heidelberg 2007

Following the above scheme, the *vector median filter* (VMF) uses the generalized Minkowski metric (L_p norm) expressed as

$$L_\beta(\mathbf{x}, \mathbf{y}) = \left(\sum_{i=1}^{N} |(x_i - y_i)|^\beta \right)^{\frac{1}{\beta}}, \tag{1}$$

and usually its particular cases the L_1 and L_2 metrics as the ρ distance function between vectors. Some approaches have been introduced with the aim of speeding up the VMF by using a linear approximation of the Euclidean distance [2], and by designing a fast algorithm when using the L_1 norm [3]. Also, the VMF has been extended to fuzzy numbers in [5] by means of *certain fuzzy distances*. Indeed, fuzzy distances have been recently proved to be very useful for image filtering tasks [4,14,15,16]. On the other hand the *basic vector directional filter* (BVDF) [19], uses the difference in direction among the image vectors as an ordering criterion. The function usually used to measure angular differences between vectors is defined as [19]

$$A(\mathbf{x}, \mathbf{y}) = cos^{-1} \left(\frac{\mathbf{x} \cdot \mathbf{y}}{||\mathbf{x}|| \cdot ||\mathbf{y}||} \right). \tag{2}$$

The BVDF uses the A function as the ρ distance function above for defining the vector ordering. Since directions of vectors are associated to their chromaticities the angular minimization may give better results than techniques based on VMF in terms of colour preservation.

The *directional distance filter* (DDF), [11], tries to minimize a combination of the aggregated distance measures used in VMF and BVDF. The accumulated distance R_k associated to each vector $\mathbf{F}_k, k = 0, \ldots, n$ in the filtering window is now calculated as follows

$$R_k = \left[\sum_{j=0}^{n} L_\beta(\mathbf{F}_k, \mathbf{F}_j) \right]^{1-q} \left[\sum_{j=0}^{n} A(\mathbf{F}_k, \mathbf{F}_j) \right]^{q}, \tag{3}$$

where L_β denotes the specific metric used, A is the angular distance function above and $q \in [0, 1]$ is a parameter which allows to tune the importance of the angle criterion versus the distance criterion. If $q = 0$, the DDF operates as the VMF, whereas for $q = 1$ DDF is equivalent to the BVDF. For $q = 0.5$ the weight is equivalent for both criteria. In this way, the DDF constitutes a generalization of the VMF and BVDF. It is useful in multichannel image processing since it inherits the properties of its ancestors [11]. The disadvantage of DDF is a relatively high computational complexity because two different aggregated measures are to be calculated.

In this paper we use a novel fuzzy metric introduced in [13] to propose a variant of the classical DDF. For this, we introduce the following novel concepts in this paper: (i) first we extend the usage of a previously studied fuzzy metric [13,14,15] to the directional domain and then (ii) we define a novel hybrid fuzzy magnitude-directional distance that allows us to define a variant of the DDF. It will be shown that the proposed filter is computationally cheaper than the DDF and that it outperforms the DDF for impulsive noise reduction in terms of objective quality measures.

The paper is organized as follows. In section 2 the novel fuzzy metric and its use in magnitude and direction vector comparison is described. Then, the proposed filters are presented. Experimental results including performance comparison are shown in section 3. Finally, conclusions are presented in section 4.

2   Novel Fuzzy Metric and Proposed Filtering

The fuzzy metric M_K, introduced in [13], which we aim to use in this paper is defined as follows. Let X be a closed real interval $[a, b]$ and let $K > |a| > 0$. The function $M_K : X^3 \times X^3 \longrightarrow]0, 1]$ given by

$$M_K(\mathbf{x}, \mathbf{y}) = \prod_{i=1}^{3} \frac{min\{x_i, y_i\} + K}{max\{x_i, y_i\} + K}, \tag{4}$$

where $\mathbf{x} = (x_1, x_2, x_3)$ and $\mathbf{y} = (y_1, y_2, y_3)$, is a stationary fuzzy metric [7,8,9] on X^3, when the t-norm $\cdot$ is the usual product in $[0, 1]$. The fuzzy metric M_K presents the particular behaviour that the given value for two distinct pairs of consecutive numbers (or vectors) may not be the same. This effect can be smoothed by increasing the value of the K parameter in Eq. (4). So, the value of K should be set high enough to reduce this effect. However, if $K \to \infty$ then $M_K(\mathbf{F}_i, \mathbf{F}_j) \to 1$, so very high values of K should also be avoided. Several experiences [13,14] have shown that for a range of values in $[0, C]$ appropriate values of K are in the range $[2C, 2^3 C]$.

If we denote by $\mathbf{F}$ a colour image and by $\mathbf{F}_k = (F_k(1), F_k(2), F_k(3))$ and $\mathbf{F}_j = (F_j(1), F_j(2), F_j(3))$ two colour image vectors at positions k and j respectively, then $M_K(\mathbf{F}_k, \mathbf{F}_j)$ is a measure of the fuzzy magnitude distance between $\mathbf{F}_k$ and $\mathbf{F}_j$, where according to above K can be set to $K = 1024$ for 24-bit RGB colour images.

Now, we denote by $\hat{\mathbf{F}}_k$ the unitary vector associated to the colour image vector $\mathbf{F}_k$. Then, we can measure directional distance between colour vectors if we use the M_K fuzzy metric between two unitary vectors as $M_{K'}(\hat{\mathbf{F}}_k, \hat{\mathbf{F}}_j)$, where the value of K' should be appropriate for unitary vectors and so, it is set to $K' = 4$.

Next, in order to approach a simultaneous fuzzy magnitude-directional distance, from a fuzzy point of view it should be appropriate to join both $M_K(\mathbf{F}_i, \mathbf{F}_j)$ and

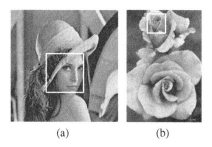

(a)   (b)

Fig. 1. Test Images: (a) Detail of Lenna image, (b) Detail of Brandy Rose image (Copyright photo courtesy of Toni Lankerd)

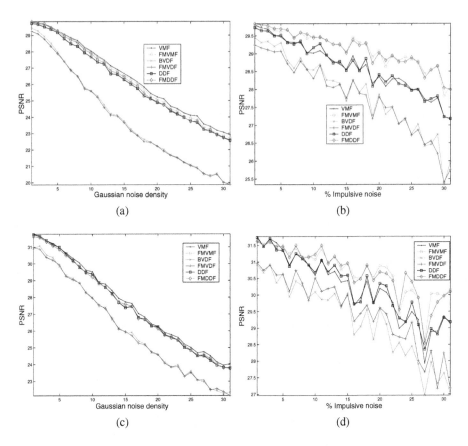

(a)   (b)

(c)   (d)

Fig. 2. PSNR performance comparison using a detail of the Lenna image (a-b) contaminated with different densities gaussian (a) and impulsive noise (b), and using a detail of the Brose image (c-d) image contaminated with different densities gaussian (c) and impulsive noise (d)

$M_{K'}(\hat{\mathbf{F}}_i, \hat{\mathbf{F}}_j)$ with an appropriate t-norm. The product t-norm will be used since it is involved in M_K then, the function

$$M_{KK'} = M_K(\mathbf{F}_i, \mathbf{F}_j) \cdot M_{K'}(\hat{\mathbf{F}}_i, \hat{\mathbf{F}}_j), \tag{5}$$

represents the fuzzy distance between the colour vectors $\mathbf{F}_i$ and $\mathbf{F}_j$ taking simultaneously into account both magnitude and directional criteria. Moreover, it is easy to verify that $M_{KK'}$ is a fuzzy metric, as well [18].

In the following, the vector filters that parallelize the VMF, BVDF, and DDF operation but using M_K, $M_{K'}$ and $M_{KK'}$ as distance criterion are named fuzzy metric vector median filter (FMVMF), fuzzy metric vector directional filter (FMVDF) and fuzzy metric directional-distance filter (FMDDF), respectively.

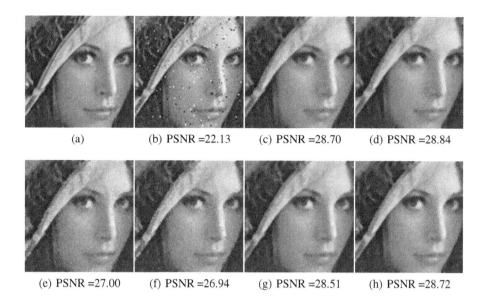

(a)	(b) PSNR =22.13	(c) PSNR =28.70	(d) PSNR =28.84
(e) PSNR =27.00	(f) PSNR =26.94	(g) PSNR =28.51	(h) PSNR =28.72

Fig. 3. Test Images: (a) Detail of the Lenna image, (b) Detail of the Lenna image contaminated with 5% Impulsive noise and $\sigma = 5$ Gaussian, (c) VMF output, (d) FMVMF output, (e) BVDF output, (f) FMVDF output, (g) DDF output, (h) FMDDF output

Notice that the main design difference between the classical VMF, BVDF and DDF and the proposed variants is that the FMDDF is sensibly faster than the classical DDF. This is due to the fact that the DDF needs to compute two accumulated distances, one in magnitude and one in direction, which are combined afterwards, whereas the FMDDF computes only one accumulation of the hybrid $M_{KK'}$ fuzzy metric. In terms of the number of computed distances we can easily see that the order of computational complexity of the VMF, FMVMF, BVDF and FMVDF is $O(n^2)$ whereas for the DDF it is $O(2n^2)$ because two accumulated distances have to be computed. However, in the case of the proposed FMDDF and due to the usage of $M_{KK'}$, this order is also $O(n^2)$.

3   Experimental Results

The classical gaussian model for the thermal noise and the impulsive noise model for the transmission noise, as defined in [17], have been used to assess the performance of the proposed filters by adding noise to the details of the images in figure 1. The *Peak Signal to Noise Ratio* (PSNR) objective quality measure has been used to assess the performance of the proposed filters.

The experimental results in figures 2-4 show that the proposed filters present a better performance than their classical versions when filtering impulsive noise and a similar performance when dealing with gaussian noise. In general, when considering mixed gaussian and impulsive noise, the results have shown that the proposed filters outperform their classical versions when the component of impulsive noise present is higher

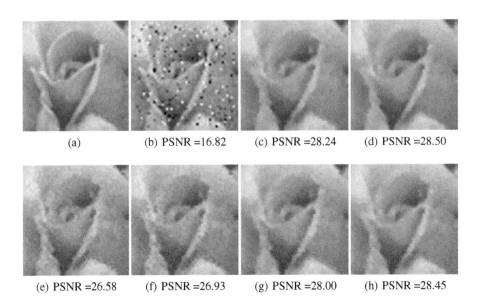

(a)	(b) PSNR =16.82	(c) PSNR =28.24	(d) PSNR =28.50
(e) PSNR =26.58	(f) PSNR =26.93	(g) PSNR =28.00	(h) PSNR =28.45

Fig. 4. Test Images: (a) Detail of the Brandy Rose image, (b) Detail of the Brandy Rose image contaminated with 15% Impulsive noise and $\sigma = 10$ Gaussian noise, (c) VMF output, (d) FMVMF output, (e) BVDF output, (f) FMVDF output, (g) DDF output, (h) FMDDF output

than the component of gaussian noise and it is similar elsewhere. Therefore, apart from the slight improvements achieved it should be stressed that the main improvement of the proposed filter is the above commented reduction of computational complexity. This approach allows to process images taking into account both magnitude and directional differences without increasing the computational load.

The improvement regarding the impulsive noise reduction is probably due to a better impulsive noise rejection that can be explained as follows. Notice that the value given by the product in Eq. (4)-(5) is always lower than or equal to the lowest term in the product. So, the lowest term is the most important one. Also, note that the presence of an impulse will be commonly associated to the lowest term in the product which corresponds to the highest difference between the components of the vectors. This implies that differences due to impulses weigh the most in the measure, which results in a better impulsive noise rejection.

4   Conclusions

In this paper, a recent fuzzy metric has been used to create variants of the classical VMF, BVDF and DDF filters. The fuzzy metric has been used to measure fuzzy magnitude distances, fuzzy directional distances and hybrid fuzzy magnitude-directional distances between image vectors. Experimental results show that the proposed filters outperform their classical versions when the impulsive noise component of the noisy images is higher than the gaussian component. Furthermore, the proposed variant of the DDF is much faster (approximately the double) than its original version thanks to the usage of the hybrid fuzzy magnitude-directional distance.

References

1. Astola, J., Haavisto, P., Neuvo, Y.: Vector Median Filters. In: Proc. IEEE. vol. 78(4), pp. 678–689 (1990)
2. Barni, M., Buti, F., Bartolini, F., Capellini, V.: A Quasi-Euclidean Norm to Speed Up Vector Median Filtering. IEEE Transactions on Image Processing 9(10), 1704–1709 (2004)
3. Barni, M.: A Fast Algorithm for 1-Norm Vector Median Filtering. IEEE Transactions on Image Processing 6(10), 1452–1455 (1997)
4. Camarena, J.G., Gregori, V., Morillas, S., Peris-Fajarnés, G.: New method for fast detection and removal of impulsive noise using fuzzy metrics. In: Campilho, A., Kamel, M. (eds.) ICIAR 2006. LNCS, vol. 4141, pp. 359–369. Springer, Heidelberg (2006)
5. Chatzis, V., Pitas, I.: Fuzzy scalar and vector median filters based on fuzzy distances. IEEE Transactions on Image Processing 8(5), 731–734 (1999)
6. David, H.A.: Order Statistics. John Wiley and Sons, New York (1981)
7. George, A., Veeramani, P.: On Some results in fuzzy metric spaces. Fuzzy Sets and Systems 64(3), 395–399 (1994)
8. Gregori, V., Romaguera, S.: Some properties of fuzzy metric spaces. Fuzzy Sets and Systems 115(3), 477–483 (2000)
9. Gregori, V., Romaguera, S.: Characterizing completable fuzzy metric spaces. Fuzzy Sets and Systems 144(3), 411–420 (2004)
10. Huber, P.S.: Robust Statistics. John Wiley and Sons, New York (1981)
11. Karakos, D.G., Trahanias, P.E.: Generalized multichannel image-filtering structure. IEEE Transactions on Image Processing 6(7), 1038–1045 (1997)
12. Lukac, R., Smolka, B., Martin, K., Plataniotis, K.N., Venetsanopoulos, A.N.: Vector Filtering for Color Imaging. IEEE Signal Processing Magazine, Special Issue on Color Image Processing 22(1), 74–86 (2005)
13. Morillas, S., Gregori, V., Peris-Fajarnés, G., Latorre, P.: A new vector median filter based on fuzzy metrics. In: Kamel, M., Campilho, A. (eds.) ICIAR 2005. LNCS, vol. 3656, pp. 81–90. Springer, Heidelberg (2005)
14. Morillas, S., Gregori, V., Peris-Fajarnés, G., Latorre, P.: A fast impulsive noise color image filter using fuzzy metrics. Real-Time Imaging 11(5-6), 417–428 (2005)
15. Morillas, S., Gregori, V., Sapena, A.: Fuzzy bilateral filtering for color images. In: Campilho, A., Kamel, M. (eds.) ICIAR 2006. LNCS, vol. 4141, pp. 138–145. Springer, Heidelberg (2006)
16. Shen, Y., Barner, K.E.: Fuzzy Vector Median Based Surface Smoothing. IEEE Transactions on Visualization and Computer Graphics 10(3), 252–265 (2004)
17. Plataniotis, K.N., Venetsanopoulos, A.N.: Color Image processing and applications. Springer, Berlin (2000)
18. Sapena, A.: A contribution to the study of fuzzy metric spaces. Appl. Gen. Topology 2(1), 63–76 (2001)
19. Trahanias, P.E., Karakos, D., Venetsanopoulos, A.N.: Directional processing of color images: theory and experimental results. IEEE Trans. Image Process 5(6), 868–880 (1996)

Color Texture Segmentation with Local Fuzzy Patterns and Spatially Constrained Fuzzy C-Means

Przemysław Górecki[1] and Laura Câponetti[2]

[1] Wydział Matematyki i Informatyki, Uniwersytet Warmińsko-Mazurski,
ul. Żołnierska 14, 10-561 Olsztyn, Poland
pgorecki@matman.uwm.edu.pl
[2] Dipartimento di Informatica, Università degli Studi di Bari,
Via E. Orabona 4, 70126 Bari, Italy
laura@di.uniba.it

Abstract. Texture and color are important cues in visual tasks such as image segmentation, classification and retrieval. In this work we propose an approach to image segmentation based on fuzzy feature distributions of color and texture information. Fuzzy C-Means clustering with spatial constraints is applied to the features extracted in the HSI color space. The effectiveness of the proposed approach is evaluated on a set of artificial and natural texture images.

Keyword: Color texture segmentation, Local Fuzzy Patterns, Fuzzy C-Means.

1 Introduction

Texture segmentation is a fundamental problem in many applications of image analysis based on local spatial variations of intensity or color. The goal is to partition an image into a set of regions which are uniform and homogeneous, with respect to some texture characteristics. Although the concept of texture is very intuitive, its definition is not definitively assessed, other than some kind of "fuzzy" determinations, like the one suggested by Sklansky [1]: "a region in a image has constant texture if a set of local statistics or other local properties are constant, slowly varying, or approximately periodic".

In this paper we propose an approach to texture segmentation based on fuzzy information extracted from color texture images. Color is an important visual cue and can be described in the three-dimensional HSI space (Hue, Saturation and Intensity). In this work the distributions of fuzzy color features extracted from the Hue and Saturation images are used to provide complementary information to the distributions of textural features extracted from the Intensity image. More specifically for a given color image we consider its representation in terms of Hue, Saturation and Intensity images: color information is coded using distributions of Hue and Saturation values and texture information is coded using Local Fuzzy Patterns and Fuzzy Contrast of the intensity values. Local fuzzy

F. Masulli, S. Mitra, and G. Pasi (Eds.): WILF 2007, LNAI 4578, pp. 362–369, 2007.

Pattern is a fuzzified version of the Local Binary Pattern operator and it has been introduced in [2] for gray level texture discrimination. Finally the segmentation is approached as a clustering problem and the Fuzzy C-Means algorithm is applied to the extracted information. The effectiveness of the proposed approach is evaluated on a set of artificial and natural texture images obtained from different texture images. The peculiarity of this work is in the application of Local Fuzzy Patterns to color images. At this aim the idea is to process separatively color information, captured by the hue and saturation components and luminance information captured by the intensity component. The paper is organized as follows. In the next section we present the feature extraction process. In section 3, the segmentation process, based on the clustering of extracted features, is presented. Section 4 presents results of the experimental session and the conclusions.

2   Texture Feature Extraction

Given a color image we characterize the color and texture information using the distributions of Hue and Saturation values and the distributions of Local Fuzzy Patterns and Fuzzy Contrast, evaluated for the intensity values. In particular, an original RGB image is at first transformed into HSI color space and divided into a grid of non-overlapping image blocks of size $W \times W$ pixels. Successively, color properties of each image block are extracted by computing fuzzy histograms of hue and saturation values. Fuzzy histograms [3] are based on the principle that any given value is uncertain, since it can be the erroneous version of another value. Thus, a given value will contribute not only to its specific bin, but also to the neighboring bins of the histogram. In practise, a fuzzy histogram is obtained by convolving the classical histogram with a smoothing kernel (i.e. triangular or Gaussian). Additionally, textural properties are extracted by computing histograms of Local Fuzzy Patterns and Fuzzy Contrast as described in the following.

Local Fuzzy Patterns

In order to capture textural properties of an image block, the histogram $f_{LFP}^{(i)}$ of the Local Fuzzy Patterns and the histogram $f_{FC}^{(i)}$ of Fuzzy Contrasts are calculated. In the following we describe a fuzzy extension of the local binary pattern operator originally introduced in [4].

Let us consider a pixel x_c and its M local neighbor pixels $\{x_i\}_{i=1}^{M}$. The difference d_i between the intensities of x_c and x_i, is characterized using two fuzzy sets $\{N, P\}$, representing negative and positive differences, respectively. The membership functions characterizing these fuzzy sets are piecewise linear as in figure 1, where the parameter e controls the amount of the fuzziness. Therefore, the neighbors of the pixel x_c can be expressed in terms of membership degrees as a set of pairs $\{(n_i, p_i)\}_{i=1}^{M}$. These membership degrees are required to characterize x_c in terms of Local Fuzzy Patterns, as explained in the following.

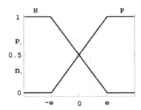

Fig. 1. Membership functions of the fuzzy sets $\{N, P\}$. The x-axis represents the amount of difference in intensity between pixels x_c and x_i.

Given M neighbors of x_c, there are 2^M unique Local Fuzzy Patterns to evaluate. Each of them is denoted as a sequence $(s_1, \ldots, s_M)$ of symbols $\{N, P\}$, indicating whether d_i is expected to be negative $(s_i = N)$, or positive $(s_i = P)$. For example, for x_c with two neighbours, four fuzzy patterns should be evaluated: $(NN), (NP), (PN), (PP)$.

If we consider he k-th fuzzy pattern $FP_k = (s_1, \ldots, s_M)$, the fulfillment degree of the pattern is calculated as:

$$F_k = \prod_{i \in I^k} p_i \prod_{j \in J^k} n_j, \quad k = 1, \ldots, 2^M. \tag{1}$$

where $I^k = \{i = 1, \ldots, M | s_i^k = P\}$ and $J^k = \{j = 1, \ldots, M | s_j^k = N\}$. Additionally, the fuzzy contrast measure FC of x_c is calculated as:

$$FC = \sum_{i=1}^M x_i p_i / \sum_{i=1}^M p_i - \sum_{i=1}^M x_i n_i / \sum_{i=1}^M n_i. \tag{2}$$

For each pixel in image block $b^{(i)}$, every computed fuzzy pattern F_k is accumulated in the k-th bin of the histogram $f_{LFP}^{(i)}$, and the value of fuzzy contrast is accumulated in the histogram $f_{FC}^{(i)}$.

Finally, an image block $b^{(i)}$ is characterized as one-dimensional feature distribution $f^{(i)}$, composed of the sequence of the calculated distributions:

$$f^{(i)} = (f_H^{(i)}, f_S^{(i)}, f_{LFP}^{(i)}, f_{FC}^{(i)}).$$

3   Spatially Constrained Clustering

Fuzzy C-Means is a well known clustering method, which has been proposed by Dunn in [5] and improved by Bezdek in [6], and it is frequently used in data clustering problems. The Fuzzy C-Means (FCM) is a partitional method, where each data sample is associated, with a certain membership degree, to each cluster centers. This method has been applied to a variety of image segmentation problems such as document image segmentation [7], medical imaging [8], or remote sensing [9].

Fuzzy C-Means is based on the minimization of the following objective function:

$$J_s = \sum_{j=1}^{m} \sum_{i=1}^{k} (u_{ij})^s \, d\,(x_i, c_j)^2, \quad 1 < s < \infty, \tag{3}$$

where $d(x, c)$ is the function expressing the distance between the observation x and the centroid c, s is the parameter determining the clustering fuzziness, m is the number of centroids, k is the number of observations, u_{ij} is the membership degree of the observation x_i belonging to the cluster c_j, calculated as following:

$$u_{ij} = \frac{1}{\sum_{l=1}^{m} \left(\dfrac{d(x_i, c_j)}{d(x_i, c_l)} \right)^{\frac{2}{s-1}}}. \tag{4}$$

The values of membership degrees are constrained to be positive and to satisfy $\sum_{j=1}^{m} u_{ij} = 1$. Given the fuzzy membthe ership matrix $U = [u_{ij}]$ of size $k \times m$, a new position of the j-th centroid is calculated as:

$$c_j = \frac{\sum_{i=1}^{k} (u_{ij})^s x_i}{\sum_{i=1}^{k} (u_{ij})^s}. \tag{5}$$

The FCM clustering is realized through an iterative approach. Given the initial parameters of the algorithm (number of centroids m and fuzziness parameter s), one iteration consists of computing the matrix U according to eq. (4), followed by updating the centroids positions, as in eq. (5). The algorithm terminates after a fixed number of iterations, or if the improvement expressed by J_s is substantially small.

Crisp data clustering can be easily obtained from the final membership matrix U by simply assigning each observation to the cluster with the highest membership degree. This may be formalized as following: a sample x_i is assigned to the cluster $c_{j^{(i)}}$, where $j^{(i)} = \arg\max_j(u_{ij})$.

The common strategy of employing FCM for image segmentation is to divide the image into regions (i.e. square blocks, pixels) and extract their feature vectors. Successively, Fuzzy C-Means algorithm is applied to the extracted features and a predefined number of clusters is obtained. This approach provides a segmented image, in which the regions are formed from the clusters obtained in the feature space.

It can be observed from eq. (3) that the Fuzzy C-Means does not incorporate any spatial dependencies between the observations, which may degrade the overall segmentation results, because the obtained regions are likely to be disjoint, irregular and noisy. However, in order to restrict the values of U to be spatially smooth,it is possible to penalize the objective function in eq. (3). This penalty should discourage spatially undesirable configurations of membership values, i.e. high membership values surrounded by low membership values of the same cluster, or by adjacent high membership values of different clusters. The following penalized objective function was proposed in [10]:

$$J'_s = \sum_{j=1}^{m}\sum_{i=1}^{k}(u_{ij})^s d(x_i, c_j)^2 + \beta \sum_{j=1}^{m}\sum_{i=1}^{k}(u_{ij})^s \sum_{l \in N_i}\sum_{o \in M_j}(u_{lo})^s, \qquad (6)$$

where N_i denotes the spatial neighbours of x_i, and $M_j = \{1, \ldots, m\}\backslash\{j\}$. The parameter β controls the spatial penalty of the objective function. In the case of β is equal to zero, no penalty is applied, while increasing β will increase also the spatial smoothness of the membership degrees will increase. The necessary condition for u_{ij}, that will minimize eq. (6), is as following:

$$u_{ij} = \frac{\left(d(x_i, c_j)^2 + \beta \sum_{l \in N_i}\sum_{o \in M_j} u_{lo}^s\right)^{-1/(s-1)}}{\sum_{q=1}^{m}\left(d(x_i, c_q)^2 + \beta \sum_{l \in N_i}\sum_{o \in M_q} u_{lo}^s\right)^{-1/(s-1)}} \qquad (7)$$

This is the only change needed in the algorithm to take into account the spatial constraints, because the penalty term in eq. (6) is not dependent on c_j. Therefore, the calculation of the centroids positions in eq. (5) remains unchanged.

Additionally, we have adopted the proposed clustering algorithm to our problem as following. Initially, each centroid is initialized to be equal to the feature vector of a random image block. Moreover, a non-parametric pseudo-metric, based on G-statistic [11] has been chosen as the distance function to compare the feature distributions:

$$d(x, c) = \sum_{i=1}^{n}(x_i \log x_i - x_i \log c_i), \qquad (8)$$

where x is the feature distribution of an image block and c is the feature distribution associated to a centroid.

4   Results and Conclusions

In order to assess the feasibility of the proposed approach, we are going to illustrate some experimental results. In particular, natural scene images were taken from Internet and the VisTex dataset [12], and the mosaic images were constructed by coloring and combining different Brodatz primitive textures [13]. The images were divided into rectangular blocks of size $W = 16$ pixels and from each image block a feature distribution was calculated. The fuzzy histograms were obtained by smoothing $f_H^{(i)}$ and $f_S^{(i)}$ images using a triangular convolution filter, with a window of size 10. Similarly, the value of the fuzzy parameter e of the Local Fuzzy Patterns was set equal to 10. Moreover, to describe patterns of each pixel, its neighborhood of $M = 8$ surrounding pixels was considered. As concerning the FCM clustering, the parameter $\beta = 0.1$ was selected empirically on the basis of the segmentation results and was constant for all the segmented images, while the parameter s, controlling the fuzziness of FCM was set equal to 2. In order to find the optimal number of clusters for a given image, the

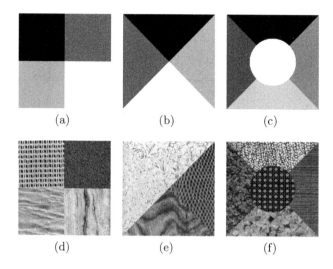

(a)   (b)   (c)

(d)   (e)   (f)

Fig. 2. Ground truth images used for generation of random mosaics: 'checker' (a), 'diagonal' (b),'circle' (c). Random texture mosaics (d-f) generated from the ground truth images.

clustering process was repeated several times with varying number of centroids. The values of the objective function were plotted against different number of centroids, and the optimal number of clusters was found by finding points of high curvature in the plot. Some of the segmentation results obtained in the experimental session are presented in figure 3.

In order to quantitatively evaluate the performance of the proposed method, a number of synthetic texture mosaic images was randomly generated on the basis of ground truth images. This is a common technique for evaluation of segmentation algorithms, because segmentation results can be easily compared with a known ground truth. In case of natural images, it is much more time consuming to produce the ground truth and typically it cannot be done unambiguously. Therefore, natural images were omitted in the quantitative evaluation.

The following procedure was employed in order to obtain a synthetic mosaic image. At first, a number of gray-scale images, were selected randomly from Brodatz album and colored at random by changing their hue and saturation values. Successively, the selected images were composed into a mosaic image of size 256×256 pixels, according to the provided ground truth image. For each type of the ground truth image, depicted in figure 2, a number of 20 mosaics were generated, therefore in total 60 different images were obtained. Next, the images were segmented and the results of segmentation were evaluated by measuring a percentage P_c of correctly segmented pixels:

$$P_c = \frac{\text{Number of correctly segmented pixels}}{\text{Number of pixels in the image}} * 100\%. \tag{9}$$

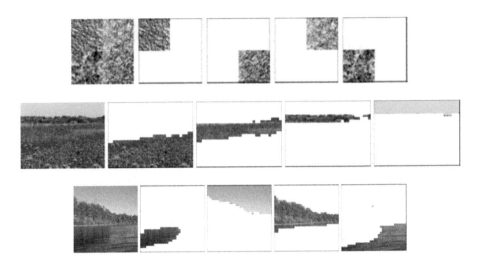

Fig. 3. Sample segmentation results obtained with our method. Input image (left) and obtained texture regions (other subimages).

Table 1. Reported segmentation accuracy [%]

| Block size | Ground truth image | | | Mean |
W	checker	diagonal	circle	accuracy
8	100,00	96,23	97,62	97,95
16	100,00	93,95	94,5	96,15
32	100,00	85,27	86,86	90,71

The experimental session was repeated for three different values of block size W. Table 1 presents the obtained segmentation accuracy, reported for different values of W and different types ground truth images used for generation of random mosaics. It can be noted that decreasing W results in better performance, because smaller blocks allow for finer localization of texture boundaries. However the segmentation is more computationally intensive due to larger number of extracted features from the blocks. The results obtained for mosaics generated from 'checker' ground truth are 100% accurate, because locations of rectangular blocks coincide with boundaries of texture.

In conclusion, the experimental session demonstrated the effectiveness of the proposed approach for the segmentation of color texture images. We have successfully segmented both artificial and natural texture images and the segmentation results are satisfactory. The segmentation accuracy is similar to the one reported in the literature [4], however our method lacks fine texture boundary localization, and implementation of this step should improve the overall segmentation accuracy.

Also, it should be noted that the method can be also applied to the segmentation of grey-scale images – in such case, the fuzzy histograms of hue and saturation would not add any additional information to the texture and could be omitted. As concerning future work, we plan to complete the segmentation method by improving the localization of regions boundaries at the pixel level. Additionally, the effectiveness of the method for the segmentation of noisy images should be investigated, as the fuzzy distributions that we employed should exhibit some natural robustness against noise.

References

1. Sklansky, J.: Image segmentation and feature extraction. IEEE Trans. Syst. Man Cybern. 8, 237–247 (1978)
2. Castiello, C., Caponetti, L., Fanelli, A., Gorecki, P.: Texture segmentation with local fuzzy patterns and neuro-fuzzy decision support. In: Gabrys, B., Howlett, R.J., Jain, L.C. (eds.) KES 2006. LNCS (LNAI), vol. 4252, pp. 34–347. Springer, Heidelberg (2006)
3. Jawahar, C., Ray, A.: Fuzzy statistics of digital images. IEEE Signal Processing Letters 3(8), 225–227 (1996)
4. Ojala, T., Pietikainen, M.: Unsupervised texture segmentation using feature distributions. Pattern Recognition 32, 477–486 (1999)
5. Dunn, J.: A fuzzy relative of the ISODATA process and its use in detecting compact well-separated clusters. Journal of Cybernetics 3, 32–57 (1974)
6. Bezdek, J.: Pattern Recognition with Fuzzy Objective Function Algorithms (Advanced Applications in Pattern Recognition). Springer, Heidelberg (1981)
7. Gorecki, P., Caponetti, L., Castiello, C.: Multiscale page segmentation using wavelet packet analysis. In: Abstracts of VII Congress Italian Society for Applied and Industrial Mathematics (SIMAI 2006), Baia Samuele (Ragusa), Italy 210 subject to revision in Word Scientific (2006)
8. Bezdek, J., Hall, L., Clarke, L.: Review of mr image segmentation techniques using pattern recognition. Med. Phys. 20, 1033–1048 (1993)
9. Rignot, E., Chellappa, R., Dubois, P.: Unsupervised segmentation of polarimetric sar data using the covariance matrix. IEEE Trans. Geosci. Remote Sensing 30(4), 697–705 (1992)
10. Pham, D.: Spatial models for fuzzy clustering. Computer Vision and Image Understanding 84, 285–297 (2001)
11. Sokal, R., Rohlf, F.: Introduction to Biostatistics. Freeman and Co, San Francisco (1987)
12. MIT: Vision texture (vistex) database. Maintained by the Vision and Modeling group at the MIT Media Lab (1995) http://whitechapel.media.mit.edu/vismod/
13. Brodatz, P.: Textures: A photographic album for artists and designers (1966)

A Flexible System for the Retrieval of Shapes in Binary Images

Gloria Bordogna, Luca Ghilardi, Simone Milesi, and Marco Pagani

Istituto per la Dinamica dei Processi Ambientali, CNR
c/o POINT, via Pasubio 5,
I-24044 Dalmine (BG) - Italy
gloria.bordogna@idpa.cnr.it

Abstract. In this paper a flexible retrieval system of shapes present in binary digital images is described: it allows customizing the retrieval function to evaluate weighted criteria constraining distinct shape characteristics of the objects in the images such as global features of contour (represented by the Fourier Coefficients), contours irregularities (represented by the Multifractal Spectrum), presence of concavities-convexities (represented by the Contour Scale Space distribution). Further also the matching function comparing the representations of the shapes can be tuned to define a more or less strict interpretation of similarity. The evaluation experiments showed that this system can be suited to different retrieval purposes, and that generally the combination of the distinct shape indexing criteria increases both Recall and Precision with respect to the application of any single indexing criterion alone.

1 Introduction

In the literature, shape retrieval systems are generally designed for specific applications, and thus they adopt an indexing method and a rigid retrieval scheme implementing a single matching function that demonstrated its effectiveness for the specific case study in the experimentation phase [1,2,3]. In this paper we present a model for the indexing and flexible retrieval of shapes present in binary images and a system implementing this model. The system is conceived for a variety of applications in which it is necessary to retrieve shapes in binary images stored in the database similar to those appearing in a visual query image.

Since we do not target a single application, we have defined the model and designed the system by considering as main requirements its flexibility, meant as the possibility to suit the retrieval results yielded by the system to fit distinct user needs. Further we did not consider a semantic indexing of the shapes but a syntactic indexing. To this end the shape retrieval system performs a Flexible Multi Criteria Decision making activity in which the alternatives are the stored shapes that can be only approximately represented by a set of descriptors; the

F. Masulli, S. Mitra, and G. Pasi (Eds.): WILF 2007, LNAI 4578, pp. 370–377, 2007.

query specifies a desired (ideal) shape together with a set of soft constraints for the retrieval; the retrieval function estimates a degree of satisfaction of the query constraints by each alternative based on a customizable partial matching function that evaluates a weighted combination of distinct satisfaction degrees of the constraints in the query.

Each soft constraint in the query specifies a twofold information: a desired qualitative characteristic of the shape that is represented by specific values for a set of descriptors, and a partial matching function for the computation of the degree of satisfaction of the soft constraint. The qualitative characteristics of the shapes we consider are:

- the number and extent of concavities and convexities on the boundary of shapes that can be qualitatively extracted from the Contour Scale Space distribution in the form of a vector of coefficients [4];
- the irregularity/linearity of the boundary that can be approximately related to the multifractal spectrum of the shape [5];
- the presence on the boundary of more or less the same global features that can be approximately described by an m-dimensional vector of Fourier Coefficients [6].

The partial matching functions evaluates the degrees of satisfaction of the soft constraints for each set of descriptors that synthesize a shape characteristics; they compute a similarity measure between the set of descriptors of each stored shape and the query shape. The flexible retrieval function is customizable: it allows a user to specify both the desired shape characteristics that must be taken into account together with their importance, and the partial matching functions to use so as to choose a more or less strict interpretation of similarity. One can either choose to specify a single shape characteristic, ex. *"retrieve shapes with similar number of concavities and convexities to the query shape"*: this corresponds to apply a matching function evaluating a "similarity measure" between the CSS descriptors. One can specify a weighted combination of several shape characteristics like in the query *"retrieve shapes with very similar global contour features with high importance and similar number of concavities and convexities with medium importance"*.

The proposed model is novel for several reasons: it applies multiple indexing techniques of the shapes; it is flexible and tunable so as to customize the retrieval behavior to different purposes and application needs, it applies fuzzy techniques to evaluate the similarity between sets of descriptors and soft fusion criteria; it is open in the sense that other sets of descriptors can be added to index other characteristics of the shapes such as the texture.

The paper is structured as follows: in the next section the main functional components of the flexible shape retrieval system are described; in section 3 the definition of the methods to compute the three sets of descriptors is presented. In section 4 the flexible retrieval function is formalized. Finally the conclusion summarizes the main achievements.

2   The Main Functional Components of the Shape Retrieval System

The shape retrieval system performs a Flexible Multi Criteria Decision making activity. Its main functional components are depicted in Figure 1.

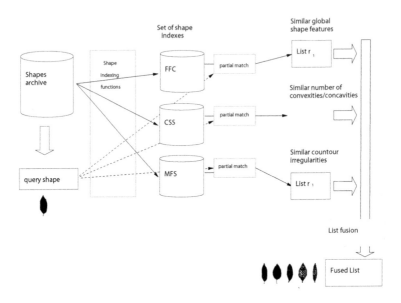

Fig. 1. Schema of the functional components of the Flexible shape retrieval system

The alternatives are the objects present in binary images that have to be identified, indexed and represented in a database. This phase has to take into account that the characteristics of the shapes of the objects can be multiple, and that can be synthesized only approximately by a set of descriptor. Since the identification of the objects present in a binary image, their representation by means of their contour coordinates, and the subsequent indexing of their shape characteristics can be costly, these operations are performed off-line, when generating the archive of the shapes. The indexes and contour data are stored into a PostgreSQL database extended with PostGIS for storing the spatial component. This way, by using any GIS software compliant with the Open Gis Consortium it is possible to easily rebuild from the stored data the objects image.

The query specifies soft constraints on the objects shapes characteristics. These constraints should be customizable by the user to a specific purpose. This requirement lead us to define a query as a binary image containing the desired (ideal) shape together with distinct shapes characteristics, their importance weights to express the desired influence on the retrieval results, and finally their partial matching functions, thus requiring a more or less strict interpretation of the soft constraints. One can then choose to perform a matching by considering just a single or multiple shape characteristics. The retrieval function is a flexible multi criteria decision function performing the evaluation of the query in two steps:

- firstly each set of descriptors associated with a desired shape characteristic are matched against those of the ideal shape in the query, independently one another. This phase produces several ranked lists in which each stored shape can appear in a different position within each list according to the similarity of its shape characteristic with respect to those of the query shape.
- Secondly, these ranked lists are fused into an overall ranked list by taking into account the positions of the shapes within each list and the importance weights of the lists, i.e., of the shape characteristics, specified by the user.

This method is independent from the kind and the number of shape characteristics used to represent the object. In the implemented system three kinds of shape characteristics have been considered to index the shapes: the presence of concavities and convexities on the contour, the irregularity/linearity of the contour and finally the overall shape features of the contour. These qualitative characteristics are represented by three vectors of positive real values computed at indexing time for the stored objects, and at retrieval time for the query object respectively. In the following section the indexing functions computing the shape descriptors are described.

3 Indexing Function of the Shape Characteristics

The number and extent of concavities and convexities on the boundary of the objects are represented by the Contour Scale Space distribution (CSS) [4]; from the CSS distribution (see Figure 2, left panel) a n-dimension vector of real values is computed in which the i-th element is the number of concavities/convexities with a curvature radius greater than σ_i. The CSS distribution is computed in a number of recursive steps by considering the vector representation of an objects contour through the coordinates of its pixels; an evolved contour is computed at each step by convolving the input contour with a Gaussian function with increasing standard deviation so as to generate a smoother contour at each step. From this CSS distributions the maxima above a noise threshold are selected to represent the concavities and convexities of the shape. This way we loose the relative position information on each concavity and convexity but achieve invariance with respect to the rotation of the object. Invariance with respect to scaling is achieved by normalizing the picks with respect to the number of contour pixels. The vector elements are in decreasing order of extent of the concavities/convexities. So the first m elements correspond with the first m greatest concavities/convexities.

The irregularity/linearity of the contour of an object is represented by the Multi-Fractal Spectrum (MFS) [5]. The MFS is computed based on the box-counting algorithm and consists in computing the fractal dimensions of the contour of an object by taking into account its variation in smooth parts and

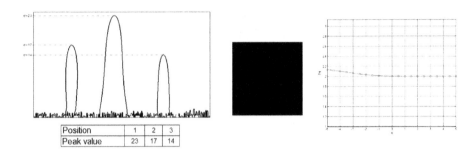

Position	1	2	3
Peak value	23	17	14

Fig. 2. (left panel) CSS distribution, the maximum corresponds to the concavities and convexities. (right panel) Multifractal Spectrum of a squared object.

irregular parts. In Figure 2 (right panel) the MFS of a square object is shown. For q=0 we have the fractal dimension. It can be seen that in this case the MSF is stationary at tends to the topological dimension of the square. The MFS is a texture descriptor of the contour of the object; we compute a 10 dimensional vector with q varying in [-5, 5].

The global shape features of a contour of an object are approximately described by the vector of Fourier Coefficients (FFC) [6]. To compute the FFC we represent the contour of an object by the discrete distance function of each contour point from the centroid of the object and apply to this function the Fast Fourier Transform. To achieve invariance with respect to rotation we consider only the module of the Fourier coefficients and to achieve invariance with respect to scaling we normalize the coefficient with respect to the continuous component. Since we are interested in achieving an approximate representation of the main shape features of the objects we only store in the database the first m coefficients, since the first ones are the most relevant in representing the shape.

4   Flexible Retrieval Function Definition

4.1   Partial Matching Functions of Sets of Descriptors

In order to provide flexibility we defined the partial matching function so as to compute a fuzzy similarity measure defined as [7]:

$$S_g = \frac{\sum_{i=1}^{N} S_i(Q_i, M_i)}{N} \text{ with } \begin{cases} 1 - \frac{d_i(Q,M)}{\max(Q_i,M_i)} & \text{if } Q_i \wedge M_i \neq 0 \\ 1 - \frac{d_i(Q,M)}{N} & \text{if } Q_i \vee M_i = 0 \\ 1 & \text{if } Q_i \wedge M_i = 0 \end{cases} \quad (1)$$

in which $Q = [Q_1, Q_2, \ldots, Q_m]$ is the query vector and $M = [M_1, M_2, \ldots, M_m]$ the object vector representing the same shape characteristic and $d_i(Q, M)$ is the difference between the i-th elements in the two vectors Q and M. N can be specified by the user at retrieval time and thus influences the interpretation of the partial matching allowing to consider all the vector elements (when $N = M$) or just the first N. The more N approaches M the more the interpretation of similarity is strict since we consider all the information in the database. By selecting small N values in the FFC and in CSS vectors we disregard the less important shape descriptors, those characterizing the shape with greatest accuracy. As far as the MFS vector is concerned, we consider the N closest values to the central element of MFS.

4.2 Fusion of Ranked Lists

The overall fusion function allows to combine the ranked lists produced by the partial matching functions by taking into account their distinct importance weights. It works on the ranks of the objects in each list ($r_{i,j} \in \mathbb{N}$ is the rank of the i-th retrieved object in the j-th list, with $j = 1, \ldots, L$, corresponding to the j-th shape characteristics). Given that w_j is the importance weight of the j characteristics the ranks fusion function is defined as:

$$S_g^i = \sum_{j=1}^{L} s_{g,j}^i = \sum_{j=1}^{L} w_j \frac{1}{\sqrt{r_{i,j}}} \qquad (2)$$

When several objects from position a to b in the same ranked list j correspond to the same partial similarity degree computed at the previous step by Formula (1) we associate a $s_{g,j}^i$ global similarity degree computed as:

$$s_{g,j}^i = \left(\frac{1}{b-a+1}\right) \sum_{k=a}^{b} w_j \frac{1}{\sqrt{k}} \qquad (3)$$

The overall similarity degree is used to rank the retrieved object shapes.

Fig. 3. Ranked leaves on the basis of FFC (above) and MFS (below): in dark grey the leaves with irregular contour and in light grey the leaves with smooth contour. On the left the query shape.

5   Experiment

We conducted the evaluations of the system [8] on two collections: a benchmark collection of 1100 shapes of marine creatures provided by the Center for Vision and Signal processing of Surrey University (UK), and a collection of leaves with distinct shapes and irregularity of the contour, some of them artificially generated so as to emphasize the irregularity of the contour to test the effect of the different sets of descriptors. Figure 3 reports the first eight ranked leaves (from left to right) by using only the FFC and the MFS respectively given the query at the left: it can be observed that with MFS we retrieve the leaves with decreasing irregularity of the contour, while with the FFC the ranking reflects a similarity of global shape features.

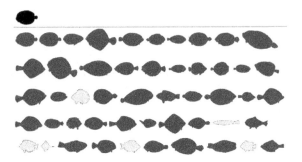

Fig. 4. Ranked shapes from top left to bottom right given the query at the top left (in light grey the shapes belonging to a wrong category)

We visually classified the marine creature into five classes according to the similarity of their shapes. We then submitted five queries by taking a fish from each category and performing the retrieval first on the basis of each single set of descriptors (FFC, CSS, MFS) and then by considering all the descriptors with the same weight, and with distinct weights emphasizing some evident characteristics of the ideal shapes (in Figure 4 we show the ranked list of shapes given the first top left shape as query and a retrieval function that takes into account all the indexing criteria with equal importance). It can be seen how only 6 out of 50 shapes belong to a different category than the query category, and the first wrong element is in 28th position. In Figure 5 we report the average R-P (Recall-Precision) graph for each applied retrieval function: it can be seen how the single indexing criteria produce worse results than by considering all the criteria with either same weight or best weights.

6   Conclusion

The system is conceived for variety of applications in which it is necessary to store in the database shapes present in binary images and to retrieve shapes similar to those appearing in a visual query image. The novelty of our approach is the use of multiple indexing criteria of the shapes characteristics and the possibility to flexibly customize the retrieval function to a specific purpose, emphasizing the role of specific indexes, and allowing the tuning of the interpretation of the matching.

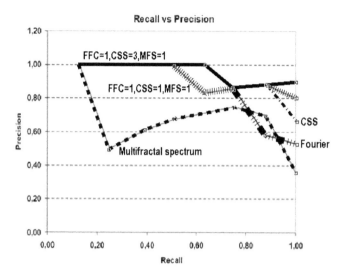

Fig. 5. Average Recall-Precision graphs by applying distinct retrieval functions

Acknowledgements

We want to thank the "Center for Vision, Speech, and Signal Processing" of the Department of Electronic and Electrical Engineering at the University of Surrey for providing the marine creatures collection.

References

1. Pratt, W.: Digital Image Processing. Wiley, Chichester (2001)
2. Vasconcelos, N., Kunt, M.: Content-based retrieval from image database: current solutions and future directions. In: Int. Conference on Image Processing. vol. 3, pp. 6–9 (2001)
3. Faloutsos, C., Barber, R., Fleekner, M., Hafne, J., Niblack, W., Petkovic, D., Equitz, W.: Efficient and effective querying by image content. Journal of Intelligent Information System 3(3–4), 1573–1675 (1994)
4. Mokhtarian, F., Macworth, A.: Theory of multi-scale curvature based shape representation for planar curves. IEEE Trans. on Pattern Analysis and Machine Intelligence 14(8), 789–805 (1992)
5. Chhabra, A.B., Jensen, R.V.: Direct determination of the f(α) singularity spectrum. Phys. Rev. Lett. 62, 1327–1330 (1989)
6. Zhang, D., Lu, G.: A comparative study on shape retrieval using Fourier descriptors with different shape signatures. In: Proc. Int. Conf. on Multimedia (2001)
7. Gadi, T., Benslimane, R., Daoudi, M., Amatusiak, S.: Fuzzy similarity measure for shape retrieval. In: Vision interface '99, Trois-Rivieres, Canada, pp. 386–389 (1999)
8. Ghilardi, L., Milesi, S.: A flexible retrieval system of shapes within digital binary images (in italian). Tesi di Laurea, Facoltà di Ingegneria, Università di Bergamo (2007)

Fuzzy C-Means Segmentation on Brain MR Slices Corrupted by RF-Inhomogeneity

Edoardo Ardizzone, Roberto Pirrone, and Orazio Gambino

Universita' degli Studi di Palermo
DINFO - Dipartimento di Ingegneria Informatica
viale delle Scienze - Edificio 6 - Terzo piano
90128 Palermo
ardizzon,pirrone@unipa.it, gambino@csai.unipa.it

Abstract. Brain MR Images corrupted by RF-Inhomogeneity exhibit brightness variations in such a way that a standard Fuzzy C-Means (*fcm*) segmentation algorithm fails. As a consequence, modified versions of the algorithm can be found in literature, which take into account the artifact. In this work we show that the application of a suitable pre-processing algorithm, already presented by the authors, followed by a standard *fcm* segmentation achieves good results also. The experimental results ones are compared with those obtained using SPM5, which can be considered the state of the art algorithm oriented to brain segmentation and bias removal.

1 Introduction

The RF-Inhomogeneity is an artifact which corrupts Magnetic Resonance Images in such a way that the brightness changes overall in the image. Such corrupted data aren't suited to a segmentation process without a pre-processing step. Some works [7][13][14] use a fuzzy based segmentation and modify the Bezek's objective function to take into account the artifact during the iteration, but they depend both on the right choice of some parameters and the starting values of the cluster centroids. Moreover, in [10] the use of Fuzzy K-means algorithm to obtain these values is suggested. In literature some works to suppress the RF-Inhomogeneity, also called bias artifact, are based on homomorphic filter[9][6][11]. The approach proposed in our paper moves from [1] where a homomorphic based method is presented. It makes use of Fuzzy C-means (*fcm*) algorithm to avoid the over-illumination artifact introduced by the filter along the boundaries, especially when it is applied on a T1-weighted image. Instead of a modified segmentation algorithm, a classic approach consisting in applying $E^2D - HUM$ as preprocessing as bias removal pre-processing followed by a standard Fuzzy C-means segmentation is presented and the results are compared with SPM5[17]. In particular, we use a bias removal approach called Exponential Entropy Driven Homomorphic Unsharp Masking ($E^2D - HUM$) which has been already presented by the authors in a previous work [1].The rest of the paper is arranged as follows. In section 2 some details are given about the $E^2D - HUM$

F. Masulli, S. Mitra, and G. Pasi (Eds.): WILF 2007, LNAI 4578, pp. 378–384, 2007.

pre-processing scheme. Section 3 deals with the use of fcm to suppress the over-illumination artifact deriving from the homomorphic filtering. Section 4 explains the segmentation scheme we used, and in section 5 the experimental results are reported. Finally, in section 6 there are some conclusions.

2 $E^2D - HUM$ Pre-processing

A medical image is often composed by a dark background and a light gray foreground. The presence of a strong edge between these two zones causes the arising of an over-illumination, called halo artifact, when a homomorphic filter is applied to the image. Guillemaud [8] proposed a homomorphic filtering scheme to compensate this over-illumination located on the boundaries using a binary image to identify the Region of Interest (ROI) which bounds the foreground. This approach can be followed because there isn't any useful information in the background: it contains only noise. In the left part of Fig.1 the filter scheme is shown.

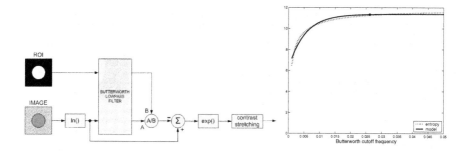

Fig. 1. Left:Guillemaud scheme. Right: Bias local entropy curve and its estimated model. The point of the curve indicates the end of the transient phase whose abscissa corresponds to the desired cutoff frequency.

There is no trace in literature about the choice of the cutoff frequency, but this parameter is very important because it controls the filter. If it is too low no effect is visible on the restored image, while for high values a strong contrast loss can be noticed. A previous work from the authors [1] the $E^2D - HUM$ algorithm has been presented. The artifact is mainly located in the lower harmonics so a part of them has to be subtracted from the image spectrum to perform the restoration. These harmonics form the Bias image, which is a slow varying one: it doesn't contain details and the image morphology isn't involved. This harmonics transferring can be regarded as an information migration so that the information content in the Bias image grows according to an increment of the cutoff frequency. The information contained in the Bias image can be measured using the Shannon's Entropy which is computed only on the foreground. Plotting the entropy amount vs. the Butterworth cutoff frequency diagram, a curve is obtained, which is an increasing monotonic function with an exponential profile.

This behavior has been approximated by the capacitor charge mathematical model and the cutoff frequency has been selected at the end of the transient phase, as depicted in the right part of Fig. 1. For more details we remaind to [1].

3   Preventing the Halo Artifact Using Fuzzy C-Means

In section 2 we introduced the Guillemaud filter [8] to avoid the halo artifact between foreground and background but it is also produced by dark tissue in the

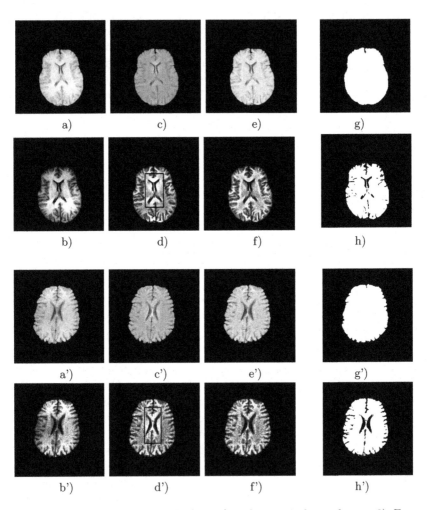

Fig. 2. Real T1-weighted image of the brain (up: dataset-1; down: dataset-2). For each group-Up:a)a')original images and b)b') their histogram equalization; c)c') restored images and d)d') their histogram equalization using Guillemaud ROI g)g'); e)e') the restored ones and f)f') their histogram equalization obtained using the masks h)h'). The dark boxes in figs d)d') indicate the halo.

foreground produces also the halo artifact on the surrounding tissues. Using the Guillemaud ROI shown in Fig.2g)g'), the halo arises as depicted in Fig.2d)d'). This is a particularly important problem in T1-weighted images, where the cerebrospinal fluid of the brain is located inside the ventricular system in the center position. As a consequence, a more careful image segmentation is required and we apply the same technique illustrated in [1]. The key idea consists in performing a *fcm* segmentation using 3 clusters (corresponding to dark, medium and light gray level) after the application of the filter with the Guillemaud ROI, so that strong shaded parts are restored. The darkest tissue, which corresponds to the cluster with the lowest centroid, is deleted from the Guillemaud ROI obtaining the masks shown in Figs.2h)h'). The filtering performed with this new ROI is shown in Figs.2f)f'), where the halos have disappeared. The experimentation has been performed on real images whose radiological parameters are shown in Table-2.

4   Image Segmentation

So far, *fcm* has been performed to avoid halos on the tissues produced by the filtering. Only gray levels in the ROI have been considered, because the background contains noise. Only the gray levels of the brain tissues are involved

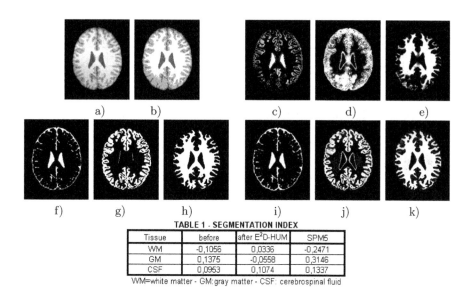

TABLE 1 - SEGMENTATION INDEX

Tissue	before	after E²D-HUM	SPM5
WM	-0,1056	0,0336	-0,2471
GM	0,1375	-0,0558	0,3146
CSF	0,0953	0,1074	0,1337

WM=white matter - GM:gray matter - CSF: cerebrospinal fluid

Fig. 3. Segmentation of slice 98 from T1-weighted Brainweb dataset with 70% of RF-Inhomogeneity. a) original corrupted image and b) its crisp representation after the application of Fuzzy C-Means. c)d)e) and i)j)k) are the spatial distributions of the clusters respectively for the Fuzzy C-Means after the application of $E^2D - HUM$ and SPM5 segmentation. f)g)h) are the labelled tissues which are also provided by Brainweb.

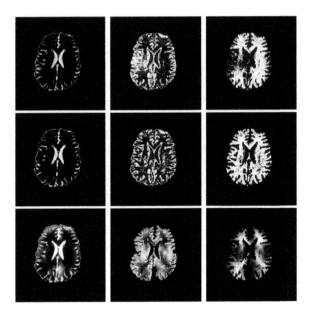

Fig. 4. Segmentation on real data. Fuzzy C-means segmentation on original image (first row) and after pre-processing (second row), the SPM5 results (third row). Here the spatial distribution of the each cluster is used instead of a crisp representation.

TABLE 2 - RADIOLOGICAL PARAMETERS OF REAL DATASETS

Dataset	Resolution	Device	M. field (Tesla)	Th. (mm.)	S. S.	Tr (msec)	Te (msec)	F. a. (degrees)
T1 brain dataset-1	256x256	PICKER MARCONI	1.50	5	SPIN ECHO	400	10	90
T1 brain dataset-2	256x256	HITACHI HIRIS2	0.30	4	SPIN ECHO	400	16	90

M.field=Megnetic field ; Th.=Thickness ; S.S.=Scanning Sequence ; Tr=Repetition Time ; Te=Echo time; F.a.=Flip angle

into the process and the algorithm speed is increased. The brain extraction can be performed using Brain Extraction Tool (BET) [5], already implemented in MRIcro [3]. A crucial task is the number of the clusters which. Usually the same number of clusters is chosen as the encephalic tissues: white matter, gray matter and cerebrospinal fluid. Using the proposed pre-processing, and a noise filter like the anisotropic diffusion filter [4] we obtain satisfactory results. Some results are shown in Fig. 3, which shows the slice n. 98 in a Brainweb simulated volume, and in Fig. 4 where a real slice is reported. The output of our implementation is the spatial distribution of the membership values of each cluster, whose values range in the interval $]0,1[$. No limitation have been encountered as regards real data. Good segmentation has been obtained also from strongly corrupted slices (see Fig.4).

5   Results Evaluation and Measures

We performed $E^2D - HUM$ followed by fcm both on simulated T1-weighted images with 70% of RF-Inhomogeneity corruption provided by Brainweb [15][16] and real data. Once a slice has been extracted from the volume of Brainweb, it has been stored as raw data and converted into Analyze format using MRIcro [3] to be processed by SPM5 [17]. The segmentation using SPM5 fails both on real (Figs. 4-3rd row) and simulated data (Figs.3c)3d)3e)), while using our method the results are quite good (see Fig.3i)3j)3k) and Fig.4-2nd row). Brainweb provides also labelled tissues shown in Fig.3f3)g)3h) so that a visual comparison with a corrected segmentation can be performed. In order to provide an objective measure of the image segmentation, we introduce a segmentation index S_i defined as follows:

$$S_i = \frac{A_e - A_r}{A_r}$$

where A_e is the area of the cluster spatial distribution; the same for A_r where it is computed on labelled tissues mentioned before. S_i measures the amount in pixels of the relative difference between the areas of the "true" segmented region (labelled in BrainWeb) and the one estimated by our algorithm. A positive value of S_i indicates an overestimation of the tissue, a negative value indicates an underestimation of the tissue and the zero value indicates a perfect identification of the cluster. Such a measure can be performed only on simulated data because we don't posses a handmade segmentation of the slices.The results in the table of figure 3 show that our approach is better in tissues estimation with respect to SPM5. The estimation error is bounded under the 10%. Similar numerical results have been obtained for all the slices in the BrainWeb simulated data set.

6   Conclusions

SPM5 doesn't use only raw image data in the file. It requires also spatial information: it is a strictly radiological tool, rather than an image processing method. SPM5 has an internal model so that a process consisting in a combination of registration, segmentation and RF-Inhomogeneity correction trying to find a best matching of the given volume with the internal atlas/model. This atlas is the result of a co-registration of statistical study performed on many subjects and provides a spatial estimation of the encephalic tissues. The presented segmentation scheme, which makes use of $E^2D - HUM$ and fcm doesn't require such sophisticated input information and provides results that are comparable with the literature state of the art.

Acknowledgements

Particular thanks to Ernesto Basilico, *eng.*; Mr. Filippo Longo; Maria Pia Pappalardo,*Md.* and all the staff of Palermo's Ospedale Civico.

References

1. Ardizzone, E., Pirrone, R., Gambino, O.: Exponential Entropy Driven HUM on Knee MR Images. In: Proc. of IEEE XXVII Engineering in Medicine and Biology Conference - 4/7 September 2005, Shanghat,China (2005)
2. Nelder, J.A., Mead, R.: A Simplex Method for Function Minimization. Comput. J. 7, 308–313 (1965)
3. http://www.sph.sc.edu/comd/rorden/mricro.html
4. Perona, P., Malik, J.: Scale-Space and Edge Detection Using Anisotropic Diffusion. IEEE Trans. on Pattern Analysis and Machine Intelligence 12(7), 629–639 (1990)
5. Smith, S.M.: Fast robust automated brain extraction. Human Brain Mapping 17(3), 143–155 (2002)
6. Johnston, B., Atkins, M.S., Mackiewich, B., Member, Anderson, M.: Segmentation of Multide Sclerosis Lesions in Intensity Corrected Multispectral MRI. IEEE Transaction On Medical Imaging 15(2) (April 1996)
7. Ahmed, M.N, Yamany, S.M., Mohamed, N.: A Modified Fuzzy C-Means Algorithm for Bias Field Estimation and Segmentation of MRI Data. IEEE Transactions on Medical Imaging 21, 193–199 (2002)
8. Guillemaud, R.: Uniformity Correction with Homomorphic filtering on Region of Interest. In: IEEE International Conference on Image Processing. vol. 2, pp. 872–875 (1998)
9. Axel, L., Costantini, J., Listerud, J.: Intensity Correction in Surface Coil MR Imaging. American Journal on Roentgenology 148, 418–420 (1987)
10. Jiang, L., Yang, W.: A Modified Fuzzy C-Means Algorithm for Segmentation of Magnetic Resonance Images. In: Sun, C., Talbot, H., Ourselin, S., Editions, A.T. (eds.) Proc. VIIth Digital Image Computing: Techniques and Applications, pp. 225–231 (2003)
11. Brinkmann, B.H., Manduca, A., Robb, R.A.: Optimized Homomorphic Unsharp Masking for MR Greyscale Inhomogeneity Correction. IEEE Transactions on Medical Imaging. 17, 161–171 (1998)
12. Likar, B., Viergever, M.A., Pernus, F.: Retrospective Correction of MR Intensity Inhomogeneity by Information Minimization. IEEE Transactions on Medical Imaging 20, 1398–1410 (2001)
13. Pham, D.L., Prince, J.L.: Adaptive Fuzzy Segmentation of Magnetic Resonance Images. IEEE Transactions on Medical Imaging 18(9), 737–752 (1999)
14. Pham, D.L., Prince, J.L.: An Adaptive Fuzzy C-Means Algorithm for Image Segmentation in the Presence of Intensity Inhomogeneities. Pattern Recognition Letters 20(1), 57–68 (1999)
15. Kwan, R.K.S., Evans, A.C., Pike, G.B.: MRI simulation-based evaluation of image-processing and classification methods. IEEE Transactions on Medical Imaging. 18(11), 1085–1097 (1999)
16. Kwan, R.K.S., Evans, A.C., Pike, G.B.: An Extensible MRI Simulator for Post-Processing Evaluation. In: Höhne, K.H., Kikinis, R. (eds.) VBC 1996. LNCS, vol. 1131, pp. 135–140. Springer, Heidelberg (1996)
17. http://www.fil.ion.ucl.ac.uk/spm/software/spm5/

Dilation and Erosion of Spatial Bipolar Fuzzy Sets

Isabelle Bloch

GET - Télécom Paris (ENST)
Dept. TSI - CNRS UMR 5141 LTCI
46 rue Barrault, 75013 Paris, France
Isabelle.Bloch@enst.fr

Abstract. Bipolarity has not been much exploited in the spatial domain yet, although it has many features to manage imprecise and incomplete information that could be interesting in this domain. This paper is a first step to address this issue, and we propose to define mathematical morphology operations on bipolar fuzzy sets (or equivalently interval valued fuzzy sets or intuitionistic fuzzy sets).

1 Introduction

In many domains, it is important to be able to deal with bipolar information [1]. Positive information represents what is granted to be possible (for instance because it has already been observed or experienced), while negative information represents what is impossible (or forbidden, or surely false). This view is supported by studies in cognitive psychology (e.g. [2]), which show that two independent types of information (positive and negative) are processed separately in the brain. The intersection of the positive information and the negative information has to be empty in order to achieve consistency of the representation, and their union does not necessarily covers the whole underlying space (i.e. there is no direct duality between both types of information).

This domain has recently motivated work in several directions. In particular, fuzzy and possibilistic formalisms for bipolar information have been proposed [1]. Interestingly enough, they are directly linked to intuitionistic fuzzy sets [3], interval-valued fuzzy sets [4] and vague sets, as shown e.g. in [5,6].

When dealing with spatial information, in image processing or for spatial reasoning applications, this bipolarity also occurs. For instance, when assessing the position of an object in space, we may have positive information expressed as a set of possible places, and negative information expressed as a set of impossible places (for instance because they are occupied by other objects). As another example, let us consider spatial relations. Human beings consider "left" and "right" as opposite relations. But this does not mean that one of them is the negation of the other one. The semantics of "opposite" captures a notion of symmetry rather than a strict complementation. In particular, there may be positions which are considered neither to the right nor to the left of some reference

F. Masulli, S. Mitra, and G. Pasi (Eds.): WILF 2007, LNAI 4578, pp. 385–393, 2007.

object, thus leaving room for some indetermination [7]. This corresponds to the idea that the union of positive and negative information does not cover all the space.

To our knowledge, bipolarity has not been much exploited in the spatial domain. The above considerations are the motivation for the present work, which aims at filling this gap by proposing formal models to manage spatial bipolar information. Additionally, imprecision has to be included, since it is an important feature of spatial information, related either to the objects themselves or to the spatial relations between them. More specifically, we consider bipolar fuzzy sets, and propose definitions of mathematical morphology operators (dilation and erosion) on these representations. To our knowledge, this is a completely new contribution in the domain of bipolar fuzzy sets.

In Section 2, we recall some definitions on bipolar fuzzy sets. Then we introduce definitions of algebraic dilations and erosions of bipolar fuzzy sets in Section 3. In the spatial domain, specific forms of these operators, involving a structuring element, are particularly interesting [8]. They are called morphological dilation and erosion. Morphological erosion is then defined in Section 4. Two forms of morphological dilations are proposed in Section 5, either based on duality or on adjunction. Properties are given in Section 6.

2   Preliminaries

Let $\mathcal{S}$ be the underlying space (the spatial domain for spatial information processing). A bipolar fuzzy set on $\mathcal{S}$ is defined by a pair of functions (μ, ν) such that $\forall x \in \mathcal{S}, \mu(x) + \nu(x) \leq 1$. Note that a bipolar fuzzy set is equivalent to an intuitionistic fuzzy set [3], as shown in [5]. It is also equivalent to an interval-valued fuzzy set [4], where the interval at each point x is $[\mu(x), 1 - \nu(x)]$ [5]. Although there has been a lot of discussion about terminology in this domain recently [5,9], we use the bipolarity terminology in this paper, for its appropriate semantics, as explained in our motivation. For each point x, $\mu(x)$ defines the degree to which x belongs to the bipolar fuzzy set (positive information) and $\nu(x)$ the non-membership degree (negative information). This formalism allows representing both bipolarity and fuzziness.

Let us consider the set of pairs of numbers (a, b) in $[0, 1]$ such that $a + b \leq 1$. This set is a complete lattice, for the partial order defined as [10]:

$$(a_1, b_1) \preceq (a_2, b_2) \text{ iff } a_1 \leq a_2 \text{ and } b_1 \geq b_2. \tag{1}$$

The greatest element is $(1, 0)$ and the smallest element is $(0, 1)$. The supremum and infimum are respectively defined as:

$$(a_1, b_1) \vee (a_2, b_2) = (\max(a_1, a_2), \min(b_1, b_2)), \tag{2}$$

$$(a_1, b_1) \wedge (a_2, b_2) = (\min(a_1, a_2), \max(b_1, b_2)). \tag{3}$$

The partial order $\preceq$ induces a partial order on the set of bipolar fuzzy sets:

$$(\mu_1, \nu_1) \preceq (\mu_2, \nu_2) \text{ iff } \forall x \in \mathcal{S}, \mu_1(x) \leq \mu_2(x) \text{ and } \nu_1(x) \geq \nu_2(x). \tag{4}$$

Note that this corresponds to the inclusion on intuitionistic fuzzy sets defined in [3]. Similarly the supremum and the infimum are equivalent to the intuitionistic union and intersection.

It follows that, if $\mathcal{B}$ denotes the set of bipolar fuzzy sets on $\mathcal{S}$, $(\mathcal{B}, \preceq)$ is a complete lattice.

3   Algebraic Dilation and Erosion of Bipolar Fuzzy Sets

Once we have a complete lattice, it is easy to define algebraic dilations and erosions on this lattice.

Definition 1. *A* dilation *is an operator δ from $\mathcal{B}$ into $\mathcal{B}$ that commutes with the supremum:*

$$\delta((\mu, \nu) \vee (\mu', \nu')) = \delta((\mu, \nu)) \vee \delta((\mu', \nu')). \tag{5}$$

An erosion *is an operator ε from $\mathcal{B}$ into $\mathcal{B}$ that commutes with the infimum:*

$$\varepsilon((\mu, \nu) \wedge (\mu', \nu')) = \varepsilon((\mu, \nu)) \wedge \varepsilon((\mu', \nu')). \tag{6}$$

The following result is useful for proving the next results.

Lemma 1

$$(\mu, \nu) \preceq (\mu', \nu') \Leftrightarrow \begin{cases} (\mu, \nu) \vee (\mu', \nu') = (\mu', \nu') \\ (\mu, \nu) \wedge (\mu', \nu') = (\mu, \nu) \end{cases} \tag{7}$$

The following results are directly derived from the properties of complete lattices [11].

Proposition 1. *The following results hold:*

- δ *and* ε *are increasing operators;*
- $\delta((0, 1)) = (0, 1);$
- $\varepsilon((1, 0)) = (1, 0);$
- *by denoting (μ_x, ν_x) the canonical bipolar fuzzy set associated with (μ, ν) and x such that $(\mu_x, \nu_x)(x) = (\mu(x), \nu(x))$ and $\forall y \in \mathcal{S} \setminus \{x\}, (\mu_x, \nu_x)(y) = (0, 1),$ we have $(\mu, \nu) = \bigvee_x (\mu_x, \nu_x)$ and $\delta((\mu, \nu)) = \bigvee_x \delta((\mu_x, \nu_x)).$*

The last result leads to morphological operators in case $\delta((\mu_x, \nu_x))$ has the same "shape" everywhere (and is then a bipolar fuzzy structuring element).

Definition 2. *A pair of operators (ε, δ) defines an* adjunction *on $(\mathcal{B}, \preceq)$ iff:*

$$\forall (\mu, \nu) \in \mathcal{B}, \forall (\mu', \nu') \in \mathcal{B}, \delta((\mu, \nu)) \preceq (\mu', \nu') \Leftrightarrow (\mu, \nu) \preceq \varepsilon((\mu', \nu')) \tag{8}$$

Again we can derive a series of results from the properties of complete lattices and adjunctions.

Proposition 2. *If a pair of operators (ε, δ) defines an adjunction, then the following results hold:*

- *δ is a dilation and ε is an erosion, in the sense of Definition 1;*
- *$\delta\varepsilon \preceq Id$, where Id denotes the identity mapping on $\mathcal{B}$;*
- *$Id \preceq \varepsilon\delta$;*
- *$\delta\varepsilon\delta\varepsilon = \delta\varepsilon$ and $\varepsilon\delta\varepsilon\delta = \varepsilon\delta$, i.e. the composition of a dilation and an erosion are idempotent operators.*

The following representation result also holds.

Proposition 3. *If ε is an increasing operator, it is an algebraic erosion if and only if there exists δ such that (ε, δ) is an adjunction. The operator δ is then an algebraic dilation and can be expressed as:*

$$\delta((\mu, \nu)) = \inf\{(\mu', \nu') \in \mathcal{B}, \ (\mu, \nu) \preceq \varepsilon((\mu', \nu'))\}. \tag{9}$$

A similar representation result holds for erosion.

4   Morphological Erosion of Bipolar Fuzzy Sets

We now assume that $\mathcal{S}$ is an affine space (or at least a space on which translations can be defined). The general principle underlying morphological erosions is to translate the structuring element at every position in space and check if this translated structuring element is included in the original set [8]. This principle has also been used in the main extensions of mathematical morphology to fuzzy sets [12,13,14,15,16]. Similarly, defining morphological erosions of bipolar fuzzy sets, using bipolar fuzzy structuring elements, requires to define a degree of inclusion between bipolar fuzzy sets. Such inclusion degrees have been proposed in the context of intuitionistic fuzzy sets in [17]. With our notations, a degree of inclusion of a bipolar fuzzy set (μ', ν') in another bipolar fuzzy set (μ, ν) is defined as:

$$\inf_{x \in \mathcal{S}} I((\mu'(x), \nu'(x)), (\mu(x), \nu(x))) \tag{10}$$

where I is an implication operator. Two types of implication are used in [17,18], one derived from an intuitionistic (or bipolar) t-conorm $\perp$, and one derived from a residuation principle from an intuitionistic t-norm $\top$:

$$I_N((a_1, b_1), (a_2, b_2)) = \perp((b_1, a_1), (a_2, b_2)), \tag{11}$$

$$I_R((a_1, b_1), (a_2, b_2)) = \sup\{(a_3, b_3), \top((a_1, b_1), (a_3, b_3)) \preceq (a_2, b_2)\} \tag{12}$$

where (a_i, b_i) are numbers in $[0, 1]$ such that $a_i + b_i \leq 1$ and (b_i, a_i) is the standard negation of (a_i, b_i).

Two types of t-norms and t-conorms are considered in [17] and will be considered here as well:

1. operators called t-representable t-norms and t-conorms, which can be expressed using usual t-norms t and t-conorms T:

$$\top((a_1, b_1), (a_2, b_2)) = (t(a_1, a_2), T(b_1, b_2)), \tag{13}$$

$$\bot((a_1, b_1), (a_2, b_2)) = (T(a_1, a_2), t(b_1, b_2)). \tag{14}$$

2. Lukasiewicz operators, which are not t-representable:

$$\top_W((a_1, b_1), (a_2, b_2)) = (\max(0, a_1 + a_2 - 1), \min(1, b_1 + 1 - a_2, b_2 + 1 - a_1)), \tag{15}$$

$$\bot_W((a_1, b_1), (a_2, b_2)) = (\min(1, a_1 + 1 - b_2, a_2 + 1 - b_1), \max(0, b_1 + b_2 - 1)). \tag{16}$$

The two types of implication coincide for the Lukasiewicz operators, as shown in [10].

Based on these concepts, we can now propose a definition for morphological erosion.

Definition 3. *Let (μ_B, ν_B) be a bipolar fuzzy structuring element (in $\mathcal{B}$). The erosion of any (μ, ν) in $\mathcal{B}$ by (μ_B, ν_B) is defined from an implication I as:*

$$\forall x \in \mathcal{S}, \varepsilon_{(\mu_B, \nu_B)}((\mu, \nu))(x) = \inf_{y \in \mathcal{S}} I((\mu_B(y - x), \nu_B(y - x)), (\mu(y), \nu(y))). \tag{17}$$

5 Morphological Dilation of Bipolar Fuzzy Sets

Dilation can be defined based on a duality principle or based on the adjunction property. Both approaches have been developed in the case of fuzzy sets, and the links between them and the conditions for their equivalence have been proved in [19]. Similarly we consider both approaches to define morphological dilation on $\mathcal{B}$.

Dilation by duality. The duality principle states that the dilation is equal to the complementation of the erosion, by the same structuring element, applied to the complementation of the original set. Applying this principle to the bipolar fuzzy sets using a complementation c (typically the standard negation $c((a, b)) = (b, a)$) leads to the following definition of morphological bipolar dilation.

Definition 4. *Let (μ_B, ν_B) be a bipolar fuzzy structuring element. The dilation of any (μ, ν) in $\mathcal{B}$ by (μ_B, ν_B) is defined from erosion by duality as:*

$$\delta_{(\mu_B, \nu_B)}((\mu, \nu)) = c[\varepsilon_{(\mu_B, \nu_B)}(c((\mu, \nu)))]. \tag{18}$$

Dilation by adjunction. Let us now consider the adjunction principle, as in the general algebraic case. An adjunction property can also be expressed between a bipolar t-norm and the corresponding residual implication as follows:

$$\top((a_1, b_1), (a_3, b_3)) \preceq (a_2, b_2) \Leftrightarrow (a_3, b_3) \preceq I((a_1, b_1), (a_2, b_2)) \tag{19}$$

with $I((a_1, b_1), (a_2, b_2)) = \sup\{(\alpha, \beta), \alpha + \beta \leq 1, \top((a_1, b_1), (\alpha, \beta)) \preceq (a_2, b_2)\}$.

Definition 5. *Using a residual implication for the erosion for a bipolar t-norm* $\top$, *the bipolar fuzzy dilation, adjoint of the erosion, is defined as:*

$$\delta_{(\mu_B,\nu_B)}((\mu,\nu))(x) = \inf\{(\mu',\nu')(x), (\mu,\nu)(x) \preceq \varepsilon_{(\mu_B,\nu_B)}((\mu',\nu'))(x)\}$$
$$= \sup_{y \in \mathcal{S}} \top((\mu_B(x-y), \nu_B(x-y)), (\mu(y), \nu(y))). \quad (20)$$

Links between both approaches. It is easy to show that the bipolar Lukasiewicz operators are adjoint, according to Equation 19. It has been shown in [17] that the adjoint operators are all derived from the Lukasiewicz operator, using a continuous bijective permutation on $[0, 1]$. Hence equivalence between both approaches can be achieved only for this class of operators.

6   Properties and Interpretation

Proposition 4. *All definitions are consistent: they actually provide bipolar fuzzy sets of* $\mathcal{B}$.

Let us first consider the implication defined from a t-representable bipolar t-conorm. Then the erosion writes:

$$\varepsilon_{(\mu_B,\nu_B)}((\mu,\nu))(x) = \inf_{y \in \mathcal{S}} \perp((\nu_B(y-x), \mu_B(y-x)), (\mu(y), \nu(y)))$$
$$= \inf_{y \in \mathcal{S}} (T((\nu_B(y-x), \mu(y)), t(\mu_B(y-x), \nu(y)))$$
$$= (\inf_{y \in \mathcal{S}} T((\nu_B(y-x), \mu(y)), \sup_{y \in \mathcal{S}} t(\mu_B(y-x), \nu(y))). \quad (21)$$

This resulting bipolar fuzzy set has a membership function which is exactly the fuzzy erosion of μ by the fuzzy structuring element $1 - \nu_B$, according to the definitions of [12]. The non-membership function is exactly the dilation of the fuzzy set ν by the fuzzy structuring element μ_B.

Let us now consider the derived dilation, based on the duality principle. Using the standard negation, it writes:

$$\delta_{(\mu_B,\nu_B)}((\mu,\nu))(x) = (\sup_{y \in \mathcal{S}} t(\mu_B(x-y), \mu(y)), \inf_{y \in \mathcal{S}} T((\nu_B(x-y), \nu(y))). \quad (22)$$

The first term (membership function) is exactly the fuzzy dilation of μ by μ_B, while the second one (non-membership function) is the fuzzy erosion of ν by $1 - \nu_B$, according to the definitions of [12].

This observation has a nice interpretation. Let (μ, ν) represent a spatial bipolar fuzzy set, where μ is a positive information for the location of an object for instance, and ν a negative information for this location. A bipolar structuring element can represent additional imprecision on the location, or additional possible locations. Dilating (μ, ν) by this bipolar structuring element amounts to dilate μ by μ_B, i.e. the positive region is extended by an amount represented by the positive information encoded in the structuring element. On the contrary,

the negative information is eroded by the complement of the negative information encoded in the structuring element. This corresponds well to what would be
intuitively expected in such situations. A similar interpretation can be provided
for the bipolar fuzzy erosion.

From these expressions it is easy to prove the following result.

Proposition 5. *In case the bipolar fuzzy sets are usual fuzzy sets (i.e. $\nu = 1 - \mu$
and $\nu_B = 1 - \mu_B$), the definitions lead to the usual definitions of fuzzy dilations
and erosions. Hence they are also compatible with classical morphology in case
μ and μ_B are crisp.*

Let us now consider the implication derived from the Lukasiewicz bipolar operators (Equations 15 and 16). The erosion and dilation write:

$$\forall x \in \mathcal{S}, \varepsilon_{(\mu_B,\nu_B)}((\mu,\nu))(x) =$$
$$\inf_{y \in \mathcal{S}}(\min(1, \mu(y) + 1 - \mu_B(y-x), \nu_B(y-x) + 1 - \nu(y)), \max(0, \nu(y) + \mu_B(y-x) - 1)) =$$
$$(\inf_{y \in \mathcal{S}} \min(1, \mu(y) + 1 - \mu_B(y-x), \nu_B(y-x) + 1 - \nu(y)), \sup_{y \in \mathcal{S}} \max(0, \nu(y) + \mu_B(y-x) - 1)),$$
$$(23)$$

$$\forall x \in \mathcal{S}, \delta_{(\mu_B,\nu_B)}((\mu,\nu))(x) =$$
$$(\sup_{y \in \mathcal{S}} \max(0, \mu(y) + \mu_B(x-y) - 1), \inf_{y \in \mathcal{S}} \min(1, \nu(y) + 1 - \mu_B(x-y), \nu_B(x-y) + 1 - \mu(y)).$$
$$(24)$$

Proposition 6. *If the bipolar fuzzy sets are usual fuzzy sets (i.e. $\nu = 1 - \mu$ and
$\nu_B = 1 - \mu_B$), the definitions based on the Lukasiewicz operators are equivalent to
the fuzzy erosion defined as in [12] by the infimum of a t-conorm for the classical
Lukasiewicz t-conorm, and to the fuzzy dilation defined by the supremum of a
t-norm for the classical Lukasiewicz t-norm, respectively.*

Proposition 7. *The proposed definitions of bipolar fuzzy dilations and erosions
commute respectively with the supremum and the infinum of the lattice $(\mathcal{B}, \preceq)$.*

Proposition 8. *The bipolar fuzzy dilation is extensive (i.e. $(\mu, \nu) \preceq
\delta_{(\mu_B,\nu_B)}((\mu,\nu)))$ and the bipolar fuzzy erosion is anti-extensive (i.e.
$\varepsilon_{(\mu_B,\nu_B)}((\mu,\nu)) \preceq (\mu,\nu))$ if and only if $(\mu_B,\nu_B)(0) = (1,0)$, where 0 is the origin of the space $\mathcal{S}$ (i.e. the origin completely belongs to the structuring element,
without any indetermination).*

Note that this condition is equivalent to the conditions on the structuring element found in classical and fuzzy morphology to have extensive dilations and
anti-extensive erosions [8,12].

Proposition 9. *If the dilation if defined from a t-representable t-norm, the following iterativity property holds:*

$$\delta_{(\mu_B,\nu_B)}(\delta_{(\mu'_B,\nu'_B)}((\mu,\nu))) = \delta_{(\delta_{\mu_B}(\mu'_B),1-\delta_{(1-\nu_B)}(1-\nu'_B))}((\mu,\nu)). \qquad (25)$$

7   Conclusion

New concepts on bipolar fuzzy sets are introduced in this paper, in particular algebraic and morphological dilations and erosions, for which good properties are proved and nice interpretations in terms of bipolarity in spatial reasoning can be derived. Further work aims at exploiting these new operations in concrete problems of spatial reasoning, in particular for handling the bipolarity nature of some spatial relations.

References

1. Dubois, D., Kaci, S., Prade, H.: Bipolarity in Reasoning and Decision, an Introduction. In: International Conference on Information Processing and Management of Uncertainty, IPMU'04, Perugia, Italy, pp. 959–966 (2004)
2. Cacioppo, J.T., Gardner, W.L., Berntson, G.G.: Beyond Bipolar Conceptualization and Measures: The Case of Attitudes and Evaluative Space. Personality and Social Psychology Review 1, 3–25 (1997)
3. Atanassov, K.T.: Intuitionistic Fuzzy Sets. Fuzzy Sets and Systems 20, 87–96 (1986)
4. Zadeh, L.A.: The Concept of a Linguistic Variable and its Application to Approximate Reasoning. Information Sciences 8, 199–249 (1975)
5. Dubois, D., Gottwald, S., Hajek, P., Kacprzyk, J., Prade, H.: Terminology Difficulties in Fuzzy Set Theory – The Case of "Intuitionistic Fuzzy Sets". Fuzzy Sets and Systems 156, 485–491 (2005)
6. Bustince, H., Burillo, P.: Vague Sets are Intuitionistic Fuzzy Sets. Fuzzy Sets and Systems 79, 403–405 (1996)
7. Bloch, I.: Fuzzy Relative Position between Objects in Image Processing: a Morphological Approach. IEEE Transactions on Pattern Analysis and Machine Intelligence 21, 657–664 (1999)
8. Serra, J.: Image Analysis and Mathematical Morphology. Academic Press, London (1982)
9. Atanassov, K.T., Dubois, D., Gottwald, S., Hajek, P., Kacprzyk, J., Prade's papers, H.: Terminology Difficulties in Fuzzy Set Theory – The Case of "Intuitionistic Fuzzy Sets". Fuzzy Sets and Systems 156, 496–499 (2005)
10. Cornelis, C., Kerre, E.: Inclusion Measures in Intuitionistic Fuzzy Sets. In: Nielsen, T.D., Zhang, N.L. (eds.) ECSQARU 2003. LNCS (LNAI), vol. 2711, pp. 345–356. Springer, Heidelberg (2003)
11. Heijmans, H.J.A.M., Ronse, C.: The Algebraic Basis of Mathematical Morphology – Part I: Dilations and Erosions. Computer Vision, Graphics and Image Processing 50, 245–295 (1990)
12. Bloch, I., Maître, H.: Fuzzy Mathematical Morphologies: A Comparative Study. Pattern Recognition 28, 1341–1387 (1995)
13. Sinha, D., Dougherty, E.R.: Fuzzification of Set Inclusion: Theory and Applications. Fuzzy Sets and Systems 55, 15–42 (1993)
14. de Baets, B.: Fuzzy Morphology: a Logical Approach. In: Ayyub, B., Gupta, M. (eds.) Uncertainty in Engineering and Sciences: Fuzzy Logic, Statistics and Neural Network Approach, pp. 53–67. Kluwer Academic, Boston, MA (1997)

15. Nachtegael, M., Kerre, E.E.: Classical and Fuzzy Approaches towards Mathematical Morphology. In: Kerre, E.E., Nachtegael, M. (eds.) Fuzzy Techniques in Image Processing. Studies in Fuzziness and Soft Computing, pp. 3–57. Physica-Verlag, Springer, Heidelberg (2000)
16. Deng, T.Q., Heijmans, H.: Grey-Scale Morphology Based on Fuzzy Logic. Journal of Mathematical Imaging and Vision 16, 155–171 (2002)
17. Deschrijver, G., Cornelis, C., Kerre, E.: On the Representation of Intuitionistic Fuzzy t-Norms and t-Conorms. IEEE Transactions on Fuzzy Systems 12, 45–61 (2004)
18. Cornelis, C., Deschrijver, G., Kerre, E.: Implication in Intuitionistic Fuzzy and Interval-Valued Fuzzy Set Theory: Construction, Classification, Application. International Journal of Approximate Reasoning 35, 55–95 (2004)
19. Bloch, I.: Duality vs Adjunction and General Form for Fuzzy Mathematical Morphology. In: Bloch, I., Petrosino, A., Tettamanzi, A.G.B. (eds.) WILF 2005. LNCS (LNAI), vol. 3849, pp. 354–361. Springer, Heidelberg (2006)

About the Embedding of Color Uncertainty in CBIR Systems

Fabio Di Donna, Lucia Maddalena[1], and Alfredo Petrosino[2]

[1] National Research Council, ICAR
Via P. Castellino 111, 80131 Naples, Italy
lucia.maddalena@na.icar.cnr.it
[2] University of Naples Parthenope, Department of Applied Science
Via A. De Gasperi 5, 80133 Naples, Italy
alfredo.petrosino@uniparthenope.it

Abstract. This paper focuses on the embedding of the uncertainty about color images, naturally arising from the quantization and the human perception of colors, into histogram-type descriptors, adopted as indexing mechanism. In particular, our work has led to an extension of the GIFT platform for Content Based Image Retrieval based on fuzzy color indexing in the HSV color space. To quantify the performances of this basic system, we have investigated different indexing strategies, based on classical logics and fuzzy logics. Performance improvements are shown, in terms of effectiveness, perfect/good searches, number and position of relevant images returned, especially in the case of large databases containing images with noisy interferences.

Keywords: Content Based Image Retrieval, Image Indexing, HSV Color Space, Fuzzy Color Histogram.

1   Introduction

Content Based Image Retrieval (CBIR) has received increasing attention as a result of the availability of large scale image repositories in several domains, such as video surveillance, medical image management, multimedia libraries, art collections, geographical information systems, law enforcement agencies, and journalism. CBIR has been proposed to overcome the difficulties encountered in textual annotation for large image databases [5,30]. Like a text-based search engine, a CBIR system aims to retrieve information that is relevant (or similar) to the users query, by addressing the problem of assisting a user to retrieve images from un-annotated databases, based on features that can be automatically derived from the images. Today, there exist several CBIR systems based on different methods, such as QBIC [11], Terraserver [36], VIR [37] or Excalibur [9], or a set of prototypes such as the Chabot and Galaxy's projects from the UC Berkeley [15,26], MIT's Photobook [27], CANDID [21], SCORE [3], VisualSEEK [32], or VORTEX [31].

Most of the research effort for CBIR systems has been focused on the search of powerful representation techniques for discriminating elements among the

F. Masulli, S. Mitra, and G. Pasi (Eds.): WILF 2007, LNAI 4578, pp. 394–403, 2007.

global database. Although the nature of data is a crucial factor to be taken into consideration, most often the final representation is a feature vector extracted from the raw data, which reflects somehow its content. Most systems use color features in the form of color histograms to compare images [28, 34, 35, 39]. The ability to retrieve images when color features are similar across the database is achieved by using texture features [1, 16, 17, 24]. Other important attributes employed in comparing similarity of image regions are shape [6, 7, 10, 18, 19], spatial relationships [8, 20], or a combination of them [38].

The approach more frequently adopted for CBIR systems is based on the conventional color histogram (CCH), which contains occurrences of each color obtained counting all image pixels having that color. Each pixel is associated to a specific histogram bin only on the basis of its own color, and color similarity across different bins or color dissimilarity in the same bin are not taken into account. The consequence is that: a) CCH is sensitive to noisy interferences, such as illumination changes and quantization errors; b) large dimension of CCH involves large computation on indexing. These problems could be addressed by considering color similarity of each pixel's color associated to all the histogram bins. If the color similarity is modeled through a fuzzy-set membership function, the representation leads to a fuzzy color histogram (FCH), like the one proposed in [13], although the real capabilities of such approach in the context of real CBIR systems are not completely clear, mainly when applied to large image databases. The usefulness of benchmarking is undeniable in the development of different algorithms, and recent attempts to benchmark CBIR systems in this respect have been made.

The paper is positioned in this context. We report the study made about the inclusion of uncertainty in color based indexing to augment the retrieval capabilities of the GIFT platform [12], an open source CBIR system. To quantify the benchmarking performances, we have investigated different indexing strategies, based on classical logics and fuzzy logics, on two different image databases. Performance improvements are shown, in terms of effectiveness, perfect/good searches, number and position of relevant images returned, mainly in the case of large databases containing images with noisy interferences.

The paper is organized as follows. The next Section reports the targeted CBIR and the operations involved within. Section 3 discusses the color histogram and fuzzy color histogram to make histogram based indexing mechanisms. In the last Section we present the experimental results and comparisons on two large image databases.

2   CBIR Reference Scheme

We adopt the method used in *GIFT* [12] for extracting local and global features and for retrieval as a *protocol*. GIFT (GNU Image Finding Tool) is the outcome of the *Viper* project [25]. This open source software tool uses many well-known techniques for text retrieval and a large number of color and texture features, together with their frequency statistics. The feature sets used are:

1. global color features in the form of a color histogram using HSV (18 hues, 3 saturations, 3 values, plus 4 grey levels);
2. local color features at different scales obtained by partitioning the images (scaled to 256×256 pixels) successively into four equally sized regions (four times) and taking the mode color of each region as a descriptor;
3. local texture features by partitioning the images and applying Gabor filters in 3 scales and 4 directions. Gabor responses are quantized into 10 strengths;
4. global texture features represented as a simple histogram of responses of the local Gabor filters in various directions and scales.

For the four feature groups two different weightings are used, depending on the *term frequency* tf_{ij} (frequency of occurrence of feature j in image i) and the *collection frequency* cf_j (frequency of occurrence of feature j in the entire database). Considering a query q containing N images with *relevances* $R_i \in [-1, 1], i = 1, \ldots, N$, the frequency of occurrence of feature j in the pseudo-image corresponding to q is

$$\mathrm{tf}_{qj} = \frac{1}{N} \sum_{i=1}^{N} (\mathrm{tf}_{ij} \cdot R_i).$$

The two global histogram features for each image k are weighted according to a histogram intersection [35] as:

$$\mathrm{FeatureWeight}_{kj} = \mathrm{sign}(\mathrm{tf}_{qj}) \cdot \min(|\mathrm{tf}_{qj}|, \mathrm{tf}_{kj}),$$

while the two block feature groups, that represent around 80% of the features, are weighted according to the inverse document frequency weighting:

$$\mathrm{FeatureWeight}_{kj} = \mathrm{tf}_{qj} \cdot \log^2\left(\frac{1}{cf_j}\right).$$

Then, a *score* is assigned to each possible result image k with features j, computed as:

$$\mathrm{Score}_{kq} = \sum_j (\mathrm{FeatureWeight}_{kj}).$$

Scores are calculated for all four feature groups separately and then added in a normalized way.

3   Embedding of Uncertainty About Color in CBIR

Uncertainty about color similarity has been modeled through a fuzzy-set membership function, so leading to a fuzzy representation of histogram and the indexing mechanism in the above described CBIR. Specifically, given a color space containing color bins, a fuzzy color histogram (FCH) of an image I containing N pixels can be expressed as $F(I) = [f_1, f_2, \ldots, f_n]$, with

$$f_i = \sum_{j=1}^{N} \mu_{ij} P_j = \frac{1}{N} \sum_{j=1}^{N} \mu_{ij},$$

where P_j is the probability of a pixel selected from image I being the jth pixel (which is $1/N$), and μ_{ij} is the membership value of the jth pixel in the ith color bin. In contrast with CCH, FCH considers not only the similarity of different colors from different bins but also the dissimilarity of colors assigned to the same bin. Therefore, FCH effectively alleviates the sensitivity to the noisy interference.

In order to quantify the perceptual color similarity, we consider Euclidean distance between colors represented in the HSV color space, which is perceptually uniform and therefore allows to obtain an accurate quantification of perceptual color similarity.

To compute the FCH of a color image, we adopt the method proposed in [13]. It consists in performing first a fine uniform quantization in RGB color space by mapping all pixel colors to n' histogram bins, then transforming the colors from RGB to HSV color space. Finally, obtained colors in HSV color space are classified into n clusters (with $n \ll n'$) using fuzzy C-means (FCM) clustering algorithm [4], with each cluster representing an FCH bin. Through these steps, a pixels membership value to an FCH bin can be represented by the corresponding fine color bins membership value to the coarse color bin. Membership values need to be computed only once, and they are represented as a membership matrix $M = [m_{ij}]_{n \times n'}$. Each element m_{ij} in M is the membership value of the jth fine color bin distributing to the ith coarse color bin. Thus, the FCH of an image can be directly computed from its CCH without computing membership values for each pixel. That is, given a CCH $H_{n' \times 1}$ with n' bins, the corresponding FCH $F_{n \times 1}$ with n bins can be computed as $F_{n \times 1} = M_{n \times n'} H_{n' \times 1}$, where membership matrix M is pre-computed only once and can be used to generate FCH for each database image.

In order to insert FCH into GIFT, we needed to set quantization parameters n' and n. As already mentioned in §2, the basic HSV color space quantization adopted in GIFT consists in 166 color bins. Experimental results showed that such quantization is too coarse for FCH; therefore we quantized the color space into $n' = 4100$ color bins (16 for each HSV component, plus 4 gray levels). Moreover, in order to choose the value of the number n of clusters, we conducted several tests on the considered databases, to obtain the optimal performance of the CBIR system (see §4).

4   Experimental Results

4.1   Performance Measures

The usual *recall* and *precision* measures are quite inadequate in the context of CBIR, since they do not take into account all information returned by a database query, such as the position of returned images and their similarity degree with respect to the query image.

Among several performance measures, we choose the *Effectiveness* measure [14] normalized in $[0, 1]$, defined as:

$$EFF = \frac{eff - \frac{R-1}{2E_r + R - 1}}{1 - \frac{R-1}{2E_r + R - 1}} \qquad eff = SumOptR/SumR_{All}$$

where

- R is the number of relevant images in the database,
- E_r is the number of images returned by the query,
- $SumOptR$ is the optimal sum of positions of relevant images,
- $SumR_{All} = (SumR + E_r + (E_r + 1) + \ldots + (E_r + M_r - 1))/R$,
- $SumR$ is the sum of positions of relevant returned images,
- R_r is the number of relevant images returned by the query,
- $M_r = R - R_r$ is the number of relevant images not returned by the query.

Such measure allows better than others to evaluate CBIR performance taking into account peculiarities of such systems, such as the position of images returned by a query. Moreover, as a measure of performance we considered also the number of:

- *Perfect searches*: searches which return all relevant images in first positions;
- *Good searches*: searches which return all relevant images in whatever position.

Even though a perfect search is the best attainable goal for a CBIR system, a good search is still an ambitious objective, since it means that all relevant images have been returned by the system.

4.2   Performance Evaluation

Performance of the various approaches has been tested on the public domain *Stanford10K* image database [33], consisting of about 10000 images, and on a database consisting of about 180 images from one of COREL's CD-ROMs [2], in the following referred to as *Alberta* database. Both the databases have a predetermined set of images similar to some fixed images, so that it is possible to compare results and evaluate performance.

First experiments have been devoted to the choice of the number n of clusters (see §3) in order to optimize performance. In Fig. 1 we report Effectiveness values obtained with FCH on the considered databases, varying n. In the case of Stanford10K database (Fig. 1-(a)), the maximum Effectiveness value EFF=0.31340 has been obtained for n=60, and it is better than the Effectiveness value EFF=0.30419 obtained using CCH. In the case of Alberta database (Fig. 1-(b)), the maximum Effectiveness value EFF=0.60431 has been obtained for n=50. However, in this case it is comparable (only slightly worse) to the Effectiveness value EFF=0.60518 obtained using CCH; this is mainly due to the fact that Alberta database has a small number of images, whose content is much simpler than that of the Stanford10K database, with no lighting intensity variations.

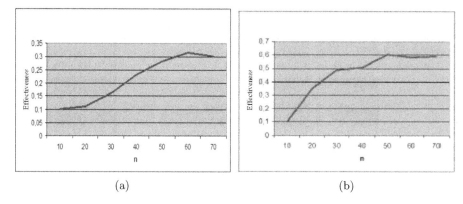

Fig. 1. Effectiveness values obtained with FCH varying the number n of clusters on: (a) Stanford10K database; (b) Alberta database

Moreover, using FCH strategy we achieved the same number of perfect and good searches obtained with CCH strategy (with optimal values for n) for both databases. Specifically, among the 32 queries predefined in Stanford10K database we obtained three perfect searches and five good searches, while among the 15 queries predefined in Alberta database we obtained one perfect search and five good searches.

The number of relevant images returned using CCH and FCH strategies was the same for almost all queries. In the case of Stanford10K database, query number 29 using FCH returned one more image than using CCH. Query image number 29 and relevant images returned with both the strategies are reported in Fig. 2. Here we can observe that the relevant image returned in position 17 by FCH was not at all returned by CCH. The content and the dominant color of such image is the same of all other relevant images; the only change, apart from shot position, is the lighting intensity. This observation confirms the superiority of FCH to CCH for image retrieval in terms of sensitivity to lighting intensity variations. In the case of Alberta database, query number 11 using FCH returned one more image than using CCH; analogous conclusions can be drawn analyzing results of such query (not reported here for space constraints).

Concerning exclusively the position of returned relevant images, we found that among the 32 queries for the Stanford10K database there were:

- 20 cases where positions are the same using CCH and FCH;
- 5 cases where positions returned with FCH are much better (more than 5 positions higher) than those returned with CCH;
- 4 cases where positions returned with FCH are better (more than 2 positions higher) than those returned with CCH;
- 3 cases where positions returned with FCH are worse (more than 2 positions lower) than those returned with CCH;

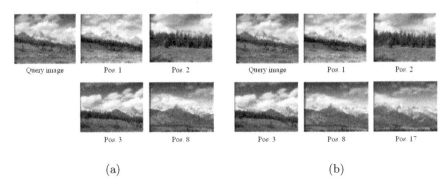

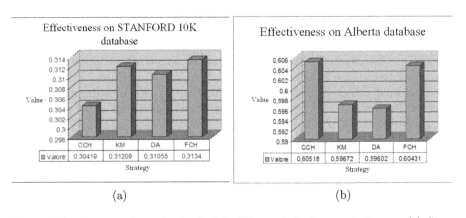

Fig. 2. Query image number 29 for Stanford10K database and relevant images returned using: (a) CCH; (b) FCH

In particular, considering Query number 16 where both CCH and FCH strategies return 5 relevant images, FCH returned a perfect search, while one of the relevant images returned by CCH is in position 9.

As a final experiment, we compared best Effectiveness values obtained with FCH with those obtained using not only CCH, but also k-Means (KM) [23] and Deterministic Annealing (DA) [29]. In Fig. 3 we report Effectiveness values obtained with all the considered strategies on both the considered image databases. In the case of Stanford10K database (3-(a)) we can observe that FCH, KM and DA attain much higher Effectiveness than CCH, with FCH reaching the best Effectiveness value. In the case of Alberta database (3-(b)) we can observe that only FCH and CCH attain high Effectiveness values.

Fig. 3. Effectiveness values obtained with different indexing strategies on: (a) Stanford10K database; (b) Alberta database

5   Conclusions and Ongoing Work

The paper concerned the inclusion of uncertainty about color in the HSV color space in the open source GIFT platform for CBIR and the benchmarking of different indexing strategies, based on classical logics and fuzzy logics, over two image databases, Stanford10K and Alberta. Specifically, the benchmarking has been made in terms of effectiveness, perfect/good searches, number and position of relevant images returned, also in presence of noisy interferences. The retrieval results are very encouraging in most cases and this proves that the use of uncertainty in CBIR is natural and desirable as long as human perception remains the key factor in judging and using the results.

References

1. Aksoy, S., Haralick, R.M.: Content-based image database retrieval using variances of gray level spatial dependencies. In: Ip, H.H.-S., Smeulders, A.W.M. (eds.) MINAR 1998. LNCS, vol. 1464, Springer, Heidelberg (1998)
2. Alberta database, http://db.cs.ualberta.ca/mn/CBIRone/
3. Aslandogan, Y.A., Thier, C., Yu, C., Liu, C., Nair, K.: Design, implementation and evaluation of SCORE (a System for COntent based REtrieval of pictures). In: Proc. of the 11th Int. Conference on Data Engineering, ICDE'95, pp. 280–287 (1995)
4. Bezdek, J.C.: Pattern Recognition with Fuzzy Objective Function Algorithms. Plenum, New York (1981)
5. Del Bimbo, A.: Visual Information Retrieval, Morgan Kaufmann Publishers, San Francisco (1999)
6. Del Bimbo, A., Pala, P.: Visual Image Retrieval by Elastic Matching of User Sketches, IEEE Trans. Pattern Analysis and Machine Intelligence 19(2), 121–132 (1997)
7. Ciocca, G., Schettini, R.: Content-based similarity retrieval of trademarks using relevance feedback. Pattern Recognition 34, 1639–1655 (2001)
8. Deng, Y., Manjunath, B.S.: An efficient low-dimensional color indexing scheme for region-based image retrieval. In: Proc. on Intl. Conf. Acoustics, Speech, and Signal Proces. (ICASSP). 6, pp. 3017–3020. IEEE Computer Society Press, Los Alamitos (1999)
9. Excalibur Tech. Corp., Excalibur, Web (2001)
10. Fleck, M.M., Forsyth, D.A., Pregler, C.: Finding naked people. In: Proc. of the Europ. Conf. on CV, pp. 593–602. Springer, Heidelberg (1996)
11. Flickner, M., et al.: Query by Image and Video Content: the QBIC system. IEEE Computer 9(10), 23–32 (1995)
12. Gnu Fundation, The GNU Image-Finding Tool, http://www.gnu.org/software/gift
13. Han, J., Ma, K.-K.: Fuzzy Color Histogram and Its Use in Color Image Retrieval. IEEE Trans. on Image Processing 11(8), 944–952 (2002)
14. Heczko, M., Keim, D., Weber, R.: Analysis of the effectiveness-efficiency dependance for image retrieval, DELOS Workshop, Zurich (2000)
15. University of California, UC Berkeley Digital Library Project, Web (2001)
16. Lin, H.-C., Wang, L.-L., Yang, S.-N.: Regular-texture image retrieval based on texture-primitive extraction. IVC 17(1), 51–63 (1999)

17. Liu, F., Picard, R.W.: Periodicity, Directionality, and Randomness: Wold Features for Image Modeling and Retrieval. IEEE Trans. Pattern Analysis and Machine Intelligence 18(7), 722–733 (1996)

18. Mehrotra, R., Gary, J.E.: Similar-Shape Retrieval in Shape Data Management. Computer 28(9), 57–62 (1995)

19. Jain, A., Vailaya, A.: Image Retrieval Using Color and Shape. Pattern Recognition 29(8), 1233–1244 (1996)

20. Kankanhalli, M.S., Mehtre, B.M., Huang, H.Y.: Color and spatial feature for content-based image retrieval. Pattern Rec. Letters 20, 109–118 (1999)

21. Kelly, P.M., Cannon, T.M., Hush, D.R.: Query by image example: the CANDID approach. In: Proc. of the SPIE, Storage and Retrieval for Image and Video Databases III 2420, SPIE, pp. 238–248 (1995)

22. Krishnapuram, R., Medasani, S., Jung, S.-H., Choi, Y.-S., Balasubramaniam, R.: Content-based image retrieval based on a fuzzy approach. IEEE Trans. on Knowledge and Data Engineering 16(10), 1185–1199 (2004)

23. MacQueen, J.B.: Some Methods for classification and Analysis of Multivariate Observations. In: Proc. of 5-th Berkeley Symposium on Mathematical Statistics and Probability, vol. 1, pp. 281-297, University of California Press,Berkeley (1967)

24. Manjunath, B.S., Ma, W.Y.: Texture Features for Browsing and Retrieval of Image Data. IEEE Trans. Pattern Analysis and Machine Intelligence 18(8), 837–842 (1996)

25. Muller, H., Squire, D.McG., Muller, W., Pun, T.: Efficient access methods for content-based image retrieval with inverted files, in: Proc. Multimedia Storage and Archiving Systems IV (VV02), Boston, Massachusetts, USA, pp. 20–22 (1999)

26. Ogle, V., Stonebraker, M.: Chabot: Retrieval from a relational database of images. IEEE Computer 28(9), 40–48 (1995)

27. Pentland, A., Picard, R.W., Sclaroff, S.: Photobook: Content-based manipulation of image databases, Tech. Rep. 255, MIT Media Laboratory Perceptual Computing (November 1993)

28. Quddus, A., et al.: Content-based object retrieval using maximum curvature points in contour images. In: Proc. of the SPIE/EI'2000, Symp. on Stor. and Retr. for Media DB, SPIE, vol. 3972, pp. 98–105 (2000)

29. Rose, K.: Deterministic annealing for clustering, compression, classification, regression, and related optimization problems. In: Proc. of IEEE, vol. 86(11), pp.2210-2239 (1998)

30. Santini, S.: Exploratory Image Databases: Content-Based Retrieval, Communications, Networking, and Multimedia. Academic Press, San Diego CA (2001)

31. Schonfeld, D., Lelescu, D.: VORTEX: Video retrieval and tracking from compressed multimedia databases-visual search engine. In: Proc. of the 32nd Hawai Int. Conference on System Sciences, IEEE, pp. 1–12 (1999)

32. Smith, J.R., Chang, S.-F.: VisualSEEk: a fully automated content-based image query system. In: ACM Multimedia'96, Boston MA, USA, pp. 87–98 (1996)

33. Stanford10K database,
http://www-db.stanford.edu/~wangz/image.vary.jpg.tar

34. Stricker, M., Orengo, M.: Similarity of Color Images. In: Niblack, W.R., Jain, R.C. (eds.) Proc. SPIE Conf. on Storage and Retrieval for Image and Video Databases III, pp. 381–392 (1995)

35. Swain, M.J., Ballard, D.H.: Color Indexing, Int. J. Computer Vision 7(1), 11–32 (1991)

36. Microsoft, Terraserver (2001)
37. Virage Inc., VIR image engine (2001), http://www.virage.com/products/image_vir.html
38. Zhong, Y., Jain, A.K.: Object localization using color, texture and shape. Pattern Recognition 33(4), 671–684 (2000)
39. Wang, J.Z., et al.: Content-based image indexing and searching using Daubechies' wavelets. Int. Journal on Digital Libraries 1, 311–328 (1997)

Evolutionary Cellular Automata Based-Approach for Edge Detection

Sihem Slatnia[1], Mohamed Batouche[2], and Kamal E. Melkemi[1]

[1] University of Biskra, Computer Science department, 07000 Biskra, Algeria
sihem.slatnia@gmail.com, melkemi@mailcity.com
[2] Computer Science department, College of Computer and Information Sciences,
University of King Saud, Saudi Arabia
batouche@yahoo.fr

Abstract. We use an evolutionary process to seek a specialized powerful rule of Cellular Automata (CA) among a set of best rules for extracting edges in a given black-white image. This best set of local rules determines the future state of CA in an asynchronous way. The Genetic Algorithm (GA) is applied to search the best CA rules that can realize better the edge detection.

Keywords: Genetic Algorithms, Evolutionary Cellular Automata, Edge Detection.

1 Introduction

We can understand the emergence like a phenomenon of producing collective behaviour by a collection of interacting elements in a complex system. The study of evolving Cellular Automata (CA) framework using evolutionary algorithms is a good example to show how evolution can create systems in which emergent computation takes place. Indeed, the actions of simple components with local information and communication give rise to coordinated global information processing [6].

In this paper, we are using Genetic Algorithms (GAs) in order to evolve CA to perform computations that require global coordination [6].

Indeed, we are interested into CA [7,1] and the edge detection [9]. Among a variety of researchers having investigated the proprieties of CA, we can't miss to cite the works of John von Neumann [2], Stephen Wolfram [3], and John Conway [4]. CA are discrete dynamical systems, which are widely applied in modelling systems in areas such as physics, biology, and sociology [8]. CA can be interpreted like a set of rules which through an Evolutionary CA (EvCA), we can find one or several appropriate rules for a definite problem. The idea of using one packet of rules in edge detection and filtering are in the merit of Rosin [1]. Indeed, it is used in restoration of black-white images. Moreover, Rosin [1] studied these best rules in details and showed the interest of each one. The result of its study showed that a single rule can remove isolated pixels in a noise black-white image.

F. Masulli, S. Mitra, and G. Pasi (Eds.): WILF 2007, LNAI 4578, pp. 404–411, 2007.

In this paper, we use a GA to find a single powerful rule for extracting efficiency edges in a given black-white image. Indeed, an EvCA is applied in order to determine the best local rules of the CA, using a GA on a population of CA candidates [6]. After this introduction, Section 2 presents the EvCA-ED approach. Experimental results are reported in Section 3. Conclusions are drawn in the last section.

2   The EvCA for Edge Detection (EvCA-ED)

The proposed EvCA-ED takes advantage of the calculating faculties of the CA, to transform the initial configurations defined by a binary image lattice as input discrete data in order to find its edges.

The execution of a simple packet of CA local rules evolved using evolutionary process [1,5] produces an emergent phenomenon. In this paper, the GA is applied to search the desirable CA rules that can realize better the edge detection. In order to explore all configurations in the research space, we regroup the rules in packets [5].

In our study, we must avoid the redundancy of a (rules/packets) during the process of evolution and the contradictory rules in the same packet (2 patch's with different transition).

In the EvCA-ED approach, we seek the best packet of transition rules for edge detection of a black-white image. The CA unit is represented by a rectangle of 9 cells. Indeed, the problem is to find the best CAs for edge detection among 2^{51} possible rules. We use a GA to find this optimal packet of rules (see Fig. 3).

The following code describes the GA to determine the best packet of transition rules that able to achieve the edge detection of binary images.

Algorithm

1. The input data: Input Image.
2. Initialization of the GA: Construction at random of rule packets extracted from the neighborhood model figured on the whole of the image (see Fig. 2).
   (a) Edge detection method: For each CA, the process: First, searches; among the current packets; the similar rule according to its neighborhood. Second, modifies the central pixel according to the defined transition.
   (b) Evaluation of the edge detection result: We compute the distance between of the edge detection result and the ideal one considered to assess the approach. We can also evaluate the error of miss-classed pixels.
3. Reproduction: Generate a new population by applying selection, crossover and mutation. We use the edge detection described above in the evaluation process.
4. The process iterates until the error $\leq$ a given threshold or a maximum of iterations.
5. The result: optimal packet of rules.

CA can be interpreted like a set of rules which through an EvCA, we can find one or several appropriate rules for a definite problem.

The idea of using one packet of rules in edge detection and filtering is reported in the work of Rosin [1]. Especially, it can be used in restoration of black-white images. Moreover, Rosin [1] studied these best rules in details and shows the interest of each one. The result of its study showed that a single rule can remove isolated pixels in a noise black-white image.

In this paper, we inspirit of this fact to seek a single powerful rule for extracting efficiency edges in a given black-white image.

We represent the transition rule of a CA by the concatenation of the cells states of the current cell neighborhood to update (see Fig. 2). Then, we add the future cell state after updating [5]. This rule (pattern) is transformed as a linear chromosome (see Fig. 1).

Fig. 1. CA rule notation and the chromosome representation the CA rule

The rule is applied when its part neighborhood coincides with a patch of the same dimension on the image. Then, we replace the central pixel of the patch by the value of the future state in the rule. The correspondence between the part neighborhood of the rule and a patch of the image is reduced according to the rotational operators (rotation to $0^0, 90^0, 180^0$ and 270^0, reversal horizontal and vertical "flip-flop"). The rules are therefore symmetrical. Each individual of the population is represented by a chromosome which is a transition vector according to a neighborhood model (see Fig. 2). We report that for the case of the black (0) and white (1) images, the numbers of the possible combinations to construct of the research space will be decreased contrary to the general case. To make the CA deterministic, we add the following constraint: Every rule of the packet must be different from the other.

To explore a vast set of configurations, the chromosome representation can be presented by two types of structure from the input image: the horizontal and the vertical. We use the horizontal one. The crossover exchanges, with given probability a genetic material between two parent chromosomes corresponding to two CA transition rules for producing two offspring. The mutation is a random change of gene in a given CA transition rule (parent). The selection process based on the edge detection assessment in EvCA represents an interdisciplinary process. Let $Err = nbr$ of $pixels$ where ($ImageED \neq ImageIdealED$), which Err and nbr are the abbreviation of error and number respectively.

The fitness function used to assess the edge detection is given by:
$F = 1 - (err/L \times H)$ where L and H represent the image width and height. The Err function computes the number of the points finds non equal in the two images: the resulted image and the ideal one.

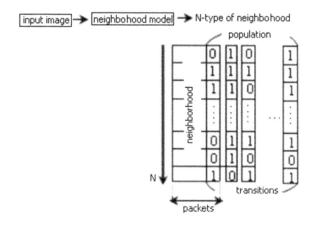

Fig. 2. Construction of the neighborhood model from an input image

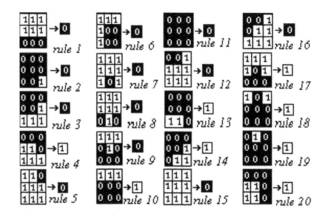

Fig. 3. A best packet of CA rules find by GA

3   Experimental Results

We present both synthetic and real results (see Figs. 4,6,8 and 10) of the EvCA-ED compared to Canny edge detector [9]. These following experiments are performed by using MATLAB on a Pentium 4, CPU 1:70 GHz with 256 MB. The EvCA-ED using the powerful rule number 15 extracts better (see Fig. 3) the edges in all the experimental results performed on a class of binary images. Consequently, for a edge detection of a class of binary images, only one powerful rule is able to give better results, what of the substantial gains give in the cost and in the qualities. We have distinguished the powerful rule number 15 (0000000001) (see Fig. 3) and its contrary (1111111110). The first rule is used for the inside edge detection and the second one for the outside edge detection.

Fig. 4. Edge detection of four characters 'A B D and H' (176×203). (a) input image (b) Canny result, (c) best packet result, (d) result using the powerful rule.

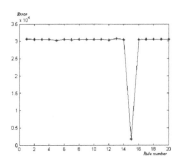

Fig. 5. The error obtained rule by rule of the characters 'A,B, H and D' experience

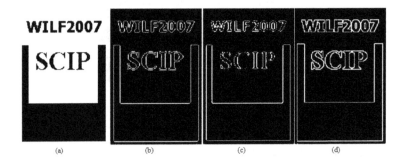

Fig. 6. Edge detection of two words 'SCIP' and 'WILF' (128×186). (a) input image (b) Canny result, (c) best packet result, (d) result using the powerful rule.

The first image (see Fig. 4) shows four characters 'A, B, H and D'. It can be seen that different edges of characters are better extracted by the powerful rule number 15 (see Fig. 3) than by Canny edge detector (see Fig. 4). The same result is presented in an edge detection of two words 'SCIP' and 'WILF' (see Fig. 6). In Fig. 8, we use a synthetic image containing different geometric shapes. It can be seen that different edges are better extracted by EvCA-ED using the powerful rule number 15 than the Canny edge detector [9] despite the interference of some shapes (see Fig. 1).

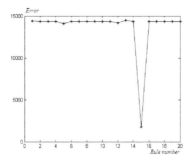

Fig. 7. The error obtained rule by rule of the SCIP-WILF experience

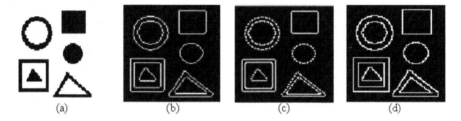

(a)   (b)   (c)   (d)

Fig. 8. Edge detection of a 100×100 image of shapes. (a) input image (b) Canny result, (c) Result by best packet, (d) Result using the powerful rule.

Table 1. Evaluation values of the experiments reported in Figs. 4, 6, 8 and 10

image of	characters		'SCIP-WILF'		shapes		cells	
ED method	Fitness	Time(Sec.)	Fitness	Time(Sec.)	Fitness	Time(Sec.)	Fitness	Time(Sec.)
Best packet	0.8590	114.916	0.9017	69.400	0.8090	22.893	0.8229	188.461
Rule 15	0.9526	4.5970	0.9999	2.984	0.8971	1.7330	0.9126	10.535

In Fig. 10, the input image represents a set of cells with a cast shadow having circle shapes. The EvCA-ED results using the rule number 15 is the adequate one comparably to the others (see Fig. 10 and Fig. 11) and better than the Canny result.

Each graph of Figs. 5, 7, 9 and 11 presents the error evaluation of the EvCA-ED of the experiments presented in 4, 6, 8 and 10 respectively. For each rule, we get the fitness value of the its result. These graphs show clearly that the rule number 15 gives the better fitness result. These results and robustness of this rule compared to the others still the same in different experiments made on black-white images.

Concerning the complexity, in spite of the implementation has made without the specialized hardware that are available [12,13], the running time of the CA using the powerful rule is better than the time of the CA using the best packet.

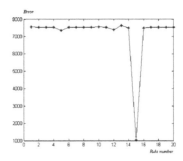

Fig. 9. The error obtained rule by rule of the shape experience

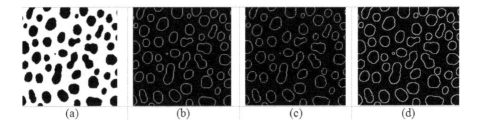

(a)	(b)	(c)	(d)

Fig. 10. Edge detection of image of cells 238×238. (a) input image (b) Canny result, (c) best packet result, (d) result using the powerful rule.

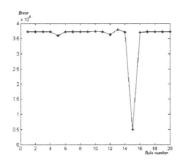

Fig. 11. The error obtained rule by rule of the best packet of the cells experience

4   Conclusion

In this paper, our proposed model of CA applied in edge detection provides insights on how evolutionary processes can be used to discover local patterns that give rise to optimal edge detection of a given binary image. Indeed, one of such local structural properties were identified via the GA allowed us to analyze the evolutionary emergence of sophisticated computation.

In this paper, we have demonstrated that the edge detection can be interpreted like an evolutionary phenomenon of a set of CA, controlled by a best packets or a single powerful rule of CA applied on a category of image. Indeed, the image can be modelled by a CA which we can implement easily.

The EvCA-ED shows the degree of specialization aspect of CA of edge detection. Indeed, the robustness of the powerful rule number 15 shows that each rule has its fitness value. Thus, we can say that for a given global computation task, the GA evolve a best packet of rules which each one has its robustness value.

The emergence phenomenon is clearly appeared in the fact that one rule is able to detect edges in a given class of image. This result illustrates that in a given task each rule has a degree of adaptation.

References

1. Rosin, P.L.: Training Cellular Automata for Image Processing. In: Kalviainen, H., Parkkinen, J., Kaarna, A. (eds.) SCIA 2005. LNCS, vol. 3540, pp. 195–204. Springer, Heidelberg (2005)
2. von Neumann, J.: Theory of Self-Reproducing Automata. University of Illinois Press, US (1966)
3. Wolfram, S.: Cellular Automata and Complexity. Addison-Wesley, London, UK (1994)
4. Gardner, M.: The fantastic combinations of John Conways new solitaire game life. Scientific American, pp. 120-123 (1970)
5. Batouche, M., Meshoul, S., Abbassene, A.: On Solving Edge Detection by Emergence, IEA/AIE, pp. 800–808 (2006)
6. Mitchell, M., Crutchfield, J.P., Das, R.: Evolving Cellular Automata with GAs: A Review of Recent Work. In: Proc. of the first Inter. Conf. on Ev. Comp. and its Appl. (EvCA'96) Moscow (1996)
7. Ganguly, N., Sikdar, B.K., Deutsch, A., Canright, G., Chaudhuri, P.P.: A Survey on Cellular Automata, Project BISON (IST-2001-38923) (2001)
8. Bar-Yam, Y.: Dynamics of Complex Systems. Addison- Wesley, Reading, MA (1997)
9. Canny, J.: A Computational Approach to Edge Detection. IEEE Trans. on PAMI, 8(6) (1986)
10. Grasemann, U., Miikkulainen, R.: Effective Image Compression using Evolved Wavelets, The University of Texas at Austin, GECCO'05, Washington, DC. 25-29 (June 2005)
11. Vezhnevets, V., Konouchine, V.: GrowCut-interactive multi-label N-D image segmentation by cellular automata, Graphicon'2005
12. Toffoli, T., Margolus, N.: Cellular Automata Machines. MIT Press, Cambridge, MA (1987)
13. Halbach, M., Hoffmann, R.: Implementing cellular automata in FPGA logic. In: Proc. 18th Int. Parallel and Distributed Processing Symp., pp. 258a-258a (2004)
14. Kotecha, K., Gambhava, N.: Solving precedence constraint traveling salesman problem using genetic algorithm. In: Nat. Conf. on Soft. Agents and Embedded Syst., Coimbatore (2003)

The Multidisciplinary Facets of Research on Humour

Rada Mihalcea[1,2]

[1] Computer Science Department, University of North Texas
[2] Computational Linguistics Group, Oxford University
rada@cs.unt.edu

1 Introduction

Humour is one of the most interesting and puzzling aspects of human behaviour, and it has been rightfully argued that it plays an important role in an individual's development, as well as in interpersonal communication. Research on this topic has received a significant amount of attention from fields as diverse as linguistics, philosophy, psychology and sociology, and recent years have also seen attempts to build computational models for humour generation and recognition.

In this paper, we summarize the main theories of humour that emerged from philosophical and modern psychological research, and survey the past and present developments in the fields of theoretical and computational linguistics. We also briefly overview related research work in the fields of psychology, sociology and neuroscience. The paper concludes with an illustration of the multidisciplinary applications of humour.

Note that we focus mainly on "verbal humour," which is the most tangible and perhaps the most widely researched form of humour. Although other forms of humour (e.g., visual or situational) have also received attention from the research community, we concentrate our work and consequently this survey on the linguistic expressions of humour.

2 Theories of Humour

There are three main theories of humour, which emerged primarily from philosophical studies and research in psychology.

2.1 Incongruity Theory

The incongruity theory suggests that humour is due to the mixing of two disparate interpretation frames in one statement. One of the earliest references to an incongruity theory of humour is perhaps due to Aristotle [1] who found that the contrast between expectation and actual outcome is often a source of humour. He is also making a distinction between surprise and incongruity, where the later is presumed to have a resolution that was initially hidden from the audience. The incongruity theory has also found a supporter in Schopenhauer

F. Masulli, S. Mitra, and G. Pasi (Eds.): WILF 2007, LNAI 4578, pp. 412–421, 2007.

[32], who emphasizes the element of surprise by suggesting that "the greater and more unexpected [...] the incongruity is, the more violent will be [the] laughter." The incongruity theory has been formalized as a necessary condition for humour and used as a basis for the Semantic Script-based Theory of Humour (SSTH) [27], and later on the General Theory of Verbal Humour (GTVH) [3].

2.2 Superiority Theory

The superiority theory argues that humour is a form of expressing the superiority of one over another. As Hobbes suggested [15], the laughter is "nothing else but sudden glory" triggered by a feeling of superiority with respect to others, or with respect to ourselves in a previous moment. A closely related theory is the one supported by Solomon [33], who suggests that humour is due to feelings of inferiority, which led to the so called "inferiority theory." Although the superiority and inferiority theories of humour have been typically perceived as diametrically opposed, they are in fact intimately related, as the "superior"/"inferior" distinctions are often due to a different point of view. In fact, it can be argued that laughter is triggered by our feelings of superiority with respect to others or ourselves in a previous moment, which are equivalent to feelings of inferiority felt by others or by ourselves in a past moment.

2.3 Relief Theory

The third major theory is the relief theory, which suggests that humour is a form of bypassing certain censors that prevent us from having "prohibited thoughts." Eluding these censors results in a release of the energy inhibited by these censors, and consequently the feeling of relief. One of the strongest supporters of the relief theory is Freud [10], who draws a connection between jokes and the unconscious, and Spencer [34], who suggests that laughter is a form of "nervous energy." Some of these ideas have been later embraced by Minsky in his theory of humour [22], to which he adds a cognitive element that attempts to explain the "faulty logic" that is typically encountered in jokes, which is normally suppressed in order to avoid "cognitive harm."

3   Linguistic Research on Humour

A significant fraction of the research on humour that has been carried out to date has concentrated on the linguistic characteristics of humour. Among the linguistic theories, the most influential is perhaps the General Theory of Verbal Humour (GTVH) [3], which is an extension of the earlier Semantic Script-based Theory of Humour (SSTH) [27].

3.1 Semantic Script-Based Theory of Humour

SSTH is based on the representation of jokes as *script opposition*, which is an idea closely related to the incongruity resolution theory. Briefly, SSTH defines the structure of a joke as consisting of a *set-up* and a *punchline*. The set-up has at least two possible interpretations out of which only one is obvious, and consequently the humorous effect is created by the punchline which triggers the second less-obvious interpretation in a surprising way.

The central hypothesis in SSTH is that a text is humorous if the following two conditions are satisfied. First, the humorous text has to be compatible with at least two different interpretations (scripts). And second, the two interpretations have to be opposed to each other. For instance, the following example taken from [27] illustrates this theory: "The first thing that strikes a stranger in New York is a big car." The set-up has two possible interpretations: strike as in "impress" or "hit," which are opposed to each other ("impress" being a positive action, and "hit" triggering negative feelings). The first interpretation is more obvious and thus initially preferred. However, the punchline "by a big car" will change the preference to the second interpretation, which generates the humorous effect.

According to SSTH, the opposition between scripts is binary, and can fall into one of the following three generic types: actual/non-actual, normal/abnormal, possible/impossible, which in turn can be broken down into more specific oppositions, such as positive/negative or good/bad.

3.2   General Theory of Verbal Humour

Following SSTH, the GTVH [3] extends the script opposition theory, and adds other possible knowledge resources for a humorous text. While SSTH was primarily focused on semantics, the GTVH is more general and includes other areas in linguistics such as pragmatics and style. GTVH defines six main knowledge resources that can be organized on six levels from concrete (low level) to abstract (high level).

- *Script opposition*, which is a knowledge source based on the main idea of SSTH of opposing interpretations that are both compatible with the text.
- *Logical mechanism*, which provides a possible resolution mechanism for the incongruity between scripts.
- *Situation*, which defines the context of the joke in terms of location, participants, and others.
- *Target*, which is the person or group of persons that are targeted by the joke.
- *Narrative strategy*, which defines the style of the joke, i.e., whether it is a dialogue, a riddle or a simple narrative.
- *Language*, which defines the "surface" of the joke in terms of linguistic aspects such as lexicon, morphology, syntax, semantics.

For example, Attardo and Raskin [3] exemplify the knowledge resources using the following joke: "How many poles does it take to screw in a light bulb? Five. One to hold the light bulb and four to turn the table he is standing on." The script opposition is formed between the expected normal behaviour of a person when screwing in a light bulb, and the "dumb" resolution proposed by the punchline; the logical mechanism is that of "reversal" of a normal behaviour;

the situation is "bulb changing"; the target of the joke are the "Poles"; and finally, the narrative structure is a "riddle" [28].

An interesting experiment centered around the GTVH theory is reported by Ruch [31], where three jokes are transformed into variants that differed from the original joke in one of the GTVH parameters. A group of 500 subjects were asked to rate the similarity between each of the variants and the original joke on a scale of 1 to 4. The findings indicate that higher similarity is observed for those variants that differ in a low level parameter in the GTVH hierarchy, thus suggesting that the higher level parameters such as script opposition and logic mechanism are more humour-related [28].

While GTVH is perhaps the most extensive linguistic theory of humour that has been proposed to date, it has been criticized by Ritchie [28] as lacking theoretical grounds. Ritchie raises doubts about the falsifiability of the GTVH, and about the lack of systematic examples where some of the GTVH knowledge resources are missing, thus resulting in a lack of humorous effect, along with humorous examples that include the missing knowledge resources.

3.3   Related Work in Linguistics

Besides the SSTH and the GTVH theories, other research work in linguistics has focused mainly on the analysis of the lexical devices used in humorous text. The syntactic ambiguity often encountered in humour is analysed by Hetzron [14], who describes the structure of jokes and punchlines, and analyses the logical devices found in verbal humour. Oaks [25] is proposing an interesting account on syntactic ambiguity in humour, and identifies several ambiguity "enablers." He focuses mainly on part-of-speech ambiguity, and identifies verbs, articles, and other parts-of-speech that can introduce ambiguity in language (e.g., *bite* that can be either a verb or a noun).

The lexical and syntactic ambiguity as a source of humour is also studied by Bucaria [6], who analyses the linguistic ambiguity in newspaper headlines. She identifies three main types of ambiguity: lexical (e.g., "Actor sent to jail for not finishing *sentence.*"), syntactic (e.g., "Eye *drops* off shelf"), and phonological (e.g., "Is there a ring of debris around *Uranus*"). She also identifies two additional schemata for humorous ambiguity, including the disjunctor/connector model (e.g. "New study on *obesity* looks for *larger* group."), and the double ambiguity model (e.g., "Farmer *Bill dies* in house."). In an analysis of 135 headlines, the lexical and syntactic forms of ambiguity were found to be dominant (71 lexical and 63 syntactic), covering a significant fraction of the corpus, and thus providing support for the incongruity theory of humour.

4   Computational Humour

While humour is relatively well studied in fields such as theoretical linguistics [2] and psychology [9,30], to date only a limited number of research contributions have been made toward the construction of computational humour prototypes.

Most of the computational approaches to date on style classification have focused on the categorization of more traditional literature genres, such as fiction, sci-tech, legal, and others [16], and much less on creative writings such as humour.

The most systematic effort in this area is perhaps Ritchie's book on the linguistic analysis of jokes, which brings together research on linguistic theories and artificial intelligence. In addition to a comprehensive overview of the main research contributions in humour, Ritchie is also proposing a classification of jokes into propositional and linguistic, and suggests a structural description of the jokes [28].

Similar to other computational linguistics research carried out on language style, there are two main research directions in computational humour: (1) *humour generation*, which attempts to build computational models to generate humorous text, and (2) *humour recognition*, which deals with the problem of identifying humour in natural language.

4.1 Humour Generation

One of the first attempts in humour generation is the work described by Binsted and Ritchie [5], where a formal model of semantic and syntactic regularities was devised, underlying some of the simplest types of puns (*punning riddles*). The model was then exploited in a system called JAPE that was able to automatically generate amusing puns.

Another humour generation project is the HAHAcronym project [35], whose goal was to develop a system able to automatically generate humorous versions of existing acronyms, or to produce a new amusing acronym constrained to be a valid vocabulary word, starting with concepts provided by the user. The comic effect was achieved mainly by exploiting incongruity theories (e.g., finding a religious variation for a technical acronym).

4.2 Humour Recognition

There are only a few studies addressing the problem of humour recognition. The study reported in [36] is devoted to the problem of humour comprehension, focusing on a restricted type of wordplays, namely the "Knock-Knock" jokes. The goal of the study was to evaluate to what extent wordplay can be automatically identified in "Knock-Knock" jokes, and if such jokes can be reliably recognized from other non-humorous text. The algorithm was based on automatically extracted structural patterns and on heuristics heavily based on the peculiar structure of this particular type of jokes. While the generic wordplay recognition gave satisfactory results (67% accuracy), the identification of wordplays that had a humorous effect turned out to be significantly more difficult (12% accuracy).

In our own previous work [20,19], humour recognition was formulated as a text classification task, and machine learning algorithms were run on large collections of humorous texts (oneliners or humorous news articles). Both content and stylistic features were evaluated, including n-gram models, alliteration, antonymy, and adult slang, with performance figures significantly higher than apriori known baselines.

Another humour recognition study was reported by Purandare and Littman [26], where the recognition experiments were performed using both content features and spoken dialogue prosody features (tempo, energy, and pitch). The experiments were run on dialogues from the TV-series "Friends," with significant improvements observed over the baseline. They also reported a gender study, with the improvement obtained for humour recognition in male dialogues being higher than the one obtained for female dialogues, suggesting perhaps that the humorous features are more prominent for males than for females.

5   Multidisciplinary Research on Humour

In addition to the research work in linguistics and the recent efforts in computational linguistics, humour has been also studied in other areas.

5.1   Sociology

In sociology, humour has been frequently associated with studies concerned with patterns of communication in different groups. For instance, Duncan [8] shows that cohesive and non-cohesive work groups have different humour patterns, suggesting a correlation between the type of humour practiced in a group and the structure of the group.

Studies have also investigated the association between gender and humour, by analysing the type and role of humour for female, male and mixed groups. Hay [12] used a taxonomy of humour in a gender-oriented analysis, which revealed the preference of women for observational humour and the tendency of male groups for insults and roleplay. Interestingly, a correlation was also observed between the gender of these groups and the function of humour; women groups used humour primarily as a social element, whereas men groups often used it as a means for increasing status. Finally, Hay's study also reported on the association between gender and humour topics, suggesting that women use more frequently humour on topics involving people, while men joke more about politics, computers and work; this observation correlates with recent conclusions drawn in corpus-based gender studies [17].

Another aspect of interest in sociology is the relation between culture and humour. Work in this area has highlighted the relation between cultural background and humour appreciation, showing that the set of values and norms of a culture largely determine the content and style of humour [13]. Focused studies have highlighted differences between various cultures, as for instance the study reported in [24], which shows how Arab and Jewish communities developed a different sense of humour explained by their diverse background and different social status.

5.2 Psychology

Humour research in psychology has been mainly concerned with the correlation between humour and individual development. There are several studies that considered the cognitive aspects of humour, and the role that humour can play in infants and children development. For instance, it has been found that humour has an important role in improving text comprehension [38].

Other studies have been concerned with the relation between personality profiles and sense of humour. Along these lines, it has been suggested that extroversion and neuroticism can be predicted from humour perception [23]. Similarly, humour was found to be related to other personality characteristics such as simplicity-complexity, intelligence, or mood [29].

5.3 Neuroscience

In recent years, given the advances made in brain imaging techniques (fMRI or MEG), researchers have started to investigate the brain activity observed during humour detection and comprehension. Recent research findings suggest that the left and the right hemispheres are both involved in humour appreciation, which is an effect that has been observed in verbal humour as well as visual humour [4]. Moreover, studies have also observed the activation of the amygdala and midbrain regions (also known as the "pleasure center"), which is probably due to the pleasurable effect created by humour [37].

It is also worth noting the study reported in [23], which shows connections between gender, personality (i.e., extroversion and neuroticism), and humour appreciation, observed using brain imaging techniques. Such associations have been typically identified through surveys conducted in psychological studies, and the study reported in [23] confirms these previous findings by identifying patterns of brain activity occurring during humour comprehension.

6   Applications of Humour

In agreement with its multidisciplinary facets, applications of humour are also found in a variety of domains, including social communication, education, health, human-computer interaction.

A few attempts were made to integrate humour into human-computer interfaces. For instance, the JAPE system [7] was integrated into a natural language robot Elmo [18] – a software agent able to carry out a dialogue that was improved with the ability of formulating humorous replies. However, since the puns used by Elmo were automatically generated, the effect was not overwhelmingly positive, as users seemed to dislike the occasional low-quality humour more than the complete absence of it.

Another attempt is the integration of oneliners into email applications. In our own previous work [21], we created an email client that was automatically adding humorous statements to emails, based on the similarity between the body of the email and the candidate oneliners. A user study conducted around the email application revealed that users found the humorous additions to be entertaining and appropriate, and considered adopting the application for their own day-by-day use.

Humour has also been used for educational purposes. For instance, the Riddles system [38] was used to improve text comprehension in children 7-11 years old. The software showed riddles to children with reading difficulties, and asked them to discuss their various possible interpretations. The interaction with the system was found to improve the reading comprehension scores for the participating children.

Finally, it is also worth mentioning the humour recommender system [11] which builds a "sense of humour" profile for the users, and consequently recommends new jokes based on the rating received from other users with a similar profile.

7   Conclusions

In this paper, we tried to bring together the main research achievements on humour in the fields of theoretical and computational linguistics, as well as in sociology, psychology and neuroscience. We hopefully demonstrated that humour is a highly multidisciplinary field of research. We believe this fact has two important implications. First, it means that research on humour can benefit from the diverse expertise of researchers working in different fields, which will broaden the perspective for understanding the role and the nature of humour. Second, because of its multidisciplinary facets, research on humour can serve as a bridge between different fields of study and consequently contribute to scientific interdisciplinarity.

References

1. Aristotle. Rhetoric. 350 BC.
2. Attardo, S.: Linguistic Theory of Humor. Mouton de Gruyter, Berlin (1994)
3. Attardo, S., Raskin, V.: Script theory revis(it)ed: Joke similarity and joke representation model. Humor: International Journal of Humor Research 4, 3–4 (1991)
4. Bartolo, A., Benuzzi, F., Nocetti, L., Baraldi, P., Nichelli, P.: Humor comprehension and appreciation: An fmri study. Journal of Cognitive Neuroscience 18 (2006)
5. Binsted, K., Ritchie, G.: Computational rules for punning riddles. Humor 10, 1 (1997)
6. Bucaria, C.: Lexical and syntactic ambiguity as a source of humor. Humor 17, 3 (2004)
7. Cawsey, A., Binsted, K., Jones, R.: An implemented model of punning riddles. In: Conference on Artificial Intelligence,Seattle (1995)
8. Duncan, W.: Perceived humor and social network patterns in a sample of task-oriented groups: A reexamination of prior research. Human Relations 37, 11 (1984)
9. Freud, S.: Der Witz und Seine Beziehung zum Unbewussten. Deutike, Vienna (1905)
10. Freud, S.: Jokes and their relation to the unconscious. Humor. International Journal of Psychoanalysis 9 (1960)

11. Goldberg, K., Roeder, T., Gupta, D., Perkins, C.: Eigentaste: A constant-time collaborative filtering algorithm. Information Retrieval 4, 2 (2001)
12. Hay, J.: Gender and humour: Beyond a joke. Master's thesis, Victoria University of Wellington (1995)
13. Hertzler, J.: Laughter: A social scientific analysis. Exposition Press, New York (1970)
14. Hetzron, R.: On the structure of punchlines. Humor: International Journal of Humor Research 4, 1 (1991)
15. Hobbes, T.: Human Nature in English Works. Molesworth (1840)
16. Kessler, B., Nunberg, G., Schuetze, H.: Automatic detection of text genre. In: *Proceedings of the 35th Annual Meeting of the Association for Computational Linguistics (ACL97)* Madrid (July 1997)
17. Liu, H., Mihalcea, R.: Of men, women, and computers: Data-driven gender modeling for improved user interfaces. In: International Conference on Weblogs and Social Media (2007)
18. Loehr, D.: An integration of a pun generator with a natural language robot. In: Colloque Linguistique-Informatique de Montreal (1996)
19. Mihalcea, R., Pulman, S.: Characterizing humour: An exploration of features in humorous texts. In: Proceedings of the Conference on Intelligent Text Processing and Computational Linguistics, Mexico City (2007)
20. Mihalcea, R., Strapparava, C.: Making computers laugh: Investigations in automatic humor recognition. In: Proceedings of the Human Language Technology / Empirical Methods in Natural Language Processing conference, Vancouver (2005)
21. Mihalcea, R., Strapparava, C.: Technologies that make you smile: Adding humor to text-based applications. IEEE Intelligent Systems 21, 5 (2006)
22. Minsky, M.: Jokes and the logic of the cognitive unconscious. Tech. rep., MIT Artificial Intelligence Laboratory (1980)
23. Mobbs, D., Hagan, C., Azim, E., Menon, V., Reiss, A.: Personality predicts activity in reward and emotional regions associated with humor. National Academy of Science 102, 45 (2005)
24. Nevo, O.: Appreciation and production of humor as an expression of aggression. Journal of Cross-Cultural Psychology 15, 2 (1984)
25. Oaks, D.: Creating structural ambiguities in humor: Getting English grammar to cooperate. Humor: International Journal of Humor 7, 4 (1994)
26. Purandare, A., Litman, D.: Humor: Prosody analysis and automatic recognition for F*R*I*E*N*D*S*. In: Proceedings of the, Conference on Empirical Methods in Natural Language Processing Sydney, Australia, pp. 208–215 (2006)
27. Raskin, V.: Semantic Mechanisms of Humor. Kluwer Academic Publications (1985)
28. Ritchie, G.: The Linguistic Analysis of Jokes. Routledge, London (2003)
29. Ruch, W.: The Sense of Humor: Explorations of a Personality Characteristic (1998)
30. Ruch, W.: Computers with a personality? lessons to be learned from studies of the psychology of humor. In: Proceedings of the The April Fools Day Workshop on Computational Humour (2002)
31. Ruch, W., Attardo, S., Raskin, V.: Toward an empirical verification of the general theory of verbal humor. Humor: International Journal of Humor Research 6, 2 (1993)
32. Schopenhauer, A.: The World as Will and Idea. Kessinger Publishing Company (1819)
33. Solomon, R.: Ethics and Values in the Information Age. Wadsworth, ch. Are the Three Stooges Funny? Soitainly! (or When is it OK to Laugh?) (2002)

34. Spencer, H.: The physiology of laughter. Macmillan's Magazine 1 (1860)
35. Stock, O., Strapparava, C.: Getting serious about the development of computational humour. In: Proceedings of the 8th International Joint Conference on Artificial Intelligence (IJCAI-03) Acapulco, Mexico (August 2003)
36. Taylor, J., Mazlack, L.: Computationally recognizing wordplay in jokes. In: Proceedings of CogSci 2004,Chicago (August 2004)
37. Watson, K., Matthews, B., Allman, J.: Brain activation during sight gags and language-dependent humor. Cerebral Cortex 17, 2 (2007)
38. Yuill, N.: A funny thing happened on the way to the classroom: Jokes, riddles and metalinguistic awareness in understanding and improving poor comprehension in children (1997)

Multi-attribute Text Classification Using the Fuzzy Borda Method and Semantic Grades

Eugene Levner[1], David Alcaide[2], and Joaquin Sicilia[2]

[1] Holon Institute of Technology, Holon, Israel
levner@hit.ac.il
[2] University of La Laguna, La Laguna, Tenerife, Spain
dalcaide@ull.es, jsicilia@ull.es

Abstract. We consider the problem of automatic classification of text documents, in particular, scientific abstracts and use two types of classifiers: ordinal and numerical. For the first type we use a fuzzy extension of the Borda voting method while for the second type we use a fuzzy Borda method in combination with the semantic grading.

1 Introduction

Text classification systems categorize documents into one or several predefined topics of interest, called categories. Text classification is of great practical importance today due to the rapid growth of information and the explosion of electronic texts from the Internet. Text classification is widely used to automatically catalogue news articles and web pages [5], classify text documents, in particular, scientific abstracts [3] and real-world data sets [12], automatically learn the reading interests of users [15], and sort electronic mail [8]. In recent years, a number of classification techniques have been applied to text categorization, including graph based classifiers [16], [17], regression models [18], nearest neighbour classifiers [7], integer programming [11], Bayesian classifiers [9], fuzzy logic based classifiers [2] and support vector machines [4].

The information that researchers use in their activities can come from many sources, such as published literature, web sites, technical reports and prospects, electronic databases, and human experts. As the amount of scientific knowledge exponentially grows, and as an increasing portion of it becomes available more easily, researchers are faced with the difficult task of finding texts relevant to their work.

Our paper addresses the question, caused by the need for processing large quantities of data: how to efficiently integrate information from different sources?

The impetus for developing the methodology reported in this paper was a desire to suggest computationally efficient and simple methods understandable to the user. We consider two types of classifiers: *ordinal*, that is, those which assign certain ranks for different papers (documents), and *numerical*, which give numerical rating of the documents. For the first type we use a fuzzy extension of the Borda voting method, while for the second type we use a fuzzy Borda method in combination with the semantic grading.

F. Masulli, S. Mitra, and G. Pasi (Eds.): WILF 2007, LNAI 4578, pp. 422–429, 2007.

The rest of the paper is organised as follows. Section 2 describes the relations between the text classification and the basic voting methods, and then introduces the Borda voting method. Section 3 describes the fuzzy Borda method supplied by semantic grading. Section 4 reports the results of our experiments. Section 5 draws the conclusion.

2   Text Classification and the Voting Methods

The goal of text categorization is the classification of documents into a fixed number of predefined categories. Using a computer-aided procedure, the objective is to do the category assignments automatically. Our text classifier consists of five steps: First, identify (a) *the set of attributes* characterizing the documents (for instance, title, keywords, abstract, bibliography, author's bio, etc.); (b) *the set of predefined categories*, and (c) *the set of classifying words and expressions* within each category. These three sets can be either fixed, or flexible being extended or decreased during the interactive classification process. Second, compute the *fitness measure* f_{ij}^k of document i to category j with respect to attribute k. The fitness f_{ij}^k is a function of two arguments: (1) the number of words in the attribute k of document i common with predefined classifying words in category j; (2) the number of classifying words such that their presence in any document in attribute k is sufficient to classify such a document into category j with maximum fitness equal 1 (this concept is explained in more detail in Section 4). At the third step, using the set of decision rules of the *if-then* type and the Borda voting method, described below, the algorithm defines weights (relative importance) v_j of categories $\{j\}$ and weights w_k of attributes $\{k\}$ which may be either linguistic variables (like *very high, high, medium, low, very low*) or crisp magnitudes ranked in intervals $[1, 100]$ or $[0, 1]$. The fourth step defines the unified fitness f_{ij} of document i to category j, by using an additive approach:

$$f_{ij} = \sum_k w_k f_{ij}^k. \tag{1}$$

Finally, the fifth step distributes the documents among the categories using standard methods of cluster-analysis aimed either to maximize the total validity of classification as in [3], [16], [17] or to maximize the total "fitness" of available documents to their assigned categories defined as follows

$$F(C) = \frac{1}{N} \sum_{i,j} v_j f_{ij} x_{ij} \times 100 \tag{2}$$

where $x_{ij} = 1$ if document i is assigned to category j and 0 otherwise, and N is the total number of documents, under predetermined constraints on the cardinality of category sets and running time of the classifying procedure.

An approach pursued at the third step of the algorithm is the Borda ranking method in combination with expert *if-then* rules serving for processing fuzzy weights. Suppose that a finite number of attributes are used in order to rank the 'fitness' of documents to different categories, and, furthermore, a finite number of sources (also called criteria, or experts' estimations) are used to evaluate the significance of different attributes. Our goal is to aggregate information for several attributes and sources in order to obtain the overall ranking of documents according to their fitness for each category as well as the overall ranking of the attributes with respect to their importance. This study will generalize the classical Borda method for the case of fuzzy data.

Our approach is hierarchical. First, we describe a fuzzy *ordinal* algorithm for ordering all the documents based on different attributes of equal weights. Next, we present a fuzzy *numerical* method permitting to aggregate the information from different sources for obtaining coordinated *different weights* of the attributes.

Let us first briefly describe the basic Borda ranking method in the case when a set of documents is to be ranked based on the information (possibly, contradicting) provided by different attributes.

Suppose that there are N documents and K attributes, and that the k-th attribute has an associated weight w_k. The original Borda method assumes that $w_k = 1$, (however, later we consider that each w_k is a positive, not necessarily integer, number). A preference order supplied by each attribute ranks the documents in each category from the most preferred to the least preferred without ties. A preference order in which x_1 is ranked first, x_2 is ranked second, and so forth, is written here as $< x_1, x_2, \ldots, x_N >$.

For each attribute, points (grades) $N - 1, N - 2, \ldots \ldots$, and 0 are independently assigned to the first-ranked, second-ranked, . . . , and last-ranked document in each attribute's preference order; then the winning document is the one with the greatest total number of points. In other words, if r_{ik} is the rank of document i by attribute k, the Borda count for document i is $b_i = \sum_k (N - r_{ik})$. The documents are then ordered according to decreasing order of these counts. The ties are handled by evaluating the rank for a tied alternative as the average of the associated rankings.

The Borda method has several advantages such as simplicity, computational efficiency and minimum of voting paradoxes, but has also some inherent limitations: (1) It is defined for equal attribute weights only; and (2) it does not permit to handle inexact, uncertain and fuzzy data. Fuzzy versions of the Borda method are capable to overcome these drawbacks.

The paper by Garcia-Lapresta and Martinez-Panero [6] considers a fuzzy Borda method based on a matrix of pairwise comparison. The matrix entries are numbers between 0 and 1 which represent their "degrees of preference". They consider incomparability of some expert estimation, but do not consider ties (indifference). In contrast, our fuzzy version of the Borda method represents expert knowledge, and permits to take into account both incomparability and indifference (ties). The generalization is done in two directions: (a) fuzzy ranking with fuzzy numbers, in which case we use the fuzzy arithmetics, and (b) fuzzy weighting of attributes and categories. These weights are linguistic variables (*very low, low, medium, high, very high, very weak, weak, medium, strong, very strong, very bad, bad, good, very good,* etc.). We call this procedure *the semantic grading* [1], [10]. When working with linguistic variables, we use AND/OR operations of the Fuzzy Logic. This approach permits to efficiently integrate the information obtained from different sources and different attributes.

3   Text Classification Using a Semantic Grading

Fuzzy inference is the process of formulating the mapping from a given input to an output using fuzzy logic. The classic process of fuzzy inference according to Mamdani [13], [14] involves five steps: (1) Fuzzify inputs and outputs, (2) Apply fuzzy operators and formulate fuzzy *if-then* expert rules, (3) Apply the implication concept, (4) Aggregate the outputs, (5) Defuzzify. In contrast, instead of using stages (3) - (5), we suggest to use a fuzzy Borda method with semantic grading.

In the text classification method suggested, the fuzzy inputs will be the following: (a) levels of contribution to text classification of category j, provided by different sources, such as the published literature, web sites, human experts, etc.: *very low, low, medium, high, very high,* (b) levels of significance for text classification of attribute k provided by different sources: again *very low, low,* etc., (c) levels of source ("expert's") confidence, competence and reliability, and (d) positions of the document d in a category (*approximately 1, approximately 2,...*). We have also the logical operators: AND and OR.

In the fuzzy *ordinal* Borda method, the fuzzy outputs are fuzzy numbers representing the fuzzy Borda's counts: *Fuzzy-Count(i) = N - (Approximate-Rank(i))*, $i = 1, \ldots, N$.

In the fuzzy *numerical* Borda method, the fuzzy outputs are the following linguistic variables: (a) levels of attribute's importance (weights) w_k (*low, medium, high*), and (b) weights of text categories v_j. The set of *if-then* rules is given a priori. Examples of the *if-then* rules are:

(*i*) If *expert's (source's) s estimation for significance of attribute k is high* and *the competence of source s is high* then *the weight of attribute k* (as seen by expert s) *is high*. The latest linguistic value (*high*) will be an entry in the corresponding semantic evaluation table (see Table 1).

(*ii*) If *expert's (source's) s estimation for contribution of category j is low* and *the competence of source s is medium* then *the weight of category j* (as seen by expert s) *is low*.

The basic idea of the semantic grading is to rate linguistic variables with numeric estimates corresponding to each variable. For example *low* will correspond to 1 and *very high* to 10. To simplify our presentation, we start with an example. We study the importance w_k of any attribute k to classify documents. Assume that there are $N = 5$ attributes (denoted A, B, C, D, and E) which characterize documents (these attributes are given at the beginning of Section 2). We wish to determine their weights (importance) according to the information that come from different sources (called "experts") (such as published literature, human experts, etc.). The expert estimates (EE) are collected in Table 1 using semantic, or linguistic, variables. The Borda counts for each attribute are computed in Table 2.

Table 1. Semantic Evaluation of Attributes by Each Expert (vh = *very high*, h = *high*, m = *medium*, l = *low*)

	EE1	EE2	EE3	EE4	EE5
Weight of A	l	l	h	l	m
Weight of B	m	l	l	h	l
Weight of C	h	vh	vh	h	vh
Weight of D	vh	h	m	vh	vh
Weight of E	m	l	h	m	m

The fuzzy variables are calibrated by their numerical values nv as follows: $nv(l) = 1$ or 2, $nv(m) = 3$ or 4, $nv(h) = 6$ or 7, $nv(vh) = 9$ or 10.

Table 2. The Borda Count (BC) for Each Attribute

	EE1	EE2	EE3	EE4	EE5	BC_k	w_k
Weight of A	1	1	6	1	4	13	0.107
Weight of B	4	1	2	1	6	14	0.116
Weight of C	6	9	10	7	6	38	0.314
Weight of D	10	6	3	9	9	37	0.306
Weight of E	4	1	6	4	4	19	0.157

The resulting Borda order of the attributes, automatically given by the voting procedure, is: $< CDEBA >$. It means that attribute C (*abstract*) is more important (relevant) than all the others. But what is most important, the procedure also provides the rating, namely 38, 37, 19, 14, and 13, and weights $\frac{13}{121} = 0.107$, $\frac{14}{121} = 0.116$, and so on. These weights, as said above, are used as steps 4 and 5 of the suggested algorithm.

4   Case Study: Classification of Conference Abstracts

The method has been used for classifying the abstracts of 412 submissions to the XXIX National Spanish Meeting of Statistics and Operations Research and III Public Statistics Journeys (SEIO 2006). Each submission has been between 70 and 600 words with average 350. The method has permitted to classify the submitted abstracts into 72 sections. It has worked in five steps: First, it identified (a) the set of five attributes characterizing the documents, (namely, *title, key-words, abstract, bibliography,* and *authors' bio*); (b) the set of 72 categories predefined by experts (for example, Mathematical Programming, Scheduling,

Graph Theory, Game Theory, Sampling, Probability) and (c) the sets of classifying words and expressions in each category, each category's set between 7 and
50 words with average 20.

Second, the algorithm automatically computed the fitness value f_{ij}^k of document i to category j with respect to attribute k; here the simple relation has
been used:

$$f_{ij}^k = \min\{1, \frac{g_{ij}^k}{\alpha_j^k}\} \tag{3}$$

where g_{ij}^k is the number of words in attribute k of document i common with
classifying words in category j; α_j^k is the number of classifying words such that
their presence in any document in attribute k is sufficient to classify such a document into category j with maximum fitness equal 1 (these values are predefined
by experts). For example, consider attribute $k = abstract$ of a document $i = i^*$,
and assume that α_j^k is defined to be 5, then if four words in k are found common
to the classifying words of category j it implies that fitness $f_{ij}^k = 0.8$. Another
example: if the attribute $k = title$ and $\alpha_j^k = 1$ then any document with at least
one classifying word of category j in its title attains $f_{ij}^k = 1$.

At the third step, using the set of decision rules of *if-then* type and the Borda
voting method, described above, the algorithm breaks ties by defining weights
(relative importance) v_j of categories and weights w_k of attributes which are linguistic variables reduced to magnitudes in interval $[0, 1]$. The fourth step defined
the complete fitness f_{ij} of each document i to category j, by using formula (1).
The fifth step finally distributed the documents among the categories using the
standard cluster-analysis algorithm aimed to maximize the total classification
quality, which, in our case, was the total fitness of available documents to their
assigned categories given by formula (2), under predetermined constraints on
the cardinality of category sets.

Two diagrams representing the quality of classification $F(C)$ (in %) are presented in Fig. 1. The first diagram represents $F(C)$ as a function of the different
strategies (each strategy is defined by a characteristic set of fixed α_j^k-values). In
our study, we selected α_j^k to be a constant, $\alpha_j^k = \alpha$ for all j, k, and the five strategies corresponded to the α-values 3, 5, 7, 10 and 12 words, respectively, with the
size S of the classifying sets equal to 50 words. The second diagram represents
$F(C)$ as a function of different sizes of the classifying sets (from 40 to 80 words)
for a fixed value $\alpha = 7$. The white column in each column series corresponds
to the automatic classification using all five attributes ($K = 5$), the black one
takes into account only two attributes *title* and *key words* ($K = 2$), and the grey
one corresponds to evaluations using attribute *title* only ($K = 1$). Notice that
in the case of $K = 1$, the corresponding values of α_j^1 for attribute *title* are small
(usually, 1, 2 or 3), which implies that the experimental average values f_{ij}^1 are
to be about 0.85. However, in fact, the total fitness $F(C)$ for $K = 1$ has been
observed between 7% and 15% (see Fig. 1), due to the presence of attribute's
weight, w_1, which is about 0.1 in our experiments.

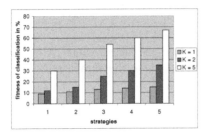 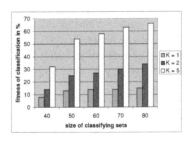

Fig. 1. Fitness of the classification (by different strategies and by different size of classifying sets)

5   Conclusions

We presented a new method for the classification of documents using the fuzzy logic. The semantic grading of linguistic variables permits to better use experts knowledge. This method has been verified for the case of the allocation of submitted abstracts into pre-assigned categories (sections of a national conference). In our future research, we intend to apply our automatic classification method to other document databases and compare it with other classification methods.

Acknowledgements

The authors wish to thank the SEIO 2006 organizers and the Spanish Statistics and Operations Research Society for providing the input data for the case study. The authors are also very grateful to Professors Paolo Rosso and Mikhail Alexandrov for their valuable comments. This work has been partially supported by the Spanish Government Research Projects DPI2001-2715-C02-02, MTM2004-07550 and MTM2006-10170, which are helped by the European Funds of Regional Development. The first author gratefully acknowledges the partial support by the Spanish Ministry of Education and Science, grant SAB2005-0161.

References

[1] Alcaide, D.: Ranking of ecological risks related to wastewater management. In: Zaidi, M.K. (ed.) Wastewater Reuse - Risk Assessment, Decision-Making and Environmental Security. Proceedings of the NATO Advanced Research Workshop, Istanbul, Turkey, 12-16 (October 2006). NATO Science for Peace and Security Series, Springer, Heidelberg (2007)

[2] Alexandrov, M., Gelbukh, A., Makagonov, P.: Some keyword-based characteristics for evaluation of thematic structure of multidisciplinary documents. In: Proc. of Intern. Conf. CICLing'2000 (2000)

[3] Alexandrov, M., Gelbukh, A., Rosso, P.: An approach to clustering abstracts, Lecture Notes in Computer Science, 3513. In: Montoyo, A., Muñoz, R., Métais, E. (eds.) NLDB 2005. LNCS, vol. 3513, pp. 275–285. Springer, Heidelberg (2005)

[4] Cortes, C., Vapnik, V.: Support vector networks. Machine learning 20, 273–297 (1995)

[5] Craven, M., DiPasquo, D., Freitag, D., McCallum, A., Mitchell, T., Nigam, K., Slattery, S.: Learning to extract symbolic knowledge from the World Wide Web. In: Proceedings of the Fifteenth National Conference on Artificial Intellligence (AAAI-98), pp. 509–516 (1994)

[6] Garcia-Lapresta, J.L., Martinez-Panero, M.: A fuzzy Borda count in multi-person decisin making. In: Trzaskalik, T., Michnik, J. (eds.) Multiple objective and goal programming: Recent Developments, Springer, Heidelberg (2002)

[7] Han, E.S., Karypis, G., Kumar, V.: Text categorization using weight adjusted k-nearest neighbour classification, Lecture Notes in Computer Science, Springer, 2035, 53-65pp. In: Cheung, D., Williams, G.J., Li, Q. (eds.) PAKDD 2001. LNCS (LNAI), vol. 2035, pp. 53–65. Springer, Heidelberg (2001)

[8] Lang, K.: Newsweeder: Learning to filter netnews. In: Machine Learning: Proceedings of the Twelfth International Conference (ICML '95), pp. 331–339 (1995)

[9] Levis, D., Ringuette, M.: A comparison of two learning algorithms for text classification.In: the 3rd Symposium on Document Analysis and Information Retrieval, pp. 81–93 (1994)

[10] Levner, E., Alcaide, D., Benayahu, Y.: Environmental risk ranking: Theory and applications for emergency planning. Scientific Israel - Technological Advantages 8(1-2), 11–21 (2006)

[11] Mahdavi, I., Sharma, R.R.K., Amiri, Z.R.: Formulation for web document classification: transforming the quadratic problem into 0-1 integer linear. International Journal of Digital Management 1 (1), 63–70 (2006)

[12] Makagonov, P., Alexandrov, M., Gelbukh, A.: Selection of typical documents in a document flow. In: Mastorakis, N., Kluev, V.(eds.) Advances in Communications and Software Technologies, pp. 197–202, WSEAS Press (2002) ISBN 960-8052-71-8

[13] Mamdani, E.H: Application of fuzzy logic to approximate reasoning using linguistic synthesis. IEEE Transactions on Computers C-26(12), 1182–1191 (1977)

[14] MATLAB 2005, Fuzzy logic toolbox user's guide The MathWorks, Inc (2005)

[15] Pazzani, M.J., Muramatsu, J., Billsus, D.: Syskill and Webert: Identifying interesting Web sites. In: Proceedings of the 13 National Conference on Artificial Intelligence, pp. 54–56 (1996)

[16] Stein, B.: Meyer zu Eissen, S. In: Günter, A., Kruse, R., Neumann, B. (eds.) KI 2003. LNCS (LNAI), vol. 2821, pp. 254–266. Springer, Heidelberg (2003)

[17] Stein, B., Niggemann, O.: On the nature of structure and its identification. In: Widmayer, P., Neyer, G., Eidenbenz, S. (eds.) WG 1999. LNCS, vol. 1665, pp. 122–134. Springer, Heidelberg (1999)

[18] Yang, Y., Pedersen, J.P.: Feature selection in statistical learning of text categorization. In: Proceedings of the Fourteenth International Conference on Machine Learning, pp. 412–420 (1997)

Approximate String Matching Techniques for Effective CLIR Among Indian Languages

Ranbeer Makin, Nikita Pandey, Prasad Pingali, and Vasudeva Varma

International Institute of Information Technology,
Hyderabad, India
{ranbeer,nikita}@students.iiit.ac.in, {pvvpr,vv}@iiit.ac.in

Abstract. Commonly used vocabulary in Indian language documents found on the web contain a number of words that have Sanskrit, Persian or English origin. However, such words may be written in different scripts with slight variations in spelling and morphology. In this paper we explore approximate string matching techniques to exploit this situation of relatively large number of cognates among Indian languages, which are higher when compared to an Indian language and a non-Indian language. We present an approach to identify cognates and make use of them for improving dictionary based CLIR when the query and documents both belong to two different Indian languages. We conduct experiments using a Hindi document collection and a set of Telugu queries and report the improvement due to cognate recognition and translation.

Keywords: Telugu-Hindi CLIR, Indian Languages, Cognate Identification.

1 Introduction

India is a multi-language, multi-script country with 22 official languages and 11 written script forms. About a billion people use these languages as their first language. A huge amount of regional news and cultural information is usually found on the web in these languages and is inaccessible to people of other regions within the country. Information access technologies such as Cross-Language Information Retrieval (CLIR) across various Indian languages remain largely unexplored. All previous CLIR research involving Indian languages were conducted in combination with English. For example, ACM TALIP[1] conducted a surprise language exercise in 2003, which focused on CLIR systems to retrieve Hindi documents for the given English queries. Similarly, ad-hoc CLIR evaluation tasks were conducted at CLEF[2] in 2006 to evaluate systems' performance to retrieve English documents for a given set of Hindi and Telugu queries[1]. Most of the Indian language texts in the print and online media have a number of words that have

---

[1] ACM Transactions on Asian Language Information Processing.
[2] Cross Language Evaluation Forum. *http://www.clef-campaign.org*

F. Masulli, S. Mitra, and G. Pasi (Eds.): WILF 2007, LNAI 4578, pp. 430–437, 2007.

originated from Sanskrit, Persian and English. While in many cases one might argue that such occurrences do not belong to an Indian language, the frequency of such usage indicates a wide acceptance of these foreign language words as Indian language words. In many cases these words are also morphologically altered as per the Indian language morphological rules to generate new variant words. We treat all such words which have a common origin as *cognates* and study how we can use approximate string matching techniques to the problem of CLIR. An example of a cognate pair for the word 'school' in English, across Indian languages is 'विद्यालय' (pronounced as 'vidyaalaya') in Hindi and 'విద్యాలయము ' (pronounced as 'vidyaalayamu') in Telugu, both of which are derived from Sanskrit. In this paper we particularly attempt to exploit the similarity among various Indian language words, which may share relatively more number of cognates when compared to an Indian language and another non-Indian language.

Some of the traditional approaches to perform query translation for CLIR include machine translation (MT), parallel or comparable corpus and machine-readable bilingual dictionary. MT and parallel corpus based approaches do not work well, in general, for CLIR [2,3][4]. Bilingual dictionaries generally contain more verbose definitions with examples which are not very suitable for retrieval. An IR system needs only direct translation of each search term [2]. In general, proper names and technical terms are absent in these dictionaries used by CLIR systems. Also, a bilingual dictionary has a greater coverage of source language words compared to that of target language. Thus, using only a bilingual dictionary approach can miss out on some of the words of the target language that might have been present in the documents. These issues of CLIR also apply in Indian language to Indian language (IL-IL) information retrieval scenario. As Indian languages exhibit significant similarity in vocabulary, we incorporate cognate identification technique in addition to using a bilingual dictionary.

Cognate identification has been found to be useful in aligning sentences [5], aligning words [6], and in translation lexicons induction [7,8]. In CLIR, Pirkola et al. [9] extracted similar terms between English and Spanish from a bilingual dictionary to assist in automatic rule generation for translation, and many studies similar to these exist in closely related languages. However, no such studies exist to study the effect of cognates in CLIR when the documents are to be retrieved from one Indian language for a given query in a different Indian language. In this paper we conduct some experiments in this direction and explore some approximate string matching techniques and their performance in the context of Indian language CLIR.

The paper is organized as follows. Section 2 gives a detailed description of the Indian language to Indian language CLIR system architecture. In Section 3 we describe the evaluation framework of our system and experimental setup, and in Section 4 we present the results of our experiments. Finally, in Section 5, we discuss the future work and conclude.

2 Indian Language CLIR System Architecture

In this paper, we report an Indian language - Indian language information retrieval system which takes a query in one Indian language (IL1) and retrieves
documents of another Indian language (IL2). The high-level architecture of this
system is depicted in Figure 1. The user issues a query in IL1 which is tokenized

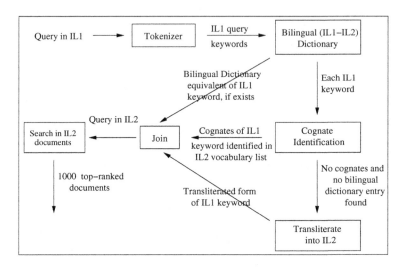

Fig. 1. High-level architectural view of Indian language - Indian language CLIR system

into keywords. These query keywords are then looked up in IL1-IL2 bilingual
dictionary to get the corresponding IL2 keywords.

The IL1 query keywords are also searched for their corresponding cognates
in IL2. For this we first extract words from an IL2 corpus to have a reasonably
good vocabulary of IL2. For each query keyword in IL1, the IL2 vocabulary list
is searched to identify its cognates. We hypothesize that the likelihood of the
two words across a pair of Indian languages to be cognates is highly correlated
with their orthographic similarity. Hence we use the string similarity metrics for
cognate identification. In this work, we make use of the *Jaro-Winkler* similarity
[10][11], which adjusts the weights of pairs s, t that share a common prefix to give
them more favorable score; the *Levenstein* distance, which is a string similarity
measure, defined as the minimum cost needed to convert a string s into another
string t; and the *Longest Common Subsequence Ratio*, or LCSR [5] which takes
the ratio of the longest common subsequence of pairs s, t to the length of the
longest string amongst the two.

Jaro-Winkler's similarity score is computed as follows:

$$JaroWinkler(s,t) = Jaro(s,t) + \left(\frac{P}{10} * (1.0 - Jaro(s,t)) \right)$$

$$Jaro(s,t) = \frac{1}{3} \left(\frac{|s\prime|}{|s|} + \frac{|t\prime|}{|t|} + \frac{|s\prime| - T_{s\prime,t\prime}}{2|s\prime|} \right)$$

where P: length of common prefix; s, t: input strings; $s\prime$: characters in s that are common with t; $t\prime$: characters in t that are common with s; $T_{s\prime,t\prime}$: number of transpositions of characters in $s\prime$ relative to $t\prime$.
And LCSR is defind as:

$$LCSR(s,t) = \frac{|LCS(s,t)|}{\max(|s|, |t|)}$$

where $LCS(s,t)$ is the longest common subsequence in strings s and t.

Since the scripts of IL1 and IL2 may differ, our cognate identification technique performs a phonetically motivated comparison of IL1 and IL2 words using the above mentioned orthographic similarity functions. This phonetic based approach allows matching to be carried out across any pair of two scripts.

The keywords, for which no bilingual dictionary equivalents and no cognates are identified, are transliterated into IL2 using a pre-determined set of mapping rules between the two scripts. The combined query resulting from all these three steps, viz. bilingual dictionary look-up, cognate identification, and transliteration, is then used to retrieve the IL2 documents using the full-featured text search engine, *Lucene*[3].The result set of documents obtained is ranked according to Lucene′s scoring criterion from which only 1000 highest-ranked documents are collected.

3   Experiments

The experiments were carried out on the two Indian languages, Hindi and Telugu. The choice of the above two languages was made because of the availability of the resources, and to ease the relevance judgment and manual translation tasks. As Hindi and Telugu are quite different in nature and the cognate identification technique is independent of the languages used, our system can work across any pair of Indian languages. The document collection for our experiments comprised of around 50,000 electronic news articles (in Hindi) published during 2003 and 2006 by the *BBC Hindi* and *Navbharat Times* websites[4]. These documents covered various domains including politics, sports, science and entertainment. The test set consisted of 50 Telugu queries framed by the native Telugu speakers, based on the guidelines that the queries should be related to the events occurred during 2003 and 2006, and should belong to the above mentioned domains.

Evaluation Framework. We used Cranfield evaluation methodology to assess the performance of our Indian Language CLIR system. Relevance judgment was manually performed by the native Hindi speakers, for which the Telugu test queries had to be translated into Hindi. These Hindi speakers were different from the people who came up with the test set.

---

[3] Text Search Engine Lucene - *http://lucene.apache.org/*
[4] *http://www.bbc.co.uk/hindi/* and *http://navbharattimes.indiatimes.com/*

Setup. In our work, we experimented with the Jaro-Winkler, Levenstein distance and LCSR similarity measures individually to identify cognates. The binary classification of cognates was done with an empirically chosen threshold[5]. The list of potential Telugu-Hindi cognate pairs thus obtained was sorted in the descending order of the scores assigned by the similarity functions. We believe that the true cognates will occur more frequently towards the top of the sorted list and decrease in frequency as we descend this list. Based on this belief, we introduced the notion of *window size*, which defines the number of cognates to be taken for every Telugu keyword. The experiments were conducted with window size varying from 1 to 10, where the maximum limit was empirically chosen.

Experiments were performed with six models, where the first three models (Jaro-Winkler, LCSR, and Levenstein) are based on orthographic similarity, and perform cross-language retrieval exclusively on the basis of cognates identified. The last three models combine the bilingual dictionary approach with each of the cognate identification techniques. To compare the performance of our system, two baseline methods were chosen, the upper baseline being the monolingual performance of our system and the lower one being the bilingual dictionary[6] method.

4 Results

We evaluated our experimental results on 11-point interpolated recall - precision averages [12], mean average precision (MAP), geometric average precision (GAP), and recall using standard *trec-eval*. Baseline-1 is the monolingual performance of the system and Baseline-2 is the bilingual dictionary approach. Model-1 is based on only the cognate identification approach using Jaro-Winkler similarity. Similarly, Model-2 corresponds to LCSR, and Model-3 to Levenstein distance. Model-4 to Model-6 combine bilingual dictionary approach with Model-1 to Model-3 respectively. In this section, we compare the six different models and analyze the performance of our CLIR system with each of these models. We then discuss the effect of varying window size on the performance of a model.

Comparisons. The Hindi monolingual run retrieved relevant documents for all the 50 queries. However, relevant documents were retrieved by only 72% (36) of the queries in the cross-lingual run using Baseline-2. Table 1 compares recall, MAP, and GAP of six different models for window size 3 (the performance of our system was comparatively better on this window size) with the baselines on the test set of 50 Telugu queries.

Surprisingly, impressive results are achieved with the cognate techniques alone. Cross-lingual retrieval based only on the cognates identified using Jaro-Winkler similarity shows an increase of 51.67% in MAP and 162.5% in GAP on comparison with Baseline-2, with only a slight decrease of 11.2% in recall.

---

[5] Thresholds chosen were 0.90 for Jaro-Winkler, and 0.85 for Levenstein and LCSR.

[6] Telugu-Hindi bilingual dictionary *http://ltrc.iiit.net/onlineServices/Dictionaries/ Tel-Hin_DictDwnld.html*

Table 1. Comparison of recall, MAP, and GAP for all the models on window size 3 and the baselines

	Baseline-1	Baseline-2	Model-1	Model-2	Model-3	Model-4	Model-5	Model-6
Recall	0.9907	0.6059	0.5381	0.4865	0.4479	0.6875	0.6628	0.6418
MAP	0.5611	0.1647	0.2498	0.1976	0.1692	0.2771	0.2449	0.2074
GAP	0.4133	0.0048	0.0126	0.0042	0.0023	0.0263	0.0186	0.0113

Table 1 also strongly suggests that combining the bilingual dictionary approach with the cognate identification techniques in Indian language - Indian language scenario yields more effective results than using these approaches individually. This is not unexpected as the drawbacks of taking only the dictionary approach, as mentioned in Section 1, are solved to a good extent by using cognates. Similarly, only cognate techniques do not perform as well as the combined approaches since there is a possibility that cognate pairs can have different meanings. Also due to partial overlap in the vocabulary of Indian languages, cognates may not necessarily exist for every word. These drawbacks are by and large compensated by the use of bilingual dictionary.

Even among the combined approaches, dictionary with Jaro-Winkler similarity computation shows better performance than the other two combined approaches. Using this Model-4, on an average, only 84% (42) of the queries retrieved relevant documents. 78.57% (33) of these 42 queries performed better

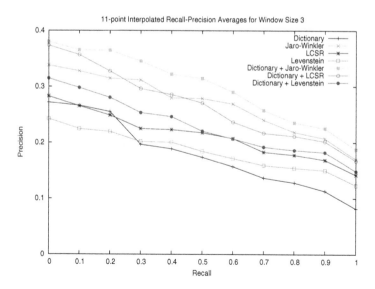

Fig. 2. 11-point interpolated recall precision curves for all the models on window size 3. X-axis represents various recall levels and Y-axis represents interpolated precision at these levels.

with this model in terms of recall and average precisions than with Baseline-2. We believe that good cognates couldn't be found for the keywords in the remaining 21.43% (9) of the queries, and hence the performance deteriorated. Out of the 14 queries for which Baseline-2 could not retrieve relevant documents, on an average Model-4 succeeded in retrieving for 50% of them. For window size 3, we observe that this model leads to a significant increase of 68.25% in MAP, 447.92% in GAP and 13.45% in recall on comparison with Baseline-2. However, its performance is still lower by 30.60% in recall, 50.61% in MAP, and 93.64% in GAP when compared with Baseline-1. This is very much expected as the monolingual retrieval performance is generally acknowledged as the practical limit.

Figure 2 gives a more detailed comparison of the effectiveness of the models on test queries for window size 3, in the form of 11-point interpolated recall-precision curves. These curves confirm to our findings above. The variations in the results obtained on varying the similarity measures are highly correlated to how well the cognates are identified by these measures.

Window Size Variation. Table 2 shows the effect of variations in window size on the combined apporach of dictionary and LCSR. We notice that significant

Table 2. Effect of varying window size from 1 to 10 on recall, MAP, and GAP using the bilingual dictionary approach with LCSR

Window Size	1	2	3	4	5	6	7	8	9	10
Recall	0.6860	0.6512	0.6628	0.6574	0.6767	0.6744	0.6775	0.6775	0.6775	0.6775
MAP	0.2313	0.2439	0.2449	0.2435	0.2336	0.2354	0.2387	0.2405	0.2404	0.2414
GAP	0.0168	0.0167	0.0186	0.0173	0.0188	0.0189	0.0213	0.0212	0.0211	0.021

variations in recall, MAP, and GAP occur when the window size is varied from 1 to 3. The variations in these measures decrease as the window size is further varied from 4 to 6. On any further increase in the window size, we observe that the variations become more or less constant. This suggests that the maximum number of true cognates get identified within window size 3, which confirms to our belief that true cognates occur near the top of the sorted cognate pairs list. Similar behavior is observed for other models as well.

5   Conclusion and Future Work

We came up with an Indian language - Indian language IR system, which exploits the significant overlap in vocabulary across the Indian languages. We identified cognates using some of the well-known similarity measures, and incorporated this technique with the traditional bilingual dictionary approach. The effectiveness of our retrieval system was compared on various models. The results show that using cognates with the existing dictionary approach leads to a significant increase in the performance of our system. Experiments have also led to the surprise finding that our Indian Language CLIR system based only on the cognates approach performs better, on an average, than the dictionary approach alone. This shows a good promise for cross-lingual retrieval across those pairs of related languages for which bilingual dictionaries do not exist.

In the future, we would like to measure the degree of similarity among other Indian languages with our CLIR system. We would also like to extend our system to perform cross-lingual retrieval across those pairs of Indian languages which have a little overlap between their vocabularies, but are significantly related to some third Indian language.

References

1. Pingali, P., Varma, V.: Hindi and Telugu to English Cross Language Information Retrieval at CLEF 2006. In: Working Notes of Cross Language Evaluation Forum 2006 (2006)
2. Hull, D., Grefenstette, G.: Querying across languages: A dictionary-based approach to multilingual information retrieval. In: Proceedings of the 19th Annual international ACM SIGIR 1996, Zurich, Switzerland, pp. 49–57 (1996)
3. Radwan, K., Fluhr, C.: Textual database lexicon used as a filter to resolve semantic ambiguity application on multilingual information retrieval. In: The 4th Symp. on Document Analysis and Information Retrieval, pp. 121–136 (1995)
4. Adriani, M., Croft, W.: The effectiveness of a dictionary-based technique for indonesion-english cross-language text retrieval. CLIR Technical Report IR-170 (1997)
5. Melamed, I.D.: Bitext maps and alignment via pattern recognition. Computational Linguistics 25(1), 107–130 (1999)
6. Tiedmann, J.: Combining clues for word alignment. In: Proceedings of the 10th Conference of the European Chapter of the ACL (EACL'03) (2003)
7. Koehn, P., Knight, K.: Knowledge sources for word-level translation models. In: Proceedings of the Conference on Empirical Methods in Natural Language Processing, pp. 27–35 (2001)
8. Mann, G.S., Yarowsky, D.: Multipath translation lexicon induction via bridge languages. In: Proceedings of NAACL 2001, pp. 151–158 (2001)
9. Pirkola, A., Toivonen, J., Keskustalo, H., Visala, K., Jarvelin, K.: Fuzzy translation of cross-lingual spelling variants. In: Proceedings of SIGIR'03, pp. 345–352 (2003)
10. Jaro, M.: Probabilistic linkage of large public health data files. Statistics in Medicine 14, 491–498 (1995)
11. Winkler, W.: The state record linkage and current research problems. Technical report, statistics of Income Division, Internal Revenue Service Publication (1999)
12. Manning, C.D., Schutze, H.: Foundations of Statistical Natural Language Processing. MIT Press, Cambridge (2001)

Using Translation Heuristics to Improve a Multimodal and Multilingual Information Retrieval System

Miguel Ángel García-Cumbreras, Maria Teresa Martín-Valdivia,
Luis Alfonso Ureña-López, Manuel Carlos Díaz-Galiano,
and Arturo Montejo-Ráez

University of Jaén. Departamento de Informática
Grupo Sistemas Inteligentes de Acceso a la Información
Campus Las Lagunillas, Ed. A3, E-23071, Jaén, Spain
{magc,maite,laurena,mcdiaz,amontejo}@ujaen.es

Abstract. Nowadays, the multimodal nature of the World Wide Web is an evidence. Web sites which include video files, pictures, music and text have become widespread. Furthermore, multimodal collections in several languages demand to apply multilingual information retrieval strategies. This paper describes a new retrieval technique applied on a multimodal and multilingual system that have been tested on two different multilingual image collections. The system applies several machine translators and implements some novel heuristics. These heuristics explore a variety of ways to combine the translations obtained from the given set of translators, and the configuration of the retrieval model by using different weighting functions, and also studying the effect of *pseudo-relevance feedback* (PRF) on this domain. Our results show interesting effects by these variations, allowing the determination of the parameters for the best retrieval model on this data and reporting the loss in performance on each language.

1 Introduction

Human communication is intrinsically multimodal, exchanging information on several media: text, audio, image or video. With the advances of technology, current communication systems are become increasingly multimodal. Content-Based Multimedia Information Retrieval (CBMIR) provides new paradigms and methods for searching on this multimodal information. Furthermore, multimodal collections that include several languages are creating the necessity of applying multilingual information retrieval strategies. The retrieval of information on these systems involves the use of the text associated to any piece of information, no matter its format, in order to provide a response to a textual query.

As a cross-language retrieval task, a multilingual image retrieval based on query translation can achieve high performance. The ad-hoc task involves the

F. Masulli, S. Mitra, and G. Pasi (Eds.): WILF 2007, LNAI 4578, pp. 438–446, 2007.

retrieval of relevant images using the text associated to each image query. This paper describes a new retrieval technique applied on a multimodal and multilingual system that works with several translators combined using different heuristics.

Given a multilingual query, the main goal is to find as many relevant images as possible from a given image collection. In our experiments, we have used the collections supplied by the CLEF[1] organization in order to accomplish the ImageCLEF[2] task. The CLEF (Cross-Language Evaluation Forum) campaign is an international meeting whose purpose is to organize a competition to evaluate different multilingual systems. Furthermore, the ImageCLEF task (the cross-language image retrieval track) includes a multimodal collection and runs as part of CLEF. Specifically, we have used two different image collections: the St. Andrews collection of historic photographs and the IAPR TC-12 image collection.

Documents in the collection are in English but the textual queries include several languages: nine different languages for the St. Andrews collection (English, Dutch, Italian, Spanish, French, German, Danish, Swedish and Russian) and seven languages for the IARP collection (Dutch, English, French, German, Italian, Portuguese and Spanish). The collections have been preprocessed using stop-words removal and the Porter's stemmer algorithm for suffix stripping. Certain tags have been selected as relevant to this task. The collections have been indexed using the LEMUR[3] Information Retrieval (IR) system. We have translated all queries into English before passing them to the IR system.

We have also developed a new translation module which combines a set of Machine Translators following some heuristics. These heuristics are, for instance, the use of the translation made by the translator by default, a combination with the translations of every translator, or a combination of the words with a higher punctuation (i.e. those words appearing in all translations get one point, and two points for those appearing in the default translation).

The proposal of this paper is to compare results with and without pseudo-relevant feedback, with or without query expansion, using different methods of query translation or using different retrieval models and weighting functions.

The paper is organized as follows. First, we present our framework and we introduce briefly the image collections used. Then, we describe the experiments accomplished and we show the results obtained. Finally, we present our conclusions and plans for future research.

2   Experimentation Framework

Our system, applied on a multimodal and multilingual environment, works with several translators combined using different heuristics.

---

[1] http://www.clef-campaign.org/
[2] http://ir.shef.ac.uk/imageclef/
[3] Available at http://www.lemurproject.org/

2.1   Collections Description

We have used two different image collections to accomplish the experiment. The first one is the St. Andrews collection of historic photographs. The St. Andrews collection contains 28,133 historic photographs provided by St. Andrews University Library[4][1], which holds one of the most important collections of historic photography in Scotland. Most of the photographs are in black and white and were taken by Scottish photographers or Scottish photographer companies. All of images in St. Andrews collection have associated textual captions written in British English. The captions consist of 8 fields including title, photographer, location, date and one or more pre-defined categories (all manually assigned by domain experts). Figure 1a shows a sample image with its corresponding annotation.

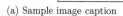

Short title: Rev Willian Swan.
Long title: Rev William Swan.
Location: fife, Scotland
Description: Seated, 3/4 face studio portrait of a man.
Date: ca.1850
Photographer: Thomas Rodger
Categories: [ministers][identified male][dress - clerical]
Notes: ALB6-85-2 jf/ pcBIOG: Rev William Swan ( ) ADD: Former owners of album: A Govan then J J? Lowson. Individuals and other subjects indicative of St Andrews provenance. By T. R. as identified by Karen A. Johnstone " Thomas Rodger 1832-1883. A biography and catalogue of selected works".

(a) Sample image caption

(b) Sample topic with title: "Woman in white dress"

Fig. 1. Samples from St. Andrews collection

We have used 28 topics with this collection. Each topic consists of a short sentence or phrase describing the search request in a few words (title), and a description of what constitutes a relevant or non-relevant image for that search request (narrative). Both topic title and narratives have been translated into the following languages: German, French, Italian, Spanish (European), Spanish (Latin American), Chinese (Simplified), Chinese (Traditional) and Japanese. Translations have also been produced for the titles only and these are available in 25 languages including Russian, Croatian, Bulgarian, Hebrew and Norwegian. All translations have been provided by native speakers and verified by at least another native speaker. Figure 1b shows a sample of a topic.

Colour information, which typically plays an important role in CBIR, is ineffective due to the nature of the St. Andrews collection (historic photographs). Also unlike typical CBIR benchmarks, the images in the St. Andrews collection are very complex containing both objects in the foreground and background which prove indistinguishable to CBIR methods. There are obvious limitations

---

[4] http://www-library.st-andrews.ac.uk/

with the existing collection: mainly black and white images, domain-specific vocabulary used in associated captions, restricted retrieval scenario (i.e. searches for historic photographs) and experiments with limited target language (English) are only possible (i.e. we cannot test further bilingual pairs). To address these issues and widen the image collections available to ImageCLEF participants, the organizers replaced the database in 2006 by a new collection of images from a personal photographic collection with associated textual descriptions in other languages, in addition to English. This new collection is the IAPR TC-12 image collection.

The IAPR TC-12 Benchmark was created under Technical Committee 12 of the International Association of Pattern Recognition (IAPR[5]). This image collection consists of 20,000 images taken from locations around the world and comprising a varying cross-section of still natural images. It includes pictures of a range of sports, actions, photographs of people, animals, cities, landscapes and many other aspects of contemporary life. The collection contains many different images of similar visual content, but varying illumination, viewing angle and background. This makes it a challenge for the successful application of visual analysis techniques. Each image in the collection has a corresponding semi-structured caption consisting of the following seven fields: a unique *identifier*, a *title*, a free-text *description* of the semantic and visual contents of the image (what we called here *narrative*), *notes* for additional information, the *provider* of the photo, *where* the photo was taken, and *when* the photo was taken. These fields are given in English and German. Figure 2a shows a sample image with its corresponding English annotation.

In order to increase the reliability of results, a total of 60 topics was provided to participants of ImageCLEF 2006. Each original topic comprised a title (a short sentence or phrase describing the search request in a few words), and a narrative (a description of what constitutes a relevant or non-relevant image for each request). In addition, three sample images were provided with each topic in order to test relevance feedback (both manual and automatic) and query-by-example searches. The topic titles were then translated into 15 languages including German, French, Spanish, Italian, Portuguese, Dutch, Russian, Japanese, and Simplified and Traditional Chinese. All translations were provided by at least one native speaker and verified by at least one another native speaker. Figure 2b shows a sample of a topic.

2.2 Preprocessing and Translation Heuristics

For both collections, a pre-processing of documents and queries was performed using stop-words removal and the Porter's stemmer algorithm for suffix stripping [4]. Resulting documents (not queries) were indexed with the LEMUR IR System. Our main objective during these two years was to test the translation module, as detailed in experiment below.

---

[5] http://www.iapr.org/

```
<DOC>
<DOCNO>annotations/16/16019.eng</DOCNO>
<TITLE>Flamingo Beach</TITLE>
<DESCRIPTION>a photo of a brown sandy beach; the
dark blue sea with small breaking waves behind
it; a dark green palm tree in the foreground on
the left; a blue sky with clouds on the horizon
in the background;
</DESCRIPTION>
<NOTES>Original name in Portuguese: "Praia do
Flamengo"; Flamingo Beach is considered as one
of the most beautiful beaches of Brazil;</NOTES>
<LOCATION>Salvador, Brazil</LOCATION>
<DATE>2 October 2004</DATE>
<IMAGE>images/16/16019.jpg</IMAGE>
<THUMBNAIL>thumbnails/16/16019.jpg</THUMBNAIL>
</DOC>
```

```
<top>
<num> Number: 14 </num>
<title> scenes of footballers in action </title>
<narr> Relevant images will show football (soccer) players in
a game situation during a match. Images with footballers that
are not playing (e.g. players posing for a group photo, warming
up before the game, celebrating after a game, sitting on the
bench, and during the half-time break) are not relevant. Images
with people not playing football (soccer) bur a different code
(American Football, Australian Football, Rugby Union, Rugby
Leage, Gaelic Football, Canadian Football, International Rules
Football, etc.) or some other sport are not relevant.
</narr>
<image> images/31/31609.jpg </image>
<image> images/31/31673.jpg </image>
<image> images/32/32467.jpg </image>
</top>
```

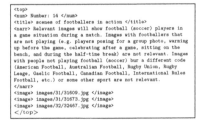

(a) Sample image caption from the IAPR TC-12 collection

(b) Sample topic with three images

Fig. 2. Samples from IAPR TC-12 collection

In the ImageCLEF 2005 evaluation forum, using the St. Andrews collection, nine languages were studied. We developed a Machine Translation Module that worked with several online machine translators to translate the queries from any language to English.

We have used some Machine Translators (in brackets the translator by default for each language):

- Epals (German and Portuguese)
- Prompt (Spanish)
- Reverso (French)
- Systran (Dutch and Italian)

The merging of translators' results has already been studied in previous research works by other authors [9,7]. In our experiments, in order to combine the translations produced by former applications, we explored the following heuristics:

- The first one is the use of the translation made by the translator by default
- The second one is a combination with the translations of every translator
- The third one is a combination of the words with a higher punctuation, where this punctuation is built using some features such as the word frequency in the translations, the named entities recognized and the translator used.

After some testing, the best heuristic was the second one and the most suitable translators were found to be Systran (for Dutch, French, German, Italian, Russian and Swedish) and Prompt (for both European and Latinoamerican Spanish).

The search space for the best set of parameters covers the use of the query title or title+narrative as final query, the weighting function to be used, such as Okapi or TFIDF, and the convenience of use of pseudo-relevance feedback (PRF). Table 1 shows a summary of experiments submitted and results obtained for all these languages [5]. The results obtained showed that in general the use of query expansion improves the results, as is displayed in Figure 3. Only one Italian experiment without query expansion got a better result. In the case of the use of only title or title + narrative, the results are not conclusive, but the use of only title seems to get better results (see figure 4 for a graphical view of this fact).

Table 1. Summary of results for the English monolingual adhoc runs and the best ones for other bilingual runs (with the Okapi weighting scheme) on the St. Andrews collection

Language	Initial Query	Expansion	MAP	% over mono.	Rank
Monolingual En(English)	title + narr	with	**0.3727**	n/a	31/70
Monolingual En(English)	title	without	0.3207	n/a	44/70
Monolingual En(English)	title	with	0.3168	n/a	45/70
Monolingual En(English)	title + narr	without	0.3135	n/a	46/70
Bilingual DeEn(German)	title	with	0.3004	58.8%	4/29
Bilingual DuEn(Dutch)	title	with	0.3397	66.5%	2/15
Bilingual FrEn(French)	title + narr	with	0.2864	56.1%	1/17
Bilingual ItEn(Italian)	title	without	0.1805	35.3%	12/19
Bilingual RuEn(Russian)	title	with	0.2229	43.6%	11/15
Bilingual SpEn(Spanish Eur)	title	with	0.2416	47.3%	5/33
Bilingual SpEn(Spanish Lat)	title	with	0.2967	58.1%	8/31
Bilingual SwEn(Swedish)	title	without	0.2074	40.6%	2/7

In 2006 the collection used was the IAPR TC-12 collection, as pointed out previously. This time a new translation module was developed, which combines the following Machine Translators and heuristics: Epals (German and Portuguese), Prompt (Spanish), Reverso (French) and Systran (Dutch and Italian). Heuristics applied are, for instance, the use of the translation made by the translator by default, a combination with the translations of every translator, or a combination of the words with a higher punctuation (scoring two points if it appears in the default translation, and one point if it appears in all of the other translations). To evaluate our framework we can summarize the results obtained at each participation of our group in the CLEF campaign.

The experiments performed over the IAPR TC-12 collection for the Image-CLEF 2006 evaluation forum show also interesting results. This time seven languages were considered in our experiments: Dutch, English, French, German, Italian, Portuguese and Spanish. In table 2, we can see the global results, for the English monolingual run and the other bilingual runs [6]. The best machine translation heuristic was the use of the translation made by the default translator (for each language pair) plus the words that appear in two or more of the other translations, obtaining the best results with pseudo-relevance feedback and Okapi a weighting function. The results show that there is a loss of MAP between the best monolingual experiment and this bilingual experiment, namely

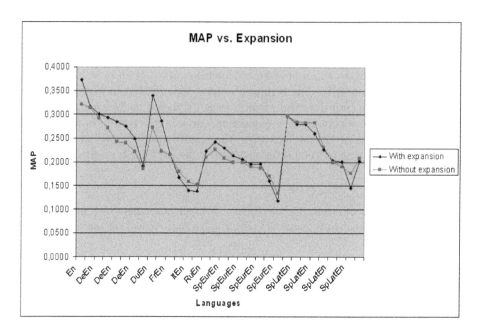

Fig. 3. Graphical view of results for different biligual experiments using the Okapi weighting scheme on the St. Andrews collection. MAP versus expansion.

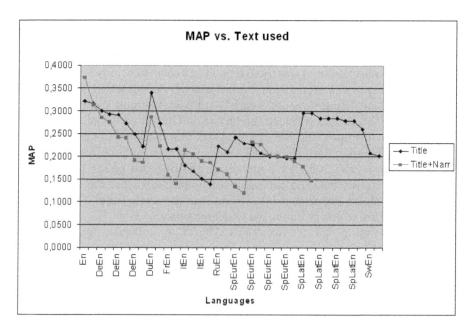

Fig. 4. Graphical view of results for different biligual experiments using the Okapi weighting scheme on the St. Andrews collection. MAP versus text used in query (title or title+narrative).

aproximately 28%. Yet, the other results in the English monolingual task are less acceptable compared to the German bilingual ones, which were found to be more robust to variations in the parametrization of the system. In general, there is a loss of precision compared to the English monolingual results. The Spanish result is the best over all bilingual experiments.

Table 2. Summary of results for the English monolingual adhoc runs and the other bilingual runs on the IAPR TC-12 corpus

Language	Initial Query	Expansion	Weight	MAP	Rank
Monolingual En(English)	title + narr	with	Okapi	**0.2234**	9/49
Monolingual En(English)	title + narr	without	Okapi	0.0845	38/49
Monolingual En(English)	title + narr	with	Tfidf	0.0846	37/49
Monolingual En(English)	title + narr	without	Tfidf	0.0823	39/49
Bilingual DeEn(German)	title + narr	with	Okapi	**0.1602**	4/8
Bilingual DeEn(German)	title + narr	without	Okapi	0.1359	7/8
Bilingual DeEn(German)	title + narr	with	Tfidf	0.1489	5/8
Bilingual DeEn(German)	title + narr	without	Tfidf	0.1369	6/8
Bilingual DuEn(Dutch)	title + narr	with	Okapi	0.1261	4/4
Bilingual FrEn(French)	title + narr	with	Okapi	0.1617	5/8
Bilingual ItEn(Italian)	title + narr	with	Okapi	0.1216	13/15
Bilingual PtEn(Portuguese)	title + narr	with	Okapi	0.0728	7/7
Bilingual SpEn(Spanish)	title + narr	with	Okapi	**0.1849**	4/7

3 Conclusions and Future Work

We have reported on our experimentation in a multimodal and multilingual environment. We have used image collections where each image has an associated text.

We have tried a new Machine Translation module. The application of some heuristics improves the bilingual results, but we consider that further study on the queries with the poorest results is needed in order to improves them. The results are quite good, but in some languages the translation is not that relevant.

Another main conclusion is that the pseudo-relevance feedback increases significantly the results, recommending its use in any case.

Our next work will be the pursuit of improvement on the results focusing on the retrieval phase, applying new techniques of query expansion (using Thesaurus or web information), investigating other heuristics for the Machine Translation module and the combination of results of the text retrieval with another module that works with image information.

Acknowledgements

This work has been partially supported by a grant from the Spanish Government, project TIMOM (TIN2006-15265-C06-03). We would like to thank the Cross-Lingual Evaluation Forum in general, and Carol Peters in particular.

References

1. Reid, N.: The photographic collections in St. Andrews University Library. Scottish Archives 5, 83–90 (1999)
2. Clough, P., Mller, H., Deselaers, T., Grubinger, M., Thomas, M.: The CLEF 2005 Cross-Language Image Retrieval Track. In: Peters, C., Gey, F.C., Gonzalo, J., Müller, H., Jones, G.J.F., Kluck, M., Magnini, B., de Rijke, M., Giampiccolo, D. (eds.) CLEF 2005. LNCS, vol. 4022, Springer, Heidelberg (2006)
3. Müller, H., Geissbhler, A., Ruch, P.: Report on the CLEF experiment: Combining image and multi-lingual search medical image retrieval. In: Peters, C., Clough, P.D., Gonzalo, J., Jones, G.J.F., Kluck, M., Magnini, B. (eds.) CLEF 2004. LNCS, vol. 3491, Springer, Heidelberg (2005)
4. Porter, M.F.: An algorithm for suffix stripping. In: Readings in information retrieval, pp. 313–316. Morgan Kaufmann Publishers, San Francisco (1997) ISBN 1-55860-454-5
5. Martín-Valdivia, M.T., García-Cumbreras, M.T., Díaz-Galiano, M.Á., Ureña-Löpez, M.C., Montejo-Ráez, A.: A.: SINAI at ImageCLEF 2005. In: Peters, C., Gey, F.C., Gonzalo, J., Müller, H., Jones, G.J.F., Kluck, M., Magnini, B., de Rijke, M., Giampiccolo, D. (eds.) CLEF 2005. LNCS, vol. 4022, Springer, Heidelberg (2006)
6. Díaz-Galiano, M.C., García-Cumbreras, M.Á., Martín-Valdivia, M.T., Montejo-Ráez, A.: Ureña-López, L.A.: SINAI at ImageCLEF 2006. In: Proceedings of the Cross Language Evaluation Forum, CLEF 2006 (2006)
7. Callison-Burch, C., Flournoy, R.: A Program for Automatically Selecting the Best Output from Multiple Machine Translation Engines. In: Proceedings of the Machine Translation Summit VIII, Santiago de Compostela, Spain (2001)
8. Gollins, T., Sanderson, M.: Improving Cross Language Retrieval with Triangulated Translation. In: SIGIR (2001)
9. Aceves-Prez, R.M., Montes-y-Gmez, M., Villaseor-Pineda, L.: Enhancing Cross-Language Question Answering by Combining Multiple Question Translations. In: Gelbukh, A. (ed.) CICLing 2007. LNCS, vol. 4394, Springer, Heidelberg (2007)
10. Dominique, L., Patrick, S., Sophie, N.: Cross lingual question answering using QRISTAL for CLEF 2005. In: Peters, C., Gey, F.C., Gonzalo, J., Müller, H., Jones, G.J.F., Kluck, M., Magnini, B., de Rijke, M., Giampiccolo, D. (eds.) CLEF 2005. LNCS, vol. 4022, Springer, Heidelberg (2006)

Ontology-Supported Text Classification Based on Cross-Lingual Word Sense Disambiguation

Dan Tufiş[1] and Svetla Koeva[2]

[1] Research Institute for Artificial Intelligence, Romanian Academy,
13, "13 Septembrie", 050711, Bucharest, Romania
[2] Institute for Bulgarian Language, Bulgarian Academy of Sciences,
52 Shipchenski prohod, 1113 Sofia, Bulgaria
tufis@racai.ro, svetla@mail.ibl.bas.bg

Abstract. The paper reports on recent experiments in cross-lingual document processing (with a case study for Bulgarian-English-Romanian language pairs) and brings evidence on the benefits of using linguistic ontologies for achieving, with a high level of accuracy, difficult tasks in NLP such as word alignment, word sense disambiguation, document classification, cross-language information retrieval, etc. We provide brief descriptions of the parallel corpus we used, the multilingual lexical ontology which supports our research, the word alignment and word sense disambiguation systems we developed and a preliminary report on an ongoing development of a system for cross-lingual text-classification which takes advantage of these multilingual technologies. Unlike the keyword-based methods in document processing, the concept-based methods are supposed to better exploit the semantic information contained in a particular document and thus to provide more accurate results.

Keywords: cross-lingual document classification, multilingual lexical ontology, parallel corpora, word alignment, word sense disambiguation.

1 Introduction

The recent advancements in corpus linguistics technologies, as well the availability of more and more textual data, demonstrated that various well established monolingual applications could achieve a higher level of accuracy when performed on parallel data. This is not surprising as human translators incorporate a great deal of linguistic and world knowledge into their translations and when this knowledge is (even partially) revealed, it represents an exceptionally useful resource for better solving challenging NLP tasks. For instance, word sense disambiguation (WSD), a very difficult task (AI-complete), has been shown to achieve superior accuracy when done on a parallel document than in a monolingual text.

This paper is organized as follows: in section 2 we introduce the parallel corpus we work with, part of a 22-languages parallel corpus, and we shortly describe the lexical ontology we rely on in processing parallel corpora. In section 3 we give

F. Masulli, S. Mitra, and G. Pasi (Eds.): WILF 2007, LNAI 4578, pp. 447–455, 2007.

an overview of the word aligning and word sense disambiguation procedures which are highly instrumental to many NLP hard problems. In section 4 we will report on an ongoing research on a concept-based document classification system. Finally, we draw some conclusions and outline future work plans.

2   JRC-Acquis and the Aligned Wordnets

Parallel corpora became recently one of the most required language resources, because they have been proved to be essential for the development of several multilingual applications such as statistical machine translation (including translation consistency checking), multilingual categorisation, extraction of multilingual dictionaries, aligning lexical ontologies, training and testing of the multilingual information extraction software and many others. JRC-Acquis [1] is a unique parallel corpus as far as the number of languages contained (22 languages) and size of the monolingual texts (an average of more than 9 million words per languages).

An additional feature of the JRC-Acquis is the fact that most texts have been manually classified into subject domains according to the EUROVOC thesaurus, which is a classification system with over 6000 hierarchically organised classes. The JRC-Acquis parallel corpus was sentence aligned for all the language pairs (210) and it is a public resource (http://wt.jrc.it/lt/acquis/), already at the version 2.2. Although the number of documents in individual languages is almost 20,000, the JRC-Acquis distribution contains a subset of the Acquis Communautaire documents because not all the existing documents are translated in all the languages. We recently created a trilingual corpus (Bg-En-Ro) containing 16291 files in Bulgarian, 7972 in English and 18291 in Romanian. The set of English documents was extracted from JRC-Acquis version 2, while the documents for Bulgarian and Romanian were downloaded from the CCVISTA server of the Technical Assistance Information Exchange Office in Brussels. The number of documents available in all three languages was 7420. We extracted various statistics from each file for all three languages and we eliminated the documents the statics of which did not correlate in the three languages. We took into account the number of paragraphs and words. The number disparities occurred because in the JRC-Acquis the annexes were eliminated while on the CCVISTA server, the documents are complete. So, we automatically filtered out the Ro and Bg documents that, unlike the En documents, included the annexes. The final number of retained documents was 4880. Table 1 displays quantitative information for the trilingual parallel corpus, before and after the correlation filtering.

Table 1. Bg-En-Ro parallel corpus before (B) and after (A) filtering

Language	Bg(B)	En(B)	Ro(B)	Bg(A)	En(A)	Ro(A)
docs	7420	7420	7420	4880	4880	4880
pars	775504	446020	820569	357654	299486	348168
words	9747796	88821220	9844904	5849462	6046003	5784323

The Romanian and Bulgarian documents were available in MS Word format and we converted them in the xml TEI format of the JRC distribution (Fig. 1). The parallel documents of our sub-corpus were sentence aligned, tokenized, lem-

```
   - <bibl>                                         - <bibl>
     Downloaded from                                  Downloaded from
       <xref url="http://ccvista.taiex.be/Fulcrum/C     <xref url="http://ccvista.taiex.be/Fulcrum/CCVista/bg/42002I
         ro.doc</xref>                                     bg.doc</xref>
     on                                               on
       <date>2005-09</date>                             <date>2006-09-11</date>
     </bibl>                                          </bibl>
   </sourceDesc>                                    </sourceDesc>
 </fileDesc>                                       </fileDesc>
 - <profileDesc>                                   - <profileDesc>
   - <textClass>                                     - <textClass>
     <classCode scheme="eurovoc">3461</classCode>      <classCode scheme="eurovoc">3461</classCode>
     <classCode scheme="eurovoc">4480</classCode>      <classCode scheme="eurovoc">4480</classCode>
     <classCode scheme="eurovoc">5343</classCode>      <classCode scheme="eurovoc">5343</classCode>
   </textClass>                                       </textClass>
 </profileDesc>                                     </profileDesc>
</teiHeader>                                       </teiHeader>
- <text id="jrc42002D0595-ro." lang="ro">         - <text id="jrc42002D0595-bg." lang="bg">
 - <body>                                          - <body>
   <p n="1">DECIZIA REPREZENTANȚILOR GUVERNEL         <p n="1">РЕШЕНИЕ НА ПРЕДСТАВИТЕЛИТЕ НА ПРАВИТЕЛСТВАТА Н
   <p n="2">din 19 iulie 2002</p>                    <p n="2">от 19 юли 2002 година</p>
   <p n="3">privind consecințele expirării Tratatului   <p n="3">ОТНОСНО последиците от изтичането на Договора за съ
     CECO</p>                                            ЕОВС международни споразумения</p>
   <p n="4">(2002/595/CE)</p>                         <p n="4">(2002/595/EO)</p>
   <p n="5">REPREZENTANȚII GUVERNELOR STATELO          <p n="5">ПРЕДСТАВИТЕЛИТЕ НА ПРАВИТЕЛСТВАТА НА ДЪРЖАВИ
   <p n="6">întrucât:</p>                                 РАМКИТЕ НА СЪВЕТА,</p>
   <p n="7">(1) În temeiul art. 97, Tratatul CECO va    <p n="6">като имат предвид, че:</p>
   <p n="8">(2) CECO a încheiat mai multe acorduri      <p n="7">(1) По силата на член 97 от него, Договорът за ЕОВС щ
   <p n="9">(3) Acordurile în cauză nu prevăd event     <p n="8">(2) ЕОВС е сключила редица международни споразуме
   <p n="10">(4) După expirarea Tratatului CECO, ot     <p n="9">(3) В тези споразумения не се предвижда евентуалнот
   <p n="11">(5) Este în interesul CECO și al sectoar   <p n="10">(4) След изтичане на срока на Договора за ЕОВС него
     să fie deci transmise Comunității Europene,</p     общност,</p>
                                                       <p n="11">(5) В интерес на ЕОВС и на съответните сектори е, ча
```

Fig. 1. Documents (Ro, Bg) encoded in compliance with the JRC-Acquis format

matized, and tagged. The tagset used is MULTEXT-EAST (nl.ijs.si/ME/) compliant. The multilingual XML encoding, exemplified in Figure 2, was inspired by XCES-Ana-Align specifications (http://www.xml-ces.org/). The XCES-Ana-Align format is the standard input for our word alignment and word disambiguation platform which will be briefly described in the section 3.

The BALKANET European project [2] created a collection of interlingually aligned wordnets for Bulgarian, Czech, Greek, Romanian, Serbian and Turkish languages, following the basic principles of EUROWORDNET [3]. The InterLingual Index (ILI) of the BALKANET wordnets is the Princeton WordNet2.0 (PWN2.0) [4]. Due to the projection of the Suggested Upper Merged (SUMO) Ontology [5] over PWN2.0, and by the multilingual equivalence linking of the BALKANET monolingual wordnets to the PWN2.0, the SUMO/MILO labelling and inference rules are directly available to any synset of any monolingual wordnet. For instance the PWN2.0 synset (*permit*:1, *allow*:2, *let*:3, *countenance*:1) tagged by the SUMO/MILO category confersRight[1] has the ID ENG20-00776433-v which uniquely identifies the Bulgarian synset (*pozvolyavam*:3,

---

[1] This is a base ontology relation described in SUMO as: "%2 %n {doesn't} &%allow %p{s}%3 to perform task of the type %1".

razreshavam:3) and the Romanian synset (*încuviinţa*:1, *îngădui*:1.1.1, *permite*: 1.2). Although both Bulgarian and Romanian wordnets are significantly smaller (currently they have about 30,000 and respectively 40,000 synsets) than Princeton WORDNET (more than 115,000 synsets) due to the development strategies adopted by the BALKANET consortium, the general texts coverage is very high, as most usual words are encoded in our wordnets.

Fig. 2. The sentence aligned, tagged and lemmatized trilingual (En-Ro-Bg) corpus

3   Word Alignment and Word Sense Disambiguation

We developed an automatic procedure for word sense disambiguation in parallel texts that takes advantage of the way the words in one language were translated in the other languages. Revealing the translators knowledge embedded in the parallel texts is achieved by a highly accurate statistics-based sentence and word alignment system[2], described elsewhere [6].

The word alignment system uses a statistical alignment model and a statistical translation dictionary. For the statistical translation dictionary we use GIZA++

---

[2] The alignment system is called COWAL, and was the best rated in the ACL 2005 Romanian-English shared task on word alignment (see: Martin, J., Mihalcea, R., Pedersen, T.: Word Alignment for Languages with Scarce Resources. In Proc. of the ACL Workshop on Building and Exploiting Parallel Texts: Data Driven Machine Translation and Beyond, Ann Arbor, MI (2005), Figure 2).

(freely available at http://www.fjoch.com/GIZA++.html) and lemmatized parallel corpora (due to strong inflectional character of Romanian and Bulgarian, in order to increase statistical confidence, the translation equivalence probabilities are computed for lemmas not for wordforms). The alignment model consists of various weights and thresholds for different features and they are supposed to work for most Indo-European languages (cognates, translation equivalence entropy, POS-affinities, locality etc.). Based on our previous translation Ro-En model and the Ro-En translation dictionary extracted from the JRC-Acquis subcorpus described in section 2, we aligned several Ro-En parallel documents. From the Bg-En sub-corpus we extracted a Bg-En translation dictionary but since we do not have yet a Bg-En word-alignment model we used the model built for English-Romanian alignment (see http://www.cse.unt.edu/~rada/wpt05/). Using the same alignment model (which was tuned for Ro-En parallel texts) for Bg-En parallel texts was motivated partly because alignment model tuning for a new pair of languages is a highly demanding task and partly because, distributionally, Ro and Bg are quite similar, in spite of belonging to different language families. Obviously, in this case, the word alignment accuracy for Bg-En parallel texts is lower than the alignment accuracy for the Ro-En parallel texts but not significantly lower (preliminary estimations at the time of this writing show an F-measure around 65%). The Bg-En texts, word-aligned this way, will be partially hand-validated and corrected (where necessary) by means of a specialized editor, part of the word-alignment and WSD platform (see Figure 3). With the corrected Bg-En lexical alignment used as training data, the alignment model will be finer tuned, with direct consequences in increased alignment accuracy of the entire corpus. We generated the Ro-Bg word alignment using the transitivity

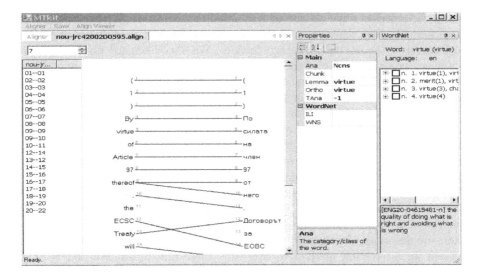

Fig. 3. The Bulgarian-English word-alignment

of the alignment links from Ro-En and En-Bg to derive the Ro-Bg alignment. The word alignment links are representations of translational equivalence between the respective tokens and we rely on the heuristics according to which if M words in language L1 are aligned to N words in the hub language L2, and these N words are aligned to Q words in language L3, then it is highly probable that the N words in language L1 are aligned to the Q words in language L3. We decided to take the hub language approach instead of the direct Bg-Ro approach for multiple reasons: it is simpler to extend to all the languages in the JRC-Acquis; for evaluations and corrections is easier to find experts understanding English and the other language; linguistic resources and the processing tools available for English, as well as the ever improving alignment technologies allow for cross-lingual annotation transfer and thus rapid prototyping of linguistic knowledge for the target language, etc. Once the parallel texts are word-aligned, the word sense disambiguation for the aligned words becomes straightforward when a multilingual lexical ontology is available for the concerned languages. Given a translation equivalence pair found by the word aligner, such as (*pozvolyavam îngădui*) the WSD system looks for unique identifiers common to the synsets containing the words *pozvolyavam* and *îngădui* respectively. If such a unique identifier is found the problem is solved: the common word sense is given by that unique ID (e.g. ENG20-00776433-v) or by the SUMO/MILO category of the unique ID (e.g. confersRight) depending on the required WSD sense granularity. It is obvious that the coarser the sense granularity, the higher the accuracy of WSD is. When using the SUMO/MILO sense inventory our WSD system has an average F-measure of more than 80%. However, as one would expect, most errors occur for the words with fewer occurrences in the corpus or for the words with a large number of distinct senses. In order to reduce the influence of semantic tagging errors we decided to consider for further processing only those words the senses of which occurred a minimal number of times (the threshold is an empirical value, depending on the documents size and the number of classes to be used in the document categorization). We also disregard words with too many senses (irrespective of their frequencies). If one agrees on the hypothesis that a word with a large number of senses is likely to be found in almost any document long enough, then it follows that the respective word would be a poor class discrimination feature for a classification system. One could see in these restrictions an analogy with the TF/IDF algorithm. With these two selectional restrictions, we estimate that the semantic tagging errors would hardly affect the final document classification performance. The reason for the optimism stems from the inherent smoothening achieved by the selection procedure of the most discriminating concepts. Our method is likely to be effective if the processed documents are not very short. For short documents one cannot afford filtering out too many words and cannot expect to see many repeated concepts. In [7] there are described the major difficulties in abstracts clustering and the authors present an interesting method to overcome these difficulties. We believe that their approach, which relies on monolingual data, could be nicely extended with a WSD method as presented here, for processing multilingual abstracts.

4   Concept-Based Text Classification

Unlike the keyword-based methods in document processing, the concept-based methods are supposed to better exploit the semantic information contained in a particular document and thus to provide more accurate results.

Having a set of before-hand classified documents, they are word sense disambiguated in terms of SUMO/MILO, and a number of concepts are selected as described in the previous section. Then, we measure the discriminative power of the selected concepts with respect to the thematic categorization of documents in terms of the majority logic operators more than n, at least n [8][3] etc. The normalized values for these thresholds give the minimum terms density of specialized lexis in the thematic reference corpora. Once these values are established, new parallel documents can be classified. Obviously, the minimum density of specialized lexis is dependent on the number of classes used for classification as well as on the sharpness of the domains differences.

In Table 2 there are summarized the observations from a preliminary experiment carried on Bulgarian data, manually sense annotated [9], where a given document could be accurately classified as belonging to one of four domains (Law, Politics, Economy and Medicine) if the density of concepts specific to that domain was at least 5%. Based on this Wizard-of-Oz experiment, we found strong motivations to automate the hand annotation part and implement a classification system based on the experimental findings. One should note that the classification mechanism based on SUMO/MILO sense tagging is more powerful than an alternative solution relying on semantic distances among the word senses in the underlying wordnets. This is because traversing wordnet relations (a paradigmatic approach) would consider semantic relatedness only among words of the same grammatical category (due to the wordnet structuring principles). The SUMO/MILO concepts labelling the wordnet synsets are insensitive to part of speech of the respective synsets. That is to say that the same SUMO/MILO concept may label words of different parts of speech (eg. the noun blow to the verb kick).

However, the wordnet structuring is complementing the SUMO/MILO ontology support. The new documents content words which are found paradigmatically related to the words tagged by a SUMO concept add relevance to the

Table 2. Frequency of domain specific lexis

Corpus vs. Lexis	Law	Politics	Economy	Medicine	Law+Economy	Law+Medicine
Law	10.3	5.4	4.2	1.1	8.4	5.9
Politics	2.9	8.3	3.4	0.5	2.9	3.6
Economy	1.2	2.0	9.2	0.6	6.5	2.5
Medicine	0.1	0.1	0.1	6.7	0.1	5.2

---

[3] The thresholds prescribed by these operators leave out most of the infrequent words liable to wrong disambiguation.

respective category. To this end, symmetric relations (antonymy), symmetric and transitive relations (also see, verb group, similar to), reverse relations (cause, derived, derivative, participle), and hierarchical relations (hyponymy, holonymy, subevent) are used to increase the density of the domain discriminating concepts. Thus for a given SUMO/MILO concept a basic list of referents is built from all the words occurrences tagged with the same concept. This list is extended with the words which are found to be paradigmatically related to the words already in the basic list. The number of words in this extended list, divided by the total number of the content words in the document to be classified represents the density of the respective concept. The category of a document is determined by the densities of the concepts in each lexis.

5   Conclusions and Further Work

The concept-based bitexts clustering and/or classification is a very promising application area of parallel data exploitation. One of the greatest advantages of our approach is that it can be used to automatically classify documents in several languages at once. That is, if we have a parallel corpus in multiple languages (such as JRC-Acquis corpus), word sense disambiguation and classification performed on any pair of them propagates to the rest via documents translation equivalence and the word alignment linkages.

We plan to evaluate the effectiveness of our method on the Bg-Ro subcorpus of the JRC-Acquis+. The Bg-Ro bitexts of JRC-Acquis+ will be automatically classified with the described method and the results will be compared to the present CELEX-based classification, used as reference data. The evaluation of the results will allow us to quantitatively evaluate the accuracy of our procedure and to detect any potential human classification errors in the CELEX database. Due to language independence of the CELEX classification, finding and correcting such classification errors will be beneficial for all the 22 languages present (now or in the future) in the JRC-Acquis+ parallel corpus.

References

1. Steinberger, R., Pouliquen, B., Widiger, A., Ignat, C., Erjavec, T., Tufiş, D.: The JRC-Acquis: A multilingual aligned parallel corpus with 20+ languages. In: proceedings of the 5th LREC Conference, Genoa, pp. 2142–2147 (2006)
2. Tufiş, D. (ed.): Special Issue on the BalkaNet Project. Romanian Journal of Information Science and Technology, vol. 7(1-2), Bucharest (2004), http://www.racai.ro/BalkanetSpecialIssue.doc
3. Vossen, P. (ed.): A Multilingual Database with Lexical Semantic Networks. Kluwer Academic Publishers, Dordrecht (1998)
4. Fellbaum, C. (ed.): WordNet: An Electronic Lexical Database. MIT Press, Cambridge (1998)
5. Niles, I., Pease, A.: Towards a Standard Upper Ontology. In: Proceedings of the 2nd International Conference on Formal Ontology in Information Systems (FOIS-2001), Ogunquit, Maine (2001)

6. Tufiş, D., Ion, R., Ceauşu, Al., Ştefănescu, D.: Improved Lexical Alignment by Combining Multiple Reified Alignments. In: Proceedings of the 11th Conference of the European Chapter of the Association for Computational Linguistics, Trento, pp. 153-160 (2006)
7. Alexandrov, M., Gelbukh, A., Rosso, P.: An Approach for Clustering Abstracts. In: Montoyo, A., Muñoz, R., Métais, E. (eds.) NLDB 2005. LNCS, vol. 3513, pp. 275–285. Springer, Heidelberg (2005)
8. Pacuit, E., Salame, S.: Majority logic. In: KR Proceedings, pp. 1–26 (2004)
9. Stoyanova, I., Koeva, S., Lesseva, S.: Applying and analysing Brown corpus model for Bulgarian (to appear)

Opinion Analysis Across Languages: An Overview of and Observations from the NTCIR6 Opinion Analysis Pilot Task

David Kirk Evans[1], Lun-Wei Ku[3], Yohei Seki[2], Hsin-Hsi Chen[3],
and Noriko Kando[1]

[1] National Institute of Informatics, Tokyo, Japan
{devans,kando}@nii.ac.jp
[2] Dept. of Information and Computer Sciences,
Toyohashi University of Technology, Japan
seki@ics.tut.ac.jp
[3] Department of Computer Science and Information Engineering, National Taiwan
University, Taipei, Taiwan
lwku@nlg.csie.ntu.edu.tw, hhchen@csie.ntu.edu.tw

Abstract. In this paper we introduce the NTCIR6 Opinion Analysis
Pilot Task, information about the Chinese, Japanese, and English data,
plans for future opinion analysis tasks at NTCIR, and a brief overview
of the evaluation results. This pilot task is a sentence-level opinion identification and polarity detection task run over data from a comparable corpus in three languages: Chinese, English, and Japanese. We have
manually annotated documents for this task in each language, producing what we believe to be the first multilingual opinion analysis data
set over comparable data. Six participants submitted Chinese system
results, three Japanese, and six English for this pilot task. We plan to
release the data to the research community, and hope to spur further research into cross-lingual opinion analysis and its use in other NLP tasks.
In particular, we look forward to researchers using this data to investigate cross-cultural perspective differences based on automatic sentiment
analysis.

1 Introduction

Opinion and sentiment analysis has been receiving a lot of attention in the
natural language processing research community recently. With the broad range
of information sources available on the web, and rapid increase in the uptake of
social community-oriented websites that foster user-generated content there has
been further interest by both commercial and governmental parties in trying to
automatically analyze and monitor the tide of prevalent attitudes on the web.
As a result, interest in automatically detecting language in which an opinion
is expressed, the polarity of the expression, targets, and opinion holders has
been receiving more attention in the research community. Applications include

F. Masulli, S. Mitra, and G. Pasi (Eds.): WILF 2007, LNAI 4578, pp. 456–463, 2007.

tracking response to and opinions about commercial products, governmental policies, tracking blog entries for potential political scandals and so on.

The NII-NACSIS Test Collection for Information Retrieval (NTCIR) Workshops have been organized to improve the state of the art in Asian and Cross-Lingual Information Retrieval, starting in 1999. [5,6] In the Sixth NTCIR Workshop to be held in Tokyo, May 2007, a new pilot task for Opinion Analysis has been introduced. The pilot task has tracks in three languages: Chinese, English, and Japanese. In this paper, we present an overview of the corpus and evaluation results.

We believe that this corpus presents a unique opportunity to expand the study of opinionated text analysis across languages due to the comparable nature of the corpus. The documents have been carefully selected based on the manual relevance judgments assigned in a cross-lingual Information Retrieval task, ensuring a high quality corpus that is relevant in all three languages. There has been earlier work in creating annotated opinion corpora, for example, [13] describes a corpus tagged at the sentence level for subjectivity and Wiebe also distributes the well-known MPQA[1] corpus. There has also been work in collaborative filtering with the MovieLens corpus[2] and other review-oriented corpora. While there has been lots of research in English opinion analysis ([1,2,9,14,8,15]) there has not been as much work in Chinese and Japanese.

Ku et al. [7] describe the construction of two Chinese corpora for opinion extraction, one based on news and one based on blog data, and also an algorithm for Chinese opinion identification at the document and sentence levels. They describe construction of a Chinese sentiment dictionary based on bootstrapping methods that also takes advantage of the ideographic nature of Chinese characters to predict polarity and strength of unknown words.

Seki et al. [10] conducted studies to build a Japanese multi-document summarizer depending on user-specified summary viewpoints. Once a set of documents is provided to the system, the user is presented with a list of topics discussed in the set and can select a topic of interest as well as the information type to focus on in the summaries, such as facts, opinions, or knowledge. The approach was then adapted to English and evaluated as part of the Document Understand Conference. [11] Kanayama et al. [3] re-cast the sentiment analysis problem into a machine translation framework, translating from free text to a more restricted set of sentiment units. They implemented systems for Japanese and English analysis based on two different transfer-based machine translations systems. Later work [4] automatically learns lexicons of polar clauses useful for domain-specific sentiment analysis.

2   NTCIR6 Opinion Analysis Pilot Task

The NTCIR-6 Opinion Analysis Pilot Task extends previous work in opinion analysis to a multilingual corpus. The initial task focuses on a simplified

---

[1] http://www.cs.pitt.edu/mpqa/
[2] http://www.grouplens.org/node/12

Table 1. Opinion Analysis task descriptions

Analysis Task	Values	Req'd?
Opinionated Sentences	YES, NO	Yes
Opinion Holders	String, multiple	Yes
Relevant Sentences	YES, NO	No
Opinionated Polarities	POS, NEG, NEU	No

sentence-level binary opinionated or not opinionated classification as opposed to more complicated contextual formulations, but we feel that starting with a simpler task will allow for wider participation from groups that may not have existing experience in opinion analysis.

The Opinion Analysis task has four subtasks, two of which are mandatory and two of which are optional. Table 1 summarizes the tasks, which are all being performed for all three languages. The two mandatory tasks are to decide whether each sentence expresses an opinion or not. For the Chinese data, all potential opinion holders are annotated whether the sentence in which the entity occurs is an opinionated sentence or not. In Japanese and English, opinion holders are only annotated for sentences that express an opinion, however, the opinion holder for a sentence can occur anywhere in the document. The annotators performed a kind of reference resolution by marking the opinion holder for the sentence, and if the opinion holder is an anaphoric reference noting the target of the anaphora. The opinionated sentences judgement is a binary decision, but in the case of opinion holders we allow for multiple opinion holders to be recorded for each sentence in the case that multiple opinions are expressed.

The two optional tasks are to decide the polarity of the opinionated sentences, and whether the sentences are relevant to the set topic or not. Each set contains documents that were found to be relevant to a particular topic, such as the one shown in Figure 1. For those participating in the relevance subtask each sentence should be judged as either relevant (Y) or non-relevant (N) to the topic. Polarity is determined for each opinionated sentence, and for sentences where more than one opinion is expressed the annotators were instructed to determine the polarity of the most main opinion expressed. In addition, the polarity is to be determined with respect to the set topic description if the sentence is relevant to the topic, and based on the attitude of the opinion if the sentence is not relevant to the topic.

Six teams participated in the Chinese opinion extraction subtask, six teams participated in the English opinion extraction subtask, and three teams participated in Japanese. Results for precision, recall, and F-measure will be presented for opinion detection and opinion holders, and optionally for sentence relevance and polarity for those participants that elected to submit results for those optional portions. Since all sentences were annotated by three annotators there is both a strict (all three annotators must have the same annotation) and a lenient standard for evaluation.

2.1 Corpus

The corpus is based on the NTCIR4 CLIR[3] documents and relevance judgments. It consists of Japanese data from 1998 to 1999 from the Yomiuri and Mainichi newspapers. The Chinese data contains data from 1998 to 1999 from the United Daily News, China Times, China Times Express, Commercial Times, China Daily News, Central and Daily News. The English data also covers from 1998 to 1999 with text from the Mainichi Daily News, Korea Times, and some data from Xinhua.

The corpus was created using about thirty queries over data from the NTCIR Cross-Lingual Information Retrieval corpus covering documents from 1998 to 2001. Document relevance for each set (query) had already been computed for the IR evaluation, so relevant documents for each language were selected based on the relevance judgements. For the Japanese and English portion of the corpus, a maximum of twenty documents were selected for each topic, while the Chinese portion might contain more than twenty documents for a topic. As an example of the topics in the NTCIR Opinion Analysis corpus, please see Figure 1, which shows topic 010, "History Textbook Controversies, World War II".

<TOPIC> <NUM>010<NUM> <SLANG>CH<SLANG> <TLANG>ENG<TLANG>
<TITLE>History Textbook Controversies, World War II</TITLE>
<DESC>Find reports on the controversial history textbook about the Second World War approved by the Japanese Ministry of Education.</DESC>
<NARR> <BACK>The Japanese Ministry of Education approved a controversial high school history textbook that allegedly glosses over Japan's atrocities during World War Two such as the Nanjing Massacre, the use of millions of Asia women as "comfort women" and the history of the annexations and colonization before the war. It was condemned by other Asian nations and Japan was asked to revise this textbook.</BACK>
<REL>Reports on the fact that the Japanese Ministry of Education approved the history textbook or its content are relevant. Reports on reflections or reactions to this issue around the world are partially relevant. Content on victims, "comfort women", or Nanjing Massacre or other wars and colonization are irrelevant. Reports on the reflections and reactions of the Japanese government and people are also irrelevant.</REL> </NARR>
<CONC>Ministry of Education, Japan, Junichiro Koizumi, textbook, comfort women, sexual slavery, Nanjing Massacre, annexation, colonization, protest, right-wing group, Lee Den Hui</CONC> </TOPIC>

Fig. 1. Topic title, description, and relevance fields for set 010

Table 2 shows the number of topics, documents, and sentences for each language, as well as the percentage of opinionated and relevant sentences. The Chinese corpus creation was started in advance of the Japanese and English

---

[3] http://research.nii.ac.jp/ntcir/permission/ntcir-4/perm-en-CLIR.html

Table 2. General information about NTCIR6 Opinion Analysis Corpus

Language	Topics	Documents	Sentences	Opinionated (Lenient / Strict)	Relevant
Chinese	32	843	8,546	62% / 25%	39% / 16%
English	28	439	8,528	30% / 7%	69% / 37%
Japanese	30	490	12,525	29% / 22%	64% / 49%

sides of the corpus, subsequently a larger number of documents was annotated whereas the English and Japanese sides of the corpus limit each topic to twenty documents.

2.2 Annotator Agreement

For English and Japanese, where three annotators were used to annotate all topics, we have computed inter-annotator agreement using Cohen's Kappa. For complete details on inter-annotator agreement, please see [12]. Table 3 shows the minimum and maximum Kappa scores between annotator pairs, as well as the average. One of the annotators in English consistently did not agree with the other two annotators, significantly lowering overall agreement scores. For Chinese, Kappa scores are computed for each topic, with the minimum, maximum, and average reported here over all 31 topics. The average Chinese Kappa agreement scores are similar to the average English scores, although the Chinese annotators are more consistent in polarity tagging. The Japanese annotators overall are much more consistent than either the Chinese or English annotators.

Table 3. Inter-annotator agreement Kappa summary

Language	Minimum	Maximum	Average
Chinese Opinionated	0.0537	0.4065	0.2328
Chinese Relevant	0.0441	0.6827	0.2885
Chinese Polarity	0.1605	0.8989	0.4733
English Opinionated	0.1704	0.4806	0.2947
English Relevant	0.0618	0.5298	0.3719
English Polarity	0.2039	0.5457	0.3380
Japanese Opinionated	0.5997	0.7681	0.6740
Japanese Relevant	0.6966	0.8394	0.7512
Japanese Polarity	0.6367	0.7875	0.7054

3 Evaluation

For a detailed description of the evaluation approach and methodology, please see [12]. Table 4 presents the results for Chinese, English, and Japanese opinion

Table 4. Chinese, English, and Japanese Opinion Analysis Lentient results

Group	L	Opinionated			Holder			Relevance			Polarity		
		P	R	F	P	R	F	P	R	F	P	R	F
CHUK	C	0.818	0.519	0.635	0.647	0.754	0.697	0.797	0.828	0.812	0.522	0.331	0.405
ISCAS	C	0.590	0.664	0.625	0.458	0.405	0.430	—	—	—	0.232	0.261	0.246
Gate-1	C	0.643	0.933	0.762	0.427	0.154	0.227	—	—	—	—	—	—
Gate-2	C	0.746	0.591	0.659	0.373	0.046	0.082	—	—	—	—	—	—
UMCP-1	C	0.645	0.974	0.776	0.241	0.410	0.303	0.683	0.516	0.588	0.292	0.441	0.351
UMCP-2	C	0.630	0.984	0.768	0.221	0.376	0.278	0.644	0.936	0.763	0.286	0.446	0.348
NTU	C	0.664	0.890	0.761	0.652	0.172	0.272	0.636	1.000	0.778	0.335	0.448	0.383
IIT-1	E	0.325	0.588	0.419	0.198	0.409	0.266	—	—	—	0.120	0.287	0.169
IIT-2	E	0.259	0.854	0.397	—	—	—	—	—	—	0.086	0.376	0.140
TUT-1	E	0.310	0.575	0.403	0.117	0.218	0.153	0.392	0.597	0.473	0.088	0.215	0.125
TUT-2	E	0.310	0.575	0.403	—	—	—	0.392	0.597	0.473	0.094	0.230	0.134
Cornell†	E	0.317	0.651	0.427	0.163	0.346	0.222	—	—	—	0.073	0.197	0.107
NII	E	0.325	0.624	0.427	0.066	0.166	0.094	0.510	0.322	0.395	0.077	0.194	0.110
GATE-1	E	0.324	0.905	0.477	0.121	0.349	0.180	0.286	0.632	0.393	—	—	—
GATE-2	E	0.324	0.905	0.477	—	—	—	0.286	0.632	0.393	—	—	—
ICU-KR	E	0.396	0.524	0.451	0.303	0.404	0.346	0.409	0.263	0.320	0.151	0.264	0.192
EHBN-1	J	0.531	0.453	0.489	0.138	0.085	0.105	—	—	—	—	—	—
EHBN-2	J	0.531	0.453	0.489	0.314	0.097	0.149	—	—	—	—	—	—
NICT-1	J	0.671	0.315	0.429	0.238	0.102	0.143	0.598	0.669	0.632	0.299	0.149	0.199
NICT-2	J	0.671	0.315	0.429	0.238	0.102	0.143	0.644	0.417	0.506	0.299	0.149	0.199
TUT	J	0.552	0.609	0.579	0.226	0.224	0.225	0.630	0.646	0.638	0.274	0.322	0.296

analysis under the lenient evaluation metric, where two of the three annotators must agree for a value to be included in the gold standard. The results from the strict evaluation have been omitted in the interest of brevity.

Performance across languages varies greatly, and due to both corpora and annotator differences are difficult to compare directly. In this pilot task, each language was evaluated independently, and actually different formulations for precision and recall were used under each language. The task overview paper presents the differences between the evaluation approaches, and also presents evaluations for each language using each approach, but the numbers reported here are the official results. Opinion Holder evaluation for English was performed semi-automatically, but due to the manual effort involved only the first priority run from each participant was evaluated. The Chinese and Japanese evaluation also used semi-automatic approaches to opinion holder evaluation, but were able to evaluate all submitted runs.

Of the groups that participated, one group (GATE) participated in both the Chinese and English task, and one group (TUT) participated in both the English and Japanese task. Despite using similar approaches, their results differ in each language in part due to the difference in annotation between the languages. An interesting question for future work is whether these differences stem more from annotator training, differences in the documents that make up the corpus, or cultural and language differences.

4 Future Work

The NTCIR Opinion Analysis Pilot task is in the first year of operation, and has started with a fairly simple task in three languages. We have proposed multiple evaluation approaches and held a workshop in May with participants discussing the evaluation results and both positive and negative experiences with this cross-lingual evaluation. We hope to foster more research into multi-lingual aspects of sentiment analysis and hope to see more sites participate in analysis for multiple languages. The next section presents the roadmap for future NTCIR Opinion Analysis Tasks.

4.1 NTCIR OAT Roadmap

We plan to conduct the Opinion Analysis Task again in NTCIR-7 and NTCIR-8. The NTCIR meetings are held every year and a half. For NTCIR-7 we plan to add a new genre to the task, reviews, in addition to the news genre used in NTCIR-6. We are currently exploring using review web sites as a source of data. NTCIR-7 and 8 will both continue to use Chinese, English, and Japanese, and while no further languages are slated for addition at this time, Korean is a possible candidate since relevance judgments for some of the topic already exist. NTCIR-7 will also add a strength of opinion and stakeholder evaluation in addition to the subjectivity, polarity, and opinion holder evaluation performed in NTCIR-6. NTCIR-8 will add a temporal evaluation, and possibly expand to clause-level subjectivity.

5 Conclusions

In this paper we have presented the NTCIR Opinion Analysis Pilot Task, the corpus used in the workshop, and an overview of the evaluation results. We look forward to future iterations of the NTCIR Opinion Analysis Task which will add new genres to the evaluation, and add further features for extraction.

References

1. Hatzivassiloglou, V., McKeown, K.R.: Predicting the semantic orientation of adjectives. In: Proceedings of the eighth conference on European chapter of the Association for Computational Linguistics, Morristown, NJ, USA, pp. 174–181 (1997)
2. Hatzivassiloglou, V., Wiebe, J.M.: Effects of adjective orientation and gradability on sentence subjectivity. In: Proceedings of the 18th International Conference on Computational Linguistics (2000)
3. Kanayama, H., Nasukawa, T.: Deeper sentiment analysis using machine translation technology. In: Proceedings of the 20th International Conference on Computational Linguistics (COLING), pp. 494–500 (2004)
4. Kanayama, H., Nasukawa, T.: Fully automatic lexicon expansion for domain-oriented sentiment analysis. In: Proceedings of the 2006 Conference on Empirical Methods in Natural Language Processing, Sydney, Australia, pp. 355–363 (July 2006)

5. Kando, N., Kuriyama, K., Nozue, T., Eguchi, K., Karo, H., Hidaka, S., Adachi, J.: The ntcir workshop: the first evaluation workshop on japanese text retrieval and cross-lingual information retrieval. In: Proceedings of the 4th International Workshop on Information Retrieval with Asian Languages (1RAL'99) (1999)

6. Kishida, K., Hua Chen, K., Lee, S., Kuriyama, K., Kando, N., Chen, H.-H., Myaeng, S.H.: Overview of clir task at the fifth ntcir workshop. In: Proceedings of the Fifth NTCIR Workshop Meeting on Evaluation of Information Access Technologies: Information Retrieval, Question Answering and Cross-Lingual Information Access, Tokyo, Japan (December 2005) (National Institute of Informatics) (2005)

7. Ku, L.-W., Liang, Y.-T., Chen, H.-H.: Opinion extraction, summarization and tracking in news and blog corpora. In: Proceedings of AAAI-2006 Spring Symposium on Computational Approaches to Analyzing Weblogs, AAAI Technical Report (2006)

8. Pang, B., Lee, L.: Seeing stars: Exploiting class relationships for sentiment categorization with respect to rating scales. In: Proceedings of the ACL, pp. 115–124 (2005)

9. Riloff, E., Wiebe, J.: Learning extraction patterns for subjective expressions. In: Proceedings of the 2003 conference on Empirical methods in natural language processing (EMNLP 2003), Sapporo, Japan, pp. 105–112 (July 2003)

10. Seki, Y., Eguchi, K., Kando, N.: Multi-document viewpoint summarization focused on facts, opinion and knowledge (chapter 24). In: Shanahan, J.G., Qu, Y., Wiebe, J. (eds.) Computing Attitude and Affect in Text: Theories and Applications, pp. 317–336. Springer, Dordrecht, The Netherlands (2005)

11. Seki, Y., Eguchi, K., Kando, N., Aono, M.: Opinion-focused Summarization and its Analysis at DUC 2006. In: Proc. of the Document Understanding Conf. Wksp. 2005 (DUC 2006) at the Human Language Technology Conf. - North American chapter of the Association for Computational Linguistics (HLT-NAACL 2006),New York Marriott pp. 122–130 (June 2006)

12. Seki, Y., Evans, D.K., Ku, L.-W., Chen, H.-H., Kando, N., Lin, C.-Y.: Overview of opinion analysis pilot task at ntcir-6. In: Proceedings of the Sixth NTCIR Workshop Meeting on Evaluation of Information Access Technologies: Information Retrieval, Question Answering and Cross-Lingual Information Access National Institute of Informatics (May 2007)

13. Wiebe, J., Bruce, R., O'Hara, T.: Development and use of a gold-standard data set for subjectivity classifications. In: Proceedings of the 37th Association of Computational Linguistics, pp. 246–253 (1999)

14. Yi, J., Nasukawa, T., Bunescu, R., Niblack, W.: Sentiment analyzer: Extracting sentiments about a given topic using natural language processing techniques. In: The Third IEEE International Conference on Data Mining, November 2003, pp. 427–343. IEEE Computer Society Press, Los Alamitos (2003)

15. Yu, H., Hatzivassiloglou, V.: Towards answering opinion questions: separating facts from opinions and identifying the polarity of opinion sentences. In: Proceedings of the conference on Empirical methods in natural language processing, (Association for Computational Linguistics), Morristown, NJ, USA (2003)

Some Experiments in Humour Recognition Using the Italian Wikiquote Collection

Davide Buscaldi and Paolo Rosso

Dpto. de Sistemas Informáticos y Computación (DSIC),
Universidad Politécnica de Valencia, Spain
{dbuscaldi,prosso}@dsic.upv.es

Abstract. In this paper we present some results obtained in humour classification over a corpus of Italian quotations manually extracted and tagged from the Wikiquote project. The experiments were carried out using both a multinomial Naïve Bayes classifier and a Support Vector Machine (SVM). The considered features range from single words to n-grams and sentence length. The obtained results show that it is possible to identify the funny quotes even with the simplest features (bag of words); the bayesian classifier performed better than the SVM. However, the size of the corpus size is too small to support definitive assertions.

1 Introduction

Nowadays, the discipline of Natural Language Processing (NLP) embraces a large quantity of specific tasks, aimed at the solution of practical problems related to the access of human users to machine-readable textual information. For instance, thanks to Machine Translation, people can read and understand documents that are written in a language they do not know; Information Retrieval techniques allow to find almost immediately some kind of information on the web or in a digital collection. Less prosaic tasks, related to emotional aspects of natural language, have, until now, obtained less attention by the NLP research community, despite their close correlation to the understanding of human language.

One of such tasks is the automatic recognition of humour. In the words of the psychologist Edward De Bono[1]:

> *Humor is by far the most significant activity of the human brain. Why has it been so neglected by traditional philosophers, psychologists and information scientists?*

The nature of humour is elusive, it is expressed in many different forms and styles; for instance, the amusing elements of jokes are not the same of irony or satire. The sense of humour is also particularly subjective. All these characteristics were considered to represent a major obstacle to process it in an automated way. The work by Mihalcea and Strapparava [2,3] in the classification of one-liners mined these beliefs, demonstrating that it is possible to apply computational approaches to the automatic recognition and use of humour.

F. Masulli, S. Mitra, and G. Pasi (Eds.): WILF 2007, LNAI 4578, pp. 464–468, 2007.

In this paper we investigated the use of Wikiquote[1] as a corpus for automatic humour recognition in Italian. Wikiquote is a section of Wikipedia[2] that stores famous quotes from a plethora of sources, from movies to writers, from anchormen to proverbs. We manually annotated a part of the quotes as humourous or not, and we used this corpus for some experiments. We used a Multinomial Naïve Bayes classifier and a Support Vector Machine (SVM) [4], as in [2].

In the following Section we describe how we selected the quotes for the corpus and its characteristics. In Section 3 we describe the experiments carried out and the obtained results.

2   Corpus Construction

The Italian Wikiquote currently contains about 4, 000 pages of quotations, aphorisms and proverbs. We decided to include only the quotations with an author assigned and Italian proverbs, that is, we excluded anonymous citations and phrases extracted from movies, television shows and category pages (for instance, *Category:Love*). A quantity of data was also removed due to formatting issues.

The quotations were extracted and presented to a human annotator by means of a simple Java interface (see Fig. 1).

Fig. 1. Interface of the Wikiquote annotation tool

The annotator had the options of skipping the quotation or the whole author, eventually adjust typos or remove exceeding informations (such as the source of the citation in Fig. 1), and label the quote as funny.

---

[1] http://en.wikiquote.org
[2] http://www.wikipedia.org

The results of such processing is a corpus consisting of $1,966$ citations from 89 authors, of which 471 labeled as "funny". For each quote we stored also the information about the author and its category. The amusing quotes include various types of humour: for instance, there are simple one-liners such as *"Per te sono ateo, ma per Dio sono una leale opposizione."* (*"To you I'm an atheist; to God, I'm the Loyal Opposition."*, by Woody Allen), and jokes such as *"Lo sa che io ho perduto due figli"* - *"Signora lei una donna piuttosto distratta"* (*"You see, I lost two sons"* - *"Madame, you are quite a scatterbrain"*, by Fabrizio De Andrè).

The corpus has been made publicly available in the web at the following direction: `http://www.dsic.upv.es/~dbuscaldi/resources/emoticorpus.xml.bz2`.

3   Experiments and Results

The experiments were carried out using the Multinomial Naïve Bayes classifier of Weka [5] and the SVM_light[3] implementation of SVM by Thorsten Joachims. The motivation of this choice is that these classifiers have been already used in the current state-of-the-art work on humour recognition [2]. Each classifier was evaluated using various sets of features: bag-of-words (the set of words in the quote, including stop-words), n-grams (from unigrams to trigrams), quotation length. For SVM we also considered using a linear and a polynomial ($d = 2$) kernel and two weight schemes for features: binary and $tf \cdot idf$. The cross-validation method used in all the experiments was the leave-one-out.

We used *precision* and *recall* as performance measures. Precision is the probability that a document predicted to be in class A truly belongs to this class. Recall is the probability that a document belonging to class A is classified into this class. We calculated also the F-measure, that is calculated as $2*p*r/(p+r)$, where p is precision and r recall.

In Table 1 we show the baselines, obtained by assigning to the whole collection all the same label, either "Humorous" or "Not-humorous".

Table 1. Baselines. BL_H is the baseline obtained by assigning to all samples the "Humourous" label. BL_N is the baseline obtained by assigning to all samples a "Non-humorous" label. p_H , r_H and F_H indicate precision, recall and F-measure over the "Humorous" set of samples, p_N , r_N and F_N indicate the same for the "Non-humorous" samples. r_O indicates overall recall.

	r_O	p_H	r_H	F_H	p_N	r_N	F_N
BL_H	0.240	0.240	1.000	0.387	0.000	0.000	0.000
BL_N	0.760	0.000	0.000	0.000	0.760	1.000	0.864

In Table 2 we show the results obtained with the Naïve Bayes classifier, using different sets of features. We used the author feature only in order to check the

---
[3] http://www.cs.cornell.edu/People/tj/svm_light/

Table 2. Multinomial Naïve Bayes results. *bow*: bag-of-words features; *n*-grams: from unigrams to trigrams; *n*-grams +*length*: *n*-grams and sentence length; *n*-grams +*author*: *n*-grams and author name.

	r_O	p_H	r_H	F_H	p_N	r_N	F_N
bow	**0.807**	0.619	0.501	0.554	0.852	0.903	**0.877**
n-grams	0.788	0.556	0.584	**0.570**	0.867	0.853	0.860
n-grams +*length*	0.796	0.584	0.516	0.548	0.853	0.884	0.868
n-grams +*author*	0.870	0.724	0.737	0.730	0.917	0.912	0.914

importance of knowing the source of a quotation. Actually, humour classification should be blind with respect to the author's name.

In Tables 2 and 4 we display the results obatined using, respectively, SVM with linear and polynomial kernels.

Table 3. Results for SVM with linear kernel. *bow*: bag-of-words features; *n*-grams: from unigrams to trigrams; *n*-grams +*length*: *n*-grams and sentence length; $tf \cdot idf$: features weighted by means of the tf · idf.

	r_O	p_H	r_H	F_H	p_N	r_N	F_N
bow	**0.796**	0.748	0.221	**0.341**	0.799	0.977	**0.879**
n-grams	0.789	0.721	0.197	0.310	0.794	0.976	0.876
n-grams +*length*	0.795	0.743	0.221	0.340	0.799	0.976	0.879
bow, $tf \cdot idf$	0.767	0.591	0.083	0.145	0.773	0.982	0.865
n-grams, $tf \cdot idf$	0.770	0.714	0.064	0.117	0.771	0.992	0.867

Table 4. Results for SVM with polynomial kernel. *bow*: bag-of-words features; *n*-grams: from unigrams to trigrams; $tf \cdot idf$: features weighted by means of the tf · idf.

	r_O	p_H	r_H	F_H	p_N	r_N	F_N
bow	0.767	0.615	0.068	0.122	0.771	0.980	0.863
n-grams	0.758	0.417	0.021	0.040	0.763	0.991	0.862
bow, $tf \cdot idf$	0.761	1.000	0.002	0.004	0.761	1.000	0.864
n-grams, $tf \cdot idf$	0.760	0.333	0.002	0.004	0.761	0.999	0.864

Generally, the obtained results are in line with those obtained by [2] for a corpus of dimensions similar to our Wikiquote-based one. The results obtained with SVMs show that they obtained a very low recall over humorous quotes; we think this is due to the nature of the corpus, that contains three times non-humorous quotes more than funny ones. Quite surprisingly, the best results were obtained with the simplest model, the Naïve Bayes with bag-of-words as features. In other words, this means that terminology is quite distinctive for humourous quotes. We suppose the *n*-grams features are more useful in other tasks where style is more important, such as authorship identification [6].

4 Conclusions and Further Work

We built a corpus of 1966 citations in Italian, extracted from Wikiquote, where each citation has been labeled as funny or not. The corpus was used to perform experiments with the leave-one-out method, using a Naïve Bayes and a SVM classifier. The results show that it is actually possible to identify the humorous quotes even with simple features such as the bag-of-words of each sentence, and that the bayesian classifier performs better than the SVM one. However, the corpus is too small (about 10% the corpus used in [2]) and the results are not decisive. Further investigation will be conditioned by the acquisition of a larger corpus, possibly by working on the English edition of Wikiquote.

Acknowledgements

We would like to thank the TIN2006-15265-C06-04 research project for partially supporting this work.

References

1. De Bono, E.: I am Right, You are Wrong: From This to the New Renaissance, From Rock Logic to Water Logic. Penguin (1991)
2. Mihalcea, R., Strapparava, C.: Computational Laughing: Automatic Recognition of Humorous One-liners. In: Proc. 27th Ann. Conf. Cognitive Science Soc (CogSci 05), Stresa, Italy, pp. 1513–1518 (2005)
3. Mihalcea, R., Strapparava, C.: Technologies That Make You Smile: Adding Humor to Text-Based Applications. IEEE Intelligent Systems 21(5), 33–39 (2006)
4. Joachims, T.: Text Categorization with Support Vector Machines: Learning with Many Relevant Features. In: Springer (ed.) Proc. 10th European Conf. on Machine Learning (ECML 98), pp. 137–142 (1998)
5. Witten, I.H., Frank, E.: Data Mining: Practical machine learning tools and techniques, 2nd edn. Morgan Kaufmann, San Francisco (2005)
6. Coyotl, R.M.: Villaseñor, L. In: Martínez-Trinidad, J.F., Carrasco Ochoa, J.A., Kittler, J. (eds.) CIARP 2006. LNCS, vol. 4225, pp. 844–853. Springer, Heidelberg (2006)

Recognizing Humor Without Recognizing Meaning

Jonas Sjöbergh and Kenji Araki

Graduate School of Information Science and Technology
Hokkaido University
Sapporo, Japan
{js,araki}@media.eng.hokudai.ac.jp

Abstract. We present a machine learning approach for classifying sentences as one-liner jokes or normal sentences. We use no deep analysis of the meaning to try to see if it is humorous, instead we rely on a combination of simple features to see if these are enough to detect humor. Features such as word overlap with other jokes, presence of words common in jokes, ambiguity and word overlap with common idioms turn out to be useful. When training and testing on equal amounts of jokes and sentences from the British National Corpus, a classification accuracy of 85% is achieved.

1 Introduction

Humor is an interesting part of human language use, usually used many times every day. Research on humor has been done in many different fields, such as psychology, philosophy, sociology and linguistics. When it comes to computational linguistics, two main approaches have been explored. One is humor generation, where systems for generating usually quite simple forms of jokes, e.g. word play jokes, have been constructed [1,2,3,4]. The second is humor recognition, where systems to recognize whether a text is a joke or not have been constructed [5,6], which is what this paper is about.

Theories of humor often state that humor appears when a setup suggests one interpretation but is followed by an ending that does not agree with this interpretation, but is consistent with some other interpretation of the setup. Thus, the listener must shift from the assumed reference frame to a new interpretation, which can be humorous.

Doing this kind of analysis automatically with current language processing techniques seems prohibitively difficult. In our experiments we instead use quite low level information sources and see if enough hints can be gathered to determine whether something is a joke or not without actually having any understanding of the meaning. Our work closely resembles the work in [6], where humor detection was treated as a text classification problem. Machine learning using content based information and some stylistic features present in many jokes gave results far above baseline performance.

F. Masulli, S. Mitra, and G. Pasi (Eds.): WILF 2007, LNAI 4578, pp. 469–476, 2007.

We also treat humor detection as text classification and use machine learning. Our method differs in what features are made available to the machine learning system. Examples of useful features are presence of words common in jokes, word overlap with known jokes and word overlap with idiomatic expressions.

2   Method for Detecting Humor

There are many machine learning algorithms available, and in many cases the performance is very similar. We put very little effort into selecting a good machine learning algorithm, instead focusing on the information features given to the machine learner. The interesting part is thus what language features can be used for classifying text as jokes or not.

The machine learning method we use is very simple. For each feature a threshold value is calculated separating the training examples into two groups. The threshold is selected so as to make the mean entropy of these as low as possible. To classify a new example, which group it belongs to is checked for each feature, and the proportion between positive and negative examples in this group used. The proportion of positive examples for each group the example belongs to is multiplied together and compared to the product in the same way for the negative examples. If the product for the positive examples is larger the example is classified as a joke, otherwise as a non-joke. This method is not very powerful, but fast.

Since we have many features that represent almost the same information, performing some feature reduction to remove redundant or useless features improves performance. It is also interesting in the respect that it shows what kind of information is useful in detecting humor.

We perform a very simplistic feature reduction. Using disjoint sets of test data (i.e. training and classifying several times), we remove one feature at a time. The feature that gives the best result when not present is then permanently removed, and the process repeated. When all features have been removed, the best result achieved in the process is found. All features that were removed when reaching this result are discarded from here on. All other features are kept and used in the tests.

The rest of this section presents the features given to the machine learner. Feature names are given in *italics*. Most features are developed in a very shallow way. This means that they might be too simplistic to capture the sought after information, but we wanted to see how well the classification could be done using only readily available and simple to use information. Many much more sophisticated features than ours could be designed and implemented, at least for narrow domains.

2.1   Text Similarity

Since we are doing text classification, it is of course useful to use common text classification features such as the closeness in some word space model between a new sentence and the labeled sentences in the training data. The first group of features contain information of this type:

Closest joke, the word overlap between the sentence to classify and the joke in the training corpus with the highest word overlap. Overlap is divided by the square root of the number of words in the sentences in the training corpus, since otherwise the overlap will tend to be higher for long sentences (since they contain more words to overlap). *Closest non-joke*, is the same but for non-joke sentences, and *closest difference*, is the difference between the two previous features.

Finally, we have the *knn* feature, a weighted vote between the five closest sentences in the training data, each with a weight equal to their word overlap. Jokes have positive sign and non-jokes have negative sign.

2.2 Joke Words

Some words are common in jokes, while some are rarely used to be funny. For instance, according to the Laughlab study [7], animals are often mentioned in jokes, especially ducks. To capture this, words that occur at least five times in the jokes in the training data and are at least five times more common in the jokes than in the non-jokes are collected in a list. Each word is given a weight that is the relative frequency of the word among the jokes divided by the relative frequency among the non-jokes.

To capture short phrases that are common in jokes, such as "change a light bulb", similar lists are constructed for word bigrams and trigrams too. To detect signs of unfunniness, the same is also done for words that are underrepresented in jokes. Using this information the following features are calculated:

Joke words, the sum of the weights of all words common in jokes. *Joke bigrams*, similarly for bigrams and *joke trigrams* for trigrams. *Joke word pairs*, the same for any pair of words occurring in the sentence, and *joke word triples* similarly for three words from the same sentence. Finally, *joke words and pairs*, the sum of *joke words* and *joke word pairs* is also used.

Non-joke words, the same as for *joke words*, except using words rare in jokes but common in non-jokes. *Non-joke bigrams*, *non-joke trigrams*, *non-joke word pairs*, *non-joke word triples*, and *non-joke words and pairs* in the same way as above.

These features are, like the previous section, fairly typical text classification features, though instead of using typical weighting schemes such as Inverse Document Frequency, we use weighting related to how common the words are in jokes compared to non-jokes. Since these lists are based on the sentences in the training data, these features of course give a much stronger separation between jokes and non-jokes in the training data than can be expected in sentences to classify later.

2.3 Ambiguity

Most theories on humor agree that ambiguity is useful in humor. A simple feature to capture this is the ambiguity of the words in the sentence. The ambiguity of a word is measured by looking up the word in the online dictionary at dictionary.com and counting the number of senses listed. Two features are based on this, *average ambiguity*, the average number of word senses of the words in the sentence, and *maximum ambiguity*, the highest ambiguity of the words in the sentence.

Of course, ambiguity is not only caused by word senses. Another measure of ambiguity is calculated by running the link parser [8] on each sentence. The number of possible parses found is then used as the feature *parse ambiguity*. To account for the fact that longer sentences generally have more possible parses, the value is divided by the sentence length in words.

2.4   Style

In a very similar study to ours [6] an analysis of the jokes in their corpus showed some possibly useful characteristics of jokes. For instance, they often contain human related words such as "you" or "I"; they often use negations, dirty words, antonymy etc. Inspired by their results, we use the following stylistic features:

Dirty, the number of dirty words present in the sentence. A list of 2,500 dirty words downloaded from the Internet was used to decide if a word is dirty or not.

Human, the number of words present from the list: "you", "your", "I", "me", "my", "man", "woman", "he", "she", "his", "her", "guy", and "girl"; and *negation*, the number of occurrences of "not" or "n't".

Using the CMU Pronunciation Dictionary[1] for finding the pronunciation of words, three features were calculated: *rimes*, the number of word pairs that have at least four letters, at least one of which is a vowel, pronounced the same way at the end of the words; *similar*, the same as *rimes* but using the beginning of the words instead of the end; and *alliteration*, the number of words that start with the same sound and have a maximum of two words in between.

The *new words* feature also uses the CMU Pronunciation Dictionary, simply counting the number of words that are not in the dictionary.

Repeated words features: *repeated words*, the number of words of at least five letters that occur more than once, and *repeated substring*, the longest substring (in letters) that occurs more than once in the sentence. *Average repeated words* and *average repeated substring* are the same but divided by sentence length.

Antonymy features look up the antonyms of a word at dictionary.com. If any of the listed antonyms are present in the sentence, a score of one divided by the number of possible antonyms is given. Two features are based on this, *maximum antonymy score*, the highest value (i.e. the antonym pair present with the fewest other possible antonyms), and *antonymy*, the sum of all antonymy scores.

2.5   Idiomatic Expressions

One-liner jokes are often amusing reformulations based on common idioms or proverbs. Searching the Internet for "English proverbs" and taking the first

---

[1] http://www.speech.cs.cmu.edu/cgi-bin/cmudict

results that contained actual collections of proverbs and idioms gave a list of 3,000 proverbs and idioms. The following features are used based on this:

Short idioms, the number of idioms of two or three words present in the sentence, and *long idioms*, similarly for those of length at least four.

Idiom overlap, the number of proverbs or idioms of at least four words that overlap with the sentence for at least four words in a row. *Vague overlap* is the same, though one non-matching word can be skipped in the middle of the match.

Longest overlap is the longest matching word sequence of any idiom, and *longest common substring* is the longest common substring (in words) between the sentence and any idiom. Both of these scores are divided by the square root of the length of the idiom, since longer idioms often overlap other sentences on common words such as prepositions.

3 Evaluation

In our evaluations we use a corpus of 6,100 jokes collected from the Internet. All jokes were automatically downloaded from collections of jokes were the classification was "oneliner". They are thus generally of the oneliner type, though some jokes that are perhaps not really oneliners (such as "What do you call 5000 dead lawyers at the bottom of the ocean? A good start!") were also downloaded if they were classified as oneliners by the original collector. All jokes are written in English.

After downloading, all jokes were manually checked to see if they were indeed jokes, removing for instance descriptions such as "Dirty one-liners section 2". Jokes with a high word overlap with other jokes in the corpus were also checked and only one version of the same joke was kept. The shortest joke is only one word long ("Contentsmaysettleduringshipping"), the longest is 80 words. On average, the jokes contain 12 words.

As non-jokes we use sentences from the British National Corpus, BNC [9], which was the hardest to distinguish from one-liners in other studies [6], where an accuracy of 79% was achieved. We use a different set of sentences from the BNC, and a different set of jokes, so results are not necessarily comparable though.

Data for training and testing was created by taking an equal number of jokes and BNC sentences to each data set. Any sentences from the BNC that were shorter than the shortest joke or longer than the longest joke were ignored. The data was divided into 95% training data and 5% test data. More training data normally gives better results with machine learning, but repeating the training and testing for each of the (in our case) 20 test sets takes quite some time. Using one in twenty was deemed a good compromise between the time required to test on a large number of examples and the amount of training data made available to the machine learner.

Five sets of test data were used for feature reduction. The system was then evaluated using the remaining 15 test data sets, which gives slightly more than 9,000 sentences to classify in the tests.

Which features were removed during the feature reduction is shown in Table 1. Since there are redundant features of several of the feature types, many are removed.

Table 1. Features that are discarded during the feature reduction

Maximum ambiguity	*Alliteration*
Maximum antonymy score	*Antonymy*
Joke word trigrams	*Joke word pairs*
Non-joke word pairs	*Human*
Average repeated words	*Negation*
Average repeated substring	*Short idiom*
Vague overlap	*Long idiom*

The general usefulness of the different feature types is shown in Table 2, where the classification accuracy based only on one group of features or when a whole group is removed is shown.

Table 2. Classification accuracy (%). Accuracy when removing or using only a single feature group is also shown.

	Only	Without
All features	85.4	50.0
Similarity	75.7	83.8
Joke words	84.1	76.8
Ambiguity	62.5	84.8
Style	59.1	85.4
Idioms	63.5	85.0

Presence of words common or rare in jokes seems to be the most useful information, giving almost as high accuracy as when using all features. This is followed by word overlap with training examples. These are fairly standard text classification features, so that they are useful in joke related text classification too is not surprising. Similarity to idioms or proverbs helps a little, as does ambiguity. The style features are sadly of little use together with the other features, though using only these is a little better than guessing, so they do provide some information.

We achieved a total classification accuracy of 85%, which is a lot better than random guessing (50%). It is also higher than previous results on similar data, though the results are not necessarily comparable. Without feature reduction, the accuracy is 81%. BNC seems to be relatively hard to distinguish from jokes, compared to other corpora. For example, a quick evaluation using sentences from the Open Mind Common Sense project [10] instead gave 93% accuracy.

4   Conclusions

We presented a text classification approach using machine learning to classify sentences as jokes or non-jokes. We made many different types of features available to the machine learner, and then did some simple feature reduction to find out what type of information is useful in detecting jokes. The classification accuracy, 85%, was higher than other reported results.

The most useful information was classical text classification features, such as word overlap with training examples or the presence of certain words. For the last type of feature, we use a novel weighting scheme, giving weight to words in proportion to how much more common or rare they are in jokes than in normal texts. Using this feature type alone gives almost as good accuracy as when using all feature types. We believe this means that jokes differ from other types of texts in what topics they treat, which agrees with other findings, such as the fact that dirty words or human related words are over represented in jokes.

We also believe that the low contribution from the other feature types is in part caused by our very shallow implementation of the features. While features such as dirty words and human related words will likely not contribute that much new information not already present in the content based features (since they too are basically content based features), other features could likely be improved. For instance, ambiguity in jokes is usually revealed by the punch line. Taking this into account, more sophisticated ambiguity features than the average number of word senses in the sentence or the total number of parses possible could be created. One example could be how much of the parse ambiguity is caused by the end of the sentence being ambiguous, another is checking the number of word senses of the last word that "make sense" in the current context or how difficult it is to determine what sense is used this time.

Other features are probably relevant for only quite few jokes, thus being largely drowned out by other examples when using our fairly simplistic machine learning system. One example is the repeated words feature. Some jokes like "Kids in the back seat cause accidents; accidents in the back seat cause kids." use a lot of repetition. These are so rare, though, that the machine learner does not consider it important to distinguish sentences with very high repetition from other sentences. Using a different machine learning system might make these features more valuable.

Acknowledgements

This work has been funded by The Japanese Society for the Promotion of Science, (JSPS).

References

1. Binsted, K.: Machine Humour: An Implemented Model of Puns. PhD thesis, University of Edinburgh, Edinburgh, United Kingdom (1996)
2. Binsted, K., Takizawa, O.: BOKE: A Japanese punning riddle generator. Journal of the Japanese Society for Artificial Intelligence 13(6), 920–927 (1998)
3. Yokogawa, T.: Generation of Japanese puns based on similarity of articulation. In: Proceedings of IFSA/NAFIPS 2001, Vancouver, Canada (2001)
4. Stark, J., Binsted, K., Bergen, B.: Disjunctor selection for one-line jokes. In: Maybury, M., Stock, O., Wahlster, W. (eds.) INTETAIN 2005. LNCS (LNAI), vol. 3814, pp. 174–182. Springer, Heidelberg (2005)
5. Taylor, J., Mazlack, L.: Toward computational recognition of humorous intent. In: Proceedings of Cognitive Science Conference 2005 (CogSci 2005), Stresa, Italy, pp. 2166–2171 (2005)
6. Mihalcea, R., Strapparava, C.: Making computers laugh: Investigations in automatic humor recognition. In: Proceedings of HLT/EMNLP, Vancouver, Canada (2005)
7. Wiseman, R.: Laughlab: The Scientific Search For The World's Funniest Joke. Random House (2002)
8. Grinberg, D., Lafferty, J., Sleator, D.: A robust parsing algorithm for link grammars. In: Proceedings of the Fourth International Workshop on Parsing Technologies, Prague, Czech Republic (1995)
9. Burnard, L.: The Users Reference Guide for the British National Corpus (1995)
10. Singh, P.: The public acquisition of commonsense knowledge. In: Proceedings of AAAI Spring Symposium on Acquiring (and Using) Linguistic (and World) Knowledge for Information Access, Palo Alto, California (2002)

Computational Humour: Utilizing Cross-Reference Ambiguity for Conversational Jokes

Hans Wim Tinholt and Anton Nijholt

University of Twente
{tinholt,anijholt}@cs.utwente.nl

Abstract. This paper presents a computer implementation that utilizes cross-reference ambiguity in utterances for simple conversational jokes. The approach is based on the SSTH. Using a simple script representation, it is shown that cross-reference ambiguities always satisfy the SSTH requirement for script overlap. To determine whether script opposition is present, we introduce a method that compares the concepts involved based on their semantic properties. When a given cross-reference ambiguity results in script opposition it is possible to generate a punchline based on this ambiguity. As a result of the low performance of the anaphora resolution algorithm and the data sparseness in ConceptNet the application performs moderately, but it does provide future prospects in generating conversational humour.

1 Introduction

Many jokes are based on ambiguity. A joke often originates from a set-up, which can be interpreted in two ways. There is an obvious interpretation, but a less obvious interpretation exists as well. The realization that this hidden meaning exists is often perceived as humorous. Natural language provides a lot of possibilities for constructing ambiguous sentences. One type of ambiguity in natural language is cross-reference ambiguity, also referred to as anaphora ambiguity. Some examples of ambiguous anaphoric references are 'they' in example 1 and 'she' in example 2.

Example 1. The cops arrested *the demonstrators* because *they* were violent.

Example 2. Mary asked *Susan* a question, and *she* gave the answer.

Sometimes a joke can be made by emphasizing the hidden interpretation of an ambiguity. In example 1 for instance, one could make a joke by asking whether the cops were violent. Whether someone considers such a joke based on cross-reference ambiguity to be humorous depends on many factors, but jokes based on some ambiguous sentences are more likely to be perceived as humorous than jokes based on others. A joke based on example 1 for instance, is likely to be

F. Masulli, S. Mitra, and G. Pasi (Eds.): WILF 2007, LNAI 4578, pp. 477–483, 2007.

considered humorous, but asking "Did Mary give the answer?" in example 2 is not particularly funny. This paper presents a system that distinguishes non-humorous cross-reference ambiguities in a conversation from ambiguities that are likely to be humorous. Whenever a humorous ambiguity is found the system generates a simple conversational joke.

2   Distinguishing Between Humorous and Non-humorous Misunderstandings

Our method to distinguish humorous anaphora misunderstandings from non-humorous ones is based on the SSTH[1]. The main hypothesis of this theory is:

> A text can be characterized as a single-joke-carrying text if both of the [following] conditions are satisfied:
> i) The text is compatible, fully or in part, with two different scripts
> ii) The two scripts with which the text is compatible are opposite (...).
> [1, p. 99]

To implement this theory a script representation is needed. Using this script representation it should be possible to generate two scripts that are compatible with a certain anaphora ambiguity. When both script overlap (condition i) and script opposition (condition ii) are present the ambiguity is humorous according to this theory and a joke can be generated. The script representation and the methods to determine whether overlap and opposition are present are discussed below.

3   Script Representation

The script representation used by us is a graph based representation, which is basically a simplified version of the representations introduced by Attardo [2]. It does not require a comprehensive interpretation of the text or the competence to understand the intentions of the persons involved. However, this representation suffices for the analysis of most anaphora jokes and it can be automatically generated based on the output of a semantic role labeller.

Figure 1 shows the two scripts that can be generated based on example 1. The script representation on the left represents the interpretation that 'they' refers to 'the demonstrators', the script representation on the right represents the interpretation that 'they' refers to 'the cops'. This type of script representations will be used to check whether both overlap and opposition exist between the two scripts involved in an anaphora ambiguity.

---

[1] Note that the SSTH has been extended to a more general theory: the GTVH. This theory allows jokes to be analyzed at different levels and it can account for joke similarity. However, for the simple computational analysis of jokes used in our system these additions do not provide much added value.

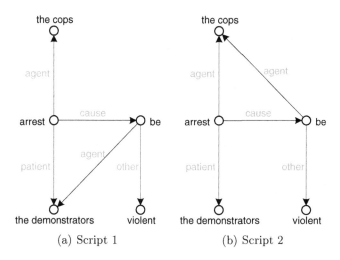

(a) Script 1
(b) Script 2

Fig. 1. Representations of the two interpretations of the anaphora ambiguity

4   Script Overlap

In the semantic network representation of scripts, two semantic network graphs are considered to be overlapping if there exists a subgraph G, such that $G \subset S_1 \& S_2$ or in other words, if they share at least one edge and two adjacent vertices [2, p. 34–35]. In the script representation of example 1 it is clear that both graphs are overlapping. Both scripts are identical, except for one edge.

The fact that the scripts of both interpretations of the anaphor are overlapping in the given example is not a coincidence. This is always the case with anaphora misunderstandings because (1) the vertex with the verb to which the anaphor is connected (in the example the vertex 'be') is always present in both graphs and (2) this verb is always preceded by a piece of text that mentions both possible antecedents (in the example 'the cops' and 'the demonstrators'). The script representation of this piece of text is exactly the same for both interpretations of the anaphora ambiguity, so it will contain at least one additional overlapping edge and an extra overlapping node.

5   Script Opposition

Now that we have established that script overlap is always present in anaphora ambiguities, the only requirement left for an ambiguity to be humorous is script opposition. It was already stated that in the case of an anaphora ambiguity, the graph representations of both possible interpretations are identical, except for one edge. Therefore this edge must play a key role in the opposition. In the example the edge that differs is the edge between 'the demonstrators' and 'be' in figure 1a and the edge between 'the cops' and 'be' in figure 1b.

'The demonstrators' and 'the cops' are both noun phrases (NPs). Intuitively one might say that these NPs are more or less opposed, but NPs do not have distinct antonyms. The approach we use to compare NPs is inspired by the statement of Fromkin et al. [3, p. 258] that two antonyms have all characteristics in common, except for one, which is present in one word, but not in the other. We use this observation to find antonyms of NPs based on the properties of both NPs. 'The cops' for example are 'human', 'alive', 'grouped', 'orderly' etc. This means that an opposite should have all properties in common, except for one, which should be opposed. This opposed property will be called the *comparison axis*. If we use the property 'alive' as comparison axis for example, then a group of dead cops can be considered to be opposed to 'the cops'.

In our computer implementation we use ConceptNet [4] to retrieve all properties of the two NPs that are involved in the scripts. If they have a sufficient number of properties in common[2] and the non-overlapping properties contain at least one antonymous pair, then the NPs are considered to be opposed. In the example 'the cops' and 'the demonstrators' actually have a lot of properties in common. There are only a few properties that differ (good, brave, orderly, rowdy and grouped) and these properties do contain a pair of antonyms: According to WordNet [5] the property 'rowdy' of 'the demonstrators' is an antonym of the property 'orderly' of 'the cops'. Based on this observation it can be concluded that both NPs are more or less opposed.

Technically speaking this method only proves that the two NPs in the ambiguous sentence are opposed. It does not prove that the complete scripts are opposed. However, the NPs are essential for the difference between the two scripts. Therefore it seems to be safe to assume that if the vertices of the NPs are opposed, the scripts are opposed as well.

6   Implementation

The presented method to distinguish humorous anaphora ambiguities from non-humorous ones was implemented in a Java application. Figure 2 shows an overview of the four modules that form this system.

The *conversation agent* is responsible for receiving input from the user and keeping the conversation with the user going. It forwards all input from the user to the rest of the system. If the system indicates that an anaphora joke can be made, then the conversation agent will make this joke. Otherwise, the conversation agent uses an AIML based chatbot [6] to formulate a response to the user. Figure 3 shows an example of a conversation with the conversation agent. Based on the first two utterances of the user the system cannot make an anaphora joke, so it uses the AIML chatbot to formulate reactions. The last utterance does contain a humorous anaphora ambiguity, so this time the conversation agent returns the joke "The cops were violent?".

---

[2] Note that the requirement that both concepts must have *all* properties in common except for one is relaxed a little. A concept that has *most* properties in common still turned out to be reasonable opposite.

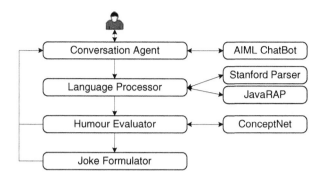

Fig. 2. System architecture

```
User: Hi.
System: What can I call you?
User: My name is John.
System: John, nice to meet you! Are you a man or a woman?
User: I am a man. Did you know that the cops arrested the demonstrators
      because they were violent?
System: The cops were violent? Or the demonstrators? :)
```

Fig. 3. Example of a conversation with the system

The analysis whether a user utterance contains humorous anaphora ambiguities is done by the *language processor* and the *humour evaluator*. The language processor uses JavaRAP [7], a Java implementation of the resolution of anaphora procedure of Lappin and Leass [8]. JavaRAP locates every pronominal anaphor in the text and returns its *real antecedent* only. For the purposes of our system it was adjusted so it returns all possible antecedents from the current and previous sentences, which are not excluded based on eliminating factors like gender and number agreement. If at least two possible antecedents are found, the anaphoric expression is ambiguous and this information is forwarded to the humour evaluator to check whether this ambiguity is humorous.

The *humour evaluator* implements the check for script opposition described earlier in this paper. Roughly this comes down to comparing the *real antecedent* of the anaphor to the possible *other candidate(s)*. The properties of both NPs are retrieved from ConceptNet. Both NPs are compared based on their properties. If they have a sufficient number of properties in common and the non-overlapping properties contain at least one pair of antonymous properties, then the scripts representing both interpretations of the text are considered to be opposite, and a joke can be formulated.

In case of a humorous anaphora ambiguity, the *joke formulator* formulates a joke. The joke is a simple clarification request that indicates that the anaphoric reference was (deliberately) misunderstood. In case of the example with the cops and the demonstrators this results in the clarification request "The cops were violent?".

7   Evaluation

The system was evaluated by having it analyze a chatterbot transcript and a simple story text. In total these texts contained 253 cross-reference ambiguities. These ambiguities were first analyzed by hand to locate all possibilities for anaphora jokes. After this manual analysis the texts were input to the system for automatic analysis. The results of the automatic analysis were then compared to the manually obtained results to evaluate the performance of the system.

In this evaluation the system achieved a precision of 15% and a recall of 15%. This shows that the system is still quite susceptible to errors. The low precision can mainly be attributed to errors in the anaphora resolution. JavaRAP has an accuracy of less than 60% when it needs to rely on imperfect parser output. This caused the system to make a significant amount of non-humorous jokes. The low recall can be attributed to three factors. Errors in the anaphora resolution caused 60% of these errors, 13% was caused by data sparseness of ConceptNet and 27% can be ascribed to limitations of our humour evaluation method. This moderate performance makes it unfeasible to use the system in existing chat applications. However, the system was able to make a number of jokes and the humour evaluation method does provide future prospects in generating conversational humour.

8   Conclusion

This paper described a first attempt at automatically generating jokes based on cross-reference ambiguity. Cross-reference ambiguity occurs frequently in texts and conversations, but it turned out that humorous cross-reference ambiguities are very rare. In fact, it was not feasible to chat with the system until it made one or several jokes. Therefore the system was evaluated by having it analyze several chat transcripts and a simple story text.

The evaluation showed that the system is susceptible to errors. Errors in the anaphora resolution and the data sparseness of ConceptNet turned out to be significant limitations. Nevertheless, the system was able to make a number of jokes from the chat transcripts and simple texts. Since many of the errors cannot be prevented without improving the anaphora resolution and the amount of information in ConceptNet, it is unfeasible to further develop the implemented system and use it in existing chat systems. However, the methods that were introduced may very well prove to be useful in future applications and the idea to utilize ambiguities in a text to construct jokes is useful as well.

References

1. Raskin, V.: Semantic Mechanisms of Humor. Dordrecht–Boston–Lancaster: D. Reidel Publishing Company (1985)
2. Attardo, S., Hempelmann, C.F., di Maio, S.: Script oppositions and logical mechanisms: Modeling incongruities and their resolutions. International Journal of Humor Research 15(1), 3–46 (2002)

3. Fromkin, V., Rodman, R., Neijt, A.: Universele taalkunde. 3e druk edn. Foris Publications, Dordrecht (1986)
4. Liu, H., Singh, P.: Commonsense reasoning in and over natural language. In: Negoita, M.G., Howlett, R.J., Jain, L.C. (eds.) KES 2004. LNCS (LNAI), vol. 3213, Springer, Heidelberg (2004)
5. Fellbaum, C.: WordNet: An Electronic Lexical Database. MIT Press, Cambridge (1998)
6. Wallace, D.R., Tomabechi, D.H., Aimless, D.D.: Chatterbots go native: Considerations for an eco-system fostering the development of artificial life forms in a human world (January 2003)
7. Qiu, L., Kan, M.Y., Chua, T.S.: A public reference implementation of the rap anaphora resolution algorithm. In: Proceedings of the Fourth International Conference on Language Resources and Evaluation (LREC 2004) vol. 1, pp. 291–294 (2004)
8. Lappin, S., Leass, H.J.: An algorithm for pronominal anaphora resolution. Computational Linguistics 20(4), 535–562 (December 1994)

Dataset Complexity and Gene Expression Based Cancer Classification

Oleg Okun[1] and Helen Priisalu[2]

[1] University of Oulu, Oulu 90014, Finland
[2] Tallinn University of Technology, Tallinn 19086, Estonia

Abstract. When applied to supervised classification problems, dataset complexity determines how difficult a given dataset to classify. Since complexity is a nontrivial issue, it is typically defined by a number of measures. In this paper, we explore complexity of three gene expression datasets used for two-class cancer classification. We demonstrate that estimating the dataset complexity before performing actual classification may provide a hint whether to apply a single best nearest neighbour classifier or an ensemble of nearest neighbour classifiers.

1 Introduction

Cancer classification based on expression levels of genes is a nontrivial task for supervised classification methods. The main source of difficulty comes from the fact that there are thousands of genes versus dozens of cases and often an independent test set is unavailable. Hence, for any classifier it is easy to overfit which implies poor generalisation to new data. In addition, there are usually many classifiers performing equally well. The latter fact prompts researchers to use ensembles of classifiers rather than a single classifier. However, an intriguing question remains: when an ensemble outperforms a single best classifier (SBC), given that both SBC and classifiers in an ensemble belong to the same model or, in other words, when increased computational efforts spent on an ensemble are worthy. In this work, we chose the nearest neighbour (NN) classifiers for study, because NNs demonstrated very good performance in many practical tasks and they do not have many parameters to set.

Our main idea is to analyse dataset complexity before actual classification in order to decide whether estimates of this complexity can be employed when choosing between an NN ensemble and SBC. The next section describes the dataset complexity in detail.

2 Dataset Complexity Measures

It is known that the performance of individual classifiers and their ensembles is strongly data-dependent. It is often difficult to give theoretical bounds on performance or these bounds are limited to few very specific cases and/or too weak

F. Masulli, S. Mitra, and G. Pasi (Eds.): WILF 2007, LNAI 4578, pp. 484–490, 2007.
© Springer-Verlag Berlin Heidelberg 2007

to be useful in practice. To gain insight into a supervised classification problem such as cancer classification, one can adopt complexity measures introduced and studied in [1]. Complexity measures described below assume two-class problems and they are classifier-independent in the sense that they can be applied to any classifier. We opted for classifier-independent measures in contrast to classifier-specific ones, because the latter do not provide an *absolute* scale for comparison. For instance, it is well known that an NN classifier can sometimes (but not always) easily deals with highly nonlinear problems.

Fisher's Discriminant Ratio (F1). Fisher's discriminant ratio is defined as $f = \frac{(\mu_1 - \mu_2)^2}{\sigma_1^2 + \sigma_2^2}$, where μ_1, μ_2, σ_1^2, σ_2^2 are the means and variances of the two classes, respectively. The higher f ($f \to \infty$ corresponds to two classes represented by two spatially separated points), the easier the classification problem. Hence $F1 = \max\{f_i\}$, $i = 1, \ldots, n$, where n is the number of features.

Volume of Overlap Region (F2). A similar measure is the overlap of the tails of the two class-conditional distributions. Let $\min(g_i, c_j)$ and $\max(g_i, c_j)$ be the minimum and maximum values of feature g_i in class c_j. Then the overlap measure $F2$ is defined to be $F2 = \Pi_{i=1}^{n} \frac{MIN(\max(g_i, c_1), \max(g_i, c_2)) - MAX(\min(g_i, c_1), \min(g_i, c_2))}{MAX(\max(g_i, c_1), \max(g_i, c_2)) - MIN(\min(g_i, c_1), \min(g_i, c_2))}$. The volume is set to zero if there is at least one feature for which value ranges of the two classes do not overlap (negative numerator of the ith component of the product above signals about this case). In other words, the smaller $F2$, the easier the dataset to classify.

Feature Efficiency (F3). This measure accounts for how much each feature individually contributes to the class separation. Each feature takes values in a certain interval. If there is an overlap of intervals of two classes, there is ambiguity of classification in the overlapping region. The larger the number of cases lying outside this region, the easier class separation. For linearly separated classes, the overlapping region is empty and therefore all cases are outside of it. For highly overlapped classes, this region is large and the number of cases lying outside is small. Thus, feature efficiency is defined as the fraction of cases outside the overlapping region. $F3$ corresponds to the maximum feature efficiency.

3   Datasets

SAGE Dataset. SAGE stands for Serial Analysis of Gene Expression [2]. This is technology alternative to microarrays (cDNAs and oligonucleotides). Though SAGE was originally conceived for use in cancer studies, there is not much research using SAGE datasets regarding ensembles of classifiers.

   In this dataset [3], there are expressions of 822 genes in 74 cases (24 cases are normal while 50 cases are cancerous) [4]. Unlike many other datasets with one or few types of cancer, it contains 9 different types of cancer. We decided to ignore the difference between cancer types and to treat all cancerous cases as belonging to a single class. No preprocessing was done.

Colon Dataset. This microarray (oligonucleotide) dataset [5], introduced in [6], contains expressions of 2,000 genes for 62 cases (22 normal and 40 colon tumour cases). Preprocessing includes the logarithmic transformation to base 10, followed by normalisation to zero mean and unit variance as usually done with this dataset.

Brain Dataset. This microarray (oligonucleotide) dataset [7] introduced in [8] is different from the previous two because it contains two classes of brain tumour instead of cancer and normal classes. The dataset (also known as Dataset B) contains 34 medulloblastoma cases, 9 of which are desmoplastic and 25 are classic. Preprocessing consists of thresholding of gene expressions with a floor of 20 and ceiling of 16,000; filtering with exclusion of genes with $max / min \leq 3$ or $max - min < 100$, where max and min refer to the maximum and minimum expressions of a certain gene across the 34 cases, respectively; base 10 logarithmic transformation; normalisation across genes to zero mean and unit variance. As a result, 5,893 out of 7,129 original genes are only retained.

4   Experiments

4.1   Complexity Estimation

Table 1 provides the values of all complexity measures estimated for all datasets. Italicised values point to the most complex dataset according to each measure.

Table 1. Summary of dataset complexity measures

Dataset	$F1$	$F2$	$F3$
SAGE	*0.35*	*2.86e-154*	*0.34*
Colon	1.39	5.15e-300	0.42
Brain	2.78	0	0.74

All three measures are well correlated in the sense that the SAGE dataset is ranked as the most complex while the Brain dataset is judged to be the least complex by all measures. The Colon dataset has the medium complexity. Close to zero values of $F2$ for all datasets imply that there are certain genes that when being selected lead to the perfect class separation. Hence, gene selection should be used prior to classification in order to boost classification performance. Having obtained complexity estimates, we are now ready to check under which circumstances an NN ensemble is superior to a single best NN classifier. We presume that ensembles are more useful for complex problems while a single strong classifier is enough to accurately classify easy data. Based on the current results, it looks as an ensemble would be the right choice for SAGE data whereas a single best classifier would suffice for Colon and Brain data.

4.2   Performance Evaluation of NN Classifiers and Their Ensembles

The following values of the number of nearest neighbours were tried: $k = 1, 3, 5$. Distance computation was done using Euclidean metric.

For gene selection, four methods also employed in [9] were chosen: pairwise gene selection (greedy-pairs and all-pairs), greedy forward selection, and individual ranking. As follows from its name, pairwise gene selection takes into account interaction between pairs of genes. Other two methods are one-gene-at-a-time methods. All the methods expect two-class data and belong to the filter model, i.e., they do not rely on a classifier when selecting genes, though they utilise class labels for this purpose[3].

A combination of gene selection followed by k-NN classification is termed the base classifier. In total, there are 12 such classifiers to fuse into an ensemble (four gene selection methods times three k-NN classifiers). Ensemble pruning was performed before generating the final ensemble according to the algorithm [10] based on diversity in predictions of individual NNs composing an ensemble[4]. This algorithm iteratively selected L out of 12 base classifiers based on the diversity criterion. The following values of L were tried: 3, 5, 7, 9, 11, and 12. For Brain data, the diversity was very small and it quickly became saturated when adding classifiers while it was the highest for SAGE data and exhibited fast growth as ensemble size increased. Finally, the base classifiers left after pruning were combined into an ensemble by 1) majority vote and 2) Naïve Bayes combination with a correction for zeroes [11].

To evaluate classification performance, a Receiver Operating Characteristic (ROC) was utilised, which is a plot of false positive rate (X-axis) versus true positive rate (Y-axis) of a binary classifier [12]. The true positive rate (TPR) is defined as the ratio of the number of correctly classified positive cases to the total number of positive cases. The false positive rate (FPR) is defined as the ratio of incorrectly classified negative cases to the total number of negative cases. Cancer cases were assumed to be the positives for both SAGE and Colon data while for Brain data the positives were classic medulloblastoma cases.

The ROC curve is a two-dimensional plot of classifier performance. To compare classifiers one typically prefers to work with a single scalar value. This value is called the Area Under Curve or AUC. It is calculated by adding the areas under the ROC curve between each pair of consecutive FPR values, using, for example, the trapezoidal rule. Because the AUC is a portion of the area of the unit square, its value will always lie between 0 and 1. The better a classifier performs, the higher its AUC.

Ensembles were generated 500 times using each combination scheme, with each classifier working with the number of genes randomly set between 1 and

---

[3] However, a decision about what gene(s) to select is made based on t-statistic.

[4] Classifiers are diverse if they make errors on different cases so that errors are uncorrelated.

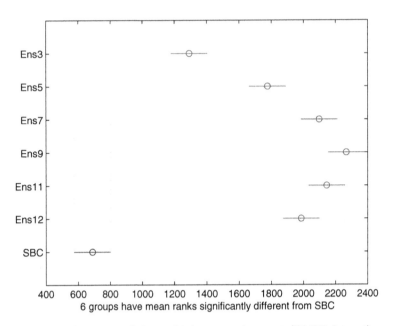

Fig. 1. Summary of the multiple comparison test (SAGE dataset)

50 so that the number of genes to be selected varied from classifier to classifier in each ensemble. The AUC values were computed for both NN ensembles of all possible configurations (six values of L above) and corresponding SBCs in each ensemble. Based on these AUC values, the nonparametric statistical tests such as the Kruskal-Wallis one-way ANOVA followed by the multiple comparisons with the Scheffé's S adjustment for the significance level α ($\alpha = 0.01$ and $\alpha = 0.05$ were tried) were carried out [13]. Both nonparametric tests operate on ranks of AUCs rather than AUC values themselves[5].

Results are summarised in Figs. 1-3. In all figures, 'Ensℓ' stands for the ensemble of ℓ base classifiers combined by the Naïve Bayes scheme, and 'mean rank' stands for the average rank of AUCs in a certain group where groups are SBC, Ens3, Ens5, Ens7, Ens9, Ens11, and Ens12.

Based on the statistical tests, NN ensembles regardless of the combination scheme fared better than SBCs for the SAGE data (mean ranks of ensembles are significantly larger than those of SBCs in Fig. 1, i.e., AUC values for ensembles tend to be larger on average than those for SBC), but not for other two datasets, where SBCs were superior to ensembles. Thus, the estimates of the dataset complexity computed above pointed to the correct choice for all datasets. Regarding two combination schemes, Naïve Bayes combination slightly outperformed majority vote on all datasets.

---

[5] Notice that lower AUC values were assigned a higher rank. For example, if there were the following values: 79, 75, and 89, then they got ranks 2, 1, and 3. Thus, the lowest AUC value is always ranked the first.

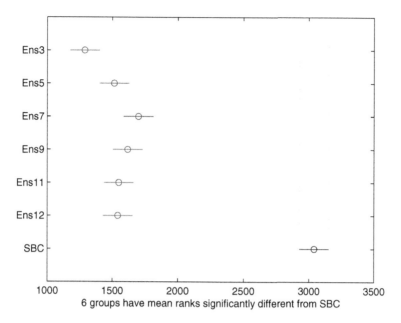

Fig. 2. Summary of the multiple comparison test (Colon dataset)

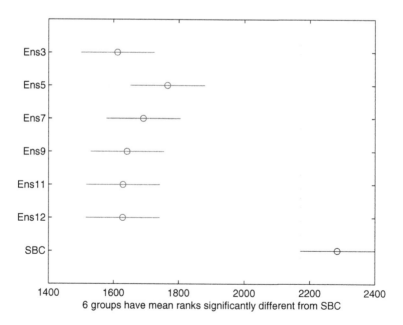

Fig. 3. Summary of the multiple comparison test (Brain dataset)

5 Conclusion

As demonstrated by our experiments, a single best NN suffices for "easy" datasets such as Colon or Brain. For complex data sets such as SAGE, an NN ensemble decisively outperforms a single best NN. The complexity measures we used well correlated with this experimental evidence. Hence, they are useful when one needs to choose between a single NN and an NN ensemble in gene expression based cancer classification.

References

1. Ho, T.K., Basu, M.: Complexity Measures of Supervised Classification Problems. IEEE Trans. Patt. Analysis and Machine Intell. 24, 289–300 (2002)
2. Velculescu, V.E., Zhang, L., Vogelstein, B., Kinzler, K.W.: Serial Analysis of Gene Expression. Science 270, 484–487 (1995)
3. http://lisp.vse.cz/challenge/ecmlpkdd2004
4. Gandrillon, O.: Guide to the Gene Expression Data. In: Berka, P., Crémilleux, B. (eds.): Proc. the ECML/PKDD Discovery Challenge Workshop, Pisa, Italy, pp. 116–120 (2004)
5. http://microarray.princeton.edu/oncology/affydata/index.html
6. Alon, U., Barkai, N., Notterman, D.A., Gish, K., Ybarra, S., Mack, D., Levine, A.J.: Broad Patterns of Gene Expression Revealed by Clustering Analysis of Tumor and Normal Colon Tissues Probed by Oligonucleotide Arrays. Proc. Natl. Acad. Sci. 96, 6745–6750 (1999)
7. http://www.broad.mit.edu/mpr/CNS/
8. Pomeroy, S.L., Tamayo, P., Gaasenbeek, M., Sturla, L.M., Angelo, M., McLaughlin, M.E., Kim, J.Y.H., Goumnerova, L.C., Black, P.M., Lau, C., Allen, J.C., Zagzag, D., Olson, J.M., Curran, T., Wetmore, C., Biegel, J.A., Poggio, T., Mukherjee, S., Rifkin, R., Califano, A., Stolovitzky, G., Louis, D.N., Mesirov, J.P., Lander, E.S., Golub, T.R.: Prediction of Central Nervous System Embryonal Tumour Outcome Based on Gene Expression. Nature 415, 436–442 (2002)
9. Bø, T.H., Jonassen, I.: Feature Subset Selection Procedures for Classification of Expression Profiles. Genome Biology 3, 0017.1–0017.11 (2002)
10. Prodromidis, A.L., Stolfo, S., Chan, P.K.: Pruning Classifiers in a Distributed Meta-Learning System. In: Proc. the 1st Panhellenic Conf. New Inf. Technologie, Athens, Greece, pp. 151–160 (1998)
11. Kuncheva, L.I.: Combining Pattern Classifiers: Methods and Algorithms. John Wiley & Sons, Inc, Hoboken, NJ (2004)
12. Fawcett, T.: An Introduction to ROC Analysis. Patt. Recogn. Letters 27, 861–874 (2006)
13. Zar, J.H.: Biostatistical Analysis. Prentice Hall, Inc., Upper Saddle River, NJ (1999)

A Novel Hybrid GMM/SVM Architecture for Protein Secondary Structure Prediction

Emad Bahrami Samani[1], M. Mehdi Homayounpour[1], and Hong Gu[2]

[1] Computer Engineering and IT Department, Amirkabir University of Technology
Tehran, Iran
bahrami@ce.aut.ac.ir, homayoun@aut.ac.ir
[2] Department of Mathematics and Statistics, Dalhousie University
Halifax, NS, Canada
hgu@mathstat.dal.ca

Abstract. The problem of secondary structure prediction can be formulated as a pattern classification problem and methods from statistics and machine learning are suitable. This paper proposes a new combination approach between Gaussian Mixture Model (GMM) and Support Vector Machine (SVM) by typical sample extraction based on a UBM/GMM system for SVM in protein secondary structure prediction. Our hybrid model achieved a good performance of **three-state overall per residue accuracy $Q_3 = 77.6\%$** which is comparable to the best techniques available.

1 Introduction

Accurate prediction of protein secondary structure is a step towards understanding the protein 3D structure which in turn determines the protein function. The problem of protein secondary structure prediction usually is formulated as classifying the residues to the structure categories of helix (H), sheet (E) or coil (C) [1].

Many approaches have been proposed to solve this problem. They can be grossly grouped into three classes: linear statistical methods based on amino acid codings of the residues or physico-chemical properties or both [10]; symbolic machine learning methods [11]; nonlinear statistical methods for prediction, where neural networks or knn (K nearest-neighbor) methods etc. are often adopted using amino acid codings of the residues or physico-chemical properties as input [7], [8]. To formulate this problem into a statistical learning problem, each residue is associated with a d-dimensional feature vector which includes the amino acid codings of the residue and its physico-chemical properties, thus each residue is viewed as a point in a d-dimensional space and will be called cases or samples henceforth. When d is large, feature selection and/or feature transformation are necessary. The goal is to choose those features and the transformations that allow cases belonging to different categories to occupy compact and disjoint regions in a transformed feature space.

In this paper, we propose a method as a combination of Gaussian Mixture Model(GMM) and Support Vector Machine (SVM). SVM has been successfully

F. Masulli, S. Mitra, and G. Pasi (Eds.): WILF 2007, LNAI 4578, pp. 491–496, 2007.

used in predicting protein secondary structures [3]. The main ideas of SVM can be viewed as that SVM maps the samples into a high dimensional space, and seeking an optimum separating hyperplane in this space. The mapping is not explicitly defined but is through the definition of a kernel function in the original d-dimensional space. The attractive point of such defined transformation is that the samples can be mapped into a space of infinite dimension but the classifier is expressed in a format of a "linear" combination of the kernel functions with only a small number of samples (which are called support vectors) with non zero coefficients α_i.

$$f(x) = \sum_{i=1}^{l} \alpha_i y_i k(x, x_i) + b \tag{1}$$

Where $x_i \in \mathbb{R}^d, 1 \leq i \leq l$ are the training data. Each point of x_i belongs to one of the two classes identified by the label $y_i \in \{-1, 1\}$. Note that the coeficients of this "linear" combination have to be learned from the data and thus it is not really linear.

We consider to fix Radial Basis Function (RBF) kernel for SVM and use GMM to preselect the samples for SVM. The main idea is to denoise the training data and provide typical and more appropriate samples for the learning of SVM classifier. In protein secondary structure prediction, the physico-chemical properties of residues play the main role in the **protein foldings**. The term "typical samples" in this area has been used for those training samples which satisfy the main constraints to form a particular 3D structure for a residue. Intuitively these "typical samples" have more concise information about the protein structures and are more proper to be based on to perform a classification task. The GMM used in selecting these typical samples has some consistency to the RBF kernels used in SVM. The results show that such pre-processing of training data improves the performance of SVM in protein secondary structure prediction.

2   The Hybrid GMM/SVM Architecture

Typically GMM is used in classifications because it is reasonably accurate in approximating a complicated distribution. Let $X^i = \{x_t, t = 1...T^i\}$ denote the set of samples from the i_{th} class (e.g., a particular structure). The joint distribution of these data can be modeled by a total number of J Gaussians as follows [6]:

$$p(X^i|\theta^i_{GMM}) = \prod_{t=1}^{T^i} \sum_{j=1}^{J} P(z_j) P_{z_j}(x_t|u_j, \Sigma_j) \tag{2}$$

where θ^i_{GMM} includes all the model parameters, i.e., $\{P(z_j), u_j, \Sigma_j, 1 \leq j \leq J\}$. $P_{z_j}(x_t|u_j, \Sigma_j)$ is the j_{th} Gaussian distribution $N(u_j, \Sigma_j)$.

Suppose three GMM models were trained on data of three protein secondary structures of helix (H), sheet (E) and coil (C), denoted as f_H, f_E and f_C respectively. According to the Bayes decision theory, a new sample x is to be assigned to the class with highest posterior probability. If the sizes of the classes are treated as the same, then the sample x is to be assigned to the class with largest log-likelihood value according to the estimated desities f_H, f_E and f_C. Here we adopt a similar idea in preprocessing the data using estimated densities. We compare the log-likelihood value of each trainning sample evaluated by the estimated density of its own class with the log-likelihood value evaluated by a mixture density estimated on the training data from all protein secondary structures, the later is called a Universal Background GMM Model (UBM/GMM). The UBM/GMM log-likelihood value is used as threshold for each sample. "Typical samples" are defined as those samples with the log-likelihood value of its own class larger than the log-likelihood values evaluated by UBM/GMM model. Only the "typical samples" will be used in trainning SVM for protein secondary structures prediction. This method strategically reduce the input number of samples and ensure the fast and accurate trainning for SVM.

In our approach a dataset of 619 protein chains from three protein secondary structures were used to train the UBM model. Figure 1 shows the framework of our hybrid architecture. First the sequence data are marked as either noise or signal using the UBM/GMM system and then the "typical samples" extracted in the first step are used as input to the SVM training.

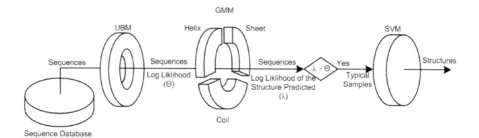

Fig. 1. Framework of the proposed hybrid GMM/SVM architecture

3   Experiments

3.1   Data Set

Two data sets were used in evaluating our system. The first dataset (RS126 dataset) consists of 126 protein chains, was presented by Rost and Sander [8]. The other larger dataset, referred as CB513 dataset by Cuff and Barton [9], contains 513 proteins.

3.2   Experimental Results

We perform the analysis by the proposed method on two data sets. The accuracy of the prediction is estimated by sevenfold cross validation on both UBM/GMM and SVM phases. The number of Gaussians in the pre-processing phase was selected as 64.

In the GMM phase, with the selected mixture, we got the best prediction accuracy of $Q_3 = 57.68\%$ having 15 as the window size for RS126 dataset and $Q_3 = 65.84\%$ for CB513 dataset by setting 13 as the window size. These results illustrate that GMM itself does not perform as well as the other techniques such as PHD and SVM which have reached the accuracy above the threshold of 70%. However, SVM by the typical samples has improved the prediction accuracy largely, which shows that GMM has done well in the typical sample extraction.

For RS126 dataset, 79.78% of the trainning samples are extracted as typical samples by using the window size as 5. Whileas for CB513 dataset, this number is 59.53%. The number of samples that have been marked as noise in CB513 dataset is much greater than that for RS126 and the extraction has been more accurate on a larger dataset. This results from the fact that the density estimation is better with a larger data set.

To optimize the performance, three tuning parameters are estimated by sevenfold cross validation grid search. They include the window size, the γ value in the kernel function and the regularization parameter C for SVM. The optimal values for these parameters are shown in Table 1.

Table 1. The optimal values of tuning parameters and the prediction accuracy

Dataset	Classifier	γ	C	Windowsize	Accuracy(%)
	$H/\tilde{H}$	0.26	1.35	11	77.69
	$E/\tilde{E}$	0.21	1.16	11	75.47
RS126	$C/\tilde{C}$	0.16	1.42	15	78.35
	H/E	0.12	1.13	13	73.98
	E/C	0.26	1.37	9	74.87
	C/H	0.17	1.46	13	75.42
	$H/\tilde{H}$	0.16	1.43	11	85.56
	$E/\tilde{E}$	0.35	1.31	11	79.27
CB513	$C/\tilde{C}$	0.23	1.36	13	83.99
	H/E	0.15	1.47	11	80.34
	E/C	0.38	1.24	15	78.22
	C/H	0.18	1.36	13	79.32

The prediction accuracies of tertiary classifiers on both data sets are shown in Table 2. The best performing tertiary classifier, measured by Q_{total} score is TREE1 having a per-residue accuracy of 77.6%.

3.3   Comparison with Other Methods

A fair comparison of different methods turns out to be difficult, because different trainning datasets and different secondary structure assignments are used[3]. However, some authors have published their experimental results estimated on

Table 2. Performance of our tertiary classifier

Dataset	TertiaryClassifier	$Q_{total}(\%)$	$Q_H(\%)$	$Q_E(\%)$	$Q_C(\%)$	C_H	C_E	C_C
	TREE1 (H-E-C)	74.69	77.33	70.29	73.83	0.61	0.53	0.54
RS126	TREE2 (E-C-H)	73.39	76.17	68.25	74.38	0.58	0.51	0.55
	TREE3 (C-H-E)	72.74	75.43	69.13	75.73	0.54	0.53	0.55
	TREE1 (H-E-C)	77.58	79.23	73.76	78.19	0.63	0.54	0.56
CB513	TREE2 (E-C-H)	74.41	77.45	71.22	78.1	0.60	0.53	0.55
	TREE3 (C-H-E)	75.22	78.71	70.05	80.21	0.60	0.53	0.57

the same datasets using the same performance measures. Comparisons between PHD method presented by Rost and Sander [8], SVM method proposed by Hua and Sun [3], and our hybrid GMM/SVM method are shown in Table 3. Note that the number of support vectors used by Hua and Sun is 43-53% and the number of support vectors in our approach is 36-44%.

Table 3. Comparison with the results of PHD and SVM

Dataset	Method	$Q_{total}(\%)$	$Q_H(\%)$	$Q_E(\%)$	$Q_C(\%)$	C_H	C_E	C_C
	PHD	70.8	72	66	72	0.60	0.52	0.51
RS126	SVM	71.2	73	58	75	0.61	0.51	0.52
	GMM/SVM	74.7	77	70	75	0.61	0.53	0.55
	PHD	72.1	70	62	79	0.63	0.53	0.52
CB513	SVM	73.5	75	60	79	0.65	0.53	0.54
	GMM/SVM	77.6	79	70	80	0.63	0.54	0.57

3.4 Tools

SVM training and scoring are performed using the software LibSVM [12]. GMM validation was performed using the open-source software HTK 3.2.1[13].

4 Conclusion

GMM and SVM are very suitable tools for data mining and machine learning applications. However, classic mixture models like GMM, which is a HMM with one state; uses the same set of mixture weights for all the training data of a specified class, which causes problems in fitting the training data accurately. On the other hand, processing a large number of feature vectors in a problem like protein secondary structure prediction is quite difficult for SVM. This paper presented a new hybrid system that fuses the advantages of both GMM and SVM for protein secondary structure prediction. Performance of 77.6% was achieved using this approach which is comparable to the best available techniques.

References

1. Baldi, P., Brunak, S.: Bioinformatics, the Machine Learning approach, 2nd edn. The MIT Press, Cambridge, MA (2001)
2. Eidhammer, I., Jonassen, I., Taylor, W.R.: Protein Bioinformatics: An algorithmic Approach to Sequence and Strcture Analysis. John Wiley & Sons, Ltd, New York (2004)
3. Hua, S., Sun, Z.: A novel method of protein secondary structure prediction with high segment overlap measure: Support vector machine approach. Jour. Mol. Biology 308, 397–407 (2001)
4. Liu, M., Xie, Y., Yao, Z., Dai, B.: A New Hybrid GMM/SVM for Speaker Verification. In: The 18th International Confrence on Pattern Recognition (ICPR 06) (2006)
5. Bredin, H., Dehak, N., Chollet, G.: GMM-based SVM for face detection. In: The 18th International Confrence on Pattern Recognition (ICPR 06)
6. Zhu, Y., Fujimura, K.: Driver Face Tracking using Gaussian Mixture Model (GMM). In: Proceedings, International IEEE conference on Image Processing. (2003)
7. Qian, N., Sejnowski, T.: Predicting the secondary structure of globular proteins using neural network models. Journal of Molecular Biology 202, 865–884 (1988)
8. Rost, B., Sander, C.: Prediction of secondary Structure at better than 70% accuracy. Journal of Molecular Biology 232, 584–599 (1993)
9. Cuff, J.A., Barton, G.J.: Evaluation and improvement of multiple sequence methods for protein secondary structure prediction. Proteins: Struct. Funct. Genet. 34, 508–519 (1999)
10. Avbelj, F., Fele, L.: Role of Main-chain Electrostatics, Hydrophobic effect and Side-chain conformational entropy in determining the secondary structure of proteins. Journal of Molecular Biology 279, 665–684 (1998)
11. Muggleton, S., King, R.D., Sternberg, M.J.E.: Protein secondary structure prediction using logic. Protein Eng. 5, 647–657 (1992)
12. Fan, R.E., Chen, P.H., Lin, C.J.: Working set selection using the second order information for training SVM. Journal of Machine Learning Research 6, 1889–1918 (2005)
13. Cambridge University Engineering Department: HTK, library modules and tools available in C source form, at :http://htk.eng.cam.ac.uk/download.shtml

A Graph Theoretic Approach to Protein Structure Selection

Marco Vassura[1], Luciano Margara[1], Piero Fariselli[2], and Rita Casadio[2]

[1] Computer Science Department, University of Bologna, Italy
[2] Biocomputing Group, Department of Biology, University of Bologna, Italy

Abstract. Protein Structure Prediction (PSP) aims to reconstruct the 3D structure of a given protein starting from its primary structure (chain of amino acids). It is a well known fact that the 3D structure of a protein only depends on its primary structure. PSP is one of the most important and still unsolved problems in computational biology. Protein Structure Selection (PSS), instead of reconstructing a 3D model for the given chain, aims to select among a given, possibly large, number of 3D structures (called decoys) those that are closer (according to a given notion of distance) to the original (unknown) one. Each decoy is represented by a set of points in $\mathbb{R}^3$. Existing methods for solving PSS make use of suitably defined energy functions which heavily rely on the primary structure of the protein and on protein chemistry. In this paper we present a completely different approach to PSS which does not take advantage at all of the knowledge of the primary structure of the protein but only relies on the graph theoretic properties of the decoys graphs (vertices represent amino acids and edges represent pairs of amino acids whose euclidean distance is less than or equal to a fixed threshold). Even if our methods only rely on approximate geometric information, experimental results show that some of the graph properties we adopt score similarly to energy-based filtering functions in selecting the best decoys. Our results show the principal role of geometric information in PSS, setting a new starting point and filtering method, for existing energy function-based techniques.

1 Introduction

One of the most important and largely unsolved problems in bioinformatics is the so called *3D protein structure prediction* (PSP) [2,5,9]. It is a well known fact that all protein molecules are uniquely identified by means of their *primary structure*, i.e., the sequence of amino acids that forms the backbone of the protein. In other words, under physiological conditions, a chain of amino acids admits a unique compact and functionally active conformation called *native structure*. PSP is the problem of computing the 3D structure of a protein, i.e., the spatial coordinates of all the amino acids, taking as input its primary structure. The output of PSP methods usually consists of a possibly large set of candidates (decoys) that are expected to approximate the given protein conformation. Protein Structure Selection problem (PSS), instead of reconstructing a 3D model for a given chain

F. Masulli, S. Mitra, and G. Pasi (Eds.): WILF 2007, LNAI 4578, pp. 497–504, 2007.

of amino acids, aims to select, among a given, possibly large, number of decoys those that are closer (according to a given notion of distance) to the original (unknown) protein 3D structure. A number of heuristics have been developed during the last few years for solving PSS (see for example [10,6,9,15]). All of them make use of the so called *energy functions*. Energy functions take as input the primary structure of the protein and the description of a decoy and yield a numerical value (score) which is expected to measure the quality of the decoy. The lowest is the energy of a decoy the closest to the 3D structure of the original protein it should be. Unfortunately, it is known that small intrinsic errors can lead to predict a high number of erroneous structures having a lower energy than the native structure [7]. In this paper we present a completely new approach to face PSS based on the analysis of some selected graph properties on suitably defined decoys graphs. We represent each decoy as an undirected graph where vertices represent amino acids (residues) and edges represent pairs of amino acids whose euclidean distance is less than or equal to a fixed threshold. Distances are actually computed between pairs of $C\alpha$ atoms which are approximately the centroids of the amino acids. Decoys graphs can be represented by contact maps: binary matrices where values equal to 1 represent pairs of amino acids whose distance is lower or equal to a threshold[1].

The main goal of this paper is to shed some light on the relations existing between decoys and graph properties. We wish to emphasize that our ranking techniques are completely independent of the primary structure of the proteins. In other words, we evaluate decoys quality according to (coarse) geometric information only. To test our methods and to make them comparable to other methods, we use one of the most widely accepted benchmark data set [15], available at the Baker Laboratory web site[2] (see Appendix 2.2). Given the data set of protein and decoy structures, we consider seven graph properties, namely *Average Degree, Contact Order, Normalized Complexity, Network Flow, Connectivity*, and a weighted version of *Network Flow* and *Connectivity*. The ability of each graph property to distinguish between correct and incorrect 3D structures is then evaluated by computing the Z score and the Enrichment score [15]. Experimental results show that the above listed properties perform similarly (if not better) to previously described methods based on backbone energy functions [15,14]. In addition, we assess the quality of our method following the MQAP CAFASP4 criteria and data sets. The Critical Assessment of Fully Automated Structure Prediction (CAFASP) experiment is a blind test that provides an objective assessment of the effectiveness of automated PSP methods. The Model Quality Assessment Programs (MQAP) category of the CAFASP4 evaluated capabilities of state of the art programs to distinguish near native structures among decoys. We show that our procedure ranks among the best MQAPs at the MQAP CAFASP4 experiment.

---

[1] Thresholds in the range from 7 to 18Å with a step of 1Å were tested, finding no correlation with the Enrichment and Z score of the best performing graph properties. For sake of brevity in this paper we show results for a fixed threshold.

[2] ftp://ftp.bakerlab.org/pub/decoys/decoys_11-14-01.tar.gz

2   Materials and Methods

2.1   Graph Properties

We selected graph properties with polynomial time complexity able to capture some of the properties of the whole protein 3D structure. The average time to compute[3] one of the following graph properties on a decoy is less than 1 second, allowing to use them as filtering tools in wide-scale computing.

Average Degree (AvgDeg). This property is obtained as the ratio of the number of edges (contacts) in the protein structure divided by the protein length. The number of edges of a given residue depends on the protein 3D structure. The greater the number of edges the more contacts each residue makes.

Contact Order (CO). Contact Order measures the average contact (edge) distributions with respect to the residue sequence separation [11]. CO is computed as: $CO = \frac{\sum^{nedges} \frac{\Delta_{ij}}{n}}{nedges}$ where the summation index runs only on the adjacent residue pairs i and j, n is the protein length, $\Delta_{ij} = |i - j|$ is the distance between residues i and j measured on the primary protein structure (sequence separation), and *nedges* is the number of edges in the graph associated to the protein contact map. A high contact order value implies that there are several adjacent residues that are far apart on the residue sequence but are close in the 3D structure.

Normalized Complexity (Ncompl). The complexity is the number of spanning trees of the graph [4], namely the number of all the trees that link all the graph vertices. It is computed as previously described in [1] using GSL libraries [8]. Values of this property are exponentially increasing at increasing number of edges per protein length (*AvgDeg*). We define *Ncompl* as the complexity of the graph divided by $AvgDeg^n$, where n is the residue number of each protein. Since *AvgDeg* is different for each structure, the information contained in *Ncompl* can be regarded as a normalized complexity.

Network Flow (Flow). *Flow* computes the maximum flow from the first (residue in position 1) to the last residue (residue in position n), i.e. the minimum number of contacts (edges) that have to be deleted in order to disconnect the first and the last residue [4]. This property is related to the protein connectivity with respect to the first and last residue and is computed with HI_PR[4], an efficient implementation of the push-relabel method [3].

Weighted Flow (Wflow). *Wflow* is the maximum flow (*Flow*) considering the graph edges (contacts) weighted by the value of the distance between adjacent residues Δ_{ij} as measured on the primary protein structure.

Connectivity (Conn). *Conn* is the edge connectivity: the minimum number of edges that have to be deleted to disconnect at least one residue from all the others [4]. It is computed as the minimum of each maximum flow from the first residue to each other residue.

---

[3] Computations were run on a system equipped with 2Gb RAM and 2.40GHz Intel(R) Xeon(TM) CPU.

[4] http://www.igsystems.com/hipr/download.html

Weighted Connectivity(Wconn) *Wconn* is similar to *Conn*, however with weights associated to edges. Weights are distances between adjacent residues Δ_{ij} as measured on the primary protein structure.

2.2   Decoy Set

The decoy set was downloaded from the Baker's Laboratory web site[5]. This set (Rosetta) was obtained with the Rosetta algorithm that routinely can generate reasonable low-resolution structures, but that cannot reliably identify the most native-like model [2]. We choose this decoys set because it is the most recent and complete in terms of number of proteins and decoys per protein[6]. In particular, the decoys were produced following four criteria: 1) containing conformations for a wide variety of different proteins; 2) containing conformations close (<0.4 nm) to the native structures; 3) consisting of conformations that are at least near local minimum of a reasonable scoring function; 4) being produced by a relatively unbiased procedure (see [15] for details). Fig. 1 shows for each protein

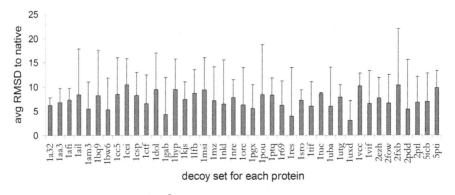

Fig. 1. Average CαRMSD (in Å) computed over the Rosetta decoy set adopted for benchmarking our method. The set is constructed to be an objective and difficult test for PSS; it consists of 41 native proteins with about 1800 decoys per native protein, for a total of about 76000 protein structures.

in the set the average CαRMSD of the decoys from the native protein together with the corresponding standard deviation.

2.3   Enrichment and Z Score

The Z score accounts for the deviation from the average distribution in standard deviation units. More formally for a graph property (see section 2.1) m:

$$Z = \frac{m_n - avg_m}{var_m}$$

---

where m_n is the value of m for the native protein 3D structure, avg and var are respectively the average and variance of m for the corresponding protein models/decoys. To compute the Z score of a set of decoys we take the average of Z scores values for each native structure (wrt corresponding decoys) in the set. The larger is the absolute Z score value, the better a specific graph property sorts out the native structure among its decoys.

The Enrichment score, as introduced by [15], accounts for the correlation between the property under examination and the CαRMSDbetween the decoys/models and the native structure. The Enrichment is computed as:

$$Enrichment = \frac{\#(First(k,m) \cap First(k, \text{C}\alpha\text{RMSD}))}{\#(First(k, Random) \cap First(k, \text{C}\alpha\text{RMSD}))}$$

where $First(k, m)$ is the subset of the first k decoys ranked according to the graph property m, at decreasing or increasing values, depending on the graph property type[7]; $First(k, \text{C}\alpha\text{RMSD})$ is the subset of the first k decoys ranked according to the CαRMSDfrom to the native structure; $First(k, Random)$ is the subset of the first k decoys ranked according to the random assignment. To compare our results with those in [15], the number of decoys found in the intersection set between the top high scoring 15% decoys (as obtained according to a given graph property), and the top 15% decoys with the lowest CαRMSDfor a given native protein is divided by the number of random assignment (the random assignment value is equal to 15% × 15% × total number of decoys in the set). This is done to highlight the performance of the graph property at hand. An Enrichment value equal to one indicates that the graph property does not perform better than a random assignment (the higher the value the better is the performance of the property at hand).

3   Results

In this paper we test our method using the Rosetta decoy set [15], computing the same accuracy scores previously described in [15]: the Z and Enrichment score (see Section 2.3 for detailed description). Results are reported in the last seven rows of Table 1: *Ncompl*, *Wflow* and *CO* are graph properties satisfactory enough to obtain an average Enrichment value higher than one (which is the Enrichment of random assignment) over the protein set. In order to effectively evaluate our graph-based properties we compare our results with methods that have been proved to be very efficient (in [14,15]). From Table 1 emerges that the graph properties perform quite similarly to existing functions, in terms of Enrichment. This is very surprising if we take into account that such accuracy is obtained without any knowledge of chemical information of the native structure, so that they are really complementary to other existing methods for PSS. On the contrary, when the Z score is considered, our graph-properties perform worse than some energy-based functions, indicating that a finer tuning is necessary to pick up the native structure among a set of very close-native decoys. These

---

[7] All properties of this work require decreasing order.

Table 1. Comparison of graph-based functions with the state of the art functions on Rosetta decoy set. The graph properties (last seven rows) perform quite similarly to existing functions in terms of Enrichment. This is surprising if we take into account that such accuracy is obtained without any knowledge of the chemical information of the protein structure.

Function/Property	Rosetta		Function/Property	Rosetta	
	Enrich.	Z score		Enrich.	Z score
All atom:			**All atom(cont.):**		
RAPDF[1]	1.23	-6.71	Effective solvent[3]	0.93	1.77
SOLV[2]	0.84	-2.96	Main chain		
HYDB[2]	1.33	-6.29	hydrogen bonding[3]	1.01	-1.16
TORS[2]	1.36	-2.09	Side chain		
FRST[2]	1.41	-3.72	hydrogen bonding[3]	0.97	-2.05
LJ attractive[3]	1.40	-1.48			
LJ attractive,			**Centroid/Backbone:**		
side chain only[3]	1.35	-1.47	Residue-environment		
LJ repulsive capped[3]	0.85	4.37	(structural)[3]	1.22	1.22
LJ repulsive linear[3]	0.87	3.10	Residue-residue (pair)[3]	1.33	1.14
LJ repulsive linear,			Hard sphere repulsion[3]	0.98	-0.53
side chain only[3]	0.78	-1.48	Strand assembly in sheets[3]	0.99	-0.18
LJ total, capped[3]	0.92	4.38	Strand orientation[3]	1.41	-1.38
LJ total, linear[3]	1.14	-2.48	Strand packing[3]	1.38	-0.98
LJ total, linear,			Helix-strand packing[3]	1.04	0.45
side chain only[3]	1.26	-2.86	$AvgDeg$[4]	1.07	0.56
Coulomb[3]	1.14	-1.52	CO[4]	1.18	0.81
Screened Coulomb[3]	0.87	-0.96	$Ncompl$[4]	1.46	0.38
GB desolvation[3]	0.63	1.51	$Flow$[4]	0.85	-0.08
GB SA[3]	1.61	-1.29	$Conn$[4]	0.58	-0.10
GB total[3]	0.63	1.08	$Wflow$[4]	1.15	0.11
SASA-ASP[3]	1.53	-1.60	$Wconn$[4]	0.69	-0.09

(1) From [12], computed using Victor/FRST software available at http://protein.cribi.unipd.it/frst/. (2) From [14], computed as 1. (3) From [15]. (4) This work.

findings show that our approach, based only on the properties computed from the protein graphs can be adopted when addressing the problem of discriminating native-like conformations in decoy sets, at least as a pre-filtering procedure.

3.1   CAFASP4

CAFASP experiment aims to evaluate the performance of fully automatic structure prediction methods. In contrast to the normal CASP procedure, CAFASP compares prediction methods without allowing any human intervention. The last CAFASP experiment (CAFASP4) automatically generated some 40000 models for 83 targets. In the CAFASP4 MQAP (Model Quality Assessment Programs) category methods to distinguish near-native structures from decoys are

Table 2. Comparison of the best performing graph property $Ncompl$ with the best 6 functions ranked at MQAP CAFASP4: N-1 rank among 86 participants, total cumulative MaxSub score, and number of correct predictions ($MaxSub > 0$). MQAP consensus is a combination of all MQAPs at CAFASP4. Note that $Ncompl$, computed without any knowledge of the protein primary structure, is ranked among the top 4 MQAPs.

Energy-based (1):	MQAP CAFASP4		
	N-1 rank	Total score	$N_{correct}$
Victor/FRST	11	25.47	52
Verify3D	13	25.38	52
Solvex	13	25.25	55
RAPDF	19	24.36	50
ProsaII	22	24.38	48
ProQ	22	24.21	51
Graph-based (2):			
Ncompl	16	24.79	49

(1) CAFASP4. (2) This work.

compared[8]. A MQAP is defined as a program that receives as input a 3D model and produces as output a real number representing the quality of the model. A blind test on the top models predicted by the other prediction methods on 70 targets was used to independently assess the quality of the 15 participating MQAPs. Three evaluation criteria were used: $N_{correct}$, N-1 rank and Total score, all based on MaxSub score. The MaxSub score [13] is the fraction of the model with CαRMSDless or equal to 3.5 Å from the native structure. It assigns scores to a model in the range 0.0 to 1.0. For each of the 70 targets the best model according to the MQAP at hand is considered. $N_{correct}$ is the number of models, among the 70 selected, with $MaxSub > 0$; the Total score is the sum of the MaxSub scores of selected models, and N-1 rank is the best ranking of the MQAP relative to other MQAPs considering only 69 targets. In other words N-1 rank is the highest rank a MQAP achieves, ordering MQAPs by decreasing Total score, in any subsets of 69 targets. Results for best MQAPs and for our best graph property $Ncompl$ are shown in Table 2. Models and details are available at the CAFASP4 web site[9]. Note that N-1 rank is relative to all 86 participants of CAFASP4 (including predictors, meta predictors and MQAPs). It is interesting to note that $Ncompl$ is ranked among the top 4 MQAPs, even if it is computed without any knowledge of the chemical structure of the target protein structures.

Acknowledgements

We thank MIUR for the following grants: PNR 2001-2003 (FIRB art.8) and PNR 2003 projects (FIRB art.8) on Bioinformatics for Genomics and Proteomics and

---

[8] http://www.cs.bgu.ac.il/~dfischer/CAFASP4/mqap.html
[9] http://www.cs.bgu.ac.il/~dfischer/CAFASP4/

LIBI-Laboratorio Internazionale di BioInformatica, both delivered to RC. This work was also supported by the Biosapiens Network of Excellence project no LSHG-CT-2003-503265 (a grant of the European Unions VI Framework Programme).

References

1. Biggs, N.: Algebraic graph theory. Cambridge University Press-VIII, Cambridge (1974)
2. Bonneau, R., Tsai, J., Ruczinski, I., Chivian, D., Rohl, C., Strauss, C.E., Baker, D.: Rosetta in CASP4: progress in ab initio protein structure prediction. Proteins 45(Suppl 5), 119–126 (2001)
3. Cherkassky, B. V., Goldberg, A. V.: On Implementing Push-Relabel Method for the Maximum Flow Problem. In: Proc. IPCO-4, pp. 157–171 (1995)
4. Cormen, T.H., Leiserson, C.E., Rivest, R.L., Stein, C.: Introduction to algorithms. The MIT Press, London (2001)
5. Fariselli, P., Casadio, R.: A neural network based predictor of residue contacts in proteins. Protein Eng. 12, 15–21 (1999)
6. Felts, A.K., Gallicchio, E., Wallqvist, A., Levy, R.M.: Distinguishing native conformations of proteins from decoys with an effective free energyestimator based on the OPLS all-atom force field and the Surface Generalized Born solvent model. Proteins 48, 404–422 (2002)
7. Finkelstein, A.V.: Protein structure: what is it possible to predict now? Curr. Opin. Struct. Biol. 7, 60–71 (1997)
8. Galassi, M., Davies, J., Theiler, J., Gough, B., Jungman, G., Booth, M., Rossi, F.: GNU Scientific Library Reference Manual - Revised 2nd edn. (2006) ISBN 0954161734
9. Hardin, C., Pogorelov, T.V., Luthey-Schulten, Z.: Ab initio protein structure prediction. Curr. Opin. Struct. Biol. 12, 176–181 (2002)
10. Park, B.H., Huang, E.S., Levitt, M.: Factors affecting the ability of energy functions to discriminate correct from incorrect folds. J. Mol. Biol. 2664, 831–846 (1997)
11. Plaxco, K.W., Simons, K.T., Baker, D.: Contact order, transition state placement and the refolding rates of single domain proteins. J. Mol. Bio. 277, 985–994 (1998)
12. Samudrala, R., Moult, J.: An all-atom distance-dependent conditional probability discriminatory function for protein structure prediction. J. Mol. Biol. 275, 895–916 (1998)
13. Siew, N., Elofsson, A., Rychlewski, L., Fischer, D.: MaxSub: An automated measure for the assessment of protein structure prediction quality. Bioinformatics 16, 776–785 (2000)
14. Tosatto, S.C.E.: The Victor/FRST Function for Model Quality Estimation. J. Comp. Biol., 12, 1316–1327 (2005)
15. Tsai, J., Bonneau, R., Morozov, A.V., Kuhlman, B., Rohl, C.A., Baker, D.: An improved protein decoy set for testing energy functions for protein structure prediction. Proteins 53, 76–87 (2003)
16. Vendruscolo, M., Dokholyan, N. V., Paci, E., Karplus, M.: Physycal review E, vol. 65(6 Pt 1):061910 (2002)

Time-Series Alignment by Non-negative Multiple Generalized Canonical Correlation Analysis

Bernd Fischer, Volker Roth, and Joachim M. Buhmann

Institute of Computational Science, ETH Zurich, Switzerland
{bernd.fischer,vroth,jbuhmann}@inf.ethz.ch,
Phone: +41-44-63 26527
Fax: +41-44-63 21562
http://www.ml.inf.ethz.ch

Abstract. For a quantitative analysis of differential protein expression, one has to overcome the problem of aligning time series of measurements from liquid chromatography coupled to mass spectrometry. When repeating experiments one typically observes that the time axis is deformed in a non-linear way. In this paper we propose a technique to align the time series based on generalized canonical correlation analysis (GCCA) for multiple datasets. The monotonicity constraint in time series alignment is incorporated in the GCCA algorithm. The alignment function is learned both in a supervised and a semi-supervised fashion. We compare our approach with previously published methods for aligning mass spectrometry data on a large proteomics dataset.

Keywords: Canonical Correlation Analysis, Time Series Alignment, Proteomics.

1 Introduction

Liquid chromatography coupled to mass spectrometry (LC/MS) has become the technology of choice for the quantitative analysis of proteins over the last years. Liquid chromatography provides a time series of measurements. A major problem when comparing two biological samples measured with LC/MS is a non-linear time deformation when comparing two experiments. The LC/MS generates peaks along the time axis. When two mass spectrometry experiments are aligned, as many peaks as possible should be matched between the two runs, while ensuring that most of the matches are correct.

One of the standard methods for aligning mass spectrometry experiments is called *correlation optimized warping* (COW) [1], where piece-wise linear functions are fitted to align the time series. A hidden Markov model [2] was proposed to align the mass spectrometry data as well as acoustic time series. Tibshirani [3] proposed hierarchical clustering for aligning. None of the previous methods, however, includes the knowledge from identified peptides that are available in tandem mass spectrometry.

F. Masulli, S. Mitra, and G. Pasi (Eds.): WILF 2007, LNAI 4578, pp. 505–511, 2007.
© Springer-Verlag Berlin Heidelberg 2007

In this paper we will extend the idea of optimizing the correlation between two experiments from piece-wise linear functions to general non-linear functions. Further we provide a multiple alignment method that employs both super- and semi-supervised learning and, thus, benefits from a larger training set: Tandem mass spectrometry allows us to identify a certain (and typically small) fraction of peaks from which we can establish sure correspondences in the two runs. In the sequel we will call those peaks that form the sure correspondences *labeled peaks*. All other peaks will be called *unlabeled*. Due to the semi-supervised nature of our approach, the inference process will include *both* types of peaks.

2   Problem Description

In quantitative proteomics one is interested in classifying a protein sample (e.g. a blood plasma sample) according to some phenotypes, e.g. distinguishing between cancer and non-cancer. Moreover, in many applications it is of particular interest to identify those proteins that are *relevant* for the actual discrimination task. In bottom-up proteomics, the proteins are first digested by an enzyme into smaller sized pieces, called peptides. Let $p_i^{(1)}$ and $p_i^{(2)}$ be the (measured) amount of ions of peptide i in sample 1 and 2. According to [4] the differential protein expression $\hat{\delta}_p$ can be estimated as

$$\hat{\delta}_p = \frac{1}{n} \sum_{i=1}^{n} \left(\log \left(p_i^{(1)} \right) - \log \left(p_i^{(2)} \right) \right) \tag{1}$$

The basis for differential protein expression estimation is a large set of peptides that are measured and identified in both samples. The LC/MS/MS measurements have two stages: In the first stage the peptides appear as peaks in a two dimensional image (see Figure 1). The first dimension is the retention time (the time when the peptides elute from the liquid chromatography column). The second dimension is the mass/charge ratio of the peptide. Figure 1 schematically shows two repeated experiments. The peptides are depicted by crosses. In a second stage a so called tandem mass spectrum is drawn, which is used to identify the underlying peptide sequence. Since this process is very time consuming, the underlying peptide sequence can only be acquired for a small (random) subset of peaks. In Figure 1, the peaks with known peptide sequence are marked by circles. There is only a small overlap of identified peptide sequences between the two experiments. It is our goal to increase the number of peptides identified jointly in both experiments and, hence, increase the number of differential protein abundance values. For this purpose we predict the retention time of peptides in one experiment which are only identified by LC/MS/MS in another experiment. While the mass/charge axis is preserved very well over different experiments, we typically observe non-linear deformations of the retention time axis. To estimate the retention time deformation, we use both supervised and unsupervised information. The supervised information is a list of time point correspondences $(x_1, y_1), \ldots (x_n, y_n)$ with known peptide sequence, where x_i are the time points in the first experiment and y_i are the time points in the second

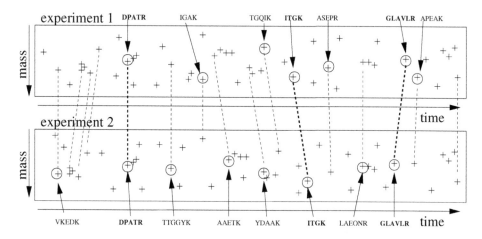

Fig. 1. A sketch of an LC/MS alignment. The crosses depict detected peaks, the circles depict identified peaks.

experiment. Unsupervised information is provided by a set of time points in the first experiment and another such set in the second experiment for which we don't know the peptide sequences and thus don't know the correspondences in the opposite experiment.

3   Alignment

3.1   Supervised Alignment by Canonical Correlation Analysis

The easiest way to estimate the time deformation function is by applying robust ridge regression [4]. Ridge regression has two disadvantages:

1. It is not symmetric in the sense that the estimated time deformation function $g_{l \to k}$ from experiment l to experiment k is not necessarily an inverse of $g_{k \to l}$.
2. The estimated function is not necessary monotone increasing. It might, thus, violate the monotonicity constraint that is inherent in temporal alignments.

To overcome the above problems of ridge regression we propose to address the alignment task by way of *canonical correlation analysis* (CCA) [5]. The two time scales are both mapped on a canonical time axis. Correlation analysis aims to find a linear projection on a canonical time axis such that the correlation between the two random variables is maximized. The time points are projected a high dimensional basis, e.g. a polynomial basis $(\phi(x_i) = (1, x_i, x_i^2, x_i^3, \ldots)^t)$. Later we will use another set of basis functions. We assume that the sample vectors $\phi(x_i)$ have zero mean and unit variance. The objective is to find parameter vectors β_1 and β_2 that maximize the correlation between the linear projections $\phi(x_i)^t \beta_1$ and $\phi(x_i)^t \beta_2$

$$\max_{\beta_1, \beta_2} \frac{\sum_{i=1}^{n} \beta_1^t \phi(x_i) \phi(y_i)^t \beta_2}{\sqrt{\sum_{i=1}^{n} (\phi(x_i)^t \beta_1)^2 \sum_{i=1}^{n} (\phi(y_i)^t \beta_2)^2}} \qquad (2)$$

The problem can directly be solved by a transformation to an eigen-value problem. In order to include the time-monotonicity constraint, however, it is advantageous to use an alternative formalization of the optimization problem, which can be equivalently restated as follows:

$$\min_{\beta_1,\beta_2} \quad \sum_{i=1}^{n} \left(\phi(x_i)^t \beta_1 - \phi(y_i)^t \beta_2\right)^2 \quad \text{s.t. } \|\beta_1\| = 1, \|\beta_2\| = 1. \quad (3)$$

The function $g_k(x_i) = \phi(x_i)^t \beta_k$ denotes the transformation from the time scale k to the canonical time scale. Even for this reformulated problem, however, we have not the guarantee that the transformation is monotonically increasing. In the case of a non-monotone function it is impossible to find an unambiguous transformation between time scales k to l, because in general g_k is not invertible.

To overcome this problem we propose two changes in the setting of canonical correlation analysis:

1. We use a set of hyperbolic tangent basis functions.
2. We introduce a non-negativity constraint on the regression parameters.

The basis functions are defined as

$$\phi(x_i) = \left(\tanh\left(\sigma(x_i - z_1)\right), \ldots, \tanh\left(\sigma(x_i - z_d)\right)\right)^t. \quad (4)$$

The set of vectors $z_1, \ldots, z_d$ can either be chosen as the set $x_1, \ldots, x_n$ or as a set of d time points equally distributed over the range of the respective time scale. The parameter σ is a scaling parameter. It controls the smoothness of the estimated alignment function.

If the parameters β_1 and β_2 are non-negative, the function $g_k(x_i) = \phi(x_i)^t \beta_k$ is monotonically increasing, because it is a linear combination of monotonically increasing (hyperbolic tangent) functions with non-negative coefficients. The alignment problem can now be defined as non-negative GCCA with hyperbolic tangent basis functions. We want to find the parameter vectors β_1 and β_2 that minimize the objective function

$$\min_{\beta_1,\beta_2} \quad \sum_{i=1}^{n} \left(\phi(x_i)^t \beta_1 - \phi(y_i)^t \beta_2\right)^2 \quad \text{s.t. } \|\beta_1\| = 1, \|\beta_2\| = 1, \beta_{k,j} \geq 0. \quad (5)$$

The problem is solved iteratively. In a first step the objective function is minimized over β_1 while keeping β_2 fixed. Then the length of the vector β_1 is normalized to fulfill the constraint $\|\beta_1\| = 1$. In a second step the objective is minimized over β_2 while keeping β_1 fixed, and β_2 is normalized accordingly. In each step of the iteration we have to solve a non-negative least-squares problem for which we use the Lawson-Hanson algorithm [6].

Using the above definition of the correlation problem we can easily extend the correlation coefficient to a *robust* version that is less sensitive to outliers. We propose to replace the squared loss by Huber's robust loss function. Optimization of the robust GCCA functional is similar to its quadratic counterpart (5), but with an additional inner loop that solves the robust non-negative least-squares problems by an iteratively re-weighted non-negative least-squares algorithm.

3.2   Multiple Canonical Correlation Analysis

Sometimes there are only a very few peptides that are measured in both runs. In the case where one has more than two experiments one can benefit from multiple datasets to increase the training dataset. The problem of canonical correlation analysis can be extended to multiple correlation analysis [7,8]. First notice that one can alternatively reformulate the two constraints $\|\beta_1\| = 1$ and $\|\beta_2\| = 1$ in equation (3) to one single constraint $\|\beta_1\| + \|\beta_2\| = 2$ [9]. A possible extension of GCCA to K time series is then defined as

$$\min_{\beta_1,\ldots,\beta_K} \sum_{1 \leq k < l \leq K} \sum_{i=1}^{m_{k,l}} \left(\phi(x_i^{(kl)})^t \beta_k - \phi(y_i^{(kl)})^t \beta_l \right)^2 \tag{6}$$

$$\text{s.t.} \sum_{k=1}^{K} \|\beta_k\| = K, \beta_{k,j} \geq 0 . \tag{7}$$

The correspondence time points between time series k and l are denoted by $x_i^{(kl)}$ and $y_i^{(kl)}$. This problem can again be solved iteratively by minimizing the objective function with respect to one vector β_k while keeping the other vectors $\beta_l, l \neq k$ fixed.

3.3   Semi-supervised Alignment

All variants of canonical correlation analysis introduced in the previous section can be combined with a *semi-supervised* alignment. The semi-supervised problem involves both a set of detected peaks for which the underlying peptide sequence is not necessarily identified and a set of identified (or *labeled*) peaks. Starting with the model that is trained exclusively on the labeled peaks, we iteratively augment this set by correspondences that can be predicted with high certainty. The augmented set of correspondences might contain some errors, but since we include in every iteration only the high-certainty correspondences we expect that the inclusion of additional training peaks is beneficial. The experiments in the next section support this hypothesis.

4   Experiments

As a test set for our aligning method we use 24 mass spectrometry experiments for proteins from an *arabidopsis thaliana* cell culture. In each experiment we have 6-8 runs (*technical replicates*) that are used to assess the quality of the alignment. For each of the experiments all pairwise alignments were computed (and the multiple alignment respectively), so that we end up with 15-28 pairwise alignments per experiment.

We compared the method using the labels of the peaks by cross validation. We separated all identified peptides in a training set and an independent test set (80% / 20%). This splitting was repeated 20 times. For the semi-supervised learning we added all detected peaks, ignoring the labels in this particular step.

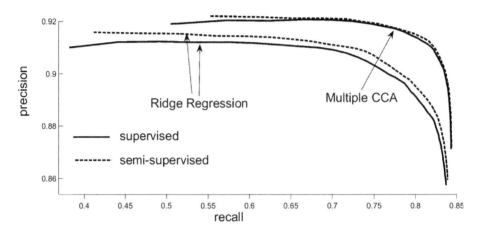

Fig. 2. Precision-Recall-Curve matching peak correspondences

All test peaks are mapped from one time series to a time point of the second time series. If there is a peak in the second time series within a window of acceptance around the predicted time point, the peak is accepted as a match. The number of matches varies with the size of a window of acceptance. For the evaluation we consider three cases:

1. **no match.** The peak is not assigned to any peak in the second time series.
2. **correct.** The peak is assigned to the peak with the same label
3. **wrong.** The peak is assigned to the peak with another label

From these categories we then compute *precision* and *recall* values as follows:

$$(\text{recall}) \quad rec = \frac{\#correct}{\#correct + \#wrong + \#nomatch} \tag{8}$$

$$(\text{precision}) \quad prec = \frac{\#correct}{\#correct + \#wrong} \tag{9}$$

In Figure 2 the precision-recall curves are plotted by varying the size of the window of acceptance. Here again multiple GCCA outperforms ridge regression.

5   Conclusion

In this paper we are concerned with one step in the data analysis process in quantitative differential proteomics experiments. If an experiment with a liquid chromatography unit is repeated, one can observe a non-linear deformation of the time measurement.

We have provided a novel technique for aligning time scales based on generalized canonical correlation analysis. With the novel technique we overcome two severe problems of previous approaches: non-symmetry of the time prediction function and a potential violation of the monotonicity constraint which is inherent in temporal alignments. Our novel technique is based on generalized canonical correlation analysis with a built-in non-negativity constraint. It is based on a set of monotonically increasing and bounded basis functions.

On a large proteomics dataset we have demonstrated that multiple generalized canonical correlation analysis outperforms ridge regression in terms of precision and recall. The number of peptide comparisons and the precision of correspondences could be improved by the novel technique. This has a direct implication on the estimation of differential protein expression values, because it increases the number of proteins and improves the estimation quality of differential protein expression values.

Acknowledgements

The authors like to thank J. Grossmann, S. Baginsky and W. Gruissem for valuable discussions and the Competence Center for Systems Physiology and Metabolic Diseases for support.

References

1. Vest Nielsen, N.-P., Carstensen, J.M., Smedsgaard, J.: Aligning of single and multiple wavelength chromatographic profiles for chemometric data analysis using correlation optimised warping. J. of Chromatography A 805, 17–35 (1998)
2. Listgarten, J., Neal, R.M., Roweis, S.T., Emili, A.: Multiple alignment of continuous time series. In: NIPS 17, pp. 817–824 (2005)
3. Tibshirani, R., Hastie, T., Narasimhan, B., Soltys, S., Shi, G., Koong, A., Le, Q.-T.: Sample classification from protein mass spectrometry, by peak probability contrasts. Bioinformatics 20, 3034–3044 (2004)
4. Fischer, B., Grossmann, J., Baginsky, S., Roth, V., Gruissem, W., Buhmann, J.M.: Semi-supervised lc/ms alignment for differential proteomics. Bioinformatics 22(14), e132–e140 (2006)
5. Hotelling, H.: Relations between two sets of variates. Biometrica 28, 321–377 (1936)
6. Lawson, C.L., Hanson, R.J.: Solving Least Square Problems. Prentice-Hall, Englewood Cliffs (1974)
7. Yamanishi, Y., Vert, J.-P., Nakaya, A., Kanehisa, M.: Extraction of correlated gene clusters from multiple genomic data by generalized kernel canonical correlation analysis. Bioinformatics 19, i323–i330 (2003)
8. Bach, F.R., Jordan, M.I.: Kernel independent component analysis. Journal of Machine Learning Research 3, 1–48 (2002)
9. Via, J., Santamaria, I., Perez, J.: Canonical correlation analysis (cca) algorithms for multiple data sets: Application to blind simo equalization. In: European Signal Processing Conference (2005)

Generative Kernels for Gene Function Prediction Through Probabilistic Tree Models of Evolution

Luca Nicotra, Alessio Micheli, and Antonina Starita

Dipartimento di Informatica, Università di Pisa
Largo B. Pontecorvo 3, 56127 Pisa, Italy
{nicotra,micheli,starita}@di.unipi.it

Abstract. In this paper we extend kernel functions defined on generative models to embed phylogenetic information into a discriminative learning approach. We describe three generative tree kernels, a Fisher kernel, a sufficient statistics kernel and a probability product kernel, whose key features are the adaptivity to the input domain and the ability to deal with structured data. In particular, kernel adaptivity is obtained through the estimation of a tree structured model of evolution starting from the phylogenetic profiles encoding the presence or absence of specific proteins in a set of fully sequenced genomes. We report preliminary results obtained by these kernels in the prediction of the functional class of the proteins of *S. Cervisae*, together with comparisons to a standard vector based kernel and to a non-adaptive tree kernel function.

1 Introduction

Phylogenetic information has extensively been used for explanation and interpretation of biological domains, and, more recently, has seen application as useful prior information for various tasks in computational biology such as gene function prediction [1,2]. Several approaches have tried to take into account evolutionary relations among species to go beyond sequence similarity when predicting gene function. Pavlidis *et al.* [3] propose the use of phylogenetic profiles, i.e., the vectors encoding the presence or absence of close homologs of specific proteins in a set of fully sequenced genomes. Their assumption is that two genes with similar phylogenetic profiles are likely to have similar functions since proteins that participate in a common structural complex or metabolic pathway will likely evolve in a similar way. In Liberales *et al.* [1] and Vert [2], taking inspiration from phylogenetic trees, i.e., hierarchical probabilistic models of the evolutionary process [4], this approach is further explored considering some form of structure among variables of the phylogenetic profile in the form of relations with hypothetical common ancestors. This determines a tree structure which can be taken into account, e.g., when computing gene similarity. More generally, it is clear that evolutionary processes embed biological data into a structured domain that is not directly usable by standard vector-based discriminative machine learning approaches. Moreover, when information about the evolutionary process characterizing the domain is available or can be inferred, it is often more natural

F. Masulli, S. Mitra, and G. Pasi (Eds.): WILF 2007, LNAI 4578, pp. 512–519, 2007.

to model biological data through generative probabilistic models [4], which can incorporate prior knowledge, hidden interactions and invariances among time and species in a principled way through Bayesian theory. The main drawback is that generative models are often dominated by less domain specific but more task oriented discriminative approaches. In particular, kernel methods [5] are emerging as the methods of choice in many areas of computational biology for their state of the art results and for their modularity. Therefore it is clear that approaches trying to combine the modeling power provided by generative models of evolution with the predictive performances of kernel methods are of practical and theoretical interest.

Generative kernels are a family of kernel functions exploiting the information encoded in generative probabilistic models to define similarity measures. Based on the way they leverage on the probabilistic models at hand, they can be divided into global and instance based approaches.

Global approaches, after adapting the parameters of an underlying probabilistic model to the whole set of available data, try to exploit the internal representation the model retains of the input data as the feature space. In particular, in Sect. 2 we describe an extension of the Fisher kernel [6] which maps each input phylogenetic profile to the gradient with respect to the parameters of the log-likelihood of a hierarchical probabilistic model. This gradient intuitively represents the relevance of each parameter for the generation of a particular input example. Similarly, we introduce a novel kernel based on another quantity well known in statistics, the so called sufficient statistics, obtaining a feature representation generally less dependent on the specific learned parameters and more directly influenced by the structure of the probabilistic model (Sect. 2).

A different approach is at the base of instance based generative kernels which employ directly the likelihood values assigned by probabilistic models trained to single input examples. Along this line the probability product kernel has been introduced [7] and it is described in Sect. 2 for the case of phylogenetic probabilistic models.

Comparison with Previous Works. The approaches presented in this paper have considerable differences from previous works from the point of view of both the model and the application.

From a model perspective, the Fisher kernel has already been used to model structured domains, but whereas so far it has been applied to data such as vectors or sequences [6] and to hierarchical domains with varying structure [8], in our generative kernels the evolutionary interactions are supposed to be known, so that a Bayesian network with a fixed structure can be used and complete non-stationariety can be introduced; similar considerations can be made for the simpler sufficient statistics kernel as well. But the advantage of a fixed structure is even more evident in the case of the probability product kernels which otherwise, in the case of trees with varying structure, would require the use of the maximum spanning tree of the whole dataset, considerably increasing the computational complexity of inference procedures.

In the application perspective previous attempts to use phylogenetic information through kernel method must be mentioned. In particular, besides approaches directly using vectorial phylogenetic profiles as input data for the kernel methods, a probabilistic tree kernel somehow analog to the kernels we describe in this paper has been introduced in Vert [2]. As other marginalized kernels, this kernel requires ad-hoc algorithms for efficient computation, while both the Fisher kernel and the sufficient statistics kernel, as explained in Sect. 2, can leverage on standard inference tools of Bayesian theory for their computation. As we explain in Sect. 2 this allows to easily vary the structure of the underlining probabilistic model. Finally, to obtain a class of adaptive kernels, we use a learning algorithm to find the optimal parameters of the probabilistic phylogenetic model. Since we believe that adaptivity is one of the strongest points characterizing generative kernels, this should be considered one main difference from previous approaches where parameters were specified a priori using biological knowledge.

2   Generative Kernel Functions

To specify what we call a *generative kernel function*, the first step is the choice of the underlining generative model. In the case of phylogenetic interactions, since there is a known direction of causality from ancestors to living organisms, directed graphical models such as Bayesian networks [4] can be employed. These are probabilistic models defined through a graph where nodes correspond to random variables and edges to causality relations between them. If we model each living or extinct specie through a random variable and suppose the absence of more complex interactions among species, a common choice consists in relying on a probabilistic Bayesian tree model. Living organisms can be represented through observed variables in the leaf nodes and hypothetical common ancestors can be represented through hidden variables in the internal nodes. In this paper we do not try to learn the structure of the generative model itself but we suppose it to be given as a biological fact or as an output of another algorithm. Besides interactions, other domain knowledge can be inserted into the model in a principled way, for instance specifying patterns of stationarity through parameters sharing. Another common choice is the inclusion of further hidden nodes which might increase the modeling power of the probabilistic tree model, representing unobserved features or non Markovian interactions between organisms. In the experiments and in the kernels formulation presented in this paper we rely on a baseline probabilistic model where no stationarity is assumed between nodes and so a different conditional probability table is assigned to each of them. In particular, if x represents a phylogenetic profile of a gene, $p(x(v)|h(pa(v)), \theta)$ is the probability of the specific gene to be present or not in the organism represented at node v given that its ancestor $pa(v)$ is in state $h(pa(v))$ and given parameters θ of the model. Moreover, in the following, we use the symbol $ch(v)$ to indicate the set of children of node v, h is a generic hidden state and s indicates the number of hidden states for ancestor nodes. Finally hidden ancestor nodes are indexed between 1 and n (with the first one, called r, being the root node), and observed living organisms are indexed between $n + 1$ and $n + m$.

Tree Fisher Kernel. The Fisher kernel [6] was one of the first proposals toward the goal of combining generative and discriminative models. In this kernel the information regarding the process generating the data is approximated by the use of a quantity well known in statistics and information theory which is called Fisher information. More precisely, given a set of learned parameters θ for the Bayesian network, for each input data x we can extract a quantity known as the *Fisher score* vector, which is defined as the gradient, with respect to the parameters of the log likelihood $\triangledown \log P(x|\theta)$. The Fisher score basically describes how much each single parameter in θ contributes to the process of generating a particular phylogenetic tree whose leaves assume the values contained in the phylogenetic profile x; this quantity preserves all structural assumptions of the model from which it is extracted, and in particular the mutual dependencies between the variables of the model. Given this mapping a natural kernel can be derived embedding $\triangledown \log P(x|\theta)$ with the standard inner product in the Euclidean space, and in the case of tree models the resulting kernel can be shown to be computable using standard inference algorithms [8]. In this case, we employ a generative model with the tree structure described in Liberales *et al.* [1], whose nodes are modeled with the set of parameters described in Sect. 2. Thus, the dimensionality of the Fisher score vector space is $s + s^2(n-1) + 2sm$ in general and 146 in the model which is concretely used in the experimental section, where the number of hidden ancestor nodes n is 13, the number of living organisms m is 24 and the number of hidden states s is 2.

The Fisher kernel for tree structured probabilistic models was introduced in [8] for the general case of varying size structures.

Tree Sufficient Statistics Kernel. The differentiability of the probabilistic model needed for the computation of the Fisher kernel can be a limit for the choice of a model of the data. A simpler choice is represented by the sufficient statistics kernel, a similarity function based on the *sufficient statistics* vector $\mathcal{T}(x)$ obtained through the concatenation of some generative model-dependent quantities, immediately available from inference, which, as in the case of the Fisher kernel, have the same dimensionality of the parameters θ of the model. The sufficient statistics are often computed as an intermediate step for parameter estimation and usually represent simple transformations of the input observations on the base of the structure of the model, somehow counting how much each conditional relation between variables occurs in a specific tree. Basically, we first learn the parameters of the Bayesian network given the whole dataset, and than, for each profile we compute the corresponding sufficient statistics vector, obtaining a domain which can be endowed with a standard inner product $\langle , \rangle$, resulting in the kernel $k^{\mathrm{suff}}(x, x') = \langle \mathcal{T}(x), \mathcal{T}(x') \rangle$. The probabilistic model used for this kernel is the same used in the case of the Fisher kernel, and hence, given the presence of hidden variables used to represent ancestor nodes, the vector of sufficient statistics is replaced with the corresponding expected sufficient statistics.

Given the conditional parameters $p(h_i(v)|h_j(pa(v)), \theta)$ or $p(x_i(v)|h_j(pa(v)), \theta)$ and a phylogenetic profile x we can obtain the corresponding expected sufficient statistics by simply applying an inference algorithm:

$$\alpha_i = p(h_i(r)|x, \theta) \text{ for } i = 1, \ldots s,$$
$$\alpha_{ij}(v) = p(h_i(v), h_j(pa(v))|x, \theta) \text{ for } i, j = 1, \ldots, s; \; v = 2, \ldots, n,$$
$$\beta_{ij}(v) = p(x_i(v), h_j(pa(v))|x, \theta) \text{ for } i = 1, 2; \; j = 1, \ldots, s; \; v = n+1, \ldots, n+m,$$

and hence the feature vector can be obtained by concatenating all these quantities

$$\mathcal{T}(x) = [\alpha_1, \ldots \alpha_s, \alpha_{11}(2), \ldots, \alpha_{ss}(n), \beta_{11}(n+1), \ldots \beta_{2s}(n+m)],$$

obtaining a feature space representation whose dimensionality is the same as for the Fisher kernel.

Tree Probability Product Kernel. Probability product kernels were introduced in Jebara *et al.* [7] and represent a way to combine generative models and discriminative methods mapping single data points to distributions over the sample space and then obtaining a similarity measure integrating the product of pairs of distributions obtained in such a way. Therefore it is often referred as a kernel between distributions. More precisely, given two phylogenetic profiles x and x' they can be used to infer the maximum likelihood estimate of the parameters of a predefined probabilistic model. If p and p' are probability distributions on a space of phylogenetic profiles obtained in this way, the probability product kernel between them is defined as $k^{\text{prob}}(p, p') = \int_x p(x)p'(x)dx$. While in general we do not need to explicitly evaluate this integral, sometimes the derivation of a practical algorithm for its computation is straightforward, in other cases it requires long derivations and even approximations. In this paper we introduce a novel extension of the probability product kernel to probabilistic phylogenetic tree models.

If we consider again a phylogenetic tree with n hidden ancestors and m living organisms we can compute the kernel $k^{\text{prob}}(p_\theta, p_{\theta'}) = \sum_x p(x|\theta)p(x|\theta')$ (where θ and θ' are the two parameters sets learned from phylogenetic profiles x and x') using the following recursive relations:

$$k^{\text{prob}}(p_\theta, p_{\theta'}) = \sum_{h(r)} \sum_{h'(r)} \prod_{w \in ch(r)} \tilde{k}_w(h(r), h'(r)),$$

$$\tilde{k}_v(h(pa(v)), h'(pa(v))) = \begin{cases} \sum_{x(v)} p(x(v)|h(pa(v)), \theta)p(x(v)|h'(pa(v)), \theta') \\ \quad \text{if } n+1 \leq v \leq n+m \quad \text{(observed)}, \\ \sum_{h(v)} \sum_{h'(v)} p(h(v)|h(pa(v)), \theta)p(h'(v)|h'(pa(v)), \theta') \\ \quad \prod_{w \in ch(v)} \tilde{k}_w(h(v), h'(v)) \quad \text{if } 2 \leq v \leq n \quad \text{(hidden)}. \end{cases}$$

It can be easily shown that the kernel is computable through a message passing algorithm which mimics the structure of belief propagation, and where messages are composed by kernel evaluations $\tilde{k}_v$.

Table 1. ROC$_{50}$ scores for the prediction of 16 functional categories by a support vector machine using (from left to right) a linear kernel (Linear), a marginalized kernel (Marg.), and the generative kernels introduced in Sect. 2, i.e., the Fisher kernel (Fish.), the sufficient statistics kernel (S. Stat) and the probability product kernel (P. Prod). In the last two columns we report, for each class, the positive examples to negative examples ratio (Pos/Neg) and the cost parameter (Balance) used on positive examples to balance support vector machine learning (see Sect. 3 for details).

Functional class	Linear	Marg.	Fish.	S. Stat.	P. Prod.	Pos/Neg	Balance
Amino-acid transporters	0.74	0.81	0.91	0.92	0.86	0.009	111.0
Fermentation	0.68	0.73	1.00	1.00	0.98	0.005	204.4
ABC transporters	0.64	0.87	0.85	0.86	0.79	0.006	153.1
C-compound, carbohydrate transport	0.59	0.68	0.72	0.94	0.09	0.012	78.52
Amino-acid biosynthesis	0.37	0.46	0.71	0.55	0.65	0.037	26.69
Amino-acid metabolism	0.35	0.32	0.48	0.48	0.45	0.068	14.60
Tricarboxylic-acid pathway	0.33	0.48	0.30	0.27	0.00	0.007	144.0
Transport facilitation	0.33	0.28	0.51	0.51	0.13	0.080	12.54
Organization of plasma membrane	0.31	0.30	0.46	0.48	0.46	0.046	21.61
Amino-acid degradation (catabolism)	0.30	0.52	0.54	0.48	0.53	0.009	106.2
Lipid and fatty-acid transport	0.29	0.52	0.52	0.49	0.53	0.005	188.6
Homeostasis of the cations	0.26	0.33	0.38	0.34	0.00	0.006	153.1
Glycolysis and gluconeogenesis	0.25	0.66	0.54	0.54	0.52	0.012	84.00
Metabolism	0.24	0.20	0.29	0.26	0.26	0.397	2.516
Cellular import	0.20	0.27	0.25	0.29	0.35	0.041	24.68
tRNA modification	0.15	0.32	0.10	0.10	0.00	0.004	245.5

3   Data and Experimental Results

We apply the generative kernels introduced in Sect. 2 to the dataset of 2465 phylogenetic profiles of the budding yeast *Saccharomyces cervisae* selected in Pavlidis *et al.* [3] for their accurate functional classification. At the same time we employ the phylogenetic tree structure proposed in Liberales *et al.* [1]. Finally, the functional categories are selected among those with at least 10 genes made available in the Munich Information Center for Protein Sequences Comprehensive Yeast Genome Databases.

For each functional category, performances were assessed through a 3-fold cross validation repeated for 50 times using a support vector machine model (SVM). The same procedure used in Vert [2] to determine the SVM cost parameter to cope with unbalanced datasets was employed. Other experimental settings include two standard practices, i.e., the use of a radial basis function as

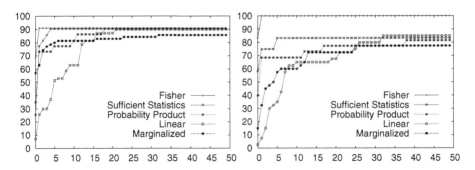

Fig. 1. ROC$_{50}$ curves for the prediction of the Amino-acid transporters (left) and Fermentation (right) classes from the phylogenetic profiles of the yeast genes with a linear, a marginalized and the three generative kernels presented in this paper.

the base dot product in the feature space of both the sufficient statistics and the Fisher kernels and kernel normalization for all the generative kernels.

The open source library Structlab (`structlab.sourceforge.net`) provides the software environment used to perform our experiments.

In Table 1 the categories obtaining the highest ROC$_{50}$ scores with a baseline linear kernel, together with the scores of the marginalized kernel presented in Vert [2], and of the different generative kernel functions are presented, while in Fig. 1 we report the plot for the ROC$_{50}$ curves of the two classes obtaining the highest performance with the linear kernel. It can be seen that a general improvement of previous results is achieved through generative kernels, with none of them clearly outperforming the others. However, while both the Fisher and the sufficient statistics kernels proved to perform at least better than the baseline in most cases, the probability product tends to perform poorly on some functional classes containing few genes. Furthermore the sufficient statistics kernel often showed to achieve results at least as good as the Fisher kernel, and hence, given its simpler definition and computation, might be preferred in this setting.

We can note that the model takes advantage of the non shared parametrization of nodes described in Sect. 2, and, trough generative parameters learning, we tend to obtain models where mutations are more probable in distant ancestors, and are less and less probable as we approach living organisms. This means that the generative kernels further penalizes mismatches between similar organisms. Both the improvements over the non-adaptive marginalized kernel and some preliminary experiments we performed using the Fisher and the sufficient statistics kernels together with generative models with fixed and prespecified parameters suggest that that a small but significant improvement of results is due to generative parameter learning.

Further experimental results will be made available through the website *http://structlab.sourceforge.net/phylogenetic-kernels.htm.*

4   Discussion

In this paper we show how kernel functions defined through probabilistic phylogenetic models offer new opportunities to represent the evolutionary process which underlies living organisms, leveraging, at the same time, on the class of kernel methods, characterized by versatility and state of the art results on many tasks in computational biology. On one hand this represents another example of how structured approaches can be useful in a biological context. On the other hand this also supports the use of hybrid generative and discriminative approaches in general. Various limitations can be pointed out in this and previous approaches, suggesting at the same time interesting research directions. While in this paper we assume to know the exact tree describing the evolution of genes a certain error should be considered in this structure. Moreover we know that a variety of evolutionary forces contributes additively in shaping proteins genetic variability. Therefore we are currently considering learning the structure of the phylogenetic trees directly from the dataset, and substituting the single tree with a distribution among trees or simply with a mixture of trees. Finally, other generative kernels are currently emerging and their use in the context of phylogenetic tree should be considered.

References

1. Liberales, D.A., Thoren, A., von Heijne, G., Eloffson, A.: The use of phylogenetic profiles for gene function prediction. Current Genomics 3, 131–137 (2002)
2. Vert, J.P.: A tree kernel to analyze phylogenetic profiles. Bioinformatics 18, s276–s284 (2002)
3. Pavlidis, P., Weston, J., Cai, J., Grundy, N.W.: Gene functional classification from heterogeneous data. In: Proceedings of the Fifth International Conference on Computational Molecular Biology, 242–248 (2001)
4. Baldi, P., Brunak, S.: Bioinformatics: the Machine Learning Approach, 2nd edn. MIT Press, Cambridge, MA (2001)
5. Shawe-Taylor, J., Cristianini, N.: Kernel Methods for Pattern Analysis. Cambridge University Press, New York, NY, USA (2004)
6. Jaakkola, T., Haussler, D.: Exploiting generative models in discriminative classifiers. In: Kearns, M.S., Solla, S.A., Cohn, D.A. (eds.) Advances in neural information processing systems, vol. 11, pp. 487–493. MIT Press, Cambridge, MA (1999)
7. Jebara, T., Kondor, R., Howard, A.: Probability product kernels. Journal of Machine Learning Research 5, 819–844 (2004)
8. Nicotra, L., Micheli, A., Starita, A.: Fisher kernel for Tree Structured Data. In: Proceedings of the IEEE International Joint Conference of Neural Networks, pp. 1917–1922. IEEE, New York (2004)

Liver Segmentation from CT Scans: A Survey

Paola Campadelli and Elena Casiraghi

Università degli Studi di Milano,
Dipartimento di Scienze dell'Informazione,
Via Comelico 39, 20135 Milano, Italy
{campadelli,casiraghi}@dsi.unimi.it

Abstract. In this paper we describe the state of the art of the semi-automatic and automatic techniques for liver volume extraction from abdominal CT. In the recent years this research focus has gained a lot of importance in the field of medical image processing since it is the first and fundamental step of any automated technique for the automatic liver disease diagnosis, liver volume measurement, and 3D liver volume rendering from CT images.

1 Introduction

Imaging techniques such as computed tomography (CT), magnetic resonance imaging (MRI), or positron emission tomography (PET) are nowadays a standard instrument for diagnosis of liver pathologies such as cirrhosis, liver cancer, fulminant hepatic failure. Among these techniques, CT images are often preferred by diagnosticians since they have high Signal-to-Noise ratio and good spatial resolution, thus giving an accurate anatomical information about the visualized structures. These good image qualities, and the advances in the digital image processing techniques, motivate the great deal of research work aimed at the development of computerized methods for the automatic liver analysis and 3D volume rendering. More precisely, the current interests are the automatic detection of liver cancer or other liver diseases [1], the measurement of the liver volume [2], which is an important index in cases of living donor liver transplantation, and the 3D liver volume rendering [3], which has been shown to be helpful for surgical planning prior to hepatic resection.

The first and fundamental step of all the systems developed with one of these aims, is the liver volume segmentation, that is the extraction of the liver volume from the CT data. This is usually done by expert radiologists who manually trace the liver contour on each slice of the CT data. Since this procedure requires more than one hour, several authors have focused on the development of semi-automatic and automatic techniques, and several papers have been presented in the literature. Unfortunately the problem is still open [4], due several factors that make the liver the most difficult organ to be automatically segmented from abdominal CT [5]. First of all, CT images have low contrast and blurred edges, due to the partial volume effects resulting from spatial averaging, patient movement, beam hardening, and reconstruction artifacts. Moreover, neighboring organs (e.g. liver, spleen and stomach) might have similar gray levels, since the gray tones in CT images are related to the tissue density, that might be similar in different

F. Masulli, S. Mitra, and G. Pasi (Eds.): WILF 2007, LNAI 4578, pp. 520–528, 2007.

organs. Besides, the same organ may exhibit different gray level values both in the same patient, due to the administration of contrast media, and in different ones, for different machine setup conditions.

This paper is a survey of recent methods presented in the literature to obtain liver segmentation. It is organized according to the image processing techniques employed, and generally chronologically within subsections. Although almost all the methods are evaluated by comparing the automatic to the manual segmentation provided by expert radiologists, the direct comparison among different systems is not possible, or at least not fair, due to the lack of a common dataset with its gold standard (i.e. a commonly accepted manual segmentation), and a unique measure of the discrepancy between the automatic and the manual segmentation (ground truth). The adopted measures can be divided into three classes: 1) **The percentage of mismatching voxels** between the automatic and manual segmentation is computed by dividing the number of mismatching voxels by the volume obtained by manual segmentation. 2) **The volume overlap** compares the computer determined areas, or volumes, to those drawn by radiologists. This measure can be computed in 2D, by measuring the percentage of error for each slice and then averaging over all the patient's slices, or in 3D by considering the percentage of error between the computer output and the manual ground truth. 3) **The 2D (3D) distance** from the points on the automatically detected liver contour (liver surface) to the points on the contour (surface) of the ground truth. The 2D (3D) distance from a point x to a contour (surface) S is usually computed as: $d_S(x, S) = min_{p \in S}(d(x, p))$, where $d(\cdot, \cdot)$ may be any 2D (3D) point-to-point distance. In the 2D case some authors employ the 3/4 Chamfer distance [6], or the city block distance [7], for they are faster to compute than the euclidean distance, which is usually used in the 3D case. The distances are then summed over all the points of the automatically obtained contour (surface), and the result is normalized with respect to either the ground truth or the computed volume. In [8], Lamecker noted that all the described performance measures miss some information, since either the ground truth or the computed volume are employed to normalize the error, while both of them should be used. Therefore, he introduces a symmetric 3D volume difference as: $1 - \frac{|V_{Aut} \cap V_{Man}|}{\frac{1}{2}(|V_{Aut}| + |V_{Man}|)}$, where V_{Aut} and V_{Man} are respectively the computed liver binary volume and the binary volume of the ground truth.

2 Live Wire Segmentation Approaches

The live wire algorithms [9] are a class of user-steered segmentation method for two-dimensional images that interpret the image as a undirected and weighted graph, and compute minimal cost paths between user defined seed points. More precisely, the vertexes of the graph represent the image pixels, the graph edges connect neighboring pixels, and their weighs represent the cost of the connections. The costs are computed as a weighted sum of different image features like gradient value, gradient direction, Laplacian zero-crossing, and the gray value. When the user initially clicks to set a starting seed point on the boundary, all the possible minimum-cost paths from this point to all other points in the image are computed via dynamic programming or the Dijkstras graph search algorithm. Subsequently, a desired boundary segment can be interactively chosen via the free point specified by the current mouse position. Indeed, as the user moves the mouse the boundary behaves like a live wire, as it erases the previous boundary points and displays the new minimum cost path that connect the free point to the seed point. When the cursor is close to the desired boundary the live wire segment finally adheres to it, and the user can input a new seed point to 'tie off' or 'freeze' the computed optimal path, up to the new seed point. This step causes the reinitialization of the boundary detection, so that new optimal paths are computed starting from the new seed point, and the procedure is repeated until the final contour is created.

This kind of segmentation technique lets the user have a full control over the segmentation process, while having the computer do most of the detail work. In this way, user interaction complements the ability of the computer to find boundaries of structures in the image, and the segmented result is always precise. For this reason different implementations of the live wire paradigm have been developed, and used for the segmentation of different types of medical images (e.g.: in [10] it has been used for brain segmentation from MRI images). In [11], the authors describe their extension of the live wire approach for the segmentation of CT images. It reduces the computation time as well as the user interaction time, by computing the cost function locally, i.e. in a tube-like area around the liver contour copied from the nearest adjacent slice already segmented. Besides a shape-based interpolation method [12] is used to reduce the number of slices that must be interactively segmented, for it can calculate all the missing contours automatically. The system is the basic step of the HepaVision software tool [13]currently used in the clinical practice by several diagnosticians, for the diagnosis of liver disease, and by several surgeons for liver surgical planning. The drawback of this method, which is common to all the semi-automatic segmentation methods, is that it still requires the user interaction time (23 minutes for each patient when using a dedicated computer). Besides, the quality of the segmentation result is heavily dependent on the skill of the operator, and it suffers from its error and biases; as a results the inter and intra observer repeatability is not higher than that obtained with manual segmentation [14].

3 Gray Level Based Liver Segmentation

The first attempts to perform automatic liver segmentation [15, 16, 17] introduce the basic processing scheme adopted in several subsequent works. At first, the liver gray levels are estimated by the statistical analysis of a subset of manually segmented slices, or by the histogram analysis in a gray level range, established by a priori knowledge about the liver density [18]. Next, simple or iterative thresholding is used to create binary images that are further processed by 2D or 3D [19] morphological operators, to separate attached organs. A priori information and the information retrieved from the previously segmented slices is then used to recognize and repair segmentation errors in the current slice. The last step smooths the boundaries in each slice by means of B-splines, or active contours (snakes). While in [16, 17] the authors provide only a visual and qualitative assessment of their results, in [15] the authors test their system on 94 slices of 4 patients and obtain a 90% 2D volume overlap.

The recent works of Lim *et al.* [20, 21, 22] are based on the above mentioned processing scheme; the authors analyze the liver intensity distribution on a subset of manually segmented CT samples, and exploit this information together with a priori knowledge about the liver location to find a coarse liver volume. Iterative morphological filtering and k-means clustering are then used to find and delete neighboring organs attached to the liver, and to define a search region where the final liver boundary is determined. To this aim the authors apply active contours that find the minimum of a cost function; this is based on the gradient direction, the intensity distribution, and the pattern features of the liver, computed by isolabel maps weighted by gradient magnitude [23]. The authors evaluate their system on 'several samples with various shapes and irregular texture of 10 patients'; the results are evaluated by comparing with the ground truth produced by experts, and the 4% of mismatching voxels is obtained.

In [24] the histogram of the whole volume is computed to identify the liver peak in a preset gray level range, so as to determine two liver thresholds, one at each side of the liver peak. These thresholds are then employed to create a liver binary volume, which is heavily processed by morphological operators to surely delete attached organs. This binary volume is used as a liver mask to select, from the result of the Canny edge detector, the external boundaries of the liver. The selected edges are input to the gradient vector flow algorithm, that helps to create an initial liver segmentation, further modified by snakes. The final step which refines the boundary requires the user to select a starting slice on which the liver has a large area profile and the segmentation result is accurate; the liver contour in this slice will be used as a mask to detect and eliminate errors, i.e. edges far beyond the liver contour, in its adjacent slices. Indeed, this is an iterative correction process that proceeds in a slice-by-slice manner, and employs the correct segmentation in the previous slice to detect and eliminate errors in the following slices. The authors evaluate their system on 20 contrast enhanced CT images, by measuring the percentage of mismatching voxels between the automatic and the manual segmentation. Note that, to ignore minor discrepancies between the manual results and the computer generated liver contour, only the mismatching regions beyond a 3 mm ring surrounding the manual results on each slice are considered as an error. The mean value of mismatching voxels over the 20 patients is 5.3%.

The problem with all the above mentioned systems relies in their first and basic step of liver gray level estimation, that does not consider the big inter-patient and intra-patient gray level variability, mentioned in the introduction. Indeed, methods based on a priori knowledge, or statistical analysis of manually segmented samples, are likely to fail when patients with completely different gray level characteristics are processed. Moreover these systems often require a lot of parameters to be experimentally set; this obviously affects their robustness.

Other approaches [25, 26, 27] try to overcome the crucial problem of liver gray levels estimation by learning the gray level features corresponding to the liver. The works in [25, 26] employ respectively a feed forward neural network trained with back propagation on liver, liver boundary and non-liver sub-images, and a unsupervised Hopfield neural network whose input are the images and a set of Haralick's texture features; unfortunately, both of them are tested on one image only and obtain really low performance. Promising results are presented in [27], where the authors experiment contextual neural networks to label the abdominal organs by an unsupervised procedure based on pixel gray levels and spatial information; to recognize and separate different organs, a set of seven fuzzy rules are then employed, based on a priori knowledge regarding the position, shape and size of each organ. Each organ boundary is further refined by analyzing the relationships among the shape of the organ in subsequent slices. To evaluate their system the authors select 10 cases among 40 patients and compute the $3/4$ Chamfer distance among manually and automatically segmented slices, obtaining an average distance of 3 pixels. Although promising results are obtained, the system still has some problems; at first, it is likely to fail when two neighboring organs have similar gray levels, since the contextual neural network cannot produce two separate labeling; second, the fuzzy rules employ experimentally set thresholds, that make the system not robust to database variations. Although its limitations, the work of Chung *et al.* is interesting in that it introduces the idea that some basic anatomical knowledge about the organs must be used.

4   Model Fitting

To simultaneously describe and capture a priori information regarding the shape, size, and position of each abdominal organ several papers have been presented, which employ deformable models, statistical shape models, and probabilistic atlases (see next section).

Gao *et al.* [28] develop parameterized 3D surface models of two abdominal organs (liver and right kidney) and describe a method to adapt them to abdominal CT data. To this aim an energy function that measures the match between the direction of the image gradient and the unit surface normal of the deformable model is defined, so that an optimal match between the parametric model and the surface in the image is found when the minimum of the energy function is reached. The algorithm is tested on 21 CT datasets for liver and kidney segmentation, but the liver segmentation results have been evaluated only visually by a radiologist, who judged the results to be without noticeable errors. Although promising and objective results have been reported for the right kidney segmentation, it has to be noted that this structure is not as difficult to be segmented as the liver; an objective liver segmentation test would better prove the efficacy and robustness of the method. Indeed, although the shape description given by deformable models includes many degrees of freedom to allow modeling of complex shapes, they must be bounded by global constraints to make them robust to noise and outliers; this is the reason why the deformable models often fail to capture the natural liver shape variability.

To overcome this limitation Montagnat *et al.* [29, 30] employ an hybrid approach that combines the classical deformable model technique, whose local deformation allow the model to freely adapt to complex shapes, with an elastic registration technique that iteratively finds the best geometric transformation between the actual model shape and the closest data points. Only few examples have been quantitatively evaluated in this work, so that the performance of the method cannot be well understood. The evaluation is performed with the mean surface distance between the automatic result and the manual segmentation, achieving an average distance value of 2 mm.

Lamecker [8] tries to achieve robustness to noise and outliers by creating a statistical shape model. The model is built with a semiautomatic mapping procedure, that requires the user to sign corresponding feature points on all the training liver volumes; these training data are input to the principal component analysis (PCA) which captures the shape variations of the liver. The model is then allowed to deform within the captured space of variations, by means of the best-matching profile technique described in [31]. This technique requires the definition of a gray level profile model of the surface normals; in this case, Lamecker formulates a simple and fixed profile model based on the gray value of the liver and its surrounding tissues. The problem of applying this method to liver segmentation comes from the fact that building a proper training set is really difficult; indeed, the training data set must have a big cardinality and the training cases must capture all the possible shapes, which is really challenging when working with the liver. As a result the system might fail when processing not standard liver shapes, or it might require too much computing time before a good matching between the model and the image data is obtained. Nevertheless, the results obtained on 33 patients seem promising since the measured symmetric 3D volume difference, ranges from 8.8 to 1.7%, with a mean value of 5.25%.

5   Probabilistic Atlases

Other noticeable works are those based on the construction of probabilistic atlases for the abdomen organs [32, 33, 34]. The first step to build the probabilistic atlas is the registration of each training CT data into a standard space defined by a small set of landmarks (manually [32, 33] or automatically [34] set for each patient). To this aim the thin plate spline is used as the warping transform, together with the mutual information as the similarity measure. The probabilistic atlas is then created by spatial averaging the registered organ surfaces, and it is incorporated into a Bayesian framework to compute, for each voxel, the probability of belonging to a certain organ. Finally, the region that maximizes the posterior probability of being the desired organ is extracted with the iterative conditional mode algorithm, or by simple thresholding. The trouble with this approach is that the generation of the probabilistic atlas requires a lot of data to be collected. Regarding the performance it is worth to be mentioned that in [33, 32, 34], results are presented respectively on 10, 20, and 80 patients. In [33] and [34] a 78% and 84% mean 3D volume overlap, between the automatic and manual liver segmentation, are reported, while Park *et al.* [32] present their results by measuring the average percentage of mismatching pixels between the automatic and manual segmentation, and obtain a 8.5% error rate.

6   Level Set Approaches

A completely different approach to segment the liver, is described by Pan *et al.* in [35]. They employ a 2D and 3D level-set approach [36] based on a novel speed function. It controls the front propagation of an implicitly defined surface toward the liver boundary; the idea is to change the speed function dynamically according to the past history of the front. In addition the propagation is constrained by simple a-priori anatomic information regarding the distance between liver and skin. Unfortunately, the authors apply their system to a rather small sample of 5 individuals. A 3D volume overlap of 94 to 96% in the 2D case and 87 to 94% in the 3D case is reported. Level set methods are also used by some authors [37, 4] as the final step of their liver segmentation, with the aim of refining the coarse liver boundary detected by the preceding steps of their system.

7 Conclusions

In this paper we have described the state of the art of the semiautomatic and automatic methods for liver volume segmentation from CT images. Although a great deal of research effort has been devoted to the development of segmentation algorithms and a great variety of image processing techniques have been experimented, the problem of automatic liver segmentation is still open. Indeed the techniques based on a liver shape model usually fail to describe the complex liver shape, while the others may be unable to correctly separate the liver from neighboring organs, such as spleen or stomach, with similar tissue appearance. Some other still require the user interaction.

A comparative evaluation of the results presented by different methods is not possible because different authors test their systems on small sets of private data and adopt self chosen error functions to assess the algorithm performance. A common test set with its gold standard traced by experts and a generally accepted performance measure are required to make any objective comparison.

References

[1] Lee, C.C., et al.: Classification of liver diseases from ct images using bp-cmac neural network. In: Proceedings of 9th International Workshop on Cellular Neural Networks and Their Applications, pp. 118–121 (2005)

[2] Nakayama, Y., et al.: Automated hepatic volumetry for living related liver transplantation at multisection ct. Radiology 240 (3), 743–748 (2006)

[3] Harms, J., et al.: Computerized ct-based 3d visualization technique in living related liver transplantation. Transplantation Proceedings 37, 1059–1062 (2005)

[4] Foruzan, A., et al.: Automated segmentation of liver from 3d ct images. In: Proceedings of CARS 2006, vol. 1(7), pp. 71–73 (2006)

[5] Camara, O., et al.: Computational modeling of thoracic and abdominal anatomy using spatial relationships for image segmentation. Real-Time Imaging 10, 263–273 (2004)

[6] Borgefors, G.: Hierarchical chamfer matching: a parametric edge matching algorithm. IEEE Transaction on Pattern Analysis and Machine Intelligence 10 (6), 849–865 (1988)

[7] Rosenfeld, A., Kak, A.: Digital Picture Processing, vol. 2, pp. 205–219 (1982)

[8] Lamecker, H., et al.: Segmentation of the liver using a 3d statistical shape model. ZIB-Report 04-09, pp. 1–25 (April 2004)

[9] Barrett, W., Mortensen, E.N.: Interactive live-wire boundary extraction. Medical Image Analysis 1(4), 331–341 (1997)

[10] O Donnell, L., et al.: Phase-based user-steered image segmentation. In: Proceedings of MICCAI 2001, pp. 1022–1030 (2001)

[11] Schenk, A., et al.: Local cost computation for efficient segmentation of 3d objects with live wire. In: Proceedings of SPIE, vol. 4322, pp. 1357–1364 (2001)

[12] Raya, S., Udupa, J.: Shape-based interpolation of multidimensional objects. IEEE Transactions on Medical Imaging 9(1), 32–42 (1990)

[13] Werkgartner, G., et al.: Augmented-reality-based liver-surgical planning system. European Surgery 36 (5), 270–274 (2004)

[14] Hermoye, L., et al.: Liver segmentation in living liver transplant donors: Comparison of semiautomatic and manual methods. Radiology 234, 171–178 (2005)

[15] Bae, K.T., et al.: Automatic segmentation of liver structure in ct images. Med. Phys. 20 (1993)

[16] Gao, L., et al.: Automatic liver segmentation technique for three-dimensional visualization of ct data. Radiology 201, 359–364 (1996)

[17] Kobashi, M., Shapiro, L.: knowledge-based organ identification from ct images. Pattern Recognition 28 (4), 475–491 (1995)

[18] Woodhouse, C., et al.: Spiral computed tomography arterial portography with three-dimensional volumetric rendering for oncologic planning: a retrospective analysis. Investigative Radiology 29, 1031–1037 (1994)

[19] Kaneko, T., et al.: Recognition of abdominal organs using 3d mathematical morphology. Systems and Computers in Japan 33 (8), 75–83 (2002)

[20] Lim, S.J., et al.: Segmentation of the liver using the deformable contour method on ct images. In: Proceedings of SPIE, vol. 3767, pp. 570–581 (2005)

[21] Lim, S.J., et al.: Automatic liver segmentation for volume measurement in ct images. Journal of Visual Communication and Image Representation 17(4), 860–875 (2006)

[22] Lim, S.J., et al.: Automatic segmentation of the liver in ct images using the watershed algorithm based on morphological filtering. In: Proceedings of SPIE, vol. 5370, pp. 1658–1666 (2004)

[23] Shiffman, S., et al.: Medical image segmentation using analysis of isolable-contour maps. IEEE Transactions on Medical Imaging 19 (11), 1064–1074 (2000)

[24] Liu, F., et al.: Liver segmentation for ct images using gvf snake. Medical Physics 32(12), 3699–3706 (2005)

[25] Tsai, D., Tanahashi, N.: Neural-network-based boundary detection of liver structure in ct images for 3-d visualization. In: Proceedings of IEEE International Conference on Neural Networks, vol. 6(1), pp. 3484–3489 (1994)

[26] Koss, J., et al.: Abdominal organ segmentation using texture transforms and a hopfield neural network. IEEE Transaction on Medical Imaging 18 (7), 640–648 (1999)

[27] Lee, C.C., et al.: Identifying multiple abdominal organs from ct image series usinmg a multimodule contextual neural network and spatial fuzzy rules. IEEE Transaction on Information Technology in Biomedicine 7, 208–217 (2003)

[28] Gao, L., et al.: Abdominal image segmentation using three-dimensional deformable models. Investigative Radiology 33 (6), 348–355 (1998)

[29] Montagnat, J., Delingette, H.: Volumetric medical images segmentation using shape constrained deformable models. In: CVRMed-MRCAS, pp. 13–22. Springer Verlag, Heidelberg (1996)

[30] Soler, L., et al.: Fully automatic anatomical, pathological, and functional segmentation from ct scans for hepatic surgery. Computed Aided Surgery 6 (3), 131–142 (2001)

[31] Cootes, T., et al.: Use of active shape models for locating structures in medical images. Image and Vision Computing 12, 355–366 (1994)

[32] Park, H., et al.: Construction of an abdominal probabilistic atlas and its application in segmentation. IEEE Transactions on Medical Imaging 22 (4), 483–492 (2003)

[33] Shimizu, A., et al.: Multi-organ segmentation in three dimensional abdominal ct images. In: Proceedings of CARS, vol. 1(7), pp. 76–78 (2006)

[34] Zhou, X., et al.: Construction of a probabilistic atlas for automated liver segmentation in non-contrast torso ct images. In: Proceedings CARS, vol. 1281, pp. 1169–1174 (2005)

[35] Pan, S., Dawant, B.: Automatic 3d segmentation of the liver from abdominal ct images: a level-set approach. In: Proceedings of SPIE, vol. 4322, pp. 128–138 (2001)

[36] Malladi, R., et al.: Shape modeling with front propagation: A level set approach. IEEE Transactions on Pattern Analysis and Machine Intelligence 17 (2), 158–175 (1995)

[37] Shimizu, A., et al.: Preliminary report of cad system competition for liver cancer extraction from 3d ct imaging and fusion of the cads. In: Proceedings of CARS, vol. 1, pp. 525–526 (2005)

Clustering Microarray Data with Space Filling Curves

Dimitrios Vogiatzis[1] and Nicolas Tsapatsoulis[2]

[1] Department of Computer Science, University of Cyprus, CY 1678, Cyprus
Phone: +357-2289-2749, Fax: +357-2289-2701;
dimitrv@cs.ucy.ac.cy
[2] Department of Telecommunications Science and Technology University of
Peloponnese Greece
ntsap@uop.gr

Abstract. We introduce a new clustering method for DNA microarray data that is based on space filling curves and wavelet denoising. The proposed method is much faster than the established fuzzy c-means clustering because clustering occurs in one dimension and it clusters cells that contain data, instead of data themselves. Moreover, preliminary evaluation results on data sets from Small Round Blue-Cell tumors, Leukemia and Lung cancer microarray experiments show that it can be equally or more accurate than fuzzy c-means clustering or a gaussian mixture model.

Keywords: clustering, space filling curve, wavelets, microarray DNA.

1 Introduction

Microarray experiments allow the simultaneous study of expression patterns of thousands of genes. Usually, microarray datasets are characterized by a large number of genes across a relatively small number of different experimental conditions [1]. The genes form a data set of a few thousands of vectors, while the experimental conditions (a few tens) constitute the dimensions of each vector. One of the reasons behind microarray experiments is to figure out the genes that have similar biological function, by comparing their expression patterns. An unaided researcher trying to make sense of these data will have a hard time. Clustering is a widely used method to group those genes that have similar expression levels into the same clusters. *Hierarchical clustering* has been widely used in microarray experiments, where smaller clusters are merged to form a hierarchical tree called the dendrogramme [2]. However, the visualisation that is offered by such a method is problematic as thousands of tiny line segments representing the genes can clutter the screen. In *Partition based clustering* the data are split into a fixed number of clusters (either crisp of fuzzy) by optimising an objective function through a series of steps. A representative is the fuzzy c-means clustering [3]. Moreover, in *Grid based clustering* the input space is first quantised into a fixed number of cells and then the clusters are formed out of cells [4]. Finally, in *Density based clustering* the aim is to find high density regions of the data space that are separated from low density regions. High density regions stand for clusters. A widely used density estimation method is through a mixture of gaussian models. Mixture models can be learnt with the expectation maximisation Algorithm (EM). A fast method for dynamically computing

F. Masulli, S. Mitra, and G. Pasi (Eds.): WILF 2007, LNAI 4578, pp. 529–536, 2007.
© Springer-Verlag Berlin Heidelberg 2007

a mixture model appeared in [5]. We refer the interested reader to a recent survey of clustering and cluster analysis for gene expression data [6].

The gene clustering method for DNA microarray we propose is based on a four step process. First, we partition (quantise) the input space. Second, we map the multidimensional gene expression vectors onto one dimension, the end result of which is a spatial signal. Then we use one dimensional discrete wavelet transform on the spatial signal to denoise the signal. Finally, we cluster the one dimensional data based on the assumption that cells that are not close belong to different clusters. Also, low density cells represent the boundaries of clusters.

To place our work into context, we would say that it has some elements of partition based clustering and it is also related to a *WaveCluster*, where wavelets are used to cluster data of very large databases. In this method low pass filter are used to remove outliers [7]. It has been shown to be very efficient and to detect arbitrary shaped clusters on benchmark datasets. However, *WaveCluster* has been applied to two dimensional data, whereas our proposal can deal with multidimensional data.

The rest of the paper is organised as follows: In Sect. 2 we introduce the concept of space filling curves, and we also present wavelet denoising. Then in Sect. 3 we present the space filling based clustering method we developed. Experiments and evaluation are presented in Sect. 4. Finally, conclusions are drawn in Sect. 5.

2   Space Filling Curves and Wavelets

A space filling curve is a one dimensional curve that can fill an entire plane [8]. There are many space filling curves, in particular we are interested in the *Z-space filling curve*. This curve is a mapping $S : \mathbb{R}^n \rightarrow \mathbb{R}$, which is constructed by interleaving bits from a point's M dimensions into a single dimension. For example, given vector $\mathbf{e} = (v_1, v_2, \ldots v_n)$, with k bits $b_1 \ldots b_k$ used to represent each dimension, with b_1 and b_k being the most and least significant bits respectively. The one dimensional projection of $\mathbf{e}$ is $e' = (b_1^{v_1} b_1^{v_2} \ldots b_1^{v_n} b_2^{v_1} b_2^{v_2} \ldots b_2^{v_n} \ldots b_k^{v_1} b_k^{v_2} \ldots b_k^{v_n})$, where b_i^j denotes the i-th ordered bit from dimension j. In Fig. 1 is depicted a two dimensional version of a Z-curve ordering of the cells in an area. In particular, we can observe a first, second and third order curve. Higher order curves represent a "denser" covering of the input space. The limit of Z-curve is the area that contains the curve.

The Z- curve has the interesting property (easier to visualise in two dimensions, but also holds for more dimensions), that it tends to preserve the locality of the data. That is data that are close together in $\mathbb{R}^n$ tend also to be close in $\mathbb{R}$, which does not hold for row major ordering. The Z-curve can be considered as a spatial signal, which can analysed with signal processing techniques, and in particular wavelets.

From the point of view of mathematics, a function can be represented as an infinite series expansion in terms of a dilated and translated version of a basis function called the *mother wavelet* denoted as $\psi(x)$ and weighted by some coefficient $b_{j,k}$: $f(t) = \sum_{j,k} b_{j,k} \psi_{j,k}(t)$ Normally, a wavelet starts at time $t = 0$ and ends at time N. Instead of time one can consider space (as it is often the case in image analysis). A shifted wavelet, denoted as ψ_{jo}, starts at time $t = k$ and ends at time $t = k + N$. A dilated wavelet w_{j0} starts at time $t = 0$ and ends at time $t = N/2^j$. A wavelet w_{jk} that

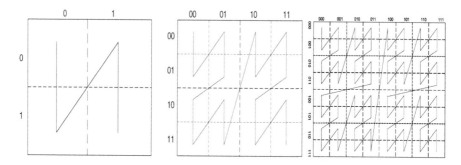

Fig. 1. The Z-space filling curve. The curve in each figure denotes the order of visitation of the cells.

is dilated j times and shifted k times is denoted as: $\psi_{j,k}(t) = \psi(2^j t - k)$. For practical purposes, we can use the discrete wavelet transform, which removes some of the redundancy found in the continuous transform. In this study we rely on *wavelet shrinkage* for denoising. The shrinkage is based on discarding some of the detail coefficients and then by reconstructing the signal based on the reduced set of coefficients. Moreover, in [9] it has been shown that the wavelet shrinkage method outperforms other methods for denoising signals.

3   Clustering with the Z-Curve

The proposed algorithm with the Z-space filling curve, henceforth called Space Filling Curve Clustering (SFCC), accepts as input a matrix of microarray data, and it assigns genes into clusters. The number of clusters are discovered by the algorithm. The steps are summarised as follows: Quantise Input space, Construct space filling curve, Smooth the curve, discover clusters. The algorithm is exposed in Table 1. The rationale of step 3 (i.e. smoothing by denoising) is based on the assumption that the limits of a cluster is marked by a high frequency component. Thus by zeroing the high frequency components we make cluster detection clearer. Step 4, says that points that belong to the same cluster must be close (determined by threshold t_1) and the cell must have a minimum amount of data density (determined by threshold t_2).

For the proposed clustering method the time complexity is the steps it takes to create the curve, to apply wavelet denoising and to cluster the data. Let N_c be the number of cells that contain data points, and N the number of data, consequently $N_c < N$. The time to create the Z-curve is $M \times nb \times N$, where nb is the number of bits used to encode each dimension. Thus $O(M \times nb \times N + N_c log N_c + N)$.

The computational complexity of the FCM algorithm is $O(Nk^2 M)$, where N is the number of data, k the number of clusters and M the number of dimensions (experiments) of the data. The important thing to notice is that the complexity of algorithm is quadratic with regard to the number of clusters.

Table 1. Clustering with the Z-curve

1. Quantise each dimension of the input space into equally spaced intervals.
2. Record the number of data in each resulting hyper rectangle
3. Construct a space filling curve $S(i)$ that passes through the created hyper rectangles (cells). Because the cell space is sparsely populated, $S(i)$ is created only for cells that contain data. $i \in \mathbb{N}$ represents the index of the cells, and $S(x)$ represents the number of data points per cell.
4. Smooth the curve by applying wavelet denoising.
5. Cluster the cells (i.e. their indices) that contain data (one dimensional clustering) as follows
   for $i = 2 \ldots i = length(S)$.
   (a) If $||S(i) - S(i-1)||_2 \leq t_1$ and $S(i) \geq t_2$ then put current cell in the existing cluster.
   (b) else if $||S(i) - S(i-1)||_2 > t_1$ and $S(i) \geq t_2$ then create a new cluster, which becomes the current cluster and put current cell into new clusters
   (c) else this cell is an outlier and ignore it.

Finally, learning gaussian mixtures with the greedyEM algorithm takes $O(N \times k^2)$ steps, under certain conditions the complexity can be reduced to $O(N \times k)$ according to [7].

4   Experiments and Evaluation

We compared the proposed method (i.e. SFCC) with FCM and greedyEM in terms of two validation indices: *figure of merit* [10] and *silhouette* [11]. The figure of merit (FOM) is defined as: $FOM(e) = \sqrt{\frac{1}{N} ||R_c(x, e) - \mu_c(e)||^2}, \forall c$ where $R_c(x, e)$ represents the e dimension of datum x that belongs in cluster c, μ_c represents the average value of $R_c(x, e)$, N is the number of data (genes), M the number of experiments (dimensions) and e is index in the experiments. The FOM index of the whole clustering is defined as:

$$FOM = \sum_{e=1}^{M} FOM(e) \tag{1}$$

Smaller values of FOM denote better clustering, for the same number of clusters by different algorithms.

The silhouette index for datum x of cluster c is defined as:

$$s_c(x) = \frac{min[b_{\forall c}(x)] - a_c(x)}{max\{a_c(x), min[b_{\forall c}(x)]\}} \tag{2}$$

where $a(x)$ is the average dissimilarity of datum x to the data of the same cluster, and $b(x)$ is the average dissimilarity of a datum x from all the data of another cluster. Dissimilarity can be defined as the eucledian distance. The silhouette index of cluster c is: $S_c = \frac{1}{|c|} \sum_{i=1}^{|c|} s_c(i)$. Finally, the silhouette index of the whole clustering is: $S = \frac{1}{k} \sum_{j=1}^{k} S_j$, where k is the number of clusters. From the definition if follows that: $s_c(x) \in [-1, 1]$. An $s(x)$ value for datum x close to 1 denotes good clustering, a value close to 0 denotes that the datum belongs to more than one clusters, and a value close to -1 denotes that x belongs to another cluster.

We have used datasets from 3 microarray DNA experiments. The first data set was obtained from "The Microarray Project cDNA Library" `http://research.nhgri.nih.gov/microarray/Supplement/`. The second and third data sets were obtained from the Gene Expression Datasets collection `http://sdmc.lit.org.sg/GEDatasets`. The first data set is about Small Round Blue-Cell tumours (SRBCT), investigated with cDNA microarrays containing 2308 genes, over a series of 83 experiments. The 83 samples included tumour biopsy material and cell lines from 4 different types: Ewing's sarcoma (EWS), rhabdomyo sarcoma (RMS), neuroblastoma (NB) and Burkitt's lymphoma (BL) [12]. The provenance of the second data set stems also is from oligonucleotide microarrays, with a view of distinguishing between acute lymphoblastic leukemia (ALL) and acute meyeloid leukemia (AML). The data set consisted of 72 bone morrow samples from 7130 human genes [13]. The third data set also stems from a microarray experiment and consists of lung malignant pleural mesothylioma (MPM) and adenocarcinoma (ADCA) samples [14]. The data set consists of 181 samples from 12534 human genes. All data sets have been normalised in the $[0, 1]$ region.

Experiments have been performed at Matlab 6.1, with the implementation of FCM from fuzzy toolbox 2.1.1, and wavelet denoising from the wavelet toolbox 2.1. The code for greedyEM was obtained from the author's site `http://www.science.uva.nl/vlassis/publications`. The code for space filling curves and evaluation was developed by the authors in matlab. In the wavelet based smoothing we employed daubechy of order 2. The wavelet smoothing is achieved by applying 4 levels of decomposition for SRBCT and Leukemia data sets and 8 levels for the Lung set. Then we set the detail coefficients to zero and we reconstructed the signal. Also, the thresholds t_1 and t_2 influence the performance of the algorithm since they define when clusters occur, thus we varied the values of t_1 and t_2 from 0.05 to 0.7 with a step of 0.01. Finally, the quantisation step for each dimension for all data sets has been set to 10. The levels of wavelet decomposition that are used to smooth the signal (i.e. the space filling curve) play a crucial role in the performance of the algorithm. Currently, the number of levels of decomposition are experimentally determined.

In Fig. 2 and we depict the results of evaluating SFCC and comparing it with FCM and greedyEM under the FOM criterion (recall that smaller values indicate better results). The FOM in the case of the space filling curve has been applied to the multi-dimensional data according to the cluster they belong to. SFCC is depicted with diamonds, FCM with rectangles and greedyEM with small dots. At the first diagramme, corresponding to the SRBC experiments, the SFCC is overall winner for a small number of clusters (2-4). At the middle diagramme (Leukemia) greedyEM is the best method. At the right most diagramme, which corresponds to Lung Cancer, it is shown that the SFCC outperforms FCM or greedy in for most cases (from 5 till 20 clusters).

Finally, in Fig. 3 we present the evaluation of SFCC, FCM and greedyEM with respect to the silhouette validation index (recall that bigger values are better and non positive values denote bad clustering). At the leftmost diagramme (SRBC data), the winner is SFCC in most cases. Considering the Leukemia data (middle diagramme) the winner in most cases is the FCM. At the rightmost diagramme (Lung Cancer), SFCC

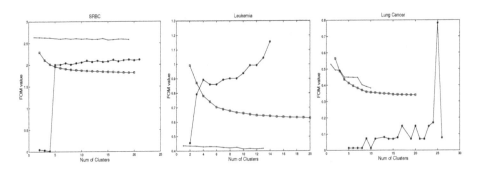

Fig. 2. Evaluation results based on comparing FOM values for the proposed method (star curve), FCM (square curve), greedyEM (small dots curves)

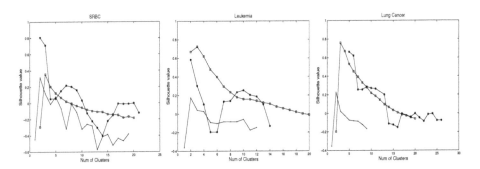

Fig. 3. Evaluation results based on comparing silhouette values for the proposed method (star curve), FCM (square curve), greedyEM (small dots curves)

and FCM have a comparable behaviour beyond three clusters, whereas greedyEM is generally worse than all the other methods.

Considering both the FOM and the silhouette validation indices, the SFCC is better or at least equally good as FCM. For the leukemia data, the two indices do not concur about the overall clustering quality of each of the clustering algorithms. In any case, we must recall that even if SFCC is equally or slightly worse than FCM, it is much faster to compute.

5   Conclusions and Future Directions

We have developed an efficient method to cluster genes from DNA microarray experiments. Our method is based on Z-space filling curve which maps multidimensional genes into one dimension and it performs clustering into one dimension which is very efficient in terms of computational complexity. It is important to emphasize that the proposed method actually does not cluster data directly, but it clusters cells into which data belong (after some partitioning). Thus it is independent of the number of data but dependent on the quantisation step. The outcome of the Z-space filling curve is a one dimensional spatial signal which can be processed as described to detect clusters. The algorithm is dependent on two thresholds, the maximum distance between two cells so that they belong to the same cluster and also on the minimum data density of a cell so as not to be considered as outlier. Of course, by clustering cells, we also cluster the data that belong to each cell. Wavelets play an important role, because they constitute a pre-processing step to the actual clustering. With wavelet shrinkage, we can denoising the spatial signal and achieve better results. Thus this paper also contributes in introducing signal processing techniques into multidimensional data. As evaluation, we have employed the FOM and silhouette criteria to compare SPCC with FCM and greedyEM, where we obtained promising results. In any case there can be no clustering method that is panacea. The clustering results will always depend on the data distribution of the samples, on the amount of noise they contain, and on the model the user tries to apply to these data.

For the future, it is important to enhance our evaluation with other measures such as the Partition Coefficient, Dunn's index and the Geometric index in order to check the validity of the derived clusters; the aforementioned indexes have been used in a work related to evaluating clusters in cDNA experiments [15]. Furthermore, all aforementioned evaluation measures are based on statistics, and we need to investigate the biological significance of the discovered clusters. For example, in [16] a clustering experiment is described, where the genes of each cluster are mapped into the functional categories of the Martinsried Institute of Protein Sciences. Then for each cluster $P-$values were calculated to measure the statistical significance of clusters.

Moreover, the space filling curve is of crucial importance in the algorithm and a basic property it must have is to preserve the locality of the data. There is enough research on such curves and there is evidence that the hilbert curve can achieve better clustering. We need to investigate that on more microarray experiments.

References

1. Macgregor, P., Squire, J.: Application of microarrays to the analysis of gene expression in cancer. Clinical Chemistry 48, 1170–1177 (2002)
2. Eisen, M., Spellman, P., Brown, P., Botsetein, D.: Cluster analysis and display of genome-wide expression patterns. In: Proceedings of the National Academy of Scienes, vol. 95 (1998)
3. Bezdek, J.: Pattern Recognition with Fuzzy Objective Function Algorithms. Plenum Press, New York (1981)
4. Hinneburg, A., Keim, D.: Optimal Grid-Clustering: Towards Breaking the Curse of Dimensionality in High-Dimensional Clustering. In: Proceedings of the 25th VLDB Conference, Edinburgh, Scotland (1999)
5. Verbeek, J., Vlassis, N., Kröse, B.: Efficient greedy learning of gaussian mixture models. Neural Computation 15, 469–485 (2002)
6. Jiang, D., Tang, C., Zhang, A.: Cluster Analysis for Gene Expression Data: A Survey. IEEE transactions on knowledge and data engineering 16, 1370–1386 (2004)
7. Sheikholeslami, G., Chatterjee, S., Zhang, A.: WaveCluster: a wavelet-based clustering approach for spatial data in very large databases. The VLDB Journal 8, 289–304 (2000)
8. Faloutsos, C., Roseman, S.: Fractals for secondary key retrieval. In: 8th ACM SIGACT-SIGMOD-SIGART Symp. Principles of Database Systems PODS, pp. 247–252 (1989)

9. Donoho, D.L., Johnstone, I.M., Kerkyacharian, G., Picard, D.: Wavelet shrinkage: Asymptopia? J. R. Statist. Soc. B. 57, 301–337 (1995)
10. Yeung, K., Haynor, D., Ruzzo, W.: Validating clustering for gene expression data. Bioinformatics 17, 309–318 (2001)
11. Rousseeuw, P.: Silhouettes: a graphical aid to the interpretation and validation of cluster analysis. J. Comp. App. Math. 20, 53–65 (1987)
12. Khan, J., Wei, J., Ringer, M., Saal, L., Ladanyi, M., Westermann, F., Berthold, F., Schwab, M., Antonescu, C., Peterson, C., Meltzer, P.: Classification and diagnostic prediction of cancers using gene expression profiling and artificial neural network. Nature Medicine 7, 673–679 (2001)
13. Golub, T.R., Slonim, D.K., Tamayo, P., Huard, C., Gaasenbeek, M., Mesirov, J.P., Coller, H., Loh, M.L., Downing, J.R., Caligiuri, M.A., Bloomfield, C.D., Lander, E.: Molecular Classification of Cancer: Class Discovery and Class Prediction by Gene Expression Monitoring. Science (1999)
14. Gordon, G., Jensen, R., Hsiao, L., Gullans, S., Blumenstock, J., Ramaswamy, S., Richard, W., Sugarbaker, D., Bueno, R.: Translation of microarray data into clinically relevant cancer diagnostic tests using gene expression ratios in lung cancer and mesothelioma. Cancer Research, 4963–4967 (2002)
15. Lam, B., Yan, H.: Cluster Validity for DNA Microarray Data using a Geometrical Index. In: Proceedings of the 4th International Conference on Machine Learning and Cybernetics (2005)
16. Tavazoie, S., Hughes, D., Campbell, M., Cho, R., Church, G.: Systematic determination of genetic network architecture. Nature Genetics 22, 281–285 (1999)

Fuzzy Ensemble Clustering for DNA Microarray Data Analysis

Roberto Avogadri and Giorgio Valentini

DSI, Dipartimento di Scienze dell' Informazione,
Università degli Studi di Milano,
Via Comelico 39, 20135 Milano, Italia
{avogadri,valentini}@dsi.unimi.it

Abstract. Two major problems related the unsupervised analysis of gene expression data are represented by the accuracy and reliability of the discovered clusters, and by the biological fact that classes of examples or classes of functionally related genes are sometimes not clearly defined. To face these items, we propose a fuzzy ensemble clustering approach to both improve the accuracy of clustering results and to take into account the inherent fuzziness of biological and bio-medical gene expression data. Preliminary results with DNA microarray data of lymphoma and adenocarcinoma patients show the effectiveness of the proposed approach.

1   Introduction

In recent years unsupervised clustering methods have been successfully applied to DNA microarray data analysis, considering in particular two main problems: the discovery of new subclasses of diseases or functionally correlated examples and the detection of subsets of co-expressed genes as a proxy of co-regulated genes [1]. Different unsupervised ensemble approaches have been proposed to improve the accuracy and the reliability of clustering results [2, 3, 4]. In bioinformatics applications, recently proposed methods based on random projections [5] have been also successfully applied to gene expression data analysis [6].

A major problem with these approaches is represented by the biological fact that classes of patients or classes of functionally related genes are sometimes not clearly defined. For instance, it is well-known that a single gene product may participate to different biological processes and as a consequence it may be at the same time expressed with different subsets of co-expressed genes.

To take into account these items we propose a fuzzy approach, in order to consider the inherent fuzziness of clusters discovered in gene expression data [7]. The main idea of this work is to combine the accuracy and the effectiveness of the ensemble clustering techniques based on random projections [5], with the expressive capacity of the fuzzy sets, to obtain clustering algorithms both reliable and able to express the uncertainty of the data. In the next section we briefly introduce random projections, then we present our proposed fuzzy ensemble clustering method, and we show some preliminary results with two DNA microarray data sets.

F. Masulli, S. Mitra, and G. Pasi (Eds.): WILF 2007, LNAI 4578, pp. 537–543, 2007.

2   Random Projections

Our proposed method perturb the original data using random projections μ : $\mathbb{R}^d \to \mathbb{R}^{d'}$ from high d-dimensional spaces to lower d'-dimensional subspaces.

A key problem consists in finding a d' such that for every pair of data $p, q \in \mathbb{R}^d$, the distances between the projections $\mu(p)$ and $\mu(q)$ are approximately preserved with high probability. A natural measure of the approximation is the distortion $dist_\mu$:

$$dist_\mu(p, q) = \frac{||\mu(p) - \mu(q)||_2}{||p - q||_2} \tag{1}$$

If $dist_\mu(p, q) = 1$, the distances are preserved; if $1 - \epsilon \le dist_\mu(p, q) \le 1 + \epsilon$, we say that an ϵ-*distortion* level is introduced.

It has been shown that using random projections that obey *Johnson-Lindenstrauss (JL) lemma* [8] we may perturb the data introducing only bounded distortions, approximately preserving the metric structure of the original data (see [9] for more details). Examples of random projections related with the JL Lemma can be found in [9, 5].

3   Fuzzy Ensemble Clustering Based on Random Projections

The general structure of the algorithm is similar to the one proposed in [5]: data are perturbed through random projections to lower dimensional subspaces and multiple clusterings are performed on the projected data; note that it is likely to obtain different clusterings, since the clustering algorithm is applied to different "views" of the data. Then the clusterings are combined, and a *consensus* ensemble clustering is computed. The main difference of our proposed method consists in using a fuzzy k-means algorithm as base clustering and in applying a fuzzy approach to the combination and the consensus steps of the ensemble algorithm.

The main steps of the fuzzy ensemble clustering algorithm can be summarized as follows:

1. *Random projections.* Multiple instances (views) of compressed data are obtained using random projections.
2. *Generation of multiple fuzzy clusterings.* The fuzzy k-means algorithm is applied to the instances of data obtained from the previous step. The output of the algorithm is a membership matrix, where each element represents the membership of an example to a particular cluster.
3. *Aggregation.* The fuzzy clusterings are combined, using a similarity matrix [2]. The generation of each element of the matrix is obtained through fuzzy t-norms.
4. *Consensus clustering.* The ensemble clustering is built up by applying the fuzzy k-means algorithm to the rows of the similarity matrix obtained in the previous step.

The *Aggregation* step is performed by using a square symmetric similarity matrix M, where each element represents the "level of agreement between" each pair of examples:

$$M_{i,j} = \sum_{s=1}^{k} \tau(\mathcal{U}_{s,i}, \mathcal{U}_{s,j});$$ (2)

where k is the number of clusters; i, j indices of the n examples, $1 \leq i, j \leq n$; $\mathcal{U}$ is a fuzzy membership matrix (where the rows are clusters and the columns examples), and finally τ is a suitable fuzzy t-norm (e.g. an algebraic product). Note that $M_{i,j}$ can be interpreted as the "common membership" of two examples i and j to the same cluster.

The similarity matrices M obtained through c repeated application of the fuzzy k-means clustering algorithm are aggregated simply by averaging: in this way we achieve the cumulative similarity matrix M^C:

$$M_{i,j}^C = \frac{1}{c} \sum_{t=1}^{c} M_{i,j}^{(t)};$$ (3)

The *Consensus clustering* step is performed by applying the fuzzy-k-means clustering to the rows of M^C, thus obtaining the *consensus membership* matrix $\mathcal{U}^C$. Indeed note that i^{th} row of M^C represents the "common membership" to the same cluster of the ith example with respect to all the other examples, averaged across multiple clusterings. In this sense the rows can be interpreted as a new "feature space" for the analyzed examples.

The *consensus clusters* can be obtained by choosing one of two classical "crispization" techniques:

Hard-clustering:

$$\chi_{ri}^H = \begin{cases} 1 & \Leftrightarrow \arg max_s \, \mathcal{U}_{si}^C = r \\ 0 & \text{otherwise.} \end{cases}$$ (4)

α-cut:

$$\chi_{ri}^\alpha = \begin{cases} 1 & \Leftrightarrow \mathcal{U}_{ji}^C \geq \alpha \\ 0 & \text{otherwise.} \end{cases}$$ (5)

where χ_{ri} is the characteristic function for the cluster r: that is $\chi_{ri} = 1$ if the ith example belongs to the rth cluster, $\chi_{ri} = 0$ otherwise; $1 \leq s \leq k; 1 \leq i \leq n$, $0 \leq \alpha \leq 1$, and $\mathcal{U}^C$ is the consensus fuzzy membership matrix obtained by applying the fuzzy k-means algorithm to M^C.

The pseudo-code of the algorithm is reported below:

Fuzzy ensemble clustering algorithm :

Input:
- a data set $X = \{x_1, x_2, \ldots, x_n\}$, stored in a $d \times n$ D matrix.
- an integer k (number of clusters)
- an integer c (number of clusterings)
- the fuzzy k-means clustering algorithm $\mathcal{C}_f$

- a procedure the realizes the randomized map μ
- an integer d' (dimension of the projected subspace)
- a function τ that defines the t-norm

```
begin algorithm
```
    (1) For each $i, j \in \{1, \ldots, n\}$ do $M_{ij} = 0$

    (2) Repeat for $t = 1$ to c

        (3) $R_t =$ Generate_projection_matrix (d', μ)

        (4) $D_t = R_t \cdot D$

        (5) $\mathcal{U}^{(t)} = \mathcal{C}_f(D_t, k, m)$

        (6) For each $i, j \in \{1, \ldots, n\}$

           $M_{ij}^{(t)} = \sum_{s=1}^{k} \tau(\mathcal{U}_{si}^{(t)}, \mathcal{U}_{sj}^{(t)})$

    end repeat

    (7) $M^C = \frac{\sum_{t=1}^{c} M^{(t)}}{c}$

    (8) $< A_1, A_2, \ldots, A_k > = \mathcal{C}_f(M^C, k, m)$

```
end algorithm.
Output:
```
- the final clustering $C = < A_1, A_2, \ldots, A_k >$
- the cumulative similarity matrix M^C.

Note that the dimension d' of the projected subspace is an input parameter of the algorithm, but it may be computed according to the *JL* lemma (Sect. 2), to approximately preserve the distances between the examples. Inside the mean loop (steps 2-6) the procedure `Generate_projection_matrix` produces a $d' \times d$ R_t matrix according to a given random map μ [5], that it is used to randomly project the original data matrix D into a $d' \times n$ D_t projected data matrix (step 4). In step (5) the fuzzy k-means algorithm $\mathcal{C}_f$ with a given fuzziness m is applied to D_t and a k-clustering represented by its $\mathcal{U}^{(t)}$ membership matrix is achieved. Hence the corresponding similarity matrix $M^{(t)}$ is computed, using a given *t-norm* (step 6). In (7) the "cumulative" similarity matrix M^C is obtained by averaging across the similarity matrices computed in the main loop. Finally, the *consensus* clustering is obtained by applying the fuzzy k-means algorithm to the rows of the similarity matrix M^C (step 8).

4   Experimental Results

4.1   Experimental Environment

We considered two DNA microarray data sets available on the web. The first one (*DLBCL-FL* data set) is composed by tumor specimens from 58 Diffuse Large B-Cell Lymphoma (DLBCL) and 19 Follicular Lymphoma (FL) patients [10]. The second one, the *Primary-Metastasis* (PM) data set, contains expression values in Affymetrix's scaled average difference units for 64 primary adenocarcinomas and 12 metastatic adenocarcinomas (lung, breast, prostate, colon, ovary, and uterus) from unmatched patients prior to any treatment [11]. In both cases we followed the same preprocessing and normalization steps described in [10] and [11].

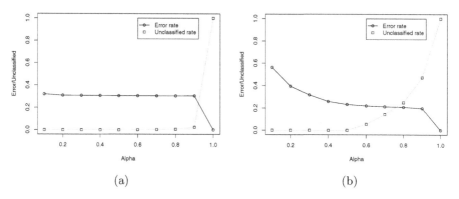

Fig. 1. *Fuzzy-Alpha* ensemble clustering error and unclassified rate with respect to α. (a) *Primary-Metastasis*; (b) *DLBCL-FL* data sets.

For each ensemble we randomly repeated the randomized projections 20 times, and each time we built fuzzy ensembles composed by 20 base clusterings (choosing projections with bounded 1 ± 0.2 distortion, according to the *JL* lemma). We compared results with corresponding "crisp" ensemble methods based on random projections proposed in [5] and with "single" clustering algorithms (hierarchical clustering and fuzzy-k-means).

Since clustering does not univocally associate a label to the examples, but only provides a set of clusters, we evaluated the error by choosing for each clustering the permutation of the classes that best matches the "a priori" known "true" classes. More precisely, considering the following clustering function:

$$f(x) : \mathcal{R}^d \rightarrow \mathcal{Y}, \text{ with } \mathcal{Y} \subseteq \{1, \ldots, k\} \tag{6}$$

where x is the sample to classify, d its dimension, k the number of the classes; the error function we applied is the following:

$$\mathcal{L}_{0/1}(Y, t) = \begin{cases} 0 \text{ if } (|Y| = 1 \wedge t \in Y) \vee Y = \{\lambda\} \\ 1 \text{ otherwise.} \end{cases} \tag{7}$$

with t the "real" label of the sample x, $Y \in \mathcal{Y}$ and $\{\lambda\}$ is the empty set. Other loss functions or measures of the performance of clustering algorithms may be applied, but we chose this modification of the 0/1 loss function to take into account the multi-label output of fuzzy k-means algorithms.

4.2   Results

To test the performance of the ensemble fuzzy algorithms proposed in this paper, we compare the results of two versions of the proposed fuzzy ensemble clustering method with other types of clustering algorithms. The two version are the *fuzzy-max* ensemble clustering, where the "defuzzifaction" of the consensus clustering is obtained through hard clustering (eq. 4), and the *fuzzy-alpha* ensemble

Table 1. *Primary-metastasis* gene expression data: compared results between fuzzy ensemble clustering methods (Fuzzy-Max and Fuzzy-Alpha) and other ensemble and "single" clustering algorithms

Algorithms	Median error	Std. Dev.
Fuzzy-Max	0.2763	0.0477
Fuzzy-Alpha	0.2763	0.0560
Rand-Clust	0.3289	0.0088
Fuzzy "single"	0.3684	–
Hierarchical "single"	0.3553	–

Table 2. *DLBCL-FL* gene expression data: compared results between fuzzy ensemble clustering methods (Fuzzy-Max and Fuzzy-Alpha) and other ensemble and "single" clustering algorithms.

Algorithms	Median error	Std. Dev.
Fuzzy-Max	0.0779	0.1163
Fuzzy-Alpha	0.2727	0.1142
Rand-Clust	0.1039	0.0023
Fuzzy "single"	0.2987	–
Hierarchical "single"	0.1039	–

clustering, where the final consensus clustering is "crispized" through the α-cut operation (eq. 5). The other clustering algorithms considered for comparison are *Rand-clust*, a crisp ensemble algorithm based on random projections proposed in [5], and other "single" clustering algorithms (hierarchical agglomerative and fuzzy k-means).

The tables 1 and 2 show the compared numerical results of the experiments on the PM data set and the DLBCL-FL data set respectively. Fuzzy ensemble methods obtain better results with respect to the other methods (considering the median error, see Tab. 1 and 2). Anyway note that the larger standard deviation (with respect to the *Rand-clust* ensemble algorithm) denotes a higher instability of the fuzzy approach, and with the *DLBCL-FL* data set *Fuzzy-Alpha* achieves significantly worse results than *Fuzzy-Max* and *Rand-clust* ensemble methods.

The graphics 1 (a) and 1 (b) represent the performance of the "fuzzy-alpha" ensemble algorithm (error rate and unclassified rate for every level of alpha-cut analyzed). The figure shows that we may obtain acceptable results with the *Fuzzy-Alpha* method too if we accept a certain rate of unclassified examples (Fig. 1(b)).

5   Conclusions

The experimental results show that our proposed fuzzy ensemble approach may be successfully applied to the analysis of gene expression data, even when we consider data sets with a single certain label for each example. Nevertheless we know that genes may belong to different biological processes or different pathways and as a consequence they may belong to different sets of co-expressed genes. We are planning new experiments with multi-label genes or examples to show more clearly the effectiveness of the proposed approach and to analyze the structure of unlabeled data when the boundaries of the clusters are uncertain.

References

[1] Dopazo, J.: Functional interpretation of microarray experiments. OMICS 3 (2006)
[2] Dudoit, S., Fridlyand, J.: Bagging to improve the accuracy of a clustering procedure. Bioinformatics 19, 1090–1099 (2003)
[3] Fern, X., Brodley, C.: Random projections for high dimensional data clustering: A cluster ensemble approach. In: Fawcett, T., Mishra, N. (eds.) Machine Learning. Proceedings of the Twentieth International Conference (ICML 2003), Washington D.C., USA, AAAI Press, Stanford, California, USA (2003)
[4] Topchy, A., Jain, A., Puch, W.: Clustering Ensembles: Models of Consensus and Weak Partitions. IEEE Transactions on Pattern Analysis and Machine Intelligence 27, 1866–1881 (2005)
[5] Bertoni, A., Valentini, G.: Ensembles based on random projections to improve the accuracy of clustering algorithms. In: Apolloni, B., Marinaro, M., Nicosia, G., Tagliaferri, R. (eds.) WIRN 2005 and NAIS 2005. LNCS, vol. 3931, pp. 31–37. Springer, Heidelberg (2006)
[6] Bertoni, A., Valentini, G.: Randomized embedding cluster ensembles for gene expression data analysis. In: SETIT 2007 - IEEE International Conf. on Sciences of Electronic, Technologies of Information and Telecommunications, Hammamet, Tunisia (2007)
[7] Gasch, P., Eisen, M.: Exploring the conditional regulation of yeast gene expression through fuzzy k-means clustering. Genome Biology 3 (2002)
[8] Johnson, W., Lindenstrauss, J.: Extensions of Lipshitz mapping into Hilbert space. In: Conference in modern analysis and probability. Contemporary Mathematics., Amer. Math. Soc., 26, 189–206 (1984)
[9] Bertoni, A., Valentini, G.: Randomized maps for assessing the reliability of patients clusters in DNA microarray data analyses. Artificial Intelligence in Medicine 37, 85–109 (2006)
[10] Shipp, M., et al.: Diffuse large B-cell lymphoma outcome prediction by geneexpression profiling and supervised machine learning. Nature Medicine 8, 68–74 (2002)
[11] Ramaswamy, S., Ross, K., Lander, E., Golub, T.: A molecular signature of metastasis in primary solid tumors. Nature Genetics 33, 49–54 (2003)

Signal Processing in Comparative Genomics

Matteo Ré and Giulio Pavesi

Dept. of Biomolecular Science and Biotechnology
University of Milan
Via Celoria 26, Milan, Italy
{matteo.re, giulio.pavesi}@unimi.it

Abstract. Comparative genomics techniques are a powerful tool for the identification of conserved functional genomic regions, but have to be coupled with methods able to assign a functional role to the regions identified. Several methods for the characterization of conserved regions have been proposed but, to our knowledge, signal processing approaches have not been applied yet in this context, despite the proven usefulness of this technique in experiments performed at single genome level. In this article we introduce the use of signal processing in comparative genomics, presenting a method for rapid classification of genomic conserved sequences as protein coding or non coding.

1 Introduction

The most important step in the early stages of the annotation of a newly sequenced genome consists in the identification of protein coding regions in the genomic sequence under investigation. Comparative genomics, that is, the comparison of the genomic sequence of different but evolutionarily related species has become the tool of election for this task. In fact, homologous regions under no selective pressure are progressively saturated of mutations, whereas regions under selective pressure retain higher levels of identity. The comparison of genomic sequences from different but close enough species can find these signatures of evolution and, consequently, one can infer which regions are more likely candidates to play a functional role. In particular, protein coding genes are usually highly conserved in different species, but other regions not coding for a protein are often found to be conserved as well: hence, the detection of conserved regions has to be coupled with some kind of prediction of their function (at least, whether they are more likely to be coding or non coding).

In any comparative genomics analysis it is of crucial importance the accurate choice of the evolutionary distance separating the genomes to be compared. It has been estimated that the rate of divergence between independently evolving vertebrate genomes is on average 0.1-0.5% per million years. This fact helps to understand why human/mouse comparisons are widely used in these experiments: the estimated 80 million years separating the two species from their last common ancestor are enough to grant the existence, at DNA sequence level, of the minimal divergence level in non functional genomic regions sufficient to

F. Masulli, S. Mitra, and G. Pasi (Eds.): WILF 2007, LNAI 4578, pp. 544–550, 2007.

single out functional conserved regions; vice versa, the divergence is not so high to result in a consistent decrease in sensitivity during comparisons aimed to find functional regions (as it is usually the case in human/fish or human/fly comparisons).

Several approaches for protein gene prediction based on comparative genomics have been proposed, ranging from TWINSCAN [1], an extension of the ab initio gene predictor GENSCAN [2] that integrates sequence conservation in the probabilistic model (GHMM) of GENSCAN, to CSTminer [3], a tool to discriminate between coding and non coding conserved sequences on the basis of the presence (or absence) of evolutionary dynamics compatible with a protein coding function.

On the other hand, another class of methods for the detection of protein coding regions rely on the analysis of DNA periodicities, exploiting techniques developed in the field of digital signal processing [4,5,6,7,8,9]. Despite the fact that these methods have been proven to be quite efficient on a single genome [10], as of today they have not been used in a comparative genomic context. Here we present a method based on signal theory that given two aligned conserved genomic sequences classifies them as coding or non coding. To assess its accuracy and sensitivity we analysed a set of pariwise human/mouse alignments of coding sequences and intergenic regions, with very encouraging results.

2   Numerical Encoding

The periodic pattern in protein coding DNA sequences is a well known phenomenon. The prominent signal detectable only in protein coding regions, often referred to as "3-periodicity", is a direct consequence of their functional role. In order to produce a new protein a flow of information has to be established from the DNA sequence to the cellular machinery responsible for protein synthesis (the ribosomes). DNA can be seen as a string of symbols belonging from a 4 letter alphabet. In order to encode for 20 amino acids the DNA has to be read in words of length 3 (the codons), and thus there are 64 (4^3) possible codons in DNA, 3 of which are used to encode the end of the translation (protein building) process. The set of rules allowing ribosomes to pair each of the 61 possible codons with the appropriate amino acid are known, in their complex, as the genetic code.

Since 20 different amino acids are encoded by 61 codons, the genetic code is redundant, and the same amino acid can be encoded by different codons (see Fig. 1). This is the key point to explain the origin of the 3-period: in families of codons encoding for the same amino acid, each member is used in coding DNA with different frequencies, leading to a codon usage pattern that is extremely specific for each organism. The presence of overrepresented codons in coding sequences results in a peak at period 3 (because of the codons' size) clearly detectable only in coding sequences and absent in non coding regions. The strength of the peak at frequency 1/3 can be easily quantified using Fourier transformation and evaluating the signal over noise ratio in the power spectrum of the DNA sequence under investigation.

Codon	AA	Codon	AA	Codon	AA	Codon	AA
TTT	Phe	TCT	Ser	TAT	Tyr	TGT	Cys
TTC	Phe	TCC	Ser	TAC	Tyr	TGC	Cys
TTA	Leu	TCA	Ser	TAA	STOP	TGA	STOP
TTG	Leu	TCG	Ser	TAG	STOP	TGG	Trp
CTT	Leu	CCT	Pro	CAT	His	CGT	Arg
CTC	Leu	CCC	Pro	CAC	His	CGC	Arg
CTA	Leu	CCA	Pro	CAA	Gln	CGA	Arg
CTG	Leu	CCG	Pro	CAG	Gln	CGG	Arg
ATT	Ile	ACT	Thr	AAT	Asn	AGT	Ser
ATC	Ile	ACC	Thr	AAC	Asn	AGC	Ser
ATA	Ile	ACA	Thr	AAA	Lys	AGA	Arg
ATG	Met*	ACG	Thr	AAG	Lys	AGG	Arg
GTT	Val	GCT	Ala	GAT	Asp	GGT	Gly
GTC	Val	GCC	Ala	GAC	Asp	GGC	Gly
GTA	Val	GCA	Ala	GAA	Glu	GGA	Gly
GTG	Val	GCG	Ala	GAG	Glu	GGG	Gly

Fig. 1. The genetic code: the 64 possible codons, and the corresponding amino acid. ATG serves both as methionine codon and translation start codon; STOP indicates codons marking the end of translation.

At primary level, a DNA sequence $S[i]$ of length N consists of a series of symbols belonging to an alphabet $\Sigma = \{A, C, G, T\}$. In single sequence signal processing techniques the sequence is mapped to four binary signals, each of which is associated with a specific nucleotide [11]. For example the DNA sequence

```
S[i] = [A T G C G T A C G C A C T G A C G C]
```

can be encoded as follows:

```
A[i] = [1 0 0 0 0 0 1 0 0 0 1 0 0 0 1 0 0 0]
```

```
C[i] = [0 0 0 1 0 0 0 1 0 1 0 1 0 0 0 1 0 1]
```

```
G[i] = [0 0 1 0 1 0 0 0 1 0 0 0 0 1 0 0 1 0]
```

```
T[i] = [0 1 0 0 0 1 0 0 0 0 0 0 1 0 0 0 0 0]
```

that is, with binary vectors indicating the presence (1) or absence (0) of each nucleotide in each position of the sequence.

Once indicated the Discrete Fourier Transform (DFT) of the signal associated to each nucleotide (e.g. A) as $\hat{A}(k)$, with $0 \leq k \leq N - 1$, the spectral energy associated with sequence $S[i]$ can be defined as follows:

$$|\hat{S}(k)|^2 = |\hat{A}(k)|^2 + |\hat{C}(k)|^2 + |\hat{G}(k)|^2 + |\hat{T}(k)|^2 \qquad (1)$$

Then, for the 3-periodicity property, in protein coding regions the spectral energy obtained by the DFT of the binary signals associated to each nucleotide shows a peak at discrete frequency $N/3$. This peak is not observed in the spectral energy of non coding DNA regions.

Instead of single sequences, in comparative genomics the objects of investigation are usually aligned sequences. The functionality of proteins encoded by DNA is directly related to their primary sequence, and therefore conserved coding regions are expected to encode for proteins having a similar amino acid sequence. Codons encoding for the same amino acid often differ only in a single nucleotide located in the third position of the codon. As a direct consequence, the probability for a substitution to be synonymous (i.e. to leave unchanged the encoded amino acid) differs according to the position of the codon where it has occurred. Thus, in a coding conserved DNA sequence under selective evolutionary pressure substitutions are more often tolerated if they occur at the third position of codons. This in turn implies that if aligned sequences are protein-coding the spectral signal of the mismatches along the alignment is expected to be maximal at frequency $N/3$, where N is the length (number of columns) of the alignment. For the alignment

```
Aquery[i]        =      [A T G A C T A A G A G A G A T C C G G]
                         | | | | |   | |   | |   | |   | |
Atarget[i]       =      [A T G A C G A A A A G C G A G C C T A]
```

we can build a binary descriptor defining the position of all the mismatches along the aligned sequences:

```
M[i]             =      [0 0 0 0 0 1 0 0 1 0 0 1 0 0 1 0 0 1 1]
```

To look for aligned regions with mismatches occurring mainly in the third position of a codon, as in [12], we can use the Position Count Function (PCF) to count the number of 1's occurring at each phase $s = \{0, 1, 2\}$ in the binary descriptor M parsed in non overlapping words of size $w = 3$:

$$C_3^M(s) = \sum_{i=0}^{(N-1)/3} M[3i + s] \tag{2}$$

Using the PCF, as shown in [12] the magnitude of the DFT $\hat{M}[k]$ at discrete frequency $N/3$ can be defined as:

$$|\hat{M}[N/3]|^2 = \frac{1}{2}[(C_3^M(0) - C_3^M(1))^2 + (C_3^M(1) - C_3^M(2))^2 + (C_3^M(2) - C_3^M(0))^2] \tag{3}$$

At this point, we need to assess of the signal strength at frequency $N/3$ with respect to the average spectral noise. The average value $|\hat{M}_{av}^{(1)}|$ of the squared magnitude $|\hat{M}[k]|^2$ of a binary descriptor, excluding the fundamental frequency component $\hat{M}[0]$, can be calculated as in [12]:

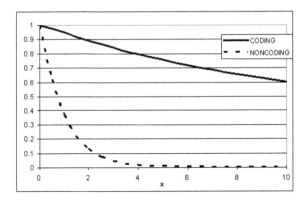

Fig. 2. Fraction of coding (continuous line) and non coding alignments (dotted line) with CP score $\geq x$

$$|\hat{M}_{av}^{(1)}|^2 = \frac{1}{(N-1)} \left(N - \sum_{s=0}^{w-1} C_w^M(s) \right) \cdot \sum_{s=0}^{w-1} C_w^M(s) \tag{4}$$

where $w = 3$. Finally, the signal (at frequency $N/3$) to noise ratio in the power spectrum representing the coding potential (CP) of the conserved sequence under investigation can be calculated using the following equation:

$$CP = \frac{|\hat{M}[N/3]|^2}{|\hat{M}_{av}^{(1)}|^2} \tag{5}$$

That is, we measure the coding potential of the alignment as the signal at frequency $N/3$ normalized with respect to the signal present at every frequency of the spectrum except for the fundamental frequency 0 (the noise).

3   Experiments

In order to assess the ability of our method to discriminate between coding and non coding conserved sequences we built two evaluation datasets. The coding dataset contained 3061 alignments obtained comparing 1580 pairs of human and mouse orthologous coding sequences retrieved from Biomart. The simplest way to obtain a non coding sequence set was to align whole genomic intergenic regions, and then to remove from the alignment sequences overlapping genomic regions annotated as coding. In particular, we employed the human genomic sequences annotated in the ENCODE project, and their alignment with the corresponding homologs in mouse. The high quality of the existing annotations for these regions allowed us to safely discriminate between alignments containing protein coding regions, even if we could not exclude a priori the presence of unknown protein coding genes or pseudogenes. The comparison of ENCODE regions and their homologs in mouse produced 4123 alignments. The comparison of genomic

Table 1. At different CP score threshold values, fraction of alignments correctly and uncorrectly classified as coding (true positives – TP, false positives – FP), and correctly and uncorrectly classified as non coding (true negatives – TN, false negatives – FN), and the corresponding sensitivity $(TP/(TP + FN))$ and specificity $(TN/(TN + FP))$ values

CP	TP	FP	TN	FN	Sens	Spec
0.0	1	1	0	0	1.00	0.00
2.0	0.89	0.14	0.86	0.11	0.89	0.86
4.0	0.80	0.02	0.98	0.20	0.80	0.98
6.0	0.72	0.00	1.00	0.28	0.72	1.00

coordinates of the alignments with the content of the ENTREZ and VEGA gene databases led to the removal 1896 alignments, 1771 of which overlapped annotated coding sequences and 125 overlapped to annotated pseudogenes. Thus, the resulting non coding set was composed by 2227 aligned sequence pairs.

Each of the alignments of the sets just described was analyzed in order to measure the signal over noise ratio introduced at frequency $N/3$ by the mutations occurring in the third position of codons. The CP index calculated as defined in Equation 5 ranged from 0.00 to 612.09 in the 3061 alignments composed only by coding sequences, and from 0 to 35.12 in the 2227 sequences of the non coding set. The cumulative distribution of CP values in coding and non coding sets is shown in Fig. 2. As we can see, CP is highly discriminative between the alignments contained in the two sets set.

Table 1 shows the number of coding sequences correctly classified (true positives), and uncorrectly classified as non coding (false negatives), and vice versa for non coding (false positives and true negatives), with the corresponding sensitivity and specificity values at different CP threshold values. For example, the CP score at threshold 4.0 is able to classify correctly 2447 coding alignments (79.94 % of coding set) yielding only 35 false positives (1.57% of the non coding set). Further examination of false positive alignments revealed that seven of the false positives obtained by the method matched transcribed regions (that is, annotations like RNAs, cDNAs, ESTs), while four overlapped proteic features (like conserved domains) indicating the possible presence of as yet unannotated genes.

4   Conclusions

The periodicity of 3 detectable at nucleotide level in coding regions has been observed by many authors, even if spectral techniques derived by this observation, to our knowledge, have never been applied to a comparative analysis. In this paper we presented the application of spectral techniques to aligned sequences and we demonstrated that the signal over noise ratio at discrete frequency $N/3$ (where N is the length of the alignment) obtained transforming a binary indicator encoding the positions of substitutions can be effectively used for discrimination between protein coding and non coding aligned sequences and that this observation is a direct effect of the characteristic selective pressure to which only functional and protein coding conserved regions are subject during evolution.

A straightforward application of our method is the annotation of newly sequenced genomes, because, once defined an appropriate cutoff value, a classification can be obtained in total absence of previous knowledge regarding the genomic regions under investigation. Because the origins of the signal we investigated in this work is the selective pressure acting on protein coding regions and because this is due to the presence of a near universal genetic code allowing the use of information encoded in DNA for protein synthesis, we expect the method to be valid for investigations in pairs of species other than human and mouse, as well as the analysis of multiple sequence alignments, or the characterization of RNA sequences as coding (mRNAs) or non coding.

References

1. Korf, I., Flicek, P., Duan, D., Brent, M.R.: Integrating genomic homology into gene structure prediction. Bioinformatics 17(suppl. 1), 140–148 (2001)
2. Burge, C., Karlin, S.: Prediction of complete gene structures in human genomic DNA. J. Mol. Biol. 268(1), 78–94 (1997)
3. Mignone, F., Grillo, G., Liuni, S., Pesole, G.: Computational identification of protein coding potential of conserved sequence tags through cross-species evolutionary analysis. Nucleic Acids Res. 31(15), 4639–4645 (2003)
4. Anastassiou, D.: Frequency-domain analysis of biomolecular sequences. Bioinformatics 16(12), 1073–1081 (2000)
5. Issac, B., Singh, H., Kaur, H., Raghava, G.P.: Locating probable genes using Fourier transform approach. Bioinformatics 18(1), 196–197 (2002)
6. Kauer, G., Blocker, H.: Applying signal theory to the analysis of biomolecules. Bioinformatics 19(16), 2016–2021 (2003)
7. Kotlar, D., Lavner, Y.: Gene prediction by spectral rotation measure: a new method for identifying protein-coding regions. Genome Res 13, 1930–1937 (2003)
8. Tiwari, S., Ramachandran, S., Bhattacharya, A., Bhattacharya, S., Ramaswamy, R.: Prediction of probable genes by Fourier analysis of genomic sequences. Comput. Appl. Biosci. 13(3), 263–270 (1997)
9. Yan, M., Lin, Z.S., Zhang, C.T.: A new Fourier transform approach for protein coding measure based on the format of the z curve. Bioinformatics 14(8), 685–690 (1998)
10. Vaidyanathan, P., Yoon, B.J.: The role of signal-processing concepts in genomics and proteomics. The Journal of The Franklin Institute 341, 111–135 (2004)
11. Voss, R.: Evolution of long-range fractal correlations and 1/f noise in DNA base sequences. Phys. Rev. Lett. 68, 3805–3808 (1992)
12. Datta, S., Asif, A.: A fast DFT based gene prediction algorithm for identification of protein coding regions. In: Proceedings of ICASSP '05, pp. 113–116 (2005)

PCA Based Feature Selection Applied to the Analysis of the International Variation in Diet

Faraz Bishehsari[1], Mahboobeh Mahdavinia[1], Reza Malekzadeh[1],
Renato Mariani-Costantini[2], Gennaro Miele[3], Francesco Napolitano[4],
Giancarlo Raiconi[4], Roberto Tagliaferri[4], and Fabio Verginelli[2]

[1] DDRC, Tehran University of Medical Sciences, Tehran, Iran
[2] DON, University G. d'Annunzio, and Ce.S.I., G. D'Annunzio Foundation, Chieti
[3] DSF, University of Naples, I-80136, via Cintia 6, Napoli, Italy
[4] DMI, University of Salerno, I-84084, via Ponte don Melillo, Fisciano (SA), Italy
{gianni, rtagliaferri}@unisa.it

Abstract. In this work we describe a clustering and feature selection technique applied to the analysis of international dietary profiles. An asymmetric entropy-based measure for assessing the similarity between two clusterizations, also taking into account subclustering relationships, is at the core of the technique, together with PCA. Then, a feature analysis of the dataset with respect to its hierarchical clusterization is performed. This way, most significant features of the dataset are found and a deep understanding of the data distribution is made possible.

1 Introduction

Somatic mutations in the p53 tumor suppressor gene are among the most frequent genetic alterations detected in colorectal cancer (CRC) [1] and are thought to reflect environmental genotoxic insults, that could be mediated through the diet, and human intestinal carcinogenesis [2][3]. With the future aim of studying relationships between p53 mutations and international dietary factors, we developed a feature selection method based on PCA and an entropy based similarity measure, which are the subjects of this paper. We apply this model to the analysis of different geographic areas in relation to local dietary profiles, as defined by percentage of energy intake from food items. The worldwide dietary data base, detailing the percentage of energy intake provided by 10 food groups (i.e., cereals, starchy roots, vegetables, fruit, meat, milk, sweeteners, added vegetable and animal fats, pulses and seeds, fish and sea-food) was obtained from the Istituto Nazionale di Ricerca per gli Alimenti e la Nutrizione (INRAN), Rome, Italy (through the courtesy of Dr. Angela Polito).

The dietary database was put through a hierarchical clustering process in order to identify groups of affine countries basing on dietary factors. A novel method of feature exploration was used to assess the stability of the clusterization and to find determinant features for the dataset. Toward this aim, the asymmetric clustering similarity measure was introduced, which is also able to detect subclustering relationships between clusterizations.

F. Masulli, S. Mitra, and G. Pasi (Eds.): WILF 2007, LNAI 4578, pp. 551–556, 2007.
© Springer-Verlag Berlin Heidelberg 2007

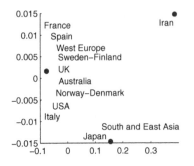

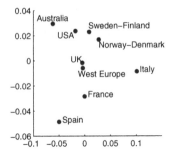

Fig. 1. MDS visualization of dataset. Many points appear superimposed.

Fig. 2. MDS visualization of the dataset of Fig. 1 without Iran, South and East Asia, and Japan points

2   The Dataset

From a mathematical point of view, the dataset appears as a 12×10 matrix of reals, expressing the percentage of energy intake provided by 10 food groups in function of the geographical area where they were collected. A useful insight over the data can be obtained from an MDS bidimensional projection of the dataset, approximating the distance between the geographical areas, as defined by the 10-dimensional dataset, with a spatial distribution of them on the plane. In such visualization Iran, Japan and South and East Asia, being relatively very far from the other points, cause the other points to appear superimposed (see Fig. 1), therefore another visualization excluding them was produced (see Fig. 2). Visually, the presence of at least two homogeneous groups of geographical areas seems evident.

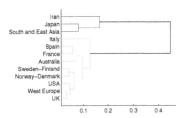

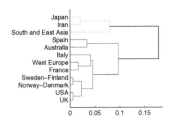

Fig. 3. Hierarchical clustering based on the whole set of features

Fig. 4. Hierarchical clustering based on features 5 and 8

Since the size of the dataset is not problematic, the use of advanced clustering techniques (as in [7]) was avoided and a simple Ward's agglomeration was performed, as shown in Fig. 3. The presence of two main groups is confirmed by the structure of the tree. To have a better understanding of the dataset, a deeper study of the features was performed, as described in the next section.

3   An Asymmetric Similarity Measure

It often happens, when dealing with the problem of data clusterizations, that two or more of them have to be compared. There are many techniques available to handle this problem [6], whose aim is generally to measure how much the two clusterizations can be superimposed. In many cases this condition can lead to miss important relations between clusterizations, like *subclustering*.

Subclustering analysis consists in studying the subclusters of each cluster. For example, in hierarchical clustering, it is equivalent to partition a cluster at a higher level of the tree into more clusters in lower levels. Another example, in supervised classification, is the case of finding all the subclusters corresponding to the same class. It is so desirable that a similarity measure could detect such relations.

3.1   Entropy-Based Subclustering Similarity

For two clusterizations to be considered identical it is necessary that, in each cluster of the first clusterization, only objects of one cluster of the second clusterization are present. The more a cluster of the first clusterization is filled with objects from different clusters of the second clusterization (*disorder*), the less is the superimposability of the two clusterizations. All the information needed to resume this phenomenon is the *confusion matrix*. Given two clusterizations A and B, where A is made of n clusters and B is made of m clusters, the confusion matrix M between A and B is an $n \times m$ matrix, in which the entry (i, j) reports the number of objects in the cluster i of the clusterization A falling into the cluster j of the clusterization B.

The obvious tool to measure the disorder of a cluster is entropy. If R_i is the i-th row of M and C_j is the j-th column of M, then $H(R_i)$ measures the disorder of the i-th cluster of A with respect to B, and $H(C_j)$ measures the disorder of the j-th cluster of B with respect to A.

We first observe that the bigger is a cluster, the more its disorder must influence the similarity between A and B. We can then compute the similarity between B and A as the *mean entropy* of the clusters of B versus A, where the a-priori probability of a cluster X, $P(X)$, can be approximated as $(number - of - objects - in - X)/(total - number - of - objects)$, giving rise to the formula:

$$S(M) = \sum_i P(X_i) \cdot H(R_i)$$

expressing the similarity of B versus A, while the similarity of A versus B can be obtained with the analogue formula on C_j, which turns to be $S(M')$. The fact that in general $S(M) \neq S(M')$ is the key of our asymmetric measure. If the clusters from A are fragmented into subclusters of B and objects from different clusters of A fall into different clusters of B, then the similarity $S(M)$ will not be affected. Actually, if the dataset is composed by m objects (remembering that B is made of m clusters), the value $S(M)$ is maximal. On the contrary, the value $S(M')$ is minimal. So the final measure of similarity between the two clusterizations lies in the trade-off between $S(M)$ and $S(M')$. We define total similarity measure S_a as follows:

$$S_a(M) = S(M) + a \cdot S(M')$$

where the real a, $0 \leq a \leq 1$, can be used to set the acceptable level of 'sub-clusteringness' of B with respect to A. When $a = 0$ no importance is given to the fragmentation level of the clusters in B. When $a = 1$ only exact matching between A and B will give rise to a maximum for S_a.

In conclusion, the S_a asymmetric similarity measure can be used to assess the similarity between two clusterizations, taking into account the possibility of a subclustering relation between them. When a is set to 1 this measures is coherent with other similarity measures found in literature but, varying a, it can be used to discover relations that other measures are blind to.

4   Feature Analysis of the Dataset

The aim of the performed feature analysis of the dataset is both assessing the stability of the clustering and having a deeper understanding of its structure. A useful information from data is given by the Principal Component Analysis [4]. Fig. 5 shows that 3 principal components are sufficient to explain 95% of the total variance of the dataset. Fig. 6 shows the sums of the absolute values of the coefficients for such principal components. Features 1, 5 and 8 explain most of the variance of the dataset. Though this is a relevant information, it is not enough to say that such features are always the most significant ones to represent the whole dataset. The approach we present can provide exact information on the ability of each subset of features to obtain the same clusterization of the previous one by using backward feature elimination. This technique is described in the following.

Different hierarchical clustering trees correspond to different selections of the features. For our purpose we can say that two dendrograms are equivalent if they can produce the same clusterization of the dataset with an opportune choice of the cut threshold. At this point we want to generalize the similarity between clusterizations to the similarity between dendrograms. Given a clusterization in one dendrogram (i.e. with all the features), chosen by the user, the similarity between it and another dendrogram can be defined as the maximum similarity between the chosen clusterization and all the clusterizations of the other dendrogram.

Therefore, the influence of each subset of features of the dataset on the final clusterization can be estimated as follows. First, a *target clusterization* is chosen from the dendrogram built on all the dataset features. Then, a hierarchical clustering tree is built for each subset of the features of the dataset and all the clusterizations derivable from such tree are compared with the target clusterization. The best similarity obtained states the ability of the chosen features subset to produce the same clusterization as the whole dataset.

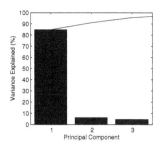

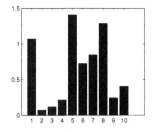

Fig. 5. First three principal components of the dataset

Fig. 6. Histogram of the sums of the absolute values of the weights related to the features for the three principal components of Fig. 5

Table 1. Worst S_1 values for each subset S of the features including feature f

Table 2. Couplings of features (f_1, f_2) giving $S_1 = 1$

$f \backslash^{|S|}$	1	2	3	4	5	6	7	8	9	10
1	0,85	0,85	0,85	0,85	0,85	0,85	0,85	0,85	0,85	1,00
2	0,59	0,59	0,59	0,59	0,59	0,59	0,69	0,69	0,85	1,00
3	0,59	0,59	0,59	0,59	0,59	0,59	0,69	0,69	0,85	1,00
4	0,59	0,59	0,59	0,59	0,59	0,59	0,69	0,69	0,85	1,00
5	0,69	0,69	0,69	0,68	0,68	0,68	0,69	0,69	0,85	1,00
6	0,82	0,73	0,69	0,68	0,68	0,68	0,69	0,69	0,85	1,00
7	0,59	0,59	0,59	0,59	0,59	0,59	0,69	0,69	0,85	1,00
8	0,75	0,73	0,72	0,73	0,73	0,73	0,73	1,00	1,00	1,00
9	0,59	0,59	0,59	0,59	0,59	0,59	0,69	0,69	0,85	1,00
10	0,60	0,59	0,59	0,59	0,59	0,59	0,69	0,69	0,85	1,00

f_1	f_2
1	4 6 8 9 10
2	-
3	-
4	1
5	8
6	1 8
7	8
8	1 5 6 7
9	1
10	1

Table 1 reports in each entry (i, j) the worst of such values obtained for each subset of j of the 12 features of the dataset, always including the i-th feature. It clearly appears that the feature 1 and 8 are able to reconstruct a good approximation of the whole feature space when considered alone or together with any combination of the other features.

Table 2 reports all the couples of features able to exactly reconstruct the features space. Coherently with data from Table 1, the features 1 and 8 achieve $S_1 = 1$ when coupled with various other features. Analogously, features 2 and 3 are not able to reach $S_1 = 1$ when coupled with any other feature.

5   Conclusions and Future Studies

In this work we performed a hierarchical clustering on a dataset containing dietary information from various nations. We showed how PCA and an entropy-based similarity measure can be exploited to perform feature analysis of the dataset. Following this way, we were able to find the most influencing features of the dataset and assess its stability with respect to the clustering process.

An analogue methodology, avoiding the exhaustive approach, is being used to successfully perform feature selection on more complex tumor-related datasets. The results of our analysis show that mutations in p53 can be associated with two major and distinct dietary patterns, corresponding to the two principal clusters of the tree. The first cluster includes the European countries along with the USA and Australia, the other cluster comprises the Asian countries, including Iran. The occurrence and type of p53 mutations in colorectal epithelium is likely to be influenced by dietary factors, both genotoxic and protective, related to the geographic origin of the patients. Further studies, presently in progress, are addressing this important issue and its correlation with other genetic factors related to p53 mutations.

References

1. Soussi, T., Beroud, C.: Significance of TP53 mutations in human cancer: a critical analysis of mutations at CpG dinucleotides. Human Mutation 21(3), 192–200 (2003)
2. Pfeifer, G.P., Denissenko, M.F.: Formation and repair of DNA lesions in the p53 gene: Relation to cancer mutations? Environmental and Molecular Mutagenesis 31(3), 197–205 (1998)
3. Olivier, Hussain, S.P., Caron de Fromentel, C., Hainaut, P., Harris, C.C.: TP53 mutation spectra and load: a tool for generating hypotheses on the etiology of cancer. IARC Sci Publ 157, 247–270 (2004)
4. Jollife, I.T.: Principal Component Analysis. Springer-Verlag, New York (1986)
5. Statistics Toolbox, Matlab, The Mathworks, Inc.
6. Ben-Hur, A., Elisseeff, A., Guyon, I.: A stability based method for discovering structure in clustered data. In: Pacific Symposium on Biocomputing (2002)
7. Ciaramella, A., Longo, G., Staiano, A., Tagliaferri, R.: NEC: A Hierarchical Agglomerative Clustering Based on Fisher and Negentropy Information. In: Apolloni, B., Marinaro, M., Nicosia, G., Tagliaferri, R. (eds.) WIRN 2005 and NAIS 2005. LNCS, vol. 3931, pp. 49–56. Springer, Heidelberg (2006)

Evaluating Switching Neural Networks for Gene Selection

Francesca Ruffino[1], Massimiliano Costacurta[2], and Marco Muselli[2]

[1] Dipartimento di Scienze dell'Informazione, Universit di Milano, Milano, Italy
`ruffino@dsi.unimi.it`
[2] Istituto di Elettronica e di Ingegneria dell'Informazione e delle Telecomunicazioni,
Consiglio Nazionale delle Ricerche, Genova, Italy
{`costacurta,muselli`}`@ieiit.cnr.it`

Abstract. A new gene selection method for analyzing microarray experiments pertaining to two classes of tissues and for determining relevant genes characterizing differences between the two classes is proposed. The new technique is based on Switching Neural Networks (SNN), learning machines that assign a relevance value to each input variable, and adopts Recursive Feature Addition (RFA) for performing gene selection.

The performances of SNN-RFA are evaluated by considering its application on two real and two artificial gene expression datasets generated according to a proper mathematical model that possesses biological and statistical plausibility. Comparisons with other two widely used gene selection methods are also shown.

1 Introduction

DNA microarrays provide the gene expression level for thousands of genes pertaining a given tissue, thus allowing to understand mechanisms regulating biological processes, such as the onset of a disease or the effects of a drug. Nevertheless, treating such a huge amount of data requires appropriate statistical and information analysis tools. An important problem in this analysis is to determine the subset of genes involved in the biological process under examination. Such problem is generally referred to as *gene selection* and several statistical and machine learning techniques have been proposed in literature to face with it.

Golub et al. [1] have obtained interesting results in discriminating two different kinds of leukemia by adopting a simple univariate statistical method, here denoted with GOLUB. More recently, Guyon et al. [2] have employed an iterative procedure, called Recursive Feature Elimination (RFE), for subsequently removing genes marked as less relevant by a specific classifier. To this end, Guyon et al. decided to employ linear Support Vector Machines (SVM), whose quality have been theoretically and experimentally demonstrated; the resulting gene selection procedure is usually referred to as SVM-RFE.

Another promising class of machine learning techniques for gene selection is rule generation methods, which solve a classification problem by generating a collection of intelligible rules in the if-then form. In particular, Switching Neural

F. Masulli, S. Mitra, and G. Pasi (Eds.): WILF 2007, LNAI 4578, pp. 557–562, 2007.
© Springer-Verlag Berlin Heidelberg 2007

Networks (SNN) [3] have been shown to obtain an excellent accuracy, when applied to solve real world problems deriving from DNA microarray [4]. This paper proposes to employ SNN for gene selection by adopting the opposite approach with respect to RFE: it subsequently adds the features considered as more relevant by a proper classifier. Since this approach is called Recursive Feature Addition (RFA), the proposed gene selection method will be denoted as SNN-RFA.

Unfortunately, real data cannot be adopted to evaluate in an objective way the quality of a gene selection method. In fact, the whole set of genes really involved in a biological process is not known: medical and biological literature provide at most a partial knowledge about it. A valid alternative consists in using the biologically plausible mathematical model described in [5], which is able to generate artificial expression data that present the same statistical behavior as data deriving from DNA microarray.

In particular, two artificial datasets possessing a statistical behavior similar to that of the datasets analyzed in [1] and in [6] have been considered for comparing the results obtained by SNN-RFA with those given by GOLUB and SVM-RFE.

2   Mathematical Model for Gene Expression Data

To derive a mathematical model for artificial data we suppose that the relationship between gene expression levels and functional state of the tissue is deterministic, i.e., no labeling error occurs during the execution of DNA-microarray experiments. Since in a real situation this is not true, the proposed model will be composed by a deterministic part, described through a function $f : \mathbb{R}^m \to \{0, 1\}$, and by a random term e corresponding to the probability that a tissue is assigned to the wrong state.

Then, for each gene g_i there exists a modulation threshold t_i such that g_i is considered to be *overexpressed* if the value x_i of its expression exceeds t_i and *underexpressed* if $x_i < -t_i$. According to the functional state in exam, a gene can be considered to be *modulated* when overexpressed or when underexpressed. Thus, it is possible to define a mapping $\boldsymbol{\beta} : \mathbb{R}^m \to \{0, 1\}^m$, which depends on the modulation thresholds t_i and returns, for each gene, the value 1 if that gene is modulated and 0 otherwise.

A biologically plausible assumption for our model implies that the output is uniquely determined by the state (modulated or not) of the m genes and does not depend on their specific expression values. Then, the function f can be written as $f(\boldsymbol{x}) = \varphi(\boldsymbol{\beta}(\boldsymbol{x}))$, where φ is a Boolean function defined on binary strings in $\{0, 1\}^m$.

Consider the case where artificial gene expression data deriving from n virtual experiments with DNA microarray are to be generated. Suppose without loss of generality that the first n_1 experiments concerns a functional state S_1 (e.g., a cancer tissue), whereas the remaining $n_2 = n - n_1$ experiments regards a different functional state S_2 (e.g., a reference tissue). We associate with S_1 and S_2 the output values $y = 1$ and $y = -1$, respectively.

Hence, each experiment is described by a pair $(\boldsymbol{x}, y)$, which must be generated according to our mathematical model. This is achieved by constructing two mappings $\boldsymbol{\beta}_1$, $\boldsymbol{\beta}_2$, one for each functional state, and two Boolean functions φ_1, φ_2. Then, n vectors $\boldsymbol{x}_1, \ldots, \boldsymbol{x}_n$ such that

$$f_1(\boldsymbol{x}_j) = \varphi_1(\boldsymbol{\beta}_1(\boldsymbol{x}_j)) = 1 , \quad f_2(\boldsymbol{x}_j) = \varphi_2(\boldsymbol{\beta}_2(\boldsymbol{x}_j)) = 0 \quad \text{for } j = 1, \ldots, n_1$$
$$f_1(\boldsymbol{x}_j) = \varphi_1(\boldsymbol{\beta}_1(\boldsymbol{x}_j)) = 0 , \quad f_2(\boldsymbol{x}_j) = \varphi_2(\boldsymbol{\beta}_2(\boldsymbol{x}_j)) = 1 \quad \text{for } j = n_1 + 1, \ldots, n$$

are generated. Finally, the output y_j for every artificial experiment is obtained by considering a random term e, corresponding to the probability that an example is assigned to the wrong state.

3 Considered Gene Selection Methods

When analyzing a gene expression dataset consisting of n vectors $\boldsymbol{x}_j$, associated with as many tissues in two different functional states S_1 and S_2, the main target is to retrieve the subset of genes that are differentially expressed in S_1 and S_2. A possible way of achieving this goal is to employ a *feature selection technique*, which aims to derive in a general classification problem the minimal subset F of inputs involved in any optimal decision function f solving the problem at hand.

Several methods of this kind can be found in the literature; however, only some of them needs a reduced computational cost, which make them suitable for treating DNA microarray data. These methods are called *gene selection techniques*; in this work we consider three of them, namely Golub's method (GOLUB), Support Vector Machines with Recursive Feature Elimination (SVM-RFE) and Switching Neural Networks with Recursive Feature Addition (SNN-RFA), focusing in particular our attention on the last one.

3.1 Golub's Method (GOLUB) [1]

GOLUB orders the genes according to the decreasing value of an appropriate relevance measure r and then builds the subset F by taking the first g genes of the list. Alternatively, a threshold θ can be considered for the relevance, including in F the genes that verifies the condition $r > \theta$. As a measure of relevance for the ith gene, Golub et al. [1] have proposed the correlation r_i with the output y_i given by the following relation:

$$r_i = \frac{(\mu_i(1) - \mu_i(0))}{(\sigma_i(1) + \sigma_i(0))} \tag{1}$$

being $\mu_i(c)$ and $\sigma_i(c)$, for $c = 0, 1$, the mean and the standard deviation of the values x_i in the tissues belonging to the class c. Positive (resp. negative) values of r_i mean a good correlation between the ith gene and the class 1 (resp. 0).

3.2 Support Vector Machines with Recursive Feature Elimination (SVM-RFE) [2]

The basic idea underlying Recursive Feature Elimination (RFE) consists in applying iteratively a given classification method on the dataset at hand, removing at each iteration the less important input, according to a proper measure of relevance. At the end of the procedure, features are ranked in increasing order, considering as most relevant the last removed input. To speed up the method, more than one feature can be removed at every iteration.

In particular, if linear Support Vector Machines (SVM) are employed as classification technique [2], a simple measure of relevance is given by the square w_i^2 of the coefficient w_i of the optimal hyperplane associated with the ith input (gene).

3.3 Switching Neural Networks with Recursive Feature Addition (SNN-RFA)

Switching Neural Networks (SNN) [3] are simple weightless connectionist models in which every neuron can only perform one of the following operations: A/D conversion, logic AND, or logic OR. The training algorithm for SNN, named *Shadow Clustering (SC)*, consists of the following three steps:

1. Every value in the dataset is converted into a binary string by using an appropriate coding which preserves the properties of distance and ordering.
2. The AND-OR expression of a positive Boolean function is built starting from the binary patterns in the coded dataset.
3. The associated SNN is built according to the positive Boolean function obtained in the previous step.

Since gene expression values are given by real numbers, the conversion at Step 1 requires a proper discretization. Once the n examples are converted into binary strings, the coded dataset can be regarded as a portion of the truth table of an unknown positive Boolean function f. SC aims to reconstruct f starting from this partial truth table, trying to generalize as well as possible the available information.

The performance of SNN in the gene selection task can be improved by adopting the complementary approach of RFE, which will be called *Recursive Feature Addition (RFA)*. This procedure applies iteratively a given classification method, specifically SNN, on the dataset at hand, removing at each iteration the most important input. At the end of the procedure features are ranked in decreasing order, taking the first removed input as the most relevant. Again, to speed up the method, more than one feature can be removed at every iteration.

4 Results

To evaluate the results obtained by GOLUB, SVM-RFE and SNN-RFA when performing gene selection on real world problems, two datasets containing gene

Table 1. Overlapping between subsets of relevant genes identified by GOLUB, SVM-RFE and SNN-RFA in the Leukemia dataset

	GOLUB Training	SNN-RFA Training	SVM-RFE Total	GOLUB Total	SNN-RFA Total	*Real Leukemia*	
	39.5%	28.5%	35%	30%	25.5%		SVM-RFE Training
GOLUB Training	37%		**44%**	26%	**54.5%**	36.5%	GOLUB Training
SNN-RFA Training	24%	**44%**		23%	37%	33.5%	SNN-RFA Training
SVM-RFE Training	33.5%	23.5%	15.5%		41.5%	40%	SVM-RFE Total
GOLUB Total	28%	**50.5%**	35.5%	29%		**59.5%**	GOLUB Total
SNN-RFA Total	22.5%	41%	34.5%	19%	**49%**		
Significant genes	23%	**37%**	32%	18.5%	**40.5%**	39%	
Artificial Leukemia	SVM-RFE Training	GOLUB Training	SNN-RFA Training	SVM-RFE Total	GOLUB Total	SNN-RFA Total	

expression levels produced by DNA microarrays have been considered: the Leukemia dataset [1] (72 experiments involving 7192 genes) and the Colon cancer dataset [6] (62 experiments involving 2000 genes). In addition, the three techniques have also been applied for the analysis of two artificial datasets generated according to the mathematical model described in Sec. 2; each of them presents statistical properties similar to those of one of the two real world problems above.

The results given by the three methods on the four datasets have been gathered into two tables; each dataset have been partitioned into a training set and a test set. The first table is related with the Leukemia dataset, for which 38 examples have been used for training and 34 for test.

The portion of the table concerning the artificial Leukemia dataset shows a significant overlapping (50.5%) between the genes selected by GOLUB on the whole dataset and those chosen by the same method on the training set only. A similar behavior characterizes the results on the real Leukemia dataset, where the overlapping reaches 54.5%. If we consider different methods upon the whole dataset, the best overlapping is given by GOLUB and SNN-RFA, both in the real and in the artificial case.

As for the artificial dataset, for which the significant genes are known, it can be noted the good agreement between the different methods and the genes really involved in determining the two classes. Best results are achieved by GOLUB and SNN-RFA, which includes in the most relevant 200 genes 81 (40.5%) and 78 (39%) genes, respectively, among the actually significant ones.

Table 2 reports the performances scored on the Colon dataset. In this case 31 tissues have been used for training and 31 for test. Again, both for the real and the artificial datasets, the best overlapping is given by the intersection between the results of GOLUB and SNN-RFA. In particular, if we consider the analysis of the whole dataset the percentages are 85% for the artificial case and 73.5% for

Table 2. Overlapping between subsets of relevant genes identified by GOLUB, SVM-RFE and SNN-RFA in the Colon dataset

	GOLUB Training	SNN-RFA Training	SVM-RFE Total	GOLUB Total	SNN-RFA Total	*Real Colon*
	41%	35.5%	36.5%	31%	32.5%	SVM-RFE Training
GOLUB Training	28.5%		**66%**	22.5%	**66.5%**	62.5% → GOLUB Training
SNN-RFA Training	27%	**81.5%**		18%	52.5%	58% → SNN-RFA Training
SVM-RFE Training	59%	28.5%	23%		25%	24.5% → SVM-RFE Total
GOLUB Total	26%	**81%**	78.5%	26%		**73.5%** → GOLUB Total
SNN-RFA Total	25.5%	78.5%	78%	24%	**85%**	
Significant genes	32.5%	**80.5%**	78%	30%	91.5%	**93.5%**
Artificial Colon	SVM-RFE Training	GOLUB Training	SNN-RFA Training	SVM-RFE Total	GOLUB Total	SNN-RFA Total

the real case, while for the training set we obtain 81.5% in the artificial problem and 66% in the real situation.

Acknowledgment

This work was partially supported by the Italian MIUR project "Laboratory of Interdisciplinary Technologies in Bioinformatics (LITBIO)".

References

1. Golub, T., et al.: Molecular classification of cancer: Class discovery and class prediction by gene expression monitoring. Science 286, 531–537 (1999)
2. Guyon, I., Weston, J., Barnhill, S.: Gene selection for cancer classification using support vectors machines. Machine Learning 46, 389–422 (2002)
3. Muselli, M.: Switching neural networks: A new connectionist model for classification. In: Apolloni, B., Marinaro, M., Nicosia, G., Tagliaferri, R. (eds.) WIRN 2005 and NAIS 2005. LNCS, vol. 3931, pp. 23–30. Springer, Heidelberg (2006)
4. Muselli, M.: Gene selection through switching neural networks. In: Proceedings of NETTAB-2003: Workshop on Bioinformatics for Microarrays, Bologna, Italy (2003)
5. Ruffino, F., Muselli, M., Valentini, G.: Gene expression modeling through positive Boolean functions. International Journal of Approximate Reasoning (to appear, 2007)
6. Alon, U., et al.: Broad patterns of gene expressions revealed by clustering analysis of tumor and normal colon tissues probed by oligonucleotide arrays. In: Proceedings of the National Academy of Science USA 96, pp. 6745–6750 (1999)

Analysis of Proteomic Spectral Data by Multi Resolution Analysis and Self-Organizing Maps

Frank-Michael Schleif[1], Thomas Villmann[1], and Barbara Hammer[2]

[1] University Leipzig, Dept. of Medicine, 04107 Leipzig, Germany
[2] TU-Clausthal, Dept. of Math. & C.S., 38678 Clausthal-Zellerfeld, Germany
{schleif,villmann}@informatik.uni-leipzig.de,+49(0)3419718896
{hammer}@in.tu-clausthal.de,+49(0)53237271[86][39]

Abstract. Analysis and visualization of high-dimensional clinical proteomic spectra obtained from mass spectrometric measurements is a complicated issue. We present a wavelet based preprocessing combined with an unsupervised and supervised analysis by Self-Organizing Maps and a fuzzy variant thereof. This leads to an optimal encoding and a robust classifier incorporating the possibility of fuzzy labels.

Keywords: fuzzy visualization, clinical proteomics, wavelet analysis, biomarker, spectra preprocessing.

1 Introduction

Applications of mass spectrometry (ms) in clinical proteomics have gained tremendous visibility in the scientific and clinical community [1,2]. One major objective is the search for potential biomarkers in complex body fluids like serum, plasma, urine, saliva, or cerebral spinal fluid. For this purpose, efficient analysis and visualization of large high-dimensional data sets derived from patient cohorts is crucial. Additionally, it is necessary to apply statistical analysis and pattern matching algorithms to attain validated signal patterns. A powerful tool for faithful data mining and visualization of potential high-dimensional data is the unsupervised self-organizing map (SOM) [3] which has been recently extended to a supervised counterpart in [4]. The later allows the determination of a prototype based fuzzy classification model (FLSOM). In contrast to the widely applied multilayer perceptron [5], prototype based classification allows an easy interpretation of the classification scheme, which is of particular interest for clinical applications. FLSOM leads to a robust fuzzy classifier where efficient learning of fuzzy labeled or partially contradictory data is possible.

Hereby a discriminative data representation is necessary. The extraction of such discriminant features is critical for spectral data and typically done by a parametric peak picking procedure. This peak picking is often focus of criticism because peaks may be insufficiently detected. To avoid this difficulties we focus on a wavelet encoding of the spectral data to get discriminative features. Thereby the obtained wavelet coefficients are sufficient to reconstruct the signal, still containing all relevant information of the spectra. However this better

F. Masulli, S. Mitra, and G. Pasi (Eds.): WILF 2007, LNAI 4578, pp. 563–570, 2007.

discriminating set of features is typically more complex and hence a robust approach to determine the desired classification model is needed.

2 Bioinformatic Methods

The classification of mass spectra involves in general the two steps peak picking to locate and quantify positions of peaks within the spectrum and feature extraction from the obtained peak list. In the first step a number of procedures as baseline correction, optional denoising, noise estimation and normalization must be applied. Upon these prepared spectra the peaks have to be identified by scanning all local maxima and the associated peak endpoints followed by a S/N thresholding such that one obtains the desired peak list.

The procedure of peak picking is standard, and has been done using Clin-ProTools for comparison in this paper (details in [2]). Here we propose an alternative which simplifies the procedure and preserves all (potentially small) peaks containing relevant information by use of the discrete wavelet transformation (DWT). The feature extraction has been done by Wavelet analysis using the Matlab Wavelet-Toolbox[1] and with ClinProTools to obtain peak lists with peak areas as final features. In that way both feature lists can be related back to original mass position in the spectral data which is essential for further biomarker analysis. In a first step a feature selection procedure using the Kolmogorov-Smirnoff test (KS-test) was applied. Thereby the test was used to identify features which show a significant ($p < 0.01$) discrimination between the two groups (cancer,control). This is done in accordance to [6] where also a generation to a multiclass experiment is given. The roughly reduced set has been further processed by FLSOM to obtain a classification model with a *small,* ranked set of features, crossvalidated by a 10-fold cross validation procedure.

2.1 Feature Extraction and Denoising with the Bi-orthogonal Discrete Wavelet Transform

Wavelets have been developed into powerful tools [7,8] used for noise removal and data compression. The discrete version of the continuous wavelet transform leads to the concept of a multiresolution analysis (MRA). This allows a fast and stable wavelet analysis and synthesis. The analysis becomes more precise if the wavelet shape is adapted to the signal to be analyzed. For this reason one can apply the so called bi-orthogonal wavelet transform[9] which uses two pairs of scaling and wavelet functions. One is for the decomposition/analysis and the other one for reconstruction/synthesis. The advantage of the bi-orthogonal wavelet transform is the higher degree of freedom for the shape of the scaling and wavelet function. In our analysis such a smooth synthesis pair was chosen to avoid artifacts. It can be expected that a signal in the time domain can be represented by a small number of a relatively large set of coefficients from the wavelet domain. The

---

[1] The Matlab Wavelet-Toolbox can be obtained from www.mathworks.com

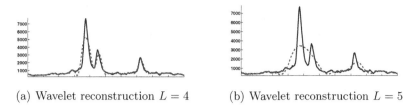

(a) Wavelet reconstruction $L = 4$ (b) Wavelet reconstruction $L = 5$

Fig. 1. Wavelet reconstruction of the spectra with $L = 4, 5$, x-mass positions, y-arbitrary unit. The original signal is plotted with the solid line. One observes that a wavelet analysis with $L = 5$ is too rough to approximate the sharp peaks.

spectra are reconstructed in dependence of a certain approximation level L of the MRA which can be considered as a hard-thresholding. The denoised spectrum looks similar to the reconstruction as depicted in Figure 1. The starting point for an argumentation is the simplest example of a MRA which can be defined by the characteristic function $\chi_{[0,1)}$. The corresponding wavelet is the so-called *Haar* wavelet. Assume that the denoised spectrum $f \in L_2(\mathbb{R})$ has a peak with endpoints $2^j k$ and $2^j(k + 1)$, the integral of the peak can be written as

$$\int_{2^j k}^{2^j(k+1)} f(t)dt = \int_{\mathbb{R}} f(t)\chi_{[2^j k, 2^j(k+1))}(t)dt$$

Obviously the right hand side is the Haar DWT scaling coefficient $c_{j,k} = \langle f, \psi_{j,k} \rangle$ at scale $a = 2^j$ and translation $b = 2^j k$. One obtains approximation- and detail-coefficients [9]. The approximation coefficients describe a generalized peak list of the denoised spectrum encoding primal spectral information and depending on the level L which is determined with respect to the measurement procedure. For linear MALDI-TOF spectra a device resolution of $500 - 800Da$ can be expected. This implies limits to the minimal peak width in the spectrum and hence, the reconstruction level of the Wavelet-Analysis should be able to model corresponding peaks. A level $L = 4$ is appropriate for our problem (see Figure 1). Applying this procedure on the spectra with an initial number of 22306 measurement points per spectrum one obtains 602 wavelet coefficients and 91 peak areas used as representative features per spectrum. Subsequently, the data were processed by FLSOM in a 10-fold cross validation procedure.

2.2   Fuzzy Labeled Self Organizing Map

The SOM is a popular unsupervised data mining and visualization method, mapping a given possibly high-dimensional data set non linearly onto a low-dimensional regular lattice, which is topology-preserving under certain conditions [3]. In the SOM formulation by Heskes [10] training of a SOM is a stochastic gradient descent on a cost function. FLSOM as given in [4] is obtained by adding a classification error term to the original cost function of Heskes, such that classification labels are taken into account for model adaptation. One obtains a supervised classification scheme based on SOM, whereby the visualization and topographic properties are preserved. In our analysis we use the scaled Euclidean metric whose parameters are adapted during the optimization (metric adaptation) in accordance to [4], [11]. Hence, prototypes, labels and the metric are optimized by a stochastic gradient descent on the FLSOM cost function.

3   Visualization and Analysis of Proteomic Data

Subsequently the proposed data processing scheme is applied to clinical ms spectra taken from a cancer study. Thereby we focus on a reliable encoding, visualization and classification model generation, indicating discriminative features.

3.1   Clinical Sample Preparation and MS Data Acquisition

Sample preparation and profile spectra analysis were carried out using the CLINPROT system [2]. Plasma samples from 45 cancer patients and 50 controls were prepared using the MB-WCX Kit. Purifications were performed according to the product description. Sample preparation onto the Anchor Chip target was done using HCCA matrix and the spectra were generated using a linear autoflex.

3.2   Analysis with SOM and FLSOM

The preprocessed set of spectra and their corresponding peak areas or wavelet coefficients were now analyzed using the SOM and the FLSOM algorithm. For complex data sets a low (2-3) dimensional visualization is complicated to achieve and simple approaches as shown in [4] are often insufficient. To overcome this, SOMs offer very powerful visualization capabilities especially for high-dimensional data. However they are not considering label information and are also not applying the concept of relevance learning which is often necessary for biomarker search [11]. The presented FLSOM algorithm allows for both directions the search for markers incorporating potentially fuzzy label information and subsequent visualization by a fuzzy labeled SOM. The results are depicted in Figure (2,3) using the obtained maps for SOM and FLSOM with peak areas or wavelet coefficients. One finds that the obtained FLSOM is well ordered with respect to the two classes separating cancer from control. In addition by calculating the first term of the topographic function [12] we found that our map is topology preserving and hence neighborings on the map indeed corresponds to neighborings in the high-dimensional feature space. The class labels for each map cell are indicated by bar plots, whereby the first bar give a possibilistic measure for class 1 (cancer) and the second bar for control respectively. For SOM these values have been obtained by a post labeling showing a clear labeling of the cells with cancer data in the lower left and control data mapped to the upper

---

[2] Devices and chemical processing by Bruker Daltonik GmbH, Bremen, Germany.

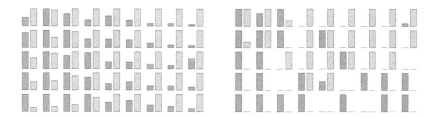

Fig. 2. Visualizations of FLSOM (left), SOM (right) using bar plots. The plots are obtained using wavelet coefficients and show that the maps are well ordered with respect to the labeling. This is also the case for SOM - due to the classwise data similarity. Within the cells the first column denotes the possibility for cancer and the second for control. While the SOM has been crisp post labeled and contains multiple empty cells, the FLSOM shows the degree of class responsibility learned during the optimization. Overlapping data regions can be identified with respect to the classification task.

right region. However one also observes a larger number of empty map cells. For FLSOM we found that the prototypes successfully learned a clear labeling from the data and hence the FLSOM map is well representing the underlying class information.

By use of a principal component analysis we projected the obtained FLSOM together with the data into the space of the two principal components (c.f. Figure (3)). There we also get a clear separation of the classes and a reliable good spreading of the FLSOM into the data space. Thereby the prototypes of the FLSOM (huge o or $\lozenge$ at the corners of the lines) are well positioned into its corresponding classes. Considering the component planes for FLSOM some relevant input dimensions are identified which are separating the two classes. This is depicted in Figure (3). The feature 414 constitutes a small peak in the original data which has not been recognized by the standard peak picking procedure but which shows good separation capabilities. Comparing the component planes for peak features with those obtained for wavelet coefficients for SOM and FLSOM similarities and dissimilarities can be observed. Especially for the wavelet coefficients a larger number of relevant feature dimensions is observed. By analyzing their origin on the original mass axis we found that multiple neighbored wavelet coefficients encoded in fact the same peak region or related peaks[3], but also new mass positions with small peaks have been found to be separating using the wavelet coefficients which were not detected using peak areas only.

The FLSOM model has been further evaluated in a 10-fold crossvalidation procedure. The models with peak areas as well as with wavelet coefficients were capable to discriminate between the two classes. For peak areas we found a recognition (training error) of 82% and a prediction (test error) of 71% wereas for wavelet coefficients the results were 78% and 75%. Hence the wavelet approach showed better generalization.

---

[3] Related peaks maybe chemically related as encodings of multiple fragments.

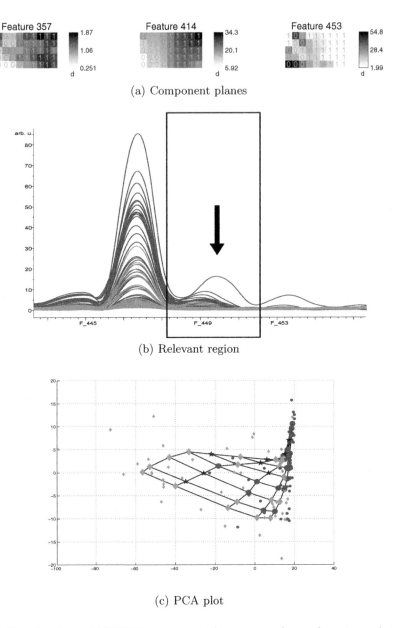

(a) Component planes

(b) Relevant region

(c) PCA plot

Fig. 3. Visualizations of FLSOM component planes using three relevant wavelet coefficients identified by the obtained relevance profile. Map cells for cancer are labeled with 0 and for control with 1, respectively. The feature 357 has been observed to be relevant for SOM (visual inspection) as well as for FLSOM. The mass position encoded by feature 453 shows that also small peaks (shown in 3(b)) are still available by the DWT. In the PCA the data and the SOM are projected in PCA space using the first two principal components. Data for controls are depicted as '◊', its prototypes by huge '◊', cancer data plotted as 'o' with huge o for prototypes, empty fields shown as '*'.

4   Conclusions

The presented initial data interpretation of proteom data demonstrate that the combined visualization and model generation of the FLSOM in combination with a wavelet based data preprocessing provides an easy and efficient detection of biomarker candidates and a very good visualization of the high-dimensional data. The usage of wavelet encoded spectra features is especially helpful in detection of small differences which maybe easily ignored by standard approaches. FLSOM was able to process high-dimensional wavelet features and observed good regularization, avoiding typical overfitting effects occuring by standard approaches. Moreover, the FLSOM visualization gives a planar representation of the high-dimensional data. If the obtained map is topological preserving one is able to identify sub-cluster of the original data space considering the receptive fields of the FLSOM cells. By use of the relevance learning we found a ranking of the features related to mass positions in the original spectrum which allows for identification of most relevant feature dimensions which was used for the identification of biomarker candidates. In future analysis it could be interesting to reduce the feature set by incorporating knowledge about fractionation of the chemical compounds leadings to multiple related peaks of the same source.

Potential biomarker peaks detected e.g. by FLSOM can be selected for indepth analysis and analyzed by tandem ms (TOF/TOF) analysis. Conclusively, wavelet based spectra encoding in combination with FLSOM is an interesting alternative to standard approaches allowing more flexibility in problem modeling as well as the control of the data processing task. It combines efficient visualization with automated data pretreatment and intuitive analysis.

Acknowledgments

The authors are grateful to M. Kostrzewa and T. Elssner for providing the clinical proteom data (both Bruker Daltonik Leipzig, Germany).

References

1. Villanueva, J., Philip, J., Entenberg, D., C.C., et al.: Serum peptide profiling by magnetic particle-assisted, automated sample processing and maldi-tof mass spectrometry. Anal. Chem. 76, 1560–1570 (2004)
2. Ketterlinus, R., Hsieh, S.Y., Teng, S.H., Lee, H., Pusch, W.: Fishing for biomarkers: analyzing mass spectrometry data with the new clinprotools software. Bio techniques 38(6), 37–40 (2005)
3. Kohonen, T.: Self-Organizing Maps. Springer Series in Information Sciences, vol. 30. Springer, Berlin, Heidelberg, (2nd Ext. Ed. 1997) (1995)
4. Schleif, F.M., Elssner, T., Kostrzewa, M., Villmann, T., Hammer, B.: Analysis and visualization of proteomic data by fuzzy labeled self organizing maps. In: Proc. of CBMS 2006, pp. 919–924 (2006)
5. Haykin, S.: Neural Networks. In: A Comp. Found. Macmillan, New York (1994)

6. Waagen, D., Cassabaum, M., Scott, C., Schmitt, H.: Exploring alternative wavelet base selection techniques with application to high resolution radar classification. In: ISIF'03. Proc. of the 6th Int. Conf. on Inf. Fusion, pp. 1078–1085. IEEE Press, New York (2003)
7. Louis, A.K., Maaß, P.A.R: Wavelets: Theory and Applications. Wiley, Chichester (1998)
8. Leung, A., Chau, F., Gao, J.: A review on applications of wavelet transform techniques in chemical analysis: 1989-1997. Chem. and Int. Lab. Sys. 43(1), 165–184(20) (1998)
9. Cohen, A., Daubechies, I., Feauveau, J.C.: Biorthogonal bases of compactly supported wavelets. Comm. Pure Appl. Math. 45(5), 485–560 (1992)
10. Heskes, T.: Energy functions for self-organizing maps. In: Oja, E., Kaski, S. (eds.) Kohonen Maps, pp. 303–316. Elsevier, Amsterdam (1999)
11. Villmann, T., Schleif, F.M., Hammer, B.: Comparison of relevance learning vector quantization with other metric adaptive classification methods. Neural Networks 19(15), 610–622 (2005)
12. Villmann, T., Der, R., Herrmann, M., Martinetz, T.: Topology Preservation in Self–Organizing Feature Maps: Exact Definition and Measurement. IEEE Transactions on Neural Networks 8(2), 256–266 (1997)

A Cost-Sensitive Approach to Feature Selection in Micro-Array Data Classification

Andrea Bosin, Nicoletta Dessì, and Barbara Pes

Università degli studi di Cagliari, Dipartimento di Matematica ed Informatica,
Via Ospedale 72, 09124 Cagliari, Italy
andrea.bosin@dsf.unica.it,{dessi,pes}@unica.it

Abstract. In analyzing gene expression data from micro-array, a major challenge is the definition of a feature selection criterion to judge the goodness of a subset of features with respect to a particular classification model. This paper presents a cost-sensitive approach feature selection that focuses on two fundamental requirements: (1) the quality of the features in order to promote the classifier accuracy and (2) the cost of computation due to the complexity that occurs during training and testing the classifier. The paper describes the approach in detail and includes a case study for a publicly available micro-array dataset. Results show that the proposed process yields state-of-art performance and uses only a small fraction of features that are generally used in competitive approaches on the same dataset.

Keywords: Data Mining, Machine Learning, Bio-informatics.

1 Introduction

DNA micro-array technology provides a powerful mean for accurate prediction and diagnosis of cancer. Realizing that datasets are large, it is necessary to perform a feature selection for the determination of genes with the most significant difference between groups of samples. The use of a subset of features not only reduces the dimensionality, but it improves the classification accuracy by eliminating redundant and/or irrelevant information, since it has been recognized that only a small number of genes are important for the distinction of tumors classes. Deciding the number of the genes to select is a first question in micro-array data analysis and finding the optimal number of genes is very difficult. Usually, one balances the effectiveness of a selected feature set with the associated classifier accuracy with respect to an evaluation criterion that generally involves two basic factors: the cost of misclassification errors and the cost of computation. That depends on the complexity of the classifier and, in turn, on the dimension of the feature set [1]. Although prior research activity indicates the feasibility of balancing the above factors, it has been recognized that the problem is further complicated when we consider a multi-classification problem [2] where the classification accuracy appears to degrade very rapidly as the number of classes increases.

F. Masulli, S. Mitra, and G. Pasi (Eds.): WILF 2007, LNAI 4578, pp. 571–579, 2007.
© Springer-Verlag Berlin Heidelberg 2007

This paper tries to encompass both the computational accuracy and the computational cost within a greedy approach that carefully considers tradeoffs between the research of an optimal set of features and the cost of computation due to the complexity that incurs during training and testing a classifier in multi-classification problems. We build and evaluate the classifier step-by-step and propose a cost function as a stopping criterion in controlling the generation of new subset of features. The paper is organized as follows. We start by introducing, in Section 2, the multi-classification techniques. Section 3 describes the proposed greedy approach. A case study is discussed in Section 4. Section 5 shows that results are comparable with recent literature and outlines future work.

2   Background

While significant progress has been made in the development of algorithms for binary classification, there is only a small amount of work on classification involving more than two classes [3], [4], [5]. Two groups of multi-class classification techniques are relevant to this paper. The first technique, here referred as Binary Classification Extension (BCE), naturally extends the binary classification algorithms to handle multi-class problems. The second one considers the strategy of breaking the original M-class problem into a set of binary sub-problems and performs classification by training and combining a family of binary classifiers with respect to one of the following decisional schemas: One-against-One (1-1), One-against-Rest (1-R), Hierarchical (HC). In the **1-1** schema, a binary classifier is trained for each distinct pair of classes, using only the training examples for those classes. This results in $M(M-1)/2$ classifiers, each predicting exactly one of the M classes. The **1-R** schema provides, for each class, a classifier that is trained for distinguishing between each class and the M-1 other remaining classes whose instances are considered as negative examples. This schema constructs M classifiers by separating the instances of each class from the rest of the classes. The HC schema builds a binary decision tree in which a binary classifier is associated with each internal node and a class label is assigned to each leaf. First, a binary classifier is trained for distinguish between the largest class L and the remaining classes. The training set is partitioned into two subset: the instances belonging to L and the instances not belonging to L for which a new classifier is built by separating the second largest class from the other remaining classes. Then, the classification process is recursively applied to each class. The possibility of ties or contradictory voting requires an overall voting procedure for the classifier outputs.

According to the survey paper [1], the problem of cost-sensitive classification has been the subject of a growing body of research. Many works [6], [7], [8] consider inductive learning methods where the costs incurred by misclassification errors vary based on the actual label of the instance. For binary classifiers, this is equivalent to consider the penalty for classifying examples in one class much different than the penalty for classifying examples in the other class. Recently, area under ROC curve (AUC) has been used in some studies [9], [10]. In this context, [11] introduces a graphical technique for visualizing cost curves for 2-class classifiers. Some works consider both the misclassification and test costs (i.e. the costs incurred by obtaining missing values of attributes) in decision tree building [12], [13]. [14] introduces a Markov decision process for sensitive learning and gives solutions in terms of optimal policies. As far as we know, the costs associated with building the classifier (and particularly multiclass-classifiers) are often ignored. The few works that consider this aspect include [1] that provides a comprehensive list if costs associated with classifier learning and [10] that analyzes the impact of the cost of training data on learning. However, the cost of building and testing a classifier can be quite substantial in learning micro-array data where the feature selection plays a major role.

3   The Proposed Approach

In a typical micro-array data analysis, the initial step is a feature selection excluding irrelevant features and reducing both the noise of the dataset and the time needed to perform the classification. Conceptually, the ideal feature selection process should traverse the feature space and evaluate all the possible subsets of features for searching the best one. Since this strategy is computationally expensive, it is necessary to find tradeoffs between the cost of computation and the quality of selected features. As regards the quality, a feature is strongly relevant if the feature cannot be removed without loss in classification accuracy and weakly relevant if its addition can increase the accuracy of classifier [15]. Being independent of the classification task, filter algorithms can be considered as "quality oriented" algorithms in that the strongly relevant features are generally highly ranked, but a crucial step is the formulation of a search strategy that controls the feature selection process i.e. the definition of a "quantitative oriented" procedure with respect to the accuracy and the computational burden.

On this premise we propose a strategy that combines a qualitative filtering approach with a cost-sensitive selection of features, seeking for the optimal subset of attributes to employ in the actual classifiers. Specifically, we denote as qualitative filtering approach a ranking procedure that orders the features by their rank within each class. Then, we propose a greedy algorithm that first considers the N top-ranked attributes, all other features being ignored. As the next step, a classifier is built with only those N attributes and its accuracy is evaluated on an independent test dataset. Then the algorithm extends the subset of selected features by greedily adding the next k top-ranked attributes. A new classifier is built on this extended subset, and its accuracy is evaluated on the independent test set. The initial number N to consider is not critical and we usually select N=1 and we next build classifiers step-by-step by setting $k = 1$. The algorithm generates a family of nested classifiers where, at each step i, the classifier C_i a more general and large model, is obtained by adding some attributes to the previous and reduced model C_{i-1}. In general, as a classifier becomes increasingly more complex by increasing the number of attributes, its fit gets better.

The basic assumptions are that we observe data x , we want to test two competing classifiers C_i and C_{i+1}, relating these data to two different sets of parameters (namely q_i and q_{i+k}), and we would like to know which of the following likelihood specifications is better: $C_i : f(x|q_i)$ or $C_{i+1} : f(x|q_{i+k})$?

More attributes always leads to a better fit of the data as well as to a higher value of the likelihood, whether or not the additional attributes are providing a significantly better fit to the data : are additional attributes justified? A classical approach to the comparison between two models is by testing the null hypothesis of no significant difference in fit by means of the likelihood ratio (LR) test [16] that is based on the fact that the asymptotic distribution of twice the logarithm of a maximum LR statistic [16] follows the chi-square distribution. More important generalization can be found in [17] and [18]. In the context of LR test, under the null that the parsimonious model generates the data, the larger model introduces noise into its forecasts by estimating parameters whose population values are zero.

It is important to note that the test is expected to be satisfactory if the probability model is "a good one", in some sense. Unfortunately, often, as in analyzing micro-array data, it is impossible to derive the model from a well established theory and there is not agreement about the model to be used. The desire for suppressing the dependence of the final choice on the prior and for easing computation has inspired various model selection criteria. These criteria are based on a measure of goodness of fit penalized by model complexity. All are associated with maximum likelihood modified by an additive penalty in order to favour parsimonious models. The best known is the Bayesian Information Criterion (BIC) in its commonly presented form [19] i.e. twice the maximized LR plus an adjustement that penalizes the model with more parameters and becomes important as the sample increases. A related criterion is the Akaike's information criterion (AIC) [20] where the penalty doubles the difference between the number of parameters. [21] discusses the difference between the LR criterion, BIC and AIC in the context of a nested model.

In this vein, we propose an evaluation criterion to judge, at each step, the goodness of the current subset of features with respect a cost function $h(C_i)$ that is formally defined as follows:

$$h(C_1) = Mis(C_1)$$
$$h(C_i) = Mis(C_i) * log(card(F_i) - card(F_{i-1})), \quad i = 2, 3, \cdots, NF$$

where C_1 is the classifier built with the first N top-ranked features at the first step (i.e. i=1), NF is the number of features in the original test set, card (F_i) is the cardinality of the subset of features that have been used for building the classifier C_i at step i, Mis (C_i) is the % number of misclassification for the classifier C_i and the logarithmic term is a penalty that balances the "quality" of the classification and the "quantitative factor" due to the computational burden. Specifically, the ranked features are considered sequentially, with low-cost classifications performed initially, followed, if necessary, by more costly and specialized classifications by greedily adding a feature one (or many) feature at a time. Each step reconsiders the costs of the previous classification for determining whether a further classification is required to gather more accuracy. According to some stopping criterion, the algorithm makes a final classification decision.

4 Experimental Results

The presented approach has been employed in evaluating the Acute Lymphoblastic Leukemia dataset [22] that contains 6 ALL sub-types (including T-ALL, E2A-PBX1, TEL-AML1, BCR-ABL, MLL, Hyperdip > 50) and consists of 327 samples, each one is described by the expression level of 12558 genes . Specifically, the dataset includes 215 training samples and 112 testing samples. All the experiments have been carried out using MDL [23] as filter method [24] and four different classification models : Naïve Bayes (NB) [25], Adaptive Naïve Bayes (ABN) [26], SVM [27], K-NN [28].

First, we carried out a BCE based classification. The filter [23] was applied for ranking features and four classification models were induced from the training set using subsets with 1, 2, and 3 · · · etc. features. For each gene subset, the performance of each classifier was evaluated on the test set which was not been used in any way in model development. Fig.1 shows results and a high error due to a small number of selected features with a gradual reduction in misclassifications as the number of genes approaches the optimal set of features. Table 1 shows the cost $h(C_i)$ of each classifier as the number of features increases. The level of misclassifications still remains relatively high (5-10%) and the cost decreases slowly, since the increasing dimension of feature sets is not balanced by the accuracy gain. Such results confirm that small sets of predictive features as well as good classification accuracy are very difficult to be achieved by a multi-target classification, as highlighted in recent literature [29], [30].

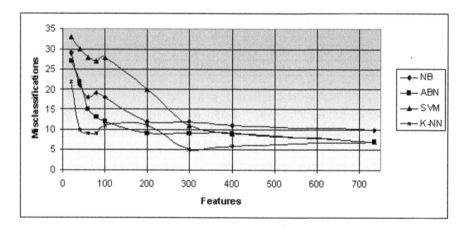

Fig. 1. Misclassifications in the BCE classification scheme

Table 1. The cost of NB, ABN, SVM,K-NN multi-target classifiers

N Classifier	20	40	60	100	200	400
NB	0,34	0,24	0,21	0,26	0,21	0,23
ABN	1,54	0,26	0,17	0,17	0,16	0,18
SVM	1,65	0,52	0,67	0,54	0,41	0,18
K-NN	1,50	0,12	0,12	0,16	0,20	0,12

Indeed, the class heterogeneity forces to select a very large number of features since the classifier is used for discriminating across all classes. Moreover, some features are effective in distinguish whether an instance is of one particular class, but they can lower the classifier accuracy in classifying instances belonging to other classes. To mitigate this problem, we analyzed the ALL-Dataset using a **1-R** classification schema. Specifically, a binary classifier between each class and the 5 other classes was trained (in total, 6 classifiers for each classification model) by separating the instances of each class from the rest of the 5 classes, whose instances were considered negative example. For each class, the features were first ranked by discriminating the features most strongly related to each class against all classes. This resulted in 6 sets of ranked features ordered by their rank within each class.

Table 2. Cardinality of the optimal set of features leading to the minimum cost classifier and number of misclassifications for each optimal set of features (in brackets), in 1-R scheme

Sub-type Classifier	T-ALL	E2A -PBX1	TEL -AML1	BCR -ABL	MLL	Hyper dip> 50	Total
NB	2(0)	2 (0)	7 (0)	12 (3)	3 (0)	30 (1)	56 (4)
ABN	6 (0)	12 (0)	7 (0)	18 (0)	3 (0)	30 (1)	76 (1)
SVM	1 (0)	1 (0)	8 (0)	6 (2)	4 (0)	16 (2)	36 (4)
k-NN	1 (0)	1 (0)	12 (0)	5 (1)	5 (0)	18 (3)	42 (4)

For each set, six binary classifiers (one for each class) were built by starting with the first top ranked feature and greedily adding features, one at a time, from the respective sets. In case of ties, the final output was the class with the largest number of training samples. At each step, the cost was evaluated and compared with the cost of the previous classification for determining whether a further classification step was required. Because the cost was observed rarely to decrease significantly $(> 0, 1)$ after the first 10 features have been added, we decided to stop adding new features if the fluctuation of the cost was less then 0,1 over the last 3 steps.

For each ALL sub-type, Table 2 shows the cardinality of the optimal sets of features best discriminating each sub-type and the corresponding number of

Table 3. Cardinality of the optimal set of features leading to the minimum cost classifier and number of misclassifications for each optimal set of features (in brackets), in HC scheme

Sub-type Classifier	T -ALL	E2A -PBX1	TEL -AML1	BCR -ABL	MLL	Hyper- dip> 50	HC
NB	2(0)	2 (0)	7 (0)	14 (3)	11 (0)	20 (1)	56 (4)
ABN	6 (0)	2 (0)	7 (0)	20 (3)	12 (0)	20 (1)	67 (4)
SVM	1 (0)	1 (0)	6 (0)	12 (3)	5 (0)	14 (1)	39 (4)
k-NN	1 (0)	1 (0)	9 (0)	3 (1)	5 (0)	20 (0)	39 (1)

misclassification (in brackets). Since our feature selection strategy is based on choosing the minimum number of most representative genes for each class and one class might be expressed more strongly than others, the cardinality of the optimal feature subsets can be different for different classifiers and different sub-subtypes with respect to the same classifiers.

Finally, the ALL dataset was classified according to the **HC scheme** in which a decision tree was grown in a recursive fashion by considering the classes with respect to the following order: T-ALL, E2A-PBX1, TEL-AML1, BCR-ABL, MLL, Hyperdip > 50. For each class, the features were ranked by discriminating the features most strongly related to the class and the classifier was built by starting with the first top ranked feature and greedily adding a feature, one at a time. As in the previous experiment, we decided to stop adding new features if the fluctuation of the cost was less then 0,1 over the last 3 steps. Table 3 shows the cardinality of the "optimal sets" of features for NB, ABN, SVM and k-NN classifiers as well as the number of misclassifications (in brackets) at each level of the decision tree.

5   Discussion and Future Work

With respect to the classification of the ALL dataset using the BCE approach, our results can be compared with [31] where the accuracy of 96% has been achieved using SVM and a correlation-based feature selection. Moreover, our results outperform [3] where, in different experimental tests, it is observed that, when the number of selected features is > 150, the variation of performance is small. Also, our results outperform [32], which proposes the use of a neural fuzzy system dataset using gene expression data.

As regards the strategy of breaking the original multi-classification problem into a set of binary problems (1-R, HC schema), our results can be compared with [2] where six different filter methods are explored and a selection heuristic is adopted that ranks attributes according to their entropy and selects features "having an entropy value less than 0.1 if these exist, or the 20 features with the lowest entropy values otherwise", up to a maximum of 20 features. The resulting NB, SVM and k-NN models respectively misclassify 7, 5 and 4 samples, while our "optimal" NB, SVM and k-NN classifiers (HC scheme) respectively result in 4, 4 and 1 misclassifications. Moreover, in [2] the threshold used to cut off top-ranked features is an arbitrary number (i.e. 20), whereas our greedy strategy enables to find, for each set of ranked features, the "optimal" cut off point.

Our emphasis throughout this paper is on the practical application of a cost-sensitive criterion in selecting the optimal set of and hence we make extensive use of experiments on the considered data set to emphasize that this approach can lead to good results. There are many future directions. First, are there better cost-sensitive criteria? Is it possible to define a cost-sensitive criteria that takes into consideration overlapping between features? Finally, how much a cost-sensitive approach is effective when ensemble methods are applied to multi-classification problems?

References

1. Turney P.D.: Types of cost in inductive concept learning, Workshop on Cost-Sensitive Learning, ICML2000, Stanford, pp. 15–21 (2000)
2. Liu, H., Li, J., Wong, L.: A Comparative Study on Feature Selection and Classification Methods Using Gene Expression Profiles and Proteomic Patterns. Genome informatics 13, 51–60 (2002)
3. Tao, L., Zhang, C., Ogihara, M.: A Comparative Study on Feature Selection and Multiclass Classification Methods for tissue classification based on gene expression. Bioinformatics 20(15), 2429–2437 (2004)
4. Bosin, A., Dessi, N., Pes, B.: High-Dimensional Micro-array Data Classification Using Minimum Description Length and Domain Expert Knowledge. In: Ali, M., Dapoigny, R. (eds.) IEA/AIE 2006. LNCS (LNAI), vol. 4031, pp. 790–799. Springer, Heidelberg (2006)
5. Bosin, A., Dessi, N., Pes, B.: Learning Classifiers for High-Dimensional Micro-Array Data. In: Bosin, A. (ed.) Applied Artificial Intelligence. Proc. of the 7th International FLINS Conference, Genova, Italy, August 29-31, 2006, pp. 29–31. World Scientific, Singapore (2006)
6. Elkan, C.: The Foundations of Cost-Sensitive Learning. In: Proceedings of IJCAI01, pp. 973-978 (2001)
7. Kai, M.T.: Inducing Cost-sensitive Trees via Instance Weighting. In: Second European Sym-posium on Principles of Data Mining and Knowledge Discovery, pp. 139–147. Springer, Heidelberg (1998)
8. Dragos, D., Margineantu, T., Dietterich, G.: Bootstrap Methods for the Cost-Sensitive Evaluation of Classifiers. ICML 2000, pp. 583–590 (2000)
9. Yan, L., Dodier, R.H., Mozer, M., Wolniewicz, R.H.: Optimizing Clas-sifier Performance via an Approximation to the Wilcoxon-Mann-Whitney Statistic. ICML 2003, pp. 848–855 (2003)
10. Weiss, G.M., Provost, F.J.: Learning When Training Data are Costly: The Effect of Class Distribution on Tree Induction. J. Artif. Intell. Res (JAIR) 19, 315–354 (2003)
11. Drummond, C., Holte, R.C.: Cost curves: An improved method for visualizing classifier performance. Machine Learning 65(1), 95–130 (2006)
12. Chai, X., Deng, L., Yang, Q., Ling, C.X.: Test-Cost Sensitive Naive Bayes Classification. In: Perner, P. (ed.) ICDM 2004. LNCS (LNAI), vol. 3275, pp. 51–58. Springer, Heidelberg (2004)

13. Ling, C.X., Yang, Q., Wang, J., Zhang, S.: Decision trees with minimal costs. ICML 2004 (2004)
14. Bayer Zubek, V., Dietterich, T.G.: Pruning Improves Heuristic Search for Cost-Sensitive Learning. ICML 2002, pp. 19–26 (2002)
15. John, G.H., Kohavi, R., Pfleger, K.: Irrelevant features and the subset selection problem. In: Proc. Eleventh International Conference on Machine Learning, San Francisco, CA (1994)
16. Pawitan, Y.: In All Likelihood: Statistical Modelling and Inference Using Likelihood, Oxford Science Publications (2001)
17. Vuong, Q.H.: Likelihood Ratio Tests for Model Selection and non-nested Hypotheses. Econometrica 57, 307–333 (1989)
18. Lo, Y., Mendell, N.R., Rubin, D.B.: Testing the number of components in a normal mixture. Biometrika 88, 767–778 (2001)
19. Schwarz, G.: Estimating the dimension of a model. Annals of Statistic 6, 461–464 (1978)
20. Aikake, H.: Information Theory as an Extension of the Maximum Likelihood Principle. In: Pro-ceedings of the Second International Symposium of Information Theory, Budapest, pp. 267–281 (1973)
21. O'Hagan, A.: Kendall's Advanced Theory of Statistics, Vol 2B: Bayesian Inference. Edward Arnold (1994)
22. http://www.stjuderesearch.org/data/ALL1/
23. Barron, A., Rissanen, J., Yu, B.: The minimum description length principle in coding and modelling. IEEE Transactions on Information Theory 44, 2743–2760 (1998)
24. Bosin, A.: Learning Bayesian Classifiers from Gene-Expression MicroArray Data. In: Bloch, I., Petrosino, A., Tettamanzi, A.G.B. (eds.) WILF 2005. LNCS (LNAI), vol. 3849, Springer, Heidelberg (2006)
25. Friedman, N., Geiger, D., Goldszmidt, M.: Bayesian Network Classifiers. Machine Learning 29, 131–161 (1997)
26. Yarmus J.S., ABN: A Fast, Greedy Bayesian Network Classifier, (2003) http://otn.oracle.com/products/bi/pdf/adaptive_bayes_net.pdf
27. Vapnik, V.: Statistical Learning Theory. Wiley-Interscience, New York, USA (1998)
28. Cover, T.M., Hart, P.E.: Nearest neighbor pattern classification. IEEE Transactions on Information Theory 13, 21–27 (1967)
29. Mukherjee, S.: Classifying Microarray Data Using Support Vector Machines. In: Mukherjee, S. (ed.) Understanding And Using Microarray Analysis Techniques: A Practical Guide, Kluwer Academic Publishers, Boston (2003)
30. Statnikov, A., et al.: A comprehensive evaluation of multicategory classification methods for microarray gene expression cancer diagnosis. Bioinformatics 21(5)(2005)
31. Yeoh, E.J., et al.: Classification, sub-type discovery, and prediction of outcome in pediatric acute lymphoblastic leukemia by gene expression profiling. Cancer Cell 1, 133–143 (2002)
32. Tung, W.L., Quek, C.: GenSo-FDSS: A neural-fuzzy decision support system for pediatric ALL cancer subtype identification using gene expression data. Artificial Intelligence in Medicine 33, 61–88 (2005)

Liknon Feature Selection for Microarrays

Erinija Pranckeviciene and Ray Somorjai

Institute for Biodiagnostics
National Research Council Canada
435 Ellice avenue, Winnipeg, MB, R3B 1Y6
{erinija.pranckevie,ray.somorjai}@nrc-cnrc.gc.ca

Abstract. Many real-world classification problems involve very sparse and high-dimensional data. The successes of LIKNON - linear programming support vector machine (LPSVM) for feature selection, motivates a more thorough analysis of the method when applied to sparse, multivariate data. Due to the sparseness, the selection of a classification model is greatly influenced by the characteristics of that particular dataset. Robust feature/model selection methods are desirable. LIKNON is claimed to have such robustness properties. Its feature selection operates by selecting the groups of features with large differences between the resultants of the two classes. The degree of desired difference is controlled by the regularization parameter. We study the practical value of LIKNON-based feature/model selection for microarray data. Our findings support the claims about the robustness of the method.

Keywords: feature selection, gene expression microarray, linear programming, support vector machine, LIKNON, regularization parameter, sample to feature ratio.

1 Introduction

Classification problems, involving very sparse, high-dimensional data, suffer from a generic difficulty due to data sparsity: the discovered classification models are greatly influenced by the peculiarities of the particular dataset under consideration. High-throughput technologies generate data with thousands of variables, but, especially for biomedical/clinical data a rather small number of exemplars. Efforts of analyzing such data are focused on the identification of sets of markers that differentiate the labelled samples of the different classes. When the sample size is small and the dimensionality high, the feature selection procedure, driven by the optimization of some criterion that ensures increasing class separation, will adapt to the peculiarities of the training set. The presence of selection bias requires proper validation (including feature selection) [1],[4], [16]. But if the monitoring set is too small, there is danger of adaptation to it [15]. The selected feature subsets will likely be different, depending on the sample sizes for the validation process and on the different selection methods. If a model selection strategy is used that takes into account the properties of the data, then we expect a more truthful, reliable model. For example, different gene subsets may

F. Masulli, S. Mitra, and G. Pasi (Eds.): WILF 2007, LNAI 4578, pp. 580–587, 2007.

be expressed under different conditions, hence methods producing a variety of identified feature subsets [5] might be useful. The problem of varying feature subsets in microarray literature is dealt with [3] by creating feature profiles. The main purpose of a feature profile is to assess how often a feature was selected. The rationale behind this approach is that if a feature was selected frequently, then it is more likely to be useful for class discrimination. An extensive analysis of various treatments of feature selection can be found in [8]. We want a procedure that is robust to bias induced by small sample sizes and: a) exhibits stability of the output in terms of error rate, b) finds subsets of features that properly reflect the true class differences.

Linear Programming (LP) Support Vector Machine (SVM) named LIKNON in [2], uses L_1 regularization, which is claimed [11] to be robust in small sample size settings. The method was initially proposed in [6], and has been applied to various classification problems [7], [14],[12] and [9]. LIKNON simultaneously identifies a feature subset and a linear discriminant associated with the subset. For a given sample size, the number of identified features is a priori constrained by the number of available samples for training (LP problem formulation). Different feature subsets and discriminants are produced, using different values of a regularization parameter, and the identification of a robust model with fewer features is relying on the proper selection of this parameter. This parameter controls the size of the bounding box (LP dual formulation). Learning by increasing the size of the bounding box may be interpreted as detecting the possibility of "early stopping" in training. Discovered in a particular learning iteration, features form a group out of the individual features having the largest differences between the resultants of the two classes (the resultant vector is a component-wise sum of a set of vectors see Equation (5)).

Here we analyze the feature selection property of LIKNON, as well its stability, when applied to a number of publicly available gene microarray datasets in the Kent Ridge Bio-medical data library [10]. Our contribution is an algorithm for inferring a classification model based on LIKNON, capitalizing on the theoretical analysis of LIKNON's feature selection property.

2   Understanding Feature Selection by LIKNON

On artificial data, with noisy features heavily masking the informative ones, we found that LIKNON is robust in detecting the "ground truth" when the number of samples is much less than the number of features (sample to feature ratio $SFR << 1$). If sample size allows, we set aside a **validation** set, which is not used until the final classification rules are identified. This is not applicable to microarrays. A training set is used in the development of the rules. In the development phase, we partition the training set into two: a balanced *training* set of size $T1 + T2$ and the remaining subset of $M1 + M2$ as a *monitoring* set. The number of splits depends on time and computational constraints.

In every split, a set of LIKNON discriminants (see Equation (1)) is identified, using the *training* set. The discriminants are found by solving the LIKNON with

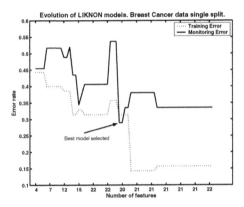

Fig. 1. Evolution of LIKNON models for a single split of the Breast Cancer data

increasing values of the regularization parameter C, as described in the following subsection. Models of increasing complexity (increasing number of features) are obtained. Gradual adaptation to the *training* set occurs, evidenced by rapidly decreasing training error. This is why we need a *monitoring* set. It is used to detect a point of possible "early stopping" and for identifying the best model for this particular split. The evolution of the procedure for single split of the Breast Cancer dataset is illustrated in Figure 1. A feature profile is created during the development, by counting the frequency of inclusion of each feature into the best discriminant. Created in this way, the profile highlights the common genes included into the discriminants obtained through different subdivisions of the data and the occurrence frequency of the common genes. In the feature profile, peaking occurs for important genes/features. If many features are selected equally frequently, this may indicate either high noise level, or many equally good features. We can assess how good or how noisy by the error rate on the monitoring set; It approaches ~ 0.5 if the data ceases to contain a learnable structure.

2.1   Formal Analysis

The formulation of LIKNON is based on using an L_1 instead of L_2 norm of the regularization term in the conventional SVM. This facilitates the use of linear programming (LP). A straightforward analysis of the constraints of the dual problem of LP and the optimality conditions suggests a way of choosing the values of the regularization parameter and provides some geometrical interpretation of its role in the feature selection. The necessary formalism was presented in [2], [12], and is briefly repeated here.

The primal minimization problem. LIKNON implements a linear rule for two-class classification:

$$y_i = sign(\boldsymbol{x}_i \boldsymbol{w}^T + w_0) \ , \tag{1}$$

where $x_i = [x_i^1, \ldots, x_i^d]$ are d-dimensional samples, y_i is the class label of sample i, and $N = N_1 + N_2$ is the total number of samples in the two classes. The important features in LIKNON are given by the large weights w_j of the vector w in (1). A component of the weight vector w_j and its absolute value are modelled through the two non-negative variables: $w_j = u_j - v_j$, $|w_j| = u_j + v_j$. Define $g_i^j = y_i x_i^j$ to merge vectors from both classes. The weights w of the separating hyperplane are found by solving an optimization problem, where C is the regularization parameter:

$$\begin{array}{c} \min\limits_{(u_1,,u_d,v_1,,v_d,\xi_1,,\xi_N)} \quad \mathbf{J}_{min} = \sum_{j=1}^{d}(u_j + v_j) + C\sum_{i=1}^{N} \xi_i, \quad \text{s.t.:} \\[2mm] \sum_{j=1}^{d} u_j g_i^j - \sum_{j=1}^{d} v_j g_i^j + u_0 - v_0 + \xi_i \geq 1, \\[2mm] \xi_i \geq 0, \quad u_j \geq 0, \quad v_j \geq 0, \quad j = 1,\ldots,d, \; i = 1,\ldots,N \; . \end{array} \quad (2)$$

The dual maximization problem. The dual of LIKNON is obtained from the primal in a straightforward manner:

$$\begin{array}{c} \max\limits_{(z_1,\ldots,z_N)} \quad \mathbf{J}_{max} = \sum_{i=1}^{N} z_i, \quad \text{s.t.:} \\[2mm] \pm g_1^j z_1 \pm \ldots \pm g_N^j z_N \leq 1, \\[2mm] y_1 z_1 + \ldots + y_N z_N = 0, \\[2mm] 0 \leq z_i \leq C, \quad i = 1,\ldots,N, \quad j = 1,\ldots,d \; . \end{array} \quad (3)$$

The optimal solution lies on a vertex of the feasible region given by the constraints in (3), and $z_i \leq C$.

Optimality conditions. The optimal solutions(*) of primal and dual satisfy the optimality conditions for every feature j and sample i:

$$u_j^* \left(\sum_{i=1}^{N} g_i^j z_i^* - 1 \right) = 0, \quad v_j^* \left(\sum_{i=1}^{N} g_i^j z_i^* + 1 \right) = 0, \quad \xi_i^* (z_i^* - C) = 0,$$
$$z_i^* \left(\sum_{j=1}^{d} g_i^j (u_j^* - v_j^*) + y_i(u_0^* - v_0^*) + \xi_i^* - 1 \right) = 0 \; . \quad (4)$$

Binding constraints determine the nonzero components w_j of w in (1), which correspond to the selected features.

Feature selection. Consider the values of the jth feature in the two classes. Denote it by vector $x^j = [x_1^j, \ldots, x_N^j]$ and project it onto the vector of class labels, then the projection represents the normalized difference between the resultants of the feature measurements of the two classes:

$$p^j = \frac{\sum_{i=1}^{N} x_i^j y_i}{\sqrt{N}} = \frac{\sum_i^{N_1} x_i^j - \sum_i^{N_2} x_i^j}{\sqrt{N}} \; . \quad (5)$$

A useful interpretation of the formulation of the dual is that all feature vectors are projected into an interval. The interpretation of the interval is as follows. We recall that we have defined $g_i^j = y_i x_i^j$ and that the constraints of the dual (3) were obtained straightforwardly from the primal corresponding to the individual features $\boldsymbol{x}^j$ just introduced. For some k and variables u_k and v_k, we explicitly write the corresponding inequalities of the dual maximization problem: $x_1^k y_1 z_1 + \ldots + x_N^k y_N z_N \leq 1$ and $x_1^k y_1 z_1 + \ldots + x_N^k y_N z_N \geq -1$. By solving the dual problem, we find vector $\boldsymbol{z} = [z_1, \ldots, z_N]$ providing a new direction of the class label vector $\boldsymbol{z}_y = [z_1 y_1, \ldots, z_N y_N]$. The length of an arbitrary vector of feature k measurements of two classes projected on $\boldsymbol{z}_y$ is:

$$x_{\boldsymbol{z}_y}^k = \frac{\sum_{i=1}^N z_i y_i x_i^k}{\|\boldsymbol{z}\|} \ . \tag{6}$$

The numerator of (6) is constrained by ± 1 (this follows from the constraints of the dual). Given a dual solution $\boldsymbol{z}^*$ and interpretation of (6), all feature vectors are projected into the interval $[\frac{-1}{\|\boldsymbol{z}^*\|} \ \frac{1}{\|\boldsymbol{z}^*\|}]$ because the numerator of (6) has to satisfy the constraints. The features selected (non-zero solutions of all u_k^* and v_k^* for some $k = 1, \ldots, K$) are on the the margins of the interval because the optimality conditions (4) have to be satisfied. The constraints of the dual (3), $z_i \leq C$, lead to $\|\boldsymbol{z}\| \leq C\sqrt{N}$ or $\frac{1}{\|\boldsymbol{z}\|} \geq \frac{1}{C\sqrt{N}}$. The size of the interval is bounded from below by $\frac{1}{C\sqrt{N}}$. If we require that the half length of the interval be no less than certain p^j given by (5), then:

$$\frac{1}{C\sqrt{N}} = \frac{\sum_{i=1}^N x_i^j y_i}{\sqrt{N}} \quad \Rightarrow \quad C = \frac{1}{\sum_{i=1}^N x_i^j y_i} \ . \tag{7}$$

By setting C small, we constrain the interval to be large, such that only some features that have large difference between the resultants are projected onto the margin. We compute C values based on (7) from the training set, sort them in ascending order, obtain a set of values in $[C_{min} : C_{max}]$ and solve LIKNON using these values. When the dimensionality is high (many features), in order to minimize the computational burden, we condense similar C values by building a histogram.

3   Main Results on Microarray Datasets

Public microarray datasets of the Kent-Ridge Bio-Medical data library were analyzed using the presented methodology. The training data were partitioned into training and monitoring sets. 31 splits were processed, discriminants identified and feature profiles produced. The summary of the experiment is in the Table 1: Dimension: dimensionality of the dataset, NTotal: total number of samples in the two classes, Class names, NTrain: sample size of the training set, NMonit- sample size of the monitoring set. Performance metrics were Sensitivity and Specificity, derived from the confusion matrixes of the models on the monitoring set, together with average confusion matrix (Avg.Confmat) for all splits. The averaged values of Sensitivity and Specificity, and standard deviations can be

Table 1. Experimental setup and LIKNON performance

Property	Leukemia	Colon cancer	Lung cancer	Prostate cancer	Breast cancer	CNS Tumor
Dimension	7129	2000	12533	12600	24481	7129
NTotal	47+25	22+40	31+150	77+59	46+51	21+39
Class name	ALL vs. AML	Positive vs. negative	MPM vs. ADCA	tumor vs. normal	relapse vs. nonrelapse	class1 vs. class2
NTrain	17+17	12+12	20+20	45+45	35+35	15+15
NMonit	30+8	10+28	11+130	32+14	11+16	6+24
Sens.% m±s	98.7±3.5	83.2±12.5	98.8±3.1	90.1±6.6	68.5±22.7	60.8±18.1
Spec.% m±s	83.5±12.4	81.9±10.5	94.4±3.5	90.6±14.3	69.7±17.6	53.4±11.3
Avg. Confmat	29.6 0.4 1.3 6.7	8.3 1.7 5.1 22.9	10.9 0.1 7.2 122.8	28.8 3.2 1.3 12.7	7.7 3.3 5.1 10.9	3.65 2.35 11.2 12.8
FNoInProfile	52	57	54	69	115	124
RangeFN	7-17	5-17	6-12	8-27	19-31	13-24
TopF1 (%) Name	1779 (80) M19507_at	119 (61) NA	7200 (90) 37157_at	12495 (94) 216_at	3591 (91) NM_004179	1054 (97) J02611_at
TopF2 (%) Name	6201 (77) Z19554_S_at	249 (58) NA	12308 (77) 769_S_at	8656 (68) 36931_at	9480 (76) NM_006217	4116 (68) X12447_at
Ens. Confmat	47 0 0 25	19 3 3 37	31 0 6 144	73 4 1 58	40 6 7 44	19 2 2 37

used as performance estimates of how the LIKNON discriminants will do on unseen data and how well the identified features discriminate the classes. The row FNoInProfile gives the total number of features included at least once in the profile. It reflects the total number of common genes appearing in different discriminants. The row RangeFN gives the range of the number of features in the subsets. In the rows TopF1, TopF2 we indicate the two common attributes most frequently found (frequency of occurrence in %) and the names when available/not available(NA) from the data repository [10]. The last row displays the confusion matrix (Ens. Confmat.) of the classification of microarray data obtained using the identified ensemble of linear discriminants. This resubstitution estimate is indeed optimistic. Nevertheless, there is good agreement between the results obtained herein with feature selection and the 10-fold crossvalidation classification results without feature selection in the previous work [13]. We were interested in the stability of the algorithm, defined by the identities of the discovered features. Though the SFR is dramatically low, the procedure consistently discovered the same features identified by the different data splits. The lowest variance of performance estimates was observed for the lung cancer data. The lowest frequency of inclusion of the attribute into the profile was for colon cancer, perhaps because of the small sample size available for training. In the CNS Tumor, although the overall performance was not as good, a single attribute occurred in almost all models. For the prostate cancer dataset, an improvement of the classification accuracy is observed, compared to the previous study [13].

When the sample size for monitoring is small, the accuracies have high variance, yet the same features appear important according to LIKNON. All classification problems with different feature subsets have different intrinsic classification errors; their accurate estimation is not possible without a large test set. Since the "ground truth", the identities of the optimal features are not known, our presented results are exploratory, subject to verification by domain experts.

4 Conclusions

We performed an exploratory analysis of LIKNON-based feature/model selection, with the goal of assessing its feature selection and stability property. The practical value of LIKNON is that it is able to discover robustly consistent differences in high-dimensional sparse data. We believe it is a useful method for creating a profile of the informative features of the data, microarrays in particular. This is because the important information we are seeking in microarrays is the expression level of a group of genes. Thus, we attempt to find the group of attributes characterized by large attribute differences between the classes. LIKNON operates by finding the groups of the most distant features, with this distance controlled by the regularization parameter. Given that microarrays have very low SFRs and present challenges for forward or backward search, LIKNON, considered as an embedded method for feature selection, is robust compared to the sequential methods. In [13], the same datasets were analyzed with simple classification models. The classification accuracies obtained therein compare very well with the results achieved by LIKNON on the monitoring sets. The biological validity of the findings has to be assessed by domain experts.

References

1. Ambroise, C., McLachlan, G.J.: Selection bias in gene extraction on the basis of microarray gene-expression data. PNAS. 99(10), 6562–6566 (2002)
2. Bhattacharyya, C., Grate, L.R., Rizki, A., et al.: Simultaneous relevant feature identification and classification in high-dimensional spaces: application to molecular profiling data. Signal Processing 83(4), 729–743 (2003)
3. Davis, C.A., Gerick, F., Hintermair, V., et al.: Reliable gene signatures for microarray classification: assessment of stability and performance. Bioinformatics 22(19), 2356–2363 (2006)
4. Berrar, D.P., Bradbury, I., Dubitzky, W.: Avoiding model selection bias in small-sample genomic datasets. Bioinformatics 22(10), 1245–1250 (2006)
5. Filippone, M., Masulli, F., Rovetta, S.: Supervised classification and gene selection using simulated annealing. In: Proc. Int. Joint Conf. on Neural Networks, pp. 6872–6877 (2006)
6. Fung, G., Mangasarian, O.: A feature selection Newton method for support vector machine classification. Computational Optimization and Applications 28, 185–202 (2004)
7. Guo, G-D., Dyer, C.: Learning from examples in the small sample case: face expression recognition. IEEE Trans. on System, Man and Cybernetics - Part B 35(3), 477–488 (2005)

8. Guyon, I., Gunn, S., Nikravesh, M., Zadeh, L. (eds.): Feature extraction, foundations and applications. Springer, Heidelberg (2006)

9. Kecman, V., Huang, T.M.: Gene extraction for cancer diagnosis by support vector machines. In: Duch, W., Kacprzyk, J., Oja, E., Zadrożny, S. (eds.) ICANN 2005. LNCS, vol. 3696, pp. 617–624. Springer, Heidelberg (2005)

10. Kent Ridge Bio-Medical data repository: `http://sdmc.lit.org.sg/GEDatasets`

11. Ng, A.: Feature selection, L_1 vs. L_2 regularization, and rotational invariance. In: Proc. 21st Int. Conf. on Machine learning. Morgan-Kaufman, Seattle, Washington, USA (2004)

12. Pranckeviciene, E., Ho, T.K., Somorjai, R.L.: Class separability in spaces reduced by feature selection. In: Int. Conf. on Pattern Recognition. vol. 3, pp. 254–257 (2006)

13. Pranckeviciene, E., Somorjai, R.: On classification models of gene expression microarrays: the simpler the better. In: Proc. Int. Joint Conf. on Neural Networks pp. 6878–6885 (2006)

14. Pranckeviciene, E., Somorjai, R., Baumgartner, R., Jeon, M.: Identification of signatures in biomedical spectra using domain knowledge. AI in Medicine 35(3), 215–226 (2005)

15. Raudys, S., Baumgartner, R., Somorjai, R.: On understanding and assessing feature selection bias. In: Miksch, S., Hunter, J., Keravnou, E.T. (eds.) AIME 2005. LNCS (LNAI), vol. 3581, pp. 468–472. Springer, Heidelberg (2005)

16. Somorjai, R., Dolenko, B., Baumgartner, R.: Class prediction and discovery using gene microarray and proteomics mass spectroscopy data: curses, cavets, cautions. Bioinformatics 19(12), 1484–1491 (2003)

An Alternative Splicing Predictor in C.Elegans Based on Time Series Analysis

Michele Ceccarelli and Antonio Maratea

Research Center On Software Technology
University of Sannio, Via Traiano 11, Benevento, Italy
(ceccarelli,amaratea)@unisannio.it

Abstract. Prediction of Alternative Splicing has been traditionally based on expressed sequences' study, helped by homology considerations and the analysis of local discriminative features. More recently, Machine Learning algorithms have been developed that try avoid the use of a priori information, with partial success. Here we approach the prediction of Alternative Splicing as a time series analysis problem and we show that it is possible to obtain results similar or better than the state of the art without any explicit modeling of homology, positions in the splice site, nor any use of other local features. As a consequence, our method has a better generality and a broader and simpler applicability with respect to previous ones. Results on pre-mRNA sequences in C.Elegans are reported.

Availability: Matlab/Octave code is available at www.scoda.unisannio.it

Keywords: Alternative Splicing, Autoregressive Model, Support Vector Machine.

1 Introduction

Alternative Splicing is one of the key mechanisms of post transcriptional modification [20]. Through it, a single gene can give rise to a number of different products rearranging its coding regions and splicing out its non coding regions in many alternative configurations. The coding regions of a gene are called Exons and the non coding regions are called Introns. Alternative Splicing (AS) happens when Exons have many different possible configurations and hence one gene can produce more than one single product (protein).

An extreme known case of AS is the gene Dscam of Drosophila, that it is know to produce more than 38000 different proteins. It is estimated that half of the human genes are alteratively spliced and this percentage does not vary much among other animals [1].

Although AS is known since the eighties there are only a few hypotesis on why it happens and traditional methods to predict it are based essentially on the study of expressed sequences, strongly helped by homology considerations and careful analysis of the splice site. Among the many possible forms of AS, the one which we will analyze here is Exon Skipping, that is the case when different gene

F. Masulli, S. Mitra, and G. Pasi (Eds.): WILF 2007, LNAI 4578, pp. 588–595, 2007.

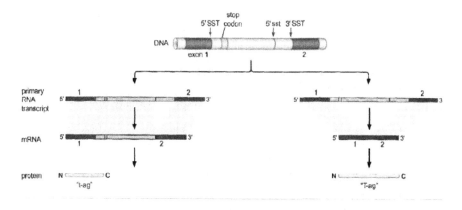

Fig. 1. *Constitutive Alternative Splicing*: two proteins are made from the same pre-mRNA sequence, skipping one Exon

products are obtained skipping one of gene's Exons. Skipped Exons are called Alternative Exons while Exons that are not skipped are called Constitutives Exons (Fig.1).

Several methods to predict AS based on the local sequence features have been proposed in literature [3,5,14,16]. Although the authors recognize many discriminative features, the most effective among them is certainly sequence homology. In spite of this result, recent studies confirm from one side that Constitutive Exons are more conserved than Alternative Exons [8] and from another side that conserved Exons are subject to species-specific AS in a significant amount [10]. The use of homology information as a discriminative feature has become hence more challenging, way beyond it's scarce availability on many sites. For this an other similar reasons traditional methods have been integrated and partially replaced by Machine Learning methods trying to infer AS on the basis of information that is always available (i.e. the crude pre-mRNA sequence).

In the work of Raetsch et al. [11] an SVM classifier based only on the pre-mRNA sequence is used as predictor for AS events in a database of C.Elegans sequences. The final classifier uses a complex kernel that's a linear combination of three terms, to model positional information togheter with information related to sequence lengths. With essentially the same task in mind, i.e. Machine Learning *ab initio* recognition of alternatively splicing Exons, our method is more general, as it does not explicitly use positions in the splice site, nor any feature derived form Exon or Intron lengths. We approach the problem as a variable length sequence classification task and extract a fixed-length set of features from the sequences to describe their dynamic nature. This approach has been already successfully applied in the analysis of gene expression patterns [6,13] and can be useful in several areas of trascriptomics. In this work, we will limit ourselves to the study of C.Elegans.

2   Method

The whole process can be resumed in three steps:

- i) coding of each exonic or intronic sequence;
- ii) feature extraction from coded sequences;
- iii) training a classifier on the features' vector previously obtained.

Trivially, coding is done substituting each of the four DNA bases A,C,G and T with one integer number from 1 to 4. Once data are coded (see Experiment), the first problem to cope with is the different length of the various sequences. We choose the parameters of an AR model as good descriptors of the dynamic of the phenomenon and use them as features. In this approach, each observed coded exonic or intronic sequence S is assumed to be the output of an order p AR model driven by a white noise process $e(n)$, that is the value in position n is assumed to be equal to a weighted sum of the p previous values plus a white noise term. The model is based on the following linear difference equations:

$$S(n) + \sum_{k}^{p} a_k S(n - k) = e(n) \tag{1}$$

where a_k is the kth AR parameter of an order p AR process. To estimate model parameters we used the classical Yule-Walker method, actually minimizing the forward prediction error in a Least-Squares sense.

At the end of process each intronic or exonic sequence S is replaced by the fixed-length vector $v = (a_1, \ldots, a_p)$ of the normalized estimate of the AR system coefficients a_k.

In step (iii) we consider Support Vector Machine (SVM). It is a classical technique for Pattern Recognition and Data Mining classification tasks [18] that has shown excellent performances in various heterogeneous fields [15]. The main advantage of SVM over i.e. Neural Networks, is that it has no local minima issues and that it has less free parameters.

Given a set of points in $\Re^k$ and a two-classes labels vector, SVM aims to find a linear surface that splits the data in two groups according to the indicated labels, maximizing the *margin*, that is the distance from *both* sets of points. This problem can be formulated as a constrained quadratic optimization problem:

$$min(\frac{1}{2}\|w\|^2) \tag{2}$$

subject to:

$$y_i(w^T x_i + b) \geq 1 \tag{3}$$

where $y_i \in \{-1, 1\}$ are classes' labels, w is the normal to the hyperplane and $2/\|w\|$ is the margin.

If the data are not linearly separable in $\Re^k$, they can be projected nonlinearly in a Hilbert space where the classification can be performed linearly, mantaining the method almost unchanged. If we look at the optimization's problem solution,

we see that data appear only in the form of dot products $x_i \cdot x_j$ and that even data transformed through a function $\Phi : \Re^k \mapsto \Gamma$ (where Γ is a space of dimension $h \geq k$) appear in the form of dot products $\Phi(x_i) \cdot \Phi(x_j)$. As a consequence, it is possible to substitute whatever dot product function $K(x_i, x_j) = \Phi(x_i) \cdot \Phi(x_j)$ in formulae and to compute the solution without even knowing the form of function Φ. Such a dot product function is called a *kernel* and there is an active field o research in the choice of the most suitable kernel for a given problem [2].
In this work we used a Gaussian kernel:

$$K(x_i, x_j) = \exp(-\gamma ||x_i - x_j||^2) \gamma > 0 \tag{4}$$

Its choice was derived mainly form the following general practical considerations [7,19]:

- the Radial Basis Function (RBF) SVM has infinite *capacity* and hence gaussian RBF SVM of sufficiently small width can classify an arbitrarily large number of training points correctly;
- the RBF kernel includes as a special case the linear kernel;
- the RBF kernel behaves like the sigmoid kernel for certain parameters' values;
- the RBF kernel has less hyperparameters than the polynomial kernel;
- the RBF kernel has less numerical difficulties than other kernels.

3   Experiment

The labeled dataset used to test our method is the same of [11]. It is a collection of 487 Exons for which EST show evidence of alternative splicing and 2531 Exons for which ther's no evidence of alternative splicing, for a total of 3018 labeled examples. All data regard C.Elegans and were obtained from the Wormbase, dbEST and UniGene [11]. As this dataset was biased towards non splicing sequences, we generated a new dataset of alternative splicing Exons resampling 5 times the original one of 487 alternative splicing sequences and obtaining a total dataset of 4966 samples.

To tune each parameter we used 5 fold cross validation. We reapetedly splitted randomly the data in five blocks and used in turn four of them as the Trainig Set and the fifth one as Testing [17]. Performances were evaluated in terms of the average AUC (Area Under Curve) index of Receiver Operating Characteristic (ROC) [4] Curves.

Using integer numbers from 1 to 4 to code the A,C,G and T DNA bases, there are 24 possible choices. We tested all of them and found no significant differences among them in terms of AUC value obtained (Fig.2).

To choose the model order, we also tested all values from 2 to 9. We couldn't use higher values due to the presence of very short sequences in data an even to reach order 9 we have been forced to remove the 20 shortest sequences from the data. It's clearly visible a regular increase of performance with the model order (Fig.3), and so we choose the maximum allowed.

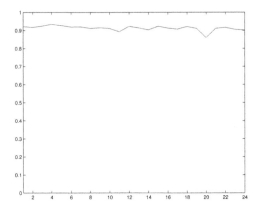

Fig. 2. Mean effect of the 24 possible codings on the AUC

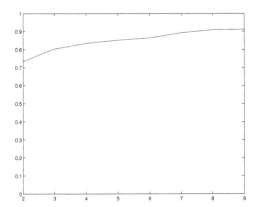

Fig. 3. Mean effect of the model order on the AUC

The last parameter, having choosen the RBF kernel, was the width of the Gaussian function σ. We tested 10 values, ranging from 0.2 to 3.8 in 0.4 steps (Fig.4) and the final choiche was $\sigma = 1.5$.

The mean variance estimate of the model error on the training sets is 1.54.

4   Results

The data matrix obtained after coding and after the AR model parameters' estimate is filled row by row by contiguous Exon triplets. Rows labeled as "AS" have the central Exon alternatively spliced, while rows labeled as "not AS" have the central Exon constitutively spliced. The matrix has $3p$ columns, as for each Exon there are p AR model coefficients. After the random division in Testing and Training sets (see Experiment) we train the SVM classifier with the labelled

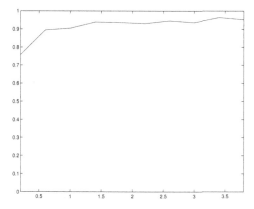

Fig. 4. Mean effect of the gaussian kernel's width

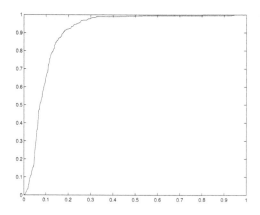

Fig. 5. ROC curve

matrix and we calculate the ROC curve and AUC on the Testing sets produced by cross validation.

The method reaches an average AUC of over 91% on Testing sets. The corresponding ROC curve does not rise immediately but has a shift from the y axis due to method's failure to classify a few high scoring points from the SVM. Ranking sequences on the base of the SVM predicted value, we noted that the top misclassified sequences at each run tend to be conserved. This fact suggests the opportunity that further biological verification is performed on these sequences, because their labeling, naturally prone to errors, may be wrong.

5 Conclusions

We have shown that a predictor for Exon skipping based only on the numerical properties of the pre-mRNA sequence in C.Elegans has similar or better performances than methods that account for homology, position whithin the splice site or length of Exons. A few top ranked sequences from the SVM are misclassified at each run and we believe these should be biologically verified, as their labels are likely to be wrong. In spite of this, we reach an average AUC of over 91% and although more data and more work are needed to validate further this result, a deeper biological understanding of the splicing mechanism seems necessary, in a close future, in order to model biological knowledge in a more effective way. Future work is in studying other organisms and in trying to predict more complex form of AS.

References

1. Brett, D., Pospisil, H., Valcrcel, J., Reich, J., Bork, P.: Alternative splicing and genome complexity. Nature Genetics 30, 29–30 (2001)
2. Cristianini, N., Shawe, J.: Kernel Methods for Pattern Analysis. Cambridge University Press, Cambridge (2004)
3. Dror, G., Sorek, R., Shamir, R.: Accurate Identification of Alternatively Spliced Exons Using Support Vector Machine. Bioinformatics 21, 897–901 (2004)
4. Egan, J.P.: Signal Detection Theory and ROC Analysis. Academic Press, New York (1975)
5. Hiller, M., Backofen, R., Heymann, S., Busch, A., Glaeber, T.M., Freytag, J.C.: Efficient prediction of alternative splice forms using protein domain homology. In: Silico Biology, vol. 4 (2004)
6. Holter, N.S., Maritan, A., Cieplak, M., Fedoroff, N.V., Banavar, J.R.: Dynamic modeling of gene expression data. In: Proceed. of Nat. Acad. Soc., vol. 98(4), pp. 1693–1698 (2001)
7. Keerthi, S.S., Lin, C.J.: Asymptotic behaviors of support vector machines with Gaussian Kernel. Neural Computation 15(7), 1667–1689 (2003)
8. Malko, D.B.B., Makeev, V.J.J., Mironov, A.A.A., Gelfand, M.S.S.: Evolution of exon-intron structure and alternative splicing in fruit flies and malarial mosquito genomes. Genome Research 6, 505–509 (2006)
9. Marple, S.L.: Digital Spectral Analysis with Applications. Prentice Hall, Englewood Cliffs (1987)
10. Pan, Q., Bakowski, M.A., Morris, Q., Zhang, W., Frey, B.J., Hughes, T.R., Blencowe, B.: Alternative splicing of conserved exons is frequently species-specific in human and mouse. Trends Genet. 21(2), 73–78 (2005)
11. Raetsch, G., Sonnenburg, S., Schoelkopf, B.: RASE: recognition of alternatively spliced exons in C.Elegans". Bioinformatics 21(Suppl. 1), 369–377 (2005)
12. Raetsch, G., Sonnenburg, S.: Accurate splice site prediction for C.Elegans. In: Raetsch, G., Sonnenburg, S. (eds.) Kernel Methods in Computational Biology, pp. 277–298. MIT press, Cambridge, MA (2003)
13. Ramoni, M., Sebastiani, P., Kohanem, I.: Cluster analysis of gene expression dynamics. In: Proceed. of Nat. Acad. Soc., vol. 99(14), pp.9121–9126 (2002)
14. Sakai, H., Skaletsky, H.J.: Extensive Search for Discriminative Features of Alternative Splicing. In: Proceedings of the Pacific Symposyum on Biocomputing, Hawaii, USA, pp. 54–65 (2000)

15. Scholkopf, B., Sung, K., Burges, C., Girosi, F., Niyogi, P., Poggio, T., Vapnik, V.: Comparing Support Vector Machines with Gaussian Kernels to Radial Basis Function Classifiers. IEEE Transactions on Signal Processing 45(11), 2758–2765 (1997)
16. Sorek, R., Ast, G.: Intronic Sequences Flanking Alternatively Spliced Exons are Conserved Between Human and Mouse. Genome Research 13, 1631–1637 (2003)
17. Stone, M.: Cross-validation: A review Mathematics. Operations and Statistics 9, 127–140 (1978)
18. Vapnik, V.: The Nature of Statistical Learning Theory. Springer-Verlag, Heidelberg (1995)
19. Verri, A., Pontil, M.: properties of support vector machines. Neural Computation 10(4), 955–974 (1998)
20. Watson, J., Baker, T., Bell, S., Gann, A., Levine, M., Losick, R.: Molecular Biology of the Gene (International Edition), 5th edn. Addison-Wesley, London, UK (2004)

Cancer Classification Based on Mass Spectrometry

Yihui Liu

School of Computer Science and Information Technology,
Shandong Institute of Light Industry,
Jinan, Shandong, China, 250353
Yihui_liu_2005@yahoo.co.uk

Abstract. In this paper wavelet analysis and Genetic Algorithm (GA) are performed to extract features and reduce dimensionality of mass spectrometry data. A set of wavelet features, which include detail coefficients and approximation coefficients, are extracted from mass spectrometry data. Detail coefficients are used to characterize the localized change of mass spectrometry data and approximation coefficients are used to compress mass spectrometry data, reducing the dimensionality. GA performs the further dimensionality reduction and optimizes the wavelet features. Experiments prove that this hybrid method of feature extraction is efficient way to characterize mass spectrometry data.

1 Introduction

Mass spectrometry is being used to generate protein profiles from human serum, and proteomic data obtained from mass spectrometry have attracted great interest for the detection of early-stage cancer. Surface enhanced laser desorption/ionization time-of-flight mass spectrometry (SELDI-TOF-MS) in combination with advanced data mining algorithms, is used to detect protein patterns associated with diseases [1,2,3,4,5]. As a kind of MS-based protein Chip technology, SELDI-TOF-MS has been successfully used to detect several disease-associated proteins in complex biological specimens such as serum [6,7,8].

The researchers [9] employ principle component analysis (PCA) for dimensionality reduction and linear discriminant analysis (LDA) coupled with a nearest centroid classifier [10] for classification. In [11], the researchers compare two feature extraction algorithms together with several classification approaches on a MALDI TOF acquired data. The T-statistic was used to rank features in terms of their relevance. Support vector machines (SVM), random forests, linear/quadratic discriminant analysis (LDA/QDA), knearest neighbors, and bagged/boosted decision trees were subsequently used to classify the data. More recently, in [12], both the GA approach and the nearest shrunken centroid approach have been found inferior to the boosting based feature selection approach. The researcher [13] examines the performance of the nearest centroid classifier coupled with the following feature selection algorithms. Student-t test, Kolmogorov-Smirnov test, and the P-test are univariate statistics used for filter-based feature ranking. Sequential forward selection and a modified version of sequential backward selection are also tested. Embedded approaches included shrunken nearest centroid and a novel version of boosting based feature selection. In

F. Masulli, S. Mitra, and G. Pasi (Eds.): WILF 2007, LNAI 4578, pp. 596–603, 2007.

addition, several dimensionality reduction approaches are also tested. Yu et al. [14] develop a novel method for dimensionality reduction and test on a published ovarian high-resolution SELDI-TOF dataset. They use a four-step strategy for data preprocessing based on: (1) binning, (2) Kolmogorov–Smirnov test, (3) restriction of coefficient of variation and (4) wavelet analysis. They use approximation coefficients. They indicated that "For the high-resolution ovarian data, the vector of detail coefficients contains almost no information for the healthy, since SVMs identify all the data as cancers". They concluded the detail coefficients do not work on high-resolution mass spectrometry using their four-step strategy method, instead of using approximation coefficients in their research. However it is wavelet detail coefficients that characterize the change of mass spectrometry data and approximation coefficients only compress the mass spectrometry. They also indicated that "Theoretically, a heavier compression rate can be achieved, at the risk of losing some useful information, by choosing a higher level of approximation coefficients". They only used 1st level wavelet approximation coefficients in their wavelet analysis. But from another view, higher level wavelet decomposition makes the "trend" of mass spectrometry data more significant and clear.

In our study we perform wavelet analysis on high dimensional mass spectrometry data to extract approximation coefficients and detail coefficients at 3rd level decomposition. GA performs the further dimensionality reduction and optimizes the wavelet features. Finally the selected GA features are used to distinguish the diagnostic classes based on linear discriminant analysis.

2 Wavelet Analysis

For one dimensional wavelet analysis, a signal can be represented as a sum of wavelets at different time shifts and scales (frequencies) using discrete wavelet analysis (DWT). The DWT is capable of extracting the features of transient signals by separating signal components in both time and frequency. According to DWT, a time-varying function (signal) $f(t) \in L^2(R)$ can be expressed in terms of $\phi(t)$ and $\psi(t)$ as follows:

$$f(t) = \sum_k c_0(k)\phi(t-k) + \sum_k \sum_{j=1} d_j(k)2^{\frac{-j}{2}}\psi(2^{-j}t-k)$$

$$= \sum_k c_{j0}(k)2^{\frac{-j0}{2}}\phi(2^{-j0}t-k) + \sum_k \sum_{j=j0} d_j(k)2^{\frac{-j}{2}}\psi(2^{-j}t-k)$$

where $\phi(t), \psi(t), c_0$, and d_j represent the scaling function, wavelet function, scaling coefficients at scale 0, and wavelet detailed coefficient at scale j, respectively. The variable k is the translation coefficient for the localization of a signal for time. The scales denote the different (high to low) frequency bands. The variable symbol j_0 is scale number selected. The wavelet decomposition tree is shown in Figure 1.

A set of wavelet approximation coefficients at different level decomposition acts as "fingerprint" of mass spectrometry data. The approximation coefficients compress high dimensional mass spectrometry data and reduce dimensionality. The purpose of detail coefficients is to detect a transient feature in one of a mass spectrometry signal's derivatives based on multilevel wavelets decomposition. The presence of noise, which is after all a fairly common situation in mass spectrometry processing, makes identification of transient change more complicated. If the first levels of the decomposition can be used to eliminate a large part of the noise, the rupture is sometimes visible at deeper levels in the decomposition. We chose approximation coefficients a_3 and detail coefficients d_3 as wavelet features. Then GA is performed to optimize the wavelet features.

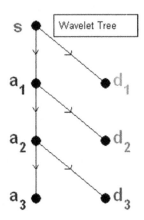

Fig. 1. Wavelet decomposition tree of mass spectrometry data. Variable s represents mass spectrometry data; a_i, d_i represent approximation coefficients and detail coefficients respectively, where $i = 1,2,3$.

3   Genetic Algorithm for Feature Selection

The Genetic Algorithm (GA) is an evolutionary computing technique that can be used to solve problems efficiently for which there are many possible solutions [15]. In our research we perform GA on wavelet features to select the best discriminant features and reduce dimensionality of wavelet feature space.

The algorithm creates initial population by ranking key features based on a two-way T-test with pooled variance estimate. We select different features in our study respectively to evaluate the performance of classification. The algorithm then creates a sequence of new populations based on different number of GA features. At each step, the algorithm uses the individuals in the current generation to create the next population. To create the new population, the algorithm performs the following steps:

a. Each member of the current population is scored by computing its fitness value. The algorithm usually selects individuals that have better fitness values as parents. A fitness function acts as selective pressure on all of the data points. This function determines which data points get passed on to or removed from each subsequent generation. To apply a genetic algorithm on the mass spectrometry data, we use a linear discriminant classifier (LDA) as fitness function to evaluate the performance how well the data gets classified [16].

b. The genetic algorithm creates three types of children for the next generation. Elite children, that are the individuals in the current generation with the best fitness values, automatically survive to the next generation. In this research two elite children are selected. Crossover children are created by combining the vectors of a pair of parents. The scattered crossover function is used in this study, which randomly selects a gene at the same coordinate from one of the two parents and assigns it to the child. The crossover fraction, which specifies the fraction of each population other than elite children, is set to 0.8. The mutation algorithm creates mutation children by randomly changing the genes of individual parents. In this study the algorithm adds a random vector from a Gaussian distribution to the parent.

c. The algorithm stops when one of the stopping criteria is met. GA uses four different criteria to determine when to stop the solver. GA stops when the maximum number of generations is reached; the maximum number of generations is set to 70 in this research. Fitness limit is considered and the algorithm stops if the best fitness value is less than or equal to the value of fitness limit. GA also detects if there is no change in the best fitness value for some time given in seconds (stall time limit=20), or for some number of generations (stall generation limit=50).

We set initial penalty parameter as 10, and penalty factor parameter as 100, which increases the penalty parameter when the problem is not solved to required accuracy and constraints are not satisfied.

4 Results

In this study we use correct rate, sensitivity, specificity, PPV, NPV and BACC to evaluate the performance. Sensitivity is defined as $\dfrac{TP}{TP+FN}$; Specificity is defined as $\dfrac{TN}{TN+FP}$; PPV (Positive Predictive Value) is defined as $\dfrac{TP}{TP+FP}$; NPV (Negative Predictive Value) is defined as $\dfrac{TN}{TN+FN}$; Correct rate is defined as $\dfrac{TP+TN}{TP+TN+FP+FN}$. Where TP, TN, FP, FN, stand for the number of true positive (cancer), true negative (control), false positive and false negative samples. BACC (Balanced Correct Rate) is defined as $\dfrac{1}{2}(\dfrac{TP}{TP+FN}+\dfrac{TN}{TN+FP})$, which is the average of sensitivity and specificity.

For the raw ovarian high-resolution SELDI-TOF, dataset composed of 95 control samples and 121 cancer samples, the dimensionality of the original feature space is 368750. They are provided by National Cancer Institute (http://home.ccr.cancer.gov/ncifdaproteomics/ppatterns.asp).

• Resample and filter mass spectrometry data

Resampling mass spectrometry data homogenizes the mass/charge (M/Z) vector in order to compare different spectra under the same reference and at the same resolution. In high resolution data sets, high resolution spectrometry contains redundant information. By resampling the signal can be decimated into a more manageable M/Z vector, preserving the information content of the spectra. Resampling mass spectrometry data select a new M/Z vector and also applies an antialias filter that prevents high frequency noise from folding into lower frequencies[17]. We resample the mass spectrometry data to 15000 M/Z points between 710 and 11900. Then we filter out mass spectrometry data with 20% variance over time. The spectra dimensionality reduces to 12000 after filtering.

• Extract wavelet features and GA features

We use Daubechies wavelet of order 7 (db7) for wavelet analysis of mass spectrometry data and the boundary values are symmetrically padded. Multilevel discrete wavelet transform (DWT) is performed on mass spectrometry data. The dimensionality of wavelet features is shown in Table 1. We perform GA feature selection on wavelet features, including approximation coefficients and detail coefficients at 3rd level decomposition. We select 15, 20, and 25 GA features to evaluate the performance. Figure 2 shows filtered mass spectra, approximation coefficients and detail coefficients at 3rd level, and 15 selected GA features.

Table 1. Feature number for high resolution ovarian dataset

	Original	resample	filtered	1st level	2nd level	3rd level
Feature number	368750	15000	12000	6006	3009	1511

• The performance of GA features

In this study we test GA features selected from 3rd level wavelet features. We run K fold cross validation experiments for each GA feature space, where K=2, 3. We run 20 times for each K fold cross validation experiments. Table 2 shows the performance of GA features selected from wavelet features.

The researcher [12] performed GA on original high resolution mass spectrometry data to select features. The "25th and 75th percentiles for test set accuracy", which are computed using two fold cross validation experiments of "Best GA" model, are 88% and 93%. Yu et al. [14] use a four-step strategy and their experimental results are shown in Table 3. They achieved 95.34% BACC for 2 fold cross validation experiment. For 2 fold cross validation experiment, we achieve 96.31% BACC based on 15 GA features selected from wavelet features. We also obtained 97.20% BACC for 3 fold cross validation based on 15 GA features, which is better than 95.88% BACC for 3 fold cross validation experiments and 96.12% BACC for 10 fold cross validation experiments in [14]. Our GA-Wavelet method outperforms their method of four-step strategy and original GA method. Our results are also better than other methods, which are shown in Table 4.

Table 2. Performance of selected GA features

FNGA	K fold	Correct rate	Sensitivity	Specificity	PPV	NPV	BACC
15	2	**0.9625**	**0.9587**	**0.9675**	**0.9740**	**0.9484**	**0.9631**
	3	**0.9716**	**0.9681**	**0.9759**	**0.9809**	**0.9601**	**0.9720**
20	2	0.9579	0.9557	0.9608	0.9688	0.9445	0.9582
	3	0.9702	0.9752	0.9639	0.9718	0.9683	0.9696
25	2	0.9583	0.9497	0.9694	0.9753	0.9380	0.9595
	3	0.9610	0.9646	0.9564	0.9657	0.9550	0.9605

This Table shows performance of high resolution ovarian dataset. PPV stands for Positive Predictive Value; NPV stands for Negative Predictive Value. BACC stands for Balanced Correct Rate. FNGA stands for selected Feature Number of GA.

Table 3. Performance of a four-step strategy [14]

K fold	Control	SD	Cancer	SD	BACC
2	0.9330	0.0174	0.9738	0.0125	0.9534
3	0.9393	0.0188	0.9783	0.0115	0.9588
10	0.9406	0.0226	0.9819	0.0113	0.9612

This Table shows performance of high-resolution ovarian dataset. BACC stands for Balanced Correct Rate. "Cancer" in [14] represents "Sensitivity"; "Control" in [14] represents "Specificity". SD strands for Standard Deviation.

Table 4. Performance of different methods [14] of high resolution ovarian dataset

Method	2 fold cross validation			10 fold cross validation		
	BACC	Control	Cancer	BACC	Control	Cancer
VP	0.9488	0.9393	0.9583	0.9587	0.9482	0.9691
QDA	0.9315	0.9202	0.9429	0.9451	0.9255	0.9647
LDA	0.9323	0.9179	0.9467	0.9388	0.9255	0.9522
MDA	0.9273	0.9392	0.9154	0.9429	0.9591	0.9267
NB	0.8997	0.8803	0.9190	0.9114	0.8979	0.9249
Bagging	0.9004	0.8835	0.9174	0.9104	0.8977	0.9232
1-NN	0.8732	0.8575	0.8889	0.8960	0.8902	0.9018
2-NN	0.8450	0.7260	0.9641	0.8904	0.8063	0.9745
ADtree	0.8558	0.8238	0.8878	0.8761	0.8498	0.9025
J48tree	0.8163	0.7818	0.8507	0.8535	0.8245	0.8825

This Table shows the performance of high-resolution ovarian dataset based on different models. BACC stands for Balanced Correct Rate. "Cancer" in [14] represents "Sensitivity"; "Control" in [14] represents "Specificity". VP stands for Voted Perceptron; QDA stands for Quadratic Discriminant Analysis; LDA stands for Linear

Discriminant Analysis; MDA stands for Mahalanobis Discriminant Analysis; k-NN stands for *k*-Nearest Neighbor; NB stands for Naïve Bayes; Bagging stands for Bootstrap aggregating; ADtree stands for Alternating Decision Trees; J48tree is a version of C4.5 in Weka classifier package.

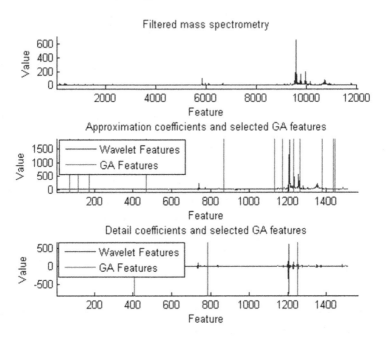

Fig. 2. Features for high resolution ovarian mass spectrometry data. This Figure shows filtered mass spectrometry data, approximation coefficients and detail coefficients at 3rd level, and selected GA features.

5   Conclusions

In this paper we perform wavelet analysis on high dimensional mass spectrometry data. We use approximation coefficients and detail coefficients at 3rd level decomposition to characterize mass spectrometry data and reduce dimensionality of mass spectrometry data. Approximation coefficients compress the mass spectrometry data and act as "fingerprint" of mass spectrometry data; detail coefficients characterize the localized change of mass spectrometry data using the compactness and finite energy characteristic of wavelet functions. Genetic algorithm is performed to select the best features from wavelet coefficients. Experiments prove that this hybrid method of feature extraction is efficient and robust.

Acknowledgements

This study is supported by research funds of Shandong Institute of Light Industry (12041653).

References

1. Petricoin, E., Ardekani, A.M., Hitt, B.A., Levine, P.J., Fusaro, V.A., Steinberg, S.M., Mills, G.B., Simone, C., Fishman, D.A., Kohn, E.C., Liotta, L.A.: Use of proteomic patterns in serum to identify ovarian cancer. The Lancet 359, 572–577 (2002)
2. Sorace, J.M., Zhan, M.: A data review and re-assessment of ovarian cancer serum proteomic profiling. BMC Bioinform. vol. 4 (2003)
3. Michener, C.M., Ardekani, A.M., Petricoin, E.F., Liotta III, L.A., Kohn, E.C.: Genomics and proteomics: application of novel technology to early detection and prevention of cancer. Cancer Detect Prev. 26, 249–255 (2002)
4. Petricoin, E.F., Zoon, K.C., Kohn, E.C., Barrett, J.C., Liotta, L.A.: Clinical proteomics: translating benchside promise into bedside reality. Nat. Rev. Drug. Discov. 1, 683–695 (2002)
5. Srinivas, P.R., Verma, M., Zhao, Y., Srivastava, S.: Proteomics for cancer biomarker discov-ery. Clin. Chem. 48, 1160–1169 (2002)
6. Herrmann, P.C., Liotta, L.A., Petricoin III, E.F.: Cancer proteomics: the state of the art. Dis. Markers 17, 49–57 (2001)
7. Jr, G.W., Cazares, L.H., Leung, S.M., Nasim, S., Adam, B.L., Yip, T.T., Schellhammer, P.F., Gong, L., Vlahou, A.: Proteinchip surface enhanced laser desorption/ionization (SELDI) mass spectrometry: a novel protein biochip technology for detection of prostate cancer bio-markers in complex protein mixtures. Prostate Cancer Prostatic Dis. 2, 264–276 (1999)
8. Vlahou, A., Schellhammer, P.F., Mendrinos, S., Patel, K., Kondylis, F.I., Gong, L., Nasim, S., Wright, Jr.,: Development of a novel proteomic approach for the detection of transitional cell carcinoma of the bladder in urine. Am. J. Pathol. 158, 1491–1520 (2001)
9. Lilien, R.H., Farid, H., Donald, B.R.: Probabilistic disease classification of expression-dependent proteomic data from mass spectrometry of human serum. Computational Biology 10 (2003)
10. Park, H., Jeon, M., Rosen, J.B.: Lower dimensional representation of text data based on centroids and least squares. BIT 43, 1–22 (2003)
11. Wu, B., Abbott, T., Fishman, D., McMurray, W., Mor, G., Stone, K., Ward, D., Williams, K., Zhao, H.: Comparison of statistical methods for classifcation of ovarian cancer using mass spectrometry data. BioInformatics 19 (2003)
12. Jeffries, N.O.: Performance of a genetic algorithm for mass spectrometry proteomics. BMC Bioinformatics 5 (2004)
13. Levner, I.: Feature selection and nearest centroid classification for protein mass spectrometry. BMC Bioinformatics 6 (2005)
14. Yu, J.S., Ongarello, S., Fiedler, R., Chen, X.W., Toffolo, G., Cobelli, C., Trajanoski, Z.: Ovarian cancer identification based on dimensionality reduction for high-throughput mass spectrometry data. Bioinformatics. 21, 2200–2209 (2005)
15. Holland, J.H.: Adaptation in Natural and Artificial Systems. MIT Press, Cambridge,MA (1992)
16. Li, L., Umbach, D.M., Terry, P., Taylor, J.A.: Application of the GA/KNN method to SELDI proteomics data. Bioinformatics 20, 1638–1640 (2004)
17. IEEE: Programs for Digital Signal Processing. Ch. 8. IEEE Press, John Wiley & Sons, New York (1979)

Computational Proteomics of Biomolecular Interactions in Sequence and Structure Space of the Tyrosine Kinome: Evolutionary Constraints and Protein Conformational Selection Determine Binding Signatures of Cancer Drugs

Gennady M. Verkhivker[1,2]

[1] Department of Pharmaceutical Chemistry, School of Pharmacy
and Center for Bioinformatics, The University of Kansas
2030 Becker Drive, Lawrence, KS 66047 USA
[2] Department of Pharmacology, University of California San Diego,
9500 Gilman Drive, La Jolla CA 92093-0636 USA
verk@ku.edu, gverkhiv@ucsd.edu

Abstract. The emerging insights into kinase function and evolution combined with a rapidly growing number of crystal structures of protein kinases complexes have facilitated a comprehensive structural bioinformatics analysis of sequence–structure relationships in determining the binding function of protein tyrosine kinases. We have found that evolutionary signal derived solely from the tyrosine kinase sequence conservation can not be readily translated into the ligand binding phenotype. However, fingerprinting ligand–protein interactions using in silico profiling of inhibitor binding against protein tyrosine kinases crystal structures can detect a functionally relevant kinase binding signal and reconcile the existing experimental data. In silico proteomics analysis unravels mechanisms by which structural plasticity of the tyrosine kinases is linked with the conformational preferences of cancer drugs Imatinib and Dasatinib in achieving effective drug binding with a distinct spectrum of the tyrosine kinome. While Imatinib binding is highly sensitive to the activation state of the enzyme, the computed binding profile of Dasatinib is remarkably tolerant to the conformational state of ABL. A comprehensive study of evolutionary, structural, dynamic and energetic aspects of tyrosine kinases binding with clinically important class of inhibitors provides important insights into mechanisms of sequence–structure relationships in the kinome space and molecular basis of functional adaptability towards specific binding.

1 Introduction

Comprehensive analysis of the protein kinase complement of the human genome (the "kinome") [1,2] has provided important insights into evolution and function of human protein kinases, emerging as a major class of drug targets in recent years. Understanding the molecular basis of protein kinases binding specificity presents a highly challenging biological problem as the binding specificity is

F. Masulli, S. Mitra, and G. Pasi (Eds.): WILF 2007, LNAI 4578, pp. 604–611, 2007.

not readily interpreted from chemical proteomics studies, neither it is easily discernable directly from sequence and structural information [3]. Evolutionary relationships between protein kinases are often employed to infer inhibitor binding profiles directly from sequence analysis of the kinase domain. However, the activity profiles of kinase inhibitors are not directly linked with the respective position of the protein kinase on the evolutionary dendrogram and often exhibit cross-activity to phylogenetically remote kinases. Imatinib mesylate (Gleevec) is a prime example of inherent complexity in inferring binding specificities by means of sequence homology of kinase domains, which assumes that phylogenetically similar kinases should display similar inhibitor binding profiles. By primary sequence analysis, ABL and ARG kinases are more closely related to SRC, FYN, FGR, BLK, LCK, and HCK tyrosine kinases than to PDGFR tyrosine kinase family [5]. However, Imatinib mesylate exhibits high selectivity at inhibiting PDGFR, KIT, and ABL kinases, with comparable efficiencies and is largely ineffective in suppressing the tyrosine kinase activity of SRC family. Although the catalytic domains of active protein kinases are structurally very similar, the crystal structures of inactive kinases reveal a remarkable plasticity that allows the adoption of distinct inactive confirmations [6]. Mechanism of action of Imatinib at inhibiting a small group of protein kinases has been clarified based on crystallographic studies of Imatinib bound to ABL tyrosine kinase [7], which demonstrated binding to the unique structural motif of the activation loop present in the inactive conformation of the ABL kinase. The crystal structures of Dasatinib, which has demonstrated a broad range of tyrosine kinases activities, has provided further evidence that ABL can adopt multiple conformations, suggesting that the inhibitor activity against various tyrosine kinases is largely driven by the recognition requirements dictated by multiple states of the enzyme [8,9]. The growing repertoire of protein kinases crystal structures have revealed a considerable diversity and significant conformational differences between active and inactive kinase conformations. These studies have confirmed that diverse structures of the activation loop are natural kinase conformations and dynamic equilibrium between multiple conformational states plays a critical role in molecular recognition of ABL with the kinase inhibitors and interacting proteins [6,7,8,9]. We have recently proposed a computational approach for in silico profiling of Imatinib with the tyrosine kinome by using evolutionary analysis and fingerprinting of the inhibitor–kinase interactions with multiple protein conformations [10]. In the present work, a comparative analysis of the kinase binding profiles with the clinically important Imatinib and Dasatinib inhibitors unravels functionally diverse specificity mechanisms which agree with the biochemical and proteomics data.

2   Systems and Methods

2.1   Protein Tyrosine Kinases Classification

Phylogenetic trees of the human protein tyrosine kinase family for whole-domain alignments and binding site sub-alignments were created with PHYLIP package of programs (version 3.6) [11]. This composite set of critically important contact alignment positions were compiled from all presently available tyrosine crystal structures based on residues with side chains within 4.5 Å of their respective ligands (referred to as the binding site subalignment) and was then used for phylogenetic clustering (Figure 1, panel A). We have also constructed the phylogenetic dendrogram based on the evolutionary conservation profile of the binding site residues, defined from the crystal structures of Imatinib mesylate complex with the ABL kinase. All currently available crystal structures of protein tyrosine kinases in the Protein Data Bank (PDB) are used to categorize the structural space into panels of active and inactive kinase conformations. The superposition of crystal structures from the protein tyrosine kinase family into a common reference frame is based on similarity of C_α atoms for a common set of residues defining the ATP binding site.

2.2   Monte Carlo Binding Simulations

The molecular recognition energetic model used in this study includes intramolecular energy terms, given by torsional and nonbonded contributions of the DREIDING force field [12], and the intermolecular energy contributions calculated using the AMBER force field to describe protein–protein interactions combined with an implicit solvation model. The dispersion–repulsion and electrostatic terms have been modified and include a soft core component that was originally developed in free energy simulations to remove the singularity in the potentials and improve numerical stability of the simulations. A solvation term was added to the interaction potential to account for the free energy of interactions between the explicitly modelled atoms of the protein–protein system and the implicitly modelled solvent. We have carried out equilibrium simulations with the ensembles of protein kinase conformations using parallel simulated tempering dynamics [13] with 50 replicas of the ligand-protein system attributed respectively to 50 different temperature levels that are uniformly distributed in the range between 5300K and 300K. In simulations with ensembles of multiple protein conformations, protein conformations are linearly assigned to each temperature level, that implies a consecutive assignment of protein conformations starting from the highest temperature level and allows each protein conformation from the ensemble at least once be assigned to a certain temperature level. Starting with the highest temperature, every pair of adjacent temperature configurations is tested for swapping until the final lowest value of temperature is reached. Monte Carlo moves are performed simultaneously and independently for each replica at the corresponding temperature level. After each simulation cycle, that is completed for all replicas, exchange of configurations for every pair of adjacent replicas at neighboring temperatures is introduced.

3   Results and Discussion

Evolutionary relationships are often exploited by probing sequence conservation profiles of the binding site residues, the functional subset of the protein residues

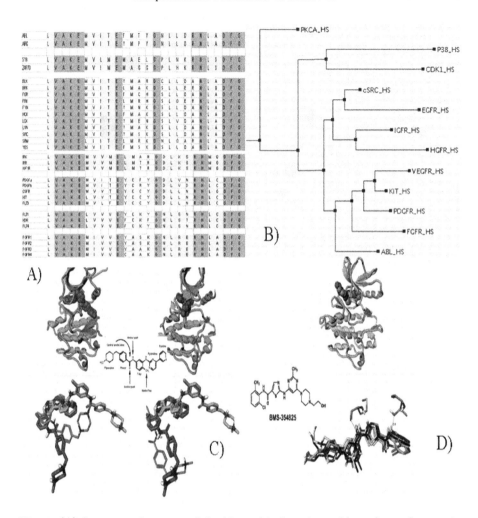

Fig. 1. (A) Sequence alignment of the kinase binding site residues shown for tyrosine kinase families. The binding site is defined by residues residing within root mean square (RMSD) of 4.5 Å from Imatinib. (B) The phylogenetic dendrogram is derived from the evolutionary conservation profile of the tyrosine kinase binding site residues determined from the crystal structure of Imatinib mesylate with the ABL kinase. (C) The crystal structure of Imatinib mesylate in the complex with the ABL inactive kinase structure (left upper) and SYK active kinase structure (right upper). The predicted conformation of Imatinib mesylate in the complex with the ABL kinase and the crystal structure conformation are virtually identical (lower panel). The predicted conformation of Imatinib mesylate (displayed in light stick) in the complex with the LCK (left lower), and SYK (right lower) kinases superimposed with the crystal structure of Imatinib bound to the SYK active kinase conformation (displayed in dark stick). (D) The predicted bound conformations of Dasatinib in the complexes with the inactive and active structures of ABL, SRC, LCK and EGFR kinases. The predicted structural models of Dasatinib are superimposed with the crystal structure of the inhibitor(displayed in stick and light blue colors).

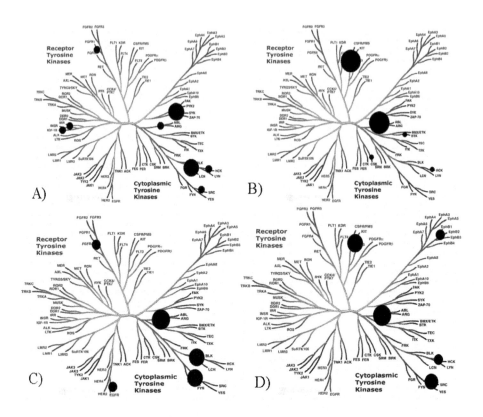

Fig. 2. The size of the filled circles mapped onto phylogenetic dendrogram of protein tyrosine kinases is proportional to the probability of respective protein kinase structure that delivers the lowest interaction energy for Imatinib with active conformations (A) and inactive conformations (B) and for Dasatinib with active conformations (C) and inactive conformations (D)

which are not necessarily near in sequence, but rather close in structural space. However, we have determined that evolutionary signal derived solely from the tyrosine kinase sequence conservation can not be readily translated into the ligand binding phenotype. Functional classification of the binding specificity based on the conservation of the binding site residues can be rather sensitive to the binding site definition and may not have a significant relationship with the respective function of these kinases to bind a particular inhibitor, unless binding site residues are defined from the crystal structure with the respective ligand. Indeed, when the binding site residues are determined from the crystal structure of Imatinib mesylate with the ABL kinase, the phylogenetic dendrogram and the evolutionary conservation profile of the ABL kinase binding site residues result in a closer proximity of ABL, CKIT and PDGFR kinases, whereas ABL and SRC kinases emerged as less similar (Figure 1). Hence, functional linkage between protein conformational diversity and sequence plasticity of the kinase binding site may be important to understand binding specificities of these cancer agents. We investigate structural and energetic aspects of Imatinib and Dasatinib a binding with the conformational states of the tyrosine kinases, using computational profiling of the inhibitor–protein interactions with an ensemble of inactive and active kinase crystal structures. The results of simulations are illustrated by comparing the phylogenetic dendrogram of the tyrosine kinome marked with the sequence location of the known active (Figure 2a,c) and inactive kinase crystal structures (Figure 2b,d) against the phylogenetic footprint mapped with the densities of respective tyrosine kinase conformations which yield the lowest energy complexes with the Imatinib (Figure 2a,b) and Dasatinib (Figure 2c,d). The high selectivity of Imatinib mesylate binding with ABL and KIT is achieved via convergence to a narrow spectrum of ABL and KIT inactive bound conformations featuring the unique binding mode of Imatinib mesylate from the crystal structure of the ABL kinase complex. Consequently, the high affinity binding of Imatinib with the ABL kinase is assured by the conformationally–specific inhibitor recognition of the ABL inactive form (Figure 1, panel C). We have also detected an alternative binding mode of Imatinib which may be recruited by the protein conformations of both SYK and LCK kinases in the active, phosphorylated form, but with much lower binding affinity (Figure 1, panel C). The alternative binding mode of Imatinib in complexes with the active tyrosine kinases structures is noticeably different from the inhibitor conformation found in the ABL kinase complex, but is structurally similar to a recently discovered crystal structure of Imatinib mesylate bound to the active conformation of SYK kinase. Computational proteomics analysis of Imatinib binding with the protein tyrosine kinases agrees with the results of recent kinase proteomics profiling study, revealing the molecular basis of inhibiting ABL, CKIT and PDGFR protein tyrosine inactive kinases structures with high efficiency and a moderate affinity with the LCK and SYK kinases [14]. In contrast, Dasatinib has revealed a broad range of promiscuous activities and a high affinity binding with the kinases from ABL and SRC families. The results of simulations with the ensemble of active kinase conformations reveal that Dasatinib inhibitor can bind to a number of tyrosine kinases, including ABL, SRC, HCK, LCK, EGFR, and FGFR active conformations (Figure 2). In agreement with the reported proteomics analysis of Dasatinib binding against a large panel of kinases, in silico profiling reproduces the spectrum of observed Dasatinib binding activities against ABL, SRC, HCK, LCK, EGFR, and FGFR active conformations. The predicted bound conformations of Dasatinib in complexes with both active and inactive conformational states of ABL, SRC, LCK and EGFR tyrosine kinases conform to the crystallographic binding mode of the inhibitors and accurately reproduce the key interactions formed in the active site. Interestingly, a conformationally tolerant Dasatinib fluctuates only within 1.5 Å from the crystal structure in order to favorably accommodate the multitude of kinase conformational states (Figure 2, panel D). We find that unlike Imatinib binding, which is highly sensitive to the activation state of the enzyme, binding promiscuity of Dasatinib may be largely determined by a remarkable adaptability of the inhibitor to structurally diverse conformational states of ABL, CKIT, SRC, and EGFR kinases with high binding affinity. These results strongly suggest that binding specificity mechanisms may be driven by conformational adaptability of the inhibitor to structurally different conformational states of the enzyme. The determined molecular basis of multi-targeted binding specificity for Dasatinib allows to better understand how effective targeted cancer therapies, including Dasatinib, exhibit their activity through inhibition of multiple tyrosine kinases. We have found that functional diversity of the tyrosine kinase binding may manifest itself in a variety of mechanisms governing specific recognition: from specific recognition only with the unique inactive form of the target (highly selective Imatinib binding with ABL) to recognition of multiple conformational states of multiple targets from a kinase family (promiscuous Dasatinib binding with ABL, CKIT, SRC, LCK).

4   Conclusions

We have shown that the molecular basis of binding specificity for tyrosine kinases may be largely driven by conformational adaptability of the inhibitors to an ensemble of structurally different conformational states of the enzyme, rather being determined by their phylogenetic proximity in the kinome space. The discovered sequence–structure relationships in the tyrosine kinome space governing binding specificity are shown to extend beyond simple phylogenetic relationships of the binding site residues and detect a functionally relevant kinase binding signal, thereby providing basis for constructing functionally relevant kinase binding trees. The presented computational approach may be also useful in complementing proteomics profiling to characterize activity signatures of small molecules against a large number of potential kinase targets.

References

1. Hunter, T., Plowman, G.D.: The protein kinases of budding yeast: six score and more. Trends Biochem. Sci. 22, 18–22 (1997)
2. Manning, G., Whyte, D.B., Martinez, R., Hunter, T., Sudarsanam, S.: The protein kinase complement of the human genome. Science 298, 1912–1934 (2002)
3. Bain, J., McLauchlan, H., Elliott, M., Cohen, P.: The specificities of protein kinase inhibitors: an update. Biochem. J. 371, 199–204 (2003)
4. Vulpetti, A., Bosotti, R.: Sequence and structural analysis of kinase ATP pocket residues. Il Farmaco 59, 759–765 (2004)
5. Wong, S., Witte, O.N.: The BCR-ABL story: bench to bedside and back. Annu. Rev. Immunol. 22, 247–306 (2004)
6. Huse, M., Kuriyan, J.: The conformational plasticity of protein kinases. Cell 109, 226–282 (2002)
7. Schindler, T., Bornmann, W., Pellicena, P., Miller, W.T., Clarkson, B., Kuriyan, J.: Structural mechanism for Imatinib mesylate inhibition of abelson tyrosine kinase. Science 289, 1938–1942 (2000)

8. Tokarski, J.S., Newitt, J.A., Chang, C.Y., Cheng, J.D., Wittekind, M., Kiefer, S.E., Kish, K., Lee, F.Y., Borzillerri, R., Lombardo, L.J., Xie, D., Zhang, Y., Klei, H.: The structure of Dasatinib (BMS-354825) bound to activated ABL kinase domain elucidates its inhibitory activity against imatinib-resistant ABL mutants. Cancer Res., 66, 5790–5797 (2006)

9. Levinson, N.M., Kuchment, O., Shen, K., Young, M.A., Koldobskiy, M., Karplus, M., Cole, P.A., Kuriyan, J.: A SRC-like inactive conformation in the ABL tyrosine kinase domain. PLoS Biol. 4, 753–767 (2006)

10. Verkhivker, G. M.: Imprint of evolutionary conservation and protein structure variation on the binding function of protein tyrosine kinases. Bioinformatics 22, 1846–1854 (2006)

11. Felsenstein, J.: PHYLIP: Phylogeny Inference Package, Version 3.6., Seattle, WA University of Washington (2002)

12. Mayo, S.L., Olafson, B.D., Goddard III, W.A.: DREIDING: a generic force field for molecular simulation. J. Phys. Chem. 94, 8897–8909 (1990)

13. Sugita, Y., Okamoto, Y.: Replica-exchange molecular dynamics method for protein folding. Chem. Phys. Lett. 314, 141–151 (1999)

14. Fabian, M.A., Biggs III, W.H., Treiber, D.K., Atteridge, C.E., Azimioara, M.D., Benedetti, M.G., Carter, T.A., Ciceri, P., Edeen, P.T., Floyd, M., Ford, J.M., Galvin, M., Gerlach, J.L., Grotzfeld, R.M., Herrgard, S., Insko, D.E., Insko, M.A., Lai, A.G., Lelias, J.M., Mehta, S.A., Milanov, Z.V., Velasco, A.M., Wodicka, L.M., Patel, H.K., Zarrinkar, P.P., Lockhart, D.J.: A small molecule-kinase interaction map for clinical kinase inhibitors. Nature Biotech., 23, 329–336 (2005)

Learning Transcriptional Regulatory Networks with Evolutionary Algorithms Enhanced with Niching

Cédric Auliac[1,2,*], Florence d'Alché–Buc[2], and Vincent Frouin[1]

[1] Service de Génomique Fonctionnelle , Commissariat à l'Energie Atomique (CEA),
Genopole, Evry, FR, Phone: 33 1 60873921
vincent.frouin@cea.fr
[2] Laboratoire Informatique Biologie Intégrative et Système Complexes
Université d'Evry-Val d'Esonne, Genopole, Evry, FR
cauliac@ibisc.univ-evry.fr, florence.dalche@ibisc.univ-evry.fr

Abstract. Reverse engineering of gene regulatory networks is a key issue for functional genomic. Indeed, unraveling complex interactions among genes is a crucial step in order to understand their role in cellular processes. High-throughput technologies such as DNA microarrays or ChIP on chip have in principle opened the door to network inference from data. However the size of available data is still limited compared to their dimension. Machine learning methods have thus to be worked out in order to respond to this challenge. In this work we focused our attention on modeling gene regulatory networks with Bayesian networks. Bayesian networks offer a probabilistic framework for the reconstruction of biological interactions networks using data, but the structure learning problem is still a bottleneck. In this paper, we use evolutionary algorithms to stochastically evolve a set of candidate Bayesian networks structures and find the model that best explains the small number of available observational data. We propose different kinds of recombination strategies and an appropriate technique of niching that ensure diversity among candidate solutions. Tests are carried out on simulated data drawn from a biorealistic network. The effect of deterministic crowding, a niching method, is compared to mutation for different kinds of recombination strategies and is shown to improve significantly the performances. Enhanced by deterministic crowding, our evolutionary approach outperforms K2, Greedy-search and MCMC, for training sets whose size is small compared to the standard in machine learning.

Keywords: gene regulatory network, evolutionary algorithms, niching.

1 Introduction

Biological functions depend on the coordinated interactions of genes as well as their products. Among the different complex regulatory mechanisms at work in

---

* Corresponding author.

F. Masulli, S. Mitra, and G. Pasi (Eds.): WILF 2007, LNAI 4578, pp. 612–619, 2007.

the cell, transcriptional regulation is one of the most important. The availability of a wide range of experimental methods and tools such as DNA-microarray, ChIP on chip or siRNA gives the modelers the opportunity to consider reverse engineering of transcriptional networks from experimental data. In this study, we focused on static Bayesian Network (BN) [1,2]. They offer a rich framework for the representation of causal dependencies between genes and allow the management of uncertainty which is necessary to account for the stochasticity of biological systems. Both the structures and the parameters of the BN are unknown and have to be learned. Most of the approaches proposed to learn BN structure are based on the search, within a candidate set, for the BN that best explains the experimental data according to a given scoring metric. It has been shown that this problem of structure learning is NP-hard [3]. Stochastic heuristics like MCMC [4,5] or evolutionary programming [6] are commonly used. They are supposed to overcome some drawbacks of deterministic search strategies, such as local optimality and dependence on the initial solution. Genetic Algorithms (GA) appear as one of the most relevant framework to deal with the exploration of such complex space in the context of regulation network inference. In this work, we studied GA using several recombination and selection strategies. Eventually, we compared our best approach to classical learning algorithms.

The paper is organized as follows : section 2 introduces Bayesian networks as the framework for modeling gene regulatory networks and develops how GA can be used to learn BN structures. Section 3 is devoted to numerical results obtained on a biorealistic network and to their analysis. In section 4, conclusions and perspectives are provided.

2   Model and Algorithm

2.1   Modeling Gene Regulatory Networks with Bayesian Networks

Gene regulatory networks may be represented by Bayesian Networks (BN). BN are defined by a tuple (G, P_{BN}). G is a Directed Acyclic Graph (DAG) where nodes are random variables $X = \{X_1, \ldots, X_n\}$ and the edges encode the conditional (in)dependencies between these variables. The graph topology defines a set of parents for each node $X_i : Pa(X_i)$. BN are used to model the true joint probability distribution on X by $P_{BN}(X)$. We consider discrete random variables to represent the gene expression levels and non parametric modeling. We use Conditional Probability Tables (CPT) referred thereafter as $\theta = \{\theta_{ik}^l\}$. They enable to express any complex regulatory interactions without requiring to fix the nature of the interactions.

$$P_{BN}(X) = \prod_{i=1}^{n} P_{BN}(X_i \mid Pa(X_i)) \ with \ P_{BN}(X_i = k \mid Pa(X_i) = l) = \theta_{ik}^l$$

2.2   Structure Evaluation Using a Scoring Metric

Given a sample of size s, $D=(x^1, \ldots, x^s)$ of n random variables $X=\{X_1, \ldots, X_n\}$, the learning algorithm must search in the set $\mathcal{G}$ the best DAG structure G, associated with corresponding CPTs, that minimizes the Bayesian Information Criterion (BIC) [7]. For the class of models we chose, the criterion can be written as follows

$$BIC(G) = \sum_i \sum_k \sum_l -2.N_{ik}^l \cdot \log(\hat{\theta}_{ik}^l) + K_G^i \log(s)$$

with K_G^i the number of parameters in the CPT of X_i. $\hat{\theta}_{ik}^l$ is the maximum likelihood estimate (MLE) of θ_{ik}^l. It can be approximated by N_{ik}^l/N_i^l where $N_i^l = \sum_k N_{ik}^l$ the number of times the X_i's parental configuration equals l . Since it relies on frequency computation, determining these MLE from data is straightforward. Note that the BIC can be read as the sum of local scores: one local score only depends on the parental set of the node for which it is computed.

2.3   Evolving DAG Structures

In GAs, candidate models are coded with (usually binary) vectors called chromosomes. Here, their constituents are termed GA-genes. Practically, GA-genes can take on multiple values (called alleles) from any finite alphabet.

Evolving BN structures is a hard task and two global strategies can be considered regarding this question : direct and indirect search. Indirect search generally performs the search in the space of n variables permutations [8,9]. Each permutation is interpreted as a precedence order over the variables such that a node in the network can only accept as parents the nodes which precede it in this ordering. Each variables ordering is usually fed to the K2 algorithm [10], a deterministic DAG builder which intend to recover the best corresponding BN structure. However, even if the space which is searched for variable ordering optimization is smaller and smoother than the space of BN structures [4], its exploration remains a hard task. In addition K2 algorithm which is based on a greedy hill-climbing method, won't necessary find the best BN structure for a given ordering. Therefore we preferred the second alternative and evolved directly BN structures as performed in [11,12,13,14]. Since the search is conducted directly over the space of DAG, we face the classical problem of producing infeasible solutions (digraph with cycle). This could be avoided by assuming a precedence order over the variables as K2 does, but such information is usually not available. In our study, the acyclicity constraint is considered *a posteriori*, using a repair function to remove cycles from new candidate structures. For computational conveniences we set an upper bound on the number of potential parents per node to 10, which limits the frequency of cycle appearance. Indeed, as mentioned in subsection 2.1, each family $(X_i, Pa(X_i))$ is associated with a CPT. For a family with m parents, assuming all nodes have the same arity noted d, $(d-1).d^m$ parameters $\hat{\theta}_{ik}^l$ have to be estimated, stored in the CPT and manipulated for subsequent computation of the objective function. Dealing with such tables becomes infeasible as the number of parents grows. Consequently, the size of the family has to be limited.

We applied paire-wise uniform recombination to the chromosomes of candidate models to perform the search in the space of BN structures. Recombination efficiency depends on its ability to manipulate meaningful information units. We considered two different coding of BN structures making use of different types of GA-genes.

Parental Recombination. The first DAG representation we considered is the parental-chromosome previously used in [13]. A parental-chromosome is composed of a sequence of n GA-genes, corresponding to a parental list Pa_j (with $j \in \{1, \ldots, n\}$). The scoring metric we used to evaluate BN structures can be expressed as the summation of local scores assessing the constituting parental lists. Thus, the search for a high fitted BN structure can be achieved by finding proper associations of high scoring parental lists. From a biological point of view, one may assume that Pa_j represents the set of regulators acting on the transcriptional activity of gene X_j which justifies exchanging it as a whole.

Link chromosomes. We also considered link-chromosomes, which enabled to exchange elementary interactions between node pairs. Link-chromosome is a ternary vector; each GA-genes ϕ_{ij} can take three values : 0 if there is no edge between X_i and X_j, 1 if $X_i \to X_j$, -1 if $X_j \to X_i$.

2.4 Maintaining the Diversity in the Population of Solutions

A fundamental characteristic of GAs is their ability to search the DAG space from multiple points in parallel. However, as the algorithm goes along, population homogenization prevents the crossover operator to explore new portions of the solution space. A common approach to fight fast homogenization is the mutation operator which introduces diversity by means of random edge additions and deletions. Alternatively the niching approach intends to maintain diversity by limiting the scope of selection process to subsets of similar individuals. In this study, we used Deterministic Crowding (DC) [15] to delay premature convergence. DC is a simple method which introduces no additional parameters: each offspring replaces the most similar parent only if it improves the score. Mutation and DC occur at two different steps of the classical progress of GA. We will compare results obtained with and without mutation on the one hand and with or without DC on the other hand. When no DC is applied, offspring replace the two worst individuals of the population if they have higher scores (elitist replacement strategy).

3   Results and Discussion

Currently there does not exist experimental dataset corresponding to completely known transcriptional regulation network. We chose the synthetic model proposed in [5], which is a biorealistic BN based on established knowledge on the insulin regulatory network (glucose homeostasis) with a moderate size (35 discrete random variables) and a limited complexity (parsimonious topology). This insulin BN provided us with our reference DAG for performance study. We generated samples with various numbers of measures for the 35 genes. The number of measures ranged from 50 to 400 corresponding to realistic biological conditions. To evaluate the performances of a structure inference algorithm, we used classical similarity measures between inferred and reference DAGs. These measures are based on the respective PDAG corresponding to the DAGs being compared (to account for the fact we obtain a similar score for any DAG belonging to the same equivalence Markov class [16]). As described in [5], PDAGs are evaluated according to the sensitivity ($\frac{tp}{tp+fn}$) and the positive predictive value (ppv)($\frac{tp}{tp+fp}$). A true positive (tp) is an edge which appears in both the learned and the reference graph. In addition, if this edge is directed in the learned graph, it must share the same orientation in the reference graph. A true negative (tn) occurs when there is no edge between two specific nodes in both the learned and reference graphs. When the previous conditions are not fulfilled, the presence and the absence of an edge in the learned graph are respectively considered as a false positive (fp) and a false negative (fn).

In Tables 1 and 2, we reported the performances of the GA optimization depending on the recombination strategies and diversity maintaining methods. In Fig.1, we compared our most promising GA implementation to some state of the art learning algorithms: Greedy search, K2 and MCMC. For both recombination methods, exchange rate was set to 0.4. We also used a small mutation rate (about 2 out of 1000 potential interactions) and a moderate population size of 200.

3.1 Evaluation of the Evolutionary Approach Enhanced by Deterministic Crowding

Whatever the mutation and selection approaches were, it appeared from Tables 1 and 2 that link-recombination outperformed the parental-recombination. Indeed, since it performs recombination at a finer level (elementary interactions) link-recombination can produce very different candidate models. This allowed the GA to escape from local minima and reach better areas of the search space before being trapped by premature convergence.

Table 1. Mean ± standard deviation of the sensitivity ($\times 100$) : a comparison of various evolutionary strategies

Recombination	NoDC/NoMut	NoDC/Mut	DC/NoMut	DC/Mut
Parental Recomb.	23 ± 7	56 ± 7	48 ± 3	66 ± 4
Link Recomb.	43 ± 4	61 ± 6	63 ± 3	68 ± 4

Table 2. Mean ± standard deviation of the PPV (×100) : a comparison of various evolutionary strategies

Recombination	NoDC/NoMut	NoDC/Mut	DC/NoMut	DC/Mut
Parental Recomb.	26 ± 8	38 ± 4	68 ± 10	69 ± 6
Link Recomb.	61 ± 12	58 ± 8	84 ± 5	74 ± 8

The introduction of niching greatly improved the performances even if mutation was used. Surprisingly, the differences we previously observed regarding the performances of the recombination strategies were smaller when we used the DC. They both performed relatively well, especially considering the positive predictive value (ppv).

Finally, DC appears to improve significantly the learning process. This advantage is obviously of greater benefit for conservative recombination methods like parental recombination, which failed to explore efficiently the solution space.

3.2 Comparison with Other Approaches

According to the previous results, we selected the GA implementing the link-recombination and the DC selection strategy. We compared it with the widely used optimization methods in the field of BN structure optimization: Greedy search, K2 [10] and MCMC [4] algorithms. All these algorithms were set up to maximize the BIC scoring metric. The K2 algorithm is a deterministic DAG builder which is provided with prior information: topological order of the nodes of the DAG. Contrarily, Greedy search and MCMC operate in the same conditions as our GA.

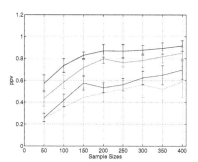 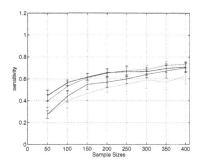

Fig. 1. PPV(left) and sensitivity(right) learning curves of various learning algorithms. The color coding is green for Greedy Search, blue for MCMC, black for K2, and red for the genetic algorithm. For each sample size, tests are performed on 10 different and independent datasets. The same datasets are used for every algorithms. Each point along the curves corresponding to a given sample size, presents the mean value and the standard deviation of the quality measurement across the 10 runs of the algorithms.

Instead of focusing on the single solution maximizing the scoring metric, MCMC yields a set of graphs obtained by sampling from the log posterior $logP(G|D)$, following the Metropolis-Hastings algorithm. After a burning of 40000 iterations, MCMC gave a set of 4000 DAG. In order to deal with the the 4000 sampled DAGs, we built a single consensus graph as described in [5].

The plots of the sensitivity and ppv against the sample size are given in Fig.1. As expected, for both ppv and sensitivity, the greedy search yielded the worst results. Indeed, it is a deterministic heuristic which converged towards local optima around the initial solutions we randomly generated. The MCMC algorithm, which relies on a stochastic and effective search strategy, gave better results. However, if we consider variability we noted that, greedy search and MCMC algorithm were relatively close.

4   Conclusions and Perspectives

We presented an evolutionary approach that is able to learn gene regulatory networks from a reasonable amount of observational data compared to the size of datasets used in machine learning. To perform this study we used synthetic gene expression data sampled from a biorealistic model of glucose homeostasis. We first compared various evolutionary strategies in order to find the one which achieved the best structure learning. We showed that recombining edges was the best reproduction strategy on the problem at hand. We emphasized the importance of the mutation operator and the necessity to promote diversity. We showed that DC improved significantly the evolutionary process thanks to its ability to postpone convergence and therefore to preserve diversity. Second, we compared our evolutionary approach with various learning algorithms. In our study, GA outperformed both greedy search and MCMC algorithms. Thanks to the node ordering at its disposal K2 yielded less false positive than GA since it considers a restricted set of potential parents for each node. However, in practice, knowledge about node ordering is never available. Other kinds of prior informations such as potential targets of transcription factors and protein-protein interactions, may be available when dealing with real networks. We showed that without prior knowledge evolutionary algorithms provide promising results. A perspective is now to extend our approach in order to exploit pieces of informations related to the biological system under study. In this case, the dataset size required for learning should be reduced. Further work will thus concern the application of this extended approach to real datasets of gene expression measurements.

References

1. Pearl, J.: Probabilistic Reasoning in Intelligent Systems: Networks of Plausible Inference. Morgan Kaufmann Publishers Inc., San Francisco, CA, USA (1988)
2. Jensen, F.V.: Bayesian Networks and Decision Graphs. Springer-Verlag New York, Inc, Secaucus, NJ, USA (2001)

3. Chickering, D.M., D.G., Heckermann, D.: Learning bayesian networks is np-complete. In: Fisher, D., Lenz, H.J. (eds.) Learning from data: AI and Statistics, New York NY, vol. 5, pp. 121–130. Springer-Verlag, Heidelberg (1996)
4. Friedman, K.: Being bayesian about network structure: A bayesian approach to structure discovery in bayesian networks. Machine Learning 50, 95–126 (2003)
5. Le, P.P., Bahl, A., Ungar, L.H.: Using prior knowledge to improve genetic network reconstruction from microarray data. In Silico Biology 4(2) (2004)
6. Wong, M.L., Lam, W., Leung, K.S.: Using evolutionary programming and minimum description length principle for data mining of bayesian networks. IEEE Transactions on Pattern Analysis and Machine Intelligence 21(2), 174–178 (1999)
7. Schwarz, G.: Estimating the dimension of a model. The Annals of Statistics 6(2), 461–464 (1978)
8. Hsu, W.H., Guo, H., Perry, B.B., Stilson, J.A.: A permutation genetic algorithm for variable ordering in learning bayesian networks from data. In: GECCO '02. Proceedings of the Genetic and Evolutionary Computation Conference, San Francisco, CA, USA, pp. 383–390. Morgan Kaufmann Publishers Inc, Seattle, Washington, USA (2002)
9. Larranaga, P., Kuijpers, C., Murga, R., Yurramendi, Y.: Learning bayesian network structures by searching for the best ordering with genetic algorithms (1996)
10. Cooper, G.F., Herskovits, E.: A bayesian method for the induction of probabilistic networks from data. Mach. Learn. 9(4), 309–347 (1992)
11. Larranaga, P., Poza, M., Yurramendi, Y., Murga, R.H., Kuijpers, C.M.H.: Structure learning of bayesian networks by genetic algorithms: A performance analysis of control parameters. IEEE Trans. Pattern Anal. Mach. Intell. 18(9), 912–926 (1996)
12. Etxeberria, R., Larranaga, P., Picaza, J.M.: Analysis of the behaviour of genetic algorithms when learning bayesian network structure from data. Pattern Recogn. Lett. 18(11-13), 1269–1273 (1997)
13. Myers, J.W., Laskey, K.B., DeJong, K.A.: Learning bayesian networks from incomplete data using evolutionary algorithms. 1 (13-17) 458–465 (1999)
14. Cotta, C., Muruzabal, J.: Towards a more efficient evolutionary induction of bayesian networks. In: PPSN VII. Proceedings of the 7th International Conference on Parallel Problem Solving from Nature, pp. 730–739. Springer-Verlag, London, UK (2002)
15. Mahfoud, S.W.: Niching methods for genetic algorithms. PhD thesis, Champaign, IL, USA (1995)
16. Verma, T., Pearl, J.: Equivalence and Synthesis of Causal Models. Elsevier Science, New York, NY (1991)

Towards a Personalized Schedule with Triplex Vaccine

Francesco Pappalardo[1,2], Santo Motta[2], Pier Luigi Lollini[3], Emilio Mastriani[2], and Marzio Pennisi[2]

[1] Faculty of Pharmacy, University of Catania, Italy
[2] Department of Mathematics and Computer Science, University of Catania, Italy
francesco@dmi.unict.it, motta@dmi.unict.it
[3] Sezione di Cancerologia, Dipartimento di Patologia Sperimentale,
and Centro Interdipartimentale di Ricerche sul Cancro "Giorgio Prodi"
University of Bologna, Italy
pierluigi.lollini@unibo.it

Abstract. The immune system is a large and complex system still incompletely understood. The synergy of biological knowledge included in data bases, mathematical and computational models and bioinformatics tools can help in gain a deeper understanding. In this paper, we try to understand how one can characterize a mouse in order to find the better vaccination protocol against mammary carcinoma for that individual. This study will be expanded in the framework of ImmunoGrid EC project.

1 Introduction

The investigation of tumor immunity has led to many clinical attempts at curing human tumors (immunotherapy). Once a therapeutic agent has demonstrated its efficacy, it can be approved for routine use by regulatory agencies. An evaluation of the preclinical results of vaccines in mouse models shows a clear dichotomy between therapeutic and prophylactic uses of vaccine. In most instances vaccination before the challenge (prophylactic vaccination) prevents tumor growth, whereas vaccination after the challenge (therapeutic vaccination) is much less effective.

Cancer immunoprevention is based on the use of immunological approaches to prevent tumor, rather than to cure cancer. This is mostly important in endogenous originated tumors in which cancer cells are continously formed from corrupted normal cells. Cancer immunoprevention vaccines are based (like all vaccines) on drugs which gives to the immune system the necessary information to recognize tumor cells as harmful. For this reason, cancer vaccines need to be administered to the host for his entire life. The vaccine cannot eliminate all tumor cells but stabilizes them to a non dangerous level.

A vaccine must be effective for the entire population and very rarely it is optimized for a single individual. Affords in cancer immunoprevention vaccines for entire pupulation started few years ago [1]. With regard to translation of cancer

F. Masulli, S. Mitra, and G. Pasi (Eds.): WILF 2007, LNAI 4578, pp. 620–626, 2007.
© Springer-Verlag Berlin Heidelberg 2007

immunopreventive approaches to human situations, it is desirable to minimize the number of vaccinations, creating a personalized schedule. In the present paper we report results from a first approach to the search of an optimal personalized schedule for a cancer immunoprevention vaccine.

Due to immune system complexity a distributed approach to database management, analysis and data mining is desiderable: GRID provides the perfect answer to these needs. The *ImmunoGrid* EC-project concerns with the implementation of virtual human immune system using grid technologies. It is the first attempt toward the simulation of the immune processes at natural scale and provides tools for applications in clinical immunology and the design of vaccines and immunotherapies. The ImmunoGrid applications will provide tools for clinicians and vaccine or immunotherapy developers for identification of optimal immunization protocols. ImmunoGrid which officially started on February, 1st 2006 and the Consortium is composed by European members - from Denmark, France, Italy, UK - and Australia.

The plan of the paper is the following. In Section 2 we briefly introduce the biological problem and we give a sketch of the present state of the Catania Mouse Model (CMM), a model & simulator (SimTriplex) of a cancer immunoprevention vaccine; in Section 3 we show how SimTriplex is applied to try to understand how one can characterize a mouse in order to find the better vaccination protocol for that individual. Finally Section 4 is devoted to conclusions and future works.

2   Modeling Immune System - Cancer - Vaccine Competition

Triplex vaccine [2,6] was designed to improve the efficacy of existing immunopreventive treatments. A complete prevention of mammary carcinogenesis with the Triplex vaccine was obtained when vaccination cycles started at 6 weeks of age and continued for the entire duration of the experiment, about one year (Chronic vaccination).

The major issue still unresolved with the Triplex vaccine is whether or not the Chronic schedule is the minimal set of vaccination yielding complete, long-term protection from mammary carcinoma. Shorter vaccination protocols failed to prevent cancer, but between shorter protocols and the Chronic one there still is an infinite set of schedules that might yield complete protection with significantly less vaccinations than the Chronic. From an experimental point of view this would require a large sets of experiments each lasting one year, a feat that discouraged the biological part of our team from the pursuit of an experimental solution *in vivo*.

Our target consists in two main points. The first is to develop a vaccine's computational model that is specifically addressed to mammary cancer whose vaccine has been studied and tested *in vivo* by the cancer immunoligists group at the University of Bologna. The second is to use the developed model to search for a schedule that is better than Chronic one.

To describe the cancer - immune system competition one needs to include all the entities (cells, molecules, adjuvants, etc.) which biologists recognize as relevant in the competition. The choice of entities was driven by the experimental data on Triplex vaccine. These entities, which are either cells or molecules, have mechanical and biological states: position, lifetime, internal states and specificity. Position and lifetime are common to all of them; internal states apply only to cellular entities, while specificity can be found both in cellular and molecular entities. The model, which has been fully described in [7,5] is implemented using a Lattice Gas Automata and includes entities (cells and molecules) of the adaptive and natural immune system, the cancer and the vaccine. The model and its computer implementation have been biologically validated against *in vivo* experiments and data. All various classes of immune functional activity, phagocytosis, immune activation, opsonization, infection, cytotoxicity and specific/aspecific recognition are described using probability functions and translated into computational rules. After appropriate tuning of the model, the *in silico* simulations were able to reproduce the *in vivo* experiments using two independent sets of 100 *virtual* different mice [7].

An interaction between two entities is a complex stochastic event which may end with a state change of one or both entities. Interactions can be *specific* or *aspecific*. Specific interactions need a *recognition phase* between the two entities (e.g. B ↔ TAA); recognition is based on Hamming distance and affinity function and is eventually enhanced by adjuvants. We refers to *positive interaction* when this first phase occurs successfully. Aspecific interaction do not have a recognition phase (e.g. DC ↔ TAA). When two entities, which may interact, lie in the same lattice site then they interact with a probabilistic law. Both specific and aspecific interactions are stochastically determined using a probability function, which depends from different parameters, computed via random number generators. Changing the seed of the random number generator one gets a different sequence of probabilistic events. This simulate the biological differences between individuals who share the same events probabilities.

3   Search for an Optimal Schedule

When a newly designed vaccine is ready to be administered for the first time *in vivo*, either to mice or to humans, the schedule is designed empirically, using a combination of immunological knowledge, vaccinological experience from previous endeavors, and practical constraints. In subsequent trials the schedule of vaccinations is then refined on the basis of the protection elicited in the first batch of subjects and of their immunological responses (e.g. kinetics of antibody titers, cell mediated response, etc.) The problem of defining optimal schedules is particularly acute in cancer immunopreventive approaches, like the Triplex vaccine, which requires a sequence of vaccine administration to keep a high level of protective immunity against a continuing generation of cancer cells for very long periods, ideally for the entire lifetime of the host.

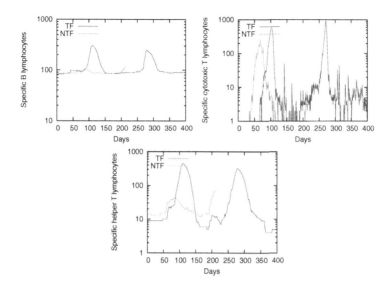

Fig. 1. Specific B (against tumor associated antigen), specific cytotoxic T lymphocytes (against peptide/major histocompatibility class I complex) and specific helper T lymphocytes (against peptide/major histocompatibility class II complex)for TF and NTF mouse

In searching for an optimal schedule, we have tried different strategies. Interested reader can found extensively review on [5,8,2,3]. In what follows, we try to understand how one can characterize a mouse in order to find the better vaccination protocol for that individual.

All the virtual mice in the model are uniquely identified by their random seeds that set the initial repertoire and the interactions with environmental variables. We ran the genetic search for optimal protocol on a single mouse, obtaining a 22 injections schedule. After that, we tried such a protocol on a set of 100 mice, obtaining a survival percentage of 27%. If we divide the initial set of virtual mice in two subset, tumor free (TF) mice and not tumor free (NTF) mice, a major question arises: are we able to identify *a priori* a mouse that will be tumor free with a specific vaccination schedule?

To find an answer to this question we firstly tried to understand if the environmental variables are meaningful in this game. We then proceeded to force all mice of the sample to have the same interactions with the environmental variables. This was simply obtained by setting environmental seed equal for all mice. As a result, we obtained a TF mice of 30%. This result led to the conclusion that the environment should be not critical. Then the difference should lie in the immunological repertoire. To highlight these differences we considered two different mice, one belonging to the TF mice and the other belonging to the NTF mice. Then we plotted (Figure 1) specific B and T lymphocytes for the two mice as functions of time (respectively $B(t)$ and $T(t)$, $t \in [0, 400]$.

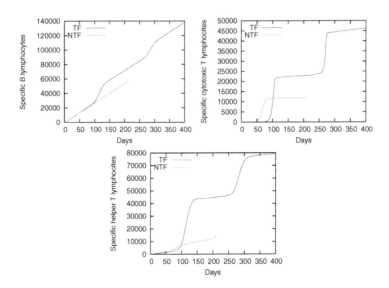

Fig. 2. Cumulative behavior for specific B (against tumor associated antigen), specific cytotoxic T lymphocytes (against peptide/major histocompatibility class I complex) and specific helper T lymphocytes (against peptide/major histocompatibility class II complex) for TF and NTF mouse

From this Figure, one can appreciate differences between the two mice. Specific B and helper T lymphocytes show clearly peaks in TF mouse while are almost flat in NTF mouse. For specific cytotoxic T lymphocytes the difference is less evident. For this reason we considered the cumulative number of B and T lymphocytes as function of time, i.e. $\int_0^t B(\tau)d\tau$ and $\int_0^t T(\tau)d\tau$ respectively. The functions are plotted in Figure 2. Figure shows that TF mouse produces a larger specific repertoire than NTF mouse and here we can better appreciate differences for the cytotoxic T lymphocytes. Results suggest that this should due to a small difference in the initial repertoire.

To find an answer to this question, we considered the cumulative number of *naive* B and T lymphocytes as function of time, i.e. lymphocytes produced by bone marrow and thymus that are not correlated with vaccination's stimuli. For T lymphocytes differences are not relevant. Figure 3 shows preliminary results for B lymphocytes.

From the figure one can envisage that TF mouse produces a higher amount of specific naive B cells than the NTF one. This probably helps the mouse in developing a more aggressive response against tumor ensuring survival with less vaccine injections. However our simulator, in its present state, has a repertoire which is too small compared with the natural one. Our next step will be to increase the size of the repertoire to investigate differences between TF and NTF mice.

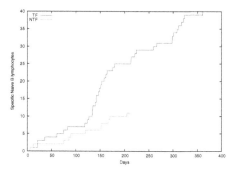

Fig. 3. Cumulative behavior for naive specific B (against tumor associated antigen) for NTF mouse

4   Conclusions and Perspectives

We presented a first trial to investigate biological differences which characterizes a set of mice respect to their response to a vaccination schedule. We found that in our case the environment is not critical. We showed that the relevant difference should lie in the specific repertoire. We plan to extend the model in order to catch differences in initial repertoire. Results in this way will be published in due course.

Acknowledgments

This work was supported under the EC contract FP6-2004-IST-4, No. 028069 (ImmunoGrid). FP and SM acknowledge partial support from University of Catania research grant and MIUR PRIN 2006. PLL acknowledges financial support from the University of Bologna, the Department of Experimental Pathology ("Pallotti" fund), MIUR and the Italian Association for Cancer Research (AIRC).

References

1. Croci, S., Nicoletti, G., Landuzzi, L., De Giovanni, C., Astolfi, A., Marini, C., Di Carlo, E., Musiani, P., Forni, G., Nanni, P., Lollini1, P.-L.: Immunological Prevention of a Multigene Cancer Syndrome. Cancer Research 64, 8428–8434 (2004)
2. De Giovanni, C., Nicoletti, G., Landuzzi, L., Astolfi, A., Croci, S., Comes, A., Ferrini, S., Meazza, R., Iezzi, M., Di Carlo, E., Musiani, P., Cavallo, F., Nanni, P., Lollini, P.-L.: Immunoprevention of HER-2/neu transgenic mammary carcinoma through an interleukin 12-engineered allogeneic cell vaccine. Cancer Res. 64(11), 4001–4009 (2004)
3. Lollini, P.-L., Motta, S., Pappalardo, F.: Discovery of cancer vaccination protocols with a genetic algorithm driving an agent based simulator, BMC Bioinformatics. vol. 7: 352, (2006) doi:10.1186/1471-2105-7-352

4. Lollini, P.-L., Motta, S., Pappalardo, F.: Modeling tumor immonology. Mathematical Models and Methods in Applied Sciences 16(Suppl. 1), 1091 (2006)
5. Motta, S., Lollini, P.-L., Castiglione, F., Pappalardo, F.: Modelling Vaccination Schedules for a Cancer Immunoprevention Vaccine. Immunome Research 1(5) (2005) doi:10.1186/1745-7580-1-5
6. Nanni, P., Nicoletti, G., De Giovanni, C., Landuzzi, L., Di Carlo, E., Cavallo, F., Pupa, S.M., Rossi, I., Colombo, M.P., Ricci, C., Astolfi, A., Musiani, P., Forni, G., Lollini, P.-L.: Combined allogeneic tumor cell vaccination and systemic interleukin 12 prevents mammary carcinogenesis in HER-2/neu transgenic mice. J. Exp. Med., 194(9), 1195–1205 (2001)
7. Pappalardo, F., Lollini, P.-L., Castiglione, F., Motta, S.: Modelling and Simulation of Cancer Immunoprevention vaccine. Bioinformatics 21(12), 2891–2897 (2005)
8. Pappalardo, F., Mastriani, E., Lollini, P.-L., Motta, S.: Genetic Algorithm against Cancer. In: Bloch, I., Petrosino, A., Tettamanzi, A.G.B. (eds.) WILF 2005. LNCS (LNAI), vol. 3849, p. 223. Springer, Heidelberg (2006)

Solving Protein Structures Using Molecular Replacement Via Protein Fragments

Jayavardhana Gubbi[1], Michael Parker[2], and Marimuthu Palaniswami[1]

[1] Department of Electrical and Electronic Engineering,
The University of Melbourne,
Victoria 3010, Australia
{jrgl, swami}@ee.unimelb.edu.au
[2] Biota Structural Biology Laboratory,
St. Vincents Institute of Medical Research, Melbourne,
Victoria 3065, Australia
mparker@svi.edu.au

Abstract. The need to determine phases is a major bottleneck in a fully automated X-ray crystallography pipeline. The problem commonly called *phasing* can be solved by a computational method called molecular replacement (MR). With the deposition of more and more proteins into the Protein Data Bank (PDB), it has been shown that the MR yields better *initial models*. In this paper, *ab initio* first model generation is addressed. A novel scheme using *PHASER* is proposed which does not require any *a priori* information about the structure. The input to the system is the target structure factors and the sequence. We created a unique set of supersecondary structure (fragment) dataset and used them in creation of the first model. The method was evaluated with log-likelihood gain (LLG) and translational Z-score (TFZ) as defined by *PHASER*. The results obtained are highly encouraging with translation Z-scores of 7 and above for the first model. The proposed scheme is tested on six proteins, two each from α, β and $\alpha + \beta$ classes with very good results.

1 Introduction

The knowledge about the three dimensional protein structure is important in understanding its function and interaction with other molecules. This will lead to the designing of new and better drugs. X-ray crystallography is the most popular technique for visualizing 3D structure of proteins. More than 80% of the known protein structures deposited in the Protein Data Bank or PDB [1] are solved using protein crystallography. The determination of protein structure via X-ray crystallography is accomplished in three stages [2]: (i) Preparation of crystals from purified protein (ii) Collection of diffraction pattern data from crystals and (iii) Construction of model from the diffraction data. The diffraction data obtained from the crystal contains only the magnitude information and the phase information is absent. The absence of phase information becomes the bottleneck in solving the protein structure from diffraction patterns. The determination of

F. Masulli, S. Mitra, and G. Pasi (Eds.): WILF 2007, LNAI 4578, pp. 627–634, 2007.
© Springer-Verlag Berlin Heidelberg 2007

phases in X-ray crystallography is called *phasing* [3,4]. Both experimental and computational methods are used to solve the phase problem [5,4].

Molecular Replacement [6] is a computational technique which is used to solve the phase problem by making use of phases from a known structure. Basically, this involves two steps (a) finding a similar structure by a standard fold recognition method [7] (b) aligning the model structure to target structure in the unit cell of the crystal. It is well accepted that if the protein sequence identity of the two proteins is greater than 35% then the proteins very likely have similar structure [8]. This knowledge is used in homology modeling to determine if a similar protein fold exists in the PDB. However this becomes challenging when the sequence identity is less than 25% [8]. The increase in the number of solved structure in PDB has led to the molecular replacement technique becoming increasingly popular for *phasing*. It is important to note that the success of molecular replacement depends on the alignment accuracy [9]. A few very popular molecular replacement methods currently supported by The Collaborative Computational Project Number 4 (CCP4) [10] are PHASER [11,12], AMORE [13], MOLREP [14], CaspR [15], MrBump [16] and BALBES [17].

A few attempts have been made in *ab initio* molecular replacement. Strop et. al. [18] have used various sized helix fragments for phasing symmetric helical membrane proteins with good success. They use different sized alpha helices and the knowledge of helical membrane proteins as constraints to generate the first model. An evolutionary computational approach to calculate the phases has been proposed by Webster and Hilgenfeld [19]. The prototype that they have developed for *ab initio* phase detection is significantly different from our approach. They use only the diffraction pattern and employ genetic algorithm to solve the phase problem. In 1998, Cowtan [20] proposed a modified translation function and applied it to molecular fragment location. In this work, he used five to ten residue helix and strand fragment to fit low quality maps. RESOLVE [21] which is a fully automated model building scheme uses helices and strands of different lengths to generate the model with Fourier transform based approaches.

Ab initio molecular replacement from protein fragments is addressed in this paper. We concentrate on generating the *first model* for proteins which have sequence identity less than 20% via super secondary fragments. The input to the system is the target diffraction pattern data and the target sequence. The output is the first model which can be used for subsequent refinement oriented in the direction similar to the target structure. As far as the authors are aware, this is the first time such an attempt has been made in *ab initio* molecular replacement using protein fragments. The method proposed uses PHASER [11,12] to accomplish the task. As compared to [20], our work involves the use of large repetitive fragments and a working strategy based on PHASER (which uses maximum likelihood). In [11], the solution of ROP four-helix bundle is obtained in a similar way as compared to the proposed scheme. In RESOLVE [21], only short helical and strand fragments are used to refine the model as compared to our super-secondary structures. In all the proposed methods so far, no single strategy to generate the first model across protein topologies has been proposed.

We have developed a working strategy to generate the first model from super secondary fragments.

2   Molecular Replacement

The idea of molecular replacement method is to obtain the unknown phases of the target using phases from a known structure in the PDB (called the model). Although these phases are not exactly the same, using further refinements, it is possible to solve the structure. It has been observed that, as the sequence identity increases above 40%, molecular replacement is almost sure to give the solution [4]. The success of MR would increase with the increase in the number of solved structures in the PDB.

Even thought the structures of the model and the target are similar, the model needs to be correctly positioned in the unit cell. Hence it becomes important to align them before using the phase information of the model in MR. All the popular molecular replacement methods like PHASER [11,12], AMORE [13] and MOLREP [14] try to achieve this task using various computational techniques. The difference between these methods is in the way they achieve the alignment. The basic idea of molecular replacement is to use a rotation function to orient the known structure to the target structure within the unit cell. Rotation is followed by the translation function which moves the given structure to match the position of the target structure. This principle is illustrated in figure 1 where 'm' is the model, 'O' is the target, 'R' is the rotation function and 'T' is the translation function. The model is first rotated with function R to get mR and mR is translated with function T to achieve the final alignment. This leads to a six parameter search, three for rotation followed by three for translation. Let $|F_{obs}|$ be the observed structure factor from the experiment and the structure factor calculated from the model be $|F_{calc}|$ [4,5]. The observed $|F_{obs}|$ and calculated $|F_{calc}|$ are compared using R-Factor given by eq. 1:

$$R = \frac{\sum ||F_{obs}| - |F_{calc}||}{\sum |F_{obs}|} \tag{1}$$

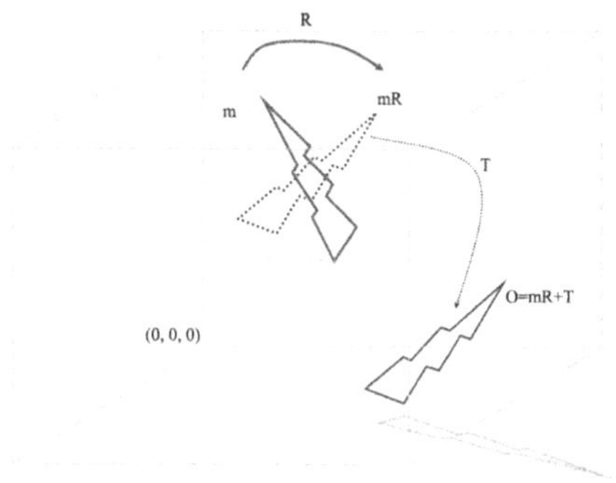

Fig. 1. Illustration of Molecular Replacement

The model which gives the R value of 0.3 to 0.4 [5] is selected as the first model to be used in further refinements. Once the initial phases α_{calc} are available, the initial electron density of the diffraction pattern is calculated using eq. 2 [5]:

$$\rho(x, y, z) = \frac{1}{V} \sum_h \sum_k \sum_l |F_{hkl}^{obs}| e^{-2\pi i (hx + ky + lz - \alpha_{hkl}^{calc})} \qquad (2)$$

where ρ is the electron density, x, y, z are the coordinates in real space; h, k, l are the coordinates in reciprocal space, $|F_{hkl}^{obs}|$ is experimentally the observed structure factor and α_{hkl}^{calc} is the calculated phase from the model. In all our experiments we use PHASER [11,12] which is based on maximum likelihood for rigid body alignment. PHASER has several modes to perform alignment tasks out of which we use MR_FRF (Fast Rotation Function) and MR_FTF (Fast Translation Function). The input to the PHASER is the target structure factors and the model protein. The output is the positioned search model.

3   Fragment Dataset

To demonstrate our proposed technique, we choose six CATH topologies [22] as shown in table 1. The dataset we chose contained 39 topologies [23] with sequence identity less than 25%. From each topology, we chose one protein randomly for testing the proposed technique. This is our preliminary fragment (super secondary structure) dataset. Totally, we extracted 17 fragments for α class, 22 fragments for β class and 16 fragments for $\alpha + \beta$ class.

Table 1. Topologies used for demonstrating the proposed method. Test protein column gives the PDB code of the test protein used from the corresponding topology.

CATH Code (C.A.T)	Topology Name	Test Protein	Number of Sequences	Class
1.10.10	Arc Repressor Mutant subunit A	1JHF	15	α
1.20.120	Four Helix Bundle (Hemerythrin (Met), subunit A)	1OQC	11	α
2.60.120	Jelly Rolls	1GNY	22	β
2.60.40	Immunoglobulin-like	1DQT	38	β
3.20.20	Bactericidal permeability-increasing protein; domain 2	1CT5	34	$\alpha + \beta$
3.40.50	Rossmann fold	1AKY	85	$\alpha + \beta$

4   Proposed Methodology

In this section, we give the description of the proposed methodology. Figure 2 gives the flow chart of the proposed technique using PHASER. The input is the diffraction data of the target, sequence of the target and the template library containing several super secondary structure templates in the form of PDB files. The fragment dataset created is arranged in decreasing order of the molecular weights. The iterative methodology proposed is as follows:

1. The first fragment is used as an ensemble and input into PHASER in
   MR_AUTO mode. If there is a successful hit with translation function Z-
   score $TFZ > 5$ and log-likelihood gain $LLG > 30$, the solution is placed
   in the solution library. If it is unsuccessful, next fragment is chosen until a
   solution is obtained. In case solution exists, the same fragment is repeated
   again to check if there are multiple fragments of the same kind. There will
   be significant increase in TFZ and LLG scores if it is true. Otherwise we
   move on to the next step.
2. In the second step, the next fragment from the template library is chosen
   and the target pattern is subjected to rotation (MR_FRF) and translation
   (MR_FTF) functions along with the previous solution. At this step, if the
   solution exists for more than 70% of the target, the TFZ score will be more
   than 10. If it is greater than 10, we stop the iteration with the final solution
   in the solution library.
3. If TFZ was not greater than 10, next fragment is chosen and step 2 is repeated populating the solution library.
4. Step 2 and 3 are continued until $TFZ > 10$ or no more fragments are left in
   the fragment dataset. If there are no fragments in the dataset, partial model
   is obtained.

The method described above is very similar to a tree search and pruning strategy [11]. However, unlike this method, we build the fragment data set and the
order of fragment usage is based on molecular weight of the fragment. The
proposed method is a more general scheme and can be used across topologies.

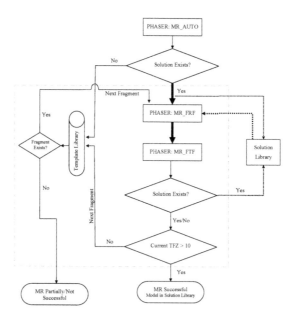

Fig. 2. Proposed MR Method using PHASER

5 Results and Discussion

The preliminary results of the proposed scheme was highly encouraging. To confirm that we are moving in the right direction, a small protein 1D0D (chain B) with 58 residues was considered. We created a reference dataset with three disjoint fragments (*helix* only, *beta-turn-beta*, *beta-turn-alpha*) from the same protein. We used the proposed scheme to generate the first model. The first model generated had a phaser score of $TFZ = 8.3$ with 86% residues aligned at 0.88 Å. The R-factor as measured with SFCHECK [10] was 0.32 with a correlation of 0.68. This little experiment motivated us to test our scheme on a large scale with super-secondary fragments.

The results for the six test proteins are summarized in table 2. The first column is the protein name as given by the authors, second column is the length of the sequence. However, the system works on multiple chains as well. Third column is the TFZ score obtained by PHASER. Fourth column is the R-factor as obtained by SFCHECK [10] and is calculated between the structure factor file and the model file generated by PHASER. As all the proteins used in our experiments are already solved, we used the final protein and the *first model* to check the alignment using DeepView [24]. Fifth and the sixth columns indicate the percentage of residues aligned and the RMSD error between the final protein and the first model generated by our scheme. The TFZ scores is more than seven for all the proteins indicating that the molecular replacement solution exists and it is valid. For 1DQT, the TFZ is the highest and the percentage of residues solved is aligned at 87%. The computational complexity of the proposed scheme is dependent on several factors. For 1CT5, the time consumed was the highest as it is a large sequence and the number of fragments required to generate the protein was more. It took approximately thirty CPU hours on a P4 2.4 GHz PC with 1.5GB of RAM. Interestingly, for 1JHF which has 191 residues, it took only eight CPU hours. The results obtained for both these proteins are very similar because of large matching fragment 3. The effect of the length of the protein fragments is also very important. If the length of the fragment is larger, the solution is comparatively faster but it becomes more specific to a particular topology. Similarly if the fragment is too small, it has the tendency to fit itself

Table 2. Results for the test set

Protein Structure	Sequence Length	TFZ score of the first model	R-factor	Residues Aligned (%)	RMSD in Å (Main Chain)
Lexa G85d Mutant (1JHF)	197	9.1	0.37	72	1.39
Augmenter Of Liver Regeneration (1OQC)	112	11.3	0.32	81	0.68
Xylan-Binding Module Cbm15 (1GNY)	153	14	0.31	86	0.8
Murine Ctla4-Cd152 (1DQT)	117	24.6	0.28	87	0.69
Yeast Hypothetical Protein (1CT5)	228	7	0.36	78	1.46
Adenylate Kinase (1AKY)	218	8.3	0.33	82	1.23

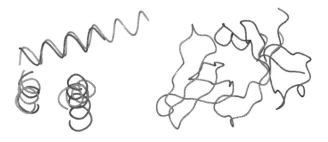

Fig. 3. Two sections of superposed target structure - 1JHF (Red) with generated model from fragments (Green)

at several positions with reasonably acceptable Z-score. Hence it is very important to choose appropriate sized fragments. In our dataset, the longest protein fragment weighs 6kDa. Due to the fact that the fragment database is arranged according to the decreasing order of molecular weight, the small fragments at the end of the search will have very few orientations left to fit themselves leading to increase in computational efficiency.

6   Conclusions

Preparation of the first model using *ab initio* molecular replacement is addressed in this paper. Protein super-secondary fragments dataset is curated from existing models in the PDB. A novel working strategy based on PHASER is proposed and is shown to successfully work on six different proteins with good result. The generated model is evaluated using log-likelihood gain (LLG) and translational Z-score (TFZ). The highest TFZ of 24.6 is obtained on Murine CTLA4-CD152 protein (1DQT). The effect of fragment length and computational complexity is discussed.

References

1. Berman, H.M., Westbrook, J., Feng, Z., Gilliland, G., Bhat, T.N., Weissig, H., Shindyalov, I.N., Bourne, P.E.: The protein data bank. Nucleic Acids Research 28, 235–242 (2000)
2. Abola, E., Kuhn, P., Earnest, T., Stevens, R.C.: Automation of x-ray crystallography. Nature structural biology, Structural Genomic Supplement, 973–977 (2000)
3. Lamzin, V.S., Perrakis, A.: Current state of automated crystallographic data analysis. Nature structural biology, Structural Genomic Supplement, 978–981 (2000)
4. Drenth, J.: Principles of Protein X-Ray Crystallography, 2nd edn. Springer, New York (1999)
5. Rhodes, G.: Crystallography Made Crystal Clear, 2nd edn. Academic Press, San Diego (2000)
6. Rossmann, M.G., Blow, D.M.: The detection of sub-units within the crystallographic asymmetric unit. Acta Crystallographica 15, 24–31 (1962)

7. Jones, D.T.: Evaluating the potential of using fold-recognition models for molecular replacement. Acta Crystallographica D57, 1428–1434 (2001)
8. Rost, B.: Twilight zone of protein sequence alignments. Protein Engineering 12(2), 85–94 (1999)
9. Schwarzenbacher, R., Godzik, A., Grzenchnik, S.K., Jaroszewski, L.: The importance of alignment accuracy for molecular replacement. Acta Crystallographica D60, 1229–1236 (2004)
10. Collaborative Computational Project Number 4. The CCP4 suite: programs for protein crystallography. Acta Crystallographica Section D, 50(5), pp.760–763 (1994)
11. McCoy, A.J.: Solving structures of protein complexes by mlecular replacement with Phaser. Acta Crystallographica D63, 32–41 (2007)
12. Read, R.J.: Pushing the boundaries of molecular replacement with maximum likelihood. Acta Crystallographica D57, 1373–1382 (2001)
13. Navaza, G.: AMORE: an automated package for molecular replacement. Acta Crystallographica A50, 157–163 (1994)
14. Vagin, A., Teplyakov, A.: MOLREP: an automated program for molecular replacement. Journal of Applied Crystallography 30, 1022–1025 (1997)
15. Claude, J.-B., Suhre, K., Notredame, C., Claverie, C., Abergel, J.M.: CaspR: a webserver for automated molecular replacement using homology modelling. Nucleic Acids Research 32, W606–W609 (2004)
16. Bahar, M., et al.: Others. SPINE workshop on automated X-ray analysis: a progress report. Acta Crystallographica D62, 1170–1183 (2006)
17. Long, F., Vagin, A.A., Murshudov, G.N.: Complete automation of molecular replacement in BALBES. CCP4 Study Weekend (Abstract, 2007)
18. Strop, P., Brzustowicz, M.R., Brunger, A.T.: Ab initio molecular replacement phasing for symmetric helical membrane proteins. Acta Crystallographica D63, 188–196 (2007)
19. Webster, G., Hilgenfeld, R.: An evolutionary computational approach to the phase problem in macromolecular X-ray crystallography. Acta Crystallographica A57, 351–358 (2001)
20. Cowtan, K.: Modified Phased Translation Functions and their application to Molecular-Fragment location. Acta Crystallographica D54, 750–756 (1998)
21. Terwilliger, T.C.: Automated main-chain model building by template matching and iterative fragment extension. Acta Crystallographica D59, 38–44 (2003)
22. Orengo, C.A., Michie, A.D., Jones, S., Jones, D.T., Swindells, M.B., Thornton, J.M.: Cath- a hierarchic classification of protein domain structures. Structure 5(8), 1093–1108 (1997)
23. Gubbi, J., Shilton, A., Parker, M., Palaniswami, M.: Protein topology classification using two-stage support vector machines. Genome Informatics 17(2), 259–269 (2006)
24. Guex, N., Peitsch, M.C.: SWISS-MODEL and the Swiss-PdbViewer: An environment for comparative protein modeling. Electrophoresis 18, 2714–2723 (1997)

An Interactive Tool for the Management and Visualization of Mass-Spectrometry Proteomics Data

Mario Cannataro[1], Giovanni Cuda[2], Marco Gaspari[2], and Pierangelo Veltri[1]

[1] Bioinformatics Laboratory
[2] Proteomics Laboratory
University Magna Græcia of Catanzaro, Italy
{cannataro, cuda, gaspari, veltri}@unicz.it

Abstract. The paper presents a software platform for the management and visualization of mass spectrometry proteomics data. MALDI-TOF and LC-MS spectra can be visualized by considering different parameters or by focusing on portions of spectra. Spectra can also be converted using the XML-based mzData standard for storing or for transmission over the network.

Keywords: Mass Spectrometry, Spectra Visualization, Proteomics, mzData.

1 Introduction

Mass spectrometry (MS) is a technique allowing to determine with high accuracy the molecular weight of chemical compounds, ranging from small molecules to large, polar biopolymers [1]. The mass spectrometer separates gas phase ions according to their m/z (mass to charge ratio) values. The output of the spectrometer, said spectrum, is a (large) sequence of value pairs. Each pair contains a measured *intensity*, which depends on the quantity of the detected biomolecule, and a mass to charge ratio (m/z), which depends on the molecular mass of the detected biomolecule.

A MS platform includes: (i) a system to input the biological sample into the spectrometer, (ii) a ionization system, (iii) a mass analyzer, (iv) a ion detector, (v) a software system to store and analyze spectra. The sample can be inserted directly into the ionization source, or can undergo some type of separation, such as Liquid Chromatography (LC), Gas Chromatography (GC), or Capillary Electrophoresis (CE), where the sample is separated into different components which enter the spectrometer sequentially for individual analysis. Concerning the MS analysis of large, polar biomolecules, commonly used ionization techniques are Electrospray Ionization (ESI) and Matrix-Assisted Laser Desorption/Ionization (MALDI), coupled with different kind of mass analyzers such as Time Of Flight (TOF) or quadrupole ion traps. Tandem mass spectrometers (MS/MS) have more than one analyzer and can be used for structural and sequencing studies.

In MS (e.g. MALDI-TOF MS) a single sample is analyzed producing a unique spectrum. In MS/MS, the first MS selects some precursor ions (e.g. those having the higher *intensity*), then they collide in a collision cell between the two spectrometers and undergo fragmentation. The resulting daughter ions are analyzed in the second MS. Thus MS/MS produces a spectrum for each precursor ion selected by the first MS. Such spectrum can be used for protein/peptide identification. For very complex and rich samples

F. Masulli, S. Mitra, and G. Pasi (Eds.): WILF 2007, LNAI 4578, pp. 635–642, 2007.
© Springer-Verlag Berlin Heidelberg 2007

a preliminary chromatographic separation eases the MS analysis. In LC-MS analysis, a sample is injected onto an LC column and separated into its various components. The components are then passed into the MS through an electrospray interface. The *retention time* of the solute is defined as the elapsed time between the time of injection of the solute and the time of elution of the maximum peak of that solute. Since different components are passed to the MS at different times, LC-MS produces a set of spectra. Usually the MS is programmed to acquire a spectrum (scan) at fixed-time intervals.

From this brief introduction it is clear that MS can produce different kind of data where a single spectrum can have different meaning according to the type of performed analysis (e.g., MS, MS/MS, LC-MS). Although spectra are more and more analyzed with semi-automatic techniques, visual inspection of graphical representation of spectra may be needed. For instance, visualization can be used if the user want to focus on specific peaks or on a portion of a spectrum, or when few spectra are available and a manual, visual inspection, is feasible. Usually, mass spectrometers provide a basic visualization tool able to load and visualize the produced spectra, but usually those tools do not support the different available spectra data formats, nor provide sophisticated visualization functions. Moreover, such software usually support proprietary file formats, that are inefficient for data sharing and transmission. The paper presents SpectraViewer, a software platform for the visualization and management of mass spectrometry proteomics data. Currently, MALDI-TOF and LC-MS spectra can be visualized by considering different parameters or by focusing on portions of spectra. Spectra can also be converted in the XML-based mzData [11] standard allowing efficient storing and transmission over the network. After introducing MS data and mzData standard in Section 2, Section 3 presents the SpectraViewer tool discussing the visualization and mzData conversion of some real spectra. Section 4 describes related work. Section 5 summarizes the paper and describes future work.

2   Mass Spectrometry Data

Mass Spectrometry can be used to perform different type of analysis: MS produces a single spectrum related to a sample, LC-MS produces different spectra related to a single sample and collected at different scan times, LC-MS/MS at each scan time selects one or more precursor ions that are then fragmented and whose spectrum is produced as output. Data mining is usually used to find discriminant peaks between healthy and diseased subjects in collection of spectra, while in MS/MS computational methods are used to identify the peptides/proteins present in the samples. Nevertheless, spectra visualization as analysis technique may be useful in many cases, for instance to compare spectra when few biological samples are available (e.g. rare diseases) or to guide the user in the inspection of single peaks.

Figure 1 shows a fragment of a LC-MS spectrum generated by the Applied Biosystems [2] QSTAR XL Hybrid LC-MS/MS system coupled with the Dionex Corporation UltiMate Nano and Capillary LC systems. The spectrum file, in proprietary WIFF format or in the standard JCAMP-DX format (file extension jdx), has been produced by

```
##TITLE=Sample001                       ##SCAN NUMBER=1          ##SCAN NUMBER=654
##JCAMP-DX=5.00                          ##BASE PEAK=519.1687     ##BASE PEAK=519.1516
##DATA TYPE=MASS SPECTRUM                ##BASE PEAK INT=1.120e+2 ##BASE~PEAK~INT=1.780e+2
##DATA CLASS=PEAKTABLE                    ##RETENTION TIME=4.04    ##RETENTION~TIME=3296.59
##DATE=May. 23 2005, 4:55:40 PM          ##TIC=5.772e+3           ##TIC=6.693e+3
##SOURCE REFERENCE=D:\name.wiff          ##NPOINTS=141            ##NPOINTS=160
##OWNER=N/A                               ##XYDATA=(XY..XY)        ##XYDATA=(XY..XY)
##IONIZATION MODE=Positive               429.0630,3.500e+1        429.0630,2.700e+1
##SPECTROMETER/DATA SYSTEM=SCIEX         429.0708,5.300e+1        429.0708,3.300e+1
##SCAN_RANGE=400.0,1200.0                429.0785,4.600e+1        429.0785,4.000e+1
##XUNITS=m/z                              ...                      ...
##YUNITS=cps                                                       ##END=
```

Fig. 1. Fragment of a LC-MS spectrum containing 654 scans

the Applied Biosystems Analyst QS software, and contains 654 scans. JCAMP-DX is a chemical spectroscopic data exchange format that can be stored as a flat text file, comprising an header containing information about the experiment (metadata), and a body containing the spectra data, usually a table of (*m/z, intensity*) couples. In Figure 1, the left column describes the main metadata of a the header, while the central and right columns contains the spectra data. A MALDI-TOF spectrum, e.g. generated by the Applied Biosystems Voyager DE-STR MALDI-TOF MS, contains just a scan. Both spectrometers are available at the Proteomics Laboratory of the University of Catanzaro, Italy.

Another important aspect in spectra management is the use of standard formats for data sharing and transmission, as well as efficient coding for data storage. *mz-Data* is an emerging XML-based data model defined by HUPO-PSI (Human Proteome Organization-Proteomics Standard Initiative) to standardize mass spectrometry-based experimental data [11]. mzData schema comprises a *description* element describing metadata about the experiment (e.g. administrative information, data about instrument and software used to generate the spectra), and a *spectrumList* element that encloses a set of *spectrum* elements. Each spectrum element stores, respectively, all the *m/z* and *intensities* values of the spectrum as Base64 encoded strings. The Base64 encoding [3] is designed to represent arbitrary sequences of octets through a 65-character alphabet, enabling 6 bits to be represented as printable character. Base64 allows to convert binary data or 8-bit characters in a format that can be transmitted over any Internet protocol and can be stored into XML documents.

3   SpectraViewer

SpectraViewer is a Java-based tool for the three-dimensional (3D) visualization of spectra data and their conversion into the mzData format. It uses the Java3D API [6] for graphic manipulation and is deployed to the user through the Java Web Start technology [7], i.e. it can be simply invoked by a web browser running the Java Virtual Machine, possibly on any hardware/software platform. The software is freely available at [13].

3.1 Spectra Visualization

The main visualization functions offered by SpectraViewer are:

1. 3D visualization of a LC-MS spectrum or of many MALDI-TOF spectra; images can be translated, zoomed, or rotated by using the mouse;
2. 2D visualization of MALDI-TOF and LC-MS spectra. The former are visualized in the (m/z, intensity) plane, while the latter can be visualized in the (m/z, intensity), (m/z, retention time), and (retention time, intensity) planes;
3. interactive visualization of ion properties on the (m/z, retention time) plane.

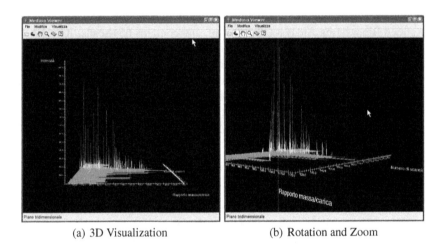

(a) 3D Visualization   (b) Rotation and Zoom

Fig. 2. 3D visualization of a LC-MS spectrum

Figure 2 shows the 3D visualization modes of SpectraViewer (images were taken by using a version of the software with Italian menu). Figure 2(a) shows the default 3D visualization, while Figure 2(b) shows the same spectrum after rotation and zoom. In particular the user may zoom, move and rotate the graphic using the mouse. The spectrum showed in Figure 2 is a LC-MS spectrum containing 654 scans with an average number of 150 peaks per scan, and occupies 2,491,472 bytes. A fragment of such spectrum is showed in Figure 1.

Figure 3 shows the main interface of SpectraViewer and the 2D visualizations of a LC-MS spectrum. Figure 3(a) shows an informative window about the loaded spectrum, while the (m/z, intensity), (retention time, intensity), and (m/z, retention time) 2D planes are respectively showed in Figure 3(b), 3(c), and 3(d). Intensity level is showed with a scale of colors, from green (low) to red (high).

An important function of SpectraViewer is its ability to interactively show information about specific ions specified by the user. Figure 4 shows the ion selection window

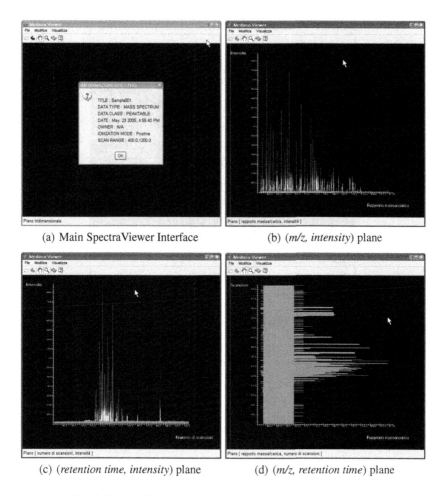

(a) Main SpectraViewer Interface   (b) (*m/z, intensity*) plane

(c) (*retention time, intensity*) plane   (d) (*m/z, retention time*) plane

Fig. 3. SpectraViewer User Interface and 2D visualization modes

where, in the (*m/z, retention time*) plane, the user can inspect the spectrum data by navigating among peaks. The lower part of the window shows the *m/z, intensity,* and *retention time* of the selected ion. The user can navigate along the *m/z* or the *retention time* axes by using the provided Left, Right, Up, and Down buttons. The user can vary the amplitude of browsing along *m/z* or *retention time* by simply providing a cursor speed parameter in the related field. When the user moves along the spectrum data, the selected ion is underlined and its *m/z, intensity,* and *retention time* are presented in the bottom part of the window. It should be noted that such information is colored according to the intensity level of the selected ion (green, yellow and red for respectively low, medium and high intensity). In such a way the user can easily find high intensity ions during spectrum navigation by observing ion color.

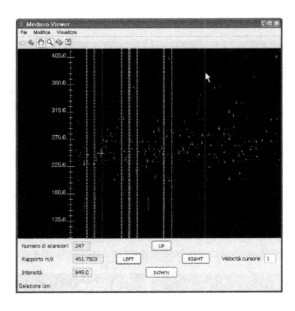

Fig. 4. Ion selection window

Table 1. Sizes and compression factors for LC-MS spectra, sizes in Bytes

Spectrum No	jdx size	mzData size	Compression factor
1	864,834	494,726	57.20%
2	1,424,022	907,694	63.74%
3	2,491,472	1,511,114	60,65%

3.2   Spectra Conversion

The main functions related to spectra management and mzData conversion are:

1. loading of a JCAMP-DX file;
2. conversion and storing of the current JCAMP-DX file in mzData;
3. loading of an mzData file;
4. conversion and storing of the current mzData file in JCAMP-DX;

The conversion of a spectrum in mzData is made by mapping the header fields of JCAMP-DX into the metadata information of mzData and by converting the body data, i.e. the couples (*m/z, intensity*), in the Base64 encoding. Figure 5 shows a fragment of the mzData file obtained by converting the LC-MS spectrum of Figure 1.

In our system, 32-bit float numbers representing *m/z* and *intensity* values are grouped to form 24-bit groups that are converted in 4 characters. Compression arises since float numbers are represented as strings in the jdx file. Table 1 shows the sizes of three LC-MS spectra in jdx and mzData format. It is possible to note an average 60% decrease of the spectra size.

```
<?xml version="1.0" encoding="UTF-8"?>
<mzData version="">
 <description>
  <admin>
   <sampleName />
   <sourceFile>
    <nameOfFile>bsa-2.mzData</nameOfFile>
    <pathToFile>D:/dataset-cibb/bsa-2.mzData</pathToFile>
    <fileType>mzData</fileType>
   </sourceFile>
   <contact>
    <name>name of administrator</name>
    <institution>name of institution</institution>
    <contactInfo>email</contactInfo>
   </contact>
  </admin>
  <instrument>
   <instrumentName>name of instrument</instrumentName>
   <analyzerList count="1">
    <analyzer>name of analyzer</analyzer>
   </analyzerList>
   <detector />
   <additional>additional information</additional>
  </instrument>
 </description>
 <spectrumList count="654">
  <spectrum id="1">
   <mzArrayBinary>
    <data precision="32" endian="little" length="141">Q6r4E ...</data>
   </mzArrayBinary>
   <intenArrayBinary>
    <data precision="32" endian="little" length="141">QgwAA ...</data>
   </intenArrayBinary>
  </spectrum>

  ...
 </spectrumList>
</mzData>
```

Fig. 5. Fragment of the mzData version of a LC-MS spectrum

4   Related Work

In the following we briefly recall some existing spectra visualization or spectra conversion systems, considering their different visualization and conversion modes.

JDXview [8] displays various kinds of spectra in JCAMP-DX format. Furthermore, it allows zooming and measuring of distances on a spectrum and supports graphics output in vector graphics format. It does not support mzData conversion nor 3D visualization.

Pep3D [9,12] supports LC-MS and LC-MS/MS spectra but does not provide 3D visualization nor mzData conversion. In Pep3D data are represented as a two dimensional density plot. For MS/MS experiments using collision-induced dissociation, links are embedded in the image to the daughter spectra and the corresponding peptide sequences.

mzViewer [10] is a simple lightweight viewer that allows only 2D visualization of mzData. It is a stand alone application, but Java classes are provided for incorporating the mzViewer into other applications.

CCWiffer [5] is a short name for "Charleston Core Wiff Converter". It is a simple system that only converts proprietary WIFF data into mzData or mzXML.

In summary, among the analyzed systems the most advanced spectra visualization system is Pep3D but it does not provide 3D visualization nor mzData conversion. On the other hand, SpectraViewer does not support MS/MS data and the connection between spectra and identified peptides.

5   Conclusions and Future Work

The paper presented a software platform for the management and visualization of mass spectrometry data. The tools offers different visualization modes and the possibility to inspect ions properties, as well as the conversion to mzData format. Future work will regard the visualization of LC-MS/MS spectra and related identified peptides, and the storing of mzData files in a native XML database to support XQuery-based spectra querying. Finally, SpectraViewer will be embedded in the MS-Analyzer platform [4].

References

1. Aebersold, R., Mann, M.: Mass spectrometry-based proteomics. Nature 422, 198–207 (2003)
2. AppliedBiosystems. http://www.appliedbiosystem.com;
3. Base64. http://www.ietf.org/rfc/rfc3548.txt?number=3548
4. Cannataro, M., Veltri, P.: Ms-analyzer: preprocessing and data mining services for proteomics applications on the grid. Concurrency and Computation: Practice and Experience, Published Online: 19 Dec 2006 (2006) doi: 10.1002/cpe.1144
5. CCWiffer.:
   http://www.charlestoncore.org/docs/ccwiffer/usermanual.html
6. Java3D. http://java.sun.com/products/java-media/3D/
7. JavaWebStartTechnology. http://java.sun.com/products/javawebstart/
8. JDXview. http://merian.pch.univie.ac.at/pch/nh_info.html
9. Li, X.J., Pedrioli, P.G., Eng, J., Martin, D., Yi, E.C., Lee, H., Aebersold, R.: A tool to visualize and evaluate data obtained by liquid chromatography-electrospray ionization-mass spectrometry. Anal Chem. 76(13), 3856–3860 (2004)
10. mzViewer.
    http://www.bioinformatics.bbsrc.ac.uk/projects/mzviewer/
11. Orchard, S., Hermjakob, H., Apweiler, R.: The proteomics standards initiative. Proteomics 3(7), 1374–1376 (2003)
12. Pep3D. http://tools.proteomecenter.org/Pep3D.php
13. SpectraViewer.
    http://dns2.icar.cnr.it/cannataro/projects/SpectraViewer/

Smart Sequence Similarity Search(S4) System

Zhuo Chen, Arturo Concepcion, Anthony Metcalf,
Arokiya Joseph, and Laurence Bohannan

California State University San Bernardino,
San Bernardino, California, USA
zhuochen@hotmail.com, concep@csci.csusb.edu,
ametcalf@csusb.edu, ajoseph@csusb.edu,
bohannan@ncmir.ucsd.edu
http://www.csusb.edu

Abstract. Sequence similarity searching is commonly used to help clarify the biochemical and physiological features of newly discovered genes or proteins. An efficient similarity search relies on the choice of tools and their associated subprograms and numerous parameter settings. This could be very challenging for similarity search users, especially those at the beginner level. To assist researchers in selecting optimal search programs and parameter settings for efficient sequence similarity searches, we have developed a Web-based expert system, Smart Sequence Similarity Search (S4). The system is implemented in Java and Jess scripts, and uses the Jess Expert System as its reasoning core. The expert knowledge provided for a sequence similarity search is represented in the form of decision tree and stored in a XML file. The system also provides interfaces for expert users to improve this knowledge by extending the decision tree. With its capability to continuously improve sequence similarity searches through a decision tree, the Web-based expert system provides a solid advising tool for researchers interested in efficient sequence similarity searches.

Keywords: Sequence Similarity Search, Expert System.

1 Introduction

Molecular biologist today have come to greatly rely on the use of computers to aid in their research and help direct them down more promising paths. With methods such as large-scale sequencing, gene expression profiling, single-nucleotide polymorphism (SNP) discovery, and proteomics, scientists find thousands of novel DNA and protein sequences every month. The functions of newly discovered sequences can more easily be predicted with a comparison to the sequences of a database of well known existing proteins to which we already know the function and sequence. The strength of these predictions depends on the quality of the alignment between the sequences typically expressed as a degree of confidence. A high degree of confidence can infer structural, functional, and evolutionary relationships.

F. Masulli, S. Mitra, and G. Pasi (Eds.): WILF 2007, LNAI 4578, pp. 643–650, 2007.
© Springer-Verlag Berlin Heidelberg 2007

The three most widely used algorithms available online for such sequence similarity searching are Smith-Waterman, FASTA, and BLAST each of which, add different restrictions to the simple model of sequence evolution on which similarity searching is based. The online tools mentioned above provide a set of programs for different similarity searches based on the type of query sequences and database to search against. Also with each similarity search program there are several parameters that must be set prior to beginning the search, these include but are not limited to scoring matrices, E-value, filter, substitution matrices, databases, word size, and gap penalties. These parameters have a great influence over the results of the search; a slight variation in the word size or choosing a different scoring matrix by the user will affect the speed, sensitivity, and selectivity of the search. The choice of programs and its corresponding search parameters could become very challenging for similarity search users, especially for those who are at the beginners level. Even most experienced users cannot take full advantages of these tools, because they are usually not familiar with all the parameters available to them, or exactly how the settings would influence the results.

The Smart Sequence Similarity Search (S4) System developed at Cal State University; San Bernardino assists researchers in selecting optimal programs and parameter settings for efficient sequence similarity searches. A ruled-based expert system is utilized to provide expert knowledge to help users choose the best programs with the most reasonable settings, based on the users search interest so that optimal search results can be obtained. The initial knowledge base of the system is built using information obtained manually from user manuals and tutorials of NCBI BLAST Service, EBI FASTA Service and DDBJ SW Search Service or experts in this field. As for sequence similarity searches the program to use and parameters settings for the optimal search result are also mainly based on experimental knowledge acquired over prolonged period of time. Hence, the expert system in S4 is also designed to gather experimental knowledge from its expert users. The S4 expert system is designed to be a conglomeration of experimental knowledge of several expert users and mimic the decision making capabilities of the experts as close as possible.

This paper is organized as follows. Section 2 describes the functionality of S4. Section 3 is devoted to the software design of S4 system that describes the expert system of S4 and its decision tree. In Section 4 we show the systems functionalities by demonstrating how to traverse a decision tree and extend the functionality of the decision tree. Finally, we conclude in Section 5.

2   Functional Features of S4

The overall goal of this project is to assist bioinformatics researcher in selecting appropriate program and optimal parameters for their specific interests, needs and search requirements. However, S4 is not only intended to improve the effectiveness of sequence similarity searches, it also allows to gather the experimental knowledge several experts and experienced similarity search users would have gained over period of years and impart it as part of its decision making process. The functional features of S4 system are described as follows:

1 Conduct a Sequence Similarity Search Using Existing Knowledge. The user is allowed to input a sequence initially, and his/her search objective is inferred by a series of questions that the researcher must answer. Based on the inference the expert system generates appropriate program and a list of associated parameter settings that would be optimal for his/her search. If the researcher is not satisfied with the results of the expert system, and wishes to modify the search requirements he/she may repeat the question series and try other options for a favorable answer with the same sequence.

2 Sequence Similarity Search with the Suggested Settings. Users may connect to the program suggested by the expert system with the suggested parameter settings. The S4 system opens a new window of the suggested program with suggested parameter setting. Say for example, if the expert system suggested BLAST for the given sequence, it opens the NCBI BLAST search page with submitted sequence and suggested parameter settings.

3 Improve the System Suggestions. Experienced users, who are well acquainted with the similarity search of various programs, parameters and databases, can contribute to existing system knowledge. This requires the researcher to input a set of decision making questions and its related options. Each new option must be followed by another set of question and options until a final more accurate suggestion are derived.

4 Obtain Help Information. Users can get basic supporting information on each page that provides information to understand the basic concept and to choose the appropriate options.

3   Software Design of S4

S4 is a Web-based system that is available on the Internet. It uses Jess expert system shell as the logic processing core. The system is developed as a 3-tier distributed architecture. The first tier is the presentation tier that displays the user interface in a Web browser via HTML. It allows the user to interact with the system and also communicates the request/responses between the middle tier and first tier via HTTP protocol. The middle tier consists of the Web server, Jess Expert system(Ernest Friedman-Hill, Sandia National Laboratories) and XML data files. The Web server that uses Java Servlets or JSP pages handles requests from the presentation tier and responds after logic processing by the system application. The Web server in the middle tier communicates between the first and the third tier via HTTP protocol. Jess expert system is mainly responsible for the logic processing. The XML data files are for knowledge storage. The Jess expert system fires the system specified rules to make appropriate decisions based on the existing knowledge in XML data files. The third tier is one of the remote sequence similarity search servers which currently include NCBI, EMBL-EBI and DDBJ. Upon Jess determining the final program and settings, the system Web server will communicate with the third tier one of the remote sequence similarity servers. A new execution thread will be opened with the remote search form filled in automatically with the determined settings.

3.1 S4 Expert System

An expert system is a computer program that contains a knowledge base and a set of algorithms or rules that infer facts from stored knowledge and from incoming data. They are designed to perform at a human expert level and mimic the reasoning capabilities of experts in the given domain. Expert Systems are more powerful because its knowledge base is built on the knowledge of several experts. Hence it mimics the reasoning capability of not just one but several experts. S4 expert system is a rule-based expert system; the existing knowledge of the system is in the form of facts or rules that emulates the decision-making ability of an expert user.

In general the expert systems consist of four basic elements: database, knowledge base, inference engine, and user interface. The facts of the domain are stored in the database. As in the case of S4 system it is stored as a decision tree in an XML file. The facts and their corresponding rules make up the knowledge base of the system. The user interface derives the current facts scenario from the user and the inference engine decides which rules are satisfied by the current facts, prioritizes them and executes the rule with the highest priority. The inference engine of S4 expert system is supported by Jess expert system. The knowledge base is developed in Jess scripting language.

3.2 S4 Decision Tree

The facts and rules which make up the knowledge base are used by the inference engine. They are stored in the database as a decision tree. The S4 decision tree consists of nodes and branches. The construction of the decision tree is based on the available subprograms, databases, and functions of the three similarity search servers as well as their performance. Whether the decision tree branches at certain point is carefully determined to make the optimal suggestion as unique as possible. Each search option results in a unique path through the decision tree and the trajectory mimics the decision-making process by a real researcher. The decision tree diverges first at the subprogram level based on query sequence and purpose of the search. The next level is the databases and program-specific functions, which is followed by the sequence characteristics. The last level is the program performance. Divergence at different levels allows our decision tree to handle most of the commonly-used search options. The leaf nodes of the tree represents the final decision and has information on optimal search program and its parameter settings. All internal nodes in the tree are referred to as decision nodes. To better represent the knowledge included in the S4 decision tree, three types of decisions nodes are constructed: manual decision node, auto decision node, and option node.

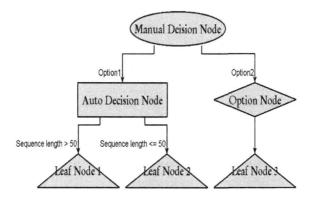

Fig. 1. *Sample Decision Tree*

Manual decision node: The location of the decision tree will move from this node to corresponding child node based on the branch the user selects.

Auto-decision node: The location of decision will move from this node to corresponding child node based on the branch automatically selected by the system using predefined branch-specific criterion.

Option node: No matter which branch the user selects, there is only one child node that the decision tree will move to. It is responsible for setting the value for a specified parameter based on the user selection.

The decision tree is presented in XML with the tree structure predefined in another XML file. Because of the large number of possible search options, there are already over 400 nodes in the populated decision tree. Whenever the user invokes the service the manual decision node, the root of the tree is the initial node. Based on the users answers the rest of the nodes(Option/Manual/Auto Decision) in the tree are traversed. See Fig 1. Whenever the expert user wishes to contribute his/her experimental knowledge, the leaf node of the decision tree will be replaced with a new sub-tree constructed with his/her new suggestions.

4   Sample Sessions

This section illustrates some of the functionalities of the S4 system by showing a sample session. First a simple sequence search is performed using a protein sequence, followed by an improvement of the existing decision tree by adding a additional manual decision node. Initially the user provides the sequence of interest to the system, the system then tries to determine which type of sequence it is. It displays the amino acid sequence query goal page to the user, see Fig 2. After selecting a search goal option of finding similar protein sequences with comprehensive database and with specific species, the suggestion page displays the parameter settings as suggested, see Fig 3. When the suggested parameters are displayed, a new window is instantiated with the suggested program so that the user can enter the parameters for the search, in

Smart Sequence Similarity Search for Bioinformatics
California State University, San Bernardino

AMINO ACID SEQUENCE QUERY GOAL

What is your query goal?

1. ○ Identify sequence
2. ◉ Find similar amino acid sequence.
3. ○ Find similar translated nucleotide sequence.
4. ○ Input peptide mixtures to find protein contains the peptides.

[CONTINUE]

Fig. 2. Amino Acid Sequence Query Goal Selection Page

Smart Sequence Similarity Search for Bioinformatics
California State University, San Bernardino

Suggestions

Sequence Name:	gi|23111051 sorting nexin 6 isoform b; tumor necrosis factor receptor-associated factor 4(TRAF4)-associated factor 2 [Homo sapiens]
Sequence Input:	MMEGLDDGPDFLSEEDRGLKAINVDLQSDAALQVDISDALSERDKVKFTVHTKSSLPNFK QNEFSVVRQHEEFIWLHDSFVENEDYAGYIIPPAPPRPDFDASREKLQKLGEGEGSMTKE EFTKMKQELEAEYLAIFKKTVAMHEVFLCRVAAHPILRRDLNFHVFLEYNQDVSVRGKNK KEKLEDFFKNMVKSADGVIVSGVKDVDDFFEHERTFLLEYHNRVKDASAKSDRMTRSHKS AADDYNRIGSSLYALGTQDSTDICKFFLKVSELFDKTRKIEARVSADEDLKLSDLLKYYL RESQAAKDLLYRRSRSLVDYENANKALDKARAKNKDVLQAETSQQLCCQKFEKISESAKQ ELIDFKTRRVAAFRKNLVELAELELKHAKGNLQLLQNCLAVLNGDT
Sequence type:	amino acid
Sequence length:	406
Program	BLAST(BLASTP)
Database	nr
ALIGNMENTS	50
WORD_SIZE	3
MATRIX_NAME	BLOSUM62
EXPECT	10
GAPCOSTS	11+1

Fig. 3. Suggestion Page for Searching Similar Proteins from a Specific Species

this case, the parameters will be automatically entered on the BLASTP search page(www.ncbi.nlm.nih.gov/blast.cgi).If the user is not satisfied by the results and decides to adjust the search goal to find similarly translated DNA sequences from bacteria or archea, but limited to the most recent updated database, the user simply chooses the try again function from the suggestion page. After the desired options are selected a new suggestion page is displayed to the user again.

The experts can also improve the performance of S4 system by including their expert knowledge of sequence similarity search. The decision tree can be easily extended by replacing a leaf node with interior nodes. For instance, an experienced user may not be satisfied with the search results that were returned in our example and may wish to update the decision tree. In such case, the page will allow the users to input the name, the title and the question to display. The options and associated parameters should also be provided by the users. Based on this information a new subtree is created and replaces the current leaf node. A new option selection page reflecting the updated decision tree is displayed. The user then may either decide to store the changes permanently or ignore them. This feature allows the decision tree to grow based on additional knowledge that the user experiences while using S4.

5   Conclusion and Future Directions

Sequence similarity search has been widely used by biologists in discovering functions, structure, and biochemical properties of novel biological sequences. An efficient similarity search relies on the choice of tools and their associated subprograms and numerous parameter settings. This could be very challenging for similarity search users, especially those at the beginner level. S4 is a Web-based expert system on biological sequence similarity search implemented in Java and Jess. It aims to help biologists choose optimal search program and corresponding parameters while conducting sequence similarity search. Several well-known online services included in the project are BLAST search from NCBI, FASTA from EBI and Smith-Waterman search from DDBJ. The decision tree with four types of nodes is chosen as an ideal data structure to store the knowledge. The knowledge is initially stored in XML format, considering its clear tree-structure data representation and high readability suitable for biologists to update knowledge directly. User interfaces are generated by servlet or JSP.

5.1   Significance and Impact

Many biologists may not have the ability nor the desire to read all the documentation that is available for sequence similarity searches. Many may find it difficult to keep pace with other advanced researchers that use sequence similarity search tools in their everyday procedures. The development of the S4 system aids the molecular biologist to reduce the learning curve for searching sequence similarity. All the sequence similarity knowledge from documents as well as experts is converted to simple easy-to-follow questions and options, allowing any researchers with basic biological knowledge to conduct a sequence similarity search. The improved accuracy of search results for researcher will be reflected in reduced experimentation research time. A powerful and useful functionality of the S4 system is its knowledge base expandability that allows improvement of the S4 expert system, functions and interfaces for incorporating advanced knowledge from expert users. S4 may lead to great improvements in the instruction, dissemination, and full utilization of sequence similarity searches techniques and parameters.

5.2   Future Work

The project is an initial step in providing a Web-based expert system on biological knowledge. It can be improved in several aspects. First of all, for more personalized searches, users can have their own decision trees. In such a case we can also prevent the decision tree from becoming erroneous if users input conflicting knowledge while updating the decision tree.Second, we currently use XML file to store all the knowledge. This was chosen because of the high readability of XML file. However if proper decision tree edit interfaces are implemented, a relational database, which is considered as a more efficient knowledge storage platform should be included into the system, while the existing XML format can be used in data exchange. Finally, our expert knowledge is represented in the form of a decision tree, which can grow very fast when more nodes are added. Large decision tree can attenuate the system performance significantly. Novel knowledge-based structures should be developed to allow for better performance such as ontologies where knowledge among users and experts can be shared effectively.

References

1. Smith, T.F., Waterman, M.S.: 'Identification of common molecular subsequences. J. Mol. Biol., 147(1), 195–197 (1981)
2. Pearson, W.R., Lipman, D.J.: Improved tools for biological sequence comparison. Proc. Natl. Acad. Sci. U.S.A 85(8), 2444–2448 (1988)
3. Altschul, S.F., Gish, W., Miller, W., Myers, E.W., Lipman, D.J.: Basic local alignment search tool. J. Mol. Biol., 215(3), 403–410 (1990)
4. Chao, K.M., Pearson, W.R., Miller, W.: Aligning two sequences within a specified diagonal band. Comput. Appl. Biosci., 8(5), 481–487 (1992)
5. Altschul, S.F., Madden, T.L., Schaffer, A.A., Zhang, J., Zhang, Z., Miller, W., Lipman, D.J.: Gapped BLAST and PSI-BLAST: a new generation of protein database search programs. Nucleic Acids Res. 25(17), 3389–3402 (1997)
6. Giarratano, J.C., Riley, G.: Expert Systems: Principles and Programming, 3rd edn. (1998)
7. Smith, D.H., Gray, N.A.B., Nourse, J.G., Crandell, C.W.: Applications of Artificial-Intelligence for Chemical Inference.38. the Dendral Project - Recent Advances in Computer-Assisted Structure Elucidation, Analytica Chimica Acta-Computer Techniques and Optimization, vol. 5(4), pp. 471–497 (1981)

Prediction of over Represented Transcription Factor Binding Sites in Co-regulated Genes Using Whole Genome Matching Statistics

Giulio Pavesi and Federico Zambelli

Dept. of Biomolecular Science and Biotechnology
University of Milan
Via Celoria 26, Milan, Italy
{giulio.pavesi,federico.zambelli}@unimi.it

Abstract. The identification of binding sites for transcription factors regulating gene transcription is one of the most important and challenging problems in molecular biology and bioinformatics. Here we present an algorithm that, given a set of promoters from co–regulated genes, identifies over-represented binding sites by using profiles (position specific frequency matrices) defining the sequence binding specificity of known TFs as well as matching statistics on a whole–genome level, bypassing the need of defining matching thresholds and/or the use of homologous sequences. Preliminary tests performed on experimentally validated sequence sets are very promising; moreover, the same algorithm is suitable also for the use with any model of the binding specificity of TFs.

1 Introduction

One of the most relevant issues in modern molecular biology is the understanding of the complex mechanisms regulating gene expression. In particular, the first step in the process, transcription, is modulated by *transcription factors* (TFs), which bind the DNA in a sequence–specific manner usually (but not only) near the start site of transcription (i.e. within the promoter region).

Ideally, the final goal would be to have a complete genomic map of the sites (*transcription factor binding sites*, TFBSs) recognized by each of the TFs encoded in a genome, or, vice versa, for any annotated gene the list of the TFs that modulate its transcription and the corresponding sites. This, in turn, would permit the unraveling of the complex pathways of gene activation and expression in response for example to developemental stage, cell type, external stimuli, cell cycle phase, and so on.

Unfortunately, the experimental in vivo or in vitro identification of binding sites for a given TF is a long and expensive work, that can be complemented with good results by the introduction of bioinformatic techniques and algorithms [1].

F. Masulli, S. Mitra, and G. Pasi (Eds.): WILF 2007, LNAI 4578, pp. 651–658, 2007.

>YAL038W	ATTCC
>YAL038W	CTTCC
>YAL038W	CTTCC
>YCR012W	CTTCC
>YCR012W	CTTCC
>YCR012W	CTTCC
>YDR050C	CATCC
>YDR050C	CATCC
>YDR050C	CTTCC
>YDR050C	CTTCC
>YHR174W	CATCC
>YOL086C	CTTCC

	1	2	3	4	5
A |	0.08	0.25	0.0	0.0	0.0
C |	0.92	0.0	0.0	1.0	1.0
G |	0.0	0.0	0.0	0.0	0.0
T |	0.0	0.75	1.0	0.0	0.0

Fig. 1. A set of binding sites for yeast factor GCR1, and the corresponding profile

2   Describing Transcription Factor Binding Sites

All transcription factors bind the DNA double helix in a sequence–specific manner, but they allow for variation in the DNA sequence (sites) they recognize. In other words, TFBSs for the same factor are short (about 6–20 nts) and similar but not identical *oligonucleotides*. Several collections of experimentally validated binding sites for TFs in species ranging from bacteria to human are now available in specialized databases like TRANSFAC [2] or Jaspar [3].

The next logical step is, given a set of sites for the same TF, to build a *descriptor* of the binding specificity of the TF, that in turn can be used to predict additional candidate sites. The simplest way is to align available sites (usually, without gaps) and describe their alignment with a *profile* (or *position specific frequency matrix*) [4]. An alignment profile is a $4 \times m$ matrix, defining the frequency with which each of the four nucleotides appears in each of the m columns of the alignment (see Figure 1). Thus, in this way, we can obtain a description of the nucleotide preference for the TF in each of the positions of the sites. The frequencies at each position can also be seen as probabilities, to assess, given a nucleotide sequence s, how it fits the profile description, or, in other words, the probability of the sequence to be generated by using the profile as a source. Usually, the nucleotide frequencies of the profile are compared by computing a log–odds ratio to the expected frequencies of the four nucleotides in the sequences investigated. However, as we will show in the next section, we used whole genome oligonucleotide statistics as expected frequencies, so for single nucleotides we chose to employ only raw frequency values.

Assuming that $s = s_1 s_2 \ldots s_m$ is a nucleotide sequence and $M = \{i, j\}$ is a $4 \times m$ profile obtained from the alignment of TFBSs for a given factor, we can define:

$$P(s|M) = \prod_{i=1}^{m} M(s_i, i) \tag{1}$$

where $M(s_i, i)$ is the value in the i–th column corresponding to nucleotide s_i. Typically, to avoid getting probability zero in correspondence of nucleotides absent from an alignment column, *pseudocounts* are added to each column (that is, one assumes that missing nucleotides could appear in each column of the alignment with very low frequency). Also, to avoid having to deal with values very close to zero, logarithms of the frequencies are usually applied:

$$MS(s|M) = \log P(s|M) \qquad (2)$$

Finally, the log–values for a given profile are transformed into relative values. In other words, let $Max(M)$ and $Min(M)$ the logarithm of the maximum and minimum probability values that can be obtained from a matrix M on any given oligo (obtained by using the maximum and minimum values of each column, respectively). For any nucleotide sequence s, the $MS(s|M)$, the *binding value* for s with respect to profile M is defined as:

$$B(s|M) = 100 \times \frac{MS(s|M) - Min(M)}{Max(M) - Min(M)} \qquad (3)$$

Binding values thus range from 0 to 100, giving an estimate of the likelihood of a given sequence to represent a site recognized by the transcription factor, by comparing it to the "best" and "worst" possible instances.

2.1   Predicting Transcription Factor Binding Sites

The main drawback of the use of profiles or similar techniques is the independence assumption: in other words, in this model the nucleotides appearing at any given position do not influence in any way the other positions of the sites, as can be easily observed in reality. This fact, coupled with the usually low level of conservation obtained in the profiles themselves, has the effect that on a typical 500-1000 bp sequence like a promoter (the region located immediately upstream of the transcription start site of a gene) a very large number of false positive matches are produced, making virtually impossible to obtain feasible results from the analysis of a single sequence, also by extending the above approach to the comparison of each nucleotide frequency in each position with a background expected value.

One possible solution is to process a promoter by comparing it to promoters obtained from homologous genes in other species, and check whether a putative site matching a matrix is conserved by evolution. But, quite naturally, one cannot expect to have every binding site in a promoter to be conserved in other species: different studies, for example, have shown that a percentage of about 65-70% of human sites are conserved in mouse (see [5] and references therein), and the degree of conservation changes significantly according to the TF involved. Thus, in this case, the problem becomes the opposite, that is, to have false negative predictions.

Another solution is to build a dataset of sequences from co–regulated (by the same TFs) genes: if the number of putative TFBSs for one or more TFs is found to be significantly higher than expected, then the TFs can be singled out as possible regulators for the genes. Given a set of sequences, and a set of profiles defining the binding specificity of a set of TFs, the usual strategy can be summarized in the following steps: first, a relative matching threshold τ (usually, 75%–85%) is chosen; then, for each available profile, the number of matches above the threshold obtained in the sequences investigated and in a random sequence set are computed; finally, the two match counts are compared, and evaluated according to some measure of statistical significance.

The input sequence set can also in this case augmented with homologous sequences so to increase the signal to noise ratio. This strategy, that has been implemented with a few differences in several algorithms (see among many others [6,7,8]), has two main weak points. The first one is the pre–selection of a unique matching threshold for all the matrices, that has strong implications on the sensitivity and the specificity of the algorithms. For some matrices 85% is too high a threshold, for others 75% yields a deluge of false positive matches. The second is the choice of a random model to which the results are compared: random sequences with oligo composition similar to real promoters can be constructed, or, alternatively a selection of random promoters can be taken. In both cases, however, the definition of "random" is far from being straightforward, and can have significant impact on the reliability of the predictions.

The approach we present in this work mainly addresses the two problems just mentioned. Our idea is that in most of the cases a set of promoters from co–regulated genes of a given species is a sample of a sequence population, that is, the collection of all the promoters (or a large number thereof) from the same species. Starting from this idea, we propose a method that does not need a matching threshold (and thus avoids the "yes–or–no" decision at the base of the current methods), and in which the "random" model is constituted by the whole set of promoters available.

3   The Algorithm

Let M be a profile obtained from the alignment of sites for a given TF, and let $\mathcal{S} = \{S_1, S_2, \ldots, S_n\}$ a very large set (or the whole collection) of promoters of the same size from the same species of the TF. We first use the set $\mathcal{S}$ to obtain the matching statistics of profile M. Let $B(M, i)$ the highest scoring binding value that can be obtained from sequence S_i, on either strand, computing according to Equation 3. Although picking only the best match in each sequence disregards the fact that TFs can (and often do) have multiple sites within the same promoter, we believe that the large number of sequences employed (usually thousands) in this step can balance any negative effect on the performance of the algorithm. The $B(M, i)$ values can be used to obtain the mean and the standard deviation of the matching values of M on the sequence set $\mathcal{S}$, that we will denote as $\mu(M, \mathcal{S})$ and $\sigma(M, \mathcal{S})$.

Now, let $\mathcal{P} = \{P_1, \ldots, P_k\}$ be a set of k promoters of the same length and species of $\mathcal{S}$. P is indeed a sub–set of $\mathcal{S}$: in other words, we have a sample from the population of the whole promoter set. We first compute the mean $\mu(M, \mathcal{P})$ of the $B(M, i)$ values of M over the sequence set $\mathcal{P}$. Then, since $\mathcal{P}$ is a sample taken from $\mathcal{S}$, we can use a z–test to assess whether the difference between $\mu(M, \mathcal{P})$ and $\mu(M, \mathcal{S})$ is statistically significant. That is, if the sequence set $\mathcal{P}$ is derived from a set of genes co–regulated by a TF described by M, then we can expect $\mu(M, \mathcal{P})$ to be significantly higher than its expected value $\mu(M, \mathcal{S})$. Let $\sigma(M, \mathcal{P})$ be the standard error of $\mu(M, \mathcal{P})$, that can be defined as:

$$\sigma(M, \mathcal{P}) = \frac{\sigma(M, \mathcal{S})}{\sqrt{k}}$$

where k is the size of the promoter sample. The z–score for matrix M, given the sample $\mathcal{P}$ and the population $\mathcal{S}$ is thus given by:

$$z(M, \mathcal{P}, \mathcal{S}) = \frac{\mu(M, \mathcal{P}) - \mu(M, \mathcal{S})}{\sigma(M, \mathcal{P})}$$

The z values follow a normal standard distribution: we can thus associate with them a p–value estimating the significance of the difference between the sample and the population mean by using the normal cumulative distribution function.

For any given species for which the whole genomic sequence with reliable gene annotations are available (typically for human, rodents, fly and yeast, that are nevertheless the most widely investigated species) and any matrix M available in specific databases like TRANSFAC and JASPAR mean and standard deviation values over the whole promoter sets can be computed beforehand for the most typical sequence sizes (500–1000 bps). Then, given and input sample $\mathcal{P}$ from genes suspected to be co–regulated, the algorithm computes the corresponding mean and standard error values for the available profiles and ranks them in order of significance. TFs whose associated p–value is significantly low are finally good candidates to be co–regulators of the genes investigated.

In this way, we can bypass the need of pre–defining a score threshold for the profile matches. Moreover, the same idea is suitable not only for profiles, but also for any kind of descriptor built from a collection of sites.

4   Experimental Evaluation

To test the performance of the algorithm, we employed studies in which the binding of a given TF to DNA was determined experimentally on large scale, with techniques like Chromatin Immunoprecipitation (ChIP) on Chip. In particular, we extracted those genes whose promoter (usually defined as the region 1000 bps upstream of the gene) was reported to be bound by the TF, using it as a sample and comparing it to the "universe" of the whole set of promoters from the same organism: in the tests presented here, the regions upstream of the transcription start site of the annotated human RefSeq genes, filtered to avoid redundant sequences, resulting in more than 20,000 promoter sequences.

In mammals, there are five members of the NF-kB TF family, namely c-Rel, RelA, RelB, NF-kB1, and NF-kB2, which share very similar binding sites (variations of oligo GGAAATTTC). We took from [8] a list 111 human genes regulated by NF-kB, for which we ran the algorithm on promoters of size 500 and 1000 by using the 87 matrices available in the JASPAR database for vertebrate factors. Unsurprisingly, in both cases the most significant matrices were NFKB, NFKB1, REL and RELA (the four profiles available for members of the family, which are very similar to each other), with p–values lower than 10^{-10}. The next matrix in the list was TBP (describing the TATA-box), with a much higher p–value of .002. Clearly, this was a "perfect" test, in which virtually all the input genes were actually co–regulated. In practice, what researchers have at their disposal are sets of co–expressed genes, deriving for example from microarray experiments. Co–expression does not imply co–regulation, and one can expect to have just subsets of a co–expressed set of genes to be actually regulated by the same TF(s). Thus, we assessed the performance of the algorithm by perturbing the original gene set replacing genes with others picked at random from the human genome. For each replacement value from 1 to 111 we chose at random the genes to be replaced and the replacing genes 100 times. The results are summarized in Figure 2(a), showing the percentage of times in which a matrix of the NF-kB family was the most significant one reported by the algorithm at different perturbation levels on promoter sequences of size 500. Quite strikingly, the algorithm identified NF-kB profiles as the highest ranking (and significantly enriched) when more than two thirds of the original genes were replaced by random ones, at very low p–value thresholds. Moreover, the performance did not seem to be influenced by the promoter size chosen (results for promoters of size 1000 were virtually the same).

A similar set comprised 100 genes whose promoters were identified as target of factor NRF-1 in human by ChIP on Chip [9]. For this test, we used the whole collection of vertebrate matrices available at the TRANSFAC database (549 in all, since JASPAR does not contain a profile for NRF-1, whose binds variations of oligo GCATGCGC). In this case, the p–value obtained was much lower than in the previous example (virtually zero for sequences of 500 and 1000 bps). Interestingly enough, other matrices had significantly low p–values associated with them, namely those deriving from sites bound by E2F and MYC. As a matter of fact, the cooperation between NRF-1 and E2F in known for the regulation of several genes [9], while the association of NRF-1 with MYC (whose binding specificity is somewhat similar) has already been reported [10]. NRF-1 always remained the highest scoring profile, with very low p–values, even at 75-80% of perturbation (only one fourth of the genes were actually co–regulated, see Fig. 2(b)).

These results are on the other hand complemented by low false positive rates: on completely random sequence sets of the same size of the experiments just presented the algorithm reported profiles with p–value $\leq 10^{-4}$ less than in 1% of the cases, and less than 5% at 10^{-3}. However, since the algorithm seems to be able to detect TFs regulating small subsets of the genes, the fact that a few of the genes picked at random were actually co–regulated could not be completely ruled out.

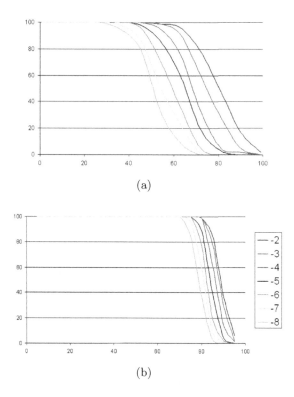

(a)

(b)

Fig. 2. Percentage of times in which the highest ranking profile belonged to the NF-kB family (y axis, figure a) or NRF-1 (y axis, figure b), at different perturbation levels (percentage of genes in the original set replaced by random genes, x axis), and at different p–value thresholds ($\log_{10}$ of the p–value). See text for further explanations.

5 Conclusions

We introduced a novel method for the identification of over–represented TFBSs in promoters from co–regulated genes. Our main contribution is the usage of unfiltered matching scores coupled with the introduction of genome–wide statistics for the assessment of the significance of the results. The results obtained in the tests we presented, as well as many others that we had to omit for sake of space, some of which are currently undergoing experimental validation, are very encouraging. Clearly, the results depend also on the reliability of the profiles employed, some of which are sometimes very poorly conserved (have a low information content), and make virtually impossible a feasible discrimination of more likely functional sites. However, the same algorithm can be applied as it is on different and more involved models of TFBSs, like position–dependent matrices or mixtures of matrices, or, vice versa, for the optimization of a descriptor or the choice of the best model for a set of sites.

References

1. MacIsaac, K.D., Fraenkel, E.: Practical strategies for discovering regulatory DNA sequence motifs. PLoS Comput. Biol. 2(4), e36 (2006)
2. Matys, V., Kel-Margoulis, O.V., Fricke, E., Liebich, I., Land, S., Barre-Dirrie, A., Reuter, I., Chekmenev, D., Krull, M., Hornischer, K., Voss, N., Stegmaier, P., Lewicki-Potapov, B., Saxel, H., Kel, A.E., Wingender, E.: TRANSFAC and its module TRANSCompel: transcriptional gene regulation in eukaryotes. Nucleic Acids Res 34, D108–110 (2006) (Database issue)
3. Sandelin, A., Alkema, W., Engstrom, P., Wasserman, W.W., Lenhard, B.: JASPAR: an open-access database for eukaryotic transcription factor binding profiles. Nucleic Acids Res 32, 91–94 (2004) (Database issue)
4. Stormo, G.D.: DNA binding sites: representation and discovery. Bioinformatics 16(1), 16–23 (2000)
5. Sauer, T., Shelest, E., Wingender, E.: Evaluating phylogenetic footprinting for human-rodent comparisons. Bioinformatics 22(4), 430–437 (2006)
6. Frith, M.C., Fu, Y., Yu, L., Chen, J.F., Hansen, U., Weng, Z.: Detection of functional DNA motifs via statistical over-representation. Nucleic Acids Res 32(4), 1372–1381 (2004)
7. Ho Sui, S.J., Mortimer, J.R., Arenillas, D.J., Brumm, J., Walsh, C.J., Kennedy, B.P., Wasserman, W.W.: opossum: identification of over-represented transcription factor binding sites in co-expressed genes. Nucleic Acids Res 33(10), 3154–3164 (2005)
8. Defrance, M., Touzet, H.: Predicting transcription factor binding sites using local over-representation and comparative genomics. BMC Bioinformatics 7, 396 (2006)
9. Cam, H., Balciunaite, E., Blais, A., Spektor, A., Scarpulla, R.C., Young, R., Kluger, Y., Dynlacht, B.D.: A common set of gene regulatory networks links metabolism and growth inhibition. Mol Cell 16(3), 399–411 (2004)
10. Elkon, R., Zeller, K.I., Linhart, C., Dang, C.V., Shamir, R., Shiloh, Y.: silico identification of transcriptional regulators associated with c-Myc. Nucleic Acids Res 32(17), 4955–4961 (2004)

Unsupervised Haplotype Reconstruction and LD Blocks Discovery in a Hidden Markov Framework

Alessandro Perina[1], Marco Cristani[1], Giovanni Malerba[2], Luciano Xumerle[2],
Vittorio Murino[1], and Pier Franco Pignatti[2]

[1] Dipartimento di Informatica,
Università degli Studi di Verona,
Strada le Grazie 15, 37134 Verona, Italia
{perina,cristanm,murino}@sci.univr.it
[2] Dipartimento Materno Infantile e di Biologia-Genetica,
Università degli Studi di Verona,
Strada le Grazie 8, 37134 Verona, Italia
{luciano.xumerle,giovanni.malerba,pignatti}@medgen.univr.it

Abstract. In the last years *haplotype reconstruction* and *haplotype blocks discovery*, *i.e.*, the estimation of patterns of linkage disequilibrium (LD) in the haplotypes, riveted the attention of the computer scientists due to the involved strong computational aspects. Such tasks are usually faced separately; recently, statistical generative techniques permitted to solve them jointly. Following this trend, we propose a generative framework based on hidden Markov processes, equipped with two novel inference strategies. The first strategy estimates finely haplotypes, while the second provides a quantitative measure to estimate LD blocks boundaries. Comparative real data results validate the proposed framework.

1 Introduction

Estimating haplotype[1] frequencies becomes increasingly important in the mapping of complex disease genes, as large numbers of closely linked single nucleotide polymorphisms (SNPs) can be genotyped. SNPs are single base pair differences between individuals in a population. Association studies work on the premise that SNP genotypes are correlated with a disease phenotype. Numerous studies have shown that human genome contains regions of high *linkage disequilibrium* (LD) with low haplotype diversity [1]: these regions are called *haplotype blocks* or *LD blocks*, where LD is a non-random association of alleles between adjacent loci. It is worth noting that SNPs or haplotype in LD blocks may serve as proxy for causative alleles: therefore, an accurate study on the blocks diversity became a key factor in genome wide association studies [2]. Unfortunately, allele phase of multilocus genotype in unrelated individuals is unknown and haplotypes needs to be reconstructed [3], before the discovery of haplotype blocks [4].

---

[1] *Haplotypes* are combinations of DNA marker alleles in a single chromosome.

F. Masulli, S. Mitra, and G. Pasi (Eds.): WILF 2007, LNAI 4578, pp. 659–665, 2007.
© Springer-Verlag Berlin Heidelberg 2007

In this paper, we propose a statistical framework aimed at the simultaneous haplotype reconstruction and block discovery. Simultaneous statistical strategies have been recently introduced [5]: the idea is to perform the two operations iteratively, providing temporary solutions (reconstructed haplotypes and blocks) which can be re-evaluated until a global data fitness criteria is met. Our framework is based on a hidden Markov setting similarly to [5], drawn here more correctly in terms of connection between fully non homogeneous hidden Markov models (FNH-HMM); differently to what carried out before, we do not add any a-priori knowledge (such as family data for reconstruction or block boundary hotspots) because this knowledge is not always recoverable. Most important, we introduce a simple way to reconstruct haplotypes and a novel inference to robustly individuate blocks. The idea is to first estimate from data relevant hidden "ancestral" patterns, i.e. allele patterns which represent high frequency haplotypes fragments. In this way, reconstructed haplotypes can be realized as the most probable path among these ancestral patterns, mimicking biological theories [3]. Frequent splits and joins among paths indicates block boundaries. The proposed strategy is compared with state-of-the-art methods and applied on real data; biological results attest the goodness of the strategy.

The paper continues as follows: Sec.2 gives preliminary notions; Sec.3 explains our framework and Sec.4 shows experimental results and draws some conclusions.

2 Preliminaries

2.1 Fully Non homogeneous Hidden Markov Model

Let us suppose to have a set $\mathbf{O}$ of J mono-dimensional observation sequences $\{\mathbf{O}_j\}, j = 1, \ldots, J$, of length N, formed by symbols from a finite vocabulary V. Formally, a FNH-HMM (depicted in Fig.1a) is a set $\mathbf{\Theta_h}$ of (hidden) parameters $(\{\mathbf{A}_k, \mathbf{B}_k, \boldsymbol{\pi}\})$, i.e., a site-dependent transition matrix $\mathbf{A}_k = \{a_k^{mn}\}$ with $a_k^{mn} = P(S_{k+1} = n | S_k = m)$, $1 \leq m, n \leq L$ and $k = 1, \ldots N$; a site-dependent emission matrix $\mathbf{B}_k = \{b_k^m(v)\}$ where $b_k^m(v) = P(v | S_k = m), v \in V$ and an initial state distribution $\boldsymbol{\pi} = \{\pi_n\}$.

Assuming the learning of a HMM as known, we propose the learning of a FNH-HMM as a modified version of the Baum-Welch algorithm (BW) [6] considered here as specialization of the Expectation-Maximization (EM) iterative procedure [7]. In the FNH-HMM learning, the E-step consists in first calculating the standard forward and backward variables, paying attention that all the transition and emission probabilities involved are site dependent (i.e., dependent on k). From these variables key quantities can be obtained, such as the conditional probability of two consecutive hidden states in an observation sequence at site k, i.e., $P(S_k = m, S_{k+1} = n | \mathbf{O}_j) = \xi_{k,j}(m, n)$ and the conditional $P(S_k = m | \mathbf{O}_j) = \sum_{n=1}^{L} \xi_{k,j}(m, n) = \gamma_{k,j}(m)$. In the M-step the parameters are updated using these quantities. The transition $\mathbf{A}_k$ and the emission $\mathbf{B}_k$ matrices are updated as follows:

$$a_k^{mn} = \frac{\sum_{j=1}^{J} \xi_{k,j}(m,n)}{\sum_{j=1}^{J} \sum_{n=1}^{L} \xi_{k,j}(m,n)} \qquad b_k^m(v) = \frac{\sum_{j=1}^{J} \gamma_{k,j}(m)}{\sum_{j=1}^{J} \sum_{n=1}^{L} \xi_{k,j}(m,n)} \tag{1}$$

with $s.t. x_k = v \in V$.

Differences with respect to the HMM framework are that here the statistics are collected for each site k individually, i.e. no summation over k is present.

3   The Proposed Model: Connection Between FNH-HMMs

In our framework, $\mathbf{O}$ is formed by J observation *samples*. Each sample represents the genotype of the j-th human subject, *i.e.*, a sequence of N allele pairs; each k-th pair, $k = 1, \ldots, N$, is formed by unordered variables $\{x_k, y_k\}$ taking values from $\{A, C, G, T\}$.

Assuming that in the samples every k-th SNP takes two symbols from two *hidden ancestral patterns*, we instantiate two independent state variables s_k and t_k that represent the k-th sites of such patterns [2]. These variables take pattern indexes values $1, \ldots, L$ by considering a first-order Markov property, i.e. considering the states s_{k-1} and t_{k-1} (Fig.1c, step 1, *Pattern choice*)[3]. Then, to each state is associated a probability of emission of a particular nucleotide symbol x_k and y_k (Fig.1c, step 1, *Symbols emission*). Now, in order to simulate the allele

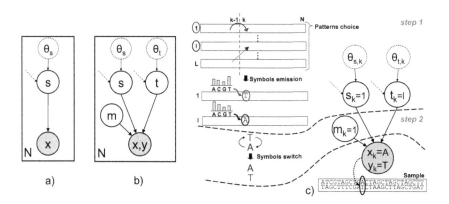

Fig. 1. a) FNH-HMM and b) FNH-HMM *double net*: nodes in a solid box indicate that they are replicated the number of times indicated in the bottom left corner; point-dashed arrows mean 1-st order Markov dependency. Filled (unfilled) circles mean observed (unobserved) random variables; dotted circle indicate the parameter set of the variable linked by the arrow; c) SNPs generative process: the picture is divided in two steps. Each step shows a portion of the process, drawn in an intuitive fashion (left) and in a formal graphical way (right).

---

[2] In the rest of the paper, we use indistinctively the terms *states* or *patterns*.

[3] Choosing the "right" L is an unsolved issue in this context; driven by biological issues, and setting $7 \le L \le 15$, very similar results have been achieved.

phasing that produces the final SNP pair, we add a switch variable m_k that decides the order of the alleles (Fig.1c, step 2, *Symbols switch*). We call this model FNH-HMM *double net*.

The joint distribution of the model over the samples is $\prod_{j=1}^{J} P_j(\{x_k,y_k,m_k, s_k,t_k\})$, $k = 1,\ldots,N$. Its factorization mirrors formally the above mentioned generative process, with a simplification done to make the learning process tractable. First of all, it is reasonable to consider samples as i.i.d. generated; so, in the following, we consider only the joint distribution P over a single sample, which can be written as:

$$P = P(x_1, y_1|m_1, s_1, t_1)P(m_1|s_1, t_1)P(s_1)P(t_1)\cdot$$
$$\prod_{k=2}^{N} P(x_k, y_k|m_k, s_k, t_k)P(m_k|s_k, t_k)P(s_k|s_{k-1})P(t_k|t_{k-1})$$

Here we note that each sample is considered as formed by two independent fully non homogeneous hidden Markov processes of states s_k and t_k, coupled at the level of the emission probability $P(x_k, y_k|m_k, s_k, t_k)$ plus the presence of the phasing distribution $P(m_k|s_k, t_k)$. The emission distribution can be further factorized, making clear the meaning of the switching variable $m_k \in \{0,1\}$, which determines the phase of the chromosome pair $\{x_k, y_k\}$. If $m_k = 1$, the state s_k (t_k) generates symbol x_k (y_k), viceversa if $m_k = 0$; in formulae this becomes

$$P(x_k, y_k|m_k, s_k, t_k) = (P(x_k|s_k)P(y_k|t_k))^{m_k}(P(y_k|s_k)P(s_k|t_k))^{1-m_k} \quad (2)$$

Finally, in order to ease the learning step, $P(m_k|s_k, t_k) = P(m_k)$, *i.e.*, we assume the switching variable only dependent on the sample site k.

The learning step, performed by a generalized EM, consists in iteratively evaluating for each k the parameters of 1) the switch distributions $P(m_k)$, which permit to estimate haplotypes; 2) the emission distributions $P(\cdot|s_k)$, $P(\cdot|t_k)$, and the transition distributions, which are useful to estimate haplotype blocks. In Eq.1 we show how to find the transition and the emission parameters; in [5], Sec.3.1, the update of $P(m_k)$ is shown.

After the model learning, the haplotype reconstruction strategy consists in evaluating for each sample $\mathbf{O}_j$ the related probability values of the masks $P(\{m_k\})$. If at site k $P(m_k) < 0.5$, then the input order of the allele couple is $< x_k, y_k >$, otherwise it is switched. This provides two haplotypes for each genotype $\mathbf{O}_j$.

As written above, the hidden patterns $1,\ldots,L$ model ancestral haplotype sequences which are fragmented and blocks-recombined in the human history, producing all the observed haplotypes. As first step toward the block discovery, we estimate, for each reconstructed haplotype sequence, the most probable pathway through these hidden patterns. This is done with a non-homogeneous version of the Viterbi algorithm applied on the learned model, designed with the same intuition used in the learning step (*i.e.*, paying attention to use site dependent transition and emission parameters). All the Viterbi paths are then disposed on a lattice $L \times N$ (Fig.2a). In this way, at each allele site k we can distinguish W_k distinct paths, each one of them indicated with $w_k(i), i = 1,\ldots,W_k$; $\| w_k(i) \|$ indicates the number of haplotypes traversing $w_k(i)$ (see Fig.2b).

We are now able to perform blocks discovery. The idea is that if two paths $w_k(i)$ and $w_k(i')$ do join, they represent two sets of haplotypes which have highly

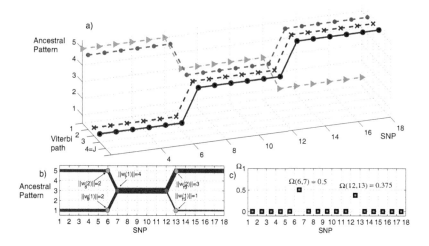

Fig. 2. Toy example (J=4 haplotypes): a) Viterbi paths b) paths over the lattice structure; note that b) is projection of a) over the SNPs-"Pattern Number" plane. c) Ω plot: between sites 6 and 7 there is a boundary "stronger" than the one present between sites 12 and 13.

different haplotype fragments up to k, becoming similar after site k; therefore, a block boundary exists between k and $k+1$. Similar reasoning holds for a split site (see Fig.2b). We translate this intuition with the *boundary presence strength* measure $\Omega(k, k+1) \in [0,1)$, which models the existence of a block boundary between sites k and $k+1$, which is

$$\Omega(k, k+1) = \mathbf{1}_{\text{Join}}(k)G(k) + \mathbf{1}_{\text{Split}}(k+1)G(k+1) \qquad (3)$$

where $\mathbf{1}_{\text{Join}}(k)$ ($\mathbf{1}_{\text{Split}}(k+1)$) equals 1 when a join (split) is present at time k ($k+1$), and $G(\cdot)$ is the *Gini* index [8]

$$G(k) = 1 - \sum_{i=1\ldots W_k} \left(\frac{\| w_k(i) \|}{W_k} \right)^2 \qquad (4)$$

Gini index can be used to describe whether a graph join or split is well balanced or not. For example, a split at site k is well balanced if the cardinalities $\{\| w_k \|\}$ of the child paths $\{w_k\}$ are similar; the idea is that the higher is $\Omega(k)$, the more likely is the presence of a block boundary between site k and $k+1$; viceversa, a low $\Omega(k)$ means that in the join (split) site k, a dominant path (*i.e.*, with a high number of haplotypes associated) merges (splits) with one ore more irrelevant paths (see Fig.2b). Given a threshold τ_Ω we can assign a block boundary to the site k when $\Omega(k) > \tau_\Omega$; in all the experiments we set $\tau_\Omega = 0.2$.

4   Experimental Results

Our framework has been tested on different data sets; here we report two explicative tests. For what concerns the initialization, no a-priori knowledge has

Table 1. Haplotype frequencies obtained with a training set composed by 60 geno-types of 25 SNPs. FNH-HMM *double net* reports the mean values over more than 100 experiments.

Haplotypes	Haplotype Frequencies		
	Groundtruth	Phase	FNH-HMM *double net*
C A C G C C C T A T G T T A G A C T C A G G T T A	0.475000	0.4760	0.475000
C G T A T G C T A T G T C G G A C T C T A A C A A	0.183333	0.1833	0.176655
C G T A T G C T A T G T C G G A C T C A A G C T A	0.116667	0.1167	0.109999
G A C G T C C T A T G T C A G A C T C A A G C A A	0.066667	0.0667	0.066667
C A C G C C C C A T G T T A G A C T C A G G T T A	0.058333	0.0583	0.056754
C A C G T C C T A T A T C G G A C T C A A G C T A	0.041667	0.0407	0.039054
C G T A T G C C A T G T C G G A C T C T A A C A A	0.025000	0.0250	0.018000
C A C G C C C T A T G T T A G A C T T A G G T T A	0.016667	0.0157	0.014444
C G T A T G C T A T A T C G G A C T C A A G C T A	0.008333	0.0083	0.007566
C A C G C C C T A T G T T A G A C C C A G G T T A	0.008333	0.0083	0.006454
C A C G T C C T A T A T C G G A C T T A A G C T A	-	0.0010	-

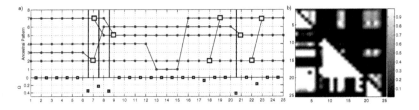

Fig. 3. a) Viterbi paths (top) and correspondent Ω plot (bottom). Splits/Joins are indicated with yellow rectangles; block boundaries are shown with a bar; b) pairwise LD table: D' (left diagonal elements) and r^2 (right diagonal elements) values confirm block boundaries found with our method.

been used, *i.e.*, for every site k, transition matrices $\{\mathbf{A}_k\}$ have been initialized to favor staying in the same state($a_k^{ii} > 0.5$) while mask distributions $P(m_k)$ have been initialized uniformly to 0.5.

The first data set is taken from the HAPMAP project (www.hapmap.org) on chromosome 7 from SNP marker *rs323917* to SNP *rs324375*. In table 1 we show haplotype reconstruction results. Please note that our approach obtains results comparable with **Phase** [3], which is the best algorithm for haplotype recon-struction. Its computational complexity ranges from $O(N^2)$ to $O(N^3)$, while our method is $O(L^2N)$. Moreover, Phase is built on a (visible) Markov model of variable order, and does not perform blocks discovery, while our method is built on a (hidden) first-order Markov model and it performs blocks discovery. In this sense, we believe that augmenting the order of the (hidden) Markov process can improve the overall performances.

Blocks discovery results are shown in Fig.3; in Fig.3b the Pairwise LD table [4] is reported[4], where the pairwise measures D' (Fig.3b - left diagonal elements) and r^2 (Fig.3b - right diagonal elements) summarize the Linkage Disequilibrium in the region; high D' or r^2 values indicate in position m, n a block relation

---

[4] Pairwise LD table is a widely used method for block-discovery, that needs *exact* haplotypes to accurately estimate blocks, *scarcely* robust to reconstruction errors.

Fig. 4. a) Viterbi paths over the ancestral patterns. No splits or joins are present.

between the site m and n. The table, built using exact reconstructed haplotypes with a-priori knowledge, confirms our results.

The second data set used consists of 11 SNPs taken from interlukin-1 cluster on human chromosome 2q12-2q14 presented in [9]. In figure 4, are all depicted the paths over the ancestral patterns inferred after the model training. No splits or joins are present, thus only a haplotype block is present here, as confirmed by a-priori knowledge on the data. Haplotype reconstruction results are optimal, but not reported here due to the lack of space.

References

1. Gabriel, S.B., et al.: The structure of haplotype blocks in the human genome. Science 296, 2225–2229 (2002)
2. Zhang, K., et al.: Haplotype block structure and its application to association studies: Power and study designs. Am. J. Hum. Genet. 71, 1386–1394 (2002)
3. Stephens, M., Donnelly, P.: A comparison of bayesian methods for haplotype reconstruction from population genotype data. Am. J. Hum. Genet. 73, 1162–1169 (2003)
4. Chen, Y., Lin, C.H., Sabatti, C.: Volume measures for linkage disequilibrium. BMC Genetics 7, 54 (2006)
5. Jojic, V., Jojic, N.: Joint discovery of haplotype blocks and complex trait associations from snp sequences. In: Proceedings of the UAI-04 (Arlington, Virginia)
6. Rabiner, L.: A tutorial on Hidden Markov Models and selected applications in speech recognition. In: Proc. of IEEE, vol. 77, pp. 257–286 (1989)
7. Dempster, A., Laird, N., Rubin, D.: Maximum likelihood from incomplete data via the EM algorithm. J. Roy. Statist. Soc. B 39, 1–38 (1977)
8. Duda, R., Hart, P., Stork, D.: Pattern Classification. John Wiley&sons, New York (2001)
9. Gohlke, H., Illig, T., et al.: Association of the interleukin-1 receptor antagonist gene with asthma. Am J Respir Crit Care Med 169, 1217–1223 (2004)

Multi-class Protein Fold Recognition Through a Symbolic-Statistical Framework

Marenglen Biba, Floriana Esposito, Stefano Ferilli,
Teresa M.A. Basile, and Nicola Di Mauro

Department of Computer Science, University of Bari, Italy
{biba,esposito,ferilli,basile,ndm}@di.uniba.it

Abstract. Protein fold recognition is an important problem in molecular biology. Machine learning symbolic approaches have been applied to automatically discover local structural signatures and relate these to the concept of fold in SCOP. However, most of these methods cannot handle uncertainty being therefore not able to solve multiple prediction problems. In this paper we present an application of the symbolic-statistical framework PRISM to a multi-class protein fold recognition problem. We compare the proposed approach to a symbolic-only technique and show that the hybrid framework outperforms the symbolic-only one in terms of predictive accuracy in the multiple prediction problem.

1 Introduction

Proteins form the very basis of life. They are responsible for regulating a variety of activities in all known organisms, from replication of the genetic code to transporting oxygen or regulating the cellular machinery. Proteins accomplish their task by three-dimensional tertiary and quaternary interactions between various substrates such as DNA and RNA, and other proteins. Therefore knowing the structure of a protein is an essential prerequisite to gain a thorough understanding of the protein's function. However, once the protein sequence has been determined, deducing its unique three-dimensional native structure is a very hard task. For this reason, many efforts have been made to develop methods for predicting proteins' structure given their amino acid sequence. Important competitions such as CASP and CAFASP2 [1] have given rise to many computational methods for the protein structure prediction problem. Despite the large amount of effort expended, the protein folding or protein structure prediction problem remains largely unsolved. Thus, there is strong motivation to continue working on the many remaining open problems that the protein structure modeling area poses.

Protein folding is the process by which a protein assumes its characteristic functional shape or tertiary structure, also known as the native state. All protein molecules are linear heteropolymers composed of amino acids and this sequence is known as the primary structure. Most proteins can carry out their biological functions only when folding has been completed, because three-dimensional

F. Masulli, S. Mitra, and G. Pasi (Eds.): WILF 2007, LNAI 4578, pp. 666–673, 2007.

shape of the proteins in the native state is critical to their function. A particular fold is adopted by a certain protein sequence/structure following several constraints which can be local or global. Local signatures, which are those dealt with in this paper, relate to a short region that may involve a particular sequence or arrangement of secondary structures. Structural signatures are hard to classify and although several automated methods have been proposed, knowledge about structural signatures depends primarily on human expertise. However, with the increase of the number of protein structures, intensive efforts have been made for the development of automated methods.

In the field of machine learning, approaches such as artificial neural networks or hidden markov models have been applied successfully to several problems of molecular biology [2]. However most of these techniques, being not able to model long range interactions, have had their best results on sequence data, while the problem of dealing with the three-dimensional structure has not been tackled very much. On the other side, symbolic approaches based on first-order logic representations have the power to deal with such complex domains and are very suitable to model rich structures and relations between objects. One of these approaches is ILP (Inductive Logic Programming) [3] that learns rules from examples and background knowledge. This technique, being able to model relations, has been applied successfully to some problems in structural molecular biology [4]. However, a major drawback of this symbolic approach is the limited ability to handle uncertainty. Rules in ILP are deterministic and there is no way to handle the uncertainty that may characterize a certain problem.

In this paper, we consider a previous study [5] in the protein folding area that uses ILP to automatically discover structural signatures of protein fold and function. A problem that arises in this previous work is that of multiple predictions, i.e. an example which represents a protein domain is predicted to be in several folds. We apply to the same problem the symbolic-statistical framework PRISM [6] in order to solve the multi-class classification problem and show that the hybrid approach outperforms the symbolic one in terms of predictive accuracy.

The paper is organized as follows. In Section 2 we report a brief introduction of ILP and its application on the structural signatures performed in [5]. Section 3 presents PRISM as a symbolic-statistical framework. Section 4 presents the modeling of the problem in [5] in the framework PRISM and the experiments. Section 5 contains conclusions and future work.

2 Multi-relational Learning for Structural Signatures of Proteins

Multi-relational data mining applications in biological domains [4] have exploited the expressive power of logic to represent complex structures. As pointed out in [5], since structures consist of interactions among objects and sub-structures and since ILP is suitable to learn logical representations, it can be applied to problems encountered in protein structure. Moreover, one of the most powerful advantages of ILP is that of using background knowledge and since great amount of knowledge has been gathered during years of research on protein structure, all this expert knowledge can be used in ILP to discover principles of protein fold. Another advantage of ILP is that rules are amenable to human interpretation.

In ILP, the model learned from the data is a set of rules. The data consist of the examples, while the background knowledge expresses what the expert already knows about a certain problem. An application of ILP to automatically discover the structural signatures of protein folds and function has been presented in [5]. In this work sets of rules were learned for each protein fold, in particular 59 signatures (rules) were learned from 20 populated folds. Positive examples were derived from SCOP [7] by selecting representative domains for the fold under study while the negative examples were derived by selecting domains from different folds of the same class where the classes are all-α, all-β, α/β and $\alpha + \beta$. For each positive and negative example, it was derived structural information (attributes such as total number of residues), relational information (adjacency of the secondary structure) and local information (such as average hydrophobicity of each secondary structure element and the presence of proline residues). In the following, we show part of the background knowledge that is used in the experiments to represent the three-dimensional structure information of the protein domains which represent the examples for the learning task.

adjacent(D, A, B, Pos, TypA, TypB): this predicate indicates that the secondary structures A and B are consecutive. Furthermore, their respective types are TypA and TypB each of which can be one of the known types of secondary structure. Pos is the serial number of the secondary structure element A. Helices and strands are numbered separately.

coil(A,B,Length): bounds Length to the length of the loop between secondary structures A and B or is true if loop has Length ±50%. A brief description of two of the signatures (rules) learned is given below, consisting of the Prolog representation and the corresponding translation in English where the symbol ":-" stands for "if...then...".

Rule (lambda repressor): The protein is between 53 and 88 residues long. Helix A at position 3 is followed by helix B. The coil between A and B is about six residues long.

fold('lambda repressor', X) :- total_length ($53 < X < 88$), adjacent(X, A, B, 3, h, h), length_loop(A, B, 6).

Rule(Rossman fold): Strand A at position 1 is followed by helix B. Strand C at position 6 is followed by helix D. The length_loop between A and B is about one residue long.

fold('NAD(P)-binding Rossmann-fold', X) :- adjacent(X, A, B, 1, e, h), adjacent(X, C, D, 6, e, h), length_loop(A, B, 1).

Since protein folding is a complex phenomenon, a problem that arises in [5] are multiple predictions. Many examples are predicted to be in different folds i.e. signatures of different folds explain the same example. For instance, the protein domain "d1hslb_" is predicted to be in three folds: "DNA-binding 3-helical bundle", "Periplasmic binding protein-like II" and "beta-Grasp" while in fact it belongs only to the fold "Periplasmic binding protein-like II". A large number of examples are involved in the multiple prediction problem hence a ranking mechanism is needed so that different folds can have different importance towards an example. We decided to use probability to model the uncertainty that arises when multiple predictions exist. On the other side, we want to preserve the expressive power of logical representations. Therefore, we need a framework that is able to provide expressive power and uncertainty handling. PRISM provides both the logic language and the ability to incorporate probability in logical descriptions. Moreover, providing learning capabilities for estimating parameters from observations (examples), it represents a suitable framework to deal with uncertainty when classifying examples with multiple potential predictions.

3   The Symbolic-Statistical Framework PRISM

PRISM (PRogramming In Statistical Modeling) [6] is a symbolic-statistical modeling language that integrates logic programming with learning algorithms for probabilistic programs. PRISM programs are not only just a probabilistic extension of logic programs but are also able to learn from examples through the EM (Expectation-Maximization) algorithm which is built-in in the language. PRISM represents a formal knowledge representation language for modeling scientific hypotheses about phenomena which are governed by rules and probabilities. The parameter learning algorithm [8], provided by the language, is a new EM algorithm called graphical EM algorithm that when combined with the tabulated search has the same time complexity as existing EM algorithms, i.e. the Baum-Welch algorithm for HMMs (Hidden Markov Models), the Inside-Outside algorithm for PCFGs (Probabilistic Context-Free Grammars), and the one for singly connected BNs (Bayesian Networks) that have been developed independently in each research field. Since PRISM programs can be arbitrarily complex (no restriction on the form or size), the most popular probabilistic modeling formalisms such as HMMs, PCFGs and BNs can be described by these programs.

PRISM programs are defined as logic programs with a probability distribution given to facts that is called basic distribution. Formally a PRISM program is $P = F \cup R$ where R is a set of logical rules working behind the observations and F is a set of facts that models observations' uncertainty with a probability distribution. Through the built-in graphical EM algorithm the parameters (probabilities) of F are learned and through the rules this learned probability distribution over the facts induces a probability distribution over the observations. As an example, we present a hidden markov model with two states slightly modified from that in [8]:

```
values(init,[s0,s1]).          % State initialization
values(out(_),[a,b]).          % Symbol emission
values(tr(_),[s0,s1]).         % State transition

hmm(L) :-                      % To observe a string L
      str_length(N),           % Get the string length as N
      msw(init,S),             % Choose an initial state randomly
      hmm(1,N,S,L).            % Start stochastic transition (loop)

hmm(T,N,_,[ ]) :- T > N,!.        % Stop the loop
hmm(T,N,S,[Ob | Y]) :-         % Loop: current state is S, current time is T
      msw(out(S),Ob),          % Output Ob at the state S
      msw(tr(S),Next),         % Transit from S to Next.
      T1 is T+1,               % Count up time
      hmm(T1,N,Next,Y).        % Go next (recursion)
str_length(10).                % String length is 10
set_params :- set_sw(init, [0.9,0.1]), set_sw(tr(s0), [0.2,0.8]), set_sw(tr(s1),
[0.8,0.2]), set_sw(out(s0),[0.5,0.5]), set_sw(out(s1),[0.6,0.4]).
```

The most appealing feature of PRISM is that it allows the users to use random switches to make probabilistic choices. A random switch has a name, a
space of possible outcomes, and a probability distribution. In the program above,
msw(init,S) probabilistically determines the initial state from which to start by
tossing a coin. The predicate set_sw(init, [0.9,0.1]), states that the probability
of starting from state s0 is 0.9 and from s1 is 0.1. The predicate learn in PRISM
is used to learn from examples (a set of strings) the parameters (probabilities of
init, out and tr) so that the ML (Maximum-Likelihood) is reached. For example,
the learned parameters from a set of examples can be: switch init: s0 (0.6570),
s1 (0.3429); switch out(s0): a (0.3257), b (0.6742); switch out(s1): a (0.7048),
b (0.2951); switch tr(s0): s0 (0.2844), s1 (0.7155); switch tr(s1): s0 (0.5703), s1
(0.4296). After learning these ML parameters, we can calculate the probability of
a certain observation using the predicate prob: prob(hmm([a,a,a,a,a,b,b,b,b,b])
= 0.000117528. This way, we are able to define a probability distribution over the
strings that we observe. Therefore from the basic distribution we have induced
a probability distribution over the observations.

4   PRISM Modeling of Structural Signatures

What we need to model in PRISM the structural signatures of protein domains
is a set of rules and a set of facts with a probability distribution over them.
The set of 59 rules learned in [5] can be used without any changes. We have to
define the random switches and learn for them a probability distribution which
models the uncertainty about the protein domains for their classification. In
the predicate adjacent(D, A, B, Pos, TypA, TypB) that is used as background

knowledge, we define a random switch that probabilistically assigns the values e or h (strand or helix) to TypA. What we have modeled in this way is a probability distribution over secondary structures that are of type e or h. Therefore after learning the parameters for this random switch we have two values that represent the probability that a secondary structure is of type e or h in the dataset of training. Another random switch that we define is that based on the length of the secondary structure. This represents the probability that a certain secondary structure has a certain length. The possible values of the length of the secondary structure define the space of possible outcomes for this second random switch.

We used as training data the dataset used in [5] and performed the experiments in PRISM version 1.10 through a 5-fold cross-validation on 381 examples. After learning the parameters for the two random switches we calculated the probability for each of the observations. Now we explain how these probabilities can be used to solve the problem of multiple predictions. In multi-relational data mining, cases of multi-class classifications are treated by assigning a test example with multiple predictions to the fold which covers the maximum number of examples. For example, if for the fold "DNA-binding 3-helical bundle" have been learned 4 rules which together cover (explain) 74 training examples and for the fold "Periplasmic binding protein-like II" have been learned 3 rules which together cover 30 examples, then the protein domain "d1hslb_" is assigned to the fold which covers more examples. In this case the prediction is wrong since the protein domain "d1hslb_" in reality belongs to the fold "Periplasmic binding protein-like II". If the number of the examples covered by the folds is equal, the example is assigned randomly. This has proven to be not an optimal solution and generally has produced low predictive accuracy in multi-class classification problems. In order to model the uncertainty of which fold to choose in case of multiple predictions we use the probabilities of the observations that we compute in PRISM. We sum the probabilities of the observations (training examples) that belong to the same fold. In this way we rank the folds with a probability instead of the number of the examples covered and in case of a multiple prediction for an example of testing we assign the example to the fold with a greater probability.

We have performed two experiments. In the first we used as a classification criterion the number of covered examples for each fold, i.e. examples with multiple predictions (covered by rules belonging to different folds) were assigned to the fold with the greatest number of covered examples. While in the second experiment we used the probability of each fold to solve multiple predictions, i.e. an example with multiple predictions was assigned to the fold with the highest probability. Table 1 contains the results of these experiments. Each column corresponds to one of the datasets in the 5-fold cross-validation and contains for each row the test results, i.e. number of correct classified examples towards the number of all the examples of testing. The number of examples with multiple predictions is about 63 % of the total number of examples.

As we can see from the table, in the Experiment 2 where we used the system PRISM and modeled the uncertainty with the probabilities of the observations, we obtained a predictive accuracy of 65,35 % towards 49,6 % of the Experiment

Table 1. Results of the 5-fold cross-validation

	Dataset 1	Dataset 2	Dataset 3	Dataset 4	Dataset 5	Overall
Exp. 1	37/76	34/76	45/76	40/76	33/77	189/381
Exp. 2	54/76	50/76	51/76	52/76	42/77	249/381

1 where we do not use probabilities. The difference in predictive accuracy is significant at the 0,005 level in a paired t-test. Analyzing the experiments' results, we observed that the significant difference in accuracy among the two experiments is due to the fact that for many examples with multiple predictions, their classification in the fold with the greatest probability was correct. This shows that fold's probability provides a more principled and robust method for handling the uncertainty of multiple predictions against the fold's number of covered examples.

The experiments validate our approach of handling the uncertainty of multiple predictions through fold probabilities. Using PRISM it was possible to learn fold probabilities from observations (training examples) and therefore better identify the most probable fold for a test example with multiple predictions. What we have learned from this application is that hybrid symbolic-statistical approaches can solve problems for which single symbolic approaches fail, such as problems where uncertainty must be dealt with.

5   Conclusions and Future Work

In this paper we have applied the symbolic-statistical framework PRISM to a multi-class protein fold recognition problem. We have exploited the ability of PRISM to represent proteins' three-dimensional structures through logic programs and to model the uncertainty about observations through learning switch probabilities. In dealing with a multi-class prediction problem we have used probability of protein folds to correctly classify test examples with multiple predictions. We have shown that the proposed method outperforms the symbolic-only approach in terms of predictive accuracy. This is to the best of our knowledge the first application of the framework PRISM to a problem of protein folding and multi-class prediction.

As future work we intend to apply PRISM to other datasets for protein fold recognition problems. We believe that PRISM, having the expressive power of a logic-based language and the ability to deal with uncertainty in a robust manner through EM based learning algorithms, provides a valid framework for dealing with structural domains with intrinsic uncertainty. Moreover, we intend to evaluate the performance of our approach towards other methods that have been applied to multi-class classification problems such as support vector machines and neural networks [9] which are among the state-of-the-art discriminative methods that have produced accurate results for the multi-class protein fold recognition problem.

References

1. Moult, J.: Rigorous Performance Evaluation in Protein Structure Modeling and Implications for Computational Biology. Phil. Trans. R. Soc. B 361, 453–458 (2006)
2. Baldi, P., Brunak, S.: Bioinformatics: The Machine Learning Approach, 2nd edn. MIT Press, Cambridge (2001)
3. Muggleton, S.H., De Raedt, L.: Inductive logic programming: Theory and methods. Journal of Logic Programming 19(20), 629–679 (1994)
4. Page, D., Craven, M.: Biological Applications of Multi-Relational Data Mining. Appears In: SIGKDD Explorations, special issue on Multi-Relational Data Mining (2003)
5. Turcotte, M., Muggleton, S.H., Sternberg, M.J.E.: Automated discovery of structural signatures of protein fold and function. Journal of Molecular Biology 306, 591–605 (2001)
6. Sato, T., Kameya, Y.: PRISM: A symbolic-statistical modeling language. In: Proceedings of the 15th International Joint Conference on Artificial Intelligence, pp. 1330–1335 (1997)
7. LoConte, L., Ailey, B., Hubbard, T.J.P., Brenner, S.E., Murzin, A.G., Chothia, C.: SCOP: a structural classification of proteins database. Nucl. Acids Res. 28, 257–259 (2000)
8. Sato, T., Kameya, Y.: Parameter learning of logic programs for symbolic-statistical modeling. Journal of Artificial Intelligence Research 15, 391–454 (2001)
9. Ding, C.H., Dubchak, I.: Multi-class protein fold recognition using support vector machines and neural networks. Bioinformatics 17(4), 349–358 (2001)

Assessment of Common Regions and Specific Footprints of DNA Copy Number Aberrations Across Multiple Affymetrix SNP Mapping Arrays

Roberta Spinelli[1,2], Ingrid Cifola[1,2], Stefano Ferrero[3], Luca Beltrame[1,2],
Paolo Mocarelli[4], and Cristina Battaglia[2]

[1] Institute of Biomedical Technologies (ITB),
National Research Council (CNR), Milan
[2] Dept. of Science and Biomedical Technologies and CISI, University of Milan, Milan
[3] Department of Medicine, Surgery and Dentistry, University of Milan, Milan
[4] Desio Hospital, University of Milan Bicocca, Milan

Abstract. The application of genome-wide approaches to the molecular characterization of cancer was investigated, identifying footprints that can potentially assist in the subclassification of tumors in order to contribute to diagnosis and clinical management of patients. High resolution DNA copy number analysis by single nucleotide polymorphism mapping array technology has been widely applied to study copy number aberrations and to distinguish among different loss of heterozigosity mechanisms associated with or without copy number changes in tumors. However, assessment of statistically significant common aberrations across the whole data set or a subset of tumor samples is still an open problem. Therefore, we adapted the recently developed STAC algorithm, previously applied to comparative genomic hybridization data, to identify common copy number aberrations in renal carcinoma samples using Affymetrix 100K SNP arrays. SNP copy number data were processed by a homebrew pipeline implemented in R and analyzed using STAC.

Keywords: SNP, copy number, SNP mapping array, aberration.

1 Introduction

Knowledge of DNA copy number aberration (CNA) can have a significant role in clinical management of oncological diseases. Many studies observed that some chromosomal gains and losses are related to cancer progression and that association with prognosis has been found for a variety of tumor types [1,2]. High resolution DNA copy number analysis using Affymetrix GeneChip[®] SNP mapping technology has been widely employed to study CNA and to distinguish between different loss of heterozygosity (LOH) mechanisms associated with or without copy number (CN) changes in tumors [3,4]. Many reports demonstrated

F. Masulli, S. Mitra, and G. Pasi (Eds.): WILF 2007, LNAI 4578, pp. 674–681, 2007.

the usefulness of GeneChip® Human Mapping SNP arrays to reveal LOH and allelic imbalances associated with clinical features in many tumor types [5,6].

SNP data can be used either to analyze genome-wide genomic profile of a single patient or to find common patterns of CNA in a tumor sample set using freely available software such as dChip [7] , CNAG [8], SNPscan [9], Ideogram-Browser [10] and CNAT (http://www.affymetrix.com/products/software/specific/cnat.affx). A major limitation is related to the lack of computational approaches to calculate common patterns or specific genomic footprints of CNA among multiple samples. Although dChip provides common LOH patterns associated to a score, to our knowledge no statistical methods are available to analyze CN profiles from multiple Affymetrix SNP arrays. Recently, a new statistical method (STAC) was proposed to perform multi-array analysis on array CGH data and to identify a consistent aberrations across multiple samples [11]. This algorithm tests the significance of frequency of aberration at predefined marker locations (which can span from one megabase to full-length BAC clones) across the whole sample set, determines the significance of the statistics and assigns a p-value to each location on the genome using a multiple testing corrected permutation approach.

We used the STAC algorithm as statistical approach to find common regions of CN gain or loss across a collection of 27 renal cell carcinoma (RCC) samples analyzed using Affymetrix 100K SNP arrays. We implemented a data processing pipeline to find common regions of CNA and specific footprints in subsets of RCC tumor samples using an unsupervised approach.

2   Methods

SNP Copy Number Aberrations Profiling

The combination of data from two GeneChip® Human Mapping 50K Xba and 50K Hind arrays, referred to as 100K SNP mapping array set, allowed the genotyping of 116,204 individual SNPs. 27 RCC tissue samples (tumor) and the corresponding blood samples (normal) were analyzed to produce CNA profiles. Genomic DNA from paired RCC samples were prepared for genome-wide SNP mapping analysis using both GeneChip® Human Mapping 50K Xba and 50K Hind assay kits (Affymetrix), according to the manufacturer's protocols. Briefly, 250 ng genomic DNA was digested separately with Xba I and Hind III restriction enzymes, ligated to synthetic adapters and amplified by PCR using a universal primer that anneals to the adapter sequence. After hybridization on GeneChip® arrays, fluorescent images of microarrays were acquired using the GeneChip® Scanner 3000 and analyzed with GTYPE 4.0 (Affymetrix) for quantification of signal intensities and assignment of genotype calls for each SNP. To obtain SNP copy number values for each sample, we used the dChip2006 software (http://dchip.org). At the same time, we used the IdeogramBrowser software (http://www.informatik.uni-ulm.de/ni/staff/HKestler/ideo/) with CNAT 3.0 copy number data from the 27 tumor samples, using genomic smoothed copy number value (GSA-CN) as display value. To identify common regions of CN gain or loss across the whole sample set we set the following tunable parameters: filtering method set as pre-filtering, lower and upper bound at 1.35 and 3 respectively, minimal DNA region length equal to 0.5 megabases (Mb), group limit at 3, consensus mode at 3.

SNP Copy Number Data Processing

In order to use SNP copy number data from each tumor sample for analysis with STAC, we implemented a data processing pipeline comprising 3 main steps:

1. **CN smoothing process** using Kernel regression smoothing function with global plug-in bandwidth selection fixed at 1Mb (*glkerns* function of *lokern* R package, freely available at http://www.sourcekeg.co.uk/cran/src/contrib/Descriptions/lokern.html). Starting from CN values of a single SNP, we assigned a CN value to genomic regions of 1Mb ("nodes"). Using the Human Genome NCBI Build 35.1 annotation, we ordered SNP copy number data according to the corresponding SNP chromosome position, and converted them to smoothed CN scores, using the *glkerns* regression smoothing function applied to each chromosome [12]. We produced a table reporting 2,858 nodes across all 22 autosomes and their corresponding smoothed CN values for tumor and normal samples.
2. **Categorization of CN values.** CN values for each node were associated to gain or loss classes as follows: in "Gain" class, each node with $CN > 2$ was flagged with 1(presence) otherwise with 0 (absence); in "Loss" class, each node with $CN < 1.8$ was flagged with 1 (presence), otherwise with 0 (absence).
3. **Application of STAC to gain and loss data to identify common CNA and specific footprints .** Due to STAC requirements, we processed gain and loss binary data separately and performed analysis for single chromosomes. Briefly, STAC identified aberrant genomic regions as series of consecutive 1s and, performing permutations, calculated their statistical significance (p-value) across the entire dataset by two robust statistics: the frequency and footprint statistic. We performed 10,000 permutations and we set footprint and frequency statistic thresholds at p-value < 0.05. Tables for gain and loss statistics for each chromosome were combined in a single data set comprising nodes, frequency p-value, footprint p-value and chromosome. Nodes were linked to corresponding chromosomal cytobands with the UCSC database (http://genome.ucsc.edu) for further bioinformatical investigation.

All the processing steps were implemented in R (http://www.r-project.org).

3   Results

We combined GeneChip® 50K Xba and 50K Hind array data and performed pairwise comparisons (tumor tissue vs blood control) on the entire dataset.

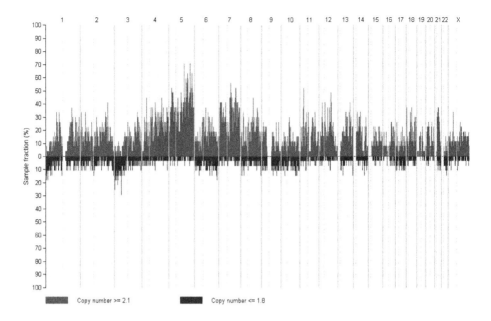

Fig. 1. Frequency of SNP copy number gain (CN$\geq$ 2.1, red bars) and loss (CN$\leq$ 1.8, blue bars) were calculated over all the 27 tumor samples by dChip2006 software. Percentages were displayed for each chromosomal arms (chromosome from 1 to X; in each chromosome, vertical dotted line divides p arm from q arm).

Using dChip2006, we plotted the frequencies of SNP copy number gain and loss occurring along each chromosome over all the 27 tumor samples, obtaining a global indication of the most frequent affected chromosomes and type of aberrations (Fig. 1). Specifically, all chromosomes showed both occurrence of CN gain and loss and principally the number of CN gain for each chromosomal arm was greater than that of CN loss, with the exception of chromosomes 1p, 3p and 22q where CN loss was the most frequent alteration. Considering only CN gain, the most affected chromosomes were chromosomes 5 (19 out of 27 samples, 70%), 4, 7, 11 and 12 (10 out of 27 samples, 40%); considering only CN loss, the most frequent altered chromosome was 3 (5 out of 27 samples, 20%).

Analysis of SNP array data with IdeogramBrowser allowed interactive visualization of all chromosomes simultaneously for all samples. Individual chromosome inspection allowed the identification of common regions of CNA in the tumor dataset, as showed for loss regions on chromosome 1 and gain regions on chromosome 5 (Fig. 2). This analysis confirmed the heterogeneous distribution of CNA in all chromosomes, making the setting of tunable software parameters difficult. However, it allows a detailed exploration of aberrant regions in terms of cytobands, genomic length and associated genes.

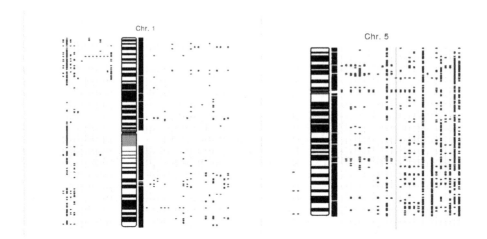

Fig. 2. IdeogramBrowser visualization of chromosome 1 (left) and chromosome 5 (right). Red lines indicate regions of CN gain for each sample, and green lines show regions of CN loss. Genes are marked with blue bars on the right hand side of chromosomes.

Combining our data processing and STAC analysis we found many significantly amplified or deleted chromosomal regions, common to a number of samples ranging from 6 to 12. The length of these aberrations was variable, with some chromosomes affected in one single node (1Mb) and other showing amplifications or deletions in more than three nodes (more than 3Mb). Specifically, on chromosome 1 and 5, we observed a specific footprint of common CN loss and gain regions, respectively (Fig. 3).

Thus, common CNA patterns were identified by an analysis without any user-tunable threshold bias. Such modified STAC analysis allowed us to identify a subset of patients carrying novel genomic aberrations never previously observed in this type of tumor. Finally, taking advantage of a robust statistical approach we found common aberrant regions which were in agreement with data obtained from dChip or IdeogramBrowser.

4   Discussion and Conclusions

dChip2006 is a multi purpose tool for the analysis of Affymetrix GeneChip® microarray data, to perform high-throughput analysis of RNA and DNA profiles with either supervised or unsupervised methods. It is also one of the most used for SNP array data analysis [3], [13]. However, it has some limitations with regards to DNA copy number analysis, because it does not provide a statistical evaluation for common aberrant genomic regions. Therefore, due to the amount of genomic aberrations present in our RCC data set, it was impossible to extract a common CNA pattern affecting specific chromosomal regions. On the other hand, IdeogramBrowser, which is a novel open source software specifically designed to

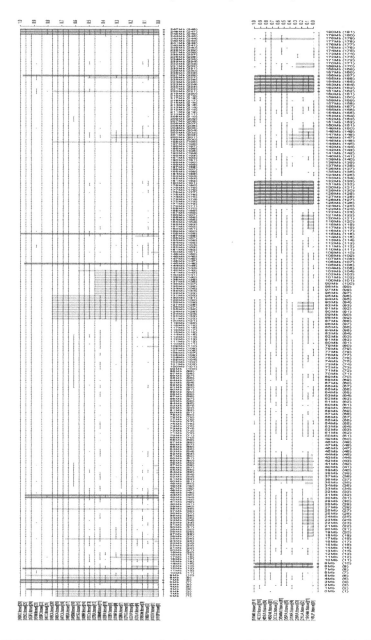

Fig. 3. STAC statistics visualization for chromosome 1 (left) and 5 (right). Samples are listed vertically. For each equally spaced node (placed horizontally), black dots represent the presence of an aberration, lines represent intervals of aberration, grey bars show frequency and footprint confidence. The chromosome is represented from p to q arm (left to right).

deal with Affymetrix SNP array data, provided a very useful visualization of common aberrant regions for multiple samples. There are several user-adjustable parameters to identify common aberrant regions, which could unfortunately lead to an improper analysis due to operator bias. Both dChip2006 and Ideogram Browser can display an interactive, virtual karyotype of multiple samples with direct links to GeneCards and the NCBI genomic database. However, neither provided a statistical based testing to identify common aberrant regions.

As a consequence, we have proposed a pipeline to use SNP copy number data with STAC to obtain statistically significant common regions of CNA within a heterogeneous sample set, as typically occurring in tumor samples. We believe that STAC analysis is a method to find specific CNA signature between tumor samples with high complex genomic profiling. Further improvements are in progress to optimize the smoothing and preprocessing methods to convert the CN of single SNPs into CN of the corresponding genes and to combine the DNA copy number profile with gene expression data [14],[15]. The combination of DNA copy number analysis and gene profiling in oncogenomic studies provides novel, powerful approach to investigate and understand the molecular mechanisms underlying cancer etiology.

Acknowledgements. This work was supported by MIUR-FIRB grants no. RBNE01HCKF, no. RBNE01TZZ8 and COFIN no. 2005069853.

References

1. Paris, P.L., Andaya, A., Fridly, J., Jain, A.N., Weinberg, V., Kowbel, D., Brebner, J.H., Simko, J., Watson, J.E., Volik, S., et al.: Whole genome scanning identifies genotypes associated with recurrence and metastasis in prostate tumors. Hum. Mol. Genet. 13(13), 1303–1313 (2004)
2. Weiss, M.M., Kuipers, E.J., Postma, C., Snijders, A.M., Pinkel, D., Meuwissen, S.G., Albertson, D., Meijer, G.A.: Genomic alterations in primary gastric adenocarcinomas correlate with clinicopathological characteristics and survival. Cell. Oncol 26(5-6), 307–317 (2004)
3. Zhao, X., Li, C., Paez, J.G., Chin, K., Janne P.A., et al.: An integrated view of copy number and allelic alterations in the cancer genome using single nucleotide polymorphism arrays. Cancer Res. 64: 30603071 (2004)
4. Liu, W., Chang, B., Sauvageot, J., Dimitrov, L., Gielzak, M., Li, T., Yan, G., Sun, J., Sun, J., Adams, T.S., et al.: Comprehensive assessment of DNA copy number alterations in human prostate cancers using Affymetrix 100K SNP mapping array. Genes Chromosomes Cancer 45(11), 1018–1032 (2006)
5. Lindblad-Toh, K., Tanenbaum, D.M., Daly, M.J., Winchester, E., Lui, W.O., Villapakkam, A., Stanton, S.E., Larsson, C., Hudson, T.J., Johnson, B.E., et al.: Loss-of-heterozygosity analysis of small-cell lung carcinomas using single-nucleotide polymorphism arrays. Nat. Biotechnol 18(9), 1001–1005 (2000)
6. Zhou, X., Li, C., Mok, S.C., Chen, Z., Wong, D.T.: Whole genome loss of heterozygosity profiling on oral squamous cell carcinoma by high-density single nucleotide polymorphic allele (SNP) array. Cancer Genet Cytogenet 151(1), 82–84 (2004)

7. Lin, M., Wei, L.-J., Sellers, W.R., Lieberfarb, M., Wong*, W.H., Li*, C.: dChipSNP: Significance Curve and Clustering of SNP-Array-Based Loss-of-Heterozygosity Data. Bioinformatics 20, 1233–1240 (2004)
8. Nannya, Y., Sanada, M., Nakazaki, K., Hosoya, N., Wang, L., Hangaishi, A., Kurokawa, M., Chiba, S., Bailey, D.K., Kennedy, G.C., et al.: A robust algorithm for copy number detection using high-density oligonucleotide single nucleotide polymorphism genotyping arrays. Cancer Res. 65(14), 6071–6079 (2005)
9. Ting, J.C., Ye, Y., Thomas, G.H., Ruczinski, I., Pevsner, J.: Analysis and visualization of chromosomal abnormalities in SNP data with SNPscan. BMC Bioinformatics 7(1), 25 (2006)
10. Muller, A., Holzmann, K., Kestler, H.A.: Visualization of genomic aberrations using Affymetrix SNP arrays. Bioinformatics 23(4), 496–497, Epub 2006 (November 30 2007)
11. Diskin, S.J., Eck, T., Greshock, J., Mosse, Y.P., Naylor, T., Stoeckert Jr., C.J., Weber, B.L., Maris, J.M., Grant, G.R.: STAC: A method for testing the significance of DNA copy number aberrations across multiple array-CGH experiments. Genome Res. 16, 000-000. (2006)
12. Gasser, T., Mller, H.: Kernel estimation of regression functions. Smoothing Techniques for Curve Estimation. In: Lecture Notes in Math., vol. 757, pp. 23–68. Springer, New York (1979)
13. Lieberfarb, M.E., Lin, M., Lechpammer, M., Li, C., Tanenbaum, D.M., Febbo, P.G., Wright, R.L., Shim, J., Kantoff, P.W., Loda, M., et al.: Genome-wide loss of heterozygosity analysis from laser capture microdissected prostate cancer using single nucleotide polymorphic allele (SNP) arrays and a novel bioinformatics platform dChipSNP. Cancer Res. 63(16), 4781–4785 (2003)
14. Garraway, L.A., Widlund, H.R., Rubin, M.A., Getz, G., Berger, A.J., Ramaswamy, S., Beroukhim, R., Milner, D.A., Granter, S.R., Du, J., et al.: Integrative genomic analyses identify MITF as a lineage survival oncogene amplified in malignant melanoma. Nature 436(7047), 117–122 (2005)
15. Tsafrir, D., Bacolod, M., Selvanayagam, Z., Tsafrir, I., Shia, J., Zeng, Z., Liu, H., Krier, C., Stengel, R.F., Barany, F., et al.: Relationship of gene expression and chromosomal abnormalities in colorectal cancer. Cancer Res. 66(4), 2129–2137 (2006)

Locally Adaptive Statistical Procedures for the Integrative Analysis on Genomic and Transcriptional Data

Mattia Zampieri[1], Ingrid Cifola[2], Dario Basso[1], Roberta Spinelli[2],
Luca Beltrame[2], Clelia Peano[3], Cristina Battaglia[2], and Silvio Bicciato[1,*]

[1] Dept. of Chemical Engineering Processes, University of Padova
via Marzolo 9 Padova Italy
tel.: +39-049-827-5002
fax: +39-049-827-5555
silvio.bicciato@unipd.it

[2] Dept. of Science and Biomedical Technologies and CISI, University of Milan
via Fantoli 16/15 Milano Italy

[3] Institute of Biomedical Technologies (ITB), National Research Council (CNR)
Via Fantoli 16/15 Milano Italy

Abstract. The systematic integration of expression profiles and other types of gene information, such as copy number, chromosomal localization, and sequence characteristics, still represents a challenge in the genomic arena. In particular, the integrative analysis of genomic and transcriptional data in context of the physical location of genes in a genome appears promising in detecting chromosomal regions with structural and transcriptional imbalances often characterizing cancer.

A computational framework based on locally adaptive statistical procedures (Global Smoothing Copy Number, GLSCN, and Locally Adaptive Statistical Procedure, LAP), which incorporate genomic and transcriptional data with structural information for the identification of imbalanced chromosomal regions, is described. Both GLSCN and LAP accounts for variations in the distance between genes and in gene density by smoothing standard statistics on gene position before testing the significance of copy number and gene expression signals. The application of GLSCN and LAP to the integrative analysis of a human metastatic clear cell renal carcinoma cell line (Caki-1) allowed identifying chromosomal regions that are directly involved in known chromosomal aberrations characteristic of tumors.

Keywords: gene expression, genotyping, microarray, integrative genomics.

1   Introduction

High-throughput genomic data represents a fundamental discovery tool to understand and reconstruct biological mechanisms and regulatory networks. The

---

* Corresponding author.

F. Masulli, S. Mitra, and G. Pasi (Eds.): WILF 2007, LNAI 4578, pp. 682–689, 2007.

massive and rapid accumulation of structural and functional information has required the development of computational frameworks able to turn genomic data into accurate and robust biological hypotheses about the genetic and epigenetic mechanisms regulating the transcriptional machinery [1]. Moreover, recent studies on the relationships between gene structure and gene function in eukaryotic genomes showed how groups of physically contiguous genes are characterized by similar, coordinated transcriptional profiles [2,3] and suggested a relationship between genomic structural abnormalities and expression imbalances (under- or over-expression). In particular, Caron et al (2001) illustrated how whole chromosome views reveal a higher order organization of the genome, as there is a strong clustering of expressed genes with most chromosomes presenting large regions of highly transcribed genes, called RIDGEs (regions of increased gene expression), interspersed with regions where gene expression is low. Similarly, the pioneering study by Garraway and colleagues [4] illustrated how the combination of gene expression profiles with genome-wide copy number data can lead to the identification of novel lineage-specific oncogenes associated with copy number gain in tumor specimens. Only recently, however, have single studies reported the simultaneous generation of genome-wide maps of copy number alterations (CNAs) and transcriptional activity to study the global effects of chromosomal instability on gene expression [5,6]. Indeed, genomic instability in human samples can now be monitored using microarray-based techniques, in particular array comparative genomic hybridization (CGH) and high-density single nucleotide polymorphism (SNP)-mapping arrays [7]. These oligonucleotide arrays permit the simultaneous genotyping of more than 100,000 SNPs and thus provide information on loss of heterozygosity (LOH) and chromosomal alterations with a detection limit reaching 20 kb. More importantly, when copy number profiles of chromosomal instability are confronted with transcriptional data in various tumor samples, a clear impact of DNA copy number change on gene expression can be observed.

Given these experimental evidences, the integration of high-throughput genomic and transcriptional data with gene structural information (i.e., chromosomal localization) and functional characteristics represents a major challenge for bioinformatics and computational biology. Indeed, an integrated approach would allow deciphering how the structural organization of genomes influences its functional utilization, identifying how transcription factors regulate gene expression through target genes, and discover novel cancer biomarkers. Few computational approaches have been adopted to identify chromosomal regions of increased or decreased expression from transcriptional data [1,7,8,9]. All these methods score differentially expressed genes using standard statistics and then scan an array-based gene map using windows of fixed length or containing a pre-selected number of genes.

The purpose of this work is to present two non-parametric, model-free bioinformatics tools to identify genomic regions characterized by concomitant alterations in copy number (CN) and in regional transcriptional activity. Global Smoothing Copy Number (GLSCN) and Locally Adaptive Statistical Procedure (LAP, [11]) account for variations in gene distance and density and are based on the computation of a standard statistic as a measure of the difference in genomic and gene expression patterns between groups of samples, assessed on high-density microarrays. For each chromosome, the statistic is locally smoothed using non-parametric estimation of regression function over the positional coordinate. Chromosomal regions with CN alterations and transcriptional imbalances are identified using an empirical null distribution obtained by permutation procedure.

2   Methods

Global Smoothing Copy Number (GLSCN) analyzes copy number values for individual array probes (SNPs). Copy number data can be generated from Affymetrix mapping arrays using Copy Number Analysis Tool (CNAT, v3.0, Affymetrix). GLSCN subjects CN data to a hypothesis test, in which the null and alternative hypotheses are formulated respectively as:

$$H_0 : CN_i = median(CN_{tot})$$
$$H_1 : CN_i \neq median(CN_{tot})$$

where CN_i is the copy number value of each SNP, the median CN was calculated over the entire dataset, and variance was assumed to be constant.

CN data are then converted to smoothed CN scores using a kernel regression estimator with fixed or automatically adapted local plug-in bandwidth. As described in [9,11], smoothing of the statistic can be formally stated as a non-parametric regression problem where the score is to be estimated over the chromosomal coordinate. Non-parametric regression problems can be approached using various methods and GLSCN uses the *lokern* function adapted from the Gasser-Müller type estimator [12,13] (*lokern* R package is freely available at http://www.sourcekeg.co.uk/cran/src/contrib/Descriptions/lokern.html). Specifically, given n independent and identically distributed bivariate random variables, (T_i, Y_i) sample points, a kernel function K of order k and a bandwidth h, the unknown regression function r can be estimated as:

$$\hat{r}_2(t; h_t) = \sum_{i=1}^{n} \int_{S_{i-1}}^{S_i} \frac{1}{h_t} K\left(\frac{t-u}{h_t}\right) du Y_i \tag{1}$$

$$t \in [a + h_t, b - h_t]$$
$$s_0 = a$$
$$s_i = \frac{1}{2}(t_i + t_{i+1}), \quad i = 1, \ldots, n-1$$
$$s_n = b.$$

In the case of CNAs, a fixed bandwidth of 1 Mb was chosen in consideration of the relatively homogeneous distribution of SNP probes along the chromosomes.

Chromosomal regions with smoothed CN scores significantly different from the median CN value are finally identified using a permutation procedure. Specifically, the statistics are randomly assigned to the array SNP locations over B permutations (e.g., 100,000) and smoothed over the chromosomal coordinate each time. The smoothed statistic for each SNP S_i is compared to the null smoothed statistic S_i^0 on the same SNP and p-values are computed as the probability that the random null statistic exceeded the observed statistic over the permutations:

$$p_i = \frac{\#\{b : |S_i^{0b}| \geq |S_i|, b = 1, \dots, B\}}{B}. \tag{2}$$

This p-value has the peculiarity to be local since the observed smoothed statistic is compared only with null statistics smoothed on the same neighborhood of chromosomal position i. Indeed, during the permutation process, the chromosomal position is conserved while the statistics are randomly shuffled. Once the distribution of empirical p-values had been generated, q-value is used to identify chromosomal regions affected by CNAs [15]. Q-values allow quantifying significance in light of thousands of simultaneous tests and can be calculated using R qvalue package (http://faculty.washington.edu/ jstorey/qvalue/).

Similarly to GLSCN, LAP calculates a statistic for ranking probes in order of strength of the evidence for differential expression; smoothes the statistic after sorting the statistical scores according to the chromosomal position of the corresponding genes, and applies a permutation test to identify differentially expressed chromosomal regions. In particular, given a matrix $\mathbf{X}$ of normalized expression levels x_{ij} for gene i in sample j ($i = 1, 2, \dots, G; j = 1, 2, \dots, n$) and $\mathbf{Y}$ a response vector y_j ($j = 1, 2, \dots, n$) for n samples, the statistic d_i can be defined as the ratio of change in gene expression r_i to the standard deviation in the data set si for each probe set i:

$$d_i = \frac{r_i}{s_i + s_0} \tag{3}$$

where the estimates of gene-specific variance over repeated measurements are stabilized by a fudge factor s_0 (see [14] and SAM technical manual for details).

LAP smoothing is based on a local variable bandwidth kernel estimator. In this case, given the heterogeneous gene distances and densities on the chromosomes, the optimal bandwidths are estimated iteratively minimizing the asymptotic mean squared error. Finally, a permutation scheme is used to identify differentially expressed regions under the assumption that each gene has a unique neighborhood and that the corresponding smoothed statistic is not comparable with any statistic smoothed in other regions of the genome. The G statistic values d_i are first randomly assigned to G chromosomal locations through permutations and then, for each permutation, smoothed over the chromosomal coordinate. Thus, observed and null statistics are smoothed and compared exactly over the same region, taking into account variations in the gene distances and in gene density. The permutation process, over B random assignments, allows defining the null smoothed statistic for gene i. The significance of the differentially expressed genes, i.e., the p-value p_i for gene i, is computed as the probability that the random null statistic exceeds the observed statistic over B permutations. Once the distribution of empirical p-values has been generated, the q-value is used to identify differentially expressed chromosomal regions.

3   Results

In the context of a research project focused on the identification of clinical bio-markers for renal cell carcinoma (RCC), we applied both GLSCN and LAP to the analysis of human metastatic RCC cell line (Caki-1). Using Affymetrix high-density oligonucleotide microarray technology, a genome-wide SNP-mapping of CNAs (on GeneChip Human Mapping 100K SNP arrays) and a transcriptional profiling (on GeneChip Human Genome U133 Plus 2.0 arrays) were performed.

The analysis with GLSCN of combined dataset from 50K Xba and 50K Hind arrays (comprising the 100K SNP array set) generated a high-resolution genomic map (Figure. 1a). Overall, CNAs were detected in 19 chromosomes. Among them, four chromosomes (chr. 1, 3, 17 and 18) had regions of both DNA gain and loss, while the remaining chromosomes had regions of either CN gain (chr. 4, 5, 7, 8, 10, 11, 12 and 16) or CN loss (chr. 9, 13, 14, 15, 20, 21 and 22). Only two chromosomes (chr. 2 and 6) had no variations in DNA copy number (chromosomes 2 and 6). In parallel, the regional transcriptional activity profile of Caki-1, calculated with LAP, revealed that up- and down-regulated genes tended to cluster in specific genomic regions (Figure 1b).

To evaluate the relationship between CNA and transcriptional activity, the relative statistic scores for 16,473 well annotated chromosomal positions (genes) were categorized into three classes: increased (gain of CN or up-regulated), unchanged and decreased (loss of CN or down-regulated). Setting q = 0 for CNA analysis and q < 0.05 for transcriptional activity analysis, the concordance of categorization was 56%. Specifically, 2,871 genes (17%) were both up-regulated and localized in areas of CN gain (increased class), 4,689 genes (29%) were classified as unchanged, and 1,699 genes (10%) were both down-regulated and localized in areas of CN loss (decreased class). When data were simplified into two categories (increased vs. other two classes, or decreased vs. other two classes), a strong association both between CN gain and up-regulation ($\chi^2 = 5,290$, p < 0.0001) and between CN loss and down-regulation ($\chi^2 = 1,501$, p < 0.0001) was observed.

Moreover, odds ratios (OR) of 16.8 (95% CI, 15.4-18.4) for the likelihood that gene expression is up-regulated when the genomic region is amplified, and of 5.7 (95% CI, 5.2-6.3) for the likelihood that gene expression is down-regulated when the genomic region is deleted, were calculated. Overall, these results demonstrate a striking association between CNA profile and regional transcriptional activity in Caki-1 cells. Moreover, since 69% of up-regulated genes had concomitant CN gain but only 29% of down-regulated genes were associated with CN loss, it appears that the two types of gene expression variation have different powers to predict CNAs.

4   Discussion and Conclusions

A novel mathematical and statistical framework to combine microarray profiles of copy number alterations (CNAs) and transcriptional activity at genome level has been developed and applied to study the Caki-1 cell line as a model for

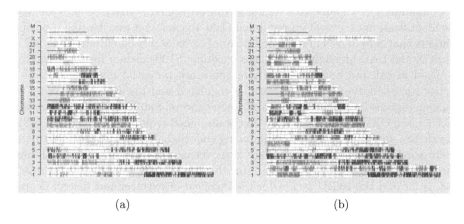

(a)   (b)

Fig. 1. Whole genome plot of the chromosomal regions with CNAs, (a), and gene expression imbalances, (b), at a q-value=0 a q-value<0.05 for CN and gene expression data, respectively.The white bars indicate locations and orientations of all probe sets in the microarray, the red perpendicular lines represent the exact chromosomal locations and orientations of genes with CN gain or up-regulated, and the green lines the location of probes with CN loss or down-regulated. The positions for both the sense and antisense strands are expressed in numbers of base pairs measured from the p (5′ end of the sense strand) to q (3′ end of the sense strand) arms; upper and lower bars stand for genes on sense and antisense strands, respectively.

renal carcinoma. The analysis of genomic and transcriptional data using locally adaptive statistical procedures allowed identifying a strong association between DNA copy number changes and regional gene expression levels. These peculiar chromosomal regions, presenting concomitant alterations in genomic and transcriptomic profiles, could be tumor-specific regions containing candidate clinical biomarkers.

To our knowledge, this is the first computational platform able to directly combine SNP-based CN data and transcriptional profiles at the level of gene loci, while for instance freely available VAMP software has been recently implemented to integrate CGH data with transcriptional profiles [16]. This bioinformatics framework highlighted a strong association between CNA profile and regional transcriptional activity map. In particular, 69% of up-regulated genes localized to areas of CN gain, while only 29% of down-regulated genes were associated with CN loss. These results indicate that differential gene expression data are more powerful for inferring CN gain rather than loss. Therefore, we conclude that CN gain has a stronger influence on regional transcriptional activity than CN loss. The observation that gene amplification greatly affects genes, enhancing their expression, is supported by much evidence from mammalian cell lines and tumors. On the contrary, there are many aneuploidy-independent mechanisms leading to down-modulation of transcriptional activity (e.g. mutation, promoter hypermethylation). These observations should be taken into consideration when chromosomal instability is inferred from transcriptomic profiles.

Combining CNA maps with regional transcriptional activity profiles allowed the identification of several up-regulated Caki-1 genes that may be RCC-specific markers that may have clinical application. For example, on chromosome 1q21, GLSCN and LAP highlighted six genes encoding S100 calcium-binding proteins involved in calcium homeostasis; these genes are potential markers of Caki-1 metastatic phenotype, since they are up-regulated and involved in the onset of bone metastasis in breast, ovarian and colon cancers. Similarly, the up-regulated CXCL1 and CXCL5 genes, selected on the amplified region of chromosome 4q21, encode pro-angiogenic chemokines inducing endothelial cell migration and tumor microvessel formation; these genes are also over-expressed in non-small cell lung and colorectal cancers. Furthermore, on the statistically relevant region 5q31-q33, is located the EGR1 gene which is involved in extracellular matrix degradation, thus promoting tumor spreading and metastasis. Noticeably, in the same region is located osteonectin, which is known to be associated with increased tumor cell motility and invasion. Since SPARC serum levels are higher in patients with certain tumors than in healthy persons, it has been proposed as a tumor biomarker detectable in biological fluids.

Acknowledgements

This work was supported by grants from the Italian Ministry of University and Research (MIUR-FIRB RBNE01HCKF1 and RBNE01TZZ8, COFIN 2005069853, and ONCOSUISSE Collaborative Cancer Research Project OCS 01517022004).

References

1. Beer, M.A., Tavazoie, S.: Predicting gene expression from sequence. Cell. 117, 185–198 (2004)
2. Caron, H., van Schaik, B., van der Mee, M., Baas, F., Riggins, G., van Sluis, P., Hermus, M.C., van Asperen, R., Boon, K., Voute, P.A., Heisterkamp, S., van Kampen, A., Versteeg, R.: The human transcriptome map: clustering of highly expressed genes in chromosomal domains. Science 291, 1289–1292 (2001)
3. Versteeg, R., van Schaik, B.D., van Batenburg, M.F., Roos, M., Monajemi, R., Caron, H., Bussemaker, H.J., van Kampen, A.H.: The human transcriptome map reveals extremes in gene density, intron length, GC content, and repeat pattern for domains of highly and weakly expressed genes. Genome Res. 13, 1998–2004 (2003)
4. Garraway, L.A., Widlund, H.R., Rubin, M.A., Getz, G., Berger, A.J., Ramaswamy, S., Beroukhim, R., Milner, D.A., Granter, S.R., Du, J., et al.: Integrative genomic analyses identify MITF as a lineage survival oncogene amplified in malignant melanoma. Nature 436(7047), 117–122 (2005)
5. Tsafrir, D., Bacolod, M., Selvanayagam, Z., Tsafrir, I., Shia, J., Zeng, Z., Liu, H., Krier, C., Stengel, R.F., Barany, F., et al.: Relationship of gene expression and chromosomal abnormalities in colorectal cancer. Cancer Res. 66(4), 2129–2137 (2006)

6. Kotliarov, Y., Steed, M.E., Christopher, N., Walling, J., Su, Q., Center, A., Heiss, J., Rosenblum, M., Mikkelsen, T., Zenklusen, J.C., et al.: High-resolution Global Genomic Survey of 178 Gliomas Reveals Novel Regions of Copy Number Alteration and Allelic Imbalances. Cancer Res. 66(19), 9428–9436 (2006)

7. Bignell, G.R., Huang, J., Greshock, J., Watt, S., Butler, A., West, S., Grigorova, M., Jones, K.W., Wei, W., Stratton, M.R., et al.: High-resolution analysis of DNA copy number using oligonucleotide microarrays. Genome Res. 14(2), 287–295 (2004)

8. Crawley, J.J., Furge K.A.: Identification of frequent cytogenetic aberrations in hepatocellular carcinoma using gene-expression microarray data. Genome Biology 3, RESEARCH0075 (2002)

9. Toedling, J., Schmeier, S., Heinigm, M., Georgi, B., Roepcke, S.: MACAT microarray chromosome analysis tool. Bioinformatics 21(9), 2112–2113 (2005)

10. Levin, A.M., Ghosh, D., Cho, K.R., Kardia, S.L.: A model-based scan statistic for identifying extreme chromosomal regions of gene expression in human tumors. Bioinformatics 21(12), 2867–2874 (2005)

11. Callegaro, A., Basso, D., Bicciato, S.A.: locally adaptive statistical procedure (LAP) to identify differentially expressed chromosomal regions. Bioinformatics 22(21), 2658–2666 (2006)

12. Herrmann, E.: Local bandwidth choice in kernel regression estimation. Journal of Graphical and Computational Statistics 6, 35–54 (1997)

13. Gasser, T., Mller, H.G.: Kernel estimation of regression functions. Smoothing Techniques for Curve Estimation. In: Lecture Notes in Math., vol. 757, pp. 23–68. springer, Heidelberg

14. Tusher, V.G., Tibshirani, R., Chu, G.: Significance analysis of microarrays applied to the ionizing radiation response. Proc. Natl. Acad. Sci. USA 98(9), 5116–5121 (2001)

15. Storey, J.D., Tibshirani, R.: Statistical significance for genome-wide experiments. Proc. Natl. Acad. Sci. USA 100(16), 9440–9445 (2003)

16. La Rosa, P., Viara, E., Hupe, P., Pierron, G., Liva, S., Neuvial, P., Brito, I., Lair, S., Servant, N., Robine, N., et al.: VAMP: visualization and analysis of array-CGH, transcriptome and other molecular profiles. Bioinformatics 22(17), 2066–2073 (2006)

Author Index

Lecture Notes in Artificial Intelligence (LNAI)